ACCOUNTING

Tools for Business Decision Making

Sixth Edition

Custom Volume 2

KIMMEL • WEYGANDT • KIESO

Indiana State University
Principles of Accounting II
BUS 202

Wiley Custom Learning Solutions

Printing identification and country of origin will either be included on this page and/or the end of the book. In addition, if the ISBN on this page and the back cover do not match, the ISBN on the back cover should be considered the correct ISBN.

Printed in the United States of America.

ISBN 978-1-119-33365-4
Printed and bound by Quad/Graphics.

V10005816_110218

CONTENTS

12	Statement of Cash Flows	590
13	Financial Analysis: The Big Picture	646
14	Managerial Accounting	702
15	Job Order Costing	746
16	Process Costing	788
17	Activity-Based Costing	834
18	Cost-Volume-Profit	882
19	Cost-Volume-Profit Analysis: Additional Issues	922
20	Incremental Analysis	974
21	Budgetary Planning	1014
22	Budgetary Control and Responsibility Accounting	1064
23	Standard Costs and Balanced Scorecard	1118
24	Planning for Capital Investments	1166

APPENDICES

A	Specimen Financial Statements: Apple Inc.	A-1
B	Specimen Financial Statements: Columbia Sportswear Company	B-1
C	Specimen Financial Statements: VF Corporation	C-1
D	Specimen Financial Statements: Amazon.com, Inc.	D-1
E	Specimen Financial Statements: Wal-Mart Stores, Inc.	E-1
F	Specimen Financial Statements: Louis Vuitton	F-1
G	Time Value of Money	G-1
H	Reporting and Analyzing Investments	H-1
I	Payroll Accounting	I-1
J	Subsidiary Ledgers and Special Journals	J-1
K	Accounting for Partnerships	K-1
L	Accounting for Sole Proprietorships	L-1
M	Pricing	M-1

Company Index CI-1
Subject Index SI-1

kimmel
weygandt
kieso
team for success

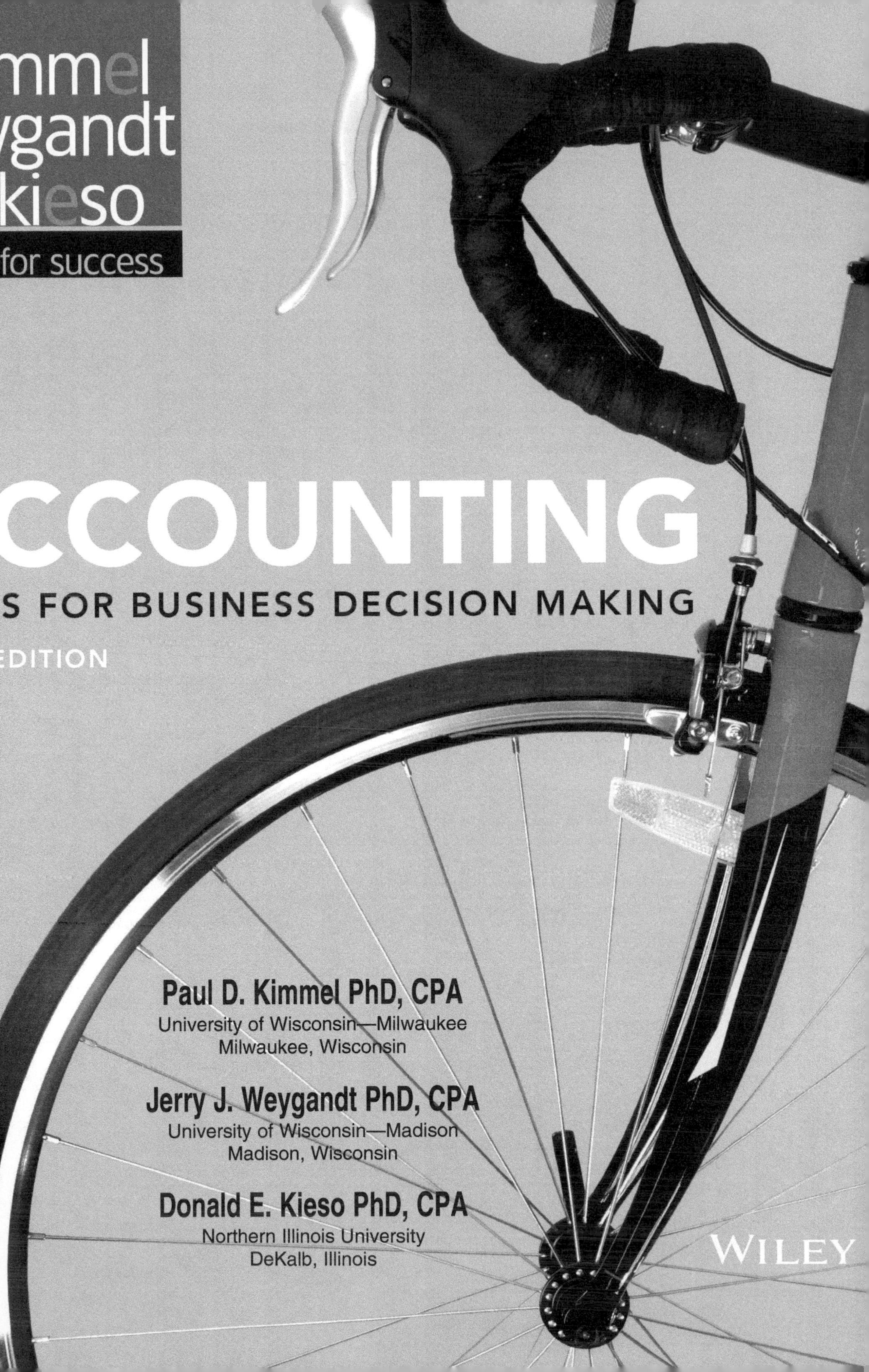

ACCOUNTING

TOOLS FOR BUSINESS DECISION MAKING

SIXTH EDITION

Paul D. Kimmel PhD, CPA
University of Wisconsin—Milwaukee
Milwaukee, Wisconsin

Jerry J. Weygandt PhD, CPA
University of Wisconsin—Madison
Madison, Wisconsin

Donald E. Kieso PhD, CPA
Northern Illinois University
DeKalb, Illinois

WILEY

DEDICATED TO

the Wiley sales representatives who sell our books and service our adopters in a professional and ethical manner, and to Merlynn, Enid, and Donna

Vice President and Director	George Hoffman
Executive Editor	Michael McDonald
Development Editor	Ed Brislin
Editorial Supervisor	Terry Ann Tatro
Editorial Associate	Margaret Thompson
Senior Content Manager	Dorothy Sinclair
Senior Production Editor	Suzie Pfister
Executive Marketing Manager	Karolina Zarychta Honsa
Senior Product Designer	Allison Morris
Product Designer	Matt Origoni
Media Specialist	Elena Santa Maria
Design Director	Harry Nolan
Cover Design	Maureen Eide
Interior Design	Maureen Eide
Senior Photo Editor	Mary Ann Price
Editorial Assistant	Elizabeth Kearns
Cover and title page	kledge/Getty Images

This book was set in New Aster LT Std by Aptara®, Inc. and printed and bound by Quad/Graphics Versailles. The cover was printed by Quad/Graphics Versailles.

Founded in 1807, John Wiley & Sons, Inc. has been a valued source of knowledge and understanding for more than 200 years, helping people around the world meet their needs and fulfill their aspirations. Our company is built on a foundation of principles that include responsibility to the communities we serve and where we live and work. In 2008, we launched a Corporate Citizenship Initiative, a global effort to address the environmental, social, economic, and ethical challenges we face in our business. Among the issues we are addressing are carbon impact, paper specifications and procurement, ethical conduct within our business and among our vendors, and community and charitable support. For more information, please visit our website: www.wiley.com/go/citizenship.

EVAL ISBN-13 978-1-119-22280-4

Binder-Ready Version ISBN 978-1-119-19167-4

The inside back cover will contain printing identification and country of origin if omitted from this page. In addition, if the ISBN on the back cover differs from the ISBN on this page, the one on the back cover is correct

Printed in the United States of America

Brief Contents

1 Introduction to Financial Statements 2
2 A Further Look at Financial Statements 44
3 The Accounting Information System 90
4 Accrual Accounting Concepts 150
5 Merchandising Operations and the Multiple-Step Income Statement 214
6 Reporting and Analyzing Inventory 266
7 Fraud, Internal Control, and Cash 316
8 Reporting and Analyzing Receivables 374
9 Reporting and Analyzing Long-Lived Assets 422
10 Reporting and Analyzing Liabilities 478
11 Reporting and Analyzing Stockholders' Equity 536
12 Statement of Cash Flows 590
13 Financial Analysis: The Big Picture 646
14 Managerial Accounting 702
15 Job Order Costing 746
16 Process Costing 788
17 Activity-Based Costing 834
18 Cost-Volume-Profit 882
19 Cost-Volume-Profit Analysis: Additional Issues 922
20 Incremental Analysis 974
21 Budgetary Planning 1014
22 Budgetary Control and Responsibility Accounting 1064
23 Standard Costs and Balanced Scorecard 1118
24 Planning for Capital Investments 1166

APPENDICES

A Specimen Financial Statements: Apple Inc. A-1
B Specimen Financial Statements: Columbia Sportswear Company B-1
C Specimen Financial Statements: VF Corporation C-1
D Specimen Financial Statements: Amazon.com, Inc. D-1
E Specimen Financial Statements: Wal-Mart Stores, Inc. E-1
F Specimen Financial Statements: Louis Vuitton F-1
G Time Value of Money G-1
H Reporting and Analyzing Investments H-1
*I Payroll Accounting I-1
*J Subsidiary Ledgers and Special Journals J-1
*K Accounting for Partnerships K-1
*L Accounting for Sole Proprietorships L-1
*M Pricing M-1

*Cases for Managerial Decision-Making

---

*Available online at www.wiley.com/college/kimmel

From the Authors

Dear Student,

Why This Course? *Remember your biology course in high school? Did you have one of those "invisible man" models (or maybe something more high-tech than that) that gave you the opportunity to look "inside" the human body? This accounting course offers something similar. To understand a business, you have to understand the financial insides of a business organization. An accounting course will help you understand the essential financial components of businesses. Whether you are looking at a large multinational company like Apple or Starbucks or a single-owner software consulting business or coffee shop, knowing the fundamentals of accounting will help you understand what is happening. As an employee, a manager, an investor, a business owner, or a director of your own personal finances—any of which roles you will have at some point in your life—you will make better decisions for having taken this course.*

> "Whether you are looking at a large multinational company like Apple or Starbucks or a single-owner software consulting business or coffee shop, knowing the fundamentals of accounting will help you understand what is happening."

Why This Book? *Hundreds of thousands of students have used this textbook. Your instructor has chosen it for you because of its trusted reputation. The authors have worked hard to keep the book fresh, timely, and accurate.*

How to Succeed? *We've asked many students and many instructors whether there is a secret for success in this course. The nearly unanimous answer turns out to be not much of a secret: "Do the homework." This is one course where doing is learning. The more time you spend on the homework assignments—using the various tools that this textbook provides—the more likely you are to learn the essential concepts, techniques, and methods of accounting. Besides the textbook itself, WileyPLUS and the book's companion website also offer various support resources.*

Good luck in this course. We hope you enjoy the experience and that you put to good use throughout a lifetime of success the knowledge you obtain in this course. We are sure you will not be disappointed.

Paul D. Kimmel
Jerry J. Weygandt
Donald E. Kieso

Author Commitment

Paul Kimmel

PAUL D. KIMMEL, PhD, CPA, received his bachelor's degree from the University of Minnesota and his doctorate in accounting from the University of Wisconsin. He is an Associate Professor at the University of Wisconsin—Milwaukee, and has public accounting experience with Deloitte & Touche (Minneapolis). He was the recipient of the UWM School of Business Advisory Council Teaching Award, the Reggie Taite Excellence in Teaching Award and a three-time winner of the Outstanding Teaching Assistant Award at the University of Wisconsin. He is also a recipient of the Elijah Watts Sells Award for Honorary Distinction for his results on the CPA exam. He is a member of the American Accounting Association and the Institute of Management Accountants and has published articles in *Accounting Review, Accounting Horizons, Advances in Management Accounting, Managerial Finance, Issues in Accounting Education, Journal of Accounting Education,* as well as other journals. His research interests include accounting for financial instruments and innovation in accounting education. He has published papers and given numerous talks on incorporating critical thinking into accounting education, and helped prepare a catalog of critical thinking resources for the Federated Schools of Accountancy.

Jerry Weygandt

JERRY J. WEYGANDT, PhD, CPA, is Arthur Andersen Alumni Emeritus Professor of Accounting at the University of Wisconsin—Madison. He holds a Ph.D. in accounting from the University of Illinois. Articles by Professor Weygandt have appeared in the Accounting Review, Journal of Accounting Research, Accounting Horizons, Journal of Accountancy, and other academic and professional journals. These articles have examined such financial reporting issues as accounting for price-level adjustments, pensions, convertible securities, stock option contracts, and interim reports. Professor Weygandt is author of other accounting and financial reporting books and is a member of the American Accounting Association, the American Institute of Certified Public Accountants, and the Wisconsin Society of Certified Public Accountants. He has served on numerous committees of the American Accounting Association and as a member of the editorial board of the Accounting Review; he also has served as President and Secretary-Treasurer of the American Accounting Association. In addition, he has been actively involved with the American Institute of Certified Public Accountants and has been a member of the Accounting Standards Executive Committee (AcSEC) of that organization. He has served on the FASB task force that examined the reporting issues related to accounting for income taxes and served as a trustee of the Financial Accounting Foundation. Professor Weygandt has received the Chancellor's Award for Excellence in Teaching and the Beta Gamma Sigma Dean's Teaching Award. He is on the board of directors of M & I Bank of Southern Wisconsin. He is the recipient of the Wisconsin Institute of CPA's Outstanding Educator's Award and the Lifetime Achievement Award. In 2001 he received the American Accounting Association's Outstanding Educator Award.

Don Kieso

DONALD E. KIESO, PhD, CPA, received his bachelor's degree from Aurora University and his doctorate in accounting from the University of Illinois. He has served as chairman of the Department of Accountancy and is currently the KPMG Emeritus Professor of Accountancy at Northern Illinois University. He has public accounting experience with Price Waterhouse & Co. (San Francisco and Chicago) and Arthur Andersen & Co. (Chicago) and research experience with the Research Division of the American Institute of Certified Public Accountants (New York). He has done postdoctoral work as a Visiting Scholar at the University of California at Berkeley and is a recipient of NIU's Teaching Excellence Award and four Golden Apple Teaching Awards. Professor Kieso is the author of other accounting and business books and is a member of the American Accounting Association, the American Institute of Certified Public Accountants, and the Illinois CPA Society. He has served as a member of the Board of Directors of the Illinois CPA Society, then AACSB's Accounting Accreditation Committees, the State of Illinois Comptroller's Commission, as Secretary-Treasurer of the Federation of Schools of Accountancy, and as Secretary-Treasurer of the American Accounting Association. Professor Kieso is currently serving on the Board of Trustees and Executive Committee of Aurora University, as a member of the Board of Directors of Kishwaukee Community Hospital, and as Treasurer and Director of Valley West Community Hospital. From 1989 to 1993 he served as a charter member of the national Accounting Education Change Commission. He is the recipient of the Outstanding Accounting Educator Award from the Illinois CPA Society, the FSA's Joseph A. Silvoso Award of Merit, the NIU Foundation's Humanitarian Award for Service to Higher Education, a Distinguished Service Award from the Illinois CPA Society, and in 2003 an honorary doctorate from Aurora University.

WileyPLUS with ORION

Quickly identify areas of strength and weakness before the first exam, and use the information to build a learning path to success.

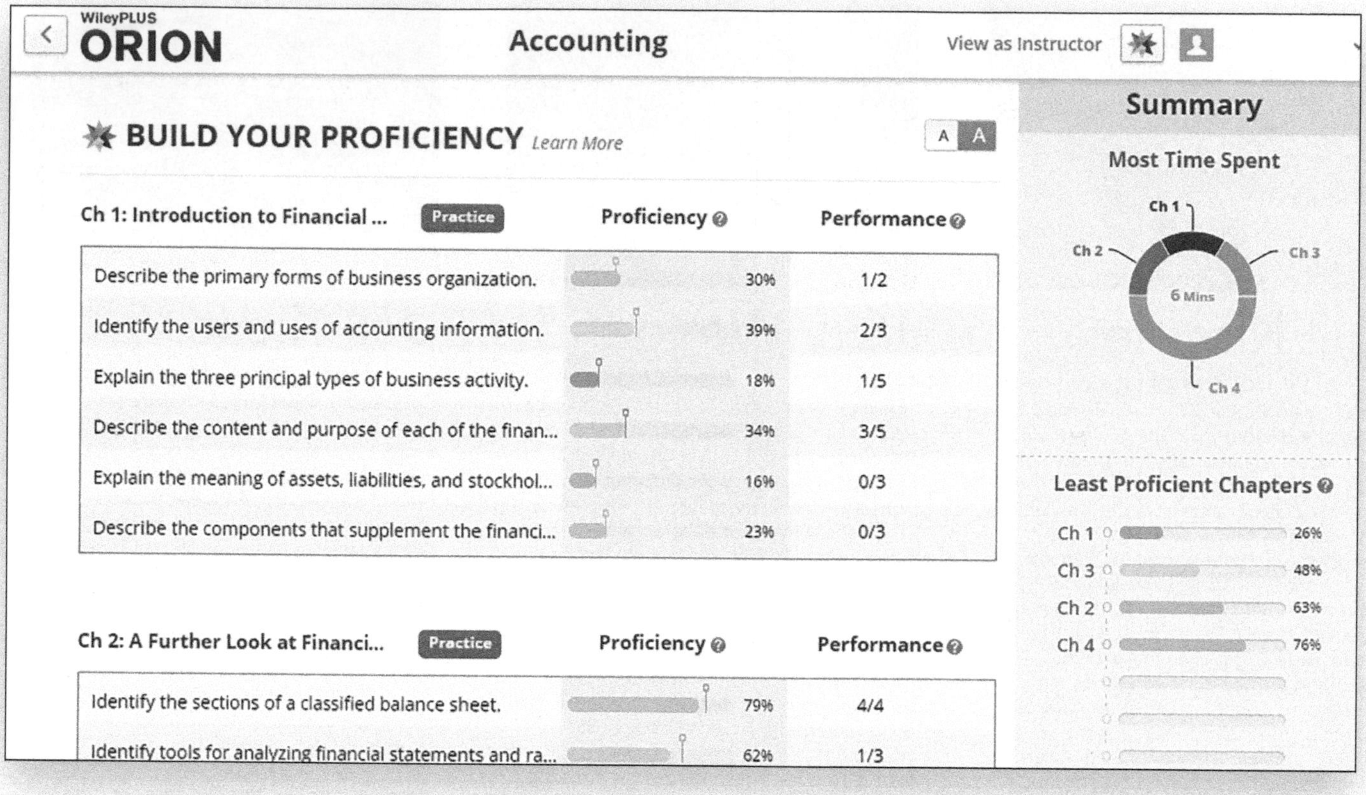

A little time with ORION goes a long way.

Based on usage data, students who engage in ORION adaptive practice—just a few minutes per week—get better outcomes. In fact, students who used ORION five or more times over the course of a semester reported the following results:

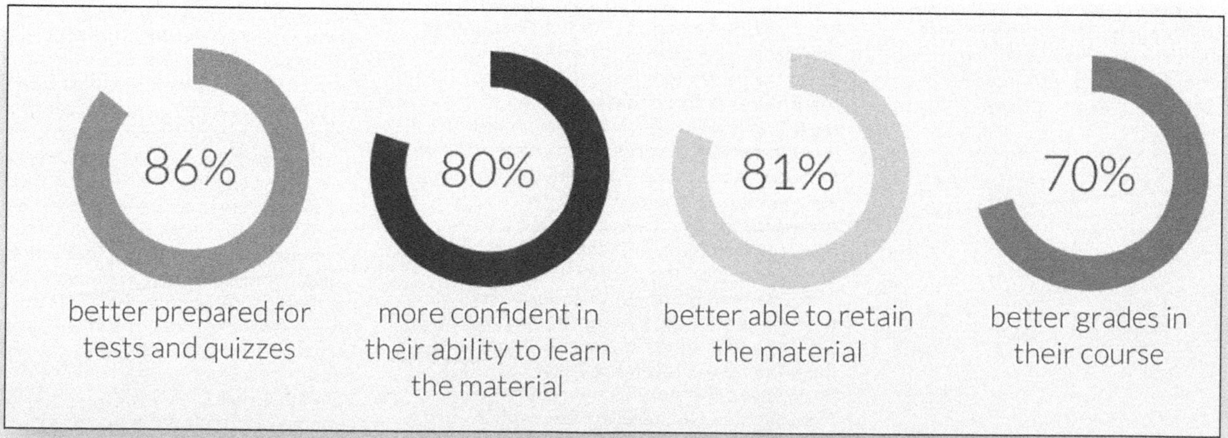

Developing effective problem solving skills requires practice, relevant feedback, and insightful examples.

New PRACTICE QUESTIONS WITH SOLUTIONS include:

- **BRIEF EXERCISES**
- **EXERCISES**
- **DO IT! Exercises**
- **PROBLEMS**

All new practice questions provide **assessment,** helping students see what they understand and where they can improve.

Algorithmic versions of the questions allow students to revisit practice questions until they understand a topic completely.

CALCULATOR | PRINTER VERSION | ◂BACK | NEXT▸

ASSIGNMENT RESOURCES

Chapter 07 Do It! Drill

Do It! Review 7-1

Do It! Review 7-3

Do It! Review 7-4

Review Score

RESET

Do It! Review 7-3

Your answer is partially correct. Try again.

Wilkinson Company established a $105 petty cash fund on August 1. On August 31, the fund had $7 cash remaining and petty cash receipts for postage $36, office supplies $31, and miscellaneous expense $28.

Prepare journal entries to establish the fund on August 1 and replenish the fund on August 31. *(Credit account titles are automatically indented when amount is entered. Do not indent manually.)*

Date	Account Titles and Explanation	Debit	Credit
Aug. 1	Petty Cash	105	
	Cash		105
Aug. 31	Postage Expense	36	
	Supplies	31	
	Miscellaneous Expense	28	
	Cash Over and Short		3

SOLUTIONS TO PRACTICE EXERCISES

1. (a)

Activity Cost Pools	Cost Drivers	Estimated Overhead
Cutting	Machine hours	$400,000
Design	Number of setups	555,000

Activity-based overhead rates:

Cutting: $\frac{\$400,000}{200,000} = \$2$ per machine hour

Design: $\frac{\$555,000}{1,500} = \$370$ per setup

	Wool	Cotton
Activity-based costing		
Cutting		
100,000 × $2	$200,000	
100,000 × $2		$200,000
Design		
1,000 × $370	370,000	
500 × $370		185,000
Total cost allocated	$570,000	$385,000

(b) $\frac{\text{Estimated overhead}}{\text{Direct labors hours}} = \frac{\$955,000}{477,500} = \$2$ per direct labor hour

Solutions to select exercises and problems are now available at the end of each chapter

REVIEW AND PRACTICE

▶ LEARNING OBJECTIVES REVIEW

1 Discuss how to classify and determine inventory. Merchandisers need only one inventory classification, merchandise inventory, to describe the different items that make up total inventory. Manufacturers, on the other hand, usually classify inventory into three categories: finished goods, work in process, and raw materials. To determine inventory quantities, manufacturers (1) take a physical inventory of goods on hand and (2) determine the ownership of goods in transit or on consignment.

2 Apply inventory cost flow methods and discuss their financial effects. The primary basis of accounting for inventories is cost. Cost includes all expenditures necessary to acquire goods and place them in a condition ready for sale. Cost of goods available for sale includes (a) cost of beginning inventory and (b) cost of goods purchased. The inventory cost flow methods are specific identification and three assumed cost flow methods—FIFO, LIFO, and average-cost.

The cost of goods available for sale may be allocated to cost of goods sold and ending inventory by specific identification or by a method based on an assumed cost flow. When prices are rising, the first-in, first-out (FIFO) method results in lower cost of goods sold and higher net income than the average-cost and the last-in, first-out (LIFO) methods. The reverse is true when prices are falling. In the balance sheet, FIFO results in an ending inventory that is closest to current value, whereas the inventory under LIFO is the farthest from current value. LIFO

Inventory turnover is calculated as cost of goods sold divided by average inventory. It can be converted to average days in inventory by dividing 365 days by the inventory turnover. A higher inventory turnover or lower average days in inventory suggests that management is trying to keep inventory levels low relative to its sales level.

The LIFO reserve represents the difference between ending inventory using LIFO and ending inventory if FIFO were employed instead. For some companies this difference can be significant, and ignoring it can lead to inappropriate conclusions when using the current ratio or inventory turnover.

***4** Apply inventory cost flow methods to perpetual inventory records. Under FIFO, the cost of the earliest goods on hand prior to each sa… Under LIFO, the cost of… sale is charged to cost… cost method, a new ave… purchase.

***5** Indicate the effects … cial statements. *In the … year:* (1) An error in … reverse effect on net … inventory results in un… vice versa). (2) An err… a similar effect on ne… inventory results in o… ending inventory error…

INSTRUCTIONS

Prepare a schedule to determine the correct inventory amount. Provide explanations for each item above, saying why you did or did not make an adjustment for each item.

SOLUTION

1. Ending inventory—as reported	$650,000
1. Subtract from inventory: The goods belong to Bosnia Corporation. Sergei is merely holding them for Bosnia.	(200,000)
2. Add to inventory: The goods belong to Sergei when they were shipped.	40,000
3. Subtract from inventory: Office supplies should be carried in a separate account. They are not considered inventory held for resale.	(15,000)
4. Add to inventory: The goods belong to Sergei until they are shipped (Jan. 1).	30,000

SOLUTIONS

1. **(d)** A physical inventory is usually taken when a limited number of goods are being sold or received, and at the end of the company's fiscal year. Choice (a) is incorrect because a physical inventory count is usually taken when the company has the least, not greatest, amount of inventory. Choices (b) and (c) are correct, but (d) is the better answer.
2. **(a)** Goods held on consignment should not be included because another company has title (ownership) to the goods. The other choices are incorrect because (b) goods shipped on consignment to another company and (c) goods in transit from another company shipped FOB shipping point should be included in a company's ending inventory. Choice (d) is incorrect because (a) is not included in the physical inventory.
3. **(b)** The inventory held on consignment by Rogers should be included in Railway's inventory balance at cost ($35,000). The purchased goods of $13,000 should not be included in inventory until January 3 because the goods are shipped FOB destination. Therefore, the correct amount of inventory is $215,000 ($180,000 + $35,000), not (a) $230,000, (c) $228,000, or (d) $193,000.
4. **(c)** Under FIFO, ending inventory will consist of 5,000 units from the Nov. 8 purchase and 4,000 units from the June 19 purchase. Therefore, ending inventory is (5,000 × $13) + (4,000 × $12) = $113,000, not (a) $99,000, (b) $108,000, or (d) $117,000.
5. **(d)** Under LIFO, ending inventory will consist of 8,000 units from the inventory at Jan. 1 and 1,000 units from the June 19 purchase. Therefore, ending inventory is (8,000 × $11) + (1,000 × $12) = $100,000, not (a) $113,000, (b) $108,000, or (c) $99,000.

What's New?

Focus on the Accounting Cycle

To help students master accounting cycle concepts, we added (1) new, recurring illustrations that show students the big picture of the accounting cycle, (2) new comprehensive accounting cycle exercises and problems, and (3) new accounting cycle questions in the Test Bank and **WileyPLUS with ORION**.

Student Practice and Solutions

New practice opportunities with solutions are integrated throughout the textbook and WileyPLUS course. Each textbook chapter now provides students with a **Review and Practice** section that includes learning objective summaries, multiple-choice questions with feedback for each answer choice, practice exercises with solutions, and a practice problem with a solution. Also, all learning objective modules in the textbook are followed by a DO IT! exercise with an accompanying solution.

In **WileyPLUS**, two brief exercises, two DO IT! exercises, two exercises, and a new problem are available for practice with each chapter. All of the new practice questions are algorithmic, providing students with multiple opportunities for advanced practice. WileyPLUS assessment now includes new narrative student feedback.

WileyPLUS with ORION

Over 5,000 questions, including new medium-level, computational, and accounting-cycle-based questions, are available for practice and review. **WileyPLUS with ORION** is an adaptive study and practice tool that helps students build proficiency in course topics.

WileyPLUS Videos

Over 350 videos are available in WileyPLUS. More than 150 of the videos are new to the Sixth Edition. The videos walk students through relevant homework problems and solutions, review important concepts, provide overviews of Excel skills, and explore topics in a real-world context.

Updated Content and Design

We scrutinized all content to find new ways to engage students and help them learn accounting concepts.
A new learning objective structure helps students practice their understanding of concepts with DO IT! exercises before they move on to different topics in other learning objectives. Coupled with a new interior design, revised infographics, and the newly designed interactive chapter tutorials, the new outcomes-oriented approach motivates students and helps them make the best use of their time.

Real World Context: Feature Stories and Comprehensive Problems

New feature stories frame chapter topics in a real-world company example. Also, the feature stories now closely correlate with the Using Decision Tools problem at the end of each chapter. In WileyPLUS, real-world Insight boxes now have questions that can be assigned as homework.

Excel

New Excel skill videos help students understand Excel features they can apply in their accounting studies. A continuing Excel tutorial is also available at the end of each managerial chapter.

More information about the Sixth Edition is available on the book's website at **www.wiley.com/college/kimmel**.

Table of Contents

1 Introduction to Financial Statements 2

Knowing the Numbers 3
LO 1: Study the forms of business organization and the uses of accounting information. 4
Forms of Business Organization 4
Users and Uses of Financial Information 5
Ethics in Financial Reporting 7
LO 2: Explain the three principal types of business activity. 8
Financing Activities 9
Investing Activities 9
Operating Activities 9
LO 3: Describe the four financial statements and how they are prepared. 11
Income Statement 11
Retained Earnings Statement 12
Balance Sheet 13
Statement of Cash Flows 14
Interrelationships of Statements 15
Other Elements of an Annual Report 18
A Look at IFRS 42

2 A Further Look at Financial Statements 44

Just Fooling Around? 45
LO 1: Identity the sections of a classified balance sheet. 46
Current Assets 46
Long-Term Investments 48
Property, Plant, and Equipment 48
Intangible Assets 48
Current Liabilities 50
Long-Term Liabilities 50
Stockholders' Equity 50
LO 2: Use ratios to evaluate a company's profitability, liquidity, and solvency. 51
Ratio Analysis 51
Using the Income Statement 52
Using a Classified Balance Sheet 53
Using the Statement of Cash Flows 57
LO 3: Discuss financial reporting concepts. 58
The Standard-Setting Environment 58
Qualities of Useful Information 59
Assumptions in Financial Reporting 60
Principles in Financial Reporting 61
Cost Constraint 62
A Look at IFRS 87

3 The Accounting Information System 90

Accidents Happen 91
LO 1: Analyze the effect of business transactions on the basic accounting equation. 92
Accounting Transactions 92
Analyzing Transactions 93
Summary of Transactions 99
LO 2: Explain how accounts, debits, and credits are used to record business transactions. 100
Debits and Credits 101
Debit and Credit Procedures 101
Stockholders' Equity Relationships 104
Summary of Debit/Credit Rules 105
LO 3: Indicate how a journal is used in the recording process. 106
The Recording Process 106
The Journal 106
LO 4: Explain how a ledger and posting help in the recording process. 109
The Ledger 109
Chart of Accounts 109
Posting 110
The Recording Process Illustrated 111
Summary Illustration of Journalizing and Posting 117
LO 5: Prepare a trial balance. 119
Limitations of a Trial Balance 119
A Look at IFRS 148

4 Accrual Accounting Concepts 150

Keeping Track of Groupons 151
LO 1: Explain the accrual basis of accounting and the reasons for adjusting entries. 152
The Revenue Recognition Principle 152
The Expense Recognition Principle 152
Accrual versus Cash Basis of Accounting 153
The Need for Adjusting Entries 154
Types of Adjusting Entries 155
LO 2: Prepare adjusting entries for deferrals. 156
Prepaid Expenses 156
Unearned Revenues 160
LO 3: Prepare adjusting entries for accruals. 163
Accrued Revenues 163
Accrued Expenses 164
Summary of Basic Relationships 167

LO 4: Prepare an adjusted trial balance and closing entries. 170
Preparing the Adjusted Trial Balance 170
Preparing Financial Statements 171
Quality of Earnings 172
Closing the Books 175
Summary of the Accounting Cycle 177
LO *5: APPENDIX 4A: Describe the purpose and the basic form of a worksheet. 182
A Look at IFRS 212

5 Merchandising Operations and the Multiple-Step Income Statement 214

Buy Now, Vote Later 215
LO 1: Describe merchandising operations and inventory systems. 216
Operating Cycles 216
Flow of Costs 217
LO 2: Record purchases under a perpetual inventory system. 219
Freight Costs 221
Purchase Returns and Allowances 221
Purchase Discounts 222
Summary of Purchasing Transactions 223
LO 3: Record sales under a perpetual inventory system. 224
Sales Returns and Allowances 225
Sales Discounts 226
LO 4: Prepare a multiple-step income statement and a comprehensive income statement. 227
Single-Step Income Statement 227
Multiple-Step Income Statement 228
Comprehensive Income Statement 231
LO 5: Determine cost of goods sold under a periodic inventory system. 233
LO 6: Compute and analyze gross profit rate and profit margin. 234
Gross Profit Rate 234
Profit Margin 235
LO *7: APPENDIX 5A: Record purchases and sales of inventory under a periodic inventory system. 239
Recording Merchandise Transactions 239
Recording Purchases of Merchandise 239
Freight Costs 240
Recording Sales of Merchandise 240
Comparison of Entries—Perpetual vs. Periodic 241
A Look at IFRS 264

6 Reporting and Analyzing Inventory 266

"Where Is That Spare Bulldozer Blade?" 267
LO 1: Discuss how to classify and determine inventory. 268
Classifying Inventory 268
Determining Inventory Quantities 269
LO 2: Apply inventory cost flow methods and discuss their financial effects. 271
Specific Identification 272
Cost Flow Assumptions 273
Financial Statement and Tax Effects of Cost Flow Methods 277
Using Inventory Cost Flow Methods Consistently 280
LO 3: Explain the statement presentation and analysis of inventory. 281
Presentation 281
Lower-of-Cost-or-Market 281
Analysis 283
Adjustments for LIFO Reserve 284
LO *4: APPENDIX 6A: Apply inventory cost flow methods to perpetual inventory records. 287
First-In, First-Out (FIFO) 287
Last-In, First-Out (LIFO) 288
Average-Cost 289
LO *5: APPENDIX 6B: Indicate the effects of inventory errors on the financial statements. 289
Income Statement Effects 289
Balance Sheet Effects 290
A Look at IFRS 314

7 Fraud, Internal Control, and Cash 316

Minding the Money in Madison 317
LO 1: Define fraud and the principles of internal control. 318
Fraud 318
The Sarbanes-Oxley Act 318
Internal Control 319
Principles of Internal Control Activities 320
Limitations of Internal Control 326
LO 2: Apply internal control principles to cash. 327
Cash Receipts Controls 328
Cash Disbursements Controls 330
LO 3: Identify the control features of a bank account. 333
Electronic Funds Transfer (EFT) System 333
Bank Statements 333
Reconciling the Bank Account 334

LO 4: Explain the reporting of cash and the basic principles of cash management. 340
Reporting Cash 340
Managing and Monitoring Cash 341
Cash Budgeting 344
LO *5: APPENDIX 7A: Explain the operation of a petty cash fund. 347
Establishing the Petty Cash Fund 347
Making Payments from Petty Cash 347
Replenishing the Petty Cash Fund 348
A Look at IFRS 371

8 Reporting and Analyzing Receivables 374

What's Cooking? 375
LO 1: Explain how companies recognize accounts receivable. 376
Types of Receivables 376
Recognizing Accounts Receivable 376
LO 2: Describe how companies value accounts receivable and record their disposition. 378
Valuing Accounts Receivable 378
Disposing of Accounts Receivable 385
LO 3: Explain how companies recognize, value, and dispose of notes receivable. 387
Determining the Maturity Date 388
Computing Interest 388
Recognizing Notes Receivable 388
Valuing Notes Receivable 389
Disposing of Notes Receivable 389
LO 4: Describe the statement presentation of receivables and the principles of receivables management. 391
Financial Statement Presentation of Receivables 391
Managing Receivables 392
Evaluating Liquidity of Receivables 394
Accelerating Cash Receipts 396
A Look at IFRS 419

9 Reporting and Analyzing Long-Lived Assets 422

A Tale of Two Airlines 423
LO 1: Explain the accounting for plant asset expenditures. 424
Determining the Cost of Plant Assets 424
Expenditures During Useful Life 427
To Buy or Lease? 428
LO 2: Apply depreciation methods to plant assets. 429
Factors in Computing Depreciation 430
Depreciation Methods 430
Revising Periodic Depreciation 435
Impairments 436
LO 3: Explain how to account for the disposal of plant assets. 437
Sale of Plant Assets 437
Retirement of Plant Assets 438
LO 4: Identity the basic issues related to reporting intangible assets. 439
Accounting for Intangible Assets 440
Types of Intangible Assets 440
LO 5: Discuss how long-lived assets are reported and analyzed. 443
Presentation 443
Analysis 444
LO *6: APPENDIX 9A: Compute periodic depreciation using the declining-balance method and the units-of-activity method. 449
Declining-Balance Method 449
Units-of-Activity Method 450
A Look at IFRS 475

10 Reporting and Analyzing Liabilities 478

And Then There Were Two 479
LO 1: Explain how to account for current liabilities. 480
What Is a Current Liability? 480
Notes Payable 480
Sales Taxes Payable 481
Unearned Revenues 481
Current Maturities of Long-Term Debt 482
Payroll and Payroll Taxes Payable 483
LO 2: Describe the major characteristics of bonds. 485
Types of Bonds 486
Issuing Procedures 486
Determining the Market Price of Bonds 486
LO 3: Explain how to account for bond transactions. 489
Issuing Bonds at Face Value 489
Discount or Premium on Bonds 489
Issuing Bonds at a Discount 490
Issuing Bonds at a Premium 492
Redeeming Bonds at Maturity 493
Redeeming Bonds before Maturity 493
LO 4: Discuss how liabilities are reported and analyzed. 495
Presentation 495
Analysis 496
LO *5: APPENDIX 10A: Apply the straight-line method of amortizing bond discount and bond premium. 502
Amortizing Bond Discount 502
Amortizing Bond Premium 503

LO *6: APPENDIX 10B: Apply the effective-interest method of amortizing bond discount and bond premium. 504
Amortizing Bond Discount 505
Amortizing Bond Premium 506
LO *7: APPENDIX 10C: Describe the accounting for long-term notes payable. 507
A Look at IFRS 533

11 Reporting and Analyzing Stockholders' Equity 536

Oh Well, I Guess I'll Get Rich 537
LO 1: Discuss the major characteristics of a corporation. 538
Characteristics of a Corporation 538
Forming a Corporation 541
Stockholder Rights 541
Stock Issue Considerations 542
Corporate Capital 544
LO 2: Explain how to account for the issuance of common and preferred stock, and the purchase of treasury stock. 545
Accounting for Common Stock 545
Accounting for Preferred Stock 546
Treasury Stock 547
LO 3: Explain how to account for cash dividends and describe the effect of stock dividends and stock splits. 549
Cash Dividends 549
Dividend Preferences 552
Stock Dividends 553
Stock Splits 555
LO 4: Discuss how stockholders' equity is reported and analyzed. 557
Retained Earnings 557
Retained Earnings Restrictions 558
Balance Sheet Presentation of Stockholders' Equity 558
Analysis of Stockholders' Equity 560
Debt versus Equity Decision 562
LO *5: APPENDIX 11A: Prepare entries for stock dividends. 565
A Look at IFRS 587

12 Statement of Cash Flows 590

Got Cash? 591
LO 1: Discuss the usefulness and format of the statement of cash flows. 592
Usefulness of the Statement of Cash Flows 592
Classification of Cash Flows 592
Significant Noncash Activities 593
Format of the Statement of Cash Flows 594
LO 2: Prepare a statement of cash flows using the indirect method. 595
Indirect and Direct Methods 596
Indirect Method—Computer Services Company 596
Step 1: Operating Activities 598
Summary of Conversion to Net Cash Provided by Operating Activities–Indirect Method 601
Step 2: Investing and Financing Activities 603
Step 3: Net Change in Cash 604
LO 3: Use the statement of cash flows to evaluate a company. 607
The Corporate Life Cycle 607
Free Cash Flow 609
LO *4: APPENDIX 12A: Prepare a statement of cash flows using the direct method. 611
Step 1: Operating Activities 613
Step 2: Investing and Financing Activities 617
Step 3: Net Change in Cash 618
LO *5: APPENDIX 12B: Use the T-account approach to prepare a statement of cash flows. 618
A Look at IFRS 643

13 Financial Analysis: The Big Picture 646

It Pays to Be Patient 647
LO 1: Apply the concept of sustainable income and quality of earnings. 648
Sustainable Income 648
Quality of Earnings 652
LO 2: Apply horizontal analysis and vertical analysis. 654
Horizontal Analysis 655
Vertical Analysis 657
LO 3: Analyze a company's performance using ratio analysis. 660
Price-Earnings Ratio 660
Liquidity Ratios 660
Solvency Ratios 661
Profitability Ratios 661
LO *4: APPENDIX 13A: Evaluate a company comprehensively using ratio analysis. 666
Liquidity Ratios 668
Solvency Ratios 670
Profitability Ratios 672
A Look at IFRS 699

14 Managerial Accounting 702

Just Add Water . . . and Paddle 703

LO 1: Identify the features of managerial accounting and the functions of management. 704
- Comparing Managerial and Financial Accounting 704
- Management Functions 704
- Organizational Structure 706

LO 2: Describe the classes of manufacturing costs and the differences between product and period costs. 708
- Manufacturing Costs 708
- Product Versus Period Costs 710
- Illustration of Cost Concepts 710

LO 3: Demonstrate how to compute cost of goods manufactured and prepare financial statements for a manufacturer. 712
- Income Statement 712
- Cost of Goods Manufactured 713
- Cost of Goods Manufactured Schedule 714
- Balance Sheet 714

LO 4: Discuss trends in managerial accounting. 716
- Service Industries 716
- Focus on the Value Chain 717
- Balanced Scorecard 718
- Business Ethics 719
- Corporate Social Responsibility 720

15 Job Order Costing 746

Profiting from the Silver Screen 747

LO 1: Describe cost systems and the flow of costs in a job order system. 748
- Process Cost System 748
- Job Order Cost System 748
- Job Order Cost Flow 749
- Accumulating Manufacturing Costs 750

LO 2: Use a job cost sheet to assign costs to work in process. 752
- Raw Materials Costs 753
- Factory Labor Costs 755

LO 3: Demonstrate how to determine and use the predetermined overhead rate. 757

LO 4: Prepare entries for manufacturing and service jobs completed and sold. 760
- Assigning Costs to Finished Goods 760
- Assigning Costs to Cost of Goods Sold 761
- Summary of Job Order Cost Flows 761
- Job Order Costing for Service Companies 763
- Advantages and Disadvantages of Job Order Costing 764

LO 5: Distinguish between under- and overapplied manufacturing overhead. 765
- Under- or Overapplied Manufacturing Overhead 766

16 Process Costing 788

The Little Guy Who Could 789

LO 1: Discuss the uses of a process cost system and how it compares to a job order system. 790
- Uses of Process Cost Systems 790
- Process Costing for Service Companies 791
- Similarities and Differences Between Job Order Cost and Process Cost Systems 791

LO 2: Explain the flow of costs in a process cost system and the journal entries to assign manufacturing costs. 793
- Process Cost Flow 793
- Assigning Manufacturing Costs—Journal Entries 793

LO 3: Compute equivalent units. 796
- Weighted-Average Method 796
- Refinements on the Weighted-Average Method 797

LO 4: Complete the four steps to prepare a production cost report. 799
- Compute the Physical Unit Flow (Step 1) 800
- Compute the Equivalent Units of Production (Step 2) 800
- Compute Unit Production Costs (Step 3) 801
- Prepare a Cost Reconciliation Schedule (Step 4) 802
- Preparing the Production Cost Report 802
- Costing Systems—Final Comments 803

LO *5: APPENDIX 16A: Compute equivalent units using the FIFO method. 806
- Equivalent Units Under FIFO 806
- Comprehensive Example 807
- FIFO and Weighted-Average 811

17 Activity-Based Costing 834

Precor Is on Your Side 835

LO 1: Discuss the difference between traditional costing and activity-based costing. 836
- Traditional Costing Systems 836
- Illustration of a Traditional Costing System 836
- The Need for a New Approach 837
- Activity-Based Costing 837

LO 2: Apply activity-based costing to a manufacturer. 840
- Identify and Classify Activities and Assign Overhead to Cost Pools (Step 1) 840
- Identify Cost Drivers (Step 2) 840
- Compute Activity-Based Overhead Rates (Step 3) 841
- Allocate Overhead Costs to Products (Step 4) 841
- Comparing Unit Costs 842

LO 3: Explain the benefits and limitations of activity-based costing. 845
- The Advantage of Multiple Cost Pools 845
- The Advantage of Enhanced Cost Control 846

The Advantage of Better Management Decisions 848
Some Limitations and Knowing When to Use ABC 849
LO 4: Apply activity-based costing to service industries. 850
Traditional Costing Example 851
Activity-Based Costing Example 852
LO *5: APPENDIX 4A: Explain just-in-time (JIT) processing. 855
Objective of JIT Processing 856
Elements of JIT Processing 856
Benefits of JIT Processing 856

18 Cost-Volume-Profit 882

Don't Worry—Just Get Big 883
LO 1: Explain variable, fixed, and mixed costs and the relevant range. 884
Variable Costs 884
Fixed Costs 885
Relevant Range 886
Mixed Costs 887
LO 2: Apply the high-low method to determine the components of mixed costs. 888
High-Low Method 889
Importance of Identifying Variable and Fixed Costs 891
LO 3: Prepare a CVP income statement to determine contribution margin. 892
Basic Components 892
CVP Income Statement 892
LO 4: Compute the break-even point using three approaches. 896
Mathematical Equation 896
Contribution Margin Technique 897
Graphic Presentation 898
LO 5: Determine the sales required to earn target net income and determine margin of safety. 899
Target Net Income 899
Margin of Safety 901

19 Cost-Volume-Profit Analysis: Additional Issues 922

Not Even a Flood Could Stop It 923
LO 1: Apply basic CVP concepts. 924
Basic Concepts 924
Basic Computations 925
CVP and Changes in the Business Environment 926
LO 2: Explain the term sales mix and its effects on break-even sales. 929
Break-Even Sales in Units 929
Break-Even Sales in Dollars 931
LO 3: Determine sales mix when a company has limited resources. 933
LO 4: Indicate how operating leverage affects profitability. 935
Effect on Contribution Margin Ratio 936
Effect on Break-Even Point 936
Effect on Margin of Safety Ratio 937
Operating Leverage 937
LO *5: APPENDIX 19A: Explain the differences between absorption costing and variable costing. 940
Example: Comparing Absorption Costing with Variable Costing 940
Net Income Effects 942
Decision-Making Concerns 946
Potential Advantages of Variable Costing 948

20 Incremental Analysis 974

Keeping It Clean 975
LO 1: Describe management's decision-making process and incremental analysis. 976
Incremental Analysis Approach 976
How Incremental Analysis Works 977
Qualitative Factors 978
Relationship of Incremental Analysis and Activity-Based Costing 978
Types of Incremental Analysis 979
LO 2: Analyze the relevant costs in accepting an order at a special price. 979
LO 3: Analyze the relevant costs in a make-or-buy decision. 981
Opportunity Cost 982
LO 4: Analyze the relevant costs in determining whether to sell or process materials further. 983
Single-Product Case 984
Multiple-Product Case 984
LO 5: Analyze the relevant costs to be considered in repairing, retaining, or replacing equipment. 987
LO 6: Analyze the relevant costs in deciding whether to eliminate an unprofitable segment or product. 988

21 Budgetary Planning 1014

What's in Your Cupcake? 1015
LO 1: State the essentials of effective budgeting and the components of the master budget. 1016
Budgeting and Accounting 1016
The Benefits of Budgeting 1016
Essentials of Effective Budgeting 1016
The Master Budget 1019
LO 2: Prepare budgets for sales, production, and direct materials. 1021
Sales Budget 1021

Production Budget 1022
Direct Materials Budget 1023
LO 3: Prepare budgets for direct labor, manufacturing overhead, and selling and administrative expenses, and a budgeted income statement. 1026
Direct Labor Budget 1026
Manufacturing Overhead Budget 1027
Selling and Administrative Expense Budget 1028
Budgeted Income Statement 1028
LO 4: Prepare a cash budget and a budgeted balance sheet. 1030
Cash Budget 1030
Budgeted Balance Sheet 1033
LO 5: Apply budgeting principles to nonmanufacturing companies. 1035
Merchandisers 1035
Service Companies 1036
Not-for-Profit Organizations 1037

22 Budgetary Control and Responsibility Accounting 1064

Pumpkin Madeleines and a Movie 1065
LO 1: Describe budgetary control and static budget reports. 1066
Budgetary Control 1066
Static Budget Reports 1067
LO 2: Prepare flexible budget reports. 1069
Why Flexible Budgets? 1069
Developing the Flexible Budget 1072
Flexible Budget—A Case Study 1072
Flexible Budget Reports 1074
LO 3: Apply responsibility accounting to cost and profit centers. 1076
Controllable Versus Noncontrollable Revenues and Costs 1078
Principles of Performance Evaluation 1078
Responsibility Reporting System 1080
Types of Responsibility Centers 1082
LO 4: Evaluate performance in investment centers. 1085
Return on Investment (ROI) 1085
Responsibility Report 1086
Judgmental Factors in ROI 1087
Improving ROI 1087
LO *5: APPENDIX 22A: Explain the difference between ROI and residual income. 1091
Residual Income Compared to ROI 1091
Residual Income Weakness 1092

23 Standard Costs and Balanced Scorecard 1118

80,000 Different Caffeinated Combinations 1119
LO 1: Describe standard costs. 1120
Distinguishing Between Standards and Budgets 1121
Setting Standard Costs 1121
LO 2: Determine direct materials variances. 1125
Analyzing and Reporting Variances 1125
Direct Materials Variances 1126
LO 3: Determine direct labor and total manufacturing overhead variances. 1129
Direct Labor Variances 1129
Manufacturing Overhead Variances 1131
LO 4: Prepare variance reports and balanced scorecards. 1133
Reporting Variances 1133
Income Statement Presentation of Variances 1134
Balanced Scorecard 1135
LO *5: APPENDIX 23A: Identify the features of a standard cost accounting system. 1139
Journal Entries 1139
Ledger Accounts 1141
LO *6: APPENDIX 23B: Compute overhead controllable and volume variances. 1142
Overhead Controllable Variance 1142
Overhead Volume Variance 1143

24 Planning for Capital Investments 1166

Floating Hotels 1167
LO 1: Describe capital budgeting inputs and apply the cash payback technique. 1168
Cash Flow Information 1168
Illustrative Data 1169
Cash Payback 1169
LO 2: Use the net present value method. 1171
Equal Annual Cash Flows 1172
Unequal Annual Cash Flows 1173
Choosing a Discount Rate 1174
Simplifying Assumptions 1175
Comprehensive Example 1175
LO 3: Identify capital budgeting challenges and refinements. 1176
Intangible Benefits 1176
Profitability Index for Mutually Exclusive Projects 1178
Risk Analysis 1180
Post-Audit of Investment Projects 1180
LO 4: Use the internal rate of return method. 1182
Comparing Discounted Cash Flow Methods 1183
LO 5: Use the annual rate of return method. 1184

A Specimen Financial Statements: Apple Inc. A-1

B Specimen Financial Statements: Columbia Sportswear Company B-1

C Specimen Financial Statements: VF Corporation C-1

D Specimen Financial Statements: Amazon.com, Inc. D-1

E Specimen Financial Statements: Wal-Mart Stores, Inc. E-1

F Specimen Financial Statements: Louis Vuitton F-1

G Time Value of Money G-1

LO 1: Compute interest and future values. G-1
- Nature of Interest G-1
- Future Value of a Single Amount G-3
- Future Value of an Annuity G-4

LO 2: Compute present values. G-7
- Present Value Variables G-7
- Present Value of a Single Amount G-7
- Present Value of an Annuity G-9
- Time Periods and Discounting G-11
- Present Value of a Long-Term Note or Bond G-11

LO 3: Use a financial calculator to solve time value of money problems. G-13
- Present Value of a Single Sum G-14
- Present Value of an Annuity G-15
- Useful Applications of the Financial Calculator G-15

H Reporting and Analyzing Investments H-1

LO 1: Explain how to account for debt investments. H-1
- Why Corporations Invest H-1
- Accounting for Debt Investments H-3

LO 2: Explain how to account for stock investments. H-4
- Holdings of Less than 20% H-4
- Holdings Between 20% and 50% H-5
- Holdings of More than 50% H-6

LO 3: Discuss how debt and stock investments are reported in the financial statements. H-7
- Categories of Securities H-7
- Balance Sheet Presentation H-10
- Presentation of Realized and Unrealized Gain or Loss H-11
- Statement of Cash Flows Presentation H-12

*I Payroll Accounting I-1

LO 1: Record the payroll for a pay period. I-1
- Determining the Payroll I-2
- Recording the Payroll I-5

LO 2: Record employer payroll taxes. I-8
- FICA Taxes I-8
- Federal Unemployment Taxes I-8
- State Unemployment Taxes I-8
- Recording Employer Payroll Taxes I-9
- Filing and Remitting Payroll Taxes I-9

LO 3: Discuss the objectives of internal control for payroll. I-10

*J Subsidiary Ledgers and Special Journals J-1

LO 1: Describe the nature and purpose of a subsidiary ledger. J-1
- Subsidiary Ledger Example J-2
- Advantages of Subsidiary Ledgers J-3

LO 2: Record transactions in special journals. J-4
- Sales Journal J-4
- Cash Receipts Journal J-7
- Purchases Journal J-11
- Cash Payments Journal J-13
- Effects of Special Journals on the General Journal J-16
- Cyber Security: A Final Comment J-17

*K Accounting for Partnerships K-1

LO 1: Discuss and account for the formation of a partnerships. K-1
- Characteristics of Partnerships K-2
- Organizations with Partnerships K-3
- Advantages and Disadvantages of Partnerships K-3
- The Partnership Agreement K-5
- Accounting for a Partnership Formation K-5

LO 2: Explain how to account for net income or net loss of a partnership. K-6
- Dividing Net Income or Net Loss K-6
- Partnership Financial Statements K-9

LO 3: Explain how to account for the liquidation of a partnerships. K-10
- No Capital Deficiency K-11
- Capital Deficiency K-12

LO 4: Prepare Journal entries when a partner is either admitted or withdraws. K-14
- Admission of a Partner K-14
- Withdrawal of a Partner K-18

*Available online.

*L Accounting for Sole Proprietorships L-1

LO 1: Identify the differences in equity accounts between a corporation and a sole proprietorship. L-1

LO 2: Understand what accounts increase and decrease owner's equity. L-2

Owner's Equity in a Sole Proprietorship L-2

Recording Transactions of a Proprietorship L-3

LO 3: Describe the differences between a retained earnings statement and an owner's equity statement. L-3

LO 4: Explain the process of closing the books for a sole proprietorship. L-4

Preparing a Post-Closing Trail Balance for a Proprietorship L-7

*M Pricing M-1

LO 1: Compute a target cost when the market determines a product price. M-2

Target Costing M-3

LO 2: Compute a target selling price using cost-plus pricing. M-3

Cost-Plus Pricing M-3

Variable-Cost Pricing M-6

LO 3: Use time-and-material pricing to determine the cost of services provided. M-7

LO 4: Determine a transfer price using the negotiated, cost-based, and market-based approaches. M-9

Negotiated Transfer Prices M-10

Cost-Based Transfer Prices M-13

Market-Based Transfer Prices M-14

Effect of Outsourcing on Transfer Pricing M-15

Transfers Between Divisions in Different Countries M-15

LO 5: Determine prices using absorption-cost pricing and variable-cost pricing. M-15

Absorption-Cost Pricing M-16

Variable-Cost Pricing M-17

Company Index CI-1

Subject Index SI-1

*Available online.

Acknowledgments

Accounting has benefited greatly from the input of focus group participants, manuscript reviewers, those who have sent comments by letter or e-mail, ancillary authors, and proofers. We greatly appreciate the constructive suggestions and innovative ideas of reviewers and the creativity and accuracy of the ancillary authors and checkers.

Sixth Edition

Joe Atallah
Coastline Community College

Dennis Avola
Northeastern University

Melody Barta
Evergreen Valley College

Thomas Bednarcik
Robert Morris University Illinois

Martin Blaine
Columbus State Community College

Bradley Blaylock
Oklahoma State University

Gary Bower
Community College of Rhode Island

Robert Braun
Southeastern Louisiana University

Lou Bravo
North Lake College

Ann K Brooks
University of New Mexico

Robert Brown
Evergreen Valley College

Myra Bruegger
Southeastern Community College

Barry Buchoff
Towson University

Melodi Bunting
Edgewood College

Matthew Calderisi
Fairleigh Dickinson University

Julia Camp
Providence College

Marian Canada
Ivy Tech Community College at Franklin

Sandy Cereola
James Madison University

James Chiafery
University of Massachusetts—Boston

Bea Chiang
The College of New Jersey

Colleen Chung
Miami Dade College

Shifei Chung
Rowan University

Tony Cioffi
Lorain County Community College

Cheryl Clark
Point Park University

Leslie Cohen
University of Arizona

Maxine Cohen
Bergen Community College

Stephen Collins
University of Massachusetts—Lowell

Solveg Cooper
Cuesta College

William Cooper
North Carolina A&T State University

Jim Coughlin
Robert Morris University

Patricia Crenny
Villanova University

Dori Danko
Grand Valley State University

Alan E. Davis
Community College of Philadelphia

Mingcherng Deng
Baruch College

Michael Deschamps
MiraCosta College

Bettye Desselle
Texas Southern University

Cyril Dibie
Tarrant County College—Arlington

Jean Dunn
Rady School of Management at University of California—San Diego

Kathy Dunne
Rider University

Barbara Durham
University of Central Florida

Dennis Elam
Texas A&M University—San Antonio

David Emerson
Salisbury University

James Emig
Villanova University

Caroline Falconetti
Nassau Community College

Nancy Fan
California State Polytechnic University, Pomona

Magdy Farag
California State Polytechnic University, Pomona

Linda Flaming
Monmouth University

Joseph Fournier
University of Rhode Island

Jeanne Franco
Paradise Valley Community College

Patrick Geer
Hawkeye Community College

Amy Geile
University of Arizona

Alan Glaser
Franklin & Marshall College

J. D. Golub
Northeastern University

Rita Grant
Grand Valley State University

Steve Groves
Ivy Tech Community College

Konrad Gunderson
Missouri Western State University

Marcye Hampton
University of Central Florida

Qian Hao
Wilkes University

Huong Higgins
Worcester Polytechnic Institute

John Hogan
Fisher College

Yongtao Hong
North Dakota State University

M.A. Houston
Wright State University

Jeff Hsu
St. Louis Community College—Meramec

Robert Hurst
Franklin University

Wayne Ingalls
University of Maine

Janet Jamieson
University of Dubuque

Jennifer Joe
University of Delaware

James B. Johnson
Community College of Philadelphia

Patricia Johnson
Canisius College

Kevin Jones
Drexel University

Jordan Kanter
University of Rhode Island

Ann Galligan Kelley
Providence College

Robert Kenny
The College of New Jersey

Emil Koren
Saint Leo University

Lynn Krausse
Bakersfield College

Steven LaFave
Augsburg College

Faith Lamprey
Providence College

Gary Laycock
Ivy Tech Community College

Charles Leflar
University of Arkansas

Jennifer LeSure
Ivy Tech Community College

Claudia Lubaski
Lorain County Community College

Yuanyuan Ma
University of Minnesota

Suneel Maheshwari
Marshall University

Diane Marker
University of Toledo

Christian Mastilak
Xavier University

Josephine Mathias
Mercer County Community College

Don McFall
Hiram College

Edward McGinnis
American River College

Allison McLeod
University of North Texas

Mary Michel
Manhattan College

Joan Miller
William Paterson University

Maha Mitrelis
Providence College

Syed Moiz
University of Wisconsin—Platteville

Louella Moore
Washburn University

Johnna Murray
University of Missouri—St. Louis

Sia Nassiripour
William Paterson University

Joseph Nesi
Monmouth University

Lee Nicholas
University of Northern Iowa

Cindy Nye
Bellevue University

Obeua Parsons
Rider University

Glenn Pate
Palm Beach State College

Suzy Pearse
Clemson University

Nori Pearson
Washington State University

Joe Pecore
Rady School of Management at University of California—San Diego

Rachel Pernia
Essex County College

Timothy Peterson
Gustavus Adolphus College

George Psaras
Aurora University

Patrick Reihing
Nassau Community College

Jim Resnik
Bergen Community College

John Ribezzo
Community College of Rhode Island

Vernon Richardson
University of Arkansas

Patrick Rogan
Consumnes River College

Juan Roman
Saint Leo University

Jorge Romero
Towson University

Maria Roxas
Central Connecticut State University

John Rude
Bloomsburg University

Martin Rudnick
William Paterson University

Susan Sadowski
Shippensburg University

August Saibeni
Consumnes River College

Barbara Sandler
Queens College

Barbara Scofield
Washburn University

Chris Severson
Franklin University

Suzanne Seymoure
Saint Leo University

Abdus Shahid
The College of New Jersey

Mike Shapeero
Bloomsburg University

Todd Shawver
Bloomsburg University

Eileen Shifflett
James Madison University

Ladd Simms
Mississippi Valley State University

Karyn Smith
Georgia Perimeter College

Patrick Stegman
College of Lake County

Richard Steingart
San Jose State University

Doug Stives
Monmouth University

Gracelyn Stuart-Tuggle
Palm Beach State University

Karen Tabak
Maryville University

Tom Thompson
Savannah Technical College

Karen Tower
Ivy Tech Community College

Daniel Tschopp
Saint Leo University

Mike Tyler
Barry University

Jin Ulmer
Angelina College

Mark Ulrich
St. John's University

Linda Vaello
University of Texas—San Antonio

Manuel Valle
City College of San Francisco

Huey L. Van Dine
Bergen Community College

Claire Veal
University of Texas—San Antonio

Sheila Viel
University of Wisconsin—Milwaukee

Dan Way
Central Piedmont Community College

Nancy Wilburn
Northern Arizona University

Wayne W. Williams
Community College of Philadelphia

Hannah Wong
William Paterson University

Kenneth Zheng
University at Buffalo

Ancillary Authors, Contributors, Proofers, and Accuracy Checkers

We sincerely thank the following individuals for their hard work in preparing the content that accompanies this textbook:

Ellen Bartley
St. Joseph's College

LuAnn Bean
Florida Institute of Technology

Jack Borke
University of Wisconsin—Platteville

Melanie Bunting
Edgewood College

Bea Chiang
The College of New Jersey

Sandra Cohen
Columbia College—Chicago

James M. Emig
Villanova University

Larry R. Falcetto
Emporia State University

Heidi Hansel
Kirkwood Community College

Coby Harmon
University of California, Santa Barbara

Derek Jackson
St. Mary's University of Minnesota

DeAnna Kirchen
Golden West College

Kirk Lynch
Sandhills Community College

Kevin McNelis
New Mexico State University

Jill Misuraca
University of Tampa

Jill Mitchell
Northern Virginia Community College

Barb Muller
Arizona State University

Yvonne Phang
Borough of Manhattan Community College

George Psarsas
Aurora University

Laura Prosser
Black Hills State University

Alice Sineath
Forsyth Technical Community College

Teresa Speck
Saint Mary's University of Minnesota

Lynn Stallworth
Appalachian State University

Diane Tanner
University of North Florida

Mark Ulrich
St. John's University

Sheila Viel
University of Wisconsin—Milwaukee

Dick D. Wasson
Southwestern College

Melanie Yon

Lori Grady Zeher
Bucks County Community College

Advisory Board

Robert Braun
Southeastern Louisiana University

Jimmy Carmenate
Florida International University

Sandra Cereola
James Madison University

Rita Grant
Grand Valley State University

Marcye Hampton
University of Central Florida

Norma Holter
Towson University

Frank Ilett
Boise State University

Christine Kloezeman
Glendale Community College

Michelle Moshier
State University of New York—Albany

Johnna Murray
University of Missouri—St. Louis

Courtney Naismith
Collin College

Michael Newman
University of Houston

Nori Pearson
Washington State University

Pamela Rouse
Butler University

Karen Russom
Lone Star College—Greenspoint

Joel Sneed
University of Oregon

Chris Solomon
Trident Technical College

We thank Benjamin Huegel and Teresa Speck of St. Mary's University for their extensive efforts in the preparation of the homework materials related to Current Designs. We also appreciate the considerable support provided to us by the following people at Current Designs: Mike Cichanowski, Jim Brown, Diane Buswell, and Jake Greseth. We also benefited from the assistance and suggestions provided to us by Joan Lee in the preparation of materials related to sustainability.

We appreciate the exemplary support and commitment given to us by executive editor Michael McDonald, executive marketing manager Karolina Zarychta Honsa, development editor Ed Brislin, editorial assistant Elizabeth Kearns, development editors Terry Ann Tatro and Margaret Thompson, senior product designer Allie Morris, product designer Matt Origoni, designer Maureen Eide, photo editor Mary Ann Price, and Dennis Free at Aptara. All of these professionals provided innumerable services that helped the textbook take shape.

Finally, our thanks to Amy Scholz, George Hoffman, Tim Stookesberry, Douglas Reiner, Brent Gordon, and Mark Allin for their support and leadership in Wiley's Global Education. We will appreciate suggestions and comments from users—instructors and students alike. You can send your thoughts and ideas about the textbook to us via email at: *AccountingAuthors@yahoo.com*.

Paul D. Kimmel
Milwaukee, Wisconsin

Jerry J. Weygandt
Madison, Wisconsin

Donald E. Kieso
DeKalb, Illinois

12

Statement of Cash Flows

CHAPTER PREVIEW

The balance sheet, income statement, and retained earnings statement do not always show the whole picture of the financial condition of a company or institution. In fact, looking at the financial statements of some well-known companies, a thoughtful investor might ask questions like these: How did Eastman Kodak finance cash dividends of $649 million in a year in which it earned only $17 million? How could United Air Lines purchase new planes that cost $1.9 billion in a year in which it reported a net loss of over $2 billion? How did the companies that spent a combined fantastic $3.4 trillion on mergers and acquisitions in a recent year finance those deals? Answers to these and similar questions can be found in this chapter, which presents the statement of cash flows.

CHAPTER OUTLINE

LEARNING OBJECTIVES		PRACTICE
1 Discuss the usefulness and format of the statement of cash flows.	• Usefulness of the statement of cash flows • Classification of cash flows • Significant noncash activities • Format of the statement of cash flows	DO IT! 1 Cash Flow Activities
2 Prepare a statement of cash flows using the indirect method.	• Indirect and direct methods • Indirect method—Computer Services Company • Step 1: Operating activities • Summary of conversion to net cash provided by operating activities • Step 2: Investing and financing activities • Step 3: Net change in cash	DO IT! 2 2a Net Cash Provided by Operating Activities 2b Indirect Method
3 Use the statement of cash flows to evaluate a company.	• The corporate life cycle • Free cash flow	DO IT! 3 Free Cash Flow

Go to the ***REVIEW AND PRACTICE*** section at the end of the chapter for a targeted summary and exercises with solutions.

Visit **WileyPLUS** for additional tutorials and practice opportunities.

TonyV3112/Shutterstock

FEATURE STORY

Got Cash?

Companies must be ready to respond to changes quickly in order to survive and thrive. This requires careful management of cash. One company that managed cash successfully in its early years was Microsoft. During those years, the company paid much of its payroll by giving employees stock options (rights to purchase company stock in the future at a given price) instead of cash. This conserved cash and turned more than a thousand of its employees into millionaires.

In recent years, Microsoft has had a different kind of cash problem. Now that it has reached a more "mature" stage in life, it generates so much cash—roughly $1 billion per month—that it cannot always figure out what to do with it. At one time, Microsoft had accumulated $60 billion.

The company said it was accumulating cash to invest in new opportunities, buy other companies, and pay off pending lawsuits. Microsoft's stockholders complained that holding all this cash was putting a drag on the company's profitability. Why? Because Microsoft had the cash invested in very low-yielding government securities. Stockholders felt that the company either should find new investment projects that would bring higher returns, or return some of the cash to stockholders.

Finally, Microsoft announced a plan to return cash to stockholders by paying a special one-time $32 billion dividend. This special dividend was so large that, according to the U.S. Commerce Department, it caused total personal income in the United States to rise by 3.7% in one month—the largest increase ever recorded by the agency. (It also made the holiday season brighter, especially for retailers in the Seattle area.) Microsoft also doubled its regular annual dividend to $3.50 per share. Further, it announced that it would spend another $30 billion buying treasury stock.

Apple has also encountered this cash "problem." Apple recently had nearly $100 billion in liquid assets (cash, cash equivalents, and investment securities). It was generating $37 billion of cash per year from its operating activities but spending only about $7 billion on plant assets and purchases of patents. In response to shareholder pressure, Apple announced that it would begin to pay a quarterly dividend of $2.65 per share and buy back up to $10 billion of its stock. Analysts noted that the dividend consumes only $10 billion of cash per year. This leaves Apple wallowing in cash. The rest of us should have such problems.

Source: "Business: An End to Growth? Microsoft's Cash Bonanza," *The Economist* (July 23, 2005), p. 61.

LEARNING OBJECTIVE 1

Discuss the usefulness and format of the statement of cash flows.

The balance sheet, income statement, and retained earnings statement provide only limited information about a company's cash flows (cash receipts and cash payments). For example, comparative balance sheets show the increase in property, plant, and equipment during the year. But, they do not show how the additions were financed or paid for. The income statement shows net income. But, it does not indicate the amount of cash generated by operating activities. The retained earnings statement shows cash dividends declared but not the cash dividends paid during the year. None of these statements presents a detailed summary of where cash came from and how it was used.

USEFULNESS OF THE STATEMENT OF CASH FLOWS

The **statement of cash flows** reports the cash receipts and cash payments from operating, investing, and financing activities during a period, in a format that reconciles the beginning and ending cash balances. The information in a statement of cash flows helps investors, creditors, and others assess the following.

1. **The entity's ability to generate future cash flows.** By examining relationships between items in the statement of cash flows, investors make predictions of the amounts, timing, and uncertainty of future cash flows better than they can from accrual-basis data.
2. **The entity's ability to pay dividends and meet obligations.** If a company does not have adequate cash, it cannot pay employees, settle debts, or pay dividends. Employees, creditors, and stockholders should be particularly interested in this statement because it alone shows the flows of cash in a business.
3. **The reasons for the difference between net income and net cash provided (used) by operating activities.** Net income provides information on the success or failure of a business enterprise. However, some financial statement users are critical of accrual-basis net income because it requires many estimates. As a result, users often challenge the reliability of the number. Such is not the case with cash. Many readers of the statement of cash flows want to know the reasons for the difference between net income and net cash provided by operating activities. Then they can assess for themselves the reliability of the income number.
4. **The cash investing and financing transactions during the period.** By examining a company's investing and financing transactions, a financial statement reader can better understand why assets and liabilities changed during the period.

ETHICS NOTE
Though we would discourage reliance on cash flows to the exclusion of accrual accounting, comparing net cash provided by operating activities to net income can reveal important information about the "quality" of reported net income. Such a comparison can reveal the extent to which net income provides a good measure of actual performance.

CLASSIFICATION OF CASH FLOWS

The statement of cash flows classifies cash receipts and cash payments as operating, investing, and financing activities. Transactions and other events characteristic of each kind of activity are as follows.

1. **Operating activities** include the cash effects of transactions that create revenues and expenses. They thus enter into the determination of net income.
2. **Investing activities** include (a) cash transactions that involve the purchase or disposal of investments and property, plant, and equipment, and (b) lending money and collecting the loans.
3. **Financing activities** include (a) obtaining cash from issuing debt and repaying the amounts borrowed, and (b) obtaining cash from stockholders, repurchasing shares, and paying dividends.

The operating activities category is the most important. It shows the cash provided by company operations. This source of cash is generally considered to be the best measure of a company's ability to generate sufficient cash to continue as a going concern.

Illustration 12-1 lists typical cash receipts and cash payments within each of the three classifications. **Study the list carefully.** It will be very useful in solving homework exercises and problems.

ILLUSTRATION 12-1
Typical receipt and payment classifications

Types of Cash Inflows and Outflows

Operating activities—**Income statement items**
Cash inflows:
From sale of goods or services.
From interest received and dividends received.
Cash outflows:
To suppliers for inventory.
To employees for wages.
To government for taxes.
To lenders for interest.
To others for expenses.

Investing activities—**Changes in investments and long-term assets**
Cash inflows:
From sale of property, plant, and equipment.
From sale of investments in debt or equity securities of other entities.
From collection of principal on loans to other entities.
Cash outflows:
To purchase property, plant, and equipment.
To purchase investments in debt or equity securities of other entities.
To make loans to other entities.

Financing activities—**Changes in long-term liabilities and stockholders' equity**
Cash inflows:
From sale of common stock.
From issuance of debt (bonds and notes).
Cash outflows:
To stockholders as dividends.
To redeem long-term debt or reacquire capital stock (treasury stock).

Operating activities

Investing activities

Financing activities

Note the following general guidelines:

1. Operating activities involve income statement items.
2. Investing activities involve cash flows resulting from changes in investments and long-term asset items.
3. Financing activities involve cash flows resulting from changes in long-term liability and stockholders' equity items.

Companies classify as operating activities some cash flows related to investing or financing activities. For example, receipts of investment revenue (interest and dividends) are classified as operating activities. So are payments of interest to lenders. Why are these considered operating activities? **Because companies report these items in the income statement, where results of operations are shown.**

SIGNIFICANT NONCASH ACTIVITIES

Not all of a company's significant activities involve cash. Examples of significant noncash activities are:

1. Direct issuance of common stock to purchase assets.
2. Conversion of bonds into common stock.
3. Direct issuance of debt to purchase assets.
4. Exchanges of plant assets.

INTERNATIONAL NOTE
The statement of cash flows is very similar under GAAP and IFRS. One difference is that, under IFRS, noncash investing and financing activities are not reported in the statement of cash flows but instead are reported in the notes to the financial statements.

▼ **HELPFUL HINT**
Do not include **noncash** investing and financing activities in the body of the statement of cash flows. Report this information in a separate schedule below the statement of cash flows.

Companies do not report in the body of the statement of cash flows significant financing and investing activities that do not affect cash. Instead, they report these activities in either a **separate schedule** at the bottom of the statement of cash flows or in a **separate note or supplementary schedule** to the financial statements. The reporting of these noncash activities in a separate schedule satisfies the **full disclosure principle**.

In solving homework assignments, you should present significant noncash investing and financing activities in a separate schedule at the bottom of the statement of cash flows. (See the last entry in Illustration 12-2 for an example.)

ACCOUNTING ACROSS THE ORGANIZATION Target Corporation

Darren McCollester/Getty Images, Inc.

Net *What?*

Net income is not the same as net cash provided by operating activities. Below are some results from recent annual reports (dollars in millions), including Target Corporation. Note how the numbers differ greatly across the list even though all these companies engage in retail merchandising.

Company	Net Income	Net Cash Provided by Operating Activities
Kohl's Corporation	$ 889	$ 1,884
Wal-Mart Stores, Inc.	16,669	25,591
J. C. Penney Company, Inc.	(1,388)	(1,814)
Costco Wholesale Corp.	20,391	3,437
Target Corporation	1,971	6,520

In general, why do differences exist between net income and net cash provided by operating activities? (Go to **WileyPLUS** for this answer and additional questions.)

FORMAT OF THE STATEMENT OF CASH FLOWS

The general format of the statement of cash flows presents the results of the three activities discussed previously—operating, investing, and financing—plus the significant noncash investing and financing activities. Illustration 12–2 shows a widely used form of the statement of cash flows.

ILLUSTRATION 12-2
Format of statement of cash flows

COMPANY NAME
Statement of Cash Flows
For the Period Covered

Cash flows from operating activities		
(List of individual items)	XX	
Net cash provided (used) by operating activities		XXX
Cash flows from investing activities		
(List of individual inflows and outflows)	XX	
Net cash provided (used) by investing activities		XXX
Cash flows from financing activities		
(List of individual inflows and outflows)	XX	
Net cash provided (used) by financing activities		XXX
Net increase (decrease) in cash		XXX
Cash at beginning of period		XXX
Cash at end of period		XXX
Noncash investing and financing activities		
(List of individual noncash transactions)		XXX

The cash flows from operating activities section always appears first, followed by the investing activities section and then the financing activities section. The sum of the operating, investing, and financing activities sections equals the net increase or decrease in cash for the period. This amount is added to the beginning cash balance to arrive at the ending cash balance—the same amount reported on the balance sheet.

DO IT! ▶1 Cash Flow Activities

During its first week, Duffy & Stevenson Company had these transactions.

1. Issued 100,000 shares of $5 par value common stock for $800,000 cash.
2. Borrowed $200,000 from Castle Bank, signing a 5-year note bearing 8% interest.
3. Purchased two semi-trailer trucks for $170,000 cash.
4. Paid employees $12,000 for salaries and wages.
5. Collected $20,000 cash for services performed.

Classify each of these transactions by type of cash flow activity. (*Hint:* Refer to Illustration 12-1.)

SOLUTION

1. Financing activity
2. Financing activity
3. Investing activity
4. Operating activity
5. Operating activity

Related exercise material: **BE12-1, BE12-2, BE12-3, DO IT! 12-1, E12-1,** and **E12-2.**

Action Plan

- ✔ Identify the three types of activities used to report all cash inflows and outflows.
- ✔ Report as operating activities the cash effects of transactions that create revenues and expenses and enter into the determination of net income.
- ✔ Report as investing activities transactions that (a) acquire and dispose of investments and productive long-lived assets and (b) lend money and collect loans.
- ✔ Report as financing activities transactions that (a) obtain cash from issuing debt and repay the amounts borrowed and (b) obtain cash from stockholders and pay them dividends.

LEARNING OBJECTIVE ▶2 Prepare a statement of cash flows using the indirect method.

Companies prepare the statement of cash flows differently from the three other basic financial statements. First, it is not prepared from an adjusted trial balance. It requires detailed information concerning the changes in account balances that occurred between two points in time. An adjusted trial balance will not provide the necessary data. Second, the statement of cash flows deals with cash receipts and payments. As a result, the company **adjusts** the effects of the use of accrual accounting **to determine cash flows**.

The information to prepare this statement usually comes from three sources:

- **Comparative balance sheets.** Information in the comparative balance sheets indicates the amount of the changes in asset, liability, and stockholders' equity accounts from the beginning to the end of the period.
- **Current income statement.** Information in this statement helps determine the amount of net cash provided or used by operating activities during the period.
- **Additional information.** Such information includes transaction data that are needed to determine how cash was provided or used during the period.

Preparing the statement of cash flows from these data sources involves three major steps, explained in Illustration 12-3.

ILLUSTRATION 12-3
Three major steps in preparing the statement of cash flows

STEP 1: Determine net cash provided/used by operating activities by converting net income from an accrual basis to a cash basis.

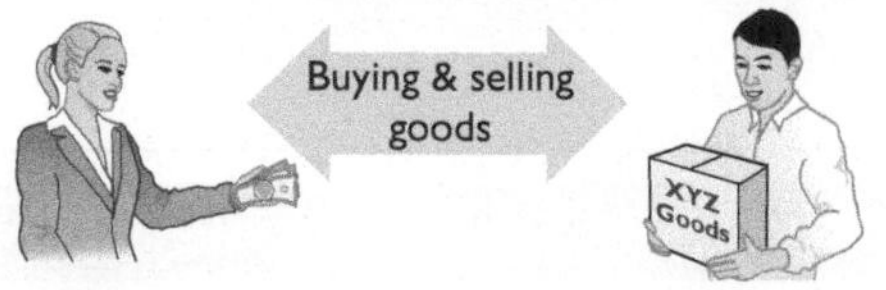

This step involves analyzing not only the current year's income statement but also comparative balance sheets and selected additional data.

STEP 2: Analyze changes in noncurrent asset and liability accounts and record as investing and financing activities, or disclose as noncash transactions.

This step involves analyzing comparative balance sheet data and selected additional information for their effects on cash.

STEP 3: Compare the net change in cash on the statement of cash flows with the change in the Cash account reported on the balance sheet to make sure the amounts agree.

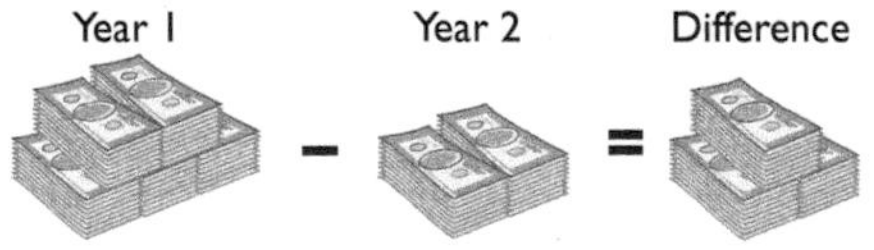

The difference between the beginning and ending cash balances can be easily computed from comparative balance sheets.

INDIRECT AND DIRECT METHODS

In order to perform Step 1, a company **must convert net income from an accrual basis to a cash basis**. This conversion may be done by either of two methods: (1) the indirect method or (2) the direct method. **Both methods arrive at the same total amount** for "Net cash provided by operating activities." They differ in **how** they arrive at the amount.

The **indirect method** adjusts net income for items that do not affect cash to determine net cash provided by operating activities. A great majority of companies (98%) use this method. Companies favor the indirect method for two reasons: (1) it is easier and less costly to prepare, and (2) it focuses on the differences between net income and net cash flow from operating activities.

The **direct method** shows operating cash receipts and payments. It is prepared by adjusting each item in the income statement from the accrual basis to the cash basis. The FASB has expressed a preference for the direct method but allows the use of either method.

The next section illustrates the more popular indirect method. Appendix 12A illustrates the direct method. Appendix 12B demonstrates an approach that employs T-accounts to prepare the statement of cash flows. Many students find the T-account approach provides a useful structure. We encourage you to give it a try as you walk through the Computer Services example.

INDIRECT METHOD—COMPUTER SERVICES COMPANY

To explain how to prepare a statement of cash flows using the indirect method, we use financial information from Computer Services Company. Illustration 12-4 presents Computer Services' current- and previous-year balance sheets, its current-year income statement, and related financial information.

ILLUSTRATION 12-4
Comparative balance sheets, income statement, and additional information for Computer Services Company

COMPUTER SERVICES COMPANY
Comparative Balance Sheets
December 31

Assets	2017	2016	Change in Account Balance Increase/Decrease
Current assets			
Cash	$ 55,000	$ 33,000	$ 22,000 Increase
Accounts receivable	20,000	30,000	10,000 Decrease
Inventory	15,000	10,000	5,000 Increase
Prepaid expenses	5,000	1,000	4,000 Increase
Property, plant, and equipment			
Land	130,000	20,000	110,000 Increase
Buildings	160,000	40,000	120,000 Increase
Accumulated depreciation—buildings	(11,000)	(5,000)	6,000 Increase
Equipment	27,000	10,000	17,000 Increase
Accumulated depreciation—equipment	(3,000)	(1,000)	2,000 Increase
Total assets	$398,000	$138,000	
Liabilities and Stockholders' Equity			
Current liabilities			
Accounts payable	$ 28,000	$ 12,000	$ 16,000 Increase
Income taxes payable	6,000	8,000	2,000 Decrease
Long-term liabilities			
Bonds payable	130,000	20,000	110,000 Increase
Stockholders' equity			
Common stock	70,000	50,000	20,000 Increase
Retained earnings	164,000	48,000	116,000 Increase
Total liabilities and stockholders' equity	$398,000	$138,000	

COMPUTER SERVICES COMPANY
Income Statement
For the Year Ended December 31, 2017

Sales revenue		$507,000
Cost of goods sold	$150,000	
Operating expenses (excluding depreciation)	111,000	
Depreciation expense	9,000	
Loss on disposal of plant assets	3,000	
Interest expense	42,000	315,000
Income before income tax		192,000
Income tax expense		47,000
Net income		$145,000

Additional information for 2017:

1. Depreciation expense was comprised of $6,000 for building and $3,000 for equipment.
2. The company sold equipment with a book value of $7,000 (cost $8,000, less accumulated depreciation $1,000) for $4,000 cash.
3. Issued $110,000 of long-term bonds in direct exchange for land.
4. A building costing $120,000 was purchased for cash. Equipment costing $25,000 was also purchased for cash.
5. Issued common stock for $20,000 cash.
6. The company declared and paid a $29,000 cash dividend.

We now apply the three steps to the information provided for Computer Services.

STEP 1: OPERATING ACTIVITIES

DETERMINE NET CASH PROVIDED/USED BY OPERATING ACTIVITIES BY CONVERTING NET INCOME FROM AN ACCRUAL BASIS TO A CASH BASIS

To determine net cash provided by operating activities under the indirect method, companies **adjust net income in numerous ways**. A useful starting point is to understand **why** net income must be converted to net cash provided by operating activities.

Under generally accepted accounting principles, most companies use the accrual basis of accounting. As you have learned, this basis requires that a company record revenue when the performance obligation is satisfied and record expenses when incurred. Revenues include credit sales for which the company has not yet collected cash. Expenses incurred include some items that it has not yet paid in cash. Thus, under the accrual basis of accounting, net income is not the same as net cash provided by operating activities.

Therefore, under the **indirect method**, companies must adjust net income to convert certain items to the cash basis. The indirect method (or reconciliation method) starts with net income and converts it to net cash provided by operating activities. Illustration 12-5 lists the three types of adjustments.

ILLUSTRATION 12-5
Three types of adjustments to convert net income to net cash provided by operating activities

Net Income +/−	Adjustments	=	Net Cash Provided/ Used by Operating Activities
	• **Add back noncash expenses,** such as depreciation expense and amortization expense. • **Deduct gains and add losses** that resulted from investing and financing activities. • **Analyze changes** to noncash current asset and current liability accounts.		

We explain the three types of adjustments in the next three sections.

▼ **HELPFUL HINT**
Depreciation is similar to any other expense in that it reduces net income. It differs in that it does not involve a current cash outflow. That is why it must be added back to net income to arrive at net cash provided by operating activities.

Depreciation Expense

Computer Services' income statement reports depreciation expense of $9,000. Although depreciation expense reduces net income, it does not reduce cash. In other words, depreciation expense is a noncash charge. The company must add it back to net income to arrive at net cash provided by operating activities. Computer Services reports depreciation expense as follows in the statement of cash flows.

ILLUSTRATION 12-6
Adjustment for depreciation

Cash flows from operating activities	
Net income	$145,000
Adjustments to reconcile net income to net cash provided by operating activities:	
Depreciation expense	9,000
Net cash provided by operating activities	$154,000

As the first adjustment to net income in the statement of cash flows, companies frequently list depreciation and similar noncash charges such as amortization of intangible assets and bad debt expense.

Loss on Disposal of Plant Assets

Illustration 12-1 states that cash received from the sale of plant assets is reported in the investing activities section. Because of this, **companies eliminate from net income all gains and losses resulting from investing activities, to arrive at net cash provided by operating activities.**

In our example, Computer Services' income statement reports a $3,000 loss on the disposal of plant assets (book value $7,000, less cash received from sale of equipment $4,000). The company's loss of $3,000 is eliminated in the operating activities section of the statement of cash flows. Illustration 12-7 shows that the $3,000 loss is eliminated by adding $3,000 back to net income to arrive at net cash provided by operating activities.

ILLUSTRATION 12-7
Adjustment for loss on disposal of plant assets

Cash flows from operating activities		
Net income		$145,000
Adjustments to reconcile net income to net cash provided by operating activities:		
Depreciation expense	$9,000	
Loss on disposal of plant assets	3,000	12,000
Net cash provided by operating activities		$157,000

If a gain on sale occurs, the company deducts the gain from net income in order to determine net cash provided by operating activities. **In the case of either a gain or a loss, companies report the actual amount of cash received from the sale, in this case $4,000, as a source of cash in the investing activities section of the statement of cash flows.**

Changes to Noncash Current Asset and Current Liability Accounts

A final step to reconcile net income to net cash provided by operating activities involves examining all changes in current asset and current liability accounts. The accrual-accounting process records revenues in the period in which the performance obligation is satisfied and expenses in the period incurred. For example, Accounts Receivable reflects amounts owed to the company for sales that have been made but for which cash collections have not yet been received. Prepaid Insurance reflects insurance that has been paid for but which has not yet expired and therefore has not been expensed. Similarly, Salaries and Wages Payable reflects salaries expense that has been incurred but has not been paid.

As a result, we need to adjust net income for these accruals and prepayments to determine net cash provided by operating activities. Thus, we must analyze the change in each current asset and current liability account to determine its impact on net income and cash.

CHANGES IN NONCASH CURRENT ASSETS. The adjustments required for changes in noncash current asset accounts are as follows. **Deduct from net income increases in current asset accounts, and add to net income decreases in current asset accounts, to arrive at net cash provided by operating activities.** We observe these relationships by analyzing the accounts of Computer Services.

DECREASE IN ACCOUNTS RECEIVABLE Computer Services' accounts receivable decreased by $10,000 (from $30,000 to $20,000) during the period. This means that cash receipts were $10,000 higher than sales revenue. The analysis of the Accounts Receivable account in Illustration 12-8 reveals this $10,000 difference. Computer Services had $507,000 in sales revenue (as reported on the income statement), but it collected $517,000 in cash.

ILLUSTRATION 12-8
Analysis of accounts receivable

Accounts Receivable

1/1/17	Balance	30,000	Receipts from customers	517,000
	Sales revenue	507,000		
12/31/17	Balance	20,000		

As shown in Illustration 12-9, to adjust net income to net cash provided by operating activities, the company adds to net income the decrease of $10,000 in accounts receivable.

ILLUSTRATION 12-9
Adjustments for changes in current asset accounts

Cash flows from operating activities		
Net income		$145,000
Adjustments to reconcile net income to net cash provided by operating activities:		
Depreciation expense	$ 9,000	
Loss on disposal of plant assets	3,000	
Decrease in accounts receivable	10,000	
Increase in inventory	(5,000)	
Increase in prepaid expenses	(4,000)	13,000
Net cash provided by operating activities		$158,000

When the Accounts Receivable balance increases, cash receipts are lower than revenue recorded under the accrual basis. Therefore, the company deducts from net income the amount of the increase in accounts receivable, to arrive at net cash provided by operating activities.

INCREASE IN INVENTORY Computer Services' inventory increased $5,000 (from $10,000 to $15,000) during the period. The change in the Inventory account reflects the difference between the amount of inventory purchased and the amount sold. For Computer Services, this means that the cost of merchandise purchased exceeded the cost of goods sold by $5,000. As a result, cost of goods sold does not reflect $5,000 of cash payments made for merchandise. The company deducts from net income this inventory increase of $5,000 during the period, to arrive at net cash provided by operating activities (see Illustration 12-9). If inventory decreases, the company adds to net income the amount of the change, to arrive at net cash provided by operating activities.

INCREASE IN PREPAID EXPENSES Computer Services' prepaid expenses increased during the period by $4,000. This means that cash paid for expenses is higher than expenses reported on an accrual basis. In other words, the company has made cash payments in the current period but will not charge expenses to income until future periods (as charges to the income statement). To adjust net income to net cash provided by operating activities, the company deducts from net income the $4,000 increase in prepaid expenses (see Illustration 12-9).

If prepaid expenses decrease, reported expenses are higher than the expenses paid. Therefore, the company adds to net income the decrease in prepaid expense, to arrive at net cash provided by operating activities.

CHANGES IN CURRENT LIABILITIES. The adjustments required for changes in current liability accounts are as follows. **Add to net income increases in current liability accounts, and deduct from net income decreases in current liability accounts, to arrive at net cash provided by operating activities.**

INCREASE IN ACCOUNTS PAYABLE For Computer Services, accounts payable increased by $16,000 (from $12,000 to $28,000) during the period. That means the company received $16,000 more in goods than it actually paid for. As shown in Illustration 12-10, to adjust net income to determine net cash provided by operating activities, the company adds to net income the $16,000 increase in the Accounts Payable account.

DECREASE IN INCOME TAXES PAYABLE When a company incurs income tax expense but has not yet paid its taxes, it records income taxes payable. A change in the Income Taxes Payable account reflects the difference between income tax expense incurred and income taxes actually paid. Computer Services' Income Taxes Payable account decreased by $2,000. That means the $47,000 of income tax expense reported on the income statement was $2,000 less than the amount of taxes paid during the period of $49,000. As shown in Illustration 12-10, to adjust net income to a cash basis, the company must reduce net income by $2,000.

ILLUSTRATION 12-10
Adjustments for changes in current liability accounts

Cash flows from operating activities		
Net income		$145,000
Adjustments to reconcile net income to net cash provided by operating activities:		
Depreciation expense	$ 9,000	
Loss on disposal of plant assets	3,000	
Decrease in accounts receivable	10,000	
Increase in inventory	(5,000)	
Increase in prepaid expenses	(4,000)	
Increase in accounts payable	**16,000**	
Decrease in income taxes payable	**(2,000)**	27,000
Net cash provided by operating activities		$172,000

Illustration 12-10 shows that after starting with net income of $145,000, the sum of all of the adjustments to net income was $27,000. This resulted in net cash provided by operating activities of $172,000.

SUMMARY OF CONVERSION TO NET CASH PROVIDED BY OPERATING ACTIVITIES—INDIRECT METHOD

As shown in the previous illustrations, the statement of cash flows prepared by the indirect method starts with net income. Items are then added or deducted to arrive at net cash provided by operating activities. The required adjustments are of three types:

1. Noncash charges such as depreciation and amortization.

2. Gains and losses from investing and financing transactions, such as the sale of plant assets.
3. Changes in noncash current asset and current liability accounts.

Illustration 12-11 provides a summary of these changes.

ILLUSTRATION 12-11
Adjustments required to convert net income to net cash provided by operating activities

		Adjustment Required to Convert Net Income to Net Cash Provided by Operating Activities
Noncash charges	Depreciation expense	Add
	Amortization expense	Add
Gains and losses	Loss on disposal of plant assets	Add
	Gain on disposal of plant assets	Deduct
Changes in current assets and current liabilities	Increase in current asset account	Deduct
	Decrease in current asset account	Add
	Increase in current liability account	Add
	Decrease in current liability account	Deduct

ANATOMY OF A FRAUD

For more than a decade, the top executives at the Italian dairy products company Parmalat engaged in multiple frauds that overstated cash and other assets by more than $1 billion while understating liabilities by between $8 and $12 billion. Much of the fraud involved creating fictitious sources and uses of cash. Some of these activities incorporated sophisticated financial transactions with subsidiaries created with the help of large international financial institutions. However, much of the fraud employed very basic, even sloppy, forgery of documents. For example, when outside auditors requested confirmation of bank accounts (such as a fake $4.8 billion account in the Cayman Islands), documents were created on scanners, with signatures that were cut and pasted from other documents. These were then passed through a fax machine numerous times to make them look real (if difficult to read). Similarly, fictitious bills were created in order to divert funds to other businesses owned by the Tanzi family (who controlled Parmalat).

Total take: Billions of dollars

THE MISSING CONTROL

Independent internal verification. Internal auditors at the company should have independently verified bank accounts and major transfers of cash to outside companies that were controlled by the Tanzi family.

DO IT! 2a Net Cash Provided by Operating Activities

Josh's PhotoPlus reported net income of $73,000 for 2017. Included in the income statement were depreciation expense of $7,000 and a gain on disposal of plant assets of $2,500. Josh's comparative balance sheets show the following balances.

	12/31/17	12/31/16
Accounts Receivable	$21,000	$17,000
Accounts Payable	2,200	6,000

Calculate net cash provided by operating activities for Josh's PhotoPlus.

SOLUTION

Cash flows from operating activities		
Net income		$73,000
Adjustments to reconcile net income to net cash provided by operating activities:		
Depreciation expense	$ 7,000	
Gain on disposal of plant assets	(2,500)	
Increase in accounts receivable	(4,000)	
Decrease in accounts payable	(3,800)	(3,300)
Net cash provided by operating activities		$69,700

Related exercise material: **BE12-4, BE12-5, BE12-6, DO IT! 12-2a, E12-3,** and **E12-4.**

Action Plan

- ✔ Add noncash charges such as depreciation back to net income to compute net cash provided by operating activities.
- ✔ Deduct gains and add back losses from the disposal of plant assets to compute net cash provided by operating activities.
- ✔ Use changes in noncash current asset and current liability accounts to compute net cash provided by operating activities.

STEP 2: INVESTING AND FINANCING ACTIVITIES

ANALYZE CHANGES IN NONCURRENT ASSET AND LIABILITY ACCOUNTS AND RECORD AS INVESTING AND FINANCING ACTIVITIES, OR DISCLOSE AS NONCASH TRANSACTIONS

INCREASE IN LAND As indicated from the change in the Land account and the additional information, Computer Services purchased land of $110,000 by directly exchanging bonds for land. The exchange of bonds payable for land has no effect on cash. But, it is a significant noncash investing and financing activity that merits disclosure in a separate schedule. (See Illustration 12–13, page 604.)

INCREASE IN BUILDINGS As the additional data indicate, Computer Services acquired an office building for $120,000 cash. This is a cash outflow reported in the investing activities section. (See Illustration 12–13.)

INCREASE IN EQUIPMENT The Equipment account increased $17,000. The additional information explains that this was a net increase that resulted from two transactions: (1) a purchase of equipment of $25,000, and (2) the sale for $4,000 of equipment costing $8,000. These transactions are both investing activities. The company should report each transaction separately. Thus, it reports the purchase of equipment as an outflow of cash for $25,000. It reports the sale as an inflow of cash for $4,000. The T-account below shows the reasons for the change in this account during the year.

▼ **HELPFUL HINT**
The investing and financing activities are measured and reported the same under both the direct and indirect methods.

ETHICS NOTE
Because investors and management bonus contracts often focus on cash flow from operations, some managers have taken unethical actions to artificially increase cash flow from operations. For example, Dynegy restated its statement of cash flows because it had improperly included in operating activities $300 million that should have been reported as financing activities. This error increased cash from operating activities by 37%.

ILLUSTRATION 12-12
Analysis of equipment

Equipment

1/1/17	Balance	10,000	Cost of equipment sold	8,000
	Purchase of equipment	**25,000**		
12/31/17	Balance	27,000		

The following entry shows the details of the equipment sale transaction.

			A	= L + SE
Cash	4,000		+4,000	
Accumulated Depreciation—Equipment	1,000		+1,000	
Loss on Disposal of Plant Assets	3,000			−3,000 Exp
Equipment		8,000	−8,000	

Cash Flows
+4,000

INCREASE IN BONDS PAYABLE The Bonds Payable account increased $110,000. As indicated in the additional information, the company acquired land by directly exchanging bonds for land. It reports this noncash transaction in a separate schedule at the bottom of the statement.

▼ HELPFUL HINT
When companies issue stocks or bonds for cash, the actual proceeds will appear in the statement of cash flows as a financing inflow (rather than the par value of the stocks or face value of bonds).

INCREASE IN COMMON STOCK The balance sheet reports an increase in Common Stock of $20,000. The additional information section notes that this increase resulted from the issuance of new shares of stock. This is a cash inflow reported in the financing activities section.

INCREASE IN RETAINED EARNINGS Retained earnings increased $116,000 during the year. This increase can be explained by two factors: (1) net income of $145,000 increased retained earnings, and (2) dividends of $29,000 decreased retained earnings. The company adjusts net income to net cash provided by operating activities in the operating activities section. Payment of the dividends (not the declaration) is a **cash outflow that the company reports as a financing activity**.

Statement of Cash Flows—2017

Using the previous information, we can now prepare a statement of cash flows for 2017 for Computer Services Company, as shown in Illustration 12-13.

ILLUSTRATION 12-13
Statement of cash flows, 2017—indirect method

COMPUTER SERVICES COMPANY
Statement of Cash Flows—Indirect Method
For the Year Ended December 31, 2017

Cash flows from operating activities		
Net income		$ 145,000
Adjustments to reconcile net income to net cash provided by operating activities:		
Depreciation expense	$ 9,000	
Loss on disposal of plant assets	3,000	
Decrease in accounts receivable	10,000	
Increase in inventory	(5,000)	
Increase in prepaid expenses	(4,000)	
Increase in accounts payable	16,000	
Decrease in income taxes payable	(2,000)	27,000
Net cash provided by operating activities		172,000
Cash flows from investing activities		
Sale of equipment	4,000	
Purchase of building	(120,000)	
Purchase of equipment	(25,000)	
Net cash used by investing activities		(141,000)
Cash flows from financing activities		
Issuance of common stock	20,000	
Payment of cash dividends	(29,000)	
Net cash used by financing activities		(9,000)
Net increase in cash		22,000
Cash at beginning of period		33,000
Cash at end of period		$ 55,000
Noncash investing and financing activities		
Issuance of bonds payable to purchase land		$ 110,000

▼ HELPFUL HINT
Note that in the investing and financing activities sections, positive numbers indicate cash inflows (receipts), and negative numbers indicate cash outflows (payments).

STEP 3: NET CHANGE IN CASH

COMPARE THE NET CHANGE IN CASH ON THE STATEMENT OF CASH FLOWS WITH THE CHANGE IN THE CASH ACCOUNT REPORTED ON THE BALANCE SHEET TO MAKE SURE THE AMOUNTS AGREE

Illustration 12-13 indicates that the net change in cash during the period was an increase of $22,000. This agrees with the change in Cash account reported on the balance sheet in Illustration 12-4 (page 597).

ACCOUNTING ACROSS THE ORGANIZATION

© Soubrette/iStockphoto

Burning Through Our Cash

Box (cloud storage), Cyan (game creator), Fireeye (cyber security), and Mobile Iron (mobile security of data) are a few of the tech companies that recently have issued or are about to issue stock to the public. Investors now have to determine whether these tech companies have viable products and high chances for success.

An important consideration in evaluating a tech company is determining its financial flexibility—its ability to withstand adversity if an economic setback occurs. One way to measure financial flexibility is to assess a company's cash burn rate, which determines how long its cash will hold out if the company is expending more cash than it is receiving.

Fireeye, for example, burned cash in excess of $50 million in 2013. But the company also had over $150 million as a cash cushion, so it would take over 30 months before it runs out of cash. And even though Box has a much lower cash burn rate than Fireeye, it still has over a year's cushion. Compare that to the tech companies in 2000, when over one-quarter of them were on track to run out of cash within a year. And many did. Fortunately, the tech companies of today seem to be better equipped to withstand an economic setback.

Source: Shira Ovide, "Tech Firms' Cash Hoards Cool Fears of a Meltdown," *Wall Street Journal* (May 14, 2014).

What implications does a company's cash burn rate have for its survival? (See **WileyPLUS** for this answer and additional questions.)

DO IT! 2b Indirect Method

Use the following information to prepare a statement of cash flows using the indirect method.

REYNOLDS COMPANY
Comparative Balance Sheets
December 31

Assets	**2017**	**2016**	**Change Increase/Decrease**
Cash	$ 54,000	$ 37,000	$ 17,000 Increase
Accounts receivable	68,000	26,000	42,000 Increase
Inventory	54,000	–0–	54,000 Increase
Prepaid expenses	4,000	6,000	2,000 Decrease
Land	45,000	70,000	25,000 Decrease
Buildings	200,000	200,000	–0–
Accumulated depreciation—buildings	(21,000)	(11,000)	10,000 Increase
Equipment	193,000	68,000	125,000 Increase
Accumulated depreciation—equipment	(28,000)	(10,000)	18,000 Increase
Totals	$569,000	$386,000	
Liabilities and Stockholders' Equity			
Accounts payable	$ 23,000	$ 40,000	$ 17,000 Decrease
Accrued expenses payable	10,000	–0–	10,000 Increase
Bonds payable	110,000	150,000	40,000 Decrease
Common stock ($1 par)	220,000	60,000	160,000 Increase
Retained earnings	206,000	136,000	70,000 Increase
Totals	$569,000	$386,000	

REYNOLDS COMPANY
Income Statement
For the Year Ended December 31, 2017

Sales revenue		$890,000
Cost of goods sold	$465,000	
Operating expenses	221,000	
Interest expense	12,000	
Loss on disposal of equipment	2,000	700,000
Income before income taxes		190,000
Income tax expense		65,000
Net income		$125,000

Additional information:

1. Operating expenses include depreciation expense of $33,000.
2. Land was sold at its book value for cash.
3. Cash dividends of $55,000 were declared and paid in 2017.
4. Equipment with a cost of $166,000 was purchased for cash. Equipment with a cost of $41,000 and a book value of $36,000 was sold for $34,000 cash.
5. Bonds of $40,000 were redeemed at their face value for cash.
6. Common stock ($1 par) of $160,000 was issued for cash.

Action Plan

✔ Determine net cash provided/used by operating activities by adjusting net income for items that did not affect cash.

✔ Determine net cash provided/used by investing activities and financing activities.

✔ Determine the net increase/decrease in cash.

SOLUTION

REYNOLDS COMPANY
Statement of Cash Flows—Indirect Method
For the Year Ended December 31, 2017

Cash flows from operating activities		
Net income		$ 125,000
Adjustments to reconcile net income to net cash provided by operating activities:		
Depreciation expense	$ 33,000	
Loss on disposal of equipment	2,000	
Increase in accounts receivable	(42,000)	
Increase in inventory	(54,000)	
Decrease in prepaid expenses	2,000	
Decrease in accounts payable	(17,000)	
Increase in accrued expenses payable	10,000	(66,000)
Net cash provided by operating activities		59,000
Cash flows from investing activities		
Sale of land	25,000	
Sale of equipment	34,000	
Purchase of equipment	(166,000)	
Net cash used by investing activities		(107,000)
Cash flows from financing activities		
Redemption of bonds	(40,000)	
Sale of common stock	160,000	
Payment of dividends	(55,000)	
Net cash provided by financing activities		65,000
Net increase in cash		17,000
Cash at beginning of period		37,000
Cash at end of period		$ 54,000

Related exercise material: **BE12-4, BE12-5, BE12-6, BE12-7, DO IT! E12-2b, E12-5, E12-6,** and **E12-7.**

LEARNING OBJECTIVE **3** Use the statement of cash flows to evaluate a company.

Traditionally, investors and creditors used ratios based on accrual accounting. These days, cash-based ratios are gaining increased acceptance among analysts. In this section, we review the corporate life cycle and free cash flow.

THE CORPORATE LIFE CYCLE

All products go through a series of phases called the **product life cycle**. The phases (in order of their occurrence) are **introductory phase**, **growth phase**, **maturity phase**, and **decline phase**. The introductory phase occurs at the beginning of a company's life, when it purchases fixed assets and begins to produce and sell products. During the growth phase, the company strives to expand its production and sales. In the maturity phase, sales and production level off. During the decline phase, sales of the product decrease due to a weakening in consumer demand.

In the same way that products have life cycles, companies have life cycles as well. Companies generally have more than one product, and not all of a company's products are in the same phase of the product life cycle at the same time. This sometimes makes it difficult to classify a company's phase. Still, we can characterize a company as being in one of the four phases because the majority of its products are in a particular phase.

Illustration 12-14 shows that the phase a company is in affects its cash flows. In the **introductory phase**, we expect that the company will not generate positive cash from operations. That is, cash used in operations will exceed cash generated by operations in the introductory phase. Also, the company spends considerable amounts to purchase productive assets such as buildings and equipment. To support its asset purchases, the company issues stock or debt. Thus, during the introductory phase, we expect negative cash from operations, negative cash from investing, and positive cash from financing.

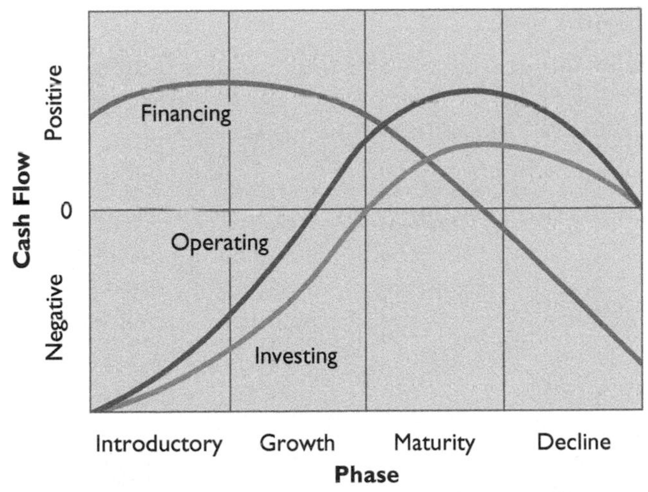

ILLUSTRATION 12-14
Impact of product life cycle on cash flows

During the **growth phase**, we expect to see the company start to generate small amounts of cash from operations. During this phase, net cash provided by operating activities on the statement of cash flows is less than net income. One reason net income exceeds cash flow from operations during this period is explained by the difference between the cash paid for inventory and the amount expensed as cost of goods sold. Since the company projects increasing sales, the size of inventory purchases increases. Thus, in the growth phase, the company expenses less inventory on an accrual basis than it purchases on a cash basis. Also, collections on accounts receivable lag behind sales, and accrual sales during a period exceed cash collections during that period. Cash needed for asset acquisitions will continue to exceed net cash provided by operating activities. The company makes up the deficiency by issuing new stock or debt. Thus, in the growth phase, the company continues to show negative cash from investing activities and positive cash from financing activities.

During the **maturity phase**, net cash provided by operating activities and net income are approximately the same. Cash generated from operations exceeds investing needs. Thus, in the maturity phase, the company starts to pay dividends, retire debt, or buy back stock.

Finally, during the **decline phase**, net cash provided by operating activities decreases. Cash from investing activities might actually become positive as the company sells off excess assets. Cash from financing activities may be negative as the company buys back stock and redeems debt.

Consider Microsoft. During its early years, it had significant product development costs and little revenue. Microsoft was lucky in that its agreement with IBM to provide the operating system for IBM PCs gave it an early steady source of cash to support growth. As noted in the Feature Story, Microsoft conserved cash by paying employees with stock options rather than cash. Today, Microsoft could be characterized as being in the maturity phase. It continues to spend considerable amounts on research and development and investment in new assets. In recent years, though, its net cash provided by operating activities has exceeded its net income. Also, cash from operations over this period exceeded cash used for investing, and common stock repurchased exceeded common stock issued. For Microsoft, as for any large company, the challenge is to maintain its growth. In the software industry, where products become obsolete very quickly, the challenge is particularly great.

INVESTOR INSIGHT

Neil Barclay/Retna

Operating with Negative Cash

Listed here are amounts (in millions) of net income and net cash provided (used) by operating, investing, and financing activities for a variety of companies at one time. The final column suggests each company's likely phase in the life cycle based on these figures.

Company	Net Income	Net Cash Provided (Used) by Operating Activities	Net Cash Provided (Used) by Investing Activities	Net Cash Provided (Used) by Financing Activities	Likely Phase in Life Cycle
Amazon.com	$ 476	$1,405	$ (42)	$ (50)	Early maturity
LDK Solar	(144)	(81)	(329)	462	Introductory/ early growth
United States Steel	879	1,745	(4,675)	(1,891)	Maturity
Kellogg	1,103	1,503	(601)	(788)	Early decline
Southwest Airlines	645	2,845	(1,529)	493	Maturity
Starbucks	673	1,331	(1,202)	(172)	Maturity

Why do companies have negative net cash provided by operating activities during the introductory phase? (Go to **WileyPLUS** for this answer and additional questions.)

FREE CASH FLOW

In the statement of cash flows, net cash provided by operating activities is intended to indicate the cash-generating capability of the company. Analysts have noted, however, that **cash provided by operating activities fails to take into account that a company must invest in new fixed assets** just to maintain its current level of operations. Companies also must at least **maintain dividends at current levels** to satisfy investors. As we discussed in Chapter 2, the measurement of free cash flow provides additional insight regarding a company's cash-generating ability. **Free cash flow** describes the net cash provided by operating activities after adjustment for capital expenditures and dividends.

DECISION TOOLS

Free cash flows helps users determine the amount of cash the company generated to expand operations or pay dividends.

Consider the following example. Suppose that MPC produced and sold 10,000 personal computers this year. It reported $100,000 cash provided by operating activities. In order to maintain production at 10,000 computers, MPC invested $15,000 in equipment. It chose to pay $5,000 in dividends. Its free cash flow was $80,000 ($100,000 − $15,000 − $5,000). The company could use this $80,000 either to purchase new assets, pay off debt, or pay an $80,000 dividend. In practice, free cash flow is often calculated with the formula in Illustration 12-15. Alternative definitions also exist.

ILLUSTRATION 12-15
Free cash flow

Free Cash Flow	=	Net Cash Provided by Operating Activities	−	Capital Expenditures	−	Cash Dividends

Illustration 12-16 provides basic information excerpted from the 2014 statement of cash flows of Apple (prior to the payment of its first dividends).

ILLUSTRATION 12-16
Apple's cash flow information ($ in millions)

Real World

APPLE INC.
Statement of Cash Flows Information (partial)
2014

Net cash provided by operating activities		$ 59,713
Cash flows from investing activities		
Additions to property and equipment and intangibles	$ (9,571)	
Purchases of investments	(217,128)	
Sales of investments	189,301	
Acquisitions of companies	(3,765)	
Maturities of investments	18,810	
Other	(226)	
Net cash used by investing activities		(22,579)
Cash paid for dividends		(11,126)

Apple's free cash flow is calculated as shown in Illustration 12-17 (in millions). Apple generated approximately $39 billion of free cash flow. This is a tremendous amount of cash generated in a single year. It is available for the acquisition of new assets, the buyback and retirement of stock or debt, or the payment of dividends.

ILLUSTRATION 12-17
Calculation of Apple's free cash flow ($ in millions)

Net cash provided by operating activities	$59,713
Less: Expenditures on property, plant, and equipment	9,571
Dividends paid	11,126
Free cash flow	$39,016

Also note that Apple's cash from operations of $59.7 billion exceeds its 2014 net income of $39.5 billion by $20.2 billion. This lends additional credibility to

Apple's income number as an indicator of potential future performance. If anything, Apple's net income might understate its actual performance.

KEEPING AN EYE ON CASH

Cash flow is closely monitored by analysts and investors for many reasons and in a variety of ways. One measure that is gaining increased attention is "price to cash flow." This is a variant of the price to earnings (P-E) ratio, which has been a staple of analysts for a long time. The difference is that rather than divide the company's stock price by its earnings per share (an accrual-accounting–based number), the price to cash flow ratio divides the company's stock price by its cash flow per share. A high measure suggests that the stock price is high relative to the company's ability to generate cash. A low measure indicates that the company's stock might be a bargain.

The following table provides values for some well-known companies in a recent year. While you should not use this measure as the sole factor in choosing a stock, it can serve as a useful screen by which to identify companies that merit further investigation.

Company	Price/Cash Flow	Price/EPS
Microsoft	55.6	62.5
Apple	11.1	12.5
Nike	19.1	24.8
Wal-Mart	9.0	15.7
Jet Blue	7.9	11.1

DO IT! 3 Free Cash Flow

Chicago Corporation issued the following statement of cash flows for 2017.

CHICAGO CORPORATION
Statement of Cash Flows—Indirect Method
For the Year Ended December 31, 2017

Cash flows from operating activities		
Net income		$ 19,000
Adjustments to reconcile net income to net cash provided by operating activities:		
Depreciation expense	$ 8,100	
Loss on disposal of plant assets	1,300	
Decrease in accounts receivable	6,900	
Increase in inventory	(4,000)	
Decrease in accounts payable	(2,000)	10,300
Net cash provided by operating activities		29,300
Cash flows from investing activities		
Sale of investments	1,100	
Purchase of equipment	(19,000)	
Net cash used by investing activities		(17,900)
Cash flows from financing activities		
Issuance of stock	10,000	
Payment on long-term note payable	(5,000)	
Payment for dividends	(9,000)	
Net cash used by financing activities		(4,000)
Net increase in cash		7,400
Cash at beginning of year		10,000
Cash at end of year		$ 17,400

(a) Compute free cash flow for Chicago Corporation. (b) Explain why free cash flow often provides better information than "Net cash provided by operating activities."

SOLUTION

(a) Free cash flow = $29,300 – $19,000 – $9,000 = $1,300

(b) Net cash provided by operating activities fails to take into account that a company must invest in new plant assets just to maintain the current level of operation. Companies must also maintain dividends at current levels to satisfy investors. The measurement of free cash flow provides additional insight regarding a company's cash-generating ability.

Action Plan

✔ Compute free cash flow as Net cash provided by operating activities – Capital expenditures – Cash dividends.

Related exercise material: **BE12-9, BE12-10, BE12-11, BE12-12, DO IT! 12-3, E12-9,** and **E12-10.**

USING DECISION TOOLS—INTEL CORPORATION

Intel Corporation is the leading producer of computer chips for personal computers. Its primary competitor is AMD. Financial statement data for Intel are provided below.

INTEL CORPORATION
Statement of Cash Flows
For the Year Ended December 31, 2014 (in millions)

	2014
Net cash provided by operating activities	$ 20,418
Net cash used for investing activities	(9,905)
Net cash used for financing activities	(13,626)
Net increase (decrease) in cash and cash equivalents	$ (3,113)

Note. Cash spent on property, plant, and equipment in 2014 was $10,105. Cash paid for dividends was $4,409.

INSTRUCTIONS

Calculate free cash flow for Intel and compare it with that of AMD (–$193 million).

SOLUTION

Intel's free cash flow is $5,904 million ($20,418 – $10,105 – $4,409). AMD's is –$193 million. This gives Intel a huge advantage in the ability to move quickly to invest in new projects.

LEARNING OBJECTIVE *4

APPENDIX 12A: Prepare a statement of cash flows using the direct method.

To explain and illustrate the direct method, we will use the transactions of Computer Services Company for 2017 to prepare a statement of cash flows. Illustration 12A-1 (page 612) presents information related to 2017 for the company.

ILLUSTRATION 12A-1
Comparative balance sheets, income statement, and additional information for Computer Services Company

COMPUTER SERVICES COMPANY
Comparative Balance Sheets
December 31

Assets	**2017**	**2016**	**Change in Account Balance Increase/Decrease**
Current assets			
Cash	$ 55,000	$ 33,000	$ 22,000 Increase
Accounts receivable	20,000	30,000	10,000 Decrease
Inventory	15,000	10,000	5,000 Increase
Prepaid expenses	5,000	1,000	4,000 Increase
Property, plant, and equipment			
Land	130,000	20,000	110,000 Increase
Buildings	160,000	40,000	120,000 Increase
Accumulated depreciation—buildings	(11,000)	(5,000)	6,000 Increase
Equipment	27,000	10,000	17,000 Increase
Accumulated depreciation—equipment	(3,000)	(1,000)	2,000 Increase
Total assets	$398,000	$138,000	
Liabilities and Stockholders' Equity			
Current liabilities			
Accounts payable	$ 28,000	$ 12,000	$ 16,000 Increase
Income taxes payable	6,000	8,000	2,000 Decrease
Long-term liabilities			
Bonds payable	130,000	20,000	110,000 Increase
Stockholders' equity			
Common stock	70,000	50,000	20,000 Increase
Retained earnings	164,000	48,000	116,000 Increase
Total liabilities and stockholders' equity	$398,000	$138,000	

COMPUTER SERVICES COMPANY
Income Statement
For the Year Ended December 31, 2017

Sales revenue		$507,000
Cost of goods sold	$150,000	
Operating expenses (excluding depreciation)	111,000	
Depreciation expense	9,000	
Loss on disposal of plant assets	3,000	
Interest expense	42,000	315,000
Income before income tax		192,000
Income tax expense		47,000
Net income		$145,000

Additional information for 2017:

1. Depreciation expense was comprised of $6,000 for building and $3,000 for equipment.
2. The company sold equipment with a book value of $7,000 (cost $8,000, less accumulated depreciation $1,000) for $4,000 cash.
3. Issued $110,000 of long-term bonds in direct exchange for land.
4. A building costing $120,000 was purchased for cash. Equipment costing $25,000 was also purchased for cash.
5. Issued common stock for $20,000 cash.
6. The company declared and paid a $29,000 cash dividend.

To prepare a statement of cash flows under the direct approach, we will apply the three steps outlined in Illustration 12-3 (page 596).

STEP 1: OPERATING ACTIVITIES

DETERMINE NET CASH PROVIDED/USED BY OPERATING ACTIVITIES BY CONVERTING NET INCOME FROM AN ACCRUAL BASIS TO A CASH BASIS

Under the **direct method**, companies compute net cash provided by operating activities by **adjusting each item in the income statement** from the accrual basis to the cash basis. To simplify and condense the operating activities section, companies **report only major classes of operating cash receipts and cash payments**. For these major classes, the difference between cash receipts and cash payments is the net cash provided by operating activities. These relationships are as shown in Illustration 12A-2.

ILLUSTRATION 12A-2
Major classes of cash receipts and payments

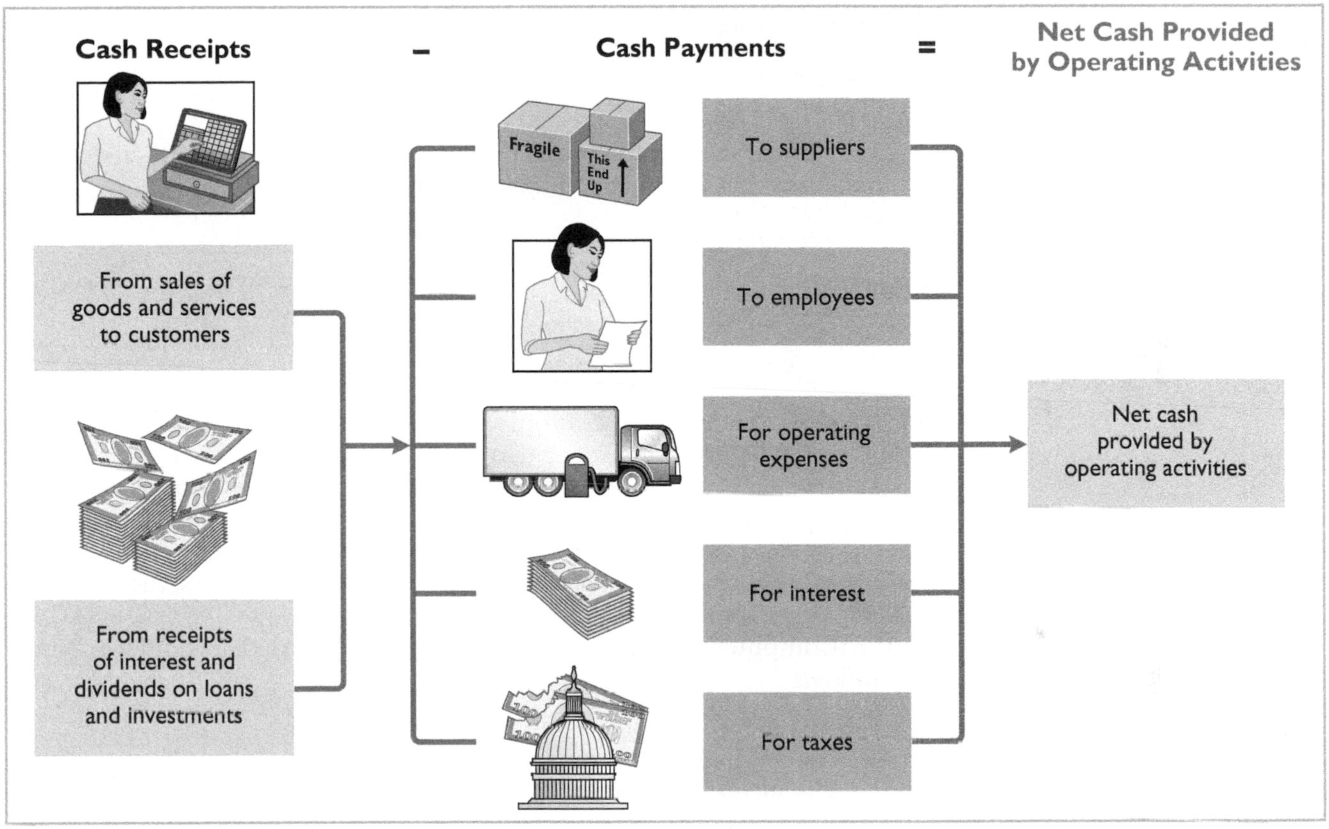

An efficient way to apply the direct method is to analyze the items reported in the income statement in the order in which they are listed. We then determine cash receipts and cash payments related to these revenues and expenses. The following pages present the adjustments required to prepare a statement of cash flows for Computer Services Company using the direct approach.

CASH RECEIPTS FROM CUSTOMERS The income statement for Computer Services reported sales revenue from customers of $507,000. How much of that was cash receipts? To answer that, companies need to consider the change in accounts receivable during the year. When accounts receivable increase during the year, revenues on an accrual basis are higher than cash receipts from customers. Operations led to revenues, but not all of these revenues resulted in cash receipts.

To determine the amount of cash receipts, the company deducts from sales revenue the increase in accounts receivable. On the other hand, there may be a decrease in accounts receivable. That would occur if cash receipts from customers exceeded sales revenue. In that case, the company adds to sales revenue the decrease in accounts receivable. For Computer Services, accounts receivable decreased $10,000. Thus, cash receipts from customers were $517,000, computed as shown in Illustration 12A-3.

ILLUSTRATION 12A-3
Computation of cash receipts from customers

Sales revenue	$ 507,000
Add: Decrease in accounts receivable	10,000
Cash receipts from customers	**$517,000**

Computer Services can also determine cash receipts from customers from an analysis of the Accounts Receivable account, as shown in Illustration 12A-4.

ILLUSTRATION 12A-4
Analysis of accounts receivable

Accounts Receivable

1/1/17	Balance	30,000	Receipts from customers	517,000
	Sales revenue	507,000		
12/31/17	Balance	20,000		

▼ **HELPFUL HINT**
The T-account shows that sales revenue plus decrease in accounts receivables equals cash receipts.

Illustration 12A-5 shows the relationships among cash receipts from customers, sales revenue, and changes in accounts receivable.

ILLUSTRATION 12A-5
Formula to compute cash receipts from customers—direct method

Cash Receipts from Customers	=	Sales Revenue	+ Decrease in Accounts Receivable or − Increase in Accounts Receivable

CASH PAYMENTS TO SUPPLIERS Computer Services reported cost of goods sold of $150,000 on its income statement. How much of that was cash payments to suppliers? To answer that, it is first necessary to find purchases for the year. To find purchases, companies adjust cost of goods sold for the change in inventory. When inventory increases during the year, purchases for the year have exceeded cost of goods sold. As a result, to determine the amount of purchases, the company adds to cost of goods sold the increase in inventory.

In 2017, Computer Services' inventory increased $5,000. It computes purchases as follows.

ILLUSTRATION 12A-6
Computation of purchases

Cost of goods sold	$ 150,000
Add: Increase in inventory	5,000
Purchases	**$155,000**

After computing purchases, a company can determine cash payments to suppliers. This is done by adjusting purchases for the change in accounts payable. When accounts payable increase during the year, purchases on an accrual basis are higher than they are on a cash basis. As a result, to determine cash payments to suppliers, a company deducts from purchases the increase in accounts payable. On the other hand, if cash payments to suppliers exceed purchases, there may be a decrease in accounts payable. In that case, a company adds to purchases the decrease in accounts payable. For Computer Services, cash payments to suppliers were $139,000, computed as follows.

ILLUSTRATION 12A-7
Computation of cash payments to suppliers

Purchases	$ 155,000
Deduct: Increase in accounts payable	16,000
Cash payments to suppliers	**$139,000**

Computer Services also can determine cash payments to suppliers from an analysis of the Accounts Payable account, as shown in Illustration 12A-8.

ILLUSTRATION 12A-8
Analysis of accounts payable

Accounts Payable

Payments to suppliers	139,000	1/1/17	Balance	12,000
			Purchases	155,000
		12/31/17	Balance	28,000

▼ **HELPFUL HINT**
The T-account shows that purchases less increase in accounts payable equals payments to suppliers.

Illustration 12A-9 shows the relationships among cash payments to suppliers, cost of goods sold, changes in inventory, and changes in accounts payable.

ILLUSTRATION 12A-9
Formula to compute cash payments to suppliers—direct method

Cash Payments to Suppliers	=	Cost of Goods Sold	+ Increase in Inventory or − Decrease in Inventory	+ Decrease in Accounts Payable or − Increase in Accounts Payable

CASH PAYMENTS FOR OPERATING EXPENSES Computer Services reported on its income statement operating expenses of $111,000. How much of that amount was cash paid for operating expenses? To answer that, we need to adjust this amount for any changes in prepaid expenses and accrued expenses payable. For example, if prepaid expenses increased during the year, cash paid for operating expenses is higher than operating expenses reported on the income statement. To convert operating expenses to cash payments for operating expenses, a company adds the increase in prepaid expenses to operating expenses. On the other hand, if prepaid expenses decrease during the year, it deducts the decrease from operating expenses.

Companies must also adjust operating expenses for changes in accrued expenses payable. When accrued expenses payable increase during the year, operating expenses on an accrual basis are higher than they are in a cash basis. As a result, to determine cash payments for operating expenses, a company deducts from operating expenses an increase in accrued expenses payable. On the other hand, a company adds to operating expenses a decrease in accrued expenses payable because cash payments exceed operating expenses.

Computer Services' cash payments for operating expenses were $115,000, computed as follows.

ILLUSTRATION 12A-10
Computation of cash payments for operating expenses

Operating expenses	$ 111,000
Add: Increase in prepaid expenses	4,000
Cash payments for operating expenses	**$115,000**

Illustration 12A-11 shows the relationships among cash payments for operating expenses, changes in prepaid expenses, and changes in accrued expenses payable.

ILLUSTRATION 12A-11
Formula to compute cash payments for operating expenses—direct method

Cash Payments for Operating Expenses	=	Operating Expenses	+ Increase in Prepaid Expense or − Decrease in Prepaid Expense	+ Decrease in Accrued Expenses Payable or − Increase in Accrued Expenses Payable

DEPRECIATION EXPENSE AND LOSS ON DISPOSAL OF PLANT ASSETS Computer Services' depreciation expense in 2017 was $9,000. Depreciation expense is not shown on a statement of cash flows under the direct method because it is a noncash charge. If the amount for operating expenses includes depreciation expense, operating expenses must be reduced by the amount of depreciation to determine cash payments for operating expenses.

The loss on disposal of plant assets of $3,000 is also a noncash charge. The loss on disposal of plant assets reduces net income, but it does not reduce cash. Thus, the loss on disposal of plant assets is not shown on the statement of cash flows under the direct method.

Other charges to expense that do not require the use of cash, such as the amortization of intangible assets and bad debt expense, are treated in the same manner as depreciation.

CASH PAYMENTS FOR INTEREST Computer Services reported on the income statement interest expense of $42,000. Since the balance sheet did not include an accrual for interest payable for 2016 or 2017, the amount reported as expense is the same as the amount of interest paid.

CASH PAYMENTS FOR INCOME TAXES Computer Services reported income tax expense of $47,000 on the income statement. Income taxes payable, however, decreased $2,000. This decrease means that income taxes paid were more than income taxes reported in the income statement. Cash payments for income taxes were, therefore, $49,000 as shown below.

ILLUSTRATION 12A-12
Computation of cash payments for income taxes

Income tax expense	$ 47,000
Add: Decrease in income taxes payable	2,000
Cash payments for income taxes	**$49,000**

Illustration 12A-13 shows the relationships among cash payments for income taxes, income tax expense, and changes in income taxes payable.

ILLUSTRATION 12A-13
Formula to compute cash payments for income taxes—direct method

Cash Payments for Income Taxes	=	**Income Tax Expense**	**+ Decrease in Income Taxes Payable** **or** **− Increase in Income Taxes Payable**

The operating activities section of the statement of cash flows of Computer Services is shown in Illustration 12A-14.

ILLUSTRATION 12A-14
Operating activities section of the statement of cash flows

Cash flows from operating activities		
Cash receipts from customers		$517,000
Less: Cash payments:		
To suppliers	$139,000	
For operating expenses	115,000	
For interest expense	42,000	
For income taxes	49,000	345,000
Net cash provided by operating activities		$172,000

When a company uses the direct method, it must also provide in a **separate schedule** (not shown here) the net cash flows from operating activities as computed under the indirect method.

STEP 2: INVESTING AND FINANCING ACTIVITIES

ANALYZE CHANGES IN NONCURRENT ASSET AND LIABILITY ACCOUNTS AND RECORD AS INVESTING AND FINANCING ACTIVITIES, OR DISCLOSE AS NONCASH TRANSACTIONS

INCREASE IN LAND As indicated from the change in the Land account and the additional information, Computer Services purchased land of $110,000 by directly exchanging bonds for land. The exchange of bonds payable for land has no effect on cash. But, it is a significant noncash investing and financing activity that merits disclosure in a separate schedule. (See Illustration 12A-16, page 618.)

▼ HELPFUL HINT
The investing and financing activities are measured and reported the same under both the direct and indirect methods.

INCREASE IN BUILDINGS As the additional data indicate, Computer Services acquired an office building for $120,000 cash. This is a cash outflow reported in the investing activities section. (See Illustration 12A-16, page 618.)

INCREASE IN EQUIPMENT The Equipment account increased $17,000. The additional information explains that this was a net increase that resulted from two transactions: (1) a purchase of equipment of $25,000, and (2) the sale for $4,000 of equipment costing $8,000. These transactions are investing activities. The company should report each transaction separately. The statement in Illustration 12A-16 reports the purchase of equipment as an outflow of cash for $25,000. It reports the sale as an inflow of cash for $4,000. The T-account below shows the reasons for the change in this account during the year.

ILLUSTRATION 12A-15
Analysis of equipment

Equipment

1/1/17	Balance	10,000	Cost of equipment sold	8,000
	Purchase of equipment	25,000		
12/31/17	Balance	27,000		

The following entry shows the details of the equipment sale transaction.

Cash	4,000	
Accumulated Depreciation—Equipment	1,000	
Loss on Disposal of Plant Assets	3,000	
Equipment		8,000

A	=	L	+	SE
+4,000				
+1,000				
				−3,000 Exp
−8,000				

Cash Flows
+4,000

INCREASE IN BONDS PAYABLE The Bonds Payable account increased $110,000. As indicated in the additional information, the company acquired land by directly exchanging bonds for land. Illustration 12A-16 reports this noncash transaction in a separate schedule at the bottom of the statement.

INCREASE IN COMMON STOCK The balance sheet reports an increase in Common Stock of $20,000. The additional information section notes that this increase resulted from the issuance of new shares of stock. This is a cash inflow reported in the financing activities section in Illustration 12A-16 (page 618).

▼ HELPFUL HINT
When companies issue stocks or bonds for cash, the actual proceeds will appear in the statement of cash flows as a financing inflow (rather than the par value of the stocks or face value of bonds).

INCREASE IN RETAINED EARNINGS Retained earnings increased $116,000 during the year. This increase can be explained by two factors: (1) net income of $145,000 increased retained earnings, and (2) dividends of $29,000 decreased retained earnings. The company adjusts net income to net cash provided by operating activities in the operating activities section. **Payment** of the dividends (not the declaration) is a **cash outflow that the company reports as a financing activity in Illustration 12A-16.**

Statement of Cash Flows—2017

Illustration 12A-16 (page 618) shows the statement of cash flows for Computer Services Company.

ILLUSTRATION 12A-16
Statement of cash flows, 2017—direct method

COMPUTER SERVICES COMPANY Statement of Cash Flows—Direct Method For the Year Ended December 31, 2017		
Cash flows from operating activities		
Cash receipts from customers		$ 517,000
Less: Cash payments:		
To suppliers	$ 139,000	
For operating expenses	115,000	
For income taxes	49,000	
For interest expense	42,000	345,000
Net cash provided by operating activities		172,000
Cash flows from investing activities		
Sale of equipment	4,000	
Purchase of building	(120,000)	
Purchase of equipment	(25,000)	
Net cash used by investing activities		(141,000)
Cash flows from financing activities		
Issuance of common stock	20,000	
Payment of cash dividends	(29,000)	
Net cash used by financing activities		(9,000)
Net increase in cash		22,000
Cash at beginning of period		33,000
Cash at end of period		$ 55,000
Noncash investing and financing activities		
Issuance of bonds payable to purchase land		$ 110,000

STEP 3: NET CHANGE IN CASH

COMPARE THE NET CHANGE IN CASH ON THE STATEMENT OF CASH FLOWS WITH THE CHANGE IN THE CASH ACCOUNT REPORTED ON THE BALANCE SHEET TO MAKE SURE THE AMOUNTS AGREE

Illustration 12A-16 indicates that the net change in cash during the period was an increase of $22,000. This agrees with the change in balances in the Cash account reported on the balance sheets in Illustration 12A-1 (page 612).

LEARNING OBJECTIVE *5

APPENDIX 12B: Use the T-account approach to prepare a statement of cash flows.

Many people like to use T-accounts to provide structure to the preparation of a statement of cash flows. The use of T-accounts is based on the accounting equation that you learned in Chapter 1. The basic equation is:

Assets = Liabilities + Equity

Now, let's rewrite the left-hand side as:

Cash + Noncash Assets = Liabilities + Equity

Next, rewrite the equation by subtracting Noncash Assets from each side to isolate Cash on the left-hand side:

Cash = Liabilities + Equity − Noncash Assets

Finally, if we insert the Δ symbol (which means "change in"), we have:

Δ Cash = Δ Liabilities + Δ Equity − Δ Noncash Assets

What this means is that the change in cash is equal to the change in all of the other balance sheet accounts. Another way to think about this is that if we analyze the changes in all of the noncash balance sheet accounts, we will explain the change in the Cash account. This, of course, is exactly what we are trying to do with the statement of cash flows.

To implement this approach, first prepare a large Cash T-account with sections for operating, investing, and financing activities. Then, prepare smaller T-accounts for all of the other noncash balance sheet accounts. Insert the beginning and ending balances for each of these accounts. Once you have done this, then walk through the steps outlined in Illustration 12-3 (page 596). As you walk through the steps, enter debit and credit amounts into the affected accounts. When all of the changes in the T-accounts have been explained, you are done. To demonstrate, we will apply this approach to the example of Computer Services Company that is presented in the chapter. Each of the adjustments in Illustration 12B-1 is numbered so you can follow them through the T-accounts.

ILLUSTRATION 12B-1
T-account approach

Cash

Operating			
(1) Net income	145,000	5,000	Inventory (5)
(2) Depreciation expense	9,000	4,000	Prepaid expenses (6)
(3) Loss on equipment	3,000	2,000	Income taxes payable (8)
(4) Accounts receivable	10,000		
(7) Accounts payable	16,000		
Net cash provided by operating activities	172,000		
Investing			
(3) Sold equipment	4,000	120,000	Purchased building (10)
		25,000	Purchased equipment (11)
		141,000	Net cash used by investing activities
Financing			
(12) Issued common stock	20,000	29,000	Dividend paid (13)
		9,000	Net cash used by financing activities
	22,000		

Accounts Receivable

30,000	10,000 (4)
20,000	

Inventory

10,000	
(5) 5,000	
15,000	

Prepaid Expenses

1,000	
(6) 4,000	
5,000	

Land

20,000	
(9) 110,000	
130,000	

Buildings

40,000	
(10) 120,000	
160,000	

Accumulated Depreciation—Buildings

	5,000
	6,000 (2)
	11,000

Equipment

10,000	
(11) 25,000	8,000 (3)
27,000	

Accumulated Depreciation—Equipment

	1,000
(3) 1,000	3,000 (2)
	3,000

Accounts Payable

	12,000
	16,000 (7)
	28,000

Income Taxes Payable

	8,000
(8) 2,000	
	6,000

Bonds Payable

	20,000
	110,000 (9)
	130,000

Common Stock

	50,000
	20,000 (12)
	70,000

Retained Earnings

	48,000
	145,000 (1)
(13) 29,000	
	164,000

1. Post net income as a debit to the operating section of the Cash T-account and a credit to Retained Earnings. Make sure to label all adjustments to the Cash T-account. It also helps to number each adjustment so you can trace all of them if you make an error.

2. Post depreciation expense as a debit to the operating section of Cash and a credit to each of the appropriate accumulated depreciation accounts.
3. Post any gains or losses on the sale of property, plant, and equipment. To do this, it is best to first prepare the journal entry that was recorded at the time of the sale and then post each element of the journal entry. For example, for Computer Services the entry was:

Cash	4,000	
Accumulated Depreciation—Equipment	1,000	
Loss on Disposal of Plant Assets	3,000	
Equipment		8,000

The $4,000 cash entry is a source of cash in the investing section of the Cash account. Accumulated Depreciation—Equipment is debited for $1,000. The Loss on Disposal of Plant Assets is a debit to the operating section of the Cash T-account. Finally, Equipment is credited for $8,000.

4–8. Next, post each of the changes to the noncash current asset and current liability accounts. For example, to explain the $10,000 decline in Computer Services' accounts receivable, credit Accounts Receivable for $10,000 and debit the operating section of the Cash T-account for $10,000.

9. Analyze the changes in the noncurrent accounts. Land was purchased by issuing bonds payable. This requires a debit to Land for $110,000 and a credit to Bonds Payable for $110,000. Note that this is a significant noncash event that requires disclosure at the bottom of the statement of cash flows.
10. Buildings is debited for $120,000, and the investing section of the Cash T-account is credited for $120,000 as a use of cash from investing.
11. Equipment is debited for $25,000 and the investing section of the Cash T-account is credited for $25,000 as a use of cash from investing.
12. Common Stock is credited for $20,000 for the issuance of shares of stock, and the financing section of the Cash T-account is debited for $20,000.
13. Retained Earnings is debited to reflect the payment of the $29,000 dividend, and the financing section of the Cash T-account is credited to reflect the use of Cash.

At this point, all of the changes in the noncash accounts have been explained. All that remains is to subtotal each section of the Cash T-account and compare the total change in cash with the change shown on the balance sheet. Once this is done, the information in the Cash T-account can be used to prepare a statement of cash flows.

REVIEW AND PRACTICE

LEARNING OBJECTIVES REVIEW

1 Discuss the usefulness and format of the statement of cash flows. The statement of cash flows provides information about the cash receipts, cash payments, and net change in cash resulting from the operating, investing, and financing activities of a company during the period.

Operating activities include the cash effects of transactions that enter into the determination of net income. Investing activities involve cash flows resulting from changes in investments and long-term asset items. Financing activities involve cash flows resulting from changes in long-term liability and stockholders' equity items.

2 Prepare a statement of cash flows using the indirect method. The preparation of a statement of cash flows involves three major steps. (1) Determine net cash provided/used by operating activities by converting net income from an accrual basis to a cash basis. (2) Analyze changes in noncurrent asset and liability accounts and record as investing and financing activities, or disclose as noncash transactions. (3) Compare the net change in cash on the statement of cash flows with the change in the Cash account reported on the balance sheet to make sure the amounts agree.

3 Use the statement of cash flows to evaluate a company. During the introductory stage, net cash provided by operating activities and net cash provided by investing activities are negative, and net cash provided by financing activities is positive. During the growth stage, net cash provided by operating activities becomes positive but is still not sufficient to meet investing needs. During the maturity stage, net cash provided by operating activities exceeds investing needs, so the company begins to retire debt. During the decline stage, net cash provided by operating activities is reduced, net cash provided by investing activities becomes positive (from selling off assets), and net cash provided by financing activities becomes more negative.

Free cash flow indicates the amount of cash a company generated during the current year that is available for the payment of dividends or for expansion.

***4 Prepare a statement of cash flows using the direct method.** The preparation of the statement of cash flows involves three major steps. (1) Determine net cash provided/used by operating activities by converting net income from an accrual basis to a cash basis. (2) Analyze changes in noncurrent asset and liability accounts and record as investing and financing activities, or disclose as noncash transactions. (3) Compare the net change in cash on the statement of cash flows with the change in the Cash account reported on the balance sheet to make sure the amounts agree. The direct method reports cash receipts less cash payments to arrive at net cash provided by operating activities.

***5 Use the T-account approach to prepare a statement of cash flows.** To use T-accounts to prepare the statement of cash flows: (1) prepare a large Cash T-account with sections for operating, investing, and financing activities; (2) prepare smaller T-accounts for all other noncash accounts; (3) insert beginning and ending balances for all accounts; and (4) follows the steps in Illustration 12-3 (page 596), entering debit and credit amounts as needed.

DECISION TOOLS REVIEW

DECISION CHECKPOINTS	INFO NEEDED FOR DECISION	TOOL TO USE FOR DECISION	HOW TO EVALUATE RESULTS
How much cash did the company generate to either expand operations or pay dividends?	Net cash provided by operating activities, cash spent on fixed assets, and cash dividends	Free cash flow = Net cash provided by operating activities − Capital expenditures − Cash dividends	Significant free cash flow indicates greater potential to finance new investment and pay additional dividends.

GLOSSARY REVIEW

Direct method A method of determining net cash provided by operating activities by adjusting each item in the income statement from the accrual basis to the cash basis. The direct method shows operating cash receipts and payments. (p. 596).

Financing activities Cash flow activities that include (a) obtaining cash from issuing debt and repaying the amounts borrowed and (b) obtaining cash from stockholders, repurchasing shares, and paying dividends. (p. 592).

Free cash flow Net cash provided by operating activities after adjusting for capital expenditures and cash dividends paid. (p. 609).

Indirect method A method of preparing a statement of cash flows in which net income is adjusted for items that do not affect cash, to determine net cash provided by operating activities. (p. 596).

Investing activities Cash flow activities that include (a) transactions that involve the purchase or disposal of investments and property, plant, and equipment using cash, and (b) lending money and collecting the loans. (p. 592).

Operating activities Cash flow activities that include the cash effects of transactions that create revenues and expenses and thus enter into the determination of net income. (p. 592).

Product life cycle A series of phases in a product's sales and cash flows over time. These phases, in order of occurrence, are introductory, growth, maturity, and decline. (p. 607).

Statement of cash flows A basic financial statement that provides information about the cash receipts and cash payments of an entity during a period, classified as operating, investing, and financing activities, in a format that reconciles the beginning and ending cash balances. (p. 592).

PRACTICE MULTIPLE-CHOICE QUESTIONS

(LO 1) 1. Which of the following is **incorrect** about the statement of cash flows?
(a) It is a fourth basic financial statement.
(b) It provides information about cash receipts and cash payments of an entity during a period.
(c) It reconciles the ending cash account balance to the balance per the bank statement.
(d) It provides information about the operating, investing, and financing activities of the business.

(LO 1) **2.** Which of the following will **not** be reported in the statement of cash flows?
(a) The net change in stockholders' equity during the year.
(b) Cash payments for plant assets during the year.
(c) Cash receipts from sales of plant assets during the year.
(d) Sources of financing during the period.

(LO 1) **3.** The statement of cash flows classifies cash receipts and cash payments by these activities:
(a) operating and nonoperating.
(b) operating, investing, and financing.
(c) financing, operating, and nonoperating.
(d) investing, financing, and nonoperating.

(LO 1) **4.** Which is an example of a cash flow from an operating activity?
(a) Payment of cash to lenders for interest.
(b) Receipt of cash from the sale of common stock.
(c) Payment of cash dividends to the company's stockholders.
(d) None of the above.

(LO 1) **5.** Which is an example of a cash flow from an investing activity?
(a) Receipt of cash from the issuance of bonds payable.
(b) Payment of cash to repurchase outstanding common stock.
(c) Receipt of cash from the sale of equipment.
(d) Payment of cash to suppliers for inventory.

(LO 1) **6.** Cash dividends paid to stockholders are classified on the statement of cash flows as:
(a) operating activities.
(b) investing activities.
(c) a combination of (a) and (b).
(d) financing activities.

(LO 1) **7.** Which is an example of a cash flow from a financing activity?
(a) Receipt of cash from sale of land.
(b) Issuance of debt for cash.
(c) Purchase of equipment for cash.
(d) None of the above

(LO 1) **8.** Which of the following is **incorrect** about the statement of cash flows?
(a) The direct method may be used to report net cash provided by operating activities.
(b) The statement shows the net cash provided (used) for three categories of activity.
(c) The operating activities section is the last section of the statement.
(d) The indirect method may be used to report net cash provided by operating activities.

Use the indirect method to solve Questions 9 through 11.

(LO 2) **9.** Net income is $132,000, accounts payable increased $10,000 during the year, inventory decreased $6,000 during the year, and accounts receivable increased $12,000 during the year. Under the indirect method, what is net cash provided by operating activities?
(a) $102,000. (c) $124,000.
(b) $112,000. (d) $136,000.

(LO 2) **10.** Items that are added back to net income in determining net cash provided by operating activities under the indirect method do **not** include:
(a) depreciation expense.
(b) an increase in inventory.
(c) amortization expense.
(d) loss on disposal of equipment.

11. The following data are available for Bill Mack Corporation. (LO 2)

Net income	$200,000
Depreciation expense	40,000
Dividends paid	60,000
Gain on sale of land	10,000
Decrease in accounts receivable	20,000
Decrease in accounts payable	30,000

Net cash provided by operating activities is:
(a) $160,000. (c) $240,000.
(b) $220,000. (d) $280,000.

12. The following are data concerning cash received or paid from various transactions for Orange Peels Corporation. (LO 2)

Sale of land	$100,000
Sale of equipment	50,000
Issuance of common stock	70,000
Purchase of equipment	30,000
Payment of cash dividends	60,000

Net cash provided by investing activities is:
(a) $120,000. (c) $150,000.
(b) $130,000. (d) $190,000.

13. The following data are available for Retique! (LO 2)

Increase in accounts payable	$ 40,000
Increase in bonds payable	100,000
Sale of investment	50,000
Issuance of common stock	60,000
Payment of cash dividends	30,000

Net cash provided by financing activities is:
(a) $90,000. (c) $160,000.
(b) $130,000. (d) $170,000.

14. Free cash flow provides an indication of a company's ability to: (LO 3)
(a) manage inventory.
(b) generate cash to pay dividends.
(c) generate cash to invest in new capital expenditures.
(d) Both (b) and (c).

15. During the introductory phase of a company's life cycle, one would normally expect to see: (LO 3)
(a) negative cash from operations, negative cash from investing, and positive cash from financing.
(b) negative cash from operations, positive cash from investing, and positive cash from financing.
(c) positive cash from operations, negative cash from investing, and negative cash from financing.
(d) positive cash from operations, negative cash from investing, and positive cash from financing.

Use the direct method to solve Questions 16 and 17.

***16.** The beginning balance in accounts receivable is $44,000, the ending balance is $42,000, and sales during the period are $129,000. What are cash receipts from customers? (LO 4)
(a) $127,000. (c) $131,000.
(b) $129,000. (d) $141,000.

***17.** Which of the following items is reported on a statement of cash flows prepared by the direct method? (LO 4)
(a) Loss on disposal of building.
(b) Increase in accounts receivable.
(c) Depreciation expense.
(d) Cash payments to suppliers.

SOLUTIONS

1. **(c)** The statement of cash flows does not reconcile the ending cash balance to the balance per the bank statement. The other choices are true statements.
2. **(a)** The net change in stockholders' equity during the year is not reported in the statement of cash flows. The other choices are true statements.
3. **(b)** Operating, investing, and financing activities are the three classifications of cash receipts and cash payments used in the statement of cash flows. The other choices are therefore incorrect.
4. **(a)** Payment of cash to lenders for interest is an operating activity. The other choices are incorrect because (b) receipt of cash from the sale of common stock is a financing activity, (c) payment of cash dividends to the company's stockholders is a financing activity, and (d) there is a correct answer.
5. **(c)** Receipt of cash from the sale of equipment is an investing activity. The other choices are incorrect because (a) the receipt of cash from the issuance of bonds payable is a financing activity, (b) payment of cash to repurchase outstanding common stock is a financing activity, and (d) payment of cash to suppliers for inventory is an operating activity.
6. **(d)** Cash dividends paid to stockholders are classified as a financing activity, not (a) an operating activity, (b) an investing activity, or (c) a combination of (a) and (b).
7. **(b)** Issuance of debt for cash is a financing activity. The other choices are incorrect because (a) the receipt of cash for the sale of land is an investing activity, (c) the purchase of equipment for cash is an investing activity, and (d) there is a correct answer.
8. **(c)** The operating section of the statement of cash flows is the first, not the last, section of the statement. The other choices are true statements.
9. **(d)** Net cash provided by operating activities is computed by adjusting net income for the changes in the three current asset/current liability accounts listed. An increase in accounts payable ($10,000) and a decrease in inventory ($6,000) are added to net income ($132,000), while an increase in accounts receivable ($12,000) is subtracted from net income, or $132,000 + $10,000 + $6,000 − $12,000 = $136,000, not (a) $102,000, (b) $112,000, or (c) $124,000.
10. **(b)** An increase in inventory is subtracted, not added, to net income in determining net cash provided by operating activities. The other choices are incorrect because (a) depreciation expense, (c) amortization expense, and (d) loss on disposal of equipment are all added back to net income in determining net cash provided by operating activities.
11. **(b)** Net cash provided by operating activities is $220,000 (Net income $200,000 + Depreciation expense $40,000 − Gain on disposal of land $10,000 + Decrease in accounts receivable $20,000 − Decrease in accounts payable $30,000), not (a) $160,000, (c) $240,000, or (d) $280,000.
12. **(a)** Net cash provided by investing activities is $120,000 (Sale of land $100,000 + Sale of equipment $50,000 − Purchase of equipment $30,000), not (b) $130,000, (c) $150,000, or (d) $190,000. Issuance of common stock and payment of cash dividends are financing activities.
13. **(b)** Net cash provided by financing activities is $130,000 (Increase in bonds payable $100,000 + Issuance of common stock $60,000 − Payment of cash dividends $30,000), not (a) $90,000, (c) $160,000, or (d) $170,000. Increase in accounts payable is an operating activity, and sale of investment is an investing activity.
14. **(d)** Free cash flow provides an indication of a company's ability to generate cash to pay dividends and to invest in new capital expenditures. Choice (a) is incorrect because other measures besides free cash flow provide the best measure of a company's ability to manage inventory. Choices (b) and (c) are true statements, but (d) is the better answer.
15. **(a)** During the introductory phase of a company's life cycle, the company will most likely finance its operations and investing activities through borrowing or the issuance of stock. This means negative cash from operations and investing, and positive cash from financing. The other choices are incorrect because during the introductory phase of a company's life cycle, the company will most likely (b) purchase long-term assets which requires a cash outflow, (c) finance its operations and investing activities through borrowing or the issuance of stock which generates cash inflows from financing, and (d) use cash to fund operations until it establishes a customer base.

*16. **(c)** Cash receipts from customers amount to $131,000 ($129,000 + $2,000). The other choices are therefore incorrect.

*17. **(d)** Cash payments to suppliers are reported on a statement of cash flows prepared by the direct method. The other choices are incorrect because (a) loss on disposal of building, (b) increase in accounts receivable, and (c) depreciation expense are reported in the operating activities section of the statement of cash flows when the indirect, not direct, method is used.

▶ PRACTICE EXERCISES

Prepare journal entries to determine effect on statement of cash flows.

(LO 2)

1. Furst Corporation had the following transactions.

1. Paid salaries of $14,000.
2. Issued 1,000 shares of $1 par value common stock for equipment worth $16,000.
3. Sold equipment (cost $10,000, accumulated depreciation $6,000) for $3,000.

4. Sold land (cost $12,000) for $16,000.
5. Issued another 1,000 shares of $1 par value common stock for $18,000.
6. Recorded depreciation of $20,000.

INSTRUCTIONS

For each transaction above, (a) prepare the journal entry and (b) indicate how it would affect the statement of cash flows. Assume the indirect method.

SOLUTION

1. 1. (a)	Salaries and Wages Expense	14,000	
	Cash		14,000

(b) Salaries and wages expense is not reported separately on the statement of cash flows. It is part of the computation of net income in the income statement and is included in the net income amount on the statement of cash flows.

2. (a)	Equipment	16,000	
	Common Stock		1,000
	Paid-in Capital in Excess of Par—Common Stock		15,000

(b) The issuance of common stock for equipment ($16,000) is reported as a noncash financing and investing activity at the bottom of the statement of cash flows.

3. (a)	Cash	3,000	
	Loss on Disposal of Plant Assets	1,000	
	Accumulated Depreciation—Equipment	6,000	
	Equipment		10,000

(b) The cash receipt ($3,000) is reported in the investing section. The loss ($1,000) is added to net income in the operating section.

4. (a)	Cash	16,000	
	Land		12,000
	Gain on Disposal of Plant Assets		4,000

(b) The cash receipt ($16,000) is reported in the investing section. The gain ($4,000) is deducted from net income in the operating section.

5. (a)	Cash	18,000	
	Common Stock		1,000
	Paid-in Capital in Excess of Par—Common Stock		17,000

(b) The cash receipt ($18,000) is reported in the financing section.

6. (a)	Depreciation Expense	20,000	
	Accumulated Depreciation—Equipment		20,000

(b) Depreciation expense ($20,000) is added to net income in the operating section.

Prepare statement of cash flows and compute free cash flow.

(LO 2, 3)

2. Strong Corporation's comparative balance sheets are presented below.

STRONG CORPORATION
Comparative Balance Sheets
December 31

	2017	2016
Cash	$ 28,200	$ 17,700
Accounts receivable	24,200	22,300
Investments	23,000	16,000
Equipment	60,000	70,000
Accumulated depreciation—equipment	(14,000)	(10,000)
Total	$ 121,400	$ 116,000
Accounts payable	$ 19,600	$ 11,100
Bonds payable	10,000	30,000
Common stock	60,000	45,000
Retained earnings	31,800	29,900
Total	$ 121,400	$ 116,000

Additional information:

1. Net income was $28,300. Dividends declared and paid were $26,400.
2. Equipment which cost $10,000 and had accumulated depreciation of $1,200 was sold for $4,300.
3. All other changes in noncurrent account balances had a direct effect on cash flows, except the change in accumulated depreciation.

INSTRUCTIONS

(a) Prepare a statement of cash flows for 2017 using the indirect method.

(b) Compute free cash flow.

SOLUTION

2. (a)

STRONG CORPORATION
Statement of Cash Flows
For the Year Ended December 31, 2017

Cash flows from operating activities		
Net income		$ 28,300
Adjustments to reconcile net income to net cash provided by operating activities:		
Depreciation expense	$ 5,200*	
Loss on sale of equipment	4,500**	
Increase in accounts payable	8,500	
Increase in accounts receivable	(1,900)	16,300
Net cash provided by operating activities		44,600
Cash flows from investing activities		
Sale of equipment	4,300	
Purchase of investments	(7,000)	
Net cash used by investing activities		(2,700)
Cash flows from financing activities		
Issuance of common stock	15,000	
Retirement of bonds	(20,000)	
Payment of dividends	(26,400)	
Net cash used by financing activities		(31,400)
Net increase in cash		10,500
Cash at beginning of period		17,700
Cash at end of period		$ 28,200

*[$14,000 – ($10,000 – $1,200)]; **[$4,300 – ($10,000 – $1,200)]

(b) $44,600 – $0 – $26,400 = $18,200

PRACTICE PROBLEM

Prepare statement of cash flows using indirect and direct methods.

(LO 2, 4)

The income statement for Kosinski Manufacturing Company contains the following condensed information.

KOSINSKI MANUFACTURING COMPANY
Income Statement
For the Year Ended December 31, 2017

Sales revenue		$6,583,000
Cost of goods sold	$2,810,000	
Operating expenses, excluding depreciation	2,086,000	
Depreciation expense	880,000	
Loss on disposal of equipment	24,000	5,800,000
Income before income taxes		783,000
Income tax expense		353,000
Net income		$ 430,000

The $24,000 loss resulting from the sale of machinery resulted from selling equipment for $270,000 cash. Machinery was purchased at a cost of $750,000. The following balances are reported on Kosinski's comparative balance sheets at December 31.

	2017	2016
Cash	$672,000	$130,000
Accounts receivable	775,000	610,000
Inventory	834,000	867,000
Accounts payable	521,000	501,000

Income tax expense of $353,000 represents the amount paid in 2017. Dividends declared and paid in 2017 totaled $200,000.

INSTRUCTIONS

(a) Prepare the statement of cash flows using the indirect method.

*(b) Prepare the statement of cash flows using the direct method.

SOLUTION

(a)

KOSINSKI MANUFACTURING COMPANY
Statement of Cash Flows—Indirect Method
For the Year Ended December 31, 2017

Cash flows from operating activities		
Net income		$ 430,000
Adjustments to reconcile net income to net cash provided by operating activities:		
Depreciation expense	$ 880,000	
Loss on disposal of plant assets	24,000	
Increase in accounts receivable	(165,000)	
Decrease in inventory	33,000	
Increase in accounts payable	20,000	792,000
Net cash provided by operating activities		1,222,000
Cash flows from investing activities		
Sale of machinery	270,000	
Purchase of machinery	(750,000)	
Net cash used by investing activities		(480,000)
Cash flows from financing activities		
Payment of cash dividends	(200,000)	
Net cash used by financing activities		(200,000)
Net increase in cash		542,000
Cash at beginning of period		130,000
Cash at end of period		$ 672,000

*(b)

KOSINSKI MANUFACTURING COMPANY
Statement of Cash Flows—Direct Method
For the Year Ended December 31, 2017

Cash flows from operating activities		
Cash collections from customers		$6,418,000*
Cash payments:		
To suppliers	$2,757,000**	
For operating expenses	2,086,000	
For income taxes	353,000	5,196,000
Net cash provided by operating activities		1,222,000
Cash flows from investing activities		
Sale of machinery	270,000	
Purchase of machinery	(750,000)	
Net cash used by investing activities		(480,000)

Cash flows from financing activities		
Payment of cash dividends	(200,000)	
Net cash used by financing activities		(200,000)
Net increase in cash		542,000
Cash at beginning of period		130,000
Cash at end of period		$ 672,000

Direct-Method Computations:	
*Computation of cash collections from customers:	
Sales revenue per the income statement	$ 6,583,000
Deduct: Increase in accounts receivable	(165,000)
Cash collections from customers	$ 6,418,000
**Computation of cash payments to suppliers	
Cost of goods sold per income statement	$ 2,810,000
Deduct: Decrease in inventories	(33,000)
Deduct: Increase in accounts payable	(20,000)
	$ 2,757,000

WileyPLUS Brief Exercises, DO IT! Exercises, Exercises, Problems, and many additional resources are available for practice in WileyPLUS.

NOTE: All asterisked Questions, Exercises, and Problems relate to material in the appendices to the chapter.

QUESTIONS

1. (a) What is a statement of cash flows?
   (b) Pat Marx maintains that the statement of cash flows is an optional financial statement. Do you agree? Explain.
2. What questions about cash are answered by the statement of cash flows?
3. Distinguish among the three activities reported in the statement of cash flows.
4. (a) What are the sources (inflows) of cash in a statement of cash flows?
   (b) What are the uses (outflows) of cash?
5. Why is it important to disclose certain noncash transactions? How should they be disclosed?
6. Helen Powell and Paul Tang were discussing the format of the statement of cash flows of Baumgarten Co. At the bottom of Baumgarten's statement of cash flows was a separate section entitled "Noncash investing and financing activities." Give three examples of significant noncash transactions that would be reported in this section.
7. Why is it necessary to use comparative balance sheets, a current income statement, and certain transaction data in preparing a statement of cash flows?
8. Contrast the advantages and disadvantages of the direct and indirect methods of preparing the statement of cash flows. Are both methods acceptable? Which method is preferred by the FASB? Which method is more popular?
9. When the total cash inflows exceed the total cash outflows in the statement of cash flows, how and where is this excess identified?
10. Describe the indirect method for determining net cash provided (used) by operating activities.
11. Why is it necessary to convert accrual-basis net income to cash-basis net income when preparing a statement of cash flows?
12. The president of Murquery Company is puzzled. During the last year, the company experienced a net loss of $800,000, yet its cash increased $300,000 during the same period of time. Explain to the president how this could occur.
13. Identify five items that are adjustments to convert net income to net cash provided by operating activities under the indirect method.
14. Why and how is depreciation expense reported in a statement of cash flows prepared using the indirect method?
15. Why is the statement of cash flows useful?
16. During 2017, Slivowitz Company exchanged $1,700,000 of its common stock for land. Indicate how the transaction would be reported on a statement of cash flows, if at all.
17. (a) What are the phases of the corporate life cycle?
    (b) What effect does each phase have on the amounts reported in a statement of cash flows?

18. Based on its statement of cash flows, in what stage of the product life cycle is Apple?

*19. Describe the direct method for determining net cash provided by operating activities.

*20. Give the formulas under the direct method for computing (a) cash receipts from customers and (b) cash payments to suppliers.

*21. Harbinger Inc. reported sales of $2 million for 2017. Accounts receivable decreased $150,000 and accounts payable increased $300,000. Compute cash receipts from customers, assuming that the receivable and payable transactions are related to operations.

*22. In the direct method, why is depreciation expense not reported in the cash flows from operating activities section?

BRIEF EXERCISES

Indicate statement presentation of selected transactions.
(LO 1), K

BE12-1 Each of these items must be considered in preparing a statement of cash flows for Irvin Co. for the year ended December 31, 2017. For each item, state how it should be shown in the statement of cash flows for 2017.
(a) Issued bonds for $200,000 cash.
(b) Purchased equipment for $180,000 cash.
(c) Sold land costing $20,000 for $20,000 cash.
(d) Declared and paid a $50,000 cash dividend.

Classify items by activities.
(LO 1), C

BE12-2 Classify each item as an operating, investing, or financing activity. Assume all items involve cash unless there is information to the contrary.
(a) Purchase of equipment.
(b) Sale of building.
(c) Redemption of bonds.
(d) Cash received from sale of goods.
(e) Payment of dividends.
(f) Issuance of capital stock.

Identify financing activity transactions.
(LO 1), AP

BE12-3 The following T-account is a summary of the Cash account of Alixon Company.

Cash (Summary Form)

Balance, Jan. 1	8,000		
Receipts from customers	364,000	Payments for goods	200,000
Dividends on stock investments	6,000	Payments for operating expenses	140,000
Proceeds from sale of equipment	36,000	Interest paid	10,000
Proceeds from issuance of		Taxes paid	8,000
bonds payable	300,000	Dividends paid	40,000
Balance, Dec. 31	316,000		

What amount of net cash provided (used) by financing activities should be reported in the statement of cash flows?

Compute net cash provided by operating activities—indirect method.
(LO 2), AP

BE12-4 Miguel, Inc. reported net income of $2.5 million in 2017. Depreciation for the year was $160,000, accounts receivable decreased $350,000, and accounts payable decreased $280,000. Compute net cash provided by operating activities using the indirect approach.

Compute net cash provided by operating activities—indirect method.
(LO 2), AP

BE12-5 The net income for Mongan Co. for 2017 was $280,000. For 2017, depreciation on plant assets was $70,000, and the company incurred a loss on disposal of plant assets of $28,000. Compute net cash provided by operating activities under the indirect method, assuming there were no other changes in the company's accounts.

Compute net cash provided by operating activities—indirect method.
(LO 2), AP

BE12-6 The comparative balance sheets for Gale Company show these changes in noncash current asset accounts: accounts receivable decreased $80,000, prepaid expenses increased $28,000, and inventories increased $40,000. Compute net cash provided by operating activities using the indirect method, assuming that net income is $186,000.

Determine cash received from sale of equipment.
(LO 2), AN

BE12-7 The T-accounts for Equipment and the related Accumulated Depreciation—Equipment for Goldstone Company at the end of 2017 are shown here.

Equipment

Beg. bal.	80,000	Disposals	22,000
Acquisitions	41,600		
End. bal.	99,600		

Accum. Depr.—Equipment

Disposals	5,100	Beg. bal.	44,500
		Depr. exp.	12,000
		End. bal.	51,400

In addition, Goldstone's income statement reported a loss on the disposal of plant assets of $3,500. What amount was reported on the statement of cash flows as "cash flow from sale of equipment"?

BE12-8
(a) Why is net cash provided by operating activities likely to be lower than reported net income during the growth phase?
(b) Why is net cash from investing activities often positive during the late maturity phase and during the decline phase?

Answer questions related to the phases of product life cycle.
(LO 3), C

BE12-9 Suppose during 2017 that Cypress Semiconductor Corporation reported net cash provided by operating activities of $89,303,000, cash used in investing of $43,126,000, and cash used in financing of $7,368,000. In addition, cash spent for fixed assets during the period was $25,823,000. No dividends were paid. Calculate free cash flow.

Calculate free cash flow.
(LO 3), AP

BE12-10 Sprouts Corporation reported net cash provided by operating activities of $412,000, net cash used by investing activities of $250,000, and net cash provided by financing activities of $70,000. In addition, cash spent for capital assets during the period was $200,000. No dividends were paid. Calculate free cash flow.

Calculate free cash flow.
(LO 3), AP

BE12-11 Suppose Canwest Global Communications Corp. reported net cash used by operating activities of $104,539,000 and sales revenue of $2,867,459,000 during 2017. Cash spent on plant asset additions during the year was $79,330,000. Calculate free cash flow.

Calculate free cash flow.
(LO 3), AP

BE12-12 The management of Uhuru Inc. is trying to decide whether it can increase its dividend. During the current year, it reported net income of $875,000. It had net cash provided by operating activities of $734,000, paid cash dividends of $92,000, and had capital expenditures of $310,000. Compute the company's free cash flow, and discuss whether an increase in the dividend appears warranted. What other factors should be considered?

Calculate and analyze free cash flow.
(LO 3), AN

***BE12-13** Suppose Columbia Sportswear Company had accounts receivable of $299,585,000 at January 1, 2017, and $226,548,000 at December 31, 2017. Assume sales revenue was $1,244,023,000 for the year 2017. What is the amount of cash receipts from customers in 2017?

Compute receipts from customers—direct method.
(LO 4), AP

***BE12-14** Hoffman Corporation reported income taxes of $370,000,000 on its 2017 income statement and income taxes payable of $277,000,000 at December 31, 2016, and $528,000,000 at December 31, 2017. What amount of cash payments were made for income taxes during 2017?

Compute cash payments for income taxes—direct method.
(LO 4), AP

***BE12-15** Pietr Corporation reports operating expenses of $90,000, excluding depreciation expense of $15,000, for 2017. During the year, prepaid expenses decreased $7,200 and accrued expenses payable increased $4,400. Compute the cash payments for operating expenses in 2017.

Compute cash payments for operating expenses—direct method.
(LO 4), AP

DO IT! EXERCISES

DO IT! 12-1 Moss Corporation had the following transactions.

1. Issued $160,000 of bonds payable.
2. Paid utilities expense.
3. Issued 500 shares of preferred stock for $45,000.
4. Sold land and a building for $250,000.
5. Loaned $30,000 to Dead End Corporation, receiving Dead End's 1-year, 12% note.

Classify each of these transactions by type of cash flow activity (operating, investing, or financing). (*Hint:* Refer to Illustration 12-1.)

Classify transactions by type of cash flow activity.
(LO 1), C

DO IT! 12-2a PK Photography reported net income of $100,000 for 2017. Included in the income statement were depreciation expense of $6,300, patent amortization expense of $4,000, and a gain on disposal of plant assets of $3,600. PK's comparative balance sheets show the following balances.

	12/31/17	12/31/16
Accounts receivable	$21,000	$27,000
Accounts payable	9,200	6,000

Calculate net cash provided by operating activities for PK Photography.

Calculate net cash from operating activities.
(LO 2), AP

Prepare statement of cash flows—indirect method.
(LO 2), AP

DO IT! 12-2b Alex Company reported the following information for 2017.

ALEX COMPANY
Comparative Balance Sheets
December 31

Assets	**2017**	**2016**	**Change Increase/Decrease**
Cash	$ 59,000	$ 36,000	$ 23,000 Increase
Accounts receivable	62,000	22,000	40,000 Increase
Inventory	44,000	–0–	44,000 Increase
Prepaid expenses	6,000	4,000	2,000 Increase
Land	55,000	70,000	15,000 Decrease
Buildings	200,000	200,000	–0–
Accumulated depreciation—buildings	(21,000)	(14,000)	7,000 Increase
Equipment	183,000	68,000	115,000 Increase
Accumulated depreciation—equipment	(28,000)	(10,000)	18,000 Increase
Totals	$560,000	$376,000	
Liabilities and Stockholders' Equity			
Accounts payable	$ 43,000	$ 40,000	$ 3,000 Increase
Accrued expenses payable	–0–	10,000	10,000 Decrease
Bonds payable	100,000	150,000	50,000 Decrease
Common stock ($1 par)	230,000	60,000	170,000 Increase
Retained earnings	187,000	116,000	71,000 Increase
Totals	$560,000	$376,000	

ALEX COMPANY
Income Statement
For the Year Ended December 31, 2017

Sales revenue		$941,000
Cost of goods sold	$475,000	
Operating expenses	231,000	
Interest expense	12,000	
Loss on disposal of equipment	2,000	720,000
Income before income taxes		221,000
Income tax expense		65,000
Net income		$156,000

Additional information:

1. Operating expenses include depreciation expense of $40,000.
2. Land was sold at its book value for cash.
3. Cash dividends of $85,000 were declared and paid in 2017.
4. Equipment with a cost of $166,000 was purchased for cash. Equipment with a cost of $51,000 and a book value of $36,000 was sold for $34,000 cash.
5. Bonds of $50,000 were redeemed at their face value for cash.
6. Common stock ($1 par) of $170,000 was issued for cash.

Use this information to prepare a statement of cash flows using the indirect method.

Compute and discuss free cash flow.
(LO 3), AP

DO IT! 12-3 Moskow Corporation issued the following statement of cash flows for 2017.

MOSKOW CORPORATION Statement of Cash Flows—Indirect Method For the Year Ended December 31, 2017		
Cash flows from operating activities		
Net income		$ 59,000
Adjustments to reconcile net income to net cash provided by operating activities:		
Depreciation expense	$ 9,100	
Decrease in accounts receivable	9,500	
Increase in inventory	(5,000)	
Decrease in accounts payable	(2,200)	
Loss on disposal of plant assets	3,300	14,700
Net cash provided by operating activities		73,700
Cash flows from investing activities		
Sale of investments	3,100	
Purchase of equipment	(24,200)	
Net cash used by investing activities		(21,100)
Cash flows from financing activities		
Issuance of stock	20,000	
Payment on long-term note payable	(10,000)	
Payment for dividends	(13,000)	
Net cash used by financing activities		(3,000)
Net increase in cash		49,600
Cash at beginning of year		13,000
Cash at end of year		$ 62,600

(a) Compute free cash flow for Moskow Corporation.
(b) Explain why free cash flow often provides better information than "Net cash provided by operating activities."

EXERCISES

Classify transactions by type of activity.

(LO 1), C

E12-1 Kiley Corporation had these transactions during 2017.
(a) Purchased a machine for $30,000, giving a long-term note in exchange.
(b) Issued $50,000 par value common stock for cash.
(c) Issued $200,000 par value common stock upon conversion of bonds having a face value of $200,000.
(d) Declared and paid a cash dividend of $13,000.
(e) Sold a long-term investment with a cost of $15,000 for $15,000 cash.
(f) Collected $16,000 from sale of goods.
(g) Paid $18,000 to suppliers.

Instructions
Analyze the transactions and indicate whether each transaction is an operating activity, investing activity, financing activity, or noncash investing and financing activity.

Classify transactions by type of activity.

(LO 1), C

E12-2 An analysis of comparative balance sheets, the current year's income statement, and the general ledger accounts of Hailey Corp. uncovered the following items. Assume all items involve cash unless there is information to the contrary.
(a) Payment of interest on notes payable.
(b) Exchange of land for patent.
(c) Sale of building at book value.
(d) Payment of dividends.
(e) Depreciation.
(f) Conversion of bonds into common stock.
(g) Receipt of interest on notes receivable.
(h) Issuance of capital stock.
(i) Amortization of patent.
(j) Issuance of bonds for land.
(k) Purchase of land.
(l) Receipt of dividends on investment in stock.
(m) Loss on disposal of plant assets.
(n) Retirement of bonds.

Instructions
Indicate how each item should be classified in the statement of cash flows (indirect method) using these four major classifications: operating activity (that is, the item would be listed among the adjustments to net income to determine net cash provided by operating activities under the indirect method), investing activity, financing activity, or significant noncash investing and financing activity.

Prepare the operating activities section—indirect method.
(LO 2), AP

E12-3 Sosa Company reported net income of $190,000 for 2017. Sosa also reported depreciation expense of $35,000 and a loss of $5,000 on the disposal of plant assets. The comparative balance sheets show an increase in accounts receivable of $15,000 for the year, a $17,000 increase in accounts payable, and a $4,000 increase in prepaid expenses.

Instructions
Prepare the operating activities section of the statement of cash flows for 2017. Use the indirect method.

Prepare the operating activities section—indirect method.
(LO 2), AP

E12-4 The current sections of Sunn Inc.'s balance sheets at December 31, 2016 and 2017, are presented here. Sunn's net income for 2017 was $153,000. Depreciation expense was $27,000.

	2017	2016
Current assets		
Cash	$105,000	$ 99,000
Accounts receivable	80,000	89,000
Inventory	168,000	172,000
Prepaid expenses	27,000	22,000
Total current assets	$380,000	$382,000
Current liabilities		
Accrued expenses payable	$ 15,000	$ 5,000
Accounts payable	85,000	92,000
Total current liabilities	$100,000	$ 97,000

Instructions
Prepare the net cash provided by operating activities section of the company's statement of cash flows for the year ended December 31, 2017, using the indirect method.

Prepare statement of cash flows—indirect method.
(LO 2), AP

E12-5 The following information is available for Stamos Corporation for the year ended December 31, 2017.

Beginning cash balance	$ 45,000
Accounts payable decrease	3,700
Depreciation expense	162,000
Accounts receivable increase	8,200
Inventory increase	11,000
Net income	284,100
Cash received for sale of land at book value	35,000
Cash dividends paid	12,000
Income taxes payable increase	4,700
Cash used to purchase building	289,000
Cash used to purchase treasury stock	26,000
Cash received from issuing bonds	200,000

Instructions
Prepare a statement of cash flows using the indirect method.

Prepare partial statement of cash flows—indirect method.
(LO 2), AN

E12-6 The following three accounts appear in the general ledger of Beiber Corp. during 2017.

Equipment

Date		Debit	Credit	Balance
Jan. 1	Balance			160,000
July 31	Purchase of equipment	70,000		230,000
Sept. 2	Cost of equipment constructed	53,000		283,000
Nov. 10	Cost of equipment sold		49,000	234,000

Accumulated Depreciation—Equipment

Date		Debit	Credit	Balance
Jan. 1	Balance			71,000
Nov. 10	Accumulated depreciation on equipment sold	16,000		55,000
Dec. 31	Depreciation for year		28,000	83,000

Retained Earnings

Date		Debit	Credit	Balance
Jan. 1	Balance			105,000
Aug. 23	Dividends (cash)	14,000		91,000
Dec. 31	Net income		72,000	163,000

Instructions

From the postings in the accounts, indicate how the information is reported on a statement of cash flows using the indirect method. The loss on disposal of plant assets was $8,000. (*Hint:* Cost of equipment constructed is reported in the investing activities section as a decrease in cash of $53,000.)

Prepare a statement of cash flows—indirect method.

(LO 2), AP

E12-7 The following are comparative balance sheets for Mitch Company.

MITCH COMPANY
Comparative Balance Sheets
December 31

Assets	2017	2016
Cash	$ 68,000	$ 22,000
Accounts receivable	88,000	76,000
Inventory	167,000	189,000
Land	80,000	100,000
Equipment	260,000	200,000
Accumulated depreciation—equipment	(66,000)	(32,000)
Total	$597,000	$555,000

Liabilities and Stockholders' Equity	2017	2016
Accounts payable	$ 39,000	$ 43,000
Bonds payable	150,000	200,000
Common stock ($1 par)	216,000	174,000
Retained earnings	192,000	138,000
Total	$597,000	$555,000

Additional information:

1. Net income for 2017 was $93,000.
2. Depreciation expense was $34,000.
3. Cash dividends of $39,000 were declared and paid.
4. Bonds payable amounting to $50,000 were redeemed for cash $50,000.
5. Common stock was issued for $42,000 cash.
6. No equipment was sold during 2017.
7. Land was sold for its book value.

Instructions

Prepare a statement of cash flows for 2017 using the indirect method.

Identify phases of product life cycle.

(LO 3), C

E12-8 The information in the table is from the statement of cash flows for a company at four different points in time (M, N, O, and P). Negative values are presented in parentheses.

	Point in Time			
	M	N	O	P
Net cash provided by operating activities	$ (60,000)	$ 30,000	$120,000	$(10,000)
Cash provided by investing activities	(100,000)	25,000	30,000	(40,000)
Cash provided by financing activities	70,000	(90,000)	(50,000)	120,000
Net income	(38,000)	10,000	100,000	(5,000)

Instructions
For each point in time, state whether the company is most likely in the introductory phase, growth phase, maturity phase, or decline phase. In each case, explain your choice.

Compare free cash flow of two companies.
(LO 3), AN

E12-9 Suppose the following is 2017 information for PepsiCo, Inc. and The Coca-Cola Company.

($ in millions)	PepsiCo	Coca-Cola
Net cash provided by operating activities	$ 6,796	$ 8,186
Average current liabilities	8,772	13,355
Net income	5,979	6,906
Sales revenue	43,232	30,990
Capital expenditures	2,128	1,993
Dividends paid	2,732	3,800

Instructions
Compute free cash flow for both companies and compare.

Compare free cash flow of two companies.
(LO 3), AN

E12-10 Information for two companies in the same industry, Merrill Corporation and Wingate Corporation, is presented here.

	Merrill Corporation	Wingate Corporation
Net cash provided by operating activities	$ 80,000	$100,000
Average current liabilities	50,000	100,000
Net income	200,000	200,000
Capital expenditures	40,000	70,000
Dividends paid	5,000	10,000

Instructions
Compute free cash flow for both companies and compare.

Compute cash provided by operating activities—direct method.
(LO 4), AP

***E12-11** Zimmer Company completed its first year of operations on December 31, 2017. Its initial income statement showed that Zimmer had sales revenue of $198,000 and operating expenses of $83,000. Accounts receivable and accounts payable at year-end were $60,000 and $23,000, respectively. Assume that accounts payable related to operating expenses. Ignore income taxes.

Instructions
Compute net cash provided by operating activity using the direct method.

Compute cash payments—direct method.
(LO 4), AP

***E12-12** Suppose the 2017 income statement for McDonald's Corporation shows cost of goods sold $5,178.0 million and operating expenses (including depreciation expense of $1,216.2 million) $10,725.7 million. The comparative balance sheets for the year show that inventory decreased $5.3 million, prepaid expenses increased $42.2 million, accounts payable (merchandise suppliers) increased $15.6 million, and accrued expenses payable increased $199.8 million.

Instructions
Using the direct method, compute (a) cash payments to suppliers and (b) cash payments for operating expenses.

Compute cash flow from operating activities—direct method.
(LO 4), AP

***E12-13** The 2017 accounting records of Megan Transport reveal these transactions and events.

Payment of interest	$ 10,000	Payment of salaries and wages	$ 53,000
Cash sales	48,000	Depreciation expense	16,000
Receipt of dividend revenue	18,000	Proceeds from sale of vehicles	812,000
Payment of income taxes	12,000	Purchase of equipment for cash	22,000
Net income	38,000	Loss on sale of vehicles	3,000
Payment for merchandise	97,000	Payment of dividends	14,000
Payment for land	74,000	Payment of operating expenses	28,000
Collection of accounts receivable	195,000		

Instructions
Prepare the cash flows from operating activities section using the direct method.

***E12-14** The following information is available for Balboa Corp. for 2017.

Prepare statement of cash flows—direct method.

(LO 4), AP

Cash used to purchase treasury stock	$ 48,100
Cash dividends paid	21,800
Cash paid for interest	22,400
Net income	464,300
Sales revenue	802,000
Cash paid for taxes	99,000
Cash received from customers	566,100
Cash received from sale of building (at book value)	197,600
Cash paid for operating expenses	77,000
Beginning cash balance	11,000
Cash paid for goods and services	279,100
Cash received from issuing common stock	355,000
Cash paid to redeem bonds at maturity	200,000
Cash paid to purchase equipment	113,200

Instructions

Prepare a statement of cash flows using the direct method.

***E12-15** The following information is taken from the 2017 general ledger of Preminger Company.

Calculate cash flows—direct method.

(LO 4), AN

Rent	Rent expense	$ 30,000
	Prepaid rent, January 1	5,900
	Prepaid rent, December 31	7,400
Salaries	Salaries and wages expense	$ 54,000
	Salaries and wages payable, January 1	2,000
	Salaries and wages payable, December 31	8,000
Sales	Sales revenue	$160,000
	Accounts receivable, January 1	16,000
	Accounts receivable, December 31	7,000

Instructions

In each case, compute the amount that should be reported in the operating activities section of the statement of cash flows under the direct method.

EXERCISES: SET B AND CHALLENGE EXERCISES

Visit the book's companion website, at **www.wiley.com/college/kimmel**, and choose the Student Companion site to access Exercises: Set B and Challenge Exercises.

PROBLEMS: SET A

P12-1A You are provided with the following information regarding events that occurred at Moore Corporation during 2017 or changes in account balances as of December 31, 2017.

Distinguish among operating, investing, and financing activities.

(LO 1, 2), AP

	(1) Statement of Cash Flow Section Affected	(2) If Operating, Did It Increase or Decrease Reported Cash from Operating Activities?
(a) Depreciation expense was $80,000.		
(b) Interest Payable account increased $5,000.		
(c) Received $26,000 from sale of plant assets.		
(d) Acquired land by issuing common stock to seller.		
(e) Paid $17,000 cash dividend to preferred stockholders.		
(f) Paid $4,000 cash dividend to common stockholders.		
(g) Accounts Receivable account decreased $10,000.		
(h) Inventory increased $2,000.		
(i) Received $100,000 from issuing bonds payable.		
(j) Acquired equipment for $16,000 cash.		

Instructions

Moore prepares its statement of cash flows using the indirect approach. Complete the first column of the table, indicating whether each item affects the operating activities section (O) (that is, the item would be listed among the adjustments to net income to determine net cash provided by operating activities under the indirect approach), investing activities section (I), financing activities section (F), or is a noncash (NC) transaction reported in a separate schedule. For those items classified as operating activities (O), indicate whether the item is added (A) or subtracted (S) from net income to determine net cash provided by operating activities.

Determine cash flow effects of changes in equity accounts.

(LO 2), AN

P12-2A The following account balances relate to the stockholders' equity accounts of Molder Corp. at year-end.

	2017	2016
Common stock, 10,500 and 10,000 shares, respectively, for 2017 and 2016	$160,800	$140,000
Preferred stock, 5,000 shares	125,000	125,000
Retained earnings	300,000	270,000

A small stock dividend was declared and issued in 2017. The market price of the shares was $8,800. Cash dividends were $20,000 in both 2017 and 2016. The common stock has no par or stated value.

Instructions

(a) Net income $58,800

(a) What was the amount of net income reported by Molder Corp. in 2017?
(b) Determine the amounts of any cash inflows or outflows related to the common stock and dividend accounts in 2017.
(c) Indicate where each of the cash inflows or outflows identified in (b) would be classified on the statement of cash flows.

Prepare the operating activities section—indirect method.

(LO 2), AP

XLS

P12-3A The income statement of Munsun Company is presented here.

MUNSUN COMPANY
Income Statement
For the Year Ended November 30, 2017

Sales revenue		$7,600,000
Cost of goods sold		
Beginning inventory	$1,900,000	
Purchases	4,400,000	
Goods available for sale	6,300,000	
Ending inventory	1,600,000	
Total cost of goods sold		4,700,000
Gross profit		2,900,000
Operating expenses		
Selling expenses	450,000	
Administrative expenses	700,000	1,150,000
Net income		$1,750,000

Additional information:

1. Accounts receivable decreased $380,000 during the year, and inventory decreased $300,000.
2. Prepaid expenses increased $150,000 during the year.
3. Accounts payable to suppliers of merchandise decreased $350,000 during the year.
4. Accrued expenses payable decreased $100,000 during the year.
5. Administrative expenses include depreciation expense of $110,000.

Instructions

Net cash provided $1,940,000

Prepare the operating activities section of the statement of cash flows for the year ended November 30, 2017, for Munsun Company, using the indirect method.

Prepare the operating activities section—direct method.

(LO 4), AP

***P12-4A** Data for Munsun Company are presented in P12-3A.

Instructions

Net cash provided—oper. act. $1,940,000

Prepare the operating activities section of the statement of cash flows using the direct method.

P12-5A Rewe Company's income statement contained the condensed information below.

Prepare the operating activities section—indirect method.

(LO 2), AP

REWE COMPANY
Income Statement
For the Year Ended December 31, 2017

Service revenue		$970,000
Operating expenses, excluding depreciation	$614,000	
Depreciation expense	55,000	
Loss on disposal of plant assets	16,000	685,000
Income before income taxes		285,000
Income tax expense		56,000
Net income		$229,000

Rewe's balance sheets contained the following comparative data at December 31.

	2017	2016
Accounts receivable	$70,000	$60,000
Accounts payable	41,000	32,000
Income taxes payable	13,000	7,000

Accounts payable pertain to operating expenses.

Instructions
Prepare the operating activities section of the statement of cash flows using the indirect method.

Net cash provided $305,000

***P12-6A** Data for Rewe Company are presented in P12-5A.

Prepare the operating activities section—direct method.

(LO 4), AP

Instructions
Prepare the operating activities section of the statement of cash flows using the direct method.

Net cash provided $305,000

P12-7A Presented below are the financial statements of Warner Company.

Prepare a statement of cash flows—indirect method, and compute free cash flow.

(LO 2, 3), AP

WARNER COMPANY
Comparative Balance Sheets
December 31

Assets	**2017**	**2016**
Cash	$ 35,000	$ 20,000
Accounts receivable	20,000	14,000
Inventory	28,000	20,000
Property, plant, and equipment	60,000	78,000
Accumulated depreciation	(32,000)	(24,000)
Total	$111,000	$108,000
Liabilities and Stockholders' Equity		
Accounts payable	$ 19,000	$ 15,000
Income taxes payable	7,000	8,000
Bonds payable	17,000	33,000
Common stock	18,000	14,000
Retained earnings	50,000	38,000
Total	$111,000	$108,000

WARNER COMPANY
Income Statement
For the Year Ended December 31, 2017

Sales revenue		$242,000
Cost of goods sold		175,000
Gross profit		67,000
Selling expenses	$18,000	
Administrative expenses	6,000	24,000
Income from operations		43,000
Interest expense		3,000
Income before income taxes		40,000
Income tax expense		8,000
Net income		$ 32,000

Additional data:

1. Depreciation expense was $17,500.
2. Dividends declared and paid were $20,000.
3. During the year equipment was sold for $8,500 cash. This equipment cost $18,000 originally and had accumulated depreciation of $9,500 at the time of sale.

(a) Net cash provided—oper. act. $38,500

Instructions

(a) Prepare a statement of cash flows using the indirect method.
(b) Compute free cash flow.

Prepare a statement of cash flows—direct method, and compute free cash flow.

(LO 3, 4), AP

***P12-8A** Data for Warner Company are presented in P12-7A. Further analysis reveals the following.

1. Accounts payable pertain to merchandise suppliers.
2. All operating expenses except for depreciation were paid in cash.
3. All depreciation expense is in the selling expense category.
4. All sales and purchases are on account.

(a) Net cash provided—oper. act. $38,500

Instructions

(a) Prepare a statement of cash flows for Warner Company using the direct method.
(b) Compute free cash flow.

Prepare a statement of cash flows—indirect method.

(LO 2), AP

P12-9A Condensed financial data of Granger Inc. follow.

GRANGER INC.
Comparative Balance Sheets
December 31

Assets	**2017**	**2016**
Cash	$ 80,800	$ 48,400
Accounts receivable	87,800	38,000
Inventory	112,500	102,850
Prepaid expenses	28,400	26,000
Long-term investments	138,000	109,000
Plant assets	285,000	242,500
Accumulated depreciation	(50,000)	(52,000)
Total	$682,500	$514,750
Liabilities and Stockholders' Equity		
Accounts payable	$102,000	$ 67,300
Accrued expenses payable	16,500	21,000
Bonds payable	110,000	146,000
Common stock	220,000	175,000
Retained earnings	234,000	105,450
Total	$682,500	$514,750

GRANGER INC.
Income Statement Data
For the Year Ended December 31, 2017

Sales revenue		$388,460
Less:		
Cost of goods sold	$135,460	
Operating expenses, excluding depreciation	12,410	
Depreciation expense	46,500	
Income tax expense	27,280	
Interest expense	4,730	
Loss on disposal of plant assets	7,500	233,880
Net income		$154,580

Additional information:

1. New plant assets costing $100,000 were purchased for cash during the year.
2. Old plant assets having an original cost of $57,500 and accumulated depreciation of $48,500 were sold for $1,500 cash.

3. Bonds payable matured and were paid off at face value for cash.
4. A cash dividend of $26,030 was declared and paid during the year.

Instructions
Prepare a statement of cash flows using the indirect method.

Net cash provided—oper. act. $176,930

Prepare a statement of cash flows—direct method.
(LO 4), AP

***P12-10A** Data for Granger Inc. are presented in P12-9A. Further analysis reveals that accounts payable pertain to merchandise creditors.

Instructions
Prepare a statement of cash flows for Granger Inc. using the direct method.

Net cash provided—oper. act. $176,930

Prepare a statement of cash flows—indirect method.
(LO 2), AP

P12-11A The comparative balance sheets for Spicer Company as of December 31 are presented below.

SPICER COMPANY
Comparative Balance Sheets
December 31

Assets	**2017**	**2016**
Cash	$ 68,000	$ 45,000
Accounts receivable	50,000	58,000
Inventory	151,450	142,000
Prepaid expenses	15,280	21,000
Land	145,000	130,000
Buildings	200,000	200,000
Accumulated depreciation—buildings	(60,000)	(40,000)
Equipment	225,000	155,000
Accumulated depreciation—equipment	(45,000)	(35,000)
Total	$749,730	$676,000
Liabilities and Stockholders' Equity		
Accounts payable	$ 44,730	$ 36,000
Bonds payable	300,000	300,000
Common stock, $1 par	200,000	160,000
Retained earnings	205,000	180,000
Total	$749,730	$676,000

Additional information:
1. Operating expenses include depreciation expense of $42,000.
2. Land was sold for cash at book value.
3. Cash dividends of $12,000 were paid.
4. Net income for 2017 was $37,000.
5. Equipment was purchased for $92,000 cash. In addition, equipment costing $22,000 with a book value of $10,000 was sold for $8,000 cash.
6. 40,000 shares of $1 par value common stock were issued in exchange for land with a fair value of $40,000.

Instructions
Prepare a statement of cash flows for the year ended December 31, 2017, using the indirect method.

Net cash provided—oper. act. $94,000

Identify the impact of transactions on free cash flow.
(LO 3), C

P12-12A You are provided with the following transactions that took place during the year.

Transactions	**Free Cash Flow ($125,000)**
(a) Recorded credit sales $2,500.	
(b) Collected $1,900 owed by customers.	
(c) Paid amount owed to suppliers $2,750.	
(d) Recorded sales returns of $500 and credited the customer's account.	
(e) Purchased new equipment $5,000; signed a long-term note payable for the cost of the equipment.	
(f) Purchased a patent and paid $65,000 cash for the asset.	

Instructions
For each transaction listed, indicate whether it will increase (I), decrease (D), or have no effect (NE) on free cash flow.

PROBLEMS: SET B AND SET C

Visit the book's companion website, at **www.wiley.com/college/kimmel**, and choose the Student Companion site to access Problems: Set B and Set C.

CONTINUING PROBLEM Cookie Creations

(*Note:* This is a continuation of the Cookie Creations problem from Chapters 1 through 11.)

CC12 Natalie has prepared the balance sheet and income statement of Cookie & Coffee Creations Inc. and would like you to prepare the statement of cash flows.

Go to the book's companion website, at **www.wiley.com/college/kimmel**, *to find the completion of this problem.*

EXPAND YOUR CRITICAL THINKING

Financial Reporting

FINANCIAL REPORTING PROBLEM: Apple Inc.

E

CT12-1 The financial statements of Apple Inc. are presented in Appendix A.

Instructions
Answer the following questions.

(a) What was the amount of net cash provided by operating activities for the year ended September 27, 2014? For the year ended September 28, 2013?
(b) What was the amount of increase or decrease in cash and cash equivalents for the year ended September 27, 2014?
(c) Which method of computing net cash provided by operating activities does Apple use?
(d) From your analysis of the September 27, 2014, statement of cash flows, was the change in accounts receivable a decrease or an increase? Was the change in inventories a decrease or an increase? Was the change in accounts payable a decrease or an increase?
(e) What was the net cash used by investing activities for the year ended September 27, 2014?
(f) What was the amount of interest paid in the year ended September 27, 2014? What was the amount of income taxes paid for the same period?

Financial Analysis

COMPARATIVE ANALYSIS PROBLEM: Columbia Sportswear Company vs. VF Corporation

E

CT12-2 Columbia Sportswear Company's financial statements are presented in Appendix B. Financial statements of VF Corporation are presented in Appendix C.

Instructions
(a) Based on the information contained in these financial statements, compute free cash flow for each company.
(b) What conclusions concerning the management of cash can be drawn from these data?

COMPARATIVE ANALYSIS PROBLEM: Amazon.com, Inc. vs. Wal-Mart Stores, Inc.

Financial Analysis

CT12-3 Amazon.com, Inc.'s financial statements are presented in Appendix D. Financial statements of Wal-Mart Stores, Inc. are presented in Appendix E. E

Instructions

(a) Based on the information contained in these financial statements, compute free cash flow for each company.
(b) What conclusions concerning the management of cash can be drawn from these data?

REAL-WORLD FOCUS

CT12-4 ***Purpose:*** Use the Internet to view SEC filings. AN

Address: **biz.yahoo.com/i**

Steps

1. Enter a company's name.
2. Choose **Quote**. Answer questions (a) and (b).
3. Choose **Profile**; then choose **SEC**. Answer questions (c) and (d).

Instructions

Answer the following questions.

(a) What company did you select?
(b) What is its stock symbol? What is its selling price?
(c) What recent SEC filings are available for your viewing?
(d) Which filing is the most recent? What is the date?

CT12-5 The March 4, 2010, edition of the *Wall Street Journal Online* contains an article by Jeffrey McCracken and Tom McGinty entitled "With Fistfuls of Cash, Firms on Hunt." AP

Instructions

Read the article and answer the following questions.

(a) How much cash did the nonfinancial (that is, nonbank-like) firms in the Standard & Poor's 500 have at the end of 2009? How big an increase in cash did this represent over the prior year?
(b) What reasons are given in the article for why companies might not want to keep hoarding cash?
(c) What steps did Alcoa take to try to increase the company's cash? Were these efforts successful?
(d) Often, companies issue shares of stock to acquire other companies. This represents a significant noncash transaction. At the time the article was written, why were many companies using cash rather than stock to acquire other companies?
(e) In addition to acquisitions, what other steps can companies take to reduce their cash balances?

CT12-6 The November 23, 2011, edition of the *Wall Street Journal Online* contains an article by John Jannarone entitled "Backlash from Netflix Buybacks." AP

Instructions

Read the article and answer the following questions.

(a) What was the stock price for the shares of common stock issued by Netflix in the article? What was the price of the stock a few months previously?
(b) Why did Netflix issue new shares at a time when its stock price was so depressed relative to previous valuations for its stock?
(c) What previous actions had Netflix taken to reduce its cash balance?
(d) What does the article say is the lesson that growth companies should learn from the Netflix example?

Financial Analysis

Writing

Group Project

DECISION-MAKING ACROSS THE ORGANIZATION

E **CT12-7** Pete Kent and Maria Robles are examining the following statement of cash flows for Sullivan Company for the year ended January 31, 2017.

SULLIVAN COMPANY
Statement of Cash Flows
For the Year Ended January 31, 2017

Sources of cash	
From sales of merchandise	$385,000
From sale of capital stock	405,000
From sale of investment (purchased below)	80,000
From depreciation	55,000
From issuance of note for truck	20,000
From interest on investments	6,000
Total sources of cash	951,000
Uses of cash	
For purchase of fixtures and equipment	320,000
For merchandise purchased for resale	258,000
For operating expenses (including depreciation)	170,000
For purchase of investment	75,000
For purchase of truck by issuance of note	20,000
For purchase of treasury stock	10,000
For interest on note payable	3,000
Total uses of cash	856,000
Net increase in cash	$ 95,000

Pete claims that Sullivan's statement of cash flows is an excellent portrayal of a superb first year with cash increasing $95,000. Maria replies that it was not a superb first year. Rather, she says, the year was an operating failure, that the statement is presented incorrectly, and that $95,000 is not the actual increase in cash. The cash balance at the beginning of the year was $140,000.

Instructions
With the class divided into groups, answer the following.
(a) Using the data provided, prepare a statement of cash flows in proper form using the indirect method. The only noncash items in the income statement are depreciation and the gain from the sale of the investment.
(b) With whom do you agree, Pete or Maria? Explain your position.

COMMUNICATION ACTIVITY

E **CT12-8** Walt Jax, the owner-president of Computer Services Company, is unfamiliar with the statement of cash flows that you, as his accountant, prepared. He asks for further explanation.

Instructions
Write him a brief memo explaining the form and content of the statement of cash flows as shown in Illustration 12-13 (page 604).

ETHICS CASE

E **CT12-9** Pendleton Automotive Corp. is a medium-sized wholesaler of automotive parts. It has 10 stockholders who have been paid a total of $1 million in cash dividends for 8 consecutive years. The board's policy requires that, for this dividend to be declared, net cash provided by operating activities as reported in Pendleton Automotive's current year's statement of cash flows must exceed $1 million. President and CEO Hans Pfizer's job is secure so long as he produces annual operating cash flows to support the usual dividend.

At the end of the current year, controller Kurt Nolte presents president Hans Pfizer with some disappointing news. The net cash provided by operating activities is calculated by the indirect method to be only $970,000. The president says to Kurt, "We must get that amount above $1 million. Isn't there some way to increase operating cash flow by another $30,000?" Kurt answers, "These figures were prepared by my assistant. I'll go back to my office and see what I can do." The president replies, "I know you won't let me down, Kurt."

Upon close scrutiny of the statement of cash flows, Kurt concludes that he can get the operating cash flows above $1 million by reclassifying a $60,000, 2-year note payable listed in the financing activities section as "Proceeds from bank loan—$60,000." He will report the note instead as "Increase in payables—$60,000" and treat it as an adjustment of net income in the operating activities section. He returns to the president, saying, "You can tell the board to declare their usual dividend. Our net cash flow provided by operating activities is $1,030,000." "Good man, Kurt! I knew I could count on you," exults the president.

Instructions

(a) Who are the stakeholders in this situation?
(b) Was there anything unethical about the president's actions? Was there anything unethical about the controller's actions?
(c) Are the board members or anyone else likely to discover the misclassification?

ALL ABOUT YOU

CT12-10 In this chapter, you learned that companies prepare a statement of cash flows in order to keep track of their sources and uses of cash and to help them plan for their future cash needs. Planning for your own short- and long-term cash needs is every bit as important as it is for a company. E

Instructions

Read the article "Financial 'Uh-oh'? No Problem," at **www.fool.com/personal-finance/saving/financial-uh-oh-no-problem.aspx**, and answer the following questions.

(a) Describe the three factors that determine how much money you should set aside for short-term needs.
(b) How many months of living expenses does the article suggest to set aside?
(c) Estimate how much you should set aside based upon your current situation. Are you closer to Cliff's scenario or to Prudence's?

FASB CODIFICATION ACTIVITY

CT12-11 If your school has a subscription to the FASB Codification, go to **http://aaahq.org/ascLogin.cfm** to log in and prepare responses to the following. Use the Master Glossary to determine the proper definitions. AN

(a) What are cash equivalents?
(b) What are financing activities?
(c) What are investing activities?
(d) What are operating activities?
(e) What is the primary objective for the statement of cash flow? Is working capital the basis for meeting this objective?
(f) Do companies need to disclose information about investing and financing activities that do not affect cash receipts or cash payments? If so, how should such information be disclosed?

A Look at IFRS

LEARNING OBJECTIVE 6 **Compare the procedures for the statement of cash flows under GAAP and IFRS.**

As in GAAP, the statement of cash flows is a required statement for IFRS. In addition, the content and presentation of an IFRS statement of cash flows is similar to the one used for GAAP. However, the disclosure requirements related to the statement of cash flows are more extensive under GAAP. *IAS 7* ("Cash Flow Statements") provides the overall IFRS requirements for cash flow information.

RELEVANT FACTS

Following are the key similarities and differences between GAAP and IFRS as related to the statement of cash flows.

Similarities

- Companies preparing financial statements under IFRS must also prepare a statement of cash flows as an integral part of the financial statements.
- Both IFRS and GAAP require that the statement of cash flows should have three major sections—operating, investing, and financing activities—along with changes in cash and cash equivalents.
- Similar to GAAP, the statement of cash flows can be prepared using either the indirect or direct method under IFRS. In both U.S. and international settings, companies choose for the most part to use the indirect method for reporting net cash flows from operating activities.
- The definition of cash equivalents used in IFRS is similar to that used in GAAP. A major difference is that in certain situations, bank overdrafts are considered part of cash and cash equivalents under IFRS (which is not the case in GAAP). Under GAAP, bank overdrafts are classified as financing activities in the statement of cash flows and are reported as liabilities on the balance sheet.

Differences

- IFRS requires that noncash investing and financing activities be excluded from the statement of cash flows. Instead, these noncash activities should be reported elsewhere. This requirement is interpreted to mean that noncash investing and financing activities should be disclosed in the notes to the financial statements instead of in the financial statements. Under GAAP, companies may present this information on the face of the statement of cash flows.
- One area where there can be substantial differences between IFRS and GAAP relates to the classification of interest, dividends, and taxes. The following table indicates the differences between the two approaches.

Item	IFRS	GAAP
Interest paid	Operating or financing	Operating
Interest received	Operating or investing	Operating
Dividends paid	Operating or financing	Financing
Dividends received	Operating or investing	Operating
Taxes paid	Operating—unless specific identification with financing or investing activity	Operating

- Under IFRS, some companies present the operating section in a single line item, with a full reconciliation provided in the notes to the financial statements. This presentation is not seen under GAAP.

LOOKING TO THE FUTURE

Presently, the FASB and the IASB are involved in a joint project on the presentation and organization of information in the financial statements. One interesting approach, revealed in a published proposal from that project, is that in the future the income statement and balance sheet would adopt headings similar to those of the statement of cash flows. That is, the income statement and balance sheet would be broken into operating, investing, and financing sections.

IFRS PRACTICE

IFRS SELF-TEST QUESTIONS

1. Under IFRS, interest paid can be reported as:
   (a) only a financing activity.
   (b) a financing activity or an investing activity.
   (c) a financing activity or an operating activity.
   (d) only an operating activity.
2. IFRS requires that noncash items:
   (a) be reported in the section to which they relate, that is, a noncash investing activity would be reported in the investing section.

(b) be disclosed in the notes to the financial statements.
(c) do not need to be reported.
(d) be treated in a fashion similar to cash equivalents.

3. In the future, it appears likely that:
(a) the income statement and balance sheet will have headings of operating, investing, and financing activities, much like the statement of cash flows.
(b) cash and cash equivalents will be combined in a single line item.
(c) the IASB will not allow companies to use the direct approach to the statement of cash flows.
(d) None of the above.

4. Under IFRS:
(a) taxes are always treated as an operating activity.
(b) the income statement uses the headings operating, investing, and financing activities.
(c) dividends received can be either an operating or investing activity.
(d) dividends paid can be either an operating or investing activity.

5. Which of the following is **correct?**
(a) Under IFRS, the statement of cash flows is optional.
(b) IFRS requires use of the direct approach in preparing the statement of cash flows.
(c) The majority of companies following GAAP and the majority following IFRS employ the indirect approach to the statement of cash flows.
(d) Under IFRS, companies offset financing activities against investing activities.

IFRS EXERCISES

IFRS12-1 Discuss the differences that exist in the treatment of bank overdrafts under GAAP and IFRS.

IFRS12-2 Describe the treatment of each of the following items under IFRS versus GAAP.

(a) Interest paid.
(b) Interest received.
(c) Dividends paid.
(d) Dividends received.

INTERNATIONAL FINANCIAL REPORTING PROBLEM: Louis Vuitton

IFRS12-3 The financial statements of Louis Vuitton are presented in Appendix F. Instructions for accessing and using the company's complete annual report, including the notes to its financial statements, are also provided in Appendix F.

Instructions
Use the company's annual report to answer the following questions.

(a) In which section (operating, investing, or financing) does Louis Vuitton report interest paid (finance costs)?
(b) In which section (operating, investing, or financing) does Louis Vuitton report dividends received?
(c) If Louis Vuitton reported under GAAP rather than IFRS, how would its treatment of bank overdrafts differ?

Answers to IFRS Self-Test Questions
1. c **2.** b **3.** a **4.** c **5.** c

13

Financial Analysis: The Big Picture

CHAPTER PREVIEW

We can all learn an important lesson from Warren Buffett: Study companies carefully if you wish to invest. Do not get caught up in fads but instead find companies that are financially healthy. Using some of the basic decision tools presented in this textbook, you can perform a rudimentary analysis on any company and draw basic conclusions about its financial health. Although it would not be wise for you to bet your life savings on a company's stock relying solely on your current level of knowledge, we strongly encourage you to practice your new skills wherever possible. Only with practice will you improve your ability to interpret financial numbers.

Before we unleash you on the world of high finance, we present a few more important concepts and techniques as well as one more comprehensive review of corporate financial statements. We use all of the decision tools presented in this textbook to analyze a single company, with comparisons to a competitor and industry averages.

CHAPTER OUTLINE

LEARNING OBJECTIVES		PRACTICE
1 Apply the concepts of sustainable income and quality of earnings.	• Sustainable income • Quality of earnings	DO IT! 1 Unusual Items
2 Apply horizontal analysis and vertical analysis.	• Horizontal analysis • Vertical analysis	DO IT! 2 Horizontal Analysis
3 Analyze a company's performance using ratio analysis.	• Price-earnings ratio • Liquidity ratios • Solvency ratios • Profitability ratios	DO IT! 3 Ratio Analysis

Go to the ***REVIEW AND PRACTICE*** section at the end of the chapter for a targeted summary and exercises with solutions.

Visit **WileyPLUS** for additional tutorials and practice opportunities.

Daniel Acker/Bloomberg/Getty Images, Inc.

It Pays to Be Patient

A recent issue of *Forbes* magazine listed Warren Buffett as the second richest person in the world. His estimated wealth was $69 billion, give or take a few million. How much is $69 billion? If you invested $69 billion in an investment earning just 4%, you could spend $7.6 million per day—every day—forever.

So, how does Buffett spend his money? Basically, he doesn't! He still lives in the same house that he purchased in Omaha, Nebraska, in 1958 for $31,500. He still drives his own car (a Cadillac DTS). And, in case you were thinking that his kids are riding the road to Easy Street, think again. Buffett has committed to donate virtually all of his money to charity before he dies.

How did Buffett amass this wealth? Through careful investing. Buffett epitomizes a "value investor." He applies the basic techniques he learned in the 1950s from the great value investor Benjamin Graham. He looks for companies that have good long-term potential but are currently underpriced. He invests in companies that have low exposure to debt and that reinvest their earnings for future growth. He does not get caught up in fads or the latest trends.

For example, Buffett sat out on the dot-com mania in the 1990s. When other investors put lots of money into fledgling high-tech firms, Buffett didn't bite because he did not find dot-com companies that met his criteria. He didn't get to enjoy the stock price boom on the way up, but on the other hand, he didn't have to ride the price back down to Earth. When the dot-com bubble burst, everyone else was suffering from investment shock. Buffett swooped in and scooped up deals on companies that he had been following for years.

In 2012, the stock market had again reached near record highs. Buffett's returns had been significantly lagging the market. Only 26% of his investments at that time were in stock, and he was sitting on $38 billion in cash. One commentator noted that "if the past is any guide, just when Buffett seems to look most like a loser, the party is about to end."

If you think you want to follow Buffett's example and transform your humble nest egg into a mountain of cash, be warned. His techniques have been widely circulated and emulated, but never practiced with the same degree of success. You should probably start by honing your financial analysis skills. A good way for you to begin your career as a successful investor is to master the fundamentals of financial analysis discussed in this chapter.

Source: Jason Zweig, "Buffett Is Out of Step," *Wall Street Journal* (May 7, 2012).

LEARNING OBJECTIVE 1

Apply the concepts of sustainable income and quality of earnings.

SUSTAINABLE INCOME

The value of a company like Google is a function of the amount, timing, and uncertainty of its future cash flows. Google's current and past income statements are particularly useful in helping analysts predict these future cash flows. In using this approach, analysts must make sure that Google's past income numbers reflect its **sustainable income**, that is, do not include unusual (out-of-the-ordinary) revenues, expenses, gains, and losses. **Sustainable income** is, therefore, the most likely level of income to be obtained by a company in the future. Sustainable income differs from actual net income by the amount of unusual revenues, expenses, gains, and losses included in the current year's income. Analysts are interested in sustainable income because it helps them derive an estimate of future earnings without the "noise" of unusual items.

Fortunately, an income statement provides information on sustainable income by separating operating transactions from nonoperating transactions. This statement also highlights intermediate components of income such as income from operations, income before income taxes, and income from continuing operations. In addition, information on unusual items such as gains or losses on discontinued items and components of other comprehensive income are disclosed.

Illustration 13-1 presents a statement of comprehensive income for Cruz Company for the year 2017. A statement of comprehensive income includes not only net income but a broader measure of income called comprehensive income. (Recall that in Chapter 5 we instead presented comprehensive income in a separate statement called a comprehensive income statement. Both approaches are allowed under GAAP.) The two major unusual items in this statement are discontinued operations and other comprehensive income (highlighted in red). When estimating future cash flows, analysts must consider the implications of each of these components.

ILLUSTRATION 13-1
Statement of comprehensive income

CRUZ COMPANY
Statement of Comprehensive Income
For the year ended 2017

Sales revenue	$900,000
Cost of goods sold	650,000
Gross profit	250,000
Operating expenses	100,000
Income from operations	150,000
Other revenues (expenses) and gains (losses)	20,000
Income before income taxes	170,000
Income tax expense	24,000
Income from continuing operations	146,000
Discontinued operations (net of tax)	**30,000**
Net income	176,000
Other comprehensive income items (net of tax)	**10,000**
Comprehensive income	$186,000

In looking at Illustration 13-1, note that Cruz Company's two major types of unusual items, discontinued operations and other comprehensive income, are reported net of tax. That is, Cruz first calculates income tax expense before income from continuing operations. Then, it calculates income tax expense related to the discontinued operations and other comprehensive income. The general concept is, "Let the tax follow the income or loss." We discuss discontinued operations and other comprehensive income in more detail next.

Discontinued Operations

Discontinued operations refers to the disposal of a **significant component** of a business, such as the elimination of a major class of customers or an entire activity. For example, to downsize its operations, General Dynamics Corp. sold its missile business to Hughes Aircraft Co. for $450 million. In its statement of comprehensive income, General Dynamics reported the sale in a separate section entitled "Discontinued operations."

DECISION TOOLS

The discontinued operations section alerts users to the sale of any of a company's major components of its business.

Following the disposal of a significant component, the company should report on its statement both income from continuing operations and income (or loss) from discontinued operations. **The income (loss) from discontinued operations consists of two parts: the income (loss) from operations** and **the gain (loss) on disposal of the component.**

To illustrate, assume that during 2017 Acro Energy Inc. has income before income taxes of $800,000. During 2017, Acro discontinued and sold its unprofitable chemical division. The loss in 2017 from chemical operations (net of $60,000 taxes) was $140,000. The loss on disposal of the chemical division (net of $30,000 taxes) was $70,000. Assuming a 30% tax rate on income, Illustration 13-2 shows Acro's statement of comprehensive income presentation.

ILLUSTRATION 13-2
Statement presentation of discontinued operations

ACRO ENERGY INC.
Statement of Comprehensive Income (partial)
For the Year Ended December 31, 2017

Income before income taxes		$800,000
Income tax expense		240,000
Income from continuing operations		560,000
Discontinued operations		
Loss from operation of chemical division, net of $60,000 income tax savings	$140,000	
Loss from disposal of chemical division, net of $30,000 income tax savings	70,000	210,000
Net income		$350,000

▼ **HELPFUL HINT**
Observe the dual disclosures: (1) the results of operation of the discontinued division must be eliminated from the results of continuing operations, and (2) the company must also report the disposal of the division.

Note that the statement uses the caption "Income from continuing operations" and adds a new section "Discontinued operations." **The new section reports both the operating loss and the loss on disposal net of applicable income taxes.** This presentation clearly indicates the separate effects of continuing operations and discontinued operations on net income.

INVESTOR INSIGHT

© Andrey Armyagov/iStockphoto

What Does "Non-Recurring" Really Mean?

Many companies incur restructuring charges as they attempt to reduce costs. They often label these items in the income statement as "non-recurring" charges, to suggest that they are isolated events, unlikely to occur in future periods. The question for analysts is, are these costs really one-time, "non-recurring events" or do they reflect problems that the company will be facing for many periods in the future? If they are one-time events, then they can be largely ignored when trying to predict future earnings.

But, some companies report "one-time" restructuring charges over and over again. For example, Procter & Gamble reported a restructuring charge in 12 consecutive quarters, and Motorola had "special" charges in 14 consecutive quarters. On the other hand, other companies have a restructuring charge only once in a 5- or 10-year period. There appears to be no substitute for careful analysis of the numbers that comprise net income.

If a company takes a large restructuring charge, what is the effect on the company's current income statement versus future ones? (Go to **WileyPLUS** for this answer and additional questions.)

Comprehensive Income

Most revenues, expenses, gains, and losses are included in net income. However, as discussed in earlier chapters, certain gains and losses that bypass net income are reported as part of a more inclusive earnings measure called comprehensive income. **Comprehensive income** is the sum of net income and other comprehensive income items.[1]

ILLUSTRATION OF COMPREHENSIVE INCOME Accounting standards require that companies adjust most investments in stocks and bonds up or down to their market price at the end of each accounting period. For example, assume that during 2017, its first year of operations, Stassi Corporation purchased IBM stock for $10,000 as an investment. At the end of 2017, Stassi was still holding the investment, but the stock's market price was now $8,000. In this case, Stassi is required to reduce the recorded value of its IBM investment by $2,000. The $2,000 difference is an unrealized loss.

Should Stassi include this $2,000 unrealized loss in net income? It depends on whether Stassi classifies the IBM stock as a trading security or an available-for-sale security. A **trading security** is bought and held primarily for sale in the near term to generate income on short-term price differences. Companies report unrealized losses on trading securities in the "Other expenses and losses" section of the income statement. The rationale: It is likely that the company will realize the unrealized loss (or an unrealized gain), so the company should report the loss (gain) as part of net income.

If Stassi did not purchase the investment for trading purposes, it is classified as available-for-sale. **Available-for-sale securities** are held with the intent of selling them sometime in the future. Companies do not include unrealized gains or losses on available-for-sale securities in net income. Instead, they report them as part of "Other comprehensive income." Other comprehensive income is not included in net income.

FORMAT As shown in Chapter 5, one format for reporting other comprehensive income is to report a separate comprehensive income statement. For example, assuming that Stassi Corporation has a net income of $300,000, the unrealized loss would be reported below net income as follows.

ILLUSTRATION 13-3
Lower portion of combined statement of income and comprehensive income

STASSI CORPORATION
Comprehensive Income Statement
For the Year Ended December 31, 2017

Net income	$300,000
Other comprehensive income	
Unrealized loss on available-for-sale securities	2,000
Comprehensive income	$298,000

As discussed in Chapter 11, companies report the cumulative amount of other comprehensive income from all years as a separate component of stockholders' equity. To illustrate, assume Stassi has common stock of $3,000,000, retained earnings of $300,000, and accumulated other comprehensive loss of $2,000. (To simplify, we are assuming that this is Stassi's first year of operations. Since it has only operated for one year, the cumulative amount of other comprehensive income is this year's loss of $2,000.) Illustration 13-4 shows the balance sheet presentation of the accumulated other comprehensive loss.

[1]The FASB'S Conceptual Framework describes comprehensive income as including all changes in stockholders' equity during a period except those changes resulting from investments by stockholders and distributions to stockholders.

ILLUSTRATION 13-4
Unrealized loss in stockholders' equity section

STASSI CORPORATION Balance Sheet (partial)	
Stockholders' equity	
Common stock	$3,000,000
Retained earnings	300,000
Total paid-in capital and retained earnings	3,300,000
Accumulated other comprehensive loss	**(2,000)**
Total stockholders' equity	$3,298,000

Note that the presentation of the accumulated other comprehensive loss is similar to the presentation of the cost of treasury stock in the stockholders' equity section. (An unrealized gain would be added in this section of the balance sheet.)

COMPLETE STATEMENT OF COMPREHENSIVE INCOME As seen in Illustration 13-1, as an alternative to preparing a separate comprehensive income statement, many companies report net income and other comprehensive income in a combined statement of comprehensive income. (*For your homework in this chapter, use this combined format*.) The statement of comprehensive income for Pace Corporation in Illustration 13-5 presents the types of items found on this statement, such as net sales, cost of goods sold, operating expenses, and income taxes. In addition, it shows how companies report discontinued operations and other comprehensive income (highlighted in red).

ILLUSTRATION 13-5
Complete statement of comprehensive income

PACE CORPORATION Statement of Comprehensive Income For the Year Ended December 31, 2017		
Net sales		$440,000
Cost of goods sold		260,000
Gross profit		180,000
Operating expenses		110,000
Income from operations		70,000
Other revenues and gains		5,600
Other expenses and losses		9,600
Income before income taxes		66,000
Income tax expense ($66,000 × 30%)		19,800
Income from continuing operations		46,200
Discontinued operations		
Loss from operation of plastics division, net of income tax savings $18,000 ($60,000 × 30%)	**$42,000**	
Gain on disposal of plastics division, net of $15,000 income taxes ($50,000 × 30%)	**35,000**	**7,000**
Net income		**39,200**
Other comprehensive income		
Unrealized gain on available-for-sale securities, net of income taxes ($15,000 × 30%)		**10,500**
Comprehensive income		**$ 49,700**

Changes in Accounting Principle

For ease of comparison, users of financial statements expect companies to prepare their statements on a basis **consistent** with the preceding period. A **change in accounting principle** occurs when the principle used in the current year is different from the one used in the preceding year. An example is a change in inventory costing methods (such as FIFO to average-cost). Accounting rules permit a change when management can show that the new principle is preferable to the old principle.

DECISION TOOLS

Informing users of a change in accounting principle helps them determine the effect of this change on current and prior periods.

Companies report most changes in accounting principle retroactively.[2] That is, they report both the current period and previous periods using the new principle. As a result, the same principle applies in all periods. This treatment improves the ability to compare results across years.

INVESTOR INSIGHT United Parcel Service (UPS)

Larry MacDougal/AP/Wide World Photos

More Frequent Ups and Downs

In the past, U.S. companies used a method to account for their pension plans that smoothed out the gains and losses on their pension portfolios by spreading gains and losses over multiple years. Many felt that this approach was beneficial because it reduced the volatility of reported net income. However, recently some companies have opted to adopt a method that comes closer to recognizing gains and losses in the period in which they occur. Some of the companies that have adopted this approach are United Parcel Service (UPS), Honeywell International, IBM, AT&T, and Verizon Communications. The CFO at UPS said he favored the new approach because "events that occurred in prior years will no longer distort current-year results. It will result in better transparency by eliminating the noise of past plan performance." When UPS switched, it resulted in a charge of $827 million from the change in accounting principle.

Source: Bob Sechler and Doug Cameron, "UPS Alters Pension-Plan Accounting," *Wall Street Journal* (January 30, 2012).

When predicting future earnings, how should analysts treat the one-time charge that results from a switch to the different approach for accounting for pension plans? (Go to **WileyPLUS** for this answer and additional questions.)

QUALITY OF EARNINGS

The quality of a company's earnings is of extreme importance to analysts. A company that has a high **quality of earnings** provides full and transparent information that will not confuse or mislead users of the financial statements.

Recent accounting scandals suggest that some companies are spending too much time managing their income and not enough time managing their business. Here are some of the factors affecting quality of earnings.

Alternative Accounting Methods

Variations among companies in the application of generally accepted accounting principles may hamper comparability and reduce quality of earnings. For example, suppose one company uses the FIFO method of inventory costing, while another company in the same industry uses LIFO. If inventory is a significant asset to both companies, it is unlikely that their current ratios are comparable. For example, if General Motors Corporation used FIFO instead of LIFO for inventory valuation, its inventories in a recent year would have been 26% higher, which significantly affects the current ratio (and other ratios as well).

In addition to differences in inventory costing methods, differences also exist in reporting such items as depreciation and amortization. Although these differences in accounting methods might be detectable from reading the notes to the financial statements, adjusting the financial data to compensate for the different methods is often difficult, if not impossible.

Pro Forma Income

Companies whose stock is publicly traded are required to present their income statement following generally accepted accounting principles (GAAP). In recent

[2]An exception to the general rule is a change in depreciation methods. The effects of this change are reported in current and future periods. Discussion of this approach is left for more advanced courses.

years, many companies have been also reporting a second measure of income, called pro forma income. **Pro forma income** usually excludes items that the company thinks are unusual or non-recurring. For example, in a recent year, Cisco Systems (a high-tech company) reported a quarterly net loss under GAAP of $2.7 billion. Cisco reported pro forma income for the same quarter as a profit of $230 million. This large difference in profits between GAAP income numbers and pro forma income is not unusual. For example, during one nine-month period, the 100 largest companies on the Nasdaq stock exchange reported a total pro forma income of $19.1 billion but a total loss as measured by GAAP of $82.3 billion—a difference of about $100 billion!

To compute pro forma income, companies generally exclude any items they deem inappropriate for measuring their performance. Many analysts and investors are critical of the practice of using pro forma income because these numbers often make companies look better than they really are. As the financial press noted, pro forma numbers might be called "earnings before bad stuff." Companies, on the other hand, argue that pro forma numbers more clearly indicate sustainable income because they exclude unusual and non-recurring expenses. "Cisco's technique gives readers of financial statements a clear picture of Cisco's normal business activities," the company said in a statement issued in response to questions about its pro forma income accounting.

Recently, the SEC provided some guidance on how companies should present pro forma information. Stay tuned: Everyone seems to agree that pro forma numbers can be useful if they provide insights into determining a company's sustainable income. However, many companies have abused the flexibility that pro forma numbers allow and have used the measure as a way to put their companies in a more favorable light.

Improper Recognition

Because some managers feel pressure from Wall Street to continually increase earnings, they manipulate earnings numbers to meet these expectations. The most common abuse is the improper recognition of revenue. One practice that some companies use is called **channel stuffing**. Offering deep discounts, companies encourage customers to buy early (stuff the channel) rather than later. This boosts earnings in the current period, but it often leads to a disaster in subsequent periods because customers have no need for additional goods. To illustrate, Bristol-Myers Squibb at one time indicated that it used sales incentives to encourage wholesalers to buy more drugs than they needed. As a result, the company had to issue revised financial statements showing corrected revenues and income.

Another practice is the improper capitalization of operating expenses. WorldCom capitalized over $7 billion of operating expenses in order to report positive net income. In other situations, companies fail to report all their liabilities. Enron promised to make payments on certain contracts if financial difficulty developed, but these guarantees were not reported as liabilities. In addition, disclosure was so lacking in transparency that it was impossible to understand what was happening at the company.

DO IT! ▶1 Unusual Items

In its proposed 2017 income statement, AIR Corporation reports income before income taxes $400,000, unrealized gain on available-for-sale securities $100,000, income taxes $120,000 (not including unusual items), loss from operation of discontinued flower division $50,000, and loss on disposal of discontinued flower division $90,000. The income tax rate is 30%. Prepare a correct statement of comprehensive income, beginning with "Income before income taxes."

Action Plan

✔ Show discontinued operations and other comprehensive income net of tax.

SOLUTION

AIR CORPORATION Statement of Comprehensive Income (partial) For the Year Ended December 31, 2017		
Income before income taxes		$400,000
Income tax expense		120,000
Income from continuing operations		280,000
Discontinued operations		
Loss from operation of flower division, net of $15,000 income tax savings	$35,000	
Loss on disposal of flower division, net of $27,000 income tax savings	63,000	98,000
Net income		182,000
Other comprehensive income		
Unrealized gain on available-for-sale securities, net of $30,000 income taxes		70,000
Comprehensive income		$252,000

Related exercise material: **BE13-1, BE13-2, DO IT! 13-1, E13-1,** and **E13-2.**

LEARNING OBJECTIVE 2

Apply horizontal analysis and vertical analysis.

As indicated, in assessing the financial performance of a company, investors are interested in the core or sustainable earnings of a company. In addition, investors are interested in making comparisons from period to period. Throughout this textbook, we have relied on three types of comparisons to improve the decision-usefulness of financial information:

1. **Intracompany basis.** Comparisons within a company are often useful to detect changes in financial relationships and significant trends. For example, a comparison of Kellogg's current year's cash amount with the prior year's cash amount shows either an increase or a decrease. Likewise, a comparison of Kellogg's year-end cash amount with the amount of its total assets at year-end shows the proportion of total assets in the form of cash.
2. **Intercompany basis.** Comparisons with other companies provide insight into a company's competitive position. For example, investors can compare Kellogg's total sales for the year with the total sales of its competitors in the breakfast cereal area, such as General Mills.
3. **Industry averages.** Comparisons with industry averages provide information about a company's relative position within the industry. For example, financial statement readers can compare Kellogg's financial data with the averages for its industry compiled by financial rating organizations such as Dun & Bradstreet, Moody's, and Standard & Poor's, or with information provided on the Internet by organizations such as Yahoo! on its financial site.

INTERNATIONAL NOTE

As more countries adopt IFRS, the ability of analysts to compare companies from different countries should improve. However, IFRSs are open to widely varying interpretations. In addition, some countries adopt IFRS "with modifications." As a consequence, most cross-country comparisons are still not as transparent as within-country comparisons.

We use three basic tools in financial statement analysis to highlight the significance of financial statement data:

1. Horizontal analysis
2. Vertical analysis
3. Ratio analysis

In previous chapters, we relied primarily on ratio analysis, supplemented with some basic horizontal and vertical analysis. In the remainder of this section, we introduce more formal forms of horizontal and vertical analysis. In the next section, we review ratio analysis in some detail.

HORIZONTAL ANALYSIS

DECISION TOOLS

Horizontal analysis helps users compare a company's financial position and operating results with those of the previous period.

Horizontal analysis, also known as trend analysis, is a technique for evaluating a series of financial statement data over a period of time. Its purpose is to determine the increase or decrease that has taken place, expressed as either an amount or a percentage. For example, here are recent net sales figures (in thousands) of Chicago Cereal Company:

2014	2013	2012	2011	2010
$11,776	$10,907	$10,177	$9,614	$8,812

If we assume that 2010 is the base year, we can measure all percentage increases or decreases relative to this base-period amount with the formula shown in Illustration 13-6.

ILLUSTRATION 13-6
Horizontal analysis—computation of changes since base period

$$\frac{\text{Change Since}}{\text{Base Period}} = \frac{\text{Current-Year Amount} - \text{Base-Year Amount}}{\text{Base-Year Amount}}$$

For example, we can determine that net sales for Chicago Cereal increased approximately 9.1% [($9,614 − $8,812) ÷ $8,812] from 2010 to 2011. Similarly, we can also determine that net sales increased by 33.6% [($11,776 − $8,812) ÷ $8,812] from 2010 to 2014.

Alternatively, we can express current-year sales as a percentage of the base period. To do so, we would divide the current-year amount by the base-year amount, as shown in Illustration 13-7.

ILLUSTRATION 13-7
Horizontal analysis—computation of current year in relation to base year

$$\frac{\text{Current Results in}}{\text{Relation to Base Period}} = \frac{\text{Current-Year Amount}}{\text{Base-Year Amount}}$$

Current-period sales expressed as a percentage of the base period for each of the five years, using 2010 as the base period, are shown in Illustration 13-8.

ILLUSTRATION 13-8
Horizontal analysis of net sales

CHICAGO CEREAL COMPANY
Net Sales (in thousands)
Base Period 2010

2014	2013	2012	2011	2010
$11,776	$10,907	$10,177	$9,614	$8,812
133.6%	123.8%	115.5%	109.1%	100%

The large increase in net sales during 2011 would raise questions regarding possible reasons for such a significant change. Chicago Cereal's 2011 notes to the financial statements explain that the company completed an acquisition of Elf Foods Company during 2011. This major acquisition would help explain the increase in sales highlighted by horizontal analysis.

To further illustrate horizontal analysis, we use the financial statements of Chicago Cereal Company. Its two-year condensed balance sheets for 2014 and 2013, showing dollar and percentage changes, are presented in Illustration 13-9 (page 656).

ILLUSTRATION 13-9
Horizontal analysis of balance sheets

CHICAGO CEREAL COMPANY
Condensed Balance Sheets
December 31 (in thousands)

			Increase (Decrease) during 2014	
Assets	**2014**	**2013**	**Amount**	**Percent**
Current assets	$ 2,717	$ 2,427	$ 290	11.9
Property assets (net)	2,990	2,816	174	6.2
Other assets	5,690	5,471	219	4.0
Total assets	$11,397	$10,714	$683	6.4
Liabilities and Stockholders' Equity				
Current liabilities	$ 4,044	$ 4,020	$ 24	0.6
Long-term liabilities	4,827	4,625	202	4.4
Total liabilities	8,871	8,645	226	2.6
Stockholders' equity				
Common stock	493	397	96	24.2
Retained earnings	3,390	2,584	806	31.2
Treasury stock (cost)	(1,357)	(912)	(445)	48.8
Total stockholders' equity	2,526	2,069	457	22.1
Total liabilities and stockholders' equity	$11,397	$10,714	$ 683	6.4

▼ **HELPFUL HINT**
When using horizontal analysis, be sure to examine both dollar amount changes and percentage changes. It is not necessarily bad if a company's earnings are growing at a declining rate. The amount of increase may be the same as or more than the base year, but the percentage change may be less because the base is greater each year.

The comparative balance sheets show that a number of changes occurred in Chicago Cereal's financial position from 2013 to 2014. In the assets section, current assets increased $290,000, or 11.9% ($290 ÷ $2,427), and property assets (net) increased $174,000, or 6.2%. Other assets increased $219,000, or 4.0%. In the liabilities section, current liabilities increased $24,000, or 0.6%, while long-term liabilities increased $202,000, or 4.4%. In the stockholders' equity section, we find that retained earnings increased $806,000, or 31.2%.

Illustration 13-10 presents two-year comparative income statements of Chicago Cereal Company for 2014 and 2013, showing dollar and percentage changes.

ILLUSTRATION 13-10
Horizontal analysis of income statements

CHICAGO CEREAL COMPANY
Condensed Income Statements
For the Years Ended December 31 (in thousands)

			Increase (Decrease) during 2014	
	2014	**2013**	**Amount**	**Percent**
Net sales	$11,776	$10,907	$869	8.0
Cost of goods sold	6,597	6,082	515	8.5
Gross profit	5,179	4,825	354	7.3
Selling and administrative expenses	3,311	3,059	252	8.2
Income from operations	1,868	1,766	102	5.8
Interest expense	319	307	12	3.9
Other income (expense), net	(2)	13	(15)	(115.4)
Income before income taxes	1,547	1,472	75	5.1
Income tax expense	444	468	(24)	(5.1)
Net income	$ 1,103	$ 1,004	$ 99	9.9

▼ **HELPFUL HINT**
Note that, in a horizontal analysis, while the amount column is additive (the total is $99,000), the percentage column is not additive (9.9% is not a total).

Horizontal analysis of the income statements shows the following changes. Net sales increased $869,000, or 8.0% ($869 ÷ $10,907). Cost of goods sold increased $515,000, or 8.5% ($515 ÷ $6,082). Selling and administrative expenses increased $252,000, or 8.2% ($252 ÷ $3,059). Overall, gross profit increased 7.3% and net income increased 9.9%. The increase in net income can be attributed to the increase in net sales and a decrease in income tax expense.

The measurement of changes from period to period in percentages is relatively straightforward and quite useful. However, complications can result in making the computations. If an item has no value in a base year or preceding year and a value in the next year, no percentage change can be computed. Likewise, no percentage change can be computed if a negative amount appears in the base or preceding period and a positive amount exists the following year.

VERTICAL ANALYSIS

Vertical analysis, also called common-size analysis, is a technique for evaluating financial statement data that expresses each item in a financial statement as a **percentage of a base amount**. For example, on a balance sheet we might express current assets as 22% of total assets (total assets being the base amount). Or, on an income statement we might express selling expenses as 16% of net sales (net sales being the base amount).

DECISION TOOLS

Vertical analysis helps users compare relationships between financial statement items with those of last year or of competitors.

Presented in Illustration 13-11 are the comparative balance sheets of Chicago Cereal for 2014 and 2013, analyzed vertically. The base for the asset items is **total assets**, and the base for the liability and stockholders' equity items is **total liabilities and stockholders' equity**.

ILLUSTRATION 13-11
Vertical analysis of balance sheets

CHICAGO CEREAL COMPANY
Condensed Balance Sheets
December 31 (in thousands)

	2014		2013	
Assets	**Amount**	**Percent***	**Amount**	**Percent***
Current assets	$ 2,717	23.8	$ 2,427	22.6
Property assets (net)	2,990	26.2	2,816	26.3
Other assets	5,690	50.0	5,471	51.1
Total assets	$11,397	100.0	$10,714	100.0
Liabilities and Stockholders' Equity				
Current liabilities	$ 4,044	35.5	$ 4,020	37.5
Long-term liabilities	4,827	42.4	4,625	43.2
Total liabilities	8,871	77.9	8,645	80.7
Stockholders' equity				
Common stock	493	4.3	397	3.7
Retained earnings	3,390	29.7	2,584	24.1
Treasury stock (cost)	(1,357)	(11.9)	(912)	(8.5)
Total stockholders' equity	2,526	22.1	2,069	19.3
Total liabilities and stockholders' equity	$11,397	100.0	$10,714	100.0

*Numbers have been rounded to total 100%.

In addition to showing the relative size of each category on the balance sheets, vertical analysis can show the percentage change in the individual asset, liability, and stockholders' equity items. In this case, current assets increased $290,000 from 2013 to 2014, and they increased from 22.6% to 23.8% of total assets. Property assets (net) decreased from 26.3% to 26.2% of total assets. Other assets decreased from 51.1% to 50.0% of total assets. Also, retained earnings increased by $806,000 from 2013 to 2014, and total stockholders' equity increased from 19.3% to 22.1% of total liabilities and stockholders' equity. This switch to a higher percentage of equity financing has two causes. First, while total liabilities increased by $226,000, the percentage of liabilities declined from 80.7% to 77.9% of total liabilities and stockholders' equity. Second, retained earnings increased by $806,000, from 24.1% to 29.7% of total liabilities and stockholders' equity. Thus, the company shifted toward equity financing by relying less on debt and by increasing the amount of retained earnings.

Vertical analysis of the comparative income statements of Chicago Cereal, shown in Illustration 13-12, reveals that cost of goods sold **as a percentage of net sales** increased from 55.8% to 56.0%, and selling and administrative expenses increased from 28.0% to 28.1%. Net income as a percentage of net sales increased from 9.1% to 9.4%. Chicago Cereal's increase in net income as a percentage of sales is due primarily to the decrease in interest expense and income tax expense as a percentage of sales.

ILLUSTRATION 13-12
Vertical analysis of income statements

CHICAGO CEREAL COMPANY
Condensed Income Statements
For the Years Ended December 31 (in thousands)

	2014		2013	
	Amount	**Percent***	**Amount**	**Percent***
Net sales	$11,776	100.0	$10,907	100.0
Cost of goods sold	6,597	56.0	6,082	55.8
Gross profit	5,179	44.0	4,825	44.2
Selling and administrative expenses	3,311	28.1	3,059	28.0
Income from operations	1,868	15.9	1,766	16.2
Interest expense	319	2.7	307	2.8
Other income (expense), net	(2)	.0	13	.0
Income before income taxes	1,547	13.2	1,472	13.4
Income tax expense	444	3.8	468	4.3
Net income	$ 1,103	9.4	$ 1,004	9.1

*Numbers have been rounded to total 100%.

Vertical analysis also enables you to compare companies of different sizes. For example, one of Chicago Cereal's competitors is General Mills. General Mills' sales are 1,000 times larger than those of Chicago Cereal. Vertical analysis enables us to meaningfully compare the condensed income statements of Chicago Cereal and General Mills, as shown in Illustration 13-13.

ILLUSTRATION 13-13
Intercompany comparison by vertical analysis

CONDENSED INCOME STATEMENTS
For the Years Ended December 31, 2014 (Chicago Cereal), and May 25, 2014 (General Mills)

	Chicago Cereal (in thousands)		General Mills, Inc. (in millions)	
	Amount	**Percent***	**Amount**	**Percent***
Net sales	$11,776	100.0	$17,910	100.0
Cost of goods sold	6,597	56.0	11,540	64.4
Gross profit	5,179	44.0	6,370	35.6
Selling and administrative expenses	3,311	28.1	3,474	19.4
Non-recurring charges and (gains)	0	—	(62)	(0.3)
Income from operations	1,868	15.9	2,958	16.5
Other expenses and revenues (including income taxes)	765	6.5	1,134	6.3
Net income	$ 1,103	9.4	$ 1,824	10.2

*Numbers have been rounded to total 100%.

Although Chicago Cereal's net sales are much less than those of General Mills, vertical analysis eliminates the impact of this size difference for our analysis. Chicago Cereal has a higher gross profit percentage 44.0%, compared to 35.6% for General Mills. But, Chicago Cereal's selling and administrative expenses are 28.1% of net sales, while those of General Mills are 19.4% of net sales. Looking at net income, we see that General Mills' percentage is higher. Chicago Cereal's net income as a percentage of net sales is 9.4%, compared to 10.2% for General Mills.

ANATOMY OF A FRAUD

This final *Anatomy of a Fraud* box demonstrates that sometimes relationships between numbers can be used to detect fraud. Financial ratios that appear abnormal or statistical abnormalities in the numbers themselves can reveal fraud. For example, the fact that WorldCom's line costs, as a percentage of either total expenses or revenues, differed very significantly from its competitors should have alerted people to the possibility of fraud. Or, consider the case of a bank manager, who cooperated with a group of his friends to defraud the bank's credit card department. The manager's friends would apply for credit cards and then run up balances of slightly less than $5,000. The bank had a policy of allowing bank personnel to write-off balances of less than $5,000 without seeking supervisor approval. The fraud was detected by applying statistical analysis based on Benford's Law. Benford's Law states that in a random collection of numbers, the frequency of lower digits (e.g., 1, 2, or 3) should be much higher than higher digits (e.g., 7, 8, or 9). In this case, bank auditors analyzed the first two digits of amounts written off. There was a spike at 48 and 49, which was not consistent with what would be expected if the numbers were random.

Total take: Thousands of dollars

THE MISSING CONTROL

Independent internal verification. While it might be efficient to allow employees to write off accounts below a certain level, it is important that these write-offs be reviewed and verified periodically. Such a review would likely call attention to an employee with large amounts of write-offs, or in this case, write-offs that were frequently very close to the approval threshold.

Source: Mark J. Nigrini, "I've Got Your Number," *Journal of Accountancy Online* (May 1999).

DO IT! 2 Horizontal Analysis

Summary financial information for Rosepatch Company is as follows.

	December 31, 2017	December 31, 2016
Current assets	$234,000	$180,000
Plant assets (net)	756,000	420,000
Total assets	$990,000	$600,000

Compute the amount and percentage changes in 2017 using horizontal analysis, assuming 2016 is the base year.

SOLUTION

	Increase in 2017	
	Amount	Percent
Current assets	$ 54,000	30% [($234,000 − $180,000) ÷ $180,000]
Plant assets (net)	336,000	80% [($756,000 − $420,000) ÷ $420,000]
Total assets	$390,000	65% [($990,000 − $600,000) ÷ $600,000]

Action Plan

✔ Find the percentage change by dividing the amount of the increase by the 2016 amount (base year).

Related exercise material: **BE13-4, BE13-6, BE13-7, BE13-9, DO IT! 13-2, E13-3, E13-5,** and **E13-6.**

LEARNING OBJECTIVE 3

Analyze a company's performance using ratio analysis.

In previous chapters, we presented many ratios used for evaluating the financial health and performance of a company. Here, we introduce one more ratio, the price-earnings ratio, and then we provide a summary listing of all ratios presented in the textbook. (Page references to prior discussions are provided if you feel you need to review any individual ratios.) Appendix 13A provides an example of a comprehensive financial analysis employing these ratios.

PRICE-EARNINGS RATIO

Earnings per share is net income available to common stockholders divided by the average number of common shares outstanding. The market price of a company's stock changes based on investors' expectations about a company's future earnings per share. To compare market prices and earnings across firms, investors calculate the **price-earnings (P-E) ratio**. The P-E ratio divides the market price of a share of common stock by earnings per share.

ILLUSTRATION 13-14
Formula for price-earnings (P-E) ratio

$$\text{Price-Earnings (P-E) Ratio} = \frac{\text{Market Price per Share}}{\text{Earnings per Share}}$$

The P-E ratio reflects investors' assessment of a company's future earnings. The ratio of price to earnings will be higher if investors think that earnings will increase substantially in the future and therefore are willing to pay more per share of stock. A low price-earnings ratio often signifies that investors think the company's future earnings will not be strong. In addition, sometimes a low P-E ratio reflects the market's belief that a company has poor-quality earnings.

To illustrate, assume that two identical companies each have earnings per share of $5. Suppose one of the companies manipulated its accounting numbers to achieve the $5 figure. If investors perceive that firm has lower-quality earnings, this perception will be reflected in a lower stock price and, consequently, a lower P-E.

Illustration 13-15 shows earnings per share and P-E ratios for five companies for a recent year.

ILLUSTRATION 13-15
Earnings per share and P-E ratios of various companies

Company	Earnings per Share	Price-Earnings Ratio
Southwest Airlines	$ 1.65	19.5
Google	29.80	27.0
Apple	6.49	15.6
Skechers USA	2.74	34.0
Nike	3.05	28.7

LIQUIDITY RATIOS

Liquidity ratios (Illustration 13-16) measure the short-term ability of the company to pay its maturing obligations and to meet unexpected needs for cash. Short-term creditors such as bankers and suppliers are particularly interested in assessing liquidity.

ILLUSTRATION 13-16
Summary of liquidity ratios

Liquidity Ratios		
Working capital	Current assets − Current liabilities	p. 54
Current ratio	$\frac{\text{Current assets}}{\text{Current liabilities}}$	p. 54
Inventory turnover	$\frac{\text{Cost of goods sold}}{\text{Average inventory}}$	p. 283
Days in inventory	$\frac{\text{365 days}}{\text{Inventory turnover}}$	p. 283
Accounts receivable turnover	$\frac{\text{Net credit sales}}{\text{Average net accounts receivable}}$	p. 395
Average collection period	$\frac{\text{365 days}}{\text{Accounts receivable turnover}}$	p. 395

INVESTOR INSIGHT

Nova Stock/SuperStock

How to Manage the Current Ratio

The apparent simplicity of the current ratio can have real-world limitations because adding equal amounts to both the numerator and the denominator causes the ratio to decrease.

Assume, for example, that a company has $2,000,000 of current assets and $1,000,000 of current liabilities. Its current ratio is 2:1. If it purchases $1,000,000 of inventory on account, it will have $3,000,000 of current assets and $2,000,000 of current liabilities. Its current ratio decreases to 1.5:1. If, instead, the company pays off $500,000 of its current liabilities, it will have $1,500,000 of current assets and $500,000 of current liabilities. Its current ratio increases to 3:1. Thus, any trend analysis should be done with care because the ratio is susceptible to quick changes and is easily influenced by management.

How might management influence a company's current ratio? (Go to **WileyPLUS** for this answer and additional questions.)

SOLVENCY RATIOS

Solvency ratios (Illustration 13-17) measure the ability of the company to survive over a long period of time. Long-term creditors and stockholders are interested in a company's long-run solvency, particularly its ability to pay interest as it comes due and to repay the balance of debt at its maturity.

ILLUSTRATION 13-17
Summary of solvency ratios

Solvency Ratios		
Debt to assets ratio	$\frac{\text{Total liabilities}}{\text{Total assets}}$	p. 56
Times interest earned	$\frac{\text{Net income + Interest expense + Income tax expense}}{\text{Interest expense}}$	p. 497
Free cash flow	Net cash provided by operating activities − Capital expenditures − Cash dividends	p. 57

PROFITABILITY RATIOS

Profitability ratios (Illustration 13-18 on page 662) measure the income or operating success of a company for a given period of time. A company's income, or lack of it, affects its ability to obtain debt and equity financing, its liquidity position, and its ability to grow. As a consequence, creditors and investors alike are interested in evaluating profitability. Profitability is frequently used as the ultimate test of management's operating effectiveness.

ILLUSTRATION 13-18
Summary of profitability ratios

Profitability Ratios		
Earnings per share	$\frac{\text{Net income} - \text{Preferred dividends}}{\text{Weighted-average common shares outstanding}}$	p. 53
Price-earnings ratio	$\frac{\text{Market price per share}}{\text{Earnings per share}}$	p. 660
Gross profit rate	$\frac{\text{Gross profit}}{\text{Net sales}}$	p. 234
Profit margin	$\frac{\text{Net income}}{\text{Net sales}}$	p. 235
Return on assets	$\frac{\text{Net income}}{\text{Average total assets}}$	p. 444
Asset turnover	$\frac{\text{Net sales}}{\text{Average total assets}}$	p. 446
Payout ratio	$\frac{\text{Cash dividends declared on common stock}}{\text{Net income}}$	p. 560
Return on common stockholders' equity	$\frac{\text{Net income} - \text{Preferred dividends}}{\text{Average common stockholders' equity}}$	p. 561

INVESTOR INSIGHT

© Ferran Traite Soler/iStockphoto

High Ratings Can Bring Low Returns

Moody's, Standard & Poor's, and Fitch are three big firms that perform financial analysis on publicly traded companies and then publish ratings of the companies' creditworthiness. Investors and lenders rely heavily on these ratings in making investment and lending decisions. Some people feel that the collapse of the financial markets was worsened by inadequate research reports and ratings provided by the financial rating agencies. Critics contend that the rating agencies were reluctant to give large companies low ratings because they feared that by offending them they would lose out on business opportunities. For example, the rating agencies gave many so-called mortgage-backed securities ratings that suggested that they were low risk. Later, many of these very securities became completely worthless. Steps have been taken to reduce the conflicts of interest that lead to these faulty ratings.

Source: Aaron Lucchetti and Judith Burns, "Moody's CEO Warned Profit Push Posed a Risk to Quality of Ratings," *Wall Street Journal Online* (October 23, 2008).

Why are credit rating agencies important to the financial markets? (Go to **WileyPLUS** for this answer and additional questions.)

DO IT! ▶3 Ratio Analysis

The condensed financial statements of John Cully Company, for the years ended June 30, 2017 and 2016, are presented on the next page.

JOHN CULLY COMPANY
Balance Sheets
June 30

	(in thousands) 2017	2016
Assets		
Current assets		
Cash and cash equivalents	$ 553.3	$ 611.6
Accounts receivable (net)	776.6	664.9
Inventory	768.3	653.5
Prepaid expenses and other current assets	204.4	269.2
Total current assets	2,302.6	2,199.2
Investments	12.3	12.6
Property, plant, and equipment (net)	694.2	647.0
Intangibles and other assets	876.7	849.3
Total assets	$3,885.8	$3,708.1
Liabilities and Stockholders' Equity		
Current liabilities	$1,497.7	$1,322.0
Long-term liabilities	679.5	637.1
Stockholders' equity—common	1,708.6	1,749.0
Total liabilities and stockholders' equity	$3,885.8	$3,708.1

JOHN CULLY COMPANY
Income Statements
For the Year Ended June 30

	(in thousands) 2017	2016
Sales revenue	$6,336.3	$5,790.4
Costs and expenses		
Cost of goods sold	1,617.4	1,476.3
Selling and administrative expenses	4,007.6	3,679.0
Interest expense	13.9	27.1
Total costs and expenses	5,638.9	5,182.4
Income before income taxes	697.4	608.0
Income tax expense	291.3	232.6
Net income	$ 406.1	$ 375.4

Compute the following ratios for 2017 and 2016.

(a) Current ratio.

(b) Inventory turnover. (Inventory on 6/30/15 was $599.0.)

(c) Profit margin.

(d) Return on assets. (Assets on 6/30/15 were $3,349.9.)

(e) Return on common stockholders' equity. (Stockholders' equity on 6/30/15 was $1,795.9.)

(f) Debt to assets ratio.

(g) Times interest earned.

Action Plan

✔ Remember that the current ratio includes all current assets.

✔ Use average balances for turnover ratios like inventory, accounts receivable, and return on assets.

SOLUTION

	2017	2016
(a) Current ratio:		
$2,302.6 ÷ $1,497.7 =	1.5:1	
$2,199.2 ÷ $1,322.0 =		1.7:1
(b) Inventory turnover:		
$1,617.4 ÷ [($768.3 + $653.5) ÷ 2] =	2.3 times	
$1,476.3 ÷ [($653.5 + $599.0) ÷ 2] =		2.4 times
(c) Profit margin:		
$406.1 ÷ $6,336.3 =	6.4%	
$375.4 ÷ $5,790.4 =		6.5%
(d) Return on assets:		
$406.1 ÷ [($3,885.8 + $3,708.1) ÷ 2] =	10.7%	
$375.4 ÷ [($3,708.1 + $3,349.9) ÷ 2] =		10.6%
(e) Return on common stockholders' equity:		
($406.1 − $0) ÷ [($1,708.6 + $1,749.0) ÷ 2] =	23.5%	
($375.4 − $0) ÷ [($1,749.0 + $1,795.9) ÷ 2] =		21.2%
(f) Debt to assets ratio:		
($1,497.7 + $679.5) ÷ $3,885.8 =	56.0%	
($1,322.0 + $637.1) ÷ $3,708.1 =		52.8%
(g) Times interest earned:		
($406.1 + $13.9 + $291.3) ÷ $13.9 =	51.2 times	
($375.4 + $27.1 + $232.6) ÷ $27.1 =		23.4 times

Related exercise material: **BE13-10, BE13-11, BE13-12, BE13-13, BE13-14, BE13-15, DO IT! 13-3, E13-7, E13-8, E13-9, E13-10, E13-11, E13-12,** and **E13-13.**

USING DECISION TOOLS—KELLOGG COMPANY

In analyzing a company, you should always investigate an extended period of time in order to determine whether the condition and performance of the company are changing. The condensed financial statements of Kellogg Company for 2014 and 2013 are presented here.

KELLOGG COMPANY, INC.
Balance Sheets
January 3, 2015, and December 28, 2013
(in millions)

Assets	**2014**	**2013**
Current assets		
Cash	$ 443	$ 273
Accounts receivable (net)	1,276	1,423
Inventories	1,279	1,248
Other current assets	342	323
Total current assets	3,340	3,267
Property (net)	3,769	3,856
Other assets	8,044	8,351
Total assets	$15,153	$15,474
Liabilities and Stockholders' Equity		
Current liabilities	$ 4,364	$ 3,835
Long-term liabilities	7,938	8,032
Stockholders' equity—common	2,851	3,607
Total liabilities and stockholders' equity	$15,153	$15,474

KELLOGG COMPANY, INC.
Condensed Income Statements
For the Years Ended January 3, 2015, and December 28, 2013
(in millions)

	2014	2013
Net sales	$14,580	$14,792
Cost of goods sold	9,517	8,689
Gross profit	5,063	6,103
Selling and administrative expenses	4,039	3,266
Income from operations	1,024	2,837
Interest expense	209	235
Other (income) expense, net	(3)	3
Income before income taxes	818	2,599
Income tax expense	186	792
Net income	$ 632	$ 1,807

INSTRUCTIONS

Compute the following ratios for Kellogg for 2014 and discuss your findings (2013 values are provided for comparison).

1. Liquidity:
   (a) Current ratio (2013: .85:1).
   (b) Inventory turnover (2013: 6.7 times).
2. Solvency:
   (a) Debt to assets ratio (2013: 77%).
   (b) Times interest earned (2013: 12.1 times).
3. Profitability:
   (a) Return on assets (2013: 11.8%).
   (b) Profit margin (2013: 12.2%).
   (c) Return on common stockholders' equity (2013: 60%).

SOLUTION

1. Liquidity
   (a) Current ratio:

   2014: $\frac{\$3,340}{\$4,364} = .77:1$ 2013: .85:1

   (b) Inventory turnover:

   2014: $\frac{\$9,517}{(\$1,279 + \$1,248)/2} = 7.5$ times 2013: 6.7 times

   We see that between 2013 and 2014, the current ratio declined, which suggests a decline in liquidity. The inventory turnover increased, which suggests an improvement in liquidity.

2. Solvency
   (a) Debt to assets ratio:

   2014: $\frac{\$4,364 + \$7,938}{\$15,153} = 81\%$ 2013: 77%

   (b) Times interest earned:

   2014: $\frac{\$632 + \$209 + \$186}{\$209} = 4.9$ times 2013: 12.1 times

   Kellogg's solvency as measured by the debt to assets ratio decreased in 2014, and its times interest earned declined as well.

3. Profitability

(a) Return on assets:

$$2014: \frac{\$632}{(\$15,153 + \$15,474)/2} = 4.1\% \qquad 2013: \; 11.8\%$$

(b) Profit margin:

$$2014: \frac{\$632}{\$14,580} = 4.3\% \qquad 2013: \; 12.2\%$$

(c) Return on common stockholders' equity:

$$2014: \frac{\$632}{(\$2,851 + \$3,607)/2} = 20\% \qquad 2013: \; 60\%$$

Kellogg's return on assets declined. Its profit margin and return on stockholders' equity also declined. The company experienced a sharp drop in net income.

LEARNING OBJECTIVE *4

APPENDIX 13A: Evaluate a company comprehensively using ratio analysis.

In previous chapters, we presented many ratios used for evaluating the financial health and performance of a company. In this appendix, we provide a comprehensive review of those ratios and discuss some important relationships among them. Since earlier chapters demonstrated the calculation of each of these ratios, in this appendix we instead focus on their interpretation. Page references to prior discussions point you to any individual ratios you feel you need to review.

We used the financial information in Illustrations 13A-1 through 13A-4 to calculate Chicago Cereal Company's 2014 ratios. You can use these data to review the computations.

ILLUSTRATION 13A-1
Chicago Cereal Company's balance sheets

CHICAGO CEREAL COMPANY
Balance Sheets
December 31 (in thousands)

Assets	2014	2013
Current assets		
Cash	$ 524	$ 411
Accounts receivable	1,026	945
Inventory	924	824
Prepaid expenses and other current assets	243	247
Total current assets	2,717	2,427
Property assets (net)	2,990	2,816
Intangibles and other assets	5,690	5,471
Total assets	$11,397	$10,714
Liabilities and Stockholders' Equity		
Current liabilities	$ 4,044	$ 4,020
Long-term liabilities	4,827	4,625
Stockholders' equity—common	2,526	2,069
Total liabilities and stockholders' equity	$11,397	$10,714

ILLUSTRATION 13A-2 Chicago Cereal Company's income statements

CHICAGO CEREAL COMPANY
Condensed Income Statements
For the Years Ended December 31 (in thousands)

	2014	2013
Net sales	$11,776	$10,907
Cost of goods sold	6,597	6,082
Gross profit	5,179	4,825
Selling and administrative expenses	3,311	3,059
Income from operations	1,868	1,766
Interest expense	319	307
Other income (expense), net	(2)	13
Income before income taxes	1,547	1,472
Income tax expense	444	468
Net income	$ 1,103	$ 1,004

ILLUSTRATION 13A-3 Chicago Cereal Company's statements of cash flows

CHICAGO CEREAL COMPANY
Condensed Statements of Cash Flows
For the Years Ended December 31 (in thousands)

	2014	2013
Cash flows from operating activities		
Cash receipts from operating activities	$11,695	$10,841
Cash payments for operating activities	10,192	9,431
Net cash provided by operating activities	1,503	1,410
Cash flows from investing activities		
Purchases of property, plant, and equipment	(472)	(453)
Other investing activities	(129)	8
Net cash used in investing activities	(601)	(445)
Cash flows from financing activities		
Issuance of common stock	163	218
Issuance of debt	2,179	721
Reductions of debt	(2,011)	(650)
Payment of dividends	(475)	(450)
Repurchase of common stock and other items	(645)	(612)
Net cash provided (used) by financing activities	(789)	(773)
Increase (decrease) in cash and cash equivalents	113	192
Cash and cash equivalents at beginning of year	411	219
Cash and cash equivalents at end of year	$ 524	$ 411

ILLUSTRATION 13A-4 Additional information for Chicago Cereal Company

Additional information:

	2014	2013
Average number of shares (thousands)	418.7	418.5
Stock price at year-end	$52.92	$50.06

As indicated in the chapter, we can classify ratios into three types for analysis of the primary financial statements:

1. **Liquidity ratios.** Measures of the short-term ability of the company to pay its maturing obligations and to meet unexpected needs for cash.
2. **Solvency ratios.** Measures of the ability of the company to survive over a long period of time.
3. **Profitability ratios.** Measures of the income or operating success of a company for a given period of time.

As a tool of analysis, ratios can provide clues to underlying conditions that may not be apparent from an inspection of the individual components of a particular ratio. But, a single ratio by itself is not very meaningful. Accordingly, in this discussion we use the following three comparisons.

1. **Intracompany comparisons** covering two years for Chicago Cereal (using comparative financial information from Illustrations 13A-1 through 13A-4).
2. **Intercompany comparisons** using General Mills as one of Chicago Cereal's competitors.
3. **Industry average comparisons** based on MSN.com median ratios for manufacturers of flour and other grain mill products and comparisons with other sources. For some of the ratios that we use, industry comparisons are not available (denoted "na").

LIQUIDITY RATIOS

Liquidity ratios measure the short-term ability of the company to pay its maturing obligations and to meet unexpected needs for cash. Short-term creditors such as bankers and suppliers are particularly interested in assessing liquidity. The measures used to determine the company's short-term debt-paying ability are the current ratio, the accounts receivable turnover, the average collection period, the inventory turnover, and days in inventory.

1. **Current ratio.** The **current ratio** expresses the relationship of current assets to current liabilities, computed by dividing current assets by current liabilities. It is widely used for evaluating a company's liquidity and short-term debt-paying ability. The 2014 and 2013 current ratios for Chicago Cereal and comparative data are shown in Illustration 13A-5.

ILLUSTRATION 13A-5
Current ratio

Ratio	Formula	Indicates	Chicago Cereal 2014	Chicago Cereal 2013	General Mills 2014	Industry 2014	Page in Textbook
Current ratio	$\frac{\text{Current assets}}{\text{Current liabilities}}$	Short-term debt-paying ability	.67	.60	.67	1.06	54

What do the measures tell us? Chicago Cereal's 2013 current ratio of .67 means that for every dollar of current liabilities, it has $0.67 of current assets. We sometimes state such ratios as .67:1 to reinforce this interpretation. Its current ratio—and therefore its liquidity—increased significantly in 2014. It is well below the industry average but the same as that of General Mills.

2. **Accounts receivable turnover.** Analysts can measure liquidity by how quickly a company converts certain assets to cash. Low values of the previous ratios can sometimes be compensated for if some of the company's current assets are highly liquid.

   How liquid, for example, are the receivables? The ratio used to assess the liquidity of the receivables is the **accounts receivable turnover**, which measures the number of times, on average, a company collects receivables during the period. The accounts receivable turnover is computed by dividing net credit sales (net sales less cash sales) by average net accounts receivable during the year. The accounts receivable turnover for Chicago Cereal is shown in Illustration 13A-6.

ILLUSTRATION 13A-6
Accounts receivable turnover

Ratio	Formula	Indicates	Chicago Cereal 2014	Chicago Cereal 2013	General Mills 2014	Industry 2014	Page in Textbook
Accounts receivable turnover	$\frac{\text{Net credit sales}}{\text{Average net accounts receivable}}$	Liquidity of receivables	11.9	12.0	12.2	11.2	395

In computing the rate, we assumed that all Chicago Cereal's sales are credit sales. Its accounts receivable turnover declined slightly in 2014. The turnover of 11.9 times is higher than the industry average of 11.2 times, and slightly lower than General Mills' turnover of 12.2 times.

3. **Average collection period.** A popular variant of the accounts receivable turnover converts it into an **average collection period** in days. This is done by dividing the accounts receivable turnover into 365 days. The average collection period for Chicago Cereal is shown in Illustration 13A-7.

ILLUSTRATION 13A-7
Average collection period

Ratio	Formula	Indicates	Chicago Cereal 2014	Chicago Cereal 2013	General Mills 2014	Industry 2014	Page in Textbook
Average collection period	$\dfrac{\text{365 days}}{\text{Accounts receivable turnover}}$	Liquidity of receivables and collection success	30.7	30.4	29.9	32.6	395

Chicago Cereal's 2014 accounts receivable turnover of 11.9 times is divided into 365 days to obtain approximately 31 days. This means that the average collection period for receivables is about 31 days. Its average collection period is slightly longer than that of General Mills and shorter than that of the industry.

Analysts frequently use the average collection period to assess the effectiveness of a company's credit and collection policies. The general rule is that the collection period should not greatly exceed the credit term period (i.e., the time allowed for payment).

4. **Inventory turnover.** The **inventory turnover** measures the number of times average inventory was sold during the period. Its purpose is to measure the liquidity of the inventory. A high measure indicates that inventory is being sold and replenished frequently. The inventory turnover is computed by dividing the cost of goods sold by the average inventory during the period. Unless seasonal factors are significant, average inventory can be computed from the beginning and ending inventory balances. Chicago Cereal's inventory turnover is shown in Illustration 13A-8.

ILLUSTRATION 13A-8
Inventory turnover

Ratio	Formula	Indicates	Chicago Cereal 2014	Chicago Cereal 2013	General Mills 2014	Industry 2014	Page in Textbook
Inventory turnover	$\dfrac{\text{Cost of goods sold}}{\text{Average inventory}}$	Liquidity of inventory	7.5	7.9	7.4	6.7	283

Chicago Cereal's inventory turnover decreased slightly in 2014. The turnover of 7.5 times is higher than the industry average of 6.7 times and similar to that of General Mills. Generally, the faster the inventory turnover, the less cash is tied up in inventory and the less the chance of inventory becoming obsolete. Of course, a downside of high inventory turnover is that it sometimes results in lost sales because if a company keeps less inventory on hand, it is more likely to run out of inventory when it is needed.

5. **Days in inventory.** A variant of the inventory turnover is the **days in inventory**, which measures the average number of days inventory is held. The days in inventory for Chicago Cereal is shown in Illustration 13A-9 (page 670).

Ratio	Formula	Indicates	Chicago Cereal 2014	Chicago Cereal 2013	General Mills 2014	Industry 2014	Page in Textbook
Days in inventory	$\frac{\text{365 days}}{\text{Inventory turnover}}$	Liquidity of inventory and inventory management	48.7	46.2	49.3	54.5	283

ILLUSTRATION 13A-9
Days in inventory

Chicago Cereal's 2014 inventory turnover of 7.5 divided into 365 is approximately 49 days. An average selling time of 49 days is faster than the industry average and similar to that of General Mills. Some of this difference might be explained by differences in product lines across the two companies, although in many ways the types of products of these two companies are quite similar.

Inventory turnovers vary considerably among industries. For example, grocery store chains have a turnover of 10 times and an average selling period of 37 days. In contrast, jewelry stores have an average turnover of 1.3 times and an average selling period of 281 days. Within a company, there may even be significant differences in inventory turnover among different types of products. Thus, in a grocery store the turnover of perishable items such as produce, meats, and dairy products is faster than the turnover of soaps and detergents.

To conclude, nearly all of these liquidity measures suggest that Chicago Cereal's liquidity changed little during 2014. Its liquidity appears acceptable when compared to the industry as a whole and when compared to General Mills.

SOLVENCY RATIOS

Solvency ratios measure the ability of the company to survive over a long period of time. Long-term creditors and stockholders are interested in a company's long-run solvency, particularly its ability to pay interest as it comes due and to repay the face value of debt at maturity. The debt to assets ratio and times interest earned provide information about debt-paying ability. In addition, free cash flow provides information about the company's solvency and its ability to pay additional dividends or invest in new projects.

6. **Debt to assets ratio.** The **debt to assets ratio** measures the percentage of total financing provided by creditors. It is computed by dividing total liabilities (both current and long-term debt) by total assets. This ratio indicates the degree of financial leveraging. It also provides some indication of the company's ability to withstand losses without impairing the interests of its creditors. The higher the percentage of debt to assets, the greater the risk that the company may be unable to meet its maturing obligations. Thus, from the creditors' point of view, a low ratio of debt to assets is desirable. Chicago Cereal's debt to assets ratio is shown in Illustration 13A-10.

ILLUSTRATION 13A-10
Debt to assets ratio

Ratio	Formula	Indicates	Chicago Cereal 2014	Chicago Cereal 2013	General Mills 2014	Industry 2014	Page in Textbook
Debt to assets ratio	$\frac{\text{Total liabilities}}{\text{Total assets}}$	Percentage of total assets provided by creditors	78%	81%	55%	55%	56

Chicago Cereal's 2014 ratio of 78% means that creditors have provided financing sufficient to cover 78% of the company's total assets. Alternatively, it says that it would have to liquidate 78% of its assets at their book value in order to pay off all of its debts. Its ratio is above the industry average of 55%, as well as that of General Mills. This suggests that it is less solvent than the industry average and General Mills. Chicago Cereal's solvency improved slightly during the year.

The adequacy of this ratio is often judged in light of the company's earnings. Generally, companies with relatively stable earnings, such as public utilities, have higher debt to assets ratios than cyclical companies with widely fluctuating earnings, such as many high-tech companies.

Another ratio with a similar meaning is the **debt to equity ratio**. It shows the relative use of borrowed funds (total liabilities) compared with resources invested by the owners. Because this ratio can be computed in several ways, be careful when making comparisons with it. Debt may be defined to include only the noncurrent portion of liabilities, and intangible assets may be excluded from stockholders' equity (which would equal tangible net worth). If debt and assets are defined as above (all liabilities and all assets), then when the debt to assets ratio equals 50%, the debt to equity ratio is 1:1.

7. **Times interest earned.** The **times interest earned** (also called interest coverage) indicates the company's ability to meet interest payments as they come due. It is computed by dividing the sum of net income, interest expense, and income tax expense by interest expense. Note that this ratio uses income before interest expense and income taxes because this amount represents what is available to cover interest. Chicago Cereal's times interest earned is shown in Illustration 13A-11.

ILLUSTRATION 13A-11
Times interest earned

Ratio	Formula	Indicates	Chicago Cereal 2014	Chicago Cereal 2013	General Mills 2014	Industry 2014	Page in Textbook
Times interest earned	$\dfrac{\text{Net Income} + \text{Interest expense} + \text{Income tax expense}}{\text{Interest expense}}$	Ability to meet interest payments as they come due	5.8	5.8	9.9	5.5	497

For Chicago Cereal, the 2014 interest coverage was 5.8, which indicates that income before interest and taxes was 5.8 times the amount needed for interest expense. This is less than the rate for General Mills, but it slightly exceeds the rate for the industry. The debt to assets ratio decreased for Chicago Cereal during 2014, and its times interest earned held constant.

8. **Free cash flow.** One indication of a company's solvency, as well as of its ability to pay dividends or expand operations, is the amount of excess cash it generated after investing in capital expenditures and paying dividends. This amount is referred to as **free cash flow**. For example, if you generate \$100,000 of net cash provided by operating activities but you spend \$30,000 on capital expenditures and pay \$10,000 in dividends, you have \$60,000 (\$100,000 − \$30,000 − \$10,000) to use either to expand operations, pay additional dividends, or pay down debt. Chicago Cereal's free cash flow is shown in Illustration 13A-12.

ILLUSTRATION 13A-12
Free cash flow

Ratio	Formula	Indicates	Chicago Cereal 2014	Chicago Cereal 2013	General Mills 2014	Industry 2014	Page in Textbook
Free cash flow	Net cash provided by operating activities − Capital expenditures − Cash dividends	Cash available for paying dividends or expanding operations	\$556 (in thousands)	\$507 (in thousands)	\$895 (in millions)	na	57

Chicago Cereal's free cash flow increased slightly from 2013 to 2014. During both years, the net cash provided by operating activities was more than enough to allow it to acquire additional productive assets and maintain dividend payments. It could have used the remaining cash to reduce debt if necessary. Given that Chicago Cereal is much smaller than General Mills, we would expect its free cash flow to be substantially smaller, which it is.

PROFITABILITY RATIOS

Profitability ratios measure the income or operating success of a company for a given period of time. A company's income, or the lack of it, affects its ability to obtain debt and equity financing, its liquidity position, and its ability to grow. As a consequence, creditors and investors alike are interested in evaluating profitability. Analysts frequently use profitability as the ultimate test of management's operating effectiveness.

Throughout this textbook, we have introduced numerous measures of profitability. The relationships among measures of profitability are very important. Understanding them can help management determine where to focus its efforts to improve profitability. Illustration 13A-13 diagrams these relationships. Our discussion of Chicago Cereal's profitability is structured around this diagram.

ILLUSTRATION 13A-13
Relationships among profitability measures

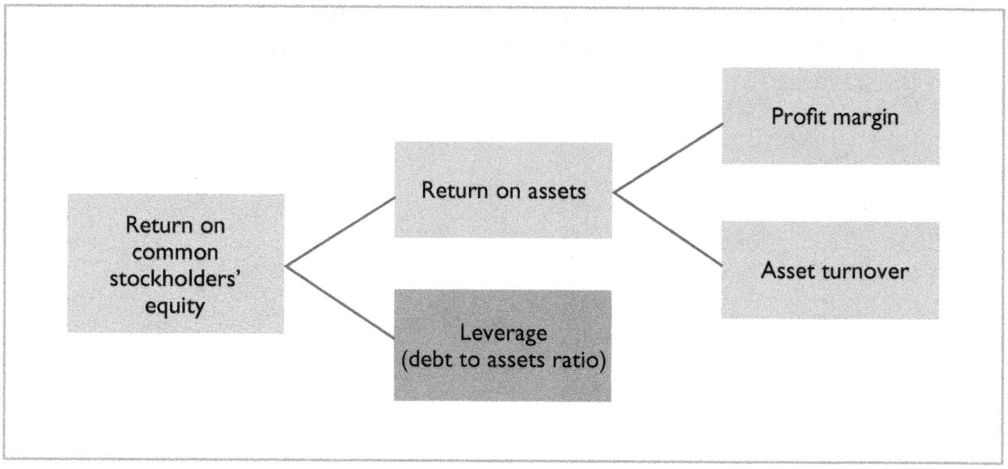

9. **Return on common stockholders' equity (ROE).** A widely used measure of profitability from the common stockholder's viewpoint is the **return on common stockholders' equity (ROE)**. This ratio shows how many dollars of net income the company earned for each dollar invested by the owners. It is computed by dividing net income minus any preferred dividends—that is, income available to common stockholders—by average common stockholders' equity. The return on common stockholders' equity for Chicago Cereal is shown in Illustration 13A-14.

ILLUSTRATION 13A-14
Return on common stockholders' equity

Ratio	Formula	Indicates	Chicago Cereal 2014	Chicago Cereal 2013	General Mills 2014	Industry 2014	Page in Textbook
Return on common stockholders' equity	$\frac{\text{Net Income} - \text{Preferred dividends}}{\text{Average common stockholders' equity}}$	Profitability of common stockholders' investment	48%	46%	25%	19%	561

Chicago Cereal's 2014 return on common stockholders' equity is unusually high at 48%. The industry average is 19% and General Mills' return is 25%. In the subsequent sections, we investigate the causes of this high return.

10. Return on assets. The return on common stockholders' equity is affected by two factors: the **return on assets** and the degree of leverage. The return on assets measures the overall profitability of assets in terms of the income earned on each dollar invested in assets. It is computed by dividing net income by average total assets. Chicago Cereal's return on assets is shown in Illustration 13A-15.

ILLUSTRATION 13A-15
Return on assets

Ratio	Formula	Indicates	Chicago Cereal 2014	Chicago Cereal 2013	General Mills 2014	Industry 2014	Page in Textbook
Return on assets	$\frac{\text{Net income}}{\text{Average total assets}}$	Overall profitability of assets	10.0%	9.4%	6.2%	5.3%	444

Chicago Cereal had a 10.0% return on assets in 2014. This rate is significantly higher than that of General Mills and the industry average.

Note that its rate of return on common stockholders' equity (48%) is substantially higher than its rate of return on assets (10%). The reason is that it has made effective use of **leverage**. **Leveraging** or **trading on the equity** at a gain means that the company has borrowed money at a lower rate of interest than the rate of return it earns on the assets it purchased with the borrowed funds. Leverage enables management to use money supplied by nonowners to increase the return to owners.

A comparison of the rate of return on assets with the rate of interest paid for borrowed money indicates the profitability of trading on the equity. If you borrow money at 8% and your rate of return on assets is 11%, you are trading on the equity at a gain. Note, however, that trading on the equity is a two-way street. For example, if you borrow money at 11% and earn only 8% on it, you are trading on the equity at a loss.

Chicago Cereal earns more on its borrowed funds than it has to pay in interest. Thus, the return to stockholders exceeds the return on assets because of the positive benefit of leverage. Recall from our earlier discussion that Chicago Cereal's percentage of debt financing, as measured by the ratio of debt to assets (or debt to equity), was higher than General Mills' and the industry average. It appears that Chicago Cereal's high return on common stockholders' equity is due in part to its use of leverage.

11. Profit margin. The return on assets is affected by two factors, the first of which is the profit margin. The **profit margin**, or rate of return on sales, is a measure of the percentage of each dollar of sales that results in net income. It is computed by dividing net income by net sales for the period. Chicago Cereal's profit margin is shown in Illustration 13A-16.

ILLUSTRATION 13A-16
Profit margin

Ratio	Formula	Indicates	Chicago Cereal 2014	Chicago Cereal 2013	General Mills 2014	Industry 2014	Page in Textbook
Profit margin	$\frac{\text{Net income}}{\text{Net sales}}$	Net income generated by each dollar of sales	9.4%	9.2%	8.2%	6.1%	235

Chicago Cereal experienced a slight increase in its profit margin from 2013 to 2014 of 9.2% to 9.4%. Its profit margin was higher than the industry average and that of General Mills.

High-volume (high inventory turnover) businesses such as grocery stores and pharmacy chains generally have low profit margins. Low-volume businesses such as jewelry stores and airplane manufacturers have high profit margins.

12. Asset turnover. The other factor that affects the return on assets is the asset turnover. The **asset turnover** measures how efficiently a company uses its assets to generate sales. It is determined by dividing net sales by average total assets for the period. The resulting number shows the dollars of sales produced by each dollar invested in assets. Illustration 13A-17 shows the asset turnover for Chicago Cereal.

ILLUSTRATION 13A-17
Asset turnover

Ratio	Formula	Indicates	Chicago Cereal 2014	Chicago Cereal 2013	General Mills 2014	Industry 2014	Page in Textbook
Asset turnover	Net sales / Average total assets	How efficiently assets are used to generate sales	1.07	1.02	.76	.87	446

The asset turnover shows that in 2014, Chicago Cereal generated sales of $1.07 for each dollar it had invested in assets. The ratio rose from 2013 to 2014. Its asset turnover is above the industry average and that of General Mills.

Asset turnovers vary considerably among industries. The average asset turnover for utility companies is .45, for example, while the grocery store industry has an average asset turnover of 3.49.

In summary, Chicago Cereal's return on assets increased from 9.4% in 2013 to 10.0% in 2014. Underlying this increase was an increased profitability on each dollar of sales (as measured by the profit margin) and a rise in the sales-generating efficiency of its assets (as measured by the asset turnover). We can analyze the combined effects of profit margin and asset turnover on return on assets for Chicago Cereal as shown in Illustration 13A-18.

ILLUSTRATION 13A-18
Composition of return on assets

Ratios:	Profit Margin	×	Asset Turnover	=	Return on Assets
	Net Income / Net Sales	×	Net Sales / Average Total Assets	=	Net Income / Average Total Assets
Chicago Cereal					
2014	9.4%	×	1.07 times	=	10.1%*
2013	9.2%	×	1.02 times	=	9.4%

*Difference from value in Illustration 13A-15 due to rounding.

13. Gross profit rate. One factor that strongly influences the profit margin is the gross profit rate. The **gross profit rate** is determined by dividing gross profit (net sales less cost of goods sold) by net sales. This rate indicates a company's ability to maintain an adequate selling price above its cost of goods sold.

As an industry becomes more competitive, this ratio declines. For example, in the early years of the personal computer industry, gross profit rates were quite high. Today, because of increased competition and a belief that most brands of personal computers are similar in quality, gross profit rates have become thin. Analysts should closely monitor gross profit rates over time. Illustration 13A-19 shows Chicago Cereal's gross profit rate.

Ratio	Formula	Indicates	Chicago Cereal 2014	Chicago Cereal 2013	General Mills 2014	Industry 2014	Page in Textbook
Gross profit rate	Gross profit / Net sales	Margin between selling price and cost of goods sold	44%	44%	34%	30%	234

ILLUSTRATION 13A-19
Gross profit rate

Chicago Cereal's gross profit rate remained constant from 2013 to 2014.

14. **Earnings per share (EPS).** Stockholders usually think in terms of the number of shares they own or plan to buy or sell. Expressing net income earned on a per share basis provides a useful perspective for determining profitability. **Earnings per share** is a measure of the net income earned on each share of common stock. It is computed by dividing net income by the average number of common shares outstanding during the year.

    The terms "net income per share" or "earnings per share" refer to the amount of net income applicable to each share of **common stock**. Therefore, when we compute earnings per share, if there are preferred dividends declared for the period, we must deduct them from net income to arrive at income available to the common stockholders. Chicago Cereal's earnings per share is shown in Illustration 13A-20.

ILLUSTRATION 13A-20
Earnings per share

Ratio	Formula	Indicates	Chicago Cereal 2014	Chicago Cereal 2013	General Mills 2014	Industry 2014	Page in Textbook
Earnings per share (EPS)	(Net income − Preferred dividends) / Weighted-average common shares outstanding	Net income earned on each share of common stock	$2.63	$2.40	$2.90	na	53

Note that no industry average is presented in Illustration 13A-20. Industry data for earnings per share are not reported, and in fact the Chicago Cereal and General Mills ratios should not be compared. Such comparisons are not meaningful because of the wide variations in the number of shares of outstanding stock among companies. Chicago Cereal's earnings per share increased 23 cents per share in 2014. This represents a 9.6% increase from the 2013 EPS of $2.40.

15. **Price-earnings ratio.** The **price-earnings ratio** is an oft-quoted statistic that measures the ratio of the market price of each share of common stock to the earnings per share. The price-earnings (P-E) ratio reflects investors' assessments of a company's future earnings. It is computed by dividing the market price per share of the stock by earnings per share. Chicago Cereal's price-earnings ratio is shown in Illustration 13A-21.

ILLUSTRATION 13A-21
Price-earnings ratio

Ratio	Formula	Indicates	Chicago Cereal 2014	Chicago Cereal 2013	General Mills 2014	Industry 2014	Page in Textbook
Price-earnings ratio	Market price per share / Earnings per share	Relationship between market price per share and earnings per share	20.1	20.9	24.3	35.8	660

At the end of 2014 and 2013, the market price of Chicago Cereal's stock was $52.92 and $50.06, respectively.

In 2014, each share of Chicago Cereal's stock sold for 20.1 times the amount that was earned on each share. Chicago Cereal's price-earnings ratio is lower than General Mills' ratio of 24.3 and lower than the industry average of 35.8 times. Its lower P-E ratio suggests that the market is less optimistic about Chicago Cereal than about General Mills. However, it might also signal that Chicago Cereal's stock is underpriced.

16. **Payout ratio.** The **payout ratio** measures the percentage of earnings distributed in the form of cash dividends. It is computed by dividing cash dividends declared on common stock by net income. Companies that have high growth rates are characterized by low payout ratios because they reinvest most of their net income in the business. The payout ratio for Chicago Cereal is shown in Illustration 13A-22.

ILLUSTRATION 13A-22
Payout ratio

Ratio	Formula	Indicates	Chicago Cereal 2014	Chicago Cereal 2013	General Mills 2014	Industry 2014	Page in Textbook
Payout ratio	Cash dividends declared on common stock / Net income	Percentage of earnings distributed in the form of cash dividends	43%	45%	54%	37%	560

The 2014 and 2013 payout ratios for Chicago Cereal are slightly lower than that of General Mills (54%) but higher than the industry average (37%).

Management has some control over the amount of dividends paid each year, and companies are generally reluctant to reduce a dividend below the amount paid in a previous year. Therefore, the payout ratio will actually increase if a company's net income declines but the company keeps its total dividend payment the same. Of course, unless the company returns to its previous level of profitability, maintaining this higher dividend payout ratio is probably not possible over the long run.

Before drawing any conclusions regarding Chicago Cereal's dividend payout ratio, we should calculate this ratio over a longer period of time to evaluate any trends and also try to find out whether management's philosophy regarding dividends has changed recently. The "Selected Financial Data" section of Chicago Cereal's Management Discussion and Analysis shows that over a 5-year period, earnings per share rose 45%, while dividends per share grew only 19%.

In terms of the types of financial information available and the ratios used by various industries, what can be practically covered in this textbook gives you only the "Titanic approach." That is, you are seeing only the tip of the iceberg compared to the vast databases and types of ratio analysis that are available on computers. The availability of information is not a problem. The real trick is to be discriminating enough to perform relevant analysis and select pertinent comparative data.

REVIEW AND PRACTICE

▶ LEARNING OBJECTIVES REVIEW

1 Apply the concepts of sustainable income and quality of earnings. Sustainable income analysis is useful in evaluating a company's performance. Sustainable income is the most likely level of income to be obtained by the company in the future. Discontinued operations and other comprehensive income are presented on the statement of comprehensive income to highlight their unusual nature. Items below income from continuing operations must be presented net of tax.

A high quality of earnings provides full and transparent information that will not confuse or mislead users of the financial statements. Issues related to quality of earnings are (1) alternative accounting methods, (2) pro forma income, and (3) improper recognition.

2 Apply horizontal analysis and vertical analysis. Horizontal analysis is a technique for evaluating a series of data over a period of time to determine the increase or decrease that has taken place, expressed as either an amount or a percentage.

Vertical analysis is a technique that expresses each item in a financial statement as a percentage of a relevant total or a base amount

3 Analyze a company's performance using ratio analysis. The price-earnings (P-E) ratio reflects investors' assessment of a company's future earnings potential. Financial ratios are provided in Illustration 13-16 (liquidity), Illustration 13-17 (solvency), and Illustration 13-18 (profitability).

***4 Evaluate a company comprehensively using ratio analysis.** To evaluate a company, ratios (liquidity, solvency, and profitability) provide clues to underlying conditions, but intracompany, intercompany, and industry average comparisons are also needed.

DECISION TOOLS REVIEW

DECISION CHECKPOINTS	INFO NEEDED FOR DECISION	TOOL TO USE FOR DECISION	HOW TO EVALUATE RESULTS
Has the company sold any major components of its business?	Discontinued operations section of income statement	Anything reported in this section indicates that the company has discontinued a major component of its business.	If a major component has been discontinued, its results during the current period should not be included in estimates of future net income.
Has the company changed any of its accounting principles?	Effect of change in accounting principle on current and prior periods	Management indicates that the new principle is preferable to the old principle.	Examine current and prior years' reported income, using new-principle basis to assess trends for estimating future income.
How do the company's financial position and operating results compare with those of the previous period?	Income statement and balance sheet	Comparative financial statements should be prepared over at least two years, with the first year reported being the base year. Changes in each line item relative to the base year should be presented both by amount and by percentage. This is called **horizontal analysis**.	Significant changes should be investigated to determine the reason for the change.
How do the relationships between items in this year's financial statements compare with those of last year or those of competitors?	Income statement and balance sheet	Each line item on the income statement should be presented as a percentage of net sales, and each line item on the balance sheet should be presented as a percentage of total assets or total liabilities and stockholders' equity. These percentages should be investigated for differences either across years in the same company or in the same year across different companies. This is called **vertical analysis**.	Any significant differences either across years or between companies should be investigated to determine the cause.

GLOSSARY REVIEW

***Accounts receivable turnover** A measure of the liquidity of receivables; computed as net credit sales divided by average net accounts receivable. (p. 668).

***Asset turnover** A measure of how efficiently a company uses its assets to generate sales; computed as net sales divided by average total assets. (p. 674).

Available-for-sale securities Securities that are held with the intent of selling them sometime in the future. (p. 650).

***Average collection period** The average number of days that receivables are outstanding; calculated as accounts receivable turnover divided into 365 days. (p. 669).

Change in accounting principle Use of an accounting principle in the current year different from the one used in the preceding year. (p. 651).

Comprehensive income The sum of net income and other comprehensive income items. (p. 650).

***Current ratio** A measure used to evaluate a company's liquidity and short-term debt-paying ability; calculated as current assets divided by current liabilities. (p. 668).

***Days in inventory** A measure of the average number of days inventory is held; computed as inventory turnover divided into 365 days. (p. 669).

***Debt to assets ratio** A measure of the percentage of total financing provided by creditors; computed as total liabilities divided by total assets. (p. 670).

Discontinued operations The disposal of a significant component of a business. (p. 649).

***Earnings per share** The net income earned by each share of common stock; computed as net income less preferred dividends divided by the weighted-average common shares outstanding. (p. 675).

***Free cash flow** A measure of solvency. Cash remaining from operating activities after adjusting for capital expenditures and dividends paid. (p. 671).

***Gross profit rate** Gross profit expressed as a percentage of sales; computed as gross profit divided by net sales. (p. 674).

Horizontal analysis A technique for evaluating a series of financial statement data over a period of time to determine the increase (decrease) that has taken place, expressed as either an amount or a percentage. (p. 655).

***Inventory turnover** A measure of the liquidity of inventory. Measures the number of times average inventory was sold during the period; computed as cost of goods sold divided by average inventory. (p. 669).

***Leveraging** Borrowing money at a lower rate of interest than can be earned by using the borrowed money; also referred to as *trading on the equity*. (p. 673).

Liquidity ratios Measures of the short-term ability of the company to pay its maturing obligations and to meet unexpected needs for cash. (p. 660).

***Payout ratio** A measure of the percentage of earnings distributed in the form of cash dividends; calculated as cash dividends declared on common stock divided by net income. (p. 676).

Price-earnings (P-E) ratio A comparison of the market price of each share of common stock to the earnings per share; computed as the market price of the stock divided by earnings per share. (pp. 660, 675).

Profitability ratios Measures of the income or operating success of a company for a given period of time. (p. 661).

***Profit margin** A measure of the net income generated by each dollar of sales; computed as net income divided by net sales. (p. 673).

Pro forma income A measure of income that usually excludes items that a company thinks are unusual or nonrecurring. (p. 653).

Quality of earnings Indicates the level of full and transparent information that is provided to users of the financial statements. (p. 652).

***Return on assets** A profitability measure that indicates the amount of net income generated by each dollar of assets; calculated as net income divided by average total assets. (p. 673).

***Return on common stockholders' equity (ROE)** A measure of the dollars of net income earned for each dollar invested by the owners; computed as income available to common stockholders divided by average common stockholders' equity. (p. 672).

Solvency ratios Measures of the ability of a company to survive over a long period of time, particularly to pay interest as it comes due and to repay the balance of debt at its maturity. (p. 661).

Sustainable income The most likely level of income to be obtained by a company in the future. (p. 648).

***Times interest earned** A measure of a company's solvency and ability to meet interest payments as they come due; calculated as the sum of net income, interest expense, and income tax expense divided by interest expense. (p. 671).

***Trading on the equity** *See leveraging*. (p. 673).

Trading securities Securities bought and held primarily for sale in the near term to generate income on short-term price differences. (p. 650).

Vertical analysis A technique for evaluating financial statement data that expresses each item in a financial statement as a percentage of a base amount. (p. 657).

PRACTICE MULTIPLE-CHOICE QUESTIONS

All of the Practice Multiple-Choice Questions in this chapter employ decision tools.

(LO 1) 1. In reporting discontinued operations, the income statement should show in a special section:

(a) gains on the disposal of the discontinued component.
(b) losses on the disposal of the discontinued component.
(c) Neither (a) nor (b).
(d) Both (a) and (b).

2. Cool Stools Corporation has income before taxes of $400,000 and a loss on discontinued operations of $100,000. If the income tax rate is 25% on all items, the statement of comprehensive income should show income from continuing operations and discontinued operations, respectively, of (LO 1)

(a) $325,000 and $100,000.
(b) $325,000 and $75,000.
(c) $300,000 and $100,000.
(d) $300,000 and $75,000.

(LO 1) **3.** Which of the following would be considered an "Other comprehensive income" item?
(a) Gain on disposal of discontinued operations.
(b) Unrealized loss on available-for-sale securities.
(c) Loss related to flood.
(d) Net income.

(LO 1) **4.** Which situation below might indicate a company has a low quality of earnings?
(a) The same accounting principles are used each year.
(b) Revenue is recognized when the performance obligation is satisfied.
(c) Maintenance costs are capitalized and then depreciated.
(d) The company's P-E ratio is high relative to competitors.

(LO 2) **5.** In horizontal analysis, each item is expressed as a percentage of the:
(a) net income amount.
(b) stockholders' equity amount.
(c) total assets amount.
(d) base-year amount.

(LO 2) **6.** Adams Corporation reported net sales of $300,000, $330,000, and $360,000 in the years 2015, 2016, and 2017, respectively. If 2015 is the base year, what percentage do 2017 sales represent of the base?
(a) 77%. (c) 120%.
(b) 108%. (d) 130%.

(LO 2) **7.** The following schedule is a display of what type of analysis?

	Amount	Percent
Current assets	$200,000	25%
Property, plant, and equipment	600,000	75%
Total assets	$800,000	

(a) Horizontal analysis. (c) Vertical analysis.
(b) Differential analysis. (d) Ratio analysis.

(LO 2) **8.** In vertical analysis, the base amount for depreciation expense is generally:
(a) net sales.
(b) depreciation expense in a previous year.
(c) gross profit.
(d) fixed assets.

(LO 3) **9.** Which measure is an evaluation of a company's ability to pay current liabilities?
(a) Accounts receivable turnover.
(b) Current ratio.
(c) Both (a) and (b).
(d) None of the above.

10. Which measure is useful in evaluating the efficiency in managing inventories? (LO 3)
(a) Inventory turnover.
(b) Days in inventory.
(c) Both (a) and (b).
(d) None of the above.

11. Which of these is **not** a liquidity ratio? (LO 3)
(a) Current ratio.
(b) Asset turnover.
(c) Inventory turnover.
(d) Accounts receivable turnover.

12. Plano Corporation reported net income $24,000, net sales $400,000, and average assets $600,000 for 2017. What is the 2017 profit margin? (LO 3)
(a) 6%. (c) 40%.
(b) 12%. (d) 200%.

Use the following financial statement information as of the end of each year to answer Questions 13–17.

	2017	2016
Inventory	$ 54,000	$ 48,000
Current assets	81,000	106,000
Total assets	382,000	326,000
Current liabilities	27,000	36,000
Total liabilities	102,000	88,000
Common stockholders' equity	240,000	198,000
Net sales	784,000	697,000
Cost of goods sold	306,000	277,000
Net income	134,000	90,000
Income tax expense	22,000	18,000
Interest expense	12,000	12,000
Dividends paid to preferred stockholders	4,000	4,000
Dividends paid to common stockholders	15,000	10,000

13. Compute the days in inventory for 2017. (LO 3)
(a) 64.4 days. (c) 6 days.
(b) 60.8 days. (d) 24 days.

14. Compute the current ratio for 2017. (LO 3)
(a) 1.26:1. (c) 0.80:1.
(b) 3.0:1. (d) 3.75:1.

15. Compute the profit margin for 2017. (LO 3)
(a) 17.1%. (c) 37.9%.
(b) 18.1%. (d) 5.9%.

16. Compute the return on common stockholders' equity for 2017. (LO 3)
(a) 54.2%. (c) 61.2%.
(b) 52.5%. (d) 59.4%.

17. Compute the times interest earned for 2017. (LO 3)
(a) 11.2 times. (c) 14.0 times.
(b) 65.3 times. (d) 13.0 times.

SOLUTIONS

1. **(d)** Gains and losses from the operations of a discontinued segment and gains and losses on the disposal of the discontinued segment are shown in a separate section immediately after continuing operations in the income statement. Choices (a) and (b) are correct, but (d) is the better answer. Choice (c) is wrong as there is a correct answer.
2. **(d)** Income tax expense = 25% × $400,000 = $100,000; therefore, income from continuing operations = $400,000 − $100,000 = $300,000. The loss on discontinued operations is shown net of tax, $100,000 × 75% = $75,000. The other choices are therefore incorrect.
3. **(b)** Unrealized gains and losses on available-for-sale securities are part of other comprehensive income. The other choices are incorrect because (a) a gain on the disposal of discontinued operations is reported as an unusual item, (c) loss related to a flood is reported among other expenses and losses, and (d) net income is a separate line item.

4. **(c)** Capitalizing and then depreciating maintenance costs suggests that a company is trying to avoid expensing certain costs by deferring them to future accounting periods to increase current-period income. The other choices are incorrect because (a) using the same accounting principles each year and (b) recognizing revenue when the performance obligation is satisfied is in accordance with GAAP. Choice (d) is incorrect because a high P-E ratio does not suggest that a firm has low quality of earnings.
5. **(d)** Horizontal analysis converts each succeeding year's balance to a percentage of the base year amount, not (a) net income amount, (b) stockholders' equity amount, or (c) total assets amount.
6. **(c)** The trend percentage for 2017 is 120% ($360,000/$300,000), not (a) 77%, (b) 108%, or (d) 130%.
7. **(c)** The data in the schedule is a display of vertical analysis because the individual asset items are expressed as a percentage of total assets. The other choices are therefore incorrect. Horizontal analysis is a technique for evaluating a series of data over a period of time.
8. **(a)** In vertical analysis, net sales is used as the base amount for income statement items, not (b) depreciation expense in a previous year, (c) gross profit, or (d) fixed assets.
9. **(c)** Both the accounts receivable turnover and the current ratio measure a firm's ability to pay current liabilities. Choices (a) and (b) are correct but (c) is the better answer. Choice (d) is incorrect because there is a correct answer.
10. **(c)** Both inventory turnover and days in inventory measure a firm's efficiency in managing inventories. Choices (a) and (b) are correct but (c) is the better answer. Choice (d) is incorrect because there is a correct answer.
11. **(b)** Asset turnover is a measure of profitability. The other choices are incorrect because the (a) current ratio, (c) inventory turnover, and (d) accounts receivable turnover are all measures of a firm's liquidity.
12. **(a)** Profit margin = Net income ($24,000) ÷ Net sales ($400,000) = 6%, not (b) 12%, (c) 40%, or (d) 200%.
13. **(b)** Inventory turnover = Cost of goods sold/Average inventory {$306,000/[($54,000 + $48,000)/2]} = 6 times. Thus, days in inventory = 60.8 (365/6), not (a) 64.4, (c) 6, or (d) 24 days.
14. **(b)** Current ratio = Current assets/Current liabilities ($81,000/$27,000) = 3.0:1, not (a) 1.26:1, (c) 0.80:1, or (d) 3.75:1.
15. **(a)** Profit margin = Net income/Net sales ($134,000/$784,000) = 17.1%, not (b) 18.1%, (c) 37.9%, or (d) 5.9%.
16. **(d)** Return on common stockholders' equity = Net income ($134,000) − Dividends to preferred stockholders ($4,000)/ Average common stockholders' equity [($240,000 + $198,000)/2] = 59.4%, not (a) 54.2%, (b) 52.5%, or (c) 61.2%.
17. **(c)** Times interest earned = Net income + Interest expense + Income tax expense divided by Interest expense [($134,000 + $12,000 + $22,000)/$12,000] = 14.0 times, not (a) 11.2, (b) 65.3, or (d) 13.0 times.

PRACTICE EXERCISES

Prepare horizontal and vertical analysis.

(LO 2)

1. The comparative condensed balance sheets of Roadway Corporation are presented below.

ROADWAY CORPORATION
Condensed Balance Sheets
December 31

	2017	2016
Assets		
Current assets	$ 76,000	$ 80,000
Property, plant, and equipment (net)	99,000	90,000
Intangibles	25,000	40,000
Total assets	$200,000	$210,000
Liabilities and Stockholders' Equity		
Current liabilities	$ 40,800	$ 48,000
Long-term liabilities	143,000	150,000
Stockholders' equity	16,200	12,000
Total liabilities and stockholders' equity	$200,000	$210,000

INSTRUCTIONS

(a) Prepare a horizontal analysis of the balance sheet data for Roadway Corporation using 2016 as a base.

(b) Prepare a vertical analysis of the balance sheet data for Roadway Corporation in columnar form for 2017.

SOLUTION

1. (a)

ROADWAY CORPORATION
Condensed Balance Sheets
December 31

	2017	2016	Increase (Decrease)	Percent Change from 2016
Assets				
Current assets	$ 76,000	$ 80,000	$ (4,000)	(5.0%)
Property, plant, and equipment (net)	99,000	90,000	9,000	10.0%
Intangibles	25,000	40,000	(15,000)	(37.5%)
Total assets	$200,000	$210,000	$(10,000)	(4.8%)
Liabilities and Stockholders' Equity				
Current liabilities	$ 40,800	$ 48,000	$ (7,200)	(15.0%)
Long-term liabilities	143,000	150,000	(7,000)	(4.7%)
Stockholders' equity	16,200	12,000	4,200	35.0%
Total liabilities and stockholders' equity	$200,000	$210,000	$(10,000)	(4.8%)

(b)

ROADWAY CORPORATION
Condensed Balance Sheet
December 31, 2017

	Amount	Percent
Assets		
Current assets	$ 76,000	38.0%
Property, plant, and equipment (net)	99,000	49.5%
Intangibles	25,000	12.5%
Total assets	$200,000	100.0%
Liabilities and Stockholders' Equity		
Current liabilities	$ 40,800	20.4%
Long-term liabilities	143,000	71.5%
Stockholders' equity	16,200	8.1%
Total liabilities and stockholders' equity	$200,000	100.0%

Compute ratios.
(LO 3)

2. Rondo Corporation's comparative balance sheets are presented below.

RONDO CORPORATION
Balance Sheets
December 31

	2017	2016
Cash	$ 5,300	$ 3,700
Accounts receivable	21,200	23,400
Inventory	9,000	7,000
Land	20,000	26,000
Buildings	70,000	70,000
Accumulated depreciation—buildings	(15,000)	(10,000)
Total	$110,500	$120,100
Accounts payable	$ 10,370	$ 31,100
Common stock	75,000	69,000
Retained earnings	25,130	20,000
Total	$110,500	$120,100

Rondo's 2017 income statement included net sales of $120,000, cost of goods sold of $70,000, and net income of $14,000.

INSTRUCTIONS

Compute the following ratios for 2017.

(a) Current ratio.
(b) Accounts receivable turnover.
(c) Inventory turnover.
(d) Profit margin.
(e) Asset turnover.
(f) Return on assets.
(g) Return on common stockholders' equity.
(h) Debt to assets ratio.

SOLUTION

2. (a) ($5,300 + $21,200 + $9,000)/$10,370 = 3.42
(b) $120,000/[($21,200 + $23,400)/2] = 5.38
(c) $70,000/[($9,000 + $7,000)/2] = 8.8
(d) $14,000/$120,000 = 11.7%
(e) $120,000/[($110,500 + $120,100)/2] = 1.04
(f) $14,000/[($110,500 + $120,100)/2] = 12.1%
(g) $14,000/[($100,130 + $89,000)/2] = 14.8%
(h) $10,370/$110,500 = 9.4%

PRACTICE PROBLEM

Prepare a statement of comprehensive income.

(LO 1)

The events and transactions of Dever Corporation for the year ending December 31, 2017, resulted in the following data.

Cost of goods sold	$2,600,000
Net sales	4,400,000
Other expenses and losses	9,600
Other revenues and gains	5,600
Selling and administrative expenses	1,100,000
Income from operations of plastics division	70,000
Gain from disposal of plastics division	500,000
Unrealized loss on available-for-sale securities	60,000

Analysis reveals the following:

1. All items are before the applicable income tax rate of 30%.
2. The plastics division was sold on July 1.
3. All operating data for the plastics division have been segregated.

INSTRUCTIONS

Prepare a statement of comprehensive income for the year.

SOLUTION

DEVER CORPORATION
Statement of Comprehensive Income
For the Year Ended December 31, 2017

Net sales	$4,400,000
Cost of goods sold	2,600,000
Gross profit	1,800,000
Selling and administrative expenses	1,100,000
Income from operations	700,000
Other revenues and gains	5,600
Other expenses and losses	9,600
Income before income taxes	696,000
Income tax expense ($696,000 × 30%)	208,800
Income from continuing operations	487,200

Discontinued operations		
Income from operation of plastics division, net of $21,000 income taxes ($70,000 × 30%)	49,000	
Gain from disposal of plastics division, net of $150,000 income taxes ($500,000 × 30%)	350,000	399,000
Net income		886,200
Unrealized loss on available-for-sale securities, net of $18,000 income tax savings ($60,000 × 30%)		42,000
Comprehensive income		$844,200

WileyPLUS Brief Exercises, DO IT! Exercises, Exercises, Problems, and many additional resources are available for practice in WileyPLUS.

NOTE: All asterisked Questions, Exercises, and Problems relate to material in the appendix to the chapter.

QUESTIONS

All of the Questions in this chapter employ decision tools.

1. Explain sustainable income. What relationship does this concept have to the treatment of discontinued operations on the income statement?
2. Hogan Inc. reported 2016 earnings per share of $3.26 and had no discontinued operations. In 2017, earnings per share on income from continuing operations was $2.99, and earnings per share on net income was $3.49. Do you consider this trend to be favorable? Why or why not?
3. Moosier Inc. has been in operation for 3 years and uses the FIFO method of pricing inventory. During the fourth year, Moosier changes to the average-cost method for all its inventory. How will Moosier report this change?
4. What amount did Apple report as "Other comprehensive earnings" in its consolidated statement of comprehensive income ending September 27, 2014? By what percentage did Apple's "Comprehensive income" differ from its "Net income"?
5. Identify and explain factors that affect quality of earnings.
6. Explain how the choice of one of the following accounting methods over the other raises or lowers a company's net income during a period of continuing inflation.
   (a) Use of FIFO instead of LIFO for inventory costing.
   (b) Use of a 6-year life for machinery instead of a 9-year life.
   (c) Use of straight-line depreciation instead of declining-balance depreciation.
7. Two popular methods of financial statement analysis are horizontal analysis and vertical analysis. Explain the difference between these two methods.
8. (a) If Erin Company had net income of $300,000 in 2016 and it experienced a 24.5% increase in net income for 2017, what is its net income for 2017?
   (b) If 6 cents of every dollar of Erin's revenue is net income in 2016, what is the dollar amount of 2016 revenue?
9. (a) Gina Jaimes believes that the analysis of financial statements is directed at two characteristics of a company: liquidity and profitability. Is Gina correct? Explain.
   (b) Are short-term creditors, long-term creditors, and stockholders interested in primarily the same characteristics of a company? Explain.
10. (a) Distinguish among the following bases of comparison: intracompany, intercompany, and industry averages.
    (b) Give the principal value of using each of the three bases of comparison.
11. Name the major ratios useful in assessing (a) liquidity and (b) solvency.
12. Vern Thoms is puzzled. His company had a profit margin of 10% in 2017. He feels that this is an indication that the company is doing well. Tina Amos, his accountant, says that more information is needed to determine the company's financial well-being. Who is correct? Why?
13. What does each type of ratio measure?
    (a) Liquidity ratios.
    (b) Solvency ratios.
    (c) Profitability ratios.
14. What is the difference between the current ratio and working capital?
15. Handi Mart, a retail store, has an accounts receivable turnover of 4.5 times. The industry average is 12.5 times. Does Handi Mart have a collection problem with its receivables?

16. Which ratios should be used to help answer each of these questions?
(a) How efficient is a company in using its assets to produce sales?
(b) How near to sale is the inventory on hand?
(c) How many dollars of net income were earned for each dollar invested by the owners?
(d) How able is a company to meet interest charges as they fall due?

17. At year-end, the price-earnings ratio of General Motors was 11.3, and the price-earnings ratio of Microsoft was 28.14. Which company did the stock market favor? Explain.

18. What is the formula for computing the payout ratio? Do you expect this ratio to be high or low for a growth company?

19. Holding all other factors constant, indicate whether each of the following changes generally signals good or bad news about a company.
(a) Increase in profit margin.
(b) Decrease in inventory turnover.
(c) Increase in current ratio.
(d) Decrease in earnings per share.
(e) Increase in price-earnings ratio.
(f) Increase in debt to assets ratio.
(g) Decrease in times interest earned.

20. The return on assets for Ayala Corporation is 7.6%. During the same year, Ayala's return on common stockholders' equity is 12.8%. What is the explanation for the difference in the two rates?

21. Which two ratios do you think should be of greatest interest in each of the following cases?
(a) A pension fund considering the purchase of 20-year bonds.
(b) A bank contemplating a short-term loan.
(c) A common stockholder.

22. Keanu Inc. has net income of $200,000, average shares of common stock outstanding of 40,000, and preferred dividends for the period of $20,000. What is Keanu's earnings per share of common stock? Fred Tyme, the president of Keanu, believes that the computed EPS of the company is high. Comment.

BRIEF EXERCISES

All of the Brief Exercises in this chapter employ decision tools.

Prepare a discontinued operations section of an income statement.
(LO 1), AP

BE13-1 On June 30, Flores Corporation discontinued its operations in Mexico. On September 1, Flores disposed of the Mexico facility at a pretax loss of $640,000. The applicable tax rate is 25%. Show the discontinued operations section of Flores's statement of comprehensive income.

Prepare statement of comprehensive income including unusual items.
(LO 1), AP

BE13-2 An inexperienced accountant for Silva Corporation showed the following in the income statement: income before income taxes $450,000 and unrealized gain on available-for-sale securities (before taxes) $70,000. The unrealized gain on available-for-sale securities and income before income taxes are both subject to a 25% tax rate. Prepare a correct statement of comprehensive income.

Indicate how a change in accounting principle is reported.
(LO 1), C

BE13-3 On January 1, 2017, Bryce Inc. changed from the LIFO method of inventory pricing to the FIFO method. Explain how this change in accounting principle should be treated in the company's financial statements.

Prepare horizontal analysis.
(LO 2), AP

BE13-4 Using these data from the comparative balance sheet of Rollaird Company, perform horizontal analysis.

	December 31, 2017	December 31, 2016
Accounts receivable	$ 460,000	$ 400,000
Inventory	780,000	650,000
Total assets	3,164,000	2,800,000

Prepare vertical analysis.
(LO 2), AP

BE13-5 Using the data presented in BE13-4 for Rollaird Company, perform vertical analysis.

Calculate percentage of change.
(LO 2), AP

BE13-6 Net income was $500,000 in 2015, $485,000 in 2016, and $518,400 in 2017. What is the percentage of change from (a) 2015 to 2016, and (b) from 2016 to 2017? Is the change an increase or a decrease?

Calculate net income.
(LO 2), AP

BE13-7 If Coho Company had net income of $382,800 in 2017 and it experienced a 16% increase in net income over 2016, what was its 2016 net income?

Analyze change in net income.
(LO 2), AP

BE13-8 Vertical analysis (common-size) percentages for Palau Company's sales revenue, cost of goods sold, and expenses are listed here.

Vertical Analysis	2017	2016	2015
Sales revenue	100.0%	100.0%	100.0%
Cost of goods sold	60.5	62.9	64.8
Expenses	26.0	26.6	27.5

Did Palau's net income as a percent of sales increase, decrease, or remain unchanged over the 3-year period? Provide numerical support for your answer.

BE13-9 Horizontal analysis (trend analysis) percentages for Phoenix Company's sales revenue, cost of goods sold, and expenses are listed here.

Analyze change in net income.
(LO 2), AP

Horizontal Analysis	2017	2016	2015
Sales revenue	96.2%	104.8%	100.0%
Cost of goods sold	101.0	98.0	100.0
Expenses	105.6	95.4	100.0

Explain whether Phoenix's net income increased, decreased, or remained unchanged over the 3-year period.

BE13-10 Suppose these selected condensed data are taken from recent balance sheets of Bob Evans Farms (in thousands).

Calculate current ratio.
(LO 3), AP

	2017	2016
Cash	$ 13,606	$ 7,669
Accounts receivable	23,045	19,951
Inventory	31,087	31,345
Other current assets	12,522	11,909
Total current assets	$ 80,260	$ 70,874
Total current liabilities	$245,805	$326,203

Compute the current ratio for each year and comment on your results.

BE13-11 The following data are taken from the financial statements of Colby Company.

Evaluate collection of accounts receivable.
(LO 3), AN

	2017	2016
Accounts receivable (net), end of year	$ 550,000	$ 540,000
Net sales on account	4,300,000	4,000,000
Terms for all sales are 1/10, n/45		

Compute for each year (a) the accounts receivable turnover and (b) the average collection period. What conclusions about the management of accounts receivable can be drawn from these data? At the end of 2015, accounts receivable was $520,000.

BE13-12 The following data were taken from the income statements of Mydorf Company.

Evaluate management of inventory.
(LO 3), AN

	2017	2016
Sales revenue	$6,420,000	$6,240,000
Beginning inventory	960,000	840,000
Purchases	4,840,000	4,661,000
Ending inventory	1,020,000	960,000

Compute for each year (a) the inventory turnover and (b) days in inventory. What conclusions concerning the management of the inventory can be drawn from these data?

BE13-13 Staples, Inc. is one of the largest suppliers of office products in the United States. Suppose it had net income of $738.7 million and sales of $24,275.5 million in 2017. Its total assets were $13,073.1 million at the beginning of the year and $13,717.3 million at the end of the year. What is Staples, Inc.'s (a) asset turnover and (b) profit margin? (Round to two decimals.) Provide a brief interpretation of your results.

Calculate profitability ratios.
(LO 3), AN

Calculate profitability ratios.
(LO 3), AN

BE13-14 Hollie Company has stockholders' equity of $400,000 and net income of $72,000. It has a payout ratio of 18% and a return on assets of 20%. How much did Hollie pay in cash dividends, and what were its average total assets?

Calculate and analyze free cash flow.
(LO 3), AN

BE13-15 Selected data taken from a recent year's financial statements of trading card company Topps Company, Inc. are as follows (in millions).

Net sales	$326.7
Current liabilities, beginning of year	41.1
Current liabilities, end of year	62.4
Net cash provided by operating activities	10.4
Total liabilities, beginning of year	65.2
Total liabilities, end of year	73.2
Capital expenditures	3.7
Cash dividends	6.2

Compute the free cash flow. Provide a brief interpretation of your results.

DO IT! EXERCISES

Prepare statement of comprehensive income including unusual items.
(LO 1), AP

DO IT! 13-1 In its proposed 2017 income statement, Hrabik Corporation reports income before income taxes $500,000, income taxes $100,000 (not including unusual items), loss on operation of discontinued music division $60,000, gain on disposal of discontinued music division $40,000, and unrealized loss on available-for-sale securities $150,000. The income tax rate is 20%. Prepare a correct statement of comprehensive income, beginning with income before income taxes.

Prepare horizontal analysis.
(LO 2), AP

DO IT! 13-2 Summary financial information for Gandaulf Company is as follows.

	Dec. 31, 2017	Dec. 31, 2016
Current assets	$ 200,000	$ 220,000
Plant assets	1,040,000	780,000
Total assets	$1,240,000	$1,000,000

Compute the amount and percentage changes in 2017 using horizontal analysis, assuming 2016 is the base year.

Compute ratios.
(LO 3), AP

DO IT! 13-3 The condensed financial statements of Murawski Company for the years 2016 and 2017 are presented as follows. (Amounts in thousands.)

MURAWSKI COMPANY
Balance Sheets
December 31

	2017	2016
Current assets		
Cash and cash equivalents	$ 330	$ 360
Accounts receivable (net)	470	400
Inventory	460	390
Prepaid expenses	120	160
Total current assets	1,380	1,310
Investments	10	10
Property, plant, and equipment	420	380
Intangibles and other assets	530	510
Total assets	$2,340	$2,210
Current liabilities	$ 900	$ 790
Long-term liabilities	410	380
Stockholders' equity—common	1,030	1,040
Total liabilities and stockholders' equity	$2,340	$2,210

MURAWSKI COMPANY
Income Statements
For the Years Ended December 31

	2017	2016
Sales revenue	$3,800	$3,460
Costs and expenses		
Cost of goods sold	955	890
Selling & administrative expenses	2,400	2,330
Interest expense	25	20
Total costs and expenses	3,380	3,240
Income before income taxes	420	220
Income tax expense	126	66
Net income	$ 294	$ 154

Compute the following ratios for 2017 and 2016.

(a) Current ratio.
(b) Inventory turnover. (Inventory on 12/31/15 was $340.)
(c) Profit margin.
(d) Return on assets. (Assets on 12/31/15 were $1,900.)
(e) Return on common stockholders' equity. (Stockholders' equity on 12/31/15 was $900.)
(f) Debt to assets ratio.
(g) Times interest earned.

EXERCISES

E13-1 For its fiscal year ending October 31, 2017, Haas Corporation reports the following partial data shown below.

Prepare a correct statement of comprehensive income.

(LO 1), AP

Income before income taxes	$540,000
Income tax expense (20% × $420,000)	84,000
Income from continuing operations	456,000
Loss on discontinued operations	120,000
Net income	$336,000

The loss on discontinued operations was comprised of a $50,000 loss from operations and a $70,000 loss from disposal. The income tax rate is 20% on all items.

Instructions

(a) Prepare a correct statement of comprehensive income beginning with income before income taxes.
(b) Explain in memo form why the income statement data are misleading.

E13-2 Trayer Corporation has income from continuing operations of $290,000 for the year ended December 31, 2017. It also has the following items (before considering income taxes).

Prepare statement of comprehensive income.

(LO 1), AP

1. An unrealized loss of $80,000 on available-for-sale securities.
2. A gain of $30,000 on the discontinuance of a division (comprised of a $10,000 loss from operations and a $40,000 gain on disposal).
3. A correction of an error in last year's financial statements that resulted in a $20,000 understatement of 2016 net income.

Assume all items are subject to income taxes at a 20% tax rate.

Instructions

Prepare a statement of comprehensive income, beginning with income from continuing operations.

Prepare horizontal analysis.
(LO 2), AP

XLS

E13-3 Here is financial information for Glitter Inc.

	December 31, 2017	December 31, 2016
Current assets	$106,000	$ 90,000
Plant assets (net)	400,000	350,000
Current liabilities	99,000	65,000
Long-term liabilities	122,000	90,000
Common stock, $1 par	130,000	115,000
Retained earnings	155,000	170,000

Instructions

Prepare a schedule showing a horizontal analysis for 2017, using 2016 as the base year.

Prepare vertical analysis.
(LO 2), AP

XLS

E13-4 Operating data for Joshua Corporation are presented below.

	2017	2016
Sales revenue	$800,000	$600,000
Cost of goods sold	520,000	408,000
Selling expenses	120,000	72,000
Administrative expenses	60,000	48,000
Income tax expense	30,000	24,000
Net income	70,000	48,000

Instructions

Prepare a schedule showing a vertical analysis for 2017 and 2016.

Prepare horizontal and vertical analyses.
(LO 2), AP

E13-5 Suppose the comparative balance sheets of Nike, Inc. are presented here.

NIKE, INC.
Comparative Balance Sheets
May 31
($ in millions)

Assets	2017	2016
Current assets	$ 9,734	$ 8,839
Property, plant, and equipment (net)	1,958	1,891
Other assets	1,558	1,713
Total assets	$13,250	$12,443
Liabilities and Stockholders' Equity		
Current liabilities	$ 3,277	$ 3,322
Long-term liabilities	1,280	1,296
Stockholders' equity	8,693	7,825
Total liabilities and stockholders' equity	$13,250	$12,443

Instructions

(a) Prepare a horizontal analysis of the balance sheet data for Nike, using 2016 as a base. (Show the amount of increase or decrease as well.)

(b) Prepare a vertical analysis of the balance sheet data for Nike for 2017.

Prepare horizontal and vertical analyses.
(LO 2), AP

E13-6 Here are the comparative income statements of Delaney Corporation.

DELANEY CORPORATION
Comparative Income Statements
For the Years Ended December 31

	2017	2016
Net sales	$598,000	$500,000
Cost of goods sold	477,000	420,000
Gross profit	121,000	80,000
Operating expenses	80,000	44,000
Net income	$ 41,000	$ 36,000

Instructions

(a) Prepare a horizontal analysis of the income statement data for Delaney Corporation, using 2016 as a base. (Show the amounts of increase or decrease.)
(b) Prepare a vertical analysis of the income statement data for Delaney Corporation for both years.

E13-7 Nordstrom, Inc. operates department stores in numerous states. Suppose selected financial statement data (in millions) for 2017 are presented below.

Compute liquidity ratios. (LO 3), AP

	End of Year	Beginning of Year
Cash and cash equivalents	$ 795	$ 72
Accounts receivable (net)	2,035	1,942
Inventory	898	900
Other current assets	326	303
Total current assets	$4,054	$3,217
Total current liabilities	$2,014	$1,601

For the year, net credit sales were $8,258 million, cost of goods sold was $5,328 million, and net cash provided by operating activities was $1,251 million.

Instructions

Compute the current ratio, accounts receivable turnover, average collection period, inventory turnover, and days in inventory at the end of the current year.

E13-8 Gwynn Incorporated had the following transactions involving current assets and current liabilities during February 2017.

Perform current ratio analysis. (LO 3), AP

Feb.	3	Collected accounts receivable of $15,000.
	7	Purchased equipment for $23,000 cash.
	11	Paid $3,000 for a 1-year insurance policy.
	14	Paid accounts payable of $12,000.
	18	Declared cash dividends, $4,000.

Additional information:
As of February 1, 2017, current assets were $120,000 and current liabilities were $40,000.

Instructions

Compute the current ratio as of the beginning of the month and after each transaction.

E13-9 Lendell Company has these comparative balance sheet data:

Compute selected ratios. (LO 3), AP

LENDELL COMPANY
Balance Sheets
December 31

	2017	2016
Cash	$ 15,000	$ 30,000
Accounts receivable (net)	70,000	60,000
Inventory	60,000	50,000
Plant assets (net)	200,000	180,000
	$345,000	$320,000
Accounts payable	$ 50,000	$ 60,000
Mortgage payable (15%)	100,000	100,000
Common stock, $10 par	140,000	120,000
Retained earnings	55,000	40,000
	$345,000	$320,000

Additional information for 2017:

1. Net income was $25,000.
2. Sales on account were $375,000. Sales returns and allowances amounted to $25,000.
3. Cost of goods sold was $198,000.
4. Net cash provided by operating activities was $48,000.
5. Capital expenditures were $25,000, and cash dividends were $10,000.

Instructions
Compute the following ratios at December 31, 2017.

(a) Current ratio.
(b) Accounts receivable turnover.
(c) Average collection period.
(d) Inventory turnover.
(e) Days in inventory.
(f) Free cash flow.

Compute selected ratios.
(LO 3), AP

E13-10 Suppose selected comparative statement data for the giant bookseller Barnes & Noble are presented here. All balance sheet data are as of the end of the fiscal year (in millions).

	2017	2016
Net sales	$5,121.8	$5,286.7
Cost of goods sold	3,540.6	3,679.8
Net income	75.9	135.8
Accounts receivable	81.0	107.1
Inventory	1,203.5	1,358.2
Total assets	2,993.9	3,249.8
Total common stockholders' equity	921.6	1,074.7

Instructions
Compute the following ratios for 2017.

(a) Profit margin.
(b) Asset turnover.
(c) Return on assets.
(d) Return on common stockholders' equity.
(e) Gross profit rate.

Compute selected ratios.
(LO 3), AP

E13-11 Here is the income statement for Myers, Inc.

MYERS, INC.
Income Statement
For the Year Ended December 31, 2017

Sales revenue	$400,000
Cost of goods sold	230,000
Gross profit	170,000
Expenses (including $16,000 interest and $24,000 income taxes)	98,000
Net income	$ 72,000

Additional information:

1. Common stock outstanding January 1, 2017, was 32,000 shares, and 40,000 shares were outstanding at December 31, 2017.
2. The market price of Myers stock was $14 in 2017.
3. Cash dividends of $21,000 were paid, $5,000 of which were to preferred stockholders.

Instructions
Compute the following measures for 2017.

(a) Earnings per share.
(b) Price-earnings ratio.
(c) Payout ratio.
(d) Times interest earned.

Compute amounts from ratios.
(LO 3), AP

E13-12 Panza Corporation experienced a fire on December 31, 2017, in which its financial records were partially destroyed. It has been able to salvage some of the records and has ascertained the following balances.

	December 31, 2017	December 31, 2016
Cash	$ 30,000	$ 10,000
Accounts receivable (net)	72,500	126,000
Inventory	200,000	180,000
Accounts payable	50,000	90,000
Notes payable	30,000	60,000
Common stock, $100 par	400,000	400,000
Retained earnings	113,500	101,000

Additional information:

1. The inventory turnover is 3.8 times.
2. The return on common stockholders' equity is 22%. The company had no additional paid-in capital.
3. The accounts receivable turnover is 11.2 times.
4. The return on assets is 18%.
5. Total assets at December 31, 2016, were $605,000.

Instructions

Compute the following for Panza Corporation.

(a) Cost of goods sold for 2017.
(b) Net credit sales for 2017.
(c) Net income for 2017.
(d) Total assets at December 31, 2017.

E13-13 The condensed financial statements of Ness Company for the years 2016 and 2017 are presented below.

Compute ratios.

(LO 3), AP

NESS COMPANY
Balance Sheets
December 31 (in thousands)

	2017	**2016**
Current assets		
Cash and cash equivalents	$ 330	$ 360
Accounts receivable (net)	470	400
Inventory	460	390
Prepaid expenses	130	160
Total current assets	1,390	1,310
Property, plant, and equipment (net)	410	380
Investments	10	10
Intangibles and other assets	530	510
Total assets	$2,340	$2,210
Current liabilities	$ 820	$ 790
Long-term liabilities	480	380
Stockholders' equity—common	1,040	1,040
Total liabilities and stockholders' equity	$2,340	$2,210

NESS COMPANY
Income Statements
For the Year Ended December 31 (in thousands)

	2017	**2016**
Sales revenue	$3,800	$3,460
Costs and expenses		
Cost of goods sold	970	890
Selling & administrative expenses	2,400	2,330
Interest expense	10	20
Total costs and expenses	3,380	3,240
Income before income taxes	420	220
Income tax expense	168	88
Net income	$ 252	$ 132

Compute the following ratios for 2017 and 2016.

(a) Current ratio.
(b) Inventory turnover. (Inventory on December 31, 2015, was $340.)
(c) Profit margin.
(d) Return on assets. (Assets on December 31, 2015, were $1,900.)
(e) Return on common stockholders' equity. (Equity on December 31, 2015, was $900.)
(f) Debt to assets ratio.
(g) Times interest earned.

EXERCISES: SET B AND CHALLENGE EXERCISES

Visit the book's companion website, at **www.wiley.com/college/kimmel**, and choose the Student Companion site to access Exercises: Set B and Challenge Exercises.

PROBLEMS: SET A

All of the Problems in this chapter employ decision tools.

Prepare vertical analysis and comment on profitability.

(LO 2, 3), AN

P13-1A Here are comparative statement data for Duke Company and Lord Company, two competitors. All balance sheet data are as of December 31, 2017, and December 31, 2016.

	Duke Company		Lord Company	
	2017	**2016**	**2017**	**2016**
Net sales	$1,849,000		$546,000	
Cost of goods sold	1,063,200		289,000	
Operating expenses	240,000		82,000	
Interest expense	6,800		3,600	
Income tax expense	62,000		28,000	
Current assets	325,975	$312,410	83,336	$ 79,467
Plant assets (net)	526,800	500,000	139,728	125,812
Current liabilities	66,325	75,815	35,348	30,281
Long-term liabilities	113,990	90,000	29,620	25,000
Common stock, $10 par	500,000	500,000	120,000	120,000
Retained earnings	172,460	146,595	38,096	29,998

Instructions

(a) Prepare a vertical analysis of the 2017 income statement data for Duke Company and Lord Company.

(b) Comment on the relative profitability of the companies by computing the 2017 return on assets and the return on common stockholders' equity for both companies.

Compute ratios from balance sheets and income statements.

(LO 3), AP

P13-2A The comparative statements of Wahlberg Company are presented here.

WAHLBERG COMPANY
Income Statements
For the Years Ended December 31

	2017	2016
Net sales	$1,890,540	$1,750,500
Cost of goods sold	1,058,540	1,006,000
Gross profit	832,000	744,500
Selling and administrative expenses	500,000	479,000
Income from operations	332,000	265,500
Other expenses and losses		
Interest expense	22,000	20,000
Income before income taxes	310,000	245,500
Income tax expense	92,000	73,000
Net income	$ 218,000	$ 172,500

WAHLBERG COMPANY
Balance Sheets
December 31

Assets	2017	2016
Current assets		
Cash	$ 60,100	$ 64,200
Debt investments (short-term)	74,000	50,000
Accounts receivable	117,800	102,800
Inventory	126,000	115,500
Total current assets	377,900	332,500
Plant assets (net)	649,000	520,300
Total assets	$1,026,900	$852,800

Liabilities and Stockholders' Equity	2017	2016
Current liabilities		
Accounts payable	$ 160,000	$145,400
Income taxes payable	43,500	42,000
Total current liabilities	203,500	187,400
Bonds payable	220,000	200,000
Total liabilities	423,500	387,400
Stockholders' equity		
Common stock ($5 par)	290,000	300,000
Retained earnings	313,400	165,400
Total stockholders' equity	603,400	465,400
Total liabilities and stockholders' equity	$1,026,900	$852,800

All sales were on account. Net cash provided by operating activities for 2017 was $220,000. Capital expenditures were $136,000, and cash dividends were $70,000.

Instructions

Compute the following ratios for 2017.

(a) Earnings per share.
(b) Return on common stockholders' equity.
(c) Return on assets.
(d) Current ratio.
(e) Accounts receivable turnover.
(f) Average collection period.
(g) Inventory turnover.
(h) Days in inventory.
(i) Times interest earned.
(j) Asset turnover.
(k) Debt to assets ratio.
(l) Free cash flow.

P13-3A Condensed balance sheet and income statement data for Jergan Corporation are presented here.

Perform ratio analysis, and discuss changes in financial position and operating results.

(LO 3), AN

XLS

JERGAN CORPORATION
Balance Sheets
December 31

	2017	2016	2015
Cash	$ 30,000	$ 20,000	$ 18,000
Accounts receivable (net)	50,000	45,000	48,000
Other current assets	90,000	95,000	64,000
Investments	55,000	70,000	45,000
Plant and equipment (net)	500,000	370,000	358,000
	$725,000	$600,000	$533,000
Current liabilities	$ 85,000	$ 80,000	$ 70,000
Long-term debt	145,000	85,000	50,000
Common stock, $10 par	320,000	310,000	300,000
Retained earnings	175,000	125,000	113,000
	$725,000	$600,000	$533,000

JERGAN CORPORATION
Income Statements
For the Years Ended December 31

	2017	2016
Sales revenue	$740,000	$600,000
Less: Sales returns and allowances	40,000	30,000
Net sales	700,000	570,000
Cost of goods sold	425,000	350,000
Gross profit	275,000	220,000
Operating expenses (including income taxes)	180,000	150,000
Net income	$ 95,000	$ 70,000

Additional information:

1. The market price of Jergan's common stock was $7.00, $7.50, and $8.50 for 2015, 2016, and 2017, respectively.
2. You must compute dividends paid. All dividends were paid in cash.

Instructions

(a) Compute the following ratios for 2016 and 2017.
   (1) Profit margin.
   (2) Gross profit rate.
   (3) Asset turnover.
   (4) Earnings per share.
   (5) Price-earnings ratio.
   (6) Payout ratio.
   (7) Debt to assets ratio.

(b) Based on the ratios calculated, discuss briefly the improvement or lack thereof in the financial position and operating results from 2016 to 2017 of Jergan Corporation.

Compute ratios; comment on overall liquidity and profitability.
(LO 3), AN

P13-4A The following financial information is for Priscoll Company.

PRISCOLL COMPANY
Balance Sheets
December 31

Assets	**2017**	**2016**
Cash	$ 70,000	$ 65,000
Debt investments (short-term)	55,000	40,000
Accounts receivable	104,000	90,000
Inventory	230,000	165,000
Prepaid expenses	25,000	23,000
Land	130,000	130,000
Building and equipment (net)	260,000	185,000
Total assets	$874,000	$698,000
Liabilities and Stockholders' Equity		
Notes payable	$170,000	$120,000
Accounts payable	65,000	52,000
Accrued liabilities	40,000	40,000
Bonds payable, due 2020	250,000	170,000
Common stock, $10 par	200,000	200,000
Retained earnings	149,000	116,000
Total liabilities and stockholders' equity	$874,000	$698,000

PRISCOLL COMPANY
Income Statements
For the Years Ended December 31

	2017	**2016**
Sales revenue	$882,000	$790,000
Cost of goods sold	640,000	575,000
Gross profit	242,000	215,000
Operating expenses	190,000	167,000
Net income	$ 52,000	$ 48,000

Additional information:

1. Inventory at the beginning of 2016 was $115,000.
2. Accounts receivable (net) at the beginning of 2016 were $86,000.
3. Total assets at the beginning of 2016 were $660,000.
4. No common stock transactions occurred during 2016 or 2017.
5. All sales were on account.

Instructions

(a) Indicate, by using ratios, the change in liquidity and profitability of Priscoll Company from 2016 to 2017. (*Note:* Not all profitability ratios can be computed nor can cash-basis ratios be computed.)

(b) The following are three independent situations and a ratio that may be affected. For each situation, compute the affected ratio (1) as of December 31, 2017, and (2) as of December 31, 2018, after giving effect to the situation. Net income for 2018 was $54,000. Total assets on December 31, 2018, were $900,000.

Situation	Ratio
1. 18,000 shares of common stock were sold at par on July 1, 2018.	Return on common stockholders' equity
2. All of the notes payable were paid in 2018.	Debt to assets ratio
3. The market price of common stock was $9 and $12 on December 31, 2017 and 2018, respectively.	Price-earnings ratio

P13-5A Suppose selected financial data of Target and Wal-Mart for 2017 are presented here (in millions).

Compute selected ratios, and compare liquidity, profitability, and solvency for two companies.

(LO 3), AN

	Target Corporation	Wal-Mart Stores, Inc.
	Income Statement Data for Year	
Net sales	$65,357	$408,214
Cost of goods sold	45,583	304,657
Selling and administrative expenses	15,101	79,607
Interest expense	707	2,065
Other income (expense)	(94)	(411)
Income tax expense	1,384	7,139
Net income	$ 2,488	$ 14,335
	Balance Sheet Data (End of Year)	
Current assets	$18,424	$ 48,331
Noncurrent assets	26,109	122,375
Total assets	$44,533	$170,706
Current liabilities	$11,327	$ 55,561
Long-term debt	17,859	44,089
Total stockholders' equity	15,347	71,056
Total liabilities and stockholders' equity	$44,533	$170,706
	Beginning-of-Year Balances	
Total assets	$44,106	$163,429
Total stockholders' equity	13,712	65,682
Current liabilities	10,512	55,390
Total liabilities	30,394	97,747
	Other Data	
Average net accounts receivable	$ 7,525	$ 4,025
Average inventory	6,942	33,836
Net cash provided by operating activities	5,881	26,249
Capital expenditures	1,729	12,184
Dividends	496	4,217

Instructions

(a) For each company, compute the following ratios.

(1) Current ratio.
(2) Accounts receivable turnover.
(3) Average collection period.
(4) Inventory turnover.
(5) Days in inventory.
(6) Profit margin.
(7) Asset turnover.
(8) Return on assets.
(9) Return on common stockholders' equity.
(10) Debt to assets ratio.
(11) Times interest earned.
(12) Free cash flow.

(b) Compare the liquidity, solvency, and profitability of the two companies.

▶ PROBLEMS: SET B AND SET C

Visit the book's companion website, at **www.wiley.com/college/kimmel**, and choose the Student Companion site to access Problems: Set B and Set C.

CONTINUING PROBLEM Cookie Creations

© leungchopan/ Shutterstock

(*Note:* This is a continuation of the Cookie Creations problem from Chapters 1 through 12.)

CC13 Natalie and Curtis have comparative balance sheets and income statements for Cookie & Coffee Creations Inc. They have been told that they can use these financial statements to prepare horizontal and vertical analyses, to calculate financial ratios, to analyze how their business is doing, and to make some decisions they have been considering.

Go to the book's companion website, at **www.wiley.com/college/kimmel**, *to find the completion of this problem.*

EXPAND YOUR CRITICAL THINKING

Financial Reporting

FINANCIAL REPORTING PROBLEM: Apple Inc.

AN

CT13-1 Your parents are considering investing in Apple Inc. common stock. They ask you, as an accounting expert, to make an analysis of the company for them. Financial statements of Apple are presented in Appendix A. Instructions for accessing and using the company's complete annual report, including the notes to its financial statements, are also provided in Appendix A.

Instructions

(a) Make a 5-year trend analysis, using 2010 as the base year, of (1) net sales and (2) net income. Comment on the significance of the trend results.
(b) Compute for 2014 and 2013 the (1) debt to assets ratio and (2) times interest earned. (See Note 3 for interest expense.) How would you evaluate Apple's long-term solvency?
(c) Compute for 2014 and 2013 the (1) profit margin, (2) asset turnover, (3) return on assets, and (4) return on common stockholders' equity. How would you evaluate Apple's profitability? Total assets at September 29, 2012, were \$176,064 million and total stockholders' equity at September 29, 2012, was \$118,210 million.
(d) What information outside the annual report may also be useful to your parents in making a decision about Apple?

Financial Analysis

COMPARATIVE ANALYSIS PROBLEM: Columbia Sportswear Company vs. VF Corporation

AN

CT13-2 The financial statements of Columbia Sportswear Company are presented in Appendix B. Financial statements of VF Corporation are presented in Appendix C.

Instructions

(a) Based on the information in the financial statements, determine each of the following for each company:
    (1) The percentage increase (i) in net sales and (ii) in net income from 2013 to 2014.
    (2) The percentage increase (i) in total assets and (ii) in total stockholders' equity from 2013 to 2014.
    (3) The basic earnings per share for 2014.
(b) What conclusions concerning the two companies can be drawn from these data?

Financial Analysis

COMPARATIVE ANALYSIS PROBLEM: Amazon.com, Inc. vs. Wal-Mart Stores, Inc.

AN

CT13-3 The financial statements of Amazon.com, Inc. are presented in Appendix D. Financial statements of Wal-Mart Stores, Inc. are presented in Appendix E.

Instructions

(a) Based on the information in the financial statements, determine each of the following for each company:
    (1) The percentage increase (i) in net sales and (ii) in net income from 2013 to 2014.
    (2) The percentage increase (i) in total assets and (ii) in total stockholders' equity from 2013 to 2014.
    (3) The basic earnings per share for 2014.
(b) What conclusions concerning the two companies can be drawn from these data?

INTERPRETING FINANCIAL STATEMENTS

Financial Analysis

AN

CT13-4 The Coca-Cola Company and PepsiCo, Inc. provide refreshments to every corner of the world. Suppose selected data from recent consolidated financial statements for The Coca-Cola Company and for PepsiCo, Inc. are presented here (in millions).

	Coca-Cola	PepsiCo
Total current assets	$17,551	$12,571
Total current liabilities	13,721	8,756
Net sales	30,990	43,232
Cost of goods sold	11,088	20,099
Net income	6,824	5,946
Average (net) accounts receivable for the year	3,424	4,654
Average inventories for the year	2,271	2,570
Average total assets	44,595	37,921
Average common stockholders' equity	22,636	14,556
Average current liabilities	13,355	8,772
Average total liabilities	21,960	23,466
Total assets	48,671	39,848
Total liabilities	23,872	23,044
Income taxes	2,040	2,100
Interest expense	355	397
Net cash provided by operating activities	8,186	6,796
Capital expenditures	1,993	2,128
Cash dividends	3,800	2,732

Instructions

(a) Compute the following liquidity ratios for Coca-Cola and for PepsiCo and comment on the relative liquidity of the two competitors.
  (1) Current ratio.
  (2) Accounts receivable turnover.
  (3) Average collection period.
  (4) Inventory turnover.
  (5) Days in inventory.

(b) Compute the following solvency ratios for the two companies and comment on the relative solvency of the two competitors.
  (1) Debt to assets ratio.
  (2) Times interest earned.
  (3) Free cash flow.

(c) Compute the following profitability ratios for the two companies and comment on the relative profitability of the two competitors.
  (1) Profit margin.
  (2) Asset turnover.
  (3) Return on assets.
  (4) Return on common stockholders' equity.

REAL-WORLD FOCUS

CT13-5 ***Purpose:*** To employ comparative data and industry data to evaluate a company's performance and financial position. E

Address: **http://www.msn.com/en-us/money**, or go to **www.wiley.com/college/kimmel**

Steps

(1) Identify two competing companies.
(2) Go to the above address.
(3) Type in the first company's stock symbol or name. (Use "symbol look-up.")
(4) Under the "Fundamentals" heading, use the Growth, Profitability, Financial health, Price ratios, and Management effectiveness tabs to answer parts (a), (b), and (c) below.

Instructions

(a) Evaluate the company's liquidity relative to the industry averages and to the competitor that you chose.
(b) Evaluate the company's solvency relative to the industry averages and to the competitor that you chose.
(c) Evaluate the company's profitability relative to the industry averages and to the competitor that you chose.

E **CT13-6** The April 25, 2012, edition of the *Wall Street Journal* contains an article by Spencer Jakab entitled "Amazon's Valuation Is Hard to Justify."

Instructions

Read the article and answer the following questions.

(a) Explain what is meant by the statement that "On a split-adjusted basis, today's share price is the equivalent of $1,166."

(b) The article says that Amazon.com nearly doubled its capital spending on items such as fulfillment centers (sophisticated warehouses where it finds, packages, and ships goods to customers). Discuss the implications that this spending would have on the company's return on assets in the short-term and in the long-term.

(c) How does Amazon's P-E ratio compare to that of Apple, Netflix, and Wal-Mart? What does this suggest about investors' expectations about Amazon's future earnings?

(d) What factor does the article cite as a possible hurdle that might reduce Amazon's ability to raise its operating margin back to previous levels?

DECISION-MAKING ACROSS THE ORGANIZATION

Financial Analysis

Writing

Group Project

CT13-7 You are a loan officer for White Sands Bank of Taos. Paul Jason, president of P. Jason Corporation, has just left your office. He is interested in an 8-year loan to expand the company's operations. The borrowed funds would be used to purchase new equipment. As evidence of the company's debt-worthiness, Jason provided you with the following facts.

E

	2017	2016
Current ratio	3.1	2.1
Asset turnover	2.8	2.2
Net income	Up 32%	Down 8%
Earnings per share	$3.30	$2.50

Jason is a very insistent (some would say pushy) man. When you told him that you would need additional information before making your decision, he acted offended and said, "What more could you possibly want to know?" You responded that, at a minimum, you would need complete, audited financial statements.

Instructions

With the class divided into groups, answer the following.

(a) Explain why you would want the financial statements to be audited.

(b) Discuss the implications of the ratios provided for the lending decision you are to make. That is, does the information paint a favorable picture? Are these ratios relevant to the decision?

(c) List three other ratios that you would want to calculate for this company, and explain why you would use each.

COMMUNICATION ACTIVITY

E **CT13-8** Larry Dundee is the chief executive officer of Palmer Electronics. Dundee is an expert engineer but a novice in accounting. Dundee asks you, as an accounting student, to explain (a) the bases for comparison in analyzing Palmer's financial statements and (b) the limitations, if any, in financial statement analysis.

Instructions

Write a memo to Larry Dundee that explains the basis for comparison and the factors affecting quality of earnings.

ETHICS CASE

E **CT13-9** René Kelly, president of RL Industries, wishes to issue a press release to bolster her company's image and maybe even its stock price, which has been gradually falling. As controller, you have been asked to provide a list of 20 financial ratios and other operating statistics for RL Industries' first-quarter financials and operations.

Two days after you provide the data requested, Erin Lourdes, the public relations director of RL, asks you to prove the accuracy of the financial and operating data contained in the press release written by the president and edited by Erin. In the news release, the president highlights the sales increase of 25% over last year's first quarter and the positive change in the current ratio from 1.5:1 last year to 3:1 this year. She also emphasizes that production was up 50% over the prior year's first quarter.

You note that the release contains only positive or improved ratios and none of the negative or deteriorated ratios. For instance, no mention is made that the debt to assets ratio has increased from 35% to 55%, that inventories are up 89%, and that although the current ratio improved, the accounts receivable turnover fell from 12 to 9. Nor is there any mention that the reported profit for the quarter would have been a loss had not the estimated lives of RL plant and machinery been increased by 30%. Erin emphasized, "The Pres wants this release by early this afternoon."

Instructions

(a) Who are the stakeholders in this situation?
(b) Is there anything unethical in the president's actions?
(c) Should you as controller remain silent? Does Erin have any responsibility?

ALL ABOUT YOU

CT13-10 In this chapter, you learned how to use many tools for performing a financial analysis of a company. When making personal investments, however, it is most likely that you won't be buying stocks and bonds in individual companies. Instead, when most people want to invest in stock, they buy mutual funds. By investing in a mutual fund, you reduce your risk because the fund diversifies by buying the stock of a variety of different companies, bonds, and other investments, depending on the stated goals of the fund. E

Before you invest in a fund, you will need to decide what type of fund you want. For example, do you want a fund that has the potential of high growth (but also high risk), or are you looking for lower risk and a steady stream of income? Do you want a fund that invests only in U.S. companies, or do you want one that invests globally? Many resources are available to help you with these types of decisions.

Instructions

Go to **http://web.archive.org/web/20050210200843/http://www.cnb1.com/invallocmdl.htm** and complete the investment allocation questionnaire. Add up your total points to determine the type of investment fund that would be appropriate for you.

FASB CODIFICATION ACTIVITY

CT13-11 If your school has a subscription to the FASB Codification, go to **http://aaahq.org/ascLogin.cfm** to log in and prepare responses to the following. Use the Master Glossary for determining the proper definitions. AP

(a) Discontinued operations.
(b) Comprehensive income.

A Look at IFRS

LEARNING OBJECTIVE 5

Compare financial statement analysis and income statement presentation under GAAP and IFRS.

The tools of financial statement analysis are the same throughout the world. Techniques such as vertical and horizontal analysis, for example, are tools used by analysts regardless of whether GAAP- or IFRS-related financial statements are being evaluated. In addition, the ratios provided in the textbook are the same ones that are used internationally.

The beginning of this chapter relates to the income statement. As in GAAP, the income statement is a required statement under IFRS. In addition, the content and presentation of an IFRS income statement is similar to the one used for GAAP. *IAS 1* (revised), "Presentation of Financial Statements," provides general guidelines for the reporting of income statement information. In general, the differences in the presentation of financial statement information are relatively minor.

RELEVANT FACTS

Following are the key similarities between GAAP and IFRS as related to financial statement analysis and income statement presentation. There are no significant differences between the two standards.

- The tools of financial statement analysis covered in this chapter are universal and therefore no significant differences exist in the analysis methods used.
- The basic objectives of the income statement are the same under both GAAP and IFRS. As indicated in the textbook, a very important objective is to ensure that users of the income statement can evaluate the sustainable income of the company. Thus, both the IASB and the FASB are interested in distinguishing normal levels of income from unusual items in order to better predict a company's future profitability.
- The basic accounting for discontinued operations is the same under IFRS and GAAP.
- The accounting for changes in accounting principles and changes in accounting estimates are the same for both GAAP and IFRS.
- Both GAAP and IFRS follow the same approach in reporting comprehensive income.

LOOKING TO THE FUTURE

The FASB and the IASB are working on a project that would rework the structure of financial statements. Recently, the IASB decided to require a statement of comprehensive income, similar to what was required under GAAP. In addition, another part of this project addresses the issue of how to classify various items in the income statement. A main goal of this new approach is to provide information that better represents how businesses are run. In addition, the approach draws attention away from one number—net income.

IFRS Practice

IFRS SELF-TEST QUESTIONS

1. The basic tools of financial analysis are the same under both GAAP and IFRS **except** that:
   (a) horizontal analysis cannot be done because the format of the statements is sometimes different.
   (b) analysis is different because vertical analysis cannot be done under IFRS.
   (c) the current ratio cannot be computed because current liabilities are often reported before current assets in IFRS statements of position.
   (d) None of the above.
2. Presentation of comprehensive income must be reported under IFRS in:
   (a) the statement of stockholders' equity.
   (b) the income statement ending with net income.
   (c) the notes to the financial statements.
   (d) a statement of comprehensive income.
3. In preparing its income statement for 2017, Parmalane assembles the following information.

Sales revenue	$500,000
Cost of goods sold	300,000
Operating expenses	40,000
Loss on discontinued operations	20,000

   Ignoring income taxes, what is Parmalane's income from continuing operations for 2017 under IFRS?
   (a) $260,000.
   (b) $250,000.
   (c) $240,000.
   (d) $160,000.

INTERNATIONAL FINANCIAL REPORTING PROBLEM: Louis Vuitton

IFRS13-1 The financial statements of Louis Vuitton are presented in Appendix F. Instructions for accessing and using the company's complete annual report, including the notes to its financial statements, are also provided in Appendix F.

Instructions

Use the company's **2014 annual report** to answer the following questions.

(a) What was the company's profit margin for 2014? Has it increased or decreased from 2013?
(b) What was the company's operating profit for 2014?
(c) The company reported comprehensive income of €3,267 billion in 2014. What are the other comprehensive gains and losses recorded in 2014?

Answers to IFRS Self-Test Questions

1. d **2.** d **3.** d

14

Managerial Accounting

CHAPTER PREVIEW

This chapter focuses on issues illustrated in the Feature Story about Current Designs and its parent company Wenonah Canoe. To succeed, the company needs to determine and control the costs of material, labor, and overhead, and understand the relationship between costs and profits. Managers often make decisions that determine their company's fate—and their own. Managers are evaluated on the results of their decisions. Managerial accounting provides tools to assist management in making decisions and to evaluate the effectiveness of those decisions.

CHAPTER OUTLINE

LEARNING OBJECTIVES		PRACTICE
1 Identify the features of managerial accounting and the functions of management.	• Comparing managerial and financial accounting • Management functions • Organizational structure	DO IT! 1 Managerial Accounting Overview
2 Describe the classes of manufacturing costs and the differences between product and period costs.	• Manufacturing costs • Product vs. period costs • Illustration of cost concepts	DO IT! 2 Managerial Cost Concepts
3 Demonstrate how to compute cost of goods manufactured and prepare financial statements for a manufacturer.	• Income statement • Cost of goods manufactured schedule • Balance sheet	DO IT! 3 Cost of Goods Manufactured
4 Discuss trends in managerial accounting.	• Service industries • Value chain • Balanced scorecard • Business ethics • Corporate social responsibility	DO IT! 4 Trends in Managerial Accounting

Go to the ***REVIEW AND PRACTICE*** section at the end of the chapter for a targeted summary and exercises with solutions.

Visit **WileyPLUS** for additional tutorials and practice opportunities.

© iNoppadal/Shutterstock

FEATURE STORY

Just Add Water ... and Paddle

Mike Cichanowski grew up on the Mississippi River in Winona, Minnesota. At a young age, he learned to paddle a canoe so he could explore the river. Before long, Mike began crafting his own canoes from bent wood and fiberglass in his dad's garage. Then, when his canoe-making shop outgrew the garage, he moved it into an old warehouse. When that was going to be torn down, Mike came to a critical juncture in his life. He took out a bank loan and built his own small shop, giving birth to the company Wenonah Canoe.

Wenonah Canoe soon became known as a pioneer in developing techniques to get the most out of new materials such as plastics, composites, and carbon fibers—maximizing strength while minimizing weight.

In the 1990s, as kayaking became popular, Mike made another critical decision when he acquired Current Designs, a premier Canadian kayak manufacturer. This venture allowed Wenonah to branch out with new product lines while providing Current Designs with much-needed capacity expansion and manufacturing expertise. Mike moved Current Designs' headquarters to Minnesota and made a big (and potentially risky) investment in a new production facility. Today, the company's 90 employees produce about 12,000 canoes and kayaks per year. These are sold across the country and around the world.

Mike will tell you that business success is "a three-legged stool." The first leg is the knowledge and commitment to make a great product. Wenonah's canoes and Current Designs' kayaks are widely regarded as among the very best. The second leg is the ability to sell your product. Mike's company started off making great canoes, but it took a little longer to figure out how to sell them. The third leg is not something that most of you would immediately associate with entrepreneurial success. It is what goes on behind the scenes—accounting. Good accounting information is absolutely critical to the countless decisions, big and small, that ensure the survival and growth of the company.

Bottom line: No matter how good your product is, and no matter how many units you sell, if you don't have a firm grip on your numbers, you are up a creek without a paddle.

Source: www.wenonah.com.

LEARNING OBJECTIVE 1

Identify the features of managerial accounting and the functions of management.

Managerial accounting provides economic and financial information for managers and other internal users. The skills that you learn in this course will be vital to your future success in business. You don't believe us? Let's look at some examples of some of the crucial activities of employees at Current Designs and where those activities are addressed in this textbook.

In order to know whether it is making a profit, Current Designs needs accurate information about the cost of each kayak (Chapters 15, 16, and 17). To be profitable, Current Designs adjusts the number of kayaks it produces in response to changes in economic conditions and consumer tastes. It needs to understand how changes in the number of kayaks it produces impact its production costs and profitability (Chapters 18 and 19). Further, Current Designs' managers often consider alternative courses of action. For example, should the company accept a special order from a customer, produce a particular kayak component internally or outsource it, or continue or discontinue a particular product line (Chapter 20)? Finally, one of the most important and most difficult decisions is what price to charge for the kayaks (Appendix M).

In order to plan for the future, Current Designs prepares budgets (Chapter 21), and it then compares its budgeted numbers with its actual results to evaluate performance and identify areas that need to change (Chapters 22 and 23). Finally, it sometimes needs to make substantial investment decisions, such as the building of a new plant or the purchase of new equipment (Chapter 24).

Someday, you are going to face decisions just like these. You may end up in sales, marketing, management, production, or finance. You may work for a company that provides medical care, produces software, or serves up mouth-watering meals. No matter what your position is and no matter what your product, the skills you acquire in this class will increase your chances of business success. Put another way, in business you can either guess or you can make an informed decision. As a CEO of Microsoft once noted: "If you're supposed to be making money in business and supposed to be satisfying customers and building market share, there are numbers that characterize those things. And if somebody can't speak to me quantitatively about it, then I'm nervous." This course gives you the skills you need to quantify information so you can make informed business decisions.

COMPARING MANAGERIAL AND FINANCIAL ACCOUNTING

There are both similarities and differences between managerial and financial accounting. First, each field of accounting deals with the economic events of a business. For example, *determining* the unit cost of manufacturing a product is part of managerial accounting. *Reporting* the total cost of goods manufactured and sold is part of financial accounting. In addition, both managerial and financial accounting require that a company's economic events be quantified and communicated to interested parties. Illustration 14-1 summarizes the principal differences between financial accounting and managerial accounting.

MANAGEMENT FUNCTIONS

Managers' activities and responsibilities can be classified into three broad functions:

1. Planning.
2. Directing.
3. Controlling.

Feature	Financial Accounting	Managerial Accounting
Primary Users of Reports	External users: stockholders, creditors, and regulators.	Internal users: officers and managers.
Types and Frequency of Reports	Financial statements. Quarterly and annually.	Internal reports. As frequently as needed.
Purpose of Reports	General-purpose.	Special-purpose for specific decisions.
Content of Reports	Pertains to business as a whole. Highly aggregated (condensed). Limited to double-entry accounting and cost data. Generally accepted accounting principles.	Pertains to subunits of the business. Very detailed. Extends beyond double-entry accounting to any relevant data. Standard is relevance to decisions.
Verification Process	Audited by CPA.	No independent audits.

ILLUSTRATION 14-1
Differences between financial and managerial accounting

In performing these functions, managers make decisions that have a significant impact on the organization.

Planning requires managers to look ahead and to establish objectives. These objectives are often diverse: maximizing short-term profits and market share, maintaining a commitment to environmental protection, and contributing to social programs. For example, Hewlett-Packard, in an attempt to gain a stronger foothold in the computer industry, greatly reduced its prices to compete with Dell. A key objective of management is to **add value** to the business under its control. Value is usually measured by the price of the company's stock and by the potential selling price of the company.

Directing involves coordinating a company's diverse activities and human resources to produce a smooth-running operation. This function relates to implementing planned objectives and providing necessary incentives to motivate employees. For example, manufacturers such as Campbell Soup Company, General Motors, and Dell need to coordinate purchasing, manufacturing, warehousing, and selling. Service corporations such as American Airlines, Federal Express, and AT&T coordinate scheduling, sales, service, and acquisitions of equipment and supplies. Directing also involves selecting executives, appointing managers and supervisors, and hiring and training employees.

The third management function, **controlling**, is the process of keeping the company's activities on track. In controlling operations, managers determine whether planned goals are met. When there are deviations from targeted objectives, managers decide what changes are needed to get back on track. Scandals at companies like Enron, Lucent, and Xerox attest to the fact that companies need adequate controls to ensure that the company develops and distributes accurate information.

How do managers achieve control? A smart manager in a very small operation can make personal observations, ask good questions, and know how to evaluate the answers. But using this approach in a larger organization would result in chaos. Imagine the president of Current Designs attempting to determine whether the company is meeting its planned objectives without some record of what has happened and what is expected to occur. Thus, large businesses typically use a formal system of evaluation. These systems include such features as budgets, responsibility centers, and performance evaluation reports—all of which are features of managerial accounting.

Decision-making is not a separate management function. Rather, it is the outcome of the exercise of good judgment in planning, directing, and controlling.

MANAGEMENT INSIGHT Louis Vuitton

© Camilia Wisbauer/iStockphoto

Even the Best Have to Get Better

Luxury-goods manufacturers used to consider stockouts to be a good thing. But recently, Louis Vuitton, a French manufacturer of high-end handbags, wallets, and suitcases, changed its attitude. The company adopted "lean" processes used by car manufacturers and electronics companies to speed up production of "hot" products. Work is done by flexible teams, with jobs organized based on how long a task takes. By reducing wasted time and eliminating bottlenecks, what used to take 20 to 30 workers eight days to do now takes only 6 to 12 workers one day.

Other efforts included organizing 10-person factory teams into U-shaped clusters. This arrangement freed up floor space, allowing Louis Vuitton to hire 300 additional employees. The company also selectively employs robots to bring items to human workers, saving valuable time. In addition, computer programs are now used to identify flaws in leather skins, enabling the company to identify the best way to cut pieces from the leather to increase quality and minimize waste.

Finally, Louis Vuitton stores around the world feed sales information to the company's headquarters in France. Production is then adjusted accordingly to ensure that would-be buyers aren't left empty-handed. With these new production processes, Louis Vuitton is already seeing improved results—returns of some products are down by two-thirds.

Sources: Christina Passariello, "Louis Vuitton Tries Modern Methods on Factory Lines," *Wall Street Journal* (October 9, 2006); and Christina Passariello, "At Vuitton, Growth in Small Batches," *Wall Street Journal* (June 27, 2011).

What are some of the steps that this company has taken in order to ensure that production meets demand? (Go to WileyPLUS for this answer and additional questions.)

ORGANIZATIONAL STRUCTURE

Most companies prepare **organization charts** to show the interrelationships of activities and the delegation of authority and responsibility within the company. Illustration 14-2 shows a typical organization chart.

ILLUSTRATION 14-2
A typical corporate organization chart

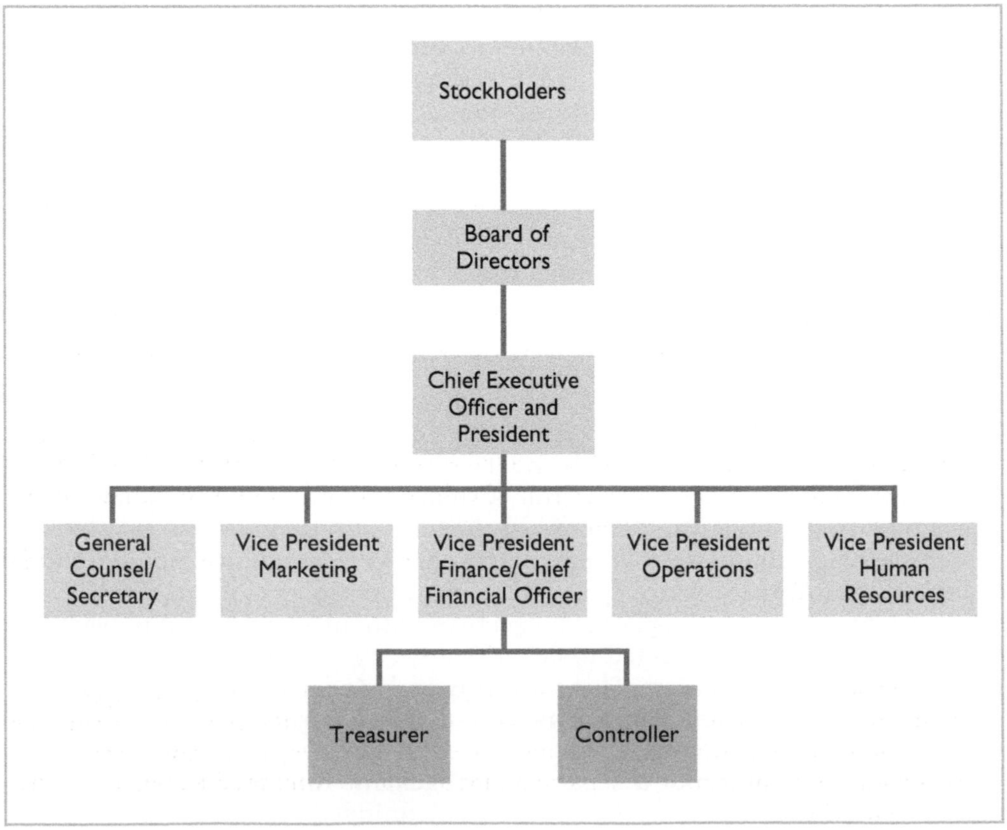

Stockholders own the corporation, but they manage it indirectly through a **board of directors** they elect. The board formulates the operating policies for the company or organization. The board also selects officers, such as a president and one or more vice presidents, to execute policy and to perform daily management functions.

The **chief executive officer (CEO)** has overall responsibility for managing the business. As the organization chart in Illustration 14-2 (page 706) shows, the CEO delegates responsibilities to other officers.

Responsibilities within the company are frequently classified as either line or staff positions. Employees with **line positions** are directly involved in the company's primary revenue-generating operating activities. Examples of line positions include the vice president of operations, vice president of marketing, plant managers, supervisors, and production personnel. Employees with **staff positions** are involved in activities that support the efforts of the line employees. In a company like General Electric or Facebook, employees in finance, legal, and human resources have staff positions. While activities of staff employees are vital to the company, these employees are nonetheless there to serve the line employees who engage in the company's primary operations.

The **chief financial officer (CFO)** is responsible for all of the accounting and finance issues the company faces. The CFO is supported by the **controller** and the **treasurer**. The controller's responsibilities include (1) maintaining the accounting records, (2) ensuring an adequate system of internal control, and (3) preparing financial statements, tax returns, and internal reports. The treasurer has custody of the corporation's funds and is responsible for maintaining the company's cash position.

Also serving the CFO is the internal audit staff. The staff's responsibilities include reviewing the reliability and integrity of financial information provided by the controller and treasurer. Staff members also ensure that internal control systems are functioning properly to safeguard corporate assets. In addition, they investigate compliance with policies and regulations. In many companies, these staff members also determine whether resources are used in the most economical and efficient fashion.

The vice president of operations oversees employees with line positions. For example, the company might have multiple plant managers, each of whom reports to the vice president of operations. Each plant also has department managers, such as fabricating, painting, and shipping, each of whom reports to the plant manager.

DO IT! ▶1 Managerial Accounting Overview

Indicate whether the following statements are true or false. If false, explain why.

1. Managerial accountants have a single role within an organization: collecting and reporting costs to management.
2. Financial accounting reports are general-purpose and intended for external users.
3. Managerial accounting reports are special-purpose and issued as frequently as needed.
4. Managers' activities and responsibilities can be classified into three broad functions: cost accounting, budgeting, and internal control.
5. Managerial accounting reports must now comply with generally accepted accounting principles (GAAP).

SOLUTION

1. False. Managerial accountants determine product costs. In addition, managerial accountants are now held responsible for evaluating how well the company employs its resources. As a result, when the company makes critical strategic decisions, managerial accountants serve as team members alongside personnel from production, marketing, and engineering.

Action Plan

✔ Understand that managerial accounting is a field of accounting that provides economic and financial information for managers and other internal users.

✔ Understand that financial accounting provides information for external users.

✔ Analyze which users require which different types of information.

2. True.
3. True.
4. False. Managers' activities are classified into three broad functions: planning, directing, and controlling. Planning requires managers to look ahead to establish objectives. Directing involves coordinating a company's diverse activities and human resources to produce a smooth-running operation. Controlling keeps the company's activities on track.
5. False. Managerial accounting reports are for internal use and thus do not have to comply with GAAP.

Related exercise material: **BE14-1, BE14-2, DO IT! 14-1,** and **E14-1.**

LEARNING OBJECTIVE 2

Describe the classes of manufacturing costs and the differences between product and period costs.

In order for managers at a company like Current Designs to plan, direct, and control operations effectively, they need good information. One very important type of information relates to costs. Managers should ask questions such as the following.

1. What costs are involved in making a product or performing a service?
2. If we decrease production volume, will costs decrease?
3. What impact will automation have on total costs?
4. How can we best control costs?

To answer these questions, managers obtain and analyze reliable and relevant cost information. The first step is to understand the various cost categories that companies use.

MANUFACTURING COSTS

Manufacturing consists of activities and processes that convert raw materials into finished goods. Contrast this type of operation with merchandising, which sells products in the form in which they are purchased. Manufacturing costs are classified as direct materials, direct labor, and manufacturing overhead.

Direct Materials

To obtain the materials that will be converted into the finished product, the manufacturer purchases raw materials. **Raw materials** are the basic materials and parts used in the manufacturing process.

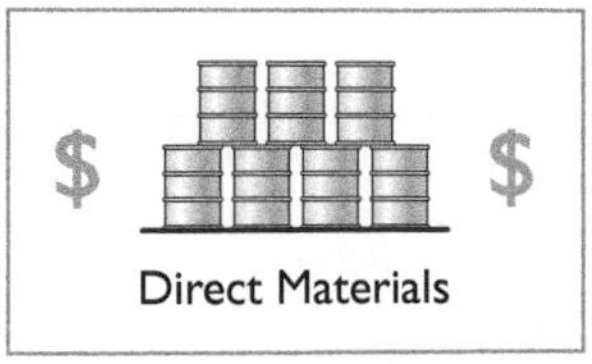

Raw materials that can be physically and directly associated with the finished product during the manufacturing process are **direct materials**. Examples include flour in the baking of bread, syrup in the bottling of soft drinks, and steel in the making of automobiles. A primary direct material of many Current Designs' kayaks is polyethylene powder. Some of its high-performance kayaks use Kevlar®.

Some raw materials cannot be easily associated with the finished product. These are called indirect materials. **Indirect materials** have one of two characteristics. (1) They do not physically become part of the finished product (such as polishing compounds used by Current Designs for the finishing touches on kayaks). Or, (2) they are impractical to trace to the finished product because their physical association with the finished product is too small in terms of cost (such as cotter pins and lock washers). Companies account for indirect materials as part of **manufacturing overhead**.

Direct Labor

The work of factory employees that can be physically and directly associated with converting raw materials into finished goods is **direct labor**. Bottlers at Coca-Cola, bakers at Sara Lee, and equipment operators at Current Designs are employees whose activities are usually classified as direct labor. **Indirect labor** refers to the work of employees that has no physical association with the finished product or for which it is impractical to trace costs to the goods produced. Examples include wages of factory maintenance people, factory time-keepers, and factory supervisors. Like indirect materials, companies classify indirect labor as **manufacturing overhead**.

Manufacturing Overhead

Manufacturing overhead consists of costs that are indirectly associated with the manufacture of the finished product. Overhead costs also include manufacturing costs that cannot be classified as direct materials or direct labor. Manufacturing overhead includes indirect materials, indirect labor, depreciation on factory buildings and machines, and insurance, taxes, and maintenance on factory facilities.

One study of manufactured goods found the following magnitudes of the three different product costs as a percentage of the total product cost: direct materials 54%, direct labor 13%, and manufacturing overhead 33%. Note that the direct labor component is the smallest. This component of product cost is dropping substantially because of automation. Companies are working hard to increase productivity by decreasing labor. In some companies, direct labor has become as little as 5% of the total cost.

ALTERNATIVE TERMINOLOGY
Some companies use terms such as *factory overhead, indirect manufacturing costs*, and *burden* instead of manufacturing overhead.

Allocating direct materials and direct labor costs to specific products is fairly straightforward. Good recordkeeping can tell a company how much plastic it used in making each type of gear, or how many hours of factory labor it took to assemble a part. But allocating overhead costs to specific products presents problems. How much of the purchasing agent's salary is attributable to the hundreds of different products made in the same plant? What about the grease that keeps the machines humming, or the computers that make sure paychecks come out on time? Boiled down to its simplest form, the question becomes: Which products cause the incurrence of which costs? In subsequent chapters, we show various methods of allocating overhead to products.

MANAGEMENT INSIGHT Whirlpool

bikeriderlondon/Shutterstock

Why Manufacturing Matters for U.S. Workers

Prior to 2010, U.S. manufacturing employment fell at an average rate of 0.1% per year for 60 years. At the same time, U.S. factory output increased by an average rate of 3.4%. As manufacturers relied more heavily on automation, the number of people they needed declined. However, factory jobs are important because the average hourly wage of a factory worker is $22, twice the average wage of employees in the service sector. Fortunately, manufacturing jobs in the United States increased by 1.2% in 2010, and they were forecast to continue to increase through at least 2015. Why? Because companies like Whirlpool, Caterpillar, and Dow are building huge new plants in the United States to replace old, inefficient U.S. facilities. For many products that are ultimately sold in the United States, it makes more sense to produce them domestically and save on the shipping costs. In addition, these efficient new plants, combined with an experienced workforce, will make it possible to compete with manufacturers in other countries, thereby increasing export potential.

Sources: Bob Tita, "Whirlpool to Invest in Tennessee Plant," *Wall Street Journal Online* (September 1, 2010); and James R. Hagerty, "U.S. Factories Buck Decline," *Wall Street Journal Online* (January 19, 2011).

In what ways does the shift to automated factories change the amount and composition of product costs? (Go to **WileyPLUS** for this answer and additional questions.)

PRODUCT VERSUS PERIOD COSTS

ALTERNATIVE TERMINOLOGY
Product costs are also called *inventoriable costs.*

Each of the manufacturing cost components—direct materials, direct labor, and manufacturing overhead—are product costs. As the term suggests, **product costs** are costs that are a necessary and integral part of producing the finished product. Companies record product costs, when incurred, as inventory. These costs do not become expenses until the company sells the finished goods inventory. At that point, the company records the expense as cost of goods sold.

Period costs are costs that are matched with the revenue of a specific time period rather than included as part of the cost of a salable product. These are non-manufacturing costs. Period costs include selling and administrative expenses. In order to determine net income, companies deduct these costs from revenues in the period in which they are incurred.

Illustration 14-3 summarizes these relationships and cost terms. Our main concern in this chapter is with product costs.

ILLUSTRATION 14-3
Product versus period costs

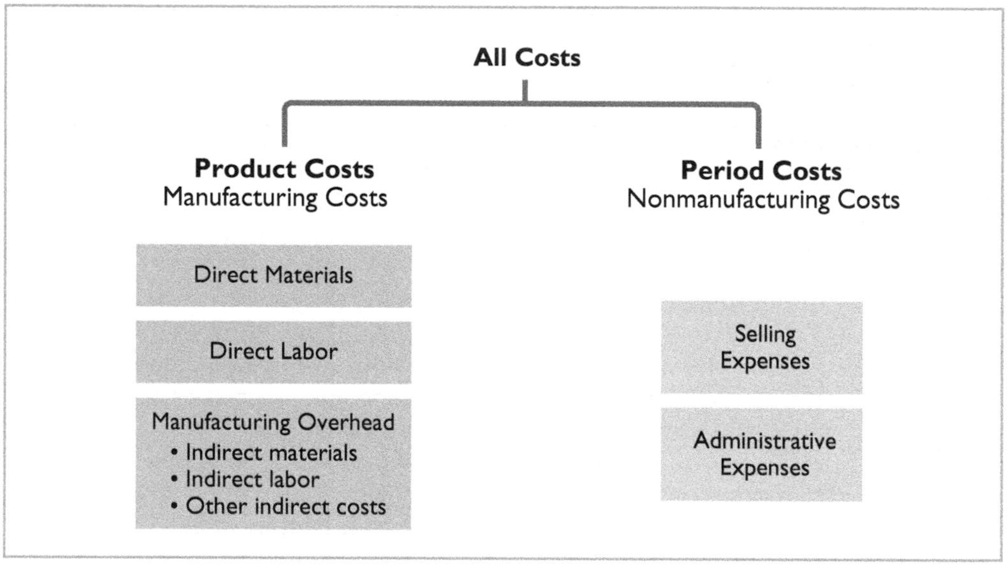

ILLUSTRATION OF COST CONCEPTS

To improve your understanding of cost concepts, we illustrate them here through an extended example. Suppose you started your own snowboard factory, Terrain Park Boards. Think that's impossible? Burton Snowboards was started by Jake Burton Carpenter, when he was only 23 years old. Jake initially experimented with 100 different prototype designs before settling on a final design. Then Jake, along with two relatives and a friend, started making 50 boards per day in Londonderry, Vermont. Unfortunately, while they made a lot of boards in their first year, they were only able to sell 300 of them. To get by during those early years, Jake taught tennis and tended bar to pay the bills.

Here are some of the costs that your snowboard factory would incur.

1. The materials cost of each snowboard (wood cores, fiberglass, resins, metal screw holes, metal edges, and ink) is $30.
2. The labor costs (for example, to trim and shape each board using jig saws and band saws) are $40.
3. Depreciation on the factory building and equipment (for example, presses, grinding machines, and lacquer machines) used to make the snowboards is $25,000 per year.
4. Property taxes on the factory building (where the snowboards are made) are $6,000 per year.

5. Advertising costs (mostly online and catalogue) are $60,000 per year.
6. Sales commissions related to snowboard sales are $20 per snowboard.
7. Salaries for factory maintenance employees are $45,000 per year.
8. The salary of the plant manager is $70,000.
9. The cost of shipping is $8 per snowboard.

Illustration 14-4 shows how Terrain Park Boards would assign these manufacturing and selling costs to the various categories.

ILLUSTRATION 14-4
Assignment of costs to cost categories

Terrain Park Boards

Cost Item	Product Costs: Direct Materials	Product Costs: Direct Labor	Product Costs: Manufacturing Overhead	Period Costs
1. Material cost ($30 per board)	X			
2. Labor costs ($40 per board)		X		
3. Depreciation on factory equipment ($25,000 per year)			X	
4. Property taxes on factory building ($6,000 per year)			X	
5. Advertising costs ($60,000 per year)				X
6. Sales commissions ($20 per board)				X
7. Maintenance salaries (factory facilities, $45,000 per year)			X	
8. Salary of plant manager ($70,000 per year)			X	
9. Cost of shipping boards ($8 per board)				X

Total manufacturing costs are the sum of the **product costs**—direct materials, direct labor, and manufacturing overhead—incurred in the current period. If Terrain Park Boards produces 10,000 snowboards the first year, the total manufacturing costs would be $846,000, as shown in Illustration 14-5.

ILLUSTRATION 14-5
Computation of total manufacturing costs

Cost Number and Item	Manufacturing Cost
1. Material cost ($30 × 10,000)	$300,000
2. Labor cost ($40 × 10,000)	400,000
3. Depreciation on factory equipment	25,000
4. Property taxes on factory building	6,000
7. Maintenance salaries (factory facilities)	45,000
8. Salary of plant manager	70,000
Total manufacturing costs	$846,000

Once it knows the total manufacturing costs, Terrain Park Boards can compute the manufacturing cost per unit. Assuming 10,000 units, the cost to produce one snowboard is $84.60 ($846,000 ÷ 10,000 units).

In subsequent chapters, we use extensively the cost concepts discussed in this chapter. So study Illustration 14-4 carefully. If you do not understand any of these classifications, go back and reread the appropriate section.

DO IT! 2 Managerial Cost Concepts

Action Plan

- ✔ Classify as direct materials any raw materials physically and directly associated with the finished product.
- ✔ Classify as direct labor the work of factory employees physically and directly associated with the finished product.
- ✔ Classify as manufacturing overhead any costs indirectly associated with the finished product.

A bicycle company has these costs: tires, salaries of employees who put tires on the wheels, factory building depreciation, advertising expenditures, lubricants, spokes, salary of factory manager, salary of accountant, handlebars, and salaries of factory maintenance employees. Classify each cost as direct materials, direct labor, overhead, or a period cost.

SOLUTION

Tires, spokes, and handlebars are direct materials. Salaries of employees who put tires on the wheels are direct labor. Factory building depreciation, lubricants, salary of factory manager, and salary of factory maintenance employees are manufacturing overhead. Advertising expenditures and salary of accountant are period costs.

Related exercise material: **BE14-3, BE14-4, BE14-5, BE14-6, DO IT! 14-2, E14-2, E14-3, E14-4, E14-5, E14-6,** and **E14-7.**

LEARNING OBJECTIVE 3 Demonstrate how to compute cost of goods manufactured and prepare financial statements for a manufacturer.

The financial statements of a manufacturer are very similar to those of a merchandiser. For example, you will find many of the same sections and same accounts in the financial statements of Procter & Gamble that you find in the financial statements of Dick's Sporting Goods. The principal differences between their financial statements occur in two places: the cost of goods sold section in the income statement and the current assets section in the balance sheet.

INCOME STATEMENT

Under a periodic inventory system, the income statements of a merchandiser and a manufacturer differ in the cost of goods sold section. Merchandisers compute cost of goods sold by adding the beginning inventory to the **cost of goods purchased** and subtracting the ending inventory. Manufacturers compute cost of goods sold by adding the beginning finished goods inventory to the **cost of goods manufactured** and subtracting the ending finished goods inventory. Illustration 14-6 shows these different methods.

A number of accounts are involved in determining the cost of goods manufactured. To eliminate excessive detail, income statements typically show only the total cost of goods manufactured. A separate statement, called a Cost of Goods Manufactured Schedule, presents the details. (See the discussion on page 714 and Illustration 14-9.)

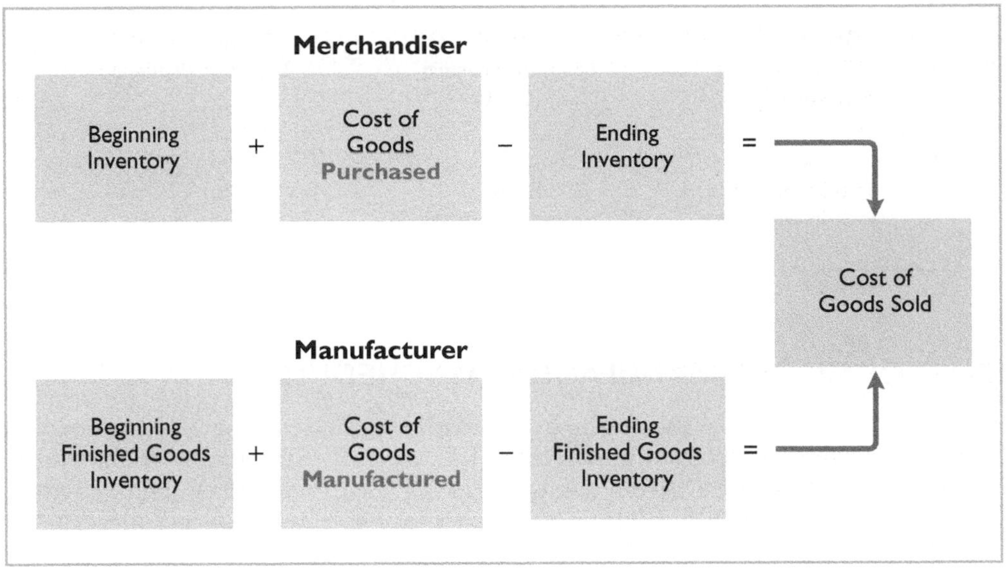

ILLUSTRATION 14-6
Cost of goods sold components

▼ **HELPFUL HINT**
We assume a periodic inventory system in this illustration.

Illustration 14-7 shows the different presentations of the cost of goods sold sections for merchandising and manufacturing companies. The other sections of an income statement are similar for merchandisers and manufacturers.

MERCHANDISING COMPANY Income Statement (partial) For the Year Ended December 31, 2017	
Cost of goods sold	
Inventory, Jan. 1	$ 70,000
Cost of goods purchased	650,000
Cost of goods available for sale	720,000
Less: Inventory, Dec. 31	400,000
Cost of goods sold	$ 320,000

MANUFACTURING COMPANY Income Statement (partial) For the Year Ended December 31, 2017	
Cost of goods sold	
Finished goods inventory, Jan. 1	$ 90,000
Cost of goods manufactured (see Illustration 14-9)	370,000
Cost of goods available for sale	460,000
Less: Finished goods inventory, Dec. 31	80,000
Cost of goods sold	$ 380,000

ILLUSTRATION 14-7
Cost of goods sold sections of merchandising and manufacturing income statements

COST OF GOODS MANUFACTURED

An example may help show how companies determine the cost of goods manufactured. Assume that on January 1, Current Designs has a number of kayaks in various stages of production. In total, these partially completed units are called **beginning work in process inventory**. The costs the company assigns to beginning work in process inventory are based on the **manufacturing costs incurred in the prior period.**

Current Designs first incurs manufacturing costs in the current year to complete the work that was in process on January 1. It then incurs manufacturing costs for production of new orders. The sum of the direct materials costs, direct labor costs, and manufacturing overhead incurred in the current year is the **total manufacturing costs** for the current period.

We now have two cost amounts: (1) the cost of the beginning work in process and (2) the total manufacturing costs for the current period. The sum of these costs is the **total cost of work in process** for the year.

At the end of the year, Current Designs may have some kayaks that are only partially completed. The costs of these units become the cost of the **ending work in process inventory**. To find the **cost of goods manufactured**, we subtract this cost from the total cost of work in process. Illustration 14-8 (page 714) shows the formula for determining the cost of goods manufactured.

ILLUSTRATION 14-8
Cost of goods manufactured formula

Beginning Work in Process Inventory	+	**Total Manufacturing Costs**	=	**Total Cost of Work in Process**
Total Cost of Work in Process	−	**Ending Inventory Work in Process**	=	Cost of Goods Manufactured

COST OF GOODS MANUFACTURED SCHEDULE

DECISION TOOLS

The cost of goods manufactured schedule helps managers determine if the company is maintaining control over the costs of production.

The **cost of goods manufactured schedule** reports cost elements used in calculating cost of goods manufactured. Illustration 14-9 shows the schedule for Current Designs (using assumed data). The schedule presents detailed data for direct materials and for manufacturing overhead.

Review Illustration 14-8 and then examine the cost of goods manufactured schedule in Illustration 14-9. You should be able to distinguish between "Total manufacturing costs" and "Cost of goods manufactured." The difference is the effect of the change in work in process during the period.

ILLUSTRATION 14-9
Cost of goods manufactured schedule

CURRENT DESIGNS
Cost of Goods Manufactured Schedule
For the Year Ended December 31, 2017

Work in process, January 1			$ 18,400
Direct materials			
Raw materials inventory, January 1	$ 16,700		
Raw materials purchases	152,500		
Total raw materials available for use	169,200		
Less: Raw materials inventory, December 31	22,800		
Direct materials used		$146,400	
Direct labor		175,600	
Manufacturing overhead			
Indirect labor	14,300		
Factory repairs	12,600		
Factory utilities	10,100		
Factory depreciation	9,440		
Factory insurance	8,360		
Total manufacturing overhead		54,800	
Total manufacturing costs			376,800
Total cost of work in process			395,200
Less: Work in process, December 31			25,200
Cost of goods manufactured			$370,000

DECISION TOOLS

The balance sheet helps managers determine whether sufficient inventory exists to meet forecasted demand.

BALANCE SHEET

The balance sheet for a merchandising company shows just one category of inventory. In contrast, the balance sheet for a manufacturer may have three inventory accounts, as shown in Illustration 14-10 for Current Designs' kayak inventory.

ILLUSTRATION 14-10
Inventory accounts for a manufacturer

Raw Materials Inventory

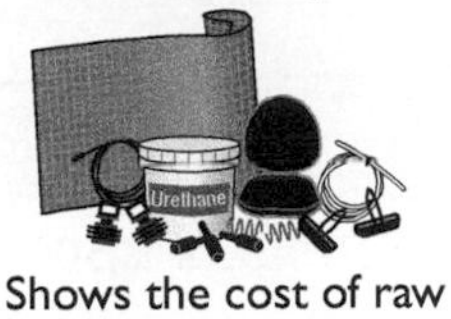

Shows the cost of raw materials on hand.

Work in Process Inventory

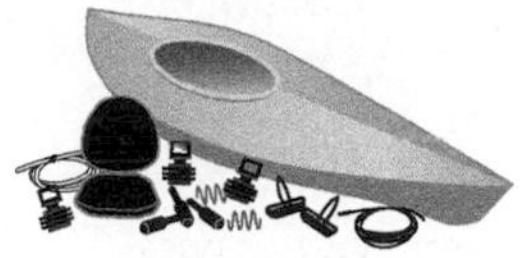

Shows the cost applicable to units that have been started into production but are only partially completed.

Finished Goods Inventory

Shows the cost of completed goods on hand.

Finished Goods Inventory is to a manufacturer what Inventory is to a merchandiser. Each of these classifications represents the goods that the company has available for sale. The current assets sections presented in Illustration 14-11 contrast the presentations of inventories for merchandising and manufacturing companies. The remainder of the balance sheet is similar for the two types of companies.

ILLUSTRATION 14-11
Current assets sections of merchandising and manufacturing balance sheets

MERCHANDISING COMPANY
Balance Sheet
December 31, 2017

Current assets	
Cash	$100,000
Accounts receivable (net)	210,000
Inventory	400,000
Prepaid expenses	22,000
Total current assets	$732,000

MANUFACTURING COMPANY
Balance Sheet
December 31, 2017

Current assets		
Cash		$180,000
Accounts receivable (net)		210,000
Inventory		
Finished goods	$80,000	
Work in process	25,200	
Raw materials	22,800	128,000
Prepaid expenses		18,000
Total current assets		$536,000

Each step in the accounting cycle for a merchandiser applies to a manufacturer. For example, prior to preparing financial statements, manufacturers make adjusting entries. The adjusting entries are essentially the same as those of a merchandiser. The closing entries are also similar for manufacturers and merchandisers.

DO IT! 3 Cost of Goods Manufactured

The following information is available for Keystone Company.

		March 1	March 31
Raw materials inventory		$12,000	$10,000
Work in process inventory		2,500	4,000
Materials purchased in March	$ 90,000		
Direct labor in March	75,000		
Manufacturing overhead in March	220,000		

Prepare the cost of goods manufactured schedule for the month of March 2017.

Action Plan

- ✔ Start with beginning work in process as the first item in the cost of goods manufactured schedule.
- ✔ Sum direct materials used, direct labor, and manufacturing overhead to determine total manufacturing costs.
- ✔ Sum beginning work in process and total manufacturing costs to determine total cost of work in process.
- ✔ Cost of goods manufactured is the total cost of work in process less ending work in process.

SOLUTION

KEYSTONE COMPANY
Cost of Goods Manufactured Schedule
For the Month Ended March 31, 2017

Work in process, March 1			$ 2,500
Direct materials			
Raw materials, March 1	$ 12,000		
Raw material purchases	90,000		
Total raw materials available for use	102,000		
Less: Raw materials, March 31	10,000		
Direct materials used		$ 92,000	
Direct labor		75,000	
Manufacturing overhead		220,000	
Total manufacturing costs			387,000
Total cost of work in process			389,500
Less: Work in process, March 31			4,000
Cost of goods manufactured			$385,500

Related exercise material: **BE14-7, BE14-8, BE14-9, BE14-10, E14-8, DO IT! 14-3, E14-9, E14-10, E14-11, E14-12, E14-13, E14-14, E14-15, E14-16,** and **E14-17.**

LEARNING OBJECTIVE 4

Discuss trends in managerial accounting.

The business environment never stands still. Regulations are always changing, global competition continues to intensify, and technology is a source of constant upheaval. In this rapidly changing world, managerial accounting needs to continue to innovate in order to provide managers with the information they need.

SERVICE INDUSTRIES

Much of the U.S. economy has shifted toward an emphasis on services. Today, more than 50% of U.S. workers are employed by service companies. Airlines, marketing agencies, cable companies, and governmental agencies are just a few examples of service companies. How do service companies differ from manufacturing companies? One difference is that services are consumed immediately. For example, when a restaurant produces a meal, that meal is not put in inventory but is instead consumed immediately. An airline uses special equipment to provide its product, but again, the output of that equipment is consumed immediately by the customer in the form of a flight. And a marketing agency performs services for its clients that are immediately consumed by the customer in the form of a marketing plan. For a manufacturing company, like Boeing, it often has a long lead time before its airplane is used or consumed by the customer.

ETHICS NOTE

Do telecommunications companies have an obligation to provide service to remote or low-user areas for a fee that may be less than the cost of the service?

This chapter's examples featured manufacturing companies because accounting for the manufacturing environment requires the use of the broadest range of accounts. That is, the accounts used by service companies represent a subset of those used by manufacturers because service companies are not producing inventory. Neither the restaurant, the airline, or the marketing agency discussed above produces an inventoriable product. However, just like a manufacturer, each needs to keep track of the costs of its services in order to know whether it is generating a profit. A successful restaurateur needs to know the cost of each offering on the menu, an airline needs to know the cost of flight service to each destination, and a marketing agency needs to know the cost to develop a marketing plan. Thus, the techniques shown in this chapter, to accumulate manufacturing costs to determine manufacturing inventory, are equally useful for determining the costs of performing services.

For example, let's consider the costs that Hewlett-Packard (HP) might incur on a consulting engagement. A significant portion of its costs would be salaries of consulting personnel. It might also incur travel costs, materials, software costs, and depreciation charges on equipment. In the same way that it needs to keep track of the cost of manufacturing its computers and printers, HP needs to know what its costs are on each consulting job. It could prepare a cost of services performed schedule similar to the cost of goods manufactured schedule in Illustration 14-9 (page 714). The structure would be essentially the same as the cost of goods manufactured schedule, but section headings would be reflective of the costs of the particular service organization.

Many of the examples we present in subsequent chapters will be based on service companies. To highlight the relevance of the techniques used in this course for service companies, we have placed a service company icon (see margin) next to those items in the text and end-of-chapter materials that relate to nonmanufacturing companies.

SERVICE COMPANY INSIGHT Allegiant Airlines

© Stephen Strathdee/iStockphoto

Low Fares but Decent Profits

When other airlines were cutting flight service due to recession, Allegiant Airlines increased capacity by 21%. Sounds crazy, doesn't it? But it must know something because while the other airlines were losing money, it was generating profits. In fact, it often has the industry's highest profit margins. Consider also that its average one-way fare is only $83. So how does it make money? As a low-budget airline, it focuses on controlling costs.

Allegiant purchases used planes for $3 million each rather than new planes for $40 million. It flies out of small towns, so wages are low and competition is nonexistent. It minimizes hotel costs by having its flight crews finish their day in their home cities. The company also only flies a route if its 150-passenger planes are nearly full (it averages about 90% of capacity). The bottom line is that Allegiant knows its costs to the penny. Knowing what your costs are might not be glamorous, but it sure beats losing money.

Sources: Susan Carey, "For Allegiant, Getaways Mean Profits," *Wall Street Journal Online* (February 18, 2009); and Scott Mayerowitz, "Tiny Allegiant Air Thrives on Low Costs, High Fees," *http://bigstory.ap.org* (June 28, 2013).

What are some of the line items that would appear in the cost of services performed schedule of an airline? (Go to **WileyPLUS** for this answer and additional questions.)

FOCUS ON THE VALUE CHAIN

The **value chain** refers to all business processes associated with providing a product or performing a service. Illustration 14-12 depicts the value chain for a manufacturer. Many of the most significant business innovations in recent years have resulted either directly, or indirectly, from a focus on the value chain. For

ILLUSTRATION 14-12
A manufacturer's value chain

example, so-called **lean manufacturing**, originally pioneered by Japanese automobile manufacturer Toyota but now widely practiced, reviews all business processes in an effort to increase productivity and eliminate waste, all while continually trying to improve quality.

Just-in-time (JIT) inventory methods, which have significantly lowered inventory levels and costs for many companies, are one innovation that resulted from the focus on the value chain. Under the JIT inventory method, goods are manufactured or purchased just in time for sale. For example, Dell can produce and deliver a custom computer within 48 hours of a customer's order. However, JIT also necessitates increased emphasis on product quality. Because JIT companies do not have excess inventory on hand, they cannot afford to stop production because of defects or machine breakdowns. If they stop production, deliveries will be delayed and customers will be unhappy. For example, a design flaw in an Intel computer chip was estimated to cost the company $1 billion in repairs and reduced revenue. As a consequence, many companies now focus on **total quality management (TQM)** to reduce defects in finished products, with the goal of zero defects. The TQM philosophy has been employed by some of the most successful businesses to improve all aspects of the value chain.

Another innovation, the **theory of constraints**, involves identification of "bottlenecks"—constraints within the value chain that limit a company's profitability. Once a major constraint has been identified and eliminated, the company moves on to fix the next most significant constraint. General Motors found that by eliminating bottlenecks, it improved its use of overtime labor while meeting customer demand. An application of the theory of constraints is presented in Chapter 19.

Technology has played a big role in the focus on the value chain and the implementation of lean manufacturing. For example, **enterprise resource planning (ERP) systems**, such as those provided by SAP, provide a comprehensive, centralized, integrated source of information to manage all major business processes—from purchasing, to manufacturing, to sales, to human resources. ERP systems have, in some large companies, replaced as many as 200 individual software packages. In addition, the focus on improving efficiency in the value chain has also resulted in adoption of automated manufacturing processes. Many companies now use computer-integrated manufacturing. These systems often reduce the reliance on manual labor by using robotic equipment. This increases overhead costs as a percentage of total product costs.

As overhead costs increased because of factory automation, the accuracy of overhead cost allocation to specific products became more important. Managerial accounting devised an approach, called **activity-based costing (ABC)**, which allocates overhead based on each product's use of particular activities in making the product. In addition to providing more accurate product costing, ABC also can contribute to increased efficiency in the value chain. For example, suppose one of a company's overhead pools is allocated based on the number of setups that each product requires. If a particular product's cost is high because it is allocated a lot of overhead due to a high number of setups, management will be motivated to try to reduce the number of setups and thus reduce its overhead allocation. ABC is discussed further in Chapter 17.

BALANCED SCORECARD

As companies implement various business practice innovations, managers sometimes focus too enthusiastically on the latest innovation, to the detriment of other areas of the business. For example, by focusing on total quality management, companies sometimes lose sight of cost/benefit considerations. Similarly, in focusing on reducing inventory levels through just-in-time inventory methods, companies sometimes lose sales due to inventory shortages. The **balanced scorecard** corrects for this limited perspective: This approach uses both financial and nonfinancial measures to evaluate all aspects of a company's operations in an integrated fashion. The performance measures are linked in a cause-and-effect fashion to ensure that they all tie to the company's overall objectives. For example, to increase return on assets, the company could try to increase sales. To increase sales, the company could try to increase customer satisfaction. To increase customer satisfaction, the company could try to reduce product defects. Finally, to reduce product defects, the company could increase employee training. The balanced scorecard, which is discussed further in Chapter 23, is now used by many companies, including Hilton Hotels, Wal-Mart Stores, Inc., and HP.

BUSINESS ETHICS

All employees within an organization are expected to act ethically in their business activities. Given the importance of ethical behavior to corporations and their owners (stockholders), an increasing number of organizations provide codes of business ethics for their employees.

Creating Proper Incentives

Companies like Amazon.com, IBM, and Nike use complex systems to monitor, control, and evaluate the actions of managers. Unfortunately, these systems and controls sometimes unwittingly create incentives for managers to take unethical actions. For example, because budgets are also used as an evaluation tool, some managers try to "game" the budgeting process by underestimating their division's predicted performance so that it will be easier to meet their performance targets. On the other hand, if budgets are set at unattainable levels, managers sometimes take unethical actions to meet the targets in order to receive higher compensation or, in some cases, to keep their jobs.

For example, at one time, airline manufacturer Boeing was plagued by a series of scandals including charges of over-billing, corporate espionage, and illegal conflicts of interest. Some long-time employees of Boeing blamed the decline in ethics on a change in the corporate culture that took place after Boeing merged with McDonnell Douglas. They suggested that evaluation systems implemented after the merger to evaluate employee performance gave employees the impression that they needed to succeed no matter what actions were required to do so.

As another example, manufacturing companies need to establish production goals for their processes. Again, if controls are not effective and realistic, problems develop. To illustrate, Schering-Plough, a pharmaceutical manufacturer, found that employees were so concerned with meeting production quantity standards that they failed to monitor the quality of the product, and as a result the dosages were often wrong.

Code of Ethical Standards

In response to corporate scandals, the U.S. Congress enacted the **Sarbanes-Oxley Act (SOX)** to help prevent lapses in internal control. One result of SOX was to clarify top management's responsibility for the company's financial statements. CEOs and CFOs are now required to certify that financial statements give a fair presentation of the company's operating results and its financial condition. In addition, top managers must certify that the company maintains an adequate system of internal controls to safeguard the company's assets and ensure accurate financial reports.

Another result of SOX is that companies now pay more attention to the composition of the board of directors. In particular, the audit committee of the board of directors must be comprised entirely of independent members (that is, non-employees) and must contain at least one financial expert. Finally, the law substantially increases the penalties for misconduct.

To provide guidance for managerial accountants, the Institute of Management Accountants (IMA) has developed a code of ethical standards, entitled *IMA Statement of Ethical Professional Practice.* Management accountants should not commit acts in violation of these standards. Nor should they condone such acts by others within their organizations. Throughout the textbook, we will address various ethical issues managers face.

CORPORATE SOCIAL RESPONSIBILITY

The balanced scorecard attempts to take a broader, more inclusive view of corporate profitability measures. Many companies, however, have begun to evaluate not just corporate profitability but also **corporate social responsibility**. In addition to profitability, corporate social responsibility considers a company's efforts to employ sustainable business practices with regard to its employees, society, and the environment. This is sometimes referred to as the **triple bottom line** because it evaluates a company's performance with regard to **people, planet, and profit**. Recent reports indicate that over 50% of the 500 largest U.S. companies provide sustainability reports. Make no mistake, these companies are still striving to maximize profits—in a competitive world, they won't survive long if they don't. In fact, you might recognize a few of the names on a recent Forbes.com list of the 100 most sustainable companies in the world. Are you surprised that General Electric, adidas, Toyota, Coca-Cola, or Starbucks made the list? These companies have learned that with a long-term, sustainable approach, they can maximize profits while also acting in the best interest of their employees, their communities, and the environment. At various points within this textbook, we will discuss situations where real companies use the very skills that you are learning to evaluate decisions from a sustainable perspective, such as in the following Insight box.

PEOPLE, PLANET, AND PROFIT INSIGHT Phantom Tac

Geanina Bechea/Shutterstock

People Matter

Many clothing factories in developing countries are known for unsafe buildings, poor working conditions, and wage and labor violations. One of the owners of Phantom Tac, a clothing manufacturer in Bangladesh, did make efforts to develop sustainable business practices. This owner, David Mayor, provided funding for a training program for female workers. He also developed a website to educate customers about the workers' conditions. But Phantom Tac also had to make a profit. Things got tight when one of its customers canceled orders because Phantom Tac failed a social compliance audit. The company had to quit funding the training program and the website.

Recently, Bangladesh's textile industry has seen some significant improvements in working conditions and safety standards. As Brad Adams, Asia director of Human Rights Watch, notes, "The (Dhaka) government has belatedly begun to register unions, which is an important first step, but it now needs to ensure that factory owners stop persecuting their leaders and actually allow them to function."

Sources: Jim Yardley, "Clothing Brands Sidestep Blame for Safety Lapses," *The New York Times Online* (December 30, 2013); and Palash Ghosh, "Despite Low Pay, Poor Work Conditions, Garment Factories Empowering Millions of Bangladeshi Women," *International Business Times* (March 25, 2014).

What are some of the common problems for many clothing factories in developing countries? (Go to WileyPLUS for this answer and additional questions.)

Sustainable business practices present numerous issues for management and managerial accountants. First, companies need to decide what items need to be measured, generally those that are of utmost importance to its stakeholders. For example, a particular company might be most concerned with minimizing water pollution or maximizing employee safety. Then, for each item identified, the company determines measurable attributes that provide relevant information regarding the company's performance with regard to that item, such as the amount of waste released into public waterways or the number of accidents per 1,000 hours worked. Finally, the company needs to consider the materiality of the item, the cost of measuring these attributes, and the reliability of the measurements. If the company uses this information to make decisions, then accuracy is critical. Of particular concern is whether the measurements can be verified by an outside third party.

Unlike financial reporting, which is overseen by the Financial Accounting Standards Board, the reporting of sustainable business practices currently has no agreed-upon standard-setter. A number of organizations have, however, published guidelines. The guidelines published by the Global Reporting Initiative are among the most widely recognized and followed. Illustration 14-13 provides a list of major categories provided by the Global Reporting Initiative for sustainability reporting and a sample of aspects that companies might consider within each category.

ILLUSTRATION 14-13
Sample categories in Global Reporting Initiative guidelines

		Social			
Economic	**Environmental**	**Labor Practices and Decent Work**	**Human Rights**	**Society**	**Product Responsibility**
Economic performance Market presence Indirect economic impacts Procurement practices	Energy Biodiversity Effluents and waste Compliance	Occupational health and safety Training and education Diversity and equal opportunity Labor practices grievance mechanisms	Non-discrimination Child labor Indigenous rights Supplier human rights assessment	Anti-corruption Anti-competitive behavior Supplier assessment for impacts on society Grievance mechanisms for impacts on society	Customer health and safety Product and service labeling Marketing communi-cations Customer privacy

Source: Global Reporting Initiative, *G4 Sustainability Reporting Guidelines,* p. 9. The full report is available at *www.globalreporting.org.*

DO IT! 4 Trends in Managerial Accounting

Match the descriptions that follow with the corresponding terms.

Descriptions:

1. ________ All activities associated with providing a product or performing a service.
2. ________ A method of allocating overhead based on each product's use of activities in making the product.
3. ________ Systems implemented to reduce defects in finished products with the goal of achieving zero defects.
4. ________ A performance-measurement approach that uses both financial and nonfinancial measures, tied to company objectives, to evaluate a company's operations in an integrated fashion.
5. ________ Inventory system in which goods are manufactured or purchased just as they are needed for use.
6. ________ A company's efforts to employ sustainable business practices with regards to its employees, society, and the environment.
7. ________ A code of ethical standards developed by the Institute of Management Accountants.

Terms:

a. Activity-based costing
b. Balanced scorecard
c. Corporate social responsibility
d. Just-in-time (JIT) inventory
e. Total quality management (TQM)
f. Statement of Ethical Professional Practice
g. Value chain

Action Plan

✔ **Develop a forward-looking view, in order to advise and provide information to various members of the organization.**

✔ **Understand current business trends and issues.**

SOLUTION

1. g 2. a 3. e 4. b 5. d 6. c 7. f

Related exercise material: **BE14-11, DO IT! 14-4,** and **E14-18.**

USING DECISION TOOLS—CURRENT DESIGNS

Current Designs faces many situations where it needs to apply the decision tools in this chapter, such as analyzing the balance sheet for optimal inventory levels. For example, assume that the market has responded enthusiastically to a new Current Designs' model, the Otter. As a result, the company has established a separate manufacturing facility to produce these kayaks. Now assume that the company produces 1,000 of these kayaks per month. Current Designs' monthly manufacturing costs and other data for the Otter are as follows.

1. Rent on manufacturing equipment (lease cost)	$2,000/month
2. Insurance on manufacturing building	$750/month
3. Raw materials (plastic, fiberglass, etc.)	$180/kayak
4. Utility costs for manufacturing facility	$1,000/month
5. Supplies for administrative office	$800/month
6. Wages for assembly line workers in manufacturing facility	$130/kayak
7. Depreciation on office equipment	$650/month
8. Miscellaneous manufacturing materials (lubricants, solders, etc.)	$12/kayak
9. Property taxes on manufacturing building	$24,000/year
10. Manufacturing supervisor's salary	$5,000/month
11. Advertising for the Otter	$30,000/year
12. Sales commissions	$30/kayak
13. Depreciation on manufacturing building	$4,000/month

INSTRUCTIONS

(a) Prepare an answer sheet with the following column headings.

Cost Item	Product Costs			Period Costs
	Direct Materials	Direct Labor	Manufacturing Overhead	

Enter each cost item on your answer sheet, placing an "X" mark under the appropriate headings.

(b) Compute total manufacturing costs for the month.

SOLUTION

(a)

Cost Item	Product Costs			Period Costs
	Direct Materials	Direct Labor	Manufacturing Overhead	
1. Rent on manufacturing equipment ($2,000/month)			X	
2. Insurance on manufacturing building ($750/month)			X	
3. Raw materials ($180/kayak)	X			
4. Manufacturing utilities ($1,000/month)			X	
5. Office supplies ($800/month)				X
6. Wages for assembly workers ($130/kayak)		X		
7. Depreciation on office equipment ($650/month)				X
8. Miscellaneous manufacturing materials ($12/kayak)			X	
9. Property taxes on manufacturing building ($24,000/year)			X	

Cost Item	Direct Materials (Product Costs)	Direct Labor (Product Costs)	Manufacturing Overhead (Product Costs)	Period Costs
10. Manufacturing supervisor's salary ($5,000/month)			X	
11. Advertising cost ($30,000/year)				X
12. Sales commissions ($30/kayak)				X
13. Depreciation on manufacturing building ($4,000/month)			X	

(b)

Cost Item	Manufacturing Cost
Rent on manufacturing equipment	$ 2,000
Insurance on manufacturing building	750
Raw materials ($180 × 1,000)	180,000
Manufacturing utilities	1,000
Labor ($130 × 1,000)	130,000
Miscellaneous materials ($12 × 1,000)	12,000
Property taxes on manufacturing building ($24,000 ÷ 12)	2,000
Manufacturing supervisor's salary	5,000
Depreciation on manufacturing building	4,000
Total manufacturing costs	$336,750

Current Designs' monthly manufacturing cost to produce 1,000 Otters is $336,750.

REVIEW AND PRACTICE

LEARNING OBJECTIVES REVIEW

1 Identify the features of managerial accounting and the functions of management. The *primary users* of managerial accounting reports, issued as frequently as needed, are internal users, who are officers, department heads, managers, and supervisors in the company. The purpose of these reports is to provide special-purpose information for a particular user for a specific decision. The content of managerial accounting reports pertains to subunits of the business. It may be very detailed, and may extend beyond the double-entry accounting system. The reporting standard is relevant to the decision being made. No independent audits are required in managerial accounting.

The functions of management are planning, directing, and controlling. Planning requires management to look ahead and to establish objectives. Directing involves coordinating the diverse activities and human resources of a company to produce a smooth-running operation. Controlling is the process of keeping the activities on track.

2 Describe the classes of manufacturing costs and the differences between product and period costs. Manufacturing costs are typically classified as either (1) direct materials, (2) direct labor, or (3) manufacturing overhead. Raw materials that can be physically and directly associated with the finished product during the manufacturing process are called direct materials. The work of factory employees that can be physically and directly associated with converting raw materials into finished goods is considered direct labor. Manufacturing overhead consists of costs that are indirectly associated with the manufacture of the finished product.

Product costs are costs that are a necessary and integral part of producing the finished product. Product costs are also called inventoriable costs. These costs do not become expenses until the company sells the finished goods inventory. Period costs are costs that are identified with a specific time period rather than with a salable product. These costs relate to nonmanufacturing costs and therefore are not inventoriable costs.

3 Demonstrate how to compute cost of goods manufactured and prepare financial statements for a manufacturer. Companies add the cost of the beginning work in process to the total manufacturing costs for the current year to arrive at the total cost of work in process for the year. They then subtract the ending work in process from the total cost of work in process to arrive at the cost of goods manufactured.

The difference between a merchandising and a manufacturing income statement is in the cost of goods sold section. A manufacturing cost of goods sold section shows beginning and ending finished goods inventories and the cost of goods manufactured.

The difference between a merchandising and a manufacturing balance sheet is in the current assets section. The current assets section of a manufacturing company's balance sheet presents three inventory accounts: finished goods inventory, work in process inventory, and raw materials inventory.

4 Discuss trends in managerial accounting. Managerial accounting has experienced many changes in recent years, including a shift toward service companies as well as an emphasis on ethical behavior. Improved practices include a focus on managing the value chain through techniques such as just-in-time inventory, total quality management, activity-based costing, and theory of constraints. The balanced scorecard is now used by many companies in order to attain a more comprehensive view of the company's operations. Finally, companies are now evaluating their performance with regard to their corporate social responsibility.

DECISION TOOLS REVIEW

DECISION CHECKPOINTS	INFO NEEDED FOR DECISION	TOOL TO USE FOR DECISION	HOW TO EVALUATE RESULTS
Is the company maintaining control over the costs of production?	Cost of material, labor, and overhead	Cost of goods manufactured schedule	Compare the cost of goods manufactured to revenue expected from product sales.
What is the composition of a manufacturing company's inventory?	Amount of raw materials, work in process, and finished goods inventories	Balance sheet	Determine whether there are sufficient finished goods, raw materials, and work in process inventories to meet forecasted demand.

GLOSSARY REVIEW

Activity-based costing (ABC) A method of allocating overhead based on each product's use of activities in making the product. (p. 718).

Balanced scorecard A performance-measurement approach that uses both financial and nonfinancial measures, tied to company objectives, to evaluate a company's operations in an integrated fashion. (p. 718).

Board of directors The group of officials elected by the stockholders of a corporation to formulate operating policies and select officers who will manage the company. (p. 707).

Chief executive officer (CEO) Corporate officer who has overall responsibility for managing the business and delegates responsibilities to other corporate officers. (p. 707).

Chief financial officer (CFO) Corporate officer who is responsible for all of the accounting and finance issues of the company. (p. 707).

Controller Financial officer responsible for a company's accounting records, system of internal control, and preparation of financial statements, tax returns, and internal reports. (p. 707).

Corporate social responsibility The efforts of a company to employ sustainable business practices with regard to its employees, society, and the environment. (p. 720).

Cost of goods manufactured Total cost of work in process less the cost of the ending work in process inventory. (p. 713).

Direct labor The work of factory employees that can be physically and directly associated with converting raw materials into finished goods. (p. 709).

Direct materials Raw materials that can be physically and directly associated with manufacturing the finished product. (p. 708).

Enterprise resource planning (ERP) system Software that provides a comprehensive, centralized, integrated source of information used to manage all major business processes. (p. 718).

Indirect labor Work of factory employees that has no physical association with the finished product or for which it is impractical to trace the costs to the goods produced. (p. 709).

Indirect materials Raw materials that do not physically become part of the finished product or for which it is impractical to trace to the finished product because their physical association with the finished product is too small. (p. 708).

Just-in-time (JIT) inventory Inventory system in which goods are manufactured or purchased just in time for sale. (p. 718).

Line positions Jobs that are directly involved in a company's primary revenue-generating operating activities. (p. 707).

Managerial accounting A field of accounting that provides economic and financial information for managers and other internal users. (p. 704).

Manufacturing overhead Manufacturing costs that are indirectly associated with the manufacture of the finished product. (p. 709).

Period costs Costs that are matched with the revenue of a specific time period and charged to expense as incurred. (p. 710).

Product costs Costs that are a necessary and integral part of producing the finished product. (p. 710).

Sarbanes-Oxley Act (SOX) Law passed by Congress intended to reduce unethical corporate behavior. (p. 719).

Staff positions Jobs that support the efforts of line employees. (p. 707).

Theory of constraints A specific approach used to identify and manage constraints in order to achieve the company's goals. (p. 718).

Total cost of work in process Cost of the beginning work in process plus total manufacturing costs for the current period. (p. 713).

Total manufacturing costs The sum of direct materials, direct labor, and manufacturing overhead incurred in the current period. (p. 711).

Total quality management (TQM) Systems implemented to reduce defects in finished products with the goal of achieving zero defects. (p. 718).

Treasurer Financial officer responsible for custody of a company's funds and for maintaining its cash position. (p. 707).

Triple bottom line The evaluation of a company's social responsibility performance with regard to people, planet, and profit. (p. 720).

Value chain All business processes associated with providing a product or performing a service. (p. 717).

PRACTICE MULTIPLE-CHOICE QUESTIONS

(LO 1) **1.** Managerial accounting:
- (a) is governed by generally accepted accounting principles.
- (b) places emphasis on special-purpose information.
- (c) pertains to the entity as a whole and is highly aggregated.
- (d) is limited to cost data.

(LO 1) **2.** The management of an organization performs several broad functions. They are:
- (a) planning, directing, and selling.
- (b) planning, directing, and controlling.
- (c) planning, manufacturing, and controlling.
- (d) directing, manufacturing, and controlling.

(LO 2) **3.** Direct materials are a:

	Product Cost	Manufacturing Overhead Cost	Period Cost
(a)	Yes	Yes	No
(b)	Yes	No	No
(c)	Yes	Yes	Yes
(d)	No	No	No

(LO 2) **4.** Which of the following costs would a computer manufacturer include in manufacturing overhead?
- (a) The cost of the disk drives.
- (b) The wages earned by computer assemblers.
- (c) The cost of the memory chips.
- (d) Depreciation on testing equipment.

(LO 2) **5.** Which of the following is **not** an element of manufacturing overhead?
- (a) Sales manager's salary.
- (b) Plant manager's salary.
- (c) Factory repairman's wages.
- (d) Product inspector's salary.

6. Indirect labor is a: (LO 2)
- (a) nonmanufacturing cost.
- (b) raw material cost.
- (c) product cost.
- (d) period cost.

7. Which of the following costs are classified as a period cost? (LO 2)
- (a) Wages paid to a factory custodian.
- (b) Wages paid to a production department supervisor.
- (c) Wages paid to a cost accounting department supervisor.
- (d) Wages paid to an assembly worker.

8. For the year, Redder Company has cost of goods manufactured of $600,000, beginning finished goods inventory of $200,000, and ending finished goods inventory of $250,000. The cost of goods sold is: (LO 3)
- (a) $450,000. (b) $500,000.
- (c) $550,000. (d) $600,000.

9. Cost of goods available for sale is a step in the calculation of cost of goods sold of: (LO 3)
- (a) a merchandising company but not a manufacturing company.
- (b) a manufacturing company but not a merchandising company.

(c) a merchandising company and a manufacturing company.
(d) neither a manufacturing company nor a merchandising company.

(LO 3) **10.** A cost of goods manufactured schedule shows beginning and ending inventories for:
(a) raw materials and work in process only.
(b) work in process only.
(c) raw materials only.
(d) raw materials, work in process, and finished goods.

(LO 3) **11.** The formula to determine the cost of goods manufactured is:
(a) Beginning raw materials inventory + Total manufacturing costs − Ending work in process inventory.
(b) Beginning work in process inventory + Total manufacturing costs − Ending finished goods inventory.
(c) Beginning finished good inventory + Total manufacturing costs − Ending finished goods inventory.
(d) Beginning work in process inventory + Total manufacturing costs − Ending work in process inventory.

(LO 4) **12.** After passage of the Sarbanes-Oxley Act:
(a) reports prepared by managerial accountants must by audited by CPAs.
(b) CEOs and CFOs must certify that financial statements give a fair presentation of the company's operating results.
(c) the audit committee, rather than top management, is responsible for the company's financial statements.
(d) reports prepared by managerial accountants must comply with generally accepted accounting principles (GAAP).

13. Which of the following managerial accounting techniques attempts to allocate manufacturing overhead in a more meaningful fashion? (LO 4)
(a) Just-in-time inventory.
(b) Total quality management.
(c) Balanced scorecard.
(d) Activity-based costing.

14. Corporate social responsibility refers to: (LO 4)
(a) the practice by management of reviewing all business processes in an effort to increase productivity and eliminate waste.
(b) an approach used to allocate overhead based on each product's use of activities.
(c) the attempt by management to identify and eliminate constraints within the value chain.
(d) efforts by companies to employ sustainable business practices with regard to employees and the environment.

SOLUTIONS

1. **(b)** Managerial accounting emphasizes special-purpose information. The other choices are incorrect because (a) financial accounting is governed by generally accepted accounting principles, (c) financial accounting pertains to the entity as a whole and is highly aggregated, and (d) cost accounting and cost data are a subset of management accounting.
2. **(b)** Planning, directing, and controlling are the broad functions performed by the management of an organization. The other choices are incorrect because (a) selling is performed by the sales group in the organization, not by management; (c) manufacturing is performed by the manufacturing group in the organization, not by management; and (d) manufacturing is performed by the manufacturing group in the organization, not by management.
3. **(b)** Direct materials are a product cost only. Therefore, choices (a), (c), and (d) are incorrect as direct materials are not manufacturing overhead or a period cost.
4. **(d)** Depreciation on testing equipment would be included in manufacturing overhead because it is indirectly associated with the finished product. The other choices are incorrect because (a) disk drives would be direct materials, (b) computer assembler wages would be direct labor, and (c) memory chips would be direct materials.
5. **(a)** The sales manager's salary is not directly or indirectly associated with the manufacture of the finished product. The other choices are incorrect because (b) the plant manager's salary, (c) the factory repairman's wages, and (d) the product inspector's salary are all elements of manufacturing overhead.
6. **(c)** Indirect labor is a product cost because it is part of the effort required to produce a product. The other choices are incorrect because (a) indirect labor is a manufacturing cost because it is part of the effort required to produce a product, (b) indirect labor is not a raw material cost because raw material costs only include direct materials and indirect materials, and (d) indirect labor is not a period cost because it is part of the effort required to produce a product.
7. **(c)** Wages paid to a cost accounting department supervisor would be included in administrative expenses and classified as a period cost. The other choices are incorrect because (a) factory custodian wages are indirect labor which is manufacturing overhead and a product cost, (b) production department supervisor wages are indirect labor which is manufacturing overhead and a product cost, and (d) assembly worker wages is direct labor and is a product cost.
8. **(c)** Cost of goods sold is computed as Beginning finished goods inventory ($200,000) + Cost of goods manufactured ($600,000) − Ending finished goods inventory ($250,000), or $200,000 + $600,000 − $250,000 = $550,000. Therefore, choices (a) $450,000, (b) $500,000, and (d) $600,000 are incorrect.
9. **(c)** Both a merchandising company and a manufacturing company use cost of goods available for sale to calculate cost of goods sold. Therefore, choices (a) only a merchandising company, (b) only a manufacturing company, and (d) neither a manufacturing company or a merchandising company are incorrect.

10. **(a)** A cost of goods manufactured schedule shows beginning and ending inventories for raw materials and work in process only. Therefore, choices (b) work in process only and (c) raw materials only are incorrect. Choice (d) is incorrect because it does not include finished goods.
11. **(d)** The formula to determine the cost of goods manufactured is Beginning work in process inventory + Total manufacturing costs − Ending work in process inventory. The other choices are incorrect because (a) raw material inventory, (b) ending finished goods inventory, and (c) beginning finished goods inventory and ending finished goods inventory are not part of the computation.
12. **(b)** CEOs and CFOs must certify that financial statements give a fair presentation of the company's operating results. The other choices are incorrect because (a) reports prepared by financial (not managerial) accountants must be audited by CPAs; (c) SOX clarifies that top management, not the audit committee, is responsible for the company's financial statements; and (d) reports by financial (not managerial) accountants must comply with GAAP.
13. **(d)** Activity-based costing attempts to allocate manufacturing overhead in a more meaningful fashion. Therefore, choices (a) just-in-time inventory, (b) total quality management, and (c) balanced scorecard are incorrect.
14. **(d)** Corporate social responsibility refers to efforts by companies to employ sustainable business practices with regard to employees and the environment. The other choices are incorrect because (a) defines lean manufacturing, (b) refers to activity-based costing, and (c) describes the theory of constraints.

PRACTICE EXERCISES

Determine the total amount of various types of costs.

(LO 2)

1. Fredricks Company reports the following costs and expenses in May.

Factory utilities	$ 15,600	Direct labor	$89,100
Depreciation on factory equipment	12,650	Sales salaries	46,400
Depreciation on delivery trucks	8,800	Property taxes on factory building	2,500
Indirect factory labor	48,900	Repairs to office equipment	2,300
Indirect materials	80,800	Factory repairs	2,000
Direct materials used	137,600	Advertising	18,000
Factory manager's salary	13,000	Office supplies used	5,640

INSTRUCTIONS

From the information, determine the total amount of:

(a) Manufacturing overhead.
(b) Product costs.
(c) Period costs.

SOLUTION

1. (a)	Factory utilities	$ 15,600
	Depreciation on factory equipment	12,650
	Indirect factory labor	48,900
	Indirect materials	80,800
	Factory manager's salary	13,000
	Property taxes on factory building	2,500
	Factory repairs	2,000
	Manufacturing overhead	$175,450
(b)	Direct materials	$137,600
	Direct labor	89,100
	Manufacturing overhead	175,450
	Product costs	$402,150
(c)	Depreciation on delivery trucks	$ 8,800
	Sales salaries	46,400
	Repairs to office equipment	2,300
	Advertising	18,000
	Office supplies used	5,640
	Period costs	$ 81,140

Compute cost of goods manufactured and sold.

(LO 3)

2. Tommi Corporation incurred the following costs while manufacturing its product.

Materials used in product	$120,000	Advertising expense	$45,000
Depreciation on plant	60,000	Property taxes on plant	19,000
Property taxes on store	7,500	Delivery expense	21,000
Labor costs of assembly-line workers	110,000	Sales commissions	35,000
Factory supplies used	25,000	Salaries paid to sales clerks	50,000

Work-in-process inventory was $10,000 at January 1 and $14,000 at December 31. Finished goods inventory was $60,500 at January 1 and $50,600 at December 31.

INSTRUCTIONS

(a) Compute cost of goods manufactured.

(b) Compute cost of goods sold.

SOLUTION

2. (a) Work-in-process, 1/1			$ 10,000
Direct materials used		$120,000	
Direct labor		110,000	
Manufacturing overhead			
Depreciation on plant	$60,000		
Factory supplies used	25,000		
Property taxes on plant	19,000		
Total manufacturing overhead		104,000	
Total manufacturing costs			334,000
Total cost of work-in-process			344,000
Less: Ending work-in-process			14,000
Cost of goods manufactured			$330,000
(b) Finished goods, 1/1			$ 60,500
Cost of goods manufactured			330,000
Cost of goods available for sale			390,500
Less: Finished goods, 12/31			50,600
Cost of goods sold			$339,900

PRACTICE PROBLEM

Prepare a cost of goods manufactured schedule, an income statement, and a partial balance sheet.

(LO 3)

Superior Company has the following cost and expense data for the year ending December 31, 2017.

Raw materials, 1/1/17	$ 30,000	Insurance, factory	$ 14,000
Raw materials, 12/31/17	20,000	Property taxes, factory building	6,000
Raw materials purchases	205,000	Sales revenue	1,500,000
Indirect materials	15,000	Delivery expenses	100,000
Work in process, 1/1/17	80,000	Sales commissions	150,000
Work in process, 12/31/17	50,000	Indirect labor	90,000
Finished goods, 1/1/17	110,000	Factory machinery rent	40,000
Finished goods, 12/31/17	120,000	Factory utilities	65,000
Direct labor	350,000	Depreciation, factory building	24,000
Factory manager's salary	35,000	Administrative expenses	300,000

INSTRUCTIONS

(a) Prepare a cost of goods manufactured schedule for Superior Company for 2017.

(b) Prepare an income statement for Superior Company for 2017.

(c) Assume that Superior Company's accounting records show the balances of the following current asset accounts: Cash $17,000, Accounts Receivable (net) $120,000, Prepaid Expenses $13,000, and Short-Term Investments $26,000. Prepare the current assets section of the balance sheet for Superior Company as of December 31, 2017.

SOLUTION

(a)

SUPERIOR COMPANY
Cost of Goods Manufactured Schedule
For the Year Ended December 31, 2017

Work in process, 1/1			$ 80,000
Direct materials			
Raw materials inventory, 1/1	$ 30,000		
Raw materials purchases	205,000		
Total raw materials available for use	235,000		
Less: Raw materials inventory, 12/31	20,000		
Direct materials used		$215,000	
Direct labor		350,000	
Manufacturing overhead			
Indirect labor	90,000		
Factory utilities	65,000		
Factory machinery rent	40,000		
Factory manager's salary	35,000		
Depreciation, factory building	24,000		
Indirect materials	15,000		
Insurance, factory	14,000		
Property taxes, factory building	6,000		
Total manufacturing overhead		289,000	
Total manufacturing costs			854,000
Total cost of work in process			934,000
Less: Work in process, 12/31			50,000
Cost of goods manufactured			$ 884,000

(b)

SUPERIOR COMPANY
Income Statement
For the Year Ended December 31, 2017

Sales revenue		$1,500,000
Cost of goods sold		
Finished goods inventory, January 1	$110,000	
Cost of goods manufactured	884,000	
Cost of goods available for sale	994,000	
Less: Finished goods inventory, December 31	120,000	
Cost of goods sold		874,000
Gross profit		626,000
Operating expenses		
Administrative expenses	300,000	
Sales commissions	150,000	
Delivery expenses	100,000	
Total operating expenses		550,000
Net income		$ 76,000

(c)

SUPERIOR COMPANY
Balance Sheet (partial)
December 31, 2017

Current assets		
Cash		$ 17,000
Short-term investments		26,000
Accounts receivable (net)		120,000
Inventory		
Finished goods	$120,000	
Work in process	50,000	
Raw materials	20,000	190,000
Prepaid expenses		13,000
Total current assets		$366,000

WileyPLUS Brief Exercises, DO IT! Exercises, Exercises, Problems, and many additional resources are available for practice in WileyPLUS.

QUESTIONS

1. (a) "Managerial accounting is a field of accounting that provides economic information for all interested parties." Do you agree? Explain.
   (b) Joe Delong believes that managerial accounting serves only manufacturing firms. Is Joe correct? Explain.
2. Distinguish between managerial and financial accounting as to (a) primary users of reports, (b) types and frequency of reports, and (c) purpose of reports.
3. How do the content of reports and the verification of reports differ between managerial and financial accounting?
4. Linda Olsen is studying for the next accounting midterm examination. Summarize for Linda what she should know about management functions.
5. "Decision-making is management's most important function." Do you agree? Why or why not?
6. Explain the primary difference between line positions and staff positions, and give examples of each.
7. Tony Andres is studying for his next accounting examination. Explain to Tony what he should know about the differences between the income statements for a manufacturing and for a merchandising company.
8. Jerry Lang is unclear as to the difference between the balance sheets of a merchandising company and a manufacturing company. Explain the difference to Jerry.
9. How are manufacturing costs classified?
10. Mel Finney claims that the distinction between direct and indirect materials is based entirely on physical association with the product. Is Mel correct? Why?
11. Tina Burke is confused about the differences between a product cost and a period cost. Explain the differences to Tina.
12. Identify the differences in the cost of goods sold section of an income statement between a merchandising company and a manufacturing company.
13. The determination of the cost of goods manufactured involves the following factors: (A) beginning work in process inventory, (B) total manufacturing costs, and (C) ending work in process inventory. Identify the meaning of x in the following formulas:
    (a) $A + B = x$
    (b) $A + B - C = x$
14. Sealy Company has beginning raw materials inventory \$12,000, ending raw materials inventory \$15,000, and raw materials purchases \$170,000. What is the cost of direct materials used?
15. Tate Inc. has beginning work in process \$26,000, direct materials used \$240,000, direct labor \$220,000, total manufacturing overhead \$180,000, and ending work in process \$32,000. What are the total manufacturing costs?
16. Using the data in Question 15, what are (a) the total cost of work in process and (b) the cost of goods manufactured?
17. In what order should manufacturing inventories be listed in a balance sheet?
18. How does the output of manufacturing operations differ from that of service operations?
19. Discuss whether the product costing techniques discussed in this chapter apply equally well to manufacturers and service companies.
20. What is the value chain? Describe, in sequence, the main components of a manufacturer's value chain.
21. What is an enterprise resource planning (ERP) system? What are its primary benefits?
22. Why is product quality important for companies that implement a just-in-time inventory system?
23. Explain what is meant by "balanced" in the balanced scorecard approach.
24. In what ways can the budgeting process create incentives for unethical behavior?
25. What new rules were enacted under the Sarbanes-Oxley Act to address unethical accounting practices?
26. What is activity-based costing, and what are its potential benefits?

BRIEF EXERCISES

Distinguish between managerial and financial accounting.
(LO 1), C

BE14-1 Complete the following comparison table between managerial and financial accounting.

	Financial Accounting	Managerial Accounting
Primary users of reports		
Types of reports		
Frequency of reports		
Purpose of reports		
Content of reports		
Verification process		

BE14-2 Listed below are the three functions of the management of an organization.

Identify the three management functions.
(LO 1), C

1. Planning 2. Directing 3. Controlling

Identify which of the following statements best describes each of the above functions.

(a) ______ requires management to look ahead and to establish objectives. A key objective of management is to add value to the business.
(b) ______ involves coordinating the diverse activities and human resources of a company to produce a smooth-running operation. This function relates to the implementation of planned objectives.
(c) ______ is the process of keeping the activities on track. Management determines whether goals are being met and what changes are necessary when there are deviations.

BE14-3 Determine whether each of the following costs should be classified as direct materials (DM), direct labor (DL), or manufacturing overhead (MO).

Classify manufacturing costs.
(LO 2), C

(a) ______ Frames and tires used in manufacturing bicycles.
(b) ______ Wages paid to production workers.
(c) ______ Insurance on factory equipment and machinery.
(d) ______ Depreciation on factory equipment.

BE14-4 Indicate whether each of the following costs of an automobile manufacturer would be classified as direct materials, direct labor, or manufacturing overhead.

Classify manufacturing costs.
(LO 2), C

(a) ______ Windshield.
(b) ______ Engine.
(c) ______ Wages of assembly line worker.
(d) ______ Depreciation of factory machinery.
(e) ______ Factory machinery lubricants.
(f) ______ Tires.
(g) ______ Steering wheel.
(h) ______ Salary of painting supervisor.

BE14-5 Identify whether each of the following costs should be classified as product costs or period costs.

Identify product and period costs.
(LO 2), C

(a) ______ Manufacturing overhead.
(b) ______ Selling expenses.
(c) ______ Administrative expenses.
(d) ______ Advertising expenses.
(e) ______ Direct labor.
(f) ______ Direct materials.

BE14-6 Presented below are Rook Company's monthly manufacturing cost data related to its tablet computer product.

Classify manufacturing costs.
(LO 2), C

(a) Utilities for manufacturing equipment	$116,000
(b) Raw material (CPU, chips, etc.)	$ 85,000
(c) Depreciation on manufacturing building	$880,000
(d) Wages for production workers	$191,000

Enter each cost item in the following table, placing an "X" under the appropriate headings.

	Product Costs		
	Direct Materials	**Direct Labor**	**Factory Overhead**
(a)			
(b)			
(c)			
(d)			

BE14-7 Francum Company has the following data: direct labor $209,000, direct materials used $180,000, total manufacturing overhead $208,000, and beginning work in process $25,000. Compute (a) total manufacturing costs and (b) total cost of work in process.

Compute total manufacturing costs and total cost of work in process.
(LO 3), AP

BE14-8 In alphabetical order below are current asset items for Roland Company's balance sheet at December 31, 2017. Prepare the current assets section (including a complete heading).

Prepare current assets section.
(LO 3), AP

Accounts receivable	$200,000
Cash	62,000
Finished goods	91,000
Prepaid expenses	38,000
Raw materials	83,000
Work in process	87,000

Determine missing amounts in computing total manufacturing costs.

(LO 3), AP

BE14-9 Presented below are incomplete manufacturing cost data. Determine the missing amounts for three different situations.

	Direct Materials Used	Direct Labor Used	Factory Overhead	Total Manufacturing Costs
(1)	$40,000	$61,000	$ 50,000	?
(2)	?	$75,000	$140,000	$296,000
(3)	$55,000	?	$111,000	$310,000

Determine missing amounts in computing cost of goods manufactured.

(LO 3), AP

BE14-10 Use the same data from BE14–9 above and the data below. Determine the missing amounts.

	Total Manufacturing Costs	Work in Process (1/1)	Work in Process (12/31)	Cost of Goods Manufactured
(1)	?	$120,000	$82,000	?
(2)	$296,000	?	$98,000	$331,000
(3)	$310,000	$463,000	?	$715,000

Identify important regulatory changes.

(LO 3), C

BE14-11 The Sarbanes-Oxley Act (SOX) has important implications for the financial community. Explain two implications of SOX.

DO IT! ▶ EXERCISES

Identify managerial accounting concepts.

(LO 1), C

DO IT! 14-1 Indicate whether the following statements are true or false.

1. Managerial accounting reports focus on manufacturing and nonmanufacturing costs, but are also used in the budget process.
2. Financial accounting reports pertain to subunits of the business and are very detailed.
3. Managerial accounting reports must follow GAAP and are audited by CPAs.
4. Managers' activities and responsibilities can be classified into three broad functions: planning, directing, and controlling.

Identify managerial cost classifications.

(LO 2), C

DO IT! 14-2 A music company has these costs:

Advertising	Paper inserts for CD cases
Blank CDs	CD plastic cases
Depreciation of CD image burner	Salaries of sales representatives
Salary of factory manager	Salaries of factory maintenance employees
Factory supplies used	Salaries of employees who burn music onto CDs

Classify each cost as a period or a product cost. Within the product cost category, indicate if the cost is part of direct materials (DM), direct labor (DL), or manufacturing overhead (MO).

Prepare cost of goods manufactured schedule.

(LO 3), AP

DO IT! 14-3 The following information is available for Tomlin Company.

	April 1	April 30
Raw materials inventory	$10,000	$14,000
Work in process inventory	5,000	3,500

Materials purchased in April	$ 98,000
Direct labor in April	80,000
Manufacturing overhead in April	160,000

Prepare the cost of goods manufactured schedule for the month of April.

DO IT! 14-4 Match the descriptions that follow with the corresponding terms.

Identify trends in managerial accounting.

(LO 4), C

Descriptions:

1. ______ Inventory system in which goods are manufactured or purchased just as they are needed for sale.
2. ______ A method of allocating overhead based on each product's use of activities in making the product.
3. ______ Systems that are especially important to firms adopting just-in-time inventory methods.
4. ______ Provides guidelines for companies to describe their sustainable business practices to external parties.
5. ______ Part of the value chain for a manufacturing company.
6. ______ The U.S. economy is trending toward this.
7. ______ A performance-measurement approach that uses both financial and nonfinancial measures, tied to company objectives, to evaluate a company's operations in an integrated fashion.
8. ______ Requires that top managers certify that the company maintains an adequate system of internal controls.

Terms:

(a) Activity-based costing	(e) Service industries
(b) Balanced scorecard	(f) Just-in-time (JIT) inventory
(c) Total quality management (TQM)	(g) Sarbanes-Oxley Act (SOX)
(d) Research and development, and product design	(h) Global Reporting Initiative

▶ EXERCISES

E14-1 Justin Bleeber has prepared the following list of statements about managerial accounting, financial accounting, and the functions of management.

Identify distinguishing features of managerial accounting.

(LO 1), C

1. Financial accounting focuses on providing information to internal users.
2. Staff positions are directly involved in the company's primary revenue-generating activities.
3. Preparation of budgets is part of financial accounting.
4. Managerial accounting applies only to merchandising and manufacturing companies.
5. Both managerial accounting and financial accounting deal with many of the same economic events.
6. Managerial accounting reports are prepared only quarterly and annually.
7. Financial accounting reports are general-purpose reports.
8. Managerial accounting reports pertain to subunits of the business.
9. Managerial accounting reports must comply with generally accepted accounting principles.
10. The company treasurer reports directly to the vice president of operations.

Instructions

Identify each statement as true or false. If false, indicate how to correct the statement.

E14-2 Presented below is a list of costs and expenses usually incurred by Barnum Corporation, a manufacturer of furniture, in its factory.

Classify costs into three classes of manufacturing costs.

(LO 2), C

1. Salaries for assembly line inspectors.
2. Insurance on factory machines.
3. Property taxes on the factory building.
4. Factory repairs.
5. Upholstery used in manufacturing furniture.
6. Wages paid to assembly line workers.
7. Factory machinery depreciation.
8. Glue, nails, paint, and other small parts used in production.
9. Factory supervisors' salaries.
10. Wood used in manufacturing furniture.

Instructions

Classify the above items into the following categories: (a) direct materials, (b) direct labor, and (c) manufacturing overhead.

Identify types of cost and explain their accounting.

(LO 2), C

E14-3 Trak Corporation incurred the following costs while manufacturing its bicycles.

Bicycle components	$100,000	Advertising expense	$45,000
Depreciation on plant	60,000	Property taxes on plant	14,000
Property taxes on store	7,500	Delivery expense	21,000
Labor costs of assembly-line workers	110,000	Sales commissions	35,000
Factory supplies used	13,000	Salaries paid to sales clerks	50,000

Instructions

(a) Identify each of the above costs as direct materials, direct labor, manufacturing overhead, or period costs.

(b) Explain the basic difference in accounting for product costs and period costs.

Determine the total amount of various types of costs.

(LO 2), AP

E14-4 Knight Company reports the following costs and expenses in May.

Factory utilities	$ 15,500	Direct labor	$69,100
Depreciation on factory equipment	12,650	Sales salaries	46,400
Depreciation on delivery trucks	3,800	Property taxes on factory building	2,500
Indirect factory labor	48,900	Repairs to office equipment	1,300
Indirect materials	80,800	Factory repairs	2,000
Direct materials used	137,600	Advertising	15,000
Factory manager's salary	8,000	Office supplies used	2,640

Instructions

From the information, determine the total amount of:

(a) Manufacturing overhead.

(b) Product costs.

(c) Period costs.

Classify various costs into different cost categories.

(LO 2), C

E14-5 Gala Company is a manufacturer of laptop computers. Various costs and expenses associated with its operations are as follows.

1. Property taxes on the factory building.
2. Production superintendents' salaries.
3. Memory boards and chips used in assembling computers.
4. Depreciation on the factory equipment.
5. Salaries for assembly-line quality control inspectors.
6. Sales commissions paid to sell laptop computers.
7. Electrical components used in assembling computers.
8. Wages of workers assembling laptop computers.
9. Soldering materials used on factory assembly lines.
10. Salaries for the night security guards for the factory building.

The company intends to classify these costs and expenses into the following categories: (a) direct materials, (b) direct labor, (c) manufacturing overhead, and (d) period costs.

Instructions

List the items (1) through (10). For each item, indicate the cost category to which it belongs.

Classify various costs into different cost categories.

(LO 2), C

E14-6 The administrators of Crawford County's Memorial Hospital are interested in identifying the various costs and expenses that are incurred in producing a patient's X-ray. A list of such costs and expenses is presented below.

1. Salaries for the X-ray machine technicians.
2. Wages for the hospital janitorial personnel.
3. Film costs for the X-ray machines.
4. Property taxes on the hospital building.
5. Salary of the X-ray technicians' supervisor.
6. Electricity costs for the X-ray department.
7. Maintenance and repairs on the X-ray machines.
8. X-ray department supplies.
9. Depreciation on the X-ray department equipment.
10. Depreciation on the hospital building.

The administrators want these costs and expenses classified as (a) direct materials, (b) direct labor, or (c) service overhead.

Instructions

List the items (1) through (10). For each item, indicate the cost category to which the item belongs.

E14-7 National Express reports the following costs and expenses in June 2017 for its delivery service.

Classify various costs into different cost categories.

(LO 2), AP

Indirect materials	$ 6,400	Drivers' salaries	$16,000
Depreciation on delivery equipment	11,200	Advertising	4,600
Dispatcher's salary	5,000	Delivery equipment repairs	300
Property taxes on office building	870	Office supplies	650
CEO's salary	12,000	Office utilities	990
Gas and oil for delivery trucks	2,200	Repairs on office equipment	180

Instructions

Determine the total amount of (a) delivery service (product) costs and (b) period costs.

E14-8 Lopez Corporation incurred the following costs while manufacturing its product.

Compute cost of goods manufactured and sold.

(LO 3), AP

Materials used in product	$120,000	Advertising expense	$45,000
Depreciation on plant	60,000	Property taxes on plant	14,000
Property taxes on store	7,500	Delivery expense	21,000
Labor costs of assembly-line workers	110,000	Sales commissions	35,000
Factory supplies used	23,000	Salaries paid to sales clerks	50,000

Work in process inventory was $12,000 at January 1 and $15,500 at December 31. Finished goods inventory was $60,000 at January 1 and $45,600 at December 31.

Instructions

(a) Compute cost of goods manufactured.
(b) Compute cost of goods sold.

E14-9 An incomplete cost of goods manufactured schedule is presented below.

Determine missing amounts in cost of goods manufactured schedule.

(LO 3), AP

HOBBIT COMPANY
Cost of Goods Manufactured Schedule
For the Year Ended December 31, 2017

Work in process (1/1)		$210,000	
Direct materials			
Raw materials inventory (1/1)	$?		
Add: Raw materials purchases	158,000		
Total raw materials available for use	?		
Less: Raw materials inventory (12/31)	22,500		
Direct materials used		$180,000	
Direct labor		?	
Manufacturing overhead			
Indirect labor	18,000		
Factory depreciation	36,000		
Factory utilities	68,000		
Total overhead		122,000	
Total manufacturing costs			?
Total cost of work in process			?
Less: Work in process (12/31)			81,000
Cost of goods manufactured			$540,000

Instructions

Complete the cost of goods manufactured schedule for Hobbit Company.

Determine the missing amount of different cost items.
(LO 3), AN

E14-10 Manufacturing cost data for Copa Company are presented below.

	Case A	Case B	Case C
Direct materials used	$ (a)	$68,400	$130,000
Direct labor	57,000	86,000	(g)
Manufacturing overhead	46,500	81,600	102,000
Total manufacturing costs	195,650	(d)	253,700
Work in process 1/1/17	(b)	16,500	(h)
Total cost of work in process	221,500	(e)	337,000
Work in process 12/31/17	(c)	11,000	70,000
Cost of goods manufactured	185,275	(f)	(i)

Instructions
Indicate the missing amount for each letter (a) through (i).

Determine the missing amount of different cost items, and prepare a condensed cost of goods manufactured schedule.
(LO 3), AN

E14-11 Incomplete manufacturing cost data for Horizon Company for 2017 are presented as follows for four different situations.

	Direct Materials Used	Direct Labor Used	Manufacturing Overhead	Total Manufacturing Costs	Work in Process 1/1	Work in Process 12/31	Cost of Goods Manufactured
(1)	$117,000	$140,000	$ 87,000	$ (a)	$33,000	$ (b)	$360,000
(2)	(c)	200,000	132,000	450,000	(d)	40,000	470,000
(3)	80,000	100,000	(e)	265,000	60,000	80,000	(f)
(4)	70,000	(g)	75,000	288,000	45,000	(h)	270,000

Instructions
(a) Indicate the missing amount for each letter.
(b) Prepare a condensed cost of goods manufactured schedule for situation (1) for the year ended December 31, 2017.

Prepare a cost of goods manufactured schedule and a partial income statement.
(LO 3), AP

E14-12 Cepeda Corporation has the following cost records for June 2017.

Indirect factory labor	$ 4,500	Factory utilities	$ 400
Direct materials used	20,000	Depreciation, factory equipment	1,400
Work in process, 6/1/17	3,000	Direct labor	40,000
Work in process, 6/30/17	3,800	Maintenance, factory equipment	1,800
Finished goods, 6/1/17	5,000	Indirect materials	2,200
Finished goods, 6/30/17	7,500	Factory manager's salary	3,000

Instructions
(a) Prepare a cost of goods manufactured schedule for June 2017.
(b) Prepare an income statement through gross profit for June 2017 assuming sales revenue is $92,100.

Classify various costs into different categories and prepare cost of services performed schedule.
(LO 2, 3), AP

E14-13 Keisha Tombert, the bookkeeper for Washington Consulting, a political consulting firm, has recently completed a managerial accounting course at her local college. One of the topics covered in the course was the cost of goods manufactured schedule. Keisha wondered if such a schedule could be prepared for her firm. She realized that, as a service-oriented company, it would have no work in process inventory to consider.

Listed below are the costs her firm incurred for the month ended August 31, 2017.

Supplies used on consulting contracts	$ 1,700
Supplies used in the administrative offices	1,500
Depreciation on equipment used for contract work	900
Depreciation used on administrative office equipment	1,050
Salaries of professionals working on contracts	15,600
Salaries of administrative office personnel	7,700
Janitorial services for professional offices	700
Janitorial services for administrative offices	500
Insurance on contract operations	800
Insurance on administrative operations	900
Utilities for contract operations	1,400
Utilities for administrative offices	1,300

Instructions

(a) Prepare a schedule of cost of contract services performed (similar to a cost of goods manufactured schedule) for the month.
(b) For those costs not included in (a), explain how they would be classified and reported in the financial statements.

E14-14 The following information is available for Aikman Company.

Prepare a cost of goods manufactured schedule and a partial income statement.

(LO 3), AP

	January 1, 2017	2017	December 31, 2017
Raw materials inventory	$21,000		$30,000
Work in process inventory	13,500		17,200
Finished goods inventory	27,000		21,000
Materials purchased		$150,000	
Direct labor		220,000	
Manufacturing overhead		180,000	
Sales revenue		910,000	

Instructions

(a) Compute cost of goods manufactured.
(b) Prepare an income statement through gross profit.
(c) Show the presentation of the ending inventories on the December 31, 2017, balance sheet.
(d) How would the income statement and balance sheet of a merchandising company be different from Aikman's financial statements?

E14-15 University Company produces collegiate apparel. From its accounting records, it prepares the following schedule and financial statements on a yearly basis.

Indicate in which schedule or financial statement(s) different cost items will appear.

(LO 3), C

(a) Cost of goods manufactured schedule.
(b) Income statement.
(c) Balance sheet.

The following items are found in its ledger and accompanying data.

1. Direct labor
2. Raw materials inventory, 1/1
3. Work in process inventory, 12/31
4. Finished goods inventory, 1/1
5. Indirect labor
6. Depreciation on factory machinery
7. Work in process, 1/1
8. Finished goods inventory, 12/31
9. Factory maintenance salaries
10. Cost of goods manufactured
11. Depreciation on delivery equipment
12. Cost of goods available for sale
13. Direct materials used
14. Heat and electricity for factory
15. Repairs to roof of factory building
16. Cost of raw materials purchases

Instructions

List the items (1)–(16). For each item, indicate by using the appropriate letter or letters, the schedule and/or financial statement(s) in which the item will appear.

E14-16 An analysis of the accounts of Roberts Company reveals the following manufacturing cost data for the month ended June 30, 2017.

Prepare a cost of goods manufactured schedule, and present the ending inventories on the balance sheet.

(LO 3), AP

Inventory	Beginning	Ending
Raw materials	$9,000	$13,100
Work in process	5,000	7,000
Finished goods	9,000	8,000

Costs incurred: raw materials purchases $54,000, direct labor $47,000, and manufacturing overhead $19,900. The specific overhead costs were indirect labor $5,500, factory insurance $4,000, machinery depreciation $4,000, machinery repairs $1,800, factory utilities $3,100, and miscellaneous factory costs $1,500. Assume that all raw materials used were direct materials.

Instructions

(a) Prepare the cost of goods manufactured schedule for the month ended June 30, 2017.
(b) Show the presentation of the ending inventories on the June 30, 2017, balance sheet.

Determine the amount of cost to appear in various accounts, and indicate in which financial statements these accounts would appear.

(LO 3), AP

E14-17 McQueen Motor Company manufactures automobiles. During September 2017, the company purchased 5,000 head lamps at a cost of $15 per lamp. McQueen withdrew 4,650 lamps from the warehouse during the month. Fifty of these lamps were used to replace the head lamps in autos used by traveling sales staff. The remaining 4,600 lamps were put in autos manufactured during the month.

Of the autos put into production during September 2017, 90% were completed and transferred to the company's storage lot. Of the cars completed during the month, 70% were sold by September 30.

Instructions

(a) Determine the cost of head lamps that would appear in each of the following accounts at September 30, 2017: Raw Materials, Work in Process, Finished Goods, Cost of Goods Sold, and Selling Expenses.

(b) Write a short memo to the chief accountant, indicating whether and where each of the accounts in (a) would appear on the income statement or on the balance sheet at September 30, 2017.

Identify various managerial accounting practices.

(LO 4), C

E14-18 The following is a list of terms related to managerial accounting practices.

1. Activity-based costing.
2. Just-in-time inventory.
3. Balanced scorecard.
4. Value chain.

Instructions

Match each of the terms with the statement below that best describes the term.

(a) ______ A performance-measurement technique that attempts to consider and evaluate all aspects of performance using financial and nonfinancial measures in an integrated fashion.

(b) ______ The group of activities associated with providing a product or performing a service.

(c) ______ An approach used to reduce the cost associated with handling and holding inventory by reducing the amount of inventory on hand.

(d) ______ A method used to allocate overhead to products based on each product's use of the activities that cause the incurrence of the overhead cost.

EXERCISES: SET B AND CHALLENGE EXERCISES

Visit the book's companion website, at **www.wiley.com/college/kimmel**, and choose the Student Companion site to access Exercises: Set B and Challenge Exercises.

PROBLEMS: SET A

Classify manufacturing costs into different categories and compute the unit cost.

(LO 2), AP

P14-1A Ohno Company specializes in manufacturing a unique model of bicycle helmet. The model is well accepted by consumers, and the company has enough orders to keep the factory production at 10,000 helmets per month (80% of its full capacity). Ohno's monthly manufacturing cost and other expense data are as follows.

Rent on factory equipment	$11,000
Insurance on factory building	1,500
Raw materials (plastics, polystyrene, etc.)	75,000
Utility costs for factory	900
Supplies for general office	300
Wages for assembly line workers	58,000
Depreciation on office equipment	800
Miscellaneous materials (glue, thread, etc.)	1,100
Factory manager's salary	5,700
Property taxes on factory building	400
Advertising for helmets	14,000
Sales commissions	10,000
Depreciation on factory building	1,500

Instructions

(a) Prepare an answer sheet with the following column headings.

	Product Costs			
Cost Item	Direct Materials	Direct Labor	Manufacturing Overhead	Period Costs

Enter each cost item on your answer sheet, placing the dollar amount under the appropriate headings. Total the dollar amounts in each of the columns.

(b) Compute the cost to produce one helmet.

(a) DM $75,000
DL $58,000
MO $22,100
PC $25,100

P14-2A Bell Company, a manufacturer of audio systems, started its production in October 2017. For the preceding 3 years, Bell had been a retailer of audio systems. After a thorough survey of audio system markets, Bell decided to turn its retail store into an audio equipment factory.

Classify manufacturing costs into different categories and compute the unit cost.

(LO 2), AP

Raw materials cost for an audio system will total $74 per unit. Workers on the production lines are on average paid $12 per hour. An audio system usually takes 5 hours to complete. In addition, the rent on the equipment used to assemble audio systems amounts to $4,900 per month. Indirect materials cost $5 per system. A supervisor was hired to oversee production; her monthly salary is $3,000.

Factory janitorial costs are $1,300 monthly. Advertising costs for the audio system will be $9,500 per month. The factory building depreciation expense is $7,800 per year. Property taxes on the factory building will be $9,000 per year.

Instructions

(a) Prepare an answer sheet with the following column headings.

	Product Costs			
Cost Item	Direct Materials	Direct Labor	Manufacturing Overhead	Period Costs

Assuming that Bell manufactures, on average, 1,500 audio systems per month, enter each cost item on your answer sheet, placing the dollar amount per month under the appropriate headings. Total the dollar amounts in each of the columns.

(b) Compute the cost to produce one audio system.

(a) DM $111,000
DL $ 90,000
MO $ 18,100
PC $ 9,500

P14-3A Incomplete manufacturing costs, expenses, and selling data for two different cases are as follows.

Indicate the missing amount of different cost items, and prepare a condensed cost of goods manufactured schedule, an income statement, and a partial balance sheet.

(LO 3), AN

	Case 1	Case 2
Direct materials used	$ 9,600	$ (g)
Direct labor	5,000	8,000
Manufacturing overhead	8,000	4,000
Total manufacturing costs	(a)	16,000
Beginning work in process inventory	1,000	(h)
Ending work in process inventory	(b)	3,000
Sales revenue	24,500	(i)
Sales discounts	2,500	1,400
Cost of goods manufactured	17,000	24,000
Beginning finished goods inventory	(c)	3,300
Goods available for sale	22,000	(j)
Cost of goods sold	(d)	(k)
Ending finished goods inventory	3,400	2,500
Gross profit	(e)	7,000
Operating expenses	2,500	(l)
Net income	(f)	5,000

Instructions

(a) Indicate the missing amount for each letter.

(b) Prepare a condensed cost of goods manufactured schedule for Case 1.

(c) Prepare an income statement and the current assets section of the balance sheet for Case 1. Assume that in Case 1 the other items in the current assets section are as follows: Cash $3,000, Receivables (net) $15,000, Raw Materials $600, and Prepaid Expenses $400.

(b) Ending WIP $ 6,600
(c) Current assets $29,000

Prepare a cost of goods manufactured schedule, a partial income statement, and a partial balance sheet.

(LO 3), AP

XLS

P14-4A The following data were taken from the records of Clarkson Company for the fiscal year ended June 30, 2017.

Raw Materials Inventory 7/1/16	$ 48,000	Factory Insurance	$ 4,600
Raw Materials Inventory 6/30/17	39,600	Factory Machinery Depreciation	16,000
Finished Goods Inventory 7/1/16	96,000	Factory Utilities	27,600
Finished Goods Inventory 6/30/17	75,900	Office Utilities Expense	8,650
Work in Process Inventory 7/1/16	19,800	Sales Revenue	534,000
Work in Process Inventory 6/30/17	18,600	Sales Discounts	4,200
Direct Labor	139,250	Plant Manager's Salary	58,000
Indirect Labor	24,460	Factory Property Taxes	9,600
Accounts Receivable	27,000	Factory Repairs	1,400
		Raw Materials Purchases	96,400
		Cash	32,000

Instructions

(a) Prepare a cost of goods manufactured schedule. (Assume all raw materials used were direct materials.)

(b) Prepare an income statement through gross profit.

(c) Prepare the current assets section of the balance sheet at June 30, 2017.

(a) CGM $386,910

(b) Gross profit $122,790

(c) Current assets $193,100

Prepare a cost of goods manufactured schedule and a correct income statement.

(LO 3), AN

XLS

P14-5A Empire Company is a manufacturer of smart phones. Its controller resigned in October 2017. An inexperienced assistant accountant has prepared the following income statement for the month of October 2017.

EMPIRE COMPANY
Income Statement
For the Month Ended October 31, 2017

Sales revenue		$780,000
Less: Operating expenses		
Raw materials purchases	$264,000	
Direct labor cost	190,000	
Advertising expense	90,000	
Selling and administrative salaries	75,000	
Rent on factory facilities	60,000	
Depreciation on sales equipment	45,000	
Depreciation on factory equipment	31,000	
Indirect labor cost	28,000	
Utilities expense	12,000	
Insurance expense	8,000	803,000
Net loss		$ (23,000)

Prior to October 2017, the company had been profitable every month. The company's president is concerned about the accuracy of the income statement. As her friend, you have been asked to review the income statement and make necessary corrections. After examining other manufacturing cost data, you have acquired additional information as follows.

1. Inventory balances at the beginning and end of October were:

	October 1	October 31
Raw materials	$18,000	$29,000
Work in process	20,000	14,000
Finished goods	30,000	50,000

2. Only 75% of the utilities expense and 60% of the insurance expense apply to factory operations. The remaining amounts should be charged to selling and administrative activities.

Instructions

(a) Prepare a schedule of cost of goods manufactured for October 2017.
(b) Prepare a correct income statement for October 2017.

(a) CGM $581,800
(b) NI $ 2,000

▶ PROBLEMS: SET B AND SET C

Visit the book's companion website, at **www.wiley.com/college/kimmel**, and choose the Student Companion site to access Problems: Set B and Set C.

▶ CONTINUING PROBLEMS

CURRENT DESIGNS

*Chapters 14–24 include a hypothetical exercise featuring **Current Designs**, the company described at the beginning of this chapter. Students can also work through this exercise following an **Excel tutorial** available in **WileyPlus** and the book's companion website. Each chapter's tutorial focuses on a different Excel function or feature.*

EXCEL TUTORIAL

CD14 Mike Cichanowski founded Wenonah Canoe and later purchased Current Designs, a company that designs and manufactures kayaks. The kayak-manufacturing facility is located just a few minutes from the canoe company's headquarters in Winona, Minnesota.

Current Designs makes kayaks using two different processes. (See *www.cdkayak.com/craftsmanship/index.php* for the details of each method.) The rotational molding process uses high temperature to melt polyethylene powder in a closed rotating metal mold to produce a complete kayak hull and deck in a single piece. These kayaks are less labor-intensive and less expensive for the company to produce and sell.

Its other kayaks use the vacuum-bagged composite lamination process (which we will refer to as the composite process). Layers of fiberglass or Kevlar® are carefully placed by hand in a mold and are bonded with resin. Then, a high-pressure vacuum is used to eliminate any excess resin that would otherwise add weight and reduce strength of the finished kayak. These kayaks require a great deal of skilled labor as each boat is individually finished. The exquisite finish of the vacuum-bagged composite kayaks gave rise to Current Designs' tag line, "A work of art, made for life."

Current Designs has the following managers:

Mike Cichanowski, CEO
Diane Buswell, Controller
Deb Welch, Purchasing Manager
Bill Johnson, Sales Manager
Dave Thill, Kayak Plant Manager
Rick Thrune, Production Manager for Composite Kayaks

Instructions

(a) What are the primary information needs of each manager?
(b) Name one special-purpose management accounting report that could be designed for each manager. Include the name of the report, the information it would contain, and how frequently it should be issued.
(c) When Diane Buswell, controller for Current Designs, reviewed the accounting records for a recent period, she noted the following items. Classify each item as a product cost or a period cost. If an item is a product cost, note if it is a direct materials, direct labor, or manufacturing overhead item.

Current Designs.xls

	A	B	C			D
1						
2			Product Costs			Period Costs
3	Payee	Purpose	Direct Materials	Direct Labor	Manufacturing Overhead	
4	Winona Agency	Property insurance for the manufacturing plant				
5	Bill Johnson (sales manager)	Payroll check—payment to sales manager				
6	Xcel Energy	Electricity for manufacturing plant				
7	Winona Printing	Price lists for salespeople				
8	Jim Kaiser (sales representative)	Sales commissions				
9	Dave Thill (plant manager)	Payroll check—payment to plant manager				
10	Dana Schultz (kayak assembler)	Payroll check—payment to kayak assembler				
11	Composite One	Bagging film used when kayaks are assembled; it is discarded after use				
12	Fastenal	Shop supplies—brooms, paper towels, etc.				
13	Ravago	Polyethylene powder which is the main ingredient for the rotational molded kayaks				
14	Winona County	Property taxes on manufacturing plant				
15	North American Composites	Kevlar® fabric for composite kayaks				
16	Waste Management	Trash disposal for the company office building				
17	None	Journal entry to record depreciation of manufacturing equipment				

*The **Waterways problem** starts in this chapter and continues in every remaining chapter. You will find the complete problem for each chapter at the book's companion website.*

WATERWAYS

WP14 Waterways Corporation is a private corporation formed for the purpose of providing the products and the services needed to irrigate farms, parks, commercial projects, and private lawns. It has a centrally located factory in a U.S. city that manufactures the products it markets to retail outlets across the nation. It also maintains a division that performs installation and warranty servicing in six metropolitan areas.

The mission of Waterways is to manufacture quality parts that can be used for effective irrigation projects that also conserve water. By that effort, the company hopes to satisfy its customers, perform rapid and responsible service, and serve the community and the employees who represent them in each community.

The company has been growing rapidly, so management is considering new ideas to help the company continue its growth and maintain the high quality of its products.

Waterways was founded by Will Winkman, who is the company president and chief executive officer (CEO). Working with him from the company's inception is Will's brother, Ben, whose sprinkler designs and ideas about the installation of proper systems have been a major basis of the company's success. Ben is the vice president who oversees all aspects of design and production in the company.

The factory itself is managed by Todd Senter who hires his line managers to supervise the factory employees. The factory makes all of the parts for the irrigation systems. The purchasing department is managed by Helen Hines.

The installation and training division is overseen by vice president Henry Writer, who supervises the managers of the six local installation operations. Each of these local managers hires his or her own local service people. These service employees are trained by the home office under Henry Writer's direction because of the uniqueness of the company's products.

There is a small human resources department under the direction of Sally Fenton, a vice president who handles the employee paperwork, though hiring is actually performed by the separate departments. Teresa Totter is the vice president who heads the sales and marketing area; she oversees 10 well-trained salespeople.

The accounting and finance division of the company is run by Ann Headman, who is the chief financial officer (CFO) and a company vice president. She is a member of the Institute of Management Accountants and holds a certificate in management accounting. She has a small staff of accountants, including a controller and a treasurer, and a staff of accounting input operators who maintain the financial records.

A partial list of Waterways' accounts and their balances for the month of November follows.

Accounts Receivable	$ 275,000
Advertising Expenses	54,000
Cash	260,000
Depreciation—Factory Equipment	16,800
Depreciation—Office Equipment	2,400
Direct Labor	42,000
Factory Supplies Used	16,800
Factory Utilities	10,200
Finished Goods Inventory, November 30	68,800
Finished Goods Inventory, October 31	72,550
Indirect Labor	48,000
Office Supplies Expense	1,600
Other Administrative Expenses	72,000
Prepaid Expenses	41,250
Raw Materials Inventory, November 30	52,700
Raw Materials Inventory, October 31	38,000
Raw Materials Purchases	184,500
Rent—Factory Equipment	47,000
Repairs—Factory Equipment	4,500
Salaries	325,000
Sales Revenue	1,350,000
Sales Commissions	40,500
Work in Process Inventory, October 31	52,700
Work in Process Inventory, November 30	42,000

Instructions

(a) Based on the information given, construct an organizational chart of Waterways Corporation.

(b) A list of accounts and their values are given above. From this information, prepare a cost of goods manufactured schedule, an income statement, and a partial balance sheet for Waterways Corporation for the month of November.

EXPAND YOUR CRITICAL THINKING

DECISION-MAKING ACROSS THE ORGANIZATION

Group Project

CT14-1 Wendall Company specializes in producing fashion outfits. On July 31, 2017, a tornado touched down at its factory and general office. The inventories in the warehouse and the factory were completely destroyed as was the general office nearby. Next morning, through a careful search of the disaster site, however, Bill Francis, the company's controller, and Elizabeth Walton, the cost accountant, were able to recover a small part of manufacturing cost data for the current month. E

"What a horrible experience," sighed Bill "And the worst part is that we may not have enough records to use in filing an insurance claim."

"It was terrible," replied Elizabeth. "However, I managed to recover some of the manufacturing cost data that I was working on yesterday afternoon. The data indicate that our direct labor cost in July totaled $250,000 and that we had purchased $365,000 of raw materials. Also, I recall that the amount of raw materials used for July was $350,000. But I'm not sure this information will help. The rest of our records are blown away."

"Well, not exactly," said Bill. "I was working on the year-to-date income statement when the tornado warning was announced. My recollection is that our sales in July were $1,240,000 and our gross profit ratio has been 40% of sales. Also, I can remember that our cost of goods available for sale was $770,000 for July."

"Maybe we can work something out from this information!" exclaimed Elizabeth. "My experience tells me that our manufacturing overhead is usually 60% of direct labor."

"Hey, look what I just found," cried Elizabeth. "It's a copy of this June's balance sheet, and it shows that our inventories as of June 30 are Finished goods $38,000, Work in process $25,000, and Raw materials $19,000."

"Super," yelled Bill. "Let's go work something out."

In order to file an insurance claim, Wendall Company needs to determine the amount of its inventories as of July 31, 2017, the date of the tornado touchdown.

Instructions

With the class divided into groups, determine the amount of cost in the Raw Materials, Work in Process, and Finished Goods inventory accounts as of the date of the tornado touchdown.

MANAGERIAL ANALYSIS

E **CT14-2** Tenrack is a fairly large manufacturing company located in the southern United States. The company manufactures tennis rackets, tennis balls, tennis clothing, and tennis shoes, all bearing the company's distinctive logo, a large green question mark on a white flocked tennis ball. The company's sales have been increasing over the past 10 years.

The tennis racket division has recently implemented several advanced manufacturing techniques. Robot arms hold the tennis rackets in place while glue dries, and machine vision systems check for defects. The engineering and design team uses computerized drafting and testing of new products. The following managers work in the tennis racket division:

Jason Dennis, Sales Manager (supervises all sales representatives)
Peggy Groneman, Technical Specialist (supervises computer programmers)
Dave Marley, Cost Accounting Manager (supervises cost accountants)
Kevin Carson, Production Supervisor (supervises all manufacturing employees)
Sally Renner, Engineer (supervises all new-product design teams)

Instructions

(a) What are the primary information needs of each manager?
(b) Which, if any, financial accounting report(s) is each likely to use?
(c) Name one special-purpose management accounting report that could be designed for each manager. Include the name of the report, the information it would contain, and how frequently it should be issued.

REAL-WORLD FOCUS

AN **CT14-3 The Institute of Management Accountants** (IMA) is an organization dedicated to excellence in the practice of management accounting and financial management.

Address: **www.imanet.org**, or go to **www.wiley.com/college/kimmel**

Instructions

At the IMA's home page, locate the answers to the following questions.

(a) How many members does the IMA have, and what are their job titles?
(b) What are some of the benefits of joining the IMA as a student?
(c) Use the chapter locator function to locate the IMA chapter nearest you, and find the name of the chapter president.

Writing

COMMUNICATION ACTIVITY

E **CT14-4** Refer to P14–5A and add the following requirement.

Prepare a letter to the president of the company, Shelly Phillips, describing the changes you made. Explain clearly why net income is different after the changes. Keep the following points in mind as you compose your letter.

1. This is a letter to the president of a company, who is your friend. The style should be generally formal, but you may relax some requirements. For example, you may call the president by her first name.

2. Executives are very busy. Your letter should tell the president your main results first (for example, the amount of net income).
3. You should include brief explanations so that the president can understand the changes you made in the calculations.

ETHICS CASE

CT14-5 Steve Morgan, controller for Newton Industries, was reviewing production cost reports for the year. One amount in these reports continued to bother him—advertising. During the year, the company had instituted an expensive advertising campaign to sell some of its slower-moving products. It was still too early to tell whether the advertising campaign was successful. E

There had been much internal debate as how to report advertising cost. The vice president of finance argued that advertising costs should be reported as a cost of production, just like direct materials and direct labor. He therefore recommended that this cost be identified as manufacturing overhead and reported as part of inventory costs until sold. Others disagreed. Morgan believed that this cost should be reported as an expense of the current period, so as not to overstate net income. Others argued that it should be reported as prepaid advertising and reported as a current asset.

The president finally had to decide the issue. He argued that these costs should be reported as inventory. His arguments were practical ones. He noted that the company was experiencing financial difficulty and expensing this amount in the current period might jeopardize a planned bond offering. Also, by reporting the advertising costs as inventory rather than as prepaid advertising, less attention would be directed to it by the financial community.

Instructions

(a) Who are the stakeholders in this situation?
(b) What are the ethical issues involved in this situation?
(c) What would you do if you were Steve Morgan?

ALL ABOUT YOU

CT14-6 The primary purpose of managerial accounting is to provide information useful for management decisions. Many of the managerial accounting techniques that you learn in this course will be useful for decisions you make in your everyday life. AP

Instructions

For each of the following managerial accounting techniques, read the definition provided and then give an example of a personal situation that would benefit from use of this technique.

(a) Break-even point (page 893).
(b) Budget (page 1016).
(c) Balanced scorecard (page 1136).
(d) Capital budgeting (page 1166).

CONSIDERING YOUR COSTS AND BENEFITS

CT14-7 As noted in this chapter, because of global competition, companies have become increasingly focused on reducing costs. To reduce costs and remain competitive, many companies are turning to outsourcing. Outsourcing means hiring an outside supplier to provide elements of a product or service rather than producing them internally. E

Suppose you are the managing partner in a CPA firm with 30 full-time staff. Larger firms in your community have begun to outsource basic tax-return preparation work to India. Should you outsource your basic tax-return work to India as well? You estimate that you would have to lay off six staff members if you outsource the work. The basic arguments for and against are as follows.

> **YES:** The wages paid to Indian accountants are very low relative to U.S. wages. You will not be able to compete unless you outsource.
>
> **NO:** Tax-return data is highly sensitive. Many customers will be upset to learn that their data is being emailed around the world.

Instructions

Write a response indicating your position regarding this situation. Provide support for your view.

15

Job Order Costing

CHAPTER PREVIEW

The Feature Story about Disney describes how important accurate costing is to movie studios. In order to submit accurate bids on new film projects and to know whether it profited from past films, the company needs a good costing system. This chapter illustrates how costs are assigned to specific jobs, such as the production of *The Avengers 2*. We begin the discussion in this chapter with an overview of the flow of costs in a job order cost accounting system. We then use a case study to explain and illustrate the documents, entries, and accounts in this type of cost accounting system.

CHAPTER OUTLINE

LEARNING OBJECTIVES		PRACTICE
1 Describe cost systems and the flow of costs in a job order system.	• Process cost system • Job order cost system • Job order cost flow • Accumulating costs	DO IT! 1 Accumulating Manufacturing Costs
2 Use a job cost sheet to assign costs to work in process.	• Raw materials costs • Factory labor costs	DO IT! 2 Work in Process
3 Demonstrate how to determine and use the predetermined overhead rate.		DO IT! 3 Predetermined Overhead Rate
4 Prepare entries for manufacturing and service jobs completed and sold.	• Finished goods • Cost of goods sold • Summary • Job order for service companies • Pros and cons of job order costing	DO IT! 4 Completion and Sale of Jobs
5 Distinguish between under- and over-applied manufacturing overhead.	• Under- or overapplied manufacturing overhead	DO IT! 5 Applied Manufacturing Overhead

Go to the ***REVIEW AND PRACTICE*** section at the end of the chapter for a targeted summary and exercises with solutions.

Visit **WileyPLUS** for additional tutorials and practice opportunities.

© Pictorial Press Ltd/Alamy

FEATURE STORY

Profiting from the Silver Screen

Have you ever had the chance to tour a movie studio? There's a lot going on! Lots of equipment and lots of people with a variety of talents. Running a film studio, whether as an independent company or part of a major corporation, is a complex and risky business. Consider Disney, which has produced such classics as *Snow White and the Seven Dwarfs* and such colossal successes as *Frozen*. The movie studio has, however, also seen its share of losses. Disney's *Lone Ranger* movie brought in revenues of $260 million, but its production and marketing costs were a combined $375 million—a loss of $115 million.

Every time Disney or another movie studio makes a new movie, it is creating a unique product. Ideally, each new movie should be able to stand on its own, that is, the film should generate revenues that exceed its costs. And in order to know whether a particular movie is profitable, the studio must keep track of all of the costs incurred to make and market the film. These costs include such items as salaries of the writers, actors, director, producer, and production team (e.g., film crew); licensing costs; depreciation on equipment; music; studio rental; and marketing and distribution costs. If you've ever watched the credits at the end of a movie, you know the list goes on and on.

The movie studio isn't the only one with an interest in knowing a particular project's profitability. Many of the people involved in making the movie, such as the screenwriters, actors, and producers, have at least part of their compensation tied to its profitability. As such, complaints about inaccurate accounting are common in the movie industry.

In particular, a few well-known and widely attended movies reported low profits, or even losses, once the accountants got done with them. How can this be? The issue is that a large portion of a movie's costs are overhead costs that can't be directly traced to a film, such as depreciation of film equipment and sets, facility maintenance costs, and executives' salaries. Actors and others often suggest that these overhead costs are overallocated to their movie and therefore negatively affect their compensation.

To reduce the risk of financial flops, many of the big studios now focus on making sequels of previous hits. This might explain why, shortly after losing money on the *Lone Ranger*, Disney announced plans to make *The Avengers 2*—a much safer bet.

LEARNING OBJECTIVE 1

Describe cost systems and the flow of costs in a job order system.

Cost accounting involves measuring, recording, and reporting product costs. Companies determine both the total cost and the unit cost of each product. The accuracy of the product cost information is critical to the success of the company. Companies use this information to determine which products to produce, what prices to charge, and how many units to produce. Accurate product cost information is also vital for effective evaluation of employee performance.

A **cost accounting system** consists of accounts for the various manufacturing costs. These accounts are fully integrated into the general ledger of a company. An important feature of a cost accounting system is the use of **a perpetual inventory system**. Such a system **provides immediate, up-to-date information on the cost of a product**.

There are two basic types of cost accounting systems: (1) a process cost system and (2) a job order cost system. Although cost accounting systems differ widely from company to company, most involve one of these two traditional product costing systems.

PROCESS COST SYSTEM

A company uses a **process cost system** when it manufactures a large volume of similar products. Production is continuous. Examples of a process cost system are the manufacture of cereal by Kellogg, the refining of petroleum by ExxonMobil, and the production of ice cream by Ben & Jerry's. Process costing accumulates product-related costs **for a period of time** (such as a week or a month) instead of assigning costs to specific products or job orders. In process costing, companies assign the costs to departments or processes for the specified period of time. Illustration 15-1 shows examples of the use of a process cost system. We will discuss the process cost system further in Chapter 16.

ILLUSTRATION 15-1
Process cost system

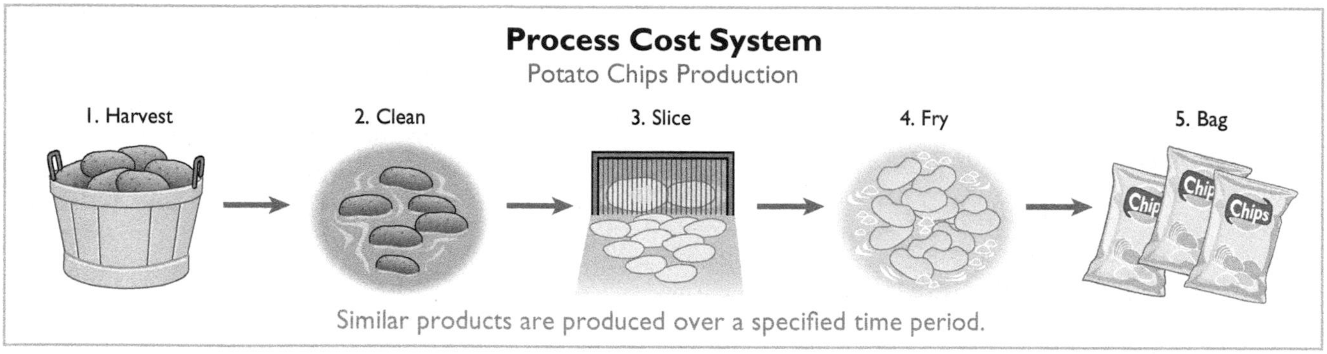

JOB ORDER COST SYSTEM

Under a **job order cost system**, the company assigns costs to each **job** or to each **batch** of goods. An example of a job is the manufacture of a jet by Boeing, the production of a movie by Disney, or the making of a fire truck by American LaFrance. An example of a batch is the printing of 225 wedding invitations by a local print shop, or the printing of a weekly issue of *Fortune* magazine by a high-tech printer such as Quad Graphics.

An important feature of job order costing is that each job or batch has its own distinguishing characteristics. For example, each house is custom built, each consulting engagement by a CPA firm is unique, and each printing job is different. **The objective is to compute the cost per job**. At each point in manufacturing a product or performing a service, the company can identify the job and its associated costs. A job order cost system measures costs for each completed job, rather than for set time periods. Illustration 15-2 shows the recording of costs in a job order cost system for Disney as it produced two different films at the same time: an animated film and an action thriller.

ILLUSTRATION 15-2
Job order cost system for Disney

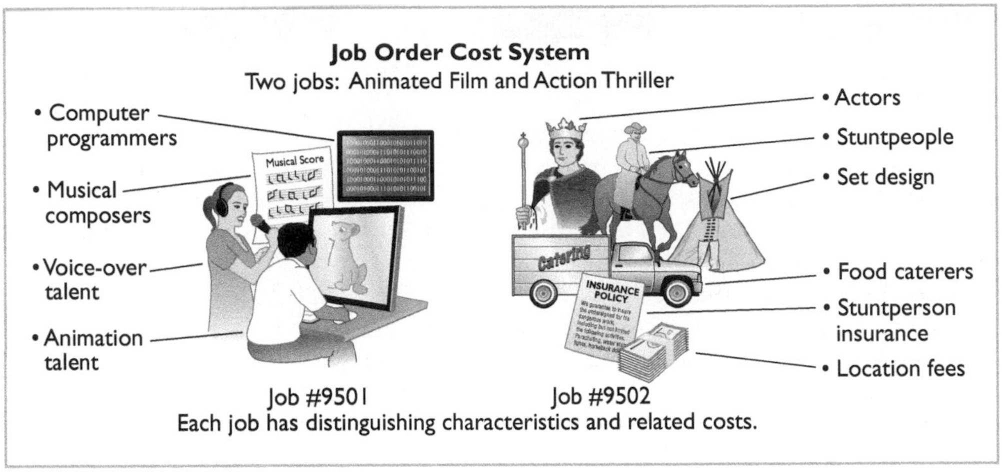

Can a company use both types of cost systems? Yes. For example, General Motors uses process cost accounting for its standard model cars, such as Malibus and Corvettes, and job order cost accounting for a custom-made limousine for the President of the United States.

The objective of both cost accounting systems is to provide unit cost information for product pricing, cost control, inventory valuation, and financial statement presentation.

MANAGEMENT INSIGHT

© Tony Tremblay/iStockphoto

Jobs Won, Money Lost

Many companies suffer from poor cost accounting. As a result, they sometimes make products they should not be selling at all, or they buy product components that they could more profitably make themselves. Also, inaccurate cost data leads companies to misallocate capital and frustrates efforts by plant managers to improve efficiency.

For example, consider the case of a diversified company in the business of rebuilding diesel locomotives. The managers thought they were making money, but a consulting firm found that the company had seriously underestimated costs. The company bailed out of the business and not a moment too soon. Says the consultant who advised the company, "The more contracts it won, the more money it lost." Given that situation, a company cannot stay in business very long!

What type of costs do you think the company had been underestimating? (Go to **WileyPLUS** for this answer and additional questions.)

JOB ORDER COST FLOW

The flow of costs (direct materials, direct labor, and manufacturing overhead) in job order cost accounting parallels the physical flow of the materials as they are converted into finished goods. As shown in Illustration 15-3 (page 750), companies first **accumulate** manufacturing costs in the form of raw materials, factory labor, or manufacturing overhead. They then **assign** manufacturing costs to the Work in Process Inventory account. When a job is completed, the company transfers the cost of the job to Finished Goods Inventory. Later when the goods are sold, the company transfers their cost to Cost of Goods Sold.

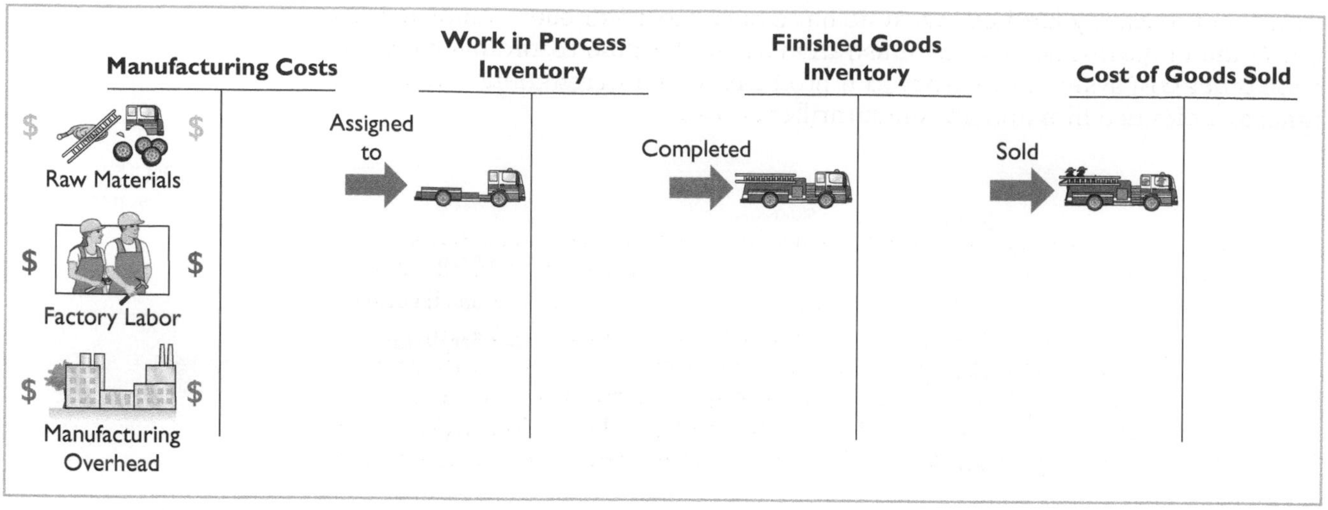

ILLUSTRATION 15-3
Flow of costs in job order costing

Illustration 15-3 provides a basic overview of the flow of costs in a manufacturing setting for production of a fire truck. A more detailed presentation of the flow of costs is summarized near the end of this chapter in Illustration 15-15. There are two major steps in the flow of costs: (1) *accumulating* the manufacturing costs incurred, and (2) *assigning* the accumulated costs to the work done. The following discussion shows that the company accumulates manufacturing costs incurred by debits to Raw Materials Inventory, Factory Labor, and Manufacturing Overhead. When the company incurs these costs, it does not attempt to associate the costs with specific jobs. The company makes additional entries to assign manufacturing costs incurred to specific jobs. In the remainder of this chapter, we will use a case study to explain how a job order cost system operates.

ACCUMULATING MANUFACTURING COSTS

To illustrate a job order cost system, we will use the January transactions of Wallace Company, which makes custom electronic sensors for corporate safety applications (such as fire and carbon monoxide) and security applications (such as theft and corporate espionage).

Raw Materials Costs

When Wallace receives the raw materials it has purchased, **it debits the cost of the materials to Raw Materials Inventory**. The company debits this account for the invoice cost of the raw materials and freight costs chargeable to the purchaser. It credits the account for purchase discounts taken and purchase returns and allowances. Wallace makes **no effort at this point to associate the cost of materials with specific jobs or orders**.

To illustrate, assume that Wallace purchases 2,000 lithium batteries (Stock No. AA2746) at $5 per unit ($10,000) and 800 electronic modules (Stock No. AA2850) at $40 per unit ($32,000) for a total cost of $42,000 ($10,000 + $32,000). The entry to record this purchase on January 4 is:

Raw Materials Inventory	
42,000	

(1)[1]

Jan. 4	Raw Materials Inventory	42,000	
	Accounts Payable		42,000
	(Purchase of raw materials on account)		

[1]The numbers placed above the entries for Wallace Company are used for reference purposes in the summary provided in Illustration 15-15.

At this point, Raw Materials Inventory has a balance of $42,000, as shown in the T-account in the margin. As we will explain later in the chapter, the company subsequently assigns direct raw materials inventory to work in process and indirect raw materials inventory to manufacturing overhead.

Factory Labor Costs

Some of a company's employees are involved in the manufacturing process, while others are not. As discussed in Chapter 14, wages and salaries of nonmanufacturing employees are expensed as period costs (e.g., Salaries and Wages Expense). Costs related to manufacturing employees are accumulated in Factory Labor to ensure their treatment as product costs. Factory labor consists of three costs: (1) gross earnings of factory workers, (2) employer payroll taxes on these earnings, and (3) fringe benefits (such as sick pay, pensions, and vacation pay) incurred by the employer. **Companies debit labor costs to Factory Labor as they incur those costs.**

To illustrate, assume that Wallace incurs $32,000 of factory labor costs. Of that amount, $27,000 relates to wages payable and $5,000 relates to payroll taxes payable in February. The entry to record factory labor for the month is:

	(2)		
Jan. 31	Factory Labor	32,000	
	Factory Wages Payable		27,000
	Employer Payroll Taxes Payable		5,000
	(To record factory labor costs)		

Factory Labor	
32,000	

At this point, Factory Labor has a balance of $32,000, as shown in the T-account in the margin. The company subsequently assigns direct factory labor to work in process and indirect factory labor to manufacturing overhead.

Manufacturing Overhead Costs

A company has many types of overhead costs. If these overhead costs, such as property taxes, depreciation, insurance, and repairs, relate to overhead costs of a nonmanufacturing facility, such as an office building, then these costs are expensed as period costs (e.g., Property Tax Expense, Depreciation Expense, Insurance Expense, and Maintenance and Repairs Expense). If the costs relate to the manufacturing process, then they are accumulated in Manufacturing Overhead to ensure their treatment as product costs.

Using assumed data, the summary entry for manufacturing overhead in Wallace Company is:

	(3)		
Jan. 31	Manufacturing Overhead	13,800	
	Utilities Payable		4,800
	Prepaid Insurance		2,000
	Accounts Payable (for repairs)		2,600
	Accumulated Depreciation		3,000
	Property Taxes Payable		1,400
	(To record overhead costs)		

Manufacturing Overhead	
13,800	

At this point, Manufacturing Overhead has a balance of $13,800, as shown in the T-account in the margin. The company subsequently assigns manufacturing overhead to work in process.

DO IT! 1 Accumulating Manufacturing Costs

During the current month, Ringling Company incurs the following manufacturing costs:

(a) Raw material purchases of $4,200 on account.

(b) Factory labor of $18,000. Of that amount, $15,000 relates to wages payable and $3,000 relates to payroll taxes payable.

(c) Factory utilities of $2,200 are payable, prepaid factory insurance of $1,800 has expired, and depreciation on the factory building is $3,500.

Prepare journal entries for each type of manufacturing cost.

Action Plan

✔ In accumulating manufacturing costs, debit at least one of three accounts: Raw Materials Inventory, Factory Labor, and Manufacturing Overhead.

✔ Manufacturing overhead costs may be recognized daily. Or, manufacturing overhead may be recorded periodically through a summary entry.

SOLUTION

(a) Raw Materials Inventory	4,200	
Accounts Payable		4,200
(Purchases of raw materials on account)		
(b) Factory Labor	18,000	
Factory Wages Payable		15,000
Employer Payroll Taxes Payable		3,000
(To record factory labor costs)		
(c) Manufacturing Overhead	7,500	
Utilities Payable		2,200
Prepaid Insurance		1,800
Accumulated Depreciation		3,500
(To record overhead costs)		

Related exercise material: **BE15-1, BE15-2, E15-1, E15-7, E15-8, E15-11,** and **DO IT! 15-1.**

LEARNING OBJECTIVE 2 Use a job cost sheet to assign costs to work in process.

Assigning manufacturing costs to work in process results in the following entries.

1. **Debits** made to Work in Process Inventory.
2. **Credits** made to Raw Materials Inventory, Factory Labor, and Manufacturing Overhead.

DECISION TOOLS

A completed job cost sheet helps managers to compare costs to both those of previous periods and of competitors to ensure that costs are in line.

An essential accounting record in assigning costs to jobs is a **job cost sheet**, as shown in Illustration 15-4. A **job cost sheet** is a form used to record the costs chargeable to a specific job and to determine the total and unit costs of the completed job.

Companies keep a separate job cost sheet for each job. The job cost sheets constitute the subsidiary ledger for the Work in Process Inventory account. A **subsidiary ledger** consists of individual records for each individual item—in this case, each job. The Work in Process account is referred to as a **control account** because it summarizes the detailed data regarding specific jobs contained in the job cost sheets. **Each entry to Work in Process Inventory must be accompanied by a corresponding posting to one or more job cost sheets.**

ILLUSTRATION 15-4
Job cost sheet

Job Cost Sheet

Job No. ____________ Quantity ____________
Item ____________ Date Requested ____________
For ____________ Date Completed ____________

Date	Direct Materials	Direct Labor	Manufacturing Overhead

Cost of completed job	
Direct materials	$ ________
Direct labor	________
Manufacturing overhead	________
Total cost	$ ________
Unit cost (total dollars ÷ quantity)	$ ________

▼ **HELPFUL HINT**
Companies typically maintain job cost sheets as computer files.

RAW MATERIALS COSTS

Companies assign raw materials costs to jobs when their materials storeroom issues the materials in response to requests. Requests for issuing raw materials are made on a prenumbered **materials requisition slip**. The materials issued may be used directly on a job, or they may be considered indirect materials. As Illustration 15-5 shows, the requisition should indicate the quantity and type of materials withdrawn and the account to be charged. The company will charge direct materials to Work in Process Inventory, and indirect materials to Manufacturing Overhead.

ETHICS NOTE
Approvals are an important internal control feature of a requisition slip because they establish individual accountability over inventory.

ILLUSTRATION 15-5
Materials requisition slip

Wallace Company
Materials Requisition Slip

Deliver to: Assembly Department Req. No. R247
Charge to: Work in Process—Job No. 101 Date: 1/6/17

Quantity	Description	Stock No.	Cost per Unit	Total
200	Lithium batteries	AA2746	$5.00	$1,000

Requested by *Bruce Howart* Received by *Herb Crowley*
Approved by *Kap Shin* Costed by *Heather Remmers*

▼ **HELPFUL HINT**
Note the specific job (in this case, Job No. 101) to be charged.

ETHICS NOTE
The internal control principle of documentation includes prenumbering to enhance accountability.

The company may use any of the inventory costing methods (FIFO, LIFO, or average-cost) in costing the requisitions **to the individual job cost sheets**.

Periodically, the company journalizes the requisitions. For example, if Wallace uses $24,000 of direct materials and $6,000 of indirect materials in January, the entry is:

	(4)		
Jan. 31	Work in Process Inventory	24,000	
	Manufacturing Overhead	6,000	
	Raw Materials Inventory		30,000
	(To assign materials to jobs and overhead)		

This entry reduces Raw Materials Inventory by $30,000, increases Work in Process Inventory by $24,000, and increases Manufacturing Overhead by $6,000, as shown below.

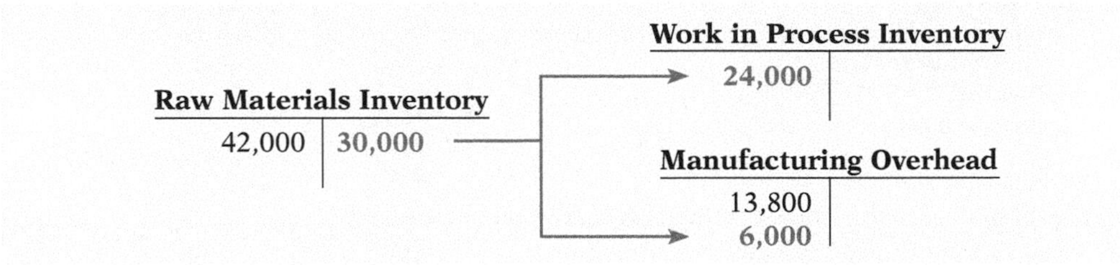

Illustration 15-6 shows the posting of requisition slip R247 to Job No. 101 and other assumed postings to the job cost sheets for materials. The requisition slips provide the basis for total direct materials costs of $12,000 for Job No. 101, $7,000 for Job No. 102, and $5,000 for Job No. 103. After the company has completed all postings, the sum of the direct materials columns of the job cost sheets

ILLUSTRATION 15-6
Job cost sheets–posting of direct materials

▼ **HELPFUL HINT**
Companies post to control accounts monthly, and post to job cost sheets daily.

▼ **HELPFUL HINT**
Prove the $24,000 direct materials charge to Work in Process Inventory by totaling the charges by jobs:

101	$12,000
102	7,000
103	5,000
	$24,000

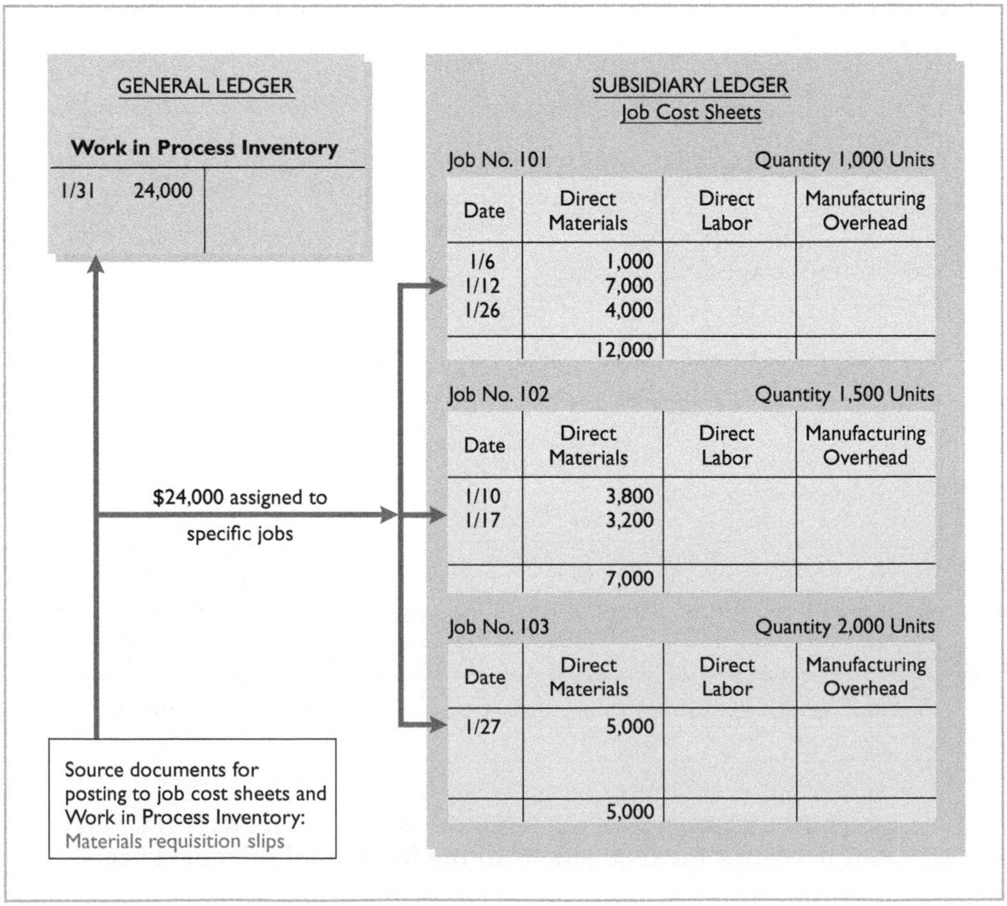

(the subsidiary account amounts of $12,000, $7,000, and $5,000) should equal the direct materials debited to Work in Process Inventory (the control account amount of $24,000).

MANAGEMENT INSIGHT iSuppli

© TommL/iStockphoto

The Cost of an iPhone? Just Tear One Apart

All companies need to know what it costs to make their own products—but a lot of companies would also like to know the cost of their competitors' products as well. That's where iSuppli steps in. For a price, iSuppli will tear apart sophisticated electronic devices to tell you what it would cost to replicate. In the case of smartphones, which often have more than 1,000 tiny components, that is no small feat. As shown in the chart to the right, the components of a recent iPhone model cost about $170. Assembly adds only about another $6.50. However, the difference between what you pay (about double the total component cost) and the "cost" is not all profit. You also have to consider the additional nonproduction costs of research, design, marketing, patent fees, and selling costs.

Components	Apple iPhone[a]
Integrated circuits	$ 91.38
Display/touchscreen	34.65
Mechanical[b]	17.80
Camera	9.35
Battery	5.07
Other	11.82
Total	**$170.07**

[a]Latest data available. [b]Includes electromechanical.
Source: iSuppli.

Source: "The Business of Dissecting Electronics: The Lowdown on Teardowns," *The Economist.com* (January 21, 2010).

What type of costs are marketing and selling costs, and how are they treated for accounting purposes? (Go to **WileyPLUS** for this answer and additional questions.)

FACTORY LABOR COSTS

Companies assign factory labor costs to jobs on the basis of time tickets prepared when the work is performed. The **time ticket** indicates the employee, the hours worked, the account and job to be charged, and the total labor cost. Many companies accumulate these data through the use of bar coding and scanning devices. When they start and end work, employees scan bar codes on their identification badges and bar codes associated with each job they work on. When direct labor is involved, the time ticket must indicate the job number, as shown in Illustration 15-7. The employee's supervisor should approve all time tickets.

ILLUSTRATION 15-7
Time ticket

Wallace Company
Time Ticket

Date: 1/6/17
Employee: John Nash — Employee No. 124
Charge to: Work in Process — Job No. 101

Time			Hourly Rate	Total Cost
Start	Stop	Total Hours		
0800	1200	4	10.00	40.00

Approved by Bob Kadler — Costed by M. Chen

The time tickets are later sent to the payroll department, which applies the employee's hourly wage rate and computes the total labor cost. Finally, the company journalizes the time tickets. It debits the account Work in Process Inventory for direct labor and debits Manufacturing Overhead for indirect labor. For example, if the $32,000 total factory labor cost consists of $28,000 of direct labor and $4,000 of indirect labor, the entry is:

(5)

Jan. 31	Work in Process Inventory	28,000	
	Manufacturing Overhead	4,000	
	Factory Labor		32,000
	(To assign labor to jobs and overhead)		

As a result of this entry, Factory Labor is reduced by $32,000 so it has a zero balance, and labor costs are assigned to the appropriate manufacturing accounts. The entry increases Work in Process Inventory by $28,000 and increases Manufacturing Overhead by $4,000, as shown below.

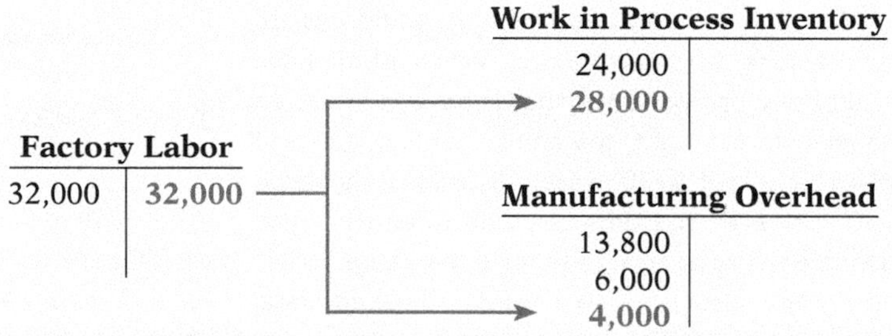

Let's assume that the labor costs chargeable to Wallace's three jobs are $15,000, $9,000, and $4,000. Illustration 15-8 shows the Work in Process Inventory

ILLUSTRATION 15-8
Job cost sheets–direct labor

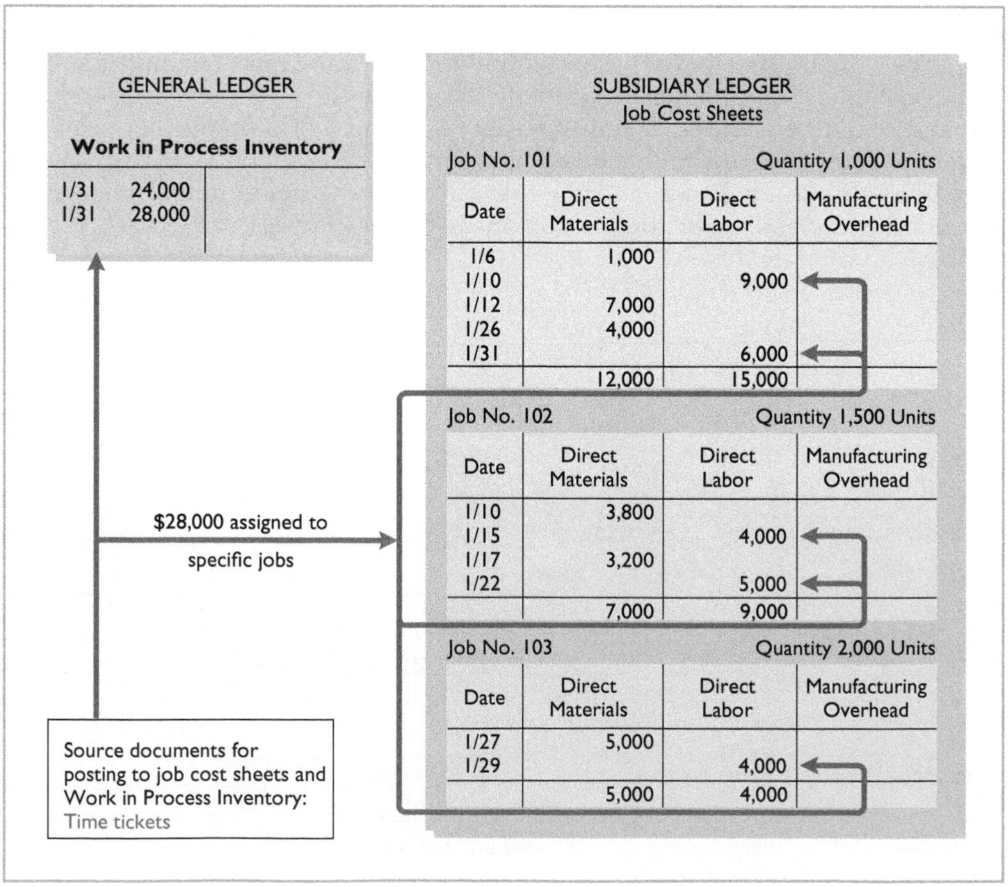

▼ **HELPFUL HINT**
Prove the $28,000 direct labor charge to Work in Process Inventory by totaling the charges by jobs:

101	$15,000
102	9,000
103	4,000
	$28,000

and job cost sheets after posting. As in the case of direct materials, the postings to the direct labor columns of the job cost sheets should equal the posting of direct labor to Work in Process Inventory.

DO IT! 2 Work in Process

Danielle Company is working on two job orders. The job cost sheets show the following:

Direct materials—Job 120 $6,000; Job 121 $3,600
Direct labor—Job 120 $4,000; Job 121 $2,000
Manufacturing overhead—Job 120 $5,000; Job 121 $2,500

Prepare the three summary entries to record the assignment of costs to Work in Process from the data on the job cost sheets.

SOLUTION

The three summary entries are:

Work in Process Inventory ($6,000 + $3,600)	9,600	
Raw Materials Inventory		9,600
(To assign materials to jobs)		
Work in Process Inventory ($4,000 + $2,000)	6,000	
Factory Labor		6,000
(To assign labor to jobs)		
Work in Process Inventory ($5,000 + $2,500)	7,500	
Manufacturing Overhead		7,500
(To assign overhead to jobs)		

Action Plan

- ✔ Recognize that Work in Process Inventory is the control account for all unfinished job cost sheets.
- ✔ Debit Work in Process Inventory for the materials, labor, and overhead charged to the job cost sheets.
- ✔ Credit the accounts that were debited when the manufacturing costs were accumulated.

Related exercise material: **BE15-3, BE15-4, BE15-5, E15-2, E15-7, E15-8,** and **DO IT! 15-2.**

LEARNING OBJECTIVE 3 Demonstrate how to determine and use the predetermined overhead rate.

Companies charge the actual costs of direct materials and direct labor to specific jobs. In contrast, manufacturing **overhead** relates to production operations **as a whole**. As a result, overhead costs cannot be assigned to specific jobs on the basis of actual costs incurred. Instead, companies assign manufacturing overhead to work in process and to specific jobs **on an estimated basis through the use of a predetermined overhead rate**.

The **predetermined overhead rate** is based on the relationship between estimated annual overhead costs and expected annual operating activity, expressed in terms of a common **activity base**. The company may state the activity in terms of direct labor costs, direct labor hours, machine hours, or any other measure that will provide an equitable basis for applying overhead costs to jobs. Companies establish the predetermined overhead rate at the beginning of the year. Small companies often use a single, company-wide predetermined overhead rate. Large companies often use rates that vary from department to department. The formula for a predetermined overhead rate is as follows.

Estimated Annual Overhead Costs	÷	Expected Annual Operating Activity	=	Predetermined Overhead Rate

ILLUSTRATION 15-9
Formula for predetermined overhead rate

Overhead relates to production operations as a whole. To know what "the whole" is, the logical thing is to wait until the end of the year's operations. At that time, the company knows all of its costs for the period. As a practical matter, though, managers cannot wait until the end of the year. To price products effectively as they are completed, managers need information about product costs of specific jobs completed during the year. Using a predetermined overhead rate enables a cost to be determined for the job immediately. Illustration 15-10 indicates how manufacturing overhead is assigned to work in process.

ILLUSTRATION 15-10
Using predetermined overhead rates

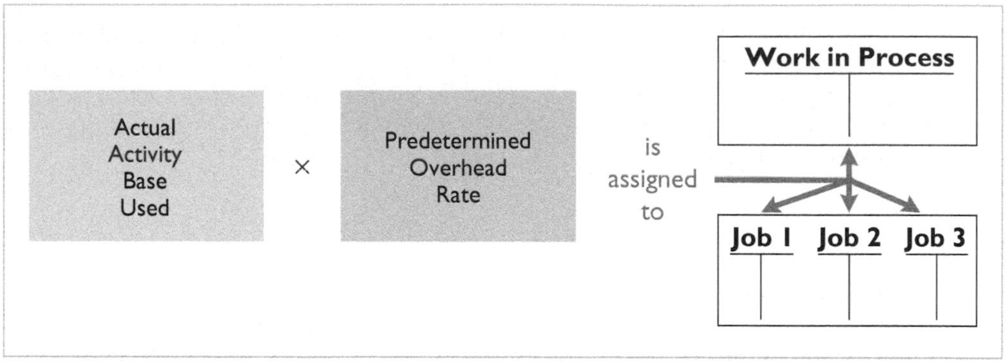

Wallace Company uses direct labor cost as the activity base. Assuming that the company expects annual overhead costs to be $280,000 and direct labor costs for the year to be $350,000, the overhead rate is 80%, computed as follows.

ILLUSTRATION 15-11
Calculation of predetermined overhead rate

Estimated Annual Overhead Costs	÷	Expected Direct Labor Cost	=	Predetermined Overhead Rate
$280,000	÷	$350,000	=	80%

This means that for every dollar of direct labor, Wallace will assign 80 cents of manufacturing overhead to a job. The use of a predetermined overhead rate enables the company to determine the approximate total cost of each job **when it completes the job**.

Historically, companies used direct labor costs or direct labor hours as the activity base. The reason was the relatively high correlation between direct labor and manufacturing overhead. Today, more companies are using **machine hours as the activity base, due to increased reliance on automation in manufacturing operations**. Or, as mentioned in Chapter 14 (and discussed more fully in Chapter 17), many companies now use activity-based costing to more accurately allocate overhead costs based on the activities that give rise to the costs.

A company may use more than one activity base. For example, if a job is manufactured in more than one factory department, each department may have its own overhead rate. In the Feature Story, Disney might use two bases in assigning overhead to film jobs: direct materials dollars for indirect materials, and direct labor hours for such costs as insurance and supervisor salaries.

Wallace Company applies manufacturing overhead to work in process when it assigns direct labor costs. It also applies manufacturing overhead to specific jobs at the same time. For January, Wallace applied overhead of $22,400 in response to its assignment of $28,000 of direct labor costs (direct labor cost of $28,000 × 80%). The following entry records this application.

(6)

Jan. 31	Work in Process Inventory	22,400	
	Manufacturing Overhead		22,400
	(To assign overhead to jobs)		

This entry reduces the balance in Manufacturing Overhead and increases Work in Process Inventory by $22,400, as shown below.

Manufacturing Overhead		Work in Process Inventory	
13,800	22,400	24,000	
6,000		28,000	
4,000		22,400	

The overhead that Wallace applies to each job will be 80% of the direct labor cost of the job for the month. Illustration 15-12 shows the Work in Process Inventory account and the job cost sheets after posting. Note that the debit of $22,400 to Work in Process Inventory equals the sum of the overhead applied to jobs: Job No. 101 $12,000 + Job No. 102 $7,200 + Job No. 103 $3,200.

ILLUSTRATION 15-12
Job cost sheets–manufacturing overhead applied

GENERAL LEDGER

Work in Process Inventory

1/31	24,000	
1/31	28,000	
1/31	22,400	

$22,400 assigned to specific jobs

Source documents for posting to job cost sheets: Predetermined overhead rate (80% of direct labor cost)

SUBSIDIARY LEDGER
Job Cost Sheets

Job No. 101 — Quantity 1,000 Units

Date	Direct Materials	Direct Labor	Manufacturing Overhead	Total
1/6	1,000			
1/10		9,000	7,200	
1/12	7,000			
1/26	4,000			
1/31		6,000	4,800	
	12,000	15,000	12,000	39,000

Job No. 102 — Quantity 1,500 Units

Date	Direct Materials	Direct Labor	Manufacturing Overhead	Total
1/10	3,800			
1/15		4,000	3,200	
1/17	3,200			
1/22		5,000	4,000	
	7,000	9,000	7,200	23,200

Job No. 103 — Quantity 2,000 Units

Date	Direct Materials	Direct Labor	Manufacturing Overhead	Total
1/27	5,000			
1/29		4,000	3,200	
	5,000	4,000	3,200	12,200

At the end of each month, the **balance in Work in Process Inventory should equal the sum of the costs shown on the job cost sheets of unfinished jobs.** Illustration 15-13 presents proof of the agreement of the control and subsidiary accounts in Wallace. (It assumes that all jobs are still in process.)

ILLUSTRATION 15-13
Proof of job cost sheets to work in process inventory

Work in Process Inventory			Job Cost Sheets	
Jan. 31	24,000		No. 101	$ 39,000
31	28,000		102	23,200
31	22,400		103	12,200
	74,400			$74,400

DO IT! 3 Predetermined Overhead Rate

Action Plan

✔ Predetermined overhead rate is estimated annual overhead cost divided by expected annual operating activity.

✔ Assignment of overhead to jobs is determined by multiplying the actual activity base used by the predetermined overhead rate.

✔ The entry to record the assignment of overhead transfers an amount out of Manufacturing Overhead into Work in Process Inventory.

Stanley Company produces specialized safety devices. For the year, manufacturing overhead costs are expected to be $160,000. Expected machine usage is 40,000 hours. The company assigns overhead based on machine hours. Job No. 302 used 2,000 machine hours.

Compute the predetermined overhead rate, determine the amount of overhead to allocate to Job No. 302, and prepare the entry to assign overhead to Job No. 302 on March 31.

SOLUTION

Predetermined overhead rate = $160,000 ÷ 40,000 hours = $4.00 per machine hour

Amount of overhead assigned to Job No. 302 = 2,000 hours × $4.00 = $8,000

The entry to record the assignment of overhead to Job No. 302 on March 31 is:

Work in Process Inventory	8,000	
Manufacturing Overhead		8,000
(To assign overhead to jobs)		

Related exercise material: **BE15-6, BE15-7, E15-5, E15-6,** and **DO IT! 15-3.**

LEARNING OBJECTIVE 4 Prepare entries for manufacturing and service jobs completed and sold.

ASSIGNING COSTS TO FINISHED GOODS

When a job is completed, Wallace Company summarizes the costs and completes the lower portion of the applicable job cost sheet. For example, if we assume that Wallace completes Job No. 101, a batch of electronic sensors, on January 31, the job cost sheet appears as shown in Illustration 15-14.

ILLUSTRATION 15-14
Completed job cost sheet

Job Cost Sheet

Job No. 101 — Quantity 1,000
Item Electronic Sensors — Date Requested January 5
For Tanner Company — Date Completed January 31

Date	Direct Materials	Direct Labor	Manufacturing Overhead
1/6	$ 1,000		
1/10		$ 9,000	$ 7,200
1/12	7,000		
1/26	4,000		
1/31		6,000	4,800
	$12,000	$15,000	$12,000

Cost of completed job	
Direct materials	$ 12,000
Direct labor	15,000
Manufacturing overhead	12,000
Total cost	$ 39,000
Unit cost ($39,000 ÷ 1,000)	$ 39.00

When a job is finished, Wallace makes an entry to transfer its total cost to finished goods inventory. The entry is as follows.

(7)

Jan. 31	Finished Goods Inventory	39,000	
	Work in Process Inventory		39,000
	(To record completion of Job No. 101)		

This entry increases Finished Goods Inventory and reduces Work in Process Inventory by $39,000, as shown in the T-accounts below.

Work in Process Inventory			Finished Goods Inventory	
24,000	39,000	→	39,000	
28,000				
22,400				

Finished Goods Inventory is a control account. It controls individual finished goods records in a finished goods subsidiary ledger.

ASSIGNING COSTS TO COST OF GOODS SOLD

Companies recognize cost of goods sold when each sale occurs. To illustrate the entries a company makes when it sells a completed job, assume that on January 31 Wallace Company sells on account Job No. 101. The job cost $39,000, and it sold for $50,000. The entries to record the sale and recognize cost of goods sold are:

(8)

Jan. 31	Accounts Receivable	50,000	
	Sales Revenue		50,000
	(To record sale of Job No. 101)		
31	Cost of Goods Sold	39,000	
	Finished Goods Inventory		39,000
	(To record cost of Job No. 101)		

This entry increases Cost of Goods Sold and reduces Finished Goods Inventory by $39,000, as shown in the T-accounts below.

Finished Goods Inventory			Cost of Goods Sold	
39,000	39,000	→	39,000	

SUMMARY OF JOB ORDER COST FLOWS

Illustration 15-15 (page 762) shows a completed flowchart for a job order cost accounting system. All postings are keyed to entries 1–8 in the example presented in the previous pages for Wallace Company.

The cost flows in the diagram can be categorized as one of four types:

- **Accumulation.** The company first accumulates costs by (1) purchasing raw materials, (2) incurring labor costs, and (3) incurring manufacturing overhead costs.
- **Assignment to jobs.** Once the company has incurred manufacturing costs, it must assign them to specific jobs. For example, as it uses raw materials on specific jobs (4), the company assigns them to work in process or treats them as manufacturing overhead if the raw materials cannot be associated with a specific job. Similarly, the company either assigns factory labor (5) to work in process or treats it as manufacturing overhead if the factory labor cannot be associated with a specific job. Finally the company assigns manufacturing

overhead (6) to work in process using a *predetermined overhead rate*. This deserves emphasis: **Do not assign overhead using actual overhead costs but instead use a predetermined rate.**

- **Completed jobs.** As jobs are completed (7), the company transfers the cost of the completed job out of work in process inventory into finished goods inventory.
- **When goods are sold.** As specific items are sold (8), the company transfers their cost out of finished goods inventory into cost of goods sold.

ILLUSTRATION 15-15
Flow of costs in a job order cost system

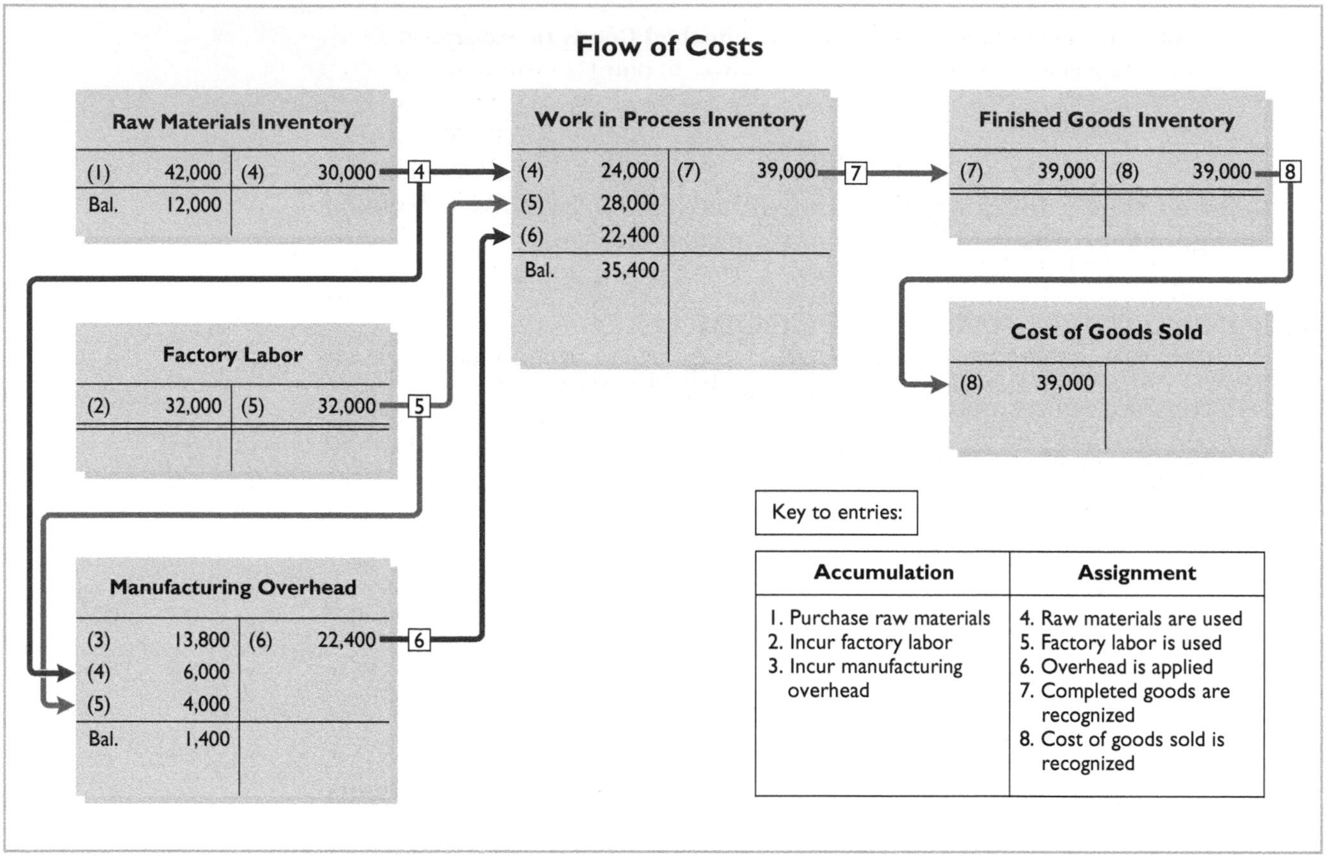

ILLUSTRATION 15-16
Flow of documents in a job order cost system

Illustration 15-16 summarizes the flow of documents in a job order cost system.

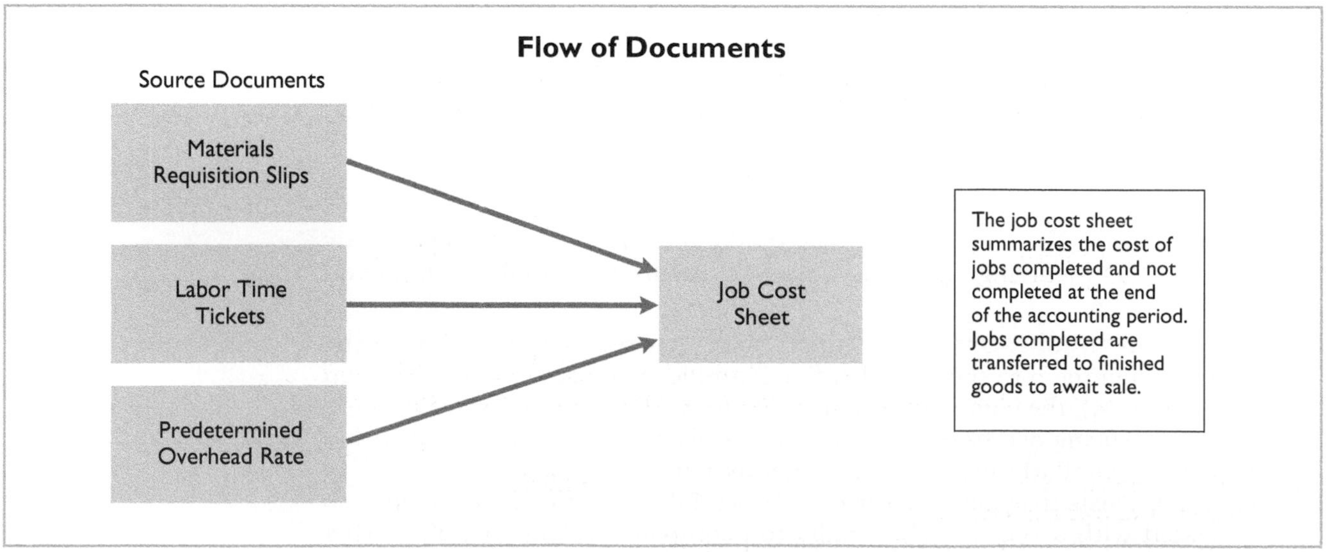

JOB ORDER COSTING FOR SERVICE COMPANIES

Our extended job order costing example focuses on a manufacturer so that you see the flow of costs through the inventory accounts. It is important to understand, however, that job order costing is also commonly used by service companies. While service companies do not have inventory, the techniques of job order costing are still quite useful in many service-industry environments. Consider, for example, the Mayo Clinic (healthcare), PriceWaterhouseCoopers (accounting), and Goldman Sachs (investment banking). These companies need to keep track of the cost of jobs performed for specific customers to evaluate the profitability of medical treatments, audits, or investment banking engagements.

Many service organizations bill their customers using cost-plus contracts. Cost-plus contracts mean that the customer's bill is the sum of the costs incurred on the job, plus a profit amount that is calculated as a percentage of the costs incurred. In order to minimize conflict with customers and reduce potential contract disputes, service companies that use cost-plus contracts must maintain accurate and up-to-date costing records. Up-to-date cost records enable a service company to immediately notify a customer of cost overruns due to customer requests for changes to the original plan or unexpected complications. Timely recordkeeping allows the contractor and customer to consider alternatives before it is too late.

A service company that uses a job order cost system does not have inventory accounts. It does, however, use an account similar to Work in Process Inventory, referred to here as Service Contracts in Process, to record job costs prior to completion. To illustrate the journal entries for a service company under a job order cost system, consider the following transactions for Dorm Decor, an interior design company. The entry to record the assignment of $9,000 of supplies to projects ($7,000 direct and $2,000 indirect) is:

Service Contracts in Process	7,000	
Operating Overhead	2,000	
Supplies		9,000
(To assign supplies to projects)		

The entry to record the assignment of service salaries and wages of $100,000 ($84,000 direct and $16,000 indirect) is:

Service Contracts in Process	84,000	
Operating Overhead	16,000	
Service Salaries and Wages		100,000
(To assign personnel costs to projects)		

Dorm Decor applies operating overhead at a rate of 50% of direct labor costs. The entry to record the application of overhead ($84,000 × 50%) based on the direct labor costs is:

Service Contracts in Process	42,000	
Operating Overhead		42,000
(To assign operating overhead to projects)		

Upon completion of a design project (for State University) the job cost sheet shows a total cost of $34,000. The entry to record completion of this project is:

Cost of Completed Service Contracts	34,000	
Service Contracts in Process		34,000
(To record completion of State University project)		

Job cost sheets for a service company keep track of materials, labor, and overhead used on a particular job similar to a manufacturer. Several exercises at the end of this chapter apply job order costing to service companies.

SERVICE COMPANY INSIGHT General Electric

© Christian Lagereek/iStockphoto

Sales Are Nice, but Service Revenue Pays the Bills

Jet engines are one of the many products made by the industrial operations division of General Electric (GE). At prices as high as $30 million per engine, you can bet that GE does its best to keep track of costs. It might surprise you that GE doesn't make much profit on the sale of each engine. So why does it bother making them? For the service revenue. During one recent year, about 75% of the division's revenues came from servicing its own products. One estimate is that the $13 billion in aircraft engines sold during a recent three-year period will generate about $90 billion in service revenue over the 30-year life of the engines. Because of the high product costs, both the engines themselves and the subsequent service are most likely accounted for using job order costing. Accurate service cost records are important because GE needs to generate high profit margins on its service jobs to make up for the low margins on the original sale. It also needs good cost records for its service jobs in order to control its costs. Otherwise, a competitor, such as Pratt and Whitney, might submit lower bids for service contracts and take lucrative service jobs away from GE.

Source: Paul Glader, "GE's Focus on Services Faces Test," *Wall Street Journal Online* (March 3, 2009).

Explain why GE would use job order costing to keep track of the cost of repairing a malfunctioning engine for a major airline. (Go to **WileyPLUS** for this answer and additional questions.)

ADVANTAGES AND DISADVANTAGES OF JOB ORDER COSTING

Job order costing is more precise in the assignment of costs to projects than process costing. For example, assume that a construction company, Juan Company, builds 10 custom homes a year at a total cost of $2,000,000. One way to determine the cost of the homes is to divide the total construction cost incurred during the year by the number of homes produced during the year. For Juan Company, an average cost of $200,000 ($2,000,000 ÷ 10) is computed. If the homes are nearly identical, then this approach is adequate for purposes of determining profit per home. But if the homes vary in terms of size, style, and material types, using the average cost of $200,000 to determine profit per home is inappropriate. Instead, Juan Company should use a job order cost system to determine the specific cost incurred to build each home and the amount of profit made on each. Thus, job order costing provides more useful information for determining the profitability of particular projects and for estimating costs when preparing bids on future jobs.

However, job order costing requires a significant amount of data entry. For Juan Company, it is much easier to simply keep track of total costs incurred during the year than it is to keep track of the costs incurred on each job (home built). Recording this information is time-consuming, and if the data is not entered accurately, then the product costs are incorrect. In recent years, technological advances, such as bar-coding devices for both labor costs and materials, have increased the accuracy and reduced the effort needed to record costs on specific jobs. These innovations expand the opportunities to apply job order costing in a wider variety of business settings, thus improving management's ability to control costs and make better informed decisions.

A common problem of all costing systems is how to allocate overhead to the finished product. Overhead often represents more than 50% of a product's cost, and this cost is often difficult to allocate meaningfully to the product. How, for example, is the salary of a project manager at Juan Company allocated to the various homes, which may differ in size, style, and cost of materials used? The accuracy of the job order cost system is largely dependent on the accuracy of the overhead allocation process. Even if the company does a good job of keeping track of the specific amounts of materials and labor used on each job, if the overhead costs are not allocated to individual jobs in a meaningful way, the product costing information is not useful. We address this issue in more detail in Chapter 17.

DO IT! 4 Completion and Sale of Jobs

During the current month, Onyx Corporation completed Job 109 and Job 112. Job 109 cost $19,000 and Job 112 cost $27,000. Job 112 was sold on account for $42,000. Journalize the entries for the completion of the two jobs and the sale of Job 112.

SOLUTION

Finished Goods Inventory	46,000	
Work in Process Inventory		46,000
(To record completion of Job 109, costing $19,000 and Job 112, costing $27,000)		
Accounts Receivable	42,000	
Sales Revenue		42,000
(To record sale of Job 112)		
Cost of Goods Sold	27,000	
Finished Goods Inventory		27,000
(To record cost of goods sold for Job 112)		

Action Plan

✔ **Debit Finished Goods Inventory for the cost of completed jobs.**

✔ **Debit Cost of Goods Sold for the cost of jobs sold.**

Related exercise material: **BE15-9, BE15-10, E15-2, E15-3, E15-6, E15-7, E15-10,** and **DO IT! 15-4.**

LEARNING OBJECTIVE 5 Distinguish between under- and overapplied manufacturing overhead.

At the end of a period, companies prepare financial statements that present aggregate data on all jobs manufactured and sold. The cost of goods manufactured schedule in job order costing is the same as in Chapter 14 with one exception: **The schedule shows manufacturing overhead applied, rather than actual overhead costs. The company adds this amount to direct materials and direct labor to determine total manufacturing costs.**

Companies prepare the cost of goods manufactured schedule directly from the Work in Process Inventory account. Illustration 15-17 (page 766) shows a condensed schedule for Wallace Company for January.

▼ HELPFUL HINT
Companies usually prepare monthly financial statements for management use only.

ILLUSTRATION 15-17
Cost of goods manufactured schedule

WALLACE COMPANY
Cost of Goods Manufactured Schedule
For the Month Ending January 31, 2017

Work in process, January 1		$ –0–
Direct materials used	$ 24,000	
Direct labor	28,000	
Manufacturing overhead applied	22,400	
Total manufacturing costs		74,400
Total cost of work in process		74,400
Less: Work in process, January 31		35,400
Cost of goods manufactured		$39,000

Note that the cost of goods manufactured ($39,000) agrees with the amount transferred from Work in Process Inventory to Finished Goods Inventory in journal entry No. 7 in Illustration 15-15 (page 762).

The income statement and balance sheet are the same as those illustrated in Chapter 14. For example, Illustration 15-18 shows the partial income statement for Wallace for the month of January.

ILLUSTRATION 15-18
Partial income statement

WALLACE COMPANY
Income Statement (partial)
For the Month Ending January 31, 2017

Sales revenue		$50,000
Cost of goods sold		
Finished goods inventory, January 1	$ –0–	
Cost of goods manufactured (see Illustration 15-17)	39,000	
Cost of goods available for sale	39,000	
Less: Finished goods inventory, January 31	–0–	
Cost of goods sold		39,000
Gross profit		$11,000

UNDER- OR OVERAPPLIED MANUFACTURING OVERHEAD

DECISION TOOLS

The Manufacturing Overhead account helps managers determine if overhead applied exceeded or was less than actual overhead costs.

Recall that overhead is applied based on an estimate of total annual overhead costs. This estimate will rarely be exactly equal to actual overhead incurred. Therefore, at the end of the year, after overhead has been applied to specific jobs, the Manufacturing Overhead account will likely have a remaining balance.

When Manufacturing Overhead has a **debit balance**, overhead is said to be underapplied. **Underapplied overhead** means that the overhead assigned to work in process is less than the overhead incurred. Conversely, when manufacturing overhead has a **credit balance**, overhead is overapplied. **Overapplied overhead** means that the overhead assigned to work in process is greater than the overhead incurred. Illustration 15-19 shows these concepts.

ILLUSTRATION 15-19
Under- and overapplied overhead

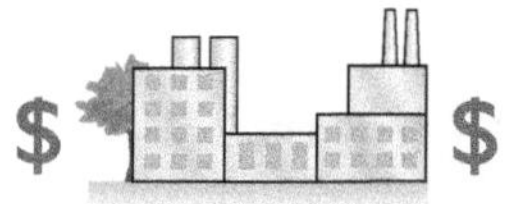

Manufacturing Overhead

Manufacturing Overhead	
Actual (Costs incurred)	Applied (Costs assigned)

If actual is **greater** than applied, manufacturing overhead is underapplied.

If actual is **less** than applied, manufacturing overhead is overapplied.

Year-End Balance

At the end of the year, all manufacturing overhead transactions are complete. There is no further opportunity for offsetting events to occur. At this point, Wallace Company eliminates any balance in Manufacturing Overhead by an adjusting entry. It considers under- or overapplied overhead to be an **adjustment to cost of goods sold**. Thus, Wallace **debits underapplied overhead to Cost of Goods Sold.** It **credits overapplied overhead to Cost of Goods Sold**.

To illustrate, assume that Wallace has a $2,500 credit balance in Manufacturing Overhead at December 31. The adjusting entry for the overapplied overhead is:

Dec. 31	Manufacturing Overhead	2,500	
	Cost of Goods Sold		2,500
	(To transfer overapplied overhead to cost of goods sold)		

After Wallace posts this entry, Manufacturing Overhead has a zero balance. In preparing an income statement for the year, Wallace reports cost of goods sold **after adjusting it** for either under- or overapplied overhead.

Conceptually, some argue that under- or overapplied overhead at the end of the year should be allocated among ending work in process, finished goods, and cost of goods sold. The discussion of this possible allocation approach is left to more advanced courses.

DO IT! ▶5 Applied Manufacturing Overhead

For Karr Company, the predetermined overhead rate is 140% of direct labor cost. During the month, Karr incurred $90,000 of factory labor costs, of which $80,000 is direct labor and $10,000 is indirect labor. Actual overhead incurred was $119,000.

Compute the amount of manufacturing overhead applied during the month. Determine the amount of under- or overapplied manufacturing overhead.

Action Plan

- ✔ Calculate the amount of overhead applied by multiplying the predetermined overhead rate by actual activity.
- ✔ If actual manufacturing overhead is greater than applied, manufacturing overhead is underapplied.
- ✔ If actual manufacturing overhead is less than applied, manufacturing overhead is overapplied.

SOLUTION

Manufacturing overhead applied = (140% × $80,000) = $112,000
Underapplied manufacturing overhead = ($119,000 − $112,000) = $7,000

Related exercise material: **BE15-10, E15-4, E15-5, E15-12, E15-13,** and **DO IT! 15-5.**

USING DECISION TOOLS—DISNEY

Disney faces many situations where it needs to apply the decision tools learned in this chapter, such as using a job cost sheet to determine a film's profitability. For example, assume Disney uses a job order cost system and applies overhead to production of its films on the basis of direct labor cost. In computing a predetermined overhead rate for the year 2017, the company estimated film production overhead to be $24 million and direct labor costs to be $20 million. In addition, it developed the following information.

Actual Costs Incurred During 2017	
Direct materials used	$30,000,000
Direct labor cost incurred	21,000,000
Insurance, studio	500,000
Indirect labor	7,500,000
Studio maintenance	1,000,000
Rent on studio building	11,000,000
Depreciation on studio equipment	2,000,000

INSTRUCTIONS

Answer each of the following.

(a) Why is Disney using a job order cost system?

(b) On what basis does Disney allocate its film production overhead? Compute the predetermined overhead rate for 2017.

(c) Compute the amount of the under- or overapplied overhead for 2017.

(d) Disney had balances in the beginning and ending films in process and finished films accounts as follows.

	1/1/17	12/31/17
Films in process	$ 5,000,000	$ 4,000,000
Finished films	13,000,000	11,000,000

Determine the (1) cost of films produced and (2) cost of films sold for Disney during 2017. Assume that any under- or overapplied overhead should be included in the cost of films sold.

(e) During 2017, Film G408 (a short documentary film produced for a customer) was started and completed. Its cost sheet showed a total cost of $100,000, and Disney prices its film at 50% above its cost. What is the price to the customer if the company follows this pricing strategy?

SOLUTION

(a) Disney is using a job order cost system because it produces films. Each film is unique, with its own distinguishing characteristics.

(b) Disney allocates its overhead on the basis of direct labor cost. The predetermined overhead rate is 120%, computed as follows: $24,000,000 ÷ 20,000,000 = 120%.

(c)

Actual film production overhead	$22,000,000*
Applied overhead cost ($21,000,000 × 120%)	25,200,000
Overapplied overhead	$ 3,200,000

*$500,000 + $7,500,000 + $1,000,000 + $11,000,000 + $2,000,000

(d) (1)

Films in process, 1/1/17		$ 5,000,000
Direct materials used	$30,000,000	
Direct labor	21,000,000	
Film production overhead applied	25,200,000	
Total film production costs		76,200,000
Total cost of films in process		81,200,000
Less: Films in process, 12/31/17		4,000,000
Cost of films produced		$77,200,000

(2)

Finished films, 1/1/17	$13,000,000
Cost of films produced (see above)	77,200,000
Cost of films available for sale	90,200,000
Finished films, 12/31/17	11,000,000
Cost of films sold (unadjusted)	79,200,000
Less: Overapplied overhead	3,200,000
Cost of films sold	$76,000,000

(e)

Film G408 cost	$ 100,000
Markup percentage	× 50%
Markup	$ 50,000

Price to customer: $150,000 ($100,000 + $50,000)

REVIEW AND PRACTICE

LEARNING OBJECTIVES REVIEW

1 Describe cost systems and the flow of costs in a job order system. Cost accounting involves the procedures for measuring, recording, and reporting product costs. From the data accumulated, companies determine the total cost and the unit cost of each product. The two basic types of cost accounting systems are process cost and job order cost.

In job order costing, companies first accumulate manufacturing costs in three accounts: Raw Materials Inventory, Factory Labor, and Manufacturing Overhead. They then assign the accumulated costs to Work in Process Inventory and eventually to Finished Goods Inventory and Cost of Goods Sold.

2 Use a job cost sheet to assign costs to work in process. A job cost sheet is a form used to record the costs chargeable to a specific job and to determine the total and unit costs of the completed job. Job cost sheets constitute the subsidiary ledger for the Work in Process Inventory control account.

3 Demonstrate how to determine and use the predetermined overhead rate. The predetermined overhead rate is based on the relationship between estimated annual overhead costs and expected annual operating activity. This is expressed in terms of a common activity base, such as direct labor cost. Companies use this rate to assign overhead costs to work in process and to specific jobs.

4 Prepare entries for manufacturing and service jobs completed and sold. When jobs are completed, companies debit the cost to Finished Goods Inventory and credit it to Work in Process Inventory. When a job is sold, the entries are (a) debit Cash or Accounts Receivable and credit Sales Revenue for the selling price, and (b) debit Cost of Goods Sold and credit Finished Goods Inventory for the cost of the goods.

5 Distinguish between under- and overapplied manufacturing overhead. Underapplied manufacturing overhead indicates that the overhead assigned to work in process is less than the overhead incurred. Overapplied overhead indicates that the overhead assigned to work in process is greater than the overhead incurred.

DECISION TOOLS REVIEW

DECISION CHECKPOINTS	INFO NEEDED FOR DECISION	TOOL TO USE FOR DECISION	HOW TO EVALUATE RESULTS
What is the cost of a job?	Cost of material, labor, and overhead assigned to a specific job	Job cost sheet	Compare costs to those of previous periods and to those of competitors to ensure that costs are in line. Compare costs to expected selling price or service fees charged to determine overall profitability.
Has the company over- or underapplied overhead for the period?	Actual overhead costs and overhead applied	Manufacturing Overhead account	If the account balance is a credit, overhead applied exceeded actual overhead costs. If the account balance is a debit, overhead applied was less than actual overhead costs.

GLOSSARY REVIEW

Cost accounting An area of accounting that involves measuring, recording, and reporting product costs. (p. 748).

Cost accounting system Manufacturing-cost accounts that are fully integrated into the general ledger of a company. (p. 748).

Job cost sheet A form used to record the costs chargeable to a specific job and to determine the total and unit costs of the completed job. (p. 752).

Job order cost system A cost accounting system in which costs are assigned to each job or batch. (p. 748).

Materials requisition slip A document authorizing the issuance of raw materials from the storeroom to production. (p. 753).

Overapplied overhead A situation in which overhead assigned to work in process is greater than the overhead incurred. (p. 766).

Predetermined overhead rate A rate based on the relationship between estimated annual overhead costs and expected annual operating activity, expressed in terms of a common activity base. (p. 757).

Process cost system A cost accounting system used when a company manufactures a large volume of similar products. (p. 748).

Time ticket A document that indicates the employee, the hours worked, the account and job to be charged, and the total labor cost. (p. 755).

Underapplied overhead A situation in which overhead assigned to work in process is less than the overhead incurred. (p. 766).

PRACTICE MULTIPLE-CHOICE QUESTIONS

(LO 1) **1.** Cost accounting involves the measuring, recording, and reporting of:
(a) product costs.
(b) future costs.
(c) manufacturing processes.
(d) managerial accounting decisions.

(LO 1) **2.** A company is more likely to use a job order cost system if:
(a) it manufactures a large volume of similar products.
(b) its production is continuous.
(c) it manufactures products with unique characteristics.
(d) it uses a periodic inventory system.

(LO 1) **3.** In accumulating raw materials costs, companies debit the cost of raw materials purchased in a perpetual system to:
(a) Raw Materials Purchases.
(b) Raw Materials Inventory.
(c) Purchases.
(d) Work in Process.

(LO 1) **4.** When incurred, factory labor costs are debited to:
(a) Work in Process.
(b) Factory Wages Expense.
(c) Factory Labor.
(d) Factory Wages Payable.

(LO 1) **5.** The flow of costs in job order costing:
(a) begins with work in process inventory and ends with finished goods inventory.
(b) begins as soon as a sale occurs.
(c) parallels the physical flow of materials as they are converted into finished goods.
(d) is necessary to prepare the cost of goods manufactured schedule.

(LO 2) **6.** Raw materials are assigned to a job when:
(a) the job is sold.
(b) the materials are purchased.
(c) the materials are received from the vendor.
(d) the materials are issued by the materials storeroom.

(LO 2) **7.** The source of information for assigning costs to job cost sheets are:
(a) invoices, time tickets, and the predetermined overhead rate.
(b) materials requisition slips, time tickets, and the actual overhead costs.
(c) materials requisition slips, payroll register, and the predetermined overhead rate.
(d) materials requisition slips, time tickets, and the predetermined overhead rate.

8. In recording the issuance of raw materials in a job order cost system, it would be **incorrect** to: (LO 2)
(a) debit Work in Process Inventory.
(b) debit Finished Goods Inventory.
(c) debit Manufacturing Overhead.
(d) credit Raw Materials Inventory.

9. The entry when direct factory labor is assigned to jobs is a debit to: (LO 2)
(a) Work in Process Inventory and a credit to Factory Labor.
(b) Manufacturing Overhead and a credit to Factory Labor.
(c) Factory Labor and a credit to Manufacturing Overhead.
(d) Factory Labor and a credit to Work in Process Inventory.

10. The formula for computing the predetermined manufacturing overhead rate is estimated annual overhead costs divided by an expected annual operating activity, expressed as: (LO 3)
(a) direct labor cost.
(b) direct labor hours.
(c) machine hours.
(d) Any of the above.

11. In Crawford Company, the predetermined overhead rate is 80% of direct labor cost. During the month, Crawford incurs $210,000 of factory labor costs, of which $180,000 is direct labor and $30,000 is indirect labor. Actual overhead incurred was $200,000. The amount of overhead debited to Work in Process Inventory should be: (LO 3)
(a) $200,000.
(b) $144,000.
(c) $168,000.
(d) $160,000.

12. Mynex Company completes Job No. 26 at a cost of $4,500 and later sells it for $7,000 cash. A **correct** entry is: (LO 4)
(a) debit Finished Goods Inventory $7,000 and credit Work in Process Inventory $7,000.
(b) debit Cost of Goods Sold $7,000 and credit Finished Goods Inventory $7,000.

(c) debit Finished Goods Inventory $4,500 and credit Work in Process Inventory $4,500.
(d) debit Accounts Receivable $7,000 and credit Sales Revenue $7,000.

(LO 5) **13.** At the end of an accounting period, a company using a job order cost system calculates the cost of goods manufactured:
(a) from the job cost sheet.
(b) from the Work in Process Inventory account.
(c) by adding direct materials used, direct labor incurred, and manufacturing overhead incurred.
(d) from the Cost of Goods Sold account.

(LO 4) **14.** Which of the following statements is **true**?
(a) Job order costing requires less data entry than process costing.
(b) Allocation of overhead is easier under job order costing than process costing.
(c) Job order costing provides more precise costing for custom jobs than process costing.
(d) The use of job order costing has declined because more companies have adopted automated accounting systems.

15. At end of the year, a company has a $1,200 debit balance in Manufacturing Overhead. The company: (LO 5)
(a) makes an adjusting entry by debiting Manufacturing Overhead Applied for $1,200 and crediting Manufacturing Overhead for $1,200.
(b) makes an adjusting entry by debiting Manufacturing Overhead Expense for $1,200 and crediting Manufacturing Overhead for $1,200.
(c) makes an adjusting entry by debiting Cost of Goods Sold for $1,200 and crediting Manufacturing Overhead for $1,200.
(d) makes no adjusting entry because differences between actual overhead and the amount applied are a normal part of job order costing and will average out over the next year.

16. Manufacturing overhead is underapplied if: (LO 5)
(a) actual overhead is less than applied.
(b) actual overhead is greater than applied.
(c) the predetermined rate equals the actual rate.
(d) actual overhead equals applied overhead.

SOLUTIONS

1. **(a)** Cost accounting involves the measuring, recording, and reporting of product costs, not (b) future costs, (c) manufacturing processes, or (d) managerial accounting decisions.
2. **(c)** A job costing system is more likely for products with unique characteristics. The other choices are incorrect because a process cost system is more likely for (a) large volumes of similar products or (b) if production is continuous. (d) is incorrect because the choice of a costing system is not dependent on whether a periodic or perpetual inventory system is used.
3. **(b)** In a perpetual system, purchases of raw materials are debited to Raw Materials Inventory, not (a) Raw Materials Purchases, (c) Purchases, or (d) Work in Process.
4. **(c)** When factory labor costs are incurred, they are debited to Factory Labor, not (a) Work in Process, (b) Factory Wages Expense, or (d) Factory Wages Payable (they are debited to Factory Labor and credited to Factory Wages Payable).
5. **(c)** Job order costing parallels the physical flow of materials as they are converted into finished goods. The other choices are incorrect because job order costing begins (a) with raw materials, not work in process, and ends with finished goods; and (b) as soon as raw materials are purchased, not when the sale occurs. (d) is incorrect because the cost of goods manufactured schedule is prepared from the Work in Process account and is only a portion of the costs in a job order system.
6. **(d)** Raw materials are assigned to a job when the materials are issued by the materials storeroom, not when (a) the job is sold, (b) the materials are purchased, or (c) the materials are received from the vendor.
7. **(d)** Materials requisition slips are used to assign direct materials, time tickets are used to assign direct labor, and the predetermined overhead rate is used to assign manufacturing overhead to job cost sheets. The other choices are incorrect because (a) materials requisition slips, not invoices, are used to assign direct materials; (b) the predetermined overhead rate, not the actual overhead costs, is used to assign manufacturing overhead; and (c) time tickets, not the payroll register, are used to assign direct labor.
8. **(b)** Finished Goods Inventory is debited when goods are transferred from work in process to finished goods, not when raw materials are issued for a job. Choices (a), (c), and (d) are true statements.
9. **(a)** When direct factory labor is assigned to jobs, the entry is a debit to Work in Process Inventory and a credit to Factory Labor. The other choices are incorrect because (b) Work in Process Inventory, not Manufacturing Overhead, is debited; (c) Work in Process Inventory, not Factory Labor, is debited and Factory Labor, not Manufacturing Overhead, is credited; and (d) Work in Process Inventory, not Factory Labor, is debited and Factory Labor, not Work in Process Inventory, is credited.
10. **(d)** Any of the activity measures mentioned can be used in computing the predetermined manufacturing overhead rate. Choices (a) direct labor cost, (b) direct labor hours, and (c) machine hours can all be used in computing the predetermined manufacturing overhead rate, but (d) is a better answer.
11. **(b)** Work in Process Inventory should be debited for $144,000 ($180,000 × 80%), the amount of manufacturing overhead applied, not (a) $200,000, (c) $168,000, or (d) $160,000.
12. **(c)** When a job costing $4,500 is completed, Finished Goods Inventory is debited and Work in Process Inventory is credited for $4,500. Choices (a) and (b) are incorrect because the amounts should be for the cost of the job ($4,500), not the sale amount ($7,000). Choice (d) is incorrect because the debit should be to Cash, not Accounts Receivable.

13. **(b)** At the end of an accounting period, a company using a job costing system prepares the cost of goods manufactured from the Work in Process Inventory account, not (a) the job cost sheet; (c) by adding direct materials used, direct labor incurred, and manufacturing overhead incurred; or (d) from the Cost of Goods Sold Account.
14. **(c)** Job order costing provides more precise costing for custom jobs than process costing. The other choices are incorrect because (a) job order costing often requires significant data entry, (b) overhead allocation is a problem for all costing systems, and (d) the use of job order costing has increased due to automated accounting systems.
15. **(c)** The company would make an adjusting entry for the underapplied overhead by debiting Cost of Goods Sold for $1,200 and crediting Manufacturing Overhead for $1,200, not by debiting (a) Manufacturing Overhead Applied for $1,200 or (b) Manufacturing Overhead Expense for $1,200. Choice (d) is incorrect because at the end of the year, a company makes an entry to eliminate any balance in Manufacturing Overhead.
16. **(b)** Manufacturing overhead is underapplied if actual overhead is greater than applied overhead. The other choices are incorrect because (a) if actual overhead is less than applied, then manufacturing overhead is overapplied; (c) if the predetermined rate equals the actual rate, the actual overhead costs incurred equal the overhead costs applied, neither over- nor underapplied; and (d) if the actual overhead equals the applied overhead, neither over- nor underapplied occurs.

PRACTICE EXERCISES

Analyze a job cost sheet and prepare entries for manufacturing costs.

(LO 1, 2, 3, 4)

1. A job order cost sheet for Michaels Company is shown below.

Job No. 92			**For 2,000 Units**
Date	Direct Materials	Direct Labor	Manufacturing Overhead
Beg. bal. Jan. 1	3,925	6,000	4,200
8	6,000		
12		8,500	6,375
25	2,000		
27		4,000	3,000
	11,925	18,500	13,575

Cost of completed job:	
Direct materials	$11,925
Direct labor	18,500
Manufacturing overhead	13,575
Total cost	$44,000
Unit cost ($44,000 ÷ 2,000)	$ 22.00

INSTRUCTIONS

(a) Answer the following questions.

(1) What was the balance in Work in Process Inventory on January 1 if this was the only unfinished job?

(2) If manufacturing overhead is applied on the basis of direct labor cost, what overhead rate was used in each year?

(b) Prepare summary entries at January 31 to record the current year's transactions pertaining to Job No. 92.

SOLUTION

1. (a) 1. $14,125, or ($3,925 + $6,000 + $4,200).
2. Last year 70%, or ($4,200 ÷ $6,000); this year 75% (either $6,375 ÷ $8,500 or $3,000 ÷ $4,000).

(b) Jan. 31	Work in Process Inventory Raw Materials Inventory ($6,000 + $2,000)	8,000	 8,000
31	Work in Process Inventory Factory Labor ($8,500 + $4,000)	12,500	 12,500
31	Work in Process Inventory Manufacturing Overhead ($6,375 + $3,000)	9,375	 9,375
31	Finished Goods Inventory Work in Process Inventory	44,000	 44,000

2. Kwik Kopy Company applies operating overhead to photocopying jobs on the basis of machine hours used. Overhead costs are expected to total $290,000 for the year, and machine usage is estimated at 125,000 hours.

Compute the overhead rate and under- or overapplied overhead.

(LO 3, 5)

For the year, $295,000 of overhead costs are incurred and 130,000 hours are used.

INSTRUCTIONS

(a) Compute the service overhead rate for the year.

(b) What is the amount of under- or overapplied overhead at December 31?

(c) Assuming the under- or overapplied overhead for the year is not allocated to inventory accounts, prepare the adjusting entry to assign the amount to cost of jobs finished.

SOLUTION

2. (a) $2.32 per machine hour ($290,000 ÷ 125,000).

(b) ($295,000) – ($2.32 × 130,000 machine hours)
$295,000 – $301,600 = $6,600 overapplied

(c) Operating Overhead	6,600	
Cost of Goods Sold		6,600

PRACTICE PROBLEM

Cardella Company applies overhead on the basis of direct labor costs. The company estimates annual overhead costs will be $760,000 and annual direct labor costs will be $950,000. During February, Cardella works on two jobs: A16 and B17. Summary data concerning these jobs are as follows.

Compute predetermined overhead rate, apply overhead, and calculate under- or overapplied overhead.

(LO 3, 5)

Manufacturing Costs Incurred

Purchased $54,000 of raw materials on account.
Factory labor $76,000, plus $4,000 employer payroll taxes.
Manufacturing overhead exclusive of indirect materials and indirect labor $59,800.

Assignment of Costs

Direct materials: Job A16 $27,000, Job B17 $21,000
Indirect materials: $3,000
Direct labor: Job A16 $52,000, Job B17 $26,000
Indirect labor: $2,000

The company completed Job A16 and sold it on account for $150,000. Job B17 was only partially completed.

INSTRUCTIONS

(a) Compute the predetermined overhead rate.
(b) Journalize the February transactions in the sequence followed in the chapter.
(c) What was the amount of under- or overapplied manufacturing overhead?

SOLUTION

(a)

Estimated annual overhead costs	÷	Expected annual operating activity	=	Predetermined overhead rate
$760,000	÷	$950,000	=	80%

(b)

Date	Account Titles and Explanation	Debit	Credit
	(1)		
Feb. 28	Raw Materials Inventory	54,000	
	Accounts Payable		54,000
	(Purchase of raw materials on account)		
	(2)		
28	Factory Labor	80,000	
	Factory Wages Payable		76,000
	Employer Payroll Taxes Payable		4,000
	(To record factory labor costs)		
	(3)		
28	Manufacturing Overhead	59,800	
	Accounts Payable, Accumulated Depreciation, and Prepaid Insurance		59,800
	(To record overhead costs)		
	(4)		
28	Work in Process Inventory	48,000	
	Manufacturing Overhead	3,000	
	Raw Materials Inventory		51,000
	(To assign raw materials to production)		
	(5)		
28	Work in Process Inventory	78,000	
	Manufacturing Overhead	2,000	
	Factory Labor		80,000
	(To assign factory labor to production)		
	(6)		
28	Work in Process Inventory	62,400	
	Manufacturing Overhead		62,400
	(To assign overhead to jobs— 80% × $78,000)		
	(7)		
28	Finished Goods Inventory	120,600	
	Work in Process Inventory		120,600
	(To record completion of Job A16: direct materials $27,000, direct labor $52,000, and manufacturing overhead $41,600)		
	(8)		
28	Accounts Receivable	150,000	
	Sales Revenue		150,000
	(To record sale of Job A16)		
28	Cost of Goods Sold	120,600	
	Finished Goods Inventory		120,600
	(To record cost of sale for Job A16)		

(c) Manufacturing Overhead has a debit balance of $2,400 as shown below.

Manufacturing Overhead

(3)	59,800	(6)	62,400
(4)	3,000		
(5)	2,000		
Bal.	2,400		

Thus, manufacturing overhead is underapplied for the month.

WileyPLUS Brief Exercises, DO IT! Exercises, Exercises, Problems, and many additional resources are available for practice in WileyPLUS.

QUESTIONS

1. (a) Mary Barett is not sure about the difference between cost accounting and a cost accounting system. Explain the difference to Mary.
   (b) What is an important feature of a cost accounting system?
2. (a) Distinguish between the two types of cost accounting systems.
   (b) Can a company use both types of cost accounting systems?
3. What type of industry is likely to use a job order cost system? Give some examples.
4. What type of industry is likely to use a process cost system? Give some examples.
5. Your roommate asks your help in understanding the major steps in the flow of costs in a job order cost system. Identify the steps for your roommate.
6. There are three inventory control accounts in a job order system. Identify the control accounts and their subsidiary ledgers.
7. What source documents are used in accumulating direct labor costs?
8. "Entries to Manufacturing Overhead normally are only made daily." Do you agree? Explain.
9. Stan Kaiser is confused about the source documents used in assigning materials and labor costs. Identify the documents and give the entry for each document.
10. What is the purpose of a job cost sheet?
11. Indicate the source documents that are used in charging costs to specific jobs.
12. Explain the purpose and use of a "materials requisition slip" as used in a job order cost system.
13. Sam Bowden believes actual manufacturing overhead should be charged to jobs. Do you agree? Why or why not?
14. What elements are involved in computing a predetermined overhead rate?
15. How can the agreement of Work in Process Inventory and job cost sheets be verified?
16. Jane Neff believes that the cost of goods manufactured schedule in job order cost accounting is the same as shown in Chapter 14. Is Jane correct? Explain.
17. Matt Litkee is confused about under- and overapplied manufacturing overhead. Define the terms for Matt, and indicate the balance in the manufacturing overhead account applicable to each term.
18. "At the end of the year, under- or overapplied overhead is closed to Income Summary." Is this correct? If not, indicate the customary treatment of this amount.

BRIEF EXERCISES

BE15-1 Dieker Company begins operations on January 1. Because all work is done to customer specifications, the company decides to use a job order cost system. Prepare a flowchart of a typical job order system with arrows showing the flow of costs. Identify the eight transactions.

Prepare a flowchart of a job order cost accounting system and identify transactions.
(LO 1), C

BE15-2 During January, its first month of operations, Dieker Company accumulated the following manufacturing costs: raw materials $4,000 on account, factory labor $6,000 of which $5,200 relates to factory wages payable and $800 relates to payroll taxes payable, and utilities payable $2,000. Prepare separate journal entries for each type of manufacturing cost.

Prepare entries in accumulating manufacturing costs.
(LO 1), AP

BE15-3 In January, Dieker Company requisitions raw materials for production as follows: Job 1 $900, Job 2 $1,200, Job 3 $700, and general factory use $600. Prepare a summary journal entry to record raw materials used.

Prepare entry for the assignment of raw materials costs.
(LO 2), AP

BE15-4 Factory labor data for Dieker Company is given in BE15-2. During January, time tickets show that the factory labor of $6,000 was used as follows: Job 1 $2,200, Job 2 $1,600, Job 3 $1,400, and general factory use $800. Prepare a summary journal entry to record factory labor used.

Prepare entry for the assignment of factory labor costs.
(LO 2), AP

BE15-5 Data pertaining to job cost sheets for Dieker Company are given in BE15-3 and BE15-4. Prepare the job cost sheets for each of the three jobs. (*Note:* You may omit the column for Manufacturing Overhead.)

Prepare job cost sheets.
(LO 2), AP

Compute predetermined overhead rates.
(LO 3), AP

BE15-6 Marquis Company estimates that annual manufacturing overhead costs will be $900,000. Estimated annual operating activity bases are direct labor cost $500,000, direct labor hours 50,000, and machine hours 100,000. Compute the predetermined overhead rate for each activity base.

Assign manufacturing overhead to production.
(LO 3), AP

BE15-7 During the first quarter, Francum Company incurs the following direct labor costs: January $40,000, February $30,000, and March $50,000. For each month, prepare the entry to assign overhead to production using a predetermined rate of 70% of direct labor cost.

Prepare entries for completion and sale of completed jobs.
(LO 4), AP

BE15-8 In March, Stinson Company completes Jobs 10 and 11. Job 10 cost $20,000 and Job 11 $30,000. On March 31, Job 10 is sold to the customer for $35,000 in cash. Journalize the entries for the completion of the two jobs and the sale of Job 10.

Prepare entries for service salaries and wages and operating overhead.
(LO 4), AP

BE15-9 Ruiz Engineering Contractors incurred service salaries and wages of $36,000 ($28,000 direct and $8,000 indirect) on an engineering project. The company applies overhead at a rate of 25% of direct labor. Record the entries to assign service salaries and wages and to apply overhead.

Prepare adjusting entries for under- and overapplied overhead.
(LO 5), C

BE15-10 At December 31, balances in Manufacturing Overhead are Shimeca Company—debit $1,200, Garcia Company—credit $900. Prepare the adjusting entry for each company at December 31, assuming the adjustment is made to cost of goods sold.

DO IT! ▶ EXERCISES

Prepare journal entries for manufacturing costs.
(LO 1), AP

DO IT! 15-1 During the current month, Wacholz Company incurs the following manufacturing costs.

(a) Purchased raw materials of $18,000 on account.
(b) Incurred factory labor of $40,000. Of that amount, $31,000 relates to wages payable and $9,000 relates to payroll taxes payable.
(c) Factory utilities of $3,100 are payable, prepaid factory property taxes of $2,700 have expired, and depreciation on the factory building is $9,500.

Prepare journal entries for each type of manufacturing cost. (Use a summary entry to record manufacturing overhead.)

Assign costs to work in process.
(LO 2), AP

DO IT! 15-2 Milner Company is working on two job orders. The job cost sheets show the following.

	Job 201	**Job 202**
Direct materials	$7,200	$9,000
Direct labor	4,000	8,000
Manufacturing overhead	5,200	9,800

Prepare the three summary entries to record the assignment of costs to Work in Process from the data on the job cost sheets.

Compute and apply the predetermined overhead rate.
(LO 3), AP

DO IT! 15-3 Washburn Company produces earbuds. During the year, manufacturing overhead costs are expected to be $200,000. Expected machine usage is 2,500 hours. The company assigns overhead based on machine hours. Job No. 551 used 90 machine hours. Compute the predetermined overhead rate, determine the amount of overhead to allocate to Job No. 551, and prepare the entry to assign overhead to Job No. 551 on January 15.

Prepare entries for completion and sale of jobs.
(LO 4), AP

DO IT! 15-4 During the current month, Standard Corporation completed Job 310 and Job 312. Job 310 cost $70,000 and Job 312 cost $50,000. Job 312 was sold on account for $90,000. Journalize the entries for the completion of the two jobs and the sale of Job 312.

Apply manufacturing overhead and determine under- or overapplication.
(LO 5), AN

DO IT! 15-5 For Eckstein Company, the predetermined overhead rate is 130% of direct labor cost. During the month, Eckstein incurred $100,000 of factory labor costs, of which $85,000 is direct labor and $15,000 is indirect labor. Actual overhead incurred was $115,000. Compute the amount of manufacturing overhead applied during the month. Determine the amount of under- or overapplied manufacturing overhead.

EXERCISES

Prepare entries for factory labor.
(LO 1, 2), AP

E15-1 The gross earnings of the factory workers for Larkin Company during the month of January are $76,000. The employer's payroll taxes for the factory payroll are $8,000. The fringe benefits to be paid by the employer on this payroll are $6,000. Of the total accumulated cost of factory labor, 85% is related to direct labor and 15% is attributable to indirect labor.

Instructions

(a) Prepare the entry to record the factory labor costs for the month of January.
(b) Prepare the entry to assign factory labor to production.

Prepare journal entries for manufacturing costs.
(LO 1, 2, 3, 4), AP

E15-2 Stine Company uses a job order cost system. On May 1, the company has a balance in Work in Process Inventory of $3,500 and two jobs in process: Job No. 429 $2,000, and Job No. 430 $1,500. During May, a summary of source documents reveals the following.

Job Number	Materials Requisition Slips		Labor Time Tickets	
429	$2,500		$1,900	
430	3,500		3,000	
431	4,400	$10,400	7,600	$12,500
General use		800		1,200
		$11,200		$13,700

Stine Company applies manufacturing overhead to jobs at an overhead rate of 60% of direct labor cost. Job No. 429 is completed during the month.

Instructions

(a) Prepare summary journal entries to record (1) the requisition slips, (2) the time tickets, (3) the assignment of manufacturing overhead to jobs, and (4) the completion of Job No. 429.
(b) Post the entries to Work in Process Inventory, and prove the agreement of the control account with the job cost sheets. (Use a T-account.)

Analyze a job cost sheet and prepare entries for manufacturing costs.
(LO 1, 2, 3, 4), AP

E15-3 A job order cost sheet for Ryan Company is shown below.

Job No. 92			**For 2,000 Units**
Date	Direct Materials	Direct Labor	Manufacturing Overhead
Beg. bal. Jan. 1	5,000	6,000	4,200
8	6,000		
12		8,000	6,400
25	2,000		
27		4,000	3,200
	13,000	18,000	13,800
Cost of completed job:			
Direct materials			$13,000
Direct labor			18,000
Manufacturing overhead			13,800
Total cost			$44,800
Unit cost ($44,800 ÷ 2,000)			$22.40

Instructions

(a) On the basis of the foregoing data, answer the following questions.
    (1) What was the balance in Work in Process Inventory on January 1 if this was the only unfinished job?
    (2) If manufacturing overhead is applied on the basis of direct labor cost, what overhead rate was used in each year?
(b) Prepare summary entries at January 31 to record the current year's transactions pertaining to Job No. 92.

Analyze costs of manufacturing and determine missing amounts.

(LO 1, 5), AN

E15-4 Manufacturing cost data for Orlando Company, which uses a job order cost system, are presented below.

	Case A	Case B	Case C
Direct materials used	$ (a)	$ 83,000	$ 63,150
Direct labor	50,000	140,000	(h)
Manufacturing overhead applied	42,500	(d)	(i)
Total manufacturing costs	145,650	(e)	213,000
Work in process 1/1/17	(b)	15,500	18,000
Total cost of work in process	201,500	(f)	(j)
Work in process 12/31/17	(c)	11,800	(k)
Cost of goods manufactured	192,300	(g)	222,000

Instructions

Indicate the missing amount for each letter. Assume that in all cases manufacturing overhead is applied on the basis of direct labor cost and the rate is the same.

Compute the manufacturing overhead rate and under- or overapplied overhead.

(LO 3, 5), AN

XLS

E15-5 Ikerd Company applies manufacturing overhead to jobs on the basis of machine hours used. Overhead costs are expected to total $300,000 for the year, and machine usage is estimated at 125,000 hours.

For the year, $322,000 of overhead costs are incurred and 130,000 hours are used.

Instructions

(a) Compute the manufacturing overhead rate for the year.
(b) What is the amount of under- or overapplied overhead at December 31?
(c) Prepare the adjusting entry to assign the under- or overapplied overhead for the year to cost of goods sold.

Analyze job cost sheet and prepare entry for completed job.

(LO 1, 2, 3, 4), AP

E15-6 A job cost sheet of Sandoval Company is given below.

Job Cost Sheet

JOB NO. 469 — Quantity 2,500
ITEM White Lion Cages — Date Requested 7/2
FOR Todd Company — Date Completed 7/31

Date	Direct Materials	Direct Labor	Manufacturing Overhead
7/10	700		
12	900		
15		440	550
22		380	475
24	1,600		
27	1,500		
31		540	675

Cost of completed job:
 Direct materials ______
 Direct labor ______
 Manufacturing overhead ______
Total cost ______
Unit cost ______

Instructions

(a) Answer the following questions.
 (1) What are the source documents for direct materials, direct labor, and manufacturing overhead costs assigned to this job?
 (2) What is the predetermined manufacturing overhead rate?
 (3) What are the total cost and the unit cost of the completed job? (Round unit cost to nearest cent.)
(b) Prepare the entry to record the completion of the job.

Prepare entries for manufacturing and nonmanufacturing costs.

(LO 1, 2, 3, 4), AP

E15-7 Crawford Corporation incurred the following transactions.

1. Purchased raw materials on account $46,300.
2. Raw materials of $36,000 were requisitioned to the factory. An analysis of the materials requisition slips indicated that $6,800 was classified as indirect materials.

3. Factory labor costs incurred were $59,900, of which $51,000 pertained to factory wages payable and $8,900 pertained to employer payroll taxes payable.
4. Time tickets indicated that $54,000 was direct labor and $5,900 was indirect labor.
5. Manufacturing overhead costs incurred on account were $80,500.
6. Depreciation on the company's office building was $8,100.
7. Manufacturing overhead was applied at the rate of 150% of direct labor cost.
8. Goods costing $88,000 were completed and transferred to finished goods.
9. Finished goods costing $75,000 to manufacture were sold on account for $103,000.

Instructions
Journalize the transactions. (Omit explanations.)

Prepare entries for manufacturing and nonmanufacturing costs.

(LO 1, 2, 3, 4), AP

E15-8 Enos Printing Corp. uses a job order cost system. The following data summarize the operations related to the first quarter's production.

1. Materials purchased on account $192,000, and factory wages incurred $87,300.
2. Materials requisitioned and factory labor used by job:

Job Number	Materials	Factory Labor
A20	$ 35,240	$18,000
A21	42,920	22,000
A22	36,100	15,000
A23	39,270	25,000
General factory use	4,470	7,300
	$158,000	$87,300

3. Manufacturing overhead costs incurred on account $49,500.
4. Depreciation on factory equipment $14,550.
5. Depreciation on the company's office building was $14,300.
6. Manufacturing overhead rate is 90% of direct labor cost.
7. Jobs completed during the quarter: A20, A21, and A23.

Instructions
Prepare entries to record the operations summarized above. (Prepare a schedule showing the individual cost elements and total cost for each job in item 7.)

Prepare a cost of goods manufactured schedule and partial financial statements.

(LO 1, 5), AP

XLS

E15-9 At May 31, 2017, the accounts of Lopez Company show the following.

1. May 1 inventories—finished goods $12,600, work in process $14,700, and raw materials $8,200.
2. May 31 inventories—finished goods $9,500, work in process $15,900, and raw materials $7,100.
3. Debit postings to work in process were direct materials $62,400, direct labor $50,000, and manufacturing overhead applied $40,000.
4. Sales revenue totaled $215,000.

Instructions
(a) Prepare a condensed cost of goods manufactured schedule.
(b) Prepare an income statement for May through gross profit.
(c) Indicate the balance sheet presentation of the manufacturing inventories at May 31, 2017.

Compute work in process and finished goods from job cost sheets.

(LO 2, 4), AP

E15-10 Tierney Company begins operations on April 1. Information from job cost sheets shows the following.

Job Number	Manufacturing Costs Assigned: April	May	June	Month Completed
10	$5,200	$4,400		May
11	4,100	3,900	$2,000	June
12	1,200			April
13		4,700	4,500	June
14		5,900	3,600	Not complete

Job 12 was completed in April. Job 10 was completed in May. Jobs 11 and 13 were completed in June. Each job was sold for 25% above its cost in the month following completion.

Instructions
(a) What is the balance in Work in Process Inventory at the end of each month?
(b) What is the balance in Finished Goods Inventory at the end of each month?
(c) What is the gross profit for May, June, and July?

Prepare entries for costs of services provided.
(LO 1, 3, 4), AP

E15-11 The following are the job cost related accounts for the law firm of Colaw Associates and their manufacturing equivalents:

Law Firm Accounts	Manufacturing Firm Accounts
Supplies	Raw Materials
Salaries and Wages Payable	Factory Wages Payable
Operating Overhead	Manufacturing Overhead
Service Contracts in Process	Work in Process
Cost of Completed Service Contracts	Cost of Goods Sold

Cost data for the month of March follow.

1. Purchased supplies on account $1,800.
2. Issued supplies $1,200 (60% direct and 40% indirect).
3. Assigned labor costs based on time cards for the month which indicated labor costs of $70,000 (80% direct and 20% indirect).
4. Operating overhead costs incurred for cash totaled $40,000.
5. Operating overhead is applied at a rate of 90% of direct labor cost.
6. Work completed totaled $75,000.

Instructions
(a) Journalize the transactions for March. (Omit explanations.)
(b) Determine the balance of the Service Contracts in Process account. (Use a T-account.)

Determine cost of jobs and ending balance in work in process and overhead accounts.
(LO 2, 3, 4), AP

E15-12 Don Lieberman and Associates, a CPA firm, uses job order costing to capture the costs of its audit jobs. There were no audit jobs in process at the beginning of November. Listed below are data concerning the three audit jobs conducted during November.

	Lynn	Brian	Mike
Direct materials	$600	$400	$200
Auditor labor costs	$5,400	$6,600	$3,375
Auditor hours	72	88	45

Overhead costs are applied to jobs on the basis of auditor hours, and the predetermined overhead rate is $50 per auditor hour. The Lynn job is the only incomplete job at the end of November. Actual overhead for the month was $11,000.

Instructions
(a) Determine the cost of each job.
(b) Indicate the balance of the Service Contracts in Process account at the end of November.
(c) Calculate the ending balance of the Operating Overhead account for November.

Determine predetermined overhead rate, apply overhead, and determine whether balance under- or overapplied.
(LO 3, 5), AP

E15-13 Tombert Decorating uses a job order cost system to collect the costs of its interior decorating business. Each client's consultation is treated as a separate job. Overhead is applied to each job based on the number of decorator hours incurred. Listed below are data for the current year.

Estimated overhead	$960,000
Actual overhead	$982,800
Estimated decorator hours	40,000
Actual decorator hours	40,500

The company uses Operating Overhead in place of Manufacturing Overhead.

Instructions
(a) Compute the predetermined overhead rate.
(b) Prepare the entry to apply the overhead for the year.
(c) Determine whether the overhead was under- or overapplied and by how much.

EXERCISES: SET B AND CHALLENGE EXERCISES

Visit the book's companion website, at **www.wiley.com/college/kimmel**, and choose the Student Companion site to access Exercises: Set B and Challenge Exercises.

PROBLEMS: SET A

Prepare entries in a job order cost system and job cost sheets.

(LO 1, 2, 3, 4, 5), AP

P15-1A Lott Company uses a job order cost system and applies overhead to production on the basis of direct labor costs. On January 1, 2017, Job 50 was the only job in process. The costs incurred prior to January 1 on this job were as follows: direct materials $20,000, direct labor $12,000, and manufacturing overhead $16,000. As of January 1, Job 49 had been completed at a cost of $90,000 and was part of finished goods inventory. There was a $15,000 balance in the Raw Materials Inventory account.

During the month of January, Lott Company began production on Jobs 51 and 52, and completed Jobs 50 and 51. Jobs 49 and 50 were also sold on account during the month for $122,000 and $158,000, respectively. The following additional events occurred during the month.

1. Purchased additional raw materials of $90,000 on account.
2. Incurred factory labor costs of $70,000. Of this amount $16,000 related to employer payroll taxes.
3. Incurred manufacturing overhead costs as follows: indirect materials $17,000, indirect labor $20,000, depreciation expense on equipment $12,000, and various other manufacturing overhead costs on account $16,000.
4. Assigned direct materials and direct labor to jobs as follows.

Job No.	Direct Materials	Direct Labor
50	$10,000	$ 5,000
51	39,000	25,000
52	30,000	20,000

Instructions

(a) Calculate the predetermined overhead rate for 2017, assuming Lott Company estimates total manufacturing overhead costs of $840,000, direct labor costs of $700,000, and direct labor hours of 20,000 for the year.

(b) Open job cost sheets for Jobs 50, 51, and 52. Enter the January 1 balances on the job cost sheet for Job 50.

(c) Prepare the journal entries to record the purchase of raw materials, the factory labor costs incurred, and the manufacturing overhead costs incurred during the month of January.

(d) Prepare the journal entries to record the assignment of direct materials, direct labor, and manufacturing overhead costs to production. In assigning manufacturing overhead costs, use the overhead rate calculated in (a). Post all costs to the job cost sheets as necessary.

(e) Total the job cost sheets for any job(s) completed during the month. Prepare the journal entry (or entries) to record the completion of any job(s) during the month.

(e) Job 50, $69,000
Job 51, $94,000

(f) Prepare the journal entry (or entries) to record the sale of any job(s) during the month.

(g) What is the balance in the Finished Goods Inventory account at the end of the month? What does this balance consist of?

(h) What is the amount of over- or underapplied overhead?

Prepare entries in a job order cost system and partial income statement.

(LO 1, 2, 3, 4, 5), AN

P15-2A For the year ended December 31, 2017, the job cost sheets of Cinta Company contained the following data.

Job Number	Explanation	Direct Materials	Direct Labor	Manufacturing Overhead	Total Costs
7640	Balance 1/1	$25,000	$24,000	$28,800	$ 77,800
	Current year's costs	30,000	36,000	43,200	109,200
7641	Balance 1/1	11,000	18,000	21,600	50,600
	Current year's costs	43,000	48,000	57,600	148,600
7642	Current year's costs	58,000	55,000	66,000	179,000

Other data:

1. Raw materials inventory totaled $15,000 on January 1. During the year, $140,000 of raw materials were purchased on account.
2. Finished goods on January 1 consisted of Job No. 7638 for $87,000 and Job No. 7639 for $92,000.
3. Job No. 7640 and Job No. 7641 were completed during the year.
4. Job Nos. 7638, 7639, and 7641 were sold on account for $530,000.
5. Manufacturing overhead incurred on account totaled $120,000.
6. Other manufacturing overhead consisted of indirect materials $14,000, indirect labor $18,000, and depreciation on factory machinery $8,000.

Instructions

(a) $179,000; Job 7642: $179,000

(a) Prove the agreement of Work in Process Inventory with job cost sheets pertaining to unfinished work. (*Hint:* Use a single T-account for Work in Process Inventory.) Calculate each of the following, then post each to the T-account: (1) beginning balance, (2) direct materials, (3) direct labor, (4) manufacturing overhead, and (5) completed jobs.

(b) Amount = $6,800

(b) Prepare the adjusting entry for manufacturing overhead, assuming the balance is allocated entirely to Cost of Goods Sold.

(c) $158,600

(c) Determine the gross profit to be reported for 2017.

Prepare entries in a job order cost system and cost of goods manufactured schedule.

(LO 1, 2, 3, 4, 5), AP

XLS

P15-3A Case Inc. is a construction company specializing in custom patios. The patios are constructed of concrete, brick, fiberglass, and lumber, depending upon customer preference. On June 1, 2017, the general ledger for Case Inc. contains the following data.

Raw Materials Inventory	$4,200	Manufacturing Overhead Applied	$32,640
Work in Process Inventory	$5,540	Manufacturing Overhead Incurred	$31,650

Subsidiary data for Work in Process Inventory on June 1 are as follows.

Job Cost Sheets

	Customer Job		
Cost Element	**Rodgers**	**Stevens**	**Linton**
Direct materials	$ 600	$ 800	$ 900
Direct labor	320	540	580
Manufacturing overhead	400	675	725
	$1,320	$2,015	$2,205

During June, raw materials purchased on account were $4,900, and all wages were paid. Additional overhead costs consisted of depreciation on equipment $900 and miscellaneous costs of $400 incurred on account.

A summary of materials requisition slips and time tickets for June shows the following.

Customer Job	Materials Requisition Slips	Time Tickets
Rodgers	$ 800	$ 850
Koss	2,000	800
Stevens	500	360
Linton	1,300	1,200
Rodgers	300	390
	4,900	3,600
General use	1,500	1,200
	$6,400	$4,800

Overhead was charged to jobs at the same rate of $1.25 per dollar of direct labor cost. The patios for customers Rodgers, Stevens, and Linton were completed during June and sold for a total of $18,900. Each customer paid in full.

Instructions

(a) Journalize the June transactions: (1) for purchase of raw materials, factory labor costs incurred, and manufacturing overhead costs incurred; (2) assignment of direct materials, labor, and overhead to production; and (3) completion of jobs and sale of goods.

(b) Post the entries to Work in Process Inventory.
(c) Reconcile the balance in Work in Process Inventory with the costs of unfinished jobs.
(d) Prepare a cost of goods manufactured schedule for June.

(d) Cost of goods manufactured $14,740

Compute predetermined overhead rates, apply overhead, and calculate under- or overapplied overhead.

(LO 3, 5), AP

P15-4A Agassi Company uses a job order cost system in each of its three manufacturing departments. Manufacturing overhead is applied to jobs on the basis of direct labor cost in Department D, direct labor hours in Department E, and machine hours in Department K.

In establishing the predetermined overhead rates for 2017, the following estimates were made for the year.

	Department		
	D	E	K
Manufacturing overhead	$1,200,000	$1,500,000	$900,000
Direct labor costs	$1,500,000	$1,250,000	$450,000
Direct labor hours	100,000	125,000	40,000
Machine hours	400,000	500,000	120,000

During January, the job cost sheets showed the following costs and production data.

	Department		
	D	E	K
Direct materials used	$140,000	$126,000	$78,000
Direct labor costs	$120,000	$110,000	$37,500
Manufacturing overhead incurred	$ 99,000	$124,000	$79,000
Direct labor hours	8,000	11,000	3,500
Machine hours	34,000	45,000	10,400

Instructions

(a) Compute the predetermined overhead rate for each department.
(b) Compute the total manufacturing costs assigned to jobs in January in each department.
(c) Compute the under- or overapplied overhead for each department at January 31.

(a) 80%, $12, $7.50
(b) $356,000, $368,000, $193,500
(c) $3,000, $(8,000), $1,000

Analyze manufacturing accounts and determine missing amounts.

(LO 1, 2, 3, 4, 5), AN

P15-5A Phillips Corporation's fiscal year ends on November 30. The following accounts are found in its job order cost accounting system for the first month of the new fiscal year.

Raw Materials Inventory

Dec. 1	Beginning balance	(a)	Dec. 31	Requisitions	16,850
31	Purchases	17,225			
Dec. 31	Ending balance	7,975			

Work in Process Inventory

Dec. 1	Beginning balance	(b)	Dec. 31	Jobs completed	(f)
31	Direct materials	(c)			
31	Direct labor	8,400			
31	Overhead	(d)			
Dec. 31	Ending balance	(e)			

Finished Goods Inventory

Dec. 1	Beginning balance	(g)	Dec. 31	Cost of goods sold	(i)
31	Completed jobs	(h)			
Dec. 31	Ending balance	(j)			

Factory Labor

Dec. 31	Factory wages	12,025	Dec. 31	Wages assigned	(k)

Manufacturing Overhead

Dec. 31	Indirect materials	2,900	Dec. 31	Overhead applied	(m)
31	Indirect labor	(l)			
31	Other overhead	1,245			

Other data:

1. On December 1, two jobs were in process: Job No. 154 and Job No. 155. These jobs had combined direct materials costs of $9,750 and direct labor costs of $15,000. Overhead was applied at a rate that was 75% of direct labor cost.
2. During December, Job Nos. 156, 157, and 158 were started. On December 31, Job No. 158 was unfinished. This job had charges for direct materials $3,800 and direct labor $4,800, plus manufacturing overhead. All jobs, except for Job No. 158, were completed in December.
3. On December 1, Job No. 153 was in the finished goods warehouse. It had a total cost of $5,000. On December 31, Job No. 157 was the only job finished that was not sold. It had a cost of $4,000.
4. Manufacturing overhead was $1,470 underapplied in December.

(c) $13,950
(f) $52,450
(i) $53,450

Instructions
List the letters (a) through (m) and indicate the amount pertaining to each letter.

PROBLEMS: SET B AND SET C

Visit the book's companion website, at **www.wiley.com/college/kimmel**, and choose the Student Companion site to access Problems: Set B and Set C.

CONTINUING PROBLEMS

EXCEL TUTORIAL

XLS

CURRENT DESIGNS

CD15 Huegel Hollow Resort has ordered 20 rotomolded kayaks from Current Designs. Each kayak will be formed in the rotomolded oven, cooled, and then the excess plastic trimmed away. Then, the hatches, seat, ropes, and bungees will be attached to the kayak.

Dave Thill, the kayak plant manager, knows that manufacturing each kayak requires 54 pounds of polyethylene powder and a finishing kit (rope, seat, hardware, etc.). The polyethylene powder used in these kayaks costs $1.50 per pound, and the finishing kits cost $170 each. Each kayak will use two kinds of labor: 2 hours of more-skilled type I labor from people who run the oven and trim the plastic, and 3 hours of less-skilled type II labor from people who attach the hatches and seat and other hardware. The type I employees are paid $15 per hour, and the type II employees are paid $12 per hour. For purposes of this problem, assume that overhead is allocated to all jobs at a rate of 150% of direct labor costs.

Instructions
Determine the total cost of the Huegel Hollow order and the cost of each individual kayak in the order. Identify costs as direct materials, direct labor, or manufacturing overhead.

WATERWAYS

(*Note:* This is a continuation of the Waterways problem from Chapter 14.)

WP15 Waterways has two major public-park projects to provide with comprehensive irrigation in one of its service locations this month. Job J57 and Job K52 involve 15 acres of landscaped terrain which will require special-order sprinkler heads to meet the specifications of the project. This problem asks you to help Waterways use a job order cost system to account for production of these parts.

Go to the book's companion website, at **www.wiley.com/college/kimmel**, *to find the completion of this problem.*

COMPREHENSIVE CASE

Greetings Inc., a nationally recognized retailer of greeting cards and small gift items, decides to employ Internet technology to expand its sales opportunities. For this case, you will employ traditional job order costing techniques and then evaluate the resulting product costs.

Go to the book's companion website, at **www.wiley.com/college/kimmel**, *for complete case details and instructions.*

EXPAND YOUR CRITICAL THINKING

DECISION-MAKING ACROSS THE ORGANIZATION

Group Project

AP

CT15-1 Khan Products Company uses a job order cost system. For a number of months, there has been an ongoing rift between the sales department and the production department concerning a special-order product, TC-1. TC-1 is a seasonal product that is manufactured in batches of 1,000 units. TC-1 is sold at cost plus a markup of 40% of cost.

The sales department is unhappy because fluctuating unit production costs significantly affect selling prices. Sales personnel complain that this has caused excessive customer complaints and the loss of considerable orders for TC-1.

The production department maintains that each job order must be fully costed on the basis of the costs incurred during the period in which the goods are produced. Production personnel maintain that the only real solution is for the sales department to increase sales in the slack periods.

Andrea Parley, president of the company, asks you as the company accountant to collect quarterly data for the past year on TC-1. From the cost accounting system, you accumulate the following production quantity and cost data.

	Quarter			
Costs	**1**	**2**	**3**	**4**
Direct materials	$100,000	$220,000	$ 80,000	$200,000
Direct labor	60,000	132,000	48,000	120,000
Manufacturing overhead	105,000	153,000	97,000	125,000
Total	$265,000	$505,000	$225,000	$445,000
Production in batches	5	11	4	10
Unit cost (per batch)	$ 53,000	$ 45,909	$ 56,250	$ 44,500

Instructions

With the class divided into groups, answer the following questions.

(a) What manufacturing cost element is responsible for the fluctuating unit costs? Why?

(b) What is your recommended solution to the problem of fluctuating unit cost?

(c) Restate the quarterly data on the basis of your recommended solution.

MANAGERIAL ANALYSIS

AN

CT15-2 In the course of routine checking of all journal entries prior to preparing year-end reports, Betty Eller discovered several strange entries. She recalled that the president's son Joe had come in to help out during an especially busy time and that he had recorded some journal entries. She was relieved that there were only a few of his entries, and even more relieved that he had included rather lengthy explanations. The entries Joe made were:

(1)

Work in Process Inventory	25,000	
Cash		25,000

(This is for materials put into process. I don't find the record that we paid for these, so I'm crediting Cash because I know we'll have to pay for them sooner or later.)

(2)

Manufacturing Overhead	12,000	
Cash		12,000

(This is for bonuses paid to salespeople. I know they're part of overhead, and I can't find an account called "Non-Factory Overhead" or "Other Overhead" so I'm putting it in Manufacturing Overhead. I have the check stubs, so I know we paid these.)

(3)

Wages Expense	120,000	
Cash		120,000

(This is for the factory workers' wages. I have a note that employer payroll taxes are $18,000. I still think that's part of wages expense and that we'll have to pay it all in cash sooner or later, so I credited Cash for the wages and the taxes.)

(4)

Work in Process Inventory	3,000	
Raw Materials Inventory		3,000

(This is for the glue used in the factory. I know we used this to make the products, even though we didn't use very much on any one of the products. I got it out of inventory, so I credited an inventory account.)

Instructions

(a) How should Joe have recorded each of the four events?

(b) If the entry was not corrected, which financial statements (income statement or balance sheet) would be affected? What balances would be overstated or understated?

REAL-WORLD FOCUS

C **CT15-3** The Institute of Management Accountants sponsors a certification for management accountants, allowing them to obtain the title of Certified Management Accountant.

Address: **www.imanet.org**, or go to **www.wiley.com/college/kimmel**

Steps

1. Go to the site shown above.
2. Choose **CMA Certification**, then **Become a CMA**, and then **How to Get Started**. Answer part (a) below.
3. Choose **CMA Resource Center** and then **Continuing Education for CMAs**. Answer part (b) below.

Instructions

(a) What is the experience qualification requirement?

(b) How many hours of continuing education are required, and what types of courses qualify?

Writing

COMMUNICATION ACTIVITY

E **CT15-4** You are the management accountant for Williams Company. Your company does custom carpentry work and uses a job order cost system. Williams sends detailed job cost sheets to its customers, along with an invoice. The job cost sheets show the date materials were used, the dollar cost of materials, and the hours and cost of labor. A predetermined overhead application rate is used, and the total overhead applied is also listed.

Nancy Kopay is a customer who recently had custom cabinets installed. Along with her check in payment for the work done, she included a letter. She thanked the company for including the detailed cost information but questioned why overhead was estimated. She stated that she would be interested in knowing exactly what costs were included in overhead, and she thought that other customers would, too.

Instructions

Prepare a letter to Ms. Kopay (address: 123 Cedar Lane, Altoona, KS 66651) and tell her why you did not send her information on exact costs of overhead included in her job. Respond to her suggestion that you provide this information.

ETHICS CASE

E **CT15-5** LRF Printing provides printing services to many different corporate clients. Although LRF bids most jobs, some jobs, particularly new ones, are negotiated on a "cost-plus" basis. Cost-plus means that the buyer is willing to pay the actual cost plus a return (profit) on these costs to LRF.

Alice Reiley, controller for LRF, has recently returned from a meeting where LRF's president stated that he wanted her to find a way to charge more costs to any project that was on a cost-plus basis. The president noted that the company needed more profits to meet its stated goals this period. By charging more costs to the cost-plus projects and therefore fewer costs to the jobs that were bid, the company should be able to increase its profit for the current year.

Alice knew why the president wanted to take this action. Rumors were that he was looking for a new position and if the company reported strong profits, the president's opportunities would be enhanced. Alice also recognized that she could probably increase the cost of certain jobs by changing the basis used to allocate manufacturing overhead.

Instructions

(a) Who are the stakeholders in this situation?
(b) What are the ethical issues in this situation?
(c) What would you do if you were Alice Reiley?

ALL ABOUT YOU

CT15-6 Many of you will work for a small business. Some of you will even own your own business. In order to operate a small business, you will need a good understanding of managerial accounting, as well as many other skills. Much information is available to assist people who are interested in starting a new business. A great place to start is the website provided by the Small Business Administration, which is an agency of the federal government whose purpose is to support small businesses. C

Instructions

Go to **www.sba.gov/smallbusinessplanner/index.html** and in the Small Business Planner, Plan Your Business link, review the material under "Get Ready." Answer the following questions.

(a) What are some of the characteristics required of a small business owner?
(b) What are the top 10 reasons given for business failure?

CONSIDERING YOUR COSTS AND BENEFITS

CT15-7 After graduating, you might decide to start a small business. As discussed in this chapter, owners of any business need to know how to calculate the cost of their products. In fact, many small businesses fail because they don't accurately calculate their product costs, so they don't know if they are making a profit or losing money—until it's too late. E

Suppose that you decide to start a landscape business. You use an old pickup truck that you've fully paid for. You store the truck and other equipment in your parents' barn, and you store trees and shrubs on their land. Your parents will not charge you for the use of these facilities for the first two years, but beginning in the third year they will charge a reasonable rent. Your mother helps you by answering phone calls and providing customers with information. She doesn't charge you for this service, but she plans on doing it for only your first two years in business. In pricing your services, should you include charges for the truck, the barn, the land, and your mother's services when calculating your product cost? The basic arguments for and against are as follows.

YES: If you don't include charges for these costs, your costs are understated and your profitability is overstated.

NO: At this point, you are not actually incurring costs related to these activities; therefore, you shouldn't record charges.

Instructions

Write a response indicating your position regarding this situation. Provide support for your view.

16

Process Costing

CHAPTER PREVIEW

As the Feature Story describes, the cost accounting system used by companies such as Jones Soda is **process cost accounting**. In contrast to job order cost accounting, which focuses on the individual job, process cost accounting focuses on the *processes* involved in mass-producing products that are identical or very similar in nature. The primary objective of this chapter is to explain and illustrate process costing.

CHAPTER OUTLINE

LEARNING OBJECTIVES		PRACTICE
1 Discuss the uses of a process cost system and how it compares to a job order system.	• Uses of process cost systems • Process costing for service companies • Comparing job order and process cost systems	DO IT! 1 Compare Job Order and Process Cost Systems
2 Explain the flow of costs in a process cost system and the journal entries to assign manufacturing costs.	• Process cost flow • Assigning manufacturing costs	DO IT! 2 Manufacturing Costs in Process Costing
3 Compute equivalent units.	• Weighted-average method • Refinements on the method	DO IT! 3 Equivalent Units
4 Complete the four steps to prepare a production cost report.	• Physical unit flow • Equivalent units of production • Unit production costs • Cost reconciliation schedule • Production cost report	DO IT! 4 Cost Reconciliation Schedule

Go to the ***REVIEW AND PRACTICE*** section at the end of the chapter for a targeted summary and exercises with solutions.

Visit **WileyPLUS** for additional tutorials and practice opportunities.

Elaine Thompson/AP Photo

FEATURE STORY

The Little Guy Who Could

It isn't easy for a small company to get a foothold in the bottled beverage business. The giants, The Coca-Cola Company and PepsiCo Inc., vigilantly defend their turf, constantly watching for new trends and opportunities. It is nearly impossible to get shelf space in stores, and consumer tastes can change faster than a bottle of soda can lose its fizz. But Jones Soda Co., headquartered in Seattle, has overcome these and other obstacles to make a name for itself. Its corporate motto is, "Run with the little guy . . . create some change."

The company started as a Canadian distributor of other companies' beverages. Soon, it decided to make its own products under the corporate name Urban Juice and Soda Company. Eventually, its name changed to Jones Soda—the name of its most popular product. From the very start, Jones Soda was different. It sold soda from machines placed in tattoo parlors and piercing shops, and it sponsored a punk rock band as well as surfers and snowboarders. At one time, the company's product was the official drink at the Seattle Seahawks' stadium and was served on Alaskan Airlines.

Today, Jones Soda makes a wide variety of products: soda-flavored candy, energy drinks, and product-promoting gear that includes t-shirts, sweatshirts, caps, shorts, and calendars. Its most profitable product is still its multi-flavored, pure cane soda with its creative labeling. If you've seen Jones Soda on a store shelf, then you know that it appears to have an infinite variety of labels. The bottle labels are actually created by customers and submitted on the company's website. (To see some of the best labels from the past, see the Gallery at *www.jonessoda.com*.) If you would like some soda with a custom label of your own, you can design and submit a label and order a 12-pack.

Because Jones Soda has a dizzying array of product variations, keeping track of costs is of vital importance. Recently, management developed a reorganization plan that involved cost-cutting from top to bottom and eliminating unprofitable products. No matter how good your products are, if you don't keep your costs under control, you are likely to fail. Jones Soda's managers need accurate cost information regarding each primary product and each variation to ensure profitability. So while its marketing approach differs dramatically from the giants, Jones Soda needs the same kind of cost information as the big guys.

LEARNING OBJECTIVE 1

Discuss the uses of a process cost system and how it compares to a job order system.

USES OF PROCESS COST SYSTEMS

Companies use **process cost systems** to apply costs to similar products that are mass-produced in a continuous fashion. Jones Soda Co. uses a process cost system: Production of the soda, once it begins, continues until the soda emerges. The processing is the same for the entire run—with precisely the same amount of materials, labor, and overhead. Each finished bottle of soda is indistinguishable from another.

A company such as USX uses process costing in the manufacturing of steel. Kellogg and General Mills use process costing for cereal production; ExxonMobil uses process costing for its oil refining. Sherwin Williams uses process costing for its paint products. At a bottling company like Jones Soda, the manufacturing process begins with the blending of ingredients. Next, automated machinery moves the bottles into position and fills them. The production process then caps, packages, and forwards the bottles to the finished goods warehouse. Illustration 16-1 shows this process.

ILLUSTRATION 16-1
Manufacturing processes

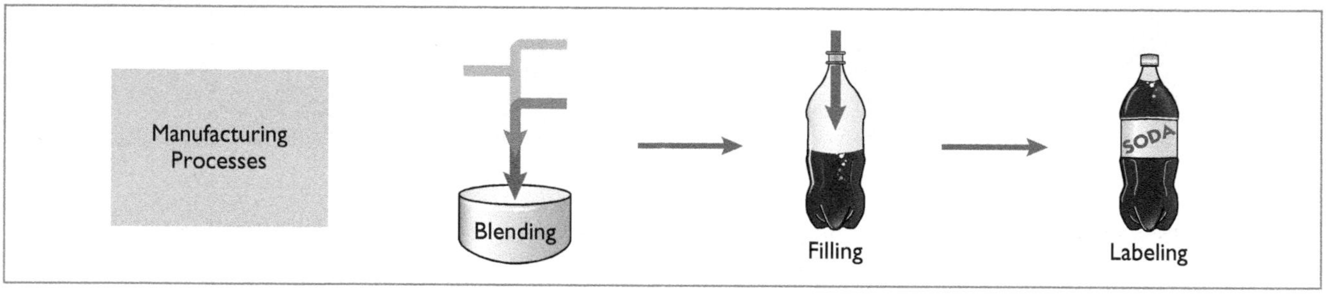

For Jones Soda, as well as the other companies just mentioned, once production begins, it continues until the finished product emerges. Each unit of finished product is like every other unit.

In comparison, a job order cost system assigns costs to a *specific job*. Examples are the construction of a customized home, the making of a movie, or the manufacturing of a specialized machine. Illustration 16-2 provides examples of companies that primarily use either a process cost system or a job order cost system.

ILLUSTRATION 16-2
Process cost and job order cost companies and products

Process Cost System: Company	Process Cost System: Product	Job Order Cost System: Company	Job Order Cost System: Product
Jones Soda, PepsiCo	Soft drinks	Young & Rubicam, J. Walter Thompson	Advertising
ExxonMobil, Royal Dutch Shell	Oil	Disney, Warner Brothers	Movies
Intel, Advanced Micro Devices	Computer chips	Center Ice Consultants, Ice Pro	Ice rinks
Dow Chemical, DuPont	Chemicals	Kaiser, Mayo Clinic	Patient health care

PROCESS COSTING FOR SERVICE COMPANIES

When considering service companies, you might initially think of specific, nonroutine tasks, such as rebuilding an automobile engine, consulting on a business acquisition, or defending a major lawsuit. However, many service companies perform repetitive, routine work. For example, Jiffy Lube regularly performs oil changes. H&R Block focuses on the routine aspects of basic tax practice. Service companies that perform individualized, nonroutine services will probably benefit from using a job order cost system. Those that perform routine, repetitive services will probably be better off with a process cost system.

SIMILARITIES AND DIFFERENCES BETWEEN JOB ORDER COST AND PROCESS COST SYSTEMS

In a job order cost system, companies assign costs to each job. In a process cost system, companies track costs through a series of connected manufacturing processes or departments, rather than by individual jobs. Thus, companies use process cost systems when they produce a large volume of uniform or relatively homogeneous products. Illustration 16-3 shows the basic flow of costs in these two systems.

ILLUSTRATION 16-3
Job order cost and process cost flow

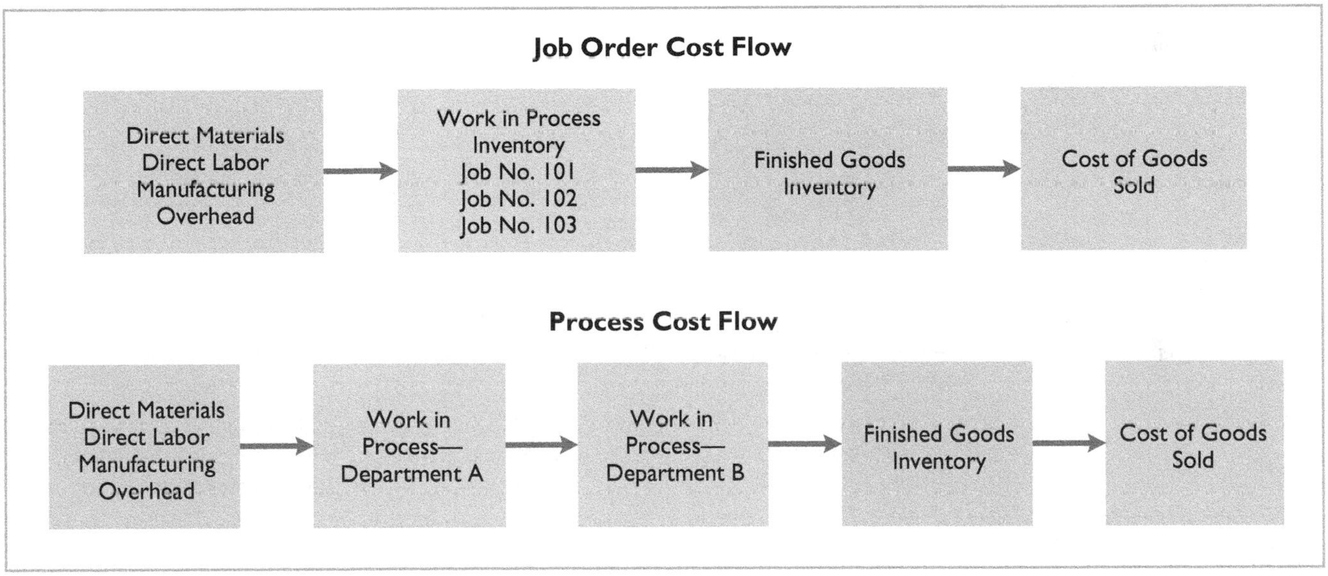

The following analysis highlights the basic similarities and differences between these two systems.

Similarities

Job order cost and process cost systems are similar in three ways:

1. **The manufacturing cost elements.** Both costing systems track three manufacturing cost elements—direct materials, direct labor, and manufacturing overhead.
2. **The accumulation of the costs of materials, labor, and overhead.** Both costing systems debit raw materials to Raw Materials Inventory, factory labor to Factory Labor, and manufacturing overhead costs to Manufacturing Overhead.

3. **The flow of costs.** As noted above, both systems accumulate all manufacturing costs by debits to Raw Materials Inventory, Factory Labor, and Manufacturing Overhead. Both systems then assign these costs to the same accounts—Work in Process, Finished Goods Inventory, and Cost of Goods Sold. **The methods of assigning costs, however, differ significantly.** These differences are explained and illustrated later in the chapter.

Differences

The differences between a job order cost and a process cost system are as follows.

1. **The number of work in process accounts used.** A job order cost system uses only one work in process account. A process cost system uses multiple work in process accounts.
2. **Documents used to track costs.** A job order cost system charges costs to individual jobs and summarizes them in a job cost sheet. A process cost system summarizes costs in a production cost report for each department.
3. **The point at which costs are totaled.** A job order cost system totals costs when the job is completed. A process cost system totals costs at the end of a period of time.
4. **Unit cost computations.** In a job order cost system, the unit cost is the total cost per job divided by the units produced. In a process cost system, the unit cost is total manufacturing costs for the period divided by the equivalent units produced during the period.

Illustration 16-4 summarizes the major differences between a job order cost and a process cost system.

ILLUSTRATION 16-4
Job order versus process cost systems

Feature	Job Order Cost System	Process Cost System
Work in process accounts	One work in process account	Multiple work in process accounts
Documents used	Job cost sheets	Production cost reports
Determination of total manufacturing costs	Each job	Each period
Unit-cost computations	Cost of each job ÷ Units produced for the job	Total manufacturing costs ÷ Equivalent units produced during the period

DO IT! ▶1 Compare Job Order and Process Cost Systems

Indicate whether each of the following statements is true or false.

1. A law firm is likely to use process costing for major lawsuits.
2. A manufacturer of paintballs is likely to use process costing.
3. Both job order and process costing determine product costs at the end of a period of time, rather than when a product is completed.
4. Process costing does not keep track of manufacturing overhead.

Action Plan

✔ Use job order costing in situations where unit costs are high, unit volume is low, and products are unique.

✔ Use process costing when there is a large volume of relatively homogeneous products.

SOLUTION

1. False. 2. True. 3. False. 4. False.

Related exercise material: **E16-1** and DO IT! **16-1.**

LEARNING OBJECTIVE 2

Explain the flow of costs in a process cost system and the journal entries to assign manufacturing costs.

PROCESS COST FLOW

Illustration 16-5 shows the flow of costs in the process cost system for Tyler Company. Tyler manufactures roller blade and skateboard wheels that it sells to manufacturers and retail outlets. Manufacturing consists of two processes: machining and assembly. The Machining Department shapes, hones, and drills the raw materials. The Assembly Department assembles and packages the parts.

ILLUSTRATION 16-5
Flow of costs in process cost system

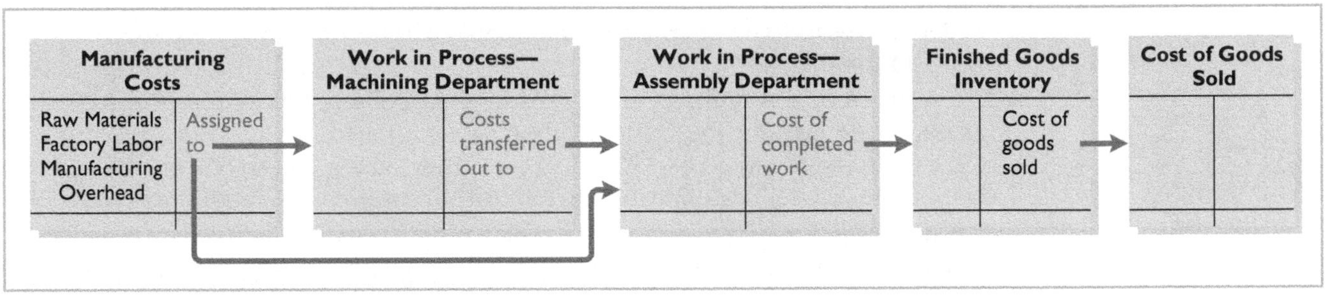

As the flow of costs indicates, the company can add materials, labor, and manufacturing overhead in both the Machining and Assembly Departments. When it finishes its work, the Machining Department transfers the partially completed units to the Assembly Department. The Assembly Department finishes the goods and then transfers them to the finished goods inventory. Upon sale, Tyler removes the goods from the finished goods inventory. Within each department, a similar set of activities is performed on each unit processed.

ASSIGNING MANUFACTURING COSTS—JOURNAL ENTRIES

As indicated, the accumulation of the costs of materials, labor, and manufacturing overhead is the same in a process cost system as in a job order cost system. That is, both systems follow these procedures:

- Companies debit all raw materials to Raw Materials Inventory at the time of purchase.
- They debit all factory labor to Factory Labor as the labor costs are incurred.
- They debit overhead costs to Manufacturing Overhead as these costs are incurred.

However, the assignment of the three manufacturing cost elements to Work in Process in a process cost system is different from a job order cost system. Here we'll look at how companies assign these manufacturing cost elements in a process cost system.

Materials Costs

All raw materials issued for production are a materials cost to the producing department. A process cost system may use materials requisition slips, but **it generally requires fewer requisitions than in a job order cost system. The materials are used for processes rather than for specific jobs** and therefore typically are for larger quantities.

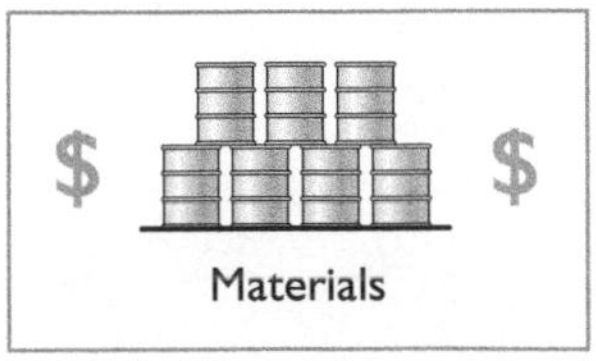

At the beginning of the first process, a company usually adds most of the materials needed for production. However, other materials may be added at various points. For example, in the manufacture of Hershey candy bars, the chocolate and other ingredients are added at the beginning of the first process, and the wrappers and cartons are added at the end of the packaging process. Tyler Company adds materials at the beginning of each process. Tyler makes the following entry to record the materials used.

Work in Process—Machining	XXXX	
Work in Process—Assembly	XXXX	
Raw Materials Inventory		XXXX
(To record materials used)		

Ice cream maker Ben & Jerry's adds materials in three departments: milk and flavoring in the mixing department, extras such as cherries and dark chocolate in the prepping department, and cardboard containers in the pinting (packaging) department.

Factory Labor Costs

In a process cost system, as in a job order cost system, companies may use time tickets to determine the cost of labor assignable to production departments. Since they assign labor costs to a process rather than a job, they can obtain, from the payroll register or departmental payroll summaries, the labor cost chargeable to a process.

Labor costs for the Machining Department include the wages of employees who shape, hone, and drill the raw materials. The entry to assign labor costs to machining and assembly for Tyler Company is:

Work in Process—Machining	XXXX	
Work in Process—Assembly	XXXX	
Factory Labor		XXXX
(To assign factory labor to production)		

Manufacturing Overhead Costs

The objective in assigning overhead in a process cost system is to allocate the overhead costs to the production departments on an objective and equitable basis. That basis is the activity that "drives" or causes the costs. A primary driver of overhead costs in continuous manufacturing operations is **machine time used**, not direct labor. Thus, companies **widely use machine hours** in allocating manufacturing overhead costs using predetermined overhead rates. Tyler Company's entry to allocate overhead to the two processes is:

Work in Process—Machining	XXXX	
Work in Process—Assembly	XXXX	
Manufacturing Overhead		XXXX
(To assign overhead to production)		

MANAGEMENT INSIGHT Caterpillar

© SweetyMommy/iStockphoto

Choosing a Cost Driver

In one of its automated cost centers, Caterpillar feeds work into the cost center, where robotic machines process it and transfer the finished job to the next cost center without human intervention. One person tends all of the machines and spends more time maintaining machines than operating them. In such cases, overhead rates based on direct labor hours may be misleading. Surprisingly, some companies continue to assign manufacturing overhead on the basis of direct labor despite the fact that there is no cause-and-effect relationship between labor and overhead.

What is the result if a company uses the wrong "cost driver" to assign manufacturing overhead? (Go to WileyPLUS for this answer and additional questions.)

Transfer to Next Department

At the end of the month, Tyler Company needs an entry to record the cost of the goods transferred out of the Machining Department. In this case, the transfer is to the Assembly Department, and Tyler makes the following entry.

Work in Process—Assembly	XXXXX	
Work in Process—Machining		XXXXX
(To record transfer of units to the Assembly Department)		

Transfer to Finished Goods

When the Assembly Department completes the units, it transfers them to the finished goods warehouse. The entry for this transfer is as follows.

Finished Goods Inventory	XXXXX	
Work in Process—Assembly		XXXXX
(To record transfer of units to finished goods)		

Transfer to Cost of Goods Sold

When Tyler Company sells the finished goods, it records the cost of goods sold as follows.

Cost of Goods Sold	XXXXX	
Finished Goods Inventory		XXXXX
(To record cost of units sold)		

DO IT! 2 Manufacturing Costs in Process Costing

Ruth Company manufactures ZEBO through two processes: blending and bottling. In June, raw materials used were Blending $18,000 and Bottling $4,000. Factory labor costs were Blending $12,000 and Bottling $5,000. Manufacturing overhead costs were Blending $6,000 and Bottling $2,500. The company transfers units completed at a cost of $19,000 in the Blending Department to the Bottling Department. The Bottling Department transfers units completed at a cost of $11,000 to Finished Goods. Journalize the assignment of these costs to the two processes and the transfer of units as appropriate.

SOLUTION

The entries are:

Work in Process—Blending	18,000	
Work in Process—Bottling	4,000	
Raw Materials Inventory		22,000
(To record materials used)		
Work in Process—Blending	12,000	
Work in Process—Bottling	5,000	
Factory Labor		17,000
(To assign factory labor to production)		
Work in Process—Blending	6,000	
Work in Process—Bottling	2,500	
Manufacturing Overhead		8,500
(To assign overhead to production)		
Work in Process—Bottling	19,000	
Work in Process—Blending		19,000
(To record transfer of units to the Bottling Department)		
Finished Goods Inventory	11,000	
Work in Process—Bottling		11,000
(To record transfer of units to finished goods)		

Action Plan

- ✔ In process cost accounting, keep separate work in process accounts for each process.
- ✔ When the costs are assigned to production, debit the separate work in process accounts.
- ✔ Transfer cost of completed units to the next process or to Finished Goods.

Related exercise material: **BE16-1, BE16-2, BE16-3, E16-2, E16-4,** and DO IT! **16-2.**

LEARNING OBJECTIVE 3

Compute equivalent units.

Suppose you have a work-study job in the office of your college's president, and she asks you to compute the cost of instruction per full-time equivalent student at your college. The college's vice president for finance provides the following information.

ILLUSTRATION 16-6
Information for full-time student example

Costs:	
Total cost of instruction	$9,000,000
Student population:	
Full-time students	900
Part-time students	1,000

Part-time students take 60% of the classes of a full-time student during the year. To compute the number of full-time equivalent students per year, you would make the following computation.

ILLUSTRATION 16-7
Full-time equivalent unit computation

Full-Time Students	+	Equivalent Units of Part-Time Students	=	Full-Time Equivalent Students
900	+	(1,000 × 60%)	=	1,500

The cost of instruction per full-time equivalent student is therefore the total cost of instruction ($9,000,000) divided by the number of full-time equivalent students (1,500), which is $6,000 ($9,000,000 ÷ 1,500).

A process cost system uses the same idea, called equivalent units of production. **Equivalent units of production** measure the work done during the period, expressed in fully completed units. Companies use this measure to determine the cost per unit of completed product.

WEIGHTED-AVERAGE METHOD

The formula to compute equivalent units of production is as follows.

ILLUSTRATION 16-8
Equivalent units of production formula

Units Completed and Transferred Out	+	Equivalent Units of Ending Work in Process	=	Equivalent Units of Production

To better understand this concept of equivalent units, consider the following two separate examples.

Example 1. In a specific period, the entire output of Sullivan Company's Blending Department consists of ending work in process of 4,000 units which are 60% complete as to materials, labor, and overhead. The equivalent units of production for the Blending Department are therefore 2,400 units (4,000 × 60%).

Example 2. The output of Kori Company's Packaging Department during the period consists of 10,000 units completed and transferred out, and 5,000 units in ending work in process which are 70% completed. The equivalent units of production are therefore 13,500 [10,000 + (5,000 × 70%)].

This method of computing equivalent units is referred to as the **weighted-average method**. It considers the degree of completion (weighting) of the units completed and transferred out and the ending work in process.

REFINEMENTS ON THE WEIGHTED-AVERAGE METHOD

Kellogg Company has produced Eggo® Waffles since 1970. Three departments produce these waffles: Mixing, Baking, and Freezing/Packaging. The Mixing Department combines dry ingredients, including flour, salt, and baking powder, with liquid ingredients, including eggs and vegetable oil, to make waffle batter. Illustration 16-9 provides information related to the Mixing Department at the end of June.

MIXING DEPARTMENT

		Percentage Complete	
	Physical Units	**Materials**	**Conversion Costs**
Work in process, June 1	100,000	100%	70%
Started into production	800,000		
Total units	900,000		
Units transferred out	700,000		
Work in process, June 30	200,000	100%	60%
Total units	900,000		

ILLUSTRATION 16-9
Information for Mixing Department

▼ HELPFUL HINT
Separate unit cost computations are needed for materials and conversion costs whenever the two types of costs do not occur in the process at the same time.

Illustration 16-9 indicates that the beginning work in process is 100% complete as to materials cost and 70% complete as to conversion costs. **Conversion costs are the sum of labor costs and overhead costs.** In other words, Kellogg adds both the dry and liquid ingredients (materials) at the beginning of the waffle-making process, and the conversion costs (labor and overhead) related to the mixing of these ingredients are incurred uniformly and are 70% complete. The ending work in process is 100% complete as to materials cost and 60% complete as to conversion costs.

ETHICS NOTE
An unethical manager might use incorrect completion percentages when determining equivalent units. This results in either raising or lowering costs. Since completion percentages are somewhat subjective, this form of income manipulation can be difficult to detect.

We then use the Mixing Department information to determine equivalent units. **In computing equivalent units, the beginning work in process is not part of the equivalent-units-of-production formula.** The units transferred out to the Baking Department are fully complete as to both materials and conversion costs. The ending work in process is fully complete as to materials, but only 60% complete as to conversion costs. We therefore need to make **two equivalent unit computations**: one for materials, and the other for conversion costs. Illustration 16-10 shows these computations.

MIXING DEPARTMENT

	Equivalent Units	
	Materials	**Conversion Costs**
Units transferred out	700,000	700,000
Work in process, June 30		
200,000 × 100%	200,000	
200,000 × 60%		120,000
Total equivalent units	900,000	820,000

ILLUSTRATION 16-10
Computation of equivalent units—Mixing Department

We can refine the earlier formula used to compute equivalent units of production (Illustration 16-8, page 796) to show the computations for materials and for conversion costs, as follows.

ILLUSTRATION 16-11
Refined equivalent units of production formula

Units Completed and Transferred Out—Materials	+	Equivalent Units of Ending Work in Process—Materials	=	Equivalent Units of Production—Materials
Units Completed and Transferred Out—Conversion Costs	+	Equivalent Units of Ending Work in Process—Conversion Costs	=	Equivalent Units of Production—Conversion Costs

PEOPLE, PLANET, AND PROFIT INSIGHT General Electric

© Nicole Hofmann/iStockphoto

Haven't I Seen That Before?

For a variety of reasons, many companies, including General Electric, are making a big push to remanufacture goods that have been thrown away. Items getting a second chance include cell phones, computers, home appliances, car parts, vacuum cleaners, and medical equipment. Businesses have figured out that profit margins on remanufactured goods are significantly higher than on new goods. As commodity prices such as copper and steel increase, reusing parts makes more sense. Also, as more local governments initiate laws requiring that electronics and appliances be recycled rather than thrown away, the cost of remanufacturing declines because the gathering of used goods becomes far more efficient. Besides benefitting the manufacturer, remanufacturing provides goods at a much lower price to consumers, reduces waste going to landfills, saves energy, reuses scarce resources, and reduces emissions. For example, it was estimated that a remanufactured car starter results in about 50% less carbon dioxide emissions than making a new one.

Source: James R. Hagerty and Paul Glader, "From Trash Heap to Store Shelf," *Wall Street Journal Online* (January 24, 2011).

In what ways might the relative composition (materials, labor, and overhead) of a remanufactured product's cost differ from that of a newly made product? (Go to WileyPLUS for this answer and additional questions.)

DO IT! ▶3 Equivalent Units

The Fabricating Department for Outdoor Essentials has the following production and cost data for the current month.

Beginning Work in Process	Units Transferred Out	Ending Work in Process
-0-	15,000	10,000

Materials are entered at the beginning of the process. The ending work in process units are 30% complete as to conversion costs. Compute the equivalent units of production for (a) materials and (b) conversion costs.

Action Plan

- ✔ To measure the work done during the period, expressed in fully completed units, compute equivalent units of production.
- ✔ Use the appropriate formula: Units completed and transferred out + Equivalent units of ending work in process = Equivalent units of production.

SOLUTION

(a) Since materials are entered at the beginning of the process, the equivalent units of ending work in process are 10,000. Thus, 15,000 units + 10,000 units = 25,000 equivalent units of production for materials.

(b) Since ending work in process is only 30% complete as to conversion costs, the equivalent units of ending work in process are 3,000 (10,000 units × 30%). Thus, 15,000 units + 3,000 units = 18,000 equivalent units of production for conversion costs.

Related exercise material: **BE16-4, BE16-5, E16-5, E16-6, E16-8, E16-9, E16-10, E16-11, E16-13, E16-14, E16-15,** and **DO IT! 16-3.**

LEARNING OBJECTIVE 4

Complete the four steps to prepare a production cost report.

As mentioned earlier, companies prepare a production cost report for each department. A **production cost report** is the key document that management uses to understand the activities in a department; it shows the production quantity and cost data related to that department. For example, in producing Eggo® Waffles, Kellogg Company uses three production cost reports: Mixing, Baking, and Freezing/Packaging. Illustration 16-12 shows the flow of costs to make an Eggo® Waffle and the related production cost reports for each department.

ILLUSTRATION 16-12
Flow of costs in making Eggo® Waffles

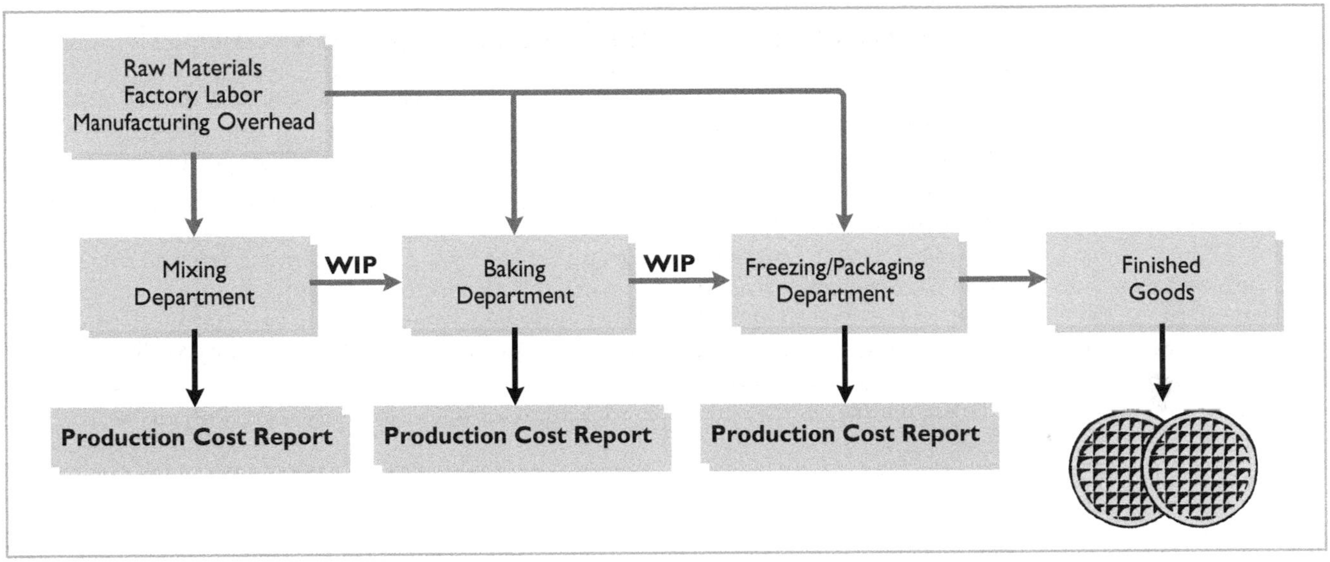

In order to complete a production cost report, the company must perform four steps, which as a whole make up the process cost system.

1. Compute the physical unit flow.
2. Compute the equivalent units of production.
3. Compute unit production costs.
4. Prepare a cost reconciliation schedule.

Illustration 16-13 shows assumed data for the Mixing Department at Kellogg Company for the month of June. We will use this information to complete a production cost report for the Mixing Department.

ILLUSTRATION 16-13
Unit and cost data—Mixing Department

MIXING DEPARTMENT	
Units	
Work in process, June 1	100,000
Direct materials: 100% complete	
Conversion costs: 70% complete	
Units started into production during June	800,000
Units completed and transferred out to Baking Department	700,000
Work in process, June 30	200,000
Direct materials: 100% complete	
Conversion costs: 60% complete	

ILLUSTRATION 16-13
(cont'd.)

Costs	
Work in process, June 1	
Direct materials: 100% complete	$ 50,000
Conversion costs: 70% complete	35,000
Cost of work in process, June 1	$ 85,000
Costs incurred during production in June	
Direct materials	$400,000
Conversion costs	170,000
Costs incurred in June	$570,000

COMPUTE THE PHYSICAL UNIT FLOW (STEP 1)

Physical units are the actual units to be accounted for during a period, irrespective of any work performed. To keep track of these units, add the units started (or transferred) into production during the period to the units in process at the beginning of the period. This amount is referred to as the **total units to be accounted for.**

The total units then are accounted for by the output of the period. The output consists of units transferred out during the period and any units in process at the end of the period. This amount is referred to as the **total units accounted for.** Illustration 16-14 shows the flow of physical units for Kellogg's Mixing Department for the month of June.

ILLUSTRATION 16-14
Physical unit flow—Mixing Department

MIXING DEPARTMENT	
	Physical Units
Units to be accounted for	
Work in process, June 1	100,000
Started (transferred) into production	800,000
Total units	900,000
Units accounted for	
Completed and transferred out	700,000
Work in process, June 30	200,000
Total units	900,000

The records indicate that the Mixing Department must account for 900,000 units. Of this sum, 700,000 units were transferred to the Baking Department and 200,000 units were still in process.

COMPUTE THE EQUIVALENT UNITS OF PRODUCTION (STEP 2)

▼ **HELPFUL HINT**
Materials are not always added at the beginning of the process. For example, materials are sometimes added uniformly during the process.

Once the physical flow of the units is established, Kellogg must measure the Mixing Department's productivity in terms of equivalent units of production. The Mixing Department adds materials at the beginning of the process, and it incurs conversion costs uniformly during the process. Thus, we need two computations of equivalent units: one for materials and one for conversion costs. The equivalent unit computation is as follows.

ILLUSTRATION 16-15
Computation of equivalent units—Mixing Department

	Equivalent Units	
	Materials	**Conversion Costs**
Units transferred out	700,000	700,000
Work in process, June 30		
200,000 × 100%	200,000	
200,000 × 60%		120,000
Total equivalent units	900,000	820,000

▼ **HELPFUL HINT**
Remember that we ignore the beginning work in process in this computation.

COMPUTE UNIT PRODUCTION COSTS (STEP 3)

Armed with the knowledge of the equivalent units of production, we can now compute the unit production costs. **Unit production costs** are costs expressed in terms of equivalent units of production. When equivalent units of production are different for materials and conversion costs, we compute three unit costs: (1) materials, (2) conversion, and (3) total manufacturing.

The computation of total materials cost related to Eggo® Waffles is as follows.

ILLUSTRATION 16-16
Total materials cost computation

Work in process, June 1	
Direct materials cost	$ 50,000
Costs added to production during June	
Direct materials cost	400,000
Total materials cost	$450,000

The computation of unit materials cost is as follows.

ILLUSTRATION 16-17
Unit materials cost computation

Total Materials Cost	÷	Equivalent Units of Materials	=	Unit Materials Cost
$450,000	÷	900,000	=	$0.50

Illustration 16-18 shows the computation of total conversion costs.

ILLUSTRATION 16-18
Total conversion costs computation

Work in process, June 1	
Conversion costs	$ 35,000
Costs added to production during June	
Conversion costs	170,000
Total conversion costs	$205,000

The computation of unit conversion cost is as follows.

ILLUSTRATION 16-19
Unit conversion cost computation

Total Conversion Costs	÷	Equivalent Units of Conversion Costs	=	Unit Conversion Cost
$205,000	÷	820,000	=	$0.25

Total manufacturing cost per unit is therefore computed as shown in Illustration 16-20 (page 802).

ILLUSTRATION 16-20
Total manufacturing cost per unit

Unit Materials Cost	+	Unit Conversion Cost	=	Total Manufacturing Cost per Unit
$0.50	+	$0.25	=	$0.75

PREPARE A COST RECONCILIATION SCHEDULE (STEP 4)

We are now ready to determine the cost of goods transferred out of the Mixing Department to the Baking Department and the costs in ending work in process. Kellogg charged total costs of $655,000 to the Mixing Department in June, calculated as follows.

ILLUSTRATION 16-21
Costs charged to Mixing Department

Costs to be accounted for	
Work in process, June 1	$ 85,000
Started into production	570,000
Total costs	$655,000

The company then prepares a cost reconciliation schedule to assign these costs to (a) units transferred out to the Baking Department and (b) ending work in process.

ILLUSTRATION 16-22
Cost reconciliation schedule—Mixing Department

MIXING DEPARTMENT
Cost Reconciliation Schedule

Costs accounted for		
Transferred out (700,000 × $0.75)		$ 525,000
Work in process, June 30		
Materials (200,000 × $0.50)	$100,000	
Conversion costs (120,000 × $0.25)	30,000	130,000
Total costs		$655,000

Kellogg uses the total manufacturing cost per unit, $0.75, in costing the **units completed** and transferred to the Baking Department. In contrast, the unit cost of materials and the unit cost of conversion are needed in costing **ending units in process**. The **cost reconciliation schedule** shows that the **total costs accounted for** (Illustration 16-22) equal the **total costs to be accounted for** (Illustration 16-21).

PREPARING THE PRODUCTION COST REPORT

At this point, Kellogg is ready to prepare the production cost report for the Mixing Department. As indicated earlier, this report is an internal document for management that shows production quantity and cost data for a production department. Illustration 16-23 shows the completed production cost report for the Mixing Department and identifies the four steps used in preparing it.

Production cost reports provide a basis for evaluating the productivity of a department. In addition, managers can use the cost data to assess whether unit costs and total costs are reasonable. By comparing the quantity and cost data with predetermined goals, top management can also judge whether current performance is meeting planned objectives.

DECISION TOOLS

A production cost report helps managers evaluate overall profitability by comparing costs to previous periods, competitors, and expected selling price.

ILLUSTRATION 16-23
Production cost report

Mixing Department.xls

	A	B	C	D	E
1	**MIXING DEPARTMENT**				
2	**Production Cost Report**				
3	**For the Month Ended June 30, 2017**				
4			Equivalent Units		
5		Physical Units	Materials	Conversion Costs	
6	**Quantities**				
7	Units to be accounted for	Step 1	Step 2		
8	Work in process, June 1	100,000			
9	Started into production	800,000			
10	Total units	900,000			
11	Units accounted for				
12	Transferred out	700,000	700,000	700,000	
13	Work in process, June 30	200,000	200,000	120,000	(200,000 × 60%)
14	Total units	900,000	900,000	820,000	
15	**Costs**				
16	Unit costs Step 3		Materials	Conversion Costs	Total
17	Total cost	(a)	$450,000	$205,000	$655,000
18	Equivalent units	(b)	900,000	820,000	
19	Unit costs [(a) ÷ (b)]		$0.50	$0.25	$0.75
20	Costs to be accounted for				
21	Work in process, June 1				$ 85,000
22	Started into production				570,000
23	Total costs				$655,000
24	**Cost Reconciliation Schedule** Step 4				
25	Costs accounted for				
26	Transferred out (700,000 × $0.75)				$525,000
27	Work in process, June 30				
28	Materials (200,000 × $0.50)			$100,000	
29	Conversion costs (120,000 × $0.25)			30,000	130,000
30	Total costs				$655,000
31					

▼ **HELPFUL HINT**
The four steps in preparing a production cost report:

1. Compute the physical unit flow.
2. Compute the equivalent units of production.
3. Compute unit production costs.
4. Prepare a cost reconciliation schedule.

COSTING SYSTEMS—FINAL COMMENTS

Companies often use a combination of a process cost and a job order cost system. Called **operations costing**, this hybrid system is similar to process costing in its assumption that standardized methods are used to manufacture the product. At the same time, the product may have some customized, individual features that require the use of a job order cost system.

Consider, for example, Ford Motor Company. Each vehicle at a given plant goes through the same assembly line, but Ford uses different materials (such as seat coverings, paint, and tinted glass) for different vehicles. Similarly, Kellogg's Pop-Tarts® toaster pastries go through numerous standardized processes—mixing, filling, baking, frosting, and packaging. The pastry dough, though, comes in different flavors—plain, chocolate, and graham—and fillings include Smucker's® real fruit, chocolate fudge, vanilla creme, brown sugar cinnamon, and s'mores.

A cost-benefit trade-off occurs as a company decides which costing system to use. A job order cost system, for example, provides detailed information related to the cost of the product. Because each job has its own distinguishing characteristics, the system can provide an accurate cost per job. This information is useful in controlling costs and pricing products. However, the cost of implementing a job order cost system is often expensive because of the accounting costs involved.

DECISION TOOLS
A cost-benefit trade-off helps managers determine which costing system to use.

On the other hand, for a company like Intel, is there a benefit in knowing whether the cost of the one-hundredth computer chip produced is different from the one-thousandth chip produced? Probably not. An average cost of the product will suffice for control and pricing purposes.

In summary, when deciding to use one of these systems or a combination system, a company must weigh the costs of implementing the system against the benefits from the additional information provided.

DO IT! 4 Cost Reconciliation Schedule

In March, Rodayo Manufacturing had the following unit production costs: materials $6 and conversion costs $9. On March 1, it had no work in process. During March, Rodayo transferred out 12,000 units. As of March 31, 800 units that were 25% complete as to conversion costs and 100% complete as to materials were in ending work in process. Assign the costs to the units transferred out and in process.

Action Plan

- ✔ **Assign the total manufacturing cost of $15 per unit to the 12,000 units transferred out.**
- ✔ **Assign the materials cost and conversion costs based on equivalent units of production to units in ending work in process.**

SOLUTION

The assignment of costs is as follows.

Costs accounted for		
Transferred out (12,000 × $15)		$180,000
Work in process, March 31		
Materials (800 × $6)	$4,800	
Conversion costs (200* × $9)	1,800	6,600
Total costs		$186,600

*800 × 25%

Related exercise material: **BE16-6, BE16-7, BE16-8, BE16-9, E16-3, E16-5, E16-6, E16-7, E16-8, E16-9, E16-10, E16-11, E16-13, E16-14, E16-15,** and **DO IT! 16-4.**

USING DECISION TOOLS—JONES SODA

Jones Soda Co. faces many situations where it needs to apply the decision tools learned in this chapter, such as using a production cost report to evaluate profitability. For example, suppose Jones Soda manufactures a high-end organic fruit soda, called Eternity, in 10-ounce plastic bottles. Because the market for beverages is highly competitive, the company is very concerned about keeping its costs under control. Eternity is manufactured through three processes: blending, filling, and labeling. Materials are added at the beginning of the process, and labor and overhead are incurred uniformly throughout each process. The company uses a weighted-average method to cost its product. A partially completed production cost report for the month of May for the Blending Department is shown below.

JONES SODA
Blending Department
Production Cost Report
For the Month Ended May 31, 2017

		Equivalent Units	
Quantities	**Physical Units**	**Materials**	**Conversion Costs**
Units to be accounted for	Step 1	Step 2	
Work in process, May 1	1,000		
Started into production	2,000		
Total units	3,000		
Units accounted for			
Transferred out	2,200	?	?
Work in process, May 31	800	?	?
Total units	3,000	?	?

Costs		**Materials**	**Conversion Costs**	**Total**
Unit costs Step 3				
Total cost	(a)	?	?	?
Equivalent units	(b)	?	?	
Unit costs [(a) ÷ (b)]		?	?	?
Costs to be accounted for				
Work in process, May 1				$ 56,300
Started into production				119,320
Total costs				$175,620

Cost Reconciliation Schedule Step 4		
Costs accounted for		
Transferred out		?
Work in process, May 31		
Materials	?	
Conversion costs	?	?
Total costs		?

Additional information:		
Work in process, May 1, 1000 units		
Materials cost, 1,000 units (100% complete)	$49,100	
Conversion costs, 1,000 units (70% complete)	7,200	$ 56,300
Materials cost for May, 2,000 units		$100,000
Work in process, May 31, 800 units, 100% complete as to materials and 50% complete as to conversion costs		

INSTRUCTIONS

(a) Prepare a production cost report for the Blending Department for the month of May.

(b) Prepare the journal entry to record the transfer of goods from the Blending Department to the Filling Department.

(c) Explain why Jones Soda is using a process cost system to account for its costs.

SOLUTION

(a) A completed production cost report for the Blending Department is shown below. Computations to support the amounts reported follow the report.

JONES SODA
Blending Department
Production Cost Report
For the Month Ended May 31, 2017

		Equivalent Units	
Quantities	**Physical Units**	**Materials**	**Conversion Costs**
Units to be accounted for	Step 1	Step 2	
Work in process, May 1	1,000		
Started into production	2,000		
Total units	3,000		
Units accounted for			
Transferred out	2,200	2,200	2,200
Work in process, May 31	800	800	400 (800 × 50%)
Total units	3,000	3,000	2,600

Costs				
Unit costs Step 3		**Materials**	**Conversion Costs**	**Total**
Total cost	(a)	$149,100*	$26,520**	$175,620
Equivalent units	(b)	3,000	2,600	
Unit costs [(a) ÷ (b)]		$49.70	$10.20	$59.90
Costs to be accounted for				
Work in process, May 1				$ 56,300
Started into production				119,320
Total costs				$175,620

*Materials cost—$49,100 + $100,000

**Conversion costs—$7,200 + $19,320 ($119,320 − $100,000)

Cost Reconciliation Schedule Step 4		
Costs accounted for		
Transferred out (2,200 × $59.90)		$131,780
Work in process, May 31		
Materials (800 × $49.70)	$39,760	
Conversion costs (400 × $10.20)	4,080	43,840
Total costs		$175,620

(b) Work in Process—Filling	131,780	
Work in Process—Blending		131,780

(c) Companies use process cost systems to apply costs to similar products that are mass-produced in a continuous fashion. Jones Soda uses a process cost system because production of the fruit soda, once it begins, continues until the soda emerges. The processing is the same for the entire run—with precisely the same amount of materials, labor, and overhead. Each bottle of Eternity soda is indistinguishable from another.

LEARNING OBJECTIVE *5

APPENDIX 16A: Compute equivalent units using the FIFO method.

In this chapter, we demonstrated the weighted-average method of computing equivalent units. Some companies use a different method, referred to as the **first-in, first-out (FIFO) method**, to compute equivalent units. The purpose of this appendix is to illustrate how companies use the FIFO method to prepare a production cost report.

EQUIVALENT UNITS UNDER FIFO

Under the FIFO method, companies compute equivalent units on a first-in, first-out basis. Some companies favor the FIFO method because the FIFO cost assumption usually corresponds to the actual physical flow of the goods. Under the FIFO method, companies therefore assume that the beginning work in process is completed before new work is started.

Using the FIFO method, equivalent units are the sum of the work performed to:

1. Finish the units of beginning work in process inventory.
2. Complete the units started into production during the period (referred to as the **units started and completed**).
3. Start, but only partially complete, the units in ending work in process inventory.

Normally, in a process cost system, some units will always be in process at both the beginning and end of the period.

Illustration

Illustration 16A-1 shows the physical flow of units for the Assembly Department of Shutters Inc. In addition, it indicates the degree of completion of the work in process accounts in regard to conversion costs.

ILLUSTRATION 16A-1
Physical unit flow—Assembly Department

ASSEMBLY DEPARTMENT	Physical Units
Units to be accounted for	
Work in process, June 1 (40% complete)	500
Started (transferred) into production	8,000
Total units	8,500
Units accounted for	
Completed and transferred out	8,100
Work in process, June 30 (75% complete)	400
Total units	8,500

In Illustration 16A-1, the units completed and transferred out (8,100) plus the units in ending work in process (400) equal the total units to be accounted for (8,500). Using FIFO, we then compute equivalent units as follows.

1. The 500 units of beginning work in process were 40% complete. Thus, 300 equivalent units (500 units × 60%) were required to complete the beginning inventory.
2. The units started and completed during the current month are **the units transferred out minus the units in beginning work in process**. For the Assembly Department, units started and completed are 7,600 (8,100 − 500).
3. The 400 units of ending work in process were 75% complete. Thus, equivalent units were 300 (400 × 75%).

Equivalent units for the Assembly Department are 8,200, computed as follows.

ILLUSTRATION 16A-2
Computation of equivalent units—FIFO method

ASSEMBLY DEPARTMENT			
Production Data	Physical Units	Work Added This Period	Equivalent Units
Work in process, June 1	500	60%	300
Started and completed	7,600	100%	7,600
Work in process, June 30	400	75%	300
Total	8,500		8,200

COMPREHENSIVE EXAMPLE

To provide a complete illustration of the FIFO method, we will use the data for the Mixing Department at Kellogg Company for the month of June, as shown in Illustration 16A-3 (page 808).

ILLUSTRATION 16A-3
Unit and cost data—Mixing Department

MIXING DEPARTMENT	
Units	
Work in process, June 1	100,000
Direct materials: 100% complete	
Conversion costs: 70% complete	
Units started into production during June	800,000
Units completed and transferred out to Baking Department	700,000
Work in process, June 30	200,000
Direct materials: 100% complete	
Conversion costs: 60% complete	
Costs	
Work in process, June 1	
Direct materials: 100% complete	$ 50,000
Conversion costs: 70% complete	35,000
Cost of work in process, June 1	$ 85,000
Costs incurred during production in June	
Direct materials	$400,000
Conversion costs	170,000
Costs incurred in June	$570,000

Compute the Physical Unit Flow (Step 1)

Illustration 16A-4 shows the physical flow of units for Kellogg's Mixing Department for the month of June.

ILLUSTRATION 16A-4
Physical unit flow—Mixing Department

MIXING DEPARTMENT	Physical Units
Units to be accounted for	
Work in process, June 1	100,000
Started (transferred) into production	800,000
Total units	900,000
Units accounted for	
Completed and transferred out	700,000
Work in process, June 30	200,000
Total units	900,000

Under the **FIFO** method, companies often expand the physical units schedule, as shown in Illustration 16A-5, to explain the transferred-out section. As a result, this section reports the beginning work in process and the units started and completed. These two items further explain the completed and transferred-out section.

ILLUSTRATION 16A-5
Physical unit flow (FIFO)—Mixing Department

MIXING DEPARTMENT	Physical Units
Units to be accounted for	
Work in process, June 1	100,000
Started (transferred) into production	800,000
Total units	900,000
Units accounted for	
Completed and transferred out	
Work in process, June 1	**100,000**
Started and completed	**600,000**
	700,000
Work in process, June 30	200,000
Total units	900,000

The records indicate that the Mixing Department must account for 900,000 units. Of this sum, 700,000 units were transferred to the Baking Department and 200,000 units were still in process.

Compute Equivalent Units of Production (Step 2)

As with the method presented in the chapter, once it determines the physical flow of the units, a company needs to determine equivalent units of production. The Mixing Department adds materials at the beginning of the process, and it incurs conversion costs uniformly during the process. Thus, Kellogg must make two computations of equivalent units: one for materials and one for conversion costs.

▼ **HELPFUL HINT**
As noted earlier, materials are not always added at the beginning of the process. For example, companies sometimes add materials uniformly during the process.

EQUIVALENT UNITS FOR MATERIALS Since Kellogg adds materials at the beginning of the process, no additional materials costs are required to complete the beginning work in process. In addition, 100% of the materials costs has been incurred on the ending work in process. Thus, the computation of equivalent units for materials is as follows.

ILLUSTRATION 16A-6
Computation of equivalent units—materials

MIXING DEPARTMENT—MATERIALS

Production Data	Physical Units	Materials Added This Period	Equivalent Units
Work in process, June 1	100,000	-0-	-0-
Started and finished	600,000	100%	600,000
Work in process, June 30	200,000	100%	200,000
Total	900,000		800,000

EQUIVALENT UNITS FOR CONVERSION COSTS The 100,000 units of beginning work in process were 70% complete in terms of conversion costs. Thus, the Mixing Department required 30,000 equivalent units (100,000 units × 30%) of conversion costs to complete the beginning inventory. In addition, the 200,000 units of ending work in process were 60% complete in terms of conversion costs. Thus, the equivalent units for conversion costs is 750,000, computed as follows.

ILLUSTRATION 16A-7
Computation of equivalent units—conversion costs

MIXING DEPARTMENT—CONVERSION COSTS

Production Data	Physical Units	Work Added This Period	Equivalent Units
Work in process, June 1	100,000	30%	30,000
Started and finished	600,000	100%	600,000
Work in process, June 30	200,000	60%	120,000
Total	900,000		750,000

Compute Unit Production Costs (Step 3)

Armed with the knowledge of the equivalent units of production, Kellogg can now compute the unit production costs. Unit production costs are costs expressed in terms of equivalent units of production. When equivalent units of production are different for materials and conversion costs, companies compute three unit costs: (1) materials, (2) conversion, and (3) total manufacturing.

Under the FIFO method, the unit costs of production are based entirely on the production costs incurred during the month. Thus, the costs in the beginning work in process are not relevant, because they were incurred on work done in the preceding month. As Illustration 16A-3 (page 808) indicated, the costs incurred during production in June were as follows.

ILLUSTRATION 16A-8
Costs incurred during production in June

Direct materials	$400,000
Conversion costs	170,000
Total costs	$570,000

Illustration 16A-9 shows the computation of unit materials cost, unit conversion costs, and total unit cost related to Eggo® Waffles.

ILLUSTRATION 16A-9
Unit cost formulas and computations—Mixing Department

(1)	**Total Materials Cost**	÷	**Equivalent Units of Materials**	=	**Unit Materials Cost**
	$400,000	÷	800,000	=	$0.50
(2)	**Total Conversion Costs**	÷	**Equivalent Units of Conversion Costs**	=	**Unit Conversion Cost**
	$170,000	÷	750,000	=	$0.227 (rounded)*
(3)	**Unit Materials Cost**	+	**Unit Conversion Cost**	=	**Total Manufacturing Cost per Unit**
	$0.50	+	$0.227	=	$0.727

**For homework problems, round unit costs to three decimal places.*

As shown, the unit costs are $0.50 for materials, $0.227 for conversion costs, and $0.727 for total manufacturing costs.

Prepare a Cost Reconciliation Schedule (Step 4)

Kellogg is now ready to determine the cost of goods transferred out of the Mixing Department to the Baking Department and the costs in ending work in process. The total costs charged to the Mixing Department in June are $655,000, calculated as follows.

ILLUSTRATION 16A-10
Costs charged to Mixing Department

Costs to be accounted for	
Work in process, June 1	$ 85,000
Started into production	570,000
Total costs	$655,000

Kellogg next prepares a cost reconciliation to assign these costs to (1) units transferred out to the Baking Department and (2) ending work in process. Under the FIFO method, the first goods to be completed during the period are the units in beginning work in process. Thus, the cost of the beginning work in process is always assigned to the goods transferred to the next department (or finished goods, if processing is complete). Under the FIFO method, ending work in process also will be assigned only the production costs incurred in the current period. Illustration 16A-11 shows a cost reconciliation schedule for the Mixing Department.

ILLUSTRATION 16A-11
Cost reconciliation report

MIXING DEPARTMENT
Cost Reconciliation Schedule

Costs accounted for		
Transferred out		
Work in process, June 1		$ 85,000
Costs to complete beginning work in process		
Conversion costs (30,000 × $0.227)		6,810
Total costs		91,810
Units started and completed (600,000 × $0.727)		435,950*
Total costs transferred out		527,760
Work in process, June 30		
Materials (200,000 × $0.50)	$100,000	
Conversion costs (120,000 × $0.227)	27,240	127,240
Total costs		$655,000

*Any rounding errors should be adjusted in the "Units started and completed" calculation.

As you can see, the total costs accounted for ($655,000 from Illustration 16A-11) equal the total costs to be accounted for ($655,000 from Illustration 16A-10).

Preparing the Production Cost Report

At this point, Kellogg is ready to prepare the production cost report for the Mixing Department. This report is an internal document for management that shows production quantity and cost data for a production department.

As discussed on page 799, there are four steps in preparing a production cost report:

1. Compute the physical unit flow.
2. Compute the equivalent units of production.
3. Compute unit production costs.
4. Prepare a cost reconciliation schedule.

Illustration 16A-12 (page 812) shows the production cost report for the Mixing Department, with the four steps identified in the report.

As indicated in the chapter, production cost reports provide a basis for evaluating the productivity of a department. In addition, managers can use the cost data to assess whether unit costs and total costs are reasonable. By comparing the quantity and cost data with predetermined goals, top management can also judge whether current performance is meeting planned objectives.

▼ **HELPFUL HINT**
The two self-checks in the report are (1) total physical units accounted for must equal the total units to be accounted for, and (2) total costs accounted for must equal the total costs to be accounted for.

FIFO AND WEIGHTED-AVERAGE

The weighted-average method of computing equivalent units has **one major advantage**: It is simple to understand and apply. In cases where prices do not fluctuate significantly from period to period, the weighted-average method will be very similar to the FIFO method. In addition, companies that have been using just-in-time procedures effectively for inventory control purposes will have minimal inventory balances. Therefore, differences between the weighted-average and the FIFO methods will not be material.

Conceptually, the FIFO method is superior to the weighted-average method because it measures **current performance** using only costs incurred in the current period. Managers are, therefore, not held responsible for costs from prior periods over which they may not have had control. In addition, the FIFO method **provides current cost information**, which the company can use to establish **more accurate pricing strategies** for goods manufactured and sold in the current period.

▼ **HELPFUL HINT**
The four steps in preparing a production cost report:
1. Compute the physical unit flow.
2. Compute the equivalent units of production.
3. Compute unit production costs.
4. Prepare a cost reconciliation schedule.

Mixing Department.xls

	A	B	C	D	E
1	**MIXING DEPARTMENT**				
2	**Production Cost Report**				
3	**For the Month Ended June 30, 2017**				
4			Equivalent Units		
5		Physical Units	Materials	Conversion Costs	
6	**Quantities**				
7	Units to be accounted for	Step 1	Step 2		
8	Work in process (WIP), June 1	100,000			
9	Started into production	800,000			
10	Total units	900,000			
11	Units accounted for				
12	Completed and transferred out				
13	Work in process, June 1	100,000	0	30,000	
14	Started and completed	600,000	600,000	600,000	
15	Work in process, June 30	200,000	200,000	120,000	
16	Total units	900,000	800,000	750,000	
17	**Costs**				
18	Unit costs Step 3		Materials	Conversion Costs	Total
19	Costs in June (excluding beginning WIP)	(a)	$400,000	$170,000	$570,000
20	Equivalent units	(b)	800,000	750,000	
21	Unit costs [(a) ÷ (b)]		$0.50	$0.227	$0.727
22	Costs to be accounted for				
23	Work in process, June 1				$ 85,000
24	Started into production				570,000
25	Total costs				$655,000
26	**Cost Reconciliation Schedule** Step 4				
27	Costs accounted for				
28	Transferred out				
29	Work in process, June 1			$ 85,000	
30	Costs to complete beginning work in process				
31	Conversion costs (30,000 × $0.227)			6,810	$ 91,810
32	Units started and completed (600,000 × $0.727)*				435,950
33	Total costs transferred out				527,760
34	Work in process, June 30				
35	Materials (200,000 × $0.50)			100,000	
36	Conversion costs (120,000 × $0.227)			27,240	127,240
37	Total costs				$655,000
38	*Any rounding errors should be adjusted in the "Units started and completed"				
39					

ILLUSTRATION 16A-12
Production cost report—FIFO method

REVIEW AND PRACTICE

LEARNING OBJECTIVES REVIEW

1 Discuss the uses of a process cost system and how it compares to a job order system. Companies that mass-produce similar products in a continuous fashion use process cost systems. Once production begins, it continues until the finished product emerges. Each unit of finished product is indistinguishable from every other unit.

Job order cost systems are similar to process cost systems in three ways. (1) Both systems track the same cost elements—direct materials, direct labor, and manufacturing overhead. (2) Both accumulate costs in the same accounts—Raw Materials Inventory, Factory Labor, and Manufacturing Overhead. (3) Both assign accumulated costs to the same accounts—Work in Process, Finished Goods Inventory, and Cost of Goods Sold. However, the method of assigning costs differs significantly.

There are four main differences between the two cost systems. (1) A process cost system uses separate accounts for each department or manufacturing process, rather than only one work in process account used in a job order cost system. (2) A process cost system summarizes costs in a production cost report for each department. A job order cost system charges costs to individual jobs and summarizes them in a job cost sheet. (3) Costs are totaled at the end of a time period in a process cost system but at the completion of a job in a job order cost system. (4) A process cost system calculates unit cost as Total manufacturing costs for the period ÷ Units produced during the period. A job order cost system calculates unit cost as Total cost per job ÷ Units produced.

2 Explain the flow of costs in a process cost system and the journal entries to assign manufacturing costs. A process cost system assigns manufacturing costs for raw materials, labor, and overhead to work in process accounts for various departments or manufacturing processes. It transfers the costs of partially completed units from one department to another as those units move through the manufacturing process. The system transfers the costs of completed work to Finished Goods Inventory. Finally, when inventory is sold, the system transfers the costs to Cost of Goods Sold.

Entries to assign the costs of raw materials, labor, and overhead consist of a credit to Raw Materials Inventory, Factory Labor, and Manufacturing Overhead, and a debit to Work in Process for each department. Entries to record the cost of goods transferred to another department are a credit to Work in Process for the department whose work is finished and a debit to the department to which the goods are transferred. The entry to record units completed and transferred to the warehouse is a credit to Work in Process for the department whose work is finished and a debit to Finished Goods Inventory. The entry to record the sale of goods is a credit to Finished Goods Inventory and a debit to Cost of Goods Sold.

3 Compute equivalent units. Equivalent units of production measure work done during a period, expressed in fully completed units. Companies use this measure to determine the cost per unit of completed product. Equivalent units are the sum of units completed and transferred out plus equivalent units of ending work in process.

4 Complete the four steps to prepare a production cost report. The four steps to complete a production cost report are as follows. (1) Compute the physical unit flow—that is, the total units to be accounted for. (2) Compute the equivalent units of production. (3) Compute the unit production costs, expressed in terms of equivalent units of production. (4) Prepare a cost reconciliation schedule, which shows that the total costs accounted for equal the total costs to be accounted for.

The production cost report contains both quantity and cost data for a production department. There are four sections in the report: (1) number of physical units, (2) equivalent units determination, (3) unit costs, and (4) cost reconciliation schedule.

***5 Compute equivalent units using the FIFO method.** Equivalent units under the FIFO method are the sum of the work performed to (1) finish the units of beginning work in process inventory, if any; (2) complete the units started into production during the period; and (3) start, but only partially complete, the units in ending work in process inventory.

DECISION TOOLS REVIEW

DECISION CHECKPOINTS	INFO NEEDED FOR DECISION	TOOL TO USE FOR DECISION	HOW TO EVALUATE RESULTS
What is the cost of a product?	Cost of materials, labor, and overhead assigned to processes used to make the product	Production cost report	Compare costs to previous periods, to competitors, and to expected selling price to evaluate overall profitability.
What costing method should be used?	Type of good produced or service performed	Cost of accounting system; benefits of additional information	The benefits of providing the additional information should exceed the costs of the accounting system needed to develop the information.

GLOSSARY REVIEW

Conversion costs The sum of labor costs and overhead costs. (p. 797).

Cost reconciliation schedule A schedule that shows that the total costs accounted for equal the total costs to be accounted for. (p. 802).

Equivalent units of production A measure of the work done during the period, expressed in fully completed units. (p. 796).

Operations costing A combination of a process cost and a job order cost system in which products are manufactured primarily by standardized methods, with some customization. (p. 803).

Physical units Actual units to be accounted for during a period, irrespective of any work performed. (p. 800).

Process cost system An accounting system used to apply costs to similar products that are mass-produced in a continuous fashion. (p. 790).

Production cost report An internal report for management that shows both production quantity and cost data for a production department. (p. 799).

Total units (costs) accounted for The sum of the units (costs) transferred out during the period plus the units (costs) in process at the end of the period. (p. 800).

Total units (costs) to be accounted for The sum of the units (costs) started (or transferred) into production during the period plus the units (costs) in process at the beginning of the period. (p. 800).

Unit production costs Costs expressed in terms of equivalent units of production. (p. 801).

Weighted-average method Method of computing equivalent units of production which considers the degree of completion (weighting) of the units completed and transferred out and the ending work in process. (p. 797).

PRACTICE MULTIPLE-CHOICE QUESTIONS

(LO 1) 1. Which of the following items is **not** characteristic of a process cost system?
(a) Once production begins, it continues until the finished product emerges.
(b) The products produced are heterogeneous in nature.
(c) The focus is on continually producing homogeneous products.
(d) When the finished product emerges, all units have precisely the same amount of materials, labor, and overhead.

(LO 1) 2. Indicate which of the following statements is **not** correct.
(a) Both a job order and a process cost system track the same three manufacturing cost elements—direct materials, direct labor, and manufacturing overhead.
(b) A job order cost system uses only one work in process account, whereas a process cost system uses multiple work in process accounts.
(c) Manufacturing costs are accumulated the same way in a job order and in a process cost system.
(d) Manufacturing costs are assigned the same way in a job order and in a process cost system.

(LO 2) 3. In a process cost system, the flow of costs is:
(a) work in process, cost of goods sold, finished goods.
(b) finished goods, work in process, cost of goods sold.
(c) finished goods, cost of goods sold, work in process.
(d) work in process, finished goods, cost of goods sold.

(LO 2) 4. In making journal entries to assign raw materials costs, a company using process costing:
(a) debits Finished Goods Inventory.
(b) often debits two or more work in process accounts.
(c) generally credits two or more work in process accounts.
(d) credits Finished Goods Inventory.

5. In a process cost system, manufacturing overhead: (LO 2)
(a) is assigned to finished goods at the end of each accounting period.
(b) is assigned to a work in process account for each job as the job is completed.
(c) is assigned to a work in process account for each production department on the basis of a predetermined overhead rate.
(d) is assigned to a work in process account for each production department as overhead costs are incurred.

6. Conversion costs are the sum of: (LO 3)
(a) fixed and variable overhead costs.
(b) labor costs and overhead costs.
(c) direct material costs and overhead costs.
(d) direct labor and indirect labor costs.

7. The Mixing Department's output during the period consists of 20,000 units completed and transferred out, and 5,000 units in ending work in process 60% complete as to materials and conversion costs. Beginning inventory is 1,000 units, 40% complete as to materials and conversion costs. The equivalent units of production are: (LO 3)
(a) 22,600. (c) 24,000.
(b) 23,000. (d) 25,000.

8. In RYZ Company, there are zero units in beginning work in process, 7,000 units started into production, and 500 units in ending work in process 20% completed. The physical units to be accounted for are: (LO 4)
(a) 7,000. (c) 7,500.
(b) 7,360. (d) 7,340.

9. Mora Company has 2,000 units in beginning work in process, 20% complete as to conversion costs, 23,000 units transferred out to finished goods, and 3,000 units in ending work in process $33\frac{1}{3}\%$ complete as to conversion costs. (LO 4)

The beginning and ending inventory is fully complete as to materials costs. Equivalent units for materials and conversion costs are, respectively:
(a) 22,000, 24,000.
(b) 24,000, 26,000.
(c) 26,000, 24,000.
(d) 26,000, 26,000.

(LO 4) 10. Fortner Company has no beginning work in process; 9,000 units are transferred out and 3,000 units in ending work in process are one-third finished as to conversion costs and fully complete as to materials cost. If total materials cost is $60,000, the unit materials cost is:
(a) $5.00.
(b) $5.45 rounded.
(c) $6.00.
(d) No correct answer is given.

(LO 4) 11. Largo Company has unit costs of $10 for materials and $30 for conversion costs. If there are 2,500 units in ending work in process, 40% complete as to conversion costs, and fully complete as to materials cost, the total cost assignable to the ending work in process inventory is:
(a) $45,000.
(b) $55,000.
(c) $75,000.
(d) $100,000.

(LO 4) 12. A production cost report:
(a) is an external report.
(b) shows both the production quantity and cost data related to a department.
(c) shows equivalent units of production but not physical units.
(d) contains six sections.

(LO 4) 13. In a production cost report, units to be accounted for are calculated as:
(a) Units started into production + Units in ending work in process.
(b) Units started into production − Units in beginning work in process.
(c) Units transferred out + Units in beginning work in process.
(d) Units started into production + Units in beginning work in process.

*14. Hollins Company uses the FIFO method to compute equivalent units. It has 2,000 units in beginning work in process, 20% complete as to conversion costs, 25,000 units started and completed, and 3,000 units in ending work in process, 30% complete as to conversion costs. All units are 100% complete as to materials. Equivalent units for materials and conversion costs are, respectively: (LO 5)
(a) 28,000 and 26,600.
(b) 28,000 and 27,500.
(c) 27,000 and 26,200.
(d) 27,000 and 29,600.

*15. KLM Company uses the FIFO method to compute equivalent units. It has no beginning work in process; 9,000 units are started and completed and 3,000 units in ending work in process are one-third completed. All material is added at the beginning of the process. If total materials cost is $60,000, the unit materials cost is: (LO 5)
(a) $5.00.
(b) $6.00.
(c) $6.67 (rounded).
(d) No correct answer is given.

*16. Toney Company uses the FIFO method to compute equivalent units. It has unit costs of $10 for materials and $30 for conversion costs. If there are 2,500 units in ending work in process, 100% complete as to materials and 40% complete as to conversion costs, the total cost assignable to the ending work in process inventory is: (LO 5)
(a) $45,000.
(b) $55,000.
(c) $75,000.
(d) $100,000.

SOLUTIONS

1. **(b)** In a process cost system, the products produced are homogeneous, not heterogeneous, in nature. Choices (a), (c), and (d) are incorrect because they all represent characteristics of a process cost system.
2. **(d)** Manufacturing costs are not assigned the same way in a job order and in a process cost system. Choices (a), (b), and (c) are true statements.
3. **(d)** In a process cost system, the flow of costs is work in process, finished goods, cost of goods sold. Therefore, choices (a), (b), and (c) are incorrect.
4. **(b)** The debit is often to two or more work in process accounts, not (a) a debit to Finished Goods Inventory, (c) credits to two or more work in process accounts, or (d) a credit to Finished Goods Inventory.
5. **(c)** In a process cost system, manufacturing overhead is assigned to a work in process account for each production department on the basis of a predetermined overhead rate, not (a) a finished goods account, (b) as the job is completed, or (d) as overhead costs are incurred.
6. **(b)** Conversion costs are the sum of labor costs and overhead costs, not the sum of (a) fixed and variable overhead costs, (c) direct material costs and overhead costs, or (d) direct labor and indirect labor costs.
7. **(b)** The equivalent units of production is the sum of units completed and transferred out (20,000) and the equivalent units of ending work in process inventory (5,000 units × 60%), or 20,000 + 3,000 = 23,000 units, not (a) 22,600 units, (c) 24,000 units, or (d) 25,000 units.
8. **(a)** There are 7,000 physical units to be accounted for (0 units in beginning inventory + 7,000 units started), not (b) 7,360, (c) 7,500, or (d) 7,340.

9. **(c)** The equivalent units for materials are 26,000 (23,000 units transferred out plus 3,000 in ending work in process inventory). The equivalent units for conversion costs are 24,000 (23,000 transferred out plus $33\frac{1}{3}$% of the ending work in process inventory or 1,000). Therefore, choices (a) 22,000, 24,000; (b) 24,000, 26,000; and (d) 26,000, 26,000 are incorrect.

10. **(a)** $60,000 ÷ (9,000 + 3,000 units) = $5.00 per unit, not (b) $5.45 (rounded), (c) $6.00, or (d) no correct answer is given.

11. **(b)** [(2,500 units × 100% complete) × $10] + [(2,500 units × 40% complete) × $30] or $25,000 + $30,000 = $55,000, not (a) $45,000, (c) $75,000, or (d) $100,000.

12. **(b)** A production cost report shows costs charged to a department and costs accounted for. The other choices are incorrect because a production cost report (a) is an internal, not external, report; (c) does show physical units; and (d) is prepared in four steps and does not contain six sections.

13. **(d)** In a production cost report, units to be accounted for are calculated as Units started in production + Units in beginning work in process, not (a) Units in ending work in process, (b) minus Units in beginning work in process, or (c) Units transferred out.

*14. **(b)** The equivalent units for materials are 28,000 [25,000 started and completed + (3,000 × 100%)]. The equivalent units for conversion costs are 27,500 [(2,000 × 80%) + 25,000 + (3,000 × 30%)]. Therefore, choices (a) 28,000, 26,600; (c) 27,000, 26,200; and (d) 27,000, 29,600 are incorrect.

*15. **(a)** Unit materials cost is $5.00 [$60,000 ÷ (9,000 + 3,000)]. Therefore, choices (b) $6.00, (c) $6.67 (rounded), and (d) no correct answer are incorrect.

*16. **(b)** The total cost assignable to the ending work in process is $55,000 [($10 × 2,500) + ($30 × 2,500 × 40%)]. Therefore, choices (a) $45,000, (c) $75,000, and (d) $100,000 are incorrect.

PRACTICE EXERCISES

Journalize transactions.
(LO 2)

1. Armando Company manufactures pizza sauce through two production departments: Cooking and Canning. In each process, materials and conversion costs are incurred evenly throughout the process. For the month of April, the work in process accounts show the following debits.

	Cooking	**Canning**
Beginning work in process	$ –0–	$ 4,000
Materials	25,000	8,000
Labor	8,500	7,500
Overhead	29,000	25,800
Costs transferred in		55,000

INSTRUCTIONS

Journalize the April transactions.

SOLUTION

1. April 30	Work in Process—Cooking	25,000	
	Work in Process—Canning	8,000	
	Raw Materials Inventory		33,000
30	Work in Process—Cooking	8,500	
	Work in Process—Canning	7,500	
	Factory Labor		16,000
30	Work in Process—Cooking	29,000	
	Work in Process—Canning	25,800	
	Manufacturing Overhead		54,800
30	Work in Process—Canning	55,000	
	Work in Process—Cooking		55,000

Prepare a production cost report.
(LO 3, 4)

2. The Sanding Department of Jo Furniture Company has the following production and manufacturing cost data for March 2017, the first month of operation.

Production: 11,000 units finished and transferred out; 4,000 units started that are 100% complete as to materials and 25% complete as to conversion costs.

Manufacturing costs: Materials $48,000; labor $42,000; and overhead $36,000.

INSTRUCTIONS

Prepare a production cost report.

SOLUTION

2.

JO FURNITURE COMPANY
Sanding Department
Production Cost Report
For the Month Ended March 31, 2017

		Equivalent Units		
Quantities	**Physical Units**	**Materials**	**Conversion Costs**	
Units to be accounted for				
Work in process, March 1	0			
Started into production	15,000			
Total units	15,000			
Units accounted for				
Transferred out	11,000	11,000	11,000	
Work in process, March 31	4,000	4,000	1,000	(4,000 × 25%)
Total units	15,000	15,000	12,000	

Costs		**Materials**	**Conversion Costs**	**Total**
Unit costs				
Costs in March		$48,000	$78,000*	$126,000
Equivalent units		15,000	12,000	
Unit costs [(a) + (b)]		$3.20	$6.50	$9.70
Costs to be accounted for				
Work in process, March 1				$ 0
Started into production				126,000
Total costs				$126,000
Cost Reconciliation Schedule				
Costs accounted for				
Transferred out (11,000 × $9.70)				$106,700
Work in process, March 31				
Materials (4,000 × $3.20)			$12,800	
Conversion costs (1,000 × $6.50)			6,500	19,300
Total costs				$126,000

*$42,000 + $36,000

PRACTICE PROBLEM

Prepare a production cost report and journalize.

(LO 3, 4)

Karlene Industries produces plastic ice cube trays in two processes: heating and stamping. All materials are added at the beginning of the Heating Department process. Karlene uses the weighted-average method to compute equivalent units.

On November 1, the Heating Department had in process 1,000 trays that were 70% complete. During November, it started into production 12,000 trays. On November 30, 2017, 2,000 trays that were 60% complete were in process.

The following cost information for the Heating Department was also available.

Work in process, November 1:		Costs incurred in November:	
Materials	$ 640	Material	$3,000
Conversion costs	360	Labor	2,300
Cost of work in process, Nov. 1	$1,000	Overhead	4,050

INSTRUCTIONS

(a) Prepare a production cost report for the Heating Department for the month of November 2017, using the weighted-average method.
(b) Journalize the transfer of costs to the Stamping Department.

SOLUTION

(a)

KARLENE INDUSTRIES
Heating Department
Production Cost Report
For the Month Ended November 30, 2017

		Equivalent Units	
Quantities	**Physical Units** Step 1	**Materials** Step 2	**Conversion Costs**
Units to be accounted for			
Work in process, November 1	1,000		
Started into production	12,000		
Total units	13,000		
Units accounted for			
Transferred out	11,000	11,000	11,000
Work in process, November 30	2,000	2,000	1,200
Total units	13,000	13,000	12,200

Costs		**Materials**	**Conversion Costs**	**Total**
Unit costs Step 3				
Total cost	(a)	$ 3,640*	$ 6,710**	$10,350
Equivalent units	(b)	13,000	12,200	
Unit costs [(a) ÷ (b)]		$0.28	$0.55	$0.83
Costs to be accounted for				
Work in process, November 1				$ 1,000
Started into production				9,350
Total costs				$10,350

*$640 + $3,000
**$360 + $2,300 + $4,050

Cost Reconciliation Schedule Step 4		
Costs accounted for		
Transferred out (11,000 × $0.83)		$ 9,130
Work in process, November 30		
Materials (2,000 × $0.28)	$560	
Conversion costs (1,200 × $0.55)	660	1,220
Total costs		$10,350

(b)

	Debit	Credit
Work in Process—Stamping	9,130	
Work in Process—Heating		9,130
(To record transfer of units to the Stamping Department)		

WileyPLUS Brief Exercises, DO IT! Exercises, Exercises, Problems, and many additional resources are available for practice in WileyPLUS.

NOTE: All asterisked Questions, Exercises, and Problems relate to material in the appendix to the chapter.

QUESTIONS

1. Identify which costing system—job order or process cost—the following companies would primarily use: (a) Quaker Oats, (b) Jif Peanut Butter, (c) Gulf Craft (luxury yachts), and (d) Warner Bros. Motion Pictures.
2. Contrast the primary focus of job order cost accounting and of process cost accounting.
3. What are the similarities between a job order and a process cost system?

4. Your roommate is confused about the features of process cost accounting. Identify and explain the distinctive features for your roommate.
5. Sam Bowyer believes there are no significant differences in the flow of costs between job order cost accounting and process cost accounting. Is Bowyer correct? Explain.
6. (a) What source documents are used in assigning (1) materials and (2) labor to production in a process cost system?
   (b) What criterion and basis are commonly used in allocating overhead to processes?
7. At Ely Company, overhead is assigned to production departments at the rate of $5 per machine hour. In July, machine hours were 3,000 in the Machining Department and 2,400 in the Assembly Department. Prepare the entry to assign overhead to production.
8. Mark Haley is uncertain about the steps used to prepare a production cost report. State the procedures that are required in the sequence in which they are performed.
9. John Harbeck is confused about computing physical units. Explain to John how physical units to be accounted for and physical units accounted for are determined.
10. What is meant by the term "equivalent units of production"?
11. How are equivalent units of production computed?
12. Coats Company had zero units of beginning work in process. During the period, 9,000 units were completed, and there were 600 units of ending work in process. What were the units started into production?
13. Sanchez Co. has zero units of beginning work in process. During the period, 12,000 units were completed, and there were 500 units of ending work in process one-fifth complete as to conversion cost and 100% complete as to materials cost. What were the equivalent units of production for (a) materials and (b) conversion costs?
14. Hindi Co. started 3,000 units during the period. Its beginning inventory is 500 units one-fourth complete as to conversion costs and 100% complete as to materials costs. Its ending inventory is 300 units one-fifth complete as to conversion costs and 100% complete as to materials costs. How many units were transferred out this period?
15. Clauss Company transfers out 14,000 units and has 2,000 units of ending work in process that are 25% complete. Materials are entered at the beginning of the process and there is no beginning work in process. Assuming unit materials costs of $3 and unit conversion costs of $5, what are the costs to be assigned to units (a) transferred out and (b) in ending work in process?
16. (a) Ann Quinn believes the production cost report is an external report for stockholders. Is Ann correct? Explain.
    (b) Identify the sections in a production cost report.
17. What purposes are served by a production cost report?
18. At Trent Company, there are 800 units of ending work in process that are 100% complete as to materials and 40% complete as to conversion costs. If the unit cost of materials is $3 and the total costs assigned to the 800 units is $6,000, what is the per unit conversion cost?
19. What is the difference between operations costing and a process cost system?
20. How does a company decide whether to use a job order or a process cost system?

*21. Soria Co. started and completed 2,000 units for the period. Its beginning inventory is 800 units 25% complete and its ending inventory is 400 units 20% complete. Soria uses the FIFO method to compute equivalent units. How many units were transferred out this period?

*22. Reyes Company transfers out 12,000 units and has 2,000 units of ending work in process that are 25% complete. Materials are entered at the beginning of the process and there is no beginning work in process. Reyes uses the FIFO method to compute equivalent units. Assuming unit materials costs of $3 and unit conversion costs of $7, what are the costs to be assigned to units (a) transferred out and (b) in ending work in process?

BRIEF EXERCISES

BE16-1 Warner Company purchases $50,000 of raw materials on account, and it incurs $60,000 of factory labor costs. Journalize the two transactions on March 31, assuming the labor costs are not paid until April.

Journalize entries for accumulating costs.
(LO 2), AP

BE16-2 Data for Warner Company are given in BE16-1. Supporting records show that (a) the Assembly Department used $24,000 of raw materials and $35,000 of the factory labor, and (b) the Finishing Department used the remainder. Journalize the assignment of the costs to the processing departments on March 31.

Journalize the assignment of materials and labor costs.
(LO 2), AP

BE16-3 Factory labor data for Warner Company are given in BE16-2. Manufacturing overhead is assigned to departments on the basis of 160% of labor costs. Journalize the assignment of overhead to the Assembly and Finishing Departments.

Journalize the assignment of overhead costs.
(LO 2), AP

Compute equivalent units of production.
(LO 3), AP

BE16-4 Goode Company has the following production data for selected months.

			Ending Work in Process	
Month	**Beginning Work in Process**	**Units Transferred Out**	**Units**	**% Complete as to Conversion Cost**
January	–0–	35,000	10,000	40%
March	–0–	40,000	8,000	75
July	–0–	45,000	16,000	25

Compute equivalent units of production for materials and conversion costs, assuming materials are entered at the beginning of the process.

Compute equivalent units of production.
(LO 3), AP

BE16-5 The Smelting Department of Kiner Company has the following production data for November.

> Beginning work in process 2,000 units that are 100% complete as to materials and 20% complete as to conversion costs; units transferred out 9,000 units; and ending work in process 7,000 units that are 100% complete as to materials and 40% complete as to conversion costs.

Compute the equivalent units of production for (a) materials and (b) conversion costs for the month of November.

Compute unit costs of production.
(LO 4), AP

BE16-6 In Mordica Company, total materials costs are $33,000, and total conversion costs are $54,000. Equivalent units of production are materials 10,000 and conversion costs 12,000. Compute the unit costs for materials, conversion costs, and total manufacturing costs.

Assign costs to units transferred out and in process.
(LO 4), AP

BE16-7 Trek Company has the following production data for April: units transferred out 40,000, and ending work in process 5,000 units that are 100% complete for materials and 40% complete for conversion costs. If unit materials cost is $4 and unit conversion cost is $7, determine the costs to be assigned to the units transferred out and the units in ending work in process.

Compute unit costs.
(LO 4), AP

BE16-8 Production costs chargeable to the Finishing Department in June in Hollins Company are materials $12,000, labor $29,500, and overhead $18,000. Equivalent units of production are materials 20,000 and conversion costs 19,000. Compute the unit costs for materials and conversion costs.

Prepare cost reconciliation schedule.
(LO 4), AP

BE16-9 Data for Hollins Company are given in BE16-8. Production records indicate that 18,000 units were transferred out, and 2,000 units in ending work in process were 50% complete as to conversion costs and 100% complete as to materials. Prepare a cost reconciliation schedule.

Assign costs to units transferred out and in process.
(LO 5), AP

***BE16-10** Pix Company has the following production data for March: no beginning work in process, units started and completed 30,000, and ending work in process 5,000 units that are 100% complete for materials and 40% complete for conversion costs. Pix uses the FIFO method to compute equivalent units. If unit materials cost is $6 and unit conversion cost is $10, determine the costs to be assigned to the units transferred out and the units in ending work in process. The total costs to be assigned are $530,000.

Prepare a partial production cost report.
(LO 5), AP

***BE16-11** Using the data in BE16-10, prepare the cost section of the production cost report for Pix Company.

Compute unit costs.
(LO 5), AP

***B163-12** Production costs chargeable to the Finishing Department in May at Kim Company are materials $8,000, labor $20,000, overhead $18,000, and transferred-in costs $67,000. Equivalent units of production are materials 20,000 and conversion costs 19,000. Kim uses the FIFO method to compute equivalent units. Compute the unit costs for materials and conversion costs. Transferred-in costs are considered materials costs.

DO IT! EXERCISES

Compare job order and process cost systems.
(LO 1), C

DO IT! 16-1 Indicate whether each of the following statements is true or false.

1. Many hospitals use job order costing for small, routine medical procedures.
2. A manufacturer of computer flash drives would use a job order cost system.
3. A process cost system uses multiple work in process accounts.
4. A process cost system keeps track of costs on job cost sheets.

Assign and journalize manufacturing costs.
(LO 2), AP

DO IT! 16-2 Kopa Company manufactures CH-21 through two processes: mixing and packaging. In July, the following costs were incurred.

	Mixing	Packaging
Raw materials used	$10,000	$28,000
Factory labor costs	8,000	36,000
Manufacturing overhead costs	12,000	54,000

Units completed at a cost of $21,000 in the Mixing Department are transferred to the Packaging Department. Units completed at a cost of $106,000 in the Packaging Department are transferred to Finished Goods. Journalize the assignment of these costs to the two processes and the transfer of units as appropriate.

Compute equivalent units.
(LO 3), AP

DO IT! 16-3 The Assembly Department for Right pens has the following production data for the current month.

Beginning Work in Process	Units Transferred Out	Ending Work in Process
–0–	20,000	10,000

Materials are entered at the beginning of the process. The ending work in process units are 70% complete as to conversion costs. Compute the equivalent units of production for (a) materials and (b) conversion costs.

Prepare cost reconciliation schedule.
(LO 4), AP

DO IT! 16-4 In March, Kelly Company had the following unit production costs: materials $10 and conversion costs $8. On March 1, it had no work in process. During March, Kelly transferred out 22,000 units. As of March 31, 4,000 units that were 40% complete as to conversion costs and 100% complete as to materials were in ending work in process.

(a) Compute the total units to be accounted for.
(b) Compute the equivalent units of production.
(c) Prepare a cost reconciliation schedule, including the costs of materials transferred out and the costs of materials in process.

EXERCISES

Understand process cost accounting.
(LO 1), C

E16-1 Robert Wilkins has prepared the following list of statements about process cost accounting.

1. Process cost systems are used to apply costs to similar products that are mass-produced in a continuous fashion.
2. A process cost system is used when each finished unit is indistinguishable from another.
3. Companies that produce soft drinks, movies, and computer chips would all use process cost accounting.
4. In a process cost system, costs are tracked by individual jobs.
5. Job order costing and process costing track different manufacturing cost elements.
6. Both job order costing and process costing account for direct materials, direct labor, and manufacturing overhead.
7. Costs flow through the accounts in the same basic way for both job order costing and process costing.
8. In a process cost system, only one work in process account is used.
9. In a process cost system, costs are summarized in a job cost sheet.
10. In a process cost system, the unit cost is total manufacturing costs for the period divided by the equivalent units produced during the period.

Instructions
Identify each statement as true or false. If false, indicate how to correct the statement.

Journalize transactions.
(LO 2), AP

E16-2 Harrelson Company manufactures pizza sauce through two production departments: Cooking and Canning. In each process, materials and conversion costs are incurred evenly throughout the process. For the month of April, the work in process accounts show the following debits.

	Cooking	Canning
Beginning work in process	$ –0–	$ 4,000
Materials	21,000	9,000
Labor	8,500	7,000
Overhead	31,500	25,800
Costs transferred in		53,000

Instructions
Journalize the April transactions.

Answer questions on costs and production.
(LO 2, 3, 4), AP

E16-3 The ledger of American Company has the following work in process account.

Work in Process—Painting

5/1	Balance	3,590	5/31	Transferred out	?
5/31	Materials	5,160			
5/31	Labor	2,530			
5/31	Overhead	1,380			
5/31	Balance	?			

Production records show that there were 400 units in the beginning inventory, 30% complete, 1,600 units started, and 1,700 units transferred out. The beginning work in process had materials cost of $2,040 and conversion costs of $1,550. The units in ending inventory were 40% complete. Materials are entered at the beginning of the painting process.

Instructions
(a) How many units are in process at May 31?
(b) What is the unit materials cost for May?
(c) What is the unit conversion cost for May?
(d) What is the total cost of units transferred out in May?
(e) What is the cost of the May 31 inventory?

Journalize transactions for two processes.
(LO 2), AP

E16-4 Schrager Company has two production departments: Cutting and Assembly. July 1 inventories are Raw Materials $4,200, Work in Process—Cutting $2,900, Work in Process—Assembly $10,600, and Finished Goods $31,000. During July, the following transactions occurred.

1. Purchased $62,500 of raw materials on account.
2. Incurred $60,000 of factory labor. (Credit Wages Payable.)
3. Incurred $70,000 of manufacturing overhead; $40,000 was paid and the remainder is unpaid.
4. Requisitioned materials for Cutting $15,700 and Assembly $8,900.
5. Used factory labor for Cutting $33,000 and Assembly $27,000.
6. Applied overhead at the rate of $18 per machine hour. Machine hours were Cutting 1,680 and Assembly 1,720.
7. Transferred goods costing $67,600 from the Cutting Department to the Assembly Department.
8. Transferred goods costing $134,900 from Assembly to Finished Goods.
9. Sold goods costing $150,000 for $200,000 on account.

Instructions
Journalize the transactions. (Omit explanations.)

E16-5 In Shady Company, materials are entered at the beginning of each process. Work in process inventories, with the percentage of work done on conversion costs, and production data for its Sterilizing Department in selected months during 2017 are as follows.

Compute physical units and equivalent units of production.

(LO 3, 4), AP

	Beginning Work in Process			Ending Work in Process	
Month	**Units**	**Conversion Cost%**	**Units Transferred Out**	**Units**	**Conversion Cost%**
January	–0–	—	11,000	2,000	60
March	–0–	—	12,000	3,000	30
May	–0–	—	14,000	7,000	80
July	–0–	—	10,000	1,500	40

Instructions

(a) Compute the physical units for January and May.

(b) Compute the equivalent units of production for (1) materials and (2) conversion costs for each month.

E16-6 The Cutting Department of Cassel Company has the following production and cost data for July.

Determine equivalent units, unit costs, and assignment of costs.

(LO 3, 4), AP

Production	**Costs**	
1. Transferred out 12,000 units.	Beginning work in process	$ –0–
2. Started 3,000 units that are 60% complete as to conversion costs and 100% complete as to materials at July 31.	Materials	45,000
	Labor	16,200
	Manufacturing overhead	18,300

Materials are entered at the beginning of the process. Conversion costs are incurred uniformly during the process.

Instructions

(a) Determine the equivalent units of production for (1) materials and (2) conversion costs.

(b) Compute unit costs and prepare a cost reconciliation schedule.

E16-7 The Sanding Department of Quik Furniture Company has the following production and manufacturing cost data for March 2017, the first month of operation.

Prepare a production cost report.

(LO 3, 4), AP

XLS

Production: 7,000 units finished and transferred out; 3,000 units started that are 100% complete as to materials and 20% complete as to conversion costs.

Manufacturing costs: Materials $33,000; labor $21,000; and overhead $36,000.

Instructions

Prepare a production cost report.

E16-8 The Blending Department of Luongo Company has the following cost and production data for the month of April.

Determine equivalent units, unit costs, and assignment of costs.

(LO 3, 4), AP

Costs:	
Work in process, April 1	
Direct materials: 100% complete	$100,000
Conversion costs: 20% complete	70,000
Cost of work in process, April 1	$170,000
Costs incurred during production in April	
Direct materials	$ 800,000
Conversion costs	365,000
Costs incurred in April	$1,165,000

Units transferred out totaled 17,000. Ending work in process was 1,000 units that are 100% complete as to materials and 40% complete as to conversion costs.

Instructions

(a) Compute the equivalent units of production for (1) materials and (2) conversion costs for the month of April.
(b) Compute the unit costs for the month.
(c) Determine the costs to be assigned to the units transferred out and in ending work in process.

Determine equivalent units, unit costs, and assignment of costs.
(LO 3, 4), AP

E16-9 Baden Company has gathered the following information.

Units in beginning work in process	–0–
Units started into production	36,000
Units in ending work in process	6,000
Percent complete in ending work in process:	
Conversion costs	40%
Materials	100%
Costs incurred:	
Direct materials	$72,000
Direct labor	$61,000
Overhead	$101,000

Instructions

(a) Compute equivalent units of production for materials and for conversion costs.
(b) Determine the unit costs of production.
(c) Show the assignment of costs to units transferred out and in process.

Determine equivalent units, unit costs, and assignment of costs.
(LO 3, 4), AP

E16-10 Overton Company has gathered the following information.

Units in beginning work in process	20,000
Units started into production	164,000
Units in ending work in process	24,000
Percent complete in ending work in process:	
Conversion costs	60%
Materials	100%
Costs incurred:	
Direct materials	$101,200
Direct labor	$164,800
Overhead	$184,000

Instructions

(a) Compute equivalent units of production for materials and for conversion costs.
(b) Determine the unit costs of production.
(c) Show the assignment of costs to units transferred out and in process.

Compute equivalent units, unit costs, and costs assigned.
(LO 3, 4), AP

XLS

E16-11 The Polishing Department of Major Company has the following production and manufacturing cost data for September. Materials are entered at the beginning of the process.

Production: Beginning inventory 1,600 units that are 100% complete as to materials and 30% complete as to conversion costs; units started during the period are 42,900; ending inventory of 5,000 units 10% complete as to conversion costs.

Manufacturing costs: Beginning inventory costs, comprised of $20,000 of materials and $43,180 of conversion costs; materials costs added in Polishing during the month, $175,800; labor and overhead applied in Polishing during the month, $125,680 and $257,140, respectively.

Instructions

(a) Compute the equivalent units of production for materials and conversion costs for the month of September.
(b) Compute the unit costs for materials and conversion costs for the month.
(c) Determine the costs to be assigned to the units transferred out and in process.

E16-12 David Skaros has recently been promoted to production manager. He has just started to receive various managerial reports, including the production cost report that you prepared. It showed that his department had 2,000 equivalent units in ending inventory. His department has had a history of not keeping enough inventory on hand to meet demand. He has come to you, very angry, and wants to know why you credited him with only 2,000 units when he knows he had at least twice that many on hand.

Explain the production cost report.

(LO 4), S

Instructions

Explain to him why his production cost report showed only 2,000 equivalent units in ending inventory. Write an informal memo. Be kind and explain very clearly why he is mistaken.

E16-13 The Welding Department of Healthy Company has the following production and manufacturing cost data for February 2017. All materials are added at the beginning of the process.

Prepare a production cost report.

(LO 3, 4), AP

Manufacturing Costs		
Beginning work in process		
Materials	$18,000	
Conversion costs	14,175	$ 32,175
Materials		180,000
Labor		67,380
Overhead		61,445

Production Data	
Beginning work in process	15,000 units
	1/10 complete
Units transferred out	55,000
Units started	51,000
Ending work in process	11,000 units
	1/5 complete

Instructions

Prepare a production cost report for the Welding Department for the month of February.

E16-14 Remington Inc. is contemplating the use of process costing to track the costs of its operations. The operation consists of three segments (departments): Receiving, Shipping, and Delivery. Containers are received at Remington's docks and sorted according to the ship they will be carried on. The containers are loaded onto a ship, which carries them to the appropriate port of destination. The containers are then off-loaded and delivered to the Receiving Department.

Compute physical units and equivalent units of production.

(LO 3, 4), AP

Remington wants to begin using process costing in the Shipping Department. Direct materials represent the fuel costs to run the ship, and "Containers in transit" represents work in process. Listed below is information about the Shipping Department's first month's activity.

Containers in transit, April 1	0
Containers loaded	1,200
Containers in transit, April 30	350, 40% of direct materials and 20% of conversion costs

Instructions

(a) Determine the physical flow of containers for the month.

(b) Calculate the equivalent units for direct materials and conversion costs.

E16-15 Santana Mortgage Company uses a process cost system to accumulate costs in its Application Department. When an application is completed, it is forwarded to the Loan Department for final processing. The following processing and cost data pertain to September.

Determine equivalent units, unit costs, and assignment of costs.

(LO 3, 4), AP

1. Applications in process on September 1: 100.
2. Applications started in September: 1,000.
3. Completed applications during September: 800.
4. Applications still in process at September 30: 100% complete as to materials (forms) and 60% complete as to conversion costs.

Beginning WIP:	
Direct materials	$ 1,000
Conversion costs	3,960
September costs:	
Direct materials	$ 4,500
Direct labor	12,000
Overhead	9,520

Materials are the forms used in the application process, and these costs are incurred at the beginning of the process. Conversion costs are incurred uniformly during the process.

Instructions

(a) Determine the equivalent units of service (production) for materials and conversion costs.

(b) Compute the unit costs and prepare a cost reconciliation schedule.

Compute equivalent units, unit costs, and costs assigned.

(LO 5), AP

***E16-16** Using the data in E16-15, assume Santana Mortgage Company uses the FIFO method. Also, assume that the applications in process on September 1 were 100% complete as to materials (forms) and 40% complete as to conversion costs. Assume overhead costs were $9,620 instead of $9,520.

Instructions

(a) Determine the equivalent units of service (production) for materials and conversion costs.

(b) Compute the unit costs and prepare a cost reconciliation schedule.

Determine equivalent units, unit costs, and assignment of costs.

(LO 5), AP

***E16-17** The Cutting Department of Lasso Company has the following production and cost data for August.

Production	Costs	
1. Started and completed 10,000 units.	Beginning work in process	$ –0–
2. Started 2,000 units that are 40% completed at August 31.	Materials	45,000
	Labor	13,600
	Manufacturing overhead	16,100

Materials are entered at the beginning of the process. Conversion costs are incurred uniformly during the process. Lasso Company uses the FIFO method to compute equivalent units.

Instructions

(a) Determine the equivalent units of production for (1) materials and (2) conversion costs.

(b) Compute unit costs and show the assignment of manufacturing costs to units transferred out and in work in process.

Compute equivalent units, unit costs, and costs assigned.

(LO 5), AP

***E16-18** The Smelting Department of Polzin Company has the following production and cost data for September.

Production: Beginning work in process 2,000 units that are 100% complete as to materials and 20% complete as to conversion costs; units started and finished 9,000 units; and ending work in process 1,000 units that are 100% complete as to materials and 40% complete as to conversion costs.

Manufacturing costs: Work in process, September 1, $15,200; materials added $60,000; labor and overhead $132,000.

Polzin uses the FIFO method to compute equivalent units.

Instructions

(a) Compute the equivalent units of production for (1) materials and (2) conversion costs for the month of September.

(b) Compute the unit costs for the month.

(c) Determine the costs to be assigned to the units transferred out and in process.

Answer questions on costs and production.

(LO 5), AP

***E16-19** The ledger of Hasgrove Company has the following work in process account.

Work in Process—Painting

3/1	Balance	3,680	3/31	Transferred out	?
3/31	Materials	6,600			
3/31	Labor	2,400			
3/31	Overhead	1,150			
3/31	Balance	?			

Production records show that there were 800 units in the beginning inventory, 30% complete, 1,100 units started, and 1,500 units transferred out. The units in ending inventory were 40% complete. Materials are entered at the beginning of the painting process. Hasgrove uses the FIFO method to compute equivalent units.

Instructions

Answer the following questions.

(a) How many units are in process at March 31?
(b) What is the unit materials cost for March?
(c) What is the unit conversion cost for March?
(d) What is the total cost of units started in February and completed in March?
(e) What is the total cost of units started and finished in March?
(f) What is the cost of the March 31 inventory?

***E16-20** The Welding Department of Majestic Company has the following production and manufacturing cost data for February 2017. All materials are added at the beginning of the process. Majestic uses the FIFO method to compute equivalent units.

Prepare a production cost report for a second process.
(LO 5), AP

Manufacturing Costs		Production Data	
Beginning work in process	$ 32,175	Beginning work in process	15,000 units, 10% complete
Costs transferred in	135,000		
Materials	57,000	Units transferred out	54,000
Labor	35,100	Units transferred in	64,000
Overhead	68,400	Ending work in process	25,000 units 20% complete

Instructions

Prepare a production cost report for the Welding Department for the month of February. Transferred-in costs are considered materials costs.

EXERCISES: SET B AND CHALLENGE EXERCISES

Visit the book's companion website, at **www.wiley.com/college/kimmel**, and choose the Student Companion site to access Exercises: Set B and Challenge Exercises.

PROBLEMS: SET A

P16-1A Fire Out Company manufactures its product, Vitadrink, through two manufacturing processes: Mixing and Packaging. All materials are entered at the beginning of each process. On October 1, 2017, inventories consisted of Raw Materials $26,000, Work in Process—Mixing $0, Work in Process—Packaging $250,000, and Finished Goods $289,000. The beginning inventory for Packaging consisted of 10,000 units that were 50% complete as to conversion costs and fully complete as to materials. During October, 50,000 units were started into production in the Mixing Department and the following transactions were completed.

Journalize transactions.
(LO 2), AP

1. Purchased $300,000 of raw materials on account.
2. Issued raw materials for production: Mixing $210,000 and Packaging $45,000.
3. Incurred labor costs of $278,900.
4. Used factory labor: Mixing $182,500 and Packaging $96,400.
5. Incurred $810,000 of manufacturing overhead on account.
6. Applied manufacturing overhead on the basis of $23 per machine hour. Machine hours were 28,000 in Mixing and 6,000 in Packaging.
7. Transferred 45,000 units from Mixing to Packaging at a cost of $979,000.
8. Transferred 53,000 units from Packaging to Finished Goods at a cost of $1,315,000.
9. Sold goods costing $1,604,000 for $2,500,000 on account.

Instructions

Journalize the October transactions.

Complete four steps necessary to prepare a production cost report.
(LO 3, 4), AP

P16-2A Rosenthal Company manufactures bowling balls through two processes: Molding and Packaging. In the Molding Department, the urethane, rubber, plastics, and other materials are molded into bowling balls. In the Packaging Department, the balls are placed in cartons and sent to the finished goods warehouse. All materials are entered at the beginning of each process. Labor and manufacturing overhead are incurred uniformly throughout each process. Production and cost data for the Molding Department during June 2017 are presented below.

Production Data	June
Beginning work in process units	–0–
Units started into production	22,000
Ending work in process units	2,000
Percent complete—ending inventory	40%
Cost Data	
Materials	$198,000
Labor	53,600
Overhead	112,800
Total	$364,400

Instructions

(a) Prepare a schedule showing physical units of production.
(b) Determine the equivalent units of production for materials and conversion costs.
(c) Compute the unit costs of production.
(d) Determine the costs to be assigned to the units transferred out and in process for June.
(e) Prepare a production cost report for the Molding Department for the month of June.

(c) Materials $9.00
CC $8.00
(d) Transferred out $340,000
WIP $ 24,400

Complete four steps necessary to prepare a production cost report.
(LO 3, 4), AP

P16-3A Thakin Industries Inc. manufactures dorm furniture in separate processes. In each process, materials are entered at the beginning, and conversion costs are incurred uniformly. Production and cost data for the first process in making two products in two different manufacturing plants are as follows.

	Cutting Department	
Production Data—July	**Plant 1 T12-Tables**	**Plant 2 C10-Chairs**
Work in process units, July 1	–0–	–0–
Units started into production	20,000	18,000
Work in process units, July 31	3,000	500
Work in process percent complete	60	80
Cost Data—July		
Work in process, July 1	$ –0–	$ –0–
Materials	380,000	288,000
Labor	234,400	110,000
Overhead	104,000	104,800
Total	$718,400	$502,800

Instructions

(a) For each plant:
(1) Compute the physical units of production.
(2) Compute equivalent units of production for materials and for conversion costs.
(3) Determine the unit costs of production.
(4) Show the assignment of costs to units transferred out and in process.
(b) Prepare the production cost report for Plant 1 for July 2017.

(a) (3) T12:
Materials $19
CC $18
(4) T12:
Transferred out $629,000
WIP $ 89,400

P16-4A Rivera Company has several processing departments. Costs charged to the Assembly Department for November 2017 totaled $2,280,000 as follows.

Assign costs and prepare production cost report.

(LO 3, 4), AP

Work in process, November 1		
Materials	$79,000	
Conversion costs	48,150	$ 127,150
Materials added		1,589,000
Labor		225,920
Overhead		337,930

Production records show that 35,000 units were in beginning work in process 30% complete as to conversion costs, 660,000 units were started into production, and 25,000 units were in ending work in process 40% complete as to conversion costs. Materials are entered at the beginning of each process.

Instructions

(a) Determine the equivalent units of production and the unit production costs for the Assembly Department.
(b) Determine the assignment of costs to goods transferred out and in process.
(c) Prepare a production cost report for the Assembly Department.

(b) Transferred out $2,211,000
WIP $ 69,000

P16-5A Polk Company manufactures basketballs. Materials are added at the beginning of the production process and conversion costs are incurred uniformly. Production and cost data for the month of July 2017 are as follows.

Determine equivalent units and unit costs and assign costs.

(LO 3, 4), AP

Production Data—Basketballs		Units	Percentage Complete
Work in process units, July 1		500	60%
Units started into production		1,000	
Work in process units, July 31		600	40%
Cost Data—Basketballs			
Work in process, July 1			
Materials	$750		
Conversion costs	600	$1,350	
Direct materials		2,400	
Direct labor		1,580	
Manufacturing overhead		1,240	

Instructions

(a) Calculate the following.
  (1) The equivalent units of production for materials and conversion costs.
  (2) The unit costs of production for materials and conversion costs.
  (3) The assignment of costs to units transferred out and in process at the end of the accounting period.
(b) Prepare a production cost report for the month of July for the basketballs.

(a) (2) Materials $ 2.10
(3) Transferred out $4,590
WIP $1,980

P16-6A Hamilton Processing Company uses a weighted-average process cost system and manufactures a single product—an industrial carpet shampoo and cleaner used by many universities. The manufacturing activity for the month of October has just been completed. A partially completed production cost report for the month of October for the Mixing and Cooking Department is shown on page 830.

Compute equivalent units and complete production cost report.

(LO 3, 4), AP

Instructions

(a) Prepare a schedule that shows how the equivalent units were computed so that you can complete the "Quantities: Units accounted for" equivalent units section shown in the production cost report, and compute October unit costs.
(b) Complete the "Cost Reconciliation Schedule" part of the production cost report.

(a) Materials $ 1.60
(b) Transferred out $282,000
WIP $ 63,000

HAMILTON PROCESSING COMPANY
Mixing and Cooking Department
Production Cost Report
For the Month Ended October 31

Quantities	Physical Units	Equivalent Units: Materials	Equivalent Units: Conversion Costs
Units to be accounted for			
Work in process, October 1 (all materials, 70% conversion costs)	20,000		
Started into production	150,000		
Total units	170,000		
Units accounted for			
Transferred out	120,000	?	?
Work in process, October 31 (60% materials, 40% conversion costs)	50,000	?	?
Total units accounted for	170,000	?	?

Costs	Materials		Conversion Costs		Total
Unit costs					
Total cost	$240,000		$105,000		$345,000
Equivalent units	?		?		
Unit costs	$?	+	$?	=	$?
Costs to be accounted for					
Work in process, October 1					$ 30,000
Started into production					315,000
Total costs					$345,000

Cost Reconciliation Schedule		
Costs accounted for		
Transferred out		$?
Work in process, October 31		
Materials	$?	
Conversion costs	?	?
Total costs		$?

Determine equivalent units and unit costs and assign costs for processes; prepare production cost report.

(LO 5), AP

***P16-7A** Owen Company manufactures bicycles and tricycles. For both products, materials are added at the beginning of the production process, and conversion costs are incurred uniformly. Owen Company uses the FIFO method to compute equivalent units. Production and cost data for the month of March are as follows.

Production Data—Bicycles	Units	Percentage Complete
Work in process units, March 1	200	80%
Units started into production	1,000	
Work in process units, March 31	300	40%
Cost Data—Bicycles		
Work in process, March 1	$19,280	
Direct materials	50,000	
Direct labor	25,900	
Manufacturing overhead	30,000	

Production Data—Tricycles	Units	Percentage Complete
Work in process units, March 1	100	75%
Units started into production	1,000	
Work in process units, March 31	60	25%

Cost Data—Tricycles	
Work in process, March 1	$ 6,125
Direct materials	30,000
Direct labor	14,300
Manufacturing overhead	20,000

Instructions

(a) Calculate the following for both the bicycles and the tricycles.
  (1) The equivalent units of production for materials and conversion costs.
  (2) The unit costs of production for materials and conversion costs.
  (3) The assignment of costs to units transferred out and in process at the end of the accounting period.

(b) Prepare a production cost report for the month of March for the bicycles only.

(a) Bicycles:
(1) Materials 1,000
(2) Materials $50
(3) Transferred out $102,380
WIP $ 22,800

PROBLEMS: SET B AND SET C

Visit the book's companion website, at **www.wiley.com/college/kimmel**, and choose the Student Companion site to access Problems: Set B and Set C.

CONTINUING PROBLEMS

CURRENT DESIGNS

EXCEL TUTORIAL

CD16 Building a kayak using the composite method is a very labor-intensive process. In the Fabrication Department, the kayaks go through several steps as employees carefully place layers of Kevlar® in a mold and then use resin to fuse together the layers. The excess resin is removed with a vacuum process, and the upper shell and lower shell are removed from the molds and assembled. The seat, hatch, and other components are added in the Finishing Department.

At the beginning of April, Current Designs had 30 kayaks in process in the Fabrication Department. Rick Thrune, the production manager, estimated that about 80% of the materials costs had been added to these boats, which were about 50% complete with respect to the conversion costs. The cost of this inventory had been calculated to be $8,400 in materials and $9,000 in conversion costs.

During April, 72 boats were started. At the end of the month, the 35 kayaks in the ending inventory had 20% of the materials and 40% of the conversion costs already added to them.

A review of the accounting records for April showed that materials with a cost of $17,500 had been requisitioned by the Fabrication Department and that the conversion costs for the month were $39,600.

Instructions

Complete a production cost report for April 2017 for the Fabrication Department using the weighted-average method.

WATERWAYS

(*Note:* This is a continuation of the Waterways problem from Chapters 14–15.)

WP16 Because most of the parts for its irrigation systems are standard, Waterways handles the majority of its manufacturing as a process cost system. There are multiple process departments. Three of these departments are the Molding, Cutting, and Welding Departments. All items eventually end up in the Packaging Department, which prepares items for sale in kits or individually. This problem asks you to help Waterways calculate equivalent units and prepare a production cost report.

Go to the book's companion website, at **www.wiley.com/college/kimmel**, *to see the completion of this problem.*

EXPAND YOUR CRITICAL THINKING

Group Project

DECISION-MAKING ACROSS THE ORGANIZATION

AP **CT16-1** Florida Beach Company manufactures sunscreen, called NoTan, in 11-ounce plastic bottles. NoTan is sold in a competitive market. As a result, management is very cost-conscious. NoTan is manufactured through two processes: mixing and filling. Materials are entered at the beginning of each process, and labor and manufacturing overhead occur uniformly throughout each process. Unit costs are based on the cost per gallon of NoTan using the weighted-average costing approach.

On June 30, 2017, Mary Ritzman, the chief accountant for the past 20 years, opted to take early retirement. Her replacement, Joe Benili, had extensive accounting experience with motels in the area but only limited contact with manufacturing accounting. During July, Joe correctly accumulated the following production quantity and cost data for the Mixing Department.

Production quantities: Work in process, July 1, 8,000 gallons 75% complete; started into production 100,000 gallons; work in process, July 31, 5,000 gallons 20% complete. Materials are added at the beginning of the process.

Production costs: Beginning work in process $88,000, comprised of $21,000 of materials costs and $67,000 of conversion costs; incurred in July: materials $573,000, conversion costs $765,000.

Joe then prepared a production cost report on the basis of physical units started into production. His report showed a production cost of $14.26 per gallon of NoTan. The management of Florida Beach was surprised at the high unit cost. The president comes to you, as Mary's top assistant, to review Joe's report and prepare a correct report if necessary.

Instructions
With the class divided into groups, answer the following questions.

(a) Show how Joe arrived at the unit cost of $14.26 per gallon of NoTan.
(b) What error(s) did Joe make in preparing his production cost report?
(c) Prepare a correct production cost report for July.

MANAGERIAL ANALYSIS

AN **CT16-2** Harris Furniture Company manufactures living room furniture through two departments: Framing and Upholstering. Materials are entered at the beginning of each process. For May, the following cost data are obtained from the two work in process accounts.

	Framing	Upholstering
Work in process, May 1	$ –0–	$?
Materials	450,000	?
Conversion costs	261,000	330,000
Costs transferred in	–0–	600,000
Costs transferred out	600,000	?
Work in process, May 31	111,000	?

Instructions
Answer the following questions.

(a) If 3,000 sofas were started into production on May 1 and 2,500 sofas were transferred to Upholstering, what was the unit cost of materials for May in the Framing Department?
(b) Using the data in (a) above, what was the per unit conversion cost of the sofas transferred to Upholstering?
(c) Continuing the assumptions in (a) above, what is the percentage of completion of the units in process at May 31 in the Framing Department?

REAL-WORLD FOCUS

E **CT16-3** Paintball is now played around the world. The process of making paintballs is actually quite similar to the process used to make certain medical pills. In fact, paintballs were previously often made at the same factories that made pharmaceuticals.

Address: Go to **www.youtube.com/watch?v=2hKrv60PJKE#t=129** to access the video.

Instructions
View that video at the site listed above and then answer the following questions.

(a) Describe in sequence the primary steps used to manufacture paintballs.
(b) Explain the costs incurred by the company that would fall into each of the following categories: materials, labor, and overhead. Of these categories, which do you think would be the greatest cost in making paintballs?
(c) Discuss whether a paintball manufacturer would use job order costing or process costing.

COMMUNICATION ACTIVITY

CT16-4 Diane Barone was a good friend of yours in high school and is from your home town. While you chose to major in accounting when you both went away to college, she majored in marketing and management. You are now the accounting manager for the Snack Foods Division of Melton Enterprises. Your friend Diane was promoted to regional sales manager for the same division of Melton. Diane recently telephoned you. She explained that she was familiar with job cost sheets, which had been used by the Special Projects Division where she had formerly worked. She was, however, very uncomfortable with the production cost reports prepared by your division. She emailed you a list of her particular questions:

Writing

E

1. Since Melton occasionally prepares snack foods for special orders in the Snack Foods Division, why don't we track costs of the orders separately?
2. What is an equivalent unit?
3. Why am I getting four production cost reports? Isn't there one work in process account?

Instructions
Prepare a memo to Diane. Answer her questions and include any additional information you think would be helpful. You may write informally but do use proper grammar and punctuation.

ETHICS CASE

CT16-5 R. B. Dillman Company manufactures a high-tech component used in Bluetooth speakers that passes through two production processing departments, Molding and Assembly. Department managers are partially compensated on the basis of units of products completed and transferred out relative to units of product put into production. This was intended as encouragement to be efficient and to minimize waste.

Jan Wooten is the department head in the Molding Department, and Tony Ferneti is her quality control inspector. During the month of June, Jan had three new employees who were not yet technically skilled. As a result, many of the units produced in June had minor molding defects. In order to maintain the department's normal high rate of completion, Jan told Tony to pass through inspection and on to the Assembly Department all units that had defects nondetectable to the human eye. "Company and industry tolerances on this product are too high anyway," says Jan. "Less than 2% of the units we produce are subjected in the market to the stress tolerance we've designed into them. The odds of those 2% being any of this month's units are even less. Anyway, we're saving the company money."

Instructions
(a) Who are the potential stakeholders involved in this situation?
(b) What alternatives does Tony have in this situation? What might the company do to prevent this situation from occurring?

CONSIDERING PEOPLE, PLANET, AND PROFIT

CT16-6 In a recent year, an oil refinery in Texas City, Texas, on the Houston Ship Channel exploded. The explosion killed 14 people and sent a plume of smoke hundreds of feet into the air. The blast started as a fire in the section of the plant that increased the octane of the gasoline that was produced at the refinery. The Houston Ship Channel is the main waterway that allows commerce to flow from the Gulf of Mexico into Houston.

E

The Texas Commission on Environmental Quality expressed concern about the release of nitrogen oxides, benzene, and other known carcinogens as a result of the blast. Neighbors of the plant complained that the plant had been emitting carcinogens for years and that the regulators had ignored their complaints about emissions and unsafe working conditions.

Instructions
Answer the following questions.

(a) Outline the costs that the company now faces as a result of the accident.
(b) How could the company have reduced the costs associated with the accident?

17

Activity-Based Costing

CHAPTER PREVIEW

As indicated in the Feature Story about Precor, the traditional costing systems described in earlier chapters are not the best answer for every company. Precor suspected that the traditional system was masking significant differences in its real cost structure, so it sought a new method of assigning costs. Similar searches by other companies for ways to improve operations and gather more accurate data for decision-making have resulted in the development of powerful new management tools, including **activity-based costing (ABC)**. The primary objective of this chapter is to explain and illustrate this concept.

CHAPTER OUTLINE

LEARNING OBJECTIVES		PRACTICE
1 Discuss the difference between traditional costing and activity-based costing.	• Traditional costing systems • Illustration of a traditional system • Need for a new approach • Activity-based costing	DO IT! 1 Costing Systems
2 Apply activity-based costing to a manufacturer.	• Identify and classify activities and assign overhead • Identify cost drivers • Compute activity-based overhead rates • Allocate overhead costs • Comparing unit costs	DO IT! 2 Apply ABC to Manufacturer
3 Explain the benefits and limitations of activity-based costing.	• Advantage of multiple cost pools • Advantage of enhanced cost control • Advantage of better management decisions • Limitations of ABC	DO IT! 3 Classify Activity Levels
4 Apply activity-based costing to service industries.	• Traditional costing example • ABC example	DO IT! 4 Apply ABC to Service Company

Go to the ***REVIEW AND PRACTICE*** section at the end of the chapter for a targeted summary and exercises with solutions.

Visit **WileyPLUS** for additional tutorials and practice opportunities.

© mediaphotos/iStockphoto

FEATURE STORY

Precor Is on Your Side

Do you feel like the whole world is conspiring against your efforts to get in shape? Is it humanly possible to resist the constant barrage of advertisements and fast-food servers who pleasantly encourage us to "supersize" it? Lest we think that we have no allies in our battle against the bulge, consider Precor.

Ever since it made the first ergonomically sound rowing machine in 1980, Precor's sole mission has been to provide exercise equipment. It makes elliptical trainers, exercise bikes, rowing machines, treadmills, multi-station strength systems, and many other forms of equipment designed to erase the cumulative effects of a fast-food nation. Its equipment is widely used in Hilton hotels, Gold's Gym franchises, and even in Madonna's Hard Candy fitness center in Moscow.

Building high-quality fitness equipment requires sizable investments by Precor in buildings and machinery. For example, Precor recently moved its facilities from Valencia, California, to Greensboro, North Carolina. In order to reduce costs and minimize environmental impact, the company installed low-flow water fixtures, high-efficiency heating and cooling systems, and state-of-the-art lighting in its $26 million, 230,000-square-foot facility. As a result of these efforts, Precor's new facility received a Leadership in Energy and Efficient Design (LEED) CI Gold Certification.

Because of its huge investments in property, plant, and equipment, overhead costs represent a large percentage of the cost of Precor's exercise equipment. The combination of high overhead costs and a wide variety of products means that it is important that Precor allocates its overhead accurately to its various products. Without accurate cost information, Precor would not know whether its elliptical trainers and recumbent bicycles are making money, whether its AMT 100i adaptive motion trainer is priced high enough to cover its costs, or if its 240i Stretchtrainer is losing money.

To increase the accuracy of its costs, Precor uses a method of overhead allocation that focuses on identifying the types of activities that cause the company to incur costs. It then assigns more overhead to those products that rely most heavily on cost-incurring activities. By doing this, the allocation of overhead is less arbitrary than traditional overhead allocation methods. In short, before it can help us burn off the pounds, Precor needs to understand what drives its overhead costs.

Source: www.precor.com.

LEARNING OBJECTIVE 1

Discuss the difference between traditional costing and activity-based costing.

TRADITIONAL COSTING SYSTEMS

It is probably impossible to determine the *exact* cost of a product or service. However, in order to achieve improved management decisions, companies strive to provide decision-makers with the most accurate cost estimates they can. The most accurate estimate of product cost occurs when the costs are traceable directly to the actual product or service. Direct materials and direct labor costs are the easiest to trace directly to the product through the use of material requisition forms and payroll time sheets. Overhead costs, on the other hand, are an indirect or common cost that generally cannot be easily or directly traced to individual products or services. Instead, companies use estimates to assign overhead costs to products and services.

Often, the most difficult part of computing accurate unit costs is determining the proper amount of **overhead cost** to assign to each product, service, or job. In our coverage of job order costing in Chapter 15 and of process costing in Chapter 16, we used a single or plantwide overhead rate throughout the year for the entire factory operation. That rate was called the **predetermined overhead rate**. For job order costing, we assumed that **direct labor cost** was the relevant activity base for assigning all overhead costs to jobs. For process costing, we assumed that **machine hours** was the relevant activity base for assigning all overhead to the process or department. Illustration 17-1 displays a simplified (one-stage) traditional costing system relying on direct labor to assign overhead.

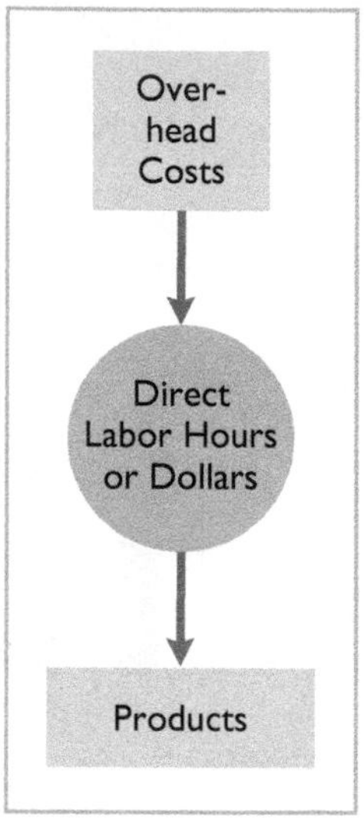

ILLUSTRATION 17-1
Traditional one-stage costing system

ILLUSTRATION OF A TRADITIONAL COSTING SYSTEM

To illustrate a traditional costing system, assume that Atlas Company produces two abdominal fitness products—the Ab Bench and the Ab Coaster. Each year, the company produces 25,000 Ab Benches but only 5,000 Ab Coasters. Each unit produced requires one hour of direct labor, for a total of 30,000 labor hours (25,000 + 5,000). The direct labor cost is $12 per unit for each product.

The direct materials cost per unit is $40 for the Ab Bench and $30 for the Ab Coaster. Therefore, the total manufacturing costs (excluding overhead) is $52 for the Ab Bench and $42 for the Ab Coaster, as shown in Illustration 17-2.

ILLUSTRATION 17-2
Direct costs per unit—traditional costing

Atlas Company.xls

	A	B	C
1	ATLAS COMPANY		
2	Manufacturing Costs	Ab Bench	Ab Coaster
3	Direct materials	$40	$30
4	Direct labor	12	12
5	Total direct cost per unit	$52	$42
6			

Atlas also expects to incur annual manufacturing overhead costs of $900,000. Atlas allocates overhead using a single predetermined overhead rate based on the 30,000 direct labor hours it expects to use. Thus, the predetermined overhead rate is $30 per direct labor hour ($900,000 / 30,000 direct labor hours).

Since both products require one direct labor hour per unit, both products are allocated overhead costs of $30 per unit under traditional costing. Illustration 17-3 shows the total unit costs for the Ab Bench and the Ab Coaster.

ILLUSTRATION 17-3
Total unit costs—traditional costing

ATLAS COMPANY		
Manufacturing Costs	Ab Bench	Ab Coaster
Direct materials	$40	$30
Direct labor	12	12
Overhead	30	30
Total direct cost per unit	$82	$72

THE NEED FOR A NEW APPROACH

As shown in Illustration 17-3, Atlas allocates the same amount of overhead costs per unit to both the Ab Bench and the Ab Coaster because these two products use the same amount of direct labor hours per unit. However, using a single rate based on direct labor hours may not be the best approach for Atlas to allocate its overhead.

Historically, the use of direct labor as the activity base made sense as direct labor made up a large portion of total manufacturing cost. Therefore, there was a high correlation between direct labor and the incurrence of overhead cost. Direct labor thus became the most popular basis for allocating overhead.

In recent years, however, manufacturers and service providers have experienced tremendous changes. Advances in computerized systems, technological innovations, global competition, and automation have altered the manufacturing environment drastically. As a result, the amount of direct labor used in many industries has greatly decreased, and total overhead costs resulting from depreciation on expensive equipment and machinery, utilities, repairs, and maintenance have significantly increased. When there is less (or no) correlation between direct labor and overhead costs incurred, plantwide predetermined overhead rates based on direct labor are misleading. Companies that use overhead rates based on direct labor when this correlation does not exist experience significant product cost distortions.

To minimize such distortions, many companies began to use machine hours instead of labor hours as the basis to allocate overhead in an automated manufacturing environment. But, even machine hours may not serve as a good basis for plantwide allocation of overhead costs. For example, product design and engineering costs are not correlated with machine hours but instead with the number of different items a company produces. Companies that have complex processes need to use multiple allocation bases to compute accurate product costs. An overhead cost allocation method that uses multiple bases is **activity-based costing**.

ACTIVITY-BASED COSTING

Activity-based costing (ABC) is an approach for allocating overhead costs. Specifically, ABC allocates overhead to multiple activity cost pools and then assigns the activity cost pools to products and services by means of cost drivers. In using ABC, you need to understand the following concepts.

KEY CONCEPTS

ACTIVITY. Any event, action, transaction, or work sequence that incurs costs when producing a product or performing a service.

ACTIVITY COST POOL. The overhead cost attributed to a distinct activity (e.g., ordering materials or setting up machines).

COST DRIVER. Any factor or activity that has a direct cause-effect relationship with the resources consumed.

Activity-based costing involves the following four steps, as shown in Illustration 17-4.

ILLUSTRATION 17-4
The four steps of activity-based costing

1. **Identify and classify the activities** involved in the manufacture of specific products and **assign overhead to cost pools.**

↓

2. **Identify the cost driver** that has a strong correlation to the costs accumulated in each cost pool.

↓

3. **Compute the activity-based overhead rate** for each cost pool.

↓

4. **Allocate overhead costs to products** using the overhead rates determined for each cost pool.

ABC allocates overhead in a two-stage process. The first stage (Step 1) assigns overhead costs to activity cost pools. (Traditional costing systems, in contrast, allocate these costs to departments or to jobs.) Examples of overhead cost pools are ordering materials, setting up machines, assembling products, and inspecting products.

The second stage (Steps 2–4) allocates the overhead in the activity cost pools to products, using cost drivers. The cost drivers measure the number of individual activities undertaken to produce goods or perform services. Examples are number of purchase orders, number of setups, labor hours, and number of inspections. Illustration 17-5 shows examples of activities, and possible cost drivers to measure them, for a company that manufactures two types of abdominal exercise equipment—Ab Benches and Ab Coasters.

In the first step (as shown at the top of Illustration 17-5), the company assigns overhead costs to activity cost pools. In this simplified example, the company has identified four activity cost pools: purchasing, storing, machining, and supervising. After the costs are assigned to the activity cost pools, the company uses cost drivers to determine the costs to allocate to the individual products based on each product's use of each activity. For example, if Ab Benches require more activity by the purchasing department, as measured by the number of required purchase orders, then more of the overhead costs from the purchasing pool are allocated to the Ab Benches.

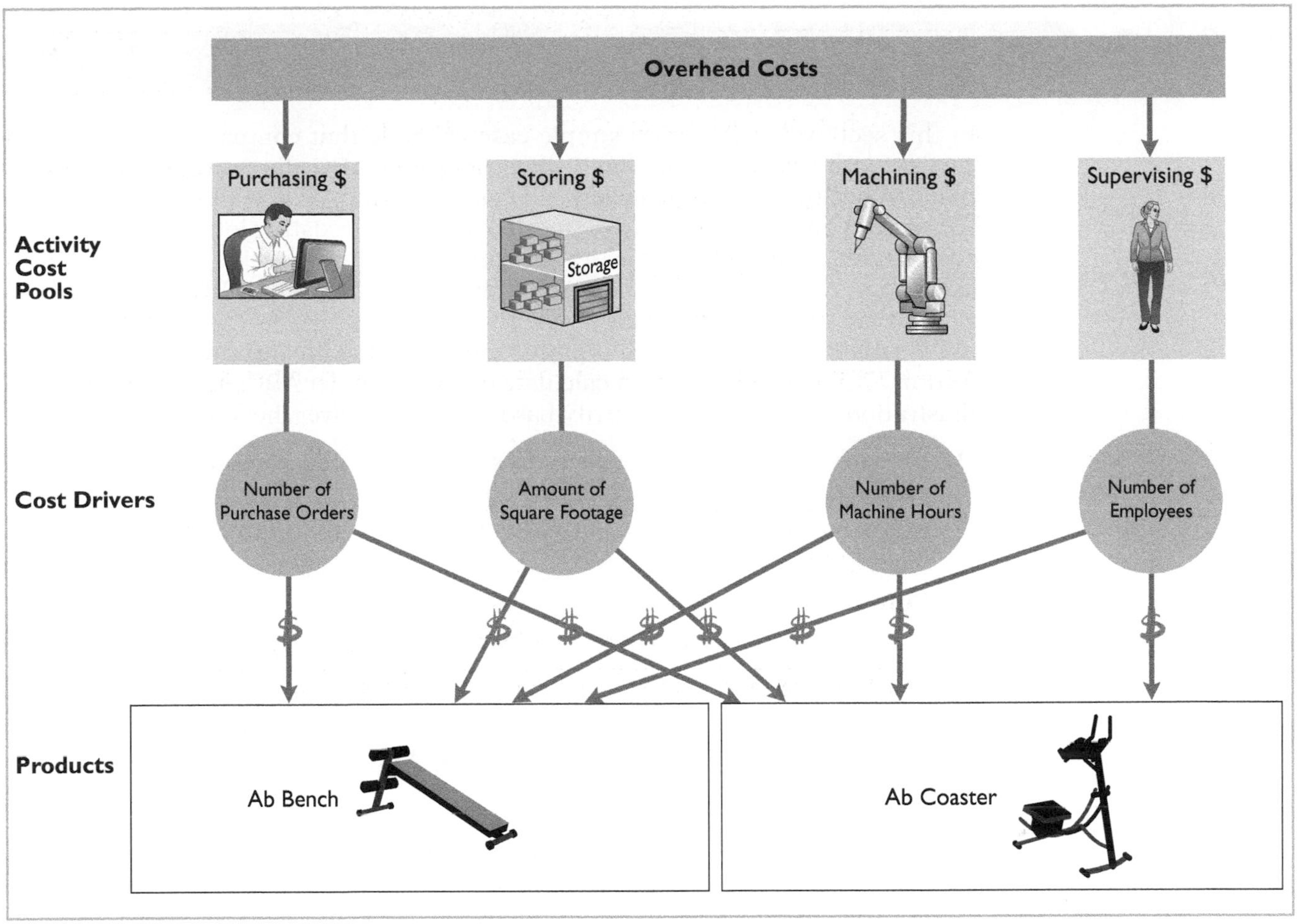

ILLUSTRATION 17-5
Activities and related cost drivers

The more complex a product's manufacturing operation, the more activities and cost drivers it is likely to have. If there is little or no correlation between changes in the cost driver and consumption of the overhead cost, inaccurate product costs are inevitable.

DO IT! ▶1 Costing Systems

Indicate whether the following statements are true or false.

1. A traditional costing system allocates overhead by means of multiple overhead rates.
2. Activity-based costing allocates overhead costs in a two-stage process.
3. Direct materials and direct labor costs are easier to trace to products than overhead.
4. As manufacturing processes have become more automated, more companies have chosen to allocate overhead on the basis of direct labor costs.
5. In activity-based costing, an activity is any event, action, transaction, or work sequence that incurs cost when producing goods or performing services.

Action Plan

✔ Understand that a traditional costing system allocates overhead on the basis of a single predetermined overhead rate.

✔ Understand that an ABC system assigns overhead to identified activity cost pools and then allocates costs to products using related cost drivers that measure the resources consumed.

SOLUTION

1. False. 2. True. 3. True. 4. False. 5. True.

Related exercise material: **BE17-1, BE17-2, E17-1, E17-2,** and **DO IT! 17-1.**

LEARNING OBJECTIVE 2

Apply activity-based costing to a manufacturer.

In this section, we present a simple case example that compares activity-based costing with traditional costing. It illustrates how ABC eliminates the distortion that can occur in traditional overhead cost allocation. As you study this example, you should understand that ABC does not *replace* an existing job order or process cost system. What ABC does is to segregate overhead into various cost pools in an effort to provide more accurate cost information. As a result, ABC supplements—rather than replaces—these cost systems.

Let's return to our Atlas Company example. Using the information from Illustration 17-3 (page 837), we can calculate unit costs under ABC. As shown earlier in Illustration 17-4 (page 838), activity-based costing involves the following four steps.

1. **Identify and classify the activities** involved in the manufacture of specific products and **assign overhead to cost pools**.
2. **Identify the cost driver** that has a strong correlation to the costs accumulated in each cost pool.
3. **Compute the activity-based overhead rate** for each cost pool.
4. **Allocate overhead costs to products** using the overhead rates determined for each cost pool.

IDENTIFY AND CLASSIFY ACTIVITIES AND ASSIGN OVERHEAD TO COST POOLS (STEP 1)

Activity-based costing starts with an analysis of the activities needed to manufacture a product or perform a service. This analysis should identify all resource-consuming activities. It requires documenting every activity undertaken to accomplish a task. Atlas Company identifies five activity cost pools: manufacturing, setups, purchase ordering, product development, and property and plant.

Next, the company assigns overhead costs directly to the appropriate activity cost pool. For example, Atlas assigns all overhead costs directly associated with machine setups (such as salaries, supplies, and depreciation) to the setup cost pool. Illustration 17-6 shows the five cost pools, along with the estimated overhead assigned to each cost pool.

ILLUSTRATION 17-6
Activity cost pools and estimated overhead

Atlas Company.xls

ATLAS COMPANY	
Activity Cost Pools	Estimated Overhead
Manufacturing	$500,000
Setups	100,000
Purchase ordering	50,000
Product development	200,000
Property and plant	50,000
Total	$900,000

IDENTIFY COST DRIVERS (STEP 2)

After costs are assigned to the activity cost pools, the company must identify the cost drivers for each cost pool. The cost driver must accurately measure the actual consumption of the activity by the various products. To achieve accurate costing, a **high degree of correlation** must exist between the cost driver and the actual consumption of the overhead costs in the cost pool.

Illustration 17-7 shows the cost drivers that Atlas Company identifies and their total expected use per activity cost pool.

ILLUSTRATION 17-7
Cost drivers and their expected use

Activity Cost Pools	Cost Drivers	Expected Use of Cost Drivers per Activity
Manufacturing	Machine hours	50,000 machine hours
Setups	Number of setups	2,000 setups
Purchase ordering	Number of purchase orders	2,500 purchase orders
Product development	Products developed	2 products developed
Property and plant	Square footage	25,000 square feet

Availability and ease of obtaining data relating to the cost driver is an important factor that must be considered in its selection.

COMPUTE ACTIVITY-BASED OVERHEAD RATES (STEP 3)

Next, the company computes an **activity-based overhead rate** per cost driver by dividing the estimated overhead per activity by the number of cost drivers expected to be used per activity. Illustration 17-8 shows the formula for this computation.

ILLUSTRATION 17-8
Formula for computing activity-based overhead rate

$$\frac{\text{Estimated Overhead per Activity}}{\text{Expected Use of Cost Drivers per Activity}} = \text{Activity-Based Overhead Rate}$$

Atlas Company computes its activity-based overhead rates by using the estimated overhead per activity cost pool, shown in Illustration 17-6, and the expected use of cost drivers per activity, shown in Illustration 17-7. These computations are presented in Illustration 17-9.

Atlas Company.xls

	A	B	C	D	E	F
1		ATLAS COMPANY				
2	Activity Cost Pools	Estimated Overhead	÷	Expected Use of Cost Drivers per Activity	=	Activity-Based Overhead Rates
3	Manufacturing	$500,000		50,000 machine hours		$10 per machine hour
4	Setups	100,000		2,000 setups		$50 per setup
5	Purchase ordering	50,000		2,500 purchase orders		$20 per order
6	Product development	200,000		2 products developed		$100,000 per product
7	Plant and property	50,000		25,000 square feet		$2 per square foot
8	Total	$900,000				
9						

ILLUSTRATION 17-9
Computation of activity-based overhead rates

ALLOCATE OVERHEAD COSTS TO PRODUCTS (STEP 4)

In allocating overhead costs, the company must know the expected use of cost drivers **for each product**. Because of its low volume and higher number of components, the Ab Coaster requires more setups and purchase orders than the

Ab Bench. Illustration 17-10 shows the expected use of cost drivers per product for each of Atlas Company's products.

ILLUSTRATION 17-10
Expected use of cost drivers per product

Activity Cost Pools	Cost Drivers	Expected Use of Cost Drivers per Activity	Expected Use of Cost Drivers per Product: Ab Bench	Ab Coaster
Manufacturing	Machine hours	50,000 machine hours	30,000	20,000
Setups	Number of setups	2,000 setups	500	1,500
Purchase ordering	Number of purchase orders	2,500 purchase orders	750	1,750
Product development	Products developed	2 products developed	1	1
Property and plant	Square footage	25,000 square feet	10,000	15,000

To allocate overhead costs to each product, Atlas multiplies the activity-based overhead rates per cost driver (Illustration 17-9) by the number of cost drivers expected to be used per product (Illustration 17-10). Illustration 17-11 shows the overhead cost allocated to each product.

ILLUSTRATION 17-11
Allocation of activity cost pools to products

Atlas Company.xls

	A	B	C	D	E	F	G	H	I	J	K	L
1						ATLAS COMPANY						
2				Ab Bench						Ab Coaster		
3	Activity Cost Pools	Expected Use of Cost Drivers per Product	×	Activity-Based Overhead Rates	=	Cost Allocated		Expected Use of Cost Drivers per Product	×	Activity-Based Overhead Rates	=	Cost Allocated
4	Manufacturing	30,000		$10		$300,000		20,000		$10		$200,000
5	Setups	500		$50		25,000		1,500		$50		75,000
6	Purchase ordering	750		$20		15,000		1,750		$20		35,000
7	Product development	1		$100,000		100,000		1		$100,000		100,000
8	Property and plant	10,000		$2.00		20,000		15,000		$2.00		30,000
9	Total costs allocated (a)					$460,000						$440,000
10	Units produced (b)					25,000						5,000
11	Overhead cost per unit [(a)÷(b)], rounded					$18.40						$88.00
12												

Under ABC, the overhead cost per unit is $18.40 for the Ab Bench and $88.00 for the Ab Coaster. We see next how this per unit amount substantially differs from that computed under a traditional costing system.

COMPARING UNIT COSTS

Illustration 17-12 compares the unit costs for Atlas Company's Ab Bench and Ab Coaster under traditional costing and ABC.

The comparison shows that unit costs under traditional costing are different and often misleading. Traditional costing overstates the cost of producing the Ab Bench by $11.60 per unit and understates the cost of producing the Ab Coaster

ILLUSTRATION 17-12
Comparison of unit product costs

	Ab Bench		Ab Coaster	
Manufacturing Costs	**Traditional Costing**	**ABC**	**Traditional Costing**	**ABC**
Direct materials	$ 40.00	$ 40.00	$ 30.00	$ 30.00
Direct labor	12.00	12.00	12.00	12.00
Overhead	30.00	18.40	30.00	88.00
Total direct cost per unit	$82.00	$70.40	$72.00	$130.00
	Overstated $11.60		Understated $58.00	

by $58 per unit. These differences are attributable to how Atlas allocates manufacturing overhead across the two systems. Using a traditional costing system, each product was allocated the same amount of overhead ($30) because both products use the same amount of the cost driver (direct labor hours). In contrast, ABC allocates overhead to products based on multiple cost drivers. For example, under ABC, Atlas allocates 75% of the costs of equipment setups to Ab Coasters because Ab Coasters were responsible for 75% (1,500 ÷ 2,000) of the total number of setups.

Note that activity-based costing does not change the amount of overhead costs. Under both traditional costing and ABC, Atlas spends the same amount of overhead—$900,000. However, ABC allocates overhead costs in a more accurate manner. Thus, ABC helps Atlas avoid some negative consequences of a traditional costing system, such as overpricing its Ab Benches and thereby possibly losing market share to competitors. Atlas has also been sacrificing profitability by underpricing the Ab Coaster.

Companies that move from traditional costing to ABC often have similar experiences as ABC shifts costs from high-volume products to low-volume products. This shift occurs because low-volume products are often more customized and require more special handling. Thus, low-volume products are frequently responsible for more overhead costs. In addition, ABC recognizes products' use of resources, which also increases the accuracy of product costs.

MANAGEMENT INSIGHT ABC Evaluated

© CGinspiration/iStockphoto

Surveys of companies often show ABC usage of approximately 50%. Yet, in recent years, articles about ABC have expressed mixed opinions regarding its usefulness. To evaluate ABC practices and user satisfaction with ABC, a survey was conducted of 348 companies worldwide. Some of the interesting findings included the following: ABC methods are widely used across the entire value chain, rather than being primarily used to allocate production-specific costs; only 25% of non-ABC companies think they are accurately tracing the costs of activities, while 70% of ABC companies think their company does this well; and respondents felt that ABC provides greater support for financial, operational, and strategic decisions. More than 87% of respondents said that their ideal costing system would include some form of ABC. Since this significantly exceeds the 50% of the respondents actually using it, ABC usage may well increase in the future.

Source: William Stratton, Denis Desroches, Raef Lawson, and Toby Hatch, "Activity-Based Costing: Is It Still Relevant?" *Management Accounting Quarterly* (Spring, 2009), pp. 31–39.

What might explain why so many companies say that ideally they would use ABC, but they haven't adopted it yet? (Go to WileyPLUS for this answer and additional questions.)

DO IT! 2 Apply ABC to Manufacturer

Casey Company has five activity cost pools and two products. It expects to produce 200,000 units of its automobile scissors jack and 80,000 units of its truck hydraulic jack. Having identified its activity cost pools and the cost drivers for each cost pool, Casey Company accumulated the following data relative to those activity cost pools and cost drivers.

Annual Overhead Data				Expected Use of Cost Drivers per Product	
Activity Cost Pools	**Cost Drivers**	**Estimated Overhead**	**Expected Use of Cost Drivers per Activity**	**Scissors Jacks**	**Hydraulic Jacks**
Ordering and receiving	Purchase orders	$ 200,000	2,500 orders	1,000	1,500
Machine setup	Setups	600,000	1,200 setups	500	700
Machining	Machine hours	2,000,000	800,000 hours	300,000	500,000
Assembling	Parts	1,800,000	3,000,000 parts	1,800,000	1,200,000
Inspecting and testing	Tests	700,000	35,000 tests	20,000	15,000
		$5,300,000			

Action Plan

✔ Determine the activity-based overhead rate by dividing the estimated overhead per activity by the expected use of cost drivers per activity.

Using the above data, do the following.

(a) Prepare a schedule showing the computations of the activity-based overhead rates per cost driver.

(b) Prepare a schedule assigning each activity's overhead cost to the two products.

(c) Compute the overhead cost per unit for each product.

(d) Comment on the comparative overhead cost per unit.

SOLUTION

(a) Computations of activity-based overhead rates per cost driver:

Activity Cost Pools	Estimated Overhead	÷	Expected Use of Cost Drivers per Activity	=	Activity-Based Overhead Rates
Ordering and receiving	$ 200,000		2,500 purchase orders		$80 per order
Machine setup	600,000		1,200 setups		$500 per setup
Machining	2,000,000		800,000 machine hours		$2.50 per machine hour
Assembling	1,800,000		3,000,000 parts		$0.60 per part
Inspecting and testing	700,000		35,000 tests		$20 per test
	$5,300,000				

(b) Assignment of each activity's overhead cost to products using ABC:

	Scissors Jacks					Hydraulic Jacks				
Activity Cost Pools	**Expected Use of Cost Drivers per Product**	×	**Activity-Based Overhead Rates**	=	**Cost Assigned**	**Expected Use of Cost Drivers per Product**	×	**Activity-Based Overhead Rates**	=	**Cost Assigned**
Ordering and receiving	1,000		$80		$ 80,000	1,500		$80		$ 120,000
Machine setup	500		$500		250,000	700		$500		350,000
Machining	300,000		$2.50		750,000	500,000		$2.50		1,250,000
Assembling	1,800,000		$0.60		1,080,000	1,200,000		$0.60		720,000
Inspecting and testing	20,000		$20		400,000	15,000		$20		300,000
Total assigned costs					$2,560,000					$2,740,000

(c) Computation of overhead cost per unit:

	Scissors Jack	Hydraulic Jack
Total costs assigned	$2,560,000	$2,740,000
Total units produced	200,000	80,000
Overhead cost per unit	$12.80	$34.25

(d) These data show that the total overhead assigned to 80,000 hydraulic jacks exceeds the overhead assigned to 200,000 scissors jacks. The overhead cost per hydraulic jack is $34.25, but it is only $12.80 per scissors jack.

Action Plan (*cont.*)

✔ Assign the overhead of each activity cost pool to the individual products by multiplying the expected use of cost driver per product times the activity-based overhead rate.

✔ Determine overhead cost per unit by dividing the overhead assigned to each product by the number of units of that product.

Related exercise material: **BE17-3, BE17-4, BE17-5, BE17-6, BE17-7, E17-3, E17-4, E17-5, E17-6, E17-7, E17-8,** and **DO IT! 17-2.**

LEARNING OBJECTIVE 3 **Explain the benefits and limitations of activity-based costing.**

ABC has three primary benefits:

1. ABC leads to more cost pools and therefore more accurate product costing.
2. ABC leads to enhanced control over overhead costs.
3. ABC leads to better management decisions.

THE ADVANTAGE OF MULTIPLE COST POOLS

The main mechanism by which ABC increases product cost accuracy is the use of multiple cost pools. Instead of one plantwide pool (or even several departmental pools) and a single cost driver, companies use numerous activity cost pools with more relevant cost drivers. Thus, costs are allocated more directly on the basis of the cost drivers used to produce each product.

Note that in the Atlas Company example, the *manufacturing* cost pool reflected multiple manufacturing activities, including machining, assembling, and painting. These activities were included in a single pool for simplicity. In many companies, the number of activities—and thus the number of pools—can be substantial. For example, Clark-Hurth (a division of Clark Equipment Company), a manufacturer of axles and transmissions, identified over 170 activities. Compumotor (a division of Parker Hannifin) identified over 80 activities in just the procurement function of its Material Control Department. Illustration 17-13 (page 846) shows a more likely "split" of the activities that were included in Atlas's manufacturing cost pool, reflecting separate pools and drivers for each of those activities.

Classification of Activity Levels

To gain the full advantage of having multiple cost pools, the costs within the pool must be correlated with the driver. To achieve this, a company's managers often characterize activities as belonging to one of the following four activity-level groups when designing an ABC system.

1. **Unit-level activities** are performed for each unit of production. For example, the assembly of cell phones is a unit-level activity because the amount of assembly the company performs increases with each additional cell phone assembled.

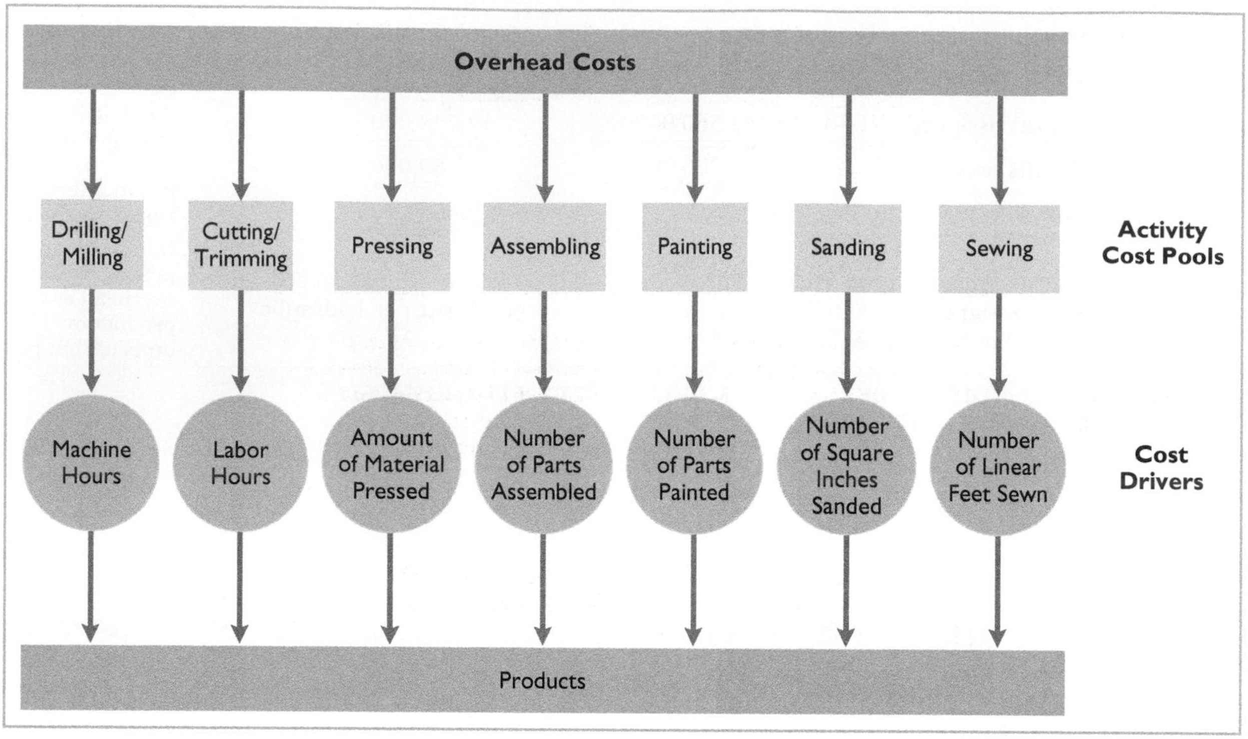

ILLUSTRATION 17-13
A more detailed view of Atlas's machining activities

2. **Batch-level activities** are performed every time a company produces another batch of a product. For example, suppose that to start processing a new batch of ice cream, an ice cream producer needs to set up its machines. The amount of time spent setting up machines increases with the number of batches produced, not with the number of units produced.
3. **Product-level activities** are performed every time a company produces a new type of product. For example, before a pharmaceutical company can produce and sell a new type of medicine, it must undergo very substantial product tests to ensure the product is effective and safe. The amount of time spent on testing activities increases with the number of products the company produces.
4. **Facility-level activities** are required to support or sustain an entire production process. Consider, for example, a hospital. The hospital building must be insured and heated, and the property taxes must be paid, no matter how many patients the hospital treats. These costs do not vary as a function of the number of units, batches, or products.

Companies may achieve greater accuracy in overhead cost allocation by recognizing these four different levels of activities and, from them, developing specific activity cost pools and their related cost drivers. Illustration 17-14 graphically displays this four-level activity hierarchy, along with the types of activities and examples of cost drivers for those activities at each level.

THE ADVANTAGE OF ENHANCED COST CONTROL

ABC leads to enhanced control over overhead costs. Under ABC, companies can trace many overhead costs directly to activities—allowing some costs previously considered to be indirect costs to be identified as direct costs. In developing an ABC system, managers increase their awareness of the activities performed by the company in its production and supporting processes. This awareness helps managers classify activities as value-added or non–value-added.

ILLUSTRATION 17-14
Hierarchy of activity levels

Four Levels	Types of Activities	Examples of Cost Drivers
Unit-Level Activities 	Machine-related Drilling, cutting, milling, trimming, pressing	Machine hours
	Labor-related Assembling, painting, sanding, sewing	Direct labor hours or cost
Batch-Level Activities 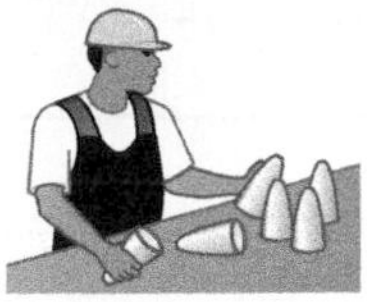	Equipment setups	Number of setups or setup time
	Purchase ordering	Number of purchase orders
	Inspection	Number of inspections or inspection time
	Materials handling	Number of material moves
Product-Level Activities 	Product design	Number of product designs
	Engineering changes	Number of changes
Facility-Level Activities 	Plant management salaries	Number of employees managed
	Plant depreciation	Square footage
	Property taxes	Square footage
	Utilities	Square footage

Value-added activities are those activities of **a company's operations** that increase the perceived value of a product or service to customers. Examples for the manufacture of Precor exercise equipment include engineering design, machining, assembly, and painting. Examples of value-added activities in a service company include performing surgery at a hospital, performing legal research at a law firm, or delivering packages by a freight company.

Non–value-added activities are those activities that, if eliminated, would not reduce the perceived value of a company's product or service. These activities simply **add cost to, or increase the time spent on, a product or service without increasing its perceived value**. One example is inventory storage. If a company **eliminated the need** to store inventory, it would not reduce the value of its product, but it would decrease its product costs. Other examples include moving materials, work in process, or finished goods from one location to another in the plant during the production process; waiting for manufacturing equipment to become available; inspecting goods; and fixing defective goods under warranty.

DECISION TOOLS

The activity flowchart helps managers identify and reduce non–value-added activities.

Companies often use **activity flowcharts** to help identify the ABC activities, such as the one shown in Illustration 17-15 (page 848). The top part of this flowchart identifies activities as value-added (highlighted in red) or non–value-added. Two rows in the lower part of the flowchart show the number of days spent on each activity. The first row shows the number of days spent on each activity under the current manufacturing process. The second row shows the number of days expected to be spent on each activity under management's proposed reengineered manufacturing process.

HEARTLAND COMPANY
Activity Flowchart

Activities

	NVA	NVA	NVA	NVA	VA		NVA	NVA	VA	NVA	NVA	NVA	VA
	Receive and Inspect Materials	Move and Store Materials	Move Materials to Production and Wait	Set Up Machines	Machining: Drill	Machining: Lathe	Inspect	Move and Wait	Assembly	Inspect and Test	Move to Storage	Store Finished Goods	Package and Ship
Current Days	1	12	2.5	1.5	2	1	0.2	6	2	0.3	0.5	14	1
Proposed Days	1	4	1.5	1.5	2	1	0.2	2	2	0.3	0.5	10	1

Total Current Average Time = 44 days

Total Proposed Average Time = 27 days

Proposed reduction in non–value-added time = 17 days

VA = Value-added NVA = Non–value-added

ILLUSTRATION 17-15
Analyzing non–value-added activities to improve operations

The proposed changes would reduce time spent on non–value-added activities by 17 days. This 17-day improvement is due entirely to moving inventory more quickly through the non–value-added processes—that is, by reducing inventory time in moving, storage, and waiting. Appendix 17A discusses a just-in-time inventory system, which some companies use to eliminate non–value-added activities related to inventory.

Not all activities labeled non–value-added are totally wasteful, nor can they be totally eliminated. For example, although inspection time is a non–value-added activity from a customer's perspective, few companies would eliminate their quality control functions. Similarly, moving and waiting time is non–value-added, but it would be impossible to completely eliminate. Nevertheless, when managers recognize the non–value-added characteristic of these activities, they are motivated to minimize them as much as possible. Attention to such matters is part of the growing practice of activity-based management, which helps managers concentrate on **continuous improvement** of operations and activities.

MANAGEMENT INSIGHT General Mills

© Action Sports Photography/ Shutterstock

What Does NASCAR Have to Do with Breakfast Cereal?

Often the best way to improve a process is to learn from observing a different process. Production-line technicians from food producer General Mills were flown to North Carolina to observe firsthand how race-car pit crews operate. In a NASCAR race, the value-added activity is driving toward the finish line; any time spent in the pit is non–value-added. Every split second saved in the pit increases the chances of winning. From what the General Mills' technicians learned at the car race, as well as other efforts, they were able to reduce setup time from 5 hours to just 20 minutes.

What are the benefits of reducing setup time? (Go to WileyPLUS for this answer and additional questions.)

THE ADVANTAGE OF BETTER MANAGEMENT DECISIONS

Some companies experiencing the benefits of activity-based costing have applied it to a broader range of management activities. **Activity-based management (ABM)** extends the use of ABC from product costing to a comprehensive management tool that focuses on reducing costs and improving processes and decision-making.

Managers extend the use of ABC via ABM for both strategic and operational decisions or perspectives. For example, returning to Atlas Company, its managers might use ABC information about its Ab Benches and Ab Coasters to improve the efficiency of its operations. For example, after realizing that both products require a high volume of setup hours—as well as the costs of these hours—they might want to reduce the hours required to set up production runs. Such information may lead managers to increase the number of units produced with each setup or to optimize production schedules for the two products.

ABC also helps managers evaluate employees, departments, and business units. Atlas, for example, might use ABC information about salespeople's activities related to customer visits, number of orders, and post-sales customer service. Such information informs managers about how much effort salespeople are exerting, as well as how efficient they are in dealing with customers. Similarly, Atlas might use ABC information about each department's use of shared resources, like inventory space. Such information lets managers know which departments are the most efficient, which in turn leads to sharing best-practices information within the company. ABC information also helps Atlas to establish **performance standards** within the company, as well as **benchmark** its performance against other companies.

The implications of ABC are not limited to operational decisions. The differences in profitability between the Ab Benches and Ab Coasters may suggest a need to change the company's product mix. Such considerations, in turn, have implications for Atlas's marketing strategy. ABM may guide managers in considering different target customer markets for the two products. Or, managers might consider bundling the two products into a "home gym" set. As another, more extreme, example, managers might consider outsourcing production for one of the products or dropping one of the product lines altogether.

It is often the case that ABM for one perspective has implications for another perspective. For instance, the strategic decision to drop a product line is usually followed by operational decisions regarding what to do with employees' time or the machinery and equipment originally used to manufacture the dropped product. Similarly, increases in employees' efficiency following from operational decisions often lead to changes in employee hiring and compensation strategy. The interrelated nature of the strategic and operational perspectives often means that a decision is not made until the cascading implications of that decision are also identified and considered.

SOME LIMITATIONS AND KNOWING WHEN TO USE ABC

ABC can be very beneficial, but it is not without its limitations. **ABC can be expensive to use**. The increased cost of identifying multiple activities and applying numerous cost drivers discourages many companies from using ABC. ABC systems are also more complex than traditional systems. So companies must ask, is the cost of implementation greater than the benefit of greater accuracy? For some companies, there may be no need to consider ABC at all because their existing system is sufficient.

Further, ABC does not offer complete accuracy as **some arbitrary allocations remain.** Even though more overhead costs can be assigned directly to products through ABC, some overhead costs still need to be allocated by arbitrary cost drivers. For example, Atlas Company assigned $50,000 of overhead pertaining to insurance and property taxes to the property and plant cost pool. Atlas allocated this $50,000 using square footage used by each product (10,000 square feet for Ab Benches and 15,000 square feet for Ab Coasters). A more accurate driver of insurance costs might be replacement costs of production equipment for each product type. However, such information may not be readily available, and Atlas must make due with square footage.

In light of these limitations, how does a company know when to use ABC? The presence of one or more of the following factors would point to possible use:

1. Product lines differ greatly in volume and manufacturing complexity.
2. Product lines are numerous and diverse, requiring various degrees of support services.
3. Overhead costs constitute a significant portion of total costs.
4. The manufacturing process or the number of products has changed significantly, for example, from labor-intensive to capital-intensive due to automation.
5. Production or marketing managers are ignoring data provided by the existing system and are instead using "bootleg" costing data or other alternative data when pricing or making other product decisions.

DECISION TOOLS

Companies replace traditional costing with ABC when ABC provides more accurate information at a reasonable cost.

Ultimately, it is important to realize that the redesign and installation of a product costing system is a significant decision that requires considerable costs and a major effort to accomplish. Therefore, financial managers need to be cautious and deliberate when initiating changes in costing systems. A key factor in implementing a successful ABC system is the support of top management, especially given that the benefits of ABC are not completely visible until *after* it has been implemented.

DO IT! ▶3 Classify Activity Levels

Morgan Toy Company manufactures six primary product lines of toys in its Morganville plant. As a result of an activity analysis, the accounting department has identified eight activity cost pools. Each of the toy products is produced in large batches, with the whole plant devoted to one product at a time. Classify each of the following activities as either unit-level, batch-level, product-level, or facility-level: (a) engineering design, (b) machine setup, (c) toy design, (d) interviews of prospective employees, (e) inspections after each setup, (f) polishing parts, (g) assembling parts, and (h) health and safety.

Action Plan

✔ You should use **unit-level** activities for each unit of product, **batch-level** activities for each batch of product, **product-level** activities for an entire product line, and **facility-level** activities for across the entire range of products.

SOLUTION

(a) Product-level. (b) Batch-level. (c) Product-level. (d) Facility-level. (e) Batch-level. (f) Unit-level. (g) Unit-level. (h) Facility-level.

Related exercise material: **BE17-10, BE17-11, BE17-12, E17-12, E17-13,** and **DO IT! 17-3.**

LEARNING OBJECTIVE ▶4 Apply activity-based costing to service industries.

Although initially developed and implemented by manufacturers, activity-based costing has been widely adopted in service industries as well. ABC is used by airlines, railroads, hotels, hospitals, banks, insurance companies, telephone companies, and financial services firms. The overall objective of ABC in service firms is no different than it is in a manufacturing company. That objective is to identify the key activities that generate costs and to keep track of how many of those activities are completed for each service performed (by job, service, contract, or customer).

The general approach to identifying activities, activity cost pools, and cost drivers is the same for service companies and for manufacturers. Also, the labeling of activities as value-added and non–value-added, and the attempt to reduce or eliminate non–value-added activities as much as possible, is just as valid in service industries as in manufacturing operations. What sometimes makes implementation of activity-based costing difficult in service industries is that, compared to manufacturers, **a larger proportion of overhead costs are company-wide costs** that cannot be directly traced to specific services performed by the company.

To illustrate the application of activity-based costing to a service company contrasted to traditional costing, we use a public accounting firm. This illustration is applicable to any service firm that performs numerous services for a client as part of a job, such as a law firm, consulting firm, or architect.

TRADITIONAL COSTING EXAMPLE

Assume that the public accounting firm of Check and Doublecheck prepares the condensed annual budget shown in Illustration 17-16. The firm engages in a number of services, including audit, tax, and computer consulting.

ILLUSTRATION 17-16
Condensed annual budget of a service firm under traditional costing

CHECK AND DOUBLECHECK, CPAS
Annual Budget

Revenue		$4,000,000
Direct labor	$1,200,000	
Overhead (expected)	600,000	
Total costs		1,800,000
Operating income		$2,200,000

$$\frac{\text{Estimated overhead}}{\text{Direct labor cost}} = \text{Predetermined overhead rate}$$

$$\frac{\$600{,}000}{\$1{,}200{,}000} = 50\%$$

Direct labor is often the professional service performed. Under traditional costing, direct labor is the basis for overhead application to each job. As shown in Illustration 17-16, the predetermined overhead rate of 50% is calculated by dividing the total estimated overhead cost by the total direct labor cost. To determine the operating income earned on any job, Check and Doublecheck applies overhead at the rate of 50% of actual direct professional labor costs incurred. For example, assume that Check and Doublecheck records $140,000 of actual direct professional labor cost during its audit of Plano Molding Company, which was billed an audit fee of $260,000. Under traditional costing, using 50% as the rate for applying overhead to the job, Check and Doublecheck would compute applied overhead and operating income related to the Plano Molding Company audit as shown in Illustration 17-17.

ILLUSTRATION 17-17
Overhead applied under traditional costing system

CHECK AND DOUBLECHECK, CPAS
Plano Molding Company Audit

Revenue		$260,000
Less: Direct professional labor	$140,000	
Applied overhead (50% × $140,000)	70,000	210,000
Operating income		$ 50,000

This example, under traditional costing, uses only one cost driver (direct labor cost) to determine the overhead application rate.

ACTIVITY-BASED COSTING EXAMPLE

Under *activity-based costing,* Check and Doublecheck distributes its estimated annual overhead costs of $600,000 to three activity cost pools. The firm computes activity-based overhead rates per cost driver by dividing each activity overhead cost pool by the expected number of cost drivers used per activity. Illustration 17-18 shows an annual overhead budget using an ABC system.

ILLUSTRATION 17-18
Condensed annual budget of a service firm under activity-based costing

CHECK AND DOUBLECHECK, CPAS
Annual Overhead Budget

Activity Cost Pools	Cost Drivers	Estimated Overhead	÷	Expected Use of Cost Drivers per Activity	=	Activity-Based Overhead Rates
Administration	Number of partner-hours	$335,000		3,350		$100 per partner-hour
Customer development	Revenue billed	160,000		$4,000,000		$0.04 per $1 of revenue
Recruiting and training	Direct professional hours	105,000		30,000		$3.50 per hour
		$600,000				

The assignment of the individual overhead activity rates to the actual number of activities used in the performance of the Plano Molding Company audit results in total overhead assigned of $57,200, as shown in Illustration 17-19.

ILLUSTRATION 17-19
Assigning overhead in a service company

Check and Doublecheck CPA.xls

Home Insert Page Layout Formulas Data Review View

P18 fx

	A	B	C	D	E
1	**CHECK AND DOUBLECHECK, CPAS**				
2	**Plano Molding Company Audit**				
3				Activity-	
4			Actual Use of	Based Overhead	Cost
5	Activity Cost Pools	Cost Drivers	Drivers	Rates	Assigned
6	Administration	Number of partner-hours	335	$100.00	$33,500
7	Customer development	Revenue billed	$260,000	$0.04	10,400
8	Recruiting and training	Direct professional hours	3,800	$3.50	13,300
9					$57,200
10					

Under activity-based costing, Check and Doublecheck assigns overhead costs of $57,200 to the Plano Molding Company audit, as compared to $70,000 under traditional costing. Illustration 17-20 compares total costs and operating margins under the two costing systems.

ILLUSTRATION 17-20
Comparison of traditional costing with ABC in a service company

CHECK AND DOUBLECHECK, CPAS
Plano Molding Company Audit

	Traditional Costing		ABC	
Revenue		$260,000		$260,000
Expenses				
Direct professional labor	$140,000		$140,000	
Applied overhead	70,000		57,200	
Total expenses		210,000		197,200
Operating income		$ 50,000		$ 62,800
Profit margin		19.2%		24.2%

Illustration 17-20 shows that the assignment of overhead costs under traditional costing and ABC is different. The total cost assigned to performing the audit of Plano Molding Company is greater under traditional costing by $12,800 ($62,800 − $50,000), and the profit margin is significantly lower. Traditional costing understates the profitability of the audit.

SERVICE COMPANY INSIGHT American Airlines

Oleksiy Maksymenko Photography/ Alamy

Traveling Light

Have you flown on American Airlines since baggage fees have been implemented? Did the fee make you so mad that you swore that the next time you flew, you would pack fewer clothes so you could use a carry-on bag instead? That is exactly how American Airlines (and the other airlines that charge baggage fees) hoped that you would react. Baggage handling is extremely labor-intensive. All that tagging, sorting, loading on carts, loading in planes, unloading, and sorting again add up to about $9 per bag. Baggage handling also involves equipment costs: sorters, carts, conveyors, tractors, and storage facilities. That's about another $4 of equipment-related overhead per bag. Finally, there is additional fuel cost of a 40-pound item—about $2 in fuel for a 3-hour flight. These costs add up to $15 ($9 + $4 + $2).

Since airlines have implemented their baggage fees, fewer customers are checking bags. Not only does this save the airlines money, it also increases the amount of space available for hauling cargo. An airline can charge at least $80 for hauling a small parcel for same-day delivery service.

Sources: Scott McCartney, "What It Costs an Airline to Fly Your Luggage," *Wall Street Journal Online* (November 25, 2008).

Why do airlines charge even higher rates for heavier bags, bags that are odd shapes (e.g., ski bags), and bags with hazardous materials in them? (Go to **WileyPLUS** for this answer and additional questions.)

DO IT! 4 Apply ABC to Service Company

We Carry It, Inc. is a trucking company. It provides local, short-haul, and long-haul services. The company has developed the following three cost pools.

Activity Cost Pools	Cost Drivers	Estimated Overhead	Expected Use of Cost Drivers per Activity
Loading and unloading	Number of pieces	$ 70,000	100,000 pieces
Travel	Miles driven	250,000	500,000 miles
Logistics	Hours	60,000	2,000 hours

(a) Compute the activity-based overhead rate for each pool.

(b) Determine the overhead allocated to Job A1027 which has 150 pieces, requires 200 miles of driving, and 0.75 hours of logistics.

SOLUTION

(a) The activity based overhead rates are as follows.

Activity Cost Pools	Estimated Overhead	÷	Expected Use of Cost Drivers per Activity	=	Activity-Based Overhead Rate
Loading and unloading	$ 70,000		100,000 pieces		$0.70 per piece
Travel	250,000		500,000 miles		$0.50 per mile
Logistics	60,000		2,000 hours		$30 per hour

(b) The overhead applied to Job A1027 is (150 × $0.70) + (200 × $0.50) + (0.75 × $30) = $227.50

Action Plan

✔ Divide the estimated overhead by the expected use of cost driver per activity to determine activity-based overhead rate.

✔ Apply the activity-based overhead rate to jobs based on actual use of drivers.

Related exercise material: **BE17-12, E17-14, E17-15, E17-17,** and DO IT! **17-4.**

USING DECISION TOOLS—PRECOR

Precor faces many situations where it needs to apply the decision tools learned in this chapter. As mentioned in the Feature Story, Precor manufactures a line of high-end exercise equipment of commercial quality. Assume that the chief accountant has proposed changing from a traditional costing system to an activity-based costing system. The financial vice president is not convinced, so she requests that the next large order for equipment be costed under both systems for purposes of comparison and analysis. A new order from Slim-Way Salons, Inc. for 150 low-impact treadmills is identified as the test case. The following cost data relate to the Slim-Way order.

Data relevant to both costing systems

Direct materials	$55,500
Direct labor hours	820
Direct labor rate per hour	$ 18.00

Data relevant to the traditional costing system

Predetermined overhead rate is 300% of direct labor cost.

Data relevant to the activity-based costing system

Activity Cost Pools	Cost Drivers	Activity-Based Overhead Rate	Expected Use of Cost Drivers for Treadmill Order
Engineering design	Engineering hours	$30 per hour	330
Machine setup	Setups	$200 per setup	22
Machining	Machine hours	$25 per hour	732
Assembly	Number of subassemblies	$8 per subassembly	1,500
Packaging and shipping	Packaging/shipping hours	$15 per hour	152
Building occupancy	Machine hours	$6 per hour	732

INSTRUCTIONS

Compute the total cost of the Slim-Way Salons, Inc. order under (a) the traditional costing system and (b) the activity-based costing system. (c) Evaluate the results.

SOLUTION

(a) Traditional costing system:

Direct materials	$ 55,500
Direct labor (820 × $18)	14,760
Overhead assigned ($14,760 × 300%)	44,280
Total costs assigned to Slim-Way order	$114,540
Number of low-impact treadmills	150
Cost per unit	$ 763.60

(b) Activity-based costing system:

Direct materials		$ 55,500
Direct labor (820 × $18)		14,760
Overhead activities costs:		
Engineering design (330 hours @ $30)	$ 9,900	
Machine setup (22 setups @ $200)	4,400	
Machining (732 machine hours @ $25)	18,300	
Assembly (1,500 subassemblies @ $8)	12,000	
Packaging and shipping (152 hours @ $15)	2,280	
Building occupancy (732 hours @ $6)	4,392	51,272
Total costs assigned to Slim-Way order		$121,532
Number of low-impact treadmills		150
Cost per unit		$ 810.21

(c) Precor will likely adopt ABC because of the difference in the cost per unit (which ABC found to be higher). More importantly, ABC provides greater insight into the sources and causes of the cost per unit. Managers are given greater insight into which activities to control in order to reduce costs. ABC will provide better product costing and greater profitability for the company.

LEARNING OBJECTIVE ***5**

APPENDIX 17A: Explain just-in-time (JIT) processing.

Traditionally, continuous process manufacturing has been based on a **just-in-case** philosophy: Inventories of raw materials are maintained *just in case* some items are of poor quality or a key supplier is shut down by a strike. Similarly, subassembly parts are manufactured and stored *just in case* they are needed later in the manufacturing process. Finished goods are completed and stored *just in case* unexpected and rush customer orders are received. This philosophy often results in a "**push approach**," in which raw materials and subassembly parts are pushed through each process. Traditional processing often results in the buildup of extensive manufacturing inventories.

Primarily in response to foreign competition, many U.S. firms have switched to **just-in-time (JIT) processing**. JIT manufacturing is dedicated to having the right amount of materials, parts, or products just as they are needed. JIT first hit the United States in the early 1980s when automobile companies adopted it to compete with foreign automakers. Many companies, including Dell, Caterpillar, and Harley-Davidson, now successfully use JIT. Under JIT processing, companies receive raw materials **just in time** for use in production, they complete subassembly parts **just in time** for use in finished goods, and they complete finished goods **just in time** to be sold. Illustration 17A-1 shows the sequence of activities in just-in-time processing.

ILLUSTRATION 17A-1
Just-in-time processing

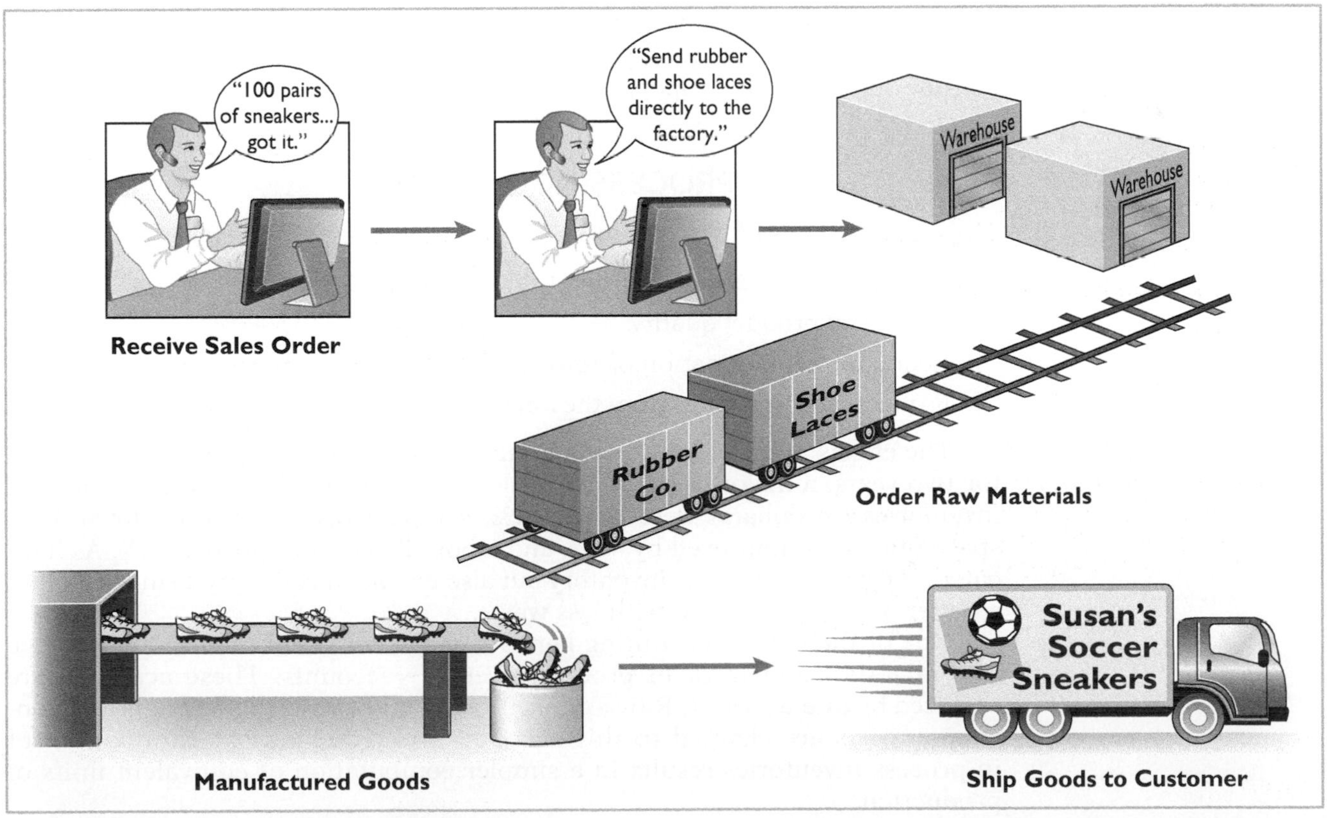

OBJECTIVE OF JIT PROCESSING

A primary objective of JIT is to eliminate all manufacturing inventories. Inventories have an adverse effect on net income because they tie up funds and storage space that could be put to more productive uses. JIT strives to eliminate inventories by using a "**pull approach**" in manufacturing. This approach begins with the customer placing an order with the company, which starts the process of pulling the product through the manufacturing process. A computer at the final workstation sends a signal to the preceding workstation. This signal indicates the exact materials (parts and subassemblies) needed to complete the production of a specified product for a specified time period, such as an eight-hour shift. The next-preceding process, in turn, sends its signal to other processes back up the line. The goal is a smooth continuous flow in the manufacturing process, with no buildup of inventories at any point.

ELEMENTS OF JIT PROCESSING

There are three important elements in JIT processing:

▼ HELPFUL HINT
Buyer leverage is important in finding dependable suppliers. Companies like GM and GE have more success than smaller companies.

1. **Dependable suppliers.** Suppliers must be willing to deliver on short notice exact quantities of raw materials according to precise quality specifications (even including multiple deliveries within the same day). Suppliers must also be willing to deliver the raw materials at specified workstations rather than at a central receiving department. This type of purchasing requires constant and direct communication. Such communication is facilitated by an online computer linkage between the company and its suppliers.
2. **A multiskilled work force.** Under JIT, machines are often strategically grouped into work cells or workstations. Much of the work is automated. As a result, one worker may operate and maintain several different types of machines.

▼ HELPFUL HINT
Without its emphasis on quality control, JIT would be impractical or even impossible. In JIT, quality is engineered into the production process.

3. **A total quality control system.** The company must establish total quality control throughout the manufacturing operations. Total quality control means **no defects**. Since the pull approach signals only required quantities, any defects at any workstation will shut down operations at subsequent workstations. Total quality control requires continuous monitoring by both line employees and supervisors at each workstation.

BENEFITS OF JIT PROCESSING

The major benefits of implementing JIT processing are as follows.

1. Significant reduction or elimination of manufacturing inventories.
2. Enhanced product quality.
3. Reduction or elimination of rework costs and inventory storage costs.
4. Production cost savings from the improved flow of goods through the processes.

The effects in many cases have been dramatic. For example, after using JIT for two years, a major division of Hewlett-Packard found that work in process inventories (in dollars) were down 82%, scrap/rework costs were down 30%, space utilization improved by 40%, and labor efficiency improved 50%. As indicated, JIT not only reduces inventory but also enables a company to manufacture a better product faster and with less waste.

One of the major accounting benefits of JIT is the elimination of separate raw materials and work in process inventory accounts. These accounts are replaced by **one account**, Raw and In-Process Inventory. All materials and conversion costs are charged to this account. The reduction (or elimination) of in-process inventories results in a simpler computation of equivalent units of production.

REVIEW AND PRACTICE

LEARNING OBJECTIVES REVIEW

1 Discuss the difference between traditional costing and activity-based costing. A traditional costing system allocates overhead to products on the basis of predetermined plantwide or departmentwide rates such as direct labor or machine hours. An ABC system allocates overhead to identified activity cost pools and then assigns costs to products using related cost drivers that measure the activities (resources) consumed.

The development of an activity-based costing system involves the following four steps. (1) Identify and classify the major activities involved in the manufacture of specific products and assign overhead to cost pools. (2) Identify the cost driver that has a strong correlation to the costs accumulated in each cost pool. (3) Compute the activity-based overhead rate for each cost pool. (4) Allocate overhead costs to products using the overhead rates determined for each cost pool.

2 Apply activity-based costing to a manufacturer. To identify activity cost pools, a company must perform an analysis of each operation or process, documenting and timing every task, action, or transaction. Cost drivers identified for assigning activity cost pools must (a) accurately measure the actual consumption of the activity by the various products and (b) have related data easily available. The overhead assigned to each activity cost pool is divided by the expected use of cost drivers to determine the activity-based overhead rate for each pool. Overhead is allocated to products by multiplying a particular product's expected use of a cost driver by the activity-based overhead rate. This is done for each activity cost pool and then summed.

3 Explain the benefits and limitations of activity-based costing. Features of ABC that make it a more accurate product costing system include (1) the increased number of cost pools used to assign overhead (including use of the activity-level hierarchy), (2) the enhanced control over overhead costs (including identification of non–value-added activities), and (3) the better management decisions it makes possible. The limitations of ABC are (1) the higher analysis and measurement costs that accompany multiple activity centers and cost drivers, and (2) the necessity still to allocate some costs arbitrarily.

4 Apply activity-based costing to service industries. The overall objective of using ABC in service industries is no different than for manufacturing industries—that is, improved costing of services performed (by job, service, contract, or customer). The general approach to costing is the same: analyze operations, identify activities, accumulate overhead costs by activity cost pools, and identify and use cost drivers to assign the cost pools to the services.

***5 Explain just-in-time (JIT) processing.** JIT is a processing system dedicated to having on hand the right materials and products just at the time they are needed, thereby reducing the amount of inventory and the time inventory is held. One of the principal accounting effects is that one account, Raw and In-Process Inventory, replaces both the raw materials and work in process inventory accounts.

DECISION TOOLS REVIEW

DECISION CHECKPOINTS	INFO NEEDED FOR DECISION	TOOL TO USE FOR DECISION	HOW TO EVALUATE RESULTS
How can activity-based management help managers?	Activities classified as value-added and non–value-added	Activity flowchart	The flowchart should motivate managers to minimize non–value-added activities. Managers should better understand the relationship between activities and the resources they consume.
When should we use ABC?	Knowledge of the products or product lines, the manufacturing process, and overhead costs	A detailed and accurate cost accounting system; cooperation between accountants and operating managers	Compare the results under both costing systems. If managers are better able to understand and control their operations using ABC and the costs are not prohibitive, the use of ABC would be beneficial.

GLOSSARY REVIEW

Activity Any event, action, transaction, or work sequence that incurs costs when producing a product or performing a service. (p. 838).

Activity-based costing (ABC) A costing system that allocates overhead to multiple activity cost pools and assigns the activity cost pools to products or services by means of cost drivers. (p. 837).

Activity-based management (ABM) Extends ABC from product costing to a comprehensive management tool that focuses on reducing costs and improving processes and decision-making. (p. 848).

Activity cost pool The overhead cost attributed to a distinct type of activity or related activities. (p. 838).

Batch-level activities Activities performed for each batch of products rather than for each unit. (p. 846).

Cost driver Any factor or activity that has a direct cause–effect relationship with the resources consumed. In ABC, cost drivers are used to assign activity cost pools to products or services. (p. 838).

Facility-level activities Activities required to support or sustain an entire production process. (p. 846).

***Just-in-time (JIT) processing** A processing system dedicated to having the right amount of materials, parts, or products arrive as they are needed, thereby reducing the amount of inventory. (p. 855).

Non–value-added activity An activity that, if eliminated, would not reduce the perceived value of a company's product or service. (p. 847).

Product-level activities Activities performed in support of an entire product line but not always performed every time a new unit or batch of products is produced. (p. 846).

Unit-level activities Activities performed for each unit of production. (p. 845).

Value-added activity An activity that increases the perceived value of a product or service to a customer. (p. 847).

PRACTICE MULTIPLE-CHOICE QUESTIONS

(LO 1) **1.** Activity-based costing (ABC):
(a) can be used only in a process cost system.
(b) focuses on units of production.
(c) focuses on activities needed to produce a good or perform a service.
(d) uses only a single basis of allocation.

(LO 1) **2.** Activity-based costing:
(a) is the initial phase of converting to a just-in-time operating environment.
(b) can be used only in a job order costing system.
(c) is a two-stage overhead cost allocation system that identifies activity cost pools and cost drivers.
(d) uses direct labor as its primary cost driver.

(LO 1, 2) **3.** Any activity that causes resources to be consumed is called a:
(a) just-in-time activity.
(b) facility-level activity.
(c) cost driver.
(d) non–value-added activity.

(LO 2) **4.** Which of the following would be the **best** cost driver for the assembling cost pool?
(a) Number of product lines.
(b) Number of parts.
(c) Number of orders.
(d) Amount of square footage.

(LO 2) **5.** The overhead rate for machine setups is $100 per setup. Products A and B have 80 and 60 setups, respectively. The overhead assigned to each product is:
(a) Product A $8,000, Product B $8,000.
(b) Product A $8,000, Product B $6,000.
(c) Product A $6,000, Product B $6,000.
(d) Product A $6,000, Product B $8,000.

6. Donna Crawford Co. has identified an activity cost pool to which it has allocated estimated overhead of $1,920,000. It has determined the expected use of cost drivers for that activity to be 160,000 inspections. Widgets require 40,000 inspections, gadgets 30,000 inspections, and targets 90,000 inspections. The overhead assigned to each product is: (LO 2)
(a) Widgets $40,000, gadgets $30,000, targets $90,000.
(b) Widgets $640,000, gadgets $640,000, targets $640,000.
(c) Widgets $360,000, gadgets $480,000, targets $1,080,000.
(d) Widgets $480,000, gadgets $360,000, targets $1,080,000.

7. A frequently cited limitation of activity-based costing is: (LO 3)
(a) ABC results in more cost pools being used to assign overhead costs to products.
(b) certain overhead costs remain to be allocated by means of some arbitrary volume-based cost driver such as labor or machine hours.
(c) ABC leads to poorer management decisions.
(d) ABC results in less control over overhead costs.

8. A company should consider using ABC if: (LO 3)
(a) overhead costs constitute a small portion of total product costs.
(b) it has only a few product lines that require similar degrees of support services.
(c) direct labor constitutes a significant part of the total product cost and a high correlation exists between direct labor and changes in overhead costs.
(d) its product lines differ greatly in volume and manufacturing complexity.

(LO 3) 9. An activity that adds costs to the product but does not increase its perceived value is a:
(a) value-added activity.
(b) cost driver.
(c) cost/benefit activity.
(d) non–value-added activity.

(LO 3) 10. The following activity is value-added:
(a) Storage of raw materials.
(b) Moving parts from machine to machine.
(c) Shaping a piece of metal on a lathe.
(d) All of the above.

(LO 3) 11. A relevant facility-level cost driver for heating costs is:
(a) machine hours.
(b) direct materials.
(c) floor space.
(d) direct labor cost.

(LO 4) 12. The first step in the development of an activity-based costing system for a service company is:
(a) identify and classify activities and allocate overhead to cost pools.
(b) assign overhead costs to products.
(c) identify cost drivers.
(d) compute overhead rates.

*13. Under just-in-time processing: (LO 5)
(a) raw materials are received just in time for use in production.
(b) subassembly parts are completed just in time for use in assembling finished goods.
(c) finished goods are completed just in time to be sold.
(d) All of the above.

*14. The primary objective of just-in-time processing is to: (LO 5)
(a) accumulate overhead in activity cost pools.
(b) eliminate or reduce all manufacturing inventories.
(c) identify relevant activity cost drivers.
(d) identify value-added activities.

SOLUTIONS

1. **(c)** Focusing on activities needed to produce a good or perform a service is an accurate statement about activity-based costing. The other choices are incorrect because ABC (a) can be used in either a process cost or a job order cost system; (b) focuses on activities performed to produce a product, not on units of production; and (d) uses multiple bases of allocation, not just a single basis of allocation.
2. **(c)** ABC is a two-stage overhead cost allocation system that identifies activity cost pools and cost drivers. The other choices are incorrect because ABC (a) is not necessarily part of the conversion to a just-in-time operating environment, (b) can be used in either a process cost or a job order cost system, and (d) uses other activities in addition to direct labor as cost drivers.
3. **(c)** Activities that cause resources to be consumed are called cost drivers, not (a) just-in-time activities, (b) facility-level activities, or (d) non–value-added activities.
4. **(b)** The number of parts would be the best cost driver for the assembling cost pool as it has a higher degree of correlation with the actual consumption of the overhead costs, that is, the assembling of parts, than (a) number of product lines, (c) number of orders, or (d) amount of square footage.
5. **(b)** The overhead assigned to Product A is $8,000 ($100 × 80) and to Product B is $6,000 ($100 × 60), not (a) $8,000, $8,000; (c) $6,000, $6,000; or (d) $6,000, $8,000.
6. **(d)** The overhead assigned to widgets is $480,000 [($1,920,000 ÷ 160,000) × 40,000], to gadgets is $360,000 [($1,920,000 ÷ 160,000) × 30,000], and to targets is $1,080,000 [($1,920,000 ÷ 160,000) × 90,000]. Therefore, choices (a) $40,000, $30,000, and $90,000; (b) $640,000, $640,000, and $640,000; and (c) $360,000, $480,000, and $1,080,000 are incorrect.
7. **(b)** A limitation of ABC is that certain overhead costs remain to be allocated by means of some arbitrary volume-based cost driver. The other choices are incorrect because (a) more cost pools is an advantage of ABC, (c) ABC can lead to better management decisions, and (d) ABC results in more control over overhead costs.
8. **(d)** A company should consider using ABC if its product lines differ greatly in volume and manufacturing complexity. For choices (a), (b), and (c), a traditional costing system should be sufficient and less expensive to implement.
9. **(d)** Non–value-added activities add costs to a product but do not increase its perceived value, not (a) value-added activities, (b) cost drivers, or (c) cost/benefit activities.
10. **(c)** Shaping a piece of metal on a lathe is a value-added activity as it is an integral part of manufacturing a product. Choices (a) and (b) are non–value-added activities, so therefore choice (d) is incorrect as well.
11. **(c)** Floor space is a relevant facility-level cost driver for heating costs. The other choices are incorrect because (a) machine hours, (b) direct materials, and (d) direct labor cost are all unit-level cost drivers.
12. **(a)** The first step in developing an ABC system is to identify and classify activities and allocate overhead to cost pools. The other choices are incorrect because (b) is Step 4, (c) is Step 2, and (d) is Step 3.

*13. **(d)** All of the choices are accurate statements about just-in-time processing.

*14. **(b)** Eliminating or reducing all manufacturing inventories is the primary objective of just-in-time processing. The other choices are incorrect because choices (a), (b), and (c) are part of the process of implementing an ABC system.

PRACTICE EXERCISES

Assign overhead using traditional costing and ABC.

(LO 1, 2)

1. Domestic Fabrics has budgeted overhead costs of $955,000. It has allocated overhead on a plantwide basis to its two products (wool and cotton) using direct labor hours which are estimated to be 477,500 for the current year. The company has decided to experiment with activity-based costing and has created two activity cost pools and related activity cost drivers. These two cost pools are Cutting (cost driver is machine hours) and Design (cost driver is number of setups). Overhead allocated to the Cutting cost pool is $400,000, and $555,000 is allocated to the Design cost pool. Additional information related to these pools is as follows.

	Wool	Cotton	Total
Machine hours	100,000	100,000	200,000
Number of setups	1,000	500	1,500

INSTRUCTIONS

(a) Determine the amount of overhead allocated to the wool product line and the cotton product line using activity-based costing.

(b) What is the difference between the allocation of overhead to the wool and cotton product lines using activity-based costing versus the traditional approach, assuming direct labor hours were incurred evenly between the wool and cotton?

SOLUTION

1. (a)

Activity Cost Pools	Cost Drivers	Estimated Overhead
Cutting	Machine hours	$400,000
Design	Number of setups	555,000

Activity-based overhead rates:

Cutting

$$\frac{\$400{,}000}{200{,}000} = \$2 \text{ per machine hour}$$

Design

$$\frac{\$555{,}000}{1{,}500} = \$370 \text{ per setup}$$

	Wool	Cotton
Activity-based costing		
Cutting		
100,000 × $2	$200,000	
100,000 × $2		$200,000
Design		
1,000 × $370	370,000	
500 × $370		185,000
Total cost allocated	$570,000	$385,000

(b) $$\frac{\text{Estimated overhead}}{\text{Direct labors hours}} = \frac{\$955{,}000}{477{,}500} = \$2 \text{ per direct labor hour}$$

	Wool	Cotton
Traditional costing		
238,750* × $2	$477,500	
238,750 × $2		$477,500

*477,500 ÷ 2

The wool product line is allocated $92,500 ($570,000 − $477,500) more overhead cost when an activity-based costing system is used. As a result, the cotton product line is allocated $92,500 ($477,500 − $385,000) less.

Assign overhead using traditional costing and ABC; classify activities as value- or non–value-added.

(LO 1, 2, 3)

2. Organic Products, Inc., uses a traditional product costing system to assign overhead costs uniformly to all products. To meet Food and Drug Administration (FDA) requirements and to assure its customers of safe, sanitary, and nutritious food, Organic engages in a high level of quality control. Organic assigns its quality-control overhead costs to all products at a rate of 20% of direct labor costs. Its direct labor cost for the month of June for its low-calorie dessert line is $55,000. In response to repeated requests from its financial vice president, Organic management agrees to adopt activity-based costing. Data relating to the low-calorie dessert line for the month of June are as follows.

Activity Cost Pools	Cost Drivers	Overhead Rate	Number of Cost Drivers Used per Activity
Inspections of material received	Number of pounds	$ 0.70 per pound	6,000 pounds
In-process inspections	Number of servings	$ 0.35 per serving	10,000 servings
FDA certification	Customer orders	$13.00 per order	450 order

INSTRUCTIONS

(a) Compute the quality-control overhead cost to be assigned to the low-calorie dessert product line for the month of June using (1) the traditional product costing system (direct labor cost is the cost driver), and (2) activity-based costing.

(b) By what amount does the traditional product costing system undercost or overcost the low-calorie dessert line?

(c) Classify each of the activities as value-added or non–value-added.

SOLUTION

2. (a) (1) Traditional product costing system:

$55,000 × .20 = $11,000. Quality-control overhead costs assigned in June to the low-calorie dessert line are $11,000.

(2) Activity-based costing system:

Activity Cost Pools	Cost Drivers Used	×	Activity-Based Overhead Rate	=	Overhead Cost Assigned
Inspections of material received	6,000		$ 0.70		$ 4,200
In-process inspections	10,000		0.35		3,500
FDA certification	450		13.00		5,850
Total assigned cost for June					$13,550

(b) As compared to ABC, the traditional costing system undercosts the quality-control overhead cost assigned to the low-calorie dessert product line by $2,550 ($13,550 − $11,000) in the month of June. That is a 23.2% ($2,550 ÷ $11,000) understatement.

(c) All three activities, as quality-control related activities, are non–value-added activities.

▶ PRACTICE PROBLEM

Assign overhead and compute unit costs.

(LO 2)

Spreadwell Paint Company manufactures two high-quality base paints: an *oil-based* paint and a *latex* paint. Both are housepaints and are manufactured only in a neutral white color. Spreadwell sells the white base paints to franchised retail paint and decorating stores where pigments are added to tint (color) the paint as the customer desires. The oil-based paint is made with organic solvents (petroleum products) such as mineral spirits or turpentine. The latex paint is made with water; synthetic resin particles are suspended in the water, and dry and harden when exposed to air.

Spreadwell uses the same processing equipment to produce both paints in different production runs. Between batches, the vats and other processing equipment must be washed and cleaned.

After analyzing the company's entire operations, Spreadwell's accountants and production managers have identified activity cost pools and accumulated annual budgeted overhead costs by pool as follows.

Activity Cost Pools	Estimated Overhead
Purchasing	$ 240,000
Processing (weighing and mixing, grinding, thinning and drying, straining)	1,400,000
Packaging (quarts, gallons, and 5-gallons)	580,000
Testing	240,000
Storage and inventory control	180,000
Washing and cleaning equipment	560,000
Total annual budgeted overhead	$3,200,000

Following further analysis, activity cost drivers were identified and their expected use by product and activity were scheduled as follows.

Activity Cost Pools	Cost Drivers	Expected Cost Drivers per Activity	Expected Use of Drivers per Product	
			Oil-Based	Latex
Purchasing	Purchase orders	1,500 orders	800	700
Processing	Gallons processed	1,000,000 gallons	400,000	600,000
Packaging	Containers filled	400,000 containers	180,000	220,000
Testing	Number of tests	4,000 tests	2,100	1,900
Storing	Avg. gals. on hand	18,000 gallons	10,400	7,600
Washing	Number of batches	800 batches	350	450

Spreadwell has budgeted 400,000 gallons of oil-based paint and 600,000 gallons of latex paint for processing during the year.

INSTRUCTIONS

(a) Prepare a schedule showing the computations of the activity-based overhead rates.

(b) Prepare a schedule assigning each activity's overhead cost pool to each product.

(c) Compute the overhead cost per unit for each product.

SOLUTION

(a) Computations of activity-based overhead rates:

Activity Cost Pools	Estimated Overhead	÷	Expected Use of Cost Drivers	=	Activity-Based Overhead Rates
Purchasing	$ 240,000		1,500 orders		$160 per order
Processing	1,400,000		1,000,000 gallons		$1.40 per gallon
Packaging	580,000		400,000 containers		$1.45 per container
Testing	240,000		4,000 tests		$60 per test
Storing	180,000		18,000 gallons		$10 per gallon
Washing	560,000		800 batches		$700 per batch
	$3,200,000				

(b) Assignment of activity cost pools to products:

	Oil-Based Paint			Latex Paint		
Activity Cost Pools	Expected Use of Drivers	Overhead Rates	Cost Assigned	Expected Use of Drivers	Overhead Rates	Cost Assigned
Purchasing	800	$160	$ 128,000	700	$160	$ 112,000
Processing	400,000	$1.40	560,000	600,000	$1.40	840,000
Packaging	180,000	$1.45	261,000	220,000	$1.45	319,000
Testing	2,100	$60	126,000	1,900	$60	114,000
Storing	10,400	$10	104,000	7,600	$10	76,000
Washing	350	$700	245,000	450	$700	315,000
Total overhead assigned			$1,424,000			$1,776,000

(c) Computation of overhead cost assigned per unit:

	Oil-Based Paint	Latex Paint
Total overhead cost assigned	$1,424,000	$1,776,000
Total gallons produced	400,000	600,000
Overhead cost per gallon	$3.56	$2.96

WileyPLUS Brief Exercises, DO IT! Exercises, Exercises, Problems, and many additional resources are available for practice in WileyPLUS.

NOTE: All asterisked Questions, Exercises, and Problems relate to material in the appendix to the chapter.

QUESTIONS

1. Under what conditions is direct labor a valid basis for allocating overhead?
2. What has happened in recent industrial history to reduce the usefulness of direct labor as the primary basis for allocating overhead to products?
3. In an automated manufacturing environment, what basis of overhead allocation is frequently more relevant than direct labor hours?
4. What is generally true about overhead allocation to high-volume products versus low-volume products under a traditional costing system?
5. What are the principal differences between activity-based costing (ABC) and traditional product costing?
6. What is the formula for computing activity-based overhead rates?
7. What steps are involved in developing an activity-based costing system?
8. Explain the preparation and use of a value-added/non–value-added activity flowchart in an ABC system.
9. What is an activity cost pool?
10. What is a cost driver?
11. What makes a cost driver accurate and appropriate?
12. What is the formula for assigning activity cost pools to products?
13. What are the benefits of activity-based costing?
14. What are the limitations of activity-based costing?
15. Under what conditions is ABC generally the superior overhead costing system?
16. What refinement has been made to enhance the efficiency and effectiveness of ABC for use in managing costs?
17. Of what benefit is classifying activities as value-added and non–value-added?
18. In what ways is the application of ABC to service industries the same as its application to manufacturing companies?
19. What is the relevance of the classification of levels of activity to ABC?

*20. (a) Describe the philosophy and approach of just-in-time processing.
(b) Identify the major elements of JIT processing.

▶ BRIEF EXERCISES

Identify differences between costing systems.
(LO 1), AP

BE17-1 Digger Inc. sells a high-speed retrieval system for mining information. It provides the following information for the year.

	Budgeted	Actual
Overhead cost	$975,000	$950,000
Machine hours	50,000	45,000
Direct labor hours	100,000	92,000

Overhead is applied on the basis of direct labor hours. (a) Compute the predetermined overhead rate. (b) Determine the amount of overhead applied for the year. (c) Explain how an activity-based costing system might differ in terms of computing a predetermined overhead rate.

Identify differences between costing systems.
(LO 1), AP

BE17-2 Finney Inc. has conducted an analysis of overhead costs related to one of its product lines using a traditional costing system (volume-based) and an activity-based costing system. Here are its results.

	Traditional Costing	ABC
Sales revenue	$600,000	$600,000
Overhead costs:		
Product RX3	$ 34,000	$ 50,000
Product Y12	36,000	20,000
	$ 70,000	$ 70,000

Explain how a difference in the overhead costs between the two systems may have occurred.

Identify cost drivers.
(LO 2), AP

BE17-3 Splash Co. identifies the following activities that pertain to manufacturing overhead for its production of water polo balls: materials handling, machine setups, factory machine maintenance, factory supervision, and quality control. For each activity, identify an appropriate cost driver.

Identify cost drivers.
(LO 2), AP

BE17-4 Mason Company manufactures four products in a single production facility. The company uses activity-based costing. The following activities have been identified through the company's activity analysis: (a) inventory control, (b) machine setups, (c) employee training, (d) quality inspections, (e) materials orderings, (f) drilling operations, and (g) building maintenance.

For each activity, name a cost driver that might be used to assign overhead costs to products.

Compute activity-based overhead rates.
(LO 2), AP

BE17-5 Morgana Company identifies three activities in its manufacturing process: machine setups, machining, and inspections. Estimated annual overhead cost for each activity is $150,000, $375,000, and $87,500, respectively. The cost driver for each activity and the expected annual usage are number of setups 2,500, machine hours 25,000, and number of inspections 1,750. Compute the overhead rate for each activity.

Compute activity-based overhead rates.
(LO 2), AP

BE17-6 Weisman, Inc. uses activity-based costing as the basis for information to set prices for its six lines of seasonal coats. Compute the activity-based overhead rates using the following budgeted data for each of the activity cost pools.

Activity Cost Pools	Estimated Overhead	Expected Use of Cost Drivers per Activity
Designing	$ 450,000	10,000 designer hours
Sizing and cutting	4,000,000	160,000 machine hours
Stitching and trimming	1,440,000	80,000 labor hours
Wrapping and packing	336,000	32,000 finished units

BE17-7 Spud, Inc. a manufacturer of gourmet potato chips, employs activity-based costing. The budgeted data for each of the activity cost pools is provided below for the year 2017.

Compute activity-based overhead rates.
(LO 2), AP

Activity Cost Pools	Estimated Overhead	Expected Use of Cost Drivers per Activity
Ordering and receiving	$ 84,000	12,000 orders
Food processing	480,000	60,000 machine hours
Packaging	1,760,000	440,000 labor hours

For 2017, the company had 11,000 orders and used 50,000 machine hours, and labor hours totaled 500,000. What is the total overhead applied?

BE17-8 Rich Novelty Company identified the following activities in its production and support operations. Classify each of these activities as either value-added or non–value-added.

Classify activities as value- or non–value-added.
(LO 3), AN

(a) Machine setup.
(b) Design engineering.
(c) Storing inventory.
(d) Moving work in process.
(e) Inspecting and testing.
(f) Painting and packing.

BE17-9 Pine and Danner is an architectural firm that is contemplating the installation of activity-based costing. The following activities are performed daily by staff architects. Classify these activities as value-added or non–value-added: (a) designing and drafting, 3 hours; (b) staff meetings, 1 hour; (c) on-site supervision, 2 hours; (d) lunch, 1 hour; (e) consultation with client on specifications, 1.5 hours; and (f) entertaining a prospective client for dinner, 2 hours.

Classify service company activities as value- or non–value-added.
(LO 3, 4), AN

BE17-10 Kwik Pix is a large digital processing center that serves 130 outlets in grocery stores, service stations, camera and photo shops, and drug stores in 16 nearby towns. Kwik Pix operates 24 hours a day, 6 days a week. Classify each of the following activity costs of Kwik Pix as either unit-level, batch-level, product-level, or facility-level.

Classify activities according to level.
(LO 3), AN

(a) Color printing materials.
(b) Photocopy paper.
(c) Depreciation of machinery.
(d) Setups for enlargements.
(e) Supervisor's salary.
(f) Ordering materials.
(g) Pickup and delivery.
(h) Commission to dealers.
(i) Insurance on building.
(j) Loading developing machines.

BE17-11 FixIt, Inc. operates 20 injection molding machines in the production of tool boxes of four different sizes, named the Apprentice, the Handyman, the Journeyman, and the Professional. Classify each of the following costs as unit-level, batch-level, product-level, or facility-level.

Classify activities according to level.
(LO 3), AP

(a) First-shift supervisor's salary.
(b) Powdered raw plastic.
(c) Dies for casting plastic components.
(d) Depreciation on injection molding machines.
(e) Changing dies on machines.
(f) Moving components to assembly department.
(g) Engineering design.
(h) Employee health and medical insurance coverage.

BE17-12 Spin Cycle Architecture uses three activity pools to apply overhead to its projects. Each activity has a cost driver used to allocate the overhead costs to the projects. The activities and related overhead costs are as follows: initial concept formation $40,000, design $300,000, and construction oversight $100,000. The cost drivers and expected use are as follows.

Compute rates and activity levels.
(LO 3, 4), AP

Activities	Cost Drivers	Expected Use of Cost Drivers per Activity
Initial concept formation	Number of project changes	20
Design	Square feet	150,000
Construction oversight	Number of months	100

(a) Compute the predetermined overhead rate for each activity. (b) Classify each of these activities as unit-level, batch-level, product-level, or facility-level.

DO IT! EXERCISES

Identify characteristics of traditional and ABC systems.

(LO 1), K

DO IT! 17-1 Indicate whether the following statements are true or false.

(a) The reasoning behind ABC cost allocation is that products consume activities and activities consume resources.
(b) Activity-based costing is an approach for allocating direct labor to products.
(c) In today's increasingly automated environment, direct labor is never an appropriate basis for allocating costs to products.
(d) A cost driver is any factor or activity that has a direct cause-effect relationship with resources consumed.
(e) Activity-based costing segregates overhead into various cost pools in an effort to provide more accurate cost information.

Compute activity-based overhead rates and assign overhead using ABC.

(LO 2), AP

DO IT! 17-2 Flynn Industries has three activity cost pools and two products. It expects to produce 3,000 units of Product BC113 and 1,500 of Product AD908. Having identified its activity cost pools and the cost drivers for each pool, Flynn accumulated the following data relative to those activity cost pools and cost drivers.

Annual Overhead Data			Expected Use of Cost Drivers per Product		
Activity Cost Pools	**Cost Drivers**	**Estimated Overhead**	**Expected Use of Cost Drivers per Activity**	**Product BC113**	**Product AD908**
Machine setup	Setups	$ 16,000	40	25	15
Machining	Machine hours	110,000	5,000	1,000	4,000
Packing	Orders	30,000	500	150	350

Using the above data, do the following:

(a) Prepare a schedule showing the computations of the activity-based overhead rates per cost driver.
(b) Prepare a schedule assigning each activity's overhead cost to the two products.
(c) Compute the overhead cost per unit for each product. (Round to nearest cent.)
(d) Comment on the comparative overhead cost per product.

Classify activities according to level.

(LO 3), C

DO IT! 17-3 Adamson Company manufactures four lines of garden tools. As a result of an activity analysis, the accounting department has identified eight activity cost pools. Each of the product lines is produced in large batches, with the whole plant devoted to one product at a time. Classify each of the following activities or costs as either unit-level, batch-level, product-level, or facility-level.

(a) Machining parts.
(b) Product design.
(c) Plant maintenance.
(d) Machine setup.
(e) Assembling parts.
(f) Purchasing raw materials.
(g) Property taxes.
(h) Painting.

Apply ABC to service company.

(LO 4), AP

DO IT! 17-4 Ready Ride is a trucking company. It provides local, short-haul, and long-haul services. It has developed the following three cost pools.

Activity Cost Pools	Cost Drivers	Estimated Overhead	Expected Use of Cost Driver per Activity
Loading and unloading	Number of pieces	$ 90,000	90,000
Travel	Miles driven	450,000	600,000
Logistics	Hours	75,000	3,000

(a) Compute the activity-based overhead rates for each pool.
(b) Determine the overhead allocated to Job XZ3275 which has 150 pieces, requires 200 miles of driving, and 0.75 hours of logistics.

▶ EXERCISES

E17-1 Saddle Inc. has two types of handbags: standard and custom. The controller has decided to use a plantwide overhead rate based on direct labor costs. The president has heard of activity-based costing and wants to see how the results would differ if this system were used. Two activity cost pools were developed: machining and machine setup. Presented below is information related to the company's operations.

Assign overhead using traditional costing and ABC.

(LO 1, 2), AP

XLS

	Standard	**Custom**
Direct labor costs	$50,000	$100,000
Machine hours	1,000	1,000
Setup hours	100	400

Total estimated overhead costs are $240,000. Overhead cost allocated to the machining activity cost pool is $140,000, and $100,000 is allocated to the machine setup activity cost pool.

Instructions

(a) Compute the overhead rate using the traditional (plantwide) approach.
(b) Compute the overhead rates using the activity-based costing approach.
(c) Determine the difference in allocation between the two approaches.

E17-2 Ayala Inc. has conducted the following analysis related to its product lines, using a traditional costing system (volume-based) and an activity-based costing system. Both the traditional and the activity-based costing systems include direct materials and direct labor costs.

Explain difference between traditional and activity-based costing.

(LO 1), AP

		Total Costs	
Products	**Sales Revenue**	**Traditional**	**ABC**
Product 540X	$180,000	$55,000	$50,000
Product 137Y	160,000	50,000	35,000
Product 249S	70,000	15,000	35,000

Instructions

(a) For each product line, compute operating income using the traditional costing system.
(b) For each product line, compute operating income using the activity-based costing system.
(c) Using the following formula, compute the percentage difference in operating income for each of the product lines of Ayala: [Operating Income (ABC) − Operating Income (traditional cost)] ÷ Operating Income (traditional cost). (Round to two decimals.)
(d) Provide a rationale as to why the costs for Product 540X are approximately the same using either the traditional or activity-based costing system.

E17-3 EcoFabrics has budgeted overhead costs of $945,000. It has allocated overhead on a plantwide basis to its two products (wool and cotton) using direct labor hours which are estimated to be 450,000 for the current year. The company has decided to experiment with activity-based costing and has created two activity cost pools and related activity cost drivers. These two cost pools are cutting (cost driver is machine hours) and design (cost driver is number of setups). Overhead allocated to the cutting cost pool is $360,000, and $585,000 is allocated to the design cost pool. Additional information related to these pools is as follows.

Assign overhead using traditional costing and ABC.

(LO 1, 2), AN

	Wool	**Cotton**	**Total**
Machine hours	100,000	100,000	200,000
Number of setups	1,000	500	1,500

Instructions

(a) Determine the amount of overhead allocated to the wool product line and the cotton product line using activity-based costing.

(b) What amount of overhead would be allocated to the wool and cotton product lines using the traditional approach, assuming direct labor hours were incurred evenly between the wool and cotton? How does this compare with the amount allocated using ABC in part (a)?

Assign overhead using traditional costing and ABC.
(LO 1, 2), AN

E17-4 Altex Inc. manufactures two products: car wheels and truck wheels. To determine the amount of overhead to assign to each product line, the controller, Robert Hermann, has developed the following information.

	Car	Truck
Estimated wheels produced	40,000	10,000
Direct labor hours per wheel	1	3

Total estimated overhead costs for the two product lines are $770,000.

Instructions

(a) Compute the overhead cost assigned to the car wheels and truck wheels, assuming that direct labor hours is used to allocate overhead costs.

(b) Hermann is not satisfied with the traditional method of allocating overhead because he believes that most of the overhead costs relate to the truck wheels product line because of its complexity. He therefore develops the following three activity cost pools and related cost drivers to better understand these costs.

Activity Cost Pools	Expected Use of Cost Drivers	Estimated Overhead Costs
Setting up machines	1,000 setups	$220,000
Assembling	70,000 labor hours	280,000
Inspection	1,200 inspections	270,000

Compute the activity-based overhead rates for these three cost pools.

(c) Compute the cost that is assigned to the car wheels and truck wheels product lines using an activity-based costing system, given the following information.

Expected Use of Cost Drivers per Product		
	Car	Truck
Number of setups	200	800
Direct labor hours	40,000	30,000
Number of inspections	100	1,100

(d) What do you believe Hermann should do?

Assign overhead using traditional costing and ABC.
(LO 1, 2), AN

E17-5 Perdon Corporation manufactures safes—large mobile safes, and large walk-in stationary bank safes. As part of its annual budgeting process, Perdon is analyzing the profitability of its two products. Part of this analysis involves estimating the amount of overhead to be allocated to each product line. The information shown below relates to overhead.

	Mobile Safes	Walk-In Safes
Units planned for production	200	50
Material moves per product line	300	200
Purchase orders per product line	450	350
Direct labor hours per product line	800	1,700

Instructions

(a) The total estimated manufacturing overhead was $260,000. Under traditional costing (which assigns overhead on the basis of direct labor hours), what amount of manufacturing overhead costs are assigned to:

(1) One mobile safe?

(2) One walk-in safe?

(b) The total estimated manufacturing overhead of $260,000 was comprised of $160,000 for materials handling costs and $100,000 for purchasing activity costs. Under activity-based costing (ABC):
   (1) What amount of materials handling costs are assigned to:
      (a) One mobile safe?
      (b) One walk-in safe?
   (2) What amount of purchasing activity costs are assigned to:
      (a) One mobile safe?
      (b) One walk-in safe?
(c) Compare the amount of overhead allocated to one mobile safe and to one walk-in safe under the traditional costing approach versus under ABC.

Identify activity cost pools and cost drivers.

(LO 2), AN

E17-6 Santana Corporation manufactures snowmobiles in its Blue Mountain, Wisconsin, plant. The following costs are budgeted for the first quarter's operations.

Machine setup, indirect materials	$ 4,000
Inspections	16,000
Tests	4,000
Insurance, plant	110,000
Engineering design	140,000
Depreciation, machinery	520,000
Machine setup, indirect labor	20,000
Property taxes	29,000
Oil, heating	19,000
Electricity, plant lighting	21,000
Engineering prototypes	60,000
Depreciation, plant	210,000
Electricity, machinery	36,000
Machine maintenance wages	19,000

Instructions

Classify the above costs of Santana Corporation into activity cost pools using the following: engineering, machinery, machine setup, quality control, factory utilities, maintenance. Next, identify a cost driver that may be used to assign each cost pool to each line of snowmobiles.

Identify activity cost drivers.

(LO 2), AN

E17-7 Rojas Vineyards in Oakville, California, produces three varieties of non-alcoholic wine: merlot, viognier, and pinot noir. The winemaster, Russel Hansen, has identified the following activities as cost pools for accumulating overhead and assigning it to products.

1. Culling and replanting. Dead or overcrowded vines are culled, and new vines are planted or relocated. (Separate vineyards by variety.)
2. Tying. The posts and wires are reset, and vines are tied to the wires for the dormant season.
3. Trimming. At the end of the harvest, the vines are cut and trimmed back in preparation for the next season.
4. Spraying. The vines are sprayed with organic pesticides for protection against insects and fungi.
5. Harvesting. The grapes are hand-picked, placed in carts, and transported to the crushers.
6. Stemming and crushing. Cartfuls of bunches of grapes of each variety are separately loaded into machines that remove stems and gently crush the grapes.
7. Pressing and filtering. The crushed grapes are transferred to presses that mechanically remove the juices and filter out bulk and impurities.
8. Fermentation. The grape juice, by variety, is fermented in either stainless-steel tanks or oak barrels.
9. Aging. The wines are aged in either stainless-steel tanks or oak barrels for one to three years depending on variety.
10. Bottling and corking. Bottles are machine-filled and corked.
11. Labeling and boxing. Each bottle is labeled, as is each nine-bottle case, with the name of the vintner, vintage, and variety.
12. Storing. Packaged and boxed bottles are stored awaiting shipment.

13. Shipping. The wine is shipped to distributors and private retailers.
14. Heating and air-conditioning of plant and offices.
15. Maintenance of buildings and equipment. Printing, repairs, replacements, and general maintenance are performed in the off-season.

Instructions

For each of Rojas Vineyards' 15 activity cost pools, identify a probable cost driver that might be used to assign overhead costs to its three wine varieties.

Identify activity cost drivers.

(LO 2), AN

E17-8 Wilmington, Inc. manufactures five models of kitchen appliances. The company is installing activity-based costing and has identified the following activities performed at its Mesa plant.

1. Designing new models.
2. Purchasing raw materials and parts.
3. Storing and managing inventory.
4. Receiving and inspecting raw materials and parts.
5. Interviewing and hiring new personnel.
6. Machine forming sheet steel into appliance parts.
7. Manually assembling parts into appliances.
8. Training all employees of the company.
9. Insuring all tangible fixed assets.
10. Supervising production.
11. Maintaining and repairing machinery and equipment.
12. Painting and packaging finished appliances.

Having analyzed its Mesa plant operations for purposes of installing activity-based costing, Wilmington, Inc. identified its activity cost centers. It now needs to identify relevant activity cost drivers in order to assign overhead costs to its products.

Instructions

Using the activities listed above, identify for each activity one or more cost drivers that might be used to assign overhead to Wilmington's five products.

Compute overhead rates and assign overhead using ABC.

(LO 2, 3), AP

E17-9 Air United, Inc. manufactures two products: missile range instruments and space pressure gauges. During April, 50 range instruments and 300 pressure gauges were produced, and overhead costs of $94,500 were estimated. An analysis of estimated overhead costs reveals the following activities.

Activities	Cost Drivers	Total Cost
1. Materials handling	Number of requisitions	$40,000
2. Machine setups	Number of setups	21,500
3. Quality inspections	Number of inspections	33,000
		$94,500

The cost driver volume for each product was as follows.

Cost Drivers	Instruments	Gauges	Total
Number of requisitions	400	600	1,000
Number of setups	200	300	500
Number of inspections	200	400	600

Instructions

(a) Determine the overhead rate for each activity.

(b) Assign the manufacturing overhead costs for April to the two products using activity-based costing.

(c) Write a memorandum to the president of Air United explaining the benefits of activity-based costing.

Assign overhead using traditional costing and ABC.

(LO 1, 2, 3), AP

E17-10 Kragan Clothing Company manufactures its own designed and labeled athletic wear and sells its products through catalog sales and retail outlets. While Kragan has for years used activity-based costing in its manufacturing activities, it has always used traditional costing in assigning its selling costs to its product lines. Selling costs have traditionally been assigned to Kragan's product lines at a rate of 70% of direct materials costs. Its direct materials costs for the month of March for Kragan's "high-intensity" line of athletic wear are $400,000. The company has decided to extend activity-based costing to its selling costs. Data relating to the "high-intensity" line of products for the month of March are as follows.

Activity Cost Pools	Cost Drivers	Overhead Rate	Number of Cost Drivers Used per Activity
Sales commissions	Dollar sales	$0.05 per dollar sales	$900,000
Advertising—TV	Minutes	$300 per minute	250
Advertising—Internet	Column inches	$10 per column inch	2,000
Catalogs	Catalogs mailed	$2.50 per catalog	60,000
Cost of catalog sales	Catalog orders	$1 per catalog order	9,000
Credit and collection	Dollar sales	$0.03 per dollar sales	900,000

Instructions

(a) Compute the selling costs to be assigned to the "high-intensity" line of athletic wear for the month of March (1) using the traditional product costing system (direct materials cost is the cost driver), and (2) using activity-based costing.

(b) By what amount does the traditional product costing system undercost or overcost the "high-intensity" product line?

Assign overhead using traditional costing and ABC; classify activities as value- or non–value-added.

(LO 1, 2, 3), AP

E17-11 Health 'R Us, Inc., uses a traditional product costing system to assign overhead costs uniformly to all its packaged multigrain products. To meet Food and Drug Administration requirements and to assure its customers of safe, sanitary, and nutritious food, Health 'R Us engages in a high level of quality control. Health 'R Us assigns its quality-control overhead costs to all products at a rate of 17% of direct labor costs. Its direct labor cost for the month of June for its low-calorie breakfast line is $70,000. In response to repeated requests from its financial vice president, Health 'R Us's management agrees to adopt activity-based costing. Data relating to the low-calorie breakfast line for the month of June are as follows.

Activity Cost Pools	Cost Drivers	Overhead Rate	Number of Cost Drivers Used per Activity
Inspections of material received	Number of pounds	$0.90 per pound	6,000 pounds
In-process inspections	Number of servings	$0.33 per serving	10,000 servings
FDA certification	Customer orders	$12.00 per order	420 orders

Instructions

(a) Compute the quality-control overhead cost to be assigned to the low-calorie breakfast product line for the month of June (1) using the traditional product costing system (direct labor cost is the cost driver), and (2) using activity-based costing.

(b) By what amount does the traditional product costing system undercost or overcost the low-calorie breakfast line?

(c) Classify each of the activities as value-added or non–value-added.

Classify activities by level.

(LO 3), AN

E17-12 Having itemized its costs for the first quarter of next year's budget, Santana Corporation desires to install an activity-based costing system. First, it identified the activity cost pools in which to accumulate factory overhead. Second, it identified the relevant cost drivers. (This was done in E17-6.)

Instructions

Using the activity cost pools identified in E17-6, classify each of those cost pools as either unit-level, batch-level, product-level, or facility-level.

Classify activities by level.

(LO 3), AN

E17-13 William Mendel & Sons, Inc. is a small manufacturing company in La Jolla that uses activity-based costing. Mendel & Sons accumulates overhead in the following activity cost pools.

1. Hiring personnel.
2. Managing parts inventory.
3. Purchasing.
4. Testing prototypes.
5. Designing products.
6. Setting up equipment.
7. Training employees.
8. Inspecting machined parts.
9. Machining.
10. Assembling.

Instructions
For each activity cost pool, indicate whether the activity cost pool would be unit-level, batch-level, product-level, or facility-level.

Assign overhead using traditional costing and ABC.
(LO 4), AP

E17-14 Venus Creations sells window treatments (shades, blinds, and awnings) to both commercial and residential customers. The following information relates to its budgeted operations for the current year.

	Commercial		Residential	
Revenues		$300,000		$480,000
Direct materials costs	$ 30,000		$ 50,000	
Direct labor costs	100,000		300,000	
Overhead costs	85,000	215,000	150,000	500,000
Operating income (loss)		$ 85,000		($ 20,000)

The controller, Peggy Kingman, is concerned about the residential product line. She cannot understand why this line is not more profitable given that the installations of window coverings are less complex for residential customers. In addition, the residential client base resides in close proximity to the company office, so travel costs are not as expensive on a per client visit for residential customers. As a result, she has decided to take a closer look at the overhead costs assigned to the two product lines to determine whether a more accurate product costing model can be developed. Here are the three activity cost pools and related information she developed:

Activity Cost Pools	Estimated Overhead	Cost Drivers
Scheduling and travel	$85,000	Hours of travel
Setup time	90,000	Number of setups
Supervision	60,000	Direct labor cost

	Expected Use of Cost Drivers per Product	
	Commercial	Residential
Scheduling and travel	750	500
Setup time	350	250

Instructions
(a) Compute the activity-based overhead rates for each of the three cost pools, and determine the overhead cost assigned to each product line.
(b) Compute the operating income for each product line, using the activity-based overhead rates.
(c) What do you believe Peggy Kingman should do?

Identify activity cost pools.
(LO 4), AP

E17-15 Snap Prints Company is a small printing and copying firm with three high-speed offset printing presses, five copiers (two color and three black-and-white), one collator, one cutting and folding machine, and one fax machine. To improve its pricing practices, owner-manager Terry Morton is installing activity-based costing. Additionally, Terry employs five employees: two printers/designers, one receptionist/bookkeeper, one salesperson/copy-machine operator, and one janitor/delivery clerk. Terry can operate any of the machines and, in addition to managing the entire operation, he performs the training, designing, selling, and marketing functions.

Instructions
As Snap Prints' independent accountant who prepares tax forms and quarterly financial statements, you have been asked to identify the activities that would be used to accumulate overhead costs for assignment to jobs and customers. Using your knowledge of a small printing and copying firm (and some imagination), identify at least 12 activity cost pools as the start of an activity-based costing system for Snap Prints Company.

Classify service company activities as value-added or non–value-added.

(LO 3), AN

E17-16 Lasso and Markowitz is a law firm that is initiating an activity-based costing system. Sam Lasso, the senior partner and strong supporter of ABC, has prepared the following list of activities performed by a typical attorney in a day at the firm.

Activities	Hours
Writing contracts and letters	1.5
Attending staff meetings	0.5
Taking depositions	1.0
Doing research	1.0
Traveling to/from court	1.0
Contemplating legal strategy	1.0
Eating lunch	1.0
Litigating a case in court	2.5
Entertaining a prospective client	1.5

Instructions

Classify each of the activities listed by Sam Lasso as value-added or non–value-added, and defend your classification. How much was value-added time and how much was non–value-added?

Apply ABC to service company.

(LO 4), AP

E17-17 Manzeck Company operates a snow-removal service. The company owns five trucks, each of which has a snow plow in the front to plow driveways and a snowthrower in the back to clear sidewalks. Because plowing snow is very tough on trucks, the company incurs significant maintenance costs. Truck depreciation and maintenance represents a significant portion of the company's overhead. The company removes snow at residential locations, in which case the drivers spend the bulk of their time walking behind the snowthrower machine to clear sidewalks. On commercial jobs, the drivers spend most of their time plowing. Manzeck allocates overhead based on labor hours. Total overhead costs for the year are $42,000. Total labor hours are 1,500 hours. The average residential property requires 0.5 hours of labor, while the average commercial property requires 2.5 hours of labor. The following additional information is available.

Activity Cost Pools	Cost Drivers	Estimated Overhead	Expected Use of Cost Drivers per Activity
Plowing	Square yards of surface plowed	$38,000	200,000
Snowthrowing	Linear feet of sidewalk cleared	$ 4,000	50,000

Instructions

(a) Determine the predetermined overhead rate under traditional costing.
(b) Determine the amount of overhead allocated to the average residential job using traditional costing based on labor hours.
(c) Determine the activity-based overhead rates for each cost pool.
(d) Determine the amount of overhead allocated to the average residential job using activity-based costing. Assume that the average residential job has 20 square yards of plowing and 60 linear feet of snowthrowing.
(e) Discuss your findings from parts (b) and (d).

EXERCISES: SET B AND CHALLENGE EXERCISES

Visit the book's companion website, at **www.wiley.com/college/kimmel**, and choose the Student Companion site to access Exercises: Set B and Challenge Exercises.

PROBLEMS: SET A

Assign overhead using traditional costing and ABC; compute unit costs; classify activities as value- or non–value-added.

(LO 1, 2, 3), AP

P17-1A Combat Fire, Inc. manufactures steel cylinders and nozzles for two models of fire extinguishers: (1) a home fire extinguisher and (2) a commercial fire extinguisher. The *home model* is a high-volume (54,000 units), half-gallon cylinder that holds 2 1/2 pounds of multi-purpose dry chemical at 480 PSI. The *commercial model* is a low-volume (10,200 units), two-gallon cylinder that holds 10 pounds of multi-purpose dry chemical at 390 PSI. Both products require 1.5 hours of direct labor for completion. Therefore, total annual direct labor hours are 96,300 or [1.5 hours × (54,000 + 10,200)]. Expected annual manufacturing overhead is $1,584,280. Thus, the predetermined overhead rate is $16.45 or ($1,584,280 ÷ 96,300) per direct labor hour. The direct materials cost per unit is $18.50 for the home model and $26.50 for the commercial model. The direct labor cost is $19 per unit for both the home and the commercial models.

The company's managers identified six activity cost pools and related cost drivers and accumulated overhead by cost pool as follows.

Activity Cost Pools	Cost Drivers	Estimated Overhead	Expected Use of Cost Drivers	Expected Use of Drivers by Product: Home	Expected Use of Drivers by Product: Commercial
Receiving	Pounds	$ 80,400	335,000	215,000	120,000
Forming	Machine hours	150,500	35,000	27,000	8,000
Assembling	Number of parts	412,300	217,000	165,000	52,000
Testing	Number of tests	51,000	25,500	15,500	10,000
Painting	Gallons	52,580	5,258	3,680	1,578
Packing and shipping	Pounds	837,500	335,000	215,000	120,000
		$1,584,280			

Instructions

(a) Unit cost—H.M. $62.18

(c) Cost assigned—H.M. $1,086,500

(d) Cost/unit—H.M. $57.62

(a) Under traditional product costing, compute the total unit cost of each product. Prepare a simple comparative schedule of the individual costs by product (similar to Illustration 17-3 on page 837).
(b) Under ABC, prepare a schedule showing the computations of the activity-based overhead rates (per cost driver).
(c) Prepare a schedule assigning each activity's overhead cost pool to each product based on the use of cost drivers. (Include a computation of overhead cost per unit, rounding to the nearest cent.)
(d) Compute the total cost per unit for each product under ABC.
(e) Classify each of the activities as a value-added activity or a non–value-added activity.
(f) Comment on (1) the comparative overhead cost per unit for the two products under ABC, and (2) the comparative total costs per unit under traditional costing and ABC.

Assign overhead to products using ABC and evaluate decision.

(LO 2), AP

XLS

P17-2A Schultz Electronics manufactures two ultra high-definition television models: the Royale which sells for $1,600, and a new model, the Majestic, which sells for $1,300. The production cost computed per unit under traditional costing for each model in 2017 was as follows.

Traditional Costing	Royale	Majestic
Direct materials	$ 700	$420
Direct labor ($20 per hour)	120	100
Manufacturing overhead ($38 per DLH)	228	190
Total per unit cost	$1,048	$710

In 2017, Schultz manufactured 25,000 units of the Royale and 10,000 units of the Majestic. The overhead rate of $38 per direct labor hour was determined by dividing total expected manufacturing overhead of $7,600,000 by the total direct labor hours (200,000) for the two models.

Under traditional costing, the gross profit on the models was Royale $552 ($1,600 − $1,048) and Majestic $590 ($1,300 − $710). Because of this difference, management is considering phasing out the Royale model and increasing the production of the Majestic model.

Before finalizing its decision, management asks Schultz's controller to prepare an analysis using activity-based costing (ABC). The controller accumulates the following information about overhead for the year ended December 31, 2017.

Activity Cost Pools	Cost Drivers	Estimated Overhead	Expected Use of Cost Drivers	Activity-Based Overhead Rate
Purchasing	Number of orders	$1,200,000	40,000	$30/order
Machine setups	Number of setups	900,000	18,000	$50/setup
Machining	Machine hours	4,800,000	120,000	$40/hour
Quality control	Number of inspections	700,000	28,000	$25/inspection

The cost drivers used for each product were:

Cost Drivers	Royale	Majestic	Total
Purchase orders	17,000	23,000	40,000
Machine setups	5,000	13,000	18,000
Machine hours	75,000	45,000	120,000
Inspections	11,000	17,000	28,000

Instructions

(a) Assign the total 2017 manufacturing overhead costs to the two products using activity-based costing (ABC) and determine the overhead cost per unit.

(b) What was the cost per unit and gross profit of each model using ABC?

(c) Are management's future plans for the two models sound? Explain.

(a) Royale $4,035,000

(b) Cost/unit—Royale $981.40

P17-3A Shaker Stairs Co. designs and builds factory-made premium wooden stairways for homes. The manufactured stairway components (spindles, risers, hangers, hand rails) permit installation of stairways of varying lengths and widths. All are of white oak wood. Budgeted manufacturing overhead costs for the year 2017 are as follows.

Assign overhead costs using traditional costing and ABC; compare results.

(LO 1, 2), AN

Overhead Cost Pools	Amount
Purchasing	$ 75,000
Handling materials	82,000
Production (cutting, milling, finishing)	210,000
Setting up machines	105,000
Inspecting	90,000
Inventory control (raw materials and finished goods)	126,000
Utilities	180,000
Total budgeted overhead costs	$868,000

For the last 4 years, Shaker Stairs Co. has been charging overhead to products on the basis of machine hours. For the year 2017, 100,000 machine hours are budgeted.

Jeremy Nolan, owner-manager of Shaker Stairs Co., recently directed his accountant, Bill Seagren, to implement the activity-based costing system that he has repeatedly proposed. At Jeremy Nolan's request, Bill and the production foreman identify the following cost drivers and their usage for the previously budgeted overhead cost pools.

Activity Cost Pools	Cost Drivers	Expected Use of Cost Drivers
Purchasing	Number of orders	600
Handling materials	Number of moves	8,000
Production (cutting, milling, finishing)	Direct labor hours	100,000
Setting up machines	Number of setups	1,250
Inspecting	Number of inspections	6,000
Inventory control (raw materials and finished goods)	Number of components	168,000
Utilities	Square feet occupied	90,000

Steve Hannon, sales manager, has received an order for 250 stairways from Community Builders, Inc., a large housing development contractor. At Steve's request, Bill prepares cost estimates for producing components for 250 stairways so Steve can submit a contract price per stairway to Community Builders. He accumulates the following data for the production of 250 stairways.

Direct materials	$103,600
Direct labor	$112,000
Machine hours	14,500
Direct labor hours	5,000
Number of purchase orders	60
Number of material moves	800
Number of machine setups	100
Number of inspections	450
Number of components	16,000
Number of square feet occupied	8,000

Instructions

(a) Compute the predetermined overhead rate using traditional costing with machine hours as the basis.

(b) Cost/stairway $1,365.84

(b) What is the manufacturing cost per stairway under traditional costing? (Round to the nearest cent.)

(c) Cost/stairway $1,139.80

(c) What is the manufacturing cost per stairway under the proposed activity-based costing? (Round to the nearest cent. Prepare all of the necessary schedules.)

(d) Which of the two costing systems is preferable in pricing decisions and why?

Assign overhead costs using traditional costing and ABC; compare results.

(LO 1, 2), AN

P17-4A Benton Corporation produces two grades of non-alcoholic wine from grapes that it buys from California growers. It produces and sells roughly 3,000,000 liters per year of a low-cost, high-volume product called CoolDay. It sells this in 600,000 5-liter jugs. Benton also produces and sells roughly 300,000 liters per year of a low-volume, high-cost product called LiteMist. LiteMist is sold in 1-liter bottles. Based on recent data, the CoolDay product has not been as profitable as LiteMist. Management is considering dropping the inexpensive CoolDay line so it can focus more attention on the LiteMist product. The LiteMist product already demands considerably more attention than the CoolDay line.

Jack Eller, president and founder of Benton, is skeptical about this idea. He points out that for many decades the company produced only the CoolDay line and that it was always quite profitable. It wasn't until the company started producing the more complicated LiteMist wine that the profitability of CoolDay declined. Prior to the introduction of LiteMist, the company had basic equipment, simple growing and production procedures, and virtually no need for quality control. Because LiteMist is bottled in 1-liter bottles, it requires considerably more time and effort, both to bottle and to label and box than does CoolDay. The company must bottle and handle 5 times as many bottles of LiteMist to sell the same quantity as CoolDay. CoolDay requires 1 month of aging; LiteMist requires 1 year. CoolDay requires cleaning and inspection of equipment every 10,000 liters; LiteMist requires such maintenance every 600 liters.

Jack has asked the accounting department to prepare an analysis of the cost per liter using the traditional costing approach and using activity-based costing. The following information was collected.

	CoolDay	LiteMist
Direct materials per liter	$0.40	$1.20
Direct labor cost per liter	$0.50	$0.90
Direct labor hours per liter	0.05	0.09
Total direct labor hours	150,000	27,000

				Expected Use of Cost Drivers per Product	
Activity Cost Pools	**Cost Drivers**	**Estimated Overhead**	**Expected Use of Cost Drivers**	**CoolDay**	**LiteMist**
Grape processing	Cart of grapes	$ 145,860	6,600	6,000	600
Aging	Total months	396,000	6,600,000	3,000,000	3,600,000
Bottling and corking	Number of bottles	270,000	900,000	600,000	300,000
Labeling and boxing	Number of bottles	189,000	900,000	600,000	300,000
Maintain and inspect equipment	Number of inspections	240,800	800	350	450
		$1,241,660			

Instructions

Answer each of the following questions. (Round all calculations to three decimal places.)

(a) Cost/liter—C.D. $1.251

(a) Under traditional product costing using direct labor hours, compute the total manufacturing cost per **liter** of both products.

(b) Under ABC, prepare a schedule showing the computation of the activity-based overhead rates (per cost driver).

(c) Cost/liter—C.D. $.241

(c) Prepare a schedule assigning each activity's overhead cost pool to each product, based on the use of cost drivers. Include a computation of overhead cost per liter.

(d) Compute the total manufacturing cost per liter for both products under ABC.

(e) Write a memo to Jack Eller discussing the implications of your analysis for the company's plans. In this memo, provide a brief description of ABC as well as an explanation of how the traditional approach can result in distortions.

Assign overhead costs to services using traditional costing and ABC; compute overhead rates and unit costs; compare results.

(LO 1, 2, 3, 4), AN

P17-5A Lewis and Stark is a public accounting firm that offers two primary services, auditing and tax-return preparation. A controversy has developed between the partners of the two service lines as to who is contributing the greater amount to the bottom line. The area of contention is the assignment of overhead. The tax partners argue for assigning overhead on the basis of 40% of direct labor dollars, while the audit partners argue for implementing activity-based costing. The partners agree to use next year's budgeted data for purposes of analysis and comparison. The following overhead data are collected to develop the comparison.

Activity Cost Pools	Cost Drivers	Estimated Overhead	Expected Use of Cost Drivers	Expected Use of Cost Drivers per Service: Audit	Expected Use of Cost Drivers per Service: Tax
Employee training	Direct labor dollars	$216,000	$1,800,000	$1,100,000	$700,000
Typing and secretarial	Number of reports/ forms	76,200	2,500	800	1,700
Computing	Number of minutes	204,000	60,000	27,000	33,000
Facility rental	Number of employees	142,500	40	22	18
Travel	Per expense reports	81,300	Direct	56,000	25,300
		$720,000			

Instructions

(a) Using traditional product costing as proposed by the tax partners, compute the total overhead cost assigned to both services (audit and tax) of Lewis and Stark.

(b) (1) Using activity-based costing, prepare a schedule showing the computations of the activity-based overhead rates (per cost driver).

(2) Prepare a schedule assigning each activity's overhead cost pool to each service based on the use of the cost drivers.

(b) (2) Cost assigned—Tax $337,441

(c) Comment on the comparative overhead cost for the two services under both traditional costing and ABC.

(c) Difference—Audit $57,441

PROBLEMS: SET B AND SET C

Visit the book's companion website, at **www.wiley.com/college/kimmel**, and choose the Student Companion site to access Problems: Set B and Set C.

CONTINUING PROBLEMS

CURRENT DESIGNS

EXCEL TUTORIAL

CD17 As you learned in the previous chapters, Current Designs has two main product lines—composite kayaks, which are handmade and very labor-intensive, and rotomolded kayaks, which require less labor but employ more expensive equipment. Current Designs' controller, Diane Buswell, is now evaluating several different methods of assigning overhead to these products. It is important to ensure that costs are appropriately assigned to the company's products. At the same time, the system that is used must not be so complex that its costs are greater than its benefits.

Diane has decided to use the following activities and costs to evaluate the methods of assigning overhead.

Current Designs Activity Cost Pools.xls

Activities	Cost
Designing new models	$121,100
Creating and testing prototypes	152,000
Creating molds for kayaks	188,500
Operating oven for the rotomolded kayaks	40,000
Operating the vacuum line for the composite kayaks	28,000
Supervising production employees	180,000
Curing time (the time that is needed for the chemical processes to finish before the next step in the production process; many of these costs are related to the space required in the building)	190,400
Total	$900,000

As Diane examines the data, she decides that the cost of operating the oven for the rotomolded kayaks and the cost of operating the vacuum line for the composite kayaks can be directly assigned to each of these product lines and do not need to be allocated with the other costs.

Instructions

For purposes of this analysis, assume that Current Designs uses $234,000 in direct labor costs to produce 1,000 composite kayaks and $286,000 in direct labor costs to produce 4,000 rotomolded kayaks each year.

(a) One method of allocating overhead would allocate the common costs to each product line by using an allocation basis such as the number of employees working on each type of kayak or the amount of factory space used for the production of each type of kayak. Diane knows that about 50% of the area of the plant and 50% of the employees work on the composite kayaks, and the remaining space and other employees work on the rotomolded kayaks. Using this information and remembering that the cost of operating the oven and vacuum line have been directly assigned, determine the total amount to be assigned to the composite kayak line and the rotomolded kayak line, and the amount to be assigned to each of the units in each line.

(b) Another method of allocating overhead is to use direct labor dollars as an allocation basis. Remembering that the costs of the oven and the vacuum line have been assigned directly to the product lines, allocate the remaining costs using direct labor dollars as the allocation basis. Then, determine the amount of overhead that should be assigned to each unit of each product line using this method.

(c) Activity-based costing requires a cost driver for each cost pool. Use the following information to assign the costs to the product lines using the activity-based costing approach.

Current Designs Cost Drivers.xls

Activity Cost Pools	Cost Drivers	Driver Amount for Composite Kayaks	Driver Amount for Rotomolded Kayaks
Designing new models	Number of models	3	1
Creating and testing prototypes	Number of prototypes	6	2
Creating molds for kayaks	Number of molds	12	1
Supervising production employees	Number of employees	12	12
Curing time	Number of days of curing time	15,000	2,000

What amount of overhead should be assigned to each composite kayak using this method? What amount of overhead should be assigned to each rotomolded kayak using this method?

(d) Which of the three methods do you think Current Designs should use? Why?

WATERWAYS

(*Note:* This is a continuation of the Waterways problem from Chapters 14–16.)

WP17 Waterways looked into ABC as a method of costing because of the variety of items it produces and the many different activities in which it is involved. This problem asks you to help Waterways use an activity-based costing system to account for its production activities.

Go to the book's companion website, at **www.wiley.com/college/kimmel**, *to find the completion of this problem.*

COMPREHENSIVE CASE

In Chapter 15, you used job order costing techniques to help Greetings Inc., a retailer of greeting cards and small gift items, expand its operations. Your next task is to help the new unit, Wall Décor, become profitable through the use of activity-based costing. In this case, you will have the opportunity to discuss the cost/benefit trade-offs between simple ABC systems versus refined systems, and the potential benefit of using capacity rather than expected sales when allocating fixed overhead costs.

Go to the book's companion website, at **www.wiley.com/college/kimmel**, *for complete case details and instructions.*

EXPAND YOUR CRITICAL THINKING

DECISION-MAKING ACROSS THE ORGANIZATION

Group Project

CT17-1 East Valley Hospital is a primary medical care facility and trauma center that serves 11 small, rural midwestern communities within a 40-mile radius. The hospital offers all the medical/surgical services of a typical small hospital. It has a staff of 18 full-time doctors and 20 part-time visiting specialists. East Valley has a payroll of 150 employees consisting of technicians, nurses, therapists, managers, directors, administrators, dieticians, secretaries, data processors, and janitors. E

Instructions

With the class divided into groups, discuss and answer the following.

(a) Using your (limited, moderate, or in-depth) knowledge of a hospital's operations, identify as many **activities** as you can that would serve as the basis for implementing an activity-based costing system.

(b) For each of the activities listed in (a), identify a **cost driver** that would serve as a valid measure of the resources consumed by the activity.

MANAGERIAL ANALYSIS

CT17-2 Ideal Manufacturing Company has supported a research and development (R&D) department that has for many years been the sole contributor to the company's new farm machinery products. The R&D activity is an overhead cost center that performs services only to in-house manufacturing departments (four different product lines), all of which produce agricultural/farm/ranch-related machinery products. E

The department has never sold its services to outside companies. But, because of its long history of success, larger manufacturers of agricultural products have approached Ideal to hire its R&D department for special projects. Because the costs of operating the R&D department have been spiraling uncontrollably, Ideal's management is considering entertaining these outside approaches to absorb the increasing costs. However, (1) management doesn't have any cost basis for charging R&D services to outsiders, and (2) it needs to gain control of its R&D costs. Management decides to implement an activity-based costing system in order to determine the charges for both outsiders and the in-house users of the department's services.

R&D activities fall into four pools with the following annual costs.

Market analysis	$1,050,000
Product design	2,350,000
Product development	3,600,000
Prototype testing	1,400,000

Activity analysis determines that the appropriate cost drivers and their usage for the four activities are:

Activities	Cost Drivers	Total Estimated Drivers
Market analysis	Hours of analysis	15,000 hours
Product design	Number of designs	2,500 designs
Product development	Number of products	90 products
Prototype testing	Number of tests	500 tests

Instructions

(a) Compute the activity-based overhead rate for each activity cost pool.

(b) How much cost would be charged to an in-house manufacturing department that consumed 1,800 hours of market analysis time, was provided 280 designs relating to 10 products, and requested 92 engineering tests?

(c) How much cost would serve as the basis for pricing an R&D bid with an outside company on a contract that would consume 800 hours of analysis time, require 178 designs relating to 3 products, and result in 70 engineering tests?

(d) What is the benefit to Ideal Manufacturing of applying activity-based costing to its R&D activity for both in-house and outside charging purposes?

REAL-WORLD FOCUS

C **CT17-3** An article in *Cost Management,* by Kocakulah, Bartlett, and Albin entitled "ABC for Calculating Mortgage Loan Servicing Expenses" (July/August 2009, p. 36), discusses a use of ABC in the financial services industry.

Instructions

Read the article and answer the following questions.

(a) What are some of the benefits of ABC that relate to the financial services industry?

(b) What are three things that the company's original costing method did not take into account?

(c) What were some of the cost drivers used by the company in the ABC approach?

ETHICS CASE

E **CT17-4** Curtis Rich, the cost accountant for Hi-Power Mower Company, recently installed activity-based costing at Hi-Power's St. Louis lawn tractor (riding mower) plant where three models—the 8-horsepower Bladerunner, the 12-horsepower Quickcut, and the 18-horsepower Supercut—are manufactured. Curtis's new product costs for these three models show that the company's traditional costing system had been significantly under-costing the 18-horsepower Supercut. This was due primarily to the lower sales volume of the Supercut compared to the Bladerunner and the Quickcut.

Before completing his analysis and reporting these results to management, Curtis is approached by his friend Ed Gray, who is the production manager for the 18-horsepower Supercut model. Ed has heard from one of Curtis's staff about the new product costs and is upset and worried for his job because the new costs show the Supercut to be losing, rather than making, money.

At first, Ed condemns the new cost system, where upon Curtis explains the practice of activity-based costing and why it is more accurate than the company's present system. Even more worried now, Ed begs Curtis, "Massage the figures just enough to save the line from being discontinued. You don't want me to lose my job, do you? Anyway, nobody will know."

Curtis holds firm but agrees to recompute all his calculations for accuracy before submitting his costs to management.

Instructions

(a) Who are the stakeholders in this situation?
(b) What, if any, are the ethical considerations in this situation?
(c) What are Curtis's ethical obligations to the company? To his friend?

ALL ABOUT YOU

CT17-5 There are many resources available on the Internet to assist people in time management. Some of these resources are designed specifically for college students.

Instructions

Do an Internet search of Dartmouth's time-management video. Watch the video and then answer the following questions.

(a) What are the main tools of time management for students, and what is each used for?
(b) At what time of day are students most inclined to waste time? What time of day is the best for studying complex topics?
(c) How can employing time-management practices be a "liberating" experience?
(d) Why is goal-setting important? What are the characteristics of good goals, and what steps should you take to help you develop your goals?

CONSIDERING YOUR COSTS AND BENEFITS

CT17-6 As discussed in the chapter, the principles underlying activity-based costing have evolved into the broader approach known as *activity-based management*. One of the common practices of activity-based management is to identify all business activities, classify each activity as either a value-added or a non–value-added activity, and then try to reduce or eliminate the time spent on non–value-added activities. Consider the implications of applying this same approach to your everyday life, at work and at school. How do you spend your time each day? How much of your day is spent on activities that help you accomplish your objectives, and how much of your day is spent on activities that do not add value?

Many "self-help" books and websites offer suggestions on how to improve your time management. Should you minimize the "non–value-added" hours in your life by adopting the methods suggested by these sources? The basic arguments for and against are as follows.

> **YES:** There are a limited number of hours in a day. You should try to maximize your chances of achieving your goals by eliminating the time that you waste.
>
> **NO:** Life is about more than working yourself to death. Being an efficiency expert doesn't guarantee that you will be happy. Schedules and daily planners are too constraining.

Instructions

Write a response indicating your position regarding this situation. Provide support for your view.

18

Cost-Volume-Profit

CHAPTER PREVIEW

As the Feature Story indicates, to manage any size business you must understand how costs respond to changes in sales volume and the effect of costs and revenues on profits. A prerequisite to understanding cost-volume-profit (CVP) relationships is knowledge of how costs behave. In this chapter, we first explain the considerations involved in cost behavior analysis. Then, we discuss and illustrate CVP analysis.

CHAPTER OUTLINE

LEARNING OBJECTIVES		PRACTICE
1 Explain variable, fixed, and mixed costs and the relevant range.	• Variable costs • Fixed costs • Relevant range • Mixed costs	DO IT! 1 Types of Costs
2 Apply the high-low method to determine the components of mixed costs.	• High-low method • Identify variable and fixed costs	DO IT! 2 High-Low Method
3 Prepare a CVP income statement to determine contribution margin.	• Basic components • CVP income statement	DO IT! 3 CVP Income Statement
4 Compute the break-even point using three approaches.	• Mathematical equation • Contribution margin technique • Graphic presentation	DO IT! 4 Break-Even Analysis
5 Determine the sales required to earn target net income and determine margin of safety.	• Target net income • Margin of safety	DO IT! 5 Break-Even, Margin of Safety, and Target Net Income

Go to the ***REVIEW AND PRACTICE*** section at the end of the chapter for a targeted summary and exercises with solutions.

Visit **WileyPLUS** for additional tutorials and practice opportunities.

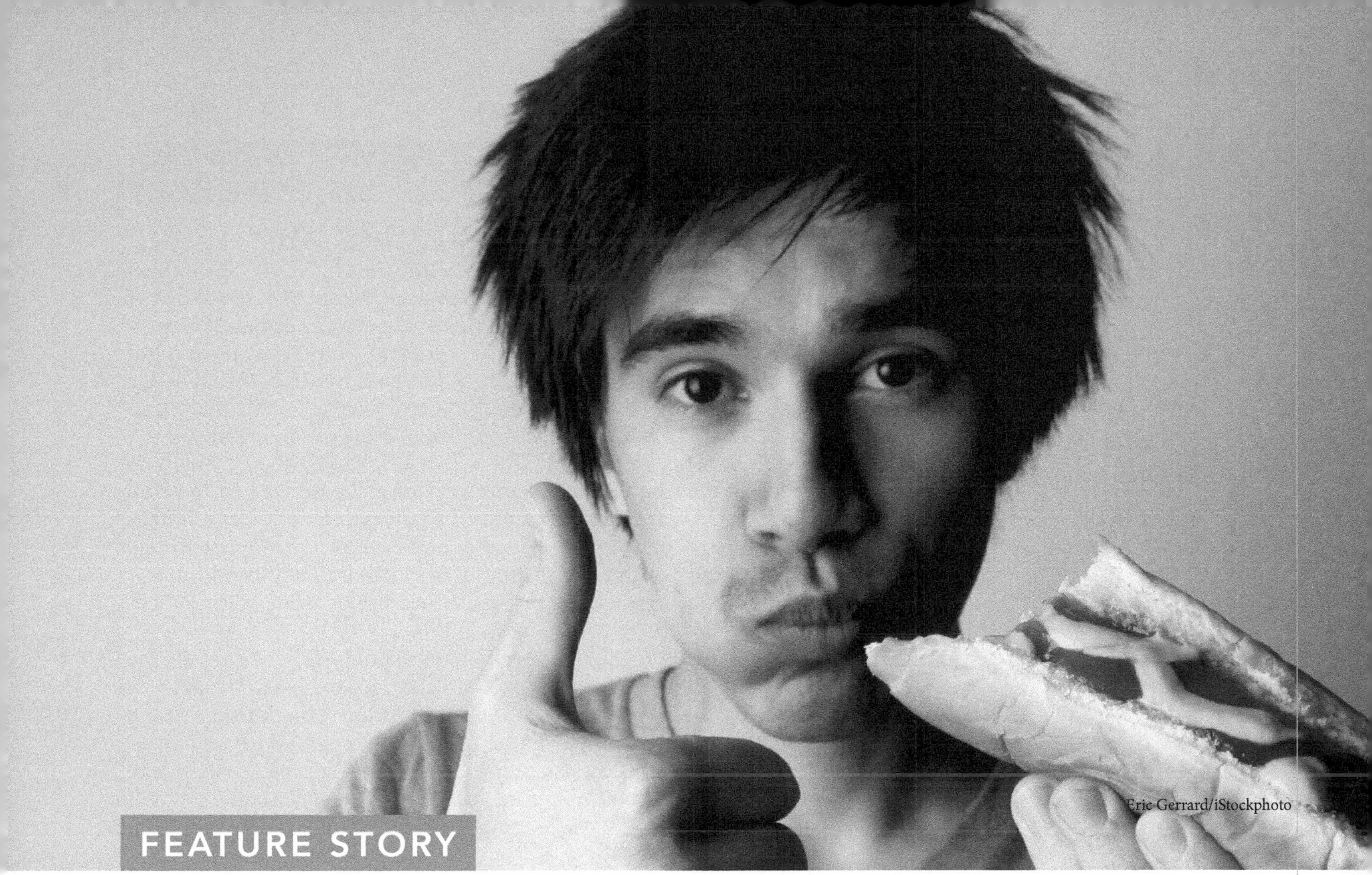

Eric Gerrard/iStockphoto

FEATURE STORY

Don't Worry— Just Get Big

It wasn't that Jeff Bezos didn't have a good job. He was a vice president at a Wall Street firm. But, he quit his job, moved to Seattle, and started an online retailer, which he named Amazon.com. Like any good entrepreneur, Jeff strove to keep his initial investment small. Operations were run out of his garage. And, to avoid the need for a warehouse, he took orders for books and had them shipped from other distributors' warehouses.

By its fourth month, Amazon was selling 100 books a day. In its first full year, it had $15.7 million in sales. The next year, sales increased eightfold. Two years later, sales were $1.6 billion.

Although its sales growth was impressive, Amazon's ability to lose money was equally amazing. One analyst nicknamed it *Amazon.bomb*, while another, predicting its demise, called it *Amazon.toast*. Why was it losing money? The company used every available dollar to reinvest in itself. It built massive warehouses and bought increasingly sophisticated (and expensive) computers and equipment to improve its distribution system. This desire to grow as fast as possible was captured in a T-shirt slogan at its company picnic, which read "Eat another hot dog, get big fast." This buying binge was increasing the company's fixed costs at a rate that exceeded its sales growth. Skeptics predicted that Amazon would soon run out of cash. It didn't.

In the fourth quarter of 2010 (only 15 years after its world headquarters was located in a garage), Amazon reported quarterly revenues of $12.95 billion and quarterly income of $416 million. But, even as it announced record profits, its share price fell by 9%. Why? Because although the company was predicting that its sales revenue in the next quarter would increase by at least 28%, it predicted that its operating profit would fall by at least 2% and perhaps by as much as 34%. The company made no apologies. It explained that it was in the process of expanding from 39 distribution centers to 52. As Amazon's finance chief noted, "You're not as productive on those assets for some time. I'm very pleased with the investments we're making and we've shown over our history that we've been able to make great returns on the capital we invest in." In other words, eat another hot dog.

Sources: Christine Frey and John Cook, "How Amazon.com Survived, Thrived and Turned a Profit," *Seattle Post* (January 28, 2008); and Stu Woo, "Sticker Shock Over Amazon Growth," *Wall Street Journal Online* (January 28, 2011).

LEARNING OBJECTIVE ▶1

Explain variable, fixed, and mixed costs and the relevant range.

Cost behavior analysis is the study of how specific costs respond to changes in the level of business activity. As you might expect, some costs change, and others remain the same. For example, for an airline company such as Southwest or United, the longer the flight, the higher the fuel costs. On the other hand, Massachusetts General Hospital's costs to staff the emergency room on any given night are relatively constant regardless of the number of patients treated. A knowledge of cost behavior helps management plan operations and decide between alternative courses of action. Cost behavior analysis applies to all types of entities.

The starting point in cost behavior analysis is measuring the key business activities. Activity levels may be expressed in terms of sales dollars (in a retail company), miles driven (in a trucking company), room occupancy (in a hotel), or dance classes taught (by a dance studio). Many companies use more than one measurement base. A manufacturer, for example, may use direct labor hours or units of output for manufacturing costs, and sales revenue or units sold for selling expenses.

For an activity level to be useful in cost behavior analysis, changes in the level or volume of activity should be correlated with changes in costs. The activity level selected is referred to as the activity (or volume) index. The **activity index** identifies the activity that causes changes in the behavior of costs. With an appropriate activity index, companies can classify the behavior of costs in response to changes in activity levels into three categories: variable, fixed, or mixed.

VARIABLE COSTS

Variable costs are costs that vary **in total** directly and proportionately with changes in the activity level. If the level increases 10%, total variable costs will increase 10%. If the level of activity decreases by 25%, variable costs will decrease 25%. Examples of variable costs include direct materials and direct labor for a manufacturer; cost of goods sold, sales commissions, and freight-out for a merchandiser; and gasoline in airline and trucking companies. A variable cost may also be defined as a cost that **remains the same *per unit* at every level of activity**.

To illustrate the behavior of a variable cost, assume that Damon Company manufactures tablet computers that contain $10 cameras. The activity index is the number of tablet computers produced. As Damon manufactures each tablet, the total cost of cameras used increases by $10. As part (a) of Illustration 18-1

ILLUSTRATION 18-1
Behavior of total and unit variable costs

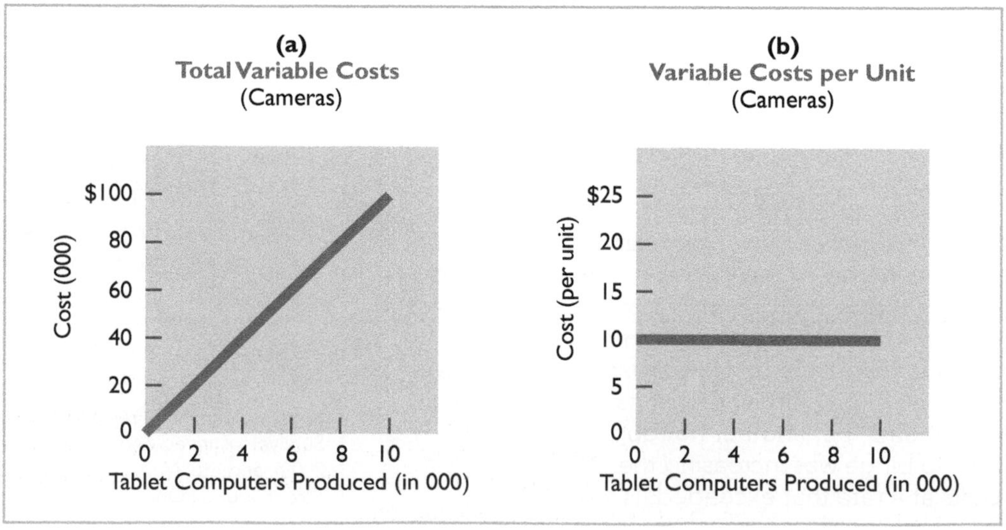

▼ **HELPFUL HINT**
Variable costs per unit remain constant at all levels of activity.

shows, total cost of the cameras will be $20,000 if Damon produces 2,000 tablets, and $100,000 when it produces 10,000 tablets. We also can see that a variable cost remains the same per unit as the level of activity changes. As part (b) of Illustration 18-1 shows, the unit cost of $10 for the cameras is the same whether Damon produces 2,000 or 10,000 tablets.

Companies that rely heavily on labor to manufacture a product, such as Nike or Reebok, or to perform a service, such as Hilton or Marriott, are likely to have many variable costs. In contrast, companies that use a high proportion of machinery and equipment in producing revenue, such as AT&T or Duke Energy Co., may have few variable costs.

FIXED COSTS

Fixed costs are costs that **remain the same in total** regardless of changes in the activity level. Examples include property taxes, insurance, rent, supervisory salaries, and depreciation on buildings and equipment. Because total fixed costs remain constant as activity changes, it follows that **fixed costs *per unit* vary inversely with activity: As volume increases, unit cost declines, and vice versa**.

To illustrate the behavior of fixed costs, assume that Damon Company leases its productive facilities at a cost of $10,000 per month. Total fixed costs of the facilities will remain constant at every level of activity, as part (a) of Illustration 18-2 shows. But, **on a per unit basis, the cost of rent will decline as activity increases**, as part (b) of Illustration 18-2 shows. At 2,000 units, the unit cost per tablet computer is $5 ($10,000 ÷ 2,000). When Damon produces 10,000 tablets, the unit cost of the rent is only $1 per tablet ($10,000 ÷ 10,000).

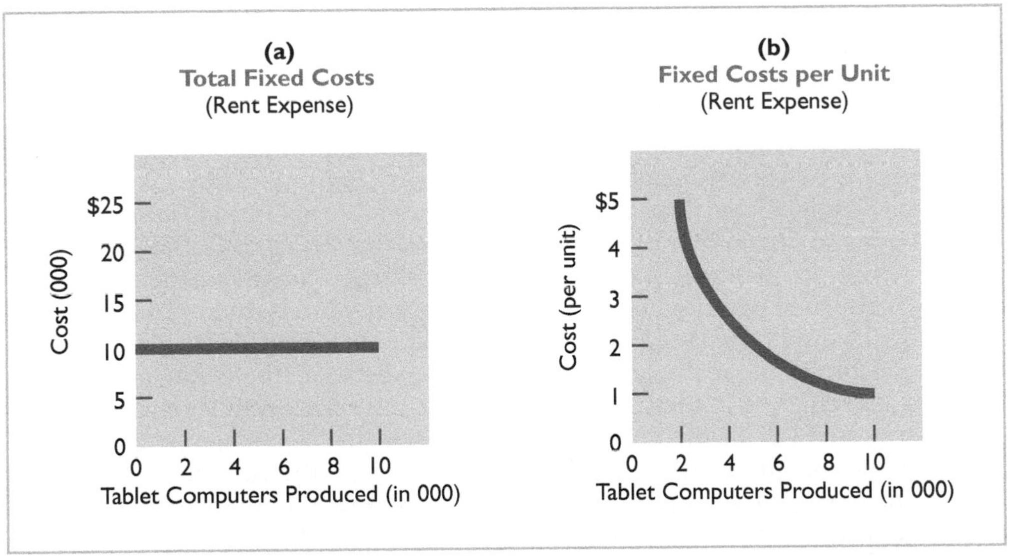

ILLUSTRATION 18-2
Behavior of total and unit fixed costs

The trend for many manufacturers is to have more fixed costs and fewer variable costs. This trend is the result of increased use of automation and less use of employee labor. As a result, depreciation and lease charges (fixed costs) increase, whereas direct labor costs (variable costs) decrease.

PEOPLE, PLANET, AND PROFIT INSIGHT **BrightFarms**

© Jani Bryson/iStockphoto

Gardens in the Sky

Because of population increases, the United Nations' Food and Agriculture Organization estimates that food production will need to increase by 70% by 2050. Also, by 2050, roughly 70% of people will live in cities, which means more food needs to be hauled further to get it to the consumer. To address the lack of farmable land and reduce the cost of transporting produce, some companies, such as New York-based BrightFarms, are building urban greenhouses.

This sounds great, but do the numbers work? Some variable costs would be reduced. For example, the use of pesticides, herbicides, fuel costs for shipping, and water would all drop. Soil erosion would be a non-issue since plants would be grown hydroponically (in a solution of water and minerals), and land requirements would be reduced because of vertical structures. But, other costs would be higher. First, there is the cost of the building. Also, any multistory building would require artificial lighting for plants on lower floors.

Until these cost challenges can be overcome, it appears that these urban greenhouses may not break even. On the other hand, rooftop greenhouses on existing city structures already appear financially viable. For example, a 15,000 square-foot rooftop greenhouse in Brooklyn already produces roughly 30 tons of vegetables per year for local residents.

Sources: "Vertical Farming: Does It Really Stack Up?" *The Economist* (December 9, 2010); and Jane Black, "BrightFarms Idea: Greenhouses That Cut Short the Path from Plant to Grocery Shelf," *The Washington Post* (May 7, 2013).

What are some of the variable and fixed costs that are impacted by hydroponic farming? (Go to WileyPLUS for this answer and additional questions.)

RELEVANT RANGE

In Illustration 18-1 part (a) (page 884), a straight line is drawn throughout the entire range of the activity index for total variable costs. In essence, the assumption is that the costs are **linear**. If a relationship is linear (that is, straight-line), then changes in the activity index will result in a direct, proportional change in the variable cost. For example, if the activity level doubles, the cost doubles.

It is now necessary to ask: Is the straight-line relationship realistic? In most business situations, a straight-line relationship **does not exist** for variable costs throughout the entire range of possible activity. At abnormally low levels of activity, it may be impossible to be cost-efficient. Small-scale operations may not allow the company to obtain quantity discounts for raw materials or to use specialized labor. In contrast, at abnormally high levels of activity, labor costs may increase sharply because of overtime pay. Also, at high activity levels, materials costs may jump significantly because of excess spoilage caused by worker fatigue.

As a result, in the real world, the relationship between the behavior of a variable cost and changes in the activity level is often **curvilinear**, as shown in part (a) of Illustration 18-3. In the curved sections of the line, a change in the activity index will not result in a direct, proportional change in the variable cost. That is, a doubling of the activity index will not result in an exact doubling of the variable cost. The variable cost may more than double, or it may be less than double.

▼ HELPFUL HINT
Fixed costs that may be changeable include research, such as new product development, and management training programs.

Total fixed costs also do not have a straight-line relationship over the entire range of activity. Some fixed costs will not change. But it is possible for management to change other fixed costs. For example, in some instances, salaried employees (fixed) are replaced with freelance workers (variable). Illustration 18-3, part (b), shows an example of the behavior of total fixed costs through all potential levels of activity.

For most companies, operating at almost zero or at 100% capacity is the exception rather than the rule. Instead, companies often operate over a somewhat narrower range, such as 40–80% of capacity. The range over which a

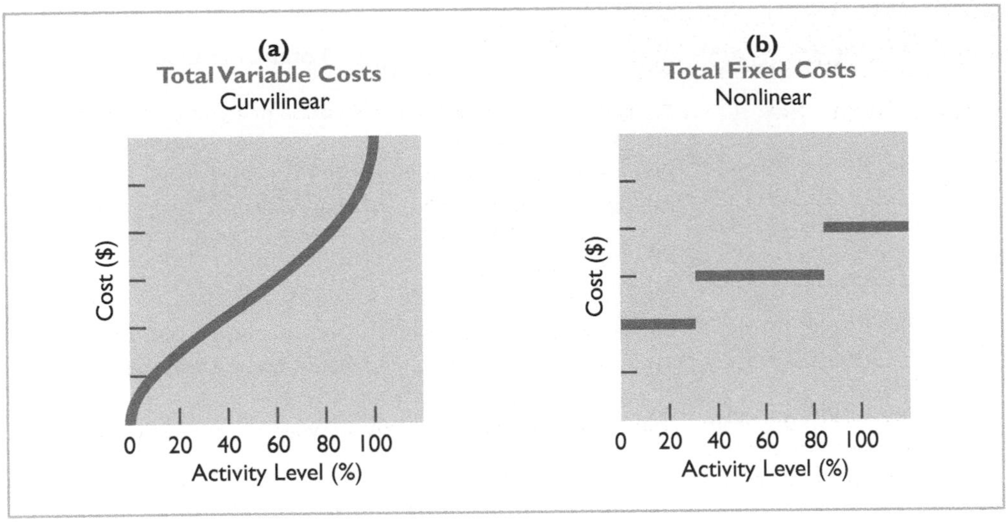

ILLUSTRATION 18-3
Nonlinear behavior of variable and fixed costs

company expects to operate during a year is called the **relevant range** of the activity index. Within the relevant range, as both diagrams in Illustration 18-4 show, a straight-line relationship generally exists for both variable and fixed costs.

ALTERNATIVE TERMINOLOGY
The relevant range is also called the *normal* or *practical range*.

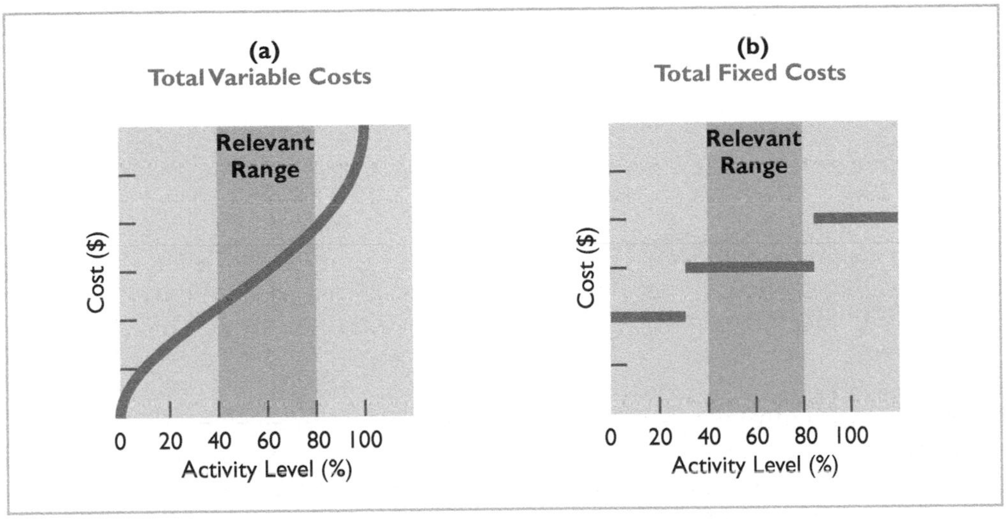

ILLUSTRATION 18-4
Linear behavior within relevant range

As you can see, although the linear (straight-line) relationship may not be completely realistic, **the linear assumption produces useful data for CVP analysis as long as the level of activity remains within the relevant range**.

MIXED COSTS

Mixed costs are costs that contain both a variable- and a fixed-cost element. **Mixed costs, therefore, change in total but not proportionately with changes in the activity level.**

The rental of a U-Haul truck is a good example of a mixed cost. Assume that local rental terms for a 17-foot truck, including insurance, are $50 per day plus 50 cents per mile. When determining the cost of a one-day rental, the per day charge is a fixed cost (with respect to miles driven), whereas the mileage charge is a variable cost. The graphic presentation of the rental cost for a one-day rental is shown in Illustration 18-5 (page 888).

ILLUSTRATION 18-5
Behavior of a mixed cost

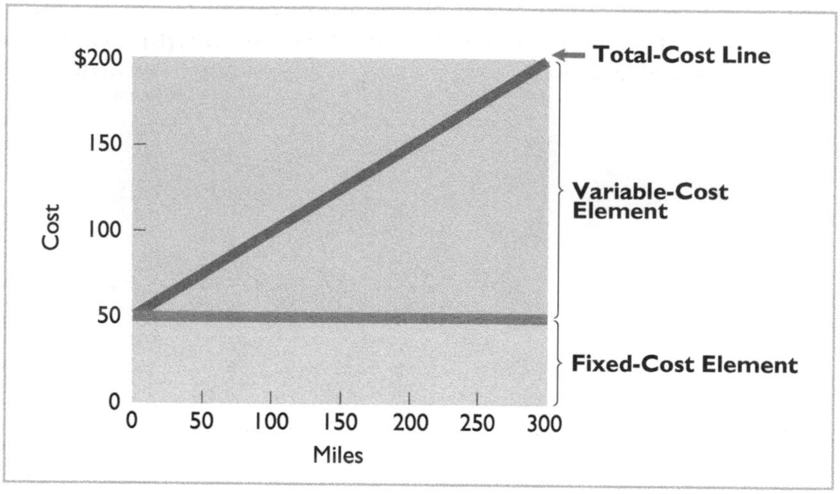

In this case, the fixed-cost element is the cost of having the service available. The variable-cost element is the cost of actually using the service. Utility costs such as for electricity are another example of a mixed cost. Each month the electric bill includes a flat service fee plus a usage charge.

DO IT! 1 Types of Costs

Helena Company reports the following total costs at two levels of production.

	10,000 Units	20,000 Units
Direct materials	$20,000	$40,000
Maintenance	8,000	10,000
Direct labor	17,000	34,000
Indirect materials	1,000	2,000
Depreciation	4,000	4,000
Utilities	3,000	5,000
Rent	6,000	6,000

Classify each cost as variable, fixed, or mixed.

Action Plan

- ✔ Recall that a variable cost varies in total directly and proportionately with each change in activity level.
- ✔ Recall that a fixed cost remains the same in total with each change in activity level.
- ✔ Recall that a mixed cost changes in total but not proportionately with each change in activity level.

SOLUTION

Direct materials, direct labor, and indirect materials are variable costs.
Depreciation and rent are fixed costs.
Maintenance and utilities are mixed costs.

Related exercise material: **BE18-1, BE18-2, E18-1, E18-2, E18-4, E18-6,** and DO IT! **18-1.**

LEARNING OBJECTIVE 2 Apply the high-low method to determine the components of mixed costs.

For purposes of cost-volume-profit analysis, **mixed costs must be classified into their fixed and variable elements**. How does management make the classification? One possibility is to determine the variable and fixed components each time a mixed cost is incurred. But because of time and cost constraints, this approach is rarely followed. Instead, the usual approach is to collect data on the behavior of the mixed costs at various levels of activity. Analysts then identify the fixed- and variable-cost components. Companies use various types of analysis. One type of analysis, called the **high-low method**, is discussed next.

HIGH-LOW METHOD

The **high-low method** uses the total costs incurred at the high and low levels of activity to classify mixed costs into fixed and variable components. The difference in costs between the high and low levels represents variable costs, since only the variable-cost element can change as activity levels change.

The steps in computing fixed and variable costs under this method are as follows.

1. Determine variable cost per unit from the following formula.

Change in Total Costs	÷	High minus Low Activity Level	=	Variable Cost per Unit

ILLUSTRATION 18-6
Formula for variable cost per unit using high-low method

To illustrate, assume that Metro Transit Company has the following maintenance costs and mileage data for its fleet of buses over a 6-month period.

Month	Miles Driven	Total Cost	Month	Miles Driven	Total Cost
January	20,000	$30,000	April	50,000	$63,000
February	40,000	48,000	May	30,000	42,000
March	35,000	49,000	June	43,000	61,000

ILLUSTRATION 18-7
Assumed maintenance costs and mileage data

The high and low levels of activity are 50,000 miles in April and 20,000 miles in January. The maintenance costs at these two levels are $63,000 and $30,000, respectively. The difference in maintenance costs is $33,000 ($63,000 − $30,000), and the difference in miles is 30,000 (50,000 − 20,000). Therefore, for Metro Transit, variable cost per unit is $1.10, computed as follows.

$$\$33,000 \div 30,000 = \$1.10$$

2. Determine the fixed costs by subtracting the total variable costs at either the high or the low activity level from the total cost at that activity level.

For Metro Transit, the computations are shown in Illustration 18-8.

Metro Transit.xls

	A	B	C	D
1		METRO TRANSIT		
2			Activity Level	
3			High	Low
4	Total cost		$63,000	$30,000
5	Less:	Variable costs		
6		50,000 × $1.10	55,000	
7		20,000 × $1.10		22,000
8	Total fixed costs		$ 8,000	$ 8,000
9				
10				

ILLUSTRATION 18-8
High-low method computation of fixed costs

Maintenance costs are therefore $8,000 per month of fixed costs plus $1.10 per mile of variable costs. This is represented by the following formula:

Maintenance costs = $8,000 + ($1.10 × Miles driven)

For example, at 45,000 miles, estimated maintenance costs would be $8,000 fixed and $49,500 variable ($1.10 × 45,000) for a total of $57,500.

The graph in Illustration 18-9 plots the 6-month data for Metro Transit Company. The red line drawn in the graph connects the high and low data points, and therefore represents the equation that we just solved using the high-low method. The red, "high-low" line intersects the y-axis at $8,000 (the fixed-cost level), and it rises by $1.10 per unit (the variable cost per unit). Note that a completely different line would result if we chose any two of the other data points. That is, by choosing any two other data points, we would end up with a different estimate of fixed costs and a different variable cost per unit. Thus, from this scatter plot, we can see that while the high-low method is simple, the result is rather arbitrary. A better approach, which uses information from all the data points to estimate fixed and variable costs, is called *regression analysis*. A discussion of regression analysis is provided in a supplement on the book's companion website.

ILLUSTRATION 18-9
Scatter plot for Metro Transit Company

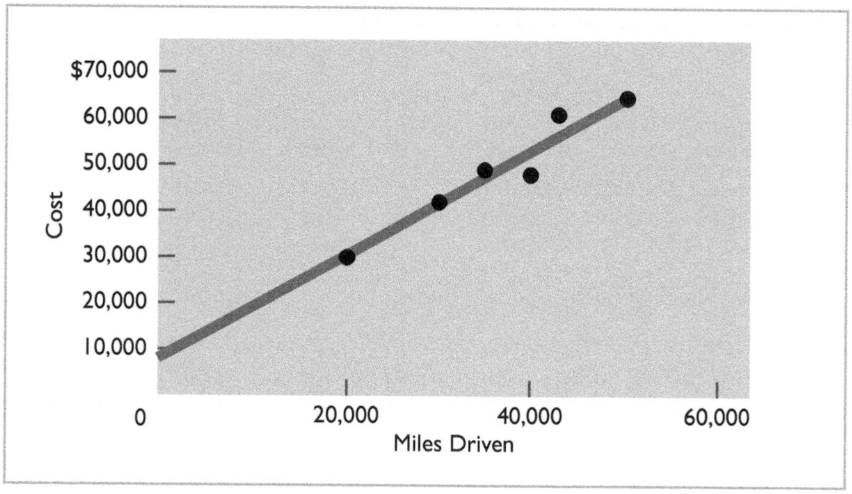

MANAGEMENT INSIGHT Tempur Sealy International

Bloomberg/Getty Images

Skilled Labor Is Truly Essential

The recent recession had devastating implications for employment. But one surprise was that for some manufacturers, the number of jobs lost was actually lower than in previous recessions. One of the main explanations for this was that in the years preceding the recession, many companies, such as Tempur Sealy International, adopted lean manufacturing practices. This meant that production relied less on large numbers of low-skilled workers and more on machines and a few highly skilled workers. As a result of this approach, a single employee supports far more dollars in sales. Thus, it requires a larger decline in sales before an employee would need to be laid-off in order for the company to continue to break even. Also, because the employees are highly skilled, employers are reluctant to lose them. Instead of lay-offs, many manufacturers now resort to cutting employees' hours when necessary.

Source: Timothy Aeppel and Justin Lahart, "Lean Factories Find It Hard to Cut Jobs Even in a Slump," *Wall Street Journal Online* (March 9, 2009).

Would you characterize labor costs as being a fixed cost, a variable cost, or something else in this situation? (Go to WileyPLUS for this answer and additional questions.)

IMPORTANCE OF IDENTIFYING VARIABLE AND FIXED COSTS

Why is it important to segregate mixed costs into variable and fixed elements? The answer may become apparent if we look at the following four business decisions.

1. If American Airlines is to make a profit when it reduces all domestic fares by 30%, what reduction in costs or increase in passengers will be required? **Answer**: To make a profit when it cuts domestic fares by 30%, American Airlines will have to increase the number of passengers or cut its variable costs for those flights. Its fixed costs will not change.
2. If Ford Motor Company meets workers' demands for higher wages, what increase in sales revenue will be needed to maintain current profit levels? **Answer**: Higher wages at Ford Motor Company will increase the variable costs of manufacturing automobiles. To maintain present profit levels, Ford will have to cut other variable costs or increase the price of its automobiles.
3. If United States Steel Corp.'s program to modernize plant facilities through significant equipment purchases reduces the work force by 50%, what will be the effect on the cost of producing one ton of steel?

   Answer: The modernizing of plant facilities at United States Steel Corp. changes the proportion of fixed and variable costs of producing one ton of steel. Fixed costs increase because of higher depreciation charges, whereas variable costs decrease due to the reduction in the number of steelworkers.
4. What happens if Kellogg's increases its advertising expenses but cannot increase prices because of competitive pressure?

   Answer: Sales volume must be increased to cover the increase in fixed advertising costs.

DO IT! 2 High-Low Method

Byrnes Company accumulates the following data concerning a mixed cost, using units produced as the activity level.

	Units Produced	Total Cost
March	9,800	$14,740
April	8,500	13,250
May	7,000	11,100
June	7,600	12,000
July	8,100	12,460

(a) Compute the variable-cost and fixed-cost elements using the high-low method.

(b) Estimate the total cost if the company produces 8,000 units.

SOLUTION

(a) Variable cost: ($14,740 − $11,100) ÷ (9,800 − 7,000) = $1.30 per unit
Fixed cost: $14,740 − $12,740* = $2,000
or $11,100 − $9,100** = $2,000

*$1.30 × 9,800 units
**$1.30 × 7,000 units

(b) Total cost to produce 8,000 units: $2,000 + $10,400 ($1.30 × 8,000 units) = $12,400

Related exercise material: **BE18-3, BE18-4, BE18-5, E18-3, E18-5,** and **DO IT! 18-2.**

Action Plan

- ✔ Determine the highest and lowest levels of activity.
- ✔ Compute variable cost per unit as Change in total costs ÷ (High − low activity level) = Variable cost per unit.
- ✔ Compute fixed cost as Total cost − (Variable cost per unit × Units produced) = Fixed cost.

LEARNING OBJECTIVE 3

Prepare a CVP income statement to determine contribution margin.

Cost-volume-profit (CVP) analysis is the study of the effects of changes in costs and volume on a company's profits. CVP analysis is important in profit planning. It also is a critical factor in such management decisions as setting selling prices, determining product mix, and maximizing use of production facilities.

BASIC COMPONENTS

CVP analysis considers the interrelationships among the components shown in Illustration 18-10.

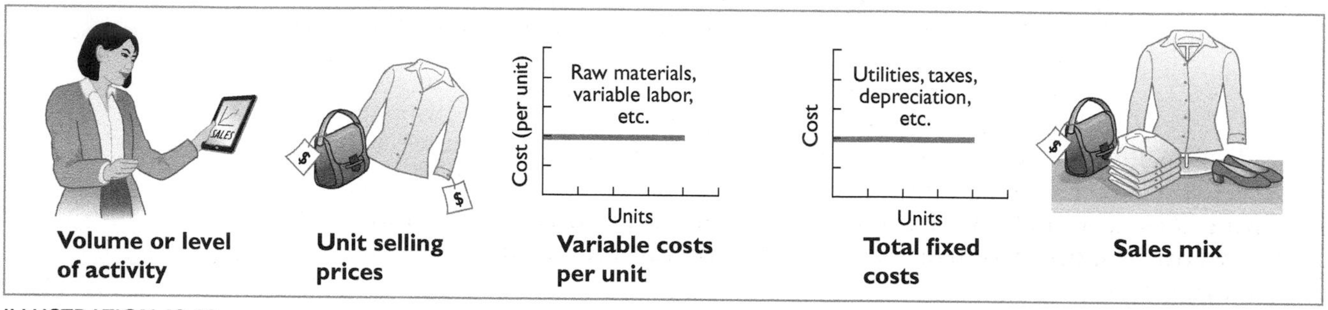

ILLUSTRATION 18-10
Components of CVP analysis

The following assumptions underlie each CVP analysis.

1. The behavior of both costs and revenues is linear throughout the relevant range of the activity index.
2. Costs can be classified accurately as either variable or fixed.
3. Changes in activity are the only factors that affect costs.
4. All units produced are sold.
5. When more than one type of product is sold, the sales mix will remain constant. That is, the percentage that each product represents of total sales will stay the same. Sales mix complicates CVP analysis because different products will have different cost relationships. In this chapter, we assume a single product. In Chapter 19, however, we examine the sales mix more closely.

When these assumptions are not valid, the CVP analysis may be inaccurate.

CVP INCOME STATEMENT

Because CVP is so important for decision-making, management often wants this information reported in a **cost-volume-profit (CVP) income statement** format for internal use. The CVP income statement classifies costs as variable or fixed and computes a contribution margin. **Contribution margin (CM)** is the amount of revenue remaining after deducting variable costs. It is often stated both as a total amount and on a per unit basis.

We will use Vargo Video Company to illustrate a CVP income statement. Vargo Video produces a high-definition digital camcorder with 15× optical zoom and a wide-screen, high-resolution LCD monitor. Relevant data for the camcorders sold by this company in June 2017 are as follows.

ILLUSTRATION 18-11
Assumed selling and cost data for Vargo Video

Unit selling price of camcorder	$500
Unit variable costs	$300
Total monthly fixed costs	$200,000
Units sold	1,600

The CVP income statement for Vargo therefore would be reported as follows.

ILLUSTRATION 18-12
CVP income statement, with net income

VARGO VIDEO COMPANY
CVP Income Statement
For the Month Ended June 30, 2017

	Total
Sales (1,600 camcorders)	$ 800,000
Variable costs	480,000
Contribution margin	320,000
Fixed costs	200,000
Net income	$120,000

A traditional income statement and a CVP income statement both report the same net income of $120,000. However, a traditional income statement does not classify costs as variable or fixed, and therefore it does not report a contribution margin. In addition, sometimes per unit amounts and percentage of sales amounts are shown in separate columns on a CVP income statement to facilitate CVP analysis. *Homework assignments specify which columns to present.*

In the applications of CVP analysis that follow, we assume that the term "cost" includes all costs and expenses related to production and sale of the product. That is, cost includes manufacturing costs plus selling and administrative expenses.

DECISION TOOLS

The unit contribution margin indicates by how much every unit sold will increase income.

Unit Contribution Margin

The formula for **unit contribution margin** and the computation for Vargo Video are as follows.

ILLUSTRATION 18-13
Formula for unit contribution margin

Unit Selling Price	−	Unit Variable Costs	=	Unit Contribution Margin
$500	−	$300	=	$200

Unit contribution margin indicates that for every camcorder sold, the selling price exceeds the variable costs by $200. Vargo generates $200 per unit sold to cover fixed costs and contribute to net income. Because Vargo has fixed costs of $200,000, it must sell 1,000 camcorders ($200,000 ÷ $200) to cover its fixed costs.

At the point where total contribution margin exactly equals fixed costs, Vargo will report net income of zero. At this point, referred to as the **break-even point**, total costs (variable plus fixed) exactly equal total revenue. Illustration 18-14 shows Vargo's CVP income statement at the point where net income equals zero. It shows a contribution margin of $200,000, and a unit contribution margin of $200 ($500 − $300).

ILLUSTRATION 18-14
CVP income statement, with zero net income

VARGO VIDEO COMPANY
CVP Income Statement
For the Month Ended June 30, 2017

	Total	Per Unit
Sales (1,000 camcorders)	$ 500,000	$ 500
Variable costs	300,000	300
Contribution margin	200,000	$200
Fixed costs	200,000	
Net income	$ -0-	

It follows that for every camcorder sold above the break-even point of 1,000 units, **net income increases by the amount of the unit contribution margin, $200**. For example, assume that Vargo sold one more camcorder, for a total of 1,001 camcorders sold. In this case, Vargo reports net income of $200, as shown in Illustration 18-15.

ILLUSTRATION 18-15
CVP income statement, with net income and per unit data

VARGO VIDEO COMPANY
CVP Income Statement
For the Month Ended June 30, 2017

	Total	Per Unit
Sales (1,001 camcorders)	$500,500	$500
Variable costs	300,300	300
Contribution margin	200,200	$200
Fixed costs	200,000	
Net income	$ 200	

Contribution Margin Ratio

Some managers prefer to use a contribution margin ratio in CVP analysis. The contribution margin ratio is the contribution margin expressed as a percentage of sales, as shown in Illustration 18-16.

ILLUSTRATION 18-16
CVP income statement, with net income and percent of sales data

VARGO VIDEO COMPANY
CVP Income Statement
For the Month Ended June 30, 2017

	Total	Percent of Sales
Sales (1,001 camcorders)	$500,500	100%
Variable costs	300,300	60
Contribution margin	200,200	40%
Fixed costs	200,000	
Net income	$ 200	

DECISION TOOLS

The contribution margin ratio indicates by how much every dollar of sales will increase income.

Alternatively, the **contribution margin ratio** can be determined by dividing the unit contribution margin by the unit selling price. For Vargo Video, the ratio is as follows.

ILLUSTRATION 18-17
Formula for contribution margin ratio

Unit Contribution Margin	÷	Unit Selling Price	=	Contribution Margin Ratio
$200	÷	$500	=	40%

The contribution margin ratio of 40% means that Vargo generates 40 cents of contribution margin with each dollar of sales. That is, $0.40 of each sales dollar (40% × $1) is available to apply to fixed costs and to contribute to net income.

This expression of contribution margin is very helpful in determining the effect of changes in sales on net income. For example, if Vargo's sales increase $100,000, net income will increase $40,000 (40% × $100,000). Thus, by using the contribution margin ratio, managers can quickly determine increases in net income from any change in sales.

We can also see this effect through a CVP income statement. Assume that Vargo's current sales are $500,000 and it wants to know the effect of a $100,000 (200-unit) increase in sales. Vargo prepares a comparative CVP income statement analysis as follows.

ILLUSTRATION 18-18
Comparative CVP income statements

VARGO VIDEO COMPANY
CVP Income Statements
For the Month Ended June 30, 2017

	No Change			With Change		
	Total	Per Unit	Percent of Sales	Total	Per Unit	Percent of Sales
Sales	$500,000	$500	100%	$600,000	$ 500	100%
Variable costs	300,000	300	60	360,000	300	60
Contribution margin	200,000	$200	40%	240,000	$200	40%
Fixed costs	200,000			200,000		
Net income	$ -0-			$ 40,000		

The $40,000 increase in net income can be calculated on either a unit contribution margin basis (200 units × $200 per unit) or using the contribution margin ratio times the increase in sales dollars (40% × $100,000). Note that the unit contribution margin and contribution margin as a percentage of sales remain unchanged by the increase in sales.

Study these CVP income statements carefully. The concepts presented in these statements are used extensively in this and later chapters.

DO IT! 3 CVP Income Statement

Ampco Industries produces and sells a cell phone-operated thermostat. Information regarding the costs and sales of thermostats during September 2017 are provided below.

Unit selling price of thermostat	$85
Unit variable costs	$32
Total monthly fixed costs	$190,000
Units sold	4,000

Prepare a CVP income statement for Ampco Industries for the month of September. Provide per unit values and total values.

SOLUTION

AMPCO INDUSTRIES
CVP Income Statement
For the Month Ended September 30, 2017

	Total	Per Unit
Sales	$340,000	$85
Variable costs	128,000	32
Contribution margin	212,000	$53
Fixed costs	190,000	
Net income	$ 22,000	

Action Plan

✔ Provide a heading with the name of the company, name of statement, and period covered.

✔ Subtract variable costs from sales to determine contribution margin. Subtract fixed costs from contribution margin to determine net income.

✔ Express sales, variable costs and contribution margin on a per unit basis.

Related exercise material: **BE18-6, BE18-7, E18-7,** and **DO IT! 18-3.**

LEARNING OBJECTIVE 4

Compute the break-even point using three approaches.

DECISION TOOLS

Break-even analysis indicates the amount of sales units or sales dollars that a company needs to cover its costs.

A key relationship in CVP analysis is the level of activity at which total revenues equal total costs (both fixed and variable)—the **break-even point**. At this volume of sales, the company will realize no income but will suffer no loss. The process of finding the break-even point is called **break-even analysis**. Knowledge of the break-even point is useful to management when it considers decisions such as whether to introduce new product lines, change sales prices on established products, or enter new market areas.

The break-even point can be:

1. Computed from a mathematical equation.
2. Computed by using contribution margin.
3. Derived from a cost-volume-profit (CVP) graph.

The break-even point can be expressed either in **sales units** or **sales dollars**.

MATHEMATICAL EQUATION

The first line of Illustration 18-19 shows a common equation used for CVP analysis. When net income is set to zero, this equation can be used to calculate the break-even point.

ILLUSTRATION 18-19
Basic CVP equation

Required Sales	−	Variable Costs	−	Fixed Costs	=	Net Income
\$500Q	−	\$300Q	−	\$200,000	=	\$0

As shown in Illustration 18-14 (page 893), net income equals zero when the contribution margin (sales minus variable costs) is equal to fixed costs.

To reflect this, Illustration 18-20 rewrites the equation with contribution margin (sales minus variable costs) on the left side, and fixed costs and net income on the right. We can compute the break-even point **in units** by **using unit selling prices** and **unit variable costs**. The computation for Vargo Video is as follows.

ILLUSTRATION 18-20
Computation of break-even point in units

Required Sales	−	Variable Costs	−	Fixed Costs	=	Net Income
\$500Q	−	\$300Q	−	\$200,000	=	\$0
\$500Q	−	\$300Q	=	\$200,000	+	\$0

$$\$200Q = \$200{,}000$$

$$Q = \frac{\$200{,}000}{\$200} = \frac{\text{Fixed Costs}}{\text{Unit Contribution Margin}}$$

$$Q = 1{,}000 \text{ units}$$

where

Q = sales volume in units
\$500 = selling price
\$300 = variable costs per unit
\$200,000 = total fixed costs

Thus, Vargo must sell 1,000 units to break even.

To find the amount of **sales dollars** required to break even, we multiply the units sold at the break-even point times the selling price per unit, as shown below.

1,000 × \$500 = \$500,000 (break-even sales dollars)

CONTRIBUTION MARGIN TECHNIQUE

Many managers employ the contribution margin to compute the break-even point.

Contribution Margin in Units

The final step in Illustration 18-20 divides fixed costs by the unit contribution margin (highlighted in red). Thus, rather than walk through all of the steps of the equation approach, we can simply employ this formula shown in Illustration 18-21.

ILLUSTRATION 18-21
Formula for break-even point in units using unit contribution margin

Fixed Costs	÷	Unit Contribution Margin	=	Break-Even Point in Units
$200,000	÷	$200	=	1,000 units

Why does this formula work? The unit contribution margin is the net amount by which each sale exceeds the variable costs per unit. Every sale generates this much money to pay off fixed costs. Consequently, if we divide fixed costs by the unit contribution margin, we know how many units we need to sell to break even.

Contribution Margin Ratio

As we will see in the next chapter, when a company has numerous products, it is not practical to determine the unit contribution margin for each product. In this case, using the contribution margin ratio is very useful for determining the break-even point in total dollars (rather than units). Recall that the contribution margin ratio is the percentage of each dollar of sales that is available to cover fixed costs and generate net income. Therefore, **to determine the sales dollars needed to cover fixed costs**, we divide fixed costs by the contribution margin ratio, as shown in Illustration 18-22.

ILLUSTRATION 18-22
Formula for break-even point in dollars using contribution margin ratio

Fixed Costs	÷	Contribution Margin Ratio	=	Break-Even Point in Dollars
$200,000	÷	40%	=	$500,000

To apply this formula to Vargo Video, consider that its 40% contribution margin ratio means that for every dollar sold, it generates 40 cents of contribution margin. The question is, how many dollars of sales does Vargo need in order to generate total contribution margin of $200,000 to pay off fixed costs? We divide the fixed costs of $200,000 by the 40 cents of contribution margin generated by each dollar of sales to arrive at $500,000 ($200,000 ÷ 40%). To prove this result, if we generate 40 cents of contribution margin for each dollar of sales, then the total contribution margin generated by $500,000 in sales is $200,000 ($500,000 × 40%).

SERVICE COMPANY INSIGHT Flightserve

Digital Vision/Getty Images

Charter Flights Offer a Good Deal

The Internet is wringing inefficiencies out of nearly every industry. While commercial aircraft spend roughly 4,000 hours a year in the air, chartered aircraft are flown only 500 hours annually. That means that they are sitting on the ground—not making any money—about 90% of the time. One company, Flightserve, saw a business opportunity in that fact. For about the same cost as a first-class ticket, Flightserve matches up executives with charter flights in small "private jets." The executive gets a more comfortable ride and avoids the hassle of big airports. Flightserve noted that the average charter jet has eight seats. When all eight seats are full, the company has an 80% profit margin. It breaks even at an average of 3.3 full seats per flight.

Source: "Jet Set Go," *The Economist* (March 18, 2000), p. 68.

How did Flightserve determine that it would break even with 3.3 seats full per flight? (Go to **WileyPLUS** for this answer and additional questions.)

GRAPHIC PRESENTATION

An effective way to find the break-even point is to prepare a break-even graph. Because this graph also shows costs, volume, and profits, it is referred to as a **cost-volume-profit (CVP) graph**.

As the CVP graph in Illustration 18-23 shows, sales volume is recorded along the horizontal axis. This axis should extend to the maximum level of expected sales. Both total revenues (sales) and total costs (fixed plus variable) are recorded on the vertical axis.

ILLUSTRATION 18-23
CVP graph

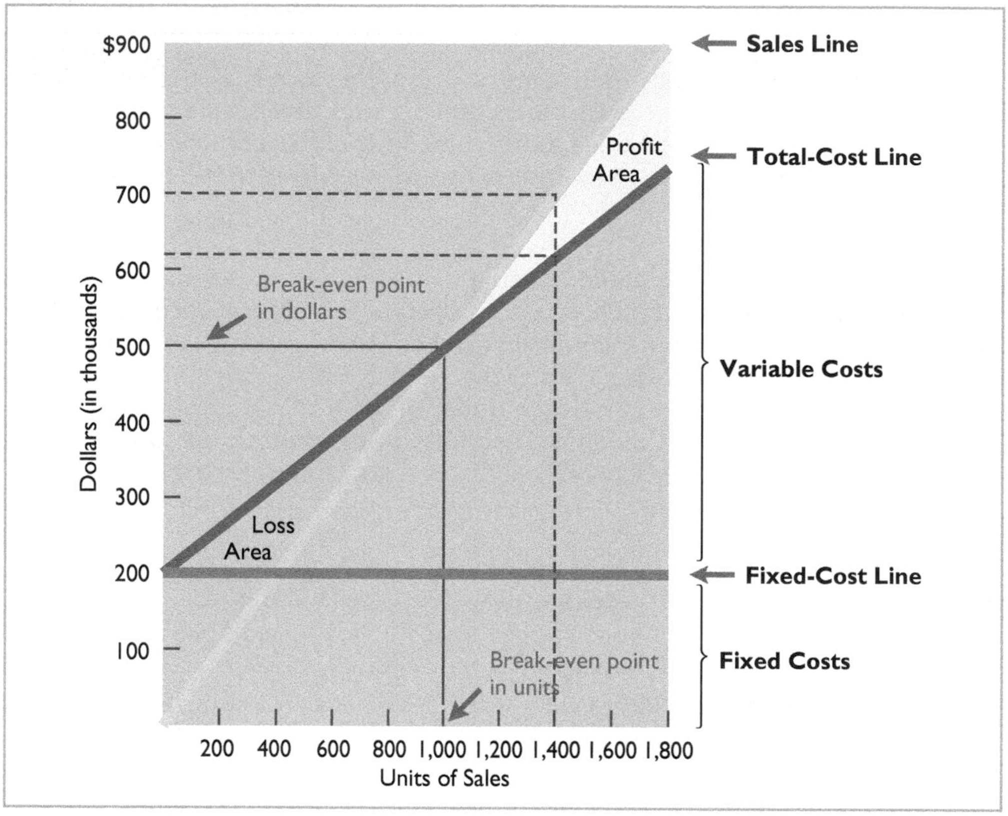

The construction of the graph, using the data for Vargo Video, is as follows.

1. Plot the sales line, starting at the zero activity level. For every camcorder sold, total revenue increases by $500. For example, at 200 units, sales are $100,000. At the upper level of activity (1,800 units), sales are $900,000. The revenue line is assumed to be linear through the full range of activity.
2. Plot the total fixed costs using a horizontal line. For the camcorders, this line is plotted at $200,000. The fixed costs are the same at every level of activity.
3. Plot the total-cost line. This starts at the fixed-cost line at zero activity. It increases by the variable costs at each level of activity. For each camcorder, variable costs are $300. Thus, at 200 units, total variable costs are $60,000 ($300 × 200) and the total cost is $260,000 ($60,000 + $200,000). At 1,800 units, total variable costs are $540,000 ($300 × 1,800) and total cost is $740,000 ($540,000 + $200,000). On the graph, the amount of the variable costs can be derived from the difference between the total-cost and fixed-cost lines at each level of activity.
4. Determine the break-even point from the intersection of the total-cost line and the sales line. The break-even point in dollars is found by drawing a horizontal line from the break-even point to the vertical axis. The break-even point

in units is found by drawing a vertical line from the break-even point to the horizontal axis. For the camcorders, the break-even point is $500,000 of sales, or 1,000 units. At this sales level, Vargo will cover costs but make no profit.

The CVP graph also shows both the net income and net loss areas. Thus, the amount of income or loss at each level of sales can be derived from the sales and total-cost lines.

A CVP graph is useful because the effects of a change in any element in the CVP analysis can be quickly seen. For example, a 10% increase in selling price will change the location of the sales line. Likewise, the effects on total costs of wage increases can be quickly observed.

DO IT! ▶4 Break-Even Analysis

Lombardi Company has a unit selling price of $400, variable costs per unit of $240, and fixed costs of $180,000. Compute the break-even point in units using (a) a mathematical equation and (b) unit contribution margin.

SOLUTION

(a) The equation is $400Q − $240Q − $180,000 = $0; ($400Q − $240Q) = $180,000. The break-even point in units is 1,125. (b) The unit contribution margin is $160 ($400 − $240). The formula therefore is $180,000 ÷ $160, and the break-even point in units is 1,125.

Related exercise material: **BE18-8, BE18-9, E18-8, E18-9, E18-10, E18-11, E18-12, E18-13, E18-16,** and **DO IT! 18-4.**

Action Plan

- ✔ **Apply the formula: Sales − Variable costs − Fixed costs = Net income.**
- ✔ **Apply the formula: Fixed costs ÷ Unit contribution margin = Break-even point in units.**

LEARNING OBJECTIVE ▶5 Determine the sales required to earn target net income and determine margin of safety.

TARGET NET INCOME

Rather than simply "breaking even," management usually sets an income objective often called **target net income**. It then determines the sales necessary to achieve this specified level of income. Companies determine the sales necessary to achieve target net income by using one of the three approaches discussed earlier.

Mathematical Equation

We know that at the break-even point no profit or loss results for the company. By adding an amount for target net income to the same basic equation, we obtain the following formula for determining required sales.

Required Sales	−	Variable Costs	−	Fixed Costs	=	Target Net Income

ILLUSTRATION 18-24
Formula for required sales to meet target net income

Recall that once the break-even point has been reached so that fixed costs are covered, each additional unit sold increases net income by the amount of the unit contribution margin. We can rewrite the equation with contribution margin (required sales minus variable costs) on the left-hand side, and fixed costs and target net income on the right. Assuming that target net income is $120,000 for Vargo Video, the computation of required sales in units is as shown in Illustration 18-25 (page 900).

ILLUSTRATION 18-25
Computation of required sales

$$\text{Required Sales} - \text{Variable Costs} - \text{Fixed Costs} = \text{Target Net Income}$$

$$\$500Q - \$300Q - \$200{,}000 = \$120{,}000$$

$$\$500Q - \$300Q = \$200{,}000 + \$120{,}000$$

$$\$200Q = \$200{,}000 + \$120{,}000$$

$$Q = \frac{\$200{,}000 + \$120{,}000}{\$200} = \frac{\text{Fixed Costs + Target Net Income}}{\text{Unit Contribution Margin}}$$

$$Q = 1{,}600$$

where

Q = sales volume
$500 = selling price
$300 = variable costs per unit
$200,000 = total fixed costs
$120,000 = target net income

Vargo must sell 1,600 units to achieve target net income of $120,000. The sales dollars required to achieve the target net income is found by multiplying the units sold by the unit selling price [(1,600 × $500) = $800,000].

Contribution Margin Technique

As in the case of break-even sales, we can compute in either units or dollars the sales required to meet target net income. The formula to compute required sales in units for Vargo Video using the unit contribution margin can be seen in the final step of the equation approach in Illustration 18-25 (shown in red). We simply divide the sum of fixed costs and target net income by the unit contribution margin. Illustration 18-26 shows this for Vargo.

ILLUSTRATION 18-26
Formula for required sales in units using unit contribution margin

(Fixed Costs + Target Net Income)	÷	Unit Contribution Margin	=	Required Sales in Units
($200,000 + $120,000)	÷	$200	=	1,600 units

To achieve its desired target net income of $120,000, Vargo must sell 1,600 camcorders.

The formula to compute the required sales in dollars for Vargo using the contribution margin ratio is shown below.

ILLUSTRATION 18-27
Formula for required sales in dollars using contribution margin ratio

(Fixed Costs + Target Net Income)	÷	Contribution Margin Ratio	=	Required Sales in Dollars
($200,000 + $120,000)	÷	40%	=	$800,000

To achieve its desired target net income of $120,000, Vargo must generate sales of $800,000.

Graphic Presentation

We also can use the CVP graph in Illustration 18-23 (on page 898) to find the sales required to meet target net income. In the profit area of the graph, the distance between the sales line and the total-cost line at any point equals net income. We can find required sales by analyzing the differences between the two lines until the desired net income is found.

For example, suppose Vargo Video sells 1,400 camcorders. Illustration 18-23 shows that a vertical line drawn at 1,400 units intersects the sales line at $700,000 and the total-cost line at $620,000. The difference between the two amounts represents the net income (profit) of $80,000.

MARGIN OF SAFETY

Margin of safety is the difference between actual or expected sales and sales at the break-even point. It measures the "cushion" that a particular level of sales provides. It tells us how far sales could fall before the company begins operating at a loss. The margin of safety is expressed in dollars or as a ratio.

The formula for stating the **margin of safety in dollars** is actual (or expected) sales minus break-even sales. Assuming that actual (expected) sales for Vargo Video are $750,000, the computation is as follows.

Actual (Expected) Sales	−	Break-Even Sales	=	Margin of Safety in Dollars
$750,000	−	$500,000	=	$250,000

ILLUSTRATION 18-28
Formula for margin of safety in dollars

Vargo's margin of safety is $250,000. Its sales could fall $250,000 before it operates at a loss.

The **margin of safety ratio** is the margin of safety in dollars divided by actual (or expected) sales. Illustration 18-29 shows the formula and computation for determining the margin of safety ratio.

Margin of Safety in Dollars	÷	Actual (Expected) Sales	=	Margin of Safety Ratio
$250,000	÷	$750,000	=	33%

ILLUSTRATION 18-29
Formula for margin of safety ratio

This means that the company's sales could fall by 33% before it operates at a loss.

The higher the dollars or the percentage, the greater the margin of safety. Management continuously evaluates the adequacy of the margin of safety in terms of such factors as the vulnerability of the product to competitive pressures and to downturns in the economy.

SERVICE COMPANY INSIGHT Rolling Stones

Yael/Retna

How a Rolling Stones' Tour Makes Money

Computations of break-even and margin of safety are important for service companies. Consider how the promoter for the Rolling Stones' tour used the break-even point and margin of safety. For example, say one outdoor show should bring 70,000 individuals for a gross of $2.45 million. The promoter guarantees $1.2 million to the Rolling Stones. In addition, 20% of gross goes to the stadium in which the performance is staged. Add another $400,000 for other expenses such as ticket takers, parking attendants, advertising, and so on. The promoter also shares in sales of T-shirts and memorabilia for which the promoter will net over $7 million during the tour. From a successful Rolling Stones' tour, the promoter could make $35 million!

What amount of sales dollars are required for the promoter to break even? (Go to **WileyPLUS** for this answer and additional questions.)

DO IT! 5 Break-Even, Margin of Safety, and Target Net Income

Zootsuit Inc. makes travel bags that sell for $56 each. For the coming year, management expects fixed costs to total $320,000 and variable costs to be $42 per unit. Compute the following: (a) break-even point in dollars using the contribution margin (CM) ratio; (b) the margin of safety and margin of safety ratio assuming actual sales are $1,382,400; and (c) the sales dollars required to earn net income of $410,000.

Action Plan

✔ Apply the formula for the break-even point in dollars.

✔ Apply the formulas for the margin of safety in dollars and the margin of safety ratio.

✔ Apply the formula for the required sales in dollars.

SOLUTION

(a) Contribution margin ratio = [($56 − $42) ÷ $56] = 25%
Break-even sales in dollars = $320,000 ÷ 25% = $1,280,000

(b) Margin of safety = $1,382,400 − $1,280,000 = $102,400
Margin of safety ratio = $102,400 ÷ $1,382,400 = 7.4%

(c) Required sales in dollars = ($320,000 + $410,000) ÷ 25% = $2,920,000

Related exercise material: **BE18-10, BE18-11, BE18-12, E18-14, E18-15, E18-17,** and **DO IT! 18-5.**

USING DECISION TOOLS—AMAZON.COM

Amazon.com faces many situations where it needs to apply the decision tools presented in this chapter, such as calculating the break-even point to determine a product's profitability. Amazon's dominance of the online retail space, selling other company's products, is well known. But not everyone may realize that Amazon also sells its own private-label electronics, including USB cables, mice, keyboards, and audio cables, under the brand name AmazonBasics. Assume that Amazon's management was provided with the following information regarding the production and sales of Bluetooth keyboards for tablet computers.

Cost Schedules

Variable costs	
Direct labor per keyboard	$ 8.00
Direct materials	4.00
Variable overhead	3.00
Variable cost per keyboard	$15.00
Fixed costs	
Manufacturing	$ 25,000
Selling	40,000
Administrative	70,000
Total fixed costs	$135,000
Selling price per keyboard	$25.00
Sales, 2017 (20,000 keyboards)	$500,000

INSTRUCTIONS

(Ignore any income tax considerations.)

(a) What is the operating income for 2017?

(b) What is the unit contribution margin for 2017?

(c) What is the break-even point in units for 2017?

(d) Assume that management set the sales target for the year 2018 at a level of $550,000 (22,000 keyboards). Amazon's management believes that to attain the sales target in 2018, the company must incur an additional selling expense of $10,000 for advertising in 2018, with all other costs remaining constant. What will be the break-even point in sales dollars for 2018 if the company spends the additional $10,000?

(e) If the company spends the additional $10,000 for advertising in 2018, what is the sales level in dollars required to equal 2017 operating income?

SOLUTION

(a) Sales			$500,000
Less:			
Variable costs (20,000 keyboards × $15)			300,000
Fixed costs			135,000
Operating income			$ 65,000
(b) Selling price per keyboard	$25		
Variable cost per keyboard	15		
Unit contribution margin	$10		

(c) Fixed costs ÷ Unit contribution margin = Break-even point in units: $135,000 ÷ $10 = 13,500 units

(d) Fixed costs ÷ Contribution margin ratio = Break-even point in dollars: $145,000* ÷ 40%** = $362,500

*Fixed costs	$135,000
Additional advertising expense	10,000
Revised fixed costs	$145,000

**Contribution margin ratio = Unit contribution margin ÷ Unit selling price: 40% = $10 ÷ $25

(e) Required sales = (Fixed costs + Target net income) ÷ Contribution margin ratio

$525,000 = ($145,000 + $65,000) ÷ 40%

REVIEW AND PRACTICE

LEARNING OBJECTIVES REVIEW

1 Explain variable, fixed, and mixed costs and the relevant range. Variable costs are costs that vary in total directly and proportionately with changes in the activity index. Fixed costs are costs that remain the same in total regardless of changes in the activity index.

The relevant range is the range of activity in which a company expects to operate during a year. It is important in CVP analysis because the behavior of costs is assumed to be linear throughout the relevant range.

Mixed costs change in total but not proportionately with changes in the activity level. For purposes of CVP analysis, mixed costs must be classified into their fixed and variable elements.

2 Apply the high-low method to determine the components of mixed costs. Determine the variable costs per unit by dividing the change in total costs at the highest and lowest levels of activity by the difference in activity at those levels. Then, determine fixed costs by subtracting total variable costs from the amount of total costs at either the highest or lowest level of activity.

3 Prepare a CVP income statement to determine contribution margin. The five components of CVP analysis are (1) volume or level of activity, (2) unit selling prices, (3) variable costs per unit, (4) total fixed costs, and (5) sales mix. Contribution margin is the amount of revenue remaining after deducting variable costs. It is identified in a CVP income statement, which classifies costs as variable or fixed. It can be expressed as a total amount, as a per unit amount, or as a ratio.

4 Compute the break-even point using three approaches. The break-even point can be (a) computed from a mathematical equation, (b) computed by using a contribution margin technique, and (c) derived from a CVP graph.

5 Determine the sales required to earn target net income and determine margin of safety. The general formula for required sales is Required sales − Variable costs − Fixed costs = Target net income. Two other formulas are (1) Required sales in units = (Fixed costs + Target net income) ÷ Unit contribution margin, and (2) Required sales in dollars = (Fixed costs + Target net income) ÷ Contribution margin ratio.

Margin of safety is the difference between actual or expected sales and sales at the break-even point. The formulas for margin of safety are (1) Actual (expected) sales − Break-even sales = Margin of safety in dollars, and (2) Margin of safety in dollars ÷ Actual (expected) sales = Margin of safety ratio.

DECISION TOOLS REVIEW

DECISION CHECKPOINTS	INFO NEEDED FOR DECISION	TOOL TO USE FOR DECISION	HOW TO EVALUATE RESULTS
What was the contribution toward fixed costs and income from each unit sold?	Selling price per unit and variable cost per unit	Unit contribution margin = Unit selling price − Unit variable cost	Every unit sold will increase income by the contribution margin.
What would be the increase in income as a result of an increase in sales?	Unit contribution margin and unit selling price	Contribution margin ratio = Unit contribution margin ÷ Unit selling cost	Every dollar of sales will increase income by the contribution margin ratio.
At what amount of sales does a company cover its costs?	Unit selling price, unit variable cost, and total fixed costs	Break-even point analysis *In units:* Break-even point = Fixed cost / Unit contribution margin *In dollars:* Break-even point = Fixed cost / Contribution margin ratio	Below the break-even point, the company is unprofitable.

GLOSSARY REVIEW

Activity index The activity that causes changes in the behavior of costs. (p. 884).

Break-even point The level of activity at which total revenue equals total costs. (p. 893).

Contribution margin (CM) The amount of revenue remaining after deducting variable costs. (p. 892).

Contribution margin ratio The percentage of each dollar of sales that is available to apply to fixed costs and contribute to net income; calculated as unit contribution margin divided by unit selling price. (p. 894).

Cost behavior analysis The study of how specific costs respond to changes in the level of business activity. (p. 884).

Cost-volume-profit (CVP) analysis The study of the effects of changes in costs and volume on a company's profits. (p. 892).

Cost-volume-profit (CVP) graph A graph showing the relationship between costs, volume, and profits. (p. 898).

Cost-volume-profit (CVP) income statement A statement for internal use that classifies costs as fixed or variable and reports contribution margin in the body of the statement. (p. 892).

Fixed costs Costs that remain the same in total regardless of changes in the activity level. (p. 885).

High-low method A mathematical method that uses the total costs incurred at the high and low levels of activity to classify mixed costs into fixed and variable components. (p. 889).

Margin of safety The difference between actual or expected sales and sales at the break-even point. (p. 901).

Mixed costs Costs that contain both a variable- and a fixed-cost element and change in total but not proportionately with changes in the activity level. (p. 887).

Relevant range The range of the activity index over which the company expects to operate during the year. (p. 887).

Target net income The income objective set by management. (p. 899).

Unit contribution margin The amount of revenue remaining per unit after deducting variable costs; calculated as unit selling price minus unit variable costs. (p. 893).

Variable costs Costs that vary in total directly and proportionately with changes in the activity level. (p. 884).

PRACTICE MULTIPLE-CHOICE QUESTIONS

(LO 1) 1. Variable costs are costs that:
(a) vary in total directly and proportionately with changes in the activity level.
(b) remain the same per unit at every activity level.
(c) Neither of the above.
(d) Both (a) and (b) above.

2. The relevant range is: (LO 1)
(a) the range of activity in which variable costs will be curvilinear.
(b) the range of activity in which fixed costs will be curvilinear.

(c) the range over which the company expects to operate during a year.
(d) usually from zero to 100% of operating capacity.

(LO 2) **3.** Mixed costs consist of a:
(a) variable-cost element and a fixed-cost element.
(b) fixed-cost element and a controllable-cost element.
(c) relevant-cost element and a controllable-cost element.
(d) variable-cost element and a relevant-cost element.

(LO 2) **4.** Your cell phone service provider offers a plan that is classified as a mixed cost. The cost per month for 1,000 minutes is $50. If you use 2,000 minutes this month, your cost will be:
(a) $50.
(b) $100.
(c) more than $100.
(d) between $50 and $100.

(LO 2) **5.** Kendra Corporation's total utility costs during the past year were $1,200 during its highest month and $600 during its lowest month. These costs corresponded with 10,000 units of production during the high month and 2,000 units during the low month. What are the fixed and variable components of its utility costs using the high-low method?
(a) $0.075 variable and $450 fixed.
(b) $0.120 variable and $0 fixed.
(c) $0.300 variable and $0 fixed.
(d) $0.060 variable and $600 fixed.

(LO 3) **6.** Which of the following is **not** involved in CVP analysis?
(a) Sales mix.
(b) Unit selling prices.
(c) Fixed costs per unit.
(d) Volume or level of activity.

(LO 3) **7.** When comparing a traditional income statement to a CVP income statement:
(a) net income will always be greater on the traditional statement.
(b) net income will always be less on the traditional statement.
(c) net income will always be identical on both.
(d) net income will be greater or less depending on the sales volume.

8. Contribution margin: (LO 3)
(a) is revenue remaining after deducting variable costs.
(b) may be expressed as unit contribution margin.
(c) is selling price less cost of goods sold.
(d) Both (a) and (b) above.

9. Cournot Company sells 100,000 wrenches for $12 a unit. Fixed costs are $300,000, and net income is $200,000. What should be reported as variable expenses in the CVP income statement? (LO 3)
(a) $700,000.
(b) $900,000.
(c) $500,000.
(d) $1,000,000.

10. Gossen Company is planning to sell 200,000 pliers for $4 per unit. The contribution margin ratio is 25%. If Gossen will break even at this level of sales, what are the fixed costs? (LO 4)
(a) $100,000.
(b) $160,000.
(c) $200,000.
(d) $300,000.

11. Brownstone Company's contribution margin ratio is 30%. If Brownstone's sales revenue is $100 greater than its break-even sales in dollars, its net income: (LO 4)
(a) will be $100.
(b) will be $70.
(c) will be $30.
(d) cannot be determined without knowing fixed costs.

12. The mathematical equation for computing required sales to obtain target net income is Required sales = (LO 5)
(a) Variable costs + Target net income.
(b) Variable costs + Fixed costs + Target net income.
(c) Fixed costs + Target net income.
(d) No correct answer is given.

13. Margin of safety is computed as: (LO 5)
(a) Actual sales − Break-even sales.
(b) Contribution margin − Fixed costs.
(c) Break-even sales − Variable costs.
(d) Actual sales − Contribution margin.

14. Marshall Company had actual sales of $600,000 when break-even sales were $420,000. What is the margin of safety ratio? (LO 5)
(a) 25%.
(b) 30%.
(c) $33\frac{1}{3}$%.
(d) 45%.

SOLUTIONS

1. **(d)** Variable costs vary in total directly and proportionately with changes in the activity level and remain the same per unit at every activity level. Choices (a) and (b) are correct, but (d) is the better and more complete answer. Since (a) and (b) are both true statements, choice (c) is incorrect.

2. **(c)** The relevant range is the range over which the company expects to operate during a year. The other choices are incorrect because the relevant range is the range over which (a) variable costs are expected to be linear, not curvilinear, and (b) the company expects fixed costs to remain the same. Choice (d) is incorrect because this answer does not specifically define relevant range.

3. **(a)** Mixed costs consist of a variable-cost element and a fixed-cost element, not (b) a controllable-cost element, (c) a relevant-cost element or a controllable-cost element, or (d) a relevant-cost element.

4. **(d)** Your cost will include the fixed-cost component (flat service fee) which does not increase plus the variable cost (usage charge) for the additional 1,000 minutes which will increase your cost to between $50 and $100. Therefore, choices (a) $50, (b) $100, and (c) more than $100 are incorrect.

5. **(a)** Variable is $0.075 [($1,200 − $600) ÷ (10,000 − 2,000)] and fixed is $450 [($1,200 − ($0.075 × 10,000)]. Therefore, choices (b) $0.120 variable and $0 fixed, (c) $0.300 variable and $0 fixed, and (d) $0.060 variable and $600 fixed are incorrect.

6. **(c)** Total fixed costs, not fixed costs per unit, are involved in CVP analysis. Choices (a) sales mix, (b) unit selling prices, and (d) volume or level of activity are all involved in CVP analysis.

7. **(c)** Net income will always be identical on both a traditional income statement and a CVP income statement. Therefore, choices (a), (b), and (d) are incorrect statements.
8. **(d)** Contribution margin is revenue remaining after deducting variable costs and it may be expressed on a per unit basis. Choices (a) and (b) are accurate, but (d) is a better answer. Choice (c) is incorrect because it defines gross margin, not contribution margin.
9. **(a)** Contribution margin is equal to fixed costs plus net income ($300,000 + $200,000 = $500,000). Since variable expenses are the difference between total sales ($1,200,000) and contribution margin ($500,000), $700,000 must be the amount of variable expenses in the CVP income statement. Therefore, choices (b) $900,000, (c) $500,000, and (d) $1,000,000 are incorrect.
10. **(c)** Unit contribution margin is $1 ($4 × 25%). Fixed costs ÷ Unit contribution margin = Break-even point in units. Solving for fixed costs, 200,000 units × $1 per unit = $200,000, not (a) $100,000, (b) $160,000, or (d) $300,000.
11. **(c)** If Brownstone's sales revenue is $100 greater than its break-even sales in dollars, its net income will be $30 or ($100 × 30%), not (a) $100 or (b) $70. Choice (d) is incorrect because net income can be determined without knowing fixed costs.
12. **(b)** The correct equation is Required sales = Variable costs + Fixed costs + Target net income. The other choices are incorrect because (a) needs fixed costs added, (c) needs variable costs added, and (d) there is a correct answer given.
13. **(a)** Margin of safety is computed as Actual sales − Break-even sales. Therefore, choices (b) Contribution margin − Fixed costs, (c) Break-even sales − Variable costs, and (d) Actual sales − Contribution margin are incorrect.
14. **(b)** The margin of safety ratio is computed by dividing the margin of safety in dollars of $180,000 ($600,000 − $420,000) by actual sales of $600,000. The result is 30% ($180,000 ÷ $600,000), not (a) 25%, (c) 33 1/3%, or (d) 45%.

PRACTICE EXERCISES

Determine fixed and variable costs using the high-low method and prepare graph.

(LO 1, 2)

1. The controller of Teton Industries has collected the following monthly expense data for use in analyzing the cost behavior of maintenance costs.

Month	Total Maintenance Costs	Total Machine Hours
January	$2,900	300
February	3,000	400
March	3,600	600
April	4,300	790
May	3,200	500
June	4,500	800

INSTRUCTIONS

(a) Determine the fixed-cost and variable-cost components using the high-low method.

(b) Prepare a graph showing the behavior of maintenance costs, and identify the fixed-cost and variable-cost elements. Use 200 unit increments and $1,000 cost increments.

SOLUTION

1. (a) **Maintenance Costs:**

$$\frac{\$4{,}500 - \$2{,}900}{800 - 300} = \frac{\$1{,}600}{500} = \$3.20 \text{ variable cost per machine hour}$$

	800 Machine Hours	300 Machine Hours
Total costs	$4,500	$2,900
Less: Variable costs		
800 × $3.20	2,560	
300 × $3.20		960
Total fixed costs	$1,940	$1,940

Thus, maintenance costs are $1,940 per month plus $3.20 per machine hour.

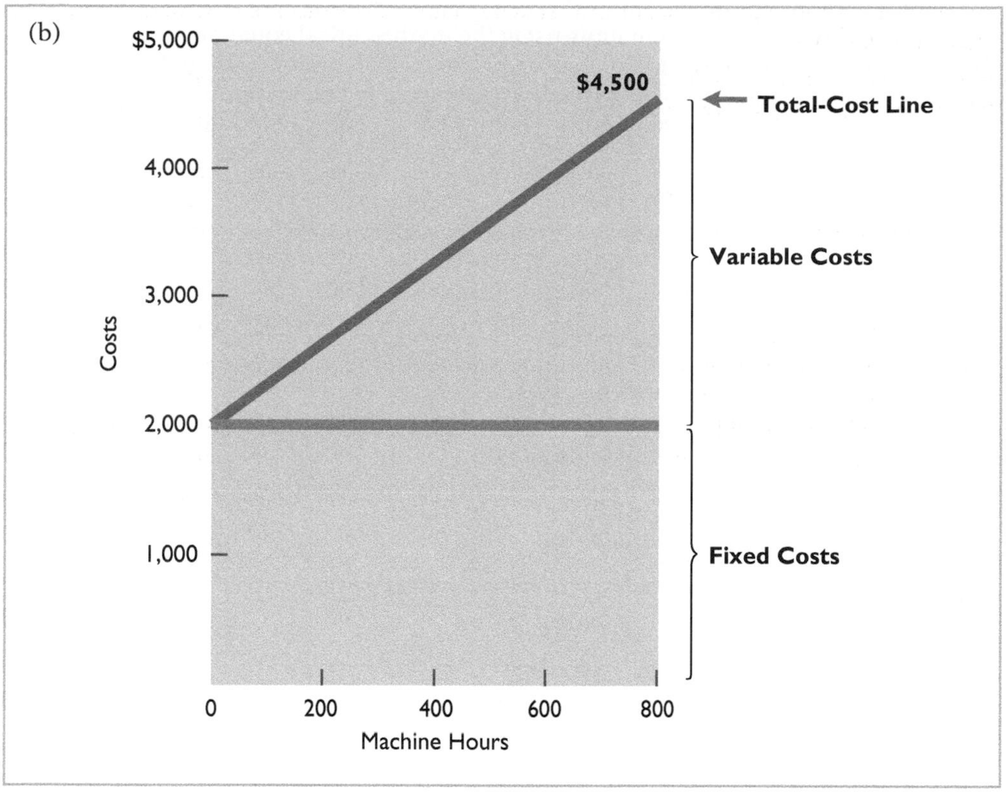

Determine contribution margin ratio, break-even point in dollars, and margin of safety.

(LO 3, 4, 5)

2. Zion Seating Co., a manufacturer of chairs, had the following data for 2017:

Sales	2,400 units
Sales price	$40 per unit
Variable costs	$15 per unit
Fixed costs	$19,500

INSTRUCTIONS

(a) What is the contribution margin ratio?

(b) What is the break-even point in dollars?

(c) What is the margin of safety in units and dollars?

(d) If the company wishes to increase its total dollar contribution margin by 40% in 2018, by how much will it need to increase its sales if all other factors remain constant?

(CGA adapted)

SOLUTION

2. (a) Contribution margin ratio = Unit contribution margin ÷ Unit selling price ($40 − $15) ÷ $40 = 62.5%

(b) Break-even in dollars: $19,500 ÷ 62.5% = $31,200

(c) Margin of safety = (2,400 × $40) − $31,200 = $64,800

$64,800 ÷ $40 = 1,620 units

(d) Current contribution margin is $40 − $15 = $25
Total contribution margin is $25 × 2,400 = $60,000
40% increase in contribution margin is $60,000 × 40% = $24,000

Total increase in sales required is $24,000 ÷ 62.5% = $38,400

▶ PRACTICE PROBLEM

Compute break-even point, contribution margin ratio, margin of safety, and sales for target net income.

(LO 4, 5)

Mabo Company makes calculators that sell for $20 each. For the coming year, management expects fixed costs to total $220,000 and variable costs to be $9 per unit.

INSTRUCTIONS

(a) Compute break-even point in units using the mathematical equation.
(b) Compute break-even point in dollars using the contribution margin (CM) ratio.
(c) Compute the margin of safety percentage assuming actual sales are $500,000.
(d) Compute the sales required in dollars to earn net income of $165,000.

SOLUTION

(a) Required sales − Variable costs − Fixed costs = Net income

$$\$20Q - \$9Q - \$220{,}000 = \$0$$
$$\$11Q = \$220{,}000$$
$$Q = 20{,}000 \text{ units}$$

(b) Unit contribution margin = Unit selling price − Unit variable costs

$$\$11 = \$20 - \$9$$

Contribution margin ratio = Unit contribution margin ÷ Unit selling price

$$55\% = \$11 \div \$20$$

Break-even point in dollars = Fixed costs ÷ Contribution margin ratio

$$= \$220{,}000 \div 55\%$$
$$= \$400{,}000$$

(c) Margin of safety $= \dfrac{\text{Actual sales} - \text{Break-even sales}}{\text{Actual sales}}$

$$= \frac{\$500{,}000 - \$400{,}000}{\$500{,}000}$$
$$= 20\%$$

(d) Required sales − Variable costs − Fixed costs = Net income

$$\$20Q - \$9Q - \$220{,}000 = \$165{,}000$$
$$\$11Q = \$385{,}000$$
$$Q = 35{,}000 \text{ units}$$

35,000 units × $20 = $700,000 required sales

WileyPLUS Brief Exercises, DO IT! Exercises, Exercises, Problems, and many additional resources are available for practice in WileyPLUS.

QUESTIONS

1. (a) What is cost behavior analysis?
   (b) Why is cost behavior analysis important to management?
2. (a) Scott Winter asks your help in understanding the term "activity index." Explain the meaning and importance of this term for Scott.
   (b) State the two ways that variable costs may be defined.
3. Contrast the effects of changes in the activity level on total fixed costs and on unit fixed costs.
4. J. P. Alexander claims that the relevant range concept is important only for variable costs.
   (a) Explain the relevant range concept.
   (b) Do you agree with J. P.'s claim? Explain.
5. "The relevant range is indispensable in cost behavior analysis." Is this true? Why or why not?
6. Adam Antal is confused. He does not understand why rent on his apartment is a fixed cost and rent on a Hertz rental truck is a mixed cost. Explain the difference to Adam.
7. How should mixed costs be classified in CVP analysis? What approach is used to effect the appropriate classification?
8. At the high and low levels of activity during the month, direct labor hours are 90,000 and 40,000, respectively. The related costs are $165,000 and $100,000. What are the fixed and variable costs at any level of activity?
9. "Cost-volume-profit (CVP) analysis is based entirely on unit costs." Do you agree? Explain.
10. Faye Dunn defines contribution margin as the amount of profit available to cover operating expenses. Is there any truth in this definition? Discuss.

11. Marshall Company's GWhiz calculator sells for $40. Variable costs per unit are estimated to be $26. What are the unit contribution margin and the contribution margin ratio?
12. "Break-even analysis is of limited use to management because a company cannot survive by just breaking even." Do you agree? Explain.
13. Total fixed costs are $26,000 for Daz Inc. It has a unit contribution margin of $15, and a contribution margin ratio of 25%. Compute the break-even sales in dollars.
14. Peggy Turnbull asks your help in constructing a CVP graph. Explain to Peggy (a) how the break-even point is plotted, and (b) how the level of activity and dollar sales at the break-even point are determined.
15. Define the term "margin of safety." If Revere Company expects to sell 1,250 units of its product at $12 per unit, and break-even sales for the product are $13,200, what is the margin of safety ratio?
16. Huang Company's break-even sales are $500,000. Assuming fixed costs are $180,000, what sales volume is needed to achieve a target net income of $90,000?
17. The traditional income statement for Pace Company shows sales $900,000, cost of goods sold $600,000, and operating expenses $200,000. Assuming all costs and expenses are 70% variable and 30% fixed, prepare a CVP income statement through contribution margin.

BRIEF EXERCISES

BE18-1 Monthly production costs in Dilts Company for two levels of production are as follows.

Classify costs as variable, fixed, or mixed.

(LO 1), C

Cost	2,000 Units	4,000 Units
Indirect labor	$10,000	$20,000
Supervisory salaries	5,000	5,000
Maintenance	4,000	6,000

Indicate which costs are variable, fixed, and mixed, and give the reason for each answer.

BE18-2 For Lodes Company, the relevant range of production is 40–80% of capacity. At 40% of capacity, a variable cost is $4,000 and a fixed cost is $6,000. Diagram the behavior of each cost within the relevant range assuming the behavior is linear.

Diagram the behavior of costs within the relevant range.

(LO 1), AN

BE18-3 For Wesland Company, a mixed cost is $15,000 plus $18 per direct labor hour. Diagram the behavior of the cost using increments of 500 hours up to 2,500 hours on the horizontal axis and increments of $15,000 up to $60,000 on the vertical axis.

Diagram the behavior of a mixed cost.

(LO 1), AN

BE18-4 Bruno Company accumulates the following data concerning a mixed cost, using miles as the activity level.

Determine variable- and fixed-cost elements using the high-low method.

(LO 2), AP

	Miles Driven	Total Cost		Miles Driven	Total Cost
January	8,000	$14,150	March	8,500	$15,000
February	7,500	13,500	April	8,200	14,490

Compute the variable- and fixed-cost elements using the high-low method.

BE18-5 Markowis Corp. has collected the following data concerning its maintenance costs for the past 6 months.

Determine variable- and fixed-cost elements using the high-low method.

(LO 2), AP

	Units Produced	Total Cost
July	18,000	$36,000
August	32,000	48,000
September	36,000	55,000
October	22,000	38,000
November	40,000	74,500
December	38,000	62,000

Compute the variable- and fixed-cost elements using the high-low method.

Determine missing amounts for contribution margin.
(LO 3), AN

BE18-6 Determine the missing amounts.

	Unit Selling Price	Unit Variable Costs	Unit Contribution Margin	Contribution Margin Ratio
1.	$640	$352	(a)	(b)
2.	$300	(c)	$93	(d)
3.	(e)	(f)	$325	25%

Prepare CVP income statement.
(LO 3), AP

BE18-7 Russell Inc. had sales of $2,200,000 for the first quarter of 2017. In making the sales, the company incurred the following costs and expenses.

	Variable	Fixed
Cost of goods sold	$920,000	$440,000
Selling expenses	70,000	45,000
Administrative expenses	86,000	98,000

Prepare a CVP income statement for the quarter ended March 31, 2017.

Compute the break-even point.
(LO 4), AP

BE18-8 Rice Company has a unit selling price of $520, variable costs per unit of $286, and fixed costs of $163,800. Compute the break-even point in units using (a) the mathematical equation and (b) unit contribution margin.

Compute the break-even point.
(LO 4), AP

BE18-9 Presto Corp. had total variable costs of $180,000, total fixed costs of $110,000, and total revenues of $300,000. Compute the required sales in dollars to break even.

Compute sales for target net income.
(LO 5), AP

BE18-10 For Flynn Company, variable costs are 70% of sales, and fixed costs are $195,000. Management's net income goal is $75,000. Compute the required sales in dollars needed to achieve management's target net income of $75,000. (Use the contribution margin approach.)

Compute the margin of safety and the margin of safety ratio.
(LO 5), AP

BE18-11 For Astoria Company, actual sales are $1,000,000, and break-even sales are $800,000. Compute (a) the margin of safety in dollars and (b) the margin of safety ratio.

Compute the required sales in units for target net income.
(LO 5), AP

BE18-12 Deines Corporation has fixed costs of $480,000. It has a unit selling price of $6, unit variable costs of $4.40, and a target net income of $1,500,000. Compute the required sales in units to achieve its target net income.

DO IT! EXERCISES

Classify types of costs.
(LO 1), C

DO IT! 18-1 Amanda Company reports the following total costs at two levels of production.

	5,000 Units	10,000 Units
Indirect labor	$ 3,000	$ 6,000
Property taxes	7,000	7,000
Direct labor	28,000	56,000
Direct materials	22,000	44,000
Depreciation	4,000	4,000
Utilities	5,000	8,000
Maintenance	9,000	11,000

Classify each cost as variable, fixed, or mixed.

DO IT! 18-2 Westerville Company accumulates the following data concerning a mixed cost, using units produced as the activity level.

Compute costs using high-low method and estimate total cost.

(LO 2), AP

	Units Produced	Total Cost
March	10,000	$18,000
April	9,000	16,650
May	10,500	18,580
June	8,800	16,200
July	9,500	17,100

(a) Compute the variable- and fixed-cost elements using the high-low method.
(b) Estimate the total cost if the company produces 9,200 units.

DO IT! 18-3 Cedar Grove Industries produces and sells a cell phone-operated home security control. Information regarding the costs and sales of security controls during May 2017 are provided below.

Prepare CVP income statement.

(LO 3), AP

Unit selling price of security control	$45
Unit variable costs	$22
Total monthly fixed costs	$120,000
Units sold	8,000

Prepare a CVP income statement for Cedar Grove Industries for the month of May. Provide per unit values and total values.

DO IT! 18-4 Snow Cap Company has a unit selling price of $250, variable costs per unit of $170, and fixed costs of $160,000. Compute the break-even point in units using (a) the mathematical equation and (b) unit contribution margin.

Compute break-even point in units.

(LO 4), AP

DO IT! 18-5 Presto Company makes radios that sell for $30 each. For the coming year, management expects fixed costs to total $220,000 and variable costs to be $18 per unit.

(a) Compute the break-even point in dollars using the contribution margin (CM) ratio.
(b) Compute the margin of safety ratio assuming actual sales are $800,000.
(c) Compute the sales dollars required to earn net income of $140,000.

Compute break-even point, margin of safety ratio, and sales for target net income.

(LO 4, 5), AP

EXERCISES

E18-1 Bonita Company manufactures a single product. Annual production costs incurred in the manufacturing process are shown below for two levels of production.

Define and classify variable, fixed, and mixed costs.

(LO 1), C

	Costs Incurred			
Production in Units	**5,000**		**10,000**	
Production Costs	**Total Cost**	**Cost/ Unit**	**Total Cost**	**Cost/ Unit**
Direct materials	$8,000	$1.60	$16,000	$1.60
Direct labor	9,500	1.90	19,000	1.90
Utilities	2,000	0.40	3,300	0.33
Rent	4,000	0.80	4,000	0.40
Maintenance	800	0.16	1,400	0.14
Supervisory salaries	1,000	0.20	1,000	0.10

Instructions

(a) Define the terms variable costs, fixed costs, and mixed costs.
(b) Classify each cost above as either variable, fixed, or mixed.

Diagram cost behavior, determine relevant range, and classify costs.

(LO 1), C

E18-2 Shingle Enterprises is considering manufacturing a new product. It projects the cost of direct materials and rent for a range of output as shown below.

Output in Units	Rent Expense	Direct Materials
1,000	$ 5,000	$ 4,000
2,000	5,000	7,200
3,000	8,000	9,000
4,000	8,000	12,000
5,000	8,000	15,000
6,000	8,000	18,000
7,000	8,000	21,000
8,000	8,000	24,000
9,000	10,000	29,300
10,000	10,000	35,000
11,000	10,000	44,000

Instructions

(a) Diagram the behavior of each cost for output ranging from 1,000 to 11,000 units.
(b) Determine the relevant range of activity for this product.
(c) Calculate the variable costs per unit within the relevant range.
(d) Indicate the fixed cost within the relevant range.

Determine fixed and variable costs using the high-low method and prepare graph.

(LO 1, 2), AP

E18-3 The controller of Norton Industries has collected the following monthly expense data for use in analyzing the cost behavior of maintenance costs.

Month	Total Maintenance Costs	Total Machine Hours
January	$2,700	300
February	3,000	350
March	3,600	500
April	4,500	690
May	3,200	400
June	5,500	700

Instructions

(a) Determine the fixed- and variable-cost components using the high-low method.
(b) Prepare a graph showing the behavior of maintenance costs, and identify the fixed- and variable-cost elements. Use 100-hour increments and $1,000 cost increments.

Classify variable, fixed, and mixed costs.

(LO 1), C

E5-18-4 Family Furniture Corporation incurred the following costs.

1. Wood used in the production of furniture.
2. Fuel used in delivery trucks.
3. Straight-line depreciation on factory building.
4. Screws used in the production of furniture.
5. Sales staff salaries.
6. Sales commissions.
7. Property taxes.
8. Insurance on buildings.
9. Hourly wages of furniture craftsmen.
10. Salaries of factory supervisors.
11. Utilities expense.
12. Telephone bill.

Instructions

Identify the costs above as variable, fixed, or mixed.

E18-5 The controller of Hall Industries has collected the following monthly expense data for use in analyzing the cost behavior of maintenance costs.

Determine fixed and variable costs using the high-low method and prepare graph.

(LO 1, 2), AP

Month	Total Maintenance Costs	Total Machine Hours
January	$2,640	3,500
February	3,000	4,000
March	3,600	6,000
April	4,500	7,900
May	3,200	5,000
June	4,620	8,000

Instructions

(a) Determine the fixed- and variable-cost components using the high-low method.

(b) Prepare a graph showing the behavior of maintenance costs and identify the fixed- and variable-cost elements. Use 2,000-hour increments and $1,000 cost increments.

E18-6 PCB Corporation manufactures a single product. Monthly production costs incurred in the manufacturing process are shown below for the production of 3,000 units. The utilities and maintenance costs are mixed costs. The fixed portions of these costs are $300 and $200, respectively.

Determine fixed, variable, and mixed costs.

(LO 1), AP

Production in Units	3,000
Production Costs	
Direct materials	$ 7,500
Direct labor	18,000
Utilities	2,100
Property taxes	1,000
Indirect labor	4,500
Supervisory salaries	1,900
Maintenance	1,100
Depreciation	2,400

Instructions

(a) Identify the above costs as variable, fixed, or mixed.

(b) Calculate the expected costs when production is 5,000 units.

E18-7 Marty Moser wants Moser Company to use CVP analysis to study the effects of changes in costs and volume on the company. Marty has heard that certain assumptions must be valid in order for CVP analysis to be useful.

Explain assumptions underlying CVP analysis.

(LO 3), K

Instructions

Prepare a memo to Marty Moser concerning the assumptions that underlie CVP analysis.

E18-8 All That Blooms provides environmentally friendly lawn services for homeowners. Its operating costs are as follows.

Compute break-even point in units and dollars.

(LO 3, 4), AP

Depreciation	$1,400 per month
Advertising	$200 per month
Insurance	$2,000 per month
Weed and feed materials	$12 per lawn
Direct labor	$10 per lawn
Fuel	$2 per lawn

All That Blooms charges $60 per treatment for the average single-family lawn.

Instructions

Determine the company's break-even point in (a) number of lawns serviced per month and (b) dollars.

Compute break-even point.
(LO 3, 4), AP

E18-9 The Palmer Acres Inn is trying to determine its break-even point during its off-peak season. The inn has 50 rooms that it rents at $60 a night. Operating costs are as follows.

Salaries	$5,900 per month
Utilities	$1,100 per month
Depreciation	$1,000 per month
Maintenance	$100 per month
Maid service	$14 per room
Other costs	$28 per room

Instructions
Determine the inn's break-even point in (a) number of rented rooms per month and (b) dollars.

Compute contribution margin and break-even point.
(LO 3, 4), AP

E18-10 In the month of March, Style Salon services 560 clients at an average price of $120. During the month, fixed costs were $21,024 and variable costs were 60% of sales.

Instructions
(a) Determine the contribution margin in dollars, per unit, and as a ratio.
(b) Using the contribution margin technique, compute the break-even point in dollars and in units.

Compute break-even point.
(LO 3, 4), AP

E18-11 Spencer Kars provides shuttle service between four hotels near a medical center and an international airport. Spencer Kars uses two 10-passenger vans to offer 12 round trips per day. A recent month's activity in the form of a cost-volume-profit income statement is shown below.

Fare revenues (1,500 fares)		$36,000
Variable costs		
Fuel	$ 5,040	
Tolls and parking	3,100	
Maintenance	860	9,000
Contribution margin		27,000
Fixed costs		
Salaries	15,700	
Depreciation	1,300	
Insurance	1,000	18,000
Net income		$ 9,000

Instructions
(a) Calculate the break-even point in (1) dollars and (2) number of fares.
(b) Without calculations, determine the contribution margin at the break-even point.

Compute variable costs per unit, contribution margin ratio, and increase in fixed costs.
(LO 3, 4), AP

E18-12 In 2016, Manhoff Company had a break-even point of $350,000 based on a selling price of $5 per unit and fixed costs of $112,000. In 2017, the selling price and the variable costs per unit did not change, but the break-even point increased to $420,000.

Instructions
(a) Compute the variable costs per unit and the contribution margin ratio for 2016.
(b) Compute the increase in fixed costs for 2017.

Prepare CVP income statements.
(LO 3, 4), AP

E18-13 Billings Company has the following information available for September 2017.

Unit selling price of video game consoles	$ 400
Unit variable costs	$ 280
Total fixed costs	$54,000
Units sold	600

Instructions
(a) Compute the unit contribution margin.
(b) Prepare a CVP income statement that shows both total and per unit amounts.
(c) Compute Billings' break-even point in units.
(d) Prepare a CVP income statement for the break-even point that shows both total and per unit amounts.

E18-14 Naylor Company had $210,000 of net income in 2016 when the selling price per unit was $150, the variable costs per unit were $90, and the fixed costs were $570,000. Management expects per unit data and total fixed costs to remain the same in 2017. The president of Naylor Company is under pressure from stockholders to increase net income by $52,000 in 2017.

Compute various components to derive target net income under different assumptions.

(LO 4, 5), AP

Instructions
(a) Compute the number of units sold in 2016.
(b) Compute the number of units that would have to be sold in 2017 to reach the stockholders' desired profit level.
(c) Assume that Naylor Company sells the same number of units in 2017 as it did in 2016. What would the selling price have to be in order to reach the stockholders' desired profit level?

E5-15 Yams Company reports the following operating results for the month of August: sales $400,000 (units 5,000), variable costs $240,000, and fixed costs $90,000. Management is considering the following independent courses of action to increase net income.

Compute net income under different alternatives.

(LO 5), AP

1. Increase selling price by 10% with no change in total variable costs or units sold.
2. Reduce variable costs to 55% of sales.

Instructions
Compute the net income to be earned under each alternative. Which course of action will produce the higher net income?

E18-16 Glacial Company estimates that variable costs will be 62.5% of sales, and fixed costs will total $600,000. The selling price of the product is $4.

Prepare a CVP graph and compute break-even point and margin of safety.

(LO 4, 5), AP

Instructions
(a) Prepare a CVP graph, assuming maximum sales of $3,200,000. (*Note:* Use $400,000 increments for sales and costs and 100,000 increments for units.)
(b) Compute the break-even point in (1) units and (2) dollars.
(c) Assuming actual sales are $2 million, compute the margin of safety in (1) dollars and (2) as a ratio.

E18-17 Felde Bucket Co., a manufacturer of rain barrels, had the following data for 2016:

Determine contribution margin ratio, break-even point in dollars, and margin of safety.

(LO 3, 4, 5), AP

Sales	2,500 units
Sales price	$40 per unit
Variable costs	$24 per unit
Fixed costs	$19,500

Instructions
(a) What is the contribution margin ratio?
(b) What is the break-even point in dollars?
(c) What is the margin of safety in dollars and as a ratio?
(d) If the company wishes to increase its total dollar contribution margin by 30% in 2017, by how much will it need to increase its sales if all other factors remain constant?

(CGA adapted)

EXERCISES: SET B AND CHALLENGE EXERCISES

Visit the book's companion website, at **www.wiley.com/college/kimmel**, and choose the Student Companion site to access Exercises: Set B and Challenge Exercises.

PROBLEMS: SET A

Determine variable and fixed costs, compute break-even point, prepare a CVP graph, and determine net income.

(LO 1, 2, 3, 4), AN

P18-1A Vin Diesel owns the Fredonia Barber Shop. He employs four barbers and pays each a base rate of $1,250 per month. One of the barbers serves as the manager and receives an extra $500 per month. In addition to the base rate, each barber also receives a commission of $4.50 per haircut.

Other costs are as follows.

Advertising	$200 per month
Rent	$1,100 per month
Barber supplies	$0.30 per haircut
Utilities	$175 per month plus $0.20 per haircut
Magazines	$25 per month

Vin currently charges $10 per haircut.

Instructions

(a) VC $5

(a) Determine the variable costs per haircut and the total monthly fixed costs.
(b) Compute the break-even point in units and dollars.
(c) Prepare a CVP graph, assuming a maximum of 1,800 haircuts in a month. Use increments of 300 haircuts on the horizontal axis and $3,000 on the vertical axis.
(d) Determine net income, assuming 1,600 haircuts are given in a month.

Prepare a CVP income statement, compute break-even point, contribution margin ratio, margin of safety ratio, and sales for target net income.

(LO 3, 4, 5), AN

P18-2A Jorge Company bottles and distributes B-Lite, a diet soft drink. The beverage is sold for 50 cents per 16-ounce bottle to retailers, who charge customers 75 cents per bottle. For the year 2017, management estimates the following revenues and costs.

Sales	$1,800,000	Selling expenses—variable	$70,000
Direct materials	430,000	Selling expenses—fixed	65,000
Direct labor	360,000	Administrative expenses—variable	20,000
Manufacturing overhead—variable	380,000	Administrative expenses—fixed	60,000
Manufacturing overhead—fixed	280,000		

Instructions

(b) (1) 2,700,000 units
(c) CM ratio 30%

(a) Prepare a CVP income statement for 2017 based on management's estimates. (Show column for total amounts only.)
(b) Compute the break-even point in (1) units and (2) dollars.
(c) Compute the contribution margin ratio and the margin of safety ratio. (Round to nearest full percent.)
(d) Determine the sales dollars required to earn net income of $180,000.

Compute break-even point under alternative courses of action.

(LO 4), E

P18-3A Tanek Corp.'s sales slumped badly in 2017. For the first time in its history, it operated at a loss. The company's income statement showed the following results from selling 500,000 units of product: sales $2,500,000, total costs and expenses $2,600,000, and net loss $100,000. Costs and expenses consisted of the amounts shown below.

	Total	Variable	Fixed
Cost of goods sold	$2,140,000	$1,590,000	$550,000
Selling expenses	250,000	92,000	158,000
Administrative expenses	210,000	68,000	142,000
	$2,600,000	$1,750,000	$850,000

Management is considering the following independent alternatives for 2018.

1. Increase unit selling price 20% with no change in costs, expenses, and sales volume.
2. Change the compensation of salespersons from fixed annual salaries totaling $150,000 to total salaries of $60,000 plus a 5% commission on sales.

Instructions
(a) Compute the break-even point in dollars for 2017.
(b) Compute the break-even point in dollars under each of the alternative courses of action. (Round all ratios to nearest full percent.) Which course of action do you recommend?

(b) Alternative 1 $2,023,810

P18-4A Mary Willis is the advertising manager for Bargain Shoe Store. She is currently working on a major promotional campaign. Her ideas include the installation of a new lighting system and increased display space that will add $24,000 in fixed costs to the $270,000 currently spent. In addition, Mary is proposing that a 5% price decrease ($40 to $38) will produce a 20% increase in sales volume (20,000 to 24,000). Variable costs will remain at $24 per pair of shoes. Management is impressed with Mary's ideas but concerned about the effects that these changes will have on the break-even point and the margin of safety.

Compute break-even point and margin of safety ratio, and prepare a CVP income statement before and after changes in business environment.

(LO 3, 4, 5), E

Instructions
(a) Compute the current break-even point in units, and compare it to the break-even point in units if Mary's ideas are used.
(b) Compute the margin of safety ratio for current operations and after Mary's changes are introduced. (Round to nearest full percent.)
(c) Prepare a CVP income statement for current operations and after Mary's changes are introduced. (Show column for total amounts only.) Would you make the changes suggested?

(b) Current margin of safety ratio 16%

P18-5A Viejol Corporation has collected the following information after its first year of sales. Sales were $1,600,000 on 100,000 units, selling expenses $250,000 (40% variable and 60% fixed), direct materials $490,000, direct labor $290,000, administrative expenses $270,000 (20% variable and 80% fixed), and manufacturing overhead $380,000 (70% variable and 30% fixed). Top management has asked you to do a CVP analysis so that it can make plans for the coming year. It has projected that unit sales will increase by 10% next year.

Compute contribution margin, fixed costs, break-even point, sales for target net income, and margin of safety ratio.

(LO 3, 4, 5), AN

Instructions
(a) Compute (1) the contribution margin for the current year and the projected year, and (2) the fixed costs for the current year. (Assume that fixed costs will remain the same in the projected year.)
(b) Compute the break-even point in units and sales dollars for the current year.
(c) The company has a target net income of $200,000. What is the required sales in dollars for the company to meet its target?
(d) If the company meets its target net income number, by what percentage could its sales fall before it is operating at a loss? That is, what is its margin of safety ratio?

(b) 120,000 units

P18-6A Kaiser Industries carries no inventories. Its product is manufactured only when a customer's order is received. It is then shipped immediately after it is made. For its fiscal year ended October 31, 2017, Kaiser's break-even point was $1.3 million. On sales of $1.2 million, its income statement showed a gross profit of $180,000, direct materials cost of $400,000, and direct labor costs of $500,000. The contribution margin was $180,000, and variable manufacturing overhead was $50,000.

Determine contribution margin ratio, break-even point, and margin of safety.

(LO 1, 3, 5), E

Instructions
(a) Calculate the following:
    (1) Variable selling and administrative expenses.
    (2) Fixed manufacturing overhead.
    (3) Fixed selling and administrative expenses.
(b) Ignoring your answer to part (a), assume that fixed manufacturing overhead was $100,000 and the fixed selling and administrative expenses were $80,000. The marketing vice president feels that if the company increased its advertising, sales could be increased by 25%. What is the maximum increased advertising cost the company can incur and still report the same income as before the advertising expenditure?

(CGA adapted)

(a) (2) $70,000

▶ PROBLEMS: SET B AND SET C

Visit the book's companion website, at **www.wiley.com/college/kimmel**, and choose the Student Companion site to access Problems: Set B and Set C.

▶ CONTINUING PROBLEMS

EXCEL TUTORIAL

XLS

CURRENT DESIGNS

CD18 Bill Johnson, sales manager, and Diane Buswell, controller, at Current Designs are beginning to analyze the cost considerations for one of the composite models of the kayak division. They have provided the following production and operational costs necessary to produce one composite kayak.

Current Designs.xls

	A	B	C
1	Kevlar®	$250 per kayak	
2	Resin and supplies	$100 per kayak	
3	Finishing kit (seat, rudder, ropes, etc.)	$170 per kayak	
4	Labor	$420 per kayak	
5	Selling and administrative expenses—variable	$400 per kayak	
6	Selling and administrative expenses—fixed	$119,700 per year	
7	Manufacturing overhead—fixed	$240,000 per year	
8			

Bill and Diane have asked you to provide a cost-volume-profit analysis, to help them finalize the budget projections for the upcoming year. Bill has informed you that the selling price of the composite kayak will be $2,000.

Instructions

(a) Calculate variable costs per unit.
(b) Determine the unit contribution margin.
(c) Using the unit contribution margin, determine the break-even point in units for this product line.
(d) Assume that Current Designs plans to earn $270,600 on this product line. Using the unit contribution margin, calculate the number of units that need to be sold to achieve this goal.
(e) Based on the most recent sales forecast, Current Designs plans to sell 1,000 units of this model. Using your results from part (c), calculate the margin of safety and the margin of safety ratio.

WATERWAYS

(*Note:* This is a continuation of the Waterways problem from Chapters 14–17.)

WP18 The Vice President for Sales and Marketing at Waterways Corporation is planning for production needs to meet sales demand in the coming year. He is also trying to determine how the company's profits might be increased in the coming year. This problem asks you to use cost-volume-profit concepts to help Waterways understand contribution margins of some of its products and decide whether to mass-produce any of them.

Go to the book's companion website, **www.wiley.com/college/kimmel**, *to find the remainder of this problem.*

EXPAND YOUR CRITICAL THINKING

Group Project ▶

DECISION-MAKING ACROSS THE ORGANIZATION

E

CT18-1 Creative Ideas Company has decided to introduce a new product. The new product can be manufactured by either a capital-intensive method or a labor-intensive method. The manufacturing method will not affect the quality of the product. The estimated manufacturing costs by the two methods are as follows.

	Capital-Intensive	Labor-Intensive
Direct materials	$5 per unit	$5.50 per unit
Direct labor	$6 per unit	$8.00 per unit
Variable overhead	$3 per unit	$4.50 per unit
Fixed manufacturing costs	$2,524,000	$1,550,000

Creative Ideas' market research department has recommended an introductory unit sales price of $32. The incremental selling expenses are estimated to be $502,000 annually plus $2 for each unit sold, regardless of manufacturing method.

Instructions

With the class divided into groups, answer the following.

(a) Calculate the estimated break-even point in annual unit sales of the new product if Creative Ideas Company uses the:
  (1) Capital-intensive manufacturing method.
  (2) Labor-intensive manufacturing method.

(b) Determine the annual unit sales volume at which Creative Ideas Company would be indifferent between the two manufacturing methods.

(c) Explain the circumstance under which Creative Ideas should employ each of the two manufacturing methods.

(CMA adapted)

MANAGERIAL ANALYSIS

CT18-2 The condensed income statement for the Peri and Paul partnership for 2017 is as follows.

PERI AND PAUL COMPANY
Income Statement
For the Year Ended December 31, 2017

Sales (240,000 units)		$1,200,000
Cost of goods sold		800,000
Gross profit		400,000
Operating expenses		
Selling	$280,000	
Administrative	150,000	430,000
Net loss		$ (30,000)

A cost behavior analysis indicates that 75% of the cost of goods sold are variable, 42% of the selling expenses are variable, and 40% of the administrative expenses are variable.

Instructions

(Round to nearest unit, dollar, and percentage, where necessary. Use the CVP income statement format in computing profits.)

(a) Compute the break-even point in total sales dollars and in units for 2017.

(b) Peri has proposed a plan to get the partnership "out of the red" and improve its profitability. She feels that the quality of the product could be substantially improved by spending $0.25 more per unit on better raw materials. The selling price per unit could be increased to only $5.25 because of competitive pressures. Peri estimates that sales volume will increase by 25%. What effect would Peri's plan have on the profits and the break-even point in dollars of the partnership? (Round the contribution margin ratio to two decimal places.)

(c) Paul was a marketing major in college. He believes that sales volume can be increased only by intensive advertising and promotional campaigns. He therefore proposed the following plan as an alternative to Peri's: (1) increase variable selling expenses to $0.59 per unit, (2) lower the selling price per unit by $0.25, and (3) increase fixed selling expenses by $40,000. Paul quoted an old marketing research report that said that sales volume would increase by 60% if these changes were made. What effect would Paul's plan have on the profits and the break-even point in dollars of the partnership?

(d) Which plan should be accepted? Explain your answer.

REAL-WORLD FOCUS

E **CT18-3** The Coca-Cola Company hardly needs an introduction. A line taken from the cover of a recent annual report says it all: If you measured time in servings of Coca-Cola, "a billion Coca-Cola's ago was yesterday morning." On average, every U.S. citizen drinks 363 8-ounce servings of Coca-Cola products each year. Coca-Cola's primary line of business is the making and selling of syrup to bottlers. These bottlers then sell the finished bottles and cans of Coca-Cola to the consumer.

In the annual report of Coca-Cola, the information shown below was provided.

THE COCA-COLA COMPANY
Management Discussion

Our gross margin declined to 61 percent this year from 62 percent in the prior year, primarily due to costs for materials such as sweeteners and packaging.

The increases [in selling expenses] in the last two years were primarily due to higher marketing expenditures in support of our Company's volume growth.

We measure our sales volume in two ways: (1) gallon shipments of concentrates and syrups and (2) unit cases of finished product (bottles and cans of Coke sold by bottlers).

Instructions
Answer the following questions.

(a) Are sweeteners and packaging a variable cost or a fixed cost? What is the impact on the contribution margin of an increase in the per unit cost of sweeteners or packaging? What are the implications for profitability?
(b) In your opinion, are Coca-Cola's marketing expenditures a fixed cost, variable cost, or mixed cost? Give justification for your answer.
(c) Which of the two measures cited for measuring volume represents the activity index as defined in this chapter? Why might Coca-Cola use two different measures?

C **CT18-4** The May 21, 2010, edition of the *Wall Street Journal* includes an article by Jeffrey Trachtenberg entitled "E-Books Rewrite Bookselling."

Instructions
Read the article and answer the following questions.

(a) What aspect of Barnes and Noble's current structure puts it at risk if electronic books become a significant portion of book sales?
(b) What was Barnes and Noble's primary competitive advantage in a "paper book" world? How has this advantage been eliminated by e-books?
(c) What event do the authors say might eventually be viewed as the big turning point for e-books?
(d) What amount does Barnes and Noble earn on a $25 hardcover book? How much would it likely earn on an e-book version of the same title? What implications does this have for Barnes and Noble versus its competitors?
(e) What two mistakes does the author suggest that Barnes and Noble made that left it ill-prepared for an e-book environment?

Writing

COMMUNICATION ACTIVITY

E **CT18-5** Your roommate asks for your help on the following questions about CVP analysis formulas.

(a) How can the mathematical equation for break-even sales show both sales units and sales dollars?
(b) How do the formulas differ for unit contribution margin and contribution margin ratio?
(c) How can contribution margin be used to determine break-even sales in units and in dollars?

Instructions
Write a memo to your roommate stating the relevant formulas and answering each question.

ETHICS CASE

CT18-6 Scott Bestor is an accountant for Westfield Company. Early this year, Scott made a highly favorable projection of sales and profits over the next 3 years for Westfield's hot-selling computer PLEX. As a result of the projections Scott presented to senior management, the company decided to expand production in this area. This decision led to dislocations of some plant personnel who were reassigned to one of the company's newer plants in another state. However, no one was fired, and in fact the company expanded its workforce slightly. E

Unfortunately, Scott rechecked his projection computations a few months later and found that he had made an error that would have reduced his projections substantially. Luckily, sales of PLEX have exceeded projections so far, and management is satisfied with its decision. Scott, however, is not sure what to do. Should he confess his honest mistake and jeopardize his possible promotion? He suspects that no one will catch the error because PLEX sales have exceeded his projections, and it appears that profits will materialize close to his projections.

Instructions

(a) Who are the stakeholders in this situation?
(b) Identify the ethical issues involved in this situation.
(c) What are the possible alternative actions for Scott? What would you do in Scott's position?

ALL ABOUT YOU

CT18-7 Cost-volume-profit analysis can also be used in making personal financial decisions. For example, the purchase of a new car is one of your biggest personal expenditures. It is important that you carefully analyze your options. E

Suppose that you are considering the purchase of a hybrid vehicle. Let's assume the following facts. The hybrid will initially cost an additional $4,500 above the cost of a traditional vehicle. The hybrid will get 40 miles per gallon of gas, and the traditional car will get 30 miles per gallon. Also, assume that the cost of gas is $3.60 per gallon.

Instructions

Using the facts above, answer the following questions.

(a) What is the variable gasoline cost of going one mile in the hybrid car? What is the variable cost of going one mile in the traditional car?
(b) Using the information in part (a), if "miles" is your unit of measure, what is the "contribution margin" of the hybrid vehicle relative to the traditional vehicle? That is, express the variable cost savings on a per-mile basis.
(c) How many miles would you have to drive in order to break even on your investment in the hybrid car?
(d) What other factors might you want to consider?

19

Cost-Volume-Profit Analysis: Additional Issues

CHAPTER PREVIEW

As the Feature Story about Whole Foods Market suggests, the relationship between a company's fixed and variable costs can have a huge impact on its profitability. In particular, the trend toward cost structures dominated by fixed costs has significantly increased the volatility of many companies' net income. The purpose of this chapter is to demonstrate additional uses of cost-volume-profit analysis in making sound business decisions.

CHAPTER OUTLINE

LEARNING OBJECTIVES		PRACTICE
1 Apply basic CVP concepts.	• Basic concepts • Basic computations • Business environment	DO IT! 1 CVP Analysis
2 Explain the term sales mix and its effects on break-even sales.	• Break-even in units • Break-even in dollars	DO IT! 2 Sales Mix Break-Even
3 Determine sales mix when a company has limited resources.		DO IT! 3 Sales Mix with Limited Resources
4 Indicate how operating leverage affects profitability.	• Contribution margin ratio • Break-even point • Margin of safety ratio • Operating leverage	DO IT! 4 Operating Leverage

Go to the ***REVIEW AND PRACTICE*** section at the end of the chapter for a targeted summary and exercises with solutions.

Visit **WileyPLUS** for additional tutorials and practice opportunities.

© bikeriderlondon/Shutterstock

FEATURE STORY

Not Even a Flood Could Stop It

America has a reputation as a country populated with people who won't buy a restaurant meal unless it can be ordered from the driver's seat of a car. Customers want to receive said "meal" 30 seconds later from a drive-up window and then consume the bagged product while driving one-handed down an 8-lane freeway. This is actually a fairly accurate depiction of the restaurant preferences (and eating habits) of one of the authors of this textbook. However, given the success of Whole Foods Market, this certainly cannot be true of all Americans.

Whole Foods Market began humbly in 1978 as a natural-foods store called SaferWay. (Get it? A play on SafeWay grocery stores.) It was founded in Austin, Texas, by 25 year-old John Mackey (a self-described college dropout) and 21 year-old Renee Lawson Hardy. They financed the first store by borrowing $45,000 from family and friends. The early days were "interesting." First, John and Renee got kicked out of their apartment for storing grocery products there. No problem—they just moved into the store. They bathed in the store's dishwasher with an attached hose. They did whatever it took to keep their costs down and the store going.

Two years later, John and Renee merged SaferWay with another store to form the first Whole Foods Market. The store's first year was very successful. Well, that is until everything in the store was completely destroyed by Austin's biggest flood in more than 70 years. They lost $400,000 in goods—and they had no insurance. But within 28 days, with tons of volunteer work and understanding creditors and vendors, the store reopened.

Today, Whole Foods operates approximately 270 stores. The size of the average store has actually declined in recent years. While huge stores (up to 80,000 square feet) were successful in a few cities, in most locations the fixed costs of such a large facility made it hard to achieve profit targets. Then, when sales became sluggish during the recession, the company determined that it could reduce its fixed costs, such as rent and utility costs, by reducing its average store size by about 20%. However, with fewer square feet, managers must keep a close eye on the sales mix. They need to be aware of the relative contribution margins of each product line to maximize the profit per square foot while still providing the products its customers want.

Why is a company as successful as Whole Foods so concerned about controlling costs? The answer is that the grocery business runs on very thin margins. So while we doubt that anybody is bathing in the store's dishwashers anymore, Whole Foods is as vigilant about its costs today as it was during its first year of operations.

LEARNING OBJECTIVE 1

Apply basic CVP concepts.

As indicated in Chapter 18, cost-volume-profit (CVP) analysis is the study of the effects of changes in costs and volume on a company's profit. CVP analysis is important to profit planning. It is also a critical factor in determining product mix, maximizing use of production facilities, and setting selling prices.

BASIC CONCEPTS

Because CVP is so important for decision-making, management often wants this information reported in a CVP income statement format for internal use. The CVP income statement classifies costs as variable or fixed, and computes a contribution margin. **Contribution margin** is the amount of revenue remaining after deducting variable costs. It is often stated both as a total amount and on a per unit basis.

Illustration 19-1 presents the CVP income statement for Vargo Video (which was shown in Illustration 18-12 on page 893). Note that Vargo sold 1,600 camcorders at $500 per unit.

ILLUSTRATION 19-1
Basic CVP income statement

VARGO VIDEO COMPANY
CVP Income Statement
For the Month Ended June 30, 2017

	Total	Per Unit
Sales (1,600 camcorders)	$ 800,000	$ 500
Variable costs	480,000	300
Contribution margin	320,000	$200
Fixed costs	200,000	
Net income	$120,000	

Companies often prepare detailed CVP income statements. The CVP income statement in Illustration 19-2 uses the same base information as that presented in Illustration 19-1 but provides more detailed information (using assumed data) about the composition of expenses.

ILLUSTRATION 19-2
Detailed CVP income statement

VARGO VIDEO COMPANY
CVP Income Statement
For the Month Ended June 30, 2017

		Total	Per Unit
Sales		$ 800,000	$ 500
Variable expenses			
Cost of goods sold	$400,000		
Selling expenses	60,000		
Administrative expenses	20,000		
Total variable expenses		480,000	300
Contribution margin		320,000	$200
Fixed expenses			
Cost of goods sold	120,000		
Selling expenses	40,000		
Administrative expenses	40,000		
Total fixed expenses		200,000	
Net income		$120,000	

▼ **HELPFUL HINT**
The appendix to this chapter provides additional discussion of income statements used for decision-making.

In the applications of CVP analysis that follow, we assume that the term "cost" includes all costs and expenses related to production and sale of the product. That is, **cost includes manufacturing costs plus selling and administrative expenses.**

BASIC COMPUTATIONS

Before we introduce additional issues of CVP analysis, let's review some of the basic concepts that you learned in Chapter 18, specifically break-even analysis, target net income, and margin of safety.

Break-Even Analysis

Vargo Video's CVP income statement (Illustration 19-2) shows that total contribution margin (sales minus variable expenses) is $320,000, and the company's unit contribution margin is $200. Recall that contribution margin can also be expressed in the form of the **contribution margin ratio** (contribution margin divided by sales), which in the case of Vargo is 40% ($200 ÷ $500).

Illustration 19-3 demonstrates how to compute Vargo's break-even point in units (using unit contribution margin).

ILLUSTRATION 19-3
Break-even point in units

Fixed Costs	÷	Unit Contribution Margin	=	Break-Even Point in Units
$200,000	÷	$200	=	1,000 units

Illustration 19-4 shows the computation for the break-even point in dollars (using contribution margin ratio).

ILLUSTRATION 19-4
Break-even point in dollars

Fixed Costs	÷	Contribution Margin Ratio	=	Break-Even Point in Dollars
$200,000	÷	.40	=	$500,000

When a company is in its early stages of operation, its primary goal is to break even. Failure to break even will lead eventually to financial failure.

Target Net Income

Once a company achieves break-even, it then sets a sales goal that will generate a target net income. For example, assume that Vargo's management has a target net income of $250,000. Illustration 19-5 shows the required sales in units to achieve its target net income.

ILLUSTRATION 19-5
Target net income in units

(Fixed Costs + Target Net Income)	÷	Unit Contribution Margin	=	Required Sales in Units
($200,000 + $250,000)	÷	$200	=	2,250 units

Illustration 19-6 uses the contribution margin ratio to compute the required sales in dollars.

ILLUSTRATION 19-6
Target net income in dollars

(Fixed Costs + Target Net Income)	÷	Contribution Margin Ratio	=	Required Sales in Dollars
($200,000 + $250,000)	÷	.40	=	$1,125,000

In order to achieve net income of $250,000, Vargo has to sell 2,250 camcorders, for a total price of $1,125,000.

Margin of Safety

Another measure managers use to assess profitability is the margin of safety. The **margin of safety** tells us **how far sales can drop** before the company will be operating at a loss. Managers like to have a sense of how much cushion they have between their current situation and operating at a loss. This can be expressed in dollars or as a ratio. In Illustration 19-2 (page 924), for example, Vargo reported sales of $800,000. At that sales level, its margin of safety in dollars and as a ratio are as follows.

ILLUSTRATION 19-7
Margin of safety in dollars

Actual (Expected) Sales	−	Break-Even Sales	=	Margin of Safety in Dollars
$800,000	−	$500,000	=	$300,000

As shown in Illustration 19-8, Vargo's sales could drop by $300,000, or 37.5%, before the company would operate at a loss.

ILLUSTRATION 19-8
Margin of safety ratio

Margin of Safety in Dollars	÷	Actual (Expected) Sales	=	Margin of Safety Ratio
$300,000	÷	$800,000	=	37.5%

CVP AND CHANGES IN THE BUSINESS ENVIRONMENT

To better understand how CVP analysis works, let's look at three independent situations that might occur at Vargo Video. Each case uses the original camcorder sales and cost data, which were as follows.

ILLUSTRATION 19-9
Original camcorder sales and cost data

Unit selling price	$500
Unit variable cost	$300
Total fixed costs	$200,000
Break-even sales	$500,000 or 1,000 units

Case I

A competitor is offering a 10% discount on the selling price of its camcorders. Management must decide whether to offer a similar discount.

Question: What effect will a 10% discount on selling price have on the break-even point for camcorders?

Answer: A 10% discount on selling price reduces the selling price per unit to $450 [$500 − ($500 × 10%)]. Variable costs per unit remain unchanged at $300. Thus, the unit contribution margin is $150. Assuming no change in fixed costs, break-even sales are 1,333 units, computed as follows.

ILLUSTRATION 19-10
Computation of break-even sales in units

Fixed Costs	÷	Unit Contribution Margin	=	Break-Even Sales
$200,000	÷	$150	=	1,333 units (rounded)

For Vargo, this change requires monthly sales to increase by 333 units, or $33\frac{1}{3}$%, in order to break even. In reaching a conclusion about offering a 10%

discount to customers, management must determine how likely it is to achieve the increased sales. Also, management should estimate the possible loss of sales if the competitor's discount price is not matched.

Case II

To meet the threat of foreign competition, management invests in new robotic equipment that will lower the amount of direct labor required to make camcorders. The company estimates that total fixed costs will increase 30% and that variable cost per unit will decrease 30%.

Question: What effect will the new equipment have on the sales volume required to break even?

Answer: Total fixed costs become \$260,000 [\$200,000 + (30% × \$200,000)]. The variable cost per unit becomes \$210 [\$300 − (30% × \$300)]. The new break-even point is approximately 897 units, computed as shown in Illustration 19-11.

ILLUSTRATION 19-11
Computation of break-even sales in units

Fixed Costs	÷	Unit Contribution Margin	=	Break-Even Sales
\$260,000	÷	(\$500 − \$210)	=	897 units (rounded)

These changes appear to be advantageous for Vargo. The break-even point is reduced by approximately 10%, or 100 units.

Case III

Vargo's principal supplier of raw materials has just announced a price increase. The higher cost is expected to increase the variable cost of camcorders by \$25 per unit. Management decides to hold the line on the selling price of the camcorders. It plans a cost-cutting program that will save \$17,500 in fixed costs per month. Vargo is currently realizing monthly net income of \$80,000 on sales of 1,400 camcorders.

Question: What increase in units sold will be needed to maintain the same level of net income?

Answer: The variable cost per unit increases to \$325 (\$300 + \$25). Fixed costs are reduced to \$182,500 (\$200,000 − \$17,500). Because of the change in variable cost, the unit contribution margin becomes \$175 (\$500 − \$325). The required number of units sold to achieve the target net income is computed as follows.

ILLUSTRATION 19-12
Computation of required sales

(Fixed Costs + Target Net Income)	÷	Unit Contribution Margin	=	Required Sales in Units
(\$182,500 + \$80,000)	÷	\$175	=	1,500

To achieve the required sales, Vargo Video will have to sell 1,500 camcorders, an increase of 100 units. If this does not seem to be a reasonable expectation, management will either have to make further cost reductions or accept less net income if the selling price remains unchanged.

We hope that the concepts reviewed in this section are now familiar to you. We are now ready to examine additional ways that companies use CVP analysis to assess profitability and to help in making effective business decisions.

MANAGEMENT INSIGHT Amazon.com

Warchi/iStockphoto

Don't Just Look—Buy Something

When analyzing an Internet business such as Amazon.com, analysts closely watch the so-called "conversion rate." This rate is calculated by dividing the number of people who actually take action at an Internet site (buy something) by the total number of people who visit the site. Average conversion rates are from 3% to 5%. A rate below 2% is poor, while a rate above 10% is great.

Conversion rates have an obvious effect on the break-even point. Suppose you spend $10,000 on your site, which then attracts 5,000 visitors. If you get a 2% conversion rate (100 purchases), your site costs $100 per purchase ($10,000 ÷ 100). A 4% conversion rate lowers your cost to $50 per transaction, and an 8% conversion rate gets you down to $25. Studies show that conversion rates increase if the site has an easy-to-use interface, fast-performing screens, a convenient ordering process, and advertising that is both clever and clear.

Sources: J. William Gurley, "The One Internet Metric That Really Counts," *Fortune* (March 6, 2000), p. 392; and Milind Mody, "Chief Mentor: How Startups Can Win Customers Online," *Wall Street Journal Online* (May 11, 2011).

Besides increasing their conversion rates, what steps can online merchants use to lower their break-even points? (Go to **WileyPLUS** for this answer and additional questions.)

DO IT! 1 CVP Analysis

Krisanne Company reports the following operating results for the month of June.

KRISANNE COMPANY
CVP Income Statement
For the Month Ended June 30, 2017

	Total	Per Unit
Sales (5,000 units)	$300,000	$60
Variable costs	180,000	36
Contribution margin	120,000	$24
Fixed expenses	100,000	
Net income	$ 20,000	

To increase net income, management is considering reducing the selling price by 10%, with no changes to unit variable costs or fixed costs. Management is confident that this change will increase unit sales by 25%.

Using the contribution margin technique, compute the break-even point in units and dollars and margin of safety in dollars (a) assuming no changes to sales price or costs, and (b) assuming changes to sales price and volume as described above. (c) Comment on your findings.

Action Plan

✔ Apply the formula for the break-even point in units.

✔ Apply the formula for the break-even point in dollars.

✔ Apply the formula for the margin of safety in dollars.

SOLUTION

(a) Assuming no changes to sales price or costs:
Break-even point in units = 4,167 units (rounded) ($100,000 ÷ $24)
Break-even point in sales dollars = $250,000 ($100,000 ÷ .40[a])
Margin of safety in dollars = $50,000 ($300,000 − $250,000)
[a]$24 ÷ $60

(b) Assuming changes to sales price and volume:
Break-even point in units = 5,556 units (rounded) ($100,000 ÷ $18[b])
Break-even point in sales dollars = $300,000 ($100,000 ÷ ($18 ÷ $54[c]))
Margin of safety in dollars = $37,500 ($337,500[d] − $300,000)
[b]$60 − (.10 × $60) − 36 = $18
[c]$60 − (.10 × $60)
[d]5,000 + (.25 × 5,000) = 6,250 units; 6,250 units × $54 = $337,500

(c) The increase in the break-even point and the decrease in the margin of safety indicate that management should not implement the proposed change. The increase in sales volume will result in a contribution margin of $112,500 (6,250 × $18), which is $7,500 less than the current amount.

Related exercise material: **BE19-3, BE19-4, BE19-5, BE19-6, E19-1, E19-2, E19-3, E19-4, E19-5**, and DO IT! **19-1.**

LEARNING OBJECTIVE 2

Explain the term sales mix and its effects on break-even sales.

To this point, our discussion of CVP analysis has assumed that a company sells only one product. However, most companies sell multiple products. When a company sells many products, it is important that management understand its sales mix.

Sales mix is the relative percentage in which a company sells its multiple products. For example, if 80% of Hewlett Packard's unit sales are printers and the other 20% are PCs, its sales mix is 80% printers to 20% PCs.

Sales mix is important to managers because different products often have substantially different contribution margins. For example, Ford's SUVs and F150 pickup trucks have higher contribution margins compared to its economy cars. Similarly, first-class tickets sold by United Airlines provide substantially higher contribution margins than coach-class tickets. Intel's sales of computer chips for netbook computers have increased, but the contribution margin on these chips is lower than for notebook and desktop PCs.

BREAK-EVEN SALES IN UNITS

Companies can compute break-even sales for a mix of two or more products by determining the **weighted-average unit contribution margin of all the products**. To illustrate, assume that Vargo Video sells not only camcorders but high-definition TVs as well. Vargo sells its two products in the following amounts: 1,500 camcorders and 500 TVs. The sales mix, expressed as a percentage of the 2,000 total units sold, is as follows.

ILLUSTRATION 19-13
Sales mix as a percentage of units sold

Camcorders	TVs
1,500 units ÷ 2,000 units = 75%	500 units ÷ 2,000 units = 25%

That is, 75% of the 2,000 units sold are camcorders, and 25% of the 2,000 units sold are TVs.

Illustration 19-14 shows additional information related to Vargo. The unit contribution margin for camcorders is $200, and for TVs it is $500. Vargo's fixed costs total $275,000.

ILLUSTRATION 19-14
Per unit data—sales mix

Unit Data	Camcorders	TVs
Selling price	$500	$1,000
Variable costs	300	500
Contribution margin	$200	$500
Sales mix—units	75%	25%
Fixed costs = $275,000		

To compute break-even for Vargo, we must determine the weighted-average unit contribution margin for the two products. We use the **weighted-average** contribution margin because Vargo sells three times as many camcorders as TVs. As a result, in determining an average unit contribution margin, three times as much weight should be placed on the contribution margin of the camcorders as on the TVs. Therefore, the camcorders must be counted three times for every TV sold. The weighted-average contribution margin for a sales mix of 75% camcorders and 25% TVs is $275, which is computed as follows.

ILLUSTRATION 19-15
Weighted-average unit contribution margin

Camcorders				TVs				
(Unit Contribution Margin	×	Sales Mix Percentage)	+	(Unit Contribution Margin	×	Sales Mix Percentage)	=	Weighted-Average Unit Contribution Margin
($200	×	.75)	+	($500	×	.25)	=	$275

DECISION TOOLS

The break-even point in units helps managers determine how many units of each product need to be sold to avoid a loss.

Similar to our calculation in the single-product setting, we can compute the break-even point in units by dividing the fixed costs by the weighted-average unit contribution margin of $275. The computation of break-even sales in units for Vargo Video, assuming $275,000 of fixed costs, is as follows.

ILLUSTRATION 19-16
Break-even point in units

Fixed Costs	÷	Weighted-Average Unit Contribution Margin	=	Break-Even Point in Units
$275,000	÷	$275	=	1,000 units

Illustration 19-16 shows the break-even point for Vargo is 1,000 units—camcorders and TVs combined. Management needs to know how many of the 1,000 units sold are camcorders and how many are TVs. Applying the sales mix percentages that we computed previously of 75% for camcorders and 25% for TVs, these 1,000 units would be comprised of 750 camcorders (.75 × 1,000 units) and 250 TVs (.25 × 1,000). This can be verified by the computations in Illustration 19-17, which shows that the total contribution margin is $275,000 when 1,000 units are sold, which equals the fixed costs of $275,000.

ILLUSTRATION 19-17
Break-even proof—sales units

Product	Unit Sales	×	Unit Contribution Margin	=	Total Contribution Margin
Camcorders	750	×	$200	=	$ 150,000
TVs	250	×	500	=	125,000
	1,000				$275,000

Management should continually review the company's sales mix. At any level of units sold, **net income will be greater if higher contribution margin units are sold rather than lower contribution margin units**. For Vargo, the TVs produce the higher contribution margin. Consequently, if Vargo sells 300 TVs and 700 camcorders, net income would be higher than in the current sales mix even though total units sold are the same.

An analysis of these relationships shows that a shift from low-margin sales to high-margin sales may increase net income even though there is a decline in total units sold. Likewise, a shift from high- to low-margin sales may result in a decrease in net income even though there is an increase in total units sold.

BREAK-EVEN SALES IN DOLLARS

The calculation of the break-even point presented for Vargo Video in the previous section works well if a company has only a *small number* of products. In contrast, consider 3M, the maker of Post-it Notes, which has more than 30,000 products. In order to calculate the break-even point for 3M using a weighted-average unit contribution margin, we would need to calculate 30,000 different unit contribution margins. That is not realistic.

Therefore, for a company with many products, we calculate the break-even point in terms of sales dollars (rather than units sold), using sales information for divisions or product lines (rather than individual products). This requires that we compute both sales mix as a percentage of total dollar sales (rather than units sold) and the contribution margin ratio (rather than unit contribution margin).

To illustrate, suppose that Kale Garden Supply Company has two divisions—Indoor Plants and Outdoor Plants. Each division has hundreds of different types of plants and plant-care products. Illustration 19-18 provides information necessary for determining the sales mix percentages for the two divisions of Kale Garden Supply.

ILLUSTRATION 19-18
Cost-volume-profit data for Kale Garden Supply

	Indoor Plant Division		Outdoor Plant Division		Company Total
Sales	$ 200,000		$ 800,000		$1,000,000
Variable costs	120,000		560,000		680,000
Contribution margin	$ 80,000		$ 240,000		$ 320,000
Sales mix percentage (Division sales ÷ Total sales)	$\frac{\$200,000}{\$1,000,000}$	= .20	$\frac{\$800,000}{\$1,000,000}$	= .80	

As shown in Illustration 19-19, the contribution margin ratio for the combined company is 32%, which is computed by dividing the total contribution margin by total sales.

ILLUSTRATION 19-19
Contribution margin ratio for each division

	Indoor Plant Division	Outdoor Plant Division	Company Total
Contribution margin ratio (Contribution margin ÷ Sales)	$\frac{\$80,000}{\$200,000} = .40$	$\frac{\$240,000}{\$800,000} = .30$	$\frac{\$320,000}{\$1,000,000} = .32$

It is useful to note that the contribution margin ratio of 32% for the total company is a weighted average of the individual contribution margin ratios of the two divisions (40% and 30%). To illustrate, in Illustration 19-20 we multiply each division's contribution margin ratio by its sales mix percentage, based on dollar sales, and then total these amounts. The calculation in Illustration 19-20 is useful because it enables us to determine how the break-even point changes when the sales mix changes.

ILLUSTRATION 19-20
Calculation of weighted-average contribution margin

Indoor Plant Division				Outdoor Plant Division				
(Contribution Margin Ratio	×	Sales Mix Percentage)	+	(Contribution Margin Ratio	×	Sales Mix Percentage)	=	Weighted-Average Contribution Margin Ratio
(.40	×	.20)	+	(.30	×	.80)	=	.32

Kale Garden Supply's break-even point in dollars is then computed by dividing its fixed costs of $300,000 by the weighted-average contribution margin ratio of 32%, as shown in Illustration 19-21 (page 932).

ILLUSTRATION 19-21
Calculation of break-even point in dollars

Fixed Costs	÷	Weighted-Average Contribution Margin Ratio	=	Break-Even Point in Dollars
$300,000	÷	.32	=	$937,500

DECISION TOOLS

The break-even point in dollars helps managers determine the sales dollars required from each division to avoid a loss.

The break-even point is based on the sales mix of 20% to 80%. We can determine the amount of sales contributed by each division by multiplying the sales mix percentage of each division by the total sales figure. Of the company's total break-even sales of $937,500, a total of $187,500 (.20 × $937,500) will come from the Indoor Plant Division, and $750,000 (.80 × $937,500) will come from the Outdoor Plant Division.

What would be the impact on the break-even point if a higher percentage of Kale Garden Supply's sales were to come from the Indoor Plant Division? Because the Indoor Plant Division enjoys a higher contribution margin ratio, this change in the sales mix would result in a higher weighted-average contribution margin ratio and consequently a lower break-even point in dollars. For example, if the sales mix changes to 50% for the Indoor Plant Division and 50% for the Outdoor Plant Division, the weighted-average contribution margin ratio would be 35% [(.40 × .50) + (.30 × .50)]. The new, lower, break-even point is $857,143 ($300,000 ÷ .35). The opposite would occur if a higher percentage of sales were expected from the Outdoor Plant Division. As you can see, the information provided using CVP analysis can help managers better understand the impact of sales mix on profitability.

SERVICE COMPANY INSIGHT Zoom Kitchen

dem10/iStockphoto

Healthy for You, and Great for the Bottom Line

Zoom Kitchen, a chain of restaurants in the Chicago area, was known for serving sizable portions of meat and potatoes. But the company's management was quite pleased when salad sales increased from 18% of its sales mix to 40%. Why were they pleased? Because the contribution margin on salads was much higher than on meat. The restaurant made a conscious effort to encourage people to buy more salads by offering an interesting assortment of salad ingredients including jicama, beets, marinated mushrooms, grilled tuna, and carved turkey. Management had to be very sensitive to contribution margin as opening up a new Zoom Kitchen restaurant was very costly.

Source: Amy Zuber, "Salad Sales 'Zoom' at Meat-and-Potatoes Specialist," *Nation's Restaurant News* (November 12, 2001), p. 26.

Why do you suppose restaurants are so eager to sell beverages and desserts? (Go to **WileyPLUS** for this answer and additional questions.)

DO IT! 2 Sales Mix Break-Even

Action Plan
- ✔ The sales mix is the relative percentage of each product sold in units.
- ✔ The weighted-average unit contribution margin is the sum of the unit contribution margins multiplied by the respective sales mix percentage.

Manzeck Bicycles International produces and sells three different types of mountain bikes. Information regarding the three models is shown below.

	Pro	Intermediate	Standard	Total
Units sold	5,000	10,000	25,000	40,000
Selling price	$800	$500	$350	
Variable costs	$500	$300	$250	

The company's total fixed costs to produce the bicycles are $7,500,000.

(a) Determine the sales mix as a function of units sold for the three products.
(b) Determine the weighted-average unit contribution margin.
(c) Determine the total number of units that the company must sell to break even.
(d) Determine the number of units of each model that the company must sell to break even.

SOLUTION

(a) The sales mix percentages as a function of units sold are:

Pro	Intermediate	Standard
5,000/40,000 = 12.5%	10,000/40,000 = 25%	25,000/40,000 = 62.5%

(b) The weighted-average unit contribution margin is:

[.125 × ($800 − $500)] + [.25 × ($500 − $300)] + [.625 × ($350 −$250)] = $150

(c) The break-even point in units is:

$7,500,000 ÷ $150 = 50,000 units

(d) The break-even units to sell for each product are:

Pro:	50,000 units × 12.5% =	6,250 units
Intermediate:	50,000 units × 25% =	12,500 units
Standard:	50,000 units × 62.5% =	31,250 units
		50,000 units

Action Plan (*cont.*)

✔ Determine the break-even point in units by dividing the fixed costs by the weighted-average unit contribution margin.

✔ Determine the number of units of each model to sell by multiplying the total break-even units by the respective sales mix percentage for each product.

Related exercise material: **BE19-7, BE19-8, BE19-9, BE19-10, E19-6, E19-7, E19-8, E19-9, E19-10,** and **DO IT! 19-2.**

LEARNING OBJECTIVE 3

Determine sales mix when a company has limited resources.

In the previous discussion, we assumed a certain sales mix and then determined the break-even point given that sales mix. We now discuss how limited resources influence the sales-mix decision.

All companies have resource limitations. The limited resource may be floor space in a retail department store, or raw materials, direct labor hours, or machine capacity in a manufacturing company. When a company has limited resources, management must decide which products to make and sell in order to maximize net income.

DECISION TOOLS

Determining the contribution margin per unit of limited resource helps managers decide which product should receive any additional capacity of the limited resource.

To illustrate, recall that Vargo Video manufactures camcorders and TVs. The limiting resource is machine capacity, which is 3,600 hours per month. Relevant data consist of the following.

	Camcorders	TVs
Unit contribution margin	$200	$500
Machine hours required per unit	.2	.625

ILLUSTRATION 19-22
Contribution margin and machine hours

The TVs may appear to be more profitable since they have a higher unit contribution margin ($500) than the camcorders ($200). However, the camcorders take fewer machine hours to produce than the TVs. Therefore, it is necessary to find the **contribution margin per unit of limited resource**—in this case, contribution margin per machine hour. This is obtained by dividing the unit contribution margin of each product by the number of units of the limited resource required for each product, as shown in Illustration 19-23.

▼ **HELPFUL HINT**
CM alone is not enough to make this decision. The key factor is CM per unit of limited resource.

	Camcorders	TVs
Unit contribution margin (a)	$200	$500
Machine hours required (b)	0.2	0.625
Contribution margin per unit of limited resource [(a) ÷ (b)]	**$1,000**	**$800**

ILLUSTRATION 19-23
Contribution margin per unit of limited resource

The computation shows that the camcorders have a higher contribution margin per unit of limited resource. This would suggest that, given sufficient demand for camcorders, Vargo should shift the sales mix to produce more camcorders or increase machine capacity.

As indicated in Illustration 19-23, the constraint for the production of the TVs is the larger number of machine hours needed to produce them. In addressing this problem, we have taken the limited number of machine hours as a given and have attempted to maximize the contribution margin given the constraint. One question that Vargo should ask, however, is whether this constraint can be reduced or eliminated. If Vargo is able to increase machine capacity from 3,600 hours to 4,200 hours, the additional 600 hours could be used to produce either the camcorders or TVs. The total contribution margin under each alternative is found by multiplying the machine hours by the contribution margin per unit of limited resource, as shown below.

ILLUSTRATION 19-24
Incremental analysis—computation of total contribution margin

	Camcorders	TVs
Machine hours (a)	600	600
Contribution margin per unit of limited resource (b)	$ 1,000	$ 800
Contribution margin [(a) × (b)]	**$600,000**	**$480,000**

From this analysis, we can see that to maximize net income, all of the increased capacity should be used to make and sell the camcorders.

Vargo's manufacturing constraint might be due to a bottleneck in production or to poorly trained machine operators. In addition to finding ways to solve those problems, the company should consider other possible solutions, such as outsourcing part of the production, acquiring additional new equipment (discussed in Chapter 24), or striving to eliminate any non–value-added activities (see Chapter 17). As discussed in Chapter 14, this approach to evaluating constraints is referred to as the theory of constraints. The **theory of constraints** is a specific approach used to identify and manage constraints in order to achieve the company's goals. According to this theory, a company must continually identify its constraints and find ways to reduce or eliminate them, where appropriate.

MANAGEMENT INSIGHT Macy's

Liv Friis-Larsen/iStockphoto

Something Smells

When fragrance sales went flat, retailers such as Macy's turned up the heat on fragrance manufacturers. They reduced the amount of floor space devoted to fragrances, leaving fragrance manufacturers fighting each other for the smaller space. The retailer doesn't just choose the fragrance with the highest contribution margin. Instead, it chooses the fragrance with the highest contribution margin per square foot for a given period of time. In this game, a product with a lower contribution margin, but a higher turnover, could well be the winner.

What is the limited resource for a retailer, and what implications does this have for sales mix? (Go to **WileyPLUS** for this answer and additional questions.)

DO IT! 3 Sales Mix with Limited Resources

Carolina Corporation manufactures and sells three different types of high-quality sealed ball bearings for mountain bike wheels. The bearings vary in terms of their quality specifications—primarily with respect to their smoothness and roundness. They are referred to as Fine, Extra-Fine, and Super-Fine bearings. Machine time is limited. More machine time is required to manufacture the Extra-Fine and Super-Fine bearings. Additional information is provided below.

	Product		
	Fine	**Extra-Fine**	**Super-Fine**
Selling price	\$6.00	\$10.00	\$16.00
Variable costs and expenses	4.00	6.50	11.00
Contribution margin	\$2.00	\$ 3.50	\$ 5.00
Machine hours required	0.02	0.04	0.08

(a) Ignoring the machine time constraint, what strategy would appear optimal?

(b) What is the contribution margin per unit of limited resource for each type of bearing?

(c) If additional machine time could be obtained, how should the additional capacity be used?

SOLUTION

(a) The Super-Fine bearings have the highest unit contribution margin. Thus, ignoring any manufacturing constraints, it would appear that the company should shift toward production of more Super-Fine units.

(b) The contribution margin per unit of limited resource (machine hours) is calculated as:

	Fine	**Extra-Fine**	**Super-Fine**
$\dfrac{\text{Unit contribution margin}}{\text{Limited resource consumed per unit}}$	$\dfrac{\$2}{.02} = \$100$	$\dfrac{\$3.5}{.04} = \$87.50$	$\dfrac{\$5}{.08} = \$62.50$

(c) The Fine bearings have the highest contribution margin per unit of limited resource even though they have the lowest unit contribution margin. Given the resource constraint, any additional capacity should be used to make Fine bearings.

Action Plan

✔ Calculate the contribution margin per unit of limited resource for each product.

✔ Apply the formula for the contribution margin per unit of limited resource.

✔ To maximize net income, shift sales mix to the product with the highest contribution margin per unit of limited resource.

Related exercise material: **BE19-11, BE19-12, E19-11, E19-12, E19-13,** and **DO IT! 19-3.**

LEARNING OBJECTIVE 4 Indicate how operating leverage affects profitability.

Cost structure refers to the relative proportion of fixed versus variable costs that a company incurs. Cost structure can have a significant effect on profitability. For example, computer equipment manufacturer Cisco Systems has substantially reduced its fixed costs by choosing to outsource much of its production. By minimizing its fixed costs, Cisco is now less susceptible to economic swings. However, as the following discussion shows, its reduced reliance on fixed costs has also reduced its ability to experience the incredible profitability that it used to have during economic booms.

The choice of cost structure should be carefully considered. There are many ways that companies can influence their cost structure. For example, by acquiring sophisticated robotic equipment, many companies have reduced their use of manual labor. Similarly, some brokerage firms, such as E*Trade, have reduced their reliance on human brokers and have instead invested heavily in computers and online technology. In so doing, they have increased their reliance on fixed costs (through depreciation on the robotic equipment or computer equipment) and reduced their reliance on variable costs (the variable employee labor cost). Alternatively, some companies have reduced their fixed costs and increased their variable costs by outsourcing their production. Nike, for example, does very little manufacturing but instead outsources the manufacture of nearly all of its shoes. It has consequently converted many of its fixed costs into variable costs and therefore changed its cost structure.

Consider the following example of Vargo Video and one of its competitors, New Wave Company. Both make camcorders. Vargo uses a traditional, labor-intensive manufacturing process. New Wave has invested in a completely automated system. The factory employees are involved only in setting up, adjusting, and maintaining the machinery. Illustration 19-25 shows CVP income statements for each company.

ILLUSTRATION 19-25
CVP income statements for two companies

	Vargo Video	New Wave Company
Sales	$800,000	$800,000
Variable costs	480,000	160,000
Contribution margin	320,000	640,000
Fixed costs	200,000	520,000
Net income	$120,000	$120,000

Both companies have the same sales and the same net income. However, because of the differences in their cost structures, they differ greatly in the risks and rewards related to increasing or decreasing sales. Let's evaluate the impact of cost structure on the profitability of the two companies.

EFFECT ON CONTRIBUTION MARGIN RATIO

First let's look at the contribution margin ratio. Illustration 19-26 shows the computation of the contribution margin ratio for each company.

ILLUSTRATION 19-26
Contribution margin ratio for two companies

	Contribution Margin	÷	Sales	=	Contribution Margin Ratio
Vargo Video	$320,000	÷	$800,000	=	.40
New Wave	$640,000	÷	$800,000	=	.80

Because of its lower variable costs, New Wave has a contribution margin ratio of 80% versus only 40% for Vargo Video. That means that with every dollar of sales, New Wave generates 80 cents of contribution margin (and thus an 80-cent increase in net income), versus only 40 cents for Vargo. However, it also means that for every dollar that sales decline, New Wave loses 80 cents in net income, whereas Vargo will lose only 40 cents. New Wave's cost structure, which relies more heavily on fixed costs, makes it more sensitive to changes in sales revenue.

EFFECT ON BREAK-EVEN POINT

The difference in cost structure also affects the break-even point. The break-even point for each company is calculated in Illustration 19-27.

ILLUSTRATION 19-27
Computation of break-even point for two companies

	Fixed Costs	÷	Contribution Margin Ratio	=	Break-Even Point in Dollars
Vargo Video	$200,000	÷	.40	=	$500,000
New Wave	$520,000	÷	.80	=	$650,000

New Wave needs to generate $150,000 ($650,000 − $500,000) more in sales than Vargo Video before it breaks even. This makes New Wave riskier than Vargo because a company cannot survive for very long unless it at least breaks even.

EFFECT ON MARGIN OF SAFETY RATIO

We can also evaluate the relative impact that changes in sales would have on the two companies by computing the margin of safety ratio. Illustration 19-28 shows the computation of the **margin of safety ratio** for the two companies.

	(Actual Sales	−	Break-Even Sales)	÷	Actual Sales	=	Margin of Safety Ratio
Vargo Video	($800,000	−	$500,000)	÷	$800,000	=	.38
New Wave	($800,000	−	$650,000)	÷	$800,000	=	.19

ILLUSTRATION 19-28
Computation of margin of safety ratio for two companies

The difference in the margin of safety ratio also reflects the difference in risk between the two companies. Vargo Video could sustain a 38% decline in sales before it would be operating at a loss. New Wave could sustain only a 19% decline in sales before it would be "in the red."

OPERATING LEVERAGE

Operating leverage refers to the extent to which a company's net income reacts to a given change in sales. Companies that have higher fixed costs relative to variable costs have higher operating leverage. When a company's sales revenue is increasing, high operating leverage is a good thing because it means that profits will increase rapidly. But when sales are declining, too much operating leverage can have devastating consequences.

DECISION TOOLS

Calculating the degree of operating leverage helps managers determine how sensitive the company's net income is to changes in sales.

Degree of Operating Leverage

How can we compare operating leverage between two companies? The **degree of operating leverage** provides a measure of a company's earnings volatility and can be used to compare companies. Degree of operating leverage is computed by dividing contribution margin by net income. This formula is presented in Illustration 19-29 and applied to our two manufacturers of camcorders.

	Contribution Margin	÷	Net Income	=	Degree of Operating Leverage
Vargo Video	$320,000	÷	$120,000	=	2.67
New Wave	$640,000	÷	$120,000	=	5.33

ILLUSTRATION 19-29
Computation of degree of operating leverage

New Wave's earnings would go up (or down) by about two times (5.33 ÷ 2.67 = 2.00) as much as Vargo Video's with an equal increase (or decrease) in sales. For example, suppose both companies experience a 10% decrease in sales. Vargo's net income will decrease by 26.7% (2.67 × 10%), while New Wave's will decrease by 53.3% (5.33 × 10%). Thus, New Wave's higher operating leverage exposes it to greater earnings volatility risk.

You should be careful not to conclude from this analysis that a cost structure that relies on higher fixed costs, and consequently has higher operating leverage, is necessarily bad. Some have suggested that Internet radio company Pandora has limited potential for growth in its profitability because it has very little operating leverage. When its revenues grow, its variable costs (fees it pays for the right to use music) grow proportionally. When used carefully, operating leverage can add considerably to a company's profitability. For example, computer equipment manufacturer Komag enjoyed a 66% increase in net income when its sales increased by only 8%. As one commentator noted, "Komag's fourth quarter illustrates the company's significant operating leverage; a small increase in sales leads to a big profit rise." However, as our illustration demonstrates, increased reliance on fixed costs increases a company's risk.

SERVICE COMPANY INSIGHT Burlington Northern Railroad

Michele Wassell/Age Fotostock America, Inc.

There Is Something About a Train

A few years ago, Warren Buffett, arguably the most successful investor in history, bought a new train set—for $44 billion. The sage from Omaha bought Burlington Northern Railroad for a price that exceeded its fair value by 31%. At a time when the rest of the investing public was obsessed with technology companies like Facebook and Twitter, what could Buffett possibly see in a railroad? What he sees is a business whose costs are between 50–60% fixed.

With such high fixed costs, railways have huge operating leverage. And because he bought the railroad at the bottom of a recession, when the economy turns around, Burlington could take off as well. Add to that the fact that railroad transport is very energy-efficient, and it has high barriers to entry. So, as energy prices increase, more people will turn to the rails, but there are a limited number of railways. Makes sense to me.

Source: Liam Denning, "Buffett's Unusual Train of Thought," *Wall Street Journal* (November 4, 2009).

Why did Warren Buffett think that this was a good time to invest in railroad stocks? (Go to WileyPLUS for this answer and additional questions.)

DO IT! 4 Operating Leverage

Rexfield Corp., a company specializing in crime scene investigations, is contemplating an investment in automated mass-spectrometers. Its current process relies on a high number of lab technicians. The new equipment would employ a computerized expert system. The company's CEO has requested a comparison of the old technology versus the new technology. The accounting department has prepared the following CVP income statements for use in your analysis.

	CSI Equipment	
	Old	**New**
Sales	$2,000,000	$2,000,000
Variable costs	1,400,000	600,000
Contribution margin	600,000	1,400,000
Fixed costs	400,000	1,200,000
Net income	$ 200,000	$ 200,000

Use the information provided above to do the following.

(a) Compute the degree of operating leverage for the company under each scenario.

(b) Discuss your results.

Action Plan

✔ Divide contribution margin by net income to determine degree of operating leverage.

✔ A higher degree of operating leverage will result in a higher change in net income with a given change in sales.

SOLUTION

(a)

	Contribution Margin	÷	Net Income	=	Degree of Operating Leverage
Old	$600,000	÷	$200,000	=	3
New	$1,400,000	÷	$200,000	=	7

(b) The degree of operating leverage measures the company's sensitivity to changes in sales. By switching to a cost structure dominated by fixed costs, the company would significantly increase its operating leverage. As a result, with a percentage change in sales, its percentage change in net income would be 2.33 (7 ÷ 3) times as much with the new technology as it would under the old.

Related exercise material: **BE19-13, BE19-14, BE19-15, E19-14, E19-15, E19-16,** and **DO IT! 19-4.**

USING DECISION TOOLS—WHOLE FOODS MARKET

Whole Foods Market faces many decisions where it needs to apply the decision tools learned in this chapter, such as determining its cost structure. For example, suppose that Whole Foods Market has been approached by a robotics company with a proposal to significantly automate one of its stores. All stocking of shelves and bagging of groceries would be done by robots. Customers would check out through self-service scanners and point-of-sale terminals. Any assistance would be provided by robots. Management has compiled the following comparative data for one average-sized store.

	Old	New
Sales	$3,600,000	$3,600,000
Variable costs	2,800,000	2,000,000
Contribution margin	800,000	1,600,000
Fixed costs	480,000	1,280,000
Net income	$ 320,000	$ 320,000

INSTRUCTIONS

Use the information provided above to do the following.

(a) Compute the degree of operating leverage for the company under each scenario, and discuss your results.

(b) Compute the break-even point in dollars and margin of safety ratio for the company under each scenario, and discuss your results.

SOLUTION

(a)

	Contribution Margin	÷	Net Income	=	Degree of Operating Leverage
Old	$800,000	÷	$320,000	=	2.5
New	$1,600,000	÷	$320,000	=	5.0

The degree of operating leverage measures the company's sensitivity to changes in sales. By switching to a cost structure with higher fixed costs, Whole Foods would significantly increase its operating leverage. As a result, with a percentage change in sales, its percentage change in net income would be 2 times as much (5 ÷ 2.5) under the new structure as it would under the old.

(b) To compute the break-even point in sales dollars, we first need to compute the contribution margin ratio under each scenario. Under the old structure, the contribution margin ratio would be .22 ($800,000 ÷ $3,600,000), and under the new it would be .44 ($1,600,000 ÷ $3,600,000).

	Fixed Costs	÷	Contribution Margin Ratio	=	Break-Even Point in Dollars
Old	$480,000	÷	.22	=	$2,181,818
New	$1,280,000	÷	.44	=	$2,909,090

Because Whole Foods' fixed costs would be substantially higher under the new cost structure, its break-even point would increase significantly, from $2,181,818 to $2,909,090. A higher break-even point is riskier because it means that the company must generate higher sales to be profitable.

The margin of safety ratio tells how far sales can fall before Whole Foods is operating at a loss.

	(Actual Sales	−	Break-Even Sales)	÷	Actual Sales	=	Margin of Safety Ratio
Old	($3,600,000	−	$2,181,818)	÷	$3,600,000	=	.39
New	($3,600,000	−	$2,909,090)	÷	$3,600,000	=	.19

Under the old structure, sales could fall by 39% before the company would be operating at a loss. Under the new structure, sales could fall by only 19%.

On the one hand, grocery store sales are more stable than most products. Sales are less inclined to fluctuate with changes in the economy. However, Whole Foods sells many organic and unique products that have higher selling prices. It may be that during a recession, its customers might choose to switch to lower cost (e.g., non-organic) substitutes at traditional, high-volume grocery stores. If Whole Foods' sales are subject to significant swings, then changes in its cost structure could significantly affect its risk profile.

LEARNING OBJECTIVE *5

APPENDIX 19A: Explain the differences between absorption costing and variable costing.

In the earlier chapters, we classified both variable and fixed manufacturing costs as product costs. In job order costing, for example, a job is assigned the costs of direct materials, direct labor, and **both** variable and fixed manufacturing overhead. This costing approach is referred to as **full** or **absorption costing**. It is so named because all manufacturing costs are charged to, or absorbed by, the product. Absorption costing is the approach used for external reporting under generally accepted accounting principles.

An alternative approach is to use **variable costing**. Under variable costing, only direct materials, direct labor, and variable manufacturing overhead costs are considered product costs. Companies recognize fixed manufacturing overhead costs as period costs (expenses) when incurred. The difference between absorption costing and variable costing is shown graphically as follows.

ILLUSTRATION 19A-1
Difference between absorption costing and variable costing

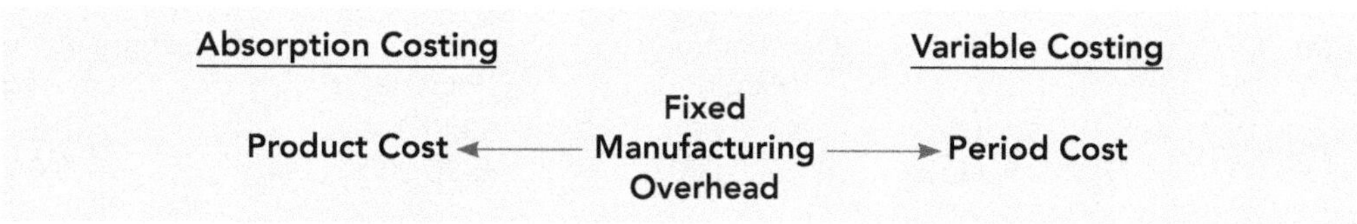

Under both absorption and variable costing, selling and administrative expenses are period costs.

Companies may not use variable costing for external financial reports because generally accepted accounting principles require that fixed manufacturing overhead be accounted for as a product cost.

EXAMPLE COMPARING ABSORPTION COSTING WITH VARIABLE COSTING

To illustrate absorption and variable costing, assume that Premium Products Corporation manufactures a polyurethane sealant, called Fix-It, for car windshields. Relevant data for Fix-It in January 2017, the first month of production, are shown in Illustration 19A-2.

ILLUSTRATION 19A-2
Sealant sales and cost data for Premium Products Corporation

Selling price	$20 per unit.
Units	Produced 30,000; sold 20,000; beginning inventory zero.
Variable unit costs	Manufacturing $9 (direct materials $5, direct labor $3, and variable overhead $1).
	Selling and administrative expenses $2.
Fixed costs	Manufacturing overhead $120,000.
	Selling and administrative expenses $15,000.

The per unit manufacturing cost under each costing approach is computed in Illustration 19A-3.

Type of Cost	Absorption Costing	Variable Costing
Direct materials	$ 5	$5
Direct labor	3	3
Variable manufacturing overhead	1	1
Fixed manufacturing overhead		
($120,000 ÷ 30,000 units produced)	4	0
Manufacturing cost per unit	$13	$9

ILLUSTRATION 19A-3
Computation of per unit manufacturing cost

The manufacturing cost per unit is $4 higher ($13 − $9) for absorption costing. This occurs because fixed manufacturing overhead costs are a product cost under absorption costing. Under variable costing, they are, instead, a period cost, and so they are expensed. Based on these data, each unit sold and each unit remaining in inventory is costed under absorption costing at $13 and under variable costing at $9.

Absorption Costing Example

Illustration 19A-4 shows the income statement for Premium Products using absorption costing. It shows that cost of goods manufactured is $390,000, computed by multiplying the 30,000 units produced times the manufacturing cost per unit of $13 (see Illustration 19A-3). Cost of goods sold is $260,000, after subtracting ending inventory of $130,000. Under absorption costing, $40,000 of the fixed overhead (10,000 units × $4) is deferred to a future period as part of the cost of ending inventory.

ILLUSTRATION 19A-4
Absorption costing income statement

PREMIUM PRODUCTS CORPORATION
Income Statement
For the Month Ended January 31, 2017
Absorption Costing

Sales (20,000 units × $20)		$400,000
Cost of goods sold		
Inventory, January 1	$ -0-	
Cost of goods manufactured (30,000 units × $13)	390,000	
Cost of goods available for sale	390,000	
Less: Inventory, January 31 (10,000 units × $13)	**130,000**	
Cost of goods sold (20,000 units × $13)		260,000
Gross profit		140,000
Variable selling and administrative expenses (20,000 × $2)	40,000	
Fixed selling and administrative expenses	15,000	55,000
Net income		**$ 85,000**

▼ **HELPFUL HINT**
The income statement format in Illustration 19A-4 is the same as that used under generally accepted accounting principles.

Variable Costing Example

As Illustration 19A-5 (page 942) shows, companies use the cost-volume-profit format in preparing a variable costing income statement. The variable manufacturing cost of $270,000 is computed by multiplying the 30,000 units produced times variable manufacturing cost of $9 per unit (see Illustration 19A-3). As in absorption costing, both variable and fixed selling and administrative expenses are treated as period costs.

ILLUSTRATION 19A-5
Variable costing income statement

▼ **HELPFUL HINT**
Note the difference in the computation of the ending inventory: $9 per unit here, $13 per unit in Illustration 19A-4.

PREMIUM PRODUCTS CORPORATION Income Statement For the Month Ended January 31, 2017 Variable Costing		
Sales (20,000 units × $20)		$400,000
Variable cost of goods sold		
Inventory, January 1	$ -0-	
Variable cost of goods manufactured (30,000 units × $9)	270,000	
Variable cost of goods available for sale	270,000	
Less: Inventory, January 31 (10,000 units × $9)	**90,000**	
Variable cost of goods sold	180,000	
Variable selling and administrative expenses (20,000 units × $2)	40,000	220,000
Contribution margin		180,000
Fixed manufacturing overhead	120,000	
Fixed selling and administrative expenses	15,000	135,000
Net income		**$ 45,000**

There is one primary difference between variable and absorption costing: Under variable costing, companies charge the fixed manufacturing overhead as an expense in the current period. Fixed manufacturing overhead costs of the current period, therefore, are not deferred to future periods through the ending inventory. As a result, absorption costing will show a **higher net income number** than variable costing **whenever units produced exceed units sold.** This difference can be seen in the income statements in Illustrations 19A-4 and 19A-5. There is a $40,000 difference in the ending inventories ($130,000 under absorption costing versus $90,000 under variable costing). Under absorption costing, $40,000 of the fixed overhead costs (10,000 units × $4) has been deferred to a future period as part of inventory. In contrast, under variable costing, all fixed manufacturing costs are expensed in the current period.

As shown, when units produced exceed units sold, income under absorption costing is *higher.* When units produced are less than units sold, income under absorption costing is *lower.* When units produced and sold are the same, net income will be *equal* under the two costing approaches. In this case, there is no increase in ending inventory. So fixed overhead costs of the current period are not deferred to future periods through the ending inventory.

NET INCOME EFFECTS

To further illustrate the concepts underlying absorption and variable costing, we will look at an extended example using Overbay Inc., a manufacturer of small airplane drones. We assume that production volume stays the same each year over the 3-year period, but the number of units sold varies each year.

2016 Results

As indicated in Illustration 19A-6, the variable manufacturing cost per drone is $240,000, and the fixed manufacturing overhead cost per drone is $60,000 (assuming 10 drones). Total manufacturing cost per drone under absorption costing is therefore $300,000 ($240,000 + $60,000). Overbay also has variable selling and administrative expenses of $5,000 per drone. The fixed selling and administrative expenses are $80,000.

ILLUSTRATION 19A-6
Information for Overbay Inc.

	2016	2017	2018
Volume information			
Drones in beginning inventory	0	0	2
Drones produced	10	10	10
Drones sold	10	8	12
Drones in ending inventory	0	2	0
Financial information			
Selling price per drone	$400,000		
Variable manufacturing cost per drone	$240,000		
Fixed manufacturing overhead for the year	$600,000		
Fixed manufacturing overhead per drone	$ 60,000 ($600,000 ÷ 10)		
Variable selling and administrative expenses per drone	$ 5,000		
Fixed selling and administrative expenses	$ 80,000		

An absorption costing income statement for 2016 for Overbay Inc. is shown in Illustration 19A-7.

ILLUSTRATION 19A-7
Absorption costing income statement—2016

OVERBAY INC.
Income Statement
For the Year Ended December 31, 2016
Absorption Costing

Sales (10 drones × $400,000)		$4,000,000
Cost of goods sold (10 drones × $300,000)		3,000,000
Gross profit		1,000,000
Variable selling and administrative expenses (10 drones × $5,000)	$50,000	
Fixed selling and administrative expenses	80,000	130,000
Net income		$ 870,000

Overbay reports net income of $870,000 under absorption costing.

Under a variable costing system, the income statement follows a cost-volume-profit (CVP) format. In this case, the manufacturing cost is comprised solely of the variable manufacturing costs of $240,000 per drone. The fixed manufacturing overhead costs of $600,000 for the year are expensed in 2016. As in absorption costing, the fixed and variable selling and administrative expenses are period costs expensed in 2016. A variable costing income statement for Overbay Inc. for 2016 is shown in Illustration 19A-8.

ILLUSTRATION 19A-8
Variable costing income statement—2016

OVERBAY INC.
Income Statement
For the Year Ended December 31, 2016
Variable Costing

Sales (10 drones × $400,000)		$4,000,000
Variable cost of goods sold (10 drones × $240,000)	$2,400,000	
Variable selling and administrative expenses (10 drones × $5,000)	50,000	2,450,000
Contribution margin		1,550,000
Fixed manufacturing overhead	600,000	
Fixed selling and administrative expenses	80,000	680,000
Net income		$ 870,000

As shown in Illustration 19A-8 (page 943), the variable costing net income of $870,000 is the same as the absorption costing net income computed in Illustration 19A-7 (page 943). **When the numbers of units produced and sold are the same, net income is equal under the two costing approaches.** Because no increase in ending inventory occurs, no fixed manufacturing overhead costs incurred in 2016 are deferred to future periods using absorption costing.

2017 Results

In 2017, Overbay produced 10 drones but sold only eight drones. As a result, there are two drones in ending inventory. The absorption costing income statement for 2017 is shown in Illustration 19A-9.

ILLUSTRATION 19A-9
Absorption costing income statement—2017

OVERBAY INC.
Income Statement
For the Year Ended December 31, 2017
Absorption Costing

Sales (8 drones × $400,000)		$3,200,000
Cost of goods sold (8 drones × $300,000)		2,400,000
Gross profit		800,000
Variable selling and administrative expenses (8 drones × $5,000)	$40,000	
Fixed selling and administrative expenses	80,000	120,000
Net income		$ 680,000

Under absorption costing, the ending inventory of two drones is $600,000 ($300,000 × 2). Each unit of ending inventory includes $60,000 of fixed manufacturing overhead. Therefore, fixed manufacturing overhead costs of $120,000 ($60,000 × 2 drones) are deferred until a future period.

The variable costing income statement for 2017 is shown in Illustration 19A-10.

ILLUSTRATION 19A-10
Variable costing income statement—2017

OVERBAY INC.
Income Statement
For the Year Ended December 31, 2017
Variable Costing

Sales (8 drones × $400,000)		$3,200,000
Variable cost of goods sold (8 drones × $240,000)	$1,920,000	
Variable selling and administrative expenses (8 drones × $5,000)	40,000	1,960,000
Contribution margin		1,240,000
Fixed manufacturing overhead	600,000	
Fixed selling and administrative expenses	80,000	680,000
Net income		$ 560,000

As shown, when units produced (10) exceeds units sold (8), net income under absorption costing ($680,000) is higher than net income under variable costing ($560,000). The reason: The cost of the ending inventory is higher under absorption costing than under variable costing. In 2017, under absorption costing, fixed manufacturing overhead of $120,000 is deferred and carried to future periods as part of inventory. Under variable costing, the $120,000 is expensed in the current period and, therefore the difference in the two net income numbers is $120,000 ($680,000 − $560,000).

2018 Results

In 2018, Overbay produced 10 drones and sold 12 (10 drones from the current year's production and 2 drones from the beginning inventory). As a result, there are no drones in ending inventory. The absorption costing income statement for 2018 is shown in Illustration 19A-11.

ILLUSTRATION 19A-11
Absorption costing income statement—2018

OVERBAY INC. Income Statement For the Year Ended December 31, 2018 Absorption Costing		
Sales (12 drones × $400,000)		$4,800,000
Cost of goods sold (12 drones × $300,000)		3,600,000
Gross profit		1,200,000
Variable selling and administrative expenses		
(12 drones × $5,000)	$60,000	
Fixed selling and administrative expenses	80,000	140,000
Net income		$1,060,000

Fixed manufacturing costs of $720,000 ($60,000 × 12 drones) are expensed as part of cost of goods sold in 2018. This $720,000 includes $120,000 of fixed manufacturing costs incurred during 2017 and included in beginning inventory, plus $600,000 of fixed manufacturing costs incurred during 2018. Given this result for the absorption costing statement, what would you now expect the result to be under variable costing? Let's take a look.

The variable costing income statement for 2018 is shown in Illustration 19A-12.

ILLUSTRATION 19A-12
Variable costing income statement—2018

OVERBAY INC. Income Statement For the Year Ended December 31, 2018 Variable Costing		
Sales (12 drones × $400,000)		$4,800,000
Variable cost of goods sold		
(12 drones × $240,000)	$2,880,000	
Variable selling and administrative expenses		
(12 drones × $5,000)	60,000	2,940,000
Contribution margin		1,860,000
Fixed manufacturing overhead	600,000	
Fixed selling and administrative expenses	80,000	680,000
Net income		$1,180,000

When drones produced (10) are less than drones sold (12), net income under absorption costing ($1,060,000) is less than net income under variable costing ($1,180,000). This difference of $120,000 ($1,180,000 − $1,060,000) results because $120,000 of fixed manufacturing overhead costs in beginning inventory are charged to 2018 under absorption costing. Under variable costing, there is no fixed manufacturing overhead cost in beginning inventory.

Illustration 19A-13 (page 946) summarizes the results of the three years.

ILLUSTRATION 19A-13
Comparison of net income under two costing approaches

	Net Income under Two Costing Approaches		
	2016	**2017**	**2018**
	Production = Sales	**Production > Sales**	**Production < Sales**
Absorption costing	$870,000	$ 680,000	$1,060,000
Variable costing	870,000	560,000	1,180,000
Difference	$ -0-	$120,000	$(120,000)

This relationship between production and sales and its effect on net income under the two costing approaches is shown graphically in Illustration 19A-14.

ILLUSTRATION 19A-14
Summary of income effects under absorption costing and variable costing

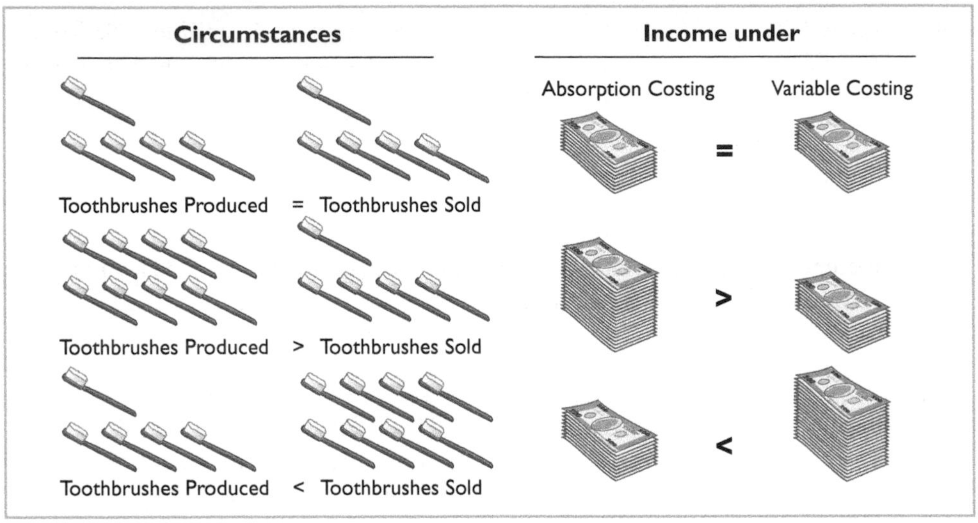

DECISION-MAKING CONCERNS

Generally accepted accounting principles require that absorption costing be used for the costing of inventory for external reporting purposes. Net income measured under GAAP (absorption costing) is often used internally to evaluate performance, justify cost reductions, or evaluate new projects. Some companies, however, have recognized that net income calculated using GAAP does not highlight differences between variable and fixed costs and may lead to poor business decisions. Consequently, these companies use variable costing for internal reporting purposes. The following discussion and example highlight a significant problem related to the use of absorption costing for decision-making purposes.

When production exceeds sales, absorption costing reports a higher net income than variable costing. The reason is that some fixed manufacturing costs are not expensed in the current period but are deferred to future periods as part of inventory. As a result, management may be tempted to overproduce in a given period in order to increase net income. Although net income will increase, this decision to overproduce may not be in the company's best interest.

Suppose, for example, a division manager's compensation is based upon the division's net income. In such a case, the manager may decide to meet the net income targets by increasing production. While this overproduction may increase the manager's compensation, the buildup of inventories in the long run will lead to additional costs to the company. Variable costing avoids this situation because net income under variable costing is unaffected by changes in production levels, as the following illustration shows.

Warren Lund, a division manager of Walker Enterprises, is under pressure to boost the performance of the Lighting Division in 2017. Unfortunately, recent profits have not met expectations. The expected sales for this year are 20,000 units. As he plans for the year, Warren has to decide whether to produce 20,000 or 30,000 units. The following facts are available for the division.

ILLUSTRATION 19A-15
Facts for Lighting Division—2017

Beginning inventory	0
Expected sales in units	20,000
Selling price per unit	$15
Variable manufacturing cost per unit	$6
Fixed manufacturing overhead cost (total)	$60,000
Fixed manufacturing overhead costs per unit	
Based on 20,000 units	$3 per unit ($60,000 ÷ 20,000 units)
Based on 30,000 units	$2 per unit ($60,000 ÷ 30,000 units)
Total manufacturing cost per unit	
Based on 20,000 units	$9 per unit ($6 variable + $3 fixed)
Based on 30,000 units	$8 per unit ($6 variable + $2 fixed)
Variable selling and administrative expenses per unit	$1
Fixed selling and administrative expenses	$15,000

Illustration 19A-16 presents the division's results based upon the two possible levels of output under absorption costing.

ILLUSTRATION 19A-16
Absorption costing income statement—2017

LIGHTING DIVISION
Income Statement
For the Year Ended December 31, 2017
Absorption Costing

	20,000 Produced	30,000 Produced
Sales (20,000 units × $15)	$300,000	$ 300,000
Cost of goods sold	180,000*	160,000**
Gross profit	120,000	140,000
Variable selling and administrative expenses (20,000 units × $1)	20,000	20,000
Fixed selling and administrative expenses	15,000	15,000
Net income	$ 85,000	$105,000

*20,000 units × $9
**20,000 units × $8

If the Lighting Division produces 20,000 units, its net income under absorption costing is $85,000. If it produces 30,000 units, its net income is $105,000. By producing 30,000 units, the division has inventory of 10,000 units. This excess inventory causes net income to increase $20,000 because $20,000 of fixed costs (10,000 units × $2) are not charged to the current year, but are deferred to future periods.

What do you think Warren Lund might do in this situation? Given his concern about the profit numbers of the Lighting Division, he may be tempted to increase production. Although this increased production will increase 2017 net income, it may be costly to the company in the long run.

Now let's evaluate the same situation under variable costing. Illustration 19A-17 (page 948) shows a variable costing income statement for production at both 20,000 and 30,000 units, using the information from Illustration 19A-15.

ILLUSTRATION 19A-17
Variable costing income statement—2017

LIGHTING DIVISION
Income Statement
For the Year Ended December 31, 2017
Variable Costing

	20,000 Produced	30,000 Produced
Sales (20,000 units × \$15)	\$300,000	\$300,000
Variable cost of goods sold (20,000 units × \$6)	120,000	120,000
Variable selling and administrative expenses (20,000 units × \$1)	20,000	20,000
Contribution margin	160,000	160,000
Fixed manufacturing overhead	60,000	60,000
Fixed selling and administrative expenses	15,000	15,000
Net income	\$ 85,000	\$ 85,000

From this example, we see that under variable costing, net income is not affected by the number of units produced. Net income is \$85,000 whether the division produces 20,000 or 30,000 units. Why? Because fixed manufacturing overhead is treated as a period expense. Unlike absorption costing, no fixed manufacturing overhead is deferred through inventory buildup. Therefore, under variable costing, production does not increase income; sales do. As a result, if the company uses variable costing, managers like Warren Lund cannot affect profitability by increasing production.

POTENTIAL ADVANTAGES OF VARIABLE COSTING

Variable costing has a number of potential advantages relative to absorption costing:

1. Net income computed under variable costing is unaffected by changes in production levels. As a result, it is much easier to understand the impact of fixed and variable costs on the computation of net income when variable costing is used.
2. The use of variable costing is consistent with the cost-volume-profit material presented in Chapters 18 and 19.
3. Net income computed under variable costing is closely tied to changes in sales levels (not production levels) and therefore provides a more realistic assessment of the company's success or failure during a period.
4. The presentation of fixed and variable cost components on the face of the variable costing income statement makes it easier to identify these costs and understand their effect on the business. Under absorption costing, the allocation of fixed costs to inventory makes it difficult to evaluate the impact of fixed costs on the company's results.

Companies that use just-in-time processing techniques to minimize their inventories will not have significant differences between absorption and variable costing net income.

DO IT! ▶5 Variable Costing

Franklin Company produces and sells tennis balls. The following costs are available for the year ended December 31, 2017. The company has no beginning inventory. In 2017, 8,000,000 units were produced, but only 7,500,000 units were sold. The unit selling price was \$0.50 per ball. Costs and expenses were as follows.

Variable costs per unit	
Direct materials	$0.10
Direct labor	0.05
Variable manufacturing overhead	0.08
Variable selling and administrative expenses	0.02
Annual fixed costs and expenses	
Manufacturing overhead	$500,000
Selling and administrative expenses	100,000

(a) Compute the manufacturing cost of one unit of product using variable costing.

(b) Prepare a 2017 income statement for Franklin Company using variable costing.

SOLUTION

(a) The cost of one unit of product under variable costing would be:

Direct materials	$0.10
Direct labor	0.05
Variable manufacturing overhead	0.08
	$0.23

(b) The variable costing income statement would be as follows.

FRANKLIN COMPANY
Income Statement
For the Year Ended December 31, 2017
Variable Costing

Sales (7,500,000 × $0.50)		$3,750,000
Variable cost of goods sold (7,500,000 × $0.23)	$1,725,000	
Variable selling and administrative expenses (7,500,000 × .02)	150,000	1,875,000
Contribution margin		1,875,000
Fixed manufacturing overhead	500,000	
Fixed selling and administrative expenses	100,000	600,000
Net income		$1,275,000

Related exercise material: **BE19-16, BE19-17, BE19-18, BE19-19, E19-17, E19-18,** and **E19-19.**

Action Plan

✔ Recall that under variable costing, only variable manufacturing costs are treated as manufacturing (product) costs.

✔ Subtract all fixed costs, both manufacturing overhead and selling and administrative expenses, as period costs.

REVIEW AND PRACTICE

▶ LEARNING OBJECTIVES REVIEW

1 Apply basic CVP concepts. The CVP income statement classifies costs and expenses as variable or fixed and reports contribution margin in the body of the statement. Contribution margin is the amount of revenue remaining after deducting variable costs. It can be expressed as a per unit amount or as a ratio. The break-even point in units is fixed costs divided by unit contribution margin. The break-even point in dollars is fixed costs divided by the contribution margin ratio. These formulas can also be used to determine units or sales dollars needed to achieve target net income, simply by adding target net income to fixed costs before dividing by the contribution margin. Margin of safety indicates how much sales can decline before the company is operating at a loss. It can be expressed in dollar terms or as a percentage.

2 Explain the term sales mix and its effects on break-even sales. Sales mix is the relative proportion in which each product is sold when a company sells more than one product. For a company with a small number of products, break-even sales in units is determined by using the weighted-average unit contribution margin of all the products. If the company sells many different products, then calculating the break-even point using unit information is not practical. Instead, in a company with many products, break-even sales in dollars is calculated using the weighted-average contribution margin ratio.

3 Determine sales mix when a company has limited resources. When a company has limited resources, it is necessary to find the contribution margin per unit of limited resource. This amount is then multiplied by the units of limited resource to determine which product maximizes net income.

4 Indicate how operating leverage affects profitability. Operating leverage refers to the degree to which a company's net income reacts to a change in sales. Operating leverage is determined by a company's relative use of fixed versus variable costs. Companies with high fixed costs relative to variable costs have high operating leverage. A company with high operating leverage experiences a sharp increase (decrease) in net income with a given increase (decrease) in sales. The degree of operating leverage is measured by dividing contribution margin by net income.

***5 Explain the differences between absorption costing and variable costing.** Under absorption costing, fixed manufacturing costs are product costs. Under variable costing, fixed manufacturing costs are period costs.

If production volume exceeds sales volume, net income under absorption costing will exceed net income under variable costing by the amount of fixed manufacturing costs included in ending inventory that results from units produced but not sold during the period. If production volume is less than sales volume, net income under absorption costing will be less than under variable costing by the amount of fixed manufacturing costs included in the units sold during the period that were not produced during the period.

The use of variable costing is consistent with cost-volume-profit analysis. Net income under variable costing is unaffected by changes in production levels. Instead, it is closely tied to changes in sales. The presentation of fixed costs in the variable costing approach makes it easier to identify fixed costs and to evaluate their impact on the company's profitability.

DECISION TOOLS REVIEW

DECISION CHECKPOINTS	INFO NEEDED FOR DECISION	TOOL TO USE FOR DECISION	HOW TO EVALUATE RESULTS
How many units of product A and product B do we need to sell to break even?	Fixed costs, weighted-average unit contribution margin, sales mix	Break-even point in units = Fixed costs / Weighted-average unit contribution margin	To determine number of units of product A and B, allocate total break-even units based on sales mix.
How many dollars of sales are required from each division in order to break even?	Fixed costs, weighted-average contribution margin ratio, sales mix	Break-even point in dollars = Fixed costs / Weighted-average contribution margin ratio	To determine the sales dollars required from each division, allocate the total break-even sales using the sales mix.
How many units of product A and B should we produce in light of a limited resource?	Unit contribution margin, limited resource required per unit	Contribution margin per unit of limited resource = Unit contribution margin / Limited resource per unit	Any additional capacity of limited resource should be applied toward the product with higher contribution margin per unit of limited resource.
How sensitive is the company's net income to changes in sales?	Contribution margin and net income	Degree of operating leverage = Contribution margin / Net income	Reports the change in net income that occurs with a given change in sales. A high degree of operating leverage means that the company's net income is very sensitive to changes in sales.

GLOSSARY REVIEW

***Absorption costing** A costing approach in which all manufacturing costs are charged to the product. (p. 940).

Cost structure The relative proportion of fixed versus variable costs that a company incurs. (p. 935).

Degree of operating leverage A measure of the extent to which a company's net income reacts to a change in sales. It is calculated by dividing contribution margin by net income. (p. 937).

Operating leverage The extent to which a company's net income reacts to a change in sales. Operating leverage is determined by a company's relative use of fixed versus variable costs. (p. 937).

Sales mix The relative percentage in which a company sells its multiple products. (p. 929).

Theory of constraints A specific approach used to identify and manage constraints in order to achieve the company's goals. (p. 934).

***Variable costing** A costing approach in which only variable manufacturing costs are product costs, and fixed manufacturing costs are period costs (expenses). (p. 940).

PRACTICE MULTIPLE-CHOICE QUESTIONS

(LO 1) 1. Which one of the following is the format of a CVP income statement?
   (a) Sales − Variable costs = Fixed costs + Net income.
   (b) Sales − Fixed costs − Variable costs − Operating expenses = Net income.
   (c) Sales − Cost of goods sold − Operating expenses = Net income.
   (d) Sales − Variable costs − Fixed costs = Net income.

(LO 1) 2. Croc Catchers calculates its contribution margin to be less than zero. Which statement is **true**?
   (a) Its fixed costs are less than the variable costs per unit.
   (b) Its profits are greater than its total costs.
   (c) The company should sell more units.
   (d) Its selling price is less than its variable costs.

(LO 1) 3. Which one of the following describes the break-even point?
   (a) It is the point where total sales equal total variable plus total fixed costs.
   (b) It is the point where the contribution margin equals zero.
   (c) It is the point where total variable costs equal total fixed costs.
   (d) It is the point where total sales equal total fixed costs.

(LO 1) 4. The following information is available for Chap Company.

Sales	$350,000
Cost of goods sold	$120,000
Total fixed expenses	$60,000
Total variable expenses	$100,000

   Which amount would you find on Chap's CVP income statement?
   (a) Contribution margin of $250,000.
   (b) Contribution margin of $190,000.
   (c) Gross profit of $230,000.
   (d) Gross profit of $190,000.

(LO 1) 5. Gabriel Corporation has fixed costs of $180,000 and variable costs of $8.50 per unit. It has a target income of $268,000. How many units must it sell at $12 per unit to achieve its target net income?
   (a) 51,429 units. (c) 76,571 units.
   (b) 128,000 units. (d) 21,176 units.

(LO 1) 6. Mackey Corporation has fixed costs of $150,000 and variable costs of $9 per unit. If sales price per unit is $12, what is break-even sales in dollars?
   (a) $200,000. (c) $480,000.
   (b) $450,000. (d) $600,000.

(LO 2) 7. Sales mix is:
   (a) important to sales managers but not to accountants.
   (b) easier to analyze on absorption costing income statements.
   (c) a measure of the relative percentage of a company's variable costs to its fixed costs.
   (d) a measure of the relative percentage in which a company's products are sold.

8. Net income will be: (LO 2)
   (a) greater if more higher-contribution margin units are sold than lower-contribution margin units.
   (b) greater if more lower-contribution margin units are sold than higher-contribution margin units.
   (c) equal as long as total sales remain equal, regardless of which products are sold.
   (d) unaffected by changes in the mix of products sold.

9. If the unit contribution margin is $15 and it takes 3.0 machine hours to produce the unit, the contribution margin per unit of limited resource is: (LO 3)
   (a) $25. (c) $4.
   (b) $5. (d) None of the answer choices are correct.

10. MEM manufactures two products. Product X has a contribution margin of $26 and requires 4 hours of machine time. Product Y has a contribution margin of $14 and requires 2 hours of machine time. Assuming that machine time is limited to 3,000 hours, how should it allocate the machine time to maximize its income? (LO 3)
   (a) Use 1,500 hours to produce X and 1,500 hours to produce Y.
   (b) Use 2,250 hours to produce X and 750 hours to produce Y.
   (c) Use 3,000 hours to produce only X.
   (d) Use 3,000 hours to produce only Y.

11. When a company has a limited resource, it should apply additional capacity of that resource to providing more units of the product or service that has: (LO 3)
   (a) the highest contribution margin.
   (b) the highest selling price.
   (c) the highest gross profit.
   (d) the highest unit contribution margin of that limited resource.

12. The degree of operating leverage: (LO 4)
   (a) can be computed by dividing total contribution margin by net income.
   (b) provides a measure of the company's earnings volatility.
   (c) affects a company's break-even point.
   (d) All of the answer choices are correct.

13. A high degree of operating leverage: (LO 4)
   (a) indicates that a company has a larger percentage of variable costs relative to its fixed costs.
   (b) is computed by dividing fixed costs by contribution margin.
   (c) exposes a company to greater earnings volatility risk.
   (d) exposes a company to less earnings volatility risk.

(LO 4) **14.** Stevens Company has a degree of operating leverage of 3.5 at a sales level of $1,200,000 and net income of $200,000. If Stevens' sales fall by 10%, Stevens can be expected to experience a:
(a) decrease in net income of $70,000.
(b) decrease in contribution margin of $7,000.
(c) decrease in operating leverage of 35%.
(d) decrease in net income of $175,000.

(LO 5) ***15.** Fixed manufacturing overhead costs are recognized as:
(a) period costs under absorption costing.
(b) product costs under absorption costing.
(c) product costs under variable costing.
(d) part of ending inventory costs under both absorption and variable costing.

***16.** Net income computed under absorption costing will be: (LO 5)
(a) higher than net income computed under variable costing in all cases.
(b) equal to net income computed under variable costing in all cases.
(c) higher than net income computed under variable costing when units produced are greater than units sold.
(d) higher than net income computed under variable costing when units produced are less than units sold.

SOLUTIONS

1. **(d)** The format of a CVP income statement is Sales − Variable costs − Fixed costs = Net income. Therefore, choices (a), (b), and (c) are incorrect.
2. **(d)** If contribution margin is less than zero, selling price is less than variable costs. The other choices are incorrect because if contribution margin is less than zero (a) selling price, not fixed costs, is less than variable costs; (b) neither profits or total costs can be determined from the contribution margin amount; and (c) selling more units will only increase the negativity of the contribution margin.
3. **(a)** The break-even point is the point where total sales equal total variable costs plus total fixed costs. Choices (b), (c), and (d) are therefore incorrect.
4. **(a)** The CVP income statement would show Sales ($350,000) − Total variable expenses ($100,000) = Contribution margin ($250,000), not (b) contribution margin of $190,000. Choices (c) and (d) are incorrect because gross profit does not appear on a CVP income statement.
5. **(b)** Required sales in units to achieve net income = ($180,000 + $268,000)/($12 − $8.50) = 128,000 units, not (a) 51,429 units, (c) 76,571 units, or (d) 21,176 units.
6. **(d)** Fixed costs ($150,000) ÷ Contribution margin ratio ($3 ÷ $12) = $600,000, not (a) $200,000, (b) $450,000, or (c) $480,000.
7. **(d)** Sales mix is the relative percentage in which a company sells its multiple products. The other choices are incorrect because (a) sales mix is also important to accountants, and (b) absorption costing income statements are not needed. Choice (c) is an incorrect definition of sales mix.
8. **(a)** Net income will be greater if more higher-contribution margin units are sold than lower-contribution units. Choices (b), (c), and (d) are therefore incorrect statements.
9. **(b)** The contribution margin per unit of limited resource is Unit contribution margin ($15) ÷ Units of limited resource (3.0 machine hours) = $5, not (a) $25, (c) $4, or (d) none of the above.
10. **(d)** Unit contribution margin of Product X ($26 ÷ 4) < unit contribution margin of Product Y ($14 ÷ 2), so the machine time should be applied toward the product with the higher unit contribution margin. Choices (a), (b), and (c) are incorrect because these options will not maximize MEM's income.
11. **(d)** The company should apply additional capacity of the limited resource to providing more units of the product or service that has the highest unit contribution margin of that limited resource, not (a) the highest contribution margin, (b) the highest selling price, or (c) the highest gross profit.
12. **(d)** All of the above statements about operating leverage are true. So while choices (a), (b), and (c) are true statements, choice (d) is the better answer.
13. **(c)** A high degree of operating leverage exposes a company to greater earnings volatility risk. The other choices are incorrect because a high degree of operating leverage (a) means a company has higher fixed costs relative to variable costs, not vice versa; (b) is computed by dividing contribution margin by net income, not fixed costs by contribution margin; and (d) exposes a company to greater, not less, earnings volatility risk.
14. **(a)** Net income ($200,000) × Operating leverage (3.5) × **Decrease** in sales (10%) = decrease in net income of $70,000, not (b) decrease in contribution margin of $7,000, (c) decrease in operating leverage of 35%, or (d) decrease in net income of $175,000.

*15. **(b)** Under absorption costing, fixed manufacturing overhead costs and variable manufacturing overhead costs are both product costs. The other choices are incorrect because (a) fixed manufacturing overhead costs are recognized as product costs under absorption costing, not period costs; (c) under variable costing, fixed manufacturing costs are recognized as period costs; and (d) fixed manufacturing costs are part of ending inventory under absorption costing only.

*16. **(c)** Net income is higher under absorption costing than under variable costing when units produced exceed units sold, not (a) higher in all cases, (b) equal to net income under variable costing in all cases, or (d) higher when units produced are less than units sold.

PRACTICE EXERCISES

Compute break-even point in units for a company with more than one product.

(LO 2)

1. Yard-King manufactures lawnmowers, weed-trimmers, and chainsaws. Its sales mix and unit contribution margins are as follows.

	Sales Mix	Unit Contribution Margin
Lawnmowers	30%	$35
Weed-trimmers	50%	$25
Chainsaws	20%	$50

Yard-King has fixed costs of $4,620,000.

INSTRUCTIONS

Compute the number of units of each product that Yard-King must sell in order to break even under this product mix.

SOLUTION

1.

	Sales Mix Percentage	Unit Contribution Margin	Weighted-Average Contribution Margin
Lawnmowers	30%	$35	$10.50
Weed-trimmers	50	25	12.50
Chainsaws	20	50	10.00
			$33.00

Total break-even sales in units = $4,620,000 ÷ $33.00 = 140,000 units

	Sales Mix Percentage		Total Break-Even Sales		Sales Needed per Product
Lawnmowers	30%	×	140,000 units	=	42,000 units
Weed-trimmers	50	×	140,000	=	70,000
Chainsaws	20	×	140,000	=	28,000
Total units					140,000 units

Compute contribution margin and determine the product to be manufactured.

(LO 3)

2. Rene Company manufactures and sells three products. Relevant per unit data concerning each product are given below.

	Product A	Product B	Product C
Selling price	$12	$13	$15
Variable costs and expenses	$ 4	$ 8	$ 9
Machine hours to produce	2	1	2

INSTRUCTIONS

(a) Compute the contribution margin per unit of limited resource (machine hours) for each product.

(b) Assuming 4,500 additional machine hours are available, which product should be manufactured?

(c) Prepare an analysis showing the total contribution margin if the additional hours are (1) divided equally among the products, and (2) allocated entirely to the product identified in (b) above.

SOLUTION

2. (a)

	Product A	Product B	Product C
Unit contribution margin (a)	$8	$5	$6
Machine hours required (b)	2	1	2
Contribution margin per unit of limited resource (a) ÷ (b)	$4	$5	$3

(b) Product B should be manufactured because it results in the highest contribution margin per machine hour.

(c) (1)

	Product A	Product B	Product C
Machine hours (a) (4,500 ÷ 3)	1,500	1,500	1,500
Contribution margin per unit of limited resource (b)	$ 4	$ 5	$ 3
Total contribution margin [(a) × (b)]	$6,000	$7,500	$4,500

The total contribution margin is $18,000 ($6,000 + $7,500 + $4,500)

(2)

	Product B
Machine hours (a)	4,500
Contribution margin per unit of limited resource (b)	$ 5
Total contribution margin [(a) × (b)]	$22,500

Compute degree of operating leverage and evaluate impact of alternative cost structures on net income.

(LO 4)

3. The CVP income statements shown below are available for Vericelli Company and Boone Company.

	Vericelli Co.	Boone Co.
Sales revenue	$600,000	$600,000
Variable costs	320,000	120,000
Contribution margin	280,000	480,000
Fixed costs	180,000	380,000
Net income	$100,000	$100,000

INSTRUCTIONS

(a) Compute the degree of operating leverage for each company and interpret your results.

(b) Assuming that sales revenue increases by 10%, prepare a variable costing income statement for each company.

(c) Discuss how the cost structure of these two companies affects their operating leverage and profitability.

SOLUTION

3. (a)

	Contribution Margin	÷	Net Income	=	Degree of Operating Leverage
Vericelli	$280,000	÷	$100,000	=	2.8
Boone	480,000	÷	100,000	=	4.8

Boone has a higher degree of operating leverage. Its earnings would increase (decrease) by a greater amount than Vericelli if each experienced an equal increase (decrease) in sales.

(b)

	Vericelli Co.	Boone Co.
Sales revenue	$660,000*	$660,000
Variable costs	352,000**	132,000***
Contribution margin	308,000	528,000
Fixed costs	180,000	380,000
Net income	$128,000	$148,000

*$600,000 × 1.1 **$320,000 × 1.1 ***$120,000 × 1.1

(c) Each company experienced a $60,000 increase in sales. However, because of Boone's higher operating leverage, it experienced a $48,000 ($148,000 − $100,000) increase in net income while Vericelli experienced only a $28,000 ($128,000 − $100,000) increase. This is what we would have expected since Boone's degree of operating leverage exceeds that of Vericelli.

PRACTICE PROBLEM

Determine sales mix with limited resources.

(LO 3)

Francis Corporation manufactures and sells three different types of water-sport wakeboards. The boards vary in terms of their quality specifications—primarily with respect to their smoothness and finish. They are referred to as Smooth, Extra-Smooth, and Super-Smooth boards. Machine time is limited. More machine time is required to manufacture the Extra-Smooth and Super-Smooth boards. Additional information is provided below.

	Product		
	Smooth	**Extra-Smooth**	**Super-Smooth**
Selling price	$60	$100	$160
Variable costs and expenses	50	75	130
Contribution margin	$10	$ 25	$ 30
Machine hours required	0.25	0.40	0.60
Total fixed costs: $234,000			

INSTRUCTIONS

Answer each of the following questions.

(a) Ignoring the machine time constraint, what strategy would appear optimal?

(b) What is the contribution margin per unit of limited resource for each type of board?

(c) If additional machine time could be obtained, how should the additional capacity be used?

SOLUTION

(a) The Super-Smooth boards have the highest unit contribution margin. Thus, ignoring any manufacturing constraints, it would appear that the company should shift toward production of more Super-Smooth units.

(b) The contribution margin per unit of limited resource is calculated as follows.

	Smooth	Extra-Smooth	Super-Smooth
$\frac{\text{Unit contribution margin}}{\text{Limited resource consumed per unit}}$	$\frac{\$10}{.25} = \$40$	$\frac{\$25}{.40} = \$62.50$	$\frac{\$30}{.60} = \$50$

(c) The Extra-Smooth boards have the highest contribution margin per unit of limited resource. Given the resource constraint, any additional capacity should be used to make Extra-Smooth boards.

WileyPLUS Brief Exercises, DO IT! Exercises, Exercises, Problems, and many additional resources are available for practice in WileyPLUS.

NOTE: All asterisked Questions, Exercises, and Problems relate to material in the appendix to the chapter.

QUESTIONS

1. What is meant by CVP analysis?
2. Provide three examples of management decisions that benefit from CVP analysis.
3. Distinguish between a traditional income statement and a CVP income statement.
4. Describe the features of a CVP income statement that make it more useful for management decision-making than the traditional income statement that is prepared for external users.
5. The traditional income statement for Wheat Company shows sales $900,000, cost of goods sold $500,000, and operating expenses $200,000. Assuming all costs and expenses are 75% variable and 25% fixed, prepare a CVP income statement through contribution margin.
6. If management chooses to reduce its selling price to match that of a competitor, how will the break-even point be affected?

7. What is meant by the term sales mix? How does sales mix affect the calculation of the break-even point?
8. Performance Company sells two types of performance tires. The lower-priced model is guaranteed for only 50,000 miles; the higher-priced model is guaranteed for 150,000 miles. The unit contribution margin on the higher-priced tire is twice as high as that of the lower-priced tire. If the sales mix shifts so that the company begins to sell more units of the lower-priced tire, explain how the company's break-even point in units will change.
9. What approach should be used to calculate the break-even point of a company that has many products?
10. How is the contribution margin per unit of limited resource computed?
11. What is the theory of constraints? Provide some examples of possible constraints for a manufacturer.
12. What is meant by "cost structure?" Explain how a company's cost structure affects its break-even point.
13. What is operating leverage? How does a company increase its operating leverage?
14. How does the replacement of manual labor with automated equipment affect a company's cost structure? What implications does this have for its operating leverage and break-even point?
15. What is a measure of operating leverage, and how is it calculated?
16. Pine Company has a degree of operating leverage of 8. Fir Company has a degree of operating leverage of 4. Interpret these measures.

*17. Distinguish between absorption costing and variable costing.

*18. (a) What is the major rationale for the use of variable costing?
(b) Discuss why variable costing may not be used for financial reporting purposes.

*19. Doc Rowan Corporation sells one product, its waterproof hiking boot. It began operations in the current year and had an ending inventory of 8,500 units. The company sold 20,000 units throughout the year. Fixed manufacturing overhead is $5 per unit, and total manufacturing cost per unit is $20 (including fixed manufacturing overhead costs). What is the difference in net income between absorption and variable costing?

*20. If production equals sales, what, if any, is the difference between net income under absorption costing versus under variable costing?

*21. If production is greater than sales, how does absorption costing net income differ from variable costing net income?

*22. In the long run, will net income be higher or lower under variable costing compared to absorption costing?

BRIEF EXERCISES

Determine missing amounts for contribution margin.
(LO 1), AN

BE19-1 Determine the missing amounts.

	Unit Selling Price	Unit Variable Costs	Unit Contribution Margin	Contribution Margin Ratio
1.	$250	$180	(a)	(b)
2.	$500	(c)	$200	(d)
3.	(e)	(f)	$330	30%

Prepare CVP income statement.
(LO 1), AP

BE19-2 Hamby Inc. has sales of $2,000,000 for the first quarter of 2017. In making the sales, the company incurred the following costs and expenses.

	Variable	Fixed
Cost of goods sold	$760,000	$600,000
Selling expenses	95,000	60,000
Administrative expenses	79,000	66,000

Prepare a CVP income statement for the quarter ended March 31, 2017.

Compute the break-even point.
(LO 1), AP

BE19-3 Eastland Corp. had total variable costs of $150,000, total fixed costs of $120,000, and total revenues of $250,000. Compute the required sales in dollars to break even.

Compute the break-even point.
(LO 1), AP

BE19-4 Dilts Company has a unit selling price of $400, variable costs per unit of $250, and fixed costs of $210,000. Compute the break-even point in units using (a) the mathematical equation and (b) unit contribution margin.

Compute sales for target net income.
(LO 1), AP

BE19-5 For Rivera Company, variable costs are 70% of sales, and fixed costs are $210,000. Management's net income goal is $60,000. Compute the required sales needed to achieve management's target net income of $60,000. (Use the mathematical equation approach.)

BE19-6 For Kosko Company, actual sales are $1,200,000 and break-even sales are $960,000. Compute (a) the margin of safety in dollars and (b) the margin of safety ratio.

Compute the margin of safety and the margin of safety ratio.

(LO 1), AP

BE19-7 NoFly Corporation sells three different models of a mosquito "zapper." Model A12 sells for $50 and has variable costs of $35. Model B22 sells for $100 and has variable costs of $70. Model C124 sells for $400 and has variable costs of $300. The sales mix of the three models is A12, 60%; B22, 15%; and C124, 25%. What is the weighted-average unit contribution margin?

Compute weighted-average unit contribution margin based on sales mix.

(LO 2), AP

BE19-8 Information for NoFly Corporation is given in BE19-7. If the company has fixed costs of $269,500, how many units of each model must the company sell in order to break even?

Compute break-even point in units for company with multiple products.

(LO 2), AP

BE19-9 Dixie Candle Supply makes candles. The sales mix (as a percentage of total dollar sales) of its three product lines is birthday candles 30%, standard tapered candles 50%, and large scented candles 20%. The contribution margin ratio of each candle type is shown below.

Compute break-even point in dollars for company with multiple product lines.

(LO 2), AP

Candle Type	Contribution Margin Ratio
Birthday	20%
Standard tapered	30%
Large scented	45%

(a) What is the weighted-average contribution margin ratio?
(b) If the company's fixed costs are $450,000 per year, what is the dollar amount of each type of candle that must be sold to break even?

BE19-10 Faune Furniture Co. consists of two divisions, Bedroom Division and Dining Room Division. The results of operations for the most recent quarter are:

Determine weighted-average contribution margin.

(LO 2), AP

	Bedroom Division	Dining Room Division	Total
Sales	$500,000	$750,000	$1,250,000
Variable costs	225,000	450,000	675,000
Contribution margin	$275,000	$300,000	$ 575,000

(a) Determine the company's sales mix.
(b) Determine the company's weighted-average contribution margin ratio.

BE19-11 In Marshall Company, data concerning two products are unit contribution margin—Product A $10, Product B $12; machine hours required for one unit—Product A 2, Product B 3. Compute the contribution margin per unit of limited resource for each product.

Show allocation of limited resources.

(LO 3), AP

BE19-12 Sage Corporation manufactures two products with the following characteristics.

Show allocation of limited resources.

(LO 3), AP

	Unit Contribution Margin	Machine Hours Required for Production
Product 1	$42	.15 hours
Product 2	$32	.10 hours

If Sage's machine hours are limited to 2,000 per month, determine which product it should produce.

BE19-13 Sam's Shingle Corporation is considering the purchase of a new automated shingle-cutting machine. The new machine will reduce variable labor costs but will increase depreciation expense. Contribution margin is expected to increase from $200,000 to $240,000. Net income is expected to be the same at $40,000. Compute the degree of operating leverage before and after the purchase of the new equipment. Interpret your results.

Compute degree of operating leverage.

(LO 4), AP

Compute break-even point with change in operating leverage.

(LO 4), AP

BE19-14 Presented below are variable costing income statements for Diggs Company and Doggs Company. They are in the same industry, with the same net incomes, but different cost structures.

	Diggs Co.	Doggs Co.
Sales	$200,000	$200,000
Variable costs	80,000	50,000
Contribution margin	120,000	150,000
Fixed costs	75,000	105,000
Net income	$ 45,000	$ 45,000

Compute the break-even point in dollars for each company and comment on your findings.

Determine contribution margin from degree of operating leverage.

(LO 4), AP

BE19-15 The degree of operating leverage for Montana Corp. and APK Co. are 1.6 and 5.4, respectively. Both have net incomes of $50,000. Determine their respective contribution margins.

Compute product costs under variable costing.

(LO 5), AP

***BE19-16** The Rock Company produces basketballs. It incurred the following costs during the year.

Direct materials	$14,400
Direct labor	$25,600
Fixed manufacturing overhead	$12,000
Variable manufacturing overhead	$29,400
Selling costs	$21,000

What are the total product costs for the company under variable costing?

Compute product costs under absorption costing.

(LO 5), AP

***BE19-17** Information concerning The Rock Company is provided in BE19-16. What are the total product costs for the company under absorption costing?

Determine manufacturing cost per unit under absorption and variable costing.

(LO 5), AP

***BE19-18** Burns Company incurred the following costs during the year: direct materials $20 per unit; direct labor $14 per unit; variable manufacturing overhead $15 per unit; variable selling and administrative costs $8 per unit; fixed manufacturing overhead $128,000; and fixed selling and administrative costs $10,000. Burns produced 8,000 units and sold 6,000 units. Determine the manufacturing cost per unit under (a) absorption costing and (b) variable costing.

Compute net income under absorption and variable costing.

(LO 5), AP

***BE19-19** Harris Company's fixed overhead costs are $4 per unit, and its variable overhead costs are $8 per unit. In the first month of operations, 50,000 units are produced, and 46,000 units are sold. Write a short memo to the chief financial officer explaining which costing approach will produce the higher income and what the difference will be.

DO IT! EXERCISES

Compute the break-even point and margin of safety under different alternatives.

(LO 1), AP

DO IT! 19-1 Victoria Company reports the following operating results for the month of April.

VICTORIA COMPANY
CVP Income Statement
For the Month Ended April 30, 2017

	Total	Per Unit
Sales (9,000 units)	$450,000	$50
Variable costs	270,000	30
Contribution margin	180,000	$20
Fixed expenses	150,000	
Net income	$ 30,000	

Management is considering the following course of action to increase net income: Reduce the selling price by 4%, with no changes to unit variable costs or fixed costs. Management is confident that this change will increase unit sales by 20%.

Using the contribution margin technique, compute the break-even point in units and dollars and margin of safety in dollars:

(a) Assuming no changes to selling price or costs, and
(b) Assuming changes to sales price and volume as described above.

Comment on your findings.

Compute sales mix, weighted-average contribution margin, and break-even point.

(LO 2), AP

DO IT! 19-2 Snow Cap Springs produces and sells water filtration systems for homeowners. Information regarding its three models is shown below.

	Basic	Basic Plus	Premium	Total
Units sold	750	450	300	1,500
Selling price	$250	$400	$800	
Variable costs	$195	$285	$415	

The company's total fixed costs to produce the filtration systems are $180,700.

(a) Determine the sales mix as a function of units sold for the three products.
(b) Determine the weighted-average unit contribution margin.
(c) Determine the total number of units that the company must produce to break even.
(d) Determine the number of units of each model that the company must produce to break even.

Determine sales mix with limited resources.

(LO 3), AP

DO IT! 19-3 Zoom Corporation manufactures and sells three different types of binoculars. They are referred to as Good, Better, and Best binoculars. Grinding and polishing time is limited. More time is required to grind and polish the lenses used in the Better and Best binoculars. Additional information is provided below.

	Product		
	Good	Better	Best
Selling price	$90.00	$330.00	$900.00
Variable costs and expenses	50.00	180.00	480.00
Contribution margin	$40.00	$150.00	$420.00
Grinding and polishing time required	0.5 hrs	1.5 hrs	6 hrs

(a) Ignoring the time constraint, what strategy would appear to be optimal?
(b) What is the contribution margin per unit of limited resource for each type of binocular?
(c) If additional grinding and polishing time could be obtained, how should the additional capacity be used?

Determine operating leverage.

(LO 4), AP

DO IT! 19-4 Bergen Hospital is contemplating an investment in an automated surgical system. Its current process relies on the a number of skilled physicians. The new equipment would employ a computer robotic system operated by a technician. The company requested an analysis of the old technology versus the new technology. The accounting department has prepared the following CVP income statements for use in your analysis.

	Old	New
Sales	$3,000,000	$3,000,000
Variable costs	1,600,000	700,000
Contribution margin	1,400,000	2,300,000
Fixed costs	1,000,000	1,900,000
Net income	$ 400,000	$ 400,000

(a) Compute the degree of operating leverage for the company under each scenario.
(b) Discuss your results.

EXERCISES

Compute break-even point and margin of safety.

(LO 1), AP

E19-1 The Soma Inn is trying to determine its break-even point. The inn has 75 rooms that are rented at $60 a night. Operating costs are as follows.

Salaries	$10,600 per month
Utilities	2,400 per month
Depreciation	1,500 per month
Maintenance	800 per month
Maid service	8 per room
Other costs	34 per room

Instructions

(a) Determine the inn's break-even point in (1) number of rented rooms per month and (2) dollars.

(b) If the inn plans on renting an average of 50 rooms per day (assuming a 30-day month), what is (1) the monthly margin of safety in dollars and (2) the margin of safety ratio?

Compute contribution margin, break-even point, and margin of safety.

(LO 1), AP

E19-2 In the month of June, Jose Hebert's Beauty Salon gave 4,000 haircuts, shampoos, and permanents at an average price of $30. During the month, fixed costs were $16,800 and variable costs were 75% of sales.

Instructions

(a) Determine the contribution margin in dollars, per unit and as a ratio.

(b) Using the contribution margin technique, compute the break-even point in dollars and in units.

(c) Compute the margin of safety in dollars and as a ratio.

Compute net income under different alternatives.

(LO 1), AP

E19-3 Barnes Company reports the following operating results for the month of August: sales $325,000 (units 5,000); variable costs $210,000; and fixed costs $75,000. Management is considering the following independent courses of action to increase net income.

1. Increase selling price by 10% with no change in total variable costs or sales volume.
2. Reduce variable costs to 58% of sales.
3. Reduce fixed costs by $15,000.

Instructions

Compute the net income to be earned under each alternative. Which course of action will produce the highest net income?

Compute break-even point and prepare CVP income statement.

(LO 1), AP

E19-4 Comfi Airways, Inc., a small two-plane passenger airline, has asked for your assistance in some basic analysis of its operations. Both planes seat 10 passengers each, and they fly commuters from Comfi's base airport to the major city in the state, Metropolis. Each month, 40 round-trip flights are made. Shown below is a recent month's activity in the form of a cost-volume-profit income statement.

Fare revenues (400 passenger flights)		$48,000
Variable costs		
Fuel	$14,000	
Snacks and drinks	800	
Landing fees	2,000	
Supplies and forms	1,200	18,000
Contribution margin		30,000
Fixed costs		
Depreciation	3,000	
Salaries	15,000	
Advertising	500	
Airport hangar fees	1,750	20,250
Net income		$ 9,750

Instructions

(a) Calculate the break-even point in (1) dollars and (2) number of passenger flights.
(b) Without calculations, determine the contribution margin at the break-even point.
(c) If ticket prices were decreased by 10%, passenger flights would increase by 25%. However, total variable costs would increase by the same percentage as passenger flights. Should the ticket price decrease be adopted?

Prepare a CVP income statement before and after changes in business environment.

(LO 1), AP

E19-5 Carey Company had sales in 2016 of $1,560,000 on 60,000 units. Variable costs totaled $900,000, and fixed costs totaled $500,000.

A new raw material is available that will decrease the variable costs per unit by 20% (or $3). However, to process the new raw material, fixed operating costs will increase by $100,000. Management feels that one-half of the decline in the variable costs per unit should be passed on to customers in the form of a sales price reduction. The marketing department expects that this sales price reduction will result in a 5% increase in the number of units sold.

Instructions

Prepare a projected CVP income statement for 2017 (a) assuming the changes have not been made, and (b) assuming that changes are made as described.

Compute break-even point in units for a company with more than one product.

(LO 2), AP

E19-6 Yard Tools manufactures lawnmowers, weed-trimmers, and chainsaws. Its sales mix and unit contribution margin are as follows.

	Sales Mix	Unit Contribution Margin
Lawnmowers	20%	$30
Weed-trimmers	50%	$20
Chainsaws	30%	$40

Yard Tools has fixed costs of $4,200,000.

Instructions

Compute the number of units of each product that Yard Tools must sell in order to break even under this product mix.

Compute service line break-even point and target net income in dollars for a company with more than one service.

(LO 2), AN

E19-7 PDQ Repairs has 200 auto-maintenance service outlets nationwide. It performs primarily two lines of service: oil changes and brake repair. Oil change–related services represent 70% of its sales and provide a contribution margin ratio of 20%. Brake repair represents 30% of its sales and provides a 40% contribution margin ratio. The company's fixed costs are $15,600,000 (that is, $78,000 per service outlet).

Instructions

(a) Calculate the dollar amount of each type of service that the company must provide in order to break even.
(b) The company has a desired net income of $52,000 per service outlet. What is the dollar amount of each type of service that must be performed by each service outlet to meet its target net income per outlet?

Compute break-even point in dollars for a company with more than one service.

(LO 2), AN

E19-8 Express Delivery is a rapidly growing delivery service. Last year, 80% of its revenue came from the delivery of mailing "pouches" and small, standardized delivery boxes (which provides a 20% contribution margin). The other 20% of its revenue came from delivering non-standardized boxes (which provides a 70% contribution margin). With the rapid growth of Internet retail sales, Express believes that there are great opportunities for growth in the delivery of non-standardized boxes. The company has fixed costs of $12,000,000.

Instructions

(a) What is the company's break-even point in total sales dollars? At the break-even point, how much of the company's sales are provided by each type of service?
(b) The company's management would like to hold its fixed costs constant but shift its sales mix so that 60% of its revenue comes from the delivery of non-standardized boxes and the remainder from pouches and small boxes. If this were to occur, what would be the company's break-even sales, and what amount of sales would be provided by each service type?

Compute break-even point in units for a company with multiple products.

(LO 2), AP

E19-9 Tiger Golf Accessories sells golf shoes, gloves, and a laser-guided range-finder that measures distance. Shown below are unit cost and sales data.

	Pairs of Shoes	Pairs of Gloves	Range-Finder
Unit sales price	$100	$30	$260
Unit variable costs	60	10	200
Unit contribution margin	$ 40	$20	$ 60
Sales mix	35%	55%	10%

Fixed costs are $620,000.

Instructions

(a) Compute the break-even point in units for the company.
(b) Determine the number of units to be sold at the break-even point for each product line.
(c) Verify that the mix of sales units determined in (b) will generate a zero net income.

Determine break-even point in dollars for two divisions.

(LO 2), AP

E19-10 Personal Electronix sells iPads and iPods. The business is divided into two divisions along product lines. CVP income statements for a recent quarter's activity are presented below.

	iPad Division	iPod Division	Total
Sales	$600,000	$400,000	$1,000,000
Variable costs	420,000	260,000	680,000
Contribution margin	$180,000	$140,000	320,000
Fixed costs			120,000
Net income			$ 200,000

Instructions

(a) Determine sales mix percentage and contribution margin ratio for each division.
(b) Calculate the company's weighted-average contribution margin ratio.
(c) Calculate the company's break-even point in dollars.
(d) Determine the sales level in dollars for each division at the break-even point.

Compute contribution margin and determine the product to be manufactured.

(LO 3), AN

E19-11 Mars Company manufactures and sells three products. Relevant per unit data concerning each product are given below.

	Product		
	A	B	C
Selling price	$9	$12	$15
Variable costs and expenses	$3	$10	$12
Machine hours to produce	2	1	2

Instructions

(a) Compute the contribution margin per unit of limited resource (machine hours) for each product.
(b) Assuming 3,000 additional machine hours are available, which product should be manufactured?
(c) Prepare an analysis showing the total contribution margin if the additional hours are (1) divided equally among the products, and (2) allocated entirely to the product identified in (b) above.

Compute contribution margin and determine the products to be manufactured.

(LO 3), AN

E19-12 Dalton Inc. produces and sells three products. Unit data concerning each product is shown below.

	Product		
	D	E	F
Selling price	$200	$300	$250
Direct labor costs	30	80	35
Other variable costs	95	80	145

The company has 2,000 hours of labor available to build inventory in anticipation of the company's peak season. Management is trying to decide which product should be produced. The direct labor hourly rate is $10.

Instructions

(a) Determine the number of direct labor hours per unit.
(b) Determine the contribution margin per direct labor hour.
(c) Determine which product should be produced and the total contribution margin for that product.

E19-13 Helena Company manufactures and sells two products. Relevant per unit data concerning each product follow.

Compute contribution margin and determine the products to be manufactured.

(LO 3), AN

	Product	
	Basic	**Deluxe**
Selling price	$40	$52
Variable costs	$22	$24
Machine hours	0.5	0.8

Instructions

(a) Compute the contribution margin per machine hour for each product.
(b) If 1,000 additional machine hours are available, which product should Helena manufacture?
(c) Prepare an analysis showing the total contribution margin if the additional hours are:
  (1) Divided equally between the products.
  (2) Allocated entirely to the product identified in part (b).

E19-14 The CVP income statements shown below are available for Armstrong Company and Contador Company.

Compute degree of operating leverage and evaluate impact of alternative cost structures on net income.

(LO 4), AN

	Armstrong Co.	Contador Co.
Sales	$500,000	$500,000
Variable costs	240,000	50,000
Contribution margin	260,000	450,000
Fixed costs	160,000	350,000
Net income	$100,000	$100,000

Instructions

(a) Compute the degree of operating leverage for each company and interpret your results.
(b) Assuming that sales revenue increases by 10%, prepare a variable costing income statement for each company.
(c) Discuss how the cost structure of these two companies affects their operating leverage and profitability.

E19-15 Casas Modernas of Juarez, Mexico, is contemplating a major change in its cost structure. Currently, all of its drafting work is performed by skilled draftsmen. Rafael Jiminez, Casas' owner, is considering replacing the draftsmen with a computerized drafting system. However, before making the change, Rafael would like to know the consequences of the change, since the volume of business varies significantly from year to year. Shown below are CVP income statements for each alternative.

Compute degree of operating leverage and evaluate impact of alternative cost structures on net income and margin of safety.

(LO 4), AN

	Manual System	Computerized System
Sales	$1,500,000	$1,500,000
Variable costs	1,200,000	600,000
Contribution margin	300,000	900,000
Fixed costs	100,000	700,000
Net income	$ 200,000	$ 200,000

Instructions

(a) Determine the degree of operating leverage for each alternative.
(b) Which alternative would produce the higher net income if sales increased by $150,000?
(c) Using the margin of safety ratio, determine which alternative could sustain the greater decline in sales before operating at a loss.

Compute degree of operating leverage and impact on net income of alternative cost structures.

(LO 4), AN

E19-16 An investment banker is analyzing two companies that specialize in the production and sale of candied yams. Traditional Yams uses a labor-intensive approach, and Auto-Yams uses a mechanized system. CVP income statements for the two companies are shown below.

	Traditional Yams	Auto-Yams
Sales	$400,000	$400,000
Variable costs	320,000	160,000
Contribution margin	80,000	240,000
Fixed costs	30,000	190,000
Net income	$ 50,000	$ 50,000

The investment banker is interested in acquiring one of these companies. However, she is concerned about the impact that each company's cost structure might have on its profitability.

Instructions

(a) Calculate each company's degree of operating leverage. Determine which company's cost structure makes it more sensitive to changes in sales volume.
(b) Determine the effect on each company's net income if sales decrease by 15% and if sales increase by 10%. Do not prepare income statements.
(c) Which company should the investment banker acquire? Discuss.

Compute product cost and prepare an income statement under variable and absorption costing.

(LO 5), AP

XLS

***E19-17** Siren Company builds custom fishing lures for sporting goods stores. In its first year of operations, 2017, the company incurred the following costs.

Variable Costs per Unit	
Direct materials	$7.50
Direct labor	$3.45
Variable manufacturing overhead	$5.80
Variable selling and administrative expenses	$3.90
Fixed Costs per Year	
Fixed manufacturing overhead	$225,000
Fixed selling and administrative expenses	$210,100

Siren Company sells the fishing lures for $25. During 2017, the company sold 80,000 lures and produced 90,000 lures.

Instructions

(a) Assuming the company uses variable costing, calculate Siren's manufacturing cost per unit for 2017.
(b) Prepare a variable costing income statement for 2017.
(c) Assuming the company uses absorption costing, calculate Siren's manufacturing cost per unit for 2017.
(d) Prepare an absorption costing income statement for 2017.

Determine ending inventory under variable costing and determine whether absorption or variable costing would result in higher net income.

(LO 5), AN

***E19-18** Langdon Company produced 9,000 units during the past year, but only 8,200 of the units were sold. The following additional information is also available.

Direct materials used	$79,000
Direct labor incurred	$30,000
Variable manufacturing overhead	$21,500
Fixed manufacturing overhead	$45,000
Fixed selling and administrative expenses	$70,000
Variable selling and administrative expenses	$10,000

There was no work in process inventory at the beginning and end of the year, nor did Langdon have any beginning finished goods inventory.

Instructions

(a) What would be Langdon Company's finished goods inventory cost on December 31 under variable costing?

(b) Which costing method, absorption or variable costing, would show a higher net income for the year? By what amount?

***E19-19** Crate Express Co. produces wooden crates used for shipping products by ocean liner. In 2017, Crate Express incurred the following costs.

Compute manufacturing cost under absorption and variable costing and explain difference.

(LO 5), AN

Wood used in crate production	$54,000
Nails (considered insignificant and a variable expense)	$ 350
Direct labor	$43,000
Utilities for the plant:	
$1,500 each month,	
plus $0.50 for each kilowatt-hour used each month	
Rent expense for the plant for the year	$21,400

Assume Crate Express used an average 500 kilowatt-hours each month over the past year.

Instructions

(a) What is Crate Express's total manufacturing cost if it uses a variable costing approach?

(b) What is Crate Express's total manufacturing cost if it uses an absorption costing approach?

(c) What accounts for the difference in manufacturing costs between these two costing approaches?

EXERCISES: SET B AND CHALLENGE EXERCISES

Visit the book's companion website, at **www.wiley.com/college/kimmel**, and choose the Student Companion site to access Exercises: Set B and Challenge Exercises.

PROBLEMS: SET A

P19-1A Midlands Inc. had a bad year in 2016. For the first time in its history, it operated at a loss. The company's income statement showed the following results from selling 80,000 units of product: net sales $2,000,000; total costs and expenses $2,235,000; and net loss $235,000. Costs and expenses consisted of the following.

Compute break-even point under alternative courses of action.

(LO 1), AN

	Total	Variable	Fixed
Cost of goods sold	$1,568,000	$1,050,000	$ 518,000
Selling expenses	517,000	92,000	425,000
Administrative expenses	150,000	58,000	92,000
	$2,235,000	$1,200,000	$1,035,000

Management is considering the following independent alternatives for 2017.

1. Increase unit selling price 25% with no change in costs and expenses.
2. Change the compensation of salespersons from fixed annual salaries totaling $200,000 to total salaries of $40,000 plus a 5% commission on net sales.
3. Purchase new high-tech factory machinery that will change the proportion between variable and fixed cost of goods sold to 50:50.

Instructions

(a) Compute the break-even point in dollars for 2017.

(b) Compute the break-even point in dollars under each of the alternative courses of action. (Round to the nearest dollar.) Which course of action do you recommend?

(b) (2) $2,500,000

Compute break-even point and margin of safety ratio, and prepare a CVP income statement before and after changes in business environment.

(LO 1), AN

P19-2A Lorge Corporation has collected the following information after its first year of sales. Sales were $1,500,000 on 100,000 units; selling expenses $250,000 (40% variable and 60% fixed); direct materials $511,000; direct labor $290,000; administrative expenses $270,000 (20% variable and 80% fixed); and manufacturing overhead $350,000 (70% variable and 30% fixed). Top management has asked you to do a CVP analysis so that it can make plans for the coming year. It has projected that unit sales will increase by 10% next year.

Instructions

(a) Compute (1) the contribution margin for the current year and the projected year, and (2) the fixed costs for the current year. (Assume that fixed costs will remain the same in the projected year.)

(b) 157,000 units

(b) Compute the break-even point in units and sales dollars for the first year.

(c) The company has a target net income of $200,000. What is the required sales in dollars for the company to meet its target?

(d) If the company meets its target net income number, by what percentage could its sales fall before it is operating at a loss? That is, what is its margin of safety ratio?

(e) (3) $1,735,714

(e) The company is considering a purchase of equipment that would reduce its direct labor costs by $104,000 and would change its manufacturing overhead costs to 30% variable and 70% fixed (assume total manufacturing overhead cost is $350,000, as above). It is also considering switching to a pure commission basis for its sales staff. This would change selling expenses to 90% variable and 10% fixed (assume total selling expense is $250,000, as above). Compute (1) the contribution margin and (2) the contribution margin ratio, and recompute (3) the break-even point in sales dollars. Comment on the effect each of management's proposed changes has on the break-even point.

Determine break-even sales under alternative sales strategies and evaluate results.

(LO 2), AN

P19-3A The Grand Inn is a restaurant in Flagstaff, Arizona. It specializes in southwestern style meals in a moderate price range. Paul Weld, the manager of Grand, has determined that during the last 2 years the sales mix and contribution margin ratio of its offerings are as follows.

	Percent of Total Sales	Contribution Margin Ratio
Appetizers	15%	50%
Main entrees	50%	25%
Desserts	10%	50%
Beverages	25%	80%

Paul is considering a variety of options to try to improve the profitability of the restaurant. His goal is to generate a target net income of $117,000. The company has fixed costs of $1,053,000 per year.

Instructions

(a) Total sales $2,600,000

(a) Calculate the total restaurant sales and the sales of each product line that would be necessary to achieve the desired target net income.

(b) Total sales $3,375,000

(b) Paul believes the restaurant could greatly improve its profitability by reducing the complexity and selling price of its entrees to increase the number of clients that it serves. It would then more heavily market its appetizers and beverages. He is proposing to reduce the contribution margin ratio on the main entrees to 10% by dropping the average selling price. He envisions an expansion of the restaurant that would increase fixed costs by $585,000. At the same time, he is proposing to change the sales mix to the following.

	Percent of Total Sales	Contribution Margin Ratio
Appetizers	25%	50%
Main entrees	25%	10%
Desserts	10%	50%
Beverages	40%	80%

Compute the total restaurant sales, and the sales of each product line that would be necessary to achieve the desired target net income.

(c) Suppose that Paul reduces the selling price on entrees and increases fixed costs as proposed in part (b), but customers are not swayed by the marketing efforts and the sales mix remains what it was in part (a). Compute the total restaurant sales and the sales of each product line that would be necessary to achieve the desired target net income. Comment on the potential risks and benefits of this strategy.

P19-4A Tanek Industries manufactures and sells three different models of wet-dry shop vacuum cleaners. Although the shop vacs vary in terms of quality and features, all are good sellers. Tanek is currently operating at full capacity with limited machine time.

Determine sales mix with limited resources.

(LO 3), AN

Sales and production information relevant to each model follows.

	Product		
	Economy	**Standard**	**Deluxe**
Selling price	$30	$50	$100
Variable costs and expenses	$16	$20	$46
Machine hours required	0.5	0.8	1.6

Instructions

(a) Ignoring the machine time constraint, which single product should Tanek Industries produce?

(b) What is the contribution margin per unit of limited resource for each product?

(c) If additional machine time could be obtained, how should the additional time be used?

(b) Economy $28

P19-5A The following CVP income statements are available for Blanc Company and Noir Company.

Compute degree of operating leverage and evaluate impact of operating leverage on financial results.

(LO 4), AN

	Blanc Company	**Noir Company**
Sales	$500,000	$500,000
Variable costs	280,000	180,000
Contribution margin	220,000	320,000
Fixed costs	170,000	270,000
Net income	$ 50,000	$ 50,000

Instructions

(a) Compute the break-even point in dollars and the margin of safety ratio (round to 3 places) for each company.

(b) Compute the degree of operating leverage for each company and interpret your results.

(c) Assuming that sales revenue increases by 20%, prepare a CVP income statement for each company.

(d) Assuming that sales revenue decreases by 20%, prepare a CVP income statement for each company.

(e) Discuss how the cost structure of these two companies affects their operating leverage and profitability.

(a) BE, Blanc $386,364
BE, Noir $421,875
(b) DOL, Blanc 4.4
DOL, Noir 6.4

P19-6A Bonita Beauty Corporation manufactures cosmetic products that are sold through a network of sales agents. The agents are paid a commission of 18% of sales. The income statement for the year ending December 31, 2017, is as follows.

Determine contribution margin, break-even point, target sales, and degree of operating leverage.

(LO 1, 4), AN

BONITA BEAUTY CORPORATION
Income Statement
For the Year Ended December 31, 2017

Sales		$75,000,000
Cost of goods sold		
Variable	$31,500,000	
Fixed	8,610,000	40,110,000
Gross margin		34,890,000
Selling and marketing expenses		
Commissions	13,500,000	
Fixed costs	10,260,000	23,760,000
Operating income		$11,130,000

The company is considering hiring its own sales staff to replace the network of agents. It will pay its salespeople a commission of 8% and incur additional fixed costs of $7.5 million.

(a) $47,175

(c) (2) 3.37

Instructions

(a) Under the current policy of using a network of sales agents, calculate the Bonita Beauty Corporation's break-even point in sales dollars for the year 2017.
(b) Calculate the company's break-even point in sales dollars for the year 2017 if it hires its own sales force to replace the network of agents.
(c) Calculate the degree of operating leverage at sales of $75 million if (1) Bonita Beauty uses sales agents, and (2) Bonita Beauty employs its own sales staff. Describe the advantages and disadvantages of each alternative.
(d) Calculate the estimated sales volume in sales dollars that would generate an identical net income for the year ending December 31, 2017, regardless of whether Bonita Beauty Corporation employs its own sales staff and pays them an 8% commission or continues to use the independent network of agents.

(CMA-Canada adapted)

Prepare income statements under absorption costing and variable costing for a company with beginning inventory, and reconcile differences.

(LO 5), AN

***P19-7A** Jackson Company produces plastic that is used for injection-molding applications such as gears for small motors. In 2016, the first year of operations, Jackson produced 4,000 tons of plastic and sold 3,500 tons. In 2017, the production and sales results were exactly reversed. In each year, the selling price per ton was $2,000, variable manufacturing costs were 15% of the sales price of units produced, variable selling expenses were 10% of the selling price of units sold, fixed manufacturing costs were $2,800,000, and fixed administrative expenses were $500,000.

(a) 2017 $2,700,000

(b) 2017 $2,350,000

Instructions

(a) Prepare income statements for each year using variable costing. (Use the format from Illustration 19A-5.)
(b) Prepare income statements for each year using absorption costing. (Use the format from Illustration 19A-4.)
(c) Reconcile the differences each year in net income under the two costing approaches.
(d) Comment on the effects of production and sales on net income under the two costing approaches.

Prepare absorption and variable costing income statements and reconcile differences between absorption and variable costing income statements when sales level and production level change. Discuss relative usefulness of absorption costing versus variable costing.

(LO 5), AN

***P19-8A** Dilithium Batteries is a division of Enterprise Corporation. The division manufactures and sells a long-life battery used in a wide variety of applications. During the coming year, it expects to sell 60,000 units for $30 per unit. Nyota Uthura is the division manager. She is considering producing either 60,000 or 90,000 units during the period. Other information is presented in the schedule.

Division Information for 2017	
Beginning inventory	0
Expected sales in units	60,000
Selling price per unit	$30
Variable manufacturing costs per unit	$12
Fixed manufacturing overhead costs (total)	$540,000
Fixed manufacturing overhead costs per unit:	
Based on 60,000 units	$9 per unit ($540,000 ÷ 60,000)
Based on 90,000 units	$6 per unit ($540,000 ÷ 90,000)
Manufacturing costs per unit:	
Based on 60,000 units	$21 per unit ($12 variable + $9 fixed)
Based on 90,000 units	$18 per unit ($12 variable + $6 fixed)
Variable selling and administrative expenses	$2
Fixed selling and administrative expenses (total)	$50,000

(a) 90,000 units: NI $550,000

Instructions

(a) Prepare an absorption costing income statement, with one column showing the results if 60,000 units are produced and one column showing the results if 90,000 units are produced.

(b) Prepare a variable costing income statement, with one column showing the results if 60,000 units are produced and one column showing the results if 90,000 units are produced.

(b) 90,000 units: NI $370,000

(c) Reconcile the difference in net incomes under the two approaches and explain what accounts for this difference.

(d) Discuss the relative usefulness of the variable costing income statements versus the absorption costing income statements for decision making and for evaluating the manager's performance.

PROBLEMS: SET B AND SET C

Visit the book's companion website, at **www.wiley.com/college/kimmel**, and choose the Student Companion site to access Problems: Set B and Set C.

CONTINUING PROBLEMS

CURRENT DESIGNS

CD19 Current Designs manufactures two different types of kayaks, rotomolded kayaks and composite kayaks. The following information is available for each product line.

EXCEL TUTORIAL

	Rotomolded	Composite
Sales price/unit	$950	$2,000
Variable costs/unit	$570	$1,340

The company's fixed costs are $820,000. An analysis of the sales mix identifies that rotomolded kayaks make up 80% of the total units sold.

Instructions

(a) Determine the weighted-average unit contribution margin for Current Designs.

(b) Determine the break-even point in units for Current Designs and identify how many units of each type of kayak will be sold at the break-even point. (Round to the nearest whole number.)

(c) Assume that the sales mix changes, and rotomolded kayaks now make up 70% of total units sold. Calculate the total number of units that would need to be sold to earn a net income of $2,000,000 and identify how many units of each type of kayak will be sold at this level of income. (Round to the nearest whole number.)

(d) Assume that Current Designs will have sales of $3,000,000 with two-thirds of the sales dollars in rotomolded kayaks and one-third of the sales dollars in composite kayaks. Assuming $660,000 of fixed costs are allocated to the rotomolded kayaks and $160,000 to the composite kayaks, prepare a CVP income statement for each product line.

(e) Using the information in part (d), calculate the degree of operating leverage for each product line and interpret your findings. (Round to two decimal places.)

WATERWAYS

(*Note:* This is a continuation of the Waterways problem from Chapters 14–18.)

WP19 This problem asks you to perform break-even analysis based on Waterways' sales mix and to make sales mix decisions related to Waterways' use of its productive facilities. An optional extension of the problem (related to the chapter appendix) also asks you to prepare a variable costing income statement and an absorption costing income statement.

Go to the book's companion website, **www.wiley.com/college/kimmel**, *to find the remainder of this problem.*

EXPAND YOUR CRITICAL THINKING

Group Project

DECISION-MAKING ACROSS THE ORGANIZATION

E **CT19-1** E-Z Seats manufactures swivel seats for customized vans. It currently manufactures 10,000 seats per year, which it sells for $500 per seat. It incurs variable costs of $200 per seat and fixed costs of $2,000,000. It is considering automating the upholstery process, which is now largely manual. It estimates that if it does so, its fixed costs will be $3,000,000, and its variable costs will decline to $100 per seat.

Instructions

With the class divided into groups, answer the following questions.

(a) Prepare a CVP income statement based on current activity.
(b) Compute contribution margin ratio, break-even point in dollars, margin of safety ratio, and degree of operating leverage based on current activity.
(c) Prepare a CVP income statement assuming that the company invests in the automated upholstery system.
(d) Compute contribution margin ratio, break-even point in dollars, margin of safety ratio, and degree of operating leverage assuming the new upholstery system is implemented.
(e) Discuss the implications of adopting the new system.

MANAGERIAL ANALYSIS

E **CT19-2** For nearly 20 years, Specialized Coatings has provided painting and galvanizing services for manufacturers in its region. Manufacturers of various metal products have relied on the quality and quick turnaround time provided by Specialized Coatings and its 20 skilled employees. During the last year, as a result of a sharp upturn in the economy, the company's sales have increased by 30% relative to the previous year. The company has not been able to increase its capacity fast enough, so Specialized Coatings has had to turn work away because it cannot keep up with customer requests.

Top management is considering the purchase of a sophisticated robotic painting booth. The booth would represent a considerable move in the direction of automation versus manual labor. If Specialized Coatings purchases the booth, it would most likely lay off 15 of its skilled painters. To analyze the decision, the company compiled production information from the most recent year and then prepared a parallel compilation assuming that the company would purchase the new equipment and lay off the workers. Those data are shown below. As you can see, the company projects that during the last year it would have been far more profitable if it had used the automated approach.

	Current Approach	Automated Approach
Sales	$2,000,000	$2,000,000
Variable costs	1,500,000	1,000,000
Contribution margin	500,000	1,000,000
Fixed costs	380,000	800,000
Net income	$ 120,000	$ 200,000

Instructions

(a) Compute and interpret the contribution margin ratio under each approach.
(b) Compute the break-even point in sales dollars under each approach. Discuss the implications of your findings.
(c) Using the current level of sales, compute the margin of safety ratio under each approach and interpret your findings.
(d) Determine the degree of operating leverage for each approach at current sales levels. How much would the company's net income decline under each approach with a 10% decline in sales?
(e) At what level of sales would the company's net income be the same under either approach?
(f) Discuss the issues that the company must consider in making this decision.

REAL-WORLD FOCUS

CT19-3 In a recent report, the Del Monte Foods Company reported three separate operating segments: consumer products (which includes a variety of canned foods including tuna, fruit, and vegetables); pet products (which includes pet food and snacks and veterinary products); and soup and infant-feeding products (which includes soup, broth, and infant feeding and pureed products). AN

In its annual report, Del Monte uses absorption costing. As a result, information regarding the relative composition of its fixed and variable costs is not available. We have assumed that $860.3 million of its total operating expenses of $1,920.3 million are fixed and have allocated the remaining variable costs across the three divisions. Sales data, along with assumed expense data, are provided below.

	(in millions)	
	Sales	**Variable Costs**
Consumer products	$1,031.8	$ 610
Pet products	837.3	350
Soup and infant-feeding products	302.0	100
	$2,171.1	$1,060

Instructions

(a) Compute each segment's contribution margin ratio and the sales mix.

(b) Using the information computed in part (a), compute the company's break-even point in dollars, and then determine the amount of sales that would be generated by each division at the break-even point.

CT19-4 The external financial statements published by publicly traded companies are based on absorption cost accounting. As a consequence, it is very difficult to gain an understanding of the relative composition of the companies' fixed and variable costs. It is possible, however, to learn about a company's sales mix and the relative profitability of its various divisions. This exercise looks at the financial statements of FedEx Corporation. AN

Address: **www.fedex.com/us/investorrelations**, or go to **www.wiley.com/college/kimmel**

Steps

1. Go to the site above.
2. Under "Financial Information," choose "Annual Reports."
3. Choose "2013 Annual Report."

Instructions

(a) Read page 9 of the report under the heading "Description of Business." What are the three primary product lines of the company? What does the company identify as the key factors affecting operating results?

(b) Page 21 of the report lists the operating expenses of FedEx Ground. Assuming that rentals, depreciation, and "other" are all fixed costs, prepare a variable costing income statement for 2013, and compute the division's contribution margin ratio and the break-even point in dollars.

(c) Page 61, Note 14 ("Business segment information") provides additional information regarding the relative profitability of the business segments.

(i) Calculate the sales mix for 2011 and 2013. (*Note:* Exclude "other" when you calculate total revenue.)

(ii) The company does not provide the contribution margin for each division, but it does provide "operating margin" (operating income divided by revenues) on pages 21, 22, and 23 for three divisions. List these for each division for 2011 and 2013.

(iii) Assuming that the "operating margin" (operating income divided by revenues) moves in parallel with each division's contribution margin, how has the shift in sales mix affected the company's profitability from 2011 to 2013?

E **CT19-5** The June 8, 2009, edition of the *Wall Street Journal* has an article by JoAnn Lublin entitled "Smart Balance Keeps Tight Focus on Creativity."

Instructions
Read the article and answer the following questions.

(a) Describe Smart Balance's approach to employment and cost structure.
(b) What function does it keep "in-house"?
(c) Based on the discussion in this chapter, what are the advantages to Smart Balance's approach?
(d) Based on the discussion in this chapter, what are the disadvantages to Smart Balance's approach?

Writing

COMMUNICATION ACTIVITY

E **CT19-6** Easton Corporation makes two different boat anchors—a traditional fishing anchor and a high-end yacht anchor—using the same production machinery. The contribution margin of the yacht anchor is three times as high as that of the other product. The company is currently operating at full capacity and has been doing so for nearly two years. Bjorn Borg, the company's CEO, wants to cut back on production of the fishing anchor so that the company can make more yacht anchors. He says that this is a "no-brainer" because the contribution margin of the yacht anchor is so much higher.

Instructions
Write a short memo to Bjorn Borg describing the analysis that the company should do before it makes this decision and any other considerations that would affect the decision.

ETHICS CASE

E ***CT19-7** Brett Stern was hired during January 2017 to manage the home products division of Hi-Tech Products. As part of his employment contract, he was told that he would get $5,000 of additional bonus for every 1% increase that the division's profits exceeded those of the previous year.

Soon after coming on board, Brett met with his plant managers and explained that he wanted the plants to be run at full capacity. Previously, the plant had employed just-in-time inventory practices and had consequently produced units only as they were needed. Brett stated that under previous management the company had missed out on too many sales opportunities because it didn't have enough inventory on hand. Because previous management had employed just-in-time inventory practices, when Brett came on board there was virtually no beginning inventory. The selling price and variable costs per unit remained the same from 2016 to 2017. Additional information is provided below.

	2016	2017
Net income	$ 300,000	$ 525,000
Units produced	25,000	30,000
Units sold	25,000	25,000
Fixed manufacturing overhead costs	$1,350,000	$1,350,000
Fixed manufacturing overhead costs per unit	$ 54	$ 45

Instructions
(a) Calculate Brett's bonus based upon the net income shown above.
(b) Recompute the 2016 and 2017 results using variable costing.
(c) Recompute Brett's 2017 bonus under variable costing.
(d) Were Brett's actions unethical? Do you think any actions need to be taken by the company?

ALL ABOUT YOU

CT19-8 Many of you will some day own your own business. One rapidly growing opportunity is no-frills workout centers. Such centers attract customers who want to take advantage of state-of-the-art fitness equipment but do not need the other amenities of full-service health clubs. One way to own your own fitness business is to buy a franchise. Snap Fitness is a Minnesota-based business that offers franchise opportunities. For a very low monthly fee ($26, without an annual contract), customers can access a Snap Fitness center 24 hours a day. E

The Snap Fitness website (*www.snapfitness.com*) indicates that start-up costs range from $60,000 to $184,000. This initial investment covers the following pre-opening costs: franchise fee, grand opening marketing, leasehold improvements, utility/rent deposits, and training.

Instructions

(a) Suppose that Snap Fitness estimates that each location incurs $4,000 per month in fixed operating expenses plus $1,460 to lease equipment. A recent newspaper article describing no-frills fitness centers indicated that a Snap Fitness site might require only 300 members to break even. Using the information provided above and your knowledge of CVP analysis, estimate the amount of variable costs. (When performing your analysis, assume that the only fixed costs are the estimated monthly operating expenses and the equipment lease.)

(b) Using the information from part (a), what would monthly sales in members and dollars have to be to achieve a target net income of $3,640 for the month?

(c) Provide five examples of variable costs for a fitness center.

(d) Go to a fitness-business website, such as Curves, Snap Fitness, or Anytime Fitness, and find information about purchasing a franchise. Summarize the franchise information needed to decide whether entering into a franchise agreement would be a good idea.

CONSIDERING PEOPLE, PLANET, AND PROFIT

CT19-9 Many politicians, scientists, economists, and businesspeople have become concerned about the potential implications of global warming. The largest source of the emissions thought to contribute to global warming is from coal-fired power plants. The cost of alternative energy has declined, but it is still higher than coal. In 1980, wind-power electricity cost 80 cents per kilowatt hour. Using today's highly efficient turbines with rotor diameters of up to 125 meters, the cost can be as low as 4 cents (about the same as coal), or as much as 20 cents in places with less wind. E

Some people have recently suggested that conventional cost comparisons are not adequate because they do not take environmental costs into account. For example, while coal is a very cheap energy source, it is also a significant contributor of greenhouse gases. Should environmental costs be incorporated into decision formulas when planners evaluate new power plants? The basic arguments for and against are as follows.

> **YES:** As long as environmental costs are ignored, renewable energy will appear to be too expensive relative to coal.

> **NO:** If one country decides to incorporate environmental costs into its decision-making process but other countries do not, the country that does so will be at a competitive disadvantage because its products will cost more to produce.

Instructions

Write a response indicating your position regarding this situation. Provide support for your view.

20

Incremental Analysis

CHAPTER PREVIEW

Companies of all sorts must make product decisions. Oral-B Laboratories opted to produce a new, higher-priced toothbrush. General Motors announced the closure of its Oldsmobile Division. This chapter explains management's decision-making process and a decision-making approach called incremental analysis. The use of incremental analysis is demonstrated in a variety of situations.

CHAPTER OUTLINE

LEARNING OBJECTIVES		PRACTICE
1 Describe management's decision-making process and incremental analysis.	• Incremental analysis approach • How incremental analysis works • Qualitative factors • Incremental analysis and ABC • Types of incremental analysis	DO IT! 1 Incremental Analysis
2 Analyze the relevant costs in accepting an order at a special price.	• Special price • Available capacity	DO IT! 2 Special Orders
3 Analyze the relevant costs in a make-or-buy decision.	• Make-or-buy • Opportunity cost	DO IT! 3 Make or Buy
4 Analyze the relevant costs in determining whether to sell or process materials further.	• Single-product case • Multiple-product case	DO IT! 4 Sell or Process Further
5 Analyze the relevant costs to be considered in repairing, retaining, or replacing equipment.	• Repair, retain, or replace equipment • Sunk costs	DO IT! 5 Repair or Replace Equipment
6 Analyze the relevant costs in deciding whether to eliminate an unprofitable segment or product.	• Unprofitable segments • Avoidable fixed costs • Effect of contribution margin	DO IT! 6 Unprofitable Segments

Go to the ***REVIEW AND PRACTICE*** section at the end of the chapter for a targeted summary and exercises with solutions.

Visit **WileyPLUS** for additional tutorials and practice opportunities.

Gabriela Hasbun/Redux

FEATURE STORY

Keeping It Clean

When you think of new, fast-growing, San Francisco companies, you probably think of fun products like smartphones, social networks, and game apps. You don't tend to think of soap. In fact, given that some of the biggest, most powerful companies in the world dominate the soap market (e.g., Proctor & Gamble, Clorox, and Unilever), starting a new soap company seems like an outrageously bad idea. But that didn't dissuade Adam Lowry and Eric Ryan from giving it a try. The long-time friends and former roommates combined their skills (Adam's chemical engineering and Eric's design and marketing) to start Method Products. Their goal: selling environmentally friendly soaps that actually remove dirt.

Within a year of its formation, the company had products on the shelves at Target stores. Within 5 years, Method was cited by numerous business publications as one of the fastest-growing companies in the country. It was easy—right? Wrong. Running a company is never easy, and given Method's commitment to sustainability, all of its business decisions are just a little more complex than usual. For example, the company wanted to use solar power to charge the batteries for the forklifts used in its factories. No problem, just put solar panels on the buildings. But because Method outsources its manufacturing, it doesn't actually own factory buildings. In fact, the company that does Method's manufacturing doesn't own the buildings either. Solution—Method parked old semi-trailers next to the factories and installed solar panels on those.

Since Method insists on using natural products and sustainable production practices, its production costs are higher than companies that don't adhere to these standards. Adam and Eric insist, however, that this actually benefits them because they have to be far more careful about controlling costs and far more innovative in solving problems. Consider Method's most recently developed laundry detergent. It is 8 times stronger than normal detergent, so it can be sold in a substantially smaller package. This reduces both its packaging and shipping costs. In fact, when the cost of the raw materials used for soap production recently jumped by as much as 40%, Method actually viewed it as an opportunity to grab market share. It determined that it could offset the cost increases in other places in its supply chain, thus absorbing the cost much easier than its big competitors.

In these and other instances, Adam and Eric identified their alternative courses of action, determined what was relevant to each choice and what wasn't, and then carefully evaluated the incremental costs of each alternative. When you are small and your competitors have some of the biggest marketing budgets in the world, you can't afford to make very many mistakes.

LEARNING OBJECTIVE 1

Describe management's decision-making process and incremental analysis.

Making decisions is an important management function. Management's decision-making process does not always follow a set pattern because decisions vary significantly in their scope, urgency, and importance. It is possible, though, to identify some steps that are frequently involved in the process. These steps are shown in Illustration 20-1.

ILLUSTRATION 20-1
Management's decision-making process

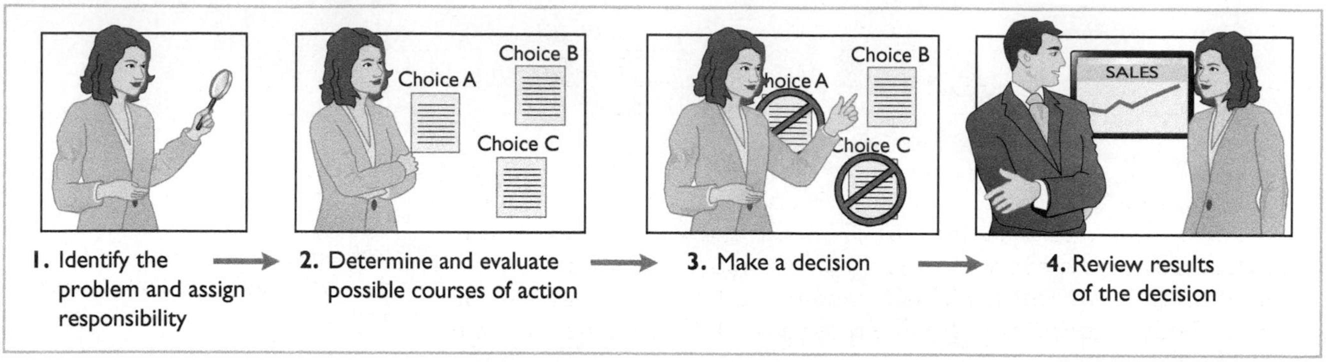

Accounting's contribution to the decision-making process occurs primarily in Steps 2 and 4—evaluating possible courses of action and reviewing results. In Step 2, for each possible course of action, relevant revenue and cost data are provided. These show the expected overall effect on net income. In Step 4, internal reports are prepared that review the actual impact of the decision.

In making business decisions, management ordinarily considers both financial and nonfinancial information. **Financial** information is related to revenues and costs and their effect on the company's overall profitability. **Nonfinancial** information relates to such factors as the effect of the decision on employee turnover, the environment, or the overall image of the company in the community. (These are considerations that we touched on in our Chapter 14 discussion of corporate social responsibility.) Although nonfinancial information can be as important as financial information, we will focus primarily on financial information that is relevant to the decision.

INCREMENTAL ANALYSIS APPROACH

Decisions involve a choice among alternative courses of action. Suppose you face the personal financial decision of whether to purchase or lease a car. The financial data relate to the cost of leasing versus the cost of purchasing. For example, leasing involves periodic lease payments; purchasing requires "up-front" payment of the purchase price. In other words, the financial information relevant to the decision are the data that vary in the future among the possible alternatives. The process used to identify the financial data that change under alternative courses of action is called **incremental analysis**. In some cases, you will find that when you use incremental analysis, both costs **and** revenues vary. In other cases, only costs **or** revenues vary.

ALTERNATIVE TERMINOLOGY
Incremental analysis is also called *differential analysis* because the analysis focuses on differences.

Just as your decision to buy or lease a car affects your future financial situation, similar decisions, on a larger scale, affect a company's future. Incremental analysis identifies the probable effects of those decisions on future earnings. Such analysis inevitably involves estimates and uncertainty. Gathering data for incremental analyses may involve market analysts, engineers, and accountants. In quantifying the data, the accountant must produce the most reliable information available.

HOW INCREMENTAL ANALYSIS WORKS

The basic approach in incremental analysis is illustrated in the following example.

ILLUSTRATION 20-2
Basic approach in incremental analysis

Incremental Analysis.xls

	A	B	C	D
1		Alternative A	Alternative B	Net Income Increase (Decrease)
2	Revenues	$125,000	$110,000	$ (15,000)
3	Costs	100,000	80,000	20,000
4	Net income	$ 25,000	$ 30,000	$ 5,000
5				

This example compares Alternative B with Alternative A. The net income column shows the differences between the alternatives. In this case, incremental revenue will be $15,000 less under Alternative B than under Alternative A. But a $20,000 incremental cost savings will be realized.[1] Thus, Alternative B will produce $5,000 more net income than Alternative A.

DECISION TOOLS

Incremental analysis helps managers choose the alternative that maximizes net income.

In the following pages, you will encounter three important cost concepts used in incremental analysis, as defined and discussed in Illustration 20-3.

ILLUSTRATION 20-3
Key cost concepts in incremental analysis

- **Relevant cost** In incremental analysis, the only factors to be considered are those costs and revenues that differ across alternatives. Those factors are called **relevant costs**. Costs and revenues that do not differ across alternatives can be ignored when trying to choose between alternatives.

- **Opportunity cost** Often in choosing one course of action, the company must give up the opportunity to benefit from some other course of action. For example, if a machine is used to make one type of product, the benefit of making another type of product with that machine is lost. This lost benefit is referred to as **opportunity cost**.

- **Sunk cost** Costs that have already been incurred and will not be changed or avoided by any present or future decisions are referred to as **sunk costs**. For example, the amount you spent in the past to purchase or repair a laptop should have no bearing on your decision whether to buy a new laptop. **Sunk costs are not relevant costs.**

[1] Although income taxes are sometimes important in incremental analysis, they are ignored in the chapter for simplicity's sake.

Incremental analysis sometimes involves changes that at first glance might seem contrary to your intuition. For example, sometimes variable costs **do not change** under the alternative courses of action. Also, sometimes fixed costs **do change**. For example, direct labor, normally a variable cost, is not an incremental cost in deciding between two new factory machines if each asset requires the same amount of direct labor. In contrast, rent expense, normally a fixed cost, is an incremental cost in a decision whether to continue occupancy of a building or to purchase or lease a new building.

It is also important to understand that **the approaches to incremental analysis discussed in this chapter do not take into consideration the time value of money**. That is, amounts to be paid or received in future years are not discounted for the cost of interest. Time value of money is addressed in Chapter 24 and Appendix G.

SERVICE COMPANY INSIGHT American Express

Tina Spruce/iStockphoto

That Letter from AmEx Might Not Be a Bill

No doubt every one of you has received an invitation from a credit card company to open a new account—some of you have probably received three in one day. But how many of you have received an offer of $300 to close out your credit card account? American Express decided to offer some of its customers $300 if they would give back their credit card. You could receive the $300 even if you hadn't paid off your balance yet, as long as you agreed to give up your credit card.

Source: Aparajita Saha-Bubna and Lauren Pollock, "AmEx Offers Some Holders $300 to Pay and Leave," *Wall Street Journal Online* (February 23, 2009).

What are the relevant costs that American Express would need to know in order to determine to whom to make this offer? (Go to **WileyPLUS** for this answer and additional questions.)

QUALITATIVE FACTORS

In this chapter, we focus primarily on the quantitative factors that affect a decision—those attributes that can be easily expressed in terms of numbers or dollars. However, many of the decisions involving incremental analysis have important qualitative features. Though not easily measured, they should not be ignored.

Consider, for example, the potential effects of the make-or-buy decision or of the decision to eliminate a line of business on existing employees and the community in which the plant is located. The cost savings that may be obtained from outsourcing or from eliminating a plant should be weighed against these qualitative attributes. One example would be the cost of lost morale that might result. Al "Chainsaw" Dunlap was a so-called "turnaround" artist who went into many companies, identified inefficiencies (using incremental analysis techniques), and tried to correct these problems to improve corporate profitability. Along the way, he laid off thousands of employees at numerous companies. As head of Sunbeam, it was Al Dunlap who lost his job because his Draconian approach failed to improve Sunbeam's profitability. It was reported that Sunbeam's employees openly rejoiced for days after his departure. Clearly, qualitative factors can matter.

RELATIONSHIP OF INCREMENTAL ANALYSIS AND ACTIVITY-BASED COSTING

In Chapter 17, we noted that many companies have shifted to activity-based costing to allocate overhead costs to products. The primary reason for using activity-based costing is that it results in a more accurate allocation of overhead. The concepts presented in this chapter are completely consistent with the use of activity-based costing. In fact, activity-based costing results in better identification of relevant costs and, therefore, better incremental analysis.

TYPES OF INCREMENTAL ANALYSIS

A number of different types of decisions involve incremental analysis. The more common types of decisions are whether to:

1. Accept an order at a special price.
2. Make or buy component parts or finished products.
3. Sell products or process them further.
4. Repair, retain, or replace equipment.
5. Eliminate an unprofitable business segment or product.

We consider each of these types of decisions in the following pages.

DO IT! 1 Incremental Analysis

Owen T Corporation is comparing two different options. The company currently follows Option 1, with revenues of $80,000 per year, maintenance expenses of $5,000 per year, and operating expenses of $38,000 per year. Option 2 provides revenues of $80,000 per year, maintenance expenses of $12,000 per year, and operating expenses of $32,000 per year. Option 1 employs a piece of equipment that was upgraded 2 years ago at a cost of $22,000. If Option 2 is chosen, it will free up resources that will increase revenues by $3,000.

Complete the following table to show the change in income from choosing Option 2 versus Option 1. Designate any sunk costs with an "S."

	Option 1	Option 2	Net Income Increase (Decrease)	Sunk (S)
Revenues				
Maintenance expenses				
Operating expenses				
Equipment upgrade				
Opportunity cost				

SOLUTION

	Option 1	Option 2	Net Income Increase (Decrease)	Sunk (S)
Revenues	$80,000	$80,000	$ 0	
Maintenance expenses	5,000	12,000	(7,000)	
Operating expenses	38,000	32,000	6,000	
Equipment upgrade	22,000	0	0	S
Opportunity cost	3,000	0	3,000	
			$ 2,000	

Action Plan

✔ Past costs that cannot be changed are sunk costs.

✔ Benefits lost by choosing one option over another are opportunity costs.

Related exercise material: **BE20-1, BE20-2, E20-1, E20-18,** and **DO IT! 20-1.**

LEARNING OBJECTIVE 2 Analyze the relevant costs in accepting an order at a special price.

Sometimes a company has an opportunity to obtain additional business if it is willing to make a price concession to a specific customer. To illustrate, assume that Sunbelt Company produces 100,000 Smoothie blenders per month, which is 80% of plant capacity. Variable manufacturing costs are $8 per unit. Fixed manufacturing costs are $400,000, or $4 per unit. The Smoothie blenders are normally sold directly to retailers at $20 each. Sunbelt has an offer from Kensington Co. (a foreign wholesaler) to purchase an additional 2,000 blenders at $11 per unit. Acceptance of the offer would not affect normal sales of the product, and the additional units can be manufactured without increasing plant capacity. What should management do?

▼ **HELPFUL HINT**
This is a good example of different costs for different purposes. In the long run all costs are relevant, but for this decision only costs that change are relevant.

If management makes its decision on the basis of the total cost per unit of $12 ($8 variable + $4 fixed), the order would be rejected because costs per unit ($12) exceed revenues per unit ($11) by $1 per unit. However, since the units can be produced within existing plant capacity, the special order **will not increase fixed costs**. Let's identify the relevant data for the decision. First, the variable manufacturing costs increase $16,000 ($8 × 2,000). Second, the expected revenue increases $22,000 ($11 × 2,000). Thus, as shown in Illustration 20-4, Sunbelt increases its net income by $6,000 by accepting this special order.

ILLUSTRATION 20-4
Incremental analysis—accepting an order at a special price

Incremental Analysis - Accepting an order at a special price.xls

Home Insert Page Layout Formulas Data Review View

P18 fx

	A	B	C	D
1		Reject Order	Accept Order	Net Income Increase (Decrease)
2	Revenues	$0	$22,000	$ 22,000
3	Costs	0	16,000	(16,000)
4	Net income	$0	$ 6,000	$ 6,000
5				

Two points should be emphasized. First, we assume that sales of the product in other markets **would not be affected by this special order**. If other sales were affected, then Sunbelt would have to consider the lost sales in making the decision. Second, if Sunbelt is operating **at full capacity**, it is likely that the special order would be rejected. Under such circumstances, the company would have to expand plant capacity. In that case, the special order would have to absorb these additional fixed manufacturing costs, as well as the variable manufacturing costs.

DO IT! 2 Special Orders

Cobb Company incurs costs of $28 per unit ($18 variable and $10 fixed) to make a product that normally sells for $42. A foreign wholesaler offers to buy 5,000 units at $25 each. The special order results in additional shipping costs of $1 per unit. Compute the increase or decrease in net income Cobb realizes by accepting the special order, assuming Cobb has excess operating capacity. Should Cobb Company accept the special order?

Action Plan

✔ Identify all revenues that change as a result of accepting the order.

✔ Identify all costs that change as a result of accepting the order, and net this amount against the change in revenues.

SOLUTION

	Reject	Accept	Net Income Increase (Decrease)
Revenues	$–0–	$125,000*	$125,000
Costs	–0–	95,000**	(95,000)
Net income	$–0–	$ 30,000	$ 30,000

*5,000 × $25
**(5,000 × $18) + (5,000 × $1)

The analysis indicates net income increases by $30,000; therefore, Cobb Company should accept the special order.

Related exercise material: **BE20-3, E20-2, E20-3, E20-4,** and **DO IT! 20-2.**

LEARNING OBJECTIVE

3 Analyze the relevant costs in a make-or-buy decision.

When a manufacturer assembles component parts in producing a finished product, management must decide whether to make or buy the components. The decision to buy parts or services is often referred to as outsourcing. For example, as discussed in the Feature Story, a company such as Method Products may either make or buy the soaps used in its products. Similarly, Hewlett-Packard Corporation may make or buy the electronic circuitry, cases, and printer heads for its printers. Boeing recently sold some of its commercial aircraft factories in an effort to cut production costs and focus on engineering and final assembly rather than manufacturing. The decision to make or buy components should be made on the basis of incremental analysis.

Baron Company makes motorcycles and scooters. It incurs the following annual costs in producing 25,000 ignition switches for scooters.

ILLUSTRATION 20-5
Annual product cost data

Direct materials	$ 50,000
Direct labor	75,000
Variable manufacturing overhead	40,000
Fixed manufacturing overhead	60,000
Total manufacturing costs	$225,000
Total cost per unit ($225,000 ÷ 25,000)	**$9.00**

Instead of making its own switches, Baron Company might purchase the ignition switches from Ignition, Inc. at a price of $8 per unit. What should management do?

At first glance, it appears that management should purchase the ignition switches for $8 rather than make them at a cost of $9. However, a review of operations indicates that if the ignition switches are purchased from Ignition, Inc., *all* of Baron's variable costs but only $10,000 of its fixed manufacturing costs will be eliminated (avoided). Thus, $50,000 of the fixed manufacturing costs remain if the ignition switches are purchased. The relevant costs for incremental analysis, therefore, are as shown below.

ILLUSTRATION 20-6
Incremental analysis—make or buy

Incremental Analysis - Make or buy.xls

Home Insert Page Layout Formulas Data Review View

P18 fx

	A	B	C	D
1		Make	Buy	Net Income Increase (Decrease)
2	Direct materials	$ 50,000	$ 0	$ 50,000
3	Direct labor	75,000	0	75,000
4	Variable manufacturing costs	40,000	0	40,000
5	Fixed manufacturing costs	60,000	50,000	10,000
6	Purchase price (25,000 × $8)	0	200,000	(200,000)
7	Total annual cost	$225,000	$250,000	$ (25,000)
8				

This analysis indicates that Baron Company incurs $25,000 of additional costs by buying the ignition switches rather than making them. Therefore, Baron should continue to make the ignition switches even though the total manufacturing

ETHICS NOTE
In the make-or-buy decision, it is important for management to take into account the social impact of its choice. For instance, buying may be the most economically feasible solution, but such action could result in the closure of a manufacturing plant that employs many good workers.

cost is $1 higher per unit than the purchase price. The primary cause of this result is that, even if the company purchases the ignition switches, it will still have fixed costs of $50,000 to absorb.

OPPORTUNITY COST

The foregoing make-or-buy analysis is complete only if it is assumed that the productive capacity used to make the ignition switches cannot be converted to another purpose. If there is an opportunity to use this productive capacity in some other manner, then this opportunity cost must be considered. As indicated earlier, **opportunity cost** is the potential benefit that may be obtained by following an alternative course of action.

To illustrate, assume that through buying the switches, Baron Company can use the released productive capacity to generate additional income of $38,000 from producing a different product. This lost income is an additional cost of continuing to make the switches in the make-or-buy decision. This opportunity cost is therefore added to the "Make" column for comparison. As shown in Illustration 20-7, it is now advantageous to buy the ignition switches. The company's income would increase by $13,000.

ILLUSTRATION 20-7
Incremental analysis—make or buy, with opportunity cost

Incremental Analysis - Make or buy with opportunity cost.xls

	A	B	C	D
1		Make	Buy	Net Income Increase (Decrease)
2	Total annual cost	$225,000	$250,000	$(25,000)
3	Opportunity cost	38,000	0	38,000
4	Total cost	$263,000	$250,000	$ 13,000
5				

The qualitative factors in this decision include the possible loss of jobs for employees who produce the ignition switches. In addition, management must assess the supplier's ability to satisfy the company's quality control standards at the quoted price per unit.

SERVICE COMPANY INSIGHT Amazon.com

iStockphoto

Giving Away the Store?

In an earlier chapter, we discussed Amazon.com's incredible growth. However, some analysts have questioned whether some of the methods that Amazon uses to increase its sales make good business sense. For example, a few years ago, Amazon initiated a "Prime" free-shipping subscription program. For a $79 fee per year, Amazon's customers get free shipping on as many goods as they want to buy. At the time, CEO Jeff Bezos promised that the program would be costly in the short-term but benefit the company in the long-term. Six years later, it was true that Amazon's sales had grown considerably. It was also estimated that its Prime customers buy two to three times as much as non-Prime customers. But, its shipping costs rose from 2.8% of sales to 4% of sales, which is remarkably similar to the drop in its gross margin from 24% to 22.3%. Perhaps even less easy to justify is a proposal by Mr. Bezos to start providing a free Internet movie-streaming service to Amazon's Prime customers. Perhaps some incremental analysis is in order?

Source: Martin Peers, "Amazon's Prime Numbers," *Wall Street Journal Online* (February 3, 2011).

What are the relevant revenues and costs that Amazon should consider relative to the decision whether to offer the Prime free-shipping subscription? (Go to WileyPLUS for this answer and additional questions.)

DO IT! 3 Make or Buy

Juanita Company must decide whether to make or buy some of its components for the appliances it produces. The costs of producing 166,000 electrical cords for its appliances are as follows.

Direct materials	$90,000	Variable overhead	$32,000
Direct labor	$20,000	Fixed overhead	$24,000

Instead of making the electrical cords at an average cost per unit of $1.00 ($166,000 ÷ 166,000), the company has an opportunity to buy the cords at $0.90 per unit. If the company purchases the cords, all variable costs and one-fourth of the fixed costs are eliminated.

(a) Prepare an incremental analysis showing whether the company should make or buy the electrical cords. (b) Will your answer be different if the released productive capacity will generate additional income of $5,000?

SOLUTION

(a)

	Make	Buy	Net Income Increase (Decrease)
Direct materials	$ 90,000	$ -0-	$ 90,000
Direct labor	20,000	-0-	20,000
Variable manufacturing costs	32,000	-0-	32,000
Fixed manufacturing costs	24,000	18,000*	6,000
Purchase price	-0-	149,400**	(149,400)
Total cost	$166,000	$167,400	$ (1,400)

*$24,000 × .75
**166,000 × $0.90

This analysis indicates that Juanita Company will incur $1,400 of additional costs if it buys the electrical cords rather than making them.

(b)

	Make	Buy	Net Income Increase (Decrease)
Total cost	$166,000	$167,400	$ (1,400)
Opportunity cost	5,000	-0-	5,000
Total cost	$171,000	$167,400	$ 3,600

Yes, the answer is different. The analysis shows that net income increases by $3,600 if Juanita Company purchases the electrical cords rather than making them.

Action Plan

✔ Look for the costs that change.
✔ Ignore the costs that do not change.
✔ Use the format in the chapter for your answer.
✔ Recognize that opportunity cost can make a difference.

Related exercise material: **BE20-4, E20-5, E20-6, E20-7, E20-8,** and **DO IT! 20-3.**

LEARNING OBJECTIVE 4 Analyze the relevant costs in determining whether to sell or process materials further.

Many manufacturers have the option of selling products at a given point in the production cycle or continuing to process with the expectation of selling them at a later point at a higher price. For example, a bicycle manufacturer such as Trek could sell its bicycles to retailers either unassembled or assembled. A furniture manufacturer such as Ethan Allen could sell its dining room sets to furniture stores either unfinished or finished. The sell-or-process-further decision should be made on the basis of incremental analysis. The basic decision rule is: **Process**

further as long as the incremental revenue from such processing exceeds the incremental processing costs.

SINGLE-PRODUCT CASE

Assume, for example, that Woodmasters Inc. makes tables. It sells unfinished tables for $50. The cost to manufacture an unfinished table is $35, computed as follows.

ILLUSTRATION 20-8
Per unit cost of unfinished table

Direct materials	$ 15
Direct labor	10
Variable manufacturing overhead	6
Fixed manufacturing overhead	4
Manufacturing cost per unit	**$35**

▼ HELPFUL HINT
Current net income is known. Net income from processing further is an estimate. In making its decision, management could add a "risk" factor for the estimate.

Woodmasters currently has unused productive capacity that is expected to continue indefinitely. Some of this capacity could be used to finish the tables and sell them at $60 per unit. For a finished table, direct materials will increase $2 and direct labor costs will increase $4. Variable manufacturing overhead costs will increase by $2.40 (60% of direct labor). No increase is anticipated in fixed manufacturing overhead.

Should the company sell the unfinished tables, or should it process them further? The incremental analysis on a per unit basis is as follows.

Incremental Analysis - Sell or process further.xls

	A	B	C	D
1		Sell Unfinished	Process Further	Net Income Increase (Decrease)
2	Sales price per unit	$50.00	$60.00	$10.00
3	Cost per unit			
4	Direct materials	15.00	17.00	(2.00)
5	Direct labor	10.00	14.00	(4.00)
6	Variable manufacturing overhead	6.00	8.40	(2.40)
7	Fixed manufacturing overhead	4.00	4.00	0.00
8	Total	35.00	43.40	(8.40)
9	Net income per unit	$15.00	$16.60	$ 1.60
10				

ILLUSTRATION 20-9
Incremental analysis—sell or process further

It would be advantageous for Woodmasters to process the tables further. The incremental revenue of $10.00 from the additional processing is $1.60 higher than the incremental processing costs of $8.40.

MULTIPLE-PRODUCT CASE

Sell-or-process-further decisions are particularly applicable to processes that produce multiple products simultaneously. In many industries, a number of end-products are produced from a single raw material and a common production process. These multiple end-products are commonly referred to as **joint products**. For example, in the meat-packing industry, Armour processes a cow or pig into meat, internal organs, hides, bones, and fat products. In the petroleum industry, ExxonMobil refines crude oil to produce gasoline, lubricating oil, kerosene, paraffin, and ethylene.

Illustration 20-10 presents a joint product situation for Marais Creamery involving a decision **to sell or process further** cream and skim milk. Cream and skim milk are joint products that result from the processing of raw milk.

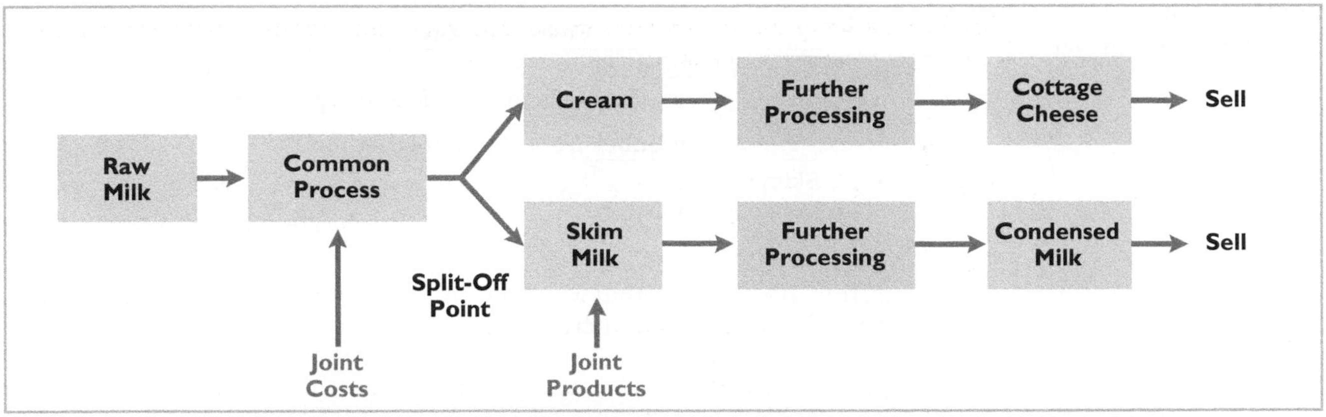

ILLUSTRATION 20-10
Joint production process—Creamery

Marais incurs many costs prior to the manufacture of the cream and skim milk. All costs incurred prior to the point at which the two products are separately identifiable (the **split-off point**) are called **joint costs**. For purposes of determining the cost of each product, joint product costs must be allocated to the individual products. This is frequently done based on the relative sales value of the joint products. While this allocation is important for determination of product cost, **it is irrelevant for any sell-or-process-further decisions**. The reason is that these **joint product costs are sunk costs**. That is, they have already been incurred, and they cannot be changed or avoided by any subsequent decision.

Illustration 20-11 provides the daily cost and revenue data for Marais Creamery related to cream and cottage cheese.

ILLUSTRATION 20-11
Cost and revenue data per day for cream

Costs (per day)	
Joint cost allocated to cream	$ 9,000
Cost to process cream into cottage cheese	10,000
Revenues from Products (per day)	
Cream	$19,000
Cottage cheese	27,000

From this information, we can determine whether the company should simply sell the cream or process it further into cottage cheese. Illustration 20-12 shows the necessary analysis. Note that the joint cost that is allocated to the cream is not included in this decision. It is not relevant to the decision because it is a sunk cost. It has been incurred in the past and will remain the same no matter whether the cream is subsequently processed into cottage cheese or not.

ILLUSTRATION 20-12
Analysis of whether to sell cream or process into cottage cheese

Incremental Analysis - Sell or process further - Cream or cottage cheese.xls

	A	B	C	D
1		Sell	Process Further	Net Income Increase (Decrease)
2	Sales per day	$19,000	$27,000	$ 8,000
3	Cost per day to process cream into cottage cheese	0	10,000	(10,000)
4		$19,000	$17,000	$ (2,000)
5				

From this analysis, we can see that Marais should not process the cream further because it will sustain an incremental loss of $2,000.

Illustration 20-13 (page 986) provides the daily cost and revenue data for the company related to skim milk and condensed milk.

ILLUSTRATION 20-13
Cost and revenue data per day for skim milk

Costs (per day)	
Joint cost allocated to skim milk	$ 5,000
Cost to process skim milk into condensed milk	8,000
Revenues from Products (per day)	
Skim milk	$11,000
Condensed milk	26,000

Illustration 20-14 shows that Marais Company should process the skim milk into condensed milk, as it will increase net income by $7,000.

Incremental Analysis - Sell or process further - Skim milk or condensed milk.xls

	A	B	C	D
1		Sell	Process Further	Net Income Increase (Decrease)
2	Sales per day	$11,000	$26,000	$15,000
3	Cost per day to process skim milk into condensed milk	0	8,000	(8,000)
4		$11,000	$18,000	$ 7,000
5				

ILLUSTRATION 20-14
Analysis of whether to sell skim milk or process into condensed milk

Again, note that the $5,000 of joint cost allocated to the skim milk is irrelevant in deciding whether to sell or process further. Why? The joint cost remains the same, whether or not further processing is performed.

These decisions need to be reevaluated as market conditions change. For example, if the price of skim milk increases relative to the price of condensed milk, it may become more profitable to sell the skim milk rather than process it into condensed milk. Consider also oil refineries. As market conditions change, the companies must constantly re-assess which products to produce from the oil they receive at their plants.

DO IT! 4 Sell or Process Further

Easy Does It manufactures unpainted furniture for the do-it-yourself (DIY) market. It currently sells a child's rocking chair for $25. Production costs are $12 variable and $8 fixed. Easy Does It is considering painting the rocking chair and selling it for $35. Variable costs to paint each chair are expected to be $9, and fixed costs are expected to be $2.

Prepare an analysis showing whether Easy Does It should sell unpainted or painted chairs.

Action Plan

✔ Identify the revenues that change as a result of painting the rocking chair.

✔ Identify all costs that change as a result of painting the rocking chair, and net the amount against the revenues.

SOLUTION

	Sell	**Process Further**	**Net Income Increase (Decrease)**
Revenues	$25	$35	$10
Variable costs	12	21[a]	(9)
Fixed costs	8	10[b]	(2)
Net income	$ 5	$ 4	$ (1)

[a]$12 + $9 [b]$8 + $2

The analysis indicates that the rocking chair should be sold unpainted because net income per chair will be $1 greater.

Related exercise material: **BE20-5, BE20-6, E20-9, E20-10, E20-11, E20-12,** and **DO IT! 20-4.**

LEARNING OBJECTIVE ▶5

Analyze the relevant costs to be considered in repairing, retaining, or replacing equipment.

Management often has to decide whether to continue using an asset, repair, or replace it. For example, Delta Airlines must decide whether to replace old jets with new, more fuel-efficient ones. To illustrate, assume that Jeffcoat Company has a factory machine that originally cost $110,000. It has a balance in Accumulated Depreciation of $70,000, so the machine's book value is $40,000. It has a remaining useful life of four years. The company is considering replacing this machine with a new machine. A new machine is available that costs $120,000. It is expected to have zero salvage value at the end of its four-year useful life. If the new machine is acquired, variable manufacturing costs are expected to decrease from $160,000 to $125,000 annually, and the old unit could be sold for $5,000. The incremental analysis for the **four-year period** is as follows.

ILLUSTRATION 20-15
Incremental analysis—retain or replace equipment

Incremental Analysis - Retain or replace equipment.xls

	Retain Equipment		Replace Equipment		Net Income Increase (Decrease)
Variable manufacturing costs	$640,000	[a]	$500,000	[b]	$140,000
New machine cost			120,000		(120,000)
Sale of old machine			(5,000)		5,000
Total	$640,000		$615,000		$ 25,000

[a](4 years × $160,000)
[b](4 years × $125,000)

In this case, it would be to the company's advantage to replace the equipment. The lower variable manufacturing costs due to replacement more than offset the cost of the new equipment. Note that the $5,000 received from the sale of the old machine is relevant to the decision because it will only be received if the company chooses to replace its equipment. In general, any trade-in allowance or cash disposal value of existing assets is relevant to the decision to retain or replace equipment.

One other point should be mentioned regarding Jeffcoat's decision: **The book value of the old machine does not affect the decision.** Book value is a **sunk cost**, which is a cost that cannot be changed by any present or future decision. **Sunk costs are not relevant in incremental analysis.** In this example, if the asset is retained, book value will be depreciated over its remaining useful life. Or, if the new unit is acquired, book value will be recognized as a loss of the current period. Thus, the effect of book value on cumulative future earnings is the same regardless of the replacement decision.

Sometimes, decisions regarding whether to replace equipment are clouded by behavioral decision-making errors. For example, suppose a manager spent $90,000 repairing a machine two months ago. Suppose that the machine now breaks down again. The manager might be inclined to think that because the company recently spent a large amount of money to repair the machine, the machine should be repaired again rather than replaced. However, the amount spent in the past to repair the machine is irrelevant to the current decision. It is a sunk cost.

Similarly, suppose a manager spent $5,000,000 to purchase a machine. Six months later, a new machine comes on the market that is significantly more efficient than the one recently purchased. The manager might be inclined to think that he or she should not buy the new machine because of the recent purchase.

In fact, the manager might fear that buying a different machine so quickly might call into question the merit of the previous decision. Again, the fact that the company recently bought a machine is not relevant. Instead, the manager should use incremental analysis to determine whether the savings generated by the efficiencies of the new machine would justify its purchase.

DO IT! 5 Repair or Replace Equipment

Rochester Roofing is faced with a decision. The company relies very heavily on the use of its 60-foot extension lift for work on large homes and commercial properties. Last year, the company spent $60,000 refurbishing the lift. It has just determined that another $40,000 of repair work is required. Alternatively, Rochester Roofing has found a newer used lift that is for sale for $170,000. The company estimates that both the old and new lifts would have useful lives of 6 years. However, the new lift is more efficient and thus would reduce operating expenses by about $20,000 per year. The company could also rent out the new lift for about $2,000 per year. The old lift is not suitable for rental. The old lift could currently be sold for $25,000 if the new lift is purchased. Prepare an incremental analysis that shows whether the company should repair or replace the equipment.

Action Plan

✔ Those costs and revenues that differ across the alternatives are relevant to the decision.

✔ Past costs that cannot be changed are sunk costs.

SOLUTION

	Retain Equipment	Replace Equipment	Net Income Increase (Decrease)
Operating expenses	$120,000*		$ 120,000
Repair costs	40,000		40,000
Rental revenue		$ (12,000)**	12,000
New machine cost		170,000	(170,000)
Sale of old machine		(25,000)	25,000
Total cost	$160,000	$133,000	$ 27,000

*(6 years × $20,000)
**(6 years × $2,000)

The analysis indicates that purchasing the new machine would increase net income for the 6-year period by $27,000.

Related exercise material: **BE20-7, E20-13, E20-14,** and **DO IT! 20-5.**

LEARNING OBJECTIVE 6 Analyze the relevant costs in deciding whether to eliminate an unprofitable segment or product.

Management sometimes must decide whether to eliminate an unprofitable business segment or product. For example, in recent years, many airlines quit servicing certain cities or cut back on the number of flights. Goodyear quit producing several brands in the low-end tire market. Again, the key is to **focus on the relevant costs—the data that change under the alternative courses of action**. To illustrate, assume that Venus Company manufactures tennis racquets in three models: Pro, Master, and Champ. Pro and Master are profitable lines. Champ (highlighted in red in the table below) operates at a loss. Condensed income statement data are as follows.

ILLUSTRATION 20-16
Segment income data

	Pro	Master	Champ	Total
Sales	$800,000	$300,000	$100,000	$1,200,000
Variable costs	520,000	210,000	90,000	820,000
Contribution margin	280,000	90,000	10,000	380,000
Fixed costs	80,000	50,000	30,000	160,000
Net income	$200,000	$ 40,000	$ (20,000)	$ 220,000

▼ **HELPFUL HINT**
A decision to discontinue a segment based solely on the bottom line—net loss—is inappropriate.

You might think that total net income will increase by $20,000 to $240,000 if the unprofitable Champ line of racquets is eliminated. However, **net income may actually decrease if the Champ line is discontinued**. The reason is that if the fixed costs allocated to the Champ racquets cannot be eliminated, they will have to be absorbed by the other products. To illustrate, assume that the $30,000 of fixed costs applicable to the unprofitable segment are allocated 2/3 to the Pro model and 1/3 to the Master model if the Champ model is eliminated. Fixed costs will increase to $100,000 ($80,000 + $20,000) in the Pro line and to $60,000 ($50,000 + $10,000) in the Master line. The revised income statement is as follows.

ILLUSTRATION 20-17
Income data after eliminating unprofitable product line

	Pro	Master	Total
Sales	$800,000	$300,000	$1,100,000
Variable costs	520,000	210,000	730,000
Contribution margin	280,000	90,000	370,000
Fixed costs	100,000	60,000	160,000
Net income	$180,000	$ 30,000	$ 210,000

Total net income has decreased $10,000 ($220,000 − $210,000). This result is also obtained in the following incremental analysis of the Champ racquets.

ILLUSTRATION 20-18
Incremental analysis—eliminating unprofitable segment with no reduction in fixed costs

Incremental Analysis - Eliminating an unprofitable segment.xls

	A	B	C	D
1		Continue	Eliminate	Net Income Increase (Decrease)
2	Sales	$100,000	$ 0	$(100,000)
3	Variable costs	90,000	0	90,000
4	Contribution margin	10,000	0	(10,000)
5	Fixed costs	30,000	30,000	0
6	Net income	$(20,000)	$(30,000)	$ (10,000)
7				

The loss in net income is attributable to the Champ line's contribution margin ($10,000) that will not be realized if the segment is discontinued.

Assume the same facts as above, except now assume that $22,000 of the fixed costs attributed to the Champ line can be eliminated if the line is discontinued. Illustration 20-19 presents the incremental analysis based on this revised assumption.

ILLUSTRATION 20-19
Incremental analysis—eliminating unprofitable segment with reduction in fixed costs

Incremental Analysis - Eliminating an unprofitable segment.xls

	A	B	C	D
1		Continue	Eliminate	Net Income Increase (Decrease)
2	Sales	$100,000	$ 0	$(100,000)
3	Variable costs	90,000	0	90,000
4	Contribution margin	10,000	0	(10,000)
5	Fixed costs	30,000	8,000	22,000
6	Net income	$(20,000)	$(8,000)	$ 12,000
7				

In this case, because the company is able to eliminate some of its fixed costs by eliminating the division, it can increase its net income by $12,000. **This occurs because the $22,000 savings that results from the eliminated fixed costs exceeds the $10,000 in lost contribution margin by $12,000 ($22,000 − $10,000).**

In deciding on the future status of an unprofitable segment, management should consider the effect of elimination on related product lines. It may be possible for continuing product lines to obtain some or all of the sales lost by the discontinued product line. In some businesses, services or products may be linked—for example, free checking accounts at a bank, or coffee at a donut shop. In addition, management should consider the effect of eliminating the product line on employees who may have to be discharged or retrained.

MANAGEMENT INSIGHT Buck Knives

Max Blain/iStockphoto

Time to Move to a New Neighborhood?

If you have ever moved, then you know how complicated and costly it can be. Now consider what it would be like for a manufacturing company with 260 employees and a 170,000-square-foot facility to move from southern California to Idaho. That is what Buck Knives did in order to save its company from financial ruin. Electricity rates in Idaho were half those in California, workers' compensation was one-third the cost, and factory wages were 20% lower. Combined, this would reduce manufacturing costs by $600,000 per year. Moving the factory would cost about $8.5 million, plus $4 million to move key employees. Offsetting these costs was the estimated $11 million selling price of the California property. Based on these estimates, the move would pay for itself in three years.

Ultimately, the company received only $7.5 million for its California property, only 58 of 75 key employees were willing to move, construction was delayed by a year which caused the new plant to increase in price by $1.5 million, and wages surged in Idaho due to low unemployment. Despite all of these complications, though, the company considers the move a great success.

Source: Chris Lydgate, "The Buck Stopped," *Inc. Magazine* (May 2006), pp. 87–95.

What were some of the factors that complicated the company's decision to move? How should the company have incorporated such factors into its incremental analysis? (Go to **WileyPLUS** for this answer and additional questions.)

DO IT! 6 Unprofitable Segments

Lambert, Inc. manufactures several types of accessories. For the year, the knit hats and scarves line had sales of $400,000, variable expenses of $310,000, and fixed expenses of $120,000. Therefore, the knit hats and scarves line had a net loss of $30,000. If Lambert eliminates the knit hats and scarves line, $20,000 of fixed costs will remain. Prepare an analysis showing whether the company should eliminate the knit hats and scarves line.

Action Plan

- ✔ Identify the revenues that change as a result of eliminating a product line.
- ✔ Identify all costs that change as a result of eliminating a product line, and net the amount against the revenues.

SOLUTION

	Continue	Eliminate	Net Income Increase (Decrease)
Sales	$400,000	$ 0	$(400,000)
Variable costs	310,000	0	310,000
Contribution margin	90,000	0	(90,000)
Fixed costs	120,000	20,000	100,000
Net income	$ (30,000)	$(20,000)	$ 10,000

The analysis indicates that Lambert should eliminate the knit hats and scarves line because net income will increase $10,000.

Related exercise material: **BE20-8, E20-15, E20-16, E20-17,** and **DO IT! 20-6.**

USING DECISION TOOLS—METHOD PRODUCTS

Method Products faces many situations where it needs to apply the decision tool learned in this chapter. For example, assume that in order to have control over the creative nature of its packaging, Method decides to manufacture (instead of outsourcing) some of its more creative soap dispensers. Suppose that the company has been approached by a plastic container manufacturer with a proposal to provide 500,000 Mickey and Minnie Mouse hand wash dispensers. Assume Method's cost of producing 500,000 of the dispensers is $110,000, broken down as follows.

Direct materials	$60,000	Variable manufacturing overhead	$12,000
Direct labor	$30,000	Fixed manufacturing overhead	$ 8,000

Instead of making the dispensers at an average cost per unit of $0.22 ($110,000 ÷ 500,000), Method has an opportunity to buy the dispensers at $0.215 per unit. If the dispensers are purchased, all variable costs and one-half of the fixed costs will be eliminated.

INSTRUCTIONS

(a) Prepare an incremental analysis showing whether Method should make or buy the dispensers.

(b) Will your answer be different if the released productive capacity resulting from the purchase of the dispensers will generate additional income of $25,000?

(c) What additional qualitative factors might Method need to consider?

SOLUTION

(a)

	Make	Buy	Net Income Increase (Decrease)
Direct materials	$ 60,000	$ -0-	$ 60,000
Direct labor	30,000	-0-	30,000
Variable manufacturing costs	12,000	-0-	12,000
Fixed manufacturing costs	8,000	4,000*	4,000
Purchase price	-0-	107,500**	(107,500)
Total cost	$110,000	$111,500	$ (1,500)

*$8,000 × .50 **$0.215 × 500,000

This analysis indicates that Method will incur $1,500 of additional costs if it buys the dispensers. Method therefore would choose to make the dispensers.

(b)

	Make	Buy	Net Income Increase (Decrease)
Total cost	$110,000	$111,500	$ (1,500)
Opportunity cost	25,000	-0-	25,000
Total cost	$135,000	$111,500	$23,500

Yes, the answer is different. The analysis shows that if additional capacity is released, net income will be increased by $23,500 if the dispensers are purchased. In this case, Method would choose to purchase the dispensers.

(c) Method is very concerned about the image of its products. It charges a higher price for many of its products than those of its larger competitors. It therefore wants to ensure that the functionality of the dispenser, as well as the appearance, are up to its standards. Also, because of Method's commitment to sustainability, it would consider numerous qualitative issues. For example, is this supplier going to use sustainable manufacturing practices? Method currently requires that its suppliers meet its expectations regarding sustainability.

REVIEW AND PRACTICE

LEARNING OBJECTIVES REVIEW

1 Describe management's decision-making process and incremental analysis. Management's decision-making process consists of (a) identifying the problem and assigning responsibility for the decision, (b) determining and evaluating possible courses of action, (c) making the decision, and (d) reviewing the results of the decision. Incremental analysis identifies financial data that change under alternative courses of action. These data are relevant to the decision because they vary across the possible alternatives.

2 Analyze the relevant costs in accepting an order at a special price. The relevant costs are those that change if the order is accepted. The relevant information in accepting an order at a special price is the difference between the variable manufacturing costs to produce the special order and expected revenues. Any changes in fixed costs, opportunity cost, or other incremental costs or savings (such as additional shipping) should be considered.

3 Analyze the relevant costs in a make-or-buy decision. In a make-or-buy decision, the relevant costs are (a) the variable manufacturing costs that will be saved as well as changes to fixed manufacturing costs, (b) the purchase price, and (c) opportunity cost.

4 Analyze the relevant costs in determining whether to sell or process materials further. The decision rule for whether to sell or process materials further is: Process further as long as the incremental revenue from processing exceeds the incremental processing costs.

5 Analyze the relevant costs to be considered in repairing, retaining, or replacing equipment. The relevant costs to be considered in determining whether equipment should be repaired, retained, or replaced are the effects on variable costs and the cost of the new equipment. Also, any disposal value of the existing asset must be considered.

6 Analyze the relevant costs in deciding whether to eliminate an unprofitable segment or product. In deciding whether to eliminate an unprofitable segment or product, the relevant costs are the variable costs that drive the contribution margin, if any, produced by the segment or product. Opportunity cost and reduction of fixed expenses must also be considered.

DECISION TOOLS REVIEW

DECISION CHECKPOINTS	INFO NEEDED FOR DECISION	TOOL TO USE FOR DECISION	HOW TO EVALUATE RESULTS
Which alternative should the company choose?	All relevant costs including opportunity cost	Compare the relevant cost of each alternative	Choose the alternative that maximizes net income.

GLOSSARY REVIEW

Incremental analysis The process of identifying the financial data that change under alternative courses of action. (p. 976).

Joint costs For joint products, all costs incurred prior to the point at which the two products are separately identifiable (known as the **split-off point**). (p. 985).

Joint products Multiple end-products produced from a single raw material and a common production process. (p. 984).

Opportunity cost The potential benefit that is lost when one course of action is chosen rather than an alternative course of action. (p. 977).

Relevant costs Those costs and revenues that differ across alternatives. (p. 977).

Sunk cost A cost that cannot be changed or avoided by any present or future decision. (p. 977).

PRACTICE MULTIPLE-CHOICE QUESTIONS

(LO 1) **1.** Three of the steps in management's decision-making process are (1) review results of decision, (2) determine and evaluate possible courses of action, and (3) make the decision. The steps are prepared in the following order:
(a) (1), (2), (3).
(b) (3), (2), (1).
(c) (2), (1), (3).
(d) (2), (3), (1).

2. Incremental analysis is the process of identifying the financial data that: (LO 1)
(a) do not change under alternative courses of action.
(b) change under alternative courses of action.
(c) are mixed under alternative courses of action.
(d) No correct answer is given.

(LO 1) **3.** In making business decisions, management ordinarily considers:
(a) quantitative factors but not qualitative factors.
(b) financial information only.
(c) both financial and nonfinancial information.
(d) relevant costs, opportunity cost, and sunk costs.

(LO 1) **4.** A company is considering the following alternatives:

	Alternative A	Alternative B
Revenues	$50,000	$50,000
Variable costs	24,000	24,000
Fixed costs	12,000	15,000

Which of the following are relevant in choosing between these alternatives?
(a) Revenues, variable costs, and fixed costs.
(b) Variable costs and fixed costs.
(c) Variable costs only.
(d) Fixed costs only.

(LO 2) **5.** It costs a company $14 of variable costs and $6 of fixed costs to produce product Z200 that sells for $30. A foreign buyer offers to purchase 3,000 units at $18 each. If the special offer is accepted and produced with unused capacity, net income will:
(a) decrease $6,000. (c) increase $12,000.
(b) increase $6,000. (d) increase $9,000.

(LO 2) **6.** It costs a company $14 of variable costs and $6 of fixed costs to produce product Z200. Product Z200 sells for $30. A buyer offers to purchase 3,000 units at $18 each. The seller will incur special shipping costs of $5 per unit. If the special offer is accepted and produced with unused capacity, net income will:
(a) increase $3,000. (c) decrease $12,000.
(b) increase $12,000. (d) decrease $3,000.

(LO 3) **7.** Jobart Company is currently operating at full capacity. It is considering buying a part from an outside supplier rather than making it in-house. If Jobart purchases the part, it can use the released productive capacity to generate additional income of $30,000 from producing a different product. When conducting incremental analysis in this make-or-buy decision, the company should:
(a) ignore the $30,000.
(b) add $30,000 to other costs in the "Make" column.
(c) add $30,000 to other costs in the "Buy" column.
(d) subtract $30,000 from the other costs in the "Make" column.

(LO 3) **8.** In a make-or-buy decision, relevant costs are:
(a) manufacturing costs that will be saved.
(b) the purchase price of the units.
(c) the opportunity cost.
(d) All of the above.

9. Derek is performing incremental analysis in a make-or-buy decision for Item X. If Derek buys Item X, he can use its released productive capacity to produce Item Z. Derek will sell Item Z for $12,000 and incur production costs of $8,000. Derek's incremental analysis should include an opportunity cost of: (LO 3)
(a) $12,000. (c) $4,000.
(b) $8,000. (d) $0.

10. The decision rule in a sell-or-process-further decision is: process further as long as the incremental revenue from processing exceeds: (LO 4)
(a) incremental processing costs.
(b) variable processing costs.
(c) fixed processing costs.
(d) No correct answer is given.

11. Walton, Inc. makes an unassembled product that it currently sells for $55. Production costs are $20. Walton is considering assembling the product and selling it for $68. The cost to assemble the product is estimated at $12. What decision should Walton make? (LO 4)
(a) Sell before assembly; net income per unit will be $12 greater.
(b) Sell before assembly; net income per unit will be $1 greater.
(c) Process further; net income per unit will be $13 greater.
(d) Process further; net income per unit will be $1 greater.

12. In a decision to retain or replace equipment, the book value of the old equipment is a (an): (LO 5)
(a) opportunity cost. (c) incremental cost.
(b) sunk cost. (d) marginal cost.

13. If an unprofitable segment is eliminated: (LO 6)
(a) net income will always increase.
(b) variable costs of the eliminated segment will have to be absorbed by other segments.
(c) fixed costs allocated to the eliminated segment will have to be absorbed by other segments.
(d) net income will always decrease.

14. A segment of Hazard Inc. has the following data. (LO 6)

Sales	$200,000
Variable expenses	140,000
Fixed expenses	100,000

If this segment is eliminated, what will be the effect on the remaining company? Assume that 50% of the fixed expenses will be eliminated and the rest will be allocated to the segments of the remaining company.
(a) $120,000 increase. (c) $50,000 increase.
(b) $10,000 decrease. (d) $10,000 increase.

SOLUTIONS

1. **(d)** The order of the steps in the decision process is (2) determine and evaluate possible courses of action, (3) make the decision, and (1) review the results of decision. Choices (a), (b), and (c) list the steps in the incorrect order.
2. **(b)** Incremental analysis is the process of identifying the financial data that change under alternative courses of action, not the financial data that (a) do not change or (c) are mixed. Choice (d) is wrong as there is a correct answer given.
3. **(c)** Management ordinarily considers both financial and nonfinancial information in making business decisions. The other choices are incorrect because they are all limited to financial data and do not consider nonfinancial information.
4. **(d)** Fixed costs is the only relevant factor, that is, the only factor that differs across Alternatives A and B. The other choices are incorrect because they list either revenues, variable costs, or both, which are the same amounts for both alternatives.
5. **(c)** If the special offer is accepted and produced with unused capacity, variable cost per unit = $14, income per unit = ($18 − $14), so net income will increase by $12,000 (3,000 × $4), not (a) decrease $6,000, (b) increase $6,000, or (d) increase $9,000.

6. **(d)** If the special offer is accepted and produced with unused capacity, variable cost per unit = $19 ($14 variable + $5 shipping costs), income per unit = −$1 ($18 − $19), so net income will decrease by $3,000 (3,000 × −$1), not (a) increase $3,000, (b) increase $12,000, or (c) decrease $12,000.
7. **(b)** Jobart Company should add $30,000 to other costs in the "Make" column as it represents lost income of continuing to make the part in-house. The other choices are incorrect because the $30,000 (a) should not be ignored as it is an opportunity cost, (c) represents potential lost income if the company continues to make the part instead of buying it so therefore should not be placed in the "Buy" column, and (d) should be added to, not subtracted from, the other costs in the "Make" column.
8. **(d)** All the costs in choices (a), (b), and (c) are relevant in a make-or-buy decision. So although choices (a), (b), and (c) are true statements, choice (d) is a better answer.
9. **(c)** Derek's opportunity cost in its make-or-buy decision is $12,000 (revenue for Item Z) − $8,000 (production costs for Item Z) = $4,000, not (a) $12,000, (b) $8,000, or (d) $0.
10. **(a)** The decision rule in a sell-or-process-further decision is to process further as long as the incremental revenue from such processing exceeds incremental processing costs, not (b) variable processing costs or (c) fixed processing costs. Choice (d) is wrong as there is a correct answer given.
11. **(d)** If Walton processes further, net income per unit will increase $13 ($68 − $55), which is $1 more than its additional production costs ($12). The other choices are therefore incorrect.
12. **(b)** In the decision to retain or replace equipment, the book value of the old equipment is a sunk cost (it reflects the original cost less accumulated depreciation, neither of which is relevant to the decision), not (a) an opportunity cost, (c) an incremental cost, or (d) a marginal cost.
13. **(c)** Even though the segment is eliminated, the fixed costs allocated to that segment will still have to be covered. This is done by having other segments absorb the fixed costs of that segment. Choices (a) and (d) are incorrect because net income can either increase or decrease if a segment is eliminated. Choice (b) is incorrect because when a segment is eliminated, the variable costs of that segment will also be eliminated and will not need to be absorbed by other segments.
14. **(b)** If the segment continues, net income = −$40,000 ($200,000 − $140,000 − $100,000). If the segment is eliminated, the contribution margin will also be eliminated but $50,000 ($100,000 × .50) of the fixed costs will remain. Therefore, the effect of eliminating the segment will be a $10,000 decrease not (a) a $120,000 increase, (c) a $50,000 increase, or (d) a $10,000 increase.

PRACTICE EXERCISES

Use incremental analysis for make-or-buy decision.

(LO 3)

1. Maningly Inc. has been manufacturing its own lampshades for its table lamps. The company is currently operating at 100% of capacity. Variable manufacturing overhead is charged to production at the rate of 50% of direct labor cost. The direct materials and direct labor cost per unit to make the lampshades are $4 and $6, respectively. Normal production is 50,000 table lamps per year.

A supplier offers to make the lampshades at a price of $13.50 per unit. If Maningly accepts the supplier's offer; all variable manufacturing costs will be eliminated, but the $50,000 of fixed manufacturing overhead currently being charged to the lampshades will have to be absorbed by other products.

INSTRUCTIONS

(a) Prepare the incremental analysis for the decision to make or buy the lampshades.

(b) Should Maningly buy the lampshades?

(c) Would your answer be different in (b) if the productive capacity released by not making the lampshades could be used to produce income of $40,000?

SOLUTION

1. (a)

	Make	Buy	Net Income Increase (Decrease)
Direct materials (50,000 × $4.00)	$200,000	$ 0	$ 200,000
Direct labor (50,000 × $6.00)	300,000	0	300,000
Variable manufacturing costs ($300,000 × 50%)	150,000	0	150,000
Fixed manufacturing costs	50,000	50,000	0
Purchase price (50,000 × $13.50)	0	675,000	(675,000)
Total annual cost	$700,000	$725,000	$ (25,000)

(b) No, Maningly should not purchase the lampshades. As indicated by the incremental analysis, it would cost the company $25,000 more to purchase the lampshades.

(c) Yes, by purchasing the lampshades, a total cost saving of $15,000 will result as shown below.

	Make	Buy	Net Income Increase (Decrease)
Total annual cost (from (a))	$700,000	$725,000	$(25,000)
Opportunity cost	40,000	0	40,000
Total cost	$740,000	$725,000	$ 15,000

2. A company manufactures three products using same production process. The costs incurred up to the split-off point are $200,000. These costs are allocated to the products on the basis of their sales value at the split-off point. The number of units produced, the selling prices per unit of the three products at the split-off point and after further processing, and the additional processing costs are as follows.

Use incremental analysis for whether to sell or process materials further.

(LO 4)

Product	Number of Units Produced	Selling Price at Split-Off	Selling Price after Processing	Additional Processing Costs
D	3,000	$11.00	$15.00	$14,000
E	6,000	12.00	16.20	16,000
F	2,000	19.40	24.00	9,000

INSTRUCTIONS

(a) Which information is relevant to the decision on whether or not to process the products further? Explain why this information is relevant.

(b) Which product(s) should be processed further and which should be sold at the split-off point?

(c) Would your decision be different if the company was using the quantity of output to allocate joint costs? Explain.

(CGA adapted)

SOLUTION

2. (a) The costs that are relevant in this decision are the incremental revenues and the incremental costs associated with processing the material past the split-off point. Any costs incurred up to the split-off point are sunk costs and therefore irrelevant to this decision.

(b) Revenue after further processing:

Product D: $45,000 (3,000 units × $15.00 per unit)
Product E: $97,200 (6,000 units × $16.20 per unit)
Product F: $48,000 (2,000 units × $24.00 per unit)

Revenue at split-off:

Product D: $33,000 (3,000 units × $11.00 per unit)
Product E: $72,000 (6,000 units × $12.00 per unit)
Product F: $38,800 (2,000 units × $19.40 per unit)

	D	E	F
Incremental revenue	$ 12,000[a]	$ 25,200[b]	$ 9,200[c]
Incremental cost	(14,000)	(16,000)	(9,000)
Increase (decrease) in profit	$ (2,000)	$ 9,200	$ 200

[a]$45,000 − $33,000; [b]$97,200 − $72,000; [c]$48,000 − $38,800

Products E and F should be processed further.

(c) The decision would remain the same. It does not matter how the joint costs are allocated because joint costs are irrelevant to this decision.

Use incremental analysis for retaining or replacing equipment.

(LO 5)

3. Tek Enterprises uses a computer to handle its sales invoices. Lately, business has been so good that it takes an extra 3 hours per night, plus every third Saturday, to keep up with the volume of sales invoices. Management is considering updating its computer with a faster model that would eliminate all of the overtime processing.

	Current Machine	New Machine
Original purchase cost	$15,000	$25,000
Accumulated depreciation	6,000	—
Estimated operating costs	25,000	20,000
Useful life	6 years	6 years

If sold now, the current machine would have a salvage value of $5,000. If operated for the remainder of its useful life, the current machine would have zero salvage value. The new machine is expected to have zero salvage value after 6 years.

INSTRUCTIONS

Should the current machine be replaced? (Ignore the time value of money.)

SOLUTION

3.

	Retain Machine	Replace Machine	Net Income Increase (Decrease)
Operating costs	$150,000*	$120,000**	$30,000
New machine cost (depr.)	0	25,000	(25,000)
Salvage value (old)	0	(5,000)	5,000
Total	$150,000	$140,000	$10,000

*$25,000 × 6
**$20,000 × 6

The current machine should be replaced. The incremental analysis shows that net income for the 6-year period will be $10,000 higher by replacing the current machine.

Use incremental analysis for elimination of division.

(LO 6)

4. Benai Lorenzo, a recent graduate of Bonita's accounting program, evaluated the operating performance of Wasson Company's six divisions. Benai made the following presentation to the Wasson board of directors and suggested the Ortiz Division be eliminated. "If the Ortiz Division is eliminated," she said, "our total profits would increase by $23,870."

	The Other Five Divisions	Ortiz Division	Total
Sales	$1,664,200	$ 96,200	$1,760,400
Cost of goods sold	978,520	76,470	1,054,990
Gross profit	685,680	19,730	705,410
Operating expenses	527,940	43,600	571,540
Net income	$ 157,740	$(23,870)	$ 133,870

In the Ortiz Division, cost of goods sold is $70,000 variable and $6,470 fixed, and operating expenses are $15,000 variable and $28,600 fixed. None of the Ortiz Division's fixed costs will be eliminated if the division is discontinued.

INSTRUCTIONS

Is Benai right about eliminating the Ortiz Division? Prepare a schedule to support your answer.

SOLUTION

4.

	Continue	Eliminate	Net Income Increase (Decrease)
Sales	$ 96,200	$ 0	$(96,200)
Variable expenses			
Cost of goods sold	70,000	0	70,000
Operating expenses	15,000	0	15,000
Total variable	85,000	0	85,000
Contribution margin	11,200	0	(11,200)
Fixed expenses			
Cost of goods sold	6,470	6,470	0
Operating expenses	28,600	28,600	0
Total fixed	35,070	35,070	0
Net income (loss)	$(23,870)	$(35,070)	$(11,200)

Benai is incorrect. The incremental analysis shows that net income will be $11,200 less if the Ortiz Division is eliminated. This amount equals the contribution margin that would be lost by discontinuing the division.

▶ PRACTICE PROBLEM

Use incremental analysis for a special order.

(LO 2)

Walston Company produces kitchen cabinets for homebuilders across the western United States. The cost of producing 5,000 cabinets is as follows.

Materials	$ 500,000
Labor	250,000
Variable overhead	100,000
Fixed overhead	400,000
Total	$1,250,000

Walston also incurs selling expenses of $20 per cabinet. Wellington Corp. has offered Walston $165 per cabinet for a special order of 1,000 cabinets. The cabinets would be sold to homebuilders in the eastern United States and thus would not conflict with Walston's current sales. Selling expenses per cabinet would be only $5 per cabinet. Walston has available capacity to do the work.

INSTRUCTIONS

(a) Prepare an incremental analysis for the special order.
(b) Should Walston accept the special order? Why or why not?

SOLUTION

(a) Relevant costs per unit would be:

Materials	$500,000/5,000 =	$100
Labor	250,000/5,000 =	50
Variable overhead	100,000/5,000 =	20
Selling expenses		5
Total relevant cost per unit		$175

	Reject Order	Accept Order	Net Income Increase (Decrease)
Revenues	$0	$165,000*	$165,000
Costs	0	175,000**	(175,000)
Net income	$0	$(10,000)	$(10,000)

*$165 × 1,000; **$175 × 1,000

(b) Walston should reject the offer. The incremental benefit of $165 per cabinet is less than the incremental cost of $175. By accepting the order, Walston's net income would actually decline by $10,000.

WileyPLUS Brief Exercises, DO IT! Exercises, Exercises, Problems, and many additional resources are available for practice in WileyPLUS.

QUESTIONS

1. What steps are frequently involved in management's decision-making process?
2. Your roommate, Anna Polis, contends that accounting contributes to most of the steps in management's decision-making process. Is your roommate correct? Explain.
3. "Incremental analysis involves the accumulation of information concerning a single course of action." Do you agree? Why?
4. Sydney Greene asks for your help concerning the relevance of variable and fixed costs in incremental analysis. Help Sydney with her problem.
5. What data are relevant in deciding whether to accept an order at a special price?
6. Emil Corporation has an opportunity to buy parts at $9 each that currently cost $12 to make. What manufacturing costs are relevant to this make-or-buy decision?
7. Define the term "opportunity cost." How may this cost be relevant in a make-or-buy decision?
8. What is the decision rule in deciding whether to sell a product or process it further?
9. What are joint products? What accounting issue results from the production process that creates joint products?
10. How are allocated joint costs treated when making a sell-or-process-further decision?
11. Your roommate, Gale Dunham, is confused about sunk costs. Explain to your roommate the meaning of sunk costs and their relevance to a decision to retain or replace equipment.
12. Huang Inc. has one product line that is unprofitable. What circumstances may cause overall company net income to be lower if the unprofitable product line is eliminated?

BRIEF EXERCISES

Identify the steps in management's decision-making process.
(LO 1), AP

BE20-1 The steps in management's decision-making process are listed in random order below. Indicate the order in which the steps should be executed.

______	Make a decision	______	Review results of the decision
______	Identify the problem and assign responsibility	______	Determine and evaluate possible courses of action

Determine incremental changes.
(LO 1), AP

BE20-2 Bogart Company is considering two alternatives. Alternative A will have revenues of $160,000 and costs of $100,000. Alternative B will have revenues of $180,000 and costs of $125,000. Compare Alternative A to Alternative B showing incremental revenues, costs, and net income.

Determine whether to accept a special order.
(LO 2), AP

BE20-3 At Bargain Electronics, it costs $30 per unit ($20 variable and $10 fixed) to make an MP3 player that normally sells for $45. A foreign wholesaler offers to buy 3,000 units at $25 each. Bargain Electronics will incur special shipping costs of $3 per unit. Assuming that Bargain Electronics has excess operating capacity, indicate the net income (loss) Bargain Electronics would realize by accepting the special order.

Determine whether to make or buy a part.
(LO 3), AP

BE20-4 Manson Industries incurs unit costs of $8 ($5 variable and $3 fixed) in making an assembly part for its finished product. A supplier offers to make 10,000 of the assembly part at $6 per unit. If the offer is accepted, Manson will save all variable costs but no fixed costs. Prepare an analysis showing the total cost saving, if any, Manson will realize by buying the part.

Determine whether to sell or process further.
(LO 4), AP

BE20-5 Pine Street Inc. makes unfinished bookcases that it sells for $62. Production costs are $36 variable and $10 fixed. Because it has unused capacity, Pine Street is considering finishing the bookcases and selling them for $70. Variable finishing costs are expected to be $6 per unit with no increase in fixed costs. Prepare an analysis on a per unit basis showing whether Pine Street should sell unfinished or finished bookcases.

BE20-6 Each day, Adama Corporation processes 1 ton of a secret raw material into two resulting products, AB1 and XY1. When it processes 1 ton of the raw material, the company incurs joint processing costs of $60,000. It allocates $25,000 of these costs to AB1 and $35,000 of these costs to XY1. The resulting AB1 can be sold for $100,000. Alternatively, it can be processed further to make AB2 at an additional processing cost of $45,000, and sold for $150,000. Each day's batch of XY1 can be sold for $95,000. Or, it can be processed further to create XY2, at an additional processing cost of $50,000, and sold for $130,000. Discuss what products Adama Corporation should make.

Determine whether to sell or process further, joint products.

(LO 4), AP

BE20-7 Bryant Company has a factory machine with a book value of $90,000 and a remaining useful life of 5 years. It can be sold for $30,000. A new machine is available at a cost of $400,000. This machine will have a 5-year useful life with no salvage value. The new machine will lower annual variable manufacturing costs from $600,000 to $500,000. Prepare an analysis showing whether the old machine should be retained or replaced.

Determine whether to retain or replace equipment.

(LO 5), AP

BE20-8 Lisah, Inc., manufactures golf clubs in three models. For the year, the Big Bart line has a net loss of $10,000 from sales $200,000, variable costs $180,000, and fixed costs $30,000. If the Big Bart line is eliminated, $20,000 of fixed costs will remain. Prepare an analysis showing whether the Big Bart line should be eliminated.

Determine whether to eliminate an unprofitable segment.

(LO 6), AP

DO IT! EXERCISES

DO IT! 20-1 Nathan T Corporation is comparing two different options. Nathan T currently uses Option 1, with revenues of $65,000 per year, maintenance expenses of $5,000 per year, and operating expenses of $26,000 per year. Option 2 provides revenues of $60,000 per year, maintenance expenses of $5,000 per year, and operating expenses of $22,000 per year. Option 1 employs a piece of equipment which was upgraded 2 years ago at a cost of $17,000. If Option 2 is chosen, it will free up resources that will bring in an additional $4,000 of revenue. Complete the following table to show the change in income from choosing Option 2 versus Option 1. Designate Sunk costs with an "S."

Determine incremental costs.

(LO 1), AN

	Option 1	Option 2	Net Income Increase (Decrease)	Sunk (S)
Revenues				
Maintenance expenses				
Operating expenses				
Equipment upgrade				
Opportunity cost				

DO IT! 20-2 Maize Company incurs a cost of $35 per unit, of which $20 is variable, to make a product that normally sells for $58. A foreign wholesaler offers to buy 6,000 units at $30 each. Maize will incur additional costs of $4 per unit to imprint a logo and to pay for shipping. Compute the increase or decrease in net income Maize will realize by accepting the special order, assuming Maize has sufficient excess operating capacity. Should Maize Company accept the special order?

Evaluate special order.

(LO 2), AN

DO IT! 20-3 Wilma Company must decide whether to make or buy some of its components. The costs of producing 60,000 switches for its generators are as follows.

Evaluate make-or-buy opportunity.

(LO 3), AN

Direct materials	$30,000	Variable overhead	$45,000
Direct labor	$42,000	Fixed overhead	$60,000

Instead of making the switches at an average cost of $2.95 ($177,000 ÷ 60,000), the company has an opportunity to buy the switches at $2.70 per unit. If the company purchases the switches, all the variable costs and one-fourth of the fixed costs will be eliminated. (a) Prepare an incremental analysis showing whether the company should make or buy the switches. (b) Would your answer be different if the released productive capacity will generate additional income of $34,000?

Sell or process further.
(LO 4), AP

DO IT! 20-4 Mesa Verde manufactures unpainted furniture for the do-it-yourself (DIY) market. It currently sells a table for $75. Production costs are $40 variable and $10 fixed. Mesa Verde is considering staining and sealing the table to sell it for $100. Variable costs to finish each table are expected to be $19, and fixed costs are expected to be $3. Prepare an analysis showing whether Mesa Verde should sell unpainted or finished tables.

Repair or replace equipment.
(LO 5), AP

DO IT! 20-5 Darcy Roofing is faced with a decision. The company relies very heavily on the use of its 60-foot extension lift for work on large homes and commercial properties. Last year, Darcy Roofing spent $60,000 refurbishing the lift. It has just determined that another $40,000 of repair work is required. Alternatively, it has found a newer used lift that is for sale for $170,000. The company estimates that both lifts would have useful lives of 6 years. The new lift is more efficient and thus would reduce operating expenses by about $20,000 per year. Darcy Roofing could also rent out the new lift for about $10,000 per year. The old lift is not suitable for rental. The old lift could currently be sold for $25,000 if the new lift is purchased. Prepare an incremental analysis showing whether the company should repair or replace the equipment.

Analyze whether to eliminate unprofitable segment.
(LO 6), AP

DO IT! 20-6 Gator Corporation manufactures several types of accessories. For the year, the gloves and mittens line had sales of $500,000, variable expenses of $370,000, and fixed expenses of $150,000. Therefore, the gloves and mittens line had a net loss of $20,000. If Gator eliminates the line, $38,000 of fixed costs will remain. Prepare an analysis showing whether the company should eliminate the gloves and mittens line.

EXERCISES

Analyze statements about decision-making and incremental analysis.
(LO 1), C

E20-1 As a study aid, your classmate Pascal Adams has prepared the following list of statements about decision-making and incremental analysis.

1. The first step in management's decision-making process is, "Determine and evaluate possible courses of action."
2. The final step in management's decision-making process is to actually make the decision.
3. Accounting's contribution to management's decision-making process occurs primarily in evaluating possible courses of action and in reviewing the results.
4. In making business decisions, management ordinarily considers only financial information because it is objectively determined.
5. Decisions involve a choice among alternative courses of action.
6. The process used to identify the financial data that change under alternative courses of action is called incremental analysis.
7. Costs that are the same under all alternative courses of action sometimes affect the decision.
8. When using incremental analysis, some costs will always change under alternative courses of action, but revenues will not.
9. Variable costs will change under alternative courses of action, but fixed costs will not.

Instructions
Identify each statement as true or false. If false, indicate how to correct the statement.

Use incremental analysis for special-order decision.
(LO 2), AN

E20-2 Gruden Company produces golf discs which it normally sells to retailers for $7 each. The cost of manufacturing 20,000 golf discs is:

Materials	$ 10,000
Labor	30,000
Variable overhead	20,000
Fixed overhead	40,000
Total	$100,000

Gruden also incurs 5% sales commission ($0.35) on each disc sold.

McGee Corporation offers Gruden $4.80 per disc for 5,000 discs. McGee would sell the discs under its own brand name in foreign markets not yet served by Gruden. If Gruden accepts the offer, its fixed overhead will increase from $40,000 to $46,000 due to the purchase of a new imprinting machine. No sales commission will result from the special order.

Instructions

(a) Prepare an incremental analysis for the special order.
(b) Should Gruden accept the special order? Why or why not?
(c) What assumptions underlie the decision made in part (b)?

Use incremental analysis for special order.
(LO 2), AN

E20-3 Moonbeam Company manufactures toasters. For the first 8 months of 2017, the company reported the following operating results while operating at 75% of plant capacity:

Sales (350,000 units)	$4,375,000
Cost of goods sold	2,600,000
Gross profit	1,775,000
Operating expenses	840,000
Net income	$ 935,000

Cost of goods sold was 70% variable and 30% fixed; operating expenses were 80% variable and 20% fixed.

In September, Moonbeam receives a special order for 15,000 toasters at $7.60 each from Luna Company of Ciudad Juarez. Acceptance of the order would result in an additional $3,000 of shipping costs but no increase in fixed costs.

Instructions

(a) Prepare an incremental analysis for the special order.
(b) Should Moonbeam accept the special order? Why or why not?

Use incremental analysis for special order.
(LO 2), AN

E20-4 Klean Fiber Company is the creator of Y-Go, a technology that weaves silver into its fabrics to kill bacteria and odor on clothing while managing heat. Y-Go has become very popular in undergarments for sports activities. Operating at capacity, the company can produce 1,000,000 Y-Go undergarments a year. The per unit and the total costs for an individual garment when the company operates at full capacity are as follows.

	Per Undergarment	Total
Direct materials	$2.00	$2,000,000
Direct labor	0.75	750,000
Variable manufacturing overhead	1.00	1,000,000
Fixed manufacturing overhead	1.50	1,500,000
Variable selling expenses	0.25	250,000
Totals	$5.50	$5,500,000

The U.S. Army has approached Klean Fiber and expressed an interest in purchasing 250,000 Y-Go undergarments for soldiers in extremely warm climates. The Army would pay the unit cost for direct materials, direct labor, and variable manufacturing overhead costs. In addition, the Army has agreed to pay an additional $1 per undergarment to cover all other costs and provide a profit. Presently, Klean Fiber is operating at 70% capacity and does not have any other potential buyers for Y-Go. If Klean Fiber accepts the Army's offer, it will not incur any variable selling expenses related to this order.

Instructions

Using incremental analysis, determine whether Klean Fiber should accept the Army's offer.

Use incremental analysis for make-or-buy decision.
(LO 3), AN

XLS

E20-5 Pottery Ranch Inc. has been manufacturing its own finials for its curtain rods. The company is currently operating at 100% of capacity, and variable manufacturing overhead is charged to production at the rate of 70% of direct labor cost. The direct materials and direct labor cost per unit to make a pair of finials are $4 and $5, respectively. Normal production is 30,000 curtain rods per year.

A supplier offers to make a pair of finials at a price of $12.95 per unit. If Pottery Ranch accepts the supplier's offer, all variable manufacturing costs will be eliminated, but the $45,000 of fixed manufacturing overhead currently being charged to the finials will have to be absorbed by other products.

Instructions

(a) Prepare the incremental analysis for the decision to make or buy the finials.
(b) Should Pottery Ranch buy the finials?
(c) Would your answer be different in (b) if the productive capacity released by not making the finials could be used to produce income of $20,000?

Use incremental analysis for make-or-buy decision.

(LO 3), E

E20-6 Jobs, Inc. has recently started the manufacture of Tri-Robo, a three-wheeled robot that can scan a home for fires and gas leaks and then transmit this information to a smartphone. The cost structure to manufacture 20,000 Tri-Robos is as follows.

	Cost
Direct materials ($50 per robot)	$1,000,000
Direct labor ($40 per robot)	800,000
Variable overhead ($6 per robot)	120,000
Allocated fixed overhead ($30 per robot)	600,000
Total	$2,520,000

Jobs is approached by Tienh Inc., which offers to make Tri-Robo for $115 per unit or $2,300,000.

Instructions

(a) Using incremental analysis, determine whether Jobs should accept this offer under each of the following independent assumptions.
 (1) Assume that $405,000 of the fixed overhead cost can be avoided.
 (2) Assume that none of the fixed overhead can be avoided. However, if the robots are purchased from Tienh Inc., Jobs can use the released productive resources to generate additional income of $375,000.
(b) Describe the qualitative factors that might affect the decision to purchase the robots from an outside supplier.

Prepare incremental analysis for make-or-buy decision.

(LO 3), E

E20-7 Riggs Company purchases sails and produces sailboats. It currently produces 1,200 sailboats per year, operating at normal capacity, which is about 80% of full capacity. Riggs purchases sails at $250 each, but the company is considering using the excess capacity to manufacture the sails instead. The manufacturing cost per sail would be $100 for direct materials, $80 for direct labor, and $90 for overhead. The $90 overhead is based on $78,000 of annual fixed overhead that is allocated using normal capacity.

The president of Riggs has come to you for advice. "It would cost me $270 to make the sails," she says, "but only $250 to buy them. Should I continue buying them, or have I missed something?"

Instructions

(a) Prepare a per unit analysis of the differential costs. Briefly explain whether Riggs should make or buy the sails.
(b) If Riggs suddenly finds an opportunity to rent out the unused capacity of its factory for $77,000 per year, would your answer to part (a) change? Briefly explain.
(c) Identify three qualitative factors that should be considered by Riggs in this make-or-buy decision.

(CGA adapted)

Prepare incremental analysis concerning make-or-buy decision.

(LO 3), E

XLS

E20-8 Innova uses 1,000 units of the component IMC2 every month to manufacture one of its products. The unit costs incurred to manufacture the component are as follows.

Direct materials	$ 65.00
Direct labor	45.00
Overhead	126.50
Total	$236.50

Overhead costs include variable material handling costs of $6.50, which are applied to products on the basis of direct material costs. The remainder of the overhead costs are applied on the basis of direct labor dollars and consist of 60% variable costs and 40% fixed costs.

A vendor has offered to supply the IMC2 component at a price of $200 per unit.

Instructions

(a) Should Innova purchase the component from the outside vendor if Innova's capacity remains idle?

(b) Should Innova purchase the component from the outside vendor if it can use its facilities to manufacture another product? What information will Innova need to make an accurate decision? Show your calculations.

(c) What are the qualitative factors that Innova will have to consider when making this decision?

(CGA adapted)

Use incremental analysis for further processing of materials decision.

(LO 4), AN

E20-9 Anna Garden recently opened her own basketweaving studio. She sells finished baskets in addition to the raw materials needed by customers to weave baskets of their own. Anna has put together a variety of raw material kits, each including materials at various stages of completion. Unfortunately, owing to space limitations, Anna is unable to carry all varieties of kits originally assembled and must choose between two basic packages.

The basic introductory kit includes undyed, uncut reeds (with dye included) for weaving one basket. This basic package costs Anna $16 and sells for $30. The second kit, called Stage 2, includes cut reeds that have already been dyed. With this kit the customer need only soak the reeds and weave the basket. Anna is able to produce the second kit by using the basic materials included in the first kit and adding one hour of her own time, which she values at $18 per hour. Because she is more efficient at cutting and dying reeds than her average customer, Anna is able to make two kits of the dyed reeds, in one hour, from one kit of undyed reeds. The Stage 2 kit sells for $36.

Instructions

Determine whether Anna's basketweaving studio should carry the basic introductory kit with undyed and uncut reeds or the Stage 2 kit with reeds already dyed and cut. Prepare an incremental analysis to support your answer.

Determine whether to sell or process further, joint products.

(LO 4), AN

E20-10 Stahl Inc. produces three separate products from a common process costing $100,000. Each of the products can be sold at the split-off point or can be processed further and then sold for a higher price. Shown below are cost and selling price data for a recent period.

	Sales Value at Split-Off Point	Cost to Process Further	Sales Value after Further Processing
Product 10	$60,000	$100,000	$190,000
Product 12	15,000	30,000	35,000
Product 14	55,000	150,000	215,000

Instructions

(a) Determine total net income if all products are sold at the split-off point.

(b) Determine total net income if all products are sold after further processing.

(c) Using incremental analysis, determine which products should be sold at the split-off point and which should be processed further.

(d) Determine total net income using the results from (c) and explain why the net income is different from that determined in (b).

Determine whether to sell or process further, joint products.

(LO 4), AN

E20-11 Kirk Minerals processes materials extracted from mines. The most common raw material that it processes results in three joint products: Spock, Uhura, and Sulu. Each of these products can be sold as is, or each can be processed further and sold for a higher price. The company incurs joint costs of $180,000 to process one batch of the raw material that produces the three joint products. The following cost and sales information is available for one batch of each product.

	Sales Value at Split-Off Point	Allocated Joint Costs	Cost to Process Further	Sales Value of Processed Product
Spock	$210,000	$40,000	$110,000	$300,000
Uhura	300,000	60,000	85,000	400,000
Sulu	455,000	80,000	250,000	800,000

Instructions

Determine whether each of the three joint products should be sold as is, or processed further.

Prepare incremental analysis for whether to sell or process materials further.

(LO 4), E

E20-12 A company manufactures three products using the same production process. The costs incurred up to the split-off point are $200,000. These costs are allocated to the products on the basis of their sales value at the split-off point. The number of units produced, the selling prices per unit of the three products at the split-off point and after further processing, and the additional processing costs are as follows.

Product	Number of Units Produced	Selling Price at Split-Off	Selling Price after Processing	Additional Processing Costs
D	4,000	$10.00	$15.00	$14,000
E	6,000	11.60	16.20	20,000
F	2,000	19.40	22.60	9,000

Instructions

(a) Which information is relevant to the decision on whether or not to process the products further? Explain why this information is relevant.

(b) Which product(s) should be processed further and which should be sold at the split-off point?

(c) Would your decision be different if the company was using the quantity of output to allocate joint costs? Explain.

(CGA adapted)

Use incremental analysis for retaining or replacing equipment decision.

(LO 5), E

E20-13 On January 2, 2016, Twilight Hospital purchased a $100,000 special radiology scanner from Bella Inc. The scanner had a useful life of 4 years and was estimated to have no disposal value at the end of its useful life. The straight-line method of depreciation is used on this scanner. Annual operating costs with this scanner are $105,000.

Approximately one year later, the hospital is approached by Dyno Technology salesperson, Jacob Cullen, who indicated that purchasing the scanner in 2016 from Bella Inc. was a mistake. He points out that Dyno has a scanner that will save Twilight Hospital $25,000 a year in operating expenses over its 3-year useful life. Jacob notes that the new scanner will cost $110,000 and has the same capabilities as the scanner purchased last year. The hospital agrees that both scanners are of equal quality. The new scanner will have no disposal value. Jacob agrees to buy the old scanner from Twilight Hospital for $50,000.

Instructions

(a) If Twilight Hospital sells its old scanner on January 2, 2017, compute the gain or loss on the sale.

(b) Using incremental analysis, determine if Twilight Hospital should purchase the new scanner on January 2, 2017.

(c) Explain why Twilight Hospital might be reluctant to purchase the new scanner, regardless of the results indicated by the incremental analysis in (b).

Use incremental analysis for retaining or replacing equipment decision.

(LO 5), AN

E20-14 Johnson Enterprises uses a computer to handle its sales invoices. Lately, business has been so good that it takes an extra 3 hours per night, plus every third Saturday, to keep up with the volume of sales invoices. Management is considering updating its computer with a faster model that would eliminate all of the overtime processing.

	Current Machine	New Machine
Original purchase cost	$15,000	$25,000
Accumulated depreciation	$ 6,000	—
Estimated annual operating costs	$25,000	$20,000
Remaining useful life	5 years	5 years

If sold now, the current machine would have a salvage value of $6,000. If operated for the remainder of its useful life, the current machine would have zero salvage value. The new machine is expected to have zero salvage value after 5 years.

Instructions

Should the current machine be replaced?

Use incremental analysis concerning elimination of division.

(LO 6), AN

XLS

E20-15 Veronica Mars, a recent graduate of Bell's accounting program, evaluated the operating performance of Dunn Company's six divisions. Veronica made the following presentation to Dunn's board of directors and suggested the Percy Division be eliminated. "If the Percy Division is eliminated," she said, "our total profits would increase by $26,000."

	The Other Five Divisions	Percy Division	Total
Sales	$1,664,200	$100,000	$1,764,200
Cost of goods sold	978,520	76,000	1,054,520
Gross profit	685,680	24,000	709,680
Operating expenses	527,940	50,000	577,940
Net income	$ 157,740	$ (26,000)	$ 131,740

In the Percy Division, cost of goods sold is $61,000 variable and $15,000 fixed, and operating expenses are $30,000 variable and $20,000 fixed. None of the Percy Division's fixed costs will be eliminated if the division is discontinued.

Instructions

Is Veronica right about eliminating the Percy Division? Prepare a schedule to support your answer.

E20-16 Cawley Company makes three models of tasers. Information on the three products is given below.

Use incremental analysis for elimination of a product line.

(LO 6), AN

	Tingler	Shocker	Stunner
Sales	$300,000	$500,000	$200,000
Variable expenses	150,000	200,000	145,000
Contribution margin	150,000	300,000	55,000
Fixed expenses	120,000	230,000	95,000
Net income	$ 30,000	$ 70,000	$ (40,000)

Fixed expenses consist of $300,000 of common costs allocated to the three products based on relative sales, and additional fixed expenses of $30,000 (Tingler), $80,000 (Shocker), and $35,000 (Stunner). The common costs will be incurred regardless of how many models are produced. The other fixed expenses would be eliminated if a model is phased out.

James Watt, an executive with the company, feels the Stunner line should be discontinued to increase the company's net income.

Instructions

(a) Compute current net income for Cawley Company.

(b) Compute net income by product line and in total for Cawley Company if the company discontinues the Stunner product line. (*Hint:* Allocate the $300,000 common costs to the two remaining product lines based on their relative sales.)

(c) Should Cawley eliminate the Stunner product line? Why or why not?

E20-17 Tharp Company operates a small factory in which it manufactures two products: C and D. Production and sales results for last year were as follows.

Prepare incremental analysis concerning keeping or dropping a product to maximize operating income.

(LO 6), AN

	C	D
Units sold	9,000	20,000
Selling price per unit	$95	$75
Variable cost per unit	50	40
Fixed cost per unit	24	24

For purposes of simplicity, the firm averages total fixed costs over the total number of units of C and D produced and sold.

The research department has developed a new product (E) as a replacement for product D. Market studies show that Tharp Company could sell 10,000 units of E next year at a price of $115; the variable cost per unit of E is $45. The introduction of product E will lead to a 10% increase in demand for product C and discontinuation of product D. If the company does not introduce the new product, it expects next year's results to be the same as last year's.

Instructions

Should Tharp Company introduce product E next year? Explain why or why not. Show calculations to support your decision.

(CMA-Canada adapted)

Identify relevant costs for different decisions.

(LO 1, 2, 3, 4, 5, 6), C

E20-18 The costs listed below relate to a variety of different decision situations.

Cost	Decision
1. Unavoidable fixed overhead	Eliminate an unprofitable segment
2. Direct labor	Make or buy
3. Original cost of old equipment	Equipment replacement
4. Joint production costs	Sell or process further
5. Opportunity cost	Accepting a special order
6. Segment manager's salary	Eliminate an unprofitable segment (manager will be terminated)
7. Cost of new equipment	Equipment replacement
8. Incremental production costs	Sell or process further
9. Direct materials	Equipment replacement (the amount of materials required does not change)
10. Rent expense	Purchase or lease a building

Instructions

For each cost listed above, indicate if it is relevant or not to the related decision. For those costs determined to be irrelevant, briefly explain why.

EXERCISES: SET B AND CHALLENGE EXERCISES

Visit the book's companion website, at **www.wiley.com/college/kimmel**, and choose the Student Companion site to access Exercises: Set B and Challenge Exercises.

PROBLEMS: SET A

Use incremental analysis for special order and identify nonfinancial factors in the decision.

(LO 2), E

P20-1A ThreePoint Sports Inc. manufactures basketballs for the Women's National Basketball Association (WNBA). For the first 6 months of 2017, the company reported the following operating results while operating at 80% of plant capacity and producing 120,000 units.

	Amount
Sales	$4,800,000
Cost of goods sold	3,600,000
Selling and administrative expenses	405,000
Net income	$ 795,000

Fixed costs for the period were cost of goods sold $960,000, and selling and administrative expenses $225,000.

In July, normally a slack manufacturing month, ThreePoint Sports receives a special order for 10,000 basketballs at $28 each from the Greek Basketball Association (GBA). Acceptance of the order would increase variable selling and administrative expenses $0.75 per unit because of shipping costs but would not increase fixed costs and expenses.

Instructions

(a) NI increase $37,500

(a) Prepare an incremental analysis for the special order.
(b) Should ThreePoint Sports Inc. accept the special order? Explain your answer.
(c) What is the minimum selling price on the special order to produce net income of $5.00 per ball?
(d) What nonfinancial factors should management consider in making its decision?

Use incremental analysis related to make or buy, consider opportunity cost, and identify nonfinancial factors.

(LO 3), E

P20-2A The management of Shatner Manufacturing Company is trying to decide whether to continue manufacturing a part or to buy it from an outside supplier. The part, called CISCO, is a component of the company's finished product.

The following information was collected from the accounting records and production data for the year ending December 31, 2017.

1. 8,000 units of CISCO were produced in the Machining Department.
2. Variable manufacturing costs applicable to the production of each CISCO unit were: direct materials $4.80, direct labor $4.30, indirect labor $0.43, utilities $0.40.
3. Fixed manufacturing costs applicable to the production of CISCO were:

Cost Item	Direct	Allocated
Depreciation	$2,100	$ 900
Property taxes	500	200
Insurance	900	600
	$3,500	$1,700

All variable manufacturing and direct fixed costs will be eliminated if CISCO is purchased. Allocated costs will have to be absorbed by other production departments.

4. The lowest quotation for 8,000 CISCO units from a supplier is $80,000.
5. If CISCO units are purchased, freight and inspection costs would be $0.35 per unit, and receiving costs totaling $1,300 per year would be incurred by the Machining Department.

Instructions

(a) Prepare an incremental analysis for CISCO. Your analysis should have columns for (1) Make CISCO, (2) Buy CISCO, and (3) Net Income Increase/(Decrease). (a) NI (decrease) $(1,160)

(b) Based on your analysis, what decision should management make?

(c) Would the decision be different if Shatner Company has the opportunity to produce $3,000 of net income with the facilities currently being used to manufacture CISCO? Show computations. (c) NI increase $1,840

(d) What nonfinancial factors should management consider in making its decision?

Determine if product should be sold or processed further.

(LO 4), AN

P20-3A Thompson Industrial Products Inc. (TIPI) is a diversified industrial-cleaner processing company. The company's Dargan plant produces two products: a table cleaner and a floor cleaner from a common set of chemical inputs (CDG). Each week, 900,000 ounces of chemical input are processed at a cost of $210,000 into 600,000 ounces of floor cleaner and 300,000 ounces of table cleaner. The floor cleaner has no market value until it is converted into a polish with the trade name FloorShine. The additional processing costs for this conversion amount to $240,000.

FloorShine sells at $20 per 30-ounce bottle. The table cleaner can be sold for $17 per 25-ounce bottle. However, the table cleaner can be converted into two other products by adding 300,000 ounces of another compound (TCP) to the 300,000 ounces of table cleaner. This joint process will yield 300,000 ounces each of table stain remover (TSR) and table polish (TP). The additional processing costs for this process amount to $100,000. Both table products can be sold for $14 per 25-ounce bottle.

The company decided not to process the table cleaner into TSR and TP based on the following analysis.

		Process Further		
	Table Cleaner	Table Stain Remover (TSR)	Table Polish (TP)	Total
Production in ounces	300,000	300,000	300,000	
Revenues	$204,000	$168,000	$168,000	$336,000
Costs:				
CDG costs	70,000*	52,500	52,500	105,000**
TCP costs	0	50,000	50,000	100,000
Total costs	70,000	102,500	102,500	205,000
Weekly gross profit	$134,000	$ 65,500	$ 65,500	$131,000

*If table cleaner is not processed further, it is allocated 1/3 of the $210,000 of CDG cost, which is equal to 1/3 of the total physical output.

**If table cleaner is processed further, total physical output is 1,200,000 ounces. TSR and TP combined account for 50% of the total physical output and are each allocated 25% of the CDG cost.

Instructions

(a) Determine if management made the correct decision to not process the table cleaner further by doing the following.

(1) Calculate the company's total weekly gross profit assuming the table cleaner is not processed further.

(2) Gross profit $186,000

(2) Calculate the company's total weekly gross profit assuming the table cleaner is processed further.

(3) Compare the resulting net incomes and comment on management's decision.

(b) Using incremental analysis, determine if the table cleaner should be processed further.

(CMA adapted)

Compute gain or loss, and determine if equipment should be replaced.

(LO 5), S

P20-4A Last year (2016), Richter Condos installed a mechanized elevator for its tenants. The owner of the company, Ron Richter, recently returned from an industry equipment exhibition where he watched a computerized elevator demonstrated. He was impressed with the elevator's speed, comfort of ride, and cost efficiency. Upon returning from the exhibition, he asked his purchasing agent to collect price and operating cost data on the new elevator. In addition, he asked the company's accountant to provide him with cost data on the company's elevator. This information is presented below.

	Old Elevator	New Elevator
Purchase price	$120,000	$160,000
Estimated salvage value	0	0
Estimated useful life	5 years	4 years
Depreciation method	Straight-line	Straight-line
Annual operating costs other than depreciation:		
Variable	$ 35,000	$ 10,000
Fixed	23,000	8,500

Annual revenues are $240,000, and selling and administrative expenses are $29,000, regardless of which elevator is used. If the old elevator is replaced now, at the beginning of 2017, Richter Condos will be able to sell it for $25,000.

Instructions

(a) Determine any gain or loss if the old elevator is replaced.

(b) Prepare a 4-year summarized income statement for each of the following assumptions:

(1) The old elevator is retained.

(b) (2) NI $539,000

(2) The old elevator is replaced.

(c) NI increase $23,000

(c) Using incremental analysis, determine if the old elevator should be replaced.

(d) Write a memo to Ron Richter explaining why any gain or loss should be ignored in the decision to replace the old elevator.

Prepare incremental analysis concerning elimination of divisions.

(LO 6), AN

P20-5A Brislin Company has four operating divisions. During the first quarter of 2017, the company reported aggregate income from operations of $213,000 and the following divisional results.

	Division			
	I	II	III	IV
Sales	$250,000	$200,000	$500,000	$450,000
Cost of goods sold	200,000	192,000	300,000	250,000
Selling and administrative expenses	75,000	60,000	60,000	50,000
Income (loss) from operations	$ (25,000)	$ (52,000)	$140,000	$150,000

Analysis reveals the following percentages of variable costs in each division.

	I	II	III	IV
Cost of goods sold	70%	90%	80%	75%
Selling and administrative expenses	40	60	50	60

Discontinuance of any division would save 50% of the fixed costs and expenses for that division.

Top management is very concerned about the unprofitable divisions (I and II). Consensus is that one or both of the divisions should be discontinued.

Instructions

(a) Compute the contribution margin for Divisions I and II. (a) I $80,000

(b) Prepare an incremental analysis concerning the possible discontinuance of (1) Division I and (2) Division II. What course of action do you recommend for each division?

(c) Prepare a columnar condensed income statement for Brislin Company, assuming Division II is eliminated. (Use the CVP format.) Division II's unavoidable fixed costs are allocated equally to the continuing divisions. (c) Income III $132,800

(d) Reconcile the total income from operations ($213,000) with the total income from operations without Division II.

PROBLEMS: SET B AND SET C

Visit the book's companion website, at **www.wiley.com/college/kimmel**, and choose the Student Companion site to access Problems: Set B and Set C.

CONTINUING PROBLEMS

CURRENT DESIGNS

EXCEL TUTORIAL

CD20 Current Designs faces a number of important decisions that require incremental analysis. Consider each of the following situations independently.

Situation 1

Recently, Mike Cichanowski, owner and CEO of Current Designs, received a phone call from the president of a brewing company. He was calling to inquire about the possibility of Current Designs producing "floating coolers" for a promotion his company was planning. These coolers resemble a kayak but are about one-third the size. They are used to float food and beverages while paddling down the river on a weekend leisure trip. The company would be interested in purchasing 100 coolers for the upcoming summer. It is willing to pay $250 per cooler. The brewing company would pick up the coolers upon completion of the order.

Mike met with Diane Buswell, controller, to identify how much it would cost Current Designs to produce the coolers. After careful analysis, the following costs were identified.

Direct materials	$80/unit	Variable overhead	$20/unit
Direct labor	$60/unit	Fixed overhead	$1,000

Current Designs would be able to modify an existing mold to produce the coolers. The cost of these modifications would be approximately $2,000.

Instructions

(a) Prepare an incremental analysis to determine whether Current Designs should accept this special order to produce the coolers.

(b) Discuss additional factors that Mike and Diane should consider if Current Designs is currently operating at full capacity.

Situation 2

Current Designs is always working to identify ways to increase efficiency while becoming more environmentally conscious. During a recent brainstorming session, one employee suggested to Diane Buswell, controller, that the company should consider replacing the current rotomold oven as a way to realize savings from reduced energy consumption. The oven operates on natural gas, using 17,000 therms of natural gas for an entire year. A new, energy-efficient rotomold oven would operate on 15,000 therms of natural gas for an entire year. After seeking out price quotes from a few suppliers, Diane determined that it would cost approximately $250,000 to purchase a new, energy-efficient rotomold oven. She determines that the expected useful life of the new oven would be 10 years, and it would have no salvage value at the end of its useful life. Current Designs would be able to sell the current oven for $10,000.

Instructions

(a) Prepare an incremental analysis to determine if Current Designs should purchase the new rotomold oven, assuming that the average price for natural gas over the next 10 years will be $0.65 per therm.

(b) Diane is concerned that natural gas prices might increase at a faster rate over the next 10 years. If the company projects that the average natural gas price of the next 10 years could be as high as $0.85 per therm, discuss how that might change your conclusion in (a).

Situation 3

One of Current Designs' competitive advantages is found in the ingenuity of its owner and CEO, Mike Cichanowski. His involvement in the design of kayak molds and production techniques has led to Current Designs being recognized as an industry leader in the design and production of kayaks. This ingenuity was evident in an improved design of one of the most important components of a kayak, the seat. The "Revolution Seating System" is a one-of-a-kind, rotating axis seat that gives unmatched, full-contact, under-leg support. It is quickly adjustable with a lever-lock system that allows for a customizable seat position that maximizes comfort for the rider.

Having just designed the "Revolution Seating System," Current Designs must now decide whether to produce the seats internally or buy them from an outside supplier. The costs for Current Designs to produce the seats are as follows.

Direct materials	$20/unit	Direct labor	$15/unit
Variable overhead	$12/unit	Fixed overhead	$20,000

Current Designs will need to produce 3,000 seats this year; 25% of the fixed overhead will be avoided if the seats are purchased from an outside vendor. After soliciting prices from outside suppliers, the company determined that it will cost $50 to purchase a seat from an outside vendor.

Instructions

(a) Prepare an incremental analysis showing whether Current Designs should make or buy the "Revolution Seating System."

(b) Would your answer in (a) change if the productive capacity released by not making the seats could be used to produce income of $20,000?

WATERWAYS

(This is a continuation of the Waterways problem from Chapters 14–19.)

WP20 Waterways Corporation is considering various business opportunities. It wants to make the best use of its production facilities to maximize income. This problem asks you to help Waterways do incremental analysis on these various opportunities.

Go to the book's companion website, **www.wiley.com/college/kimmel**, *to find the remainder of this problem.*

EXPAND YOUR CRITICAL THINKING

Group Project

DECISION-MAKING ACROSS THE ORGANIZATION

AN

CT20-1 Aurora Company is considering the purchase of a new machine. The invoice price of the machine is $140,000, freight charges are estimated to be $4,000, and installation costs are expected to be $6,000. Salvage value of the new equipment is expected to be zero after a useful life of 5 years. Existing equipment could be retained and used for an additional 5 years if the new machine is not purchased. At that time, the salvage value of the equipment would be zero. If the new machine is purchased now, the existing machine would have to be scrapped. Aurora's accountant, Lisah Huang, has accumulated the following data regarding annual sales and expenses with and without the new machine.

1. Without the new machine, Aurora can sell 12,000 units of product annually at a per unit selling price of $100. If the new machine is purchased, the number of units produced and sold would increase by 10%, and the selling price would remain the same.
2. The new machine is faster than the old machine, and it is more efficient in its usage of materials. With the old machine the gross profit rate will be 25% of sales, whereas the rate will be 30% of sales with the new machine.

3. Annual selling expenses are $180,000 with the current equipment. Because the new equipment would produce a greater number of units to be sold, annual selling expenses are expected to increase by 10% if it is purchased.
4. Annual administrative expenses are expected to be $100,000 with the old machine, and $113,000 with the new machine.
5. The current book value of the existing machine is $36,000. Aurora uses straight-line depreciation.

Instructions

With the class divided into groups, prepare an incremental analysis for the 5 years showing whether Aurora should keep the existing machine or buy the new machine. (Ignore income tax effects.)

MANAGERIAL ANALYSIS

CT20-2 MiniTek manufactures private-label small electronic products, such as alarm clocks, calculators, kitchen timers, stopwatches, and automatic pencil sharpeners. Some of the products are sold as sets, and others are sold individually. Products are studied as to their sales potential, and then cost estimates are made. The Engineering Department develops production plans, and then production begins. The company has generally had very successful product introductions. Only two products introduced by the company have been discontinued. E

One of the products currently sold is a multi-alarm clock. The clock has four alarms that can be programmed to sound at various times and for varying lengths of time. The company has experienced a great deal of difficulty in making the circuit boards for the clocks. The production process has never operated smoothly. The product is unprofitable at the present time, primarily because of warranty repairs and product recalls. Two models of the clocks were recalled, for example, because they sometimes caused an electric shock when the alarms were being shut off. The Engineering Department is attempting to revise the manufacturing process, but the revision will take another 6 months at least.

The clocks were very popular when they were introduced, and since they are private-label, the company has not suffered much from the recalls. Presently, the company has a very large order for several items from Kmart Stores. The order includes 5,000 of the multi-alarm clocks. When the company suggested that Kmart purchase the clocks from another manufacturer, Kmart threatened to rescind the entire order unless the clocks were included.

The company has therefore investigated the possibility of having another company make the clocks for them. The clocks were bid for the Kmart order based on an estimated $6.90 cost to manufacture:

Circuit board, 1 each @ $2.00	$2.00
Plastic case, 1 each @ $0.80	0.80
Alarms, 4 @ $0.15 each	0.60
Labor, 15 minutes @ $12/hour	3.00
Overhead, $2.00 per labor hour	0.50

MiniTek could purchase clocks to fill the Kmart order for $10 from Trans-Tech Asia, a Korean manufacturer with a very good quality record. Trans-Tech has offered to reduce the price to $7.50 after MiniTek has been a customer for 6 months, placing an order of at least 1,000 units per month. If MiniTek becomes a "preferred customer" by purchasing 15,000 units per year, the price would be reduced still further to $4.50.

Omega Products, a local manufacturer, has also offered to make clocks for MiniTek. They have offered to sell 5,000 clocks for $5 each. However, Omega Products has been in business for only 6 months. They have experienced significant turnover in their labor force, and the local press has reported that the owners may face tax evasion charges soon. The owner of Omega Products is an electronic engineer, however, and the quality of the clocks is likely to be good.

If MiniTek decides to purchase the clocks from either Trans-Tech or Omega, all the costs to manufacture could be avoided, except a total of $1,000 in overhead costs for machine depreciation. The machinery is fairly new, and has no alternate use.

Instructions

(a) What is the difference in profit under each of the alternatives if the clocks are to be sold for $14.50 each to Kmart?

(b) What are the most important nonfinancial factors that MiniTek should consider when making this decision?

(c) What do you think MiniTek should do in regard to the Kmart order? What should it do in regard to continuing to manufacture the multi-alarm clocks? Be prepared to defend your answer.

REAL-WORLD FOCUS

E **CT20-3** Founded in 1983 and foreclosed in 1996 Beverly Hills Fan Company was located in Woodland Hills, California. With 23 employees and sales of less than $10 million, the company was relatively small. In 1992, management felt that there was potential for growth in the upscale market for ceiling fans and lighting. They were particularly optimistic about growth in Mexican and Canadian markets.

Presented below is information from the president's letter in one of the company's last annual reports.

> **BEVERLY HILLS FAN COMPANY**
> President's Letter
>
> An aggressive product development program was initiated during the past year resulting in new ceiling fan models planned for introduction this year. Award winning industrial designer Ron Rezek created several new fan models for the Beverly Hills Fan and L.A. Fan lines, including a new Showroom Collection, designed specifically for the architectural and designer markets. Each of these models has received critical acclaim, and order commitments for this year have been outstanding. Additionally, our Custom Color and special order fans continued to enjoy increasing popularity and sales gains as more and more customers desire fans that match their specific interior decors. Currently, Beverly Hills Fan Company offers a product line of over 100 models of contemporary, traditional, and transitional ceiling fans.

Instructions

(a) What points did the company management need to consider before deciding to offer the special-order fans to customers?
(b) How would have incremental analysis been employed to assist in this decision?

C **CT20-4** Outsourcing by both manufacturers and service companies is becoming increasingly common. There are now many firms that specialize in outsourcing consulting.

Address: **www.alsbridge.com**, or go to **www.wiley.com/college/kimmel**

Instructions

Go to the Web page of Alsbridge, Inc. at the address shown above, and answer the following questions.

(a) What are some of the types of outsourcing for which the company provides assistance?
(b) What is insourcing?
(c) What are some of the potential benefits of insourcing?

Writing

COMMUNICATION ACTIVITY

E **CT20-5** Hank Jewell is a production manager at a metal fabricating plant. Last night, he read an article about a new piece of equipment that would dramatically reduce his division's costs. Hank was very excited about the prospect, and the first thing he did this morning was to bring the article to his supervisor, Preston Thiese, the plant manager. The following conversation occurred:

Hank: Preston, I thought you would like to see this article on the new PDD1130; they've made some fantastic changes that could save us millions of dollars.

Preston: I appreciate your interest, Hank, but I actually have been aware of the new machine for two months. The problem is that we just bought a new machine last year. We spent $2 million on that machine, and it was supposed to last us 12 years. If we replace it now, we would have to write its book value off of the books for a huge loss. If I go to top management now and say that I want a new machine, they will fire me. I think we should use our existing machine for a couple of years, and then when it becomes obvious that we have to have a new machine, I will make the proposal.

Instructions

Hank just completed a course in managerial accounting, and he believes that Preston is making a big mistake. Write a memo from Hank to Preston explaining Preston's decision-making error.

ETHICS CASE

CT20-6 Blake Romney became Chief Executive Officer of Peters Inc. two years ago. At the time, the company was reporting lagging profits, and Blake was brought in to "stir things up." The company has three divisions, electronics, fiber optics, and plumbing supplies. Blake has no interest in plumbing supplies, and one of the first things he did was to put pressure on his accountants to reallocate some of the company's fixed costs away from the other two divisions to the plumbing division. This had the effect of causing the plumbing division to report losses during the last two years; in the past it had always reported low, but acceptable, net income. Blake felt that this reallocation would shine a favorable light on him in front of the board of directors because it meant that the electronics and fiber optics divisions would look like they were improving. Given that these are "businesses of the future," he believed that the stock market would react favorably to these increases, while not penalizing the poor results of the plumbing division. Without this shift in the allocation of fixed costs, the profits of the electronics and fiber optics divisions would not have improved. But now the board of directors has suggested that the plumbing division be closed because it is reporting losses. This would mean that nearly 500 employees, many of whom have worked for Peters their whole lives, would lose their jobs.

Instructions

(a) If a division is reporting losses, does that necessarily mean that it should be closed?
(b) Was the reallocation of fixed costs across divisions unethical?
(c) What should Blake do?

ALL ABOUT YOU

CT20-7 Managerial accounting techniques can be used in a wide variety of settings. As we have frequently pointed out, you can use them in many personal situations. They also can be useful in trying to find solutions for societal issues that appear to be hard to solve.

Instructions

Read the Fortune article, "The Toughest Customers: How Hardheaded Business Metrics Can Help the Hard-core Homeless," by Cait Murphy, available at *http://money.cnn.com/magazines/fortune/fortune_archive/2006/04/03/8373067/index.htm*. Answer the following questions.

(a) How does the article define "chronic" homelessness?
(b) In what ways does homelessness cost a city money? What are the estimated costs of a chronic homeless person to various cities?
(c) What are the steps suggested to address the problem?
(d) What is the estimated cost of implementing this program in New York? What results have been seen?
(e) In terms of incremental analysis, frame the relevant costs in this situation.

CONSIDERING YOUR COSTS AND BENEFITS

CT20-8 School costs money. Is this an expenditure that you should have avoided? A year of tuition at a public four-year college costs about $8,655, and a year of tuition at a public two-year college costs about $1,359. If you did not go to college, you might avoid mountains of school-related debt. In fact, each year, about 600,000 students decide to drop out of school. Many of them never return. Suppose that you are working two jobs and going to college, and that you are not making ends meet. Your grades are suffering due to your lack of available study time. You feel depressed. Should you drop out of school?

> **YES:** You can always go back to school. If your grades are bad and you are depressed, what good is school doing you anyway?
>
> **NO:** Once you drop out, it is very hard to get enough momentum to go back. Dropping out will dramatically reduce your long-term opportunities. It is better to stay in school, even if you take only one class per semester. While you cannot go back and redo your initial decision, you can look at some facts to evaluate the wisdom of your decision.

Instructions

Write a response indicating your position regarding this situation. Provide support for your view.

21

Budgetary Planning

CHAPTER PREVIEW

As a student, you budget your study time and your money. Businesses use budgets in planning and controlling their operations. This chapter focuses on how budgeting is used as a planning tool by management. Through budgeting, it should be possible for management to maintain enough cash to pay creditors as well as have sufficient raw materials to meet production requirements and adequate finished goods to meet expected sales.

CHAPTER OUTLINE

LEARNING OBJECTIVES		PRACTICE
1 State the essentials of effective budgeting and the components of the master budget.	• Budgeting and accounting • Benefits of budgeting • Effective budgeting essentials • Master budget	**DO IT!** 1 Budget Terminology
2 Prepare budgets for sales, production, and direct materials.	• Sales budget • Production budget • Direct materials budget	**DO IT!** 2 Sales, Production, and Direct Materials Budgets
3 Prepare budgets for direct labor, manufacturing overhead, and selling and administrative expenses, and a budgeted income statement.	• Direct labor budget • Manufacturing overhead budget • Selling and administrative expense budget • Budgeted income statement	**DO IT!** 3 Budgeted Income Statement
4 Prepare a cash budget and a budgeted balance sheet.	• Cash budget • Budgeted balance sheet	**DO IT!** 4 Cash Budget
5 Apply budgeting principles to nonmanufacturing companies.	• Merchandisers • Service companies • Not-for-profit organizations	**DO IT!** 5 Merchandise Purchases Budget

Go to the ***REVIEW AND PRACTICE*** section at the end of the chapter for a targeted summary and exercises with solutions.

Visit **WileyPLUS** for additional tutorials and practice opportunities.

Deidre Schoo/The New York Times/Redux Pictures

FEATURE STORY

What's in Your Cupcake?

The best business plans often result from meeting a basic human need. Many people would argue that cupcakes aren't necessarily essential to support life. But if you found out that allergies were going to deprive you forever of cupcakes, you might view baked goods in a whole new light. Such was the dilemma faced by Erin McKenna. When she found that her wheat allergies prevented her from consuming most baked sweets, she decided to open a bakery that met her needs. Her vegan and kosher bakery, BabyCakes NYC, advertises that it is refined-sugar-free, gluten-free, wheat-free, soy-free, dairy-free, and egg-free. So if you're one of the more than 10 million Americans with a food allergy or some other dietary constraint, this is probably the bakery for you.

Those of you that have spent a little time in the kitchen might wonder what kind of ingredients BabyCakes uses. To avoid the gluten in wheat, the company uses Bob's Red Mill rice flour, a garbanzo/fava bean mix, or oat flours. How does BabyCakes get all those great frosting colors without artificial dyes? The company achieves pink with beets, green with chlorophyll, yellow with turmeric, and blue/purple with red cabbage. To eliminate dairy and soy, the bakers use rice and coconut milk. And finally, to accomplish over-the-top deliciousness without refined sugar, BabyCakes uses agave nectar (a sweetener derived from cactus) and evaporated cane juice (often referred to as organic or unrefined sugar).

With cupcakes priced at over $3 per item and a brisk business, you might think that making money is easy for BabyCakes. But all of these specialty ingredients don't come cheap. In addition, BabyCakes' shops are located in Manhattan, Los Angeles, and Orlando, so rent isn't exactly inexpensive either. Despite these costs, Erin's first store made a profit its first year and did even better in later years. To achieve this profitability, Erin relies on careful budgeting. First, she needs to estimate how many items she will sell. Then, she determines her needs for materials, labor, and overhead. Prices for BabyCakes' materials can fluctuate significantly, so Erin needs to update her budget accordingly. Finally, she has to budget for other products such as her cookbooks, baking kits, and T-shirts. Without a budget, Erin's business might not be so sweet.

LEARNING OBJECTIVE ▶1

State the essentials of effective budgeting and the components of the master budget.

One of management's major responsibilities is planning. As explained in Chapter 14, **planning** is the process of establishing company-wide objectives. A successful organization makes both long-term and short-term plans. These plans establish the objectives of the company and the proposed way of accomplishing them.

A **budget** is a formal written statement of management's plans for a specified future time period, expressed in financial terms. It represents the primary method of communicating agreed-upon objectives throughout the organization. Once adopted, a budget becomes an important basis for evaluating performance. It promotes efficiency and serves as a deterrent to waste and inefficiency. We consider the role of budgeting as a **control device** in Chapter 22.

BUDGETING AND ACCOUNTING

Accounting information makes major contributions to the budgeting process. From the accounting records, companies can obtain historical data on revenues, costs, and expenses. These data are helpful in formulating future budget goals.

Normally, accountants have the responsibility for presenting management's budgeting goals in financial terms. In this role, they translate management's plans and communicate the budget to employees throughout the company. They prepare periodic budget reports that provide the basis for measuring performance and comparing actual results with planned objectives. The budget itself and the administration of the budget, however, are entirely management responsibilities.

THE BENEFITS OF BUDGETING

The primary benefits of budgeting are as follows.

1. It requires all levels of management to **plan ahead** and to formalize goals on a recurring basis.
2. It provides **definite objectives** for evaluating performance at each level of responsibility.
3. It creates an **early warning system** for potential problems so that management can make changes before things get out of hand.
4. It facilitates the **coordination of activities** within the business. It does this by correlating the goals of each segment with overall company objectives. Thus, the company can integrate production and sales promotion with expected sales.
5. It results in greater **management awareness** of the entity's overall operations and the impact on operations of external factors, such as economic trends.
6. It **motivates personnel** throughout the organization to meet planned objectives.

A budget is an aid to management; it is not a *substitute* for management. A budget cannot operate or enforce itself. Companies can realize the benefits of budgeting only when managers carefully administer budgets.

ESSENTIALS OF EFFECTIVE BUDGETING

Effective budgeting depends on a **sound organizational structure**. In such a structure, authority and responsibility for all phases of operations are clearly defined. Budgets based on **research and analysis** are more likely to result in realistic goals that will contribute to the growth and profitability of a company. And, the effectiveness of a budget program is directly related to its **acceptance by all levels of management**.

Once adopted, the budget is an important tool for evaluating performance. Managers should systematically and periodically review variations between actual and expected results to determine their cause(s). However, individuals should not be held responsible for variations that are beyond their control.

Length of the Budget Period

The budget period is not necessarily one year in length. **A budget may be prepared for any period of time.** Various factors influence the length of the budget period. These factors include the type of budget, the nature of the organization, the need for periodic appraisal, and prevailing business conditions.

The budget period should be long enough to provide an attainable goal under normal business conditions. Ideally, the time period should minimize the impact of seasonal or cyclical fluctuations. On the other hand, the budget period should not be so long that reliable estimates are impossible.

The **most common budget period is one year**. The annual budget, in turn, is often supplemented by monthly and quarterly budgets. Many companies use **continuous 12-month budgets**. These budgets drop the month just ended and add a future month. One benefit of continuous budgeting is that it keeps management planning a full year ahead.

ACCOUNTING ACROSS THE ORGANIZATION

Thinkstock/Comstock/Getty Images, Inc.

Businesses Often Feel Too Busy to Plan for the Future

A study by Willard & Shullman Group Ltd. found that fewer than 14% of businesses with less than 500 employees do an annual budget or have a written business plan. For many small businesses, the basic assumption is that, "As long as I sell as much as I can, and keep my employees paid, I'm doing OK." A few small business owners even say that they see no need for budgeting and planning. Most small business owners, though, say that they understand that budgeting and planning are critical for survival and growth. But given the long hours that they already work addressing day-to-day challenges, they also say that they are "just too busy to plan for the future."

Describe a situation in which a business "sells as much as it can" but cannot "keep its employees paid." (Go to **WileyPLUS** for this answer and additional questions.)

The Budgeting Process

The development of the budget for the coming year generally starts several months before the end of the current year. The budgeting process usually begins with the collection of data from each organizational unit of the company. Past performance is often the starting point from which future budget goals are formulated.

The budget is developed within the framework of a **sales forecast**. This forecast shows potential sales for the industry and the company's expected share of such sales. Sales forecasting involves a consideration of various factors: (1) general economic conditions, (2) industry trends, (3) market research studies, (4) anticipated advertising and promotion, (5) previous market share, (6) changes in prices, and (7) technological developments. The input of sales personnel and top management is essential to the sales forecast.

In small companies like BabyCakes NYC, the budgeting process is often informal. In larger companies, a **budget committee** has responsibility for coordinating the preparation of the budget. The committee ordinarily includes the president, treasurer, chief accountant (controller), and management personnel from each of the major areas of the company, such as sales, production, and research. The budget committee serves as a review board where managers can defend their budget goals and requests. Differences are reviewed, modified if necessary, and reconciled. The budget is then put in its final form by the budget committee, approved, and distributed.

Budgeting and Human Behavior

A budget can have a significant impact on human behavior. If done well, it can inspire managers to higher levels of performance. However, if done poorly, budgets can discourage additional effort and pull down the morale of managers. Why do these diverse effects occur? The answer is found in how the budget is developed and administered.

In developing the budget, each level of management should be invited to participate. This "bottom-to-top" approach is referred to as **participative budgeting**. One benefit of participative budgeting is that lower-level managers have more detailed knowledge of their specific area and thus are able to provide more accurate budgetary estimates. Also, when lower-level managers participate in the budgeting process, they are more likely to perceive the resulting budget as fair. The overall goal is to reach agreement on a budget that the managers consider fair and achievable, but which also meets the corporate goals set by top management. When this goal is met, the budget will provide positive motivation for the managers. In contrast, if managers view the budget as unfair and unrealistic, they may feel discouraged and uncommitted to budget goals. The risk of having unrealistic budgets is generally greater when the budget is developed from top management down to lower management than vice versa. Illustration 21-1 graphically displays the flow of budget data from bottom to top under participative budgeting.

ILLUSTRATION 21-1
Flow of budget data under participative budgeting

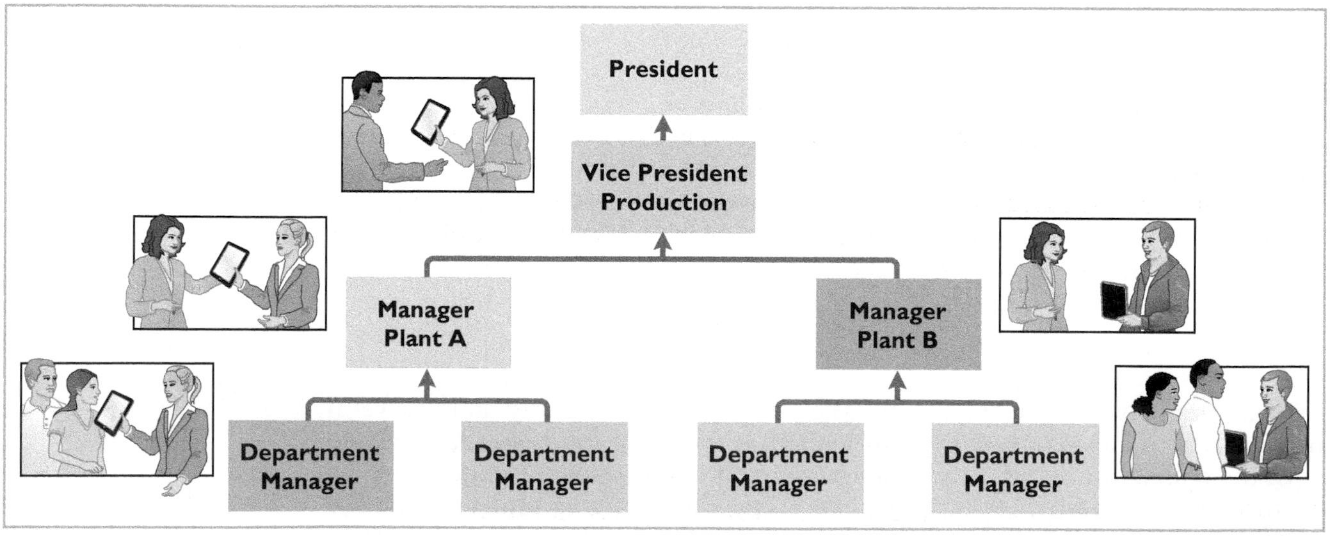

For example, at one time, in an effort to revive its plummeting stock price, Time Warner's top management determined and publicly announced bold new financial goals for the coming year. Unfortunately, these goals were not reached.

The next year, the company got a new CEO who said the company would now actually set reasonable goals that it could meet. The new budgets were developed with each operating unit setting what it felt were optimistic but attainable goals. In the words of one manager, using this approach created a sense of teamwork.

Participative budgeting does, however, have potential disadvantages. First, the "give and take" of participative budgeting is time-consuming (and thus more costly). Under a "top-down" approach, the budget is simply developed by top management and then dictated to lower-level managers. A second disadvantage is that participative budgeting can foster budgetary "gaming" through budgetary slack. **Budgetary slack** occurs when managers intentionally underestimate budgeted revenues or overestimate budgeted expenses in order to make it easier to achieve budgetary goals. To minimize budgetary slack, higher-level managers must carefully review and thoroughly question the budget projections provided to them by employees whom they supervise.

For the budget to be effective, top management must completely support the budget. The budget is an important basis for evaluating performance. It also can be used as a positive aid in achieving projected goals. The effect of an evaluation is positive when top management tempers criticism with advice and assistance. In contrast, a manager is likely to respond negatively if top management uses the budget exclusively to assess blame. A budget should not be used as a pressure device to force improved performance. In sum, a budget can be a manager's friend or foe.

ETHICS NOTE

Unrealistic budgets can lead to unethical employee behavior such as cutting corners on the job or distorting internal financial reports.

Budgeting and Long-Range Planning

Budgeting and long-range planning are not the same. One important difference is the **time period involved**. The maximum length of a budget is usually one year, and budgets are often prepared for shorter periods of time, such as a month or a quarter. In contrast, long-range planning usually encompasses a period of at least five years.

A second significant difference is in **emphasis**. Budgeting focuses on achieving specific short-term goals, such as meeting annual profit objectives. **Long-range planning**, on the other hand, identifies long-term goals, selects strategies to achieve those goals, and develops policies and plans to implement the strategies. In long-range planning, management also considers anticipated trends in the economic and political environment and how the company should cope with them.

▼ HELPFUL HINT

In comparing a budget with a long-range plan, a budget has more detail and is more concerned with short-term goals, while a long-range plan is done for a longer period of time.

The final difference between budgeting and long-range planning relates to the **amount of detail presented**. Budgets, as you will see in this chapter, can be very detailed. Long-range plans contain considerably less detail. The data in long-range plans are intended more for a review of progress toward long-term goals than as a basis of control for achieving specific results. The primary objective of long-range planning is to develop the best strategy to maximize the company's performance over an extended future period.

THE MASTER BUDGET

The term "budget" is actually a shorthand term to describe a variety of budget documents. All of these documents are combined into a master budget. The **master budget** is a set of interrelated budgets that constitutes a plan of action for a specified time period.

The master budget contains two classes of budgets. **Operating budgets** are the individual budgets that result in the preparation of the budgeted income statement. These budgets establish goals for the company's sales and production personnel. In contrast, **financial budgets** focus primarily on the cash resources needed to fund expected

DECISION TOOLS

Managers use the master budget to determine if the company met its targets for such things as sales, production expenses, selling and administrative expenses, and net income.

operations and planned capital expenditures. Financial budgets include the capital expenditure budget, the cash budget, and the budgeted balance sheet.

Illustration 21-2 shows the individual budgets included in a master budget, and the sequence in which they are prepared. The company first develops the operating budgets, beginning with the sales budget. Then, it prepares the financial budgets. We will explain and illustrate each budget shown in Illustration 21-2 except the capital expenditure budget. That budget is discussed under the topic of capital budgeting in Chapter 24.

ILLUSTRATION 21-2
Components of the master budget

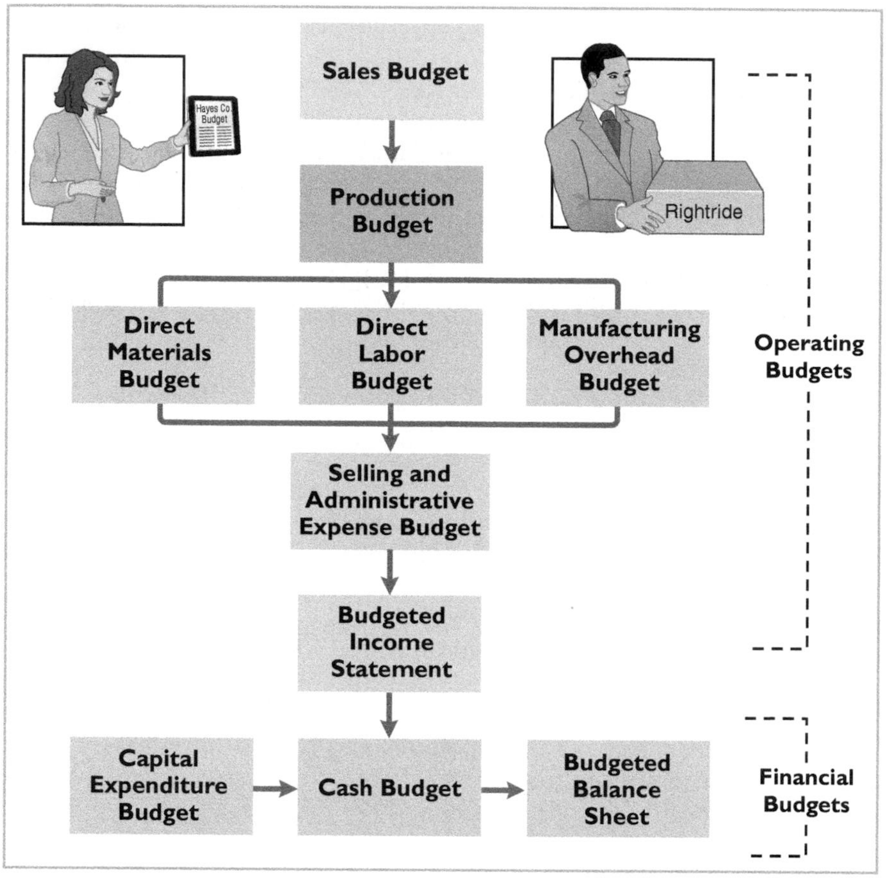

DO IT! ▶1 Budget Terminology

Use this list of terms to complete the sentences that follow.

Long-range planning	Participative budgeting
Sales forecast	Operating budgets
Master budget	Financial budgets

1. A ______________ shows potential sales for the industry and a company's expected share of such sales.
2. ______________ are used as the basis for the preparation of the budgeted income statement.
3. The ______________ is a set of interrelated budgets that constitutes a plan of action for a specified time period.
4. ______________ identifies long-term goals, selects strategies to achieve these goals, and develops policies and plans to implement the strategies.

5. Lower-level managers are more likely to perceive results as fair and achievable under a ______________ approach.
6. ______________ focus primarily on the cash resources needed to fund expected operations and planned capital expenditures.

SOLUTION

1. Sales forecast.
2. Operating budgets.
3. Master budget.
4. Long-range planning.
5. Participative budgeting.
6. Financial budgets.

Related exercise material: **BE21-1, E21-1,** and **DO IT! 21-1.**

Action Plan

✔ Understand the budgeting process, including the importance of the sales forecast.

✔ Understand the difference between an operating budget and a financial budget.

✔ Differentiate budgeting from long-range planning.

✔ Realize that the master budget is a set of interrelated budgets.

LEARNING OBJECTIVE 2

Prepare budgets for sales, production, and direct materials.

We use a case study of Hayes Company in preparing the operating budgets. Hayes manufactures and sells a single product, an ergonomically designed bike seat with multiple customizable adjustments, called the Rightride. The budgets are prepared by quarters for the year ending December 31, 2017. Hayes Company begins its annual budgeting process on September 1, 2016, and it completes the budget for 2017 by December 1, 2016. The company begins by preparing the budgets for sales, production, and direct materials.

SALES BUDGET

As shown in the master budget in Illustration 21-2, **the sales budget is prepared first**. Each of the other budgets depends on the sales budget. The **sales budget** is derived from the sales forecast. It represents management's best estimate of sales revenue for the budget period. An inaccurate sales budget may adversely affect net income. For example, an overly optimistic sales budget may result in excessive inventories that may have to be sold at reduced prices. In contrast, an unduly pessimistic sales budget may result in loss of sales revenue due to inventory shortages.

▼ **HELPFUL HINT**
For a retail or manufacturing company, the sales budget is the starting point for the master budget. It sets the level of activity for other functions such as production and purchasing.

For example, at one time Amazon.com significantly underestimated demand for its e-book reader, the Kindle. As a consequence, it did not produce enough Kindles and was completely sold out well before the holiday shopping season. Not only did this represent a huge lost opportunity for Amazon, but it exposed the company to potential competitors, who were eager to provide customers with alternatives to the Kindle.

Forecasting sales is challenging. For example, consider the forecasting challenges faced by major sports arenas, whose revenues depend on the success of the home team. Madison Square Garden's revenues from April to June were $193 million during a year when the Knicks made the NBA playoffs. But revenues were only $133.2 million a couple of years later when the team did not make the playoffs. Or, consider the challenges faced by Hollywood movie producers in predicting the complicated revenue stream produced by a new movie. Movie theater ticket sales represent only 20% of total revenue. The bulk of revenue comes from global sales, DVDs, video-on-demand, merchandising products, and videogames, all of which are difficult to forecast.

The sales budget is prepared by multiplying the expected unit sales volume for each product by its anticipated unit selling price. Hayes Company expects sales volume to be 3,000 units in the first quarter, with 500-unit increases in each succeeding quarter. Illustration 21-3 (page 1022) shows the sales budget for the year, by quarter, based on a sales price of $60 per unit.

ILLUSTRATION 21-3
Sales budget

Hayes Company Sales Budget.xls

	A	B	C	D	E	F
1			**HAYES COMPANY**			
2			**Sales Budget**			
3			**For the Year Ending December 31, 2017**			
4				Quarter		
5		1	2	3	4	Year
6	Expected unit sales	3,000	3,500	4,000	4,500	15,000
7	Unit selling price	× $60	× $60	× $60	× $60	× $60
8	Total sales	$180,000	$210,000	$240,000	$270,000	$900,000

Some companies classify the anticipated sales revenue as cash or credit sales and by geographical regions, territories, or salespersons.

SERVICE COMPANY INSIGHT

Marcela Barsse/iStockphoto

The Implications of Budgetary Optimism

Companies aren't the only ones that have to estimate revenues. Governments at all levels (e.g., local, state or federal) prepare annual budgets. Most are required to submit balanced budgets, that is, estimated revenues are supposed to cover anticipated expenditures. Unfortunately, estimating government revenues can be as difficult as, or even more difficult than, estimating company revenues. For example, during a recent year, the median state government overestimated revenues by 10.2%, with four state governments missing by more than 25%.

What makes estimation so difficult for these governments? Most states rely on income taxes, which fluctuate widely with economic gyrations. Some states rely on sales taxes, which are problematic because the laws regarding sales taxes haven't adjusted for the shift from manufacturing to service companies and from brick-and-mortar stores to online sales.

Source: Conor Dougherty, "States Fumble Revenue Forecasts," *Wall Street Journal Online* (March 2, 2011).

Why is it important that government budgets accurately estimate future revenues during economic downturns? (Go to **WileyPLUS** for this answer and additional questions.)

PRODUCTION BUDGET

The **production budget** shows the number of units of a product to produce to meet anticipated sales demand. Production requirements are determined from the following formula.[1]

ILLUSTRATION 21-4
Production requirements formula

Budgeted Sales Units	+	Desired Ending Finished Goods Units	−	Beginning Finished Goods Units	=	Required Production Units

[1]This formula ignores any work in process inventories, which are assumed to be nonexistent in Hayes Company.

A realistic estimate of ending inventory is essential in scheduling production requirements. Excessive inventories in one quarter may lead to cutbacks in production and employee layoffs in a subsequent quarter. On the other hand, inadequate inventories may result either in added costs for overtime work or in lost sales. Hayes Company believes it can meet future sales requirements by maintaining an ending inventory equal to 20% of the next quarter's budgeted sales volume. For example, the ending finished goods inventory for the first quarter is 700 units (20% × anticipated second-quarter sales of 3,500 units). Illustration 21-5 shows the production budget.

Units of Finished Goods Inventory

Beg. Inv.	Sales
Required Prod. Units	
End. Inv.	

Hayes Company Production Budget.xls

	A	B	D	F	H	J
1			HAYES COMPANY			
2			Production Budget			
3			For the Year Ending December 31, 2017			
4			Quarter			
5		1	2	3	4	Year
6	Expected unit sales (Illustration 21-3)	3,000	3,500	4,000	4,500	
7	Add: Desired ending finished goods units[a]	700	800	900	1,000[b]	
8	Total required units	3,700	4,300	4,900	5,500	
9	Less: Beginning finished goods units	600[c]	700	800	900	
10	Required production units	3,100	3,600	4,100	4,600	15,400
11						
12	[a]20% of next quarter's sales					
13	[b]Expected 2018 first-quarter sales, 5,000 units × 20%					
14	[c]20% of estimated first-quarter 2017 sales units					

Units of Finished Goods Inventory

600	
3,100	3,000
700	

ILLUSTRATION 21-5
Production budget

The production budget, in turn, provides the basis for the budgeted costs for each manufacturing cost element, as explained in the following pages.

DIRECT MATERIALS BUDGET

The **direct materials budget** shows both the quantity and cost of direct materials to be purchased. The quantities of direct materials are derived from the following formula.

Direct Materials Units Required for Production	+	Desired Ending Direct Materials Units	−	Beginning Direct Materials Units	=	Required Direct Materials Units to Be Purchased

ILLUSTRATION 21-6
Formula for direct materials quantities

After the company determines the number of units to purchase, it can compute the budgeted cost of direct materials to be purchased. It does so by multiplying the required units of direct materials by the anticipated cost per unit.

Units of Direct Materials

Beg. Inv.	
Direct Materials to Purchase	Direct Materials Required for Prod.
End. Inv.	

The desired ending inventory is again a key component in the budgeting process. For example, inadequate inventories could result in temporary shutdowns of production. Because of its close proximity to suppliers, Hayes Company maintains an ending inventory of raw materials equal to 10% of the next quarter's production requirements. The manufacture of each Rightride requires 2 pounds of raw materials, and the expected cost per pound is $4. Illustration 21-7 shows the direct materials budget. Assume that the desired ending direct materials amount is 1,020 pounds for the fourth quarter of 2017.

ILLUSTRATION 21-7
Direct materials budget

Units of Direct Materials (1st Qtr.)

620	
6,300	6,200
720	

Hayes Company Direct Materials Budget.xls

HAYES COMPANY
Direct Materials Budget
For the Year Ending December 31, 2017

	Quarter 1	2	3	4	Year
Units to be produced (Illustration 21-5)	3,100	3,600	4,100	4,600	
Direct materials per unit	× 2	× 2	× 2	× 2	
Total pounds needed for production	6,200	7,200	8,200	9,200	
Add: Desired ending direct materials (pounds)[a]	720	820	920	1,020	
Total materials required	6,920	8,020	9,120	10,220	
Less: Beginning direct materials (pounds)	620[b]	720	820	920	
Direct materials purchases	6,300	7,300	8,300	9,300	
Cost per pound	× $4	× $4	× $4	× $4	
Total cost of direct materials purchases	$25,200	$29,200	$33,200	$37,200	$124,800

[a]10% of next quarter's production requirements
[b]10% of estimated first-quarter pounds needed for production

MANAGEMENT INSIGHT

© William Wang/iStockphoto

Betting That Prices Won't Fall

Sometimes things happen that cause managers to reevaluate their normal purchasing patterns. Consider, for example, the predicament that businesses faced when the price of many raw materials recently skyrocketed. Rubber, cotton, oil, corn, wheat, steel, copper, and spices—prices for seemingly everything were going straight up. Anticipating that prices might continue to go up, many managers decided to stockpile much larger quantities of raw materials to avoid paying even higher prices in the future. For example, after cotton prices rose 92%, one manager of a printed T-shirt manufacturer decided to stockpile a huge supply of plain T-shirts in anticipation of additional price increases. While he normally has about 30 boxes of T-shirts in inventory, he purchased 2,500 boxes.

Source: Liam Pleven and Matt Wirz, "Companies Stock Up as Commodities Prices Rise," *Wall Street Journal Online* (February 3, 2011).

What are the potential downsides of stockpiling a huge amount of raw materials? (Go to **WileyPLUS** for this answer and additional questions.)

DO IT! ▶2 Sales, Production, and Direct Materials Budgets

Soriano Company is preparing its master budget for 2017. Relevant data pertaining to its sales, production, and direct materials budgets are as follows.

Sales. Sales for the year are expected to total 1,200,000 units. Quarterly sales, as a percentage of total sales, are 20%, 25%, 30%, and 25%, respectively. The sales price is expected to be $50 per unit for the first three quarters and $55 per unit beginning in the fourth quarter. Sales in the first quarter of 2018 are expected to be 10% higher than the budgeted sales for the first quarter of 2017.

Production. Management desires to maintain the ending finished goods inventories at 25% of the next quarter's budgeted sales volume.

Direct materials. Each unit requires 3 pounds of raw materials at a cost of $5 per pound. Management desires to maintain raw materials inventories at 5% of the next quarter's production requirements. Assume the production requirements for the first quarter of 2018 are 810,000 pounds.

Prepare the sales, production, and direct materials budgets by quarters for 2017.

Action Plan

- ✔ Know the form and content of the sales budget.
- ✔ Prepare the sales budget first, as the basis for the other budgets.
- ✔ Determine the units that must be produced to meet anticipated sales.
- ✔ Know how to compute the beginning and ending finished goods units.
- ✔ Determine the materials required to meet production needs.
- ✔ Know how to compute the beginning and ending direct materials units.

SOLUTION

Soriano Company Sales Budget.xls

SORIANO COMPANY
Sales Budget
For the Year Ending December 31, 2017

	Quarter				
	1	2	3	4	Year
Expected unit sales	240,000	300,000	360,000	300,000	1,200,000
Unit selling price	× $50	× $50	× $50	× $55	
Total sales	$12,000,000	$15,000,000	$18,000,000	$16,500,000	$61,500,000

Soriano Company Production Budget.xls

SORIANO COMPANY
Production Budget
For the Year Ending December 31, 2017

	Quarter				
	1	2	3	4	Year
Expected unit sales	240,000	300,000	360,000	300,000	
Add: Desired ending finished goods units[a]	75,000	90,000	75,000	66,000[b]	
Total required units	315,000	390,000	435,000	366,000	
Less: Beginning finished goods units	60,000[c]	75,000	90,000	75,000	
Required production units	255,000	315,000	345,000	291,000	1,206,000

[a]25% of next quarter's unit sales
[b]Estimated first-quarter 2018 sales units: 240,000 + (240,000 × 10%) = 264,000: 264,000 × 25%
[c]25% of estimated first-quarter 2017 sales units (240,000 × 25%)

Soriano Company Direct Materials Budget.xls

SORIANO COMPANY
Direct Materials Budget
For the Year Ending December 31, 2017

	Quarter 1	Quarter 2	Quarter 3	Quarter 4	Year
Units to be produced	255,000	315,000	345,000	291,000	
Direct materials per unit	× 3	× 3	× 3	× 3	
Total pounds needed for production	765,000	945,000	1,035,000	873,000	
Add: Desired ending direct materials (pounds)	47,250	51,750	43,650	40,500[a]	
Total materials required	812,250	996,750	1,078,650	913,500	
Less: Beginning direct materials (pounds)	38,250[b]	47,250	51,750	43,650	
Direct materials purchases	774,000	949,500	1,026,900	869,850	
Cost per pound	× $5	× $5	× $5	× $5	
Total cost of direct materials purchases	$3,870,000	$4,747,500	$5,134,500	$4,349,250	$18,101,250

[a]Estimated first-quarter 2018 production requirements: 810,000 × 5% = 40,500
[b]5% of estimated first-quarter pounds needed for production

Related exercise material: **BE21-2, BE21-3, BE21-4, E21-2, E21-3, E21-4, E21-5, E21-6, E21-7, E21-8,** and DO IT! **21-2.**

LEARNING OBJECTIVE 3

Prepare budgets for direct labor, manufacturing overhead, and selling and administrative expenses, and a budgeted income statement.

As shown in Illustration 21-2 (page 1020), the operating budgets culminate with preparation of the budgeted income statement. Before we can do that, we need to prepare budgets for direct labor, manufacturing overhead, and selling and administrative expenses.

DIRECT LABOR BUDGET

Like the direct materials budget, the **direct labor budget** contains the quantity (hours) and cost of direct labor necessary to meet production requirements. The total direct labor cost is derived from the following formula.

ILLUSTRATION 21-8
Formula for direct labor cost

Units to Be Produced × **Direct Labor Hours per Unit** × **Direct Labor Cost per Hour** = Total Direct Labor Cost

Direct labor hours are determined from the production budget. At Hayes Company, two hours of direct labor are required to produce each unit of finished goods. The anticipated hourly wage rate is $10. Illustration 21-9 shows these data.

Hayes Company Direct Labor Budget.xls

HAYES COMPANY
Direct Labor Budget
For the Year Ending December 31, 2017

	Quarter 1	Quarter 2	Quarter 3	Quarter 4	Year
Units to be produced (Illustration 21-5)	3,100	3,600	4,100	4,600	
Direct labor time (hours) per unit	× 2	× 2	× 2	× 2	
Total required direct labor hours	6,200	7,200	8,200	9,200	
Direct labor cost per hour	× $10	× $10	× $10	× $10	
Total direct labor cost	**$62,000**	**$72,000**	**$82,000**	**$92,000**	**$308,000**

ILLUSTRATION 21-9
Direct labor budget

The direct labor budget is critical in maintaining a labor force that can meet the expected levels of production.

▼ HELPFUL HINT
An important assumption in Illustration 21-9 is that the company can add to and subtract from its work force as needed so that the $10 per hour labor cost applies to a wide range of possible production activity.

MANUFACTURING OVERHEAD BUDGET

The **manufacturing overhead budget** shows the expected manufacturing overhead costs for the budget period. As Illustration 21-10 shows, **this budget distinguishes between variable and fixed overhead costs**. Hayes Company expects variable costs to fluctuate with production volume on the basis of the following rates per direct labor hour: indirect materials $1.00, indirect labor $1.40, utilities $0.40, and maintenance $0.20. Thus, for the 6,200 direct labor hours to produce 3,100 units, budgeted indirect materials are $6,200 (6,200 × $1), and budgeted indirect labor is $8,680 (6,200 × $1.40). Hayes also recognizes that some maintenance is fixed. The amounts reported for fixed costs are assumed for our example.

Hayes Company Manufacturing Overhead Budget.xls

HAYES COMPANY
Manufacturing Overhead Budget
For the Year Ending December 31, 2017

	Quarter 1	Quarter 2	Quarter 3	Quarter 4	Year
Variable costs					
Indirect materials ($1.00/hour)	$ 6,200	$ 7,200	$ 8,200	$ 9,200	$ 30,800
Indirect labor ($1.40/hour)	8,680	10,080	11,480	12,880	43,120
Utilities ($0.40/hour)	2,480	2,880	3,280	3,680	12,320
Maintenance ($0.20/hour)	1,240	1,440	1,640	1,840	6,160
Total variable costs	18,600	21,600	24,600	27,600	92,400
Fixed costs					
Supervisory salaries	20,000	20,000	20,000	20,000	80,000
Depreciation	3,800	3,800	3,800	3,800	15,200
Property taxes and insurance	9,000	9,000	9,000	9,000	36,000
Maintenance	5,700	5,700	5,700	5,700	22,800
Total fixed costs	38,500	38,500	38,500	38,500	154,000
Total manufacturing overhead	**$57,100**	**$60,100**	**$63,100**	**$66,100**	**$246,400**
Direct labor hours (Illustration 21-9)	**6,200**	**7,200**	**8,200**	**9,200**	**30,800**
Manufacturing overhead rate per direct labor hour ($246,400 ÷ 30,800)					**$8**

ILLUSTRATION 21-10
Manufacturing overhead budget

The accuracy of budgeted overhead cost estimates can be greatly improved by employing activity-based costing.

At Hayes Company, overhead is applied to production on the basis of direct labor hours. Thus, as Illustration 21-10 shows, the budgeted annual rate is $8 per hour ($246,400 ÷ 30,800).

SELLING AND ADMINISTRATIVE EXPENSE BUDGET

Hayes Company combines its operating expenses into one budget, the **selling and administrative expense budget**. This budget projects anticipated selling and administrative expenses for the budget period. This budget (Illustration 21-11) also classifies expenses as either variable or fixed. In this case, the variable expense rates per unit of sales are sales commissions $3 and freight-out $1. Variable expenses per quarter are based on the unit sales from the sales budget (see Illustration 21-3, page 1022). For example, Hayes expects sales in the first quarter to be 3,000 units. Thus, sales commissions expense is $9,000 (3,000 × $3), and freight-out is $3,000 (3,000 × $1). Fixed expenses are based on assumed data.

ILLUSTRATION 21-11
Selling and administrative expense budget

Hayes Company Manufacturing Selling and Administrative Expense Budget.xls

Home Insert Page Layout Formulas Data Review View

P18 fx

HAYES COMPANY
Selling and Administrative Expense Budget
For the Year Ending December 31, 2017

	Quarter 1	Quarter 2	Quarter 3	Quarter 4	Year
Budgeted sales in units (Illustration 21-3)	3,000	3,500	4,000	4,500	15,000
Variable expenses					
Sales commissions ($3 per unit)	$ 9,000	$10,500	$12,000	$13,500	$ 45,000
Freight-out ($1 per unit)	3,000	3,500	4,000	4,500	15,000
Total variable expenses	12,000	14,000	16,000	18,000	60,000
Fixed expenses					
Advertising	5,000	5,000	5,000	5,000	20,000
Sales salaries	15,000	15,000	15,000	15,000	60,000
Office salaries	7,500	7,500	7,500	7,500	30,000
Depreciation	1,000	1,000	1,000	1,000	4,000
Property taxes and insurance	1,500	1,500	1,500	1,500	6,000
Total fixed expenses	30,000	30,000	30,000	30,000	120,000
Total selling and administrative expenses	**$42,000**	**$44,000**	**$46,000**	**$48,000**	**$180,000**

BUDGETED INCOME STATEMENT

The **budgeted income statement** is the important end-product of the operating budgets. This budget indicates the expected profitability of operations for the budget period. The budgeted income statement provides the basis for evaluating company performance. Budgeted income statements often act as a call to action. For example, a board member at XM Satellite Radio Holdings felt that budgeted costs were too high relative to budgeted revenues. When management refused to cut its marketing and programming costs, the board member resigned. He felt that without the cuts, the company risked financial crisis.

As you would expect, the budgeted income statement is prepared from the various operating budgets. For example, to find the cost of goods sold, Hayes Company must first determine the total unit cost of producing one Rightride, as follows.

ILLUSTRATION 21-12
Computation of total unit cost

Cost of One Rightride				
Cost Element	**Illustration**	**Quantity**	**Unit Cost**	**Total**
Direct materials	21-7	2 pounds	$ 4.00	$ 8.00
Direct labor	21-9	2 hours	$10.00	20.00
Manufacturing overhead	21-10	2 hours	$ 8.00	16.00
Total unit cost				$44.00

Hayes then determines cost of goods sold by multiplying the units sold by the unit cost. Its budgeted cost of goods sold is $660,000 (15,000 × $44). All data for the income statement come from the individual operating budgets except the following: (1) interest expense is expected to be $100, and (2) income taxes are estimated to be $12,000. Illustration 21-13 shows the budgeted multiple-step income statement.

ILLUSTRATION 21-13
Budgeted multiple-step income statement

HAYES COMPANY
Budgeted Income Statement
For the Year Ending December 31, 2017

Sales (Illustration 21-3)	$900,000
Cost of goods sold (15,000 × $44)	660,000
Gross profit	240,000
Selling and administrative expenses (Illustration 21-11)	180,000
Income from operations	60,000
Interest expense	100
Income before income taxes	59,900
Income tax expense	12,000
Net income	$ 47,900

DO IT! 3 Budgeted Income Statement

Soriano Company is preparing its budgeted income statement for 2017. Relevant data pertaining to its sales, production, and direct materials budgets can be found in DO IT! 2 (page 1025).

In addition, Soriano budgets 0.5 hours of direct labor per unit, labor costs at $15 per hour, and manufacturing overhead at $25 per direct labor hour. Its budgeted selling and administrative expenses for 2017 are $12,000,000.

(a) Calculate the budgeted total unit cost. (b) Prepare the budgeted multiple-step income statement for 2017. (Ignore income taxes.)

Action Plan

✔ Recall that total unit cost consists of direct materials, direct labor, and manufacturing overhead.

✔ Recall that direct materials costs are included in the direct materials budget.

SOLUTION

(a)

Cost Element	Quantity	Unit Cost	Total
Direct materials	3.0 pounds	$ 5	$ 15.00
Direct labor	0.5 hours	$15	7.50
Manufacturing overhead	0.5 hours	$25	12.50
Total unit cost			$35.00

Action Plan (cont.)

✔ Know the form and content of the income statement.

✔ Use the total unit sales information from the sales budget to compute annual sales and cost of goods sold.

(b)

SORIANO COMPANY Budgeted Income Statement For the Year Ending December 31, 2017	
Sales (1,200,000 units from sales budget, page 1025)	$61,500,000
Cost of goods sold (1,200,000 × $35.00/unit)	42,000,000
Gross profit	19,500,000
Selling and administrative expenses	12,000,000
Net income	$ 7,500,000

Related exercise material: **BE21-8, E21-11, E21-13,** and DO IT! **21-3.**

LEARNING OBJECTIVE 4

Prepare a cash budget and a budgeted balance sheet.

As shown in Illustration 21-2 (page 1020), the financial budgets consist of the capital expenditure budget, the cash budget, and the budgeted balance sheet. We will discuss the capital expenditure budget in Chapter 24.

DECISION TOOLS

Managers use the cash budget to determine if the company needs to borrow funds in the coming period.

CASH BUDGET

The **cash budget** shows anticipated cash flows. Because cash is so vital, this budget is often considered to be the most important financial budget. The cash budget contains three sections (cash receipts, cash disbursements, and financing) and the beginning and ending cash balances, as shown in Illustration 21-14.

ILLUSTRATION 21-14
Basic form of a cash budget

Any Company Cash Budget.xls

	A	B	C
1	**ANY COMPANY**		
2	**Cash Budget**		
3	Beginning cash balance	$X,XXX	
4	Add: Cash receipts (itemized)	X,XXX	
5	Total available cash	X,XXX	
6	Less: Cash disbursements (itemized)	X,XXX	
7	Excess (deficiency) of available cash over cash disbursements	X,XXX	
8	Financing	X,XXX	
9	Ending cash balance	$X,XXX	

▼ **HELPFUL HINT**
The cash budget is prepared after the other budgets because the information generated by the other budgets dictates the expected inflows and outflows of cash.

The **cash receipts section** includes expected receipts from the company's principal source(s) of revenue. These are usually cash sales and collections from customers on credit sales. This section also shows anticipated receipts of interest and dividends, and proceeds from planned sales of investments, plant assets, and the company's capital stock.

The **cash disbursements section** shows expected cash payments. Such payments include direct materials, direct labor, manufacturing overhead, and selling and administrative expenses. This section also includes projected payments for income taxes, dividends, investments, and plant assets.

The **financing section** shows expected borrowings and the repayment of the borrowed funds plus interest. Companies need this section when there is a cash deficiency or when the cash balance is below management's minimum required balance.

Data in the cash budget are prepared in sequence. The ending cash balance of one period becomes the beginning cash balance for the next period. Companies obtain data for preparing the cash budget from other budgets and from information provided by management. In practice, cash budgets are often prepared for the year on a monthly basis.

To minimize detail, we will assume that Hayes Company prepares an annual cash budget by quarters. Its cash budget is based on the following assumptions.

1. The January 1, 2017, cash balance is expected to be $38,000. Hayes wishes to maintain a balance of at least $15,000.
2. Sales (Illustration 21-3, page 1022): 60% are collected in the quarter sold and 40% are collected in the following quarter. Accounts receivable of $60,000 at December 31, 2016, are expected to be collected in full in the first quarter of 2017.
3. Short-term investment securities are expected to be sold for $2,000 cash in the first quarter.
4. Direct materials (Illustration 21-7, page 1024): 50% are paid in the quarter purchased and 50% are paid in the following quarter. Accounts payable of $10,600 at December 31, 2016, are expected to be paid in full in the first quarter of 2017.
5. Direct labor (Illustration 21-9, page 1027): 100% is paid in the quarter incurred.
6. Manufacturing overhead (Illustration 21-10, page 1027) and selling and administrative expenses (Illustration 21-11, page 1028): All items except depreciation are paid in the quarter incurred.
7. Management plans to purchase a truck in the second quarter for $10,000 cash.
8. Hayes makes equal quarterly payments of its estimated $12,000 annual income taxes.
9. Loans are repaid in the earliest quarter in which there is sufficient cash (that is, when the cash on hand exceeds the $15,000 minimum required balance).

In preparing the cash budget, it is useful to prepare schedules for collections from customers (assumption 2) and cash payments for direct materials (assumption 4). These schedules are shown in Illustrations 21-15 and 21-16 (page 1032).

ILLUSTRATION 21-15
Collections from customers

Hayes Company.xls

Home Insert Page Layout Formulas Data Review View

P18 fx

	A	B	C	D	E	F
1	**HAYES COMPANY**					
2	**Schedule of Expected Collections from Customers**					
3			Collections by Quarter			
4		Sales[a]	1	2	3	4
5	Accounts receivable, 12/31/16		$ 60,000			
6	First quarter	$180,000	108,000[b]	$ 72,000[c]		
7	Second quarter	210,000		126,000	$ 84,000	
8	Third quarter	240,000			144,000	$ 96,000
9	Fourth quarter	270,000				162,000
10	Total collections		$168,000	$198,000	$228,000	$258,000
11						
12	[a]Per Illustration 21-3; [b]$180,000 × .60; [c]$180,000 × .40					
13						

ILLUSTRATION 21-16
Payments for direct materials

Hayes Company.xls

	Purchases[a]	Payments by Quarter 1	2	3	4
HAYES COMPANY					
Schedule of Expected Payments for Direct Materials					
Accounts payable, 12/31/16		$10,600			
First quarter	$25,200	12,600[b]	$12,600[c]		
Second quarter	29,200		14,600	$14,600	
Third quarter	33,200			16,600	$16,600
Fourth quarter	37,200				18,600
Total payments		$23,200	$27,200	$31,200	$35,200

[a]Per Illustration 21-7; [b]$25,200 × .50; [c]$25,200 × .50

Illustration 21-17 shows the cash budget for Hayes Company. The budget indicates that Hayes will need $3,000 of financing in the second quarter to maintain a minimum cash balance of $15,000. Since there is an excess of available cash over disbursements of $22,500 at the end of the third quarter, the borrowing, plus $100 interest, is repaid in this quarter.

ILLUSTRATION 21-17
Cash budget

Hayes Company Cash Budget.xls

HAYES COMPANY
Cash Budget
For the Year Ending December 31, 2017

	Assumption	Quarter 1	2	3	4
Beginning cash balance	1	$ 38,000	$ 25,500	$ 15,000	$ 19,400
Add: Receipts					
Collections from customers	2	168,000	198,000	228,000	258,000
Sale of investment securities	3	2,000	0	0	0
Total receipts		170,000	198,000	228,000	258,000
Total available cash		208,000	223,500	243,000	277,400
Less: Disbursements					
Direct materials	4	23,200	27,200	31,200	35,200
Direct labor	5	62,000	72,000	82,000	92,000
Manufacturing overhead	6	53,300[a]	56,300	59,300	62,300
Selling and administrative expenses	6	41,000[b]	43,000	45,000	47,000
Purchase of truck	7	0	10,000	0	0
Income tax expense	8	3,000	3,000	3,000	3,000
Total disbursements		182,500	211,500	220,500	239,500
Excess (deficiency) of available cash over cash disbursements		25,500	12,000	22,500	37,900
Financing					
Add: Borrowings		0	3,000	0	0
Less: Repayments including interest	9	0	0	3,100	0
Ending cash balance		$ 25,500	$ 15,000	$ 19,400	$ 37,900

[a]$57,100 − $3,800 depreciation
[b]$42,000 − $1,000 depreciation

A cash budget contributes to more effective cash management. It shows managers when additional financing is necessary well before the actual need arises. And, it indicates when excess cash is available for investments or other purposes.

SERVICE COMPANY INSIGHT Olympic Games

Marianna Day Massey/ZumaPress/NewsCom

Without a Budget, Can the Games Begin?

Behind the grandeur of the Olympic Games lies a huge financial challenge—how to keep budgeted costs in line with revenues. For example, the 2006 Winter Olympics in Turin, Italy, narrowly avoided going into bankruptcy before the Games even started. In order for the event to remain solvent, organizers cancelled glitzy celebrations and shifted promotional responsibilities to an Italian state-run agency. Despite these efforts, after the Games were over, the Italian government created a lottery game to cover its financial losses.

As another example, organizers of the 2002 Winter Olympics in Salt Lake City cut budgeted costs by $200 million shortly before the events began. According to the chief operating and financial officer, the organizers went through every line item in the budget, sorting each one into "must have" versus "nice to have." As a result, the Salt Lake City Games produced a surplus of $100 million.

Source: Gabriel Kahn and Roger Thurow, "In Turin, Paying for Games Went Down to the Wire," *Wall Street Journal* (February 10, 2006).

Why does it matter whether the Olympic Games meet their budget? (Go to **WileyPLUS** for this answer and additional questions.)

BUDGETED BALANCE SHEET

The **budgeted balance sheet** is a projection of financial position at the end of the budget period. This budget is developed from the budgeted balance sheet for the preceding year and the budgets for the current year. Pertinent data from the budgeted balance sheet at December 31, 2016, are as follows.

Buildings and equipment	$182,000	Common stock	$225,000
Accumulated depreciation	$ 28,800	Retained earnings	$ 46,480

Illustration 21-18 shows Hayes Company's budgeted classified balance sheet at December 31, 2017.

ILLUSTRATION 21-18
Budgeted classified balance sheet

HAYES COMPANY
Budgeted Balance Sheet
December 31, 2017

Assets		
Current assets		
Cash		$ 37,900
Accounts receivable		108,000
Finished goods inventory		44,000
Raw materials inventory		4,080
Total current assets		193,980
Property, plant, and equipment		
Buildings and equipment	$192,000	
Less: Accumulated depreciation	48,000	144,000
Total assets		$337,980

Liabilities and Stockholders' Equity		
Liabilities		
Accounts payable		$ 18,600
Stockholders' equity		
Common stock	$225,000	
Retained earnings	94,380	
Total stockholders' equity		319,380
Total liabilities and stockholders' equity		$337,980

The computations and sources of the amounts are explained below.

Cash: Ending cash balance $37,900, shown in the cash budget (Illustration 21-17, page 1032).

Accounts receivable: 40% of fourth-quarter sales $270,000, shown in the schedule of expected collections from customers (Illustration 21-15, page 1031).

Finished goods inventory: Desired ending inventory 1,000 units, shown in the production budget (Illustration 21-5, page 1023) times the total unit cost $44 (shown in Illustration 21-12, page 1029).

Raw materials inventory: Desired ending inventory 1,020 pounds, times the cost per pound $4, shown in the direct materials budget (Illustration 21-7, page 1024).

Buildings and equipment: December 31, 2016, balance $182,000, plus purchase of truck for $10,000 (Illustration 21-17, page 1032).

Accumulated depreciation: December 31, 2016, balance $28,800, plus $15,200 depreciation shown in manufacturing overhead budget (Illustration 21-10, page 1027) and $4,000 depreciation shown in selling and administrative expense budget (Illustration 21-11, page 1028).

Accounts payable: 50% of fourth-quarter purchases $37,200, shown in schedule of expected payments for direct materials (Illustration 21-16, page 1032).

Common stock: Unchanged from the beginning of the year.

Retained earnings: December 31, 2016, balance $46,480, plus net income $47,900, shown in budgeted income statement (Illustration 21-13, page 1029).

After budget data are entered into the computer, Hayes prepares the various budgets (sales, cash, etc.), as well as the budgeted financial statements. Using spreadsheets, management can also perform "what if" (sensitivity) analyses based on different hypothetical assumptions. For example, suppose that sales managers project that sales will be 10% higher in the coming quarter. What impact does this change have on the rest of the budgeting process and the financing needs of the business? The impact of the various assumptions on the budget is quickly determined by the spreadsheet. Armed with these analyses, managers make more informed decisions about the impact of various projects. They also anticipate future problems and business opportunities. As seen in this chapter, budgeting is an excellent use of computer spreadsheets.

DO IT! ▶4 Cash Budget

Martian Company management wants to maintain a minimum monthly cash balance of $15,000. At the beginning of March, the cash balance is $16,500, expected cash receipts for March are $210,000, and cash disbursements are expected to be $220,000. How much cash, if any, must be borrowed to maintain the desired minimum monthly balance?

SOLUTION

Martian Company Cash Budget.xls

	A	B	C
1	**MARTIAN COMPANY**		
2	**Cash Budget**		
3	**For the Month Ending March 31, 2017**		
4	Beginning cash balance	$ 16,500	
5	Add: Cash receipts for March	210,000	
6	Total available cash	226,500	
7	Less: Cash disbursements for March	220,000	
8	Excess (deficiency) of available cash over cash disbursements	6,500	
9	Financing	8,500	
10	**Ending cash balance**	$ 15,000	
11			

To maintain the desired minimum cash balance of $15,000, Martian Company must borrow $8,500 of cash.

Action Plan

✔ Write down the basic form of the cash budget, starting with the beginning cash balance, adding cash receipts for the period, deducting cash disbursements, and identifying the needed financing to achieve the desired minimum ending cash balance.

✔ Insert the data given into the outlined form of the cash budget.

Related exercise material: **BE21-9, E21-14, E21-15, E21-16,** and **DO IT! 21-4.**

LEARNING OBJECTIVE **5** **Apply budgeting principles to nonmanufacturing companies.**

Budgeting is not limited to manufacturers. Budgets are also used by merchandisers, service companies, and not-for-profit organizations.

MERCHANDISERS

As in manufacturing operations, the sales budget for a merchandiser is both the starting point and the key factor in the development of the master budget. The major differences between the master budgets of a merchandiser and a manufacturer are as follows.

1. A merchandiser **uses a merchandise purchases budget instead of a production budget**.
2. A merchandiser **does not use the manufacturing budgets (direct materials, direct labor, and manufacturing overhead)**.

The **merchandise purchases budget** shows the estimated cost of goods to be purchased to meet expected sales. The formula for determining budgeted merchandise purchases is as follows.

Budgeted Cost of Goods Sold	+	Desired Ending Merchandise Inventory	−	Beginning Merchandise Inventory	=	Required Merchandise Inventory

ILLUSTRATION 21-19
Merchandise purchases formula

To illustrate, assume that the budget committee of Lima Company is preparing the merchandise purchases budget for July 2017. It estimates that budgeted sales will be $300,000 in July and $320,000 in August. Cost of goods sold is expected to be 70% of sales—that is, $210,000 in July (.70 × $300,000) and $224,000 in August (.70 × $320,000). The company's desired ending inventory is 30% of the following month's cost of goods sold. Required merchandise purchases for July are $214,200, computed as follows.

ILLUSTRATION 21-20
Merchandise purchases budget

Lima Company Merchandise Purchases Budget.xls

	A	B
1	**LIMA COMPANY**	
2	**Merchandise Purchases Budget**	
3	**For the Month Ending July 31, 2017**	
4	Budgeted cost of goods sold ($300,000 × 70%)	$210,000
5	Add: Desired ending merchandise inventory ($224,000 × 30%)	67,200
6	Total	277,200
7	Less: Beginning merchandise inventory ($210,000 × 30%)	63,000
8	Required merchandise purchases for July	$214,200

Departmentalized budgets

When a merchandiser is departmentalized, it prepares separate budgets for each department. For example, a grocery store prepares sales budgets and purchases budgets for each of its major departments, such as meats, dairy, and produce. The store then combines these budgets into a master budget for the store. When a retailer has branch stores, it prepares separate master budgets for each store. Then, it incorporates these budgets into master budgets for the company as a whole.

SERVICE COMPANIES

In a service company, such as a public accounting firm, a law office, or a medical practice, the critical factor in budgeting is **coordinating professional staff needs with anticipated services**. If a firm is overstaffed, several problems may result: Labor costs are disproportionately high. Profits are lower because of the additional salaries. Staff turnover sometimes increases because of lack of challenging work. In contrast, if a service company is understaffed, it may lose revenue because existing and prospective client needs for service cannot be met. Also, professional staff may seek other jobs because of excessive work loads.

Suppose that Stephan Lawn and Plowing Service estimates that it will service 300 small lawns, 200 medium lawns, and 100 large lawns during the month of July. It estimates its direct labor needs as 1 hour per small lawn, 1.75 hours for a medium lawn, and 2.75 hours for a large lawn. Its average cost for direct labor is $15 per hour. Stephan prepares a direct labor budget as follows.

ILLUSTRATION 21-21
Direct labor budget for service company

Stephan Lawn and Plowing Service Direct Labor Budget.xls

	A	B	C	D	E
1	**STEPHAN LAWN AND PLOWING SERVICE**				
2	**Direct Labor Budget**				
3	**For the Month Ending July 31, 2017**				
4		Small	Medium	Large	Total
5	Lawns to be serviced	300	200	100	
6	Direct labor time (hours) per lawn	× 1	× 1.75	× 2.75	
7	Total required direct labor hours	300	350	275	
8	Direct labor cost per hour	× $15	× $15	× $15	
9	Total direct labor cost	$4,500	$5,250	$4,125	$13,875

Service companies can obtain budget data for service revenue from **expected output** or **expected input**. When output is used, it is necessary to determine the expected billings of clients for services performed. In a public accounting firm, for example, output is the sum of its billings in auditing, tax, and consulting services. When input data are used, each professional staff member projects his or her billable time. The firm then applies billing rates to billable time to produce expected service revenue.

NOT-FOR-PROFIT ORGANIZATIONS

Budgeting is just as important for not-for-profit organizations as for profit-oriented businesses. The budget process, however, is different. In most cases, not-for-profit entities budget **on the basis of cash flows (expenditures and receipts), rather than on a revenue and expense basis**. Further, the starting point in the process is usually expenditures, not receipts. For the not-for-profit entity, management's task generally is to find the receipts needed to support the planned expenditures. The activity index is also likely to be significantly different. For example, in a not-for-profit entity, such as a university, budgeted faculty positions may be based on full-time equivalent students or credit hours expected to be taught in a department.

For some governmental units, voters approve the budget. In other cases, such as state governments and the federal government, legislative approval is required. After the budget is adopted, it must be followed. Overspending is often illegal. In governmental budgets, authorizations tend to be on a line-by-line basis. That is, the budget for a municipality may have a specified authorization for police and fire protection, garbage collection, street paving, and so on. The line-item authorization of governmental budgets significantly limits the amount of discretion management can exercise. The city manager often cannot use savings from one line item, such as street paving, to cover increased spending in another line item, such as snow removal.

SERVICE COMPANY INSIGHT Museum of Contemporary Art

© ZUMA Press/Newscom/NewsCom

Budget Shortfalls as Far as the Eye Can See

All organizations need to stick to budgets. The Museum of Contemporary Art in Los Angeles learned this the hard way. Over a 10-year period, its endowment shrunk from $50 million to $6 million as its newly hired director strove to build the museum's reputation through spending. The director consistently ran budget deficits, which eventually threatened the museum's survival.

The most recent recession created budgeting challenges for nearly all governmental agencies. Tax revenues dropped rapidly as earnings declined and unemployment skyrocketed. At the same time, sources of debt financing dried up. Even Princeton University, with the largest endowment per student of any U.S. university ($2 million per student), experienced a 25% drop in the value of its endowment when the financial markets plunged. Because the endowment supports 45% of the university's $1.25 billion budget, when the endowment fell the university had to make cuts. Many raises were capped at $2,000, administrative budgets were cut by 5%, and major construction projects were put on hold.

Sources: Edward Wyatt and Jori Finkel, "Soaring in Art, Museum Trips Over Finances," Wall Street Journal Online (December 4, 2008); Stu Woo, "California's Plans to Close Gap Become More Drastic," *Wall Street Journal Online* (January 8, 2009); and John Hechinger, "Princeton Cuts Budget as Endowment Slides," *Wall Street Journal Online* (January 9, 2009).

Why would a university's budgeted scholarships probably fall when the stock market suffers a serious drop? (Go to WileyPLUS for this answer and additional questions.)

DO IT! 5 Merchandise Purchases Budget

Becker Company estimates that 2017 sales will be $15,000 in quarter 1, $20,000 in quarter 2, and $25,000 in quarter 3. Cost of goods sold is 80% of sales. Management desires to have ending finished goods inventory equal to 15% of the next quarter's expected cost of goods sold. Prepare a merchandise purchases budget by quarter for the first six months of 2017.

Action Plan

- ✔ Begin with budgeted cost of goods sold.
- ✔ Add desired ending merchandise inventory.
- ✔ Subtract beginning merchandise inventory.

SOLUTION

Becker Company Merchandise Purchases Budget.xls

	A	B	C	D
1	**BECKER COMPANY**			
2	**Merchandise Purchases Budget**			
3	**For the Six Months Ending June 30, 2017**			
4		Quarter		
5		1	2	Six Months
6	Budgeted cost of goods sold (sales × .80)	$12,000	$16,000	
7	Add: Desired ending merchandise inventory (15% of next quarter's cost of goods sold)	2,400	3,000	
8	Total	14,400	19,000	
9	Less: Beginning merchandise inventory (15% this quarter's cost of goods sold)	1,800	2,400	
10	Required merchandise purchases	$12,600	$16,600	$29,200

Related exercise material: **BE21-10, E21-19, E21-20, E21-21,** and DO IT! **21-5.**

USING DECISION TOOLS—BABYCAKES NYC

As discussed in the Feature Story, BabyCakes NYC relies on budgeting to aid in the management of its cupcake operations. Assume that BabyCakes prepares monthly cash budgets. Relevant data from assumed operating budgets for 2017 are as follows:

	January	February
Sales	$460,000	$412,000
Direct materials purchases	185,000	210,000
Direct labor	70,000	85,000
Manufacturing overhead	50,000	65,000
Selling and administrative expenses	85,000	95,000

Assume that BabyCakes sells its cupcakes in its own shops as well as to other stores. Collections are expected to be 75% in the month of sale, and 25% in the month following sale. BabyCakes pays 60% of direct materials purchases in cash in the month of purchase, and the balance due in the month following the purchase. All other items above are paid in the month incurred. (Depreciation has been excluded from manufacturing overhead and selling and administrative expenses.)

Other data:

(1) Sales: December 2016, $320,000
(2) Purchases of direct materials: December 2016, $175,000
(3) Other receipts: January—Donation received, $2,000
February—Sale of used equipment, $4,000
(4) Other disbursements: February—Purchased equipment, $10,000
(5) Repaid debt: January, $30,000

The company's cash balance on January 1, 2017, is expected to be $50,000. The company wants to maintain a minimum cash balance of $45,000.

INSTRUCTIONS

(a) Prepare schedules for (1) expected collections from customers and (2) expected payments for direct materials purchases for January and February.

(b) Prepare a cash budget for January and February in columnar form.

SOLUTION

(a) (1)

Expected Collections from Customers

	Sales	January	February
December	$320,000	$ 80,000	$ 0
January	460,000	345,000	115,000
February	412,000	0	309,000
Totals		$425,000	$424,000

(2)

Expected Payments for Direct Materials

	Purchases	January	February
December	$175,000	$ 70,000	$ 0
January	185,000	111,000	74,000
February	210,000	0	126,000
Totals		$181,000	$200,000

(b)

BABYCAKES NYC
Cash Budget
For the Two Months Ending February 28, 2017

	January	February
Beginning cash balance	$ 50,000	$ 61,000
Add: Receipts		
Collections from customers	425,000	424,000
Donations received	2,000	0
Sale of used equipment	0	4,000
Total receipts	427,000	428,000
Total available cash	477,000	489,000
Less: Disbursements		
Direct materials	181,000	200,000
Direct labor	70,000	85,000
Manufacturing overhead	50,000	65,000
Selling and administrative expenses	85,000	95,000
Purchase of equipment	0	10,000
Total disbursements	386,000	455,000
Excess (deficiency) of available cash over cash disbursements	91,000	34,000
Financing		
Add: Borrowings	0	11,000
Less: Repayments	30,000	0
Ending cash balance	$ 61,000	$ 45,000

REVIEW AND PRACTICE

LEARNING OBJECTIVES REVIEW

1 State the essentials of effective budgeting and the components of the master budget. The primary benefits of budgeting are that it (a) requires management to plan ahead, (b) provides definite objectives for evaluating performance, (c) creates an early warning system for potential problems, (d) facilitates coordination of activities, (e) results in greater management awareness, and (f) motivates personnel to meet planned objectives. The essentials of effective budgeting are (a) sound organizational structure, (b) research and analysis, and (c) acceptance by all levels of management.

The master budget consists of the following budgets: (a) sales, (b) production, (c) direct materials, (d) direct labor, (e) manufacturing overhead, (f) selling and administrative expense, (g) budgeted income statement, (h) capital expenditure budget, (i) cash budget, and (j) budgeted balance sheet.

2 Prepare budgets for sales, production, and direct materials. The sales budget is derived from sales forecasts. The production budget starts with budgeted sales units, adds desired ending finished goods inventory, and subtracts beginning finished goods inventory to arrive at the required number of production units. The direct materials budget starts with the direct materials units (e.g., pounds) required for budgeted production, adds desired ending direct materials units, and subtracts beginning direct materials units to arrive at required direct materials units to be purchased. This amount is multiplied by the direct materials cost (e.g., cost per pound) to arrive at the total cost of direct materials purchases.

3 Prepare budgets for direct labor, manufacturing overhead, and selling and administrative expenses, and a budgeted income statement. The direct labor budget starts with the units to be produced as determined in the production budget. This amount is multiplied by the direct labor hours per unit and the direct labor cost per hour to arrive at the total direct labor cost. The manufacturing overhead budget lists all of the individual types of overhead costs, distinguishing between fixed and variable costs. The selling and administrative expense budget lists all of the individual types of selling and administrative expense items, distinguishing between fixed and variable costs. The budgeted income statement is prepared from the various operating budgets. Cost of goods sold is determined by calculating the budgeted cost to produce one unit, then multiplying this amount by the number of units sold.

4 Prepare a cash budget and a budgeted balance sheet. The cash budget has three sections (receipts, disbursements, and financing) and the beginning and ending cash balances. Receipts and payments sections are determined after preparing separate schedules for collections from customers and payments to suppliers. The budgeted balance sheet is developed from the budgeted balance sheet from the preceding year and the various budgets for the current year.

5 Apply budgeting principles to nonmanufacturing companies. Budgeting may be used by merchandisers for development of a merchandise purchases budget. In service companies, budgeting is a critical factor in coordinating staff needs with anticipated services. In not-for-profit organizations, the starting point in budgeting is usually expenditures, not receipts.

DECISION TOOLS REVIEW

DECISION CHECKPOINTS	INFO NEEDED FOR DECISION	TOOL TO USE FOR DECISION	HOW TO EVALUATE RESULTS
Has the company met its targets for sales, production expenses, selling and administrative expenses, and net income?	Sales forecasts, inventory levels, projected materials, labor, overhead, and selling and administrative requirements	Master budget—a set of interrelated budgets including sales, production, materials, labor, overhead, and selling and administrative expense budgets	Results are favorable if revenues exceed budgeted amounts, or if expenses are less than budgeted amounts.
Is the company going to need to borrow funds in the coming period?	Beginning cash balance, cash receipts, cash disbursements, and desired cash balance	Cash budget	The company will need to borrow money if the cash budget indicates a projected cash deficiency.

GLOSSARY REVIEW

Budget A formal written statement of management's plans for a specified future time period, expressed in financial terms. (p. 1016).

Budgetary slack The amount by which a manager intentionally underestimates budgeted revenues or overestimates budgeted expenses in order to make it easier to achieve budgetary goals. (p. 1019).

Budget committee A group responsible for coordinating the preparation of the budget. (p. 1018).

Budgeted balance sheet A projection of financial position at the end of the budget period. (p. 1033).

Budgeted income statement An estimate of the expected profitability of operations for the budget period. (p. 1028).

Cash budget A projection of anticipated cash flows. (p. 1030).

Direct labor budget A projection of the quantity and cost of direct labor necessary to meet production requirements. (p. 1026).

Direct materials budget An estimate of the quantity and cost of direct materials to be purchased. (p. 1023).

Financial budgets Individual budgets that focus primarily on the cash resources needed to fund expected operations and planned capital expenditures. (p. 1019).

Long-range planning A formalized process of identifying long-term goals, selecting strategies to achieve those goals, and developing policies and plans to implement the strategies. (p. 1019).

Manufacturing overhead budget An estimate of expected manufacturing overhead costs for the budget period. (p. 1027).

Master budget A set of interrelated budgets that constitutes a plan of action for a specific time period. (p. 1019).

Merchandise purchases budget The estimated cost of goods to be purchased by a merchandiser to meet expected sales. (p. 1035).

Operating budgets Individual budgets that result in a budgeted income statement. (p. 1019).

Participative budgeting A budgetary approach that starts with input from lower-level managers and works upward so that managers at all levels participate. (p. 1018).

Production budget A projection of the units that must be produced to meet anticipated sales. (p. 1022).

Sales budget An estimate of expected sales revenue for the budget period. (p. 1021).

Sales forecast The projection of potential sales for the industry and the company's expected share of such sales. (p. 1017).

Selling and administrative expense budget A projection of anticipated selling and administrative expenses for the budget period. (p. 1028).

PRACTICE MULTIPLE-CHOICE QUESTIONS

(LO 1) 1. Which of the following is **not** a benefit of budgeting?
- (a) Management can plan ahead.
- (b) An early warning system is provided for potential problems.
- (c) It enables disciplinary action to be taken at every level of responsibility.
- (d) The coordination of activities is facilitated.

(LO 1) 2. A budget:
- (a) is the responsibility of management accountants.
- (b) is the primary method of communicating agreed-upon objectives throughout an organization.
- (c) ignores past performance because it represents management's plans for a future time period.
- (d) may promote efficiency but has no role in evaluating performance.

(LO 1) 3. The essentials of effective budgeting do **not** include:
- (a) top-down budgeting.
- (b) management acceptance.
- (c) research and analysis.
- (d) sound organizational structure.

(LO 1) 4. Compared to budgeting, long-range planning generally has the:
- (a) same amount of detail. (c) same emphasis.
- (b) longer time period. (d) same time period.

(LO 2) 5. A sales budget is:
- (a) derived from the production budget.
- (b) management's best estimate of sales revenue for the year.
- (c) not the starting point for the master budget.
- (d) prepared only for credit sales.

(LO 2) 6. The formula for the production budget is budgeted sales in units plus:
- (a) desired ending merchandise inventory less beginning merchandise inventory.
- (b) beginning finished goods units less desired ending finished goods units.
- (c) desired ending direct materials units less beginning direct materials units.
- (d) desired ending finished goods units less beginning finished goods units.

7. Direct materials inventories are kept in pounds in Byrd Company, and the total pounds of direct materials needed for production is 9,500. If the beginning inventory is 1,000 pounds and the desired ending inventory is 2,200 pounds, the total pounds to be purchased is: (LO 2)
- (a) 9,400. (c) 9,700.
- (b) 9,500. (d) 10,700.

8. The formula for computing the direct labor budget is to multiply the direct labor cost per hour by the: (LO 3)
- (a) total required direct labor hours.
- (b) physical units to be produced.
- (c) equivalent units to be produced.
- (d) No correct answer is given.

9. Each of the following budgets is used in preparing the budgeted income statement **except** the: (LO 3)
- (a) sales budget.
- (b) selling and administrative expense budget.
- (c) capital expenditure budget.
- (d) direct labor budget.

10. The budgeted income statement is: (LO 3)
- (a) the end-product of the operating budgets.
- (b) the end-product of the financial budgets.
- (c) the starting point of the master budget.
- (d) dependent on cash receipts and cash disbursements.

11. The budgeted balance sheet is: (LO 4)
- (a) developed from the budgeted balance sheet for the preceding year and the budgets for the current year.
- (b) the last operating budget prepared.
- (c) used to prepare the cash budget.
- (d) All of the above.

(LO 4) **12.** The format of a cash budget is:
(a) Beginning cash balance + Cash receipts + Cash from financing − Cash disbursements = Ending cash balance.
(b) Beginning cash balance + Cash receipts − Cash disbursements +/− Financing = Ending cash balance.
(c) Beginning cash balance + Net income − Cash dividends = Ending cash balance.
(d) Beginning cash balance + Cash revenues − Cash expenses = Ending cash balance.

(LO 4) **13.** Expected direct materials purchases in Read Company are $70,000 in the first quarter and $90,000 in the second quarter. Forty percent of the purchases are paid in cash as incurred, and the balance is paid in the following quarter. The budgeted cash payments for purchases in the second quarter are:
(a) $96,000. (c) $78,000.
(b) $90,000. (d) $72,000.

14. The budget for a merchandiser differs from a budget for a manufacturer because: (LO 5)
(a) a merchandise purchases budget replaces the production budget.
(b) the manufacturing budgets are not applicable.
(c) None of the above.
(d) Both (a) and (b) above.

15. In most cases, not-for-profit entities: (LO 5)
(a) prepare budgets using the same steps as those used by profit-oriented businesses.
(b) know budgeted cash receipts at the beginning of a time period, so they budget only for expenditures.
(c) begin the budgeting process by budgeting expenditures rather than receipts.
(d) can ignore budgets because they are not expected to generate net income.

SOLUTIONS

1. **(c)** Budgeting does not necessarily enable disciplinary action to be taken at every level of responsibility. The other choices are all benefits of budgeting.
2. **(b)** A budget is the primary method of communicating agreed-upon objectives throughout an organization. The other choices are incorrect because (a) a budget is the responsibility of all levels of management, not management accountants; (c) past performance is not ignored in the budgeting process but instead is the starting point from which future budget goals are formulated; and (d) the budget not only may promote efficiency but is an important tool for evaluating performance.
3. **(a)** Top-down budgeting is not one of the essentials of effective budgeting. The other choices are true statements.
4. **(b)** Long-range planning generally encompasses a period of at least 5 years whereas budgeting usually covers a period of 1 year. The other choices are incorrect because budgeting and long-range planning (a) do not have the same amount of detail, (c) do not have the same emphasis, and (d) do not cover the same time period.
5. **(b)** A sales budget is management's best estimate of sales revenue for the year. The other choices are incorrect because a sales budget (a) is the first budget prepared and is the one budget that is not derived from any other budget, (c) is the starting point for the master budget, and (d) is prepared for both cash and credit sales.
6. **(d)** The formula for the production budget is budgeted sales in units plus desired ending finished goods units less beginning finished goods units. The other choices are therefore incorrect.
7. **(d)** Pounds to be purchased = Amount needed for production (9,500) + Desired ending inventory (2,200) − Beginning inventory (1,000) = 10,700, not (a) 9,400, (b) 9,500, or (c) 9,700.
8. **(a)** Direct labor cost = Direct labor cost per hour × Total required direct labor hours. The other choices are therefore incorrect.
9. **(c)** The capital expenditure budget is not used in preparing the budgeted income statement. The other choices are true statements.
10. **(a)** The budgeted income statement is the end-product of the operating budgets, not (b) the financial budgets, (c) the starting point of the master budget, or (d) dependent on cash receipts and cash disbursements.
11. **(a)** The budgeted balance sheet is developed from the budgeted balance sheet for the preceding year and the budgets for the current year. The other choices are therefore incorrect.
12. **(b)** The format of a cash budget is Beginning cash balance + Cash receipts − Cash disbursements +/− Financing = Ending cash balance. The other choices are therefore incorrect.
13. **(c)** Budgeted cash payments for the second quarter = Purchases for the first quarter ($42,000; $70,000 × 60%) + 40% of the purchases for the second quarter ($36,000; $90,000 × 40%) = $78,000, not (a) $96,000, (b) $90,000, or (d) $72,000.
14. **(d)** The budget for a merchandiser uses a merchandise purchases budget in place of a production budget, and the manufacturing budgets are not applicable for a merchandiser. Therefore, as both choices (a) and (b) are correct, choice (d) is the best answer.
15. **(c)** In most cases, not-for-profit entities begin the budgeting process by budgeting expenditures rather than receipts. The other choices are incorrect because in most cases not-for-profit entities (a) prepare budgets using different, not the same, steps as those used by profit-oriented enterprises; (b) budget for both expenditures and receipts; and (d) cannot ignore budgets.

PRACTICE EXERCISES

Prepare production and direct materials budgets by quarter for 6 months.

(LO 2)

1. On January 1, 2017 the Heche Company budget committee has reached agreement on the following data for the 6 months ending June 30, 2017.

Sales units:	First quarter 5,000; second quarter 6,000; third quarter 7,000
Ending raw materials inventory:	40% of the next quarter's production requirements
Ending finished goods inventory:	30% of the next quarter's expected sales units
Third-quarter 2017 production:	7,500 units

The ending raw materials and finished goods inventories at December 31, 2016, follow the same percentage relationships to production and sales that occur in 2017. Two pounds of raw materials are required to make each unit of finished goods. Raw materials purchased are expected to cost $5 per pound.

INSTRUCTIONS

(a) Prepare a production budget by quarters for the 6-month period ended June 30, 2017.

(b) Prepare a direct materials budget by quarters for the 6-month period ended June 30, 2017.

SOLUTION

1. (a)

Heche Company Production Budget.xls

HECHE COMPANY
Production Budget
For the Six Months Ending June 30, 2017

	Quarter 1	Quarter 2	Six Months
Expected unit sales	5,000	6,000	
Add: Desired ending finished goods units	1,800 (1)	2,100 (2)	
Total required units	6,800	8,100	
Less: Beginning finished goods units	1,500 (3)	1,800	
Required production units	5,300	6,300	11,600

(1) 30% × 6,000; (2) 30% × 7,000; (3) 30% × 5,000

(b)

Heche Company Direct Materials Budget.xls

HECHE COMPANY
Direct Materials Budget
For the Six Months Ending June 30, 2017

	Quarter 1	Quarter 2	Six Months
Units to be produced	5,300	6,300	
Direct materials per unit	× 2	× 2	
Total pounds needed for production	10,600	12,600	
Add: Desired ending direct materials (pounds)	5,040 (1)	6,000 (2)	
Total materials required	15,640	18,600	
Less: Beginning direct materials (pounds)	4,240 (3)	5,040	
Direct materials purchase	11,400	13,560	
Cost per pound	× $5	× $5	
Total cost of direct materials purchase	$57,000	$67,800	$124,800

(1) 40% × 12,600; (2) 7,500 × (2 × 40%); (3) 40% × 10,600

Prepare a cash budget for 2 months.

(LO 4)

2. Jake Company expects to have a cash balance of $45,000 on January 1, 2017. Relevant monthly budget data for the first 2 months of 2017 are as follows.

Collections from customers: January $100,000. February $160,000.

Payments for direct materials: January $60,000, February $80,000.

Direct labor: January $30,000, February $45,000. Wages are paid in the month they are incurred.

Manufacturing overhead: January $26,000, February $31,000. These costs include depreciation of $1,000 per month. All other overhead costs are paid as incurred.

Selling and administrative expenses: January $15,000. February $20,000. These costs are exclusive of depreciation. They are paid as incurred.

Sales of marketable securities in January are expected to realize $10,000 in cash. Jake Company has a line of credit at a local bank that enables it to borrow up to $25,000. The company wants to maintain a minimum monthly cash balance of $25,000.

INSTRUCTIONS

Prepare a cash budget for January and February.

SOLUTION

2.

Jake Company Cash Budget.xls

Home Insert Page Layout Formulas Data Review View

P18 *fx*

	A	B	C
1	**JAKE COMPANY**		
2	**Cash Budget**		
3	**For the Two Months Ending February 28, 2017**		
4		January	February
5	Beginning cash balance	$ 45,000	$ 25,000
6	Add: Receipts		
7	Collections from customers	100,000	160,000
8	Sale of marketable securities	10,000	0
9	Total receipts	110,000	160,000
10	Total available cash	155,000	185,000
11	Less: Disbursements		
12	Direct materials	60,000	80,000
13	Direct labor	30,000	45,000
14	Manufacturing overhead	25,000	30,000
15	Selling and administrative expenses	15,000	20,000
16	Total disbursements	130,000	175,000
17	Excess (deficiency) of available cash over cash		
18	Disbursements	25,000	10,000
19	Financing		
20	Borrowings	0	15,000
21	Repayments	0	0
22	Ending cash balance	$ 25,000	$ 25,000
23			

▶ PRACTICE PROBLEMS

Prepare sales and production budgets.

(LO 2)

1. Asheville Company is preparing its master budget for 2017. Relevant data pertaining to its sales and production budgets are as follows.

Sales. Sales for the year are expected to total 2,100,000 units. Quarterly sales, as a percentage of total sales, are 15%, 25%, 35%, and 25%, respectively. The sales price is expected to be $70 per unit for the first three quarters and $75 per unit beginning in the fourth quarter. Sales in the first quarter of 2018 are expected to be 10% higher than the budgeted sales volume for the first quarter of 2017.

Production. Management desires to maintain ending finished goods inventories at 20% of the next quarter's budgeted sales volume.

INSTRUCTIONS

Prepare the sales budget and production budget by quarters for 2017.

SOLUTION

1.

Asheville Company Sales Budget and Production Budget.xls

	ASHEVILLE COMPANY					
	For the Year Ending December 31, 2017					
	Sales Budget					
	Quarter					
	1	2	3	4		Year
Expected unit sales	315,000	525,000	735,000	525,000		2,100,000
Unit selling price	× $70	× $70	× $70	× $75		
Total sales	$22,050,000	$36,750,000	$51,450,000	$39,375,000		$149,625,000
		Production Budget				
Expected unit sales	315,000	525,000	735,000	525,000		
Add: Desired ending finished goods units	105,000	147,000	105,000	69,300[a]		
Total required units	420,000	672,000	840,000	594,300		
Less: Beginning finished goods units	63,000[b]	105,000	147,000	105,000		
Required production units	357,000	567,000	693,000	489,300		2,106,300

[a]Estimated first-quarter 2018 sales volume 315,000 + (315,000 × 10%) = 346,500; 346,500 × 20%

[b]20% of estimated first-quarter 2017 sales units (315,000 × 20%)

Prepare budgeted cost of goods sold, income statement, and balance sheet.

(LO 3, 4)

2. Barrett Company has completed all operating budgets other than the income statement for 2017. Selected data from these budgets follow.

Sales: $300,000
Purchases of raw materials: $145,000
Ending inventory of raw materials: $15,000
Direct labor: $40,000
Manufacturing overhead: $73,000, including $3,000 of depreciation expense
Selling and administrative expenses: $36,000 including depreciation expense of $1,000
Interest expense: $1,000
Principal payment on note: $2,000
Dividends declared: $2,000
Income tax rate: 30%

Other information:

Assume that the number of units produced equals the number sold.
Year-end accounts receivable: 4% of 2017 sales.
Year-end accounts payable: 50% of ending inventory of raw materials.
Interest, direct labor, manufacturing overhead, and selling and administrative expenses other than depreciation are paid as incurred.
Dividends declared and income taxes for 2017 will not be paid until 2018.

BARRETT COMPANY
Balance Sheet
December 31, 2016

Assets		
Current assets		
Cash		$20,000
Raw materials inventory		10,000
Total current assets		30,000
Property, plant, and equipment		
Equipment	$40,000	
Less: Accumulated depreciation	4,000	36,000
Total assets		$66,000

Liabilities and Stockholders' Equity		
Liabilities		
Accounts payable	$ 5,000	
Notes payable	22,000	
Total liabilities		$27,000
Stockholders' equity		
Common stock	25,000	
Retained earnings	14,000	
Total stockholders' equity		39,000
Total liabilities and stockholders' equity		$66,000

INSTRUCTIONS

(a) Calculate budgeted cost of goods sold.

(b) Prepare a budgeted multiple-step income statement for the year ending December 31, 2017.

(c) Prepare a budgeted classified balance sheet as of December 31, 2017.

SOLUTION

2. (a) Beginning raw materials + Purchases − Ending raw materials = Cost of direct materials used ($10,000 + $145,000 − $15,000 = $140,000)
Direct materials used + Direct labor + Manufacturing overhead = Cost of goods sold ($140,000 + $40,000 + $73,000 = $253,000)

(b)

BARRETT COMPANY
Budgeted Income Statement
For the Year Ending December 31, 2017

Sales	$300,000
Cost of goods sold	253,000
Gross profit	47,000
Selling and administrative expenses	36,000
Income from operations	11,000
Interest expense	1,000
Income before income tax expense	10,000
Income tax expense (30%)	3,000
Net income	$ 7,000

(c)

BARRETT COMPANY
Budgeted Balance Sheet
December 31, 2017

Assets		
Current assets		
Cash(1)		$17,500
Accounts receivable (4% × $300,000)		12,000
Raw materials inventory		15,000
Total current assets		44,500
Property, plant and equipment		
Equipment	$40,000	
Less: Accumulated depreciation	8,000	32,000
Total assets		$76,500

(1)Beginning cash balance	$ 20,000
Add: Collections from customers (96% × $300,000 sales)	288,000
Total available cash	308,000

Less: Disbursements		
Direct materials ($5,000 + $145,000 − $7,500)	$142,500	
Direct labor	40,000	
Manufacturing overhead	70,000	
Selling and administrative expenses	35,000	
Total disbursements		287,500
Excess of available cash over cash disbursements		20,500
Financing		
Less: Repayment of principal and interest		3,000
Ending cash balance		$ 17,500

Liabilities and Stockholders' Equity

Liabilities		
Accounts payable (50% × $15,000)	$ 7,500	
Income taxes payable	3,000	
Dividends payable	2,000	
Note payable	20,000	
Total liabilities		$32,500
Stockholders' equity		
Common stock	25,000	
Retained earnings(2)	19,000	
Total stockholders' equity		44,000
Total liabilities and stockholders' equity		$76,500

(2)Beginning retained earnings + Net income − Dividends declared = Ending retained earnings ($14,000 + $7,000 − $2,000 = $19,000)

WileyPLUS Brief Exercises, DO IT! Exercises, Exercises, Problems, and many additional resources are available for practice in WileyPLUS.

QUESTIONS

1. (a) What is a budget?
   (b) How does a budget contribute to good management?
2. Kate Cey and Joe Coulter are discussing the benefits of budgeting. They ask you to identify the primary benefits of budgeting. Comply with their request.
3. Jane Gilligan asks your help in understanding the essentials of effective budgeting. Identify the essentials for Jane.
4. (a) "Accounting plays a relatively unimportant role in budgeting." Do you agree? Explain.
   (b) What responsibilities does management have in budgeting?
5. What criteria are helpful in determining the length of the budget period? What is the most common budget period?
6. Lori Wilkins maintains that the only difference between budgeting and long-range planning is time. Do you agree? Why or why not?
7. What is participative budgeting? What are its potential benefits? What are its potential disadvantages?
8. What is budgetary slack? What incentive do managers have to create budgetary slack?
9. Distinguish between a master budget and a sales forecast.
10. What budget is the starting point in preparing the master budget? What may result if this budget is inaccurate?
11. "The production budget shows both unit production data and unit cost data." Is this true? Explain.
12. Alou Company has 20,000 beginning finished goods units. Budgeted sales units are 160,000. If management desires 15,000 ending finished goods units, what are the required units of production?
13. In preparing the direct materials budget for Quan Company, management concludes that required purchases are 64,000 units. If 52,000 direct materials units are required in production and there are 9,000 units of beginning direct materials, what is the desired units of ending direct materials?

14. The production budget of Justus Company calls for 80,000 units to be produced. If it takes 45 minutes to make one unit and the direct labor rate is $16 per hour, what is the total budgeted direct labor cost?
15. Ortiz Company's manufacturing overhead budget shows total variable costs of $198,000 and total fixed costs of $162,000. Total production in units is expected to be 150,000. It takes 20 minutes to make one unit, and the direct labor rate is $15 per hour. Express the manufacturing overhead rate as (a) a percentage of direct labor cost, and (b) an amount per direct labor hour.
16. Everly Company's variable selling and administrative expenses are 12% of net sales. Fixed expenses are $50,000 per quarter. The sales budget shows expected sales of $200,000 and $240,000 in the first and second quarters, respectively. What are the total budgeted selling and administrative expenses for each quarter?
17. For Goody Company, the budgeted cost for one unit of product is direct materials $10, direct labor $20, and manufacturing overhead 80% of direct labor cost. If 25,000 units are expected to be sold at $65 each, what is the budgeted gross profit?
18. Indicate the supporting schedules used in preparing a budgeted income statement through gross profit for a manufacturer.
19. Identify the three sections of a cash budget. What balances are also shown in this budget?
20. Noterman Company has credit sales of $600,000 in January. Past experience suggests that 40% is collected in the month of sale, 50% in the month following the sale, and 10% in the second month following the sale. Compute the cash collections from January sales in January, February, and March.
21. What is the formula for determining required merchandise purchases for a merchandiser?
22. How may expected revenues in a service company be computed?

BRIEF EXERCISES

Prepare a diagram of a master budget.
(LO 1), AN

BE21-1 Maris Company uses the following budgets: balance sheet, capital expenditure, cash, direct labor, direct materials, income statement, manufacturing overhead, production, sales, and selling and administrative expense. Prepare a diagram of the interrelationships of the budgets in the master budget. Indicate whether each budget is an operating or a financial budget.

Prepare a sales budget.
(LO 2), AP

BE21-2 Paige Company estimates that unit sales will be 10,000 in quarter 1, 14,000 in quarter 2, 15,000 in quarter 3, and 18,000 in quarter 4. Using a sales price of $70 per unit, prepare the sales budget by quarters for the year ending December 31, 2017.

Prepare a production budget for 2 quarters.
(LO 2), AP

BE21-3 Sales budget data for Paige Company are given in BE21-2. Management desires to have an ending finished goods inventory equal to 25% of the next quarter's expected unit sales. Prepare a production budget by quarters for the first 6 months of 2017.

Prepare a direct materials budget for 1 month.
(LO 2), AP

BE21-4 Perine Company has 2,000 pounds of raw materials in its December 31, 2016, ending inventory. Required production for January and February of 2017 are 4,000 and 5,000 units, respectively. Two pounds of raw materials are needed for each unit, and the estimated cost per pound is $6. Management desires an ending inventory equal to 25% of next month's materials requirements. Prepare the direct materials budget for January.

Prepare a direct labor budget for 2 quarters.
(LO 3), AP

BE21-5 For Gundy Company, units to be produced are 5,000 in quarter 1 and 7,000 in quarter 2. It takes 1.6 hours to make a finished unit, and the expected hourly wage rate is $15 per hour. Prepare a direct labor budget by quarters for the 6 months ending June 30, 2017.

Prepare a manufacturing overhead budget.
(LO 3), AP

BE21-6 For Roche Inc., variable manufacturing overhead costs are expected to be $20,000 in the first quarter of 2017, with $5,000 increments in each of the remaining three quarters. Fixed overhead costs are estimated to be $40,000 in each quarter. Prepare the manufacturing overhead budget by quarters and in total for the year.

Prepare a selling and administrative expense budget.
(LO 3), AP

BE21-7 Elbert Company classifies its selling and administrative expense budget into variable and fixed components. Variable expenses are expected to be $24,000 in the first quarter, and $4,000 increments are expected in the remaining quarters of 2017. Fixed expenses are expected to be $40,000 in each quarter. Prepare the selling and administrative expense budget by quarters and in total for 2017.

Prepare a budgeted income statement for the year.
(LO 3), AP

BE21-8 North Company has completed all of its operating budgets. The sales budget for the year shows 50,000 units and total sales of $2,250,000. The total unit cost of making one unit of sales is $25. Selling and administrative expenses are expected to be $300,000. Interest is estimated to be $10,000. Income taxes are estimated to be $200,000. Prepare a budgeted multiple-step income statement for the year ending December 31, 2017.

BE21-9 Kaspar Industries expects credit sales for January, February, and March to be $220,000, $260,000, and $300,000, respectively. It is expected that 75% of the sales will be collected in the month of sale, and 25% will be collected in the following month. Compute cash collections from customers for each month.

Prepare data for a cash budget. (LO 4), AP

BE21-10 Moore Wholesalers is preparing its merchandise purchases budget. Budgeted sales are $400,000 for April and $480,000 for May. Cost of goods sold is expected to be 65% of sales. The company's desired ending inventory is 20% of the following month's cost of goods sold. Compute the required purchases for April.

Determine required merchandise purchases for 1 month. (LO 5), AP

DO IT! EXERCISES

DO IT! 21-1 Use this list of terms to complete the sentences that follow.

Identify budget terminology. (LO 1), K

Long-range plans	Participative budgeting
Sales forecast	Operating budgets
Master budget	Financial budgets

1. ___________ establish goals for the company's sales and production personnel.
2. The ___________ is a set of interrelated budgets that constitutes a plan of action for a specified time period.
3. ___________ reduces the risk of having unrealistic budgets.
4. ___________ include the cash budget and the budgeted balance sheet.
5. The budget is formed within the framework of a ___________.
6. ___________ contain considerably less detail than budgets.

DO IT! 21-2 Pargo Company is preparing its master budget for 2017. Relevant data pertaining to its sales, production, and direct materials budgets are as follows.

Prepare sales, production, and direct materials budgets. (LO 2), AP

Sales. Sales for the year are expected to total 1,000,000 units. Quarterly sales are 20%, 25%, 25%, and 30%, respectively. The sales price is expected to be $40 per unit for the first three quarters and $45 per unit beginning in the fourth quarter. Sales in the first quarter of 2018 are expected to be 20% higher than the budgeted sales for the first quarter of 2017.

Production. Management desires to maintain the ending finished goods inventories at 25% of the next quarter's budgeted sales volume.

Direct materials. Each unit requires 2 pounds of raw materials at a cost of $12 per pound. Management desires to maintain raw materials inventories at 10% of the next quarter's production requirements. Assume the production requirements for first quarter of 2018 are 450,000 pounds.

Prepare the sales, production, and direct materials budgets by quarters for 2017.

DO IT! 21-3 Pargo Company is preparing its budgeted income statement for 2017. Relevant data pertaining to its sales, production, and direct materials budgets can be found in DO IT! 21-2.

Calculate budgeted total unit cost and prepare budgeted income statement. (LO 3), AP

In addition, Pargo budgets 0.3 hours of direct labor per unit, labor costs at $15 per hour, and manufacturing overhead at $20 per direct labor hour. Its budgeted selling and administrative expenses for 2017 are $6,000,000.

(a) Calculate the budgeted total unit cost.

(b) Prepare the budgeted multiple-step income statement for 2017. (Ignore income taxes.)

DO IT! 21-4 Batista Company management wants to maintain a minimum monthly cash balance of $25,000. At the beginning of April, the cash balance is $25,000, expected cash receipts for April are $245,000, and cash disbursements are expected to be $255,000. How much cash, if any, must be borrowed to maintain the desired minimum monthly balance?

Determine amount of financing needed. (LO 4), AP

DO IT! 21-5 Zeller Company estimates that 2017 sales will be $40,000 in quarter 1, $48,000 in quarter 2, and $58,000 in quarter 3. Cost of goods sold is 50% of sales. Management desires to have ending finished goods inventory equal to 10% of the next quarter's expected cost of goods sold. Prepare a merchandise purchases budget by quarter for the first 6 months of 2017.

Prepare merchandise purchases budget. (LO 5), AP

▶ EXERCISES

Explain the concept of budgeting.
(LO 1), C

E21-1 Trusler Company has always done some planning for the future, but the company has never prepared a formal budget. Now that the company is growing larger, it is considering preparing a budget.

Instructions
Write a memo to Jim Dixon, the president of Trusler Company, in which you define budgeting, identify the budgets that comprise the master budget, identify the primary benefits of budgeting, and discuss the essentials of effective budgeting.

Prepare a sales budget for 2 quarters.
(LO 2), AP

E21-2 Edington Electronics Inc. produces and sells two models of pocket calculators, XQ-103 and XQ-104. The calculators sell for $15 and $25, respectively. Because of the intense competition Edington faces, management budgets sales semiannually. Its projections for the first 2 quarters of 2017 are as follows.

	Unit Sales	
Product	**Quarter 1**	**Quarter 2**
XQ-103	20,000	22,000
XQ-104	12,000	15,000

No changes in selling prices are anticipated.

Instructions
Prepare a sales budget for the 2 quarters ending June 30, 2017. List the products and show for each quarter and for the 6 months, units, selling price, and total sales by product and in total.

Prepare a sales budget for 4 quarters.
(LO 2), AP

E21-3 Thome and Crede, CPAs, are preparing their service revenue (sales) budget for the coming year (2017). The practice is divided into three departments: auditing, tax, and consulting. Billable hours for each department, by quarter, are provided below.

Department	Quarter 1	Quarter 2	Quarter 3	Quarter 4
Auditing	2,300	1,600	2,000	2,400
Tax	3,000	2,200	2,000	2,500
Consulting	1,500	1,500	1,500	1,500

Average hourly billing rates are auditing $80, tax $90, and consulting $110.

Instructions
Prepare the service revenue (sales) budget for 2017 by listing the departments and showing for each quarter and the year in total, billable hours, billable rate, and total revenue.

Prepare quarterly production budgets.
(LO 2), AP

E21-4 Turney Company produces and sells automobile batteries, the heavy-duty HD-240. The 2017 sales forecast is as follows.

Quarter	HD-240
1	5,000
2	7,000
3	8,000
4	10,000

The January 1, 2017, inventory of HD-240 is 2,000 units. Management desires an ending inventory each quarter equal to 40% of the next quarter's sales. Sales in the first quarter of 2018 are expected to be 25% higher than sales in the same quarter in 2017.

Instructions
Prepare quarterly production budgets for each quarter and in total for 2017.

E21-5 DeWitt Industries has adopted the following production budget for the first 4 months of 2017.

Prepare a direct materials purchases budget.

(LO 2), AP

Month	Units	Month	Units
January	10,000	March	5,000
February	8,000	April	4,000

Each unit requires 2 pounds of raw materials costing $3 per pound. On December 31, 2016, the ending raw materials inventory was 4,000 pounds. Management wants to have a raw materials inventory at the end of the month equal to 20% of next month's production requirements.

Instructions

Prepare a direct materials purchases budget by month for the first quarter.

E21-6 On January 1, 2017, the Hardin Company budget committee has reached agreement on the following data for the 6 months ending June 30, 2017.

Prepare production and direct materials budgets by quarters for 6 months.

(LO 2), AP

Sales units: First quarter 5,000; second quarter 6,000; third quarter 7,000.

Ending raw materials inventory: 40% of the next quarter's production requirements.

Ending finished goods inventory: 25% of the next quarter's expected sales units.

Third-quarter production: 7,200 units.

The ending raw materials and finished goods inventories at December 31, 2016, follow the same percentage relationships to production and sales that occur in 2017. Three pounds of raw materials are required to make each unit of finished goods. Raw materials purchased are expected to cost $4 per pound.

Instructions

(a) Prepare a production budget by quarters for the 6-month period ended June 30, 2017.
(b) Prepare a direct materials budget by quarters for the 6-month period ended June 30, 2017.

E21-7 Rensing Ltd. estimates sales for the second quarter of 2017 will be as follows.

Calculate raw materials purchases in dollars.

(LO 2), AP

Month	Units
April	2,550
May	2,675
June	2,390

The target ending inventory of finished products is as follows.

March 31	2,000
April 30	2,230
May 31	2,200
June 30	2,310

Two units of material are required for each unit of finished product. Production for July is estimated at 2,700 units to start building inventory for the fall sales period. Rensing's policy is to have an inventory of raw materials at the end of each month equal to 50% of the following month's production requirements.

Raw materials are expected to cost $4 per unit throughout the period.

Instructions

Calculate the May raw materials purchases in dollars.

(CGA adapted)

E21-8 Fuqua Company's sales budget projects unit sales of part 198Z of 10,000 units in January, 12,000 units in February, and 13,000 units in March. Each unit of part 198Z requires 4 pounds of materials, which cost $2 per pound. Fuqua Company desires its ending raw materials inventory to equal 40% of the next month's production requirements, and its ending finished goods inventory to equal 20% of the next month's expected unit sales. These goals were met at December 31, 2016.

Prepare a production and a direct materials budget.

(LO 2), AP

Instructions

(a) Prepare a production budget for January and February 2017.

(b) Prepare a direct materials budget for January 2017.

Prepare a direct labor budget.

(LO 3), AP

E21-9 Rodriguez, Inc., is preparing its direct labor budget for 2017 from the following production budget based on a calendar year.

Quarter	Units	Quarter	Units
1	20,000	3	35,000
2	25,000	4	30,000

Each unit requires 1.5 hours of direct labor.

Instructions

Prepare a direct labor budget for 2017. Wage rates are expected to be $16 for the first 2 quarters and $18 for quarters 3 and 4.

Prepare production and direct labor budgets.

(LO 2, 3), AP

E21-10 Lowell Company makes and sells artistic frames for pictures. The controller is responsible for preparing the master budget and has accumulated the following information for 2017.

	January	February	March	April	May
Estimated unit sales	12,000	14,000	13,000	11,000	11,000
Sales price per unit	$50.00	$47.50	$47.50	$47.50	$47.50
Direct labor hours per unit	2.0	2.0	1.5	1.5	1.5
Wage per direct labor hour	$8.00	$8.00	$8.00	$9.00	$9.00

Lowell has a labor contract that calls for a wage increase to $9.00 per hour on April 1. New labor-saving machinery has been installed and will be fully operational by March 1.

Lowell expects to begin the year with 17,600 frames on hand and has a policy of carrying an end-of-month inventory of 100% of the following month's sales, plus 40% of the second following month's sales.

Instructions

Prepare a production budget and a direct labor budget for Lowell Company by month and for the first quarter of the year. The direct labor budget should include direct labor hours.

(CMA-Canada adapted)

Prepare a manufacturing overhead budget for the year.

(LO 3), AP

XLS

E21-11 Atlanta Company is preparing its manufacturing overhead budget for 2017. Relevant data consist of the following.

Units to be produced (by quarters): 10,000, 12,000, 14,000, 16,000.

Direct labor: time is 1.5 hours per unit.

Variable overhead costs per direct labor hour: indirect materials $0.80; indirect labor $1.20; and maintenance $0.50.

Fixed overhead costs per quarter: supervisory salaries $35,000; depreciation $15,000; and maintenance $12,000.

Instructions

Prepare the manufacturing overhead budget for the year, showing quarterly data.

Prepare a selling and administrative expense budget for 2 quarters.

(LO 3), AP

E21-12 Kirkland Company combines its operating expenses for budget purposes in a selling and administrative expense budget. For the first 6 months of 2017, the following data are available.

1. Sales: 20,000 units quarter 1; 22,000 units quarter 2.
2. Variable costs per dollar of sales: sales commissions 5%, delivery expense 2%, and advertising 3%.
3. Fixed costs per quarter: sales salaries $12,000, office salaries $8,000, depreciation $4,200, insurance $1,500, utilities $800, and repairs expense $500.
4. Unit selling price: $20.

Instructions

Prepare a selling and administrative expense budget by quarters for the first 6 months of 2017.

E21-13 Fultz Company has accumulated the following budget data for the year 2017.

Prepare a budgeted income statement for the year.

(LO 3), AP

1. Sales: 30,000 units, unit selling price $85.
2. Cost of one unit of finished goods: direct materials 1 pound at $5 per pound, direct labor 3 hours at $15 per hour, and manufacturing overhead $5 per direct labor hour.
3. Inventories (raw materials only): beginning, 10,000 pounds; ending, 15,000 pounds.
4. Selling and administrative expenses: $170,000; interest expense: $30,000.
5. Income taxes: 30% of income before income taxes.

Instructions

(a) Prepare a schedule showing the computation of cost of goods sold for 2017.
(b) Prepare a budgeted multiple-step income statement for 2017.

E9-14 Danner Company expects to have a cash balance of $45,000 on January 1, 2017. Relevant monthly budget data for the first 2 months of 2017 are as follows.

Prepare a cash budget for 2 months.

(LO 4), AP

Collections from customers: January $85,000, February $150,000.

Payments for direct materials: January $50,000, February $75,000.

Direct labor: January $30,000, February $45,000. Wages are paid in the month they are incurred.

Manufacturing overhead: January $21,000, February $25,000. These costs include depreciation of $1,500 per month. All other overhead costs are paid as incurred.

Selling and administrative expenses: January $15,000, February $20,000. These costs are exclusive of depreciation. They are paid as incurred.

Sales of marketable securities in January are expected to realize $12,000 in cash. Danner Company has a line of credit at a local bank that enables it to borrow up to $25,000. The company wants to maintain a minimum monthly cash balance of $20,000.

Instructions

Prepare a cash budget for January and February.

E21-15 Deitz Corporation is projecting a cash balance of $30,000 in its December 31, 2016, balance sheet. Deitz's schedule of expected collections from customers for the first quarter of 2017 shows total collections of $185,000. The schedule of expected payments for direct materials for the first quarter of 2017 shows total payments of $43,000. Other information gathered for the first quarter of 2017 is sale of equipment $3,000, direct labor $70,000, manufacturing overhead $35,000, selling and administrative expenses $45,000, and purchase of securities $14,000. Deitz wants to maintain a balance of at least $25,000 cash at the end of each quarter.

Prepare a cash budget.

(LO 4), AP

Instructions

Prepare a cash budget for the first quarter.

E21-16 The controller of Trenshaw Company wants to improve the company's control system by preparing a month-by-month cash budget. The following information is for the month ending July 31, 2017.

Prepare cash budget for a month.

(LO 4), AN

June 30, 2017, cash balance	$45,000
Dividends to be declared on July 15*	12,000
Cash expenditures to be paid in July for operating expenses	40,800
Amortization expense in July	4,500
Cash collections to be received in July	90,000
Merchandise purchases to be paid in cash in July	56,200
Equipment to be purchased for cash in July	20,000

*Dividends are payable 30 days after declaration to shareholders of record on the declaration date.

Trenshaw Company wants to keep a minimum cash balance of $25,000.

Instructions

(a) Prepare a cash budget for the month ended July 31, 2017, and indicate how much money, if any, Trenshaw Company will need to borrow to meet its minimum cash requirement.
(b) Explain how cash budgeting can reduce the cost of short-term borrowing.

(CGA adapted)

Prepare schedules of expected collections and payments.

(LO 4), AP

E21-17 Nieto Company's budgeted sales and direct materials purchases are as follows.

	Budgeted Sales	Budgeted D.M. Purchases
January	$200,000	$30,000
February	220,000	36,000
March	250,000	38,000

Nieto's sales are 30% cash and 70% credit. Credit sales are collected 10% in the month of sale, 50% in the month following sale, and 36% in the second month following sale; 4% are uncollectible. Nieto's purchases are 50% cash and 50% on account. Purchases on account are paid 40% in the month of purchase, and 60% in the month following purchase.

Instructions

(a) Prepare a schedule of expected collections from customers for March.
(b) Prepare a schedule of expected payments for direct materials for March.

Prepare schedules for cash receipts and cash payments, and determine ending balances for balance sheet.

(LO 4), AP

E21-18 Green Landscaping Inc. is preparing its budget for the first quarter of 2017. The next step in the budgeting process is to prepare a cash receipts schedule and a cash payments schedule. To that end the following information has been collected.

Clients usually pay 60% of their fee in the month that service is performed, 30% the month after, and 10% the second month after receiving service.

Actual service revenue for 2016 and expected service revenues for 2017 are November 2016, $80,000; December 2016, $90,000; January 2017, $100,000; February 2017, $120,000; and March 2017, $140,000.

Purchases of landscaping supplies (direct materials) are paid 60% in the month of purchase and 40% the following month. Actual purchases for 2016 and expected purchases for 2017 are December 2016, $14,000; January 2017, $12,000; February 2017, $15,000; and March 2017, $18,000.

Instructions

(a) Prepare the following schedules for each month in the first quarter of 2017 and for the quarter in total:
  (1) Expected collections from clients.
  (2) Expected payments for landscaping supplies.
(b) Determine the following balances at March 31, 2017:
  (1) Accounts receivable.
  (2) Accounts payable.

Prepare a cash budget for 2 quarters.

(LO 4, 5), AP

E21-19 Pletcher Dental Clinic is a medium-sized dental service specializing in family dental care. The clinic is currently preparing the master budget for the first 2 quarters of 2017. All that remains in this process is the cash budget. The following information has been collected from other portions of the master budget and elsewhere.

Beginning cash balance	$ 30,000
Required minimum cash balance	25,000
Payment of income taxes (2nd quarter)	4,000
Professional salaries:	
1st quarter	140,000
2nd quarter	140,000
Interest from investments (2nd quarter)	7,000
Overhead costs:	
1st quarter	77,000
2nd quarter	100,000

Selling and administrative costs, including $2,000 depreciation:	
1st quarter	50,000
2nd quarter	70,000
Purchase of equipment (2nd quarter)	50,000
Sale of equipment (1st quarter)	12,000
Collections from patients:	
1st quarter	235,000
2nd quarter	380,000
Interest payments (2nd quarter)	200

Instructions

Prepare a cash budget for each of the first two quarters of 2017.

E21-20 In May 2017, the budget committee of Grand Stores assembles the following data in preparation of budgeted merchandise purchases for the month of June.

Prepare a purchases budget and budgeted income statement for a merchandiser.

(LO 5), AP

1. Expected sales: June $500,000, July $600,000.
2. Cost of goods sold is expected to be 75% of sales.
3. Desired ending merchandise inventory is 30% of the following (next) month's cost of goods sold.
4. The beginning inventory at June 1 will be the desired amount.

Instructions

(a) Compute the budgeted merchandise purchases for June.
(b) Prepare the budgeted multiple-step income statement for June through gross profit.

E21-21 Emeric and Ellie's Painting Service estimates that it will paint 10 small homes, 5 medium homes, and 2 large homes during the month of June 2017. The company estimates its direct labor needs as 40 hours per small home, 70 hours for a medium home, and 120 hours for a large home. Its average cost for direct labor is $18 per hour.

Prepare a direct labor budget for a service company.

(LO 5), AP

Instructions

Prepare a direct labor budget for Emeric and Ellie's Painting Service for June 2017.

EXERCISES: SET B AND CHALLENGE EXERCISES

Visit the book's companion website, at **www.wiley.com/college/kimmel**, and choose the Student Companion site to access Exercises: Set B and Challenge Exercises.

PROBLEMS: SET A

P21-1A Cook Farm Supply Company manufactures and sells a pesticide called Snare. The following data are available for preparing budgets for Snare for the first 2 quarters of 2017.

Prepare budgeted income statement and supporting budgets.

(LO 2, 3), AP

1. Sales: quarter 1, 40,000 bags; quarter 2, 56,000 bags. Selling price is $60 per bag.
2. Direct materials: each bag of Snare requires 4 pounds of Gumm at a cost of $3.80 per pound and 6 pounds of Tarr at $1.50 per pound.
3. Desired inventory levels:

Type of Inventory	January 1	April 1	July 1
Snare (bags)	8,000	15,000	18,000
Gumm (pounds)	9,000	10,000	13,000
Tarr (pounds)	14,000	20,000	25,000

4. Direct labor: direct labor time is 15 minutes per bag at an hourly rate of $16 per hour.
5. Selling and administrative expenses are expected to be 15% of sales plus $175,000 per quarter.
6. Interest expense is $100,000.
7. Income taxes are expected to be 30% of income before income taxes.

Your assistant has prepared two budgets: (1) the manufacturing overhead budget shows expected costs to be 125% of direct labor cost, and (2) the direct materials budget for Tarr shows the cost of Tarr purchases to be $297,000 in quarter 1 and $439,500 in quarter 2.

Net income $881,160
Cost per bag $33.20

Instructions

Prepare the budgeted multiple-step income statement for the first 6 months and all required operating budgets by quarters. (*Note:* Use variable and fixed in the selling and administrative expense budget.) Do not prepare the manufacturing overhead budget or the direct materials budget for Tarr.

Prepare sales, production, direct materials, direct labor, and income statement budgets.

(LO 2, 3), AP

P21-2A Deleon Inc. is preparing its annual budgets for the year ending December 31, 2017. Accounting assistants furnish the data shown below.

	Product JB 50	Product JB 60
Sales budget:		
Anticipated volume in units	400,000	200,000
Unit selling price	$20	$25
Production budget:		
Desired ending finished goods units	30,000	15,000
Beginning finished goods units	25,000	10,000
Direct materials budget:		
Direct materials per unit (pounds)	2	3
Desired ending direct materials pounds	30,000	10,000
Beginning direct materials pounds	40,000	15,000
Cost per pound	$3	$4
Direct labor budget:		
Direct labor time per unit	0.4	0.6
Direct labor rate per hour	$12	$12
Budgeted income statement:		
Total unit cost	$13	$20

An accounting assistant has prepared the detailed manufacturing overhead budget and the selling and administrative expense budget. The latter shows selling expenses of $560,000 for product JB 50 and $360,000 for product JB 60, and administrative expenses of $540,000 for product JB 50 and $340,000 for product JB 60. Interest expense is $150,000 (not allocated to products). Income taxes are expected to be 30%.

(a) Total sales $13,000,000
(b) Required production units: JB 50, 405,000 JB 60, 205,000
(c) Total cost of direct materials purchases $4,840,000
(d) Total direct labor cost $3,420,000
(e) Net income $1,295,000

Instructions

Prepare the following budgets for the year. Show data for each product. Quarterly budgets should not be prepared.

(a) Sales.
(b) Production.
(c) Direct materials.
(d) Direct labor.
(e) Multiple-step income statement (*Note:* income taxes are not allocated to the products).

Prepare sales and production budgets and compute cost per unit under two plans.

(LO 2), E

P21-3A Hill Industries had sales in 2016 of $6,800,000 and gross profit of $1,100,000. Management is considering two alternative budget plans to increase its gross profit in 2017.

Plan A would increase the selling price per unit from $8.00 to $8.40. Sales volume would decrease by 10% from its 2016 level. Plan B would decrease the selling price per unit by $0.50. The marketing department expects that the sales volume would increase by 100,000 units.

At the end of 2016, Hill has 40,000 units of inventory on hand. If Plan A is accepted, the 2017 ending inventory should be equal to 5% of the 2017 sales. If Plan B is accepted, the ending inventory should be equal to 60,000 units. Each unit produced will cost $1.80 in direct labor, $1.40 in direct materials, and $1.20 in variable overhead. The fixed overhead for 2017 should be $1,895,000.

(c) Unit cost: Plan A $6.88 Plan B $6.35
(d) Gross profit: Plan A $1,162,800 Plan B $1,092,500

Instructions

(a) Prepare a sales budget for 2017 under each plan.
(b) Prepare a production budget for 2017 under each plan.
(c) Compute the production cost per unit under each plan. Why is the cost per unit different for each of the two plans? (Round to two decimals.)
(d) Which plan should be accepted? (*Hint:* Compute the gross profit under each plan.)

P21-4A Colter Company prepares monthly cash budgets. Relevant data from operating budgets for 2017 are as follows.

Prepare cash budget for 2 months.

(LO 4), AP

	January	February
Sales	$360,000	$400,000
Direct materials purchases	120,000	125,000
Direct labor	90,000	100,000
Manufacturing overhead	70,000	75,000
Selling and administrative expenses	79,000	85,000

All sales are on account. Collections are expected to be 50% in the month of sale, 30% in the first month following the sale, and 20% in the second month following the sale. Sixty percent (60%) of direct materials purchases are paid in cash in the month of purchase, and the balance due is paid in the month following the purchase. All other items above are paid in the month incurred except for selling and administrative expenses that include $1,000 of depreciation per month.

Other data:

1. Credit sales: November 2016, $250,000; December 2016, $320,000.
2. Purchases of direct materials: December 2016, $100,000.
3. Other receipts: January—collection of December 31, 2016, notes receivable $15,000; February—proceeds from sale of securities $6,000.
4. Other disbursements: February—payment of $6,000 cash dividend.

The company's cash balance on January 1, 2017, is expected to be $60,000. The company wants to maintain a minimum cash balance of $50,000.

Instructions

(a) Prepare schedules for (1) expected collections from customers and (2) expected payments for direct materials purchases for January and February.

(b) Prepare a cash budget for January and February in columnar form.

(a) January: collections $326,000 payments $112,000

(b) Ending cash balance: January $51,000 February $50,000

P21-5A The budget committee of Suppar Company collects the following data for its San Miguel Store in preparing budgeted income statements for May and June 2017.

Prepare purchases and income statement budgets for a merchandiser.

(LO 5), AP

XLS

1. Sales for May are expected to be $800,000. Sales in June and July are expected to be 5% higher than the preceding month.
2. Cost of goods sold is expected to be 75% of sales.
3. Company policy is to maintain ending merchandise inventory at 10% of the following month's cost of goods sold.
4. Operating expenses are estimated to be as follows:

Sales salaries	$35,000 per month
Advertising	6% of monthly sales
Delivery expense	2% of monthly sales
Sales commissions	5% of monthly sales
Rent expense	$5,000 per month
Depreciation	$800 per month
Utilities	$600 per month
Insurance	$500 per month

5. Interest expense is $2,000 per month. Income taxes are estimated to be 30% of income before income taxes.

Instructions

(a) Prepare the merchandise purchases budget for each month in columnar form.

(b) Prepare budgeted multiple-step income statements for each month in columnar form. Show in the statements the details of cost of goods sold.

(a) Purchases: May $603,000 June $633,150

(b) Net income: May $36,470 June $39,830

Prepare budgeted cost of goods sold, income statement, retained earnings, and balance sheet.

(LO 3, 4), AP

P21-6A Krause Industries' balance sheet at December 31, 2016, is presented below.

KRAUSE INDUSTRIES
Balance Sheet
December 31, 2016

Assets

Current assets		
Cash		$ 7,500
Accounts receivable		73,500
Finished goods inventory (1,500 units)		24,000
Total current assets		105,000
Property, plant, and equipment		
Equipment	$40,000	
Less: Accumulated depredation	10,000	30,000
Total assets		$135,000

Liabilities and Stockholders' Equity

Liabilities		
Notes payable		$ 25,000
Accounts payable		45,000
Total liabilities		70,000
Stockholders' equity		
Common stock	$40,000	
Retained earnings	25,000	
Total stockholders' equity		65,000
Total liabilities and stockholders' equity		$135,000

Budgeted data for the year 2017 include the following.

	2017	
	Quarter 4	Total
Sales budget (8,000 units at $32)	$76,800	$256,000
Direct materials used	17,000	62,500
Direct labor	12,500	50,900
Manufacturing overhead applied	10,000	48,600
Selling and administrative expenses	18,000	75,000

To meet sales requirements and to have 2,500 units of finished goods on hand at December 31, 2017, the production budget shows 9,000 required units of output. The total unit cost of production is expected to be $18. Krause uses the first-in, first-out (FIFO) inventory costing method. Interest expense is expected to be $3,500 for the year. Income taxes are expected to be 40% of income before income taxes. In 2017, the company expects to declare and pay an $8,000 cash dividend.

The company's cash budget shows an expected cash balance of $5,880 at December 31, 2017. All sales and purchases are on account. It is expected that 60% of quarterly sales are collected in cash within the quarter and the remainder is collected in the following quarter. Direct materials purchased from suppliers are paid 50% in the quarter incurred and the remainder in the following quarter. Purchases in the fourth quarter were the same as the materials used. In 2017, the company expects to purchase additional equipment costing $9,000. $4,000 of depreciation expense on equipment is included in the budget data and split equally between manufacturing overhead and selling and administrative expenses. Krause expects to pay $8,000 on the outstanding notes payable balance plus all interest due and payable to December 31 (included in interest expense $3,500, above). Accounts payable at December 31, 2017, includes amounts due suppliers (see above) plus other accounts payable of $7,200. Unpaid income taxes at December 31 will be $5,000.

Instructions

Prepare a budgeted statement of cost of goods sold, budgeted multiple-step income statement and retained earnings statement for 2017, and a budgeted classified balance sheet at December 31, 2017.

Net income $21,900
Total assets $116,600

PROBLEMS: SET B AND SET C

Visit the book's companion website, at **www.wiley.com/college/kimmel**, and choose the Student Companion site to access Problems: Set B and Set C.

CONTINUING PROBLEMS

CURRENT DESIGNS

EXCEL TUTORIAL

CD21 Diane Buswell is preparing the 2017 budget for one of Current Designs' rotomolded kayaks. Extensive meetings with members of the sales department and executive team have resulted in the following unit sales projections for 2017.

Quarter 1	1,000 kayaks
Quarter 2	1,500 kayaks
Quarter 3	750 kayaks
Quarter 4	750 kayaks

Current Designs' policy is to have finished goods ending inventory in a quarter equal to 20% of the next quarter's anticipated sales. Preliminary sales projections for 2018 are 1,100 units for the first quarter and 1,500 units for the second quarter. Ending inventory of finished goods at December 31, 2016, will be 200 rotomolded kayaks.

Production of each kayak requires 54 pounds of polyethylene powder and a finishing kit (rope, seat, hardware, etc.). Company policy is that the ending inventory of polyethylene powder should be 25% of the amount needed for production in the next quarter. Assume that the ending inventory of polyethylene powder on December 31, 2016, is 19,400 pounds. The finishing kits can be assembled as they are needed. As a result, Current Designs does not maintain a significant inventory of the finishing kits.

The polyethylene powder used in these kayaks costs $1.50 per pound, and the finishing kits cost $170 each. Production of a single kayak requires 2 hours of time by more experienced, type I employees and 3 hours of finishing time by type II employees. The type I employees are paid $15 per hour, and the type II employees are paid $12 per hour.

Selling and administrative expenses for this line are expected to be $45 per unit sold plus $7,500 per quarter. Manufacturing overhead is assigned at 150% of labor costs.

Instructions

Prepare the production budget, direct materials budget, direct labor budget, manufacturing overhead budget, and selling and administrative budget for this product line by quarter and in total for 2017.

WATERWAYS

(*Note:* This is a continuation of the Waterways problem from Chapters 14–20.)

WP21 Waterways Corporation is preparing its budget for the coming year, 2017. The first step is to plan for the first quarter of that coming year. The company has gathered information from its managers in preparation of the budgeting process. This problem asks you to prepare the various budgets that comprise the master budget for 2017.

Go to the book's companion website, at **www.wiley.com/college/kimmel,** *to see the completion of this problem.*

COMPREHENSIVE CASES

CC21-1 Auburn Circular Club is planning a major fundraiser that it hopes will become a successful annual event: sponsoring a professional rodeo. For this case, you will encounter many managerial accounting issues that would be common for a start-up business, such as CVP analysis (Chapter 18), incremental analysis (Chapter 20), and budgetary planning (Chapter 21).

Go to the book's companion website, at **www.wiley.com/college/kimmel,** *for complete case details and instructions.*

CC21-2 Sweats Galore is a new business venture that will make custom sweatshirts using a silk-screen process. In helping the company's owner, Michael Woods, set up his business, you will have the opportunity to apply your understanding of CVP relationships (Chapter 18) and budgetary planning (Chapter 21).

Go to the book's companion website, at **www.wiley.com/college/kimmel**, *for complete case details and instructions.*

EXPAND YOUR CRITICAL THINKING

DECISION-MAKING ACROSS THE ORGANIZATION

Group Project

E

CT21-1 Palmer Corporation operates on a calendar-year basis. It begins the annual budgeting process in late August when the president establishes targets for the total dollar sales and net income before taxes for the next year.

The sales target is given first to the marketing department. The marketing manager formulates a sales budget by product line in both units and dollars. From this budget, sales quotas by product line in units and dollars are established for each of the corporation's sales districts. The marketing manager also estimates the cost of the marketing activities required to support the target sales volume and prepares a tentative marketing expense budget.

The executive vice president uses the sales and profit targets, the sales budget by product line, and the tentative marketing expense budget to determine the dollar amounts that can be devoted to manufacturing and corporate office expense. The executive vice president prepares the budget for corporate expenses. She then forwards to the production department the product-line sales budget in units and the total dollar amount that can be devoted to manufacturing.

The production manager meets with the factory managers to develop a manufacturing plan that will produce the required units when needed within the cost constraints set by the executive vice president. The budgeting process usually comes to a halt at this point because the production department does not consider the financial resources allocated to be adequate.

When this standstill occurs, the vice president of finance, the executive vice president, the marketing manager, and the production manager meet together to determine the final budgets for each of the areas. This normally results in a modest increase in the total amount available for manufacturing costs and cuts in the marketing expense and corporate office expense budgets. The total sales and net income figures proposed by the president are seldom changed. Although the participants are seldom pleased with the compromise, these budgets are final. Each executive then develops a new detailed budget for the operations in his or her area.

None of the areas has achieved its budget in recent years. Sales often run below the target. When budgeted sales are not achieved, each area is expected to cut costs so that the president's profit target can be met. However, the profit target is seldom met because costs are not cut enough. In fact, costs often run above the original budget in all functional areas (marketing, production, and corporate office).

The president is disturbed that Palmer has not been able to meet the sales and profit targets. He hired a consultant with considerable experience with companies in Palmer's industry. The consultant reviewed the budgets for the past 4 years. He concluded that the product line sales budgets were reasonable and that the cost and expense budgets were adequate for the budgeted sales and production levels.

Instructions

With the class divided into groups, answer the following.

(a) Discuss how the budgeting process employed by Palmer Corporation contributes to the failure to achieve the president's sales and profit targets.

(b) Suggest how Palmer Corporation's budgeting process could be revised to correct the problems.

(c) Should the functional areas be expected to cut their costs when sales volume falls below budget? Explain your answer.

(CMA adapted)

MANAGERIAL ANALYSIS

CT21-2 Elliot & Hesse Inc. manufactures ergonomic devices for computer users. Some of its more popular products include anti-glare filters and privacy filters (for computer monitors) and keyboard stands with wrist rests. Over the past 5 years, it experienced rapid growth, with sales of all products increasing 20% to 50% each year. E

Last year, some of the primary manufacturers of computers began introducing new products with some of the ergonomic designs, such as anti-glare filters and wrist rests, already built in. As a result, sales of Elliot & Hesse's accessory devices have declined somewhat. The company believes that the privacy filters will probably continue to show growth, but that the other products will probably continue to decline. When the next year's budget was prepared, increases were built into research and development so that replacement products could be developed or the company could expand into some other product line. Some product lines being considered are general-purpose ergonomic devices including back supports, foot rests, and sloped writing pads.

The most recent results have shown that sales decreased more than was expected for the anti-glare filters. As a result, the company may have a shortage of funds. Top management has therefore asked that all expenses be reduced 10% to compensate for these reduced sales. Summary budget information is as follows.

Direct materials	$240,000
Direct labor	110,000
Insurance	50,000
Depreciation	90,000
Machine repairs	30,000
Sales salaries	50,000
Office salaries	80,000
Factory salaries (indirect labor)	50,000
Total	$700,000

Instructions

Using the information above, answer the following questions.

(a) What are the implications of reducing each of the costs? For example, if the company reduces direct materials costs, it may have to do so by purchasing lower-quality materials. This may affect sales in the long run.

(b) Based on your analysis in (a), what do you think is the best way to obtain the $70,000 in cost savings requested? Be specific. Are there any costs that cannot or should not be reduced? Why?

REAL-WORLD FOCUS

CT21-3 Information regarding many approaches to budgeting can be found online. The following activity investigates the merits of "zero-based" budgeting, as discussed by Michael LaFaive, Director of Fiscal Policy of the Mackinac Center for Public Policy. AN

Address: **www.mackinac.org/5928,** or go to **www.wiley.com/college/kimmel**

Instructions

Read the article at the website and answer the following questions.

(a) How does zero-based budgeting differ from standard budgeting procedures?
(b) What are some potential advantages of zero-based budgeting?
(c) What are some potential disadvantages of zero-based budgeting?
(d) How often do departments in Oklahoma undergo zero-based budgeting?

COMMUNICATION ACTIVITY

Writing

CT21-4 In order to better serve their rural patients, Drs. Joe and Rick Parcells (brothers) began giving safety seminars. Especially popular were their "emergency-preparedness" talks given to farmers. Many people asked whether the "kit" of materials the doctors recommended for common farm emergencies was commercially available. E

After checking with several suppliers, the doctors realized that no other company offered the supplies they recommended in their seminars, packaged in the way they described. Their wives, Megan and Sue, agreed to make a test package by ordering supplies from various medical supply companies and assembling them into a "kit" that could be sold at the seminars. When these kits proved a runaway success, the sisters-in-law decided to market them. At the advice of their accountant, they organized this venture as a separate company, called Life Protection Products (LPP), with Megan Parcells as CEO and Sue Parcells as Secretary-Treasurer.

LPP soon started receiving requests for the kits from all over the country, as word spread about their availability. Even without advertising, LPP was able to sell its full inventory every month. However, the company was becoming financially strained. Megan and Sue had about $100,000 in savings, and they invested about half that amount initially. They believed that this venture would allow them to make money. However, at the present time, only about $30,000 of the cash remains, and the company is constantly short of cash.

Megan has come to you for advice. She does not understand why the company is having cash flow problems. She and Sue have not even been withdrawing salaries. However, they have rented a local building and have hired two more full-time workers to help them cope with the increasing demand. They do not think they could handle the demand without this additional help.

Megan is also worried that the cash problems mean that the company may not be able to support itself. She has prepared the cash budget shown below. All seminar customers pay for their products in full at the time of purchase. In addition, several large companies have ordered the kits for use by employees who work in remote sites. They have requested credit terms and have been allowed to pay in the month following the sale. These large purchasers amount to about 25% of the sales at the present time. LPP purchases the materials for the kits about 2 months ahead of time. Megan and Sue are considering slowing the growth of the company by simply purchasing less materials, which will mean selling fewer kits.

The workers are paid weekly. Megan and Sue need about $15,000 cash on hand at the beginning of the month to pay for purchases of raw materials. Right now they have been using cash from their savings, but as noted, only $30,000 is left.

LIFE PROTECTION PRODUCTS
Cash Budget
For the Quarter Ending June 30, 2017

	April	May	June
Cash balance, beginning	$15,000	$15,000	$15,000
Cash received			
From prior month sales	5,000	7,500	12,500
From current sales	15,000	22,500	37,500
Total cash on hand	35,000	45,000	65,000
Cash payments			
To employees	3,000	3,000	3,000
For products	25,000	35,000	45,000
Miscellaneous expenses	5,000	6,000	7,000
Postage	1,000	1,000	1,000
Total cash payments	34,000	45,000	56,000
Cash balance	$ 1,000	$ 0	$ 9,000
Borrow from savings	$14,000	$15,000	$ 1,000
Borrow from bank?	$ 0	$ 0	$ 5,000

Instructions

Write a response to Megan Parcells. Explain why LPP is short of cash. Will this company be able to support itself? Explain your answer. Make any recommendations you deem appropriate.

ETHICS CASE

CT21-5 You are an accountant in the budgetary, projections, and special projects department of Fernetti Conductor, Inc., a large manufacturing company. The president, Richard Brown, asks you on very short notice to prepare some sales and income projections covering the next 2 years of the company's much heralded new product lines. He wants these projections for a series of speeches he is making while on a 2-week trip to eight East Coast brokerage firms. The president hopes to bolster Fernetti's stock sales and price. E

You work 23 hours in 2 days to compile the projections, hand-deliver them to the president, and are swiftly but graciously thanked as he departs. A week later, you find time to go over some of your computations and discover a miscalculation that makes the projections grossly overstated. You quickly inquire about the president's itinerary and learn that he has made half of his speeches and has half yet to make. You are in a quandary as to what to do.

Instructions

(a) What are the consequences of telling the president of your gross miscalculations?
(b) What are the consequences of not telling the president of your gross miscalculations?
(c) What are the ethical considerations to you and the president in this situation?

ALL ABOUT YOU

CT21-6 In order to get your personal finances under control, you need to prepare a personal budget. Assume that you have compiled the following information regarding your expected cash flows for a typical month. AP

Rent payment	$ 500	Miscellaneous costs	$210
Interest income	50	Savings	50
Income tax withheld	300	Eating out	150
Electricity bill	85	Telephone and Internet costs	125
Groceries	100	Student loan payments	375
Wages earned	2,500	Entertainment costs	250
Insurance	100	Transportation costs	150

Instructions

Using the information above, prepare a personal budget. In preparing this budget, use the format found at *http://financialplan.about.com/cs/budgeting/l/blbudget.htm*. Just skip any unused line items.

CONSIDERING YOUR COSTS AND BENEFITS

CT21-7 You might hear people say that they "need to learn to live within a budget." The funny thing is that most people who say this haven't actually prepared a personal budget, nor do they intend to. Instead, what they are referring to is a vaguely defined, poorly specified collection of rough ideas of how much they should spend on various aspects of their lives. However, you can't live within or even outside of something that doesn't exist. With that in mind, let's take a look at one aspect of personal-budget templates. E

Many personal-budget worksheet templates that are provided for college students treat student loans as an income source. See, for example, the template provided at *http://financialplan.about.com/cs/budgeting/l/blmocolbud.htm*. Based on your knowledge of accounting, is this correct?

YES: Student loans provide a source of cash, which can be used to pay costs. As the saying goes, "It all spends the same." Therefore, student loans are income.

NO: Student loans must eventually be repaid; therefore, they are not income. As the name suggests, they are loans.

Instructions

Write a response indicating your position regarding this situation. Provide support for your view.

22

Budgetary Control and Responsibility Accounting

CHAPTER PREVIEW

In Chapter 21, we discussed the use of budgets for planning. We now consider how budgets are used by management to control operations. In the Feature Story on the Tribeca Grand Hotel, we see that management uses the budget to adapt to the business environment. This chapter focuses on two aspects of management control: (1) budgetary control and (2) responsibility accounting.

CHAPTER OUTLINE

LEARNING OBJECTIVES		PRACTICE
1 Describe budgetary control and static budget reports.	• Budgetary control • Static budget reports	DO IT! 1 Static Budget Reports
2 Prepare flexible budget reports.	• Why flexible budgets? • Developing the flexible budget • Flexible budget—a case study • Flexible budget reports	DO IT! 2 Flexible Budgets
3 Apply responsibility accounting to cost and profit centers.	• Controllable vs. noncontrollable revenues and costs • Principles of performance evaluation • Responsibility reporting system • Types of responsibility centers	DO IT! 3 Profit Center Responsibility Report
4 Evaluate performance in investment centers.	• Return on investment (ROI) • Responsibility report • Judgmental factors in ROI • Improving ROI	DO IT! 4 Performance Evaluation

Go to the ***REVIEW AND PRACTICE*** section at the end of the chapter for a targeted summary and exercises with solutions.

Visit **WileyPLUS** for additional tutorials and practice opportunities.

Eviled/Shutterstock

FEATURE STORY

Pumpkin Madeleines and a Movie

Perhaps no place in the world has a wider variety of distinctive, high-end accommodations than New York City. It's tough to set yourself apart in the Big Apple, but unique is what the Tribeca Grand Hotel is all about.

When you walk through the doors of this triangular-shaped building, nestled in one of Manhattan's most affluent neighborhoods, you immediately encounter a striking eight-story atrium. Although the hotel was completely renovated, it still maintains its funky mid-century charm. Just consider the always hip Church Bar. Besides serving up cocktails until 2 A.M., Church's also provides food. These are not the run-of-the-mill, chain hotel, borderline edibles. Church's chef is famous for tantalizing delectables such as duck rillettes, sea salt baked branzino, housemade pappardelle, and pumpkin madeleines.

Another thing that really sets the Tribeca Grand apart is its private screening room. As a guest, you can enjoy plush leather seating, state-of-the-art projection, and digital surround sound, all while viewing a cult classic from the hotel's film series. In fact, on Sundays, free screenings are available to guests and non-guests alike on a first-come-first-served basis.

To attract and satisfy a discerning clientele, the Tribeca Grand's management incurs higher and more unpredictable costs than those of your standard hotel. As fun as it might be to run a high-end hotel, management can't be cavalier about spending money. To maintain profitability, management closely monitors costs and revenues to make sure that they track with budgeted amounts. Further, because of unexpected fluctuations (think Hurricane Sandy or a bitterly cold stretch of winter weather), management must sometimes revise forecasts and budgets and adapt quickly. To evaluate performance when things happen that are beyond management's control, the budget needs to be flexible.

LEARNING OBJECTIVE ▶1 **Describe budgetary control and static budget reports.**

BUDGETARY CONTROL

One of management's functions is to control company operations. Control consists of the steps taken by management to see that planned objectives are met. We now ask: How do budgets contribute to control of operations?

The use of budgets in controlling operations is known as **budgetary control**. Such control takes place by means of **budget reports** that compare actual results with planned objectives. The use of budget reports is based on the belief that planned objectives lose much of their potential value without some monitoring of progress along the way. Just as your professors give midterm exams to evaluate your progress, top management requires periodic reports on the progress of department managers toward their planned objectives.

Budget reports provide management with feedback on operations. The feedback for a crucial objective, such as having enough cash on hand to pay bills, may be made daily. For other objectives, such as meeting budgeted annual sales and operating expenses, monthly budget reports may suffice. Budget reports are prepared as frequently as needed. From these reports, management analyzes any differences between actual and planned results and determines their causes. Management then takes corrective action, or it decides to modify future plans. Budgetary control involves the activities shown in Illustration 22-1.

ILLUSTRATION 22-1
Budgetary control activities

Budgetary control works best when a company has a formalized reporting system. The system does the following:

1. Identifies the name of the budget report, such as the sales budget or the manufacturing overhead budget.
2. States the frequency of the report, such as weekly or monthly.
3. Specifies the purpose of the report.
4. Indicates the primary recipient(s) of the report.

Illustration 22-2 provides a partial budgetary control system for a manufacturing company. Note the frequency of the reports and their emphasis on control. For example, there is a daily report on scrap and a weekly report on labor.

Name of Report	Frequency	Purpose	Primary Recipient(s)
Sales	Weekly	Determine whether sales goals are met	Top management and sales manager
Labor	Weekly	Control direct and indirect labor costs	Vice president of production and production department managers
Scrap	Daily	Determine efficient use of materials	Production manager
Departmental overhead costs	Monthly	Control overhead costs	Department manager
Selling expenses	Monthly	Control selling expenses	Sales manager
Income statement	Monthly and quarterly	Determine whether income goals are met	Top management

ILLUSTRATION 22-2
Budgetary control reporting system

STATIC BUDGET REPORTS

You learned in Chapter 21 that the master budget formalizes management's planned objectives for the coming year. When used in budgetary control, each budget included in the master budget is considered to be static. A **static budget** is a projection of budget data **at one level of activity**. These budgets do not consider data for different levels of activity. As a result, companies always compare actual results with budget data at the activity level that was used in developing the master budget.

Examples

To illustrate the role of a static budget in budgetary control, we will use selected data prepared for Hayes Company in Chapter 21. Budget and actual sales data for the Rightride product in the first and second quarters of 2017 are as follows.

ILLUSTRATION 22-3
Budget and actual sales data

Sales	First Quarter	Second Quarter	Total
Budgeted	$180,000	$210,000	$390,000
Actual	179,000	199,500	378,500
Difference	$ 1,000	$ 10,500	$ 11,500

The sales budget report for Hayes' first quarter is shown below. The rightmost column reports the difference between the budgeted and actual amounts.

ILLUSTRATION 22-4
Sales budget report—first quarter

Hayes Company Sales Budget Report.xls

HAYES COMPANY
Sales Budget Report
For the Quarter Ended March 31, 2017

Product Line	Budget	Actual	Difference Favorable F Unfavorable U
Rightride[a]	$180,000	$179,000	$1,000 U

[a]In practice, each product line would be included in the report.

The report shows that sales are $1,000 under budget—an unfavorable result. This difference is less than 1% of budgeted sales ($1,000 ÷ $180,000 = .0056). Top management's reaction to unfavorable differences is often influenced by the materiality (significance) of the difference. Since the difference of $1,000 is immaterial in this case, we assume that Hayes management takes no specific corrective action.

ALTERNATIVE TERMINOLOGY
The difference between budget and actual is sometimes called a *budget variance*.

Illustration 22-5 shows the budget report for the second quarter. It contains one new feature: cumulative year-to-date information. This report indicates that sales for the second quarter are $10,500 below budget. This is 5% of budgeted sales ($10,500 ÷ $210,000). Top management may now conclude that the difference between budgeted and actual sales requires investigation.

ILLUSTRATION 22-5
Sales budget report—second quarter

Hayes Company Sales Budget Report.xls

HAYES COMPANY						
Sales Budget Report						
For the Quarter Ended June 30, 2017						
	Second Quarter			Year-to-Date		
			Difference			Difference
			Favorable F			Favorable F
Product Line	Budget	Actual	Unfavorable U	Budget	Actual	Unfavorable U
Rightride	$210,000	$199,500	$10,500 U	$390,000	$378,500	$11,500 U

Management's analysis should start by asking the sales manager the cause(s) of the shortfall. Managers should consider the need for corrective action. For example, management may decide to spur sales by offering sales incentives to customers or by increasing the advertising of the product line. Or, if management concludes that a downturn in the economy is responsible for the lower sales, it may modify planned sales and profit goals for the remainder of the year.

Uses and Limitations

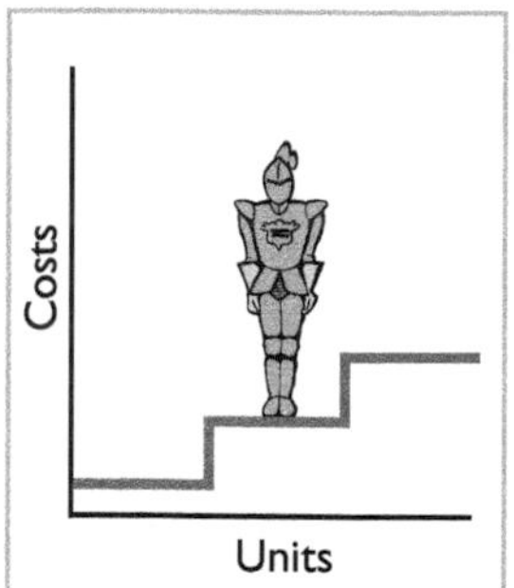

Static budgets report a single level of activity

From these examples, you can see that a master sales budget is useful in evaluating the performance of a sales manager. It is now necessary to ask: Is the master budget appropriate for evaluating a manager's performance in controlling costs? Recall that in a static budget, data are not modified or adjusted, regardless of changes in activity. It follows, then, that a static budget is appropriate in evaluating a manager's effectiveness in controlling costs when:

1. The actual level of activity closely approximates the master budget activity level, and/or
2. The behavior of the costs in response to changes in activity is fixed.

A static budget report is, therefore, appropriate for **fixed manufacturing costs** and for **fixed selling and administrative expenses**. But, as you will see shortly, static budget reports may not be a proper basis for evaluating a manager's performance in controlling variable costs.

DO IT! 1 Static Budget Reports

Lawler Company expects to produce 5,000 units of product CV93 during the current month. Budgeted variable manufacturing costs per unit are direct materials $6, direct labor $15, and overhead $24. Monthly budgeted fixed manufacturing overhead costs are $10,000 for depreciation and $5,000 for supervision.

In the current month, Lawler actually produced 5,500 units and incurred the following costs: direct materials $33,900, direct labor $74,200, variable overhead $120,500, depreciation $10,000, and supervision $5,000.

Prepare a static budget report. (*Hint:* The Budget column is based on estimated production of 5,000 units while the Actual column is the actual costs incurred during the period.) Were costs controlled? Discuss limitations of this budget.

SOLUTION

Lawler Company.xls

	A	B	C	D	
1				Difference	
2				Favorable - F	
3		Budget	Actual	Unfavorable - U	
4	Production in units	5,000	5,500		
5					
6	Variable costs				
7	Direct materials ($6)	$ 30,000	$ 33,900	$3,900	U
8	Direct labor ($15)	75,000	74,200	800	F
9	Overhead ($24)	120,000	120,500	500	U
10	Total variable costs	225,000	228,600	3,600	U
11					
12	Fixed costs				
13	Depreciation	10,000	10,000	0	
14	Supervision	5,000	5,000	0	
15	Total fixed costs	15,000	15,000	0	
16	Total costs	$240,000	$243,600	$3,600	U
17					
18					

The static budget indicates that actual variable costs exceeded budgeted amounts by $3,600. Fixed costs were exactly as budgeted. The static budget gives the impression that the company did not control its variable costs. However, the static budget does not give consideration to the fact that the company produced 500 more units than planned. As a result, the static budget is not a good tool to evaluate variable costs. It is, however, a good tool to evaluate fixed costs as those should not vary with changes in production volume.

Related exercise material: **BE22-1, BE22-2, E22-1, E22-2,** and DO IT! **22-1.**

Action Plan

✔ Classify each cost as variable or fixed.

✔ Determine the difference as favorable or unfavorable.

✔ Determine the difference in total variable costs, total fixed costs, and total costs.

LEARNING OBJECTIVE 2

Prepare flexible budget reports.

In contrast to a static budget, which is based on one level of activity, a **flexible budget** projects budget data for various levels of activity. In essence, **the flexible budget is a series of static budgets at different levels of activity**. The flexible budget recognizes that the budgetary process is more useful if it is adaptable to changed operating conditions.

Flexible budgets can be prepared for each of the types of budgets included in the master budget. For example, Marriott Hotels can budget revenues and net income on the basis of 60%, 80%, and 100% of room occupancy. Similarly, American Van Lines can budget its operating expenses on the basis of various levels of truck-miles driven. Duke Energy can budget revenue and net income on the basis of estimated billions of kwh (kilowatt hours) of residential, commercial, and industrial electricity generated. In the following pages, we will illustrate a flexible budget for manufacturing overhead.

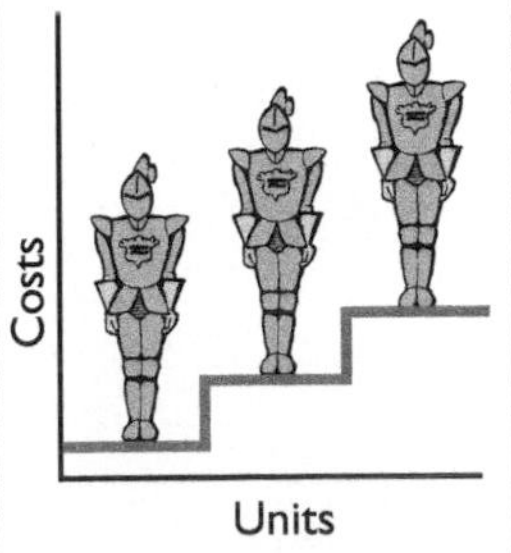

Flexible budgets are static budgets at different activity levels

WHY FLEXIBLE BUDGETS?

Assume that you are the manager in charge of manufacturing overhead in the Assembly Department of Barton Robotics. In preparing the manufacturing overhead budget for 2017, you prepare the following static budget based on a production volume of 10,000 units of robotic controls.

ILLUSTRATION 22-6
Static overhead budget

Barton Robotics.xls

BARTON ROBOTICS	
Manufacturing Overhead Budget (Static)	
Assembly Department	
For the Year Ended December 31, 2017	
Budgeted production in units (robotic controls)	10,000
Budgeted costs	
Indirect materials	$ 250,000
Indirect labor	260,000
Utilities	190,000
Depreciation	280,000
Property taxes	70,000
Supervision	50,000
	$1,100,000

▼ **HELPFUL HINT**
The master budget described in Chapter 21 is based on a static budget.

Fortunately for the company, the demand for robotic controls has increased, and Barton produces and sells 12,000 units during the year rather than 10,000. You are elated! Increased sales means increased profitability, which should mean a bonus or a raise for you and the employees in your department. Unfortunately, a comparison of Assembly Department actual and budgeted costs has put you on the spot. The budget report is shown below.

ILLUSTRATION 22-7
Overhead static budget report

Barton Robotics.xls

BARTON ROBOTICS
Manufacturing Overhead Static Budget Report
For the Year Ended December 31, 2017

	Budget	Actual	Difference Favorable - F Unfavorable - U	
Production in units	10,000	12,000		
Costs				
Indirect materials	$ 250,000	$ 295,000	$ 45,000	U
Indirect labor	260,000	312,000	52,000	U
Utilities	190,000	225,000	35,000	U
Depreciation	280,000	280,000	0	
Property taxes	70,000	70,000	0	
Supervision	50,000	50,000	0	
	$1,100,000	$1,232,000	$132,000	U

This comparison uses budget data based on the original activity level (10,000 robotic controls). It indicates that the Assembly Department is significantly **over budget** for three of the six overhead costs. There is a total unfavorable difference of $132,000, which is 12% over budget ($132,000 ÷ $1,100,000). Your supervisor is very unhappy. Instead of sharing in the company's success, you may find yourself looking for another job. What went wrong?

When you calm down and carefully examine the manufacturing overhead budget, you identify the problem: The budget data are not relevant! At the time the budget was developed, the company anticipated that only 10,000 units would be produced, **not** 12,000. Comparing actual with budgeted variable costs is meaningless. As production increases, the budget allowances for variable costs should increase proportionately. The variable costs in this example are indirect materials, indirect labor, and utilities.

Analyzing the budget data for these costs at 10,000 units, you arrive at the following per unit results.

▼ **HELPFUL HINT**
A static budget is not useful for performance evaluation if a company has substantial variable costs.

ILLUSTRATION 22-8
Variable costs per unit

Item	Total Cost	Per Unit
Indirect materials	$250,000	$25
Indirect labor	260,000	26
Utilities	190,000	19
	$700,000	$70

Illustration 22-9 calculates the budgeted variable costs at 12,000 units.

ILLUSTRATION 22-9
Budgeted variable costs, 12,000 units

Item	Computation	Total
Indirect materials	$25 × 12,000	$300,000
Indirect labor	26 × 12,000	312,000
Utilities	19 × 12,000	228,000
		$840,000

Because fixed costs do not change in total as activity changes, the budgeted amounts for these costs remain the same. Illustration 22-10 shows the budget report based on the flexible budget for 12,000 units of production. (Compare this with Illustration 22-7.)

ILLUSTRATION 22-10
Overhead flexible budget report

Barton Robotics.xls

Home Insert Page Layout Formulas Data Review View

P18 fx

	A	B	C	D	E
1	BARTON ROBOTICS				
2	Manufacturing Overhead Flexible Budget Report				
3	For the Year Ended December 31, 2017				
4				Difference	
5		Budget	Actual	Favorable - F Unfavorable - U	
6	Production in units	12,000	12,000		
7					
8	Variable costs				
9	Indirect materials ($25)	$ 300,000	$ 295,000	$5,000	F
10	Indirect labor ($26)	312,000	312,000	0	
11	Utilities ($19)	228,000	225,000	3,000	F
12	Total variable costs	840,000	832,000	8,000	F
13					
14	Fixed costs				
15	Depreciation	280,000	280,000	0	
16	Property taxes	70,000	70,000	0	
17	Supervision	50,000	50,000	0	
18	Total fixed costs	400,000	400,000	0	
19	Total costs	$1,240,000	$1,232,000	$8,000	F
20					

DECISION TOOLS

The flexible budget indicates whether cost changes resulting from different production volumes are reasonable.

This report indicates that the Assembly Department's costs are **under budget**—a favorable difference. Instead of worrying about being fired, you may be in line for a bonus or a raise after all! As this analysis shows, the only appropriate comparison is between actual costs at 12,000 units of production and budgeted costs at 12,000 units. Flexible budget reports provide this comparison.

DEVELOPING THE FLEXIBLE BUDGET

The flexible budget uses the master budget as its basis. To develop the flexible budget, management uses the following steps.

1. Identify the activity index and the relevant range of activity.
2. Identify the variable costs, and determine the budgeted variable cost per unit of activity for each cost.
3. Identify the fixed costs, and determine the budgeted amount for each cost.
4. Prepare the budget for selected increments of activity within the relevant range.

The activity index chosen should significantly influence the costs being budgeted. For manufacturing overhead costs, for example, the activity index is usually the same as the index used in developing the predetermined overhead rate—that is, direct labor hours or machine hours. For selling and administrative expenses, the activity index usually is sales or net sales.

The choice of the increment of activity is largely a matter of judgment. For example, if the relevant range is 8,000 to 12,000 direct labor hours, increments of 1,000 hours may be selected. The flexible budget is then prepared for each increment within the relevant range.

SERVICE COMPANY INSIGHT NBCUniversal

Fox BroadcastingCompany/ Album/Newscom

Just What the Doctor Ordered?

Nobody is immune from the effects of declining revenues—not even movie stars. When the number of viewers of the television show "House," a medical drama, declined by almost 20%, Fox Broadcasting said it wanted to cut the license fee that it paid to NBCUniversal by 20%. What would NBCUniversal do in response? It might cut the size of the show's cast, which would reduce the payroll costs associated with the show. Or, it could reduce the number of episodes that take advantage of the full cast. Alternatively, it might threaten to quit providing the show to Fox altogether and instead present the show on its own NBC-affiliated channels.

Source: Sam Schechner, "Media Business Shorts: NBCU, Fox Taking Scalpel to 'House'," *Wall Street Journal Online* (April 17, 2011).

Explain how the use of flexible budgets might help to identify the best solution to this problem. (Go to **WileyPLUS** for this answer and additional questions.)

FLEXIBLE BUDGET—A CASE STUDY

To illustrate the flexible budget, we use Fox Company. Fox's management uses a **flexible budget for monthly comparisons** of actual and budgeted manufacturing overhead costs of the Finishing Department. The master budget for the year ending December 31, 2017, shows expected annual operating capacity of 120,000 direct labor hours and the following overhead costs.

ILLUSTRATION 22-11
Master budget data

Variable Costs		Fixed Costs	
Indirect materials	$180,000	Depreciation	$180,000
Indirect labor	240,000	Supervision	120,000
Utilities	60,000	Property taxes	60,000
Total	$480,000	Total	$360,000

The four steps for developing the flexible budget are applied as follows.

STEP 1. Identify the activity index and the relevant range of activity. The activity index is direct labor hours. The relevant range is 8,000–12,000 direct labor hours per **month**.

STEP 2. Identify the variable costs, and determine the budgeted variable cost per unit of activity for each cost. There are three variable costs. The variable cost per unit is found by dividing each total budgeted cost by the direct labor hours used in preparing the annual master budget (120,000 hours). Illustration 22-12 shows the computations for Fox Company.

ILLUSTRATION 22-12
Computation of variable cost per direct labor hour

Variable Costs	Computation	Variable Cost per Direct Labor Hour
Indirect materials	\$180,000 ÷ 120,000	\$1.50
Indirect labor	240,000 ÷ 120,000	2.00
Utilities	60,000 ÷ 120,000	0.50
Total		\$4.00

STEP 3. Identify the fixed costs, and determine the budgeted amount for each cost. There are three fixed costs. Since Fox desires **monthly budget data**, it divides each annual budgeted cost by 12 to find the monthly amounts. Therefore, the monthly budgeted fixed costs are depreciation \$15,000, supervision \$10,000, and property taxes \$5,000.

STEP 4. Prepare the budget for selected increments of activity within the relevant range. Management prepares the budget in increments of 1,000 direct labor hours.

Illustration 22-13 shows Fox's flexible budget.

ILLUSTRATION 22-13
Monthly overhead flexible budget

Fox Company.xls

FOX COMPANY
Monthly Manufacturing Overhead Flexible Budget
Finishing Department
For Months During the Year 2017

	A	B	C	D	E	F
5	Activity level					
6	Direct labor hours	8,000	9,000	10,000	11,000	12,000
7	Variable costs					
8	Indirect materials (\$1.50)[a]	\$12,000[b]	\$13,500	\$15,000	\$16,500	\$18,000
9	Indirect labor (\$2.00)[a]	16,000[c]	18,000	20,000	22,000	24,000
10	Utilities (\$0.50)[a]	4,000[d]	4,500	5,000	5,500	6,000
11	Total variable costs	32,000	36,000	40,000	44,000	48,000
12	Fixed costs					
13	Depreciation	15,000	15,000	15,000	15,000	15,000
14	Supervision	10,000	10,000	10,000	10,000	10,000
15	Property taxes	5,000	5,000	5,000	5,000	5,000
16	Total fixed costs	30,000	30,000	30,000	30,000	30,000
17	Total costs	\$62,000	\$66,000	\$70,000	\$74,000	\$78,000

[a]Cost per direct labor hour; [b]8,000 x \$1.50; [c]8,000 x \$2.00; [d]8,000 x \$0.50

Fox uses the formula below to determine total budgeted costs at any level of activity.

ILLUSTRATION 22-14
Formula for total budgeted costs

Fixed Costs	+	Variable Costs*	=	Total Budgeted Costs

***Total variable cost per unit of activity × Activity level.**

▼ HELPFUL HINT
Using the data given for Fox, the amount of total costs to be budgeted for 10,600 direct labor hours would be \$30,000 fixed + \$42,400 variable (10,600 × \$4) = \$72,400 total.

For Fox, fixed costs are \$30,000, and total variable cost per direct labor hour is \$4 (\$1.50 + \$2.00 + \$0.50). At 9,000 direct labor hours, total budgeted costs are \$66,000 [\$30,000 + (\$4 × 9,000)]. At 8,622 direct labor hours, total budgeted costs are \$64,488 [\$30,000 + (\$4 × 8,622)].

Total budgeted costs can also be shown graphically, as in Illustration 22-15. In the graph, the horizontal axis represents the activity index, and costs are indicated on the vertical axis. The graph highlights two activity levels (10,000 and 12,000). As shown, total budgeted costs at these activity levels are \$70,000 [\$30,000 + (\$4 × 10,000)] and \$78,000 [\$30,000 + (\$4 × 12,000)], respectively.

ILLUSTRATION 22-15
Graphic flexible budget data highlighting 10,000 and 12,000 activity levels

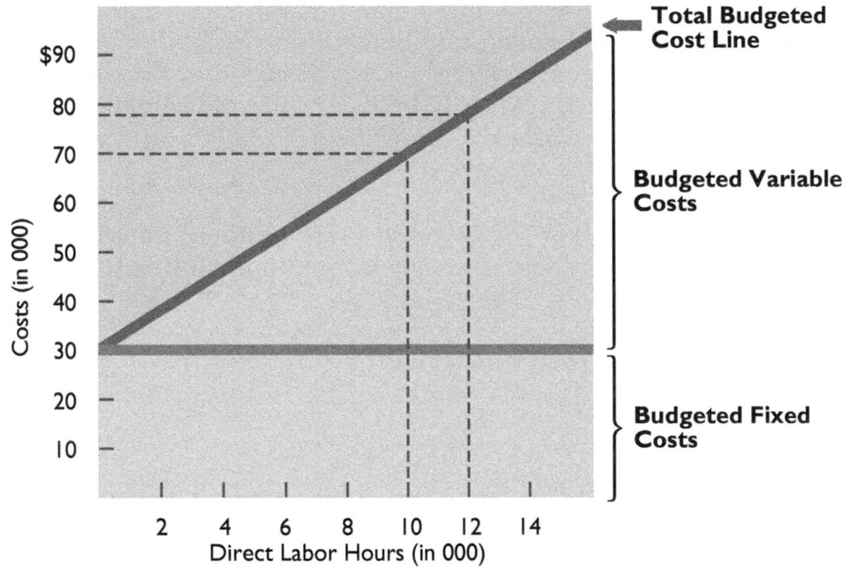

FLEXIBLE BUDGET REPORTS

Flexible budget reports are another type of internal report. The flexible budget report consists of two sections: (1) production data for a selected activity index, such as direct labor hours, and (2) cost data for variable and fixed costs. The report provides a basis for evaluating a manager's performance in two areas: production control and cost control. Flexible budget reports are widely used in production and service departments.

Illustration 22-16 shows a budget report for the Finishing Department of Fox Company for the month of January. In this month, 9,000 hours are worked. The budget data are therefore based on the flexible budget for 9,000 hours in Illustration 22-13 (page 1073). The actual cost data are assumed.

How appropriate is this report in evaluating the Finishing Department manager's performance in controlling overhead costs? The report clearly provides a reliable basis. Both actual and budget costs are based on the activity level worked during January. Since variable costs generally are incurred directly by the department, the difference between the budget allowance for those hours and the actual costs is the responsibility of the department manager.

ILLUSTRATION 22-16
Overhead flexible budget report

Fox Company.xls

FOX COMPANY
Manufacturing Overhead Flexible Budget Report
Finishing Department
For the Month Ended January 31, 2017

Direct labor hours (DLH)	Budget at 9,000 DLH	Actual costs at 9,000 DLH	Difference Favorable - F Unfavorable - U	
Variable costs				
Indirect materials ($1.50)[a]	$13,500	$14,000	$ 500	U
Indirect labor ($2.00)[a]	18,000	17,000	1,000	F
Utilities ($0.50)[a]	4,500	4,600	100	U
Total variable costs	36,000	35,600	400	F
Fixed costs				
Depreciation	15,000	15,000	0	
Supervision	10,000	10,000	0	
Property taxes	5,000	5,000	0	
Total fixed costs	30,000	30,000	0	
Total costs	$66,000	$65,600	$ 400	F

[a]Cost per direct labor hour

In subsequent months, Fox Company will prepare other flexible budget reports. For each month, the budget data are based on the actual activity level attained. In February that level may be 11,000 direct labor hours, in July 10,000, and so on.

Note that this flexible budget is based on a single cost driver. A more accurate budget often can be developed using the activity-based costing concepts explained in Chapter 17.

SERVICE COMPANY INSIGHT San Diego Zoo

Eric Isselée/iStockphoto

Budgets and the Exotic Newcastle Disease

Exotic Newcastle Disease, one of the most infectious bird diseases in the world, kills so swiftly that many victims die before any symptoms appear. When it broke out in Southern California, it could have spelled disaster for the San Diego Zoo. "We have one of the most valuable collections of birds in the world, if not *the* most valuable," says Paula Brock, CFO of the Zoological Society of San Diego, which operates the zoo.

Bird exhibits were closed to the public for several months (the disease, which is harmless to humans, can be carried on clothes and shoes). The tires of arriving delivery trucks were sanitized, as were the shoes of anyone visiting the zoo's nonpublic areas. Zookeeper uniforms had to be changed and cleaned daily. And ultimately, the zoo, with $150 million in revenues, spent almost half a million dollars on quarantine measures.

It worked: No birds got sick. Better yet, the damage to the rest of the zoo's budget was minimized by another protective measure: the monthly budget reforecast. "When we get a hit like this, we still have to find a way to make our bottom line," says Brock. Thanks to a new planning process Brock had introduced a year earlier, the zoo's scientists were able to raise the financial alarm as they redirected resources to ward off the disease. "Because we had timely awareness," she says, "we were able to make adjustments to weather the storm."

Source: Tim Reason, "Budgeting in the Real World," CFO Magazine (July 12, 2005), *www.cfodirect.com/cfopublic.nsf/vContentPrint/649A82C8FF8AB06B85257037004* (accessed July 2005).

What is the major benefit of tying a budget to the overall goals of the company? (Go to WileyPLUS for this answer and additional questions.)

DO IT! 2 Flexible Budgets

In Strassel Company's flexible budget graph, the fixed cost line and the total budgeted cost line intersect the vertical axis at $36,000. The total budgeted cost line is $186,000 at an activity level of 50,000 direct labor hours. Compute total budgeted costs at 30,000 direct labor hours.

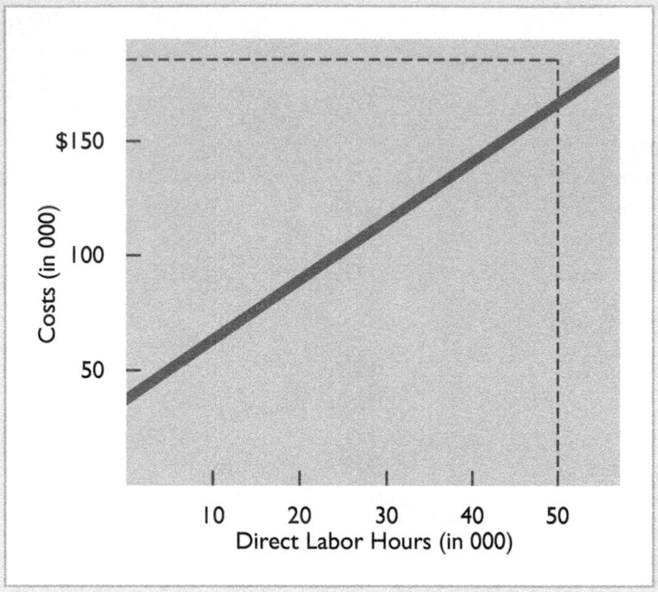

Action Plan

✔ Apply the formula: Fixed costs + Variable costs (Total variable cost per unit × Activity level) = Total budgeted costs.

SOLUTION

Using the graph, fixed costs are $36,000, and variable costs are $3 per direct labor hour [($186,000 − $36,000) ÷ 50,000]. Thus, at 30,000 direct labor hours, total budgeted costs are $126,000 [$36,000 + ($3 × 30,000)].

Related exercise material: **BE22-4, E22-3, E22-5,** and **DO IT! 22-2.**

LEARNING OBJECTIVE 3 Apply responsibility accounting to cost and profit centers.

Like budgeting, responsibility accounting is an important part of management accounting. **Responsibility accounting** involves accumulating and reporting costs (and revenues, where relevant) on the basis of the manager who has the authority to make the day-to-day decisions about the items. Under responsibility accounting, a manager's performance is evaluated on matters directly under that manager's control. Responsibility accounting can be used at every level of management in which the following conditions exist.

1. Costs and revenues can be directly associated with the specific level of management responsibility.
2. The costs and revenues can be controlled by employees at the level of responsibility with which they are associated.
3. Budget data can be developed for evaluating the manager's effectiveness in controlling the costs and revenues.

Illustration 22-17 depicts levels of responsibility for controlling costs.

Under responsibility accounting, any individual who controls a specified set of activities can be a responsibility center. Thus, responsibility accounting may

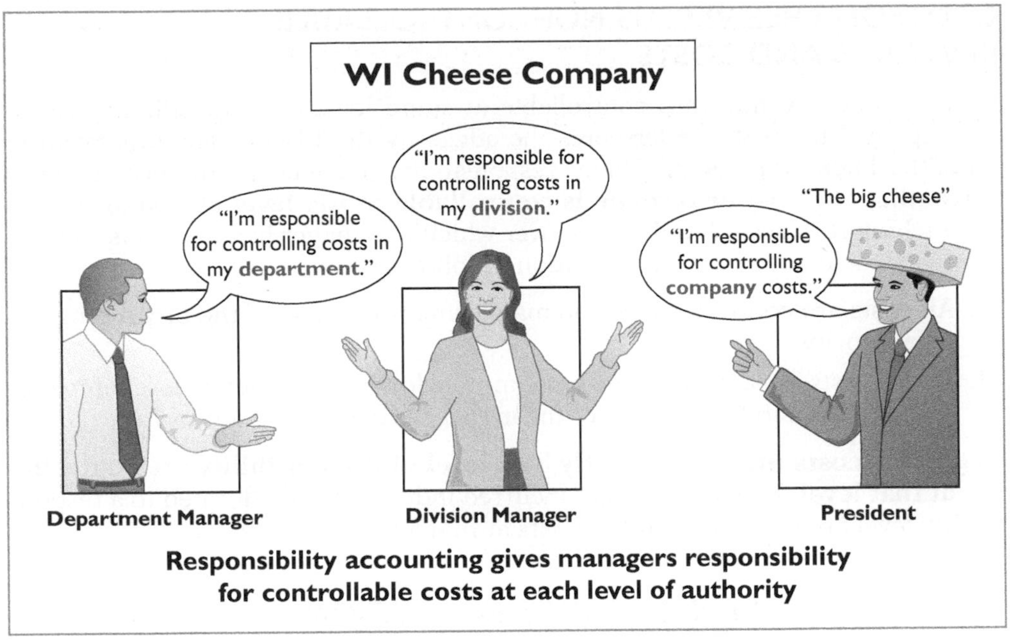

ILLUSTRATION 22-17 Responsibility for controllable costs at varying levels of management

extend from the lowest level of control to the top strata of management. Once responsibility is established, the company first measures and reports the effectiveness of the individual's performance for the specified activity. It then reports that measure upward throughout the organization.

Responsibility accounting is especially valuable in a decentralized company. **Decentralization** means that the control of operations is delegated to many managers throughout the organization. The term **segment** is sometimes used to identify an area of responsibility in decentralized operations. Under responsibility accounting, companies prepare segment reports periodically, such as monthly, quarterly, and annually, to evaluate managers' performance.

Responsibility accounting is an essential part of any effective system of budgetary control. The reporting of costs and revenues under responsibility accounting differs from budgeting in two respects:

1. A distinction is made between controllable and noncontrollable items.
2. Performance reports either emphasize or include only items controllable by the individual manager.

Responsibility accounting applies to both profit and not-for-profit entities. For-profit entities seek to maximize net income. Not-for-profit entities wish to provide services as efficiently as possible.

▼ HELPFUL HINT
All companies use responsibility accounting. Without some form of responsibility accounting, there would be chaos in discharging management's control function.

MANAGEMENT INSIGHT Procter & Gamble

Khuong Hoang/iStockphoto

Competition versus Collaboration

Many compensation and promotion programs encourage competition among employees for pay raises. To get ahead, you have to perform better than your fellow employees. While this may encourage hard work, it does not foster collaboration, and it can lead to distrust and disloyalty. Such negative effects have led some companies to believe that cooperation and collaboration, not competition, are essential in order to succeed in today's work environment.

As a consequence, many companies now explicitly include measures of collaboration in their performance measures. For example, Procter & Gamble measures collaboration in employees' annual performance reviews. At Cisco Systems, the assessment of an employee's teamwork can affect the annual bonus by as much as 20%.

Source: Carol Hymowitz, "Rewarding Competitors Over Collaboration No Longer Makes Sense," *Wall Street Journal* (February 13, 2006).

How might managers of separate divisions be able to reduce division costs through collaboration? (Go to **WileyPLUS** for this answer and additional questions.)

CONTROLLABLE VERSUS NONCONTROLLABLE REVENUES AND COSTS

▼ **HELPFUL HINT**
There are more, not fewer, controllable costs as you move to higher levels of management.

All costs and revenues are controllable at some level of responsibility within a company. This truth underscores the adage by the CEO of any organization that "the buck stops here." Under responsibility accounting, the critical issue is **whether the cost or revenue is controllable at the level of responsibility with which it is associated**. A cost over which a manager has control is called a **controllable cost**. From this definition, it follows that:

1. All costs are controllable by top management because of the broad range of its authority.
2. Fewer costs are controllable as one moves down to each lower level of managerial responsibility because of the manager's decreasing authority.

▼ **HELPFUL HINT**
The longer the time span, the more likely that the cost becomes controllable.

In general, **costs incurred directly by a level of responsibility are controllable at that level**. In contrast, costs incurred indirectly and allocated to a responsibility level are **noncontrollable costs** at that level.

PRINCIPLES OF PERFORMANCE EVALUATION

Performance evaluation is at the center of responsibility accounting. It is a management function that compares actual results with budget goals. It involves both behavioral and reporting principles.

Management by Exception

Management by exception means that top management's review of a budget report is focused either entirely or primarily on differences between actual results and planned objectives. This approach enables top management to focus on problem areas. For example, many companies now use online reporting systems for employees to file their travel and entertainment expense reports. In addition to cutting reporting time in half, the online system enables managers to quickly analyze variances from travel budgets. This cuts down on expense account "padding" such as spending too much on meals or falsifying documents for costs that were never actually incurred.

Management by exception does not mean that top management will investigate every difference. For this approach to be effective, there must be guidelines for identifying an exception. The usual criteria are materiality and controllability.

MATERIALITY Without quantitative guidelines, management would have to investigate every budget difference regardless of the amount. Materiality is usually expressed as a percentage difference from budget. For example, management may set the percentage difference at 5% for important items and 10% for other items. Managers will investigate all differences either over or under budget by the specified percentage. Costs over budget warrant investigation to determine why they were not controlled. Likewise, costs under budget merit investigation to determine whether costs critical to profitability are being curtailed. For example, if maintenance costs are budgeted at $80,000 but only $40,000 is spent, major unexpected breakdowns in productive facilities may occur in the future. Alternatively, as discussed earlier, cost might be under budget due to budgetary slack.

Alternatively, a company may specify a single percentage difference from budget for all items and supplement this guideline with a minimum dollar limit. For example, the exception criteria may be stated at 5% of budget or more than $10,000.

CONTROLLABILITY OF THE ITEM Exception guidelines are more restrictive for controllable items than for items the manager cannot control. In fact, there may be no guidelines for noncontrollable items. For example, a large unfavorable difference between actual and budgeted property tax expense may not be flagged for investigation because the only possible causes are an unexpected increase in the tax rate or in the assessed value of the property. An investigation into the difference would be useless: The manager cannot control either cause.

Behavioral Principles

The human factor is critical in evaluating performance. Behavioral principles include the following.

1. **Managers of responsibility centers should have direct input into the process of establishing budget goals of their area of responsibility.** Without such input, managers may view the goals as unrealistic or arbitrarily set by top management. Such views adversely affect the managers' motivation to meet the targeted objectives.
2. **The evaluation of performance should be based entirely on matters that are controllable by the manager being evaluated.** Criticism of a manager on matters outside his or her control reduces the effectiveness of the evaluation process. It leads to negative reactions by a manager and to doubts about the fairness of the company's evaluation policies.
3. **Top management should support the evaluation process.** As explained earlier, the evaluation process begins at the lowest level of responsibility and extends upward to the highest level of management. Managers quickly lose faith in the process when top management ignores, overrules, or bypasses established procedures for evaluating a manager's performance.
4. **The evaluation process must allow managers to respond to their evaluations.** Evaluation is not a one-way street. Managers should have the opportunity to defend their performance. Evaluation without feedback is both impersonal and ineffective.
5. **The evaluation should identify both good and poor performance.** Praise for good performance is a powerful motivating factor for a manager. This is especially true when a manager's compensation includes rewards for meeting budget goals.

Reporting Principles

Performance evaluation under responsibility accounting should be based on certain reporting principles. These principles pertain primarily to the internal reports that provide the basis for evaluating performance. Performance reports should:

1. Contain only data that are controllable by the manager of the responsibility center.
2. Provide accurate and reliable budget data to measure performance.
3. Highlight significant differences between actual results and budget goals.
4. Be tailor-made for the intended evaluation.
5. Be prepared at reasonable time intervals.

In recent years, companies have come under increasing pressure from influential shareholder groups to do a better job of linking executive pay to corporate performance. For example, software maker Siebel Systems unveiled a new incentive plan after lengthy discussions with the California Public Employees' Retirement System. One unique feature of the plan is that managers' targets will be publicly disclosed at the beginning of each year for investors to evaluate.

MANAGEMENT INSIGHT Honda

Kyodo/© AP/Wide World Photos

Flexible Manufacturing Requires Flexible Accounting

Flexible budgeting is useful because it enables managers to evaluate performance in light of changing conditions. But the ability to react quickly to changing conditions is even more important. Among automobile manufacturing facilities in the U.S., few plants are more flexible than Honda.

The manufacturing facilities of some auto companies can make slight alterations to the features of a vehicle in response to changes in demand for particular features. But for most plants, to switch from production of one type of vehicle to a completely different one typically takes months and costs hundreds of millions of dollars. At the Honda plant, however, the switch takes minutes. For example, it takes about five minutes to install different hand-like parts on the robots so they can switch from making Civic compacts to the longer, taller CR-V crossover. This ability to adjust quickly to changing demand gave Honda a huge advantage when gas prices surged and demand for more fuel-efficient cars increased quickly.

Source: Kate Linebaugh, "Honda's Flexible Plants Provide Edge," *Wall Street Journal Online* (September 23, 2008).

What implications do these improvements in production capabilities have for management accounting information and performance evaluation within the organization? (Go to **WileyPLUS** for this answer and additional questions.)

DECISION TOOLS

Responsibility reports help to hold individual managers accountable for the costs and revenues under their control.

RESPONSIBILITY REPORTING SYSTEM

A **responsibility reporting system** involves the preparation of a report for each level of responsibility in the company's organization chart. To illustrate such a system, we use the partial organization chart and production departments of Francis Chair Company in Illustration 22-18.

Report A
President sees summary data of vice presidents.

Report B
Vice president sees summary of controllable costs in his/her functional area.

Report C
Plant manager sees summary of controllable costs for each department in the plant.

Report D
Department manager sees controllable costs of his/her department.

ILLUSTRATION 22-18
Partial organization chart

The responsibility reporting system begins with the lowest level of responsibility for controlling costs and moves upward to each higher level. Illustration 22-19 details the connections between levels.

Report A
President sees summary data of vice presidents.

Report A.xls

	A	B	C	D	E
1					
2		**Report A**			
3	To President			Month: January	
4	Controllable Costs:	Budget	Actual	Fav/Unfav	
5	President	$ 150,000	$ 151,500	$ 1,500	U
6	Vice Presidents:				
7	Sales	185,000	187,000	2,000	U
8	Production	1,179,000	1,186,300	7,300	U
9	Finance	100,000	101,000	1,000	U
10	Total	$1,614,000	$1,625,800	$11,800	U
11					

Report B
Vice president sees summary of controllable costs in his/her functional area.

Report B.xls

	A	B	C	D	E
1					
2		**Report B**			
3	To Vice President Production			Month: January	
4	Controllable Costs:	Budget	Actual	Fav/Unfav	
5	VP Production	$ 125,000	$ 126,000	$ 1,000	U
6	Assembly Plants:				
7	Detroit	420,000	418,000	2,000	F
8	Chicago	304,000	309,300	5,300	U
9	St. Louis	330,000	333,000	3,000	U
10	Total	$1,179,000	$1,186,300	$ 7,300	U
11					

Report C
Plant manager sees summary of controllable costs for each department in the plant.

Report C.xls

	A	B	C	D	E
1					
2		**Report C**			
3	To Plant Manager-Chicago			Month: January	
4	Controllable Costs:	Budget	Actual	Fav/Unfav	
5	Chicago Plant	$110,000	$113,000	$3,000	U
6	Departments:				
7	Fabricating	84,000	85,300	1,300	U
8	Enameling	62,000	64,000	2,000	U
9	Assembly	48,000	47,000	1,000	F
10	Total	$304,000	$309,300	$5,300	U
11					

Report D
Department manager sees controllable costs of his/her department.

Report D.xls

	A	B	C	D	E
1					
2		**Report D**			
3	To Fabricating Dept. Manager			Month: January	
4	Controllable Costs:	Budget	Actual	Fav/Unfav	
5	Direct Materials	$20,000	$20,500	$ 500	U
6	Direct Labor	40,000	41,000	1,000	U
7	Overhead	24,000	23,800	200	F
8	Total	$84,000	$85,300	$1,300	U
9					

ILLUSTRATION 22-19
Responsibility reporting system

A brief description of the four reports for Francis Chair is as follows.

1. **Report D** is typical of reports that go to department managers. Similar reports are prepared for the managers of the Assembly and Enameling Departments.
2. **Report C** is an example of reports that are sent to plant managers. It shows the costs of the Chicago plant that are controllable at the second level of responsibility. In addition, Report C shows summary data for each department that is controlled by the plant manager. Similar reports are prepared for the Detroit and St. Louis plant managers.
3. **Report B** illustrates the reports at the third level of responsibility. It shows the controllable costs of the vice president of production and summary data on the three assembly plants for which this officer is responsible. Similar reports are prepared for the vice presidents of sales and finance.
4. **Report A** is typical of reports that go to the top level of responsibility—the president. It shows the controllable costs and expenses of this office and summary data on the vice presidents that are accountable to the president.

A responsibility reporting system permits management by exception at each level of responsibility. And, each higher level of responsibility can obtain the detailed report for each lower level of responsibility. For example, the vice president of production in Francis Chair may request the Chicago plant manager's report because this plant is $5,300 over budget.

This type of reporting system also permits comparative evaluations. In Illustration 22-19, the Chicago plant manager can easily rank the department managers' effectiveness in controlling manufacturing costs. Comparative rankings provide further incentive for a manager to control costs.

TYPES OF RESPONSIBILITY CENTERS

There are three basic types of responsibility centers: cost centers, profit centers, and investment centers. These classifications indicate the degree of responsibility the manager has for the performance of the center.

▼ HELPFUL HINT
The jewelry department of Macy's department store is a profit center, while the props department of a movie studio is a cost center.

A **cost center** incurs costs (and expenses) but does not directly generate revenues. Managers of cost centers have the authority to incur costs. They are evaluated on their ability to control costs. **Cost centers are usually either production departments or service departments.** Production departments participate directly in making the product. Service departments provide only support services. In a Ford Motor Company automobile plant, the welding, painting, and assembling departments are production departments. Ford's maintenance, cafeteria, and human resources departments are service departments. All of them are cost centers.

A **profit center** incurs costs (and expenses) and also generates revenues. Managers of profit centers are judged on the profitability of their centers. Examples of profit centers include the individual departments of a retail store, such as clothing, furniture, and automotive products, and branch offices of banks.

Like a profit center, an **investment center** incurs costs (and expenses) and generates revenues. In addition, an investment center has control over decisions regarding the assets available for use. Investment center managers are evaluated on both the profitability of the center and the rate of return earned on the funds invested. Investment centers are often associated with subsidiary companies. Utility Duke Energy has operating divisions such as electric utility, energy trading, and natural gas. Investment center managers control or significantly influence investment decisions related to such matters as plant expansion and entry into new market areas. Illustration 22-20 depicts the three types of responsibility centers.

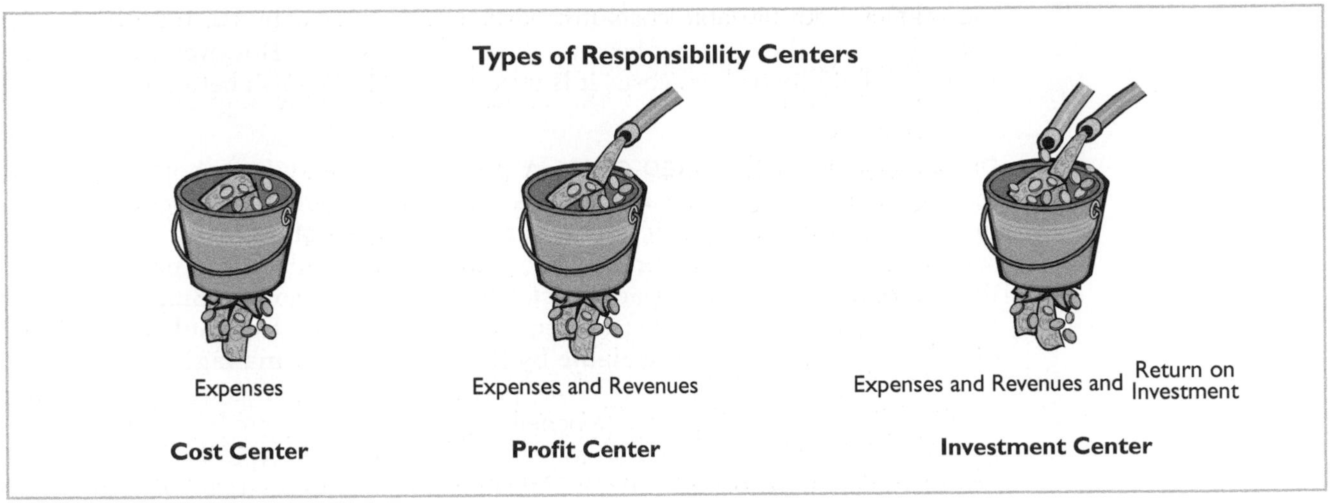

ILLUSTRATION 22-20
Types of responsibility centers

Responsibility Accounting for Cost Centers

The evaluation of a manager's performance for cost centers is based on his or her ability to meet budgeted goals for controllable costs. **Responsibility reports for cost centers compare actual controllable costs with flexible budget data.**

Illustration 22-21 shows a responsibility report. The report is adapted from the flexible budget report for Fox Company in Illustration 22-16 (page 1075). It assumes that the Finishing Department manager is able to control all manufacturing overhead costs except depreciation, property taxes, and his own monthly salary of $6,000. The remaining $4,000 ($10,000 − $6,000) of supervision costs are assumed to apply to other supervisory personnel within the Finishing Department, whose salaries are controllable by the manager.

ILLUSTRATION 22-21
Responsibility report for a cost center

Fox Company.xls

FOX COMPANY
Finishing Department
Responsibility Report
For the Month Ended January 31, 2017

Controllable Costs	Budget	Actual	Difference Favorable - F Unfavorable - U	
Indirect materials	$13,500	$14,000	$ 500	U
Indirect labor	18,000	17,000	1,000	F
Utilities	4,500	4,600	100	U
Supervision	4,000	4,000	0	
Total	$40,000	$39,600	$ 400	F

The report in Illustration 22-21 includes **only controllable costs**, and no distinction is made between variable and fixed costs. The responsibility report continues the concept of management by exception. In this case, top management may request an explanation of the $1,000 favorable difference in indirect labor and/or the $500 unfavorable difference in indirect materials.

Responsibility Accounting for Profit Centers

To evaluate the performance of a profit center manager, upper management needs detailed information about both controllable revenues and controllable costs. The operating revenues earned by a profit center, such as sales, are controllable by the manager. All variable costs (and expenses) incurred by the center are also controllable by the manager because they vary with sales. However, to determine the controllability of fixed costs, it is necessary to distinguish between direct and indirect fixed costs.

DIRECT AND INDIRECT FIXED COSTS A profit center may have both direct and indirect fixed costs. **Direct fixed costs** relate specifically to one center and are incurred for the sole benefit of that center. Examples of such costs include the salaries established by the profit center manager for supervisory personnel and the cost of a timekeeping department for the center's employees. Since these fixed costs can be traced directly to a center, they are also called **traceable costs. Most direct fixed costs are controllable by the profit center manager.**

In contrast, **indirect fixed costs** pertain to a company's overall operating activities and are incurred for the benefit of more than one profit center. Management allocates indirect fixed costs to profit centers on some type of equitable basis. For example, property taxes on a building occupied by more than one center may be allocated on the basis of square feet of floor space used by each center. Or, the costs of a company's human resources department may be allocated to profit centers on the basis of the number of employees in each center. Because these fixed costs apply to more than one center, they are also called **common costs. Most indirect fixed costs are not controllable by the profit center manager.**

▼ HELPFUL HINT
Recognize that we are emphasizing *financial* measures of performance. Companies are now making an effort to also stress *nonfinancial* performance measures such as product quality, labor productivity, market growth, materials' yield, manufacturing flexibility, and technological capability.

RESPONSIBILITY REPORT The responsibility report for a profit center shows budgeted and actual **controllable revenues and costs**. The report is prepared using the cost-volume-profit income statement explained in Chapter 18. In the report:

1. Controllable fixed costs are deducted from contribution margin.
2. The excess of contribution margin over controllable fixed costs is identified as **controllable margin**.
3. Noncontrollable fixed costs are not reported.

Illustration 22-22 shows the responsibility report for the manager of the Marine Division, a profit center of Mantle Company. For the year, the Marine Division also had $60,000 of indirect fixed costs that were not controllable by the profit center manager.

ILLUSTRATION 22-22
Responsibility report for profit center

Mantle Company.xls

MANTLE COMPANY
Marine Division
Responsibility Report
For the Year Ended December 31, 2017

	Budget	Actual	Difference Favorable - F Unfavorable - U	
Sales	$1,200,000	$1,150,000	$50,000	U
Variable costs				
Cost of goods sold	500,000	490,000	10,000	F
Selling and administrative	160,000	156,000	4,000	F
Total	660,000	646,000	14,000	F
Contribution margin	540,000	504,000	36,000	U
Controllable fixed costs				
Cost of goods sold	100,000	100,000	0	
Selling and administrative	80,000	80,000	0	
Total	180,000	180,000	0	
Controllable margin	$ 360,000	$ 324,000	$36,000	U

Controllable margin is considered to be the best measure of the manager's performance **in controlling revenues and costs.** The report in Illustration 22-22 shows that the manager's performance was below budgeted expectations by 10% (\$36,000 ÷ \$360,000). Top management would likely investigate the causes of this unfavorable result. Note that the report does not show the Marine Division's noncontrollable fixed costs of \$60,000. These costs would be included in a report on the profitability of the profit center.

Management also may choose to see **monthly** responsibility reports for profit centers. In addition, responsibility reports may include cumulative year-to-date results.

DO IT! 3 Profit Center Responsibility Report

Midwest Division operates as a profit center. It reports the following for the year:

	Budget	Actual
Sales	\$1,500,000	\$1,700,000
Variable costs	700,000	800,000
Controllable fixed costs	400,000	400,000
Noncontrollable fixed costs	200,000	200,000

Prepare a responsibility report for the Midwest Division for December 31, 2017.

SOLUTION

Midwest Division Responsibility Report.xls

MIDWEST DIVISION
Responsibility Report
For the Year Ended December 31, 2017

	Budget	Actual	Difference Favorable F Unfavorable U	
Sales	\$1,500,000	\$1,700,000	\$200,000	F
Variable costs	700,000	800,000	100,000	U
Contribution margin	800,000	900,000	100,000	F
Controllable fixed costs	400,000	400,000	0	
Controllable margin	\$ 400,000	\$ 500,000	\$100,000	F

Action Plan

- ✔ Deduct variable costs from sales to show contribution margin.
- ✔ Deduct controllable fixed costs from the contribution margin to show controllable margin.
- ✔ Do not report noncontrollable fixed costs.

Related exercise material: **BE22-7, E22-15,** and **DO IT! 22-3.**

LEARNING OBJECTIVE 4 Evaluate performance in investment centers.

As explained earlier, an investment center manager can control or significantly influence the investment funds available for use. Thus, the primary basis for evaluating the performance of a manager of an investment center is **return on investment (ROI).** The return on investment is considered to be a useful performance measurement because it shows the **effectiveness of the manager in utilizing the assets at his or her disposal.**

RETURN ON INVESTMENT (ROI)

The formula for computing ROI for an investment center, together with assumed illustrative data, is shown in Illustration 22-23 (page 1086).

ILLUSTRATION 22-23
ROI formula

Controllable Margin	÷	Average Operating Assets	=	Return on Investment (ROI)
$1,000,000	÷	$5,000,000	=	20%

DECISION TOOLS

The ROI formula helps managers determine if the investment center has used its assets effectively.

Both factors in the formula are controllable by the investment center manager. Operating assets consist of current assets and plant assets used in operations by the center and controlled by the manager. Non-operating assets such as idle plant assets and land held for future use are excluded. Average operating assets are usually based on the cost or book value of the assets at the beginning and end of the year.

RESPONSIBILITY REPORT

The scope of the investment center manager's responsibility significantly affects the content of the performance report. Since an investment center is an independent entity for operating purposes, **all fixed costs are controllable by its manager**. For example, the manager is responsible for depreciation on investment center assets. Therefore, more fixed costs are identified as controllable in the performance report for an investment center manager than in a performance report for a profit center manager. The report also shows budgeted and actual ROI below controllable margin.

To illustrate this responsibility report, we will now assume that the Marine Division of Mantle Company is an investment center. It has budgeted and actual average operating assets of $2,000,000. The manager can control $60,000 of fixed costs that were not controllable when the division was a profit center. Illustration 22-24 shows the division's responsibility report.

ILLUSTRATION 22-24
Responsibility report for investment center

Mantle Company.xls

MANTLE COMPANY
Marine Division
Responsibility Report
For the Year Ended December 31, 2017

	Budget	Actual	Difference Favorable - F Unfavorable - U	
Sales	$ 1,200,000	$ 1,150,000	$ 50,000	U
Variable costs				
Cost of goods sold	500,000	490,000	10,000	F
Selling and administrative	160,000	156,000	4,000	F
Total	660,000	646,000	14,000	F
Contribution margin	540,000	504,000	36,000	U
Controllable fixed costs				
Cost of goods sold	100,000	100,000	0	
Selling and administrative	80,000	80,000	0	
Other fixed costs	60,000	60,000	0	
Total	240,000	240,000	0	
Controllable margin	$ 300,000	$ 264,000	$ 36,000	U
Return on investment	15.0%	13.2%	1.8%	U
	(a)	(b)	(c)	

(a) $\frac{\$300,000}{\$2,000,000}$ (b) $\frac{\$264,000}{\$2,000,000}$ (c) $\frac{\$36,000}{\$2,000,000}$

The report shows that the manager's performance based on ROI was below budget expectations by 1.8% (15.0% versus 13.2%). Top management would likely want explanations for this unfavorable result.

JUDGMENTAL FACTORS IN ROI

The return on investment approach includes two judgmental factors:

1. **Valuation of operating assets.** Operating assets may be valued at acquisition cost, book value, appraised value, or fair value. The first two bases are readily available from the accounting records.
2. **Margin (income) measure.** This measure may be controllable margin, income from operations, or net income.

Each of the alternative values for operating assets can provide a reliable basis for evaluating a manager's performance as long as it is consistently applied between reporting periods. However, the use of income measures other than controllable margin will not result in a valid basis for evaluating the performance of an investment center manager.

IMPROVING ROI

The manager of an investment center can improve ROI by increasing controllable margin, and/or reducing average operating assets. To illustrate, we will use the following assumed data for the Laser Division of Berra Company.

ILLUSTRATION 22-25
Assumed data for Laser Division

Sales	$2,000,000
Variable costs	1,100,000
Contribution margin (45%)	900,000
Controllable fixed costs	300,000
Controllable margin (a)	$ 600,000
Average operating assets (b)	$5,000,000
Return on investment (a) ÷ (b)	12%

Increasing Controllable Margin

Controllable margin can be increased by increasing sales or by reducing variable and controllable fixed costs as follows.

1. **Increase sales 10%.** Sales will increase $200,000 ($2,000,000 × .10). Assuming no change in the contribution margin percentage of 45%, contribution margin will increase $90,000 ($200,000 × .45). Controllable margin will increase by the same amount because controllable fixed costs will not change. Thus, controllable margin becomes $690,000 ($600,000 + $90,000). The new ROI is 13.8%, computed as follows.

ILLUSTRATION 22-26
ROI computation—increase in sales

$$\text{ROI} = \frac{\text{Controllable margin}}{\text{Average operating assets}} = \frac{\$690,000}{\$5,000,000} = 13.8\%$$

An increase in sales benefits both the investment center and the company if it results in new business. It would not benefit the company if the increase was achieved at the expense of other investment centers.

2. **Decrease variable and fixed costs 10%.** Total costs decrease $140,000 [($1,100,000 + $300,000) × .10]. This reduction results in a corresponding increase in controllable margin. Thus, controllable margin becomes $740,000 ($600,000 + $140,000). The new ROI is 14.8%, computed as follows.

ILLUSTRATION 22-27
ROI computation—decrease in costs

$$\text{ROI} = \frac{\text{Controllable margin}}{\text{Average operating assets}} = \frac{\$740,000}{\$5,000,000} = 14.8\%$$

This course of action is clearly beneficial when the reduction in costs is the result of eliminating waste and inefficiency. But, a reduction in costs that results from cutting expenditures on vital activities, such as required maintenance and inspections, is not likely to be acceptable to top management.

Reducing Average Operating Assets

Assume that average operating assets are reduced 10% or $500,000 ($5,000,000 × .10). Average operating assets become $4,500,000 ($5,000,000 − $500,000). Since controllable margin remains unchanged at $600,000, the new ROI is 13.3%, computed as follows.

ILLUSTRATION 22-28
ROI computation—decrease in operating assets

$$\text{ROI} = \frac{\text{Controllable margin}}{\text{Average operating assets}} = \frac{\$600{,}000}{\$4{,}500{,}000} = \mathbf{13.3\%}$$

Reductions in operating assets may or may not be prudent. It is beneficial to eliminate overinvestment in inventories and to dispose of excessive plant assets. However, it is unwise to reduce inventories below expected needs or to dispose of essential plant assets.

ACCOUNTING ACROSS THE ORGANIZATION Hollywood

brentmelissa/iStockphoto

Does Hollywood Look at ROI?

If Hollywood were run like a real business, where things like return on investment mattered, there would be one unchallenged, sacred principle that studio chieftains would never violate: Make lots of G-rated movies.

No matter how you slice the movie business—by star vehicles, by budget levels, or by sequels or franchises—by far the best return on investment comes from the not-so-glamorous world of G-rated films. The problem is, these movies represent only 3% of the total films made in a typical year.

On the flip side are the R-rated films, which dominate the total releases and yet yield the worst return on investment. A whopping 646 R-rated films were released in a recent year—69% of the total output—but only four of the top-20 grossing movies of the year were R-rated films.

This trend—G-rated movies are good for business but underproduced, R-rated movies are bad for business and yet overdone—is something that has been driving economists batty for the past several years.

Source: David Grainger, "The Dysfunctional Family-Film Business," *Fortune* (January 10, 2005), pp. 20–21.

What might be the reason that movie studios do not produce G-rated movies as much as R-rated ones? (Go to **WileyPLUS** for this answer and additional questions.)

DO IT! ▶4 Performance Evaluation

The service division of Metro Industries reported the following results for 2017.

Sales	$400,000
Variable costs	320,000
Controllable fixed costs	40,800
Average operating assets	280,000

Management is considering the following independent courses of action in 2018 in order to maximize the return on investment for this division.

1. Reduce average operating assets by $80,000, with no change in controllable margin.
2. Increase sales $80,000, with no change in the contribution margin percentage.
   (a) Compute the controllable margin and the return on investment for 2017.
   (b) Compute the controllable margin and the expected return on investment for each proposed alternative.

SOLUTION

(a) Return on investment for 2017:

Sales	$400,000
Variable costs	320,000
Contribution margin	80,000
Controllable fixed costs	40,800
Controllable margin	$ 39,200

$$\text{Return on investment} \quad \frac{\$39{,}200}{\$280{,}000} = 14\%$$

(b) Expected return on investment for alternative 1:

$$\frac{\$39{,}200}{\$280{,}000 - \$80{,}000} = 19.6\%$$

Expected return on investment for alternative 2:

Sales ($400,000 + $80,000)	$480,000
Variable costs ($320,000/$400,000 × $480,000)	384,000
Contribution margin	96,000
Controllable fixed costs	40,800
Controllable margin	$ 55,200

$$\text{Return on investment} \quad \frac{\$55{,}200}{\$280{,}000} = 19.7\%$$

Action Plan

- ✔ **Recall key formulas: Sales − Variable costs = Contribution margin.**
- ✔ **Contribution margin ÷ Sales = Contribution margin percentage.**
- ✔ **Contribution margin − Controllable fixed costs = Controllable margin.**
- ✔ **Return on investment = Controllable margin ÷ Average operating assets.**

Related exercise material: **BE22-8, BE22-9, BE22-10, E22-16, E22-17,** and **DO IT! 22-4.**

USING DECISION TOOLS—TRIBECA GRAND HOTEL

The Tribeca Grand Hotel, which was discussed in the Feature Story, faces many situations where it needs to apply the decision tools learned in this chapter. For example, assume that the hotel's housekeeping budget contains the following items.

Variable costs	
Direct labor	$37,000
Laundry service	10,000
Supplies	6,000
Total variable	$53,000
Fixed costs	
Supervision	$17,000
Inspection costs	1,000
Insurance expenses	2,000
Depreciation	15,000
Total fixed	$35,000

The budget was based on an estimated 4,000-room rental for the month. During November, 3,000 rooms were actually rented, with the following costs incurred.

Variable costs	
Direct labor	$38,700
Laundry service	8,200
Supplies	5,100
Total variable	$52,000

Fixed costs	
Supervision	$19,300
Inspection costs	1,200
Insurance expenses	2,200
Depreciation	14,700
Total fixed	$37,400

INSTRUCTIONS

(a) Determine which items would be controllable by the housekeeping manager. (Assume "supervision" excludes the housekeeping manager's own salary.)

(b) How much should have been spent during the month for providing rental of 3,000 rooms?

(c) Prepare a flexible housekeeping budget report for the housekeeping manager.

(d) Prepare a responsibility report. Include only the costs that would have been controllable by the housekeeping manager.

SOLUTION

(a) The housekeeping manager should be able to control all the variable costs and the fixed costs of supervision and inspection. Insurance and depreciation ordinarily are not the responsibility of the housekeeping manager.

(b) The total variable cost per unit is $13.25 ($53,000 ÷ 4,000). The total budgeted cost during the month to provide 3,000 room rentals is variable costs $39,750 (3,000 × $13.25) plus fixed costs ($35,000), for a total of $74,750 ($39,750 + $35,000).

(c)

TRIBECA GRAND HOTEL
Housekeeping Department
Housekeeping Budget Report (Flexible)
For the Month Ended November 30, 2017

	Budget at 3,000 Rooms	**Actual at 3,000 Rooms**	**Difference Favorable F Unfavorable U**
Variable costs			
Direct labor ($9.25)*	$27,750	$38,700	$10,950 U
Laundry service ($2.50)	7,500	8,200	700 U
Supplies ($1.50)	4,500	5,100	600 U
Total variable ($13.25)	39,750	52,000	12,250 U
Fixed costs			
Supervision	17,000	19,300	2,300 U
Inspection	1,000	1,200	200 U
Insurance	2,000	2,200	200 U
Depreciation	15,000	14,700	300 F
Total fixed	35,000	37,400	2,400 U
Total costs	$74,750	$89,400	$14,650 U

*$37,000 ÷ 4,000

(d) Because a housekeeping department is a cost center, the responsibility report should include only the costs that are controllable by the housekeeping manager. In this type of report, no distinction is made between variable and fixed costs. Budget data in the report should be based on the rooms actually rented.

TRIBECA GRAND HOTEL
Housekeeping Department
Housekeeping Responsibility Report
For the Month Ended November 30, 2017

Controllable Costs	**Budget**	**Actual**	**Difference Favorable F Unfavorable U**
Direct labor	$27,750	$38,700	$10,950 U
Laundry service	7,500	8,200	700 U
Supplies	4,500	5,100	600 U
Supervision	17,000	19,300	2,300 U
Inspection	1,000	1,200	200 U
Total	$57,750	$72,500	$14,750 U

LEARNING OBJECTIVE *5

APPENDIX 22A: Explain the difference between ROI and residual income.

Although most companies use ROI to evaluate investment performance, ROI has a significant disadvantage. To illustrate, let's look at the Electronics Division of Pujols Company. It has an ROI of 20%, computed as follows.

ILLUSTRATION 22A-1
ROI formula

Controllable Margin	÷	Average Operating Assets	=	Return on Investment (ROI)
$1,000,000	÷	$5,000,000	=	20%

The Electronics Division is considering producing a new product, a GPS device (hereafter referred to as Tracker) for its boats. To produce Tracker, operating assets will have to increase $2,000,000. Tracker is expected to generate an additional $260,000 of controllable margin. Illustration 22A-2 shows how Tracker will effect ROI.

ILLUSTRATION 22A-2
ROI comparison

	Without Tracker	Tracker	With Tracker
Controllable margin (a)	$1,000,000	$ 260,000	$1,260,000
Average operating assets (b)	$5,000,000	$2,000,000	$7,000,000
Return on investment [(a) ÷ (b)]	20%	13%	18%

The investment in Tracker reduces ROI from 20% to 18%.

Let's suppose that you are the manager of the Electronics Division and must make the decision to produce or not produce Tracker. If you were evaluated using ROI, you probably would not produce Tracker because your ROI would drop from 20% to 18%. The problem with this ROI analysis is that it ignores an important variable: the minimum rate of return on a company's operating assets. The **minimum rate of return** is the rate at which the Electronics Division can cover its costs and earn a profit. Assuming that the Electronics Division has a minimum rate of return of 10%, it should invest in Tracker because its ROI of 13% is greater than 10%.

RESIDUAL INCOME COMPARED TO ROI

To evaluate performance using the minimum rate of return, companies use the residual income approach. **Residual income** is the income that remains after subtracting from the controllable margin the minimum rate of return on a company's average operating assets. The residual income for Tracker would be computed as follows.

ILLUSTRATION 22A-3
Residual income formula

Controllable Margin	−	Minimum Rate of Return × Average Operating Assets	=	Residual Income
$260,000	−	10% × $2,000,000	=	$60,000

As shown, the residual income related to the Tracker investment is $60,000. Illustration 22A-4 (page 1092) indicates how residual income changes as the additional investment is made.

ILLUSTRATION 22A-4
Residual income comparison

	Without Tracker	Tracker	With Tracker
Controllable margin (a)	$1,000,000	$260,000	$1,260,000
Average operating assets × 10% (b)	500,000	200,000	700,000
Residual income [(a) − (b)]	$ 500,000	$ 60,000	$ 560,000

This example illustrates how performance evaluation based on ROI can be misleading and can even cause managers to reject projects that would actually increase income for the company. As a result, many companies such as Coca-Cola, Briggs and Stratton, Eli Lilly, and Siemens AG use residual income (or a variant often referred to as economic value added) to evaluate investment alternatives and measure company performance.

RESIDUAL INCOME WEAKNESS

It might appear from the above discussion that the goal of any company should be to maximize the total amount of residual income in each division. This goal, however, ignores the fact that one division might use substantially fewer assets to attain the same level of residual income as another division. For example, we know that to produce Tracker, the Electronics Division of Pujols Company used $2,000,000 of average operating assets to generate $260,000 of controllable margin. Now let's say a different division produced a product called SeaDog, which used $4,000,000 to generate $460,000 of controllable margin, as shown in Illustration 22A-5.

ILLUSTRATION 22A-5
Comparison of two products

	Tracker	SeaDog
Controllable margin (a)	$260,000	$460,000
Average operating assets × 10% (b)	200,000	400,000
Residual income [(a) − (b)]	$ 60,000	$ 60,000

If the performance of these two investments were evaluated using residual income, they would be considered equal: Both products have the same total residual income. This ignores, however, the fact that SeaDog required **twice** as many operating assets to achieve the same level of residual income.

REVIEW AND PRACTICE

▶ LEARNING OBJECTIVES REVIEW

1 Describe budgetary control and static budget reports. Budgetary control consists of (a) preparing periodic budget reports that compare actual results with planned objectives, (b) analyzing the differences to determine their causes, (c) taking appropriate corrective action, and (d) modifying future plans, if necessary.

Static budget reports are useful in evaluating the progress toward planned sales and profit goals. They are also appropriate in assessing a manager's effectiveness in controlling costs when (a) actual activity closely approximates the master budget activity level, and/or (b) the behavior of the costs in response to changes in activity is fixed.

2 Prepare flexible budget reports. To develop the flexible budget it is necessary to: (a) Identify the activity index and the relevant range of activity. (b) Identify the variable costs, and determine the budgeted variable cost per unit of activity for each cost. (c) Identify the fixed costs, and determine the budgeted amount for each cost. (d) Prepare the budget for selected increments of activity within the relevant range. Flexible budget reports permit an evaluation of a manager's performance in controlling production and costs.

3 Apply responsibility accounting to cost and profit centers. Responsibility accounting involves accumulating and reporting revenues and costs on the basis of the individual manager who has the authority to make the day-to-day decisions about the items. The evaluation of a manager's performance is based on the matters directly under the manager's control. In responsibility accounting, it is necessary to distinguish between controllable and noncontrollable fixed costs and to identify three types of responsibility centers: cost, profit, and investment.

Responsibility reports for cost centers compare actual costs with flexible budget data. The reports show only controllable costs, and no distinction is made between variable and fixed costs. Responsibility reports show contribution margin, controllable fixed costs, and controllable margin for each profit center.

4 Evaluate performance in investment centers. The primary basis for evaluating performance in investment centers is return on investment (ROI). The formula for computing ROI for investment centers is Controllable margin ÷ Average operating assets.

***5 Explain the difference between ROI and residual income.** ROI is controllable margin divided by average operating assets. Residual income is the income that remains after subtracting the minimum rate of return on a company's average operating assets. ROI sometimes provides misleading results because profitable investments are often rejected when the investment reduces ROI but increases overall profitability.

DECISION TOOLS REVIEW

DECISION CHECKPOINTS	INFO NEEDED FOR DECISION	TOOL TO USE FOR DECISION	HOW TO EVALUATE RESULTS
Are the increased costs resulting from increased production reasonable?	Variable costs projected at different levels of production	Flexible budget	After taking into account different production levels, results are favorable if expenses are less than budgeted amounts.
Have the individual managers been held accountable for the costs and revenues under their control?	Relevant costs and revenues, where the individual manager has authority to make day-to-day decisions about the items	Responsibility reports focused on cost centers, profit centers, and investment centers as appropriate	Compare budget to actual costs and revenues for controllable items.
Has the investment center performed up to expectations?	Controllable margin (contribution margin minus controllable fixed costs), and average investment center operating assets	Return on investment	Compare actual ROI to expected ROI.

GLOSSARY REVIEW

Budgetary control The use of budgets to control operations. (p. 1066).

Controllable cost A cost over which a manager has control. (p. 1078).

Controllable margin Contribution margin less controllable fixed costs. (p. 1084).

Cost center A responsibility center that incurs costs but does not directly generate revenues. (p. 1082).

Decentralization Control of operations is delegated to many managers throughout the organization. (p. 1077).

Direct fixed costs Costs that relate specifically to a responsibility center and are incurred for the sole benefit of the center. (p. 1084).

Flexible budget A projection of budget data for various levels of activity. (p. 1069).

Indirect fixed costs Costs that are incurred for the benefit of more than one profit center. (p. 1084).

Investment center A responsibility center that incurs costs, generates revenues, and has control over decisions regarding the assets available for use. (p. 1082).

Management by exception The review of budget reports by top management focused entirely or primarily on differences between actual results and planned objectives. (p. 1078).

Noncontrollable costs Costs incurred indirectly and allocated to a responsibility center that are not controllable at that level. (p. 1078).

Profit center A responsibility center that incurs costs and also generates revenues. (p. 1082).

***Residual income** The income that remains after subtracting from the controllable margin the minimum rate of return on a company's average operating assets. (p. 1091).

Responsibility accounting A part of management accounting that involves accumulating and reporting revenues and costs on the basis of the manager who has the authority to make the day-to-day decisions about the items. (p. 1076).

Responsibility reporting system The preparation of reports for each level of responsibility in the company's organization chart. (p. 1080).

Return on investment (ROI) A measure of management's effectiveness in utilizing assets at its disposal in an investment center. (p. 1085).

Segment An area of responsibility in decentralized operations. (p. 1077).

Static budget A projection of budget data at one level of activity. (p. 1067).

PRACTICE MULTIPLE-CHOICE QUESTIONS

(LO 1) 1. Budgetary control involves all but one of the following:
(a) modifying future plans.
(b) analyzing differences.
(c) using static budgets but **not** flexible budgets.
(d) determining differences between actual and planned results.

(LO 1) 2. Budget reports are prepared:
(a) daily. (c) monthly.
(b) weekly. (d) All of the above.

(LO 1) 3. A production manager in a manufacturing company would most likely receive a:
(a) sales report.
(b) income statement.
(c) scrap report.
(d) shipping department overhead report.

(LO 1) 4. A static budget is:
(a) a projection of budget data at several levels of activity within the relevant range of activity.
(b) a projection of budget data at a single level of activity.
(c) compared to a flexible budget in a budget report.
(d) never appropriate in evaluating a manager's effectiveness in controlling costs.

(LO 1) 5. A static budget is useful in controlling costs when cost behavior is:
(a) mixed. (c) variable.
(b) fixed. (d) linear.

(LO 1) 6. At zero direct labor hours in a flexible budget graph, the total budgeted cost line intersects the vertical axis at $30,000. At 10,000 direct labor hours, a horizontal line drawn from the total budgeted cost line intersects the vertical axis at $90,000. Fixed and variable costs may be expressed as:
(a) $30,000 fixed plus $6 per direct labor hour variable.
(b) $30,000 fixed plus $9 per direct labor hour variable.
(c) $60,000 fixed plus $3 per direct labor hour variable.
(d) $60,000 fixed plus $6 per direct labor hour variable.

(LO 2) 7. At 9,000 direct labor hours, the flexible budget for indirect materials is $27,000. If $28,000 of indirect materials costs are incurred at 9,200 direct labor hours, the flexible budget report should show the following difference for indirect materials:
(a) $1,000 unfavorable.
(b) $1,000 favorable.
(c) $400 favorable.
(d) $400 unfavorable.

8. Under responsibility accounting, the evaluation of a manager's performance is based on matters that the manager: (LO 3)
(a) directly controls.
(b) directly and indirectly controls.
(c) indirectly controls.
(d) has shared responsibility for with another manager.

9. Responsibility centers include: (LO 3)
(a) cost centers.
(b) profit centers.
(c) investment centers.
(d) All of the above.

10. Responsibility reports for cost centers: (LO 3)
(a) distinguish between fixed and variable costs.
(b) use static budget data.
(c) include both controllable and noncontrollable costs.
(d) include only controllable costs.

11. The accounting department of a manufacturing company is an example of: (LO 3)
(a) a cost center.
(b) a profit center.
(c) an investment center.
(d) a contribution center.

12. To evaluate the performance of a profit center manager, upper management needs detailed information about: (LO 3)
(a) controllable costs.
(b) controllable revenues.
(c) controllable costs and revenues.
(d) controllable costs and revenues and average operating assets.

(LO 3) **13.** In a responsibility report for a profit center, controllable fixed costs are deducted from contribution margin to show:
(a) profit center margin.
(b) controllable margin.
(c) net income.
(d) income from operations.

(LO 4) **14.** In the formula for return on investment (ROI), the factors for controllable margin and operating assets are, respectively:
(a) controllable margin percentage and total operating assets.
(b) controllable margin dollars and average operating assets.
(c) controllable margin dollars and total assets.
(d) controllable margin percentage and average operating assets.

15. A manager of an investment center can improve ROI by: (LO 4)
(a) increasing average operating assets.
(b) reducing sales.
(c) increasing variable costs.
(d) reducing variable and/or controllable fixed costs.

SOLUTIONS

1. **(c)** Budgetary control involves using flexible budgets and sometimes static budgets. The other choices are all part of budgetary control.
2. **(d)** Budget reports are prepared daily, weekly, or monthly. The other choices are correct, but choice (d) is the better answer.
3. **(c)** A production manager in a manufacturing company would most likely receive a scrap report. The other choices are incorrect because (a) top management or a sales manager would most likely receive a sales report, (b) top management would most likely receive an income statement, and (d) a department manager would most likely receive a shipping department overhead report.
4. **(b)** A static budget is a projection of budget data at a single level of activity. The other choices are incorrect because a static budget (a) is a projection of budget data at a single level of activity, not at several levels of activity within the relevant range of activity; (c) is not compared to a flexible budget in a budget report; and (d) is appropriate in evaluating a manager's effectiveness in controlling fixed costs.
5. **(b)** A static budget is useful for controlling fixed costs. The other choices are incorrect because a static budget is not useful for controlling (a) mixed costs, (c) variable costs, or (d) linear costs.
6. **(a)** The intersection point of $90,000 is total budgeted costs, or budgeted fixed costs plus budgeted variable costs. Fixed costs are $30,000 (amount at zero direct labor hours), so budgeted variable costs are $60,000 [$90,000 (Total costs) − $30,000 (Fixed costs)]. Budgeted variable costs ($60,000) divided by total activity level (10,000 direct labor hours) gives the variable cost per unit of $6 per direct labor hour. The other choices are therefore incorrect.
7. **(d)** Budgeted indirect materials per direct labor hour (DLH) is $3 ($27,000/9,000). At an activity level of 9,200 direct labor hours, budgeted indirect materials are $27,600 (9,200 × $3 per DLH) but actual indirect materials costs are $28,000, resulting in a $400 unfavorable difference. The other choices are therefore incorrect.
8. **(a)** The evaluation of a manager's performance is based only on matters that the manager directly controls. The other choices are therefore incorrect as they include indirect controls and shared responsibility.
9. **(d)** Cost centers, profit centers, and investment centers are all responsibility centers. The other choices are correct, but choice (d) is the better answer.
10. **(d)** Responsibility reports for cost centers report only controllable costs; they (a) do not distinguish between fixed and variable costs; (b) use flexible budget data, not static budget data; and (c) do not include noncontrollable costs.
11. **(a)** The accounting department of a manufacturing company is an example of a cost center, not (b) a profit center, (c) an investment center, or (d) contribution center.
12. **(c)** To evaluate the performance of a profit center manager, upper management needs detailed information about controllable costs and revenues, not just (a) controllable costs or (b) controllable revenues. Choice (d) is incorrect because upper management does not need information about average operating assets.
13. **(b)** Contribution margin less controllable fixed costs is the controllable margin, not (a) the profit center margin, (c) net income, or (d) income from operations.
14. **(b)** The factors in the formula for ROI are controllable margin dollars and average operating assets. The other choices are therefore incorrect.
15. **(d)** Reducing variable or controllable fixed costs will cause the controllable margin to increase, which is one way a manager of an investment center can improve ROI. The other choices are incorrect because (a) increasing average operating assets will lower ROI; (b) reducing sales will cause contribution margin to go down, thereby decreasing controllable margin since there will be less contribution margin to cover controllable fixed costs and resulting in lower ROI; and (c) increasing variable costs will cause the contribution margin to be lower, thereby decreasing controllable margin and resulting in lower ROI.

PRACTICE EXERCISES

Prepare flexible manufacturing overhead budget.

(LO 2)

1. Felix Company uses a flexible budget for manufacturing overhead based on direct labor hours. Variable manufacturing overhead costs per direct labor hour are as follows.

Indirect labor	$0.70
Indirect materials	0.50
Utilities	0.40

Fixed overhead costs per month are supervision $4,000, depreciation $3,000, and property taxes $800. The company believes it will normally operate in a range of 7,000–10,000 direct labor hours per month.

INSTRUCTIONS

Prepare a monthly flexible manufacturing overhead budget for 2017 for the expected range of activity, using increments of 1,000 direct labor hours.

SOLUTION

1.

FELIX COMPANY
Monthly Flexible Manufacturing Overhead Budget
For the Year 2017

Activity level				
Direct labor hours	7,000	8,000	9,000	10,000
Variable costs				
Indirect labor ($.70)	$ 4,900	$ 5,600	$ 6,300	$ 7,000
Indirect materials ($.50)	3,500	4,000	4,500	5,000
Utilities ($.40)	2,800	3,200	3,600	4,000
Total variable costs ($1.60)	11,200	12,800	14,400	16,000
Fixed costs				
Supervision	4,000	4,000	4,000	4,000
Depreciation	3,000	3,000	3,000	3,000
Property taxes	800	800	800	800
Total fixed costs	7,800	7,800	7,800	7,800
Total costs	$19,000	$20,600	$22,200	$23,800

Compute ROI for current year and for possible future changes.

(LO 4)

2. The White Division of Mesin Company reported the following data for the current year.

Sales	$3,000,000
Variable costs	2,400,000
Controllable fixed costs	400,000
Average operating assets	5,000,000

Top management is unhappy with the investment center's return on investment (ROI). It asks the manager of the White Division to submit plans to improve ROI in the next year. The manager believes it is feasible to consider the following independent courses of action.

1. Increase sales by $300,000 with no change in the contribution margin percentage.
2. Reduce variable costs by $100,000.
3. Reduce average operating assets by 4%.

INSTRUCTIONS

(a) Compute the return on investment (ROI) for the current year.

(b) Using the ROI formula, compute the ROI under each of the proposed courses of action. (Round to one decimal.)

SOLUTION

2. (a) Controllable margin = ($3,000,000 − $2,400,000 − $400,000) = $200,000
ROI = $200,000 ÷ $5,000,000 = 4%

(b) (1) Contribution margin percentage is 20%, or ($600,000 ÷ $3,000,000)
Increase in controllable margin = $300,000 × 20% = $60,000
ROI = ($200,000 + $60,000) ÷ $5,000,000 = 5.2%

(2) ($200,000 + $100,000) ÷ $5,000,000 = 6%
(3) $200,000 ÷ [$5,000,000 − ($5,000,000 × .04)] = 4.2%

PRACTICE PROBLEM

Prepare flexible budget report. (LO 2)

Glenda Company uses a flexible budget for manufacturing overhead based on direct labor hours. For 2017, the master overhead budget for the Packaging Department based on 300,000 direct labor hours was as follows.

Variable Costs		Fixed Costs	
Indirect labor	$360,000	Supervision	$ 60,000
Supplies and lubricants	150,000	Depreciation	24,000
Maintenance	210,000	Property taxes	18,000
Utilities	120,000	Insurance	12,000
	$840,000		$114,000

During July, 24,000 direct labor hours were worked. The company incurred the following variable costs in July: indirect labor $30,200, supplies and lubricants $11,600, maintenance $17,500, and utilities $9,200. Actual fixed overhead costs were the same as monthly budgeted fixed costs.

INSTRUCTIONS

Prepare a flexible budget report for the Packaging Department for July.

SOLUTION

GLENDA COMPANY
Manufacturing Overhead Budget Report (Flexible)
Packaging Department
For the Month Ended July 31, 2017

Direct labor hours (DLH)	Budget 24,000 DLH	Actual Costs 24,000 DLH	Difference: Favorable F Unfavorable U
Variable costs			
Indirect labor ($1.20[a])	$ 28,800	$30,200	$1,400 U
Supplies and lubricants ($0.50[a])	12,000	11,600	400 F
Maintenance ($0.70[a])	16,800	17,500	700 U
Utilities ($0.40[a])	9,600	9,200	400 F
Total variable	67,200	68,500	1,300 U
Fixed costs			
Supervision	$ 5,000[b]	$ 5,000	-0-
Depreciation	2,000[b]	2,000	-0-
Property taxes	1,500[b]	1,500	-0-
Insurance	1,000[b]	1,000	-0-
Total fixed	9,500	9,500	-0-
Total costs	$ 76,700	$78,000	$1,300 U

[a]$360,000 ÷ 300,000; $150,000 ÷ 300,000; $210,000 ÷ 300,000; $120,000 ÷ 300,000.
[b]Annual cost divided by 12.

WileyPLUS Brief Exercises, DO IT! Exercises, Exercises, Problems, and many additional resources are available for practice in WileyPLUS

NOTE: All asterisked Questions, Exercises, and Problems relate to material in the appendix to the chapter.

QUESTIONS

1. (a) What is budgetary control?
   (b) Fred Barone is describing budgetary control. What steps should be included in Fred's description?
2. The following purposes are part of a budgetary reporting system: (a) Determine efficient use of materials. (b) Control overhead costs. (c) Determine whether income objectives are being met. For each purpose, indicate the name of the report, the frequency of the report, and the primary recipient(s) of the report.
3. How may a budget report for the second quarter differ from a budget report for the first quarter?
4. Ken Bay questions the usefulness of a master sales budget in evaluating sales performance. Is there justification for Ken's concern? Explain.
5. Under what circumstances may a static budget be an appropriate basis for evaluating a manager's effectiveness in controlling costs?
6. "A flexible budget is really a series of static budgets." Is this true? Why?
7. The static manufacturing overhead budget based on 40,000 direct labor hours shows budgeted indirect labor costs of $54,000. During March, the department incurs $64,000 of indirect labor while working 45,000 direct labor hours. Is this a favorable or unfavorable performance? Why?
8. A static overhead budget based on 40,000 direct labor hours shows Factory Insurance $6,500 as a fixed cost. At the 50,000 direct labor hours worked in March, factory insurance costs were $6,300. Is this a favorable or unfavorable performance? Why?
9. Megan Pedigo is confused about how a flexible budget is prepared. Identify the steps for Megan.
10. Cali Company has prepared a graph of flexible budget data. At zero direct labor hours, the total budgeted cost line intersects the vertical axis at $20,000. At 10,000 direct labor hours, the line drawn from the total budgeted cost line intersects the vertical axis at $85,000. How may the fixed and variable costs be expressed?
11. The flexible budget formula is fixed costs $50,000 plus variable costs of $4 per direct labor hour. What is the total budgeted cost at (a) 9,000 hours and (b) 12,345 hours?
12. What is management by exception? What criteria may be used in identifying exceptions?
13. What is responsibility accounting? Explain the purpose of responsibility accounting.
14. Eve Rooney is studying for an accounting examination. Describe for Eve what conditions are necessary for responsibility accounting to be used effectively.
15. Distinguish between controllable and noncontrollable costs.
16. How do responsibility reports differ from budget reports?
17. What is the relationship, if any, between a responsibility reporting system and a company's organization chart?
18. Distinguish among the three types of responsibility centers.
19. (a) What costs are included in a performance report for a cost center? (b) In the report, are variable and fixed costs identified?
20. How do direct fixed costs differ from indirect fixed costs? Are both types of fixed costs controllable?
21. Jane Nott is confused about controllable margin reported in an income statement for a profit center. How is this margin computed, and what is its primary purpose?
22. What is the primary basis for evaluating the performance of the manager of an investment center? Indicate the formula for this basis.
23. Explain the ways that ROI can be improved.
24. Indicate two behavioral principles that pertain to (a) the manager being evaluated and (b) top management.

*25. What is a major disadvantage of using ROI to evaluate investment and company performance?

*26. What is residual income, and what is one of its major weaknesses?

BRIEF EXERCISES

Prepare static budget report.
(LO 1), AP

BE22-1 For the quarter ended March 31, 2017, Croix Company accumulates the following sales data for its newest guitar, The Edge: $315,000 budget; $305,000 actual. Prepare a static budget report for the quarter.

Prepare static budget report for 2 quarters.
(LO 1), AP

BE22-2 Data for Croix Company are given in BE22-1. In the second quarter, budgeted sales were $380,000, and actual sales were $384,000. Prepare a static budget report for the second quarter and for the year to date.

BE22-3 In Rooney Company, direct labor is $20 per hour. The company expects to operate at 10,000 direct labor hours each month. In January 2017, direct labor totaling $206,000 is incurred in working 10,400 hours. Prepare (a) a static budget report and (b) a flexible budget report. Evaluate the usefulness of each report.

Show usefulness of flexible budgets in evaluating performance.

(LO 2), E

BE22-4 Gundy Company expects to produce 1,200,000 units of Product XX in 2017. Monthly production is expected to range from 80,000 to 120,000 units. Budgeted variable manufacturing costs per unit are direct materials $5, direct labor $6, and overhead $8. Budgeted fixed manufacturing costs per unit for depreciation are $2 and for supervision are $1. Prepare a flexible manufacturing budget for the relevant range value using 20,000 unit increments.

Prepare a flexible budget for variable costs.

(LO 2), AP

BE22-5 Data for Gundy Company are given in BE22-4. In March 2017, the company incurs the following costs in producing 100,000 units: direct materials $520,000, direct labor $596,000, and variable overhead $805,000. Actual fixed costs were equal to budgeted fixed costs. Prepare a flexible budget report for March. Were costs controlled?

Prepare flexible budget report.

(LO 2), AN

BE22-6 In the Assembly Department of Hannon Company, budgeted and actual manufacturing overhead costs for the month of April 2017 were as follows.

Prepare a responsibility report for a cost center.

(LO 3), AP

	Budget	Actual
Indirect materials	$16,000	$14,300
Indirect labor	20,000	20,600
Utilities	10,000	10,850
Supervision	5,000	5,000

All costs are controllable by the department manager. Prepare a responsibility report for April for the cost center.

BE22-7 Torres Company accumulates the following summary data for the year ending December 31, 2017, for its Water Division, which it operates as a profit center: sales—$2,000,000 budget, $2,080,000 actual; variable costs—$1,000,000 budget, $1,050,000 actual; and controllable fixed costs—$300,000 budget, $305,000 actual. Prepare a responsibility report for the Water Division.

Prepare a responsibility report for a profit center.

(LO 3), AP

BE22-8 For the year ending December 31, 2017, Cobb Company accumulates the following data for the Plastics Division which it operates as an investment center: contribution margin—$700,000 budget, $710,000 actual; controllable fixed costs—$300,000 budget, $302,000 actual. Average operating assets for the year were $2,000,000. Prepare a responsibility report for the Plastics Division beginning with contribution margin.

Prepare a responsibility report for an investment center.

(LO 4), AP

BE22-9 For its three investment centers, Gerrard Company accumulates the following data:

Compute return on investment using the ROI formula.

(LO 4), AP

	I	II	III
Sales	$2,000,000	$4,000,000	$ 4,000,000
Controllable margin	1,400,000	2,000,000	3,600,000
Average operating assets	5,000,000	8,000,000	10,000,000

Compute the return on investment (ROI) for each center.

BE22-10 Data for the investment centers for Gerrard Company are given in BE22-9. The centers expect the following changes in the next year: (I) increase sales 15%, (II) decrease costs $400,000, and (III) decrease average operating assets $500,000. Compute the expected return on investment (ROI) for each center. Assume center I has a controllable margin percentage of 70%.

Compute return on investment under changed conditions.

(LO 4), AP

***BE22-11** Sterling, Inc. reports the following financial information.

Compute ROI and residual income.

(LO 5), AP

Average operating assets	$3,000,000
Controllable margin	$ 630,000
Minimum rate of return	10%

Compute the return on investment and the residual income.

Compute ROI and residual income.

(LO 5), AP

***BE22-12** Presented below is information related to the Southern Division of Lumber, Inc.

Contribution margin	$1,200,000
Controllable margin	$ 800,000
Average operating assets	$4,000,000
Minimum rate of return	15%

Compute the Southern Division's return on investment and residual income.

DO IT! EXERCISES

Prepare and evaluate a static budget report.

(LO 1), AP

DO IT! 22-1 Wade Company estimates that it will produce 6,000 units of product IOA during the current month. Budgeted variable manufacturing costs per unit are direct materials $7, direct labor $13, and overhead $18. Monthly budgeted fixed manufacturing overhead costs are $8,000 for depreciation and $3,800 for supervision.

In the current month, Wade actually produced 6,500 units and incurred the following costs: direct materials $38,850, direct labor $76,440, variable overhead $116,640, depreciation $8,000, and supervision $4,000.

Prepare a static budget report. *Hint:* The Budget column is based on estimated production while the Actual column is the actual cost incurred during the period. (*Note:* You do not need to prepare the heading.) Were costs controlled? Discuss limitations of the budget.

Compute total budgeted costs in flexible budget.

(LO 2), AP

DO IT! 22-2 In Pargo Company's flexible budget graph, the fixed cost line and the total budgeted cost line intersect the vertical axis at $90,000. The total budgeted cost line is $350,000 at an activity level of 50,000 direct labor hours. Compute total budgeted costs at 65,000 direct labor hours.

Prepare a responsibility report.

(LO 3), AP

DO IT! 22-3 The Rockies Division operates as a profit center. It reports the following for the year.

	Budget	Actual
Sales	$2,000,000	$1,890,000
Variable costs	800,000	760,000
Controllable fixed costs	550,000	550,000
Noncontrollable fixed costs	250,000	250,000

Prepare a responsibility report for the Rockies Division at December 31, 2017.

Compute ROI and expected return on investments.

(LO 4), AP

DO IT! 22-4 The service division of Raney Industries reported the following results for 2017.

Sales	$500,000
Variable costs	300,000
Controllable fixed costs	75,000
Average operating assets	625,000

Management is considering the following independent courses of action in 2018 in order to maximize the return on investment for this division.

1. Reduce average operating assets by $125,000, with no change in controllable margin.
2. Increase sales $100,000, with no change in the contribution margin percentage.

(a) Compute the controllable margin and the return on investment for 2017. (b) Compute the controllable margin and the expected return on investment for each proposed alternative.

EXERCISES

Understand the concept of budgetary control.

(LO 1, 2), K

E22-1 Connie Rice has prepared the following list of statements about budgetary control.

1. Budget reports compare actual results with planned objectives.
2. All budget reports are prepared on a weekly basis.
3. Management uses budget reports to analyze differences between actual and planned results and determine their causes.

4. As a result of analyzing budget reports, management may either take corrective action or modify future plans.
5. Budgetary control works best when a company has an informal reporting system.
6. The primary recipients of the sales report are the sales manager and the production supervisor.
7. The primary recipient of the scrap report is the production manager.
8. A static budget is a projection of budget data at one level of activity.
9. Top management's reaction to unfavorable differences is not influenced by the materiality of the difference.
10. A static budget is not appropriate in evaluating a manager's effectiveness in controlling costs unless the actual activity level approximates the static budget activity level or the behavior of the costs is fixed.

Instructions

Identify each statement as true or false. If false, indicate how to correct the statement.

Prepare and evaluate static budget report.

(LO 1), AN

E22-2 Crede Company budgeted selling expenses of $30,000 in January, $35,000 in February, and $40,000 in March. Actual selling expenses were $31,200 in January, $34,525 in February, and $46,000 in March.

Instructions

(a) Prepare a selling expense report that compares budgeted and actual amounts by month and for the year to date.
(b) What is the purpose of the report prepared in (a), and who would be the primary recipient?
(c) What would be the likely result of management's analysis of the report?

Prepare flexible manufacturing overhead budget.

(LO 2), AP

E22-3 Myers Company uses a flexible budget for manufacturing overhead based on direct labor hours. Variable manufacturing overhead costs per direct labor hour are as follows.

Indirect labor	$1.00
Indirect materials	0.70
Utilities	0.40

Fixed overhead costs per month are supervision $4,000, depreciation $1,200, and property taxes $800. The company believes it will normally operate in a range of 7,000–10,000 direct labor hours per month.

Instructions

Prepare a monthly manufacturing overhead flexible budget for 2017 for the expected range of activity, using increments of 1,000 direct labor hours.

Prepare flexible budget reports for manufacturing overhead costs, and comment on findings.

(LO 2), AN

E22-4 Using the information in E22-3, assume that in July 2017, Myers Company incurs the following manufacturing overhead costs.

Variable Costs		Fixed Costs	
Indirect labor	$8,800	Supervision	$4,000
Indirect materials	5,800	Depreciation	1,200
Utilities	3,200	Property taxes	800

Instructions

(a) Prepare a flexible budget performance report, assuming that the company worked 9,000 direct labor hours during the month.
(b) Prepare a flexible budget performance report, assuming that the company worked 8,500 direct labor hours during the month.
(c) Comment on your findings.

Prepare flexible selling expense budget.

(LO 2), AP

E22-5 Fallon Company uses flexible budgets to control its selling expenses. Monthly sales are expected to range from $170,000 to $200,000. Variable costs and their percentage relationship to sales are sales commissions 6%, advertising 4%, traveling 3%, and delivery 2%. Fixed selling expenses will consist of sales salaries $35,000, depreciation on delivery equipment $7,000, and insurance on delivery equipment $1,000.

Instructions

Prepare a monthly flexible budget for each $10,000 increment of sales within the relevant range for the year ending December 31, 2017.

Prepare flexible budget reports for selling expenses.

(LO 2), AN

E22-6 The actual selling expenses incurred in March 2017 by Fallon Company are as follows.

Variable Expenses		Fixed Expenses	
Sales commissions	$11,000	Sales salaries	$35,000
Advertising	6,900	Depreciation	7,000
Travel	5,100	Insurance	1,000
Delivery	3,450		

Instructions

(a) Prepare a flexible budget performance report for March using the budget data in E22-5, assuming that March sales were $170,000.

(b) Prepare a flexible budget performance report, assuming that March sales were $180,000.

(c) Comment on the importance of using flexible budgets in evaluating the performance of the sales manager.

Prepare flexible budget report.

(LO 2), AP

E22-7 Appliance Possible Inc. (AP) is a manufacturer of toaster ovens. To improve control over operations, the president of AP wants to begin using a flexible budgeting system, rather than use only the current master budget. The following data are available for AP's expected costs at production levels of 90,000, 100,000, and 110,000 units.

Variable costs	
Manufacturing	$6 per unit
Administrative	$4 per unit
Selling	$3 per unit
Fixed costs	
Manufacturing	$160,000
Administrative	$ 80,000

Instructions

(a) Prepare a flexible budget for each of the possible production levels: 90,000, 100,000, and 110,000 units.

(b) If AP sells the toaster ovens for $16 each, how many units will it have to sell to make a profit of $60,000 before taxes?

(CGA adapted)

Prepare flexible budget report; compare flexible and static budgets.

(LO 1, 2), E

E22-8 Rensing Groomers is in the dog-grooming business. Its operating costs are described by the following formulas:

Grooming supplies (variable)	$y = \$0 + \$5x$
Direct labor (variable)	$y = \$0 + \$14x$
Overhead (mixed)	$y = \$10,000 + \$1x$

Milo, the owner, has determined that direct labor is the cost driver for all three categories of costs.

Instructions

(a) Prepare a flexible budget for activity levels of 550, 600, and 700 direct labor hours.

(b) Explain why the flexible budget is more informative than the static budget.

(c) Calculate the total cost per direct labor hour at each of the activity levels specified in part (a).

(d) The groomers at Rensing normally work a total of 650 direct labor hours during each month. Each grooming job normally takes a groomer 1.3 hours. Milo wants to earn a profit equal to 40% of the costs incurred. Determine what he should charge each pet owner for grooming.

(CGA adapted)

Prepare flexible budget report, and answer question.

(LO 1, 2), E

E22-9 As sales manager, Joe Batista was given the following static budget report for selling expenses in the Clothing Department of Soria Company for the month of October.

SORIA COMPANY
Clothing Department
Budget Report
For the Month Ended October 31, 2017

	Budget	Actual	Difference Favorable F Unfavorable U
Sales in units	8,000	10,000	2,000 F
Variable expenses			
Sales commissions	$ 2,400	$ 2,600	$ 200 U
Advertising expense	720	850	130 U
Travel expense	3,600	4,100	500 U
Free samples given out	1,600	1,400	200 F
Total variable	8,320	8,950	630 U
Fixed expenses			
Rent	1,500	1,500	–0–
Sales salaries	1,200	1,200	–0–
Office salaries	800	800	–0–
Depreciation—autos (sales staff)	500	500	–0–
Total fixed	4,000	4,000	–0–
Total expenses	$12,320	$12,950	$ 630 U

As a result of this budget report, Joe was called into the president's office and congratulated on his fine sales performance. He was reprimanded, however, for allowing his costs to get out of control. Joe knew something was wrong with the performance report that he had been given. However, he was not sure what to do, and comes to you for advice.

Instructions

(a) Prepare a budget report based on flexible budget data to help Joe.
(b) Should Joe have been reprimanded? Explain.

Prepare flexible budget and responsibility report for manufacturing overhead.

(LO 2, 3), AP

E22-10 Chubbs Inc.'s manufacturing overhead budget for the first quarter of 2017 contained the following data.

Variable Costs		Fixed Costs	
Indirect materials	$12,000	Supervisory salaries	$36,000
Indirect labor	10,000	Depreciation	7,000
Utilities	8,000	Property taxes and insurance	8,000
Maintenance	6,000	Maintenance	5,000

Actual variable costs were indirect materials $13,500, indirect labor $9,500, utilities $8,700, and maintenance $5,000. Actual fixed costs equaled budgeted costs except for property taxes and insurance, which were $8,300. The actual activity level equaled the budgeted level.

All costs are considered controllable by the production department manager except for depreciation, and property taxes and insurance.

Instructions

(a) Prepare a manufacturing overhead flexible budget report for the first quarter.
(b) Prepare a responsibility report for the first quarter.

Prepare and discuss a responsibility report.

(LO 2, 3), AP

E22-11 UrLink Company is a newly formed company specializing in high-speed Internet service for home and business. The owner, Lenny Kirkland, had divided the company into two segments: Home Internet Service and Business Internet Service. Each segment is run by its own supervisor, while basic selling and administrative services are shared by both segments.

Lenny has asked you to help him create a performance reporting system that will allow him to measure each segment's performance in terms of its profitability. To that end, the following information has been collected on the Home Internet Service segment for the first quarter of 2017.

	Budget	Actual
Service revenue	$25,000	$26,200
Allocated portion of:		
Building depreciation	11,000	11,000
Advertising	5,000	4,200
Billing	3,500	3,000
Property taxes	1,200	1,000
Material and supplies	1,600	1,200
Supervisory salaries	9,000	9,500
Insurance	4,000	3,900
Wages	3,000	3,250
Gas and oil	2,800	3,400
Equipment depreciation	1,500	1,300

Instructions

(a) Prepare a responsibility report for the first quarter of 2017 for the Home Internet Service segment.

(b) Write a memo to Lenny Kirkland discussing the principles that should be used when preparing performance reports.

State total budgeted cost formulas, and prepare flexible budget graph.

(LO 2), AP

E22-12 Venetian Company has two production departments, Fabricating and Assembling. At a department managers' meeting, the controller uses flexible budget graphs to explain total budgeted costs. Separate graphs based on direct labor hours are used for each department. The graphs show the following.

1. At zero direct labor hours, the total budgeted cost line and the fixed cost line intersect the vertical axis at $50,000 in the Fabricating Department and $40,000 in the Assembling Department.
2. At normal capacity of 50,000 direct labor hours, the line drawn from the total budgeted cost line intersects the vertical axis at $150,000 in the Fabricating Department, and $120,000 in the Assembling Department.

Instructions

(a) State the total budgeted cost formula for each department.

(b) Compute the total budgeted cost for each department, assuming actual direct labor hours worked were 53,000 and 47,000, in the Fabricating and Assembling Departments, respectively.

(c) Prepare the flexible budget graph for the Fabricating Department, assuming the maximum direct labor hours in the relevant range is 100,000. Use increments of 10,000 direct labor hours on the horizontal axis and increments of $50,000 on the vertical axis.

Prepare reports in a responsibility reporting system.

(LO 3), AP

E22-13 Fey Company's organization chart includes the president; the vice president of production; three assembly plants—Dallas, Atlanta, and Tucson; and two departments within each plant—Machining and Finishing. Budget and actual manufacturing cost data for July 2017 are as follows.

Finishing Department—Dallas: direct materials $42,500 actual, $44,000 budget; direct labor $83,400 actual, $82,000 budget; manufacturing overhead $51,000 actual, $49,200 budget.

Machining Department—Dallas: total manufacturing costs $220,000 actual, $219,000 budget.

Atlanta Plant: total manufacturing costs $424,000 actual, $420,000 budget.

Tucson Plant: total manufacturing costs $494,200 actual, $496,500 budget.

The Dallas plant manager's office costs were $95,000 actual and $92,000 budget. The vice president of production's office costs were $132,000 actual and $130,000 budget. Office costs are not allocated to departments and plants.

Instructions

Using the format shown in Illustration 22-19 (page 1081), prepare the reports in a responsibility system for:

(a) The Finishing Department—Dallas.

(b) The plant manager—Dallas.

(c) The vice president of production.

E22-14 The Mixing Department manager of Malone Company is able to control all overhead costs except rent, property taxes, and salaries. Budgeted monthly overhead costs for the Mixing Department, in alphabetical order, are:

Prepare a responsibility report for a cost center.

(LO 3), AN

Indirect labor	$12,000	Property taxes	$ 1,000
Indirect materials	7,700	Rent	1,800
Lubricants	1,675	Salaries	10,000
Maintenance	3,500	Utilities	5,000

Actual costs incurred for January 2017 are indirect labor $12,250; indirect materials $10,200; lubricants $1,650; maintenance $3,500; property taxes $1,100; rent $1,800; salaries $10,000; and utilities $6,400.

Instructions

(a) Prepare a responsibility report for January 2017.

(b) What would be the likely result of management's analysis of the report?

E22-15 Horatio Inc. has three divisions which are operated as profit centers. Actual operating data for the divisions listed alphabetically are as follows.

Compute missing amounts in responsibility reports for three profit centers, and prepare a report.

(LO 3), AN

Operating Data	Women's Shoes	Men's Shoes	Children's Shoes
Contribution margin	$270,000	(3)	$180,000
Controllable fixed costs	100,000	(4)	(5)
Controllable margin	(1)	$ 90,000	95,000
Sales	600,000	450,000	(6)
Variable costs	(2)	320,000	250,000

Instructions

(a) Compute the missing amounts. Show computations.

(b) Prepare a responsibility report for the Women's Shoes Division assuming (1) the data are for the month ended June 30, 2017, and (2) all data equal budget except variable costs which are $5,000 over budget.

E22-16 The Sports Equipment Division of Harrington Company is operated as a profit center. Sales for the division were budgeted for 2017 at $900,000. The only variable costs budgeted for the division were cost of goods sold ($440,000) and selling and administrative ($60,000). Fixed costs were budgeted at $100,000 for cost of goods sold, $90,000 for selling and administrative, and $70,000 for noncontrollable fixed costs. Actual results for these items were:

Prepare a responsibility report for a profit center, and compute ROI.

(LO 3, 4), AP

Sales	$880,000
Cost of goods sold	
Variable	408,000
Fixed	105,000
Selling and administrative	
Variable	61,000
Fixed	66,000
Noncontrollable fixed	90,000

Instructions

(a) Prepare a responsibility report for the Sports Equipment Division for 2017.

(b) Assume the division is an investment center, and average operating assets were $1,000,000. The noncontrollable fixed costs are controllable at the investment center level. Compute ROI.

E22-17 The South Division of Wiig Company reported the following data for the current year.

Compute ROI for current year and for possible future changes.

(LO 4), AP

Sales	$3,000,000
Variable costs	1,950,000
Controllable fixed costs	600,000
Average operating assets	5,000,000

Top management is unhappy with the investment center's return on investment (ROI). It asks the manager of the South Division to submit plans to improve ROI in the next year. The manager believes it is feasible to consider the following independent courses of action.

1. Increase sales by $300,000 with no change in the contribution margin percentage.
2. Reduce variable costs by $150,000.
3. Reduce average operating assets by 4%.

Instructions

(a) Compute the return on investment (ROI) for the current year.
(b) Using the ROI formula, compute the ROI under each of the proposed courses of action. (Round to one decimal.)

Prepare a responsibility report for an investment center.
(LO 4), AP

E22-18 The Dinkle and Frizell Dental Clinic provides both preventive and orthodontic dental services. The two owners, Reese Dinkle and Anita Frizell, operate the clinic as two separate investment centers: Preventive Services and Orthodontic Services. Each of them is in charge of one of the centers: Reese for Preventive Services and Anita for Orthodontic Services. Each month, they prepare an income statement for the two centers to evaluate performance and make decisions about how to improve the operational efficiency and profitability of the clinic.

Recently, they have been concerned about the profitability of the Preventive Services operations. For several months, it has been reporting a loss. The responsibility report for the month of May 2017 is shown below.

	Actual	Difference from Budget
Service revenue	$ 40,000	$1,000 F
Variable costs		
Filling materials	5,000	100 U
Novocain	3,900	100 U
Supplies	1,900	350 F
Dental assistant wages	2,500	–0–
Utilities	500	110 U
Total variable costs	13,800	40 F
Fixed costs		
Allocated portion of receptionist's salary	3,000	200 U
Dentist salary	9,800	400 U
Equipment depreciation	6,000	–0–
Allocated portion of building depreciation	15,000	1,000 U
Total fixed costs	33,800	1,600 U
Operating income (loss)	$ (7,600)	$ 560 U

In addition, the owners know that the investment in operating assets at the beginning of the month was $82,400, and it was $77,600 at the end of the month. They have asked for your assistance in evaluating their current performance reporting system.

Instructions

(a) Prepare a responsibility report for an investment center as illustrated in the chapter.
(b) Write a memo to the owners discussing the deficiencies of their current reporting system.

Prepare missing amounts in responsibility reports for three investment centers.
(LO 4), AN

E22-19 The Ferrell Transportation Company uses a responsibility reporting system to measure the performance of its three investment centers: Planes, Taxis, and Limos. Segment performance is measured using a system of responsibility reports and return on investment calculations. The allocation of resources within the company and the segment managers' bonuses are based in part on the results shown in these reports.

Recently, the company was the victim of a computer virus that deleted portions of the company's accounting records. This was discovered when the current period's responsibility reports were being prepared. The printout of the actual operating results appeared as follows.

	Planes	Taxis	Limos
Service revenue	$?	$500,000	$?
Variable costs	5,500,000	?	300,000
Contribution margin	?	250,000	480,000
Controllable fixed costs	1,500,000	?	?
Controllable margin	?	80,000	210,000
Average operating assets	25,000,000	?	1,500,000
Return on investment	12%	10%	?

Instructions

Determine the missing pieces of information above.

***E22-20** Presented below is selected information for three regional divisions of Medina Company.

Compare ROI and residual income.

(LO 5), AN

	Divisions		
	North	West	South
Contribution margin	$ 300,000	$ 500,000	$ 400,000
Controllable margin	$ 140,000	$ 360,000	$ 210,000
Average operating assets	$1,000,000	$2,000,000	$1,500,000
Minimum rate of return	13%	16%	10%

Instructions

(a) Compute the return on investment for each division.
(b) Compute the residual income for each division.
(c) Assume that each division has an investment opportunity that would provide a rate of return of 16%.
   (1) If ROI is used to measure performance, which division or divisions will probably make the additional investment?
   (2) If residual income is used to measure performance, which division or divisions will probably make the additional investment?

***E22-21** Presented below is selected financial information for two divisions of Samberg Brewing.

Fill in information related to ROI and residual income.

(LO 5), AN

	Lager	Lite Lager
Contribution margin	$500,000	$ 300,000
Controllable margin	200,000	(c)
Average operating assets	(a)	$1,200,000
Minimum rate of return	(b)	11%
Return on investment	16%	(d)
Residual income	$100,000	$ 204,000

Instructions

Supply the missing information for the lettered items.

▶ EXERCISES: SET B AND CHALLENGE EXERCISES

Visit the book's companion website, at **www.wiley.com/college/kimmel**, and choose the Student Companion site to access Exercises: Set B and Challenge Exercises.

▶ PROBLEMS: SET A

P22-1A Bumblebee Company estimates that 300,000 direct labor hours will be worked during the coming year, 2017, in the Packaging Department. On this basis, the following budgeted manufacturing overhead cost data are computed for the year.

Prepare flexible budget and budget report for manufacturing overhead.

(LO 2), AN

XLS

Fixed Overhead Costs		Variable Overhead Costs	
Supervision	$ 96,000	Indirect labor	$126,000
Depreciation	72,000	Indirect materials	90,000
Insurance	30,000	Repairs	69,000
Rent	24,000	Utilities	72,000
Property taxes	18,000	Lubricants	18,000
	$240,000		$375,000

It is estimated that direct labor hours worked each month will range from 27,000 to 36,000 hours.

During October, 27,000 direct labor hours were worked and the following overhead costs were incurred.

Fixed overhead costs: supervision $8,000, depreciation $6,000, insurance $2,460, rent $2,000, and property taxes $1,500.

Variable overhead costs: indirect labor $12,432, indirect materials $7,680, repairs $6,100, utilities $6,840, and lubricants $1,920.

(a) Total costs: DLH 27,000, $53,750; DLH 36,000, $65,000
(b) Total $1,182 U

Instructions

(a) Prepare a monthly manufacturing overhead flexible budget for each increment of 3,000 direct labor hours over the relevant range for the year ending December 31, 2017.
(b) Prepare a flexible budget report for October.
(c) Comment on management's efficiency in controlling manufacturing overhead costs in October.

Prepare flexible budget, budget report, and graph for manufacturing overhead.

(LO 2), E

P22-2A Zelmer Company manufactures tablecloths. Sales have grown rapidly over the past 2 years. As a result, the president has installed a budgetary control system for 2017. The following data were used in developing the master manufacturing overhead budget for the Ironing Department, which is based on an activity index of direct labor hours.

Variable Costs	Rate per Direct Labor Hour	Annual Fixed Costs	
Indirect labor	$0.40	Supervision	$48,000
Indirect materials	0.50	Depreciation	18,000
Factory utilities	0.30	Insurance	12,000
Factory repairs	0.20	Rent	30,000

The master overhead budget was prepared on the expectation that 480,000 direct labor hours will be worked during the year. In June, 41,000 direct labor hours were worked. At that level of activity, actual costs were as shown below.

Variable—per direct labor hour: indirect labor $0.44, indirect materials $0.48, factory utilities $0.32, and factory repairs $0.25.

Fixed: same as budgeted.

(a) Total costs: 35,000 DLH, $58,000; 50,000 DLH, $79,000
(b) Budget $66,400
Actual $70,090

Instructions

(a) Prepare a monthly manufacturing overhead flexible budget for the year ending December 31, 2017, assuming production levels range from 35,000 to 50,000 direct labor hours. Use increments of 5,000 direct labor hours.
(b) Prepare a budget report for June comparing actual results with budget data based on the flexible budget.
(c) Were costs effectively controlled? Explain.
(d) State the formula for computing the total budgeted costs for the Ironing Department.
(e) Prepare the flexible budget graph, showing total budgeted costs at 35,000 and 45,000 direct labor hours. Use increments of 5,000 direct labor hours on the horizontal axis and increments of $10,000 on the vertical axis.

State total budgeted cost formula, and prepare flexible budget reports for 2 time periods.

(LO 1, 2), AN

XLS

P22-3A Ratchet Company uses budgets in controlling costs. The August 2017 budget report for the company's Assembling Department is as follows.

RATCHET COMPANY
Budget Report
Assembling Department
For the Month Ended August 31, 2017

Manufacturing Costs	Budget	Actual	Difference Favorable F Unfavorable U
Variable costs			
Direct materials	$ 48,000	$ 47,000	$1,000 F
Direct labor	54,000	51,200	2,800 F
Indirect materials	24,000	24,200	200 U
Indirect labor	18,000	17,500	500 F
Utilities	15,000	14,900	100 F
Maintenance	12,000	12,400	400 U
Total variable	171,000	167,200	3,800 F
Fixed costs			
Rent	12,000	12,000	–0–
Supervision	17,000	17,000	–0–
Depreciation	6,000	6,000	–0–
Total fixed	35,000	35,000	–0–
Total costs	$206,000	$202,200	$3,800 F

The monthly budget amounts in the report were based on an expected production of 60,000 units per month or 720,000 units per year. The Assembling Department manager is pleased with the report and expects a raise, or at least praise for a job well done. The company president, however, is unhappy with the results for August because only 58,000 units were produced.

Instructions

(a) State the total monthly budgeted cost formula.

(b) Prepare a budget report for August using flexible budget data. Why does this report provide a better basis for evaluating performance than the report based on static budget data?

(b) Budget $200,300

(c) In September, 64,000 units were produced. Prepare the budget report using flexible budget data, assuming (1) each variable cost was 10% higher than its actual cost in August, and (2) fixed costs were the same in September as in August.

(c) Budget $217,400
Actual $218,920

P22-4A Clarke Inc. operates the Patio Furniture Division as a profit center. Operating data for this division for the year ended December 31, 2017, are as shown below.

Prepare responsibility report for a profit center.

(LO 3), AN

	Budget	Difference from Budget
Sales	$2,500,000	$50,000 F
Cost of goods sold		
Variable	1,300,000	41,000 F
Controllable fixed	200,000	3,000 U
Selling and administrative		
Variable	220,000	6,000 U
Controllable fixed	50,000	2,000 U
Noncontrollable fixed costs	70,000	4,000 U

In addition, Clarke incurs $180,000 of indirect fixed costs that were budgeted at $175,000. Twenty percent (20%) of these costs are allocated to the Patio Furniture Division.

Instructions

(a) Prepare a responsibility report for the Patio Furniture Division for the year.

(b) Comment on the manager's performance in controlling revenues and costs.

(c) Identify any costs excluded from the responsibility report and explain why they were excluded.

(a) Contribution margin $85,000 F
Controllable margin $80,000 F

Prepare responsibility report for an investment center, and compute ROI.

(LO 4), E

P22-5A Optimus Company manufactures a variety of tools and industrial equipment. The company operates through three divisions. Each division is an investment center. Operating data for the Home Division for the year ended December 31, 2017, and relevant budget data are as follows.

	Actual	Comparison with Budget
Sales	$1,400,000	$100,000 favorable
Variable cost of goods sold	665,000	45,000 unfavorable
Variable selling and administrative expenses	125,000	25,000 unfavorable
Controllable fixed cost of goods sold	170,000	On target
Controllable fixed selling and administrative expenses	80,000	On target

Average operating assets for the year for the Home Division were $2,000,000 which was also the budgeted amount.

Instructions

(a) Prepare a responsibility report (in thousands of dollars) for the Home Division.

(b) Evaluate the manager's performance. Which items will likely be investigated by top management?

(c) Compute the expected ROI in 2017 for the Home Division, assuming the following independent changes to actual data.

(1) Variable cost of goods sold is decreased by 5%.

(2) Average operating assets are decreased by 10%.

(3) Sales are increased by $200,000, and this increase is expected to increase contribution margin by $80,000.

(a) Controllable margin: Budget $330; Actual $360

Prepare reports for cost centers under responsibility accounting, and comment on performance of managers.

(LO 3), AN

P22-6A Durham Company uses a responsibility reporting system. It has divisions in Denver, Seattle, and San Diego. Each division has three production departments: Cutting, Shaping, and Finishing. The responsibility for each department rests with a manager who reports to the division production manager. Each division manager reports to the vice president of production. There are also vice presidents for marketing and finance. All vice presidents report to the president.

In January 2017, controllable actual and budget manufacturing overhead cost data for the departments and divisions were as shown below.

Manufacturing Overhead	Actual	Budget
Individual costs—Cutting Department—Seattle		
Indirect labor	$ 73,000	$ 70,000
Indirect materials	47,900	46,000
Maintenance	20,500	18,000
Utilities	20,100	17,000
Supervision	22,000	20,000
	$183,500	$171,000
Total costs		
Shaping Department—Seattle	$158,000	$148,000
Finishing Department—Seattle	210,000	205,000
Denver division	678,000	673,000
San Diego division	722,000	715,000

Additional overhead costs were incurred as follows: Seattle division production manager—actual costs $52,500, budget $51,000; vice president of production—actual costs $65,000, budget $64,000; president—actual costs $76,400, budget $74,200. These expenses are not allocated.

The vice presidents who report to the president, other than the vice president of production, had the following expenses.

Vice President	Actual	Budget
Marketing	$133,600	$130,000
Finance	109,000	104,000

Instructions

(a) Using the format on page 1081, prepare the following responsibility reports.
    (1) Manufacturing overhead—Cutting Department manager—Seattle division.
    (2) Manufacturing overhead—Seattle division manager.
    (3) Manufacturing overhead—vice president of production.
    (4) Manufacturing overhead and expenses—president.

(b) Comment on the comparative performances of:
    (1) Department managers in the Seattle division.
    (2) Division managers.
    (3) Vice presidents.

(a) (1) $12,500 U
(2) $29,000 U
(3) $42,000 U
(4) $52,800 U

Compare ROI and residual income.

(LO 5), AN

***P22-7A** Sentinel Industries has manufactured prefabricated houses for over 20 years. The houses are constructed in sections to be assembled on customers' lots. Sentinel expanded into the precut housing market when it acquired Jensen Company, one of its suppliers. In this market, various types of lumber are precut into the appropriate lengths, banded into packages, and shipped to customers' lots for assembly. Sentinel designated the Jensen Division as an investment center.

Sentinel uses return on investment (ROI) as a performance measure with investment defined as average operating assets. Management bonuses are based in part on ROI. All investments are expected to earn a minimum rate of return of 18%. Jensen's ROI has ranged from 20.1% to 23.5% since it was acquired. Jensen had an investment opportunity in 2017 that had an estimated ROI of 19%. Jensen management decided against the investment because it believed the investment would decrease the division's overall ROI.

Selected financial information for Jensen are presented below. The division's average operating assets were $12,300,000 for the year 2017.

SENTINEL INDUSTRIES
Jensen Division
Selected Financial Information
For the Year Ended December 31, 2017

Sales	$24,000,000
Contribution margin	9,100,000
Controllable margin	2,460,000

Instructions

(a) Calculate the following performance measures for 2017 for the Jensen Division.
    (1) Return on investment (ROI).
    (2) Residual income.

(b) Would the management of Jensen Division have been more likely to accept the investment opportunity it had in 2017 if residual income were used as a performance measure instead of ROI? Explain your answer.

(CMA adapted)

PROBLEMS: SET B AND SET C

Visit the book's companion website, at **www.wiley.com/college/kimmel**, and choose the Student Companion site to access Problems: Set B and Set C.

CONTINUING PROBLEMS

CURRENT DESIGNS

EXCEL TUTORIAL

CD22 The Current Designs staff has prepared the annual manufacturing budget for the rotomolded line based on an estimated annual production of 4,000 kayaks during 2017. Each kayak will require 54 pounds of polyethylene powder and a finishing kit (rope, seat, hardware, etc.). The polyethylene powder used in these kayaks costs $1.50 per pound, and the finishing kits cost $170 each. Each kayak will use two kinds of labor—2 hours of type I labor from people who run the oven and trim the plastic, and 3 hours of work from type II workers who attach the hatches and seat and other hardware. The type I employees are paid $15 per hour, and the type II are paid $12 per hour.

Manufacturing overhead is budgeted at $396,000 for 2017, broken down as follows.

Variable costs	
Indirect materials	$ 40,000
Manufacturing supplies	53,800
Maintenance and utilities	88,000
	181,800
Fixed costs	
Supervision	90,000
Insurance	14,400
Depreciation	109,800
	214,200
Total	$396,000

During the first quarter, ended March 31, 2017, 1,050 units were actually produced with the following costs.

Polyethylene powder	$ 87,000
Finishing kits	178,840
Type I labor	31,500
Type II labor	39,060
Indirect materials	10,500
Manufacturing supplies	14,150
Maintenance and utilities	26,000
Supervision	20,000
Insurance	3,600
Depreciation	27,450
Total	$438,100

Instructions

(a) Prepare the annual manufacturing budget for 2017, assuming that 4,000 kayaks will be produced.

(b) Prepare the flexible budget for manufacturing for the quarter ended March 31, 2017. Assume activity levels of 900, 1,000, and 1,050 units.

(c) Assuming the rotomolded line is treated as a profit center, prepare a flexible budget report for manufacturing for the quarter ended March 31, 2017, when 1,050 units were produced.

WATERWAYS

(*Note:* This is a continuation of the Waterways problem from Chapters 14–21.)

WP22 Waterways Corporation is continuing its budget preparations. This problem gives you static budget information as well as actual overhead costs, and asks you to calculate amounts related to budgetary control and responsibility accounting.

Go to the book's companion website, at **www.wiley.com/college/kimmel**, *to find the completion of this problem.*

EXPAND YOUR CRITICAL THINKING

Group Project

DECISION-MAKING ACROSS THE ORGANIZATION

E

CT22-1 Green Pastures is a 400-acre farm on the outskirts of the Kentucky Bluegrass, specializing in the boarding of broodmares and their foals. A recent economic downturn in the thoroughbred industry has led to a decline in breeding activities, and it has made the boarding business extremely competitive. To meet the competition, Green Pastures planned in 2017 to entertain clients, advertise more extensively, and absorb expenses formerly paid by clients such as veterinary and blacksmith fees.

The budget report for 2017 is presented below. As shown, the static income statement budget for the year is based on an expected 21,900 boarding days at $25 per mare. The variable expenses per mare per day were budgeted: feed $5, veterinary fees $3, blacksmith fees $0.25, and supplies $0.55. All other budgeted expenses were either semifixed or fixed.

During the year, management decided not to replace a worker who quit in March, but it did issue a new advertising brochure and did more entertaining of clients.[1]

GREEN PASTURES
Static Budget Income Statement
For the Year Ended December 31, 2017

	Actual	Master Budget	Difference
Number of mares	52	60	8 U
Number of boarding days	19,000	21,900	2,900 U
Sales	$380,000	$547,500	$167,500 U
Less: Variable expenses			
Feed	104,390	109,500	5,110 F
Veterinary fees	58,838	65,700	6,862 F
Blacksmith fees	4,984	5,475	491 F
Supplies	10,178	12,045	1,867 F
Total variable expenses	178,390	192,720	14,330 F
Contribution margin	201,610	354,780	153,170 U
Less: Fixed expenses			
Depreciation	40,000	40,000	–0–
Insurance	11,000	11,000	–0–
Utilities	12,000	14,000	2,000 F
Repairs and maintenance	10,000	11,000	1,000 F
Labor	88,000	95,000	7,000 F
Advertisement	12,000	8,000	4,000 U
Entertainment	7,000	5,000	2,000 U
Total fixed expenses	180,000	184,000	4,000 F
Net income	$ 21,610	$170,780	$149,170 U

Instructions

With the class divided into groups, answer the following.

(a) Based on the static budget report:
  (1) What was the primary cause(s) of the loss in net income?
  (2) Did management do a good, average, or poor job of controlling expenses?
  (3) Were management's decisions to stay competitive sound?

(b) Prepare a flexible budget report for the year.

(c) Based on the flexible budget report, answer the three questions in part (a) above.

(d) What course of action do you recommend for the management of Green Pastures?

MANAGERIAL ANALYSIS

CT22-2 Lanier Company manufactures expensive watch cases sold as souvenirs. Three of its sales departments are Retail Sales, Wholesale Sales, and Outlet Sales. The Retail Sales Department is a profit center. The Wholesale Sales Department is a cost center. Its managers merely take orders from customers who purchase through the company's wholesale AN

[1]Data for this case are based on Hans Sprohge and John Talbott, "New Applications for Variance Analysis," *Journal of Accountancy* (AICPA, New York), April 1989, pp. 137–141.

catalog. The Outlet Sales Department is an investment center because each manager is given full responsibility for an outlet store location. The manager can hire and discharge employees, purchase, maintain, and sell equipment, and in general is fairly independent of company control.

Mary Gammel is a manager in the Retail Sales Department. Stephen Flott manages the Wholesale Sales Department. Jose Gomez manages the Golden Gate Club outlet store in San Francisco. The following are the budget responsibility reports for each of the three departments.

Budget

	Retail Sales	Wholesale Sales	Outlet Sales
Sales	$ 750,000	$ 400,000	$200,000
Variable costs			
Cost of goods sold	150,000	100,000	25,000
Advertising	100,000	30,000	5,000
Sales salaries	75,000	15,000	3,000
Printing	10,000	20,000	5,000
Travel	20,000	30,000	2,000
Fixed costs			
Rent	50,000	30,000	10,000
Insurance	5,000	2,000	1,000
Depreciation	75,000	100,000	40,000
Investment in assets	1,000,000	1,200,000	800,000

Actual Results

	Retail Sales	Wholesale Sales	Outlet Sales
Sales	$ 750,000	$ 400,000	$200,000
Variable costs			
Cost of goods sold	192,000	122,000	26,500
Advertising	100,000	30,000	5,000
Sales salaries	75,000	15,000	3,000
Printing	10,000	20,000	5,000
Travel	14,000	21,000	1,500
Fixed costs			
Rent	40,000	50,000	12,300
Insurance	5,000	2,000	1,000
Depreciation	80,000	90,000	56,000
Investment in assets	1,000,000	1,200,000	800,000

Instructions

(a) Determine which of the items should be included in the responsibility report for each of the three managers.

(b) Compare the budgeted measures with the actual results. Decide which results should be called to the attention of each manager.

REAL-WORLD FOCUS

AP **CT22-3** Computer Associates International, Inc., the world's leading business software company, delivers the end-to-end infrastructure to enable e-business through innovative technology, services, and education. Recently, Computer Associates had 19,000 employees worldwide and revenue of over $6 billion.

The following information is from the company's annual report.

COMPUTER ASSOCIATES INTERNATIONAL, INC.
Management Discussion

The Company has experienced a pattern of business whereby revenue for its third and fourth fiscal quarters reflects an increase over first- and second-quarter revenue. The Company attributes this increase to clients' increased spending at the end of their calendar year budgetary periods and the culmination of its annual sales plan. Since the Company's costs do not increase proportionately with the third- and fourth-quarters' increase in revenue, the higher revenue in these quarters results in greater profit margins and income. Fourth-quarter profitability is traditionally affected by significant new hirings, training, and education expenditures for the succeeding year.

Instructions

(a) Why don't the company's costs increase proportionately as the revenues increase in the third and fourth quarters?
(b) What type of budgeting seems appropriate for the Computer Associates situation?

CT22-4 There are many useful resources regarding budgeting available on websites. The following activity investigates the results of a comprehensive budgeting study. C

Address: **http://www.accountingweb.com/whitepapers/centage_ioma.pdf,** or go to **www.wiley.com/college/kimmel**

Instructions

Go to the address above and then answer the following questions.

(a) What are cited as the two most common "pain points" of budgeting?
(b) What percentage of companies that participated in the survey said that they prepare annual budgets? Of those that prepare budgets, what percentage say that they start the budgeting process by first generating sales projections?
(c) What is the most common amount of time for the annual budgeting process?
(d) When evaluating variances from budgeted amounts, what was the most commonly defined range of acceptable tolerance levels?
(e) The study defines three types of consequences for varying from budgeted amounts. How does it describe "severe" consequences?

COMMUNICATION ACTIVITY

Writing

CT22-5 The manufacturing overhead budget for Fleming Company contains the following items. E

Variable costs		Fixed costs	
Indirect materials	$22,000	Supervision	$17,000
Indirect labor	12,000	Inspection costs	1,000
Maintenance expense	10,000	Insurance expense	2,000
Manufacturing supplies	6,000	Depreciation	15,000
Total variable	$50,000	Total fixed	$35,000

The budget was based on an estimated 2,000 units being produced. During the past month, 1,500 units were produced, and the following costs incurred.

Variable costs		Fixed costs	
Indirect materials	$22,500	Supervision	$18,400
Indirect labor	13,500	Inspection costs	1,200
Maintenance expense	8,200	Insurance expense	2,200
Manufacturing supplies	5,000	Depreciation	14,700
Total variable	$49,200	Total fixed	$36,500

Instructions

(a) Determine which items would be controllable by Fred Bedner, the production manager.
(b) How much should have been spent during the month for the manufacture of the 1,500 units?
(c) Prepare a flexible manufacturing overhead budget report for Mr. Bedner.
(d) Prepare a responsibility report. Include only the costs that would have been controllable by Mr. Bedner. Assume that the supervision cost above includes Mr. Bedner's salary of $10,000, both at budget and actual. In an attached memo, describe clearly for Mr. Bedner the areas in which his performance needs to be improved.

ETHICS CASE

E **CT22-6** American Products Corporation participates in a highly competitive industry. In order to meet this competition and achieve profit goals, the company has chosen the decentralized form of organization. Each manager of a decentralized investment center is measured on the basis of profit contribution, market penetration, and return on investment. Failure to meet the objectives established by corporate management for these measures has not been acceptable and usually has resulted in demotion or dismissal of an investment center manager.

An anonymous survey of managers in the company revealed that the managers feel the pressure to compromise their personal ethical standards to achieve the corporate objectives. For example, at certain plant locations there was pressure to reduce quality control to a level which could not assure that all unsafe products would be rejected. Also, sales personnel were encouraged to use questionable sales tactics to obtain orders, including gifts and other incentives to purchasing agents.

The chief executive officer is disturbed by the survey findings. In his opinion, such behavior cannot be condoned by the company. He concludes that the company should do something about this problem.

Instructions

(a) Who are the stakeholders (the affected parties) in this situation?
(b) Identify the ethical implications, conflicts, or dilemmas in the above described situation.
(c) What might the company do to reduce the pressures on managers and decrease the ethical conflicts?

(CMA adapted)

ALL ABOUT YOU

E **CT22-7** It is one thing to prepare a personal budget; it is another thing to stick to it. Financial planners have suggested various mechanisms to provide support for enforcing personal budgets. One approach is called "envelope budgeting."

Instructions

Read the article provided at **http://en.wikipedia.org/wiki/Envelope_budgeting**, and answer the following questions.

(a) Summarize the process of envelope budgeting.
(b) Evaluate whether you think you would benefit from envelope budgeting. What do you think are its strengths and weaknesses relative to your situation?

CONSIDERING YOUR COSTS AND BENEFITS

E **CT22-8** Preparing a personal budget is a great first step toward control over your personal finances. It is especially useful to prepare a budget when you face a big decision. For most people, the biggest decision they will ever make is whether to purchase a house. The percentage of people in the United States who own a home is high compared to many other countries. This is partially the result of U.S. government programs and incentives that encourage home ownership. For example, the interest on a home mortgage is tax-deductible.

Before purchasing a house, you should first consider whether buying it is the best choice for you. Suppose you just graduated from college and are moving to a new community. Should you immediately buy a new home?

YES: If I purchase a home, I am making my housing cost more like a "fixed cost," thus minimizing increases in my future housing costs. Also, I benefit from the appreciation in my home's value. Although recent turbulence in the economy has caused home prices in many communities to decline, I know that over the long term, home prices have increased across the country.

NO: I just moved to a new town, so I don't know the housing market. I am new to my job, so I don't know whether I will like it or my new community. Also, if my job does go well, it is likely that my income will increase in the next few years, so I will able to afford a better house if I wait. Therefore, the flexibility provided by renting is very valuable to me at this point in my life.

Instructions

Write a response indicating your position regarding this situation. Provide support for your view.

23

Standard Costs and Balanced Scorecard

CHAPTER PREVIEW

Standards are a fact of life. You met the admission standards for the school you are attending. The vehicle that you drive had to meet certain governmental emissions standards. The hamburgers and salads that you eat in a restaurant have to meet certain health and nutritional standards before they can be sold. As described in our Feature Story, Starbucks has standards for the costs of its materials, labor, and overhead. The reason for standards in these cases is very simple: They help to ensure that overall product quality is high while keeping costs under control.

In this chapter, we continue the study of controlling costs. You will learn how to evaluate performance using standard costs and a balanced scorecard.

CHAPTER OUTLINE

LEARNING OBJECTIVES		PRACTICE
1 Describe standard costs.	• Distinguishing between standards and budgets • Setting standard costs	DO IT! 1 Standard Costs
2 Determine direct materials variances.	• Analyzing and reporting variances • Direct materials variances	DO IT! 2 Direct Materials Variances
3 Determine direct labor and total manufacturing overhead variances.	• Direct labor variances • Manufacturing overhead variances	DO IT! 3 Labor and Manufacturing Overhead Variances
4 Prepare variance reports and balanced scorecards.	• Reporting variances • Income statement presentation of variances • Balanced scorecard	DO IT! 4 Reporting Variances

Go to the ***REVIEW AND PRACTICE*** section at the end of the chapter for a targeted summary and exercises with solutions.

Visit **WileyPLUS** for additional tutorials and practice opportunities.

© Jeff Greenberg 5 of 6/Alamy

FEATURE STORY

80,000 Different Caffeinated Combinations

When Howard Schultz purchased a small Seattle coffee-roasting business in 1987, he set out to create a new kind of company. He thought the company should sell coffee by the cup in its store, in addition to the bags of roasted beans it already sold. He also saw the store as a place where you could order a beverage, custom-made to your unique tastes, in an environment that would give you the sense that you had escaped, if only momentarily, from the chaos we call life. Finally, Schultz believed that the company would prosper if employees shared in its success.

In a little more than 20 years, Howard Schultz's company, Starbucks, grew from that one store to over 17,000 locations in 54 countries. That is an incredible rate of growth, and it didn't happen by accident. While Starbucks does everything it can to maximize the customer's experience, behind the scenes it needs to control costs. Consider the almost infinite options of beverage combinations and variations at Starbucks. The company must determine the most efficient way to make each beverage, it must communicate these methods in the form of standards to its employees, and it must then evaluate whether those standards are being met.

Schultz's book, *Onward: How Starbucks Fought for Its Life Without Losing Its Soul*, describes a painful period in which Starbucks had to close 600 stores and lay off thousands of employees. However, when a prominent shareholder suggested that the company eliminate its employee healthcare plan, as so many other companies had done, Schultz refused. The healthcare plan represented one of the company's most tangible commitments to employee well-being as well as to corporate social responsibility. Schultz feels strongly that providing health care to the company's employees is an essential part of the standard cost of a cup of Starbucks' coffee.

LEARNING OBJECTIVE ▶1

Describe standard costs.

Standards are common in business. Those imposed by government agencies are often called **regulations**. They include the Fair Labor Standards Act, the Equal Employment Opportunity Act, and a multitude of environmental standards. Standards established internally by a company may extend to personnel matters, such as employee absenteeism and ethical codes of conduct, quality control standards for products, and standard costs for goods and services. In managerial accounting, **standard costs** are predetermined unit costs, which companies use as measures of performance.

We focus on manufacturing operations in this chapter. But you should recognize that standard costs also apply to many types of service businesses as well. For example, a fast-food restaurant such as McDonald's knows the price it should pay for pickles, beef, buns, and other ingredients. It also knows how much time it should take an employee to flip hamburgers. If the company pays too much for pickles or if employees take too much time to prepare Big Macs, McDonald's notices the deviations and takes corrective action. Not-for-profit entities, such as universities, charitable organizations, and governmental agencies, also may use standard costs as measures of performance.

Standard costs offer a number of advantages to an organization, as shown in Illustration 23-1. The organization will realize these advantages only when standard costs are carefully established and prudently used. Using standards solely as

ILLUSTRATION 23-1
Advantages of standard costs

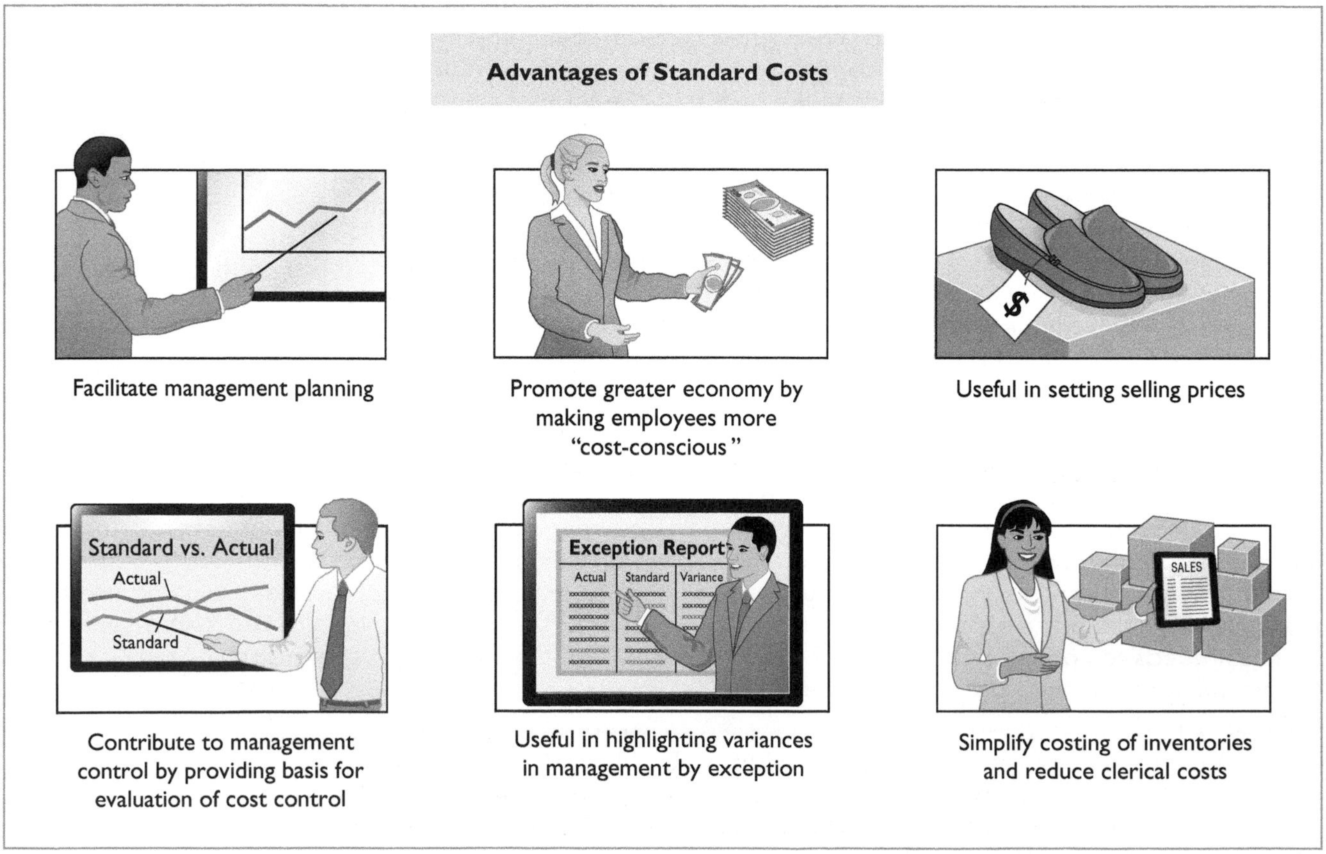

a way to place blame can have a negative effect on managers and employees. To minimize this effect, many companies offer wage incentives to those who meet the standards.

DISTINGUISHING BETWEEN STANDARDS AND BUDGETS

Both **standards** and **budgets** are predetermined costs, and both contribute to management planning and control. There is a difference, however, in the way the terms are expressed. A standard is a **unit** amount. A budget is a **total** amount. Thus, it is customary to state that the **standard cost** of direct labor for a unit of product is, say, $10. If the company produces 5,000 units of the product, the $50,000 of direct labor is the **budgeted** labor cost. A standard is the budgeted **cost per unit** of product. A standard is therefore concerned with each individual cost component that makes up the entire budget.

There are important accounting differences between budgets and standards. Except in the application of manufacturing overhead to jobs and processes, budget data are not journalized in cost accounting systems. In contrast, as we illustrate in the appendix to this chapter, standard costs may be incorporated into cost accounting systems. Also, a company may report its inventories at standard cost in its financial statements, but it would not report inventories at budgeted costs.

SETTING STANDARD COSTS

The setting of standard costs to produce a unit of product is a difficult task. It requires input from all persons who have responsibility for costs and quantities. To determine the standard cost of direct materials, management consults purchasing agents, product managers, quality control engineers, and production supervisors. In setting the standard cost for direct labor, managers obtain pay rate data from the payroll department. Industrial engineers generally determine the labor time requirements. The managerial accountant provides important input for the standard-setting process by accumulating historical cost data and by knowing how costs respond to changes in activity levels.

To be effective in controlling costs, standard costs need to be current at all times. Thus, standards are under continuous review. They should change whenever managers determine that the existing standard is not a good measure of performance. Circumstances that warrant revision of a standard include changed wage rates resulting from a new union contract, a change in product specifications, or the implementation of a new manufacturing method.

Ideal versus Normal Standards

Companies set standards at one of two levels: ideal or normal. **Ideal standards** represent optimum levels of performance under perfect operating conditions. **Normal standards** represent efficient levels of performance that are attainable under expected operating conditions.

Some managers believe ideal standards will stimulate workers to ever-increasing improvement. However, most managers believe that ideal standards lower the morale of the entire workforce because they are difficult, if not impossible, to meet. Very few companies use ideal standards.

ETHICS NOTE

When standards are set too high, employees sometimes feel pressure to consider unethical practices to meet these standards.

Most companies that use standards set them at a normal level. Properly set, normal standards should be **rigorous but attainable**. Normal standards allow for rest periods, machine breakdowns, and other "normal" contingencies in the production process. In the remainder of this chapter, we will assume that standard costs are set at a normal level.

ACCOUNTING ACROSS THE ORGANIZATION U.S. Navy

SpotX/iStockphoto

How Do Standards Help a Business?

A number of organizations, including corporations, consultants, and governmental agencies, share information regarding performance standards in an effort to create a standard set of measures for thousands of business processes. The group, referred to as the Open Standards Benchmarking Collaborative, includes IBM, Procter and Gamble, the U.S. Navy, and the World Bank. Companies that are interested in participating can go to the group's website and enter their information.

Source: Becky Partida, "Benchmark Your Manufacturing Performance," Control Engineering (February 4, 2013).

How will the creation of such standards help a business or organization? (Go to **WileyPLUS** for this answer and additional questions.)

A Case Study

To establish the standard cost of producing a product, it is necessary to establish standards for each manufacturing cost element—direct materials, direct labor, and manufacturing overhead. The standard for each element is derived from the standard price to be paid and the standard quantity to be used.

To illustrate, we use an extended example. Xonic Beverage Company uses standard costs to measure performance at the production facility of its caffeinated energy drink, Xonic Tonic. Xonic produces one-gallon containers of concentrated syrup that it sells to coffee and smoothie shops, and other retail outlets. The syrup is mixed with ice water or ice "slush" before serving. The potency of the beverage varies depending on the amount of concentrated syrup used.

DIRECT MATERIALS The **direct materials price standard** is the cost per unit of direct materials that should be incurred. This standard is based on the purchasing department's best estimate of the **cost of raw materials**. This cost is frequently based on current purchase prices. The price standard also includes an amount for related costs such as receiving, storing, and handling. The materials price standard per pound of material for Xonic Tonic is as follows.

ILLUSTRATION 23-2
Setting direct materials price standard

Item	Price
Purchase price, net of discounts	$ 2.70
Freight	0.20
Receiving and handling	0.10
Standard direct materials price per pound	**$3.00**

The **direct materials quantity standard** is the quantity of direct materials that should be used per unit of finished goods. This standard is expressed as a physical measure, such as pounds, barrels, or board feet. In setting the standard, management considers both the quality and quantity of materials required to manufacture the product. The standard includes allowances for unavoidable waste and normal spoilage. The standard quantity per unit for Xonic Tonic is shown in Illustration 23-3.

ILLUSTRATION 23-3
Setting direct materials quantity standard

Item	Quantity (Pounds)
Required materials	3.5
Allowance for waste	0.4
Allowance for spoilage	0.1
Standard direct materials quantity per unit	**4.0**

The standard direct materials cost per unit is the standard direct materials price times the standard direct materials quantity. For Xonic, the standard direct materials cost per gallon of Xonic Tonic is $12.00 ($3 × 4 pounds).

DIRECT LABOR The **direct labor price standard** is the rate per hour that should be incurred for direct labor. This standard is based on current wage rates, adjusted for anticipated changes such as cost of living adjustments (COLAs). The price standard also generally includes employer payroll taxes and fringe benefits, such as paid holidays and vacations. For Xonic, the direct labor price standard is as follows.

ALTERNATIVE TERMINOLOGY
The direct labor price standard is also called the *direct labor rate standard.*

ILLUSTRATION 23-4
Setting direct labor price standard

Item	Price
Hourly wage rate	$ 12.50
COLA	0.25
Payroll taxes	0.75
Fringe benefits	1.50
Standard direct labor rate per hour	**$15.00**

The **direct labor quantity standard** is the time that should be required to make one unit of the product. This standard is especially critical in labor-intensive companies. Allowances should be made in this standard for rest periods, cleanup, machine setup, and machine downtime. Illustration 23-5 shows the direct labor quantity standard for Xonic.

ALTERNATIVE TERMINOLOGY
The direct labor quantity standard is also called the *direct labor efficiency standard.*

ILLUSTRATION 23-5
Setting direct labor quantity standard

Item	Quantity (Hours)
Actual production time	1.5
Rest periods and cleanup	0.2
Setup and downtime	0.3
Standard direct labor hours per unit	**2.0**

The standard direct labor cost per unit is the standard direct labor rate times the standard direct labor hours. For Xonic, the standard direct labor cost per gallon is $30 ($15 × 2 hours).

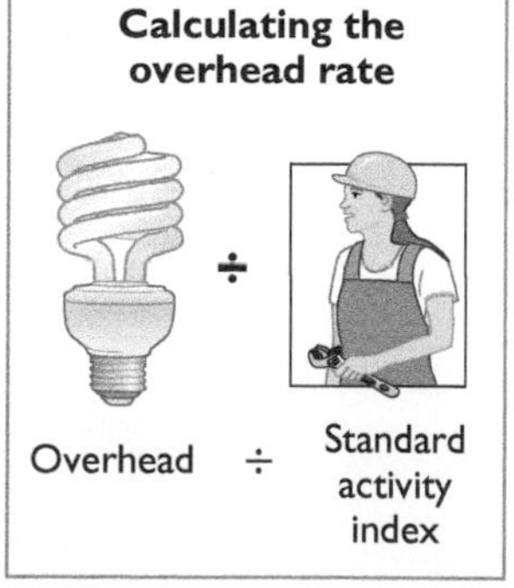

MANUFACTURING OVERHEAD For manufacturing overhead, companies use a **standard predetermined overhead rate** in setting the standard. This overhead rate is determined by dividing budgeted overhead costs by an expected standard activity index. For example, the index may be standard direct labor hours or standard machine hours.

As discussed in Chapter 17, many companies employ activity-based costing (ABC) to allocate overhead costs. Because ABC uses multiple activity indices to allocate overhead costs, it results in a better correlation between activities and costs incurred than do other methods. As a result, the use of ABC can significantly improve the usefulness of standard costing for management decision-making.

Xonic uses standard direct labor hours as the activity index. The company expects to produce 13,200 gallons of Xonic Tonic during the year at normal capacity. **Normal capacity** is the average activity output that a company should experience over the long run. Since it takes two direct labor hours for each gallon, total standard direct labor hours are 26,400 (13,200 gallons × 2 hours).

At normal capacity of 26,400 direct labor hours, overhead costs are expected to be $132,000. Of that amount, $79,200 are variable and $52,800 are fixed. Illustration 23-6 shows computation of the standard predetermined overhead rates for Xonic.

ILLUSTRATION 23-6
Computing predetermined overhead rates

Budgeted Overhead Costs	Amount	÷	Standard Direct Labor Hours	=	Overhead Rate per Direct Labor Hour
Variable	$ 79,200		26,400		$3.00
Fixed	52,800		26,400		2.00
Total	$132,000		26,400		$5.00

The standard manufacturing overhead cost per unit is the predetermined overhead rate times the activity index quantity standard. For Xonic, which uses direct labor hours as its activity index, the standard manufacturing overhead cost per gallon of Xonic Tonic is $10 ($5 × 2 hours).

TOTAL STANDARD COST PER UNIT After a company has established the standard quantity and price per unit of product, it can determine the total standard cost. The total standard cost per unit is the sum of the standard costs of direct materials, direct labor, and manufacturing overhead. The total standard cost per gallon of Xonic Tonic is $52, as shown on the following standard cost card.

ILLUSTRATION 23-7
Standard cost per gallon of Xonic Tonic

Product: Xonic Tonic **Unit Measure: Gallon**

Manufacturing Cost Elements	Standard Quantity	×	Standard Price	=	Standard Cost
Direct materials	4 pounds		$ 3.00		$12.00
Direct labor	2 hours		$15.00		30.00
Manufacturing overhead	2 hours		$ 5.00		10.00
					$52.00

The company prepares a standard cost card for each product. This card provides the basis for determining variances from standards.

DO IT! 1 Standard Costs

Ridette Inc. accumulated the following standard cost data concerning product Cty31.

Direct materials per unit: 1.5 pounds at $4 per pound
Direct labor per unit: 0.25 hours at $13 per hour.
Manufacturing overhead: allocated based on direct labor hours at a predetermined rate of $15.60 per direct labor hour.

Compute the standard cost of one unit of product Cty31.

Action Plan

- ✔ Know that standard costs are predetermined unit costs.
- ✔ To establish the standard cost of producing a product, establish the standard for each manufacturing cost element—direct materials, direct labor, and manufacturing overhead.
- ✔ Compute the standard cost for each element from the standard price to be paid and the standard quantity to be used.

SOLUTION

Manufacturing Cost Element	Standard Quantity	×	Standard Price	=	Standard Cost
Direct materials	1.5 pounds		$ 4.00		$ 6.00
Direct labor	0.25 hours		$13.00		3.25
Manufacturing overhead	0.25 hours		$15.60		3.90
Total					$13.15

Related exercise material: **BE23-2, BE23-3, E23-1, E23-2, E23-3,** and **DO IT! 23-1.**

LEARNING OBJECTIVE 2 Determine direct materials variances.

ANALYZING AND REPORTING VARIANCES

One of the major management uses of standard costs is to identify variances from standards. **Variances** are the differences between total actual costs and total standard costs.

ALTERNATIVE TERMINOLOGY In business, the term *variance* is also used to indicate differences between total budgeted and total actual costs.

To illustrate, assume that in producing 1,000 gallons of Xonic Tonic in the month of June, Xonic incurred the following costs.

ILLUSTRATION 23-8 Actual production costs

Direct materials	$13,020
Direct labor	31,080
Variable overhead	6,500
Fixed overhead	4,400
Total actual costs	$55,000

Companies determine total standard costs by multiplying the units produced by the standard cost per unit. The total standard cost of Xonic Tonic is $52,000 (1,000 gallons × $52). Thus, the total variance is $3,000, as shown below.

ILLUSTRATION 23-9 Computation of total variance

Actual costs	$55,000
Less: Standard costs	52,000
Total variance	**$ 3,000**

Note that the variance is expressed in total dollars, not on a per unit basis.

When actual costs exceed standard costs, the variance is **unfavorable**. The $3,000 variance in June for Xonic Tonic is unfavorable. An unfavorable variance has a negative connotation. It suggests that the company paid too much for one or more of the manufacturing cost elements or that it used the elements inefficiently.

If actual costs are less than standard costs, the variance is **favorable**. A favorable variance has a positive connotation. It suggests efficiencies in incurring manufacturing costs and in using direct materials, direct labor, and manufacturing overhead.

However, be careful: A favorable variance could be obtained by using inferior materials. In printing wedding invitations, for example, a favorable variance could result from using an inferior grade of paper. Or, a favorable variance might be achieved in installing tires on an automobile assembly line by tightening only half of the lug bolts. A variance is not favorable if the company has sacrificed quality control standards.

To interpret a variance, you must analyze its components. A variance can result from differences related to the cost of materials, labor, or overhead. Illustration 23-10 shows that the total variance is the sum of the materials, labor, and overhead variances.

ILLUSTRATION 23-10
Components of total variance

Materials Variance + Labor Variance + Overhead Variance = Total Variance

In the following discussion, you will see that the materials variance and the labor variance are the sum of variances resulting from price differences and quantity differences. Illustration 23-11 shows a format for computing the price and quantity variances.

ILLUSTRATION 23-11
Breakdown of materials or labor variance into price and quantity variances

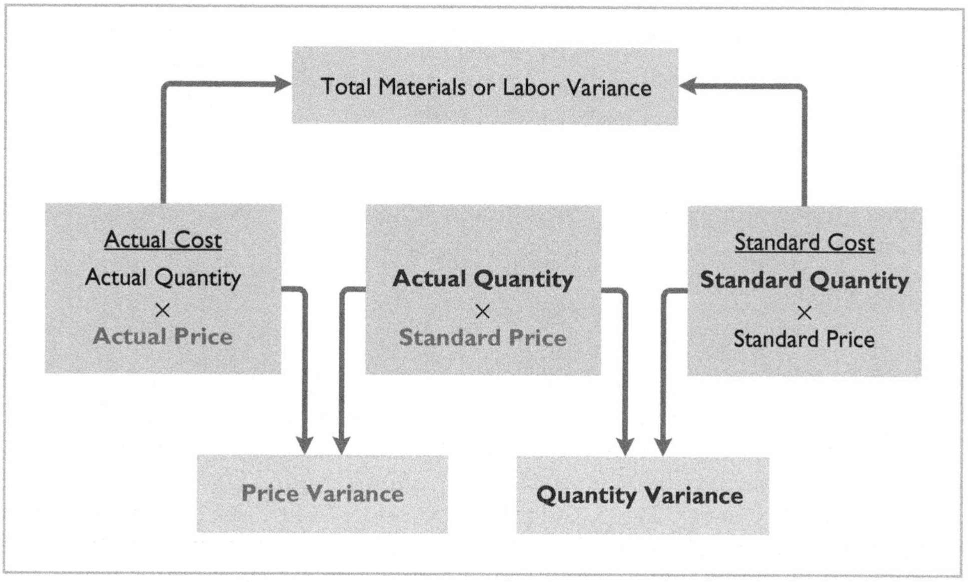

Note that the left side of the matrix is actual cost (actual quantity times actual price). The right hand is standard cost (standard quantity times standard price). The only additional element you need in order to compute the price and quantity variances is the middle element, the actual quantity at the standard price.

DIRECT MATERIALS VARIANCES

Part of Xonic's total variance of $3,000 is due to a materials variance. In completing the order for 1,000 gallons of Xonic Tonic, the company used 4,200 pounds of direct materials. The direct materials were purchased at a price of $3.10 per unit. From Illustration 23-3, we know that Xonic's standards require it to use 4 pounds of materials per gallon produced, so it should have only used 4,000 (4 × 1,000) pounds of direct materials to produce 1,000 gallons. Illustration 23-2 shows that the standard cost of each pound of direct materials is $3 instead of the $3.10 actually paid. Illustration 23-12 shows that the **total materials variance** is computed as the difference between the amount paid (actual quantity times actual price) and the amount that should have been paid based on standards (standard quantity times standard price of materials).

DECISION TOOLS

The materials price and materials quantity variances help managers determine if they have met their price and quantity objectives regarding materials.

Actual Quantity × Actual Price	−	Standard Quantity × Standard Price	=	Total Materials Variance
(AQ) × (AP)		(SQ) × (SP)		(TMV)
(4,200 × $3.10)	−	(4,000 × $3.00)	=	$1,020 U

ILLUSTRATION 23-12
Formula for total materials variance

Thus, for Xonic, the total materials variance is $1,020 ($13,020 − $12,000) unfavorable.

The total materials variance could be caused by differences in the price paid for the materials or by differences in the amount of materials used. Illustration 23-13 shows that the total materials variance is the sum of the materials price variance and the materials quantity variance.

Materials Price Variance + Materials Quantity Variance = Total Materials Variance

ILLUSTRATION 23-13
Components of total materials variance

The materials price variance results from a difference between the actual price and the standard price. Illustration 23-14 shows that the **materials price variance** is computed as the difference between the actual amount paid (actual quantity of materials times actual price) and the standard amount that should have been paid for the materials used (actual quantity of materials times standard price).[1]

Actual Quantity × Actual Price	−	Actual Quantity × Standard Price	=	Materials Price Variance
(AQ) × (AP)		(AQ) × (SP)		(MPV)
(4,200 × $3.10)	−	(4,200 × $3.00)	=	$420 U

ILLUSTRATION 23-14
Formula for materials price variance

For Xonic, the materials price variance is $420 ($13,020 − $12,600) unfavorable.

The price variance can also be computed by multiplying the actual quantity purchased by the difference between the actual and standard price per unit. The computation in this case is 4,200 × ($3.10 − $3.00) = $420 U.

▼ HELPFUL HINT
The alternative formula is:
AQ × AP − SP = MPV

As seen in Illustration 23-13, the other component of the materials variance is the quantity variance. The quantity variance results from differences between the amount of material actually used and the amount that should have been used. As shown in Illustration 23-15, the **materials quantity variance** is computed as the difference between the standard cost of the actual quantity (actual quantity times standard price) and the standard cost of the amount that should have been used (standard quantity times standard price for materials).

Actual Quantity × Standard Price	−	Standard Quantity × Standard Price	=	Materials Quantity Variance
(AQ) × (SP)		(SQ) × (SP)		(MQV)
(4,200 × $3.00)	−	(4,000 × $3.00)	=	$600 U

ILLUSTRATION 23-15
Formula for materials quantity variance

[1]Assume that all materials purchased during the period are used in production and that no units remain in inventory at the end of the period.

Thus, for Xonic, the materials quantity variance is $600 ($12,600 − $12,000) unfavorable.

▼ **HELPFUL HINT**
The alternative formula is:
SP × AQ − SQ = MQV

The quantity variance can also be computed by applying the standard price to the difference between actual and standard quantities used. The computation in this example is $3.00 × (4,200 − 4,000) = $600 U.

The total materials variance of $1,020 U, therefore, consists of the following.

ILLUSTRATION 23-16
Summary of materials variances

Materials price variance	$ 420 U
Materials quantity variance	600 U
Total materials variance	**$1,020 U**

Companies sometimes use a matrix to analyze a variance. **When the matrix is used, a company computes the amounts using the formulas for each cost element first and then computes the variances.** Illustration 23-17 shows the completed matrix for the direct materials variance for Xonic. The matrix provides a convenient structure for determining each variance.

ILLUSTRATION 23-17
Matrix for direct materials variances

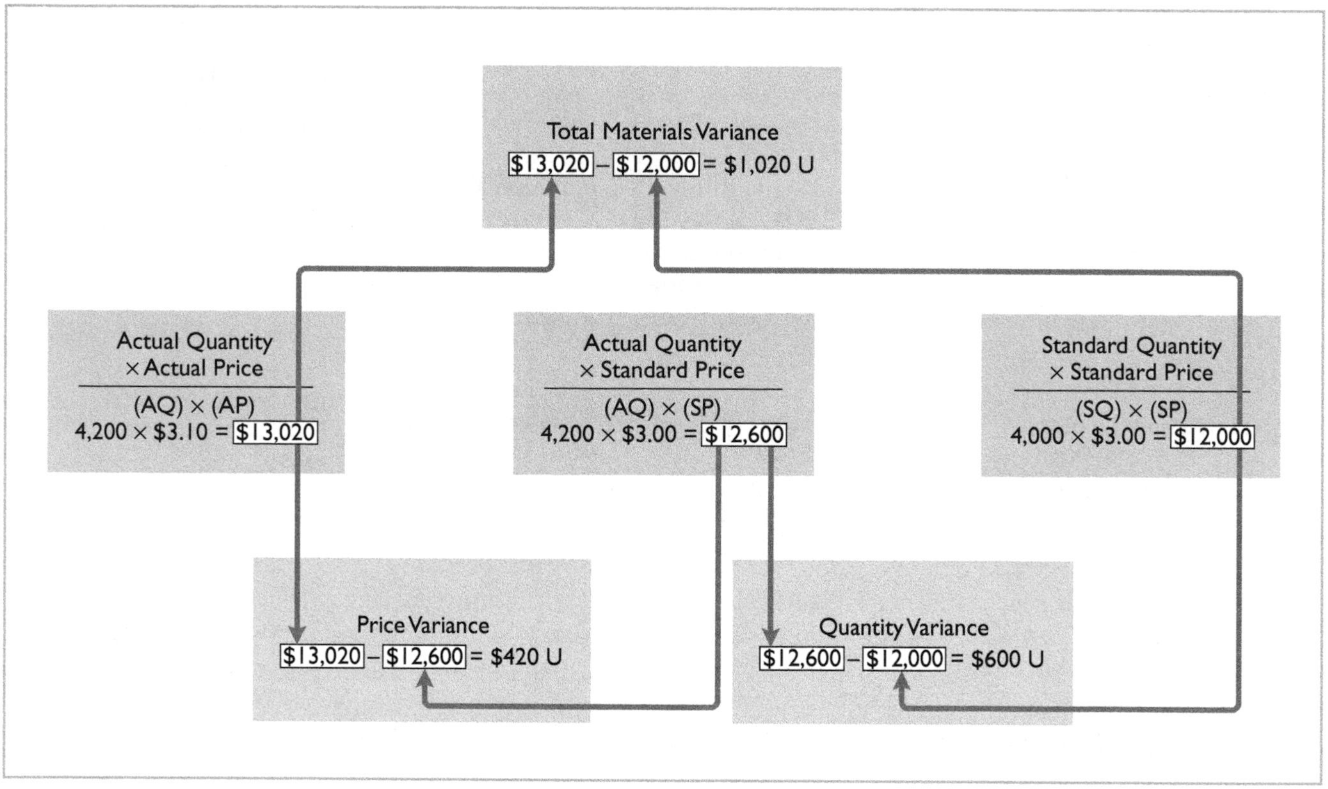

Causes of Materials Variances

What are the causes of a variance? The causes may relate to both internal and external factors. The investigation of a **materials price variance usually begins in the purchasing department**. Many factors affect the price paid for raw materials. These include availability of quantity and cash discounts, the quality of the materials requested, and the delivery method used. To the extent that these factors are considered in setting the price standard, the purchasing department is responsible for any variances.

However, a variance may be beyond the control of the purchasing department. Sometimes, for example, prices may rise faster than expected. Moreover, actions by groups over which the company has no control, such as the OPEC nations' oil price increases, may cause an unfavorable variance. For example, during a recent year, Kraft Foods and Kellogg Company both experienced unfavorable materials price variances when the cost of dairy and wheat products jumped unexpectedly. There are also times when a production department may be responsible for the price variance. This may occur when a rush order forces the company to pay a higher price for the materials.

The starting point for determining the cause(s) of a significant **materials quantity variance is in the production department**. If the variances are due to inexperienced workers, faulty machinery, or carelessness, the production department is responsible. However, if the materials obtained by the purchasing department were of inferior quality, then the purchasing department is responsible.

DO IT! 2 Direct Materials Variances

The standard cost of Wonder Walkers includes two units of direct materials at $8.00 per unit. During July, the company buys 22,000 units of direct materials at $7.50 and uses those materials to produce 10,000 Wonder Walkers. Compute the total, price, and quantity variances for materials.

Action Plan

Use the formulas for computing each of the materials variances:

- ✔ Total materials variance = (AQ × AP) − (SQ × SP)
- ✔ Materials price variance = (AQ × AP) − (AQ × SP)
- ✔ Materials quantity variance = (AQ × SP) − (SQ × SP)

SOLUTION

Standard quantity = 10,000 × 2

Substituting amounts into the formulas, the variances are:

Total materials variance = (22,000 × $7.50) − (20,000 × $8.00) = $5,000 unfavorable
Materials price variance = (22,000 × $7.50) − (22,000 × $8.00) = $11,000 favorable
Materials quantity variance = (22,000 × $8.00) − (20,000 × $8.00) = $16,000 unfavorable

Related exercise material: **BE23-4, E23-5, and DO IT! 23-2.**

LEARNING OBJECTIVE 3 Determine direct labor and total manufacturing overhead variances.

DIRECT LABOR VARIANCES

DECISION TOOLS

Labor price and labor quantity variances help managers to determine if they have met their price and quantity objectives regarding labor.

The process of determining direct labor variances is the same as for determining the direct materials variances. In completing the Xonic Tonic order, the company incurred 2,100 direct labor hours at an average hourly rate of $14.80. The standard hours allowed for the units produced were 2,000 hours (1,000 gallons × 2 hours). The standard labor rate was $15 per hour.

The total labor variance is the difference between the amount actually paid for labor versus the amount that should have been paid. Illustration 23-18 shows that the **total labor variance** is computed as the difference between the amount actually paid for labor (actual hours times actual rate) and the amount that should have been paid (standard hours times standard rate for labor).

ILLUSTRATION 23-18
Formula for total labor variance

Actual Hours × Actual Rate	−	Standard Hours × Standard Rate	=	Total Labor Variance
(AH) × (AR)		(SH) × (SR)		(TLV)
(2,100 × $14.80)	−	(2,000 × $15.00)	=	$1,080 U

The total labor variance is $1,080 ($31,080 − $30,000) unfavorable.

The total labor variance is caused by differences in the labor rate or differences in labor hours. Illustration 23-19 shows that the total labor variance is the sum of the labor price variance and the labor quantity variance.

ILLUSTRATION 23-19
Components of total labor variance

Labor Price Variance	+	**Labor Quantity Variance**	=	**Total Labor Variance**

The labor price variance results from the difference between the rate paid to workers versus the rate that was supposed to be paid. Illustration 23-20 shows that the **labor price variance** is computed as the difference between the actual amount paid (actual hours times actual rate) and the amount that should have been paid for the number of hours worked (actual hours times standard rate for labor).

ILLUSTRATION 23-20
Formula for labor price variance

Actual Hours × Actual Rate	−	**Actual Hours × Standard Rate**	=	**Labor Price Variance**
(AH) × (AR)		**(AH) × (SR)**		**(LPV)**
(2,100 × $14.80)	−	(2,100 × $15.00)	=	$420 F

▼ HELPFUL HINT
The alternative formula is:
AH × AR − SR = LPV

For Xonic, the labor price variance is $420 ($31,080 − $31,500) favorable.

The labor price variance can also be computed by multiplying actual hours worked by the difference between the actual pay rate and the standard pay rate. The computation in this example is 2,100 × ($15.00 − $14.80) = $420 F.

The other component of the total labor variance is the labor quantity variance. The labor quantity variance results from the difference between the actual number of labor hours and the number of hours that should have been worked for the quantity produced. Illustration 23-21 shows that the **labor quantity variance** is computed as the difference between the amount that should have been paid for the hours worked (actual hours times standard rate) and the amount that should have been paid for the amount of hours that should have been worked (standard hours times standard rate for labor).

ILLUSTRATION 23-21
Formula for labor quantity variance

Actual Hours × Standard Rate	−	**Standard Hours × Standard Rate**	=	**Labor Quantity Variance**
(AH) × (SR)		**(SH) × (SR)**		**(LQV)**
(2,100 × $15.00)	−	(2,000 × $15.00)	=	$1,500 U

▼ HELPFUL HINT
The alternative formula is:
SR × AH − SH = LQV

Thus, for Xonic, the labor quantity variance is $1,500 ($31,500 − $30,000) unfavorable.

The same result can be obtained by multiplying the standard rate by the difference between actual hours worked and standard hours allowed. In this case, the computation is $15.00 × (2,100 − 2,000) = $1,500 U.

The total direct labor variance of $1,080 U, therefore, consists of the following.

ILLUSTRATION 23-22
Summary of labor variances

Labor price variance	$ 420 F
Labor quantity variance	1,500 U
Total direct labor variance	**$1,080 U**

These results can also be obtained from the matrix in Illustration 23-23.

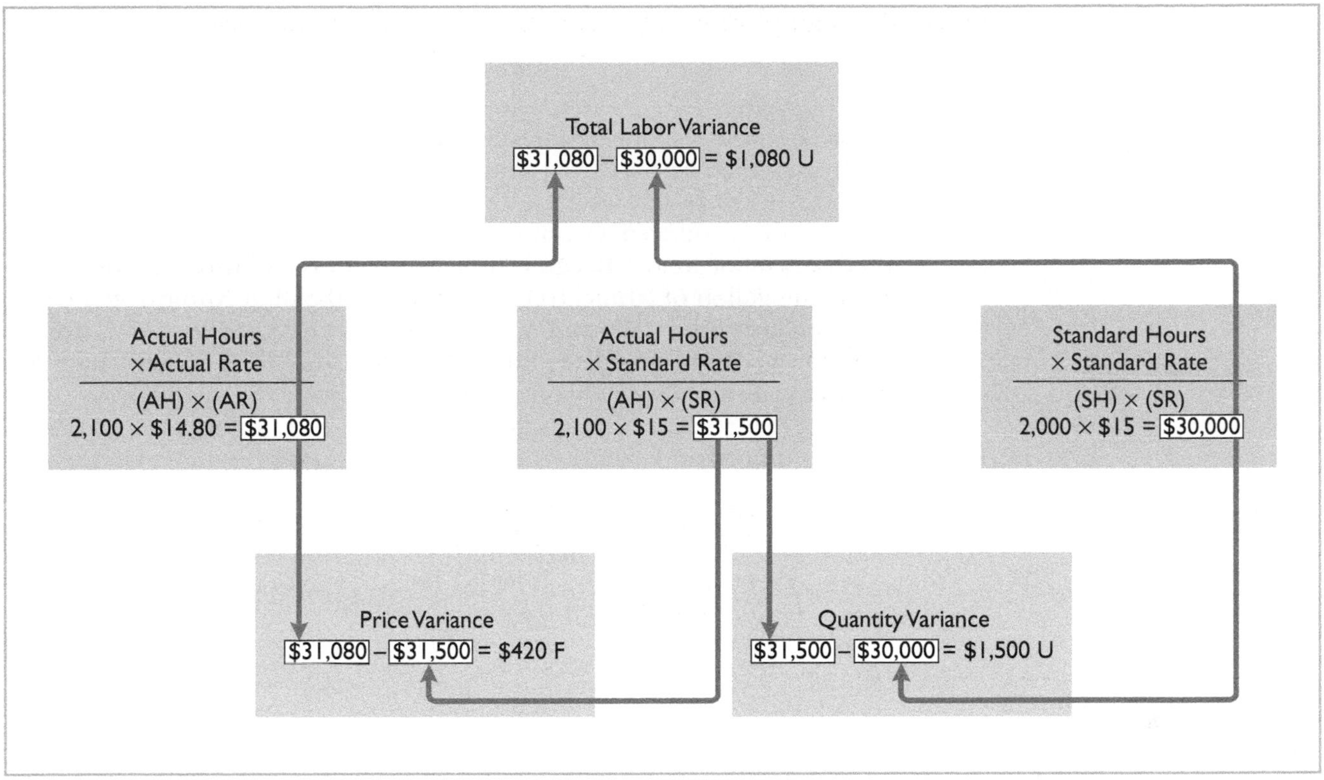

ILLUSTRATION 23-23
Matrix for direct labor variances

Causes of Labor Variances

Labor price variances usually result from two factors: (1) paying workers **different wages than expected**, and (2) **misallocation of workers**. In companies where pay rates are determined by union contracts, labor price variances should be infrequent. When workers are not unionized, there is a much higher likelihood of such variances. The responsibility for these variances rests with the manager who authorized the wage change.

Misallocation of the workforce refers to using skilled workers in place of unskilled workers and vice versa. The use of an inexperienced worker instead of an experienced one will result in a favorable price variance because of the lower pay rate of the unskilled worker. An unfavorable price variance would result if a skilled worker were substituted for an inexperienced one. The production department generally is responsible for labor price variances resulting from misallocation of the workforce.

Labor quantity variances relate to the **efficiency of workers**. The cause of a quantity variance generally can be traced to the production department. The causes of an unfavorable variance may be poor training, worker fatigue, faulty machinery, or carelessness. These causes are the responsibility of the **production department**. However, if the excess time is due to inferior materials, the responsibility falls outside the production department.

MANUFACTURING OVERHEAD VARIANCES

The **total overhead variance** is the difference between the actual overhead costs and overhead costs applied based on standard hours allowed for the amount of goods produced. As indicated in Illustration 23-8 (page 1125), Xonic incurred overhead costs of $10,900 to produce 1,000 gallons of Xonic Tonic in June. The computation of the actual overhead is comprised of a variable and a fixed component. Illustration 23-24 (page 1132) shows this computation.

ILLUSTRATION 23-24
Actual overhead costs

Variable overhead	$ 6,500
Fixed overhead	4,400
Total actual overhead	**$10,900**

DECISION TOOLS

The total manufacturing overhead variance helps managers to determine if they have met their objectives regarding manufacturing overhead.

To find the total overhead variance in a standard costing system, we determine the overhead costs applied based on standard hours allowed. **Standard hours allowed** are the hours that *should* have been worked for the units produced. Overhead costs for Xonic Tonic are applied based on direct labor hours. Because it takes two hours of direct labor to produce one gallon of Xonic Tonic, for the 1,000-gallon Xonic Tonic order, the standard hours allowed are 2,000 hours (1,000 gallons × 2 hours). We then apply the predetermined overhead rate to the 2,000 standard hours allowed.

Recall from Illustration 23-6 (page 1124) that the amount of budgeted overhead costs at normal capacity of $132,000 was divided by normal capacity of 26,400 direct labor hours, to arrive at a predetermined overhead rate of $5 ($132,000 ÷ 26,400). The predetermined rate of $5 is then multiplied by the 2,000 standard hours allowed, to determine the overhead costs applied.

Illustration 23-25 shows the formula for the total overhead variance and the calculation for Xonic for the month of June.

ILLUSTRATION 23-25
Formula for total overhead variance

Actual Overhead	−	Overhead Applied*	=	Total Overhead Variance
$10,900 ($6,500 + $4,400)	−	$10,000 ($5 × 2,000 hours)	=	$900 U

*Based on standard hours allowed.

Thus, for Xonic, the total overhead variance is $900 unfavorable.

The overhead variance is generally analyzed through a price and a quantity variance. (These computations are discussed in more detail in advanced courses.) The name usually given to the price variance is the **overhead controllable variance**; the quantity variance is referred to as the **overhead volume variance**. Appendix 23B discusses how the total overhead variance can be broken down into these two variances.

Causes of Manufacturing Overhead Variances

One reason for an overhead variance relates to over- or underspending on overhead items. For example, overhead may include indirect labor for which a company paid wages higher than the standard labor price allowed. Or, the price of electricity to run the company's machines increased, and the company did not anticipate this additional cost. Companies should investigate any spending variances to determine whether they will continue in the future. Generally, the responsibility for these variances rests with the production department.

The overhead variance can also result from the inefficient use of overhead. For example, because of poor maintenance, a number of the manufacturing machines are experiencing breakdowns on a consistent basis, leading to reduced production. Or, the flow of materials through the production process is impeded because of a lack of skilled labor to perform the necessary production tasks, due to a lack of planning. In both of these cases, the production department is responsible for the cause of these variances. On the other hand, overhead can also be underutilized because of a lack of sales orders. When the cause is a lack of sales orders, the responsibility rests outside the production department. For example, at one point Chrysler experienced a very significant unfavorable overhead variance because plant capacity was maintained at excessively high levels, due to overly optimistic sales forecasts.

PEOPLE, PLANET, AND PROFIT INSIGHT Starbucks

Archer Colin/SIPA/NewsCom

What's Brewing at Starbucks?

It's easy for a company to say it's committed to corporate social responsibility. But Starbucks actually spells out measurable goals. Recently, the company published its annual *Global Responsibility Report* in which it describes its goals, achievements, and even its shortcomings related to corporate social responsibility. For example, Starbucks achieved its goal of getting more than 50% of its electricity from renewable sources. It also has numerous goals related to purchasing coffee from sources that are certified as responsibly grown and ethically traded; providing funds for loans to coffee farmers; and fostering partnerships with Conservation International to provide training to farmers on ecologically friendly growing.

The report also candidly explains that the company did not meet its goal to cut energy consumption by 25%. It also fell far short of its goal of getting customers to reuse their cups. In those instances where it didn't achieve its goals, Starbucks set new goals and described steps it would take to achieve them. You can view the company's *Global Responsibility Report* at *www.starbucks.com*.

Source: "Starbucks Launches 10th Global Responsibility Report," *Business Wire* (April 18, 2011).

What implications does Starbucks' commitment to corporate social responsibility have for the standard cost of a cup of coffee? (Go to WileyPLUS for this answer and additional questions.)

DO IT! ▶3 Labor and Manufacturing Overhead Variances

The standard cost of Product YY includes 3 hours of direct labor at $12.00 per hour. The predetermined overhead rate is $20.00 per direct labor hour. During July, the company incurred 3,500 hours of direct labor at an average rate of $12.40 per hour and $71,300 of manufacturing overhead costs. It produced 1,200 units.

(a) Compute the total, price, and quantity variances for labor. (b) Compute the total overhead variance.

SOLUTION

Substituting amounts into the formulas, the variances are:

Total labor variance = (3,500 × $12.40) − (3,600 × $12.00) = $200 unfavorable

Labor price variance = (3,500 × $12.40) − (3,500 × $12.00) = $1,400 unfavorable

Labor quantity variance = (3,500 × $12.00) − (3,600 × $12.00) = $1,200 favorable

Total overhead variance = $71,300 − $72,000* = $700 favorable

*(1,200 × 3 hours) × $20.00

Related exercise material: **BE23-5, BE23-6, E23-4, E23-6, E23-7, E23-8, E23-11,** and **DO IT! 23-3.**

Action Plan

✔ Use the formulas for computing each of the variances:
Total labor variance = (AH × AR) − (SH × SR)
Labor price variance = (AH × AR) − (AH × SR)
Labor quantity variance = (AH × SR) − (SH × SR)
Total overhead variance = Actual overhead − Overhead applied*

*Based on standard hours allowed.

LEARNING OBJECTIVE ▶4 Prepare variance reports and balanced scorecards.

REPORTING VARIANCES

All variances should be reported to appropriate levels of management as soon as possible. The sooner managers are informed, the sooner they can evaluate problems and take corrective action.

The form, content, and frequency of variance reports vary considerably among companies. One approach is to prepare a weekly report for each department that has primary responsibility for cost control. Under this approach, materials price variances are reported to the purchasing department, and all other variances are reported to the production department that did the work. The following report for Xonic, with the materials for the Xonic Tonic order listed first, illustrates this approach.

ILLUSTRATION 23-26
Materials price variance report

XONIC
Variance Report—Purchasing Department
For Week Ended June 8, 2017

Type of Materials	Quantity Purchased	Actual Price	Standard Price	Price Variance	Explanation
X100	4,200 lbs.	$3.10	$3.00	$ 420 U	Rush order
X142	1,200 units	2.75	2.80	60 F	Quantity discount
A85	600 doz.	5.20	5.10	60 U	Regular supplier on strike
Total price variance				$420 U	

The explanation column is completed after consultation with the purchasing department manager.

Variance reports facilitate the principle of "management by exception" explained in Chapter 22. For example, the vice president of purchasing can use the report shown above to evaluate the effectiveness of the purchasing department manager. Or, the vice president of production can use production department variance reports to determine how well each production manager is controlling costs. In using variance reports, top management normally looks for **significant variances**. These may be judged on the basis of some quantitative measure, such as more than 10% of the standard or more than $1,000.

INCOME STATEMENT PRESENTATION OF VARIANCES

In income statements **prepared for management** under a standard cost accounting system, **cost of goods sold is stated at standard cost and the variances are disclosed separately**. Unfavorable variances increase cost of goods sold, while favorable variances decrease cost of goods sold. Illustration 23-27 shows

ILLUSTRATION 23-27
Variances in income statement for management

XONIC
Income Statement
For the Month Ended June 30, 2017

Sales revenue		$70,000
Cost of goods sold (at standard)		52,000
Gross profit (at standard)		18,000
Variances		
Materials price	$ 420 U	
Materials quantity	600 U	
Labor price	420 F	
Labor quantity	1,500 U	
Overhead	900 U	
Total variance unfavorable		3,000
Gross profit (actual)		15,000
Selling and administrative expenses		3,000
Net income		$12,000

the presentation of variances in an income statement. This income statement is based on the production and sale of 1,000 units of Xonic Tonic at $70 per unit. It also assumes selling and administrative costs of $3,000. Observe that each variance is shown, as well as the total net variance. In this example, variations from standard costs reduced net income by $3,000.

Standard costs may be used in financial statements prepared for stockholders and other external users. The costing of inventories at standard costs is in accordance with generally accepted accounting principles when there are no significant differences between actual costs and standard costs. Hewlett-Packard and Jostens, Inc., for example, report their inventories at standard costs. However, if there are significant differences between actual and standard costs, the financial statements must report inventories and cost of goods sold at actual costs.

It is also possible to show the variances in an income statement prepared in the variable costing (CVP) format. To do so, it is necessary to analyze the overhead variances into variable and fixed components. This type of analysis is explained in cost accounting textbooks.

BALANCED SCORECARD

Financial measures (measurement of dollars), such as variance analysis and return on investment (ROI), are useful tools for evaluating performance. However, many companies now supplement these financial measures with nonfinancial measures to better assess performance and anticipate future results. For example, airlines like Delta and United use capacity utilization as an important measure to understand and predict future performance. Companies that publish the *New York Times* and the *Chicago Tribune* newspapers use circulation figures as another measure by which to assess performance. Penske Automotive Group, the owner of 300 dealerships, rewards executives for meeting employee retention targets. Illustration 23-28 lists some key nonfinancial measures used in various industries.

ILLUSTRATION 23-28
Nonfinancial measures used in various industries

Industry		Measure
Automobiles		Capacity utilization of plants. Average age of key assets. Impact of strikes. Brand-loyalty statistics.
Computer Systems		Market profile of customer end-products. Number of new products. Employee stock ownership percentages. Number of scientists and technicians used in R&D.
Chemicals		Customer satisfaction data. Factors affecting customer product selection. Number of patents and trademarks held. Customer brand awareness.
Regional Banks	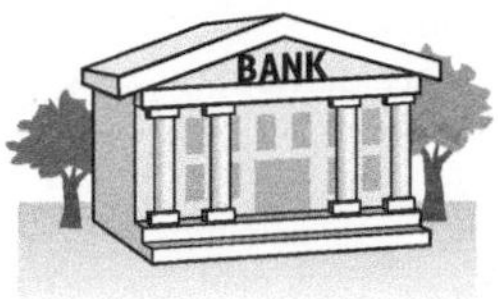	Number of ATMs by state. Number of products used by average customer. Percentage of customer service calls handled by interactive voice response units. Personnel cost per employee. Credit card retention rates.

Source: Financial Accounting Standards Board, *Business Reporting: Insights into Enhancing Voluntary Disclosures* (Norwalk, Conn.: FASB, 2001).

Most companies recognize that both financial and nonfinancial measures can provide useful insights into what is happening in the company. As a result, many companies now use a broad-based measurement approach, called the **balanced scorecard**, to evaluate performance. The **balanced scorecard** incorporates financial and nonfinancial measures in an integrated system that links performance measurement with a company's strategic goals. Nearly 50% of the largest companies in the United States, including Unilever, Chase, and Wal-Mart Stores Inc., are using the balanced scorecard approach.

The balanced scorecard evaluates company performance from a series of "perspectives." The four most commonly employed perspectives are as follows.

1. The **financial perspective** is the most traditional view of the company. It employs financial measures of performance used by most firms.
2. The **customer perspective** evaluates the company from the viewpoint of those people who buy its products or services. This view compares the company to competitors in terms of price, quality, product innovation, customer service, and other dimensions.
3. The **internal process perspective** evaluates the internal operating processes critical to success. All critical aspects of the value chain—including product development, production, delivery, and after-sale service—are evaluated to ensure that the company is operating effectively and efficiently.
4. The **learning and growth perspective** evaluates how well the company develops and retains its employees. This would include evaluation of such things as employee skills, employee satisfaction, training programs, and information dissemination.

Within each perspective, the balanced scorecard identifies objectives that contribute to attainment of strategic goals. Illustration 23-29 shows examples of objectives within each perspective.

Perspective		Objective
Financial		Return on assets. Net income. Credit rating. Share price. Profit per employee.
Customer		Percentage of customers who would recommend product. Customer retention. Response time per customer request. Brand recognition. Customer service expense per customer.
Internal Process		Percentage of defect-free products. Stockouts. Labor utilization rates. Waste reduction. Planning accuracy.
Learning and Growth		Percentage of employees leaving in less than one year. Number of cross-trained employees. Ethics violations. Training hours. Reportable accidents.

ILLUSTRATION 23-29
Examples of objectives within the four perspectives of balanced scorecard

The objectives are linked across perspectives in order to tie performance measurement to company goals. The financial-perspective objectives are normally set first, and then objectives are set in the other perspectives in order to accomplish the financial goals.

For example, within the financial perspective, a common goal is to increase profit per dollars invested as measured by ROI. In order to increase ROI, a customer-perspective objective might be to increase customer satisfaction as measured by the percentage of customers who would recommend the product to a friend. In order to increase customer satisfaction, an internal-process-perspective objective might be to increase product quality as measured by the percentage of defect-free units. Finally, in order to increase the percentage of defect-free units, the learning-and-growth-perspective objective might be to reduce factory employee turnover as measured by the percentage of employees leaving in under one year.

Illustration 23-30 illustrates this linkage across perspectives.

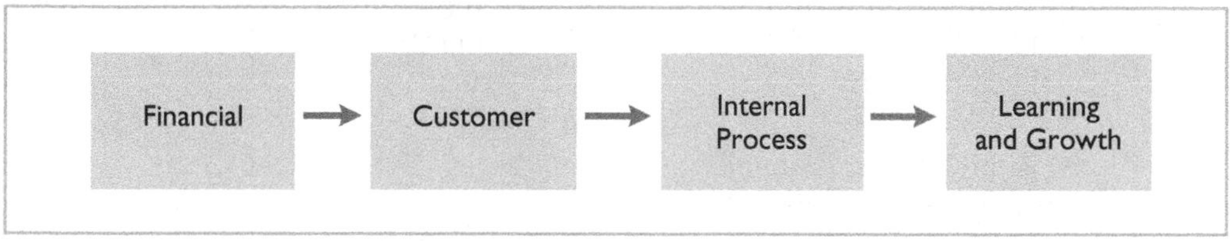

ILLUSTRATION 23-30
Linked process across balanced scorecard perspectives

Through this linked process, the company can better understand how to achieve its goals and what measures to use to evaluate performance.

In summary, the balanced scorecard does the following:

1. Employs both **financial and nonfinancial measures**. (For example, ROI is a financial measure; employee turnover is a nonfinancial measure.)
2. **Creates linkages** so that high-level corporate goals can be communicated all the way down to the shop floor.
3. **Provides measurable objectives for nonfinancial measures** such as product quality, rather than vague statements such as "We would like to improve quality."
4. Integrates all of the company's goals into a single performance measurement system, so that **an inappropriate amount of weight will not be placed on any single goal**.

SERVICE COMPANY INSIGHT United Airlines

PhotoDisc, Inc./Getty Images

It May Be Time to Fly United Again

Many of the benefits of a balanced scorecard approach are evident in the improved operations at United Airlines. At the time it filed for bankruptcy, United had a reputation for some of the worst service in the airline business. But when Glenn Tilton took over as United's chief executive officer, he recognized that things had to change.

He implemented an incentive program that allows all of United's 63,000 employees to earn a bonus of 2.5% or more of their wages if the company "exceeds its goals for on-time flight departures and for customer intent to fly United again." After instituting this program, the company's on-time departures were among the best, its customer complaints were reduced considerably, and the number of customers who said that they would fly United again was at its highest level ever.

Sources: Susan Carey, "Friendlier Skies: In Bankruptcy, United Airlines Forges a Path to Better Service," *Wall Street Journal* (June 15, 2004); and Emre Serpen, "More to Maintain," *Airline Business* (November 2012), pp. 38–40.

Which of the perspectives of a balanced scorecard were the focus of United's CEO? (Go to **WileyPLUS** for this answer and additional questions.)

DO IT! ▶4 Reporting Variances

Polar Vortex Corporation experienced the following variances: materials price $250 F, materials quantity $1,100 F, labor price $700 U, labor quantity $300 F, and overhead $800 F. Sales revenue was $102,700, and cost of goods sold (at standard) was $61,900. Determine the actual gross profit.

Action Plan

- ✔ Gross profit at standard is sales revenue less cost of goods sold at standard.
- ✔ Adjust standard gross profit by adding a net favorable variance or subtracting a net unfavorable variance.

SOLUTION

Sales revenue		$102,700
Cost of goods sold (at standard)		61,900
Standard gross profit		40,800
Variances		
Materials price	$ 250 F	
Materials quantity	1,100 F	
Labor price	700 U	
Labor quantity	300 F	
Overhead	800 F	
Total variance favorable		1,750
Gross profit (actual)		$ 42,550

Related exercise material: **E23-10, E23-14, E23-15,** and **DO IT! 23-4.**

USING DECISION TOOLS—STARBUCKS

Starbucks faces many situations where it needs to apply the decision tools learned in this chapter. Assume that during the past month, Starbucks produced 10,000 50-pound sacks of dark roast Sumatra coffee beans, with the standard cost for one 50-pound sack of dark roast Sumatra as follows.

	Standard				
Manufacturing Cost Elements	**Quantity**	×	**Price**	=	**Cost**
Direct materials (unroasted beans)	60 lbs.	×	$ 2.00	=	$120.00
Direct labor	0.25 hours	×	$16.00	=	4.00
Overhead	0.25 hours	×	$48.00	=	12.00
					$136.00

During the month, the following transactions occurred in manufacturing the 10,000 50-pound sacks of Sumatra coffee.

1. Purchased 620,000 pounds of unroasted beans at a price of $1.90 per pound for a total cost of $1,178,000.
2. All materials purchased during the period were used to make coffee during the period.
3. 2,300 direct labor hours were worked at a total labor cost of $36,340 (an average hourly rate of $15.80).
4. Variable manufacturing overhead incurred was $34,600, and fixed overhead incurred was $84,000.

The manufacturing overhead rate of $48.00 is based on a normal capacity of 2,600 direct labor hours. The total budget at this capacity is $83,980 fixed and $40,820 variable.

INSTRUCTIONS

Determine whether Starbucks met its price and quantity objectives relative to materials, labor, and overhead.

SOLUTION

To determine whether Starbucks met its price and quantity objectives, compute the total variance and the variances for direct materials and direct labor, and calculate the total variance for manufacturing overhead.

Total Variance

Actual cost incurred:	
Direct materials	$1,178,000
Direct labor	36,340
Overhead	118,600
Total actual costs	1,332,940
Less: Standard cost (10,000 × $136.00)	1,360,000
Total variance	$ 27,060 F

Direct Materials Variances

Total	= $1,178,000 (620,000 × $1.90)	− $1,200,000 (600,000 × $2.00)	= $22,000 F
Price	= $1,178,000 (620,000 × $1.90)	− $1,240,000 (620,000 × $2.00)	= $62,000 F
Quantity	= $1,240,000 (620,000 × $2.00)	− $1,200,000 (600,000 × $2.00)	= $40,000 U

Direct Labor Variances

Total	= $36,340 (2,300 × $15.80)	− $40,000 (2,500* × $16.00)	= $ 3,660 F
Price	= $36,340 (2,300 × $15.80)	− $36,800 (2,300 × $16.00)	= $ 460 F
Quantity	= $36,800 (2,300 × $16.00)	− $40,000 (2,500* × $16.00)	= $ 3,200 F

*10,000 × .25

Overhead Variance

Total	= $118,600 ($84,000 + $34,600)	− $120,000 (2,500 × $48)	= $ 1,400 F

Starbucks' total variance was a favorable $27,060. The total materials, labor, and overhead variances were favorable. The company did have an unfavorable materials quantity variance, but this was outweighed by the favorable materials price variance.

LEARNING OBJECTIVE *5

APPENDIX 23A: Identify the features of a standard cost accounting system.

A **standard cost accounting system** is a double-entry system of accounting. In this system, companies use standard costs in making entries, and they formally recognize variances in the accounts. Companies may use a standard cost system with either job order or process costing.

In this appendix, we will explain and illustrate a **standard cost, job order cost accounting system**. The system is based on two important assumptions:

1. Variances from standards are recognized at the earliest opportunity.
2. The Work in Process account is maintained exclusively on the basis of standard costs.

In practice, there are many variations among standard cost systems. The system described here should prepare you for systems you see in the "real world."

JOURNAL ENTRIES

We will use the transactions of Xonic to illustrate the journal entries. Note as you study the entries that the major difference between the entries here and those for the job order cost accounting system in Chapter 15 is the **variance accounts**.

1. Purchase raw materials on account for $13,020 when the standard cost is $12,600.

Raw Materials Inventory	12,600	
Materials Price Variance	420	
Accounts Payable		13,020
(To record purchase of materials)		

Xonic debits the inventory account for actual quantities at standard cost. This enables the perpetual materials records to show actual quantities. Xonic debits the price variance, which is unfavorable, to Materials Price Variance.

2. Incur direct labor costs of $31,080 when the standard labor cost is $31,500.

Factory Labor	31,500	
Labor Price Variance		420
Factory Wages Payable		31,080
(To record direct labor costs)		

Like the raw materials inventory account, Xonic debits Factory Labor for actual hours worked at the standard hourly rate of pay. In this case, the labor variance is favorable. Thus, Xonic credits Labor Price Variance.

3. Incur actual manufacturing overhead costs of $10,900.

Manufacturing Overhead	10,900	
Accounts Payable/Cash/Acc. Depreciation		10,900
(To record overhead incurred)		

The controllable overhead variance (see Appendix 23B) is not recorded at this time. It depends on standard hours applied to work in process. This amount is not known at the time overhead is incurred.

4. Issue raw materials for production at a cost of $12,600 when the standard cost is $12,000.

Work in Process Inventory	12,000	
Materials Quantity Variance	600	
Raw Materials Inventory		12,600
(To record issuance of raw materials)		

Xonic debits Work in Process Inventory for standard materials quantities used at standard prices. It debits the variance account because the variance is unfavorable. The company credits Raw Materials Inventory for actual quantities at standard prices.

5. Assign factory labor to production at a cost of $31,500 when standard cost is $30,000.

Work in Process Inventory	30,000	
Labor Quantity Variance	1,500	
Factory Labor		31,500
(To assign factory labor to jobs)		

Xonic debits Work in Process Inventory for standard labor hours at standard rates. It debits the unfavorable variance to Labor Quantity Variance. The credit to Factory Labor produces a zero balance in this account.

6. Apply manufacturing overhead to production $10,000.

Work in Process Inventory	10,000	
Manufacturing Overhead		10,000
(To assign overhead to jobs)		

Xonic debits Work in Process Inventory for standard hours allowed multiplied by the standard overhead rate.

7. Transfer completed work to finished goods $52,000.

Finished Goods Inventory	52,000	
Work in Process Inventory		52,000
(To record transfer of completed work to finished goods)		

In this example, both inventory accounts are at standard cost.

8. Sell the 1,000 gallons of Xonic Tonic for $70,000.

Accounts Receivable	70,000	
Cost of Goods Sold	52,000	
Sales		70,000
Finished Goods Inventory		52,000
(To record sale of finished goods and the cost of goods sold)		

The company debits Cost of Goods Sold at standard cost. Gross profit, in turn, is the difference between sales and the standard cost of goods sold.

9. Recognize unfavorable total overhead variance:

Overhead Variance	900	
Manufacturing Overhead		900
(To recognize overhead variances)		

Prior to this entry, a debit balance of $900 existed in Manufacturing Overhead. This entry therefore produces a zero balance in the Manufacturing Overhead account. The information needed for this entry is often not available until the end of the accounting period.

LEDGER ACCOUNTS

Illustration 23A-1 shows the cost accounts for Xonic after posting the entries. Note that five variance accounts are included in the ledger. The remaining accounts are the same as those illustrated for a job order cost system in Chapter 15, in which only actual costs were used.

ILLUSTRATION 23A-1
Cost accounts with variances

Raw Materials Inventory

(1) 12,600	(4) 12,600

Materials Price Variance

(1) 420	

Work in Process Inventory

(4) 12,000	(7) 52,000
(5) 30,000	
(6) 10,000	

Factory Labor

(2) 31,500	(5) 31,500

Materials Quantity Variance

(4) 600	

Finished Goods Inventory

(7) 52,000	(8) 52,000

Manufacturing Overhead

(3) 10,900	(6) 10,000
	(9) 900

Labor Price Variance

	(2) 420

Cost of Goods Sold

(8) 52,000	

Labor Quantity Variance

(5) 1,500	

Overhead Variance

(9) 900	

▼ **HELPFUL HINT**
All debit balances in variance accounts indicate unfavorable variances; all credit balances indicate favorable variances.

LEARNING OBJECTIVE *6

APPENDIX 23B: Compute overhead controllable and volume variances.

As indicated in the chapter, the total overhead variance is generally analyzed through a price variance and a quantity variance. The name usually given to the price variance is the **overhead controllable variance**; the quantity variance is referred to as the **overhead volume variance**.

OVERHEAD CONTROLLABLE VARIANCE

The **overhead controllable variance** shows whether overhead costs are effectively controlled. To compute this variance, the company compares actual overhead costs incurred with budgeted costs for the **standard hours allowed**. The budgeted costs are determined from a flexible manufacturing overhead budget. The concepts related to a flexible budget were discussed in Chapter 22.

For Xonic, the budget formula for manufacturing overhead is variable manufacturing overhead cost of $3 per hour of labor plus fixed manufacturing overhead costs of $4,400 ($52,800 ÷ 12, per Illustration 23-6 on page 1124). Illustration 23B-1 shows the monthly flexible budget for Xonic.

ILLUSTRATION 23B-1
Flexible budget using standard direct labor hours

Xonic.xls

	A	B	C	D	E
1	**XONIC**				
2	**Flexible Manufacturing Overhead Monthly Budget**				
3	Activity Index				
4	Standard direct labor hours	1,800	2,000	2,200	2,400
5					
6	Costs				
7	Variable costs				
8	Indirect materials	$1,800	$ 2,000	$ 2,200	$ 2,400
9	Indirect labor	2,700	3,000	3,300	3,600
10	Utilities	900	1,000	1,100	1,200
11	Total variable costs	5,400	6,000	6,600	7,200
12					
13	Fixed costs				
14	Supervision	3,000	3,000	3,000	3,000
15	Depreciation	1,400	1,400	1,400	1,400
16	Total fixed costs	4,400	4,400	4,400	4,400
17	Total costs	$9,800	$10,400	$11,000	$11,600

As shown, the budgeted costs for 2,000 standard hours are $10,400 ($6,000 variable and $4,400 fixed).

Illustration 23B-2 shows the formula for the overhead controllable variance and the calculation for Xonic at 1,000 units of output (2,000 standard labor hours).

ILLUSTRATION 23B-2
Formula for overhead controllable variance

Actual Overhead	−	Overhead Budgeted*	=	Overhead Controllable Variance
$10,900 ($6,500 + $4,400)	−	$10,400 ($6,000 + $4,400)	=	$500 U

*Based on standard hours allowed.

The overhead controllable variance for Xonic is $500 unfavorable.

Most controllable variances are associated with variable costs, which are controllable costs. Fixed costs are often known at the time the budget is prepared and are therefore not as likely to deviate from the budgeted amount. In Xonic's case, all of the overhead controllable variance is due to the difference between the actual variable overhead costs ($6,500) and the budgeted variable costs ($6,000).

Management can compare actual and budgeted overhead for each manufacturing overhead cost that contributes to the controllable variance. In addition, management can develop cost and quantity variances for each overhead cost, such as indirect materials and indirect labor.

OVERHEAD VOLUME VARIANCE

The **overhead volume variance** is the difference between normal capacity hours and standard hours allowed times the fixed overhead rate. The overhead volume variance relates to whether fixed costs were under- or overapplied during the year. For example, the overhead volume variance answers the question of whether Xonic effectively used its fixed costs. If Xonic produces less Xonic Tonic than normal capacity would allow, an unfavorable variance results. Conversely, if Xonic produces more Xonic Tonic than what is considered normal capacity, a favorable variance results.

The formula for computing the overhead volume variance is as follows.

Fixed Overhead Rate	×	(Normal Capacity Hours	−	Standard Hours Allowed)	=	Overhead Volume Variance

ILLUSTRATION 23B-3
Formula for overhead volume variance

To illustrate the fixed overhead rate computation, recall that Xonic budgeted fixed overhead cost for the year of $52,800 (Illustration 23-6 on page 1124). At normal capacity, 26,400 standard direct labor hours are required. The fixed overhead rate is therefore $2 per hour ($52,800 ÷ 26,400 hours).

Xonic produced 1,000 units of Xonic Tonic in June. The standard hours allowed for the 1,000 gallons produced in June is 2,000 (1,000 gallons × 2 hours). For Xonic, normal capacity for June is 1,100, so standard direct labor hours for June at normal capacity is 2,200 (26,400 annual hours ÷ 12 months). The computation of the overhead volume variance in this case is as follows.

Fixed Overhead Rate	×	(Normal Capacity Hours	−	Standard Hours Allowed)	=	Overhead Volume Variance
$2	×	(2,200	−	2,000)	=	$400 U

ILLUSTRATION 23B-4
Computation of overhead volume variance for Xonic

In Xonic's case, a $400 unfavorable volume variance results. The volume variance is unfavorable because Xonic produced only 1,000 gallons rather than the normal capacity of 1,100 gallons in the month of June. As a result, it underapplied fixed overhead for that period.

In computing the overhead variances, it is important to remember the following.

1. Standard hours allowed are used in each of the variances.
2. Budgeted costs for the controllable variance are derived from the flexible budget.
3. The controllable variance generally pertains to variable costs.
4. The volume variance pertains solely to fixed costs.

REVIEW AND PRACTICE

▶ LEARNING OBJECTIVES REVIEW

1 Describe standard costs. Both standards and budgets are predetermined costs. The primary difference is that a standard is a unit amount, whereas a budget is a total amount. A standard may be regarded as the budgeted cost per unit of product.

Standard costs offer a number of advantages. They (a) facilitate management planning, (b) promote greater economy, (c) are useful in setting selling prices, (d) contribute to management control, (e) permit "management by exception," and (f) simplify the costing of inventories and reduce clerical costs.

The direct materials price standard should be based on the delivered cost of raw materials plus an allowance for receiving and handling. The direct materials quantity standard should establish the required quantity plus an allowance for waste and spoilage.

The direct labor price standard should be based on current wage rates and anticipated adjustments such as COLAs. It also generally includes payroll taxes and fringe benefits. Direct labor quantity standards should be based on required production time plus an allowance for rest periods, cleanup, machine setup, and machine downtime.

For manufacturing overhead, a standard predetermined overhead rate is used. It is based on an expected standard activity index such as standard direct labor hours or standard machine hours.

2 Determine direct materials variances. The formulas for the direct materials variances are as follows.

$$\begin{pmatrix}\text{Actual quantity}\\ \times\ \text{Actual price}\end{pmatrix} - \begin{pmatrix}\text{Standard quantity}\\ \times\ \text{Standard price}\end{pmatrix} = \text{Total materials variance}$$

$$\begin{pmatrix}\text{Actual quantity}\\ \times\ \text{Actual price}\end{pmatrix} - \begin{pmatrix}\text{Actual quantity}\\ \times\ \text{Standard price}\end{pmatrix} = \text{Materials price variance}$$

$$\begin{pmatrix}\text{Actual quantity}\\ \times\ \text{Standard price}\end{pmatrix} - \begin{pmatrix}\text{Standard quantity}\\ \times\ \text{Standard price}\end{pmatrix} = \text{Materials quantity variance}$$

3 Determine direct labor and total manufacturing overhead variances. The formulas for the direct labor variances are as follows.

$$\begin{pmatrix}\text{Actual hours}\\ \times\ \text{Actual rate}\end{pmatrix} - \begin{pmatrix}\text{Standard hours}\\ \times\ \text{Standard rate}\end{pmatrix} = \text{Total labor variance}$$

$$\begin{pmatrix}\text{Actual hours}\\ \times\ \text{Actual rate}\end{pmatrix} - \begin{pmatrix}\text{Actual hours}\\ \times\ \text{Standard rate}\end{pmatrix} = \text{Labor price variance}$$

$$\begin{pmatrix}\text{Actual hours}\\ \times\ \text{Standard rate}\end{pmatrix} - \begin{pmatrix}\text{Standard hours}\\ \times\ \text{Standard rate}\end{pmatrix} = \text{Labor quantity variance}$$

The formula for the total manufacturing overhead variance is as follows.

$$\begin{pmatrix}\text{Actual}\\ \text{overhead}\end{pmatrix} - \begin{pmatrix}\text{Overhead}\\ \text{applied at}\\ \text{standard hours}\\ \text{allowed}\end{pmatrix} = \text{Total overhead variance}$$

4 Prepare variance reports and balanced scorecards. Variances are reported to management in variance reports. The reports facilitate management by exception by highlighting significant differences. Under a standard costing system, an income statement prepared for management will report cost of goods sold at standard cost and then disclose each variance separately.

The balanced scorecard incorporates financial and nonfinancial measures in an integrated system that links performance measurement and a company's strategic goals. It employs four perspectives: financial, customer, internal process, and learning and growth. Objectives are set within each of these perspectives that link to objectives within the other perspectives.

***5 Identify the features of a standard cost accounting system.** In a standard cost accounting system, companies journalize and post standard costs, and they maintain separate variance accounts in the ledger.

***6 Compute overhead controllable and volume variances.** The total overhead variance is generally analyzed through a price variance and a quantity variance. The name usually given to the price variance is the overhead controllable variance. The quantity variance is referred to as the overhead volume variance.

DECISION TOOLS REVIEW

DECISION CHECKPOINTS	INFO NEEDED FOR DECISION	TOOL TO USE FOR DECISION	HOW TO EVALUATE RESULTS
Has management accomplished its price and quantity objectives regarding materials?	Actual cost and standard cost of materials	Materials price and materials quantity variances	Positive (favorable) variances suggest that price and quantity objectives have been met.
Has management accomplished its price and quantity objectives regarding labor?	Actual cost and standard cost of labor	Labor price and labor quantity variances	Positive (favorable) variances suggest that price and quantity objectives have been met.
Has management accomplished its objectives regarding manufacturing overhead?	Actual cost and standard cost of manufacturing overhead	Total manufacturing overhead variance	Positive (favorable) variances suggest that manufacturing overhead objectives have been met.

GLOSSARY REVIEW

Balanced scorecard An approach that incorporates financial and nonfinancial measures in an integrated system that links performance measurement and a company's strategic goals. (p. 1136).

Customer perspective A viewpoint employed in the balanced scorecard to evaluate the company from the perspective of those people who buy and use its products or services. (p. 1136).

Direct labor price standard The rate per hour that should be incurred for direct labor. (p. 1123).

Direct labor quantity standard The time that should be required to make one unit of product. (p. 1123).

Direct materials price standard The cost per unit of direct materials that should be incurred. (p. 1122).

Direct materials quantity standard The quantity of direct materials that should be used per unit of finished goods. (p. 1122).

Financial perspective A viewpoint employed in the balanced scorecard to evaluate a company's performance using financial measures. (p. 1136).

Ideal standards Standards based on the optimum level of performance under perfect operating conditions. (p. 1121).

Internal process perspective A viewpoint employed in the balanced scorecard to evaluate the effectiveness and efficiency of a company's value chain, including product development, production, delivery, and after-sale service. (p. 1136).

Labor price variance The difference between the actual hours times the actual rate and the actual hours times the standard rate for labor. (p. 1130).

Labor quantity variance The difference between actual hours times the standard rate and standard hours times the standard rate for labor. (p. 1130).

Learning and growth perspective A viewpoint employed in the balanced scorecard to evaluate how well a company develops and retains its employees. (p. 1136).

Materials price variance The difference between the actual quantity times the actual price and the actual quantity times the standard price for materials. (p. 1127).

Materials quantity variance The difference between the actual quantity times the standard price and the standard quantity times the standard price for materials. (p. 1127).

Normal capacity The average activity output that a company should experience over the long run. (p. 1124).

Normal standards Standards based on an efficient level of performance that are attainable under expected operating conditions. (p. 1121).

***Overhead controllable variance** The difference between actual overhead incurred and overhead budgeted for the standard hours allowed. (p. 1142).

***Overhead volume variance** The difference between normal capacity hours and standard hours allowed times the fixed overhead rate. (p. 1143).

***Standard cost accounting system** A double-entry system of accounting in which standard costs are used in making entries, and variances are recognized in the accounts. (p. 1139).

Standard costs Predetermined unit costs which companies use as measures of performance. (p. 1120).

Standard hours allowed The hours that should have been worked for the units produced. (p. 1132).

Standard predetermined overhead rate An overhead rate determined by dividing budgeted overhead costs by an expected standard activity index. (p. 1123).

Total labor variance The difference between actual hours times the actual rate and standard hours times the standard rate for labor. (p. 1129).

Total materials variance The difference between the actual quantity times the actual price and the standard quantity times the standard price of materials. (p. 1127).

Total overhead variance The difference between actual overhead costs and overhead costs applied to work done, based on standard hours allowed. (p. 1131).

Variance The difference between total actual costs and total standard costs. (p. 1125).

PRACTICE MULTIPLE-CHOICE QUESTIONS

(LO 1) **1.** Standards differ from budgets in that:
(a) budgets but not standards may be used in valuing inventories.
(b) budgets but not standards may be journalized and posted.
(c) budgets are a total amount and standards are a unit amount.
(d) only budgets contribute to management planning and control.

(LO 1) **2.** Standard costs:
(a) are only imposed by governmental agencies.
(b) are predetermined unit costs which companies use as measures of performance.
(c) can be used by manufacturing companies but not by service or not-for-profit companies.
(d) All of the above.

(LO 1) **3.** The advantages of standard costs include all of the following **except**:
(a) management by exception may be used.
(b) management planning is facilitated.
(c) they may simplify the costing of inventories.
(d) management must use a static budget.

(LO 1) **4.** Normal standards:
(a) allow for rest periods, machine breakdowns, and setup time.
(b) represent levels of performance under perfect operating conditions.
(c) are rarely used because managers believe they lower workforce morale.
(d) are more likely than ideal standards to result in unethical practices.

(LO 1) **5.** The setting of standards is:
(a) a managerial accounting decision.
(b) a management decision.
(c) a worker decision.
(d) preferably set at the ideal level of performance.

(LO 2) **6.** Each of the following formulas is correct **except**:
(a) Labor price variance = (Actual hours × Actual rate) − (Actual hours × Standard rate).
(b) Total overhead variance = Actual overhead − Overhead applied.
(c) Materials price variance = (Actual quantity × Actual price) − (Standard quantity × Standard price).
(d) Labor quantity variance = (Actual hours × Standard rate) − (Standard hours × Standard rate).

(LO 2) **7.** In producing product AA, 6,300 pounds of direct materials were used at a cost of $1.10 per pound. The standard was 6,000 pounds at $1.00 per pound. The direct materials quantity variance is:
(a) $330 unfavorable. (c) $600 unfavorable.
(b) $300 unfavorable. (d) $630 unfavorable.

8. In producing product ZZ, 14,800 direct labor hours were used at a rate of $8.20 per hour. The standard was 15,000 hours at $8.00 per hour. Based on these data, the direct labor: (LO 3)
(a) quantity variance is $1,600 favorable.
(b) quantity variance is $1,600 unfavorable.
(c) price variance is $3,000 favorable.
(d) price variance is $3,000 unfavorable.

9. Which of the following is **correct** about the total overhead variance? (LO 3)
(a) Budgeted overhead and overhead applied are the same.
(b) Total actual overhead is composed of variable overhead, fixed overhead, and period costs.
(c) Standard hours actually worked are used in computing the variance.
(d) Standard hours allowed for the work done is the measure used in computing the variance.

10. The formula for computing the total overhead variance is: (LO 3)
(a) actual overhead less overhead applied.
(b) overhead budgeted less overhead applied.
(c) actual overhead less overhead budgeted.
(d) No correct answer is given.

11. Which of the following is **incorrect** about variance reports? (LO 4)
(a) They facilitate "management by exception."
(b) They should only be sent to the top level of management.
(c) They should be prepared as soon as possible.
(d) They may vary in form, content, and frequency among companies.

12. In using variance reports to evaluate cost control, management normally looks into: (LO 4)
(a) all variances.
(b) favorable variances only.
(c) unfavorable variances only.
(d) both favorable and unfavorable variances that exceed a predetermined quantitative measure such as a percentage or dollar amount.

13. Generally accepted accounting principles allow a company to: (LO 4)
(a) report inventory at standard cost but cost of goods sold must be reported at actual cost.
(b) report cost of goods sold at standard cost but inventory must be reported at actual cost.
(c) report inventory and cost of goods sold at standard cost as long as there are no significant differences between actual and standard cost.
(d) report inventory and cost of goods sold only at actual costs; standard costing is never permitted.

(LO 4) **14.** Which of the following would **not** be an objective used in the customer perspective of the balanced scorecard approach?
(a) Percentage of customers who would recommend product to a friend.
(b) Customer retention.
(c) Brand recognition.
(d) Earnings per share.

(LO 5) ***15.** Which of the following is **incorrect** about a standard cost accounting system?
(a) It is applicable to job order costing.
(b) It is applicable to process costing.
(c) It reports only favorable variances.
(d) It keeps separate accounts for each variance.

***16.** The formula to compute the overhead volume variance is: (LO 6)
(a) Fixed overhead rate × (Standard hours − Actual hours).
(b) Fixed overhead rate × (Normal capacity hours − Actual hours).
(c) Fixed overhead rate × (Normal capacity hours − Standard hours allowed).
(d) (Variable overhead rate + Fixed overhead rate) × (Normal capacity hours − Standard hours allowed).

SOLUTIONS

1. **(c)** Budgets are expressed in total amounts, and standards are expressed in unit amounts. The other choices are incorrect because (a) standards, not budgets, may be used in valuing inventories; (b) standards, not budgets, may be journalized and posted; and (d) both budgets and standards contribute to management planning and control.
2. **(b)** Standard costs are predetermined unit costs which companies use as measures of performance. The other choices are incorrect because (a) only those standard costs that are part of regulations are imposed by governmental agencies, (c) standard costs can be used by all types of companies, and (d) choices (a) and (c) are incorrect.
3. **(d)** Standard costs are separate from a static budget. The other choices are all advantages of using standard costs.
4. **(a)** Normal standards allow for rest periods, machine breakdowns, and setup time. The other choices are incorrect because they describe ideal standards, not normal standards.
5. **(b)** Standards are set by management. The other choices are incorrect because setting standards requires input from (a) managerial accountants and (c) sometimes workers, but the final decision is made by management. Choice (d) is incorrect because setting standards at the ideal level of performance is uncommon because of the perceived negative effect on worker morale.
6. **(c)** Materials price variance = (Actual quantity × Actual price) − (Actual quantity (not Standard quantity) × Standard price). The other choices are correct formulas.
7. **(b)** The direct materials quantity variance is (6,300 × $1.00) − (6,000 × $1.00) = $300. This variance is unfavorable because more material was used than prescribed by the standard. The other choices are therefore incorrect.
8. **(a)** The direct labor quantity variance is (14,800 × $8) − (15,000 × $8) = $1,600. This variance is favorable because less labor was used than prescribed by the standard. The other choices are therefore incorrect.
9. **(d)** Standard hours allowed for work done is the measure used in computing the variance. The other choices are incorrect because (a) budgeted overhead is used to calculate the predetermined overhead rate while overhead applied is equal to standard hours allowed times the predetermined overhead rate, (b) overhead is a product cost and does not include period costs, and (c) standard hours allowed, not hours actually worked, are used in computing the overhead variance.
10. **(a)** Total overhead variance equals actual overhead less overhead applied. The other choices are therefore incorrect.
11. **(b)** Variance reports should be sent to the level of management responsible for the area in which the variance occurred so it can be remedied as quickly as possible. The other choices are correct statements.
12. **(d)** In using variance reports to evaluate cost control, management normally looks into both favorable and unfavorable variances that exceed a predetermined quantitative measure such as a percentage or dollar amount. The other choices are therefore incorrect.
13. **(c)** GAAP allows a company to report both inventory and cost of goods sold at standard cost as long as there are no significant differences between actual and standard cost. The other choices are therefore incorrect.
14. **(d)** Earnings per share is not an objective used in the customer perspective of the balanced scorecard approach. The other choices are all true statements.

*15. **(c)** A standard cost accounting system reports both favorable and unfavorable variances. The other choices are all correct statements.

*16. **(c)** The formula to compute the overhead volume variance is Fixed overhead rate × (Normal capacity hours − Standard hours allowed). The other choices are therefore incorrect.

PRACTICE EXERCISES

Compute materials and labor variances.

(LO 2, 3)

1. Hector Inc., which produces a single product, has prepared the following standard cost sheet for one unit of the product.

Direct materials (6 pounds at $2.50 per pound)	$15.00
Direct labor (3.1 hours at $12.00 per hour)	$37.20

During the month of April, the company manufactures 250 units and incurs the following actual costs.

Direct materials purchased and used (1,600 pounds)	$4,192
Direct labor (760 hours)	$8,740

INSTRUCTIONS

Compute the total, price, and quantity variances for materials and labor.

SOLUTION

1. Total materials variance:

(AQ × AP)	–	(SQ × SP)	
(1,600 × $2.62*)		(1,500** × $2.50)	
$4,192	–	$3,750	= $442 U

*$4,192 ÷ 1,600 **250 × 6

Materials price variance:

(AQ × AP)	–	(AQ × SP)	
(1,600 × $2.62)		(1,600 × $2.50)	
$4,192	–	$4,000	= $192 U

Materials quantity variance:

(AQ × SP)	–	(SQ × SP)	
(1,600 × $2.50)		(1,500 × $2.50)	
$4,000	–	$3,750	= $250 U

Total labor variance:

(AH × AR)	–	(SH × SR)	
(760 × $11.50*)		(775** × $12.00)	
$8,740	–	$9,300	= $560 F

*$8,740 ÷ 760 **250 × 3.1

Labor price variance:

(AH × AR)	–	(AH × SR)	
(760 × $11.50)		(760 × $12.00)	
$8,740	–	$9,120	= $380 F

Labor quantity variance:

(AH × SR)	–	(SH × SR)	
(760 × $12.00)		(775 × $12.00)	
$9,120	–	$9,300	= $180 F

Compute overhead variance.

(LO 3)

2. Manufacturing overhead data for the production of Product H by Yamato Company are as follows.

Overhead incurred for 35,000 actual direct labor hours worked	$140,000
Overhead rate (variable $3; fixed $1) at normal capacity of 36,000 direct labor hours	$4
Standard hours allowed for work done	34,000

INSTRUCTIONS

Compute the total overhead variance.

SOLUTION

2. Total overhead variance:

Actual Overhead	−	Overhead Applied		
$140,000	−	$136,000	=	$4,000 U
		(34,000 × $4)		

▶ PRACTICE PROBLEM

Compute variances. (LO 2, 3)

Manlow Company makes a cologne called Allure. the standard cost for one bottle of Allure is as follows.

	Standard						
Manufacturing Cost Elements	**Quantity**	×	**Price**	=	**Cost**
Direct materials	6 oz.	×	$ 0.90	=	$ 5.40
Direct labor	0.5 hrs.	×	12.00	=	6.00
Manufacturing overhead	0.5 hrs.	×	4.80	=	2.40
					$13.80

During the month, the following transactions occurred in manufacturing 10,000 bottles of Allure.

1. 58,000 ounces of materials were purchased at $1.00 per ounce.
2. All the materials purchased were used to produce the 10,000 bottles of Allure.
3. 4,900 direct labor hours were worked at a total labor cost of $56,350.
4. Variable manufacturing overhead incurred was $15,000 and fixed overhead incurred was $10,400.

The manufacturing overhead rate of $4.80 is based on a normal capacity of 5,200 direct labor hours. The total budget at this capacity is $10,400 fixed and $14,560 variable.

INSTRUCTIONS

(a) Compute the total variance and the variances for direct materials and direct labor elements.

(b) Compute the total variance for manufacturing overhead.

SOLUTION

(a)

Total Variance

Actual costs incurred	
Direct materials	$ 58,000
Direct labor	56,350
Manufacturing overhead	25,400
	139,750
Standard cost (10,000 × $13.80)	138,000
Total variance	$ 1,750 U

Direct Materials Variances

Total	=	$58,000 (58,000 × $1.00)	−	$54,000 (60,000* × $0.90)	=	$4,000 U
Price	=	$58,000 (58,000 × $1.00)	−	$52,200 (58,000 × $0.90)	=	$5,800 U
Quantity	=	$52,200 (58,000 × $0.90)	−	$54,000 (60,000 × $0.90)	=	$1,800 F

*10,000 × 6

Direct Labor Variances

Total	=	$56,350 (4,900 × $11.50*)	−	$60,000 (5,000** × $12.00)	=	$3,650 F
Price	=	$56,350 (4,900 × $11.50)	−	$58,800 (4,900 × $12.00)	=	$2,450 F
Quantity	=	$58,800 (4,900 × $12.00)	−	$60,000 (5,000 × $12.00)	=	$1,200 F

*56,350 ÷ 4,900; **10,000 × 0.5

(b)

Overhead Variance

Total	=	$25,400 ($15,000 + $10,400)	−	$24,000 (5,000 × $4.80)	=	$1,400 U

WileyPLUS Brief Exercises, DO IT! Exercises, Exercises, Problems, and many additional resources are available for practice in WileyPLUS.

NOTE: All asterisked Questions, Exercises, and Problems relate to material in the appendices to the chapter.

QUESTIONS

1. (a) "Standard costs are the expected total cost of completing a job." Is this correct? Explain.
   (b) "A standard imposed by a governmental agency is known as a regulation." Do you agree? Explain.
2. (a) Explain the similarities and differences between standards and budgets.
   (b) Contrast the accounting for standards and budgets.
3. Standard costs facilitate management planning. What are the other advantages of standard costs?
4. Contrast the roles of the management accountant and management in setting standard costs.
5. Distinguish between an ideal standard and a normal standard.
6. What factors should be considered in setting (a) the direct materials price standard and (b) the direct materials quantity standard?
7. "The objective in setting the direct labor quantity standard is to determine the aggregate time required to make one unit of product." Do you agree? What allowances should be made in setting this standard?
8. How is the predetermined overhead rate determined when standard costs are used?
9. What is the difference between a favorable cost variance and an unfavorable cost variance?
10. In each of the following formulas, supply the words that should be inserted for each number in parentheses.
    (a) (Actual quantity × (1)) − (Standard quantity × (2)) = Total materials variance
    (b) ((3) × Actual price) − (Actual quantity × (4)) = Materials price variance
    (c) (Actual quantity × (5)) − ((6) × Standard price) = Materials quantity variance
11. In the direct labor variance matrix, there are three factors: (1) Actual hours × Actual rate, (2) Actual hours × Standard rate, and (3) Standard hours × Standard rate. Using the numbers, indicate the formulas for each of the direct labor variances.
12. Mikan Company's standard predetermined overhead rate is $9 per direct labor hour. For the month of June, 26,000 actual hours were worked, and 27,000 standard hours were allowed. How much overhead was applied?
13. How often should variances be reported to management? What principle may be used with variance reports?
14. What circumstances may cause the purchasing department to be responsible for both an unfavorable materials price variance and an unfavorable materials quantity variance?
15. What are the four perspectives used in the balanced scorecard? Discuss the nature of each, and how the perspectives are linked.
16. Kerry James says that the balanced scorecard was created to replace financial measures as the primary mechanism for performance evaluation. He says that it uses only nonfinancial measures. Is this true?
17. What are some examples of nonfinancial measures used by companies to evaluate performance?
18. (a) How are variances reported in income statements prepared for management? (b) May standard costs be used in preparing financial statements for stockholders? Explain.

*19. (a) Explain the basic features of a standard cost accounting system. (b) What type of balance will exist in the variance account when (1) the materials price variance is unfavorable and (2) the labor quantity variance is favorable?

*20. If the $9 per hour overhead rate in Question 12 includes $5 variable, and actual overhead costs were $248,000, what is the overhead controllable variance for June? The normal capacity hours were 28,000. Is the variance favorable or unfavorable?

*21. What is the purpose of computing the overhead volume variance? What is the basic formula for this variance?

*22. Alma Ortiz does not understand why the overhead volume variance indicates that fixed overhead costs are under- or overapplied. Clarify this matter for Alma.

*23. John Hsu is attempting to outline the important points about overhead variances on a class examination. List four points that John should include in his outline.

BRIEF EXERCISES

Distinguish between a standard and a budget.
(LO 1), AP

BE23-1 Lopez Company uses both standards and budgets. For the year, estimated production of Product X is 500,000 units. Total estimated cost for materials and labor are $1,400,000 and $1,700,000. Compute the estimates for (a) a standard cost and (b) a budgeted cost.

Set direct materials standard.
(LO 1), AP

BE23-2 Tang Company accumulates the following data concerning raw materials in making one gallon of finished product. (1) Price—net purchase price $2.30, freight-in $0.20,

and receiving and handling $0.10. (2) Quantity—required materials 3.6 pounds, allowance for waste and spoilage 0.4 pounds. Compute the following.
(a) Standard direct materials price per gallon.
(b) Standard direct materials quantity per gallon.
(c) Total standard materials cost per gallon.

BE23-3 Labor data for making one gallon of finished product in Bing Company are as follows. (1) Price—hourly wage rate $14.00, payroll taxes $0.80, and fringe benefits $1.20. (2) Quantity—actual production time 1.1 hours, rest periods and cleanup 0.25 hours, and setup and downtime 0.15 hours. Compute the following.
(a) Standard direct labor rate per hour.
(b) Standard direct labor hours per gallon.
(c) Standard labor cost per gallon.

Set direct labor standard.
(LO 1), AP

BE23-4 Simba Company's standard materials cost per unit of output is $10 (2 pounds × $5). During July, the company purchases and uses 3,200 pounds of materials costing $16,192 in making 1,500 units of finished product. Compute the total, price, and quantity materials variances.

Compute direct materials variances.
(LO 2), AP

BE23-5 Mordica Company's standard labor cost per unit of output is $22 (2 hours × $11 per hour). During August, the company incurs 2,150 hours of direct labor at an hourly cost of $10.80 per hour in making 1,000 units of finished product. Compute the total, price, and quantity labor variances.

Compute direct labor variances.
(LO 3), AP

BE23-6 In October, Pine Company reports 21,000 actual direct labor hours, and it incurs $118,000 of manufacturing overhead costs. Standard hours allowed for the work done is 20,600 hours. The predetermined overhead rate is $6 per direct labor hour. Compute the total overhead variance.

Compute total overhead variance.
(LO 3), AP

BE23-7 The four perspectives in the balanced scorecard are (1) financial, (2) customer, (3) internal process, and (4) learning and growth. Match each of the following objectives with the perspective it is most likely associated with: (a) plant capacity utilization, (b) employee work days missed due to injury, (c) return on assets, and (d) brand recognition.

Match balanced scorecard perspectives.
(LO 4), AP

***BE23-8** Journalize the following transactions for Combs Company.
(a) Purchased 6,000 units of raw materials on account for $11,500. The standard cost was $12,000.
(b) Issued 5,600 units of raw materials for production. The standard units were 5,800.

Journalize materials variances.
(LO 5), AP

***BE23-9** Journalize the following transactions for Shelton, Inc.
(a) Incurred direct labor costs of $24,000 for 3,000 hours. The standard labor cost was $24,900.
(b) Assigned 3,000 direct labor hours costing $24,000 to production. Standard hours were 3,150.

Journalize labor variances.
(LO 5), AP

***BE23-10** Some overhead data for Pine Company are given in BE23-6. In addition, the flexible manufacturing overhead budget shows that budgeted costs are $4 variable per direct labor hour and $50,000 fixed. Compute the overhead controllable variance.

Compute the overhead controllable variance.
(LO 6), AP

***BE23-11** Using the data in BE23-6 and BE23-10, compute the overhead volume variance. Normal capacity was 25,000 direct labor hours.

Compute overhead volume variance.
(LO 6), AP

DO IT! EXERCISES

DO IT! 23-1 Larkin Company accumulated the following standard cost data concerning product I-Tal.

Direct materials per unit: 2 pounds at $5 per pound
Direct labor per unit: 0.2 hours at $16 per hour
Manufacturing overhead: Allocated based on direct labor hours at a predetermined rate of $20 per direct labor hour

Compute the standard cost of one unit of product I-Tal.

Compute standard cost.
(LO 1), AP

Compute materials variance.
(LO 2), AP

DO IT! 23-2 The standard cost of product 777 includes 2 units of direct materials at $6.00 per unit. During August, the company bought 29,000 units of materials at $6.30 and used those materials to produce 16,000 units. Compute the total, price, and quantity variances for materials.

Compute labor and manufacturing overhead variances.
(LO 3), AP

DO IT! 23-3 The standard cost of product 5252 includes 1.9 hours of direct labor at $14.00 per hour. The predetermined overhead rate is $22.00 per direct labor hour. During July, the company incurred 4,000 hours of direct labor at an average rate of $14.30 per hour and $81,300 of manufacturing overhead costs. It produced 2,000 units.

(a) Compute the total, price, and quantity variances for labor. (b) Compute the total overhead variance.

Prepare variance report.
(LO 4), AP

DO IT! 23-4 Tropic Zone Corporation experienced the following variances: materials price $350 U, materials quantity $1,700 F, labor price $800 F, labor quantity $500 F, and overhead $1,200 U. Sales revenue was $92,100, and cost of goods sold (at standard) was $51,600. Determine the actual gross profit.

EXERCISES

Compute budget and standard.
(LO 1), AP

E23-1 Parsons Company is planning to produce 2,000 units of product in 2017. Each unit requires 3 pounds of materials at $5 per pound and a half-hour of labor at $16 per hour. The overhead rate is 70% of direct labor.

Instructions

(a) Compute the budgeted amounts for 2017 for direct materials to be used, direct labor, and applied overhead.
(b) Compute the standard cost of one unit of product.
(c) What are the potential advantages to a corporation of using standard costs?

Compute standard materials costs.
(LO 1), AP

XLS

E23-2 Hank Itzek manufactures and sells homemade wine, and he wants to develop a standard cost per gallon. The following are required for production of a 50-gallon batch.

3,000 ounces of grape concentrate at $0.06 per ounce
54 pounds of granulated sugar at $0.30 per pound
60 lemons at $0.60 each
50 yeast tablets at $0.25 each
50 nutrient tablets at $0.20 each
2,600 ounces of water at $0.005 per ounce

Hank estimates that 4% of the grape concentrate is wasted, 10% of the sugar is lost, and 25% of the lemons cannot be used.

Instructions

Compute the standard cost of the ingredients for one gallon of wine. (Carry computations to two decimal places.)

Compute standard cost per unit.
(LO 1), AP

E23-3 Stefani Company has gathered the following information about its product.

Direct materials. Each unit of product contains 4.5 pounds of materials. The average waste and spoilage per unit produced under normal conditions is 0.5 pounds. Materials cost $5 per pound, but Stefani always takes the 2% cash discount all of its suppliers offer. Freight costs average $0.25 per pound.

Direct labor. Each unit requires 2 hours of labor. Setup, cleanup, and downtime average 0.4 hours per unit. The average hourly pay rate of Stefani's employees is $12. Payroll taxes and fringe benefits are an additional $3 per hour.

Manufacturing overhead. Overhead is applied at a rate of $7 per direct labor hour.

Instructions

Compute Stefani's total standard cost per unit.

E23-4 Monte Services, Inc. is trying to establish the standard labor cost of a typical oil change. The following data have been collected from time and motion studies conducted over the past month.

Compute labor cost and labor quantity variance.

(LO 3), AP

Actual time spent on the oil change	1.0 hour
Hourly wage rate	$12
Payroll taxes	10% of wage rate
Setup and downtime	20% of actual labor time
Cleanup and rest periods	30% of actual labor time
Fringe benefits	25% of wage rate

Instructions

(a) Determine the standard direct labor hours per oil change.
(b) Determine the standard direct labor hourly rate.
(c) Determine the standard direct labor cost per oil change.
(d) If an oil change took 1.6 hours at the standard hourly rate, what was the direct labor quantity variance?

E23-5 The standard cost of Product B manufactured by Pharrell Company includes three units of direct materials at $5.00 per unit. During June, 29,000 units of direct materials are purchased at a cost of $4.70 per unit, and 29,000 units of direct materials are used to produce 9,400 units of Product B.

Compute materials price and quantity variances.

(LO 2), AP

Instructions

(a) Compute the total materials variance and the price and quantity variances.
(b) Repeat (a), assuming the purchase price is $5.15 and the quantity purchased and used is 28,000 units.

E23-6 Lewis Company's standard labor cost of producing one unit of Product DD is 4 hours at the rate of $12.00 per hour. During August, 40,600 hours of labor are incurred at a cost of $12.15 per hour to produce 10,000 units of Product DD.

Compute labor price and quantity variances.

(LO 3), AP

Instructions

(a) Compute the total labor variance.
(b) Compute the labor price and quantity variances.
(c) Repeat (b), assuming the standard is 4.1 hours of direct labor at $12.25 per hour.

E23-7 Levine Inc., which produces a single product, has prepared the following standard cost sheet for one unit of the product.

Compute materials and labor variances.

(LO 2, 3), AP

Direct materials (8 pounds at $2.50 per pound)	$20
Direct labor (3 hours at $12.00 per hour)	$36

During the month of April, the company manufactures 230 units and incurs the following actual costs.

Direct materials purchased and used (1,900 pounds)	$5,035
Direct labor (700 hours)	$8,120

Instructions

Compute the total, price, and quantity variances for materials and labor.

E23-8 The following direct materials and direct labor data pertain to the operations of Laurel Company for the month of August.

Compute the materials and labor variances and list reasons for unfavorable variances.

(LO 2, 3), AN

Costs		Quantities	
Actual labor rate	$13 per hour	Actual hours incurred and used	4,150 hours
Actual materials price	$128 per ton	Actual quantity of materials purchased and used	1,220 tons
Standard labor rate	$12.50 per hour	Standard hours used	4,300 hours
Standard materials price	$130 per ton	Standard quantity of materials used	1,200 tons

Instructions

(a) Compute the total, price, and quantity variances for materials and labor.
(b) Provide two possible explanations for each of the unfavorable variances calculated above, and suggest where responsibility for the unfavorable result might be placed.

Determine amounts from variance report.
(LO 2, 3), AN

E23-9 You have been given the following information about the production of Usher Co., and are asked to provide the plant manager with information for a meeting with the vice president of operations.

	Standard Cost Card
Direct materials (5 pounds at $4 per pound)	$20.00
Direct labor (0.8 hours at $10)	8.00
Variable overhead (0.8 hours at $3 per hour)	2.40
Fixed overhead (0.8 hours at $7 per hour)	5.60
	$36.00

The following is a variance report for the most recent period of operations.

		Variances	
Costs	**Total Standard Cost**	**Price**	**Quantity**
Direct materials	$410,000	$2,095 F	$9,000 U
Direct labor	164,000	3,840 U	6,000 U

Instructions

(a) How many units were produced during the period?
(b) How many pounds of raw materials were purchased and used during the period?
(c) What was the actual cost per pound of raw materials?
(d) How many actual direct labor hours were worked during the period?
(e) What was the actual rate paid per direct labor hour?

(CGA adapted)

Prepare a variance report for direct labor.
(LO 3, 4), AP

E23-10 During March 2017, Toby Tool & Die Company worked on four jobs. A review of direct labor costs reveals the following summary data.

Job	Actual		Standard		Total
Number	**Hours**	**Costs**	**Hours**	**Costs**	**Variance**
A257	221	$4,420	225	$4,500	$ 80 F
A258	450	9,450	430	8,600	850 U
A259	300	6,180	300	6,000	180 U
A260	116	2,088	110	2,200	112 F
Total variance					$838 U

Analysis reveals that Job A257 was a repeat job. Job A258 was a rush order that required overtime work at premium rates of pay. Job A259 required a more experienced replacement worker on one shift. Work on Job A260 was done for one day by a new trainee when a regular worker was absent.

Instructions

Prepare a report for the plant supervisor on direct labor cost variances for March. The report should have columns for (1) Job No., (2) Actual Hours, (3) Standard Hours, (4) Quantity Variance, (5) Actual Rate, (6) Standard Rate, (7) Price Variance, and (8) Explanation.

Compute overhead variance.
(LO 3), AN

E23-11 Manufacturing overhead data for the production of Product H by Shakira Company are as follows.

Overhead incurred for 52,000 actual direct labor hours worked	$263,000
Overhead rate (variable $3; fixed $2) at normal capacity of 54,000 direct labor hours	$5
Standard hours allowed for work done	52,000

Instructions

Compute the total overhead variance.

Compute overhead variances.

(LO 3), AP

E23-12 Byrd Company produces one product, a putter called GO-Putter. Byrd uses a standard cost system and determines that it should take one hour of direct labor to produce one GO-Putter. The normal production capacity for this putter is 100,000 units per year. The total budgeted overhead at normal capacity is $850,000 comprised of $250,000 of variable costs and $600,000 of fixed costs. Byrd applies overhead on the basis of direct labor hours.

During the current year, Byrd produced 95,000 putters, worked 94,000 direct labor hours, and incurred variable overhead costs of $256,000 and fixed overhead costs of $600,000.

Instructions

(a) Compute the predetermined variable overhead rate and the predetermined fixed overhead rate.

(b) Compute the applied overhead for Byrd for the year.

(c) Compute the total overhead variance.

Compute variances for materials.

(LO 2, 3), AP

E23-13 Ceelo Company purchased (at a cost of $10,200) and used 2,400 pounds of materials during May. Ceelo's standard cost of materials per unit produced is based on 2 pounds per unit at a cost $5 per pound. Production in May was 1,050 units.

Instructions

(a) Compute the total, price, and quantity variances for materials.

(b) Assume Ceelo also had an unfavorable labor quantity variance. What is a possible scenario that would provide one cause for the variances computed in (a) and the unfavorable labor quantity variance?

Prepare a variance report.

(LO 2, 4), AP

E23-14 Picard Landscaping plants grass seed as the basic landscaping for business campuses. During a recent month, the company worked on three projects (Remington, Chang, and Wyco). The company is interested in controlling the materials costs, namely the grass seed, for these plantings projects.

In order to provide management with useful cost control information, the company uses standard costs and prepares monthly variance reports. Analysis reveals that the purchasing agent mistakenly purchased poor-quality seed for the Remington project. The Chang project, however, received higher-than-standard-quality seed that was on sale. The Wyco project received standard-quality seed. However, the price had increased and a new employee was used to spread the seed.

Shown below are quantity and cost data for each project.

	Actual		Standard		
Project	**Quantity**	**Costs**	**Quantity**	**Costs**	**Total Variance**
Remington	500 lbs.	$1,200	460 lbs.	$1,150	$ 50 U
Chang	400	920	410	1,025	105 F
Wyco	550	1,430	480	1,200	230 U
Total variance					$175 U

Instructions

(a) Prepare a variance report for the purchasing department with the following columns: (1) Project, (2) Actual Pounds Purchased, (3) Actual Price per Pound, (4) Standard Price per Pound, (5) Price Variance, and (6) Explanation.

(b) Prepare a variance report for the production department with the following columns: (1) Project, (2) Actual Pounds, (3) Standard Pounds, (4) Standard Price per Pound, (5) Quantity Variance, and (6) Explanation.

Complete variance report.

(LO 4), AP

E23-15 Urban Corporation prepared the following variance report.

URBAN CORPORATION
Variance Report—Purchasing Department
For the Week Ended January 9, 2017

Type of Materials	Quantity Purchased	Actual Price	Standard Price	Price Variance	Explanation
Rogue11	? lbs.	$5.20	$5.00	$5,500 ?	Price increase
Storm17	7,000 oz.	?	3.30	1,050 U	Rush order
Beast29	22,000 units	0.40	?	660 F	Bought larger quantity

Instructions

Fill in the appropriate amounts or letters for the question marks in the report.

Prepare income statement for management.
(LO 4), AP

E23-16 Fisk Company uses a standard cost accounting system. During January, the company reported the following manufacturing variances.

Materials price variance	$1,200 U	Labor quantity variance	$750 U
Materials quantity variance	800 F	Overhead variance	800 U
Labor price variance	550 U		

In addition, 8,000 units of product were sold at $8 per unit. Each unit sold had a standard cost of $5. Selling and administrative expenses were $8,000 for the month.

Instructions

Prepare an income statement for management for the month ended January 31, 2017.

Identify performance evaluation terminology.
(LO 1, 4), C

E23-17 The following is a list of terms related to performance evaluation.

1. Balanced scorecard
2. Variance
3. Learning and growth perspective
4. Nonfinancial measures
5. Customer perspective
6. Internal process perspective
7. Ideal standards
8. Normal standards

Instructions

Match each of the following descriptions with one of the terms above.

(a) The difference between total actual costs and total standard costs.
(b) An efficient level of performance that is attainable under expected operating conditions.
(c) An approach that incorporates financial and nonfinancial measures in an integrated system that links performance measurement and a company's strategic goals.
(d) A viewpoint employed in the balanced scorecard to evaluate how well a company develops and retains its employees.
(e) An evaluation tool that is not based on dollars.
(f) A viewpoint employed in the balanced scorecard to evaluate the company from the perspective of those people who buy its products or services.
(g) An optimum level of performance under perfect operating conditions.
(h) A viewpoint employed in the balanced scorecard to evaluate the efficiency and effectiveness of the company's value chain.

Identity balanced scorecard perspectives.
(LO 4), C

E23-18 Indicate which of the four perspectives in the balanced scorecard is most likely associated with the objectives that follow.

1. Percentage of repeat customers.
2. Number of suggestions for improvement from employees.
3. Contribution margin.
4. Brand recognition.
5. Number of cross-trained employees.
6. Amount of setup time.

Identify balance scorecard perspectives.
(LO 4), C

E23-19 Indicate which of the four perspectives in the balanced scorecard is most likely associated with the objectives that follow.

1. Ethics violations.
2. Credit rating.
3. Customer retention.
4. Stockouts.
5. Reportable accidents.
6. Brand recognition.

Journalize entries in a standard cost accounting system.
(LO 5), AP

E23-20 Vista Company installed a standard cost system on January 1. Selected transactions for the month of January are as follows.

1. Purchased 18,000 units of raw materials on account at a cost of $4.50 per unit. Standard cost was $4.40 per unit.
2. Issued 18,000 units of raw materials for jobs that required 17,500 standard units of raw materials.
3. Incurred 15,300 actual hours of direct labor at an actual rate of $5.00 per hour. The standard rate is $5.50 per hour. (Credit Factory Wages Payable.)

4. Performed 15,300 hours of direct labor on jobs when standard hours were 15,400.
5. Applied overhead to jobs at the rate of 100% of direct labor cost for standard hours allowed.

Instructions
Journalize the January transactions.

***E23-21** Lopez Company uses a standard cost accounting system. Some of the ledger accounts have been destroyed in a fire. The controller asks your help in reconstructing some missing entries and balances.

Answer questions concerning missing entries and balances.
(LO 2, 3, 5), AN

Instructions
Answer the following questions.
(a) Materials Price Variance shows a $2,000 unfavorable balance. Accounts Payable shows $138,000 of raw materials purchases. What was the amount debited to Raw Materials Inventory for raw materials purchased?
(b) Materials Quantity Variance shows a $3,000 favorable balance. Raw Materials Inventory shows a zero balance. What was the amount debited to Work in Process Inventory for direct materials used?
(c) Labor Price Variance shows a $1,500 favorable balance. Factory Labor shows a debit of $145,000 for wages incurred. What was the amount credited to Factory Wages Payable?
(d) Factory Labor shows a credit of $145,000 for direct labor used. Labor Quantity Variance shows a $900 favorable balance. What was the amount debited to Work in Process for direct labor used?
(e) Overhead applied to Work in Process totaled $165,000. If the total overhead variance was $1,200 favorable, what was the amount of overhead costs debited to Manufacturing Overhead?

***E23-22** Data for Levine Inc. are given in E23-7.

Journalize entries for materials and labor variances.
(LO 5), AP

Instructions
Journalize the entries to record the materials and labor variances.

***E23-23** The information shown below was taken from the annual manufacturing overhead cost budget of Connick Company.

Compute manufacturing overhead variances and interpret findings.
(LO 6), AN

Variable manufacturing overhead costs	$34,650
Fixed manufacturing overhead costs	$19,800
Normal production level in labor hours	16,500
Normal production level in units	4,125
Standard labor hours per unit	4

During the year, 4,050 units were produced, 16,100 hours were worked, and the actual manufacturing overhead was $55,500. Actual fixed manufacturing overhead costs equaled budgeted fixed manufacturing overhead costs. Overhead is applied on the basis of direct labor hours.

Instructions
(a) Compute the total, fixed, and variable predetermined manufacturing overhead rates.
(b) Compute the total, controllable, and volume overhead variances.
(c) Briefly interpret the overhead controllable and volume variances computed in (b).

***E23-24** The loan department of Calgary Bank uses standard costs to determine the overhead cost of processing loan applications. During the current month, a fire occurred, and the accounting records for the department were mostly destroyed. The following data were salvaged from the ashes.

Compute overhead variances.
(LO 6), AN

Standard variable overhead rate per hour	$9
Standard hours per application	2
Standard hours allowed	2,000
Standard fixed overhead rate per hour	$6
Actual fixed overhead cost	$12,600
Variable overhead budget based on standard hours allowed	$18,000
Fixed overhead budget	$12,600
Overhead controllable variance	$ 1,200 U

Instructions

(a) Determine the following.
   (1) Total actual overhead cost.
   (2) Actual variable overhead cost.
   (3) Variable overhead costs applied.
   (4) Fixed overhead costs applied.
   (5) Overhead volume variance.

(b) Determine how many loans were processed.

Compute variances.
(LO 6), AP

***E23-25** Seacrest Company's overhead rate was based on estimates of $200,000 for overhead costs and 20,000 direct labor hours. Seacrest's standards allow 2 hours of direct labor per unit produced. Production in May was 900 units, and actual overhead incurred in May was $19,500. The overhead budgeted for 1,800 standard direct labor hours is $17,600 ($5,000 fixed and $12,600 variable).

Instructions

(a) Compute the total, controllable, and volume variances for overhead.
(b) What are possible causes of the variances computed in part (a)?

EXERCISES: SET B AND CHALLENGE EXERCISES

Visit the book's companion website, at **www.wiley.com/college/kimmel**, and choose the Student Companion site to access Exercises: Set B and Challenge Exercises.

PROBLEMS: SET A

Compute variances.
(LO 2, 3), AP

P23-1A Rogen Corporation manufactures a single product. The standard cost per unit of product is shown below.

Direct materials—1 pound plastic at $7.00 per pound	$ 7.00
Direct labor—1.6 hours at $12.00 per hour	19.20
Variable manufacturing overhead	12.00
Fixed manufacturing overhead	4.00
Total standard cost per unit	$42.20

The predetermined manufacturing overhead rate is $10 per direct labor hour ($16.00 ÷ 1.6). It was computed from a master manufacturing overhead budget based on normal production of 8,000 direct labor hours (5,000 units) for the month. The master budget showed total variable costs of $60,000 ($7.50 per hour) and total fixed overhead costs of $20,000 ($2.50 per hour). Actual costs for October in producing 4,800 units were as follows.

Direct materials (5,100 pounds)	$ 36,720
Direct labor (7,400 hours)	92,500
Variable overhead	59,700
Fixed overhead	21,000
Total manufacturing costs	$209,920

The purchasing department buys the quantities of raw materials that are expected to be used in production each month. Raw materials inventories, therefore, can be ignored.

Instructions

(a) MPV $1,020 U

(a) Compute all of the materials and labor variances.
(b) Compute the total overhead variance.

P23-2A Ayala Corporation accumulates the following data relative to jobs started and finished during the month of June 2017.

Compute variances, and prepare income statement.

(LO 2, 3, 4), AP

Costs and Production Data	Actual	Standard
Raw materials unit cost	$2.25	$2.10
Raw materials units used	10,600	10,000
Direct labor payroll	$120,960	$120,000
Direct labor hours worked	14,400	15,000
Manufacturing overhead incurred	$189,500	
Manufacturing overhead applied		$193,500
Machine hours expected to be used at normal capacity		42,500
Budgeted fixed overhead for June		$55,250
Variable overhead rate per machine hour		$3.00
Fixed overhead rate per machine hour		$1.30

Overhead is applied on the basis of standard machine hours. Three hours of machine time are required for each direct labor hour. The jobs were sold for $400,000. Selling and administrative expenses were $40,000. Assume that the amount of raw materials purchased equaled the amount used.

Instructions

(a) Compute all of the variances for (1) direct materials and (2) direct labor.

(b) Compute the total overhead variance.

(c) Prepare an income statement for management. (Ignore income taxes.)

(a) LQV $4,800 F

P23-3A Rudd Clothiers is a small company that manufactures tall-men's suits. The company has used a standard cost accounting system. In May 2017, 11,250 suits were produced. The following standard and actual cost data applied to the month of May when normal capacity was 14,000 direct labor hours. All materials purchased were used.

Compute and identify significant variances.

(LO 2, 3, 4), AN

Cost Element	Standard (per unit)	Actual
Direct materials	8 yards at $4.40 per yard	$375,575 for 90,500 yards ($4.15 per yard)
Direct labor	1.2 hours at $13.40 per hour	$200,925 for 14,250 hours ($14.10 per hour)
Overhead	1.2 hours at $6.10 per hour (fixed $3.50; variable $2.60)	$49,000 fixed overhead $37,000 variable overhead

Overhead is applied on the basis of direct labor hours. At normal capacity, budgeted fixed overhead costs were $49,000, and budgeted variable overhead was $36,400.

Instructions

(a) Compute the total, price, and quantity variances for (1) materials and (2) labor.

(b) Compute the total overhead variance.

(c) Which of the materials and labor variances should be investigated if management considers a variance of more than 4% from standard to be significant?

(a) MPV $22,625 F

P23-4A Kansas Company uses a standard cost accounting system. In 2017, the company produced 28,000 units. Each unit took several pounds of direct materials and 1.6 standard hours of direct labor at a standard hourly rate of $12.00. Normal capacity was 50,000 direct labor hours. During the year, 117,000 pounds of raw materials were purchased at $0.92 per pound. All materials purchased were used during the year.

Answer questions about variances.

(LO 2, 3), AN

Instructions

(a) If the materials price variance was $3,510 favorable, what was the standard materials price per pound?

(b) If the materials quantity variance was $4,750 unfavorable, what was the standard materials quantity per unit?

(b) 4.0 pounds

(c) What were the standard hours allowed for the units produced?

(d) If the labor quantity variance was $7,200 unfavorable, what were the actual direct labor hours worked?

(e) If the labor price variance was $9,080 favorable, what was the actual rate per hour?

(f) If total budgeted manufacturing overhead was $360,000 at normal capacity, what was the predetermined overhead rate?

(f) $7.20 per DLH

(g) What was the standard cost per unit of product?

(h) How much overhead was applied to production during the year?

(i) Using one or more answers above, what were the total costs assigned to work in process?

Compute variances, prepare an income statement, and explain unfavorable variances.

(LO 2, 3, 4), AP

P23-5A Hart Labs, Inc. provides mad cow disease testing for both state and federal governmental agricultural agencies. Because the company's customers are governmental agencies, prices are strictly regulated. Therefore, Hart Labs must constantly monitor and control its testing costs. Shown below are the standard costs for a typical test.

Direct materials (2 test tubes @ $1.46 per tube)	$ 2.92
Direct labor (1 hour @ $24 per hour)	24.00
Variable overhead (1 hour @ $6 per hour)	6.00
Fixed overhead (1 hour @ $10 per hour)	10.00
Total standard cost per test	$42.92

The lab does not maintain an inventory of test tubes. As a result, the tubes purchased each month are used that month. Actual activity for the month of November 2017, when 1,475 tests were conducted, resulted in the following.

Direct materials (3,050 test tubes)	$ 4,270
Direct labor (1,550 hours)	35,650
Variable overhead	7,400
Fixed overhead	15,000

Monthly budgeted fixed overhead is $14,000. Revenues for the month were $75,000, and selling and administrative expenses were $5,000.

Instructions

(a) LQV $1,800 U

(a) Compute the price and quantity variances for direct materials and direct labor.
(b) Compute the total overhead variance.
(c) Prepare an income statement for management.
(d) Provide possible explanations for each unfavorable variance.

Journalize and post standard cost entries, and prepare income statement.

(LO 2, 3, 4, 5), AP

***P23-6A** Jorgensen Corporation uses standard costs with its job order cost accounting system. In January, an order (Job No. 12) for 1,900 units of Product B was received. The standard cost of one unit of Product B is as follows.

Direct materials	3 pounds at $1.00 per pound	$ 3.00
Direct labor	1 hour at $8.00 per hour	8.00
Overhead	2 hours (variable $4.00 per machine hour; fixed $2.25 per machine hour)	12.50
Standard cost per unit		$23.50

Normal capacity for the month was 4,200 machine hours. During January, the following transactions applicable to Job No. 12 occurred.

1. Purchased 6,200 pounds of raw materials on account at $1.05 per pound.
2. Requisitioned 6,200 pounds of raw materials for Job No. 12.
3. Incurred 2,000 hours of direct labor at a rate of $7.80 per hour.
4. Worked 2,000 hours of direct labor on Job No. 12.
5. Incurred manufacturing overhead on account $25,000.
6. Applied overhead to Job No. 12 on basis of standard machine hours allowed.
7. Completed Job No. 12.
8. Billed customer for Job No. 12 at a selling price of $65,000.

Instructions

(a) Journalize the transactions.
(b) Post to the job order cost accounts.
(c) Prepare the entry to recognize the total overhead variance.
(d) Prepare the January 2017 income statement for management. Assume selling and administrative expenses were $2,000.

(d) NI $15,890

Compute overhead controllable and volume variances.

(LO 6), AP

***P23-7A** Using the information in P23-1A, compute the overhead controllable variance and the overhead volume variance.

Compute overhead controllable and volume variances.

(LO 6), AP

***P23-8A** Using the information in P23-2A, compute the overhead controllable variance and the overhead volume variance.

***P23-9A** Using the information in P23-3A, compute the overhead controllable variance and the overhead volume variance.

Compute overhead controllable and volume variances.

(LO 6), AP

***P23-10A** Using the information in P23-5A, compute the overhead controllable variance and the overhead volume variance.

Compute overhead controllable and volume variances.

(LO 6), AP

▶ PROBLEMS: SET B AND SET C

Visit the book's companion website, at **www.wiley.com/college/kimmel**, and choose the Student Companion site to access Problems: Set B and Set C.

▶ CONTINUING PROBLEMS

CURRENT DESIGNS

EXCEL TUTORIAL

XLS

CD23 The executive team at Current Designs has gathered to evaluate the company's operations for the last month. One of the topics on the agenda is the special order from Huegel Hollow, which was presented in CD2. Recall that Current Designs had a special order to produce a batch of 20 kayaks for a client, and you were asked to determine the cost of the order and the cost per kayak.

Mike Cichanowski asked the others if the special order caused any particular problems in the production process. Dave Thill, the production manager, made the following comments: "Since we wanted to complete this order quickly and make a good first impression on this new customer, we had some of our most experienced type I workers run the rotomold oven and do the trimming. They were very efficient and were able to complete that part of the manufacturing process even more quickly than the regular crew. However, the finishing on these kayaks required a different technique than what we usually use, so our type II workers took a little longer than usual for that part of the process."

Deb Welch, who is in charge of the purchasing function, said, "We had to pay a little more for the polyethylene powder for this order because the customer wanted a color that we don't usually stock. We also ordered a little extra since we wanted to make sure that we had enough to allow us to calibrate the equipment. The calibration was a little tricky, and we used all of the powder that we had purchased. Since the number of kayaks in the order was fairly small, we were able to use some rope and other parts that were left over from last year's production in the finishing kits. We've seen a price increase for these components in the last year, so using the parts that we already had in inventory cut our costs for the finishing kits."

Instructions

(a) Based on the comments above, predict whether each of the following variances will be favorable or unfavorable. If you don't have enough information to make a prediction, use "NEI" to indicate "Not Enough Information."

(1) Quantity variance for polyethylene powder.
(2) Price variance for polyethylene powder.
(3) Quantity variance for finishing kits.
(4) Price variance for finishing kits.
(5) Quantity variance for type I workers.
(6) Price variance for type I workers.
(7) Quantity variance for type II workers.
(8) Price variance for type II workers.

(b) Diane Buswell examined some of the accounting records and reported that Current Designs purchased 1,200 pounds of pellets for this order at a total cost of $2,040. Twenty (20) finishing kits were assembled at a total cost of $3,240. The payroll records showed that the type I employees worked 38 hours on this project at a total cost of $570. The type II finishing employees worked 65 hours at a total cost of $796.25. A total of 20 kayaks were produced for this order.

The standards that had been developed for this model of kayak were used in CD2 and are reproduced here. For each kayak:

54 pounds of polyethylene powder at $1.50 per pound

1 finishing kit (rope, seat, hardware, etc.) at $170

2 hours of type I labor from people who run the oven and trim the plastic at a standard wage rate of $15 per hour

3 hours of type II labor from people who attach the hatches and seat and other hardware at a standard wage rate of $12 per hour.

Calculate the eight variances that are listed in part (a) of this problem.

WATERWAYS

(This is a continuation of the Waterways problem from Chapters 14–22.)

WP23 Waterways Corporation uses very stringent standard costs in evaluating its manufacturing efficiency. These standards are not "ideal" at this point, but management is working toward that as a goal. This problem asks you to calculate and evaluate the company's variances.

Go to the book's companion website, at **www.wiley.com/college/kimmel**, *to find the completion of this problem.*

EXPAND YOUR CRITICAL THINKING

Group Project

DECISION-MAKING ACROSS THE ORGANIZATION

E **CT23-1** Milton Professionals, a management consulting firm, specializes in strategic planning for financial institutions. James Hahn and Sara Norton, partners in the firm, are assembling a new strategic planning model for use by clients. The model is designed for use on most personal computers and replaces a rather lengthy manual model currently marketed by the firm. To market the new model, James and Sara will need to provide clients with an estimate of the number of labor hours and computer time needed to operate the model. The model is currently being test-marketed at five small financial institutions. These financial institutions are listed below, along with the number of combined computer/labor hours used by each institution to run the model one time.

Financial Institutions	Computer/Labor Hours Required
Midland National	25
First State	45
Financial Federal	40
Pacific America	30
Lakeview National	30
Total	170
Average	34

Any company that purchases the new model will need to purchase user manuals for the system. User manuals will be sold to clients in cases of 20, at a cost of $320 per case. One manual must be used each time the model is run because each manual includes a nonreusable computer-accessed password for operating the system. Also required are specialized computer forms that are sold only by Milton. The specialized forms are sold in packages of 250, at a cost of $60 per package. One application of the model requires the use of 50 forms. This amount includes two forms that are generally wasted in each application due to printer alignment errors. The overall cost of the strategic planning model to clients is $12,000. Most clients will use the model four times annually.

Milton must provide its clients with estimates of ongoing costs incurred in operating the new planning model, and would like to do so in the form of standard costs.

Instructions

With the class divided into groups, answer the following.

(a) What factors should be considered in setting a standard for computer/labor hours?
(b) What alternatives for setting a standard for computer/labor hours might be used?
(c) What standard for computer/labor hours would you select? Justify your answer.
(d) Determine the standard materials cost associated with the user manuals and computer forms for each application of the strategic planning model.

MANAGERIAL ANALYSIS

AN ***CT23-2** Ana Carillo and Associates is a medium-sized company located near a large metropolitan area in the Midwest. The company manufactures cabinets of mahogany, oak, and other fine woods for use in expensive homes, restaurants, and hotels. Although some of the work is custom, many of the cabinets are a standard size.

One such non-custom model is called Luxury Base Frame. Normal production is 1,000 units. Each unit has a direct labor hour standard of 5 hours. Overhead is applied to production based on standard direct labor hours. During the most recent month, only 900 units were produced; 4,500 direct labor hours were allowed for standard production, but only 4,000 hours were used. Standard and actual overhead costs were as follows.

	Standard (1,000 units)	Actual (900 units)
Indirect materials	$ 12,000	$ 12,300
Indirect labor	43,000	51,000
(Fixed) Manufacturing supervisors salaries	22,500	22,000
(Fixed) Manufacturing office employees salaries	13,000	12,500
(Fixed) Engineering costs	27,000	25,000
Computer costs	10,000	10,000
Electricity	2,500	2,500
(Fixed) Manufacturing building depreciation	8,000	8,000
(Fixed) Machinery depreciation	3,000	3,000
(Fixed) Trucks and forklift depreciation	1,500	1,500
Small tools	700	1,400
(Fixed) Insurance	500	500
(Fixed) Property taxes	300	300
Total	$144,000	$150,000

Instructions

(a) Determine the overhead application rate.
(b) Determine how much overhead was applied to production.
(c) Calculate the total overhead variance, controllable variance, and volume variance.
(d) Decide which overhead variances should be investigated.
(e) Discuss causes of the overhead variances. What can management do to improve its performance next month?

REAL-WORLD FOCUS

CT23-3 Glassmaster Company is organized as two divisions and one subsidiary. One division focuses on the manufacture of filaments such as fishing line and sewing thread; the other division manufactures antennas and specialty fiberglass products. Its subsidiary manufactures flexible steel wire controls and molded control panels. E

The annual report of Glassmaster provides the following information.

GLASSMASTER COMPANY
Management Discussion

Gross profit margins for the year improved to 20.9% of sales compared to last year's 18.5%. All operations reported improved margins due in large part to improved operating efficiencies as a result of cost reduction measures implemented during the second and third quarters of the fiscal year and increased manufacturing throughout due to higher unit volume sales. Contributing to the improved margins was a favorable materials price variance due to competitive pricing by suppliers as a result of soft demand for petrochemical-based products. This favorable variance is temporary and will begin to reverse itself as stronger worldwide demand for commodity products improves in tandem with the economy. Partially offsetting these positive effects on profit margins were competitive pressures on sales prices of certain product lines. The company responded with pricing strategies designed to maintain and/or increase market share.

Instructions

(a) Is it apparent from the information whether Glassmaster utilizes standard costs?
(b) Do you think the price variance experienced should lead to changes in standard costs for the next fiscal year?

C **CT23-4** The Balanced Scorecard Institute *(www.balancedscorecard.org)* is a great resource for information about implementing the balanced scorecard. One item of interest provided at its website is an example of a balanced scorecard for a regional airline.

Address: **http://www.balancedscorecard.org/portals/0/pdf/regional_airline.pdf**, or go to **www.wiley.com/college/kimmel**

Instructions

Go to the address above and answer the following questions.

(a) What are the objectives identified for the airline for each perspective?
(b) What measures are used for the objectives in the customer perspective?
(c) What initiatives are planned to achieve the objective in the learning perspective?

AN **CT23-5** The December 22, 2009, edition of the *Wall Street Journal* has an article by Kevin Kelliker entitled "In Risky Move, GM to Run Plants Around Clock."

Instructions

Read the article and answer the following questions.

(a) According to the article, what is the normal industry standard for plants to be considered operating at full capacity?
(b) What ideal standard is the company hoping to achieve?
(c) What reasons are given in the article for why most companies do not operate a third shift? How does GM propose to overcome these issues?
(d) What are some potential drawbacks of the midnight shift? What implications does this have for variances from standards?
(e) What potential sales/marketing disadvantage does the third shift create?

Writing ▶

COMMUNICATION ACTIVITY

E **CT23-6** The setting of standards is critical to the effective use of standards in evaluating performance.

Instructions

Explain the following in a memo to your instructor.

(a) The comparative advantages and disadvantages of ideal versus normal standards.
(b) The factors that should be included in setting the price and quantity standards for direct materials, direct labor, and manufacturing overhead.

ETHICS CASE

AN **CT23-7** At Symond Company, production workers in the Painting Department are paid on the basis of productivity. The labor time standard for a unit of production is established through periodic time studies conducted by Douglas Management Consultants. In a time study, the actual time required to complete a specific task by a worker is observed. Allowances are then made for preparation time, rest periods, and cleanup time. Bill Carson is one of several veterans in the Painting Department.

Bill is informed by Douglas that he will be used in the time study for the painting of a new product. The findings will be the basis for establishing the labor time standard for the next 6 months. During the test, Bill deliberately slows his normal work pace in an effort to obtain a labor time standard that will be easy to meet. Because it is a new product, the Douglas representative who conducted the test is unaware that Bill did not give the test his best effort.

Instructions

(a) Who was benefited and who was harmed by Bill's actions?
(b) Was Bill ethical in the way he performed the time study test?
(c) What measure(s) might the company take to obtain valid data for setting the labor time standard?

ALL ABOUT YOU

E **CT23-8** From the time you first entered school many years ago, instructors have been measuring and evaluating you by imposing standards. In addition, many of you will pursue professions that administer professional examinations to attain recognized certification.

A federal commission presented proposals suggesting all public colleges and universities should require standardized tests to measure their students' learning.

Instructions

Read the article at **www.signonsandiego.com/uniontrib/20060811/news_1n11colleges.html**, and answer the following questions.

(a) What areas of concern did the panel's recommendations address?
(b) What are possible advantages of standard testing?
(c) What are possible disadvantages of standard testing?
(d) Would you be in favor of standardized tests?

CONSIDERING YOUR COSTS AND BENEFITS

CT23-9 Do you think that standard costs are used only in making products like wheel bearings and hamburgers? Think again. Standards influence virtually every aspect of our lives. For example, the next time you call to schedule an appointment with your doctor, ask the receptionist how many minutes the appointment is scheduled for. Doctors are under increasing pressure to see more patients each day, which means the time spent with each patient is shorter. As insurance companies and employers push for reduced medical costs, every facet of medicine has been standardized and analyzed. Doctors, nurses, and other medical staff are evaluated in every part of their operations to ensure maximum efficiency. While keeping medical treatment affordable seems like a worthy goal, what are the potential implications for the quality of health care? Does a focus on the bottom line result in a reduction in the quality of health care? E

A simmering debate has centered on a very basic question: To what extent should accountants, through financial measures, influence the type of medical care that you receive? Suppose that your local medical facility is in danger of closing because it has been losing money. Should the facility put in place incentives that provide bonuses to doctors if they meet certain standard-cost targets for the cost of treating specific ailments?

YES: If the facility is in danger of closing, then someone should take steps to change the medical practices to reduce costs. A closed medical facility is of no use to me, my family, or the community.

NO: I don't want an accountant deciding the right medical treatment for me. My family and I deserve the best medical care.

Instructions

Write a response indicating your position regarding this situation. Provide support for your view.

24

Planning for Capital Investments

CHAPTER PREVIEW

Companies must constantly determine how to invest their resources. For example, Dell announced plans to spend $1 billion on data centers for cloud computing. ExxonMobil announced that two wells off the Brazilian coast, which it had spent hundreds of millions of dollars to drill, would produce no oil. The process of making such capital expenditure decisions is referred to as **capital budgeting**. Capital budgeting involves choosing among various capital projects to find those that will maximize a company's return on its financial investment. The purpose of this chapter is to discuss the various techniques used to make effective capital budgeting decisions.

CHAPTER OUTLINE

LEARNING OBJECTIVES		PRACTICE
1 Describe capital budgeting inputs and apply the cash payback technique.	• Cash flow information • Cash payback	DO IT! 1 Cash Payback Period
2 Use the net present value method.	• Equal annual cash flows • Unequal annual cash flows • Choosing a discount rate • Simplifying assumptions • Comprehensive example	DO IT! 2 Net Present Value
3 Identify capital budgeting challenges and refinements.	• Intangible benefits • Profitability index for mutually exclusive projects • Risk analysis • Post-audit of investment projects	DO IT! 3 Profitability Index
4 Use the internal rate of return method.	• Comparing discounted cash flow methods	DO IT! 4 Internal Rate of Return
5 Use the annual rate of return method.	• Based on accrual-accounting data	DO IT! 5 Annual Rate of Return

Go to the ***REVIEW AND PRACTICE*** section at the end of the chapter for a targeted summary and exercises with solutions.

Visit **WileyPLUS** for additional tutorials and practice opportunities.

FEATURE STORY

© Engel & Gielen/Getty Images

Floating Hotels

Do you own a boat? Maybe it's a nice boat, but how many swimming pools, movie theaters, shopping malls, or restaurants does it have on board? If you are in the cruise-line business, like Holland America Line, you need all of these amenities and more just to stay afloat. Holland America Line is considered by many to be the leader of the premium luxury-liner segment. Carnival Corporation, which owns Holland America Line and other cruise lines, is one of the largest vacation companies in the world. During one recent three-year period, Carnival spent more than $3 billion per year on capital expenditures. That's a big number, but keep in mind that Carnival estimates that at any given time there are 270,000 people (200,000 customers and 70,000 crew) on its 100 ships somewhere in the world.

The cruise industry is a tricky business. When times are good, customers are looking for ways to splurge. But when times get tough, people are more inclined to take a trip in a minivan than a luxury yacht. So it's important to time your investment properly. For example, during one stretch of solid global economic growth, many cruise lines decided to add capacity. The industry built 14 new ships at a total price of $4.7 billion. (That's an average price of about $330 million.) But, it takes up to three years to build one of these giant vessels. Unfortunately, by the time the ships were completed, the economy was in a nose-dive.

To maintain passenger numbers, cruise prices had to be cut by up to 40%. While the lower prices attracted lots of customers, that wasn't enough to offset an overall decline in revenue of 10% in the middle of the recession. The industry had added capacity at just the wrong time.

LEARNING OBJECTIVE 1

Describe capital budgeting inputs and apply the cash payback technique.

Many companies follow a carefully prescribed process in capital budgeting. At least once a year, top management requests proposals for projects from departments, plants, and authorized personnel. A capital budgeting committee screens the proposals and submits its findings to the officers of the company. The officers, in turn, select the projects they believe to be most worthy of funding. They submit this list of projects to the board of directors. Ultimately, the directors approve the capital expenditure budget for the year. Illustration 24-1 shows this process.

ILLUSTRATION 24-1
Corporate capital budget authorization process

1. Project proposals are requested from departments, plants, and authorized personnel.
2. Proposals are screened by a capital budget committee.
3. Officers determine which projects are worthy of funding.
4. Board of directors approves capital budget.

The involvement of top management and the board of directors in the process demonstrates the importance of capital budgeting decisions. These decisions often have a significant impact on a company's future profitability. In fact, poor capital budgeting decisions can cost a lot of money. Such decisions have even led to the bankruptcy of some companies.

CASH FLOW INFORMATION

In this chapter, we will look at several methods that help companies make effective capital budgeting decisions. Most of these methods employ **cash flow numbers**, rather than accrual accounting revenues and expenses. Remember from your financial accounting course that accrual accounting records **revenues** and **expenses**, rather than cash inflows and cash outflows. In fact, revenues and expenses measured during a period often differ significantly from their cash flow counterparts. Accrual accounting has advantages over cash accounting in many contexts. **For purposes of capital budgeting, though, estimated cash inflows and outflows are the preferred inputs.** Why? Because ultimately the value of all financial investments is determined by the value of cash flows received and paid.

Sometimes cash flow information is not available. In this case, companies can make adjustments to accrual accounting numbers to estimate cash flow. Often, they estimate net annual cash flow by adding back depreciation expense to net income. Depreciation expense is added back because it is an expense that does not require an outflow of cash. By adding depreciation expense back to net income, companies approximate net annual cash flow. Suppose, for example, that Reno Company's net income of $13,000 includes a charge for depreciation expense of $26,000. Its estimated net annual cash flow would be $39,000 ($13,000 + $26,000).

Illustration 24-2 lists some typical cash outflows and inflows related to equipment purchase and replacement.

ILLUSTRATION 24-2
Typical cash flows relating to capital budgeting decisions

Cash Outflows

Initial investment
Repairs and maintenance
Increased operating costs
Overhaul of equipment

Cash Inflows

Sale of old equipment
Increased cash received from customers
Reduced cash outflows related to operating costs
Salvage value of equipment

These cash flows are the inputs that are considered relevant in capital budgeting decisions.

The capital budgeting decision, under any technique, depends in part on a variety of considerations:

- **The availability of funds:** Does the company have unlimited funds, or will it have to ration capital investments?
- **Relationships among proposed projects:** Are proposed projects independent of each other, or does the acceptance or rejection of one depend on the acceptance or rejection of another?
- **The company's basic decision-making approach:** Does the company want to produce an accept-reject decision or a ranking of desirability among possible projects?
- **The risk associated with a particular project:** How certain are the projected returns? The certainty of estimates varies with such issues as market considerations or the length of time before returns are expected.

ILLUSTRATIVE DATA

To compare the results of the various capital budgeting techniques, we will use a continuing example. Assume that Stewart Shipping Company is considering an investment of $130,000 in new equipment. The new equipment is expected to last 10 years. It will have a zero salvage value at the end of its useful life. The annual cash inflows are $200,000, and the annual cash outflows are $176,000. Illustration 24-3 summarizes these data.

ILLUSTRATION 24-3
Investment information for Stewart Shipping example

Initial investment	$130,000
Estimated useful life	10 years
Estimated salvage value	–0–
Estimated annual cash flows	
Cash inflows from customers	$200,000
Cash outflows for operating costs	176,000
Net annual cash flow	$ 24,000

In the following two sections, we will examine two popular techniques for evaluating capital investments: cash payback and the net present value method.

CASH PAYBACK

The **cash payback technique** identifies the time period required to recover the cost of the capital investment from the net annual cash flow produced by the investment. Illustration 24-4 presents the formula for computing the cash payback period assuming equal annual cash flows.

ILLUSTRATION 24-4
Cash payback formula

Cost of Capital Investment	÷	Net Annual Cash Flow	=	Cash Payback Period

▼ **HELPFUL HINT**
Net annual cash flow can also be approximated by "Net cash provided by operating activities" from the statement of cash flows.

The cash payback period in the Stewart Shipping example is 5.42 years, computed as follows.

$$\$130,000 \div \$24,000 = 5.42 \text{ years}$$

The evaluation of the payback period is often related to the expected useful life of the asset. For example, assume that at Stewart Shipping a project is unacceptable if the payback period is longer than 60% of the asset's expected useful life. The 5.42-year payback period is 54.2% (5.42 ÷ 10) of the project's expected useful life. Thus, the project is acceptable.

It follows that when the payback technique is used to decide among acceptable alternative projects, **the shorter the payback period, the more attractive the investment**. This is true for two reasons: First, the earlier the investment is recovered, the sooner the company can use the cash funds for other purposes. Second, the risk of loss from obsolescence and changed economic conditions is less in a shorter payback period.

The preceding computation of the cash payback period assumes **equal** net annual cash flows in each year of the investment's life. In many cases, this assumption is not valid. In the case of **uneven** net annual cash flows, the company determines the cash payback period when the cumulative net cash flows from the investment equal the cost of the investment.

To illustrate, assume that Chen Company proposes an investment in a new website that is estimated to cost $300,000. Illustration 24-5 shows the proposed investment cost, net annual cash flows, cumulative net cash flows, and the cash payback period.

ILLUSTRATION 24-5
Computation of cash payback period—unequal cash flows

Year	Investment	Net Annual Cash Flow	Cumulative Net Cash Flow
0	$300,000		
1		$ 60,000	$ 60,000
2		90,000	150,000
3		90,000	240,000
4		120,000	360,000
5		100,000	460,000

Cash payback period = 3.5 years

As Illustration 24-5 shows, at the end of year 3, cumulative net cash flow of $240,000 is less than the investment cost of $300,000, but at the end of year 4 the cumulative cash inflow of $360,000 exceeds the investment cost. The cash flow needed in year 4 to equal the investment cost is $60,000 ($300,000 − $240,000). Assuming the cash inflow occurred evenly during year 4, we then divide this amount by the net annual cash flow in year 4 ($120,000) to determine the point during the year when the cash payback occurs. Thus, we get 0.50 ($60,000/$120,000), or half of the year, and the cash payback period is 3.5 years.

The cash payback technique may be useful as an initial screening tool. It may be the most critical factor in the capital budgeting decision for a company that desires a fast turnaround of its investment because of a weak cash position. It also is relatively easy to compute and understand.

However, cash payback should not ordinarily be the only basis for the capital budgeting decision because it **ignores the expected profitability of the project**.

To illustrate, assume that Projects A and B have the same payback period, but Project A's useful life is double the useful life of Project B. Project A's earning power, therefore, is twice as long as Project B's. A further—and major—disadvantage of this technique is that it **ignores the time value of money**.

DO IT! ▶ 1 Cash Payback Period

Watertown Paper Corporation is considering adding another machine for the manufacture of corrugated cardboard. The machine would cost $900,000. It would have an estimated life of 6 years and no salvage value. The company estimates that annual cash inflows would increase by $400,000 and that annual cash outflows would increase by $190,000. Compute the cash payback period.

SOLUTION

Estimated annual cash inflows	$400,000
Estimated annual cash outflows	190,000
Net annual cash flow	$210,000

Cash payback period = $900,000/$210,000 = 4.3 years.

Related exercise material: **BE24-1** and **DO IT! 24-1.**

Action Plan

- ✔ Annual cash inflows − Annual cash outflows = Net annual cash flow.
- ✔ Cash payback period = Cost of capital investment/Net annual cash flow.

LEARNING OBJECTIVE ▶ 2 Use the net present value method.

Recognition of the time value of money can make a significant difference in the long-term impact of the capital budgeting decision. For example, cash flows that occur early in the life of an investment are worth more than those that occur later—because of the time value of money. Therefore, it is useful to recognize the timing of cash flows when evaluating projects.

Capital budgeting techniques that take into account both the time value of money and the estimated net cash flows from an investment are called **discounted cash flow techniques**. They are generally recognized as the most informative and best conceptual approaches to making capital budgeting decisions. The expected net cash flow used in discounting cash flows consists of the annual net cash flows plus the estimated liquidation proceeds (salvage value) when the asset is sold for salvage at the end of its useful life.

The primary discounted cash flow technique is the **net present value method**. A second method, discussed later in the chapter, is the **internal rate of return**. At this point, before you read on, **we recommend that you examine Appendix G** at the end of the book to review the time value of money concepts upon which these methods are based.

The **net present value (NPV) method** involves discounting net cash flows to their present value and then comparing that present value with the capital outlay required by the investment. The difference between these two amounts is referred to as **net present value (NPV)**. Company management determines what interest rate to use in discounting the future net cash flows. This rate, often referred to as the **discount rate** or **required rate of return**, is discussed in a later section.

The NPV decision rule is this: **A proposal is acceptable when net present value is zero or positive**. At either of those values, the rate of

DECISION TOOLS

Using the net present value method helps companies to determine whether or not to invest in proposed projects.

return on the investment equals or exceeds the **required rate of return**. This is the rate of return management expects on investments, sometimes called the discount rate or cost of capital. When net present value is negative, the project is unacceptable. Illustration 24-6 shows the net present value decision criteria.

ILLUSTRATION 24-6
Net present value decision criteria

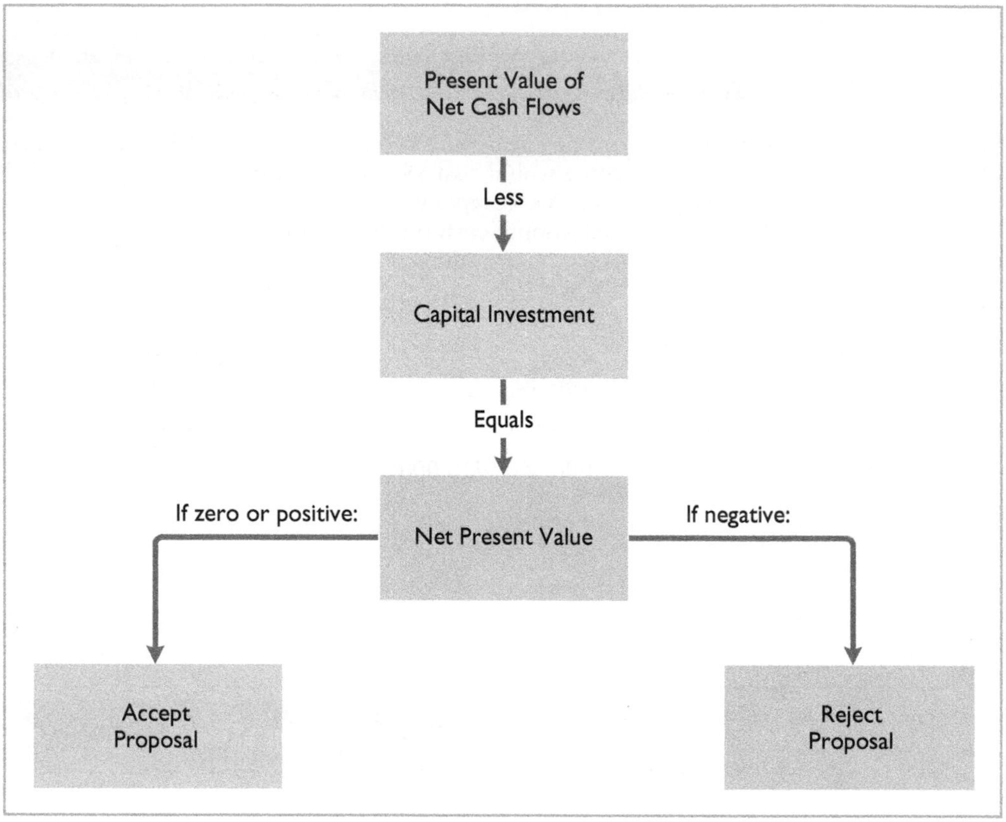

When making a selection among acceptable proposals, **the higher the positive net present value, the more attractive the investment**. The application of this method to two cases is described in the next two sections. In each case, we assume that the investment has no salvage value at the end of its useful life.

EQUAL ANNUAL CASH FLOWS

▼ HELPFUL HINT
The ABC Co. expects equal cash flows over an asset's 5-year useful life. The discount factor it should use in determining present values if management wants a 12% return is 3.60478 (using Table 4).

In our Stewart Shipping Company example, the company's net annual cash flows are $24,000. If we assume this amount **is uniform over the asset's useful life**, we can compute the present value of the net annual cash flows by using the present value of an annuity of 1 for 10 payments (from Table 4, Appendix G). Assuming a discount rate of 12%, the present value of net cash flows are as shown in Illustration 24-7 (rounded to the nearest dollar).

ILLUSTRATION 24-7
Computation of present value of equal net annual cash flows

	Present Value at 12%
Discount factor for 10 periods	5.65022
Present value of net cash flows:	
$24,000 × 5.65022	$135,605

The analysis of the proposal by the net present value method is as follows.

ILLUSTRATION 24-8
Computation of net present value—equal net annual cash flows

	12%
Present value of net cash flows	$135,605
Less: Capital investment	130,000
Net present value	**$ 5,605**

The proposed capital expenditure is acceptable at a required rate of return of 12% because the net present value is positive.

UNEQUAL ANNUAL CASH FLOWS

When net annual cash flows are unequal, we cannot use annuity tables to calculate their present value. Instead, we use tables showing the **present value of a single future amount for each annual cash flow**.

To illustrate, assume that Stewart Shipping Company expects the same total net cash flows of $240,000 over the life of the investment. But because of a declining market demand for the product over the life of the equipment, the net annual cash flows are higher in the early years and lower in the later years. The present value of the net annual cash flows is calculated as follows, using Table 3 in Appendix G.

▼ **HELPFUL HINT**
Appendix G demonstrates the use of a financial calculator to solve time value of money problems.

ILLUSTRATION 24-9
Computation of present value of unequal annual cash flows

Year	Assumed Net Annual Cash Flows	Discount Factor 12%	Present Value 12%
	(1)	(2)	(1) × (2)
1	$ 34,000	.89286	$ 30,357
2	30,000	.79719	23,916
3	27,000	.71178	19,218
4	25,000	.63552	15,888
5	24,000	.56743	13,618
6	22,000	.50663	11,146
7	21,000	.45235	9,499
8	20,000	.40388	8,078
9	19,000	.36061	6,852
10	18,000	.32197	5,795
	$240,000		$144,367

Therefore, the analysis of the proposal by the net present value method is as follows.

ILLUSTRATION 24-10
Computation of net present value—unequal annual cash flows

	12%
Present value of net cash flows	$144,367
Less: Capital investment	130,000
Net present value	**$ 14,367**

In this example, the present value of the net cash flows is greater than the $130,000 capital investment. Thus, the project is acceptable at a 12% required rate of return. The difference between the present values using the 12% rate under equal cash flows ($135,605) and unequal cash flows ($144,367) is due to the pattern of the flows. Since more money is received sooner under this particular uneven cash flow scenario, its present value is greater.

MANAGEMENT INSIGHT Verizon

Trevor Smith/iStockphoto

Can You Hear Me—Better?

What's better than 3G wireless service? 4G. But the question for wireless service providers is whether customers will be willing to pay extra for that improvement. Verizon has spent billions on upgrading its networks in the past few years, so it now offers 4G LTE service to 97% of the nation. Verizon is hoping that its investment in 4G works out better than its $23 billion investment in its FIOS fiber-wired network for TV and ultrahigh-speed Internet. One analyst estimates that the present value of each FIOS customer is $800 less than the cost of the connection.

Sources: Martin Peers, "Investors: Beware Verizon's Generation GAP," *Wall Street Journal Online* (January 26, 2010); and Chad Fraser, "What Warren Buffett Sees in Verizon," *Investing Daily* (May 30, 2014).

If customers are slow to initially adopt 4G, how might the conclusions of a cash payback analysis of Verizon's 4G investment differ from a present value analysis? (Go to WileyPLUS for this answer and additional questions.)

CHOOSING A DISCOUNT RATE

Now that you understand how companies apply the net present value method, it is logical to ask a related question: How is a discount rate (required rate of return) determined in real capital budgeting decisions? In most instances, a company uses a required rate of return equal to its **cost of capital**—that is, the rate that it must pay to obtain funds from creditors and stockholders.

▼ HELPFUL HINT
Cost of capital is the rate that management expects to pay on all borrowed and equity funds. It does not relate to the cost of funding a *specific* project.

The cost of capital is a weighted average of the rates paid on borrowed funds as well as on funds provided by investors in the company's common stock and preferred stock. If management believes a project is riskier than the company's usual line of business, the discount rate should be increased. That is, the discount rate has two elements, a cost of capital element and a risk element. Often, companies assume the risk element is equal to zero.

Using an incorrect discount rate can lead to incorrect capital budgeting decisions. Consider again the Stewart Shipping example in Illustration 24-8, where we used a discount rate of 12%. Suppose that this rate does not take into account the fact that this project is riskier than most of the company's investments. A more appropriate discount rate, given the risk, might be 15%. Illustration 24-11 compares the net present values at the two rates. At the higher, more appropriate discount rate of 15%, the net present value is negative, and the company should reject the project (discount factors from Appendix G, Table 4).

ILLUSTRATION 24-11
Comparison of net present values at different discount rates

	Present Values at Different Discount Rates	
	12%	15%
Discount factor for 10 payments	5.65022	5.01877
Present value of net cash flows:		
$24,000 × 5.65022	$135,605	
$24,000 × 5.01877		$120,450
Less: Capital investment	130,000	130,000
Positive (negative) net present value	$ 5,605	$ (9,550)

The discount rate is often referred to by alternative names, including the **required rate of return**, the **hurdle rate**, and the **cutoff rate**. Determination of the cost of capital varies somewhat depending on whether the entity is a for-profit or not-for-profit business. Calculation of the cost of capital is discussed more fully in advanced accounting and finance courses.

SIMPLIFYING ASSUMPTIONS

In our examples of the net present value method, we made a number of simplifying assumptions:

- **All cash flows come at the end of each year.** In reality, cash flows will come at uneven intervals throughout the year. However, it is far simpler to assume that all cash flows come at the end (or in some cases the beginning) of the year. In fact, this assumption is frequently made in practice.
- **All cash flows are immediately reinvested in another project that has a similar return.** In most capital budgeting situations, companies receive cash flows during each year of a project's life. In order to determine the return on the investment, some assumption must be made about how the cash flows are reinvested in the year that they are received. It is customary to assume that cash flows received are reinvested in some other project of similar return until the end of the project's life.
- **All cash flows can be predicted with certainty.** The outcomes of business investments are full of uncertainty, as the Holland America Line Feature Story shows. There is no way of knowing how popular a new product will be, how long a new machine will last, or what competitors' reactions might be to changes in a product. But, in order to make investment decisions, analysts must estimate future outcomes. In this chapter, we have assumed that future amounts are known with certainty.[1] In reality, little is known with certainty. More advanced capital budgeting techniques deal with uncertainty by considering the probability that various outcomes will occur.

COMPREHENSIVE EXAMPLE

Best Taste Foods is considering investing in new equipment to produce fat-free snack foods. Management believes that although demand for fat-free foods has leveled off, fat-free foods are here to stay. The following estimated costs, cost of capital, and cash flows were determined in consultation with the marketing, production, and finance departments.

ILLUSTRATION 24-12
Investment information for Best Taste Foods example

Initial investment	$1,000,000
Cost of equipment overhaul in 5 years	$200,000
Salvage value of equipment in 10 years	$20,000
Cost of capital (discount rate)	15%
Estimated annual cash flows	
Cash inflows received from sales	$500,000
Cash outflows for cost of goods sold	$200,000
Maintenance costs	$30,000
Other direct operating costs	$40,000

Remember that we are using cash flows in our analysis, not accrual revenues and expenses. Thus, for example, the direct operating costs would not include depreciation expense, since depreciation expense does not use cash. Illustration 24-13 presents the computation of the net annual cash flows of this project.

ILLUSTRATION 24-13
Computation of net annual cash flow

Cash inflows received from sales	$ 500,000
Cash outflows for cost of goods sold	(200,000)
Maintenance costs	(30,000)
Other direct operating costs	(40,000)
Net annual cash flow	**$230,000**

[1]One exception is a brief discussion of sensitivity analysis later in the chapter.

Illustration 24-14 shows computation of the net present value for this proposed investment (discount factors from Appendix G, Tables 3 and 4).

ILLUSTRATION 24-14
Computation of net present value for Best Taste Foods investment

Event	Time Period	Cash Flow	×	15% Discount Factor	=	Present Value
Net annual cash flow	1–10	$ 230,000	×	5.01877	=	$1,154,317
Salvage value	10	20,000		.24719		4,944
Less: Equipment purchase	0	1,000,000		1.00000		1,000,000
Less: Equipment overhaul	5	200,000		.49718		99,436
Net present value						$ 59,825

Because the net present value of the project is positive, Best Taste should accept the project.

DO IT! 2 Net Present Value

Watertown Paper Corporation is considering adding another machine for the manufacture of corrugated cardboard. The machine would cost $900,000. It would have an estimated life of 6 years and no salvage value. The company estimates that annual cash inflows would increase by $400,000 and that annual cash outflows would increase by $190,000. Management has a required rate of return of 9%. Calculate the net present value on this project and discuss whether it should be accepted.

Action Plan

- ✔ Estimated annual cash inflows − Estimated annual cash outflows = Net annual cash flow.
- ✔ Use the NPV technique to calculate the difference between net cash flows and the initial investment.
- ✔ Accept the project if the net present value is positive.

SOLUTION

Estimated annual cash inflows	$400,000
Estimated annual cash outflows	190,000
Net annual cash flow	$210,000

	Cash Flow	9% Discount Factor	Present Value
Present value of net annual cash flows	$210,000	4.48592[a]	$942,043
Less: Capital investment			900,000
Net present value			$ 42,043

[a]Table 4, Appendix G, 9%, 6 years

Since the net present value is greater than zero, Watertown should accept the project.

Related exercise material: **BE24-2, BE24-3, E24-1, E24-2, E24-3,** and **DO IT! 24-2.**

LEARNING OBJECTIVE 3 Identify capital budgeting challenges and refinements.

Now that you understand how the net present value method works, we can add some "additional wrinkles." Specifically, these are the impact of intangible benefits, a way to compare mutually exclusive projects, refinements that take risk into account, and the need to conduct post-audits of investment projects.

INTANGIBLE BENEFITS

The NPV evaluation techniques employed thus far rely on tangible costs and benefits that can be relatively easily quantified. Some investment projects, especially high-tech projects, fail to make it through initial capital budget screens because only the project's tangible benefits are considered. **Intangible benefits** might include increased quality, improved safety, or enhanced employee loyalty. By ignoring intangible benefits, capital budgeting techniques might incorrectly eliminate projects that could be financially beneficial to the company.

To avoid rejecting projects that actually should be accepted, analysts suggest two possible approaches:

1. Calculate net present value ignoring intangible benefits. Then, if the NPV is negative, ask whether the project offers any intangible benefits that are worth at least the amount of the negative NPV.
2. Project rough, conservative estimates of the value of the intangible benefits, and incorporate these values into the NPV calculation.

Example

Assume that Berg Company is considering the purchase of a new mechanical robot to be used for soldering electrical connections. Illustration 24-15 shows the estimates related to this proposed purchase (discount factor from Appendix G, Table 4).

ILLUSTRATION 24-15
Investment information for Berg Company example

Initial investment	$200,000
Annual cash inflows	$ 50,000
Annual cash outflows	20,000
Net annual cash flow	$ 30,000
Estimated life of equipment	10 years
Discount rate	12%

	Cash Flows	×	12% Discount Factor	=	Present Value
Present value of net annual cash flows	$30,000	×	5.65022	=	$169,507
Less: Initial investment					200,000
Net present value					$(30,493)

Based on the negative net present value of $30,493, the proposed project is not acceptable. This calculation, however, ignores important information. First, the company's engineers believe that purchasing this machine will dramatically improve the quality of electrical connections in the company's products. As a result, future warranty costs will be reduced. Also, the company believes that this higher quality will translate into higher future sales. Finally, the new machine will be much safer than the previous one.

Berg can incorporate this new information into the capital budgeting decision in the two ways discussed earlier. First, management might simply ask whether the reduced warranty costs, increased sales, and improved safety benefits have an estimated total present value to the company of at least $30,493. If yes, then the project is acceptable.

Alternatively, analysts can estimate the annual cash flows of these benefits. In our initial calculation, we assumed each of these benefits to have a value of zero. It seems likely that their actual values are much higher than zero. Given the difficulty of estimating these benefits, however, conservative values should be assigned to them. If, after using conservative estimates, the net present value is positive, Berg should accept the project.

To illustrate, assume that Berg estimates that improved sales will increase cash inflows by $10,000 annually as a result of an increase in perceived quality. Berg also estimates that annual cost outflows would be reduced by $5,000 as a result of lower warranty claims, reduced injury claims, and missed work. Consideration of the intangible benefits results in the following revised NPV calculation (discount factor from Appendix G, Table 4).

ILLUSTRATION 24-16
Revised investment information for Berg Company example, including intangible benefits

Initial investment	$200,000				
Annual cash inflows (revised)	$ 60,000 ($50,000 + $10,000)				
Annual cash outflows (revised)	15,000 ($20,000 − $5,000)				
Net annual cash flow	$ 45,000				
Estimated life of equipment	10 years				
Discount rate	12%				
	Cash Flows	×	**12% Discount Factor**	=	**Present Value**
Present value of net annual cash flows	$45,000	×	5.65022	=	$254,260
Less: Initial investment					200,000
Net present value					$ 54,260

Using these conservative estimates of the value of the additional benefits, Berg should accept the project.

ETHICS INSIGHT

Carol Gering/iStockphoto

It Need Not Cost an Arm and a Leg

Most manufacturers say that employee safety matters above everything else. But how many back up this statement with investments that improve employee safety? Recently, a woodworking hobbyist, who also happens to be a patent attorney with a Ph.D. in physics, invented a mechanism that automatically shuts down a power saw when the saw blade comes in contact with human flesh. The blade stops so quickly that only minor injuries result.

Power saws injure 40,000 Americans each year, and 4,000 of those injuries are bad enough to require amputation. Therefore, one might think that power-saw companies would be lined up to incorporate this mechanism into their saws. But, in the words of one power-tool company, "Safety doesn't sell." Since existing saw manufacturers were unwilling to incorporate the device into their saws, eventually the inventor started his own company to build the devices and sell them directly to businesses that use power saws.

Source: Melba Newsome, "An Edgy New Idea," *Time: Inside Business* (May 2006), p. A16.

In addition to the obvious humanitarian benefit of reducing serious injuries, how else might the manufacturer of this product convince potential customers of its worth? (Go to WileyPLUS for this answer and additional questions.)

PROFITABILITY INDEX FOR MUTUALLY EXCLUSIVE PROJECTS

In theory, companies should accept all projects with positive NPVs. However, companies rarely are able to adopt all positive-NPV proposals. First, proposals often are **mutually exclusive**. This means that if the company adopts one proposal, it would be impossible or impractical also to adopt the other proposal. For example, a company may be considering the purchase of a new packaging machine and is looking at various brands and models. It needs only one packaging machine. Once the company has determined which brand and model to purchase, the others will not be purchased—even though they also may have positive net present values.

Even in instances where projects are not mutually exclusive, managers often must choose between various positive-NPV projects because of **limited resources**. For example, the company might have ideas for two new lines of business, each of which has a projected positive NPV. However, both of these proposals require skilled personnel, and the company determines that it will not be able to find enough skilled personnel to staff both projects. Management will have to choose the project it thinks is a better option.

When choosing between alternative proposals, it is tempting simply to choose the project with the higher NPV. Consider the following example of two mutually exclusive projects. Each is assumed to have a 10-year life and a 12% discount rate (discount factors from Appendix G, Tables 3 and 4). Illustration 24-17 shows the estimates for each project and the computation of the present value of the net cash flows.

ILLUSTRATION 24-17
Investment information for mutually exclusive projects

	Project A	Project B
Initial investment	$40,000	$ 90,000
Net annual cash inflow	10,000	19,000
Salvage value	5,000	10,000
Present value of net cash flows		
($10,000 × 5.65022) + ($5,000 × .32197)	58,112	
($19,000 × 5.65022) + ($10,000 × .32197)		110,574

Illustration 24-18 computes the net present values of Project A and Project B by subtracting the initial investment from the present value of the net cash flows.

ILLUSTRATION 24-18
Net present value computation

	Project A	Project B
Present value of net cash flows	$ 58,112	$110,574
Less: Initial investment	40,000	90,000
Net present value	$18,112	$ 20,574

As Project B has the higher NPV, it would seem that the company should adopt it. However, Project B also requires more than twice the original investment of Project A. In choosing between the two projects, the company should also include in its calculations the amount of the original investment.

One relatively simple method of comparing alternative projects is the **profitability index**. This method takes into account both the size of the original investment and the discounted cash flows. The profitability index is calculated by dividing the present value of net cash flows that occur after the initial investment by the amount of the initial investment, as Illustration 24-19 shows.

ILLUSTRATION 24-19
Formula for profitability index

Present Value of Net Cash Flows	÷	Initial Investment	=	Profitability Index

The profitability index allows comparison of the relative desirability of projects that require differing initial investments. Note that any project with a positive NPV will have a profitability index above 1. The profitability index for each of the mutually exclusive projects is calculated in Illustration 24-20 (page 1180).

DECISION TOOLS

The profitability index helps a company determine which investment proposal to accept.

ILLUSTRATION 24-20
Calculation of profitability index

$$\text{Profitability Index} = \frac{\text{Present Value of Net Cash Flows}}{\text{Initial Investment}}$$

Project A	Project B
$\frac{\$58,112}{\$40,000} = \mathbf{1.45}$	$\frac{\$110,574}{\$90,000} = \mathbf{1.23}$

In this case, the profitability index of Project A exceeds that of Project B. Thus, Project A is more desirable. Again, if these were not mutually exclusive projects and if resources were not limited, then the company should invest in both projects since both have positive NPVs. Additional considerations related to preference decisions are discussed in more advanced courses.

RISK ANALYSIS

A simplifying assumption made by many financial analysts is that projected results are known with certainty. In reality, projected results are only estimates based upon the forecaster's belief as to the most probable outcome. One approach for dealing with such uncertainty is **sensitivity analysis**. Sensitivity analysis uses a number of outcome estimates to get a sense of the variability among potential returns. An example of sensitivity analysis was presented in Illustration 24-11 (page 1174), where we illustrated the impact on NPV of different discount rate assumptions. A higher-risk project would be evaluated using a higher discount rate.

Similarly, to take into account that more distant cash flows are often more uncertain, a higher discount rate can be used to discount more distant cash flows. Other techniques to address uncertainty are discussed in advanced courses.

MANAGEMENT INSIGHT Sharp

Matjaz Boncina/iStockphoto

Wide-Screen Capacity

Building a new factory to produce 60-inch TV screens can cost $4 billion. But for more than 10 years, manufacturers of these screens have continued to build new plants. By building so many plants, they have expanded productive capacity at a rate that has exceeded the demand for big-screen TVs. In fact, during one recent year, the supply of big-screen TVs was estimated to exceed demand by 12%, rising to 16% in the future. One state-of-the-art plant built by Sharp was estimated to be operating at only 50% of capacity. Experts say that prices of big-screen TVs will have to fall much further than they already have before demand may eventually catch up with productive capacity.

Source: James Simms, "Sharp's Payoff Delayed," *Wall Street Journal Online* (September 14, 2010).

What implications does the excess capacity have for the cash payback and net present value calculations of these investments? (Go to **WileyPLUS** for this answer and additional questions.)

POST-AUDIT OF INVESTMENT PROJECTS

Any well-run organization should perform an evaluation, called a **post-audit**, of its investment projects after their completion. A post-audit is a thorough evaluation of how well a project's actual performance matches the original projections. An example of a post-audit is seen in a situation that occurred at Campbell Soup. The company made the original decision to invest in the Intelligent Quisine line based on management's best estimates of future cash flows. During the development phase of the project, Campbell hired an outside consulting firm to evaluate the project's potential for success. Because actual results during the initial years were far below the estimated results and because the future also did not look promising, the project was terminated.

Performing a post-audit is important for a variety of reasons. First, if managers know that the company will compare their estimates to actual results, they will be more likely to submit reasonable and accurate data when they make investment proposals. This clearly is better for the company than for managers to submit overly optimistic estimates in an effort to get pet projects approved. Second, as seen with Campbell Soup, a post-audit provides a formal mechanism by which the company can determine whether existing projects should be supported or terminated. Third, post-audits improve future investment proposals because, by evaluating past successes and failures, managers improve their estimation techniques.

A post-audit involves the same evaluation techniques used in making the original capital budgeting decision—for example, use of the NPV method. The difference is that, in the post-audit, analysts insert actual figures, where known, and they revise estimates of future amounts based on new information. The managers responsible for the estimates used in the original proposal must explain the reasons for any significant differences between their estimates and actual results.

Post-audits are not foolproof. In the case of Campbell Soup, some observers suggested that the company was too quick to abandon the project. Industry analysts suggested that with more time and more advertising expenditures, the company might have enjoyed success.

DO IT! 3 Profitability Index

Taz Corporation has decided to invest in renewable energy sources to meet part of its energy needs for production. It is considering solar power versus wind power. After considering cost savings as well as incremental revenues from selling excess electricity into the power grid, it has determined the following.

	Solar	Wind
Present value of annual cash flows	$78,580	$168,450
Initial investment	$45,500	$125,300

Determine the net present value and profitability index of each project. Which energy source should it choose?

SOLUTION

	Solar	Wind
Present value of annual cash flows	$78,580	$168,450
Less: Initial investment	45,500	125,300
Net present value	$33,080	$ 43,150
Profitability index	1.73*	1.34**

*$78,580 ÷ $45,500
**168,450 ÷ 125,300

While the investment in wind power generates the higher net present value, it also requires a substantially higher initial investment. The profitability index favors solar power, which suggests that the additional net present value of wind is outweighed by the cost of the initial investment. The company should choose solar power.

Related exercise material: **BE24-5, E24-4,** and **DO IT! 24-3.**

Action Plan

- ✔ Determine the present value of annual cash flows of each mutually exclusive project.
- ✔ Determine profitability index by dividing the present value of annual cash flows by the amount of the initial investment.
- ✔ Choose project with highest profitability index.

LEARNING OBJECTIVE 4

Use the internal rate of return method.

The **internal rate of return method** differs from the net present value method in that it finds the **interest yield of the potential investment**. The **internal rate of return (IRR)** is the interest rate that will cause the present value of the proposed capital expenditure to equal the present value of the expected net annual cash flows (that is, NPV equal to zero). Because it recognizes the time value of money, the internal rate of return method is (like the NPV method) a discounted cash flow technique.

DECISION TOOLS

The IRR helps a company determine if it should invest in a proposed project.

How do we determine the internal rate of return? One way is to use a financial calculator (see Appendix G) or electronic spreadsheet to solve for this rate. Or, we can use a trial-and-error procedure.

To illustrate, assume that Stewart Shipping Company is considering the purchase of a new front-end loader at a cost of $244,371. Net annual cash flows from this loader are estimated to be $100,000 a year for three years. To determine the internal rate of return on this front-end loader, the company finds the discount rate that results in a net present value of zero. As Illustration 24-21 shows, at a rate of return of 10%, Stewart Shipping has a positive net present value of $4,315. At a rate of return of 12%, it has a negative net present value of $4,188. At an 11% rate, the net present value is zero. Therefore, 11% is the internal rate of return for this investment (discount factors from Appendix G, Table 3).

ILLUSTRATION 24-21
Estimation of internal rate of return

Year	Net Annual Cash Flows	Discount Factor 10%	Present Value 10%	Discount Factor 11%	Present Value 11%	Discount Factor 12%	Present Value 12%
1	$100,000	.90909	$ 90,909	.90090	$ 90,090	.89286	$ 89,286
2	$100,000	.82645	82,645	.81162	81,162	.79719	79,719
3	$100,000	.75132	75,132	.73119	73,119	.71178	71,178
			248,686		244,371		240,183
Less: Initial investment			244,371		244,371		244,371
Net present value			$ 4,315		$ –0–		$ (4,188)

An easier approach to solving for the internal rate of return can be used if the net annual cash flows are **equal**, as in the Stewart Shipping example. In this special case, we can find the internal rate of return using the following formula.

ILLUSTRATION 24-22
Formula for internal rate of return—even cash flows

Capital Investment	÷	Net Annual Cash Flows	=	Internal Rate of Return Factor

Applying this formula to the Stewart Shipping example, we find:

$$\$244{,}371 \div \$100{,}000 = 2.44371$$

We then look up the factor 2.44371 in Table 4 of Appendix G in the three-payment row and find it under 11%. Row 3 is reproduced below for your convenience.

Table 4 Present Value of an Annuity of 1

(*n*) Payments	4%	5%	6%	7%	8%	9%	10%	11%	12%	15%
3	2.77509	2.72325	2.67301	2.62432	2.57710	2.53130	2.48685	2.44371	2.40183	2.28323

Recognize that if the cash flows are **uneven**, then a trial-and-error approach or a financial calculator or computerized spreadsheet must be used.

Once managers know the internal rate of return, they compare it to the company's required rate of return (the discount rate). The IRR decision rule is as follows: **Accept the project when the internal rate of return is equal to or greater than the required rate of return. Reject the project when the internal rate of return is less than the required rate of return.** Illustration 24-23 shows these relationships. The internal rate of return method is widely used in practice, largely because most managers find the internal rate of return easy to interpret.

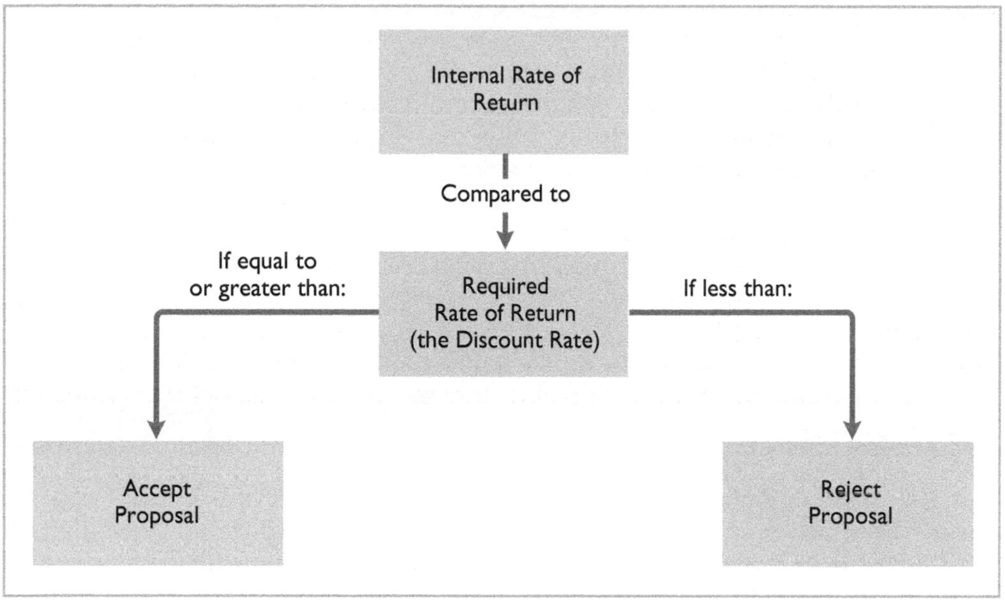

ILLUSTRATION 24-23
Internal rate of return decision criteria

COMPARING DISCOUNTED CASH FLOW METHODS

Illustration 24-24 compares the two discounted cash flow methods—net present value and internal rate of return. When properly used, either method will provide management with relevant quantitative data for making capital budgeting decisions.

ILLUSTRATION 24-24
Comparison of discounted cash flow methods

	Net Present Value	Internal Rate of Return
1. Objective	Compute net present value (a dollar amount).	Compute internal rate of return (a percentage).
2. Decision Rule	If net present value is zero or positive, accept the proposal. If net present value is negative, reject the proposal.	If internal rate of return is equal to or greater than the required rate of return, accept the proposal. If internal rate of return is less than the required rate of return, reject the proposal.

DO IT! ▶4 Internal Rate of Return

Watertown Paper Corporation is considering adding another machine for the manufacture of corrugated cardboard. The machine would cost $900,000. It would have an estimated life of 6 years and no salvage value. The company estimates that annual cash inflows would increase by $400,000 and that annual cash outflows would increase by $190,000. Management has a required rate of return of 9%. Calculate the internal rate of return on this project and discuss whether it should be accepted.

Action Plan

- ✔ Estimated annual cash inflows − Estimated annual cash outflows = Net annual cash flow.
- ✔ Capital investment/Net annual cash flows = Internal rate of return factor.
- ✔ Look up the factor in the present value of an annuity table to find the internal rate of return.
- ✔ Accept the project if the internal rate of return is equal to or greater than the required rate of return.

SOLUTION

Estimated annual cash inflows	$400,000
Estimated annual cash outflows	190,000
Net annual cash flow	$210,000

$900,000/$210,000 = 4.285714. Using Table 4 of Appendix G and the factors that correspond with the six-payment row, 4.285714 is between the factors for 10% and 11%. Since the project has an internal rate that is greater than 10% and the required rate of return is only 9%, the project should be accepted.

Related exercise material: **BE24-7, BE24-8, E24-5, E24-6, E24-7,** and **DO IT! 24-4.**

LEARNING OBJECTIVE **5**

Use the annual rate of return method.

The final capital budgeting technique we will look at is the **annual rate of return method**. It is based directly on accrual accounting data rather than on cash flows. It indicates **the profitability of a capital expenditure** by dividing expected annual net income by the average investment. Illustration 24-25 shows the formula for computing annual rate of return.

ILLUSTRATION 24-25
Annual rate of return formula

Expected Annual Net Income	÷	Average Investment	=	Annual Rate of Return

Assume that Reno Company is considering an investment of $130,000 in new equipment. The new equipment is expected to last five years and have zero salvage value at the end of its useful life. Reno uses the straight-line method of depreciation for accounting purposes. The expected annual revenues and costs of the new product that will be produced from the investment are as follows.

ILLUSTRATION 24-26
Estimated annual net income from Reno Company's capital expenditure

Sales		$200,000
Less: Costs and expenses		
Manufacturing costs (exclusive of depreciation)	$132,000	
Depreciation expense ($130,000 ÷ 5)	26,000	
Selling and administrative expenses	22,000	180,000
Income before income taxes		20,000
Income tax expense		7,000
Net income		$ 13,000

Reno's expected annual net income is $13,000. Average investment is derived from the formula shown below.

$$\frac{\text{Original Investment + Value at End of Useful Life}}{2} = \text{Average Investment}$$

ILLUSTRATION 24-27
Formula for computing average investment

The value at the end of useful life is equal to the asset's salvage value, if any. For Reno, average investment is $65,000 [($130,000 + $0) ÷ 2]. The expected annual rate of return for Reno's investment in new equipment is therefore 20%, computed as follows.

$$\$13{,}000 \div \$65{,}000 = 20\%$$

Management then compares the annual rate of return with its **required rate of return** for investments of similar risk. The required rate of return is generally based on the company's cost of capital. The decision rule is: **A project is acceptable if its rate of return is greater than management's required rate of return. It is unacceptable when the reverse is true.** When companies use the rate of return technique in deciding among several acceptable projects, **the higher the rate of return for a given risk, the more attractive the investment.**

The principal advantages of this method are the simplicity of its calculation and management's familiarity with the accounting terms used in the computation. A major limitation of the annual rate of return method is that it does not consider the time value of money. For example, no consideration is given as to whether cash inflows will occur early or late in the life of the investment. As explained in Appendix G, recognition of the time value of money can make a significant difference between the future value and the discounted present value of an investment. A second disadvantage is that this method relies on accrual accounting numbers rather than expected cash flows.

▼ HELPFUL HINT
A capital budgeting decision based on only one technique may be misleading. It is often wise to analyze an investment from a number of different perspectives.

DO IT! ▶5 Annual Rate of Return

Watertown Paper Corporation is considering adding another machine for the manufacture of corrugated cardboard. The machine would cost $900,000. It would have an estimated life of 6 years and no salvage value. The company estimates that annual revenues would increase by $400,000 and that annual expenses excluding depreciation would increase by $190,000. It uses the straight-line method to compute depreciation expense. Management has a required rate of return of 9%. Compute the annual rate of return.

SOLUTION

Revenues		$400,000
Less:		
Expenses (excluding depreciation)	$190,000	
Depreciation ($900,000/6 years)	150,000	340,000
Annual net income		$ 60,000

Average investment = ($900,000 + $0)/2 = $450,000.
Annual rate of return = $60,000/$450,000 = 13.3%.

Since the annual rate of return (13.3%) is greater than Watertown's required rate of return (9%), the proposed project is acceptable.

Related exercise material: **BE24-9, E24-8, E24-9, E24-10, E24-11,** and **DO IT! 24-5.**

Action Plan

- ✔ Expected annual net income = Annual revenues − Annual expenses (including depreciation expense).
- ✔ Average investment = (Original investment + Value at end of useful life)/2.
- ✔ Annual rate of return = Expected annual net income/Average investment.

USING DECISION TOOLS—HOLLAND AMERICA LINE

As noted in the Feature Story, Holland America Line must continually make significant capital investments in ships. Some of these decisions require comparisons of strategic alternatives. For example, not all of the company's ships are the same size. Different-sized ships offer alternative advantages and disadvantages. Suppose the company is currently trying to decide between two investment options. It is weighing the purchase of three extremely large ships for a total of $2,500,000 versus five smaller ships for a total of $1,400,000. Information regarding these two alternatives is provided below.

	Three Larger Ships	Five Smaller Ships
Initial investment	$2,500,000	$1,400,000
Estimated useful life	20 years	20 years
Annual revenues (accrual)	$500,000	$380,000
Annual expenses (accrual)	$200,000	$180,000
Annual cash inflows	$550,000	$430,000
Annual cash outflows	$222,250	$206,350
Estimated salvage value	$500,000	$0
Discount rate	9%	9%

INSTRUCTIONS

Evaluate each of these mutually exclusive proposals employing (a) cash payback, (b) net present value, (c) profitability index, (d) internal rate of return, and (e) annual rate of return. Discuss the implications of your findings.

SOLUTION

	Three Larger Ships	Five Smaller Ships
(a) Cash payback	$\frac{\$2,500,000}{\$327,750^*} = 7.63$ years	$\frac{\$1,400,000}{\$223,650^{**}} = 6.26$ years

*$550,000 − $222,250; **$430,000 − $206,350

(b) Net present value

	Three Larger Ships	Five Smaller Ships
Present value of net cash flows		
$327,750 × 9.12855 =	$2,991,882	$223,650 × 9.12855 = $2,041,600
$500,000 × 0.17843 =	89,215	
	3,081,097	
Less: Initial investment	2,500,000	1,400,000
Net present value	$ 581,097	$ 641,600

	Three Larger Ships	Five Smaller Ships
(c) Profitability index	$\frac{\$3,081,097}{\$2,500,000} = 1.23$	$\frac{\$2,041,600}{\$1,400,000} = 1.46$

(d) The internal rate of return can be approximated by experimenting with different discount rates to see which one comes the closest to resulting in a net present value of zero. Doing this, we find that the larger ships have an internal rate of return of approximately 12%, while the internal rate of return of the smaller ships is approximately 15% as shown below.

Internal rate of return

Cash Flows	×	12% Discount Factor	=	Present Value	Cash Flows	×	15% Discount Factor	=	Present Value
$327,750	×	7.46944	=	$2,448,109	$223,650	×	6.25933	=	$1,399,899
$500,000	×	0.10367	=	51,835					
				$2,499,944					
Less: Capital investment				2,500,000					1,400,000
Net present value				$ (56)					$ (101)

(e) Annual rate of return

	Three Larger Ships	Five Smaller Ships
Average investment	$\frac{(\$2{,}500{,}000 + \$500{,}000)}{2} = \$1{,}500{,}000$	$\frac{(\$1{,}400{,}000 + \$0)}{2} = \$700{,}000$
Annual rate of return	$\frac{\$300{,}000^{*}}{\$1{,}500{,}000} = .20 = 20\%$	$\frac{\$200{,}000^{**}}{\$700{,}000} = .286 = 28.6\%$

*$500,000 – $200,000; **$380,000 – $180,000

Although the annual rate of return is higher for the smaller ships, this method has the disadvantage of ignoring time value of money, as well as using accrual numbers rather than cash flows. The cash payback of the smaller ships is also shorter, but this method also ignores the time value of money. Thus, while these two methods can be used for a quick assessment, neither should be relied upon as the sole evaluation tool.

From the net present value calculation, it would appear that the two alternatives are nearly identical in their acceptability. However, the profitability index indicates that the small-ship investment is far more desirable because it generates its cash flows with a much smaller initial investment. A similar result is found by using the internal rate of return. Overall, assuming that the company will select only one alternative, it would appear that the small-ship option should be chosen.

REVIEW AND PRACTICE

LEARNING OBJECTIVES REVIEW

1 Describe capital budgeting inputs and apply the cash payback technique. Management gathers project proposals from each department; a capital budget committee screens the proposals and recommends worthy projects. Company officers decide which projects to fund, and the board of directors approves the capital budget. In capital budgeting, estimated cash inflows and outflows, rather than accrual-accounting numbers, are the preferred inputs.

The cash payback technique identifies the time period required to recover the cost of the investment. The formula when net annual cash flows are equal is Cost of capital investment ÷ Estimated net annual cash flow = Cash payback period. The shorter the payback period, the more attractive the investment.

2 Use the net present value method. The net present value method compares the present value of future cash inflows with the capital investment to determine net present value. The NPV decision rule is: Accept the project if net present value is zero or positive. Reject the project if net present value is negative.

3 Identify capital budgeting challenges and refinements. Intangible benefits are difficult to quantify and thus are often ignored in capital budgeting decisions. This can result in incorrectly rejecting some projects. One method for considering intangible benefits is to calculate the NPV, ignoring intangible benefits. If the resulting NPV is below zero, evaluate whether the benefits are worth at least the amount of the negative net present value. Alternatively, intangible benefits can be incorporated into the NPV calculation, using conservative estimates of their value.

The profitability index is a tool for comparing the relative merits of alternative capital investment opportunities. It is computed as Present value of net cash flows ÷ Initial investment. The higher the index, the more desirable the project.

A post-audit is an evaluation of a capital investment's actual performance. Post-audits create an incentive for managers to make accurate estimates. Post-audits also are useful for determining whether a company should continue, expand, or terminate a project. Finally, post-audits provide feedback that is useful for improving estimation techniques.

4 Use the internal rate of return method. The objective of the internal rate of return method is to find the interest yield of the potential investment, which is expressed as a percentage rate. The IRR decision rule is: Accept the project when the internal rate of return is equal to or greater than the required rate of return. Reject the project when the internal rate of return is less than the required rate of return.

5 Use the annual rate of return method. The annual rate of return uses accrual accounting data to indicate the profitability of a capital investment. It is calculated as Expected annual net income ÷ Amount of the average investment. The higher the rate of return, the more attractive the investment.

DECISION TOOLS REVIEW

DECISION CHECKPOINTS	INFO NEEDED FOR DECISION	TOOL TO USE FOR DECISION	HOW TO EVALUATE RESULTS
Should the company invest in a proposed project?	Cash flow estimates, discount rate	Net present value = Present value of net cash flows less capital investment	The investment is financially acceptable if net present value is zero or positive.
Which investment proposal should a company accept?	Estimated cash flows and discount rate for each proposal	$\text{Profitability index} = \dfrac{\text{Present value of net cash flows}}{\text{Initial investment}}$	The investment proposal with the highest profitability index should be accepted.
Should the company invest in a proposed project?	Estimated cash flows and the required rate of return (hurdle rate)	Internal rate of return = Interest rate that results in a net present value of zero	If the internal rate of return exceeds the required rate of return for the project, then the project is financially acceptable.

GLOSSARY REVIEW

Annual rate of return method The determination of the profitability of a capital expenditure, computed by dividing expected annual net income by the average investment. (p. 1184).

Capital budgeting The process of making capital expenditure decisions in business. (p. 1166).

Cash payback technique A capital budgeting technique that identifies the time period required to recover the cost of a capital investment from the net annual cash flow produced by the investment. (p. 1169).

Cost of capital The weighted-average rate of return that the firm must pay to obtain funds from creditors and stockholders. (p. 1174).

Discounted cash flow technique A capital budgeting technique that considers both the estimated net cash flows from the investment and the time value of money. (p. 1171).

Discount rate The interest rate used in discounting the future net cash flows to determine present value. (p. 1171).

Internal rate of return (IRR) The interest rate that will cause the present value of the proposed capital expenditure to equal the present value of the expected net annual cash flows. (p. 1182).

Internal rate of return (IRR) method A method used in capital budgeting that results in finding the interest yield of the potential investment. (p. 1182).

Net present value (NPV) The difference that results when the original capital outlay is subtracted from the discounted net cash flows. (p. 1171).

Net present value (NPV) method A method used in capital budgeting in which net cash flows are discounted to their present value and then compared to the capital outlay required by the investment. (p. 1171).

Post-audit A thorough evaluation of how well a project's actual performance matches the original projections. (p. 1180).

Profitability index A method of comparing alternative projects that takes into account both the size of the investment and its discounted net cash flows. It is computed by dividing the present value of net cash flows by the initial investment. (p. 1179).

Required rate of return The rate of return management expects on investments, sometimes called the discount rate or cost of capital. (p. 1172).

PRACTICE MULTIPLE-CHOICE QUESTIONS

(LO 1) **1.** Which of the following is **not** an example of a capital budgeting decision?
(a) Decision to build a new plant.
(b) Decision to renovate an existing facility.
(c) Decision to buy a piece of machinery.
(d) All of these are capital budgeting decisions.

(LO 1) **2.** What is the order of involvement of the following parties in the capital budgeting authorization process?
(a) Plant managers, officers, capital budget committee, board of directors.
(b) Board of directors, plant managers, officers, capital budget committee.
(c) Plant managers, capital budget committee, officers, board of directors.
(d) Officers, plant managers, capital budget committee, board of directors.

3. What is a weakness of the cash payback approach? (LO 1)
(a) It uses accrual-based accounting numbers.
(b) It ignores the time value of money.
(c) It ignores the useful life of alternative projects.
(d) Both (b) and (c) are true.

4. Siegel Industries is considering two capital budgeting projects. Project A requires an initial investment of $48,000. It is expected to produce net annual cash (LO 1)

flows of $7,000. Project B requires an initial investment of $75,000 and is expected to produce net annual cash flows of $12,000. Using the cash payback technique to evaluate the two projects, Siegel should accept:
(a) Project A because it has a shorter cash payback period.
(b) Project B because it has a shorter cash payback period.
(c) Project A because it requires a smaller initial investment.
(d) Project B because it produces a larger net annual cash flow.

(LO 2) 5. Which is a **true** statement regarding using a higher discount rate to calculate the net present value of a project?
(a) It will make it less likely that the project will be accepted.
(b) It will make it more likely that the project will be accepted.
(c) It is appropriate to use a higher rate if the project is perceived as being less risky than other projects being considered.
(d) It is appropriate to use a higher rate if the project will have a short useful life relative to other projects being considered.

(LO 2) 6. A positive net present value means that the:
(a) project's rate of return is less than the cutoff rate.
(b) project's rate of return exceeds the required rate of return.
(c) project's rate of return equals the required rate of return.
(d) project is unacceptable.

(LO 2) 7. Which of the following is **not** an alternative name for the discount rate?
(a) Hurdle rate.
(b) Required rate of return.
(c) Cutoff rate.
(d) All of these are alternative names for the discount rate.

(LO 3) 8. If a project has intangible benefits whose value is hard to estimate, the best thing to do is:
(a) ignore these benefits, since any estimate of their value will most likely be wrong.
(b) include a conservative estimate of their value.
(c) ignore their value in your initial net present value calculation, but then estimate whether their potential value is worth at least the amount of the net present value deficiency.
(d) Either (b) or (c) is correct.

(LO 3) 9. An example of an intangible benefit provided by a capital budgeting project is:
(a) the salvage value of the capital investment.
(b) a positive net present value.
(c) a decrease in customer complaints due to poor quality.
(d) an internal rate of return greater than zero.

(LO 3) 10. The following information is available for a potential capital investment.

Initial investment	$80,000
Salvage value	10,000
Net annual cash flow	14,820
Present value of net annual cash flows	98,112
Net present value	18,112
Useful life	10 years

The potential investment's profitability index (rounded to two decimals) is:
(a) 5.40. (c) 1.23.
(b) 1.19. (d) 1.40.

(LO 3) 11. A post-audit of an investment project should be performed:
(a) on all significant capital expenditure projects.
(b) on all projects that management feels might be financial failures.
(c) on randomly selected projects.
(d) only on projects that enjoy tremendous success.

(LO 4) 12. A project should be accepted if its internal rate of return exceeds:
(a) zero.
(b) the rate of return on a government bond.
(c) the company's required rate of return.
(d) the rate the company pays on borrowed funds.

(LO 4) 13. The following information is available for a potential capital investment.

Initial investment	$60,000
Net annual cash flow	15,400
Net present value	3,143
Useful life	5 years

The potential investment's internal rate of return is approximately:
(a) 5%. (c) 4%.
(b) 10%. (d) 9%.

(LO 5) 14. Which of the following is **incorrect** about the annual rate of return technique?
(a) The calculation is simple.
(b) The accounting terms used are familiar to management.
(c) The timing of the cash inflows is not considered.
(d) The time value of money is considered.

(LO 5) 15. The following information is available for a potential capital investment.

Initial investment	$120,000
Annual net income	15,000
Net annual cash flow	27,500
Salvage value	20,000
Useful life	8 years

The potential investment's annual rate of return is approximately:
(a) 21%. (c) 30%.
(b) 15%. (d) 39%.

SOLUTIONS

1. **(d)** Choices (a), (b), and (c) are all examples of capital budgeting decisions, so choice (d) is the best answer.
2. **(c)** The process of authorizing capital budget expenditures starts with plant managers, moves on to the capital budgeting committee, goes next to the officers of the firm and finally is acted upon by the board of directors. The other choices are therefore incorrect.

3. **(d)** Choices (b) and (c) are both correct; therefore, choice (d) is the best answer. Choice (a) is incorrect as the use of accrual-based accounting numbers is not a weakness of the cash payback approach.
4. **(b)** Project B ($75,000 ÷ $12,000) has a shorter cash payback period than Project A ($48,000 ÷ $7,000). The other choices are therefore incorrect.
5. **(a)** If a higher discount rate is used in calculating the net present value of a project, the resulting net present value will be lower and the project will be less likely to be accepted. The other choices are therefore incorrect.
6. **(b)** A positive net present value means that the project's rate of return exceeds the required rate of return. The other choices are therefore incorrect.
7. **(d)** Choices (a), (b), and (c) are all alternative names for the discount rate; therefore, choice (d) is the best answer.
8. **(d)** Choices (b) and (c) are both reasonable approaches to including intangible benefits in the capital budgeting process; therefore, choice (d) is the best answer. Choice (a) is incorrect because even though these intangible benefits may be hard to quantify, they should not be ignored in the capital budgeting process.
9. **(c)** A decrease in customer complaints due to poor quality is one example of an intangible benefit provided by a capital budgeting project. The other choices are incorrect because (a) salvage value, (b) net present value, and (d) internal rate of return are all quantitative measures, i.e., tangible.
10. **(c)** $98,112 ÷ $80,000 = 1.23, not (a) 5.40, (b) 1.19, or (d) 1.40.
11. **(a)** A post-audit should be performed on all significant capital expenditure projects, not just on (b) financial failures, (c) randomly selected projects, or (d) tremendous successes, because the feedback gained will help to improve the process in the future and also will give managers an incentive to be more realistic in preparing capital expenditure proposals.
12. **(c)** A project should be accepted if its internal rate of return exceeds the company's required rate of return, not (a) zero, (b) the rate of return on a government bond, or (d) the rate the company pays on borrowed funds.
13. **(d)** ($60,000 ÷ $15,400) equals 3.8961, which corresponds with approximately 9% in Table 4 of Appendix G, not (a) 5%, (b) 10%, or (c) 4%.
14. **(d)** The time value of money is not considered when applying the annual rate of return method. The other choices are correct statements.
15. **(a)** $15,000 ÷ [($120,000 + $20,000) ÷ 2] = 21%, not (b) 15%, (c) 30%, or (d) 39%.

PRACTICE EXERCISES

Calculate payback period, internal rate of return, and apply decision rules.

(LO 1, 4)

1. BTMS Inc. wants to purchase a new machine for $30,000, excluding $1,500 of installation costs. The old machine was bought five years ago and had an expected economic life of 10 years without salvage value. This old machine now has a book value of $2,000, and BTMS Inc. expects to sell it for that amount. The new machine would decrease operating costs by $8,000 each year of its economic life. The straight-line depreciation method would be used for the new machine, for a five-year period with no salvage value.

INSTRUCTIONS

(a) Determine the cash payback period.

(b) Determine the approximate internal rate of return.

(c) Assuming the company has a required rate of return of 10%, state your conclusion on whether the new machine should be purchased.

(CGA adapted)

SOLUTION

1. (a) Total net investment = $30,000 + $1,500 − $2,000 = $29,500
Annual net cash flow = $8,000
Payback period = $29,500 ÷ $8,000 = 3.7 years

(b) Net present value approximates zero when discount rate is 11%.

Item	Amount	Years	PV Factor	Present Value
Net annual cash flows	$8,000	1–5	3.69590	$29,567
Less: Capital investment				29,500
Net present value				$ 67

(c) Because the approximate internal rate of return of 11% exceeds the required rate of return of 10%, the investment should be accepted.

2. MCA Corporation is reviewing an investment proposal. The initial cost and estimates of the book value of the investment at the end of each year, the net cash flows for each year, and the net income for each year are presented in the schedule below. All cash flows are assumed to take place at the end of the year. The salvage value of the investment at the end of each year is equal to its book value. There would be no salvage value at the end of the investment's life.

Calculate payback, annual rate of return, and net present value

(LO 1, 2, 5)

Investment Proposal

Year	Initial Cost and Book Value	Annual Cash Flows	Annual Net Income
0	$105,000		
1	70,000	$45,000	$16,000
2	42,000	40,000	18,000
3	21,000	35,000	20,000
4	7,000	30,000	22,000
5	0	25,000	24,000

MCA Corporation uses a 15% target rate of return for new investment proposals.

INSTRUCTIONS

(a) What is the cash payback period for this proposal?

(b) What is the annual rate of return for the investment?

(c) What is the net present value of the investment?

(CMA-Canada adapted)

SOLUTION

2. (a)

	Year	Amount	Balance
Initial investment	0	$(105,000)	$(105,000)
Less: Cash flow	1	45,000	(60,000)
	2	40,000	(20,000)
	3	35,000	15,000

Payback period = 2 + ($20,000 ÷ $35,000) = 2.57

(b) Average annual net income = ($16,000 + $18,000 + $20,000 + $22,000 + $24,000) ÷ 5 = $20,000
Average investment = ($105,000 + $0) ÷ 2 = $52,500
Annual rate of return = $20,000 ÷ $52,500 = 38.10%

(c)

	Year	Discount Factor, 15%	Amount	Present Value
Net cash flows	1	0.86957	$45,000	$ 39,131
	2	0.75614	40,000	30,246
	3	0.65752	35,000	23,013
	4	0.57175	30,000	17,153
	5	0.49718	25,000	12,430
Present value of cash inflows				121,973
Less: Initial investment				105,000
Net present value				$ 16,973

▶ PRACTICE PROBLEM

Cornfield Company is considering a long-term capital investment project in laser equipment. This will require an investment of $280,000, and it will have a useful life of 5 years. Annual net income is expected to be $16,000 a year. Depreciation is computed by the straight-line method with no salvage value. The company's cost of capital is 10%. (*Hint:* Assume cash flows can be computed by adding back depreciation expense.)

Compute annual rate of return, cash payback, and net present value.

(LO 1, 2, 5)

INSTRUCTIONS

(Round all computations to two decimal places unless directed otherwise.)

(a) Compute the cash payback period for the project.

(b) Compute the net present value for the project. (Round to nearest dollar.)

(c) Compute the annual rate of return for the project.

(d) Should the project be accepted? Why?

SOLUTION

(a) $280,000 ÷ $72,000 ($16,000 + $56,000) = 3.89 years

(b)

	Present Value at 10%
Discount factor for 5 payments	3.79079
Present value of net cash flows:	
$72,000 × 3.79079	$272,937
Less: Capital investment	280,000
Negative net present value	$ (7,063)

(c) $16,000 ÷ $140,000 ($280,000 ÷ 2) = 11.4%

(d) The annual rate of return of 11.4% is good. However, the cash payback period is 78% of the project's useful life, and net present value is negative. The recommendation is to reject the project.

WileyPLUS Brief Exercises, DO IT! Exercises, Exercises, Problems, and many additional resources are available for practice in WileyPLUS.

QUESTIONS

1. Describe the process a company may use in screening and approving the capital expenditure budget.
2. What are the advantages and disadvantages of the cash payback technique?
3. Tom Wells claims the formula for the cash payback technique is the same as the formula for the annual rate of return technique. Is Tom correct? What is the formula for the cash payback technique?
4. Two types of present value tables may be used with the discounted cash flow techniques. Identify the tables and the circumstance(s) when each table should be used.
5. What is the decision rule under the net present value method?
6. Discuss the factors that determine the appropriate discount rate to use when calculating the net present value.
7. What simplifying assumptions were made in the chapter regarding calculation of net present value?
8. What are some examples of potential intangible benefits of investment proposals? Why do these intangible benefits complicate the capital budgeting evaluation process? What might happen if intangible benefits are ignored in a capital budgeting decision?
9. What steps can be taken to incorporate intangible benefits into the capital budget evaluation process?
10. What advantages does the profitability index provide over direct comparison of net present value when comparing two projects?
11. What is a post-audit? What are the potential benefits of a post-audit?
12. Identify the steps required in using the internal rate of return method when the net annual cash flows are equal.
13. El Cajon Company uses the internal rate of return method. What is the decision rule for this method?
14. What are the strengths of the annual rate of return approach? What are its weaknesses?
15. Your classmate, Mike Dawson, is confused about the factors that are included in the annual rate of return technique. What is the formula for this technique?
16. Sveta Pace is trying to understand the term "cost of capital." Define the term and indicate its relevance to the decision rule under the internal rate of return technique.

▶ BRIEF EXERCISES

BE24-1 Rihanna Company is considering purchasing new equipment for $450,000. It is expected that the equipment will produce net annual cash flows of $60,000 over its 10-year useful life. Annual depreciation will be $45,000. Compute the cash payback period.

Compute the cash payback period for a capital investment.
(LO 1), AP

BE24-2 Hsung Company accumulates the following data concerning a proposed capital investment: cash cost $215,000, net annual cash flows $40,000, and present value factor of cash inflows for 10 years 5.65 (rounded). Determine the net present value, and indicate whether the investment should be made.

Compute net present value of an investment.
(LO 2), AN

BE24-3 Thunder Corporation, an amusement park, is considering a capital investment in a new exhibit. The exhibit would cost $136,000 and have an estimated useful life of 5 years. It will be sold for $60,000 at that time. (Amusement parks need to rotate exhibits to keep people interested.) It is expected to increase net annual cash flows by $25,000. The company's borrowing rate is 8%. Its cost of capital is 10%. Calculate the net present value of this project to the company.

Compute net present value of an investment.
(LO 2), AP

BE24-4 Caine Bottling Corporation is considering the purchase of a new bottling machine. The machine would cost $200,000 and has an estimated useful life of 8 years with zero salvage value. Management estimates that the new bottling machine will provide net annual cash flows of $34,000. Management also believes that the new bottling machine will save the company money because it is expected to be more reliable than other machines, and thus will reduce downtime. How much would the reduction in downtime have to be worth in order for the project to be acceptable? Assume a discount rate of 9%. (*Hint:* Calculate the net present value.)

Compute net present value of an investment and consider intangible benefits.
(LO 2, 3), AN

BE24-5 McKnight Company is considering two different, mutually exclusive capital expenditure proposals. Project A will cost $400,000, has an expected useful life of 10 years, a salvage value of zero, and is expected to increase net annual cash flows by $70,000. Project B will cost $310,000, has an expected useful life of 10 years, a salvage value of zero, and is expected to increase net annual cash flows by $55,000. A discount rate of 9% is appropriate for both projects. Compute the net present value and profitability index of each project. Which project should be accepted?

Compute net present value and profitability index.
(LO 2, 3), AN

BE24-6 Quillen Company is performing a post-audit of a project completed one year ago. The initial estimates were that the project would cost $250,000, would have a useful life of 9 years, zero salvage value, and would result in net annual cash flows of $46,000 per year. Now that the investment has been in operation for 1 year, revised figures indicate that it actually cost $260,000, will have a total useful life of 11 years, and will produce net annual cash flows of $39,000 per year. Evaluate the success of the project. Assume a discount rate of 10%.

Perform a post-audit.
(LO 3), AN

BE24-7 Kanye Company is evaluating the purchase of a rebuilt spot-welding machine to be used in the manufacture of a new product. The machine will cost $176,000, has an estimated useful life of 7 years, a salvage value of zero, and will increase net annual cash flows by $35,000. What is its approximate internal rate of return?

Calculate internal rate of return.
(LO 4), AP

BE24-8 Viera Corporation is considering investing in a new facility. The estimated cost of the facility is $2,045,000. It will be used for 12 years, then sold for $716,000. The facility will generate annual cash inflows of $400,000 and will need new annual cash outflows of $150,000. The company has a required rate of return of 7%. Calculate the internal rate of return on this project, and discuss whether the project should be accepted.

Calculate internal rate of return.
(LO 4), AN

BE24-9 Swift Oil Company is considering investing in a new oil well. It is expected that the oil well will increase annual revenues by $130,000 and will increase annual expenses by $70,000 including depreciation. The oil well will cost $490,000 and will have a $10,000 salvage value at the end of its 10-year useful life. Calculate the annual rate of return.

Compute annual rate of return.
(LO 5), AP

DO IT! EXERCISES

Compute the cash payback period for an investment.
(LO 1), AP

DO IT! 24-1 Wayne Company is considering a long-term investment project called ZIP. ZIP will require an investment of $140,000. It will have a useful life of 4 years and no salvage value. Annual cash inflows would increase by $80,000, and annual cash outflows would increase by $40,000. Compute the cash payback period.

Calculate net present value of an investment.
(LO 2), AN

DO IT! 24-2 Wayne Company is considering a long-term investment project called ZIP. ZIP will require an investment of $120,000. It will have a useful life of 4 years and no salvage value. Annual cash inflows would increase by $80,000, and annual cash outflows would increase by $40,000. The company's required rate of return is 12%. Calculate the net present value on this project and discuss whether it should be accepted.

Compute profitability index.
(LO 3), AP

DO IT! 24-3 Ranger Corporation has decided to invest in renewable energy sources to meet part of its energy needs for production. It is considering solar power versus wind power. After considering cost savings as well as incremental revenues from selling excess electricity into the power grid, it has determined the following.

	Solar	Wind
Present value of annual cash flows	$52,580	$128,450
Initial investment	$39,500	$105,300

Determine the net present value and profitability index of each project. Which energy source should it choose?

Calculate internal rate of return.
(LO 4), AN

DO IT! 24-4 Wayne Company is considering a long-term investment project called ZIP. ZIP will require an investment of $120,000. It will have a useful life of 4 years and no salvage value. Annual cash inflows would increase by $80,000, and annual cash outflows would increase by $40,000. The company's required rate of return is 12%. Calculate the internal rate of return on this project and discuss whether it should be accepted.

Calculate annual rate of return.
(LO 5), AP

DO IT! 24-5 Wayne Company is considering a long-term investment project called ZIP. ZIP will require an investment of $120,000. It will have a useful life of 4 years and no salvage value. Annual revenues would increase by $80,000, and annual expenses (excluding depreciation) would increase by $41,000. Wayne uses the straight-line method to compute depreciation expense. The company's required rate of return is 12%. Compute the annual rate of return.

EXERCISES

Compute cash payback and net present value.
(LO 1, 2), AN

E24-1 Linkin Corporation is considering purchasing a new delivery truck. The truck has many advantages over the company's current truck (not the least of which is that it runs). The new truck would cost $56,000. Because of the increased capacity, reduced maintenance costs, and increased fuel economy, the new truck is expected to generate cost savings of $8,000. At the end of 8 years, the company will sell the truck for an estimated $27,000. Traditionally the company has used a rule of thumb that a proposal should not be accepted unless it has a payback period that is less than 50% of the asset's estimated useful life. Larry Newton, a new manager, has suggested that the company should not rely solely on the payback approach, but should also employ the net present value method when evaluating new projects. The company's cost of capital is 8%.

Instructions

(a) Compute the cash payback period and net present value of the proposed investment.
(b) Does the project meet the company's cash payback criteria? Does it meet the net present value criteria for acceptance? Discuss your results.

Compute cash payback period and net present value.

(LO 1, 2), AN

E24-2 Doug's Custom Construction Company is considering three new projects, each requiring an equipment investment of $22,000. Each project will last for 3 years and produce the following net annual cash flows.

Year	AA	BB	CC
1	$ 7,000	$10,000	$13,000
2	9,000	10,000	12,000
3	12,000	10,000	11,000
Total	$28,000	$30,000	$36,000

The equipment's salvage value is zero, and Doug uses straight-line depreciation. Doug will not accept any project with a cash payback period over 2 years. Doug's required rate of return is 12%.

Instructions

(a) Compute each project's payback period, indicating the most desirable project and the least desirable project using this method. (Round to two decimals and assume in your computations that cash flows occur evenly throughout the year.)

(b) Compute the net present value of each project. Does your evaluation change? (Round to nearest dollar.)

Calculate net present value and apply decision rule.

(LO 2), AN

E24-3 Hillsong Inc. manufactures snowsuits. Hillsong is considering purchasing a new sewing machine at a cost of $2.45 million. Its existing machine was purchased five years ago at a price of $1.8 million; six months ago, Hillsong spent $55,000 to keep it operational. The existing sewing machine can be sold today for $250,000. The new sewing machine would require a one-time, $85,000 training cost. Operating costs would decrease by the following amounts for years 1 to 7:

Year 1	$390,000
2	400,000
3	411,000
4	426,000
5	434,000
6	435,000
7	436,000

The new sewing machine would be depreciated according to the declining-balance method at a rate of 20%. The salvage value is expected to be $400,000. This new equipment would require maintenance costs of $100,000 at the end of the fifth year. The cost of capital is 9%.

Instructions

Use the net present value method to determine whether Hillsong should purchase the new machine to replace the existing machine, and state the reason for your conclusion.

(CGA adapted)

Compute net present value and profitability index.

(LO 2, 3), AN

E24-4 BAK Corp. is considering purchasing one of two new diagnostic machines. Either machine would make it possible for the company to bid on jobs that it currently isn't equipped to do. Estimates regarding each machine are provided below.

	Machine A	Machine B
Original cost	$75,500	$180,000
Estimated life	8 years	8 years
Salvage value	–0–	–0–
Estimated annual cash inflows	$20,000	$40,000
Estimated annual cash outflows	$5,000	$10,000

Instructions

Calculate the net present value and profitability index of each machine. Assume a 9% discount rate. Which machine should be purchased?

Determine internal rate of return.

(LO 4), AN

E24-5 Bruno Corporation is involved in the business of injection molding of plastics. It is considering the purchase of a new computer-aided design and manufacturing machine for $430,000. The company believes that with this new machine it will improve productivity and increase quality, resulting in an increase in net annual cash flows of $101,000 for the next 6 years. Management requires a 10% rate of return on all new investments.

Instructions

Calculate the internal rate of return on this new machine. Should the investment be accepted?

Calculate cash payback period, internal rate of return, and apply decision rules.

(LO 1, 4), AN

E24-6 BSU Inc. wants to purchase a new machine for $29,300, excluding $1,500 of installation costs. The old machine was bought five years ago and had an expected economic life of 10 years without salvage value. This old machine now has a book value of $2,000, and BSU Inc. expects to sell it for that amount. The new machine would decrease operating costs by $7,000 each year of its economic life. The straight-line depreciation method would be used for the new machine, for a six-year period with no salvage value.

Instructions

(a) Determine the cash payback period.
(b) Determine the approximate internal rate of return.
(c) Assuming the company has a required rate of return of 10%, state your conclusion on whether the new machine should be purchased.

(CGA adapted)

Determine internal rate of return.

(LO 4), AN

E24-7 Iggy Company is considering three capital expenditure projects. Relevant data for the projects are as follows.

Project	Investment	Annual Income	Life of Project
22A	$240,000	$15,500	6 years
23A	270,000	20,600	9 years
24A	280,000	15,700	7 years

Annual income is constant over the life of the project. Each project is expected to have zero salvage value at the end of the project. Iggy Company uses the straight-line method of depreciation.

Instructions

(a) Determine the internal rate of return for each project. Round the internal rate of return factor to three decimals.
(b) If Iggy Company's required rate of return is 10%, which projects are acceptable?

Calculate annual rate of return.

(LO 5), AP

E24-8 Pierre's Hair Salon is considering opening a new location in French Lick, California. The cost of building a new salon is $300,000. A new salon will normally generate annual revenues of $70,000, with annual expenses (including depreciation) of $41,500. At the end of 15 years the salon will have a salvage value of $80,000.

Instructions

Calculate the annual rate of return on the project.

Compute cash payback period and annual rate of return.

(LO 1, 5), AP

E24-9 Legend Service Center just purchased an automobile hoist for $32,400. The hoist has an 8-year life and an estimated salvage value of $3,000. Installation costs and freight charges were $3,300 and $700, respectively. Legend uses straight-line depreciation.

The new hoist will be used to replace mufflers and tires on automobiles. Legend estimates that the new hoist will enable his mechanics to replace five extra mufflers per week. Each muffler sells for $72 installed. The cost of a muffler is $36, and the labor cost to install a muffler is $16.

Instructions

(a) Compute the cash payback period for the new hoist.
(b) Compute the annual rate of return for the new hoist. (Round to one decimal.)

Compute annual rate of return, cash payback period, and net present value.

(LO 1, 2, 5), AP

E24-10 Vilas Company is considering a capital investment of $190,000 in additional productive facilities. The new machinery is expected to have a useful life of 5 years with no salvage value. Depreciation is by the straight-line method. During the life of the investment, annual net income and net annual cash flows are expected to be $12,000 and

$50,000, respectively. Vilas has a 12% cost of capital rate, which is the required rate of return on the investment.

Instructions

(Round to two decimals.)

(a) Compute (1) the cash payback period and (2) the annual rate of return on the proposed capital expenditure.
(b) Using the discounted cash flow technique, compute the net present value.

Calculate payback, annual rate of return, and net present value.

(LO 1, 2, 5), AP

E24-11 Drake Corporation is reviewing an investment proposal. The initial cost and estimates of the book value of the investment at the end of each year, the net cash flows for each year, and the net income for each year are presented in the schedule below. All cash flows are assumed to take place at the end of the year. The salvage value of the investment at the end of each year is equal to its book value. There would be no salvage value at the end of the investment's life.

Investment Proposal

Year	**Initial Cost and Book Value**	**Annual Cash Flows**	**Annual Net Income**
0	$105,000		
1	70,000	$45,000	$10,000
2	42,000	40,000	12,000
3	21,000	35,000	14,000
4	7,000	30,000	16,000
5	0	25,000	18,000

Drake Corporation uses an 11% target rate of return for new investment proposals.

Instructions

(a) What is the cash payback period for this proposal?
(b) What is the annual rate of return for the investment?
(c) What is the net present value of the investment?

(CMA-Canada adapted)

EXERCISES: SET B AND CHALLENGE EXERCISES

Visit the book's companion website, at **www.wiley.com/college/kimmel**, and choose the Student Companion site to access Exercises: Set B and Challenge Exercises.

PROBLEMS: SET A

Compute annual rate of return, cash payback, and net present value.

(LO 1, 2, 5), AN

XLS

P24-1A U3 Company is considering three long-term capital investment proposals. Each investment has a useful life of 5 years. Relevant data on each project are as follows.

	Project Bono	**Project Edge**	**Project Clayton**
Capital investment	$160,000	$175,000	$200,000
Annual net income:			
Year 1	14,000	18,000	27,000
2	14,000	17,000	23,000
3	14,000	16,000	21,000
4	14,000	12,000	13,000
5	14,000	9,000	12,000
Total	$ 70,000	$ 72,000	$ 96,000

Depreciation is computed by the straight-line method with no salvage value. The company's cost of capital is 15%. (Assume that cash flows occur evenly throughout the year.)

Instructions

(a) Compute the cash payback period for each project. (Round to two decimals.)
(b) Compute the net present value for each project. (Round to nearest dollar.)

(b) E $(7,312); C $2,163

(c) Compute the annual rate of return for each project. (Round to two decimals.) (*Hint:* Use average annual net income in your computation.)
(d) Rank the projects on each of the foregoing bases. Which project do you recommend?

Compute annual rate of return, cash payback, and net present value.
(LO 1, 2, 5), AN

P24-2A Lon Timur is an accounting major at a midwestern state university located approximately 60 miles from a major city. Many of the students attending the university are from the metropolitan area and visit their homes regularly on the weekends. Lon, an entrepreneur at heart, realizes that few good commuting alternatives are available for students doing weekend travel. He believes that a weekend commuting service could be organized and run profitably from several suburban and downtown shopping mall locations. Lon has gathered the following investment information.

1. Five used vans would cost a total of $75,000 to purchase and would have a 3-year useful life with negligible salvage value. Lon plans to use straight-line depreciation.
2. Ten drivers would have to be employed at a total payroll expense of $48,000.
3. Other annual out-of-pocket expenses associated with running the commuter service would include Gasoline $16,000, Maintenance $3,300, Repairs $4,000, Insurance $4,200, and Advertising $2,500.
4. Lon has visited several financial institutions to discuss funding. The best interest rate he has been able to negotiate is 15%. Use this rate for cost of capital.
5. Lon expects each van to make ten round trips weekly and carry an average of six students each trip. The service is expected to operate 30 weeks each year, and each student will be charged $12.00 for a round-trip ticket.

Instructions

(a) (1) $5,000

(b) (1) 2.5 years

(a) Determine the annual (1) net income and (2) net annual cash flows for the commuter service.
(b) Compute (1) the cash payback period and (2) the annual rate of return. (Round to two decimals.)
(c) Compute the net present value of the commuter service. (Round to the nearest dollar.)
(d) What should Lon conclude from these computations?

Compute net present value, profitability index, and internal rate of return.
(LO 2, 3, 4), AN

P24-3A Brooks Clinic is considering investing in new heart-monitoring equipment. It has two options. Option A would have an initial lower cost but would require a significant expenditure for rebuilding after 4 years. Option B would require no rebuilding expenditure, but its maintenance costs would be higher. Since the Option B machine is of initial higher quality, it is expected to have a salvage value at the end of its useful life. The following estimates were made of the cash flows. The company's cost of capital is 8%.

	Option A	Option B
Initial cost	$160,000	$227,000
Annual cash inflows	$71,000	$80,000
Annual cash outflows	$30,000	$31,000
Cost to rebuild (end of year 4)	$50,000	$0
Salvage value	$0	$8,000
Estimated useful life	7 years	7 years

Instructions

(a) (1) NPV A $16,709
(3) IRR B 12%

(a) Compute the (1) net present value, (2) profitability index, and (3) internal rate of return for each option. (*Hint:* To solve for internal rate of return, experiment with alternative discount rates to arrive at a net present value of zero.)
(b) Which option should be accepted?

Compute net present value considering intangible benefits.
(LO 2, 3), E

P24-4A Jane's Auto Care is considering the purchase of a new tow truck. The garage doesn't currently have a tow truck, and the $60,000 price tag for a new truck would represent a major expenditure. Jane Austen, owner of the garage, has compiled the estimates shown below in trying to determine whether the tow truck should be purchased.

Initial cost	$60,000
Estimated useful life	8 years
Net annual cash flows from towing	$8,000
Overhaul costs (end of year 4)	$6,000
Salvage value	$12,000

Jane's good friend, Rick Ryan, stopped by. He is trying to convince Jane that the tow truck will have other benefits that Jane hasn't even considered. First, he says, cars that need towing need to be fixed. Thus, when Jane tows them to her facility, her repair revenues will increase. Second, he notes that the tow truck could have a plow mounted on it, thus saving Jane the cost of plowing her parking lot. (Rick will give her a used plow blade for free if Jane will plow Rick's driveway.) Third, he notes that the truck will generate goodwill; people who are rescued by Jane's tow truck will feel grateful and might be more inclined to use her service station in the future or buy gas there. Fourth, the tow truck will have "Jane's Auto Care" on its doors, hood, and back tailgate—a form of free advertising wherever the tow truck goes. Rick estimates that, at a minimum, these benefits would be worth the following.

Additional annual net cash flows from repair work	$3,000
Annual savings from plowing	750
Additional annual net cash flows from customer "goodwill"	1,000
Additional annual net cash flows resulting from free advertising	750

The company's cost of capital is 9%.

Instructions

(a) Calculate the net present value, ignoring the additional benefits described by Rick. Should the tow truck be purchased? (a) NPV $(13,950)

(b) Calculate the net present value, incorporating the additional benefits suggested by Rick. Should the tow truck be purchased? (b) NPV $16,491

(c) Suppose Rick has been overly optimistic in his assessment of the value of the additional benefits. At a minimum, how much would the additional benefits have to be worth in order for the project to be accepted?

Compute net present value and internal rate of return with sensitivity analysis.

(LO 2, 3, 4), E

P24-5A Coolplay Corp. is thinking about opening a soccer camp in southern California. To start the camp, Coolplay would need to purchase land and build four soccer fields and a sleeping and dining facility to house 150 soccer players. Each year, the camp would be run for 8 sessions of 1 week each. The company would hire college soccer players as coaches. The camp attendees would be male and female soccer players ages 12–18. Property values in southern California have enjoyed a steady increase in value. It is expected that after using the facility for 20 years, Coolplay can sell the property for more than it was originally purchased for. The following amounts have been estimated.

Cost of land	$300,000
Cost to build soccer fields, dorm and dining facility	$600,000
Annual cash inflows assuming 150 players and 8 weeks	$920,000
Annual cash outflows	$840,000
Estimated useful life	20 years
Salvage value	$1,500,000
Discount rate	8%

Instructions

(a) Calculate the net present value of the project. (a) NPV $207,277

(b) To gauge the sensitivity of the project to these estimates, assume that if only 125 players attend each week, annual cash inflows will be $805,000 and annual cash outflows will be $750,000. What is the net present value using these alternative estimates? Discuss your findings.

(c) Assuming the original facts, what is the net present value if the project is actually riskier than first assumed and an 10% discount rate is more appropriate?

(d) Assume that during the first 5 years, the annual net cash flows each year were only $40,000. At the end of the fifth year, the company is running low on cash, so management decides to sell the property for $1,332,000. What was the actual internal rate of return on the project? Explain how this return was possible given that the camp did not appear to be successful. (d) IRR 12%

▶ PROBLEMS: SET B AND SET C

Visit the book's companion website, at **www.wiley.com/college/kimmel**, and choose the Student Companion site to access Problems: Set B and Set C.

CONTINUING PROBLEMS

CURRENT DESIGNS

EXCEL TUTORIAL

CD24 A company that manufactures recreational pedal boats has approached Mike Cichanowski to ask if he would be interested in using Current Designs' rotomold expertise and equipment to produce some of the pedal boat components. Mike is intrigued by the idea and thinks it would be an interesting way of complementing the present product line.

One of Mike's hesitations about the proposal is that the pedal boats are a different shape than the kayaks that Current Designs produces. As a result, the company would need to buy an additional rotomold oven in order to produce the pedal boat components. This project clearly involves risks, and Mike wants to make sure that the returns justify the risks. In this case, since this is a new venture, Mike thinks that a 15% discount rate is appropriate to use to evaluate the project.

As an intern at Current Designs, Mike has asked you to prepare an initial evaluation of this proposal. To aid in your analysis, he has provided the following information and assumptions.

1. The new rotomold oven will have a cost of $256,000, a salvage value of $0, and an 8-year useful life. Straight-line depreciation will be used.
2. The projected revenues, costs, and results for each of the 8 years of this project are as follows.

Sales		$220,000
Less:		
Manufacturing costs	$140,000	
Depreciation	32,000	
Shipping and administrative costs	22,000	194,000
Income before income taxes		26,000
Income tax expense		10,800
Net income		$ 15,200

Instructions

(a) Compute the annual rate of return. (Round to two decimal places.)

(b) Compute the payback period. (Round to two decimal places.)

(c) Compute the net present value using a discount rate of 9%. (Round to nearest dollar.) Should the proposal be accepted using this discount rate?

(d) Compute the net present value using a discount rate of 15%. (Round to nearest dollar.) Should the proposal be accepted using this discount rate?

WATERWAYS

(*Note:* This is a continuation of the Waterways problem from Chapters 14–23.)

WP24 Waterways Corporation puts much emphasis on cash flow when it plans for capital investments. The company chose its discount rate of 8% based on the rate of return it must pay its owners and creditors. Using that rate, Waterways then uses different methods to determine the best decisions for making capital outlays. Waterways is considering buying five new backhoes to replace the backhoes it now has. This problem asks you to evaluate that decision, using various capital budgeting techniques.

Go to the book's companion website, **www.wiley.com/college/kimmel**, *to find the remainder of this problem.*

COMPREHENSIVE CASES

CC24-1 For this case, revisit the Greetings Inc. company presented in earlier chapters. The company is now searching for new opportunities for growth. This case will provide you with the opportunity to evaluate a proposal based on initial estimates as well as conduct sensitivity analysis. It also requires evaluation of the underlying assumptions used in the analysis.

CC24-2 Armstrong Helmet Company needs to determine the cost for a given product. For this case, you will have the opportunity to explore cost-volume-profit relationships and prepare a set of budgets.

Go to the book's companion website, **at www.wiley.com/college/kimmel**, *for details and instructions for both cases.*

EXPAND YOUR CRITICAL THINKING

DECISION-MAKING ACROSS THE ORGANIZATION

Group Project

CT24-1 Luang Company is considering the purchase of a new machine. Its invoice price is $122,000, freight charges are estimated to be $3,000, and installation costs are expected to be $5,000. Salvage value of the new machine is expected to be zero after a useful life of 4 years. Existing equipment could be retained and used for an additional 4 years if the new machine is not purchased. At that time, the salvage value of the equipment would be zero. If the new machine is purchased now, the existing machine would be scrapped. Luang's accountant, Lisa Hsung, has accumulated the following data regarding annual sales and expenses with and without the new machine. E

1. Without the new machine, Luang can sell 10,000 units of product annually at a per unit selling price of $100. If the new unit is purchased, the number of units produced and sold would increase by 25%, and the selling price would remain the same.
2. The new machine is faster than the old machine, and it is more efficient in its usage of materials. With the old machine the gross profit rate will be 28.5% of sales, whereas the rate will be 30% of sales with the new machine. (*Note:* These gross profit rates do not include depreciation on the machines. For purposes of determining net income, treat depreciation expense as a separate line item.)
3. Annual selling expenses are $160,000 with the current equipment. Because the new equipment would produce a greater number of units to be sold, annual selling expenses are expected to increase by 10% if it is purchased.
4. Annual administrative expenses are expected to be $100,000 with the old machine, and $112,000 with the new machine.
5. The current book value of the existing machine is $40,000. Luang uses straight-line depreciation.
6. Luang's management has a required rate of return of 15% on its investment and a cash payback period of no more than 3 years.

Instructions

With the class divided into groups, answer the following. (Ignore income tax effects.)

(a) Calculate the annual rate of return for the new machine. (Round to two decimals.)
(b) Compute the cash payback period for the new machine. (Round to two decimals.)
(c) Compute the net present value of the new machine. (Round to the nearest dollar.)
(d) On the basis of the foregoing data, would you recommend that Luang buy the machine? Why?

MANAGERIAL ANALYSIS

CT24-2 Hawke Skateboards is considering building a new plant. Bob Skerritt, the company's marketing manager, is an enthusiastic supporter of the new plant. Lucy Liu, the company's chief financial officer, is not so sure that the plant is a good idea. Currently, the company purchases its skateboards from foreign manufacturers. The following figures were estimated regarding the construction of a new plant. E

Cost of plant	$4,000,000	Estimated useful life	15 years
Annual cash inflows	4,000,000	Salvage value	$2,000,000
Annual cash outflows	3,540,000	Discount rate	11%

Bob Skerritt believes that these figures understate the true potential value of the plant. He suggests that by manufacturing its own skateboards the company will benefit from a "buy American" patriotism that he believes is common among skateboarders. He also notes that the firm has had numerous quality problems with the skateboards manufactured by its suppliers. He suggests that the inconsistent quality has resulted in lost sales, increased warranty claims, and some costly lawsuits. Overall, he believes sales will be $200,000 higher than projected above, and that the savings from lower warranty costs and legal costs will be $60,000 per year. He also believes that the project is not as risky as assumed above, and that a 9% discount rate is more reasonable.

Instructions
Answer each of the following.

(a) Compute the net present value of the project based on the original projections.
(b) Compute the net present value incorporating Bob's estimates of the value of the intangible benefits, but still using the 11% discount rate.
(c) Compute the net present value using the original estimates, but employing the 9% discount rate that Bob suggests is more appropriate.
(d) Comment on your findings.

REAL-WORLD FOCUS

E **CT24-3** Tecumseh Products Company has its headquarters in Tecumseh, Michigan. It describes itself as "a global multinational corporation producing mechanical and electrical components essential to industries creating end-products for health, comfort, and convenience." The following was excerpted from the management discussion and analysis section of a recent annual report.

TECUMSEH PRODUCTS COMPANY
Management Discussion and Analysis

The company has invested approximately $50 million in a scroll compressor manufacturing facility in Tecumseh, Michigan. After experiencing setbacks in developing a commercially acceptable scroll compressor, the Company is currently testing a new generation of scroll product. The Company is unable to predict when, or if, it will offer a scroll compressor for commercial sale, but it does anticipate that reaching volume production will require a significant additional investment. Given such additional investment and current market conditions, management is currently reviewing its options with respect to scroll product improvement, cost reductions, joint ventures and alternative new products.

Instructions
Discuss issues the company should consider and techniques the company should employ to determine whether to continue pursuing this project.

AP **CT24-4** Campbell Soup Company is an international provider of soup products. Management is very interested in continuing to grow the company in its core business, while "spinning off" those businesses that are not part of its core operation.

Address: **www.campbellsoups.com**, or go to **www.wiley.com/college/kimmel**

Steps
1. Go to the home page of Campbell Soup Company at the address shown above.
2. Choose the current annual report.

Instructions
Review the financial statements and management's discussion and analysis, and answer the following questions.

(a) What was the total amount of capital expenditures in the current year, and how does this amount compare with the previous year? In your response, note what year you are using.
(b) What interest rate did the company pay on new borrowings in the current year?
(c) Assume that this year's capital expenditures are expected to increase cash flows by $50 million. What is the expected internal rate of return (IRR) for these capital expenditures? (Assume a 10-year period for the cash flows.)

Writing ▶

COMMUNICATION ACTIVITY

E **CT24-5** Refer back to E24-9 to address the following.

Instructions
Prepare a memo to Maria Fierro, your supervisor. Show your calculations from E24-9 (a) and (b). In one or two paragraphs, discuss important nonfinancial considerations. Make any assumptions you believe to be necessary. Make a recommendation based on your analysis.

ETHICS CASE

CT24-6 NuComp Company operates in a state where corporate taxes and workers' compensation insurance rates have recently doubled. NuComp's president has just assigned you the task of preparing an economic analysis and making a recommendation relative to moving the entire operation to Missouri. The president is slightly in favor of such a move because Missouri is his boyhood home and he also owns a fishing lodge there. AN

You have just completed building your dream house, moved in, and sodded the lawn. Your children are all doing well in school and sports and, along with your spouse, want no part of a move to Missouri. If the company does move, so will you because the town is a one-industry community and you and your spouse will have to move to have employment. Moving when everyone else does will cause you to take a big loss on the sale of your house. The same hardships will be suffered by your coworkers, and the town will be devastated.

In compiling the costs of moving versus not moving, you have latitude in the assumptions you make, the estimates you compute, and the discount rates and time periods you project. You are in a position to influence the decision singlehandedly.

Instructions

(a) Who are the stakeholders in this situation?
(b) What are the ethical issues in this situation?
(c) What would you do in this situation?

ALL ABOUT YOU

CT24-7 Numerous articles have been written that identify early warning signs that you might be getting into trouble with your personal debt load. You can find many good articles on this topic on the Web. E

Instructions

Find an article that identifies early warning signs of personal debt trouble. Write up a summary of the article and bring your summary and the article to class to share.

CONSIDERING YOUR COSTS AND BENEFITS

CT24-8 The March 31, 2011, edition of the *Wall Street Journal* includes an article by Russell Gold entitled "Solar Gains Traction—Thanks to Subsidies." AP

Instructions

Read the article and answer the following questions.

(a) What was the total cost of the solar panels installed? What was the "out-of-pocket" cost to the couple?
(b) Using the total annual electricity bill of $5,000 mentioned in the story, what is the cash payback of the project using the total cost? What is the cash payback based on the "out-of-pocket" cost?
(c) Solar panel manufacturers estimate that solar panels can last up to 40 years with only minor maintenance costs. Assuming no maintenance costs, a 6% rate of interest, a more conservative 20-year life, and zero salvage value, what is the net present value of the project based on the total cost? What is the net present value of the project based on the "out-of-pocket" cost?
(d) What was the wholesale price of panels per watt at the time the article was written? At what price per watt does the article say that subsidies no longer be needed? Does this price appear to be achievable?

A

Specimen Financial Statements: Apple Inc.

Once each year, a corporation communicates to its stockholders and other interested parties by issuing a complete set of audited financial statements. The **annual report**, as this communication is called, summarizes the financial results of the company's operations for the year and its plans for the future. Many annual reports are attractive, multicolored, glossy public relations pieces, containing pictures of corporate officers and directors as well as photos and descriptions of new products and new buildings. Yet the basic function of every annual report is to report financial information, almost all of which is a product of the corporation's accounting system.

The content and organization of corporate annual reports have become fairly standardized. Excluding the public relations part of the report (pictures, products, etc.), the following are the traditional financial portions of the annual report:

- Financial Highlights
- Letter to the Stockholders
- Management's Discussion and Analysis
- Financial Statements
- Notes to the Financial Statements
- Management's Responsibility for Financial Reporting
- Management's Report on Internal Control over Financial Reporting
- Report of Independent Registered Public Accounting Firm
- Selected Financial Data

The official SEC filing of the annual report is called a **Form 10-K**, which often omits the public relations pieces found in most standard annual reports. On the following pages, we present Apple Inc.'s financial statements taken from the company's 2014 Form 10-K. To access Apple's Form 10-K, including notes to the financial statements, follow these steps:

1. Go to **http://investor.apple.com**.
2. Select the Financial Information tab.
3. Select the 10-K annual report dated September 29, 2014.
4. The Notes to Consolidated Financial Statements begin on page 50.

CONSOLIDATED STATEMENTS OF OPERATIONS

(In millions, except number of shares which are reflected in thousands and per share amounts)

	Years ended		
	September 27, 2014	September 28, 2013	September 29, 2012
Net sales	$ 182,795	$ 170,910	$ 156,508
Cost of sales	112,258	106,606	87,846
Gross margin	70,537	64,304	68,662
Operating expenses:			
Research and development	6,041	4,475	3,381
Selling, general and administrative	11,993	10,830	10,040
Total operating expenses	18,034	15,305	13,421
Operating income	52,503	48,999	55,241
Other income/(expense), net	980	1,156	522
Income before provision for income taxes	53,483	50,155	55,763
Provision for income taxes	13,973	13,118	14,030
Net income	$ 39,510	$ 37,037	$ 41,733
Earnings per share:			
Basic	$ 6.49	$ 5.72	$ 6.38
Diluted	$ 6.45	$ 5.68	$ 6.31
Shares used in computing earnings per share:			
Basic	6,085,572	6,477,320	6,543,726
Diluted	6,122,663	6,521,634	6,617,483
Cash dividends declared per common share	$ 1.82	$ 1.64	$ 0.38

See accompanying Notes to Consolidated Financial Statements.

CONSOLIDATED STATEMENTS OF COMPREHENSIVE INCOME

(In millions)

	Years ended		
	September 27, 2014	September 28, 2013	September 29, 2012
Net income	$ 39,510	$ 37,037	$ 41,733
Other comprehensive income/(loss):			
Change in foreign currency translation, net of tax effects of $50, $35 and $13, respectively	(137)	(112)	(15)
Change in unrecognized gains/losses on derivative instruments:			
Change in fair value of derivatives, net of tax benefit/(expense) of $(297), $(351) and $73, respectively	1,390	522	(131)
Adjustment for net losses/(gains) realized and included in net income, net of tax expense/(benefit) of $(36), $255 and $220, respectively	149	(458)	(399)
Total change in unrecognized gains/losses on derivative instruments, net of tax	1,539	64	(530)
Change in unrealized gains/losses on marketable securities:			
Change in fair value of marketable securities, net of tax benefit/(expense) of $(153), $458 and $(421), respectively	285	(791)	715
Adjustment for net losses/(gains) realized and included in net income, net of tax expense/(benefit) of $71, $82 and $68, respectively	(134)	(131)	(114)
Total change in unrealized gains/losses on marketable securities, net of tax	151	(922)	601
Total other comprehensive income/(loss)	1,553	(970)	56
Total comprehensive income	$ 41,063	$ 36,067	$ 41,789

See accompanying Notes to Consolidated Financial Statements.

CONSOLIDATED BALANCE SHEETS

(In millions, except number of shares which are reflected in thousands and par value)

	September 27, 2014	September 28, 2013
ASSETS:		
Current assets:		
Cash and cash equivalents	$ 13,844	$ 14,259
Short-term marketable securities	11,233	26,287
Accounts receivable, less allowances of $86 and $99, respectively	17,460	13,102
Inventories	2,111	1,764
Deferred tax assets	4,318	3,453
Vendor non-trade receivables	9,759	7,539
Other current assets	9,806	6,882
Total current assets	68,531	73,286
Long-term marketable securities	130,162	106,215
Property, plant and equipment, net	20,624	16,597
Goodwill	4,616	1,577
Acquired intangible assets, net	4,142	4,179
Other assets	3,764	5,146
Total assets	$ 231,839	$ 207,000
LIABILITIES AND SHAREHOLDERS' EQUITY:		
Current liabilities:		
Accounts payable	$ 30,196	$ 22,367
Accrued expenses	18,453	13,856
Deferred revenue	8,491	7,435
Commercial paper	6,308	0
Total current liabilities	63,448	43,658
Deferred revenue – non-current	3,031	2,625
Long-term debt	28,987	16,960
Other non-current liabilities	24,826	20,208
Total liabilities	120,292	83,451
Commitments and contingencies		
Shareholders' equity:		
Common stock and additional paid-in capital, $0.00001 par value; 12,600,000 shares authorized; 5,866,161 and 6,294,494 shares issued and outstanding, respectively	23,313	19,764
Retained earnings	87,152	104,256
Accumulated other comprehensive income/(loss)	1,082	(471)
Total shareholders' equity	111,547	123,549
Total liabilities and shareholders' equity	$ 231,839	$ 207,000

See accompanying Notes to Consolidated Financial Statements.

CONSOLIDATED STATEMENTS OF SHAREHOLDERS' EQUITY
(In millions, except number of shares which are reflected in thousands)

	Common Stock and Additional Paid-In Capital		Retained Earnings	Accumulated Other Comprehensive Income/(Loss)	Total Shareholders' Equity
	Shares	Amount			
Balances as of September 24, 2011	6,504,937	$ 13,331	$ 62,841	$ 443	$ 76,615
Net income	0	0	41,733	0	41,733
Other comprehensive income/(loss)	0	0	0	56	56
Dividends and dividend equivalents declared	0	0	(2,523)	0	(2,523)
Share-based compensation	0	1,740	0	0	1,740
Common stock issued, net of shares withheld for employee taxes	69,521	200	(762)	0	(562)
Tax benefit from equity awards, including transfer pricing adjustments	0	1,151	0	0	1,151
Balances as of September 29, 2012	6,574,458	16,422	101,289	499	118,210
Net income	0	0	37,037	0	37,037
Other comprehensive income/(loss)	0	0	0	(970)	(970)
Dividends and dividend equivalents declared	0	0	(10,676)	0	(10,676)
Repurchase of common stock	(328,837)	0	(22,950)	0	(22,950)
Share-based compensation	0	2,253	0	0	2,253
Common stock issued, net of shares withheld for employee taxes	48,873	(143)	(444)	0	(587)
Tax benefit from equity awards, including transfer pricing adjustments	0	1,232	0	0	1,232
Balances as of September 28, 2013	6,294,494	19,764	104,256	(471)	123,549
Net income	0	0	39,510	0	39,510
Other comprehensive income/(loss)	0	0	0	1,553	1,553
Dividends and dividend equivalents declared	0	0	(11,215)	0	(11,215)
Repurchase of common stock	(488,677)	0	(45,000)	0	(45,000)
Share-based compensation	0	2,863	0	0	2,863
Common stock issued, net of shares withheld for employee taxes	60,344	(49)	(399)	0	(448)
Tax benefit from equity awards, including transfer pricing adjustments	0	735	0	0	735
Balances as of September 27, 2014	5,866,161	$ 23,313	$ 87,152	$ 1,082	$111,547

See accompanying Notes to Consolidated Financial Statements.

CONSOLIDATED STATEMENTS OF CASH FLOWS
(In millions)

	Years ended		
	September 27, 2014	September 28, 2013	September 29, 2012
Cash and cash equivalents, beginning of the year	$ 14,259	$ 10,746	$ 9,815
Operating activities:			
Net income	39,510	37,037	41,733
Adjustments to reconcile net income to cash generated by operating activities:			
Depreciation and amortization	7,946	6,757	3,277
Share-based compensation expense	2,863	2,253	1,740
Deferred income tax expense	2,347	1,141	4,405
Changes in operating assets and liabilities:			
Accounts receivable, net	(4,232)	(2,172)	(5,551)
Inventories	(76)	(973)	(15)
Vendor non-trade receivables	(2,220)	223	(1,414)
Other current and non-current assets	167	1,080	(3,162)
Accounts payable	5,938	2,340	4,467
Deferred revenue	1,460	1,459	2,824
Other current and non-current liabilities	6,010	4,521	2,552
Cash generated by operating activities	59,713	53,666	50,856
Investing activities:			
Purchases of marketable securities	(217,128)	(148,489)	(151,232)
Proceeds from maturities of marketable securities	18,810	20,317	13,035
Proceeds from sales of marketable securities	189,301	104,130	99,770
Payments made in connection with business acquisitions, net	(3,765)	(496)	(350)
Payments for acquisition of property, plant and equipment	(9,571)	(8,165)	(8,295)
Payments for acquisition of intangible assets	(242)	(911)	(1,107)
Other	16	(160)	(48)
Cash used in investing activities	(22,579)	(33,774)	(48,227)
Financing activities:			
Proceeds from issuance of common stock	730	530	665
Excess tax benefits from equity awards	739	701	1,351
Taxes paid related to net share settlement of equity awards	(1,158)	(1,082)	(1,226)
Dividends and dividend equivalents paid	(11,126)	(10,564)	(2,488)
Repurchase of common stock	(45,000)	(22,860)	0
Proceeds from issuance of long-term debt, net	11,960	16,896	0
Proceeds from issuance of commercial paper, net	6,306	0	0
Cash used in financing activities	(37,549)	(16,379)	(1,698)
Increase/(decrease) in cash and cash equivalents	(415)	3,513	931
Cash and cash equivalents, end of the year	$ 13,844	$ 14,259	$ 10,746
Supplemental cash flow disclosure:			
Cash paid for income taxes, net	$ 10,026	$ 9,128	$ 7,682
Cash paid for interest	$ 339	$ 0	$ 0

See accompanying Notes to Consolidated Financial Statements.

B

Specimen Financial Statements: Columbia Sportswear Company

Columbia Sportswear Company is a leader in outdoor sportswear. The following are Columbia's financial statements as presented in its 2014 annual report. To access Columbia's complete annual report, including notes to the financial statements, follow these steps:

1. Go to **www.columbia.com**.
2. Select Financial Information and then Annual Reports under the Investor Relations tab near the bottom of the page.
3. Select the 2014 Annual Report.
4. The Notes to Consolidated Financial Statements begin on page 50.

COLUMBIA SPORTSWEAR COMPANY

CONSOLIDATED STATEMENTS OF OPERATIONS
(In thousands, except per share amounts)

	Year Ended December 31, 2014	2013	2012
Net sales	$ 2,100,590	$ 1,684,996	$ 1,669,563
Cost of sales	1,145,639	941,341	953,169
Gross profit	954,951	743,655	716,394
Selling, general and administrative expenses	763,063	625,656	596,635
Net licensing income	6,956	13,795	13,769
Income from operations	198,844	131,794	133,528
Interest income, net	1,004	503	379
Interest expense on note payable to related party (Note 22)	(1,053)	—	—
Other non-operating expense	(274)	(871)	—
Income before income tax	198,521	131,426	133,907
Income tax expense (Note 11)	(56,662)	(37,823)	(34,048)
Net income	141,859	93,603	99,859
Net income (loss) attributable to non-controlling interest	4,686	(738)	—
Net income attributable to Columbia Sportswear Company	$ 137,173	$ 94,341	$ 99,859
Earnings per share attributable to Columbia Sportswear Company (Note 17):			
Basic	$ 1.97	$ 1.37	$ 1.48
Diluted	1.94	1.36	1.46
Weighted average shares outstanding (Note 17):			
Basic	69,807	68,756	67,680
Diluted	70,681	69,434	68,264

See accompanying notes to consolidated financial statements

COLUMBIA SPORTSWEAR COMPANY

CONSOLIDATED BALANCE SHEETS
(In thousands)

	December 31, 2014	December 31, 2013
ASSETS		
Current Assets:		
Cash and cash equivalents	$ 413,558	$ 437,489
Short-term investments	27,267	91,755
Accounts receivable, net (Note 6)	344,390	306,878
Inventories	384,650	329,228
Deferred income taxes (Note 11)	57,001	52,041
Prepaid expenses and other current assets	39,175	33,081
Total current assets	1,266,041	1,250,472
Property, plant, and equipment, net (Note 7)	291,563	279,373
Intangible assets, net (Notes 3, 8)	143,731	36,288
Goodwill (Notes 3, 8)	68,594	14,438
Other non-current assets	22,280	25,017
Total assets	$ 1,792,209	$ 1,605,588
LIABILITIES AND EQUITY		
Current Liabilities:		
Accounts payable	$ 214,275	$ 173,557
Accrued liabilities (Note 10)	144,288	120,397
Income taxes payable (Note 11)	14,388	7,251
Deferred income taxes (Note 11)	169	49
Total current liabilities	373,120	301,254
Note payable to related party (Note 22)	15,728	—
Other long-term liabilities (Notes 12, 13)	35,435	29,527
Income taxes payable (Note 11)	9,388	13,984
Deferred income taxes (Note 11)	3,304	7,959
Total liabilities	436,975	352,724
Commitments and contingencies (Note 14)		
Shareholders' Equity:		
Preferred stock; 10,000 shares authorized; none issued and outstanding	—	—
Common stock (no par value); 250,000 shares authorized; 69,828 and 69,190 issued and outstanding (Note 15)	72,700	52,325
Retained earnings	1,255,070	1,157,733
Accumulated other comprehensive income (Note 18)	15,833	35,360
Total Columbia Sportswear Company shareholders' equity	1,343,603	1,245,418
Non-controlling interest (Note 5)	11,631	7,446
Total equity	1,355,234	1,252,864
Total liabilities and equity	$ 1,792,209	$ 1,605,588

See accompanying notes to consolidated financial statements

COLUMBIA SPORTSWEAR COMPANY

CONSOLIDATED STATEMENTS OF COMPREHENSIVE INCOME
(In thousands)

	Year Ended December 31, 2014	2013	2012
Net income	$ 141,859	$ 93,603	$ 99,859
Other comprehensive loss:			
Unrealized holding gains (losses) on available-for-sale securities (net of tax (expense) benefit of ($5), ($2), and $4, respectively)	10	3	(7)
Unrealized gains (losses) on derivative transactions (net of tax (expense) benefit of ($1,507), $9 and ($171), respectively)	7,751	(1,261)	(4,745)
Foreign currency translation adjustments (net of tax benefit (expense) of $1,023, ($191) and ($59), respectively)	(27,789)	(9,861)	4,518
Other comprehensive loss	(20,028)	(11,119)	(234)
Comprehensive income	121,831	82,484	99,625
Comprehensive income (loss) attributable to non-controlling interest	4,185	(554)	—
Comprehensive income attributable to Columbia Sportswear Company	$ 117,646	$ 83,038	$ 99,625

See accompanying notes to consolidated financial statements

COLUMBIA SPORTSWEAR COMPANY

CONSOLIDATED STATEMENTS OF CASH FLOWS
(In thousands)

	Year Ended December 31,		
	2014	2013	2012
Cash flows from operating activities:			
Net income	$ 141,859	$ 93,603	$ 99,859
Adjustments to reconcile net income to net cash provided by operating activities:			
Depreciation and amortization	54,017	40,871	40,892
Loss on disposal or impairment of property, plant, and equipment	481	9,344	1,582
Deferred income taxes	(6,978)	8,818	7,140
Stock-based compensation	11,120	8,878	7,833
Excess tax benefit from employee stock plans	(4,927)	(1,532)	(1,016)
Changes in operating assets and liabilities:			
Accounts receivable	(31,478)	27,442	18,166
Inventories	(62,086)	34,089	2,951
Prepaid expenses and other current assets	(4,869)	5,166	(2,025)
Other assets	4,291	(4,215)	(1,259)
Accounts payable	41,941	31,711	(12,330)
Accrued liabilities	35,051	12,210	(5,199)
Income taxes payable	1,166	5,534	(11,052)
Other liabilities	6,195	2,356	3,126
Net cash provided by operating activities	185,783	274,275	148,668
Cash flows from investing activities:			
Acquisition of business, net of cash acquired	(188,467)	—	—
Purchases of short-term investments	(48,243)	(125,390)	(83,969)
Sales of short-term investments	112,895	78,636	42,319
Capital expenditures	(60,283)	(69,443)	(50,491)
Proceeds from sale of property, plant, and equipment	71	111	7,099
Net cash used in investing activities	(184,027)	(116,086)	(85,042)
Cash flows from financing activities:			
Proceeds from credit facilities	52,356	69,136	100,654
Repayments on credit facilities	(52,205)	(69,292)	(100,498)
Proceeds from issuance of common stock under employee stock plans	22,277	19,537	14,600
Tax payments related to restricted stock unit issuances	(3,141)	(2,291)	(1,486)
Excess tax benefit from employee stock plans	4,927	1,532	1,016
Repurchase of common stock	(15,000)	—	(206)
Proceeds from note payable to related party	16,072	—	—
Capital contribution from non-controlling interest	—	8,000	—
Cash dividends paid	(39,836)	(31,298)	(29,780)
Net cash used in financing activities	(14,550)	(4,676)	(15,700)
Net effect of exchange rate changes on cash	(11,137)	(6,805)	1,821
Net increase (decrease) in cash and cash equivalents	(23,931)	146,708	49,747
Cash and cash equivalents, beginning of year	437,489	290,781	241,034
Cash and cash equivalents, end of year	$ 413,558	$ 437,489	$ 290,781

Supplemental disclosures of cash flow information:			
Cash paid during the year for income taxes	$ 53,958	$ 22,771	$ 43,696
Supplemental disclosures of non-cash investing activities:			
Capital expenditures incurred but not yet paid	7,196	5,195	5,313

See accompanying notes to consolidated financial statements

COLUMBIA SPORTSWEAR COMPANY

CONSOLIDATED STATEMENTS OF EQUITY
(In thousands)

	Columbia Sportswear Company Shareholders' Equity					
	Common Stock					
	Shares Outstanding	Amount	Retained Earnings	Accumulated Other Comprehensive Income	Non-Controlling Interest	Total
BALANCE, JANUARY 1, 2012	67,276	$ 3,037	$ 1,024,611	$ 46,897	$ —	$ 1,074,545
Net income	—	—	99,859	—	—	99,859
Other comprehensive income (loss):						
Unrealized holding losses on available-for-sale securities, net	—	—	—	(7)	—	(7)
Unrealized holding losses on derivative transactions, net	—	—	—	(4,745)	—	(4,745)
Foreign currency translation adjustment, net	—	—	—	4,518	—	4,518
Cash dividends ($0.44 per share)	—	—	(29,780)	—	—	(29,780)
Issuance of common stock under employee stock plans, net	882	13,114	—	—	—	13,114
Tax adjustment from stock plans	—	1,036	—	—	—	1,036
Stock-based compensation expense	—	7,833	—	—	—	7,833
Repurchase of common stock	(8)	(206)	—	—	—	(206)
BALANCE, DECEMBER 31, 2012	68,150	24,814	1,094,690	46,663	—	1,166,167
Net income (loss)	—	—	94,341	—	(738)	93,603
Other comprehensive income (loss):						
Unrealized holding gains on available-for-sale securities, net	—	—	—	3	—	3
Unrealized holding losses on derivative transactions, net	—	—	—	(1,261)	—	(1,261)
Foreign currency translation adjustment, net	—	—	—	(10,045)	184	(9,861)
Cash dividends ($0.46 per share)	—	—	(31,298)	—	—	(31,298)
Issuance of common stock under employee stock plans, net	1,040	17,246	—	—	—	17,246
Capital contribution from non-controlling interest	—	—	—	—	8,000	8,000
Tax adjustment from stock plans	—	1,387	—	—	—	1,387
Stock-based compensation expense	—	8,878	—	—	—	8,878
BALANCE, DECEMBER 31, 2013	69,190	52,325	1,157,733	35,360	7,446	1,252,864
Net income	—	—	137,173	—	4,686	141,859
Other comprehensive income (loss):						
Unrealized holding gains on available-for-sale securities, net	—	—	—	10	—	10
Unrealized holding gains on derivative transactions, net	—	—	—	7,751	—	7,751
Foreign currency translation adjustment, net	—	—	—	(27,288)	(501)	(27,789)
Cash dividends ($0.57 per share)	—	—	(39,836)	—	—	(39,836)
Issuance of common stock under employee stock plans, net	1,059	19,136	—	—	—	19,136
Tax adjustment from stock plans	—	5,119	—	—	—	5,119
Stock-based compensation expense	—	11,120	—	—	—	11,120
Repurchase of common stock	(421)	(15,000)	—	—	—	(15,000)
BALANCE, DECEMBER 31, 2014	69,828	$ 72,700	$ 1,255,070	$ 15,833	$ 11,631	$ 1,355,234

See accompanying notes to consolidated financial statements

C

Specimen Financial Statements: VF Corporation

VF Corporation is a leader in outdoor sportswear. The following are VF's financial statements as presented in its 2014 annual report. To access VF's complete annual report, including notes to the financial statements, follow these steps:

1. Go to **www.vfc.com**.
2. Select the Investor Relations link and then select Financial Reports.
3. Select the 2014 Annual Report on Form 10-K.
4. The Notes to Consolidated Financial Statements begin on page F-10.

VF CORPORATION

Consolidated Balance Sheets

	December 2014	December 2013
	In thousands, except share amounts	
ASSETS		
Current assets		
Cash and equivalents	$ 971,895	$ 776,403
Accounts receivable, less allowance for doubtful accounts of $26,694 in 2014 and $45,350 in 2013	1,276,224	1,360,443
Inventories	1,482,804	1,399,062
Deferred income taxes	154,285	169,321
Other current assets	300,646	177,753
Total current assets	4,185,854	3,882,982
Property, plant and equipment	942,181	932,792
Intangible assets	2,433,552	2,960,201
Goodwill	1,824,956	2,021,750
Other assets	593,597	517,718
Total assets	$ 9,980,140	$ 10,315,443
LIABILITIES AND STOCKHOLDERS' EQUITY		
Current liabilities		
Short-term borrowings	$ 21,822	$ 18,810
Current portion of long-term debt	3,975	5,167
Accounts payable	690,842	638,732
Accrued liabilities	903,602	905,292
Total current liabilities	1,620,241	1,568,001
Long-term debt	1,423,581	1,426,829
Other liabilities	1,305,436	1,243,575
Commitments and contingencies		
Stockholders' equity		
Preferred Stock, par value $1; shares authorized, 25,000,000; no shares outstanding in 2014 and 2013	—	—
Common Stock, stated value $0.25; shares authorized, 1,200,000,000; 432,859,891 shares outstanding in 2014 and 440,310,370 in 2013	108,215	110,078
Additional paid-in capital	2,993,186	2,746,590
Accumulated other comprehensive income (loss)	(702,272)	(211,720)
Retained earnings	3,231,753	3,432,090
Total stockholders' equity	5,630,882	6,077,038
Total liabilities and stockholders' equity	$ 9,980,140	$ 10,315,443

See notes to consolidated financial statements.

VF CORPORATION

Consolidated Statements of Income

	Year Ended December		
	2014	2013	2012
	In thousands, except per share amounts		
Net sales	$ 12,154,784	$ 11,302,350	$ 10,766,020
Royalty income	127,377	117,298	113,835
Total revenues	12,282,161	11,419,648	10,879,855
Costs and operating expenses			
Cost of goods sold	6,288,190	5,931,469	5,817,880
Selling, general and administrative expenses	4,159,885	3,841,032	3,596,708
Impairment of goodwill and intangible assets	396,362	—	—
	10,844,437	9,772,501	9,414,588
Operating income	1,437,724	1,647,147	1,465,267
Interest income	6,911	4,141	3,353
Interest expense	(86,725)	(84,773)	(93,605)
Other income (expense), net	(5,544)	(4,025)	46,860
Income before income taxes	1,352,366	1,562,490	1,421,875
Income taxes	304,861	352,371	335,737
Net income	1,047,505	1,210,119	1,086,138
Net income attributable to noncontrolling interests	—	—	(139)
Net income attributable to VF Corporation common stockholders	$ 1,047,505	$ 1,210,119	$ 1,085,999
Earnings per common share attributable to VF Corporation common stockholders			
Basic	$ 2.42	$ 2.76	$ 2.47
Diluted	2.38	2.71	2.43
Cash dividends per common share	$ 1.1075	$ 0.9150	$ 0.7575

See notes to consolidated financial statements.

VF CORPORATION

Consolidated Statements of Comprehensive Income

	Year Ended December		
	2014	2013	2012
	In thousands		
Net income	$1,047,505	$1,210,119	$1,086,138
Other comprehensive income (loss)			
Foreign currency translation			
Gains (losses) arising during year	(469,663)	109,463	37,648
Less income tax effect	6,075	1,252	9,443
Defined benefit pension plans			
Current year actuarial gains (losses) and plan amendments	(203,234)	146,746	(173,959)
Amortization of net deferred actuarial losses	37,518	85,356	69,744
Amortization of deferred prior service costs	5,445	1,270	3,357
Less income tax effect	60,588	(90,285)	37,013
Derivative financial instruments			
Gains (losses) arising during year	88,387	(8,133)	(9,555)
Less income tax effect	(34,736)	3,196	3,976
Reclassification to net income for (gains) losses realized	32,111	(12,169)	(15,883)
Less income tax effect	(12,619)	4,782	6,199
Marketable securities			
Gains (losses) arising during year	(698)	1,239	(401)
Less income tax effect	274	(542)	—
Other comprehensive income (loss)	(490,552)	242,175	(32,418)
Comprehensive income including noncontrolling interests	556,953	1,452,294	1,053,720
Comprehensive (income) loss attributable to noncontrolling interests	—	—	(139)
Comprehensive income attributable to VF Corporation	$ 556,953	$1,452,294	$1,053,581

See notes to consolidated financial statements.

VF CORPORATION

Consolidated Statements of Cash Flows

	Year Ended December 2014	2013	2012
	In thousands		
Operating activities			
Net income	$ 1,047,505	$1,210,119	$1,086,138
Adjustments to reconcile net income to cash provided by operating activities:			
Impairment of goodwill and intangible assets	396,362	—	—
Depreciation	172,443	157,810	148,969
Amortization of intangible assets	42,061	45,787	47,929
Other amortization	60,379	49,676	41,058
Stock-based compensation	104,313	87,118	92,814
Provision for doubtful accounts	(2,198)	15,756	19,264
Pension expense less than contributions	(9,864)	(28,102)	(20,198)
Deferred income taxes	(78,064)	(12,370)	(20,797)
Gain on sale of businesses	—	—	(44,485)
Other, net	4,112	14,306	(40,931)
Changes in operating assets and liabilities, net of purchases and sales of businesses:			
Accounts receivable	854	(155,053)	(111,571)
Inventories	(130,540)	(47,240)	87,620
Accounts payable	69,807	75,073	(74,294)
Income taxes	(44,144)	16,628	26,213
Accrued liabilities	41,989	84,472	(35,912)
Other assets and liabilities	22,614	(7,939)	73,183
Cash provided by operating activities	1,697,629	1,506,041	1,275,000
Investing activities			
Capital expenditures	(234,077)	(271,153)	(251,940)
Business acquisitions, net of cash acquired	—	—	(1,750)
Proceeds from sale of businesses	—	—	72,519
Software purchases	(67,943)	(53,989)	(30,890)
Other, net	(27,235)	(25,131)	(8,230)
Cash used by investing activities	(329,255)	(350,273)	(220,291)
Financing activities			
Net increase (decrease) in short-term borrowings	4,761	9,032	(269,010)
Payments on long-term debt	(4,760)	(404,872)	(2,776)
Purchases of treasury stock	(727,795)	(282,024)	(307,282)
Cash dividends paid	(478,933)	(402,136)	(333,229)
Proceeds from issuance of Common Stock, net of shares withheld for taxes	34,869	48,029	62,770
Tax benefits of stock-based compensation	64,437	48,140	47,213
Other, net	—	—	(201)
Cash used by financing activities	(1,107,421)	(983,831)	(802,515)
Effect of foreign currency rate changes on cash and equivalents	(65,461)	7,005	4,039
Net change in cash and equivalents	195,492	178,942	256,233
Cash and equivalents — beginning of year	776,403	597,461	341,228
Cash and equivalents — end of year	$ 971,895	$ 776,403	$ 597,461

See notes to consolidated financial statements.

VF CORPORATION

Consolidated Statements of Stockholders' Equity

	VF Corporation Stockholders: Common Stock Shares	Common Stock Amounts	Additional Paid-in Capital	Accumulated Other Comprehensive Income (Loss)	Retained Earnings	Non-controlling Interests
	In thousands, except share amounts					
Balance, December 2011	442,227,924	$110,557	$2,316,107	$ (421,477)	$2,520,804	$ (816)
Net income	—	—	—	—	1,085,999	139
Dividends on Common Stock	—	—	—	—	(333,229)	—
Purchase of treasury stock	(8,072,920)	(2,018)	—	—	(297,692)	—
Stock-based compensation, net	6,663,932	1,666	211,761	—	(34,435)	—
Disposition of noncontrolling interests	—	—	—	—	—	677
Foreign currency translation	—	—	—	47,091	—	—
Defined benefit pension plans	—	—	—	(63,845)	—	—
Derivative financial instruments	—	—	—	(15,263)	—	—
Marketable securities	—	—	—	(401)	—	—
Balance, December 2012	440,818,936	$110,205	$2,527,868	$ (453,895)	$2,941,447	$ —
Net income	—	—	—	—	1,210,119	—
Dividends on Common Stock	—	—	—	—	(402,136)	—
Purchase of treasury stock	(6,849,160)	(1,712)	—	—	(280,408)	—
Stock-based compensation, net	6,340,594	1,585	218,722	—	(36,932)	—
Foreign currency translation	—	—	—	110,715	—	—
Defined benefit pension plans	—	—	—	143,087	—	—
Derivative financial instruments	—	—	—	(12,324)	—	—
Marketable securities	—	—	—	697	—	—
Balance, December 2013	440,310,370	$110,078	$2,746,590	$ (211,720)	$3,432,090	$ —
Net income	—	—	—	—	1,047,505	—
Dividends on Common Stock	—	—	—	—	(478,933)	—
Purchase of treasury stock	(12,037,000)	(3,009)	—	—	(724,786)	—
Stock-based compensation, net	4,586,521	1,146	246,596	—	(44,123)	—
Foreign currency translation	—	—	—	(463,588)	—	—
Defined benefit pension plans	—	—	—	(99,683)	—	—
Derivative financial instruments	—	—	—	73,143	—	—
Marketable securities	—	—	—	(424)	—	—
Balance, December 2014	432,859,891	$108,215	$2,993,186	$ (702,272)	$3,231,753	$ —

See notes to consolidated financial statements.

D

Specimen Financial Statements: Amazon.com, Inc.

Amazon.com, Inc. is the world's largest online retailer. It also produces consumer electronics—notably the Kindle e-book reader and the Kindle Fire Tablet computer—and is a major provider of cloud computing services. The following are Amazon's financial statements as presented in the company's 2014 annual report. To access Amazon's complete annual report, including notes to the financial statements, follow these steps:

1. Go to **www.amazon.com**.
2. Select the Investor Relations link at the bottom of the page and then select the 2014 Annual Report under Annual Reports and Proxies.
3. The Notes to Consolidated Financial Statements begin on page 43.

AMAZON.COM, INC.
CONSOLIDATED STATEMENTS OF CASH FLOWS
(in millions)

	Year Ended December 31,		
	2014	2013	2012
CASH AND CASH EQUIVALENTS, BEGINNING OF PERIOD	$ 8,658	$ 8,084	$ 5,269
OPERATING ACTIVITIES:			
Net income (loss)	(241)	274	(39)
Adjustments to reconcile net income (loss) to net cash from operating activities:			
Depreciation of property and equipment, including internal-use software and website development, and other amortization	4,746	3,253	2,159
Stock-based compensation	1,497	1,134	833
Other operating expense (income), net	129	114	154
Losses (gains) on sales of marketable securities, net	(3)	1	(9)
Other expense (income), net	62	166	253
Deferred income taxes	(316)	(156)	(265)
Excess tax benefits from stock-based compensation	(6)	(78)	(429)
Changes in operating assets and liabilities:			
Inventories	(1,193)	(1,410)	(999)
Accounts receivable, net and other	(1,039)	(846)	(861)
Accounts payable	1,759	1,888	2,070
Accrued expenses and other	706	736	1,038
Additions to unearned revenue	4,433	2,691	1,796
Amortization of previously unearned revenue	(3,692)	(2,292)	(1,521)
Net cash provided by (used in) operating activities	6,842	5,475	4,180
INVESTING ACTIVITIES:			
Purchases of property and equipment, including internal-use software and website development	(4,893)	(3,444)	(3,785)
Acquisitions, net of cash acquired, and other	(979)	(312)	(745)
Sales and maturities of marketable securities and other investments	3,349	2,306	4,237
Purchases of marketable securities and other investments	(2,542)	(2,826)	(3,302)
Net cash provided by (used in) investing activities	(5,065)	(4,276)	(3,595)
FINANCING ACTIVITIES:			
Excess tax benefits from stock-based compensation	6	78	429
Common stock repurchased	—	—	(960)
Proceeds from long-term debt and other	6,359	394	3,378
Repayments of long-term debt	(513)	(231)	(82)
Principal repayments of capital lease obligations	(1,285)	(775)	(486)
Principal repayments of finance lease obligations	(135)	(5)	(20)
Net cash provided by (used in) financing activities	4,432	(539)	2,259
Foreign-currency effect on cash and cash equivalents	(310)	(86)	(29)
Net increase (decrease) in cash and cash equivalents	5,899	574	2,815
CASH AND CASH EQUIVALENTS, END OF PERIOD	$ 14,557	$ 8,658	$ 8,084
SUPPLEMENTAL CASH FLOW INFORMATION:			
Cash paid for interest on long-term debt	$ 91	$ 97	$ 31
Cash paid for income taxes (net of refunds)	177	169	112
Property and equipment acquired under capital leases	4,008	1,867	802
Property and equipment acquired under build-to-suit leases	920	877	29

See accompanying notes to consolidated financial statements.

AMAZON.COM, INC.
CONSOLIDATED STATEMENTS OF OPERATIONS
(in millions, except per share data)

	Year Ended December 31, 2014	2013	2012
Net product sales	$ 70,080	$ 60,903	$ 51,733
Net service sales	18,908	13,549	9,360
Total net sales	88,988	74,452	61,093
Operating expenses (1):			
Cost of sales	62,752	54,181	45,971
Fulfillment	10,766	8,585	6,419
Marketing	4,332	3,133	2,408
Technology and content	9,275	6,565	4,564
General and administrative	1,552	1,129	896
Other operating expense (income), net	133	114	159
Total operating expenses	88,810	73,707	60,417
Income from operations	178	745	676
Interest income	39	38	40
Interest expense	(210)	(141)	(92)
Other income (expense), net	(118)	(136)	(80)
Total non-operating income (expense)	(289)	(239)	(132)
Income (loss) before income taxes	(111)	506	544
Provision for income taxes	(167)	(161)	(428)
Equity-method investment activity, net of tax	37	(71)	(155)
Net income (loss)	$ (241)	$ 274	$ (39)
Basic earnings per share	$ (0.52)	$ 0.60	$ (0.09)
Diluted earnings per share	$ (0.52)	$ 0.59	$ (0.09)
Weighted average shares used in computation of earnings per share:			
Basic	462	457	453
Diluted	462	465	453

(1) Includes stock-based compensation as follows:	2014	2013	2012
Fulfillment	$ 375	$ 294	$ 212
Marketing	125	88	61
Technology and content	804	603	434
General and administrative	193	149	126

See accompanying notes to consolidated financial statements.

AMAZON.COM, INC.
CONSOLIDATED STATEMENTS OF COMPREHENSIVE INCOME
(in millions)

	Year Ended December 31, 2014	2013	2012
Net income (loss)	$ (241)	$ 274	$ (39)
Other comprehensive income (loss):			
Foreign currency translation adjustments, net of tax of $(3), $(20), and $(30)	(325)	63	76
Net change in unrealized gains on available-for-sale securities:			
Unrealized gains (losses), net of tax of $1, $3, and $(3)	2	(10)	8
Reclassification adjustment for losses (gains) included in "Other income (expense), net," net of tax of $(1), $(1), and $3	(3)	1	(7)
Net unrealized gains (losses) on available-for-sale securities	(1)	(9)	1
Total other comprehensive income (loss)	(326)	54	77
Comprehensive income (loss)	$ (567)	$ 328	$ 38

See accompanying notes to consolidated financial statements.

AMAZON.COM, INC.

CONSOLIDATED BALANCE SHEETS
(in millions, except per share data)

	December 31, 2014	December 31, 2013
ASSETS		
Current assets:		
Cash and cash equivalents	$ 14,557	$ 8,658
Marketable securities	2,859	3,789
Inventories	8,299	7,411
Accounts receivable, net and other	5,612	4,767
Total current assets	31,327	24,625
Property and equipment, net	16,967	10,949
Goodwill	3,319	2,655
Other assets	2,892	1,930
Total assets	$ 54,505	$ 40,159
LIABILITIES AND STOCKHOLDERS' EQUITY		
Current liabilities:		
Accounts payable	$ 16,459	$ 15,133
Accrued expenses and other	9,807	6,688
Unearned revenue	1,823	1,159
Total current liabilities	28,089	22,980
Long-term debt	8,265	3,191
Other long-term liabilities	7,410	4,242
Commitments and contingencies (Note 8)		
Stockholders' equity:		
Preferred stock, $0.01 par value:		
Authorized shares — 500		
Issued and outstanding shares — none	—	—
Common stock, $0.01 par value:		
Authorized shares — 5,000		
Issued shares — 488 and 483		
Outstanding shares — 465 and 459	5	5
Treasury stock, at cost	(1,837)	(1,837)
Additional paid-in capital	11,135	9,573
Accumulated other comprehensive loss	(511)	(185)
Retained earnings	1,949	2,190
Total stockholders' equity	10,741	9,746
Total liabilities and stockholders' equity	$ 54,505	$ 40,159

See accompanying notes to consolidated financial statements.

AMAZON.COM, INC.

CONSOLIDATED STATEMENTS OF STOCKHOLDERS' EQUITY
(in millions)

	Common Stock Shares	Common Stock Amount	Treasury Stock	Additional Paid-In Capital	Accumulated Other Comprehensive Income (Loss)	Retained Earnings	Total Stockholders' Equity
Balance as of January 1, 2012	455	$ 5	$ (877)	$ 6,990	$ (316)	$ 1,955	$ 7,757
Net loss	—	—	—	—	—	(39)	(39)
Other comprehensive income	—	—	—	—	77	—	77
Exercise of common stock options	4	—	—	8	—	—	8
Repurchase of common stock	(5)	—	(960)	—	—	—	(960)
Excess tax benefits from stock-based compensation	—	—	—	429	—	—	429
Stock-based compensation and issuance of employee benefit plan stock	—	—	—	854	—	—	854
Issuance of common stock for acquisition activity	—	—	—	66	—	—	66
Balance as of December 31, 2012	454	5	(1,837)	8,347	(239)	1,916	8,192
Net income	—	—	—	—	—	274	274
Other comprehensive income	—	—	—	—	54	—	54
Exercise of common stock options	5	—	—	4	—	—	4
Repurchase of common stock	—	—	—	—	—	—	—
Excess tax benefits from stock-based compensation	—	—	—	73	—	—	73
Stock-based compensation and issuance of employee benefit plan stock	—	—	—	1,149	—	—	1,149
Balance as of December 31, 2013	459	5	(1,837)	9,573	(185)	2,190	9,746
Net loss	—	—	—	—	—	(241)	(241)
Other comprehensive loss	—	—	—	—	(326)	—	(326)
Exercise of common stock options	6	—	—	2	—	—	2
Excess tax benefits from stock-based compensation	—	—	—	6	—	—	6
Stock-based compensation and issuance of employee benefit plan stock	—	—	—	1,510	—	—	1,510
Issuance of common stock for acquisition activity	—	—	—	44	—	—	44
Balance as of December 31, 2014	465	$ 5	$ (1,837)	$ 11,135	$ (511)	$ 1,949	$ 10,741

See accompanying notes to consolidated financial statements.

E

Specimen Financial Statements: Wal-Mart Stores, Inc.

The following are Wal-Mart Stores, Inc.'s financial statements as presented in the company's 2015 annual report. To access Wal-Mart's complete annual report, including notes to the financial statements, follow these steps:

1. Go to **http://corporate.walmart.com**.
2. Select Financial Information and then Annual Reports & Proxies under the Investors tab.
3. Select the 2015 Annual Report (Wal-Mart's fiscal year ends January 31).
4. The Notes to Consolidated Financial Statements begin on page 40.

Wal-Mart Stores, Inc.
Consolidated Statements of Income

	Fiscal Years Ended January 31,		
(Amounts in millions, except per share data)	2015	2014	2013
Revenues:			
Net sales	$ 482,229	$ 473,076	$ 465,604
Membership and other income	3,422	3,218	3,047
Total revenues	485,651	476,294	468,651
Costs and expenses:			
Cost of sales	365,086	358,069	352,297
Operating, selling, general and administrative expenses	93,418	91,353	88,629
Operating income	27,147	26,872	27,725
Interest:			
Debt	2,161	2,072	1,977
Capital leases	300	263	272
Interest income	(113)	(119)	(186)
Interest, net	2,348	2,216	2,063
Income from continuing operations before income taxes	24,799	24,656	25,662
Provision for income taxes:			
Current	8,504	8,619	7,976
Deferred	(519)	(514)	(18)
Total provision for income taxes	7,985	8,105	7,958
Income from continuing operations	16,814	16,551	17,704
Income from discontinued operations, net of income taxes	285	144	52
Consolidated net income	17,099	16,695	17,756
Less consolidated net income attributable to noncontrolling interest	(736)	(673)	(757)
Consolidated net income attributable to Walmart	$ 16,363	$ 16,022	$ 16,999
Basic net income per common share:			
Basic income per common share from continuing operations attributable to Walmart	$ 5.01	$ 4.87	$ 5.03
Basic income per common share from discontinued operations attributable to Walmart	0.06	0.03	0.01
Basic net income per common share attributable to Walmart	$ 5.07	$ 4.90	$ 5.04
Diluted net income per common share:			
Diluted income per common share from continuing operations attributable to Walmart	$ 4.99	$ 4.85	$ 5.01
Diluted income per common share from discontinued operations attributable to Walmart	0.06	0.03	0.01
Diluted net income per common share attributable to Walmart	$ 5.05	$ 4.88	$ 5.02
Weighted-average common shares outstanding:			
Basic	3,230	3,269	3,374
Diluted	3,243	3,283	3,389
Dividends declared per common share	$ 1.92	$ 1.88	$ 1.59

See accompanying notes.

Wal-Mart Stores, Inc.
Consolidated Statements of Comprehensive Income

	Fiscal Years Ended January 31,		
(Amounts in millions)	2015	2014	2013
Consolidated net income	$ 17,099	$ 16,695	$ 17,756
Less consolidated net income attributable to nonredeemable noncontrolling interest	(736)	(606)	(684)
Less consolidated net income attributable to redeemable noncontrolling interest	—	(67)	(73)
Consolidated net income attributable to Walmart	16,363	16,022	16,999
Other comprehensive income (loss), net of income taxes			
Currency translation and other	(4,179)	(3,146)	1,042
Derivative instruments	(470)	207	136
Minimum pension liability	(69)	153	(166)
Other comprehensive income (loss), net of income taxes	(4,718)	(2,786)	1,012
Less other comprehensive income (loss) attributable to nonredeemable noncontrolling interest	546	311	(138)
Less other comprehensive income (loss) attributable to redeemable noncontrolling interest	—	66	(51)
Other comprehensive income (loss) attributable to Walmart	(4,172)	(2,409)	823
Comprehensive income, net of income taxes	12,381	13,909	18,768
Less comprehensive income (loss) attributable to nonredeemable noncontrolling interest	(190)	(295)	(822)
Less comprehensive income (loss) attributable to redeemable noncontrolling interest	—	(1)	(124)
Comprehensive income attributable to Walmart	$ 12,191	$ 13,613	$ 17,822

See accompanying notes.

Wal-Mart Stores, Inc.
Consolidated Balance Sheets

(Amounts in millions)	As of January 31, 2015	As of January 31, 2014
ASSETS		
Current assets:		
Cash and cash equivalents	$ 9,135	$ 7,281
Receivables, net	6,778	6,677
Inventories	45,141	44,858
Prepaid expenses and other	2,224	1,909
Current assets of discontinued operations	—	460
Total current assets	63,278	61,185
Property and equipment:		
Property and equipment	177,395	173,089
Less accumulated depreciation	(63,115)	(57,725)
Property and equipment, net	114,280	115,364
Property under capital leases:		
Property under capital leases	5,239	5,589
Less accumulated amortization	(2,864)	(3,046)
Property under capital leases, net	2,375	2,543
Goodwill	18,102	19,510
Other assets and deferred charges	5,671	6,149
Total assets	$ 203,706	$ 204,751
LIABILITIES, REDEEMABLE NONCONTROLLING INTEREST, AND EQUITY		
Current liabilities:		
Short-term borrowings	$ 1,592	$ 7,670
Accounts payable	38,410	37,415
Accrued liabilities	19,152	18,793
Accrued income taxes	1,021	966
Long-term debt due within one year	4,810	4,103
Obligations under capital leases due within one year	287	309
Current liabilities of discontinued operations	—	89
Total current liabilities	65,272	69,345
Long-term debt	41,086	41,771
Long-term obligations under capital leases	2,606	2,788
Deferred income taxes and other	8,805	8,017
Redeemable noncontrolling interest	—	1,491
Commitments and contingencies		
Equity:		
Common stock	323	323
Capital in excess of par value	2,462	2,362
Retained earnings	85,777	76,566
Accumulated other comprehensive income (loss)	(7,168)	(2,996)
Total Walmart shareholders' equity	81,394	76,255
Nonredeemable noncontrolling interest	4,543	5,084
Total equity	85,937	81,339
Total liabilities, redeemable noncontrolling interest, and equity	$ 203,706	$ 204,751

See accompanying notes.

Wal-Mart Stores, Inc.
Consolidated Statement of Shareholders' Equity and Redeemable Noncontrolling Interest

(Amounts in millions)	Common Stock Shares	Common Stock Amount	Capital in Excess of Par Value	Retained Earnings	Accumulated Other Comprehensive Income (Loss)	Total Walmart Shareholders' Equity	Nonredeemable Noncontrolling Interest	Total Equity	Redeemable Noncontrolling Interest
Balances as of February 1, 2012	3,418	$ 342	$ 3,692	$ 68,691	$ (1,410)	$ 71,315	$ 4,446	$ 75,761	$ 404
Consolidated net income	—	—	—	16,999	—	16,999	684	17,683	73
Other comprehensive income, net of income taxes	—	—	—	—	823	823	138	961	51
Cash dividends declared ($1.59 per share)	—	—	—	(5,361)	—	(5,361)	—	(5,361)	—
Purchase of Company stock	(115)	(11)	(357)	(7,341)	—	(7,709)	—	(7,709)	—
Nonredeemable noncontrolling interest of acquired entity	—	—	—	—	—	—	469	469	—
Other	11	1	285	(10)	—	276	(342)	(66)	(9)
Balances as of January 31, 2013	3,314	332	3,620	72,978	(587)	76,343	5,395	81,738	519
Consolidated net income	—	—	—	16,022	—	16,022	595	16,617	78
Other comprehensive loss, net of income taxes	—	—	—	—	(2,409)	(2,409)	(311)	(2,720)	(66)
Cash dividends declared ($1.88 per share)	—	—	—	(6,139)	—	(6,139)	—	(6,139)	—
Purchase of Company stock	(87)	(9)	(294)	(6,254)	—	(6,557)	—	(6,557)	—
Redemption value adjustment of redeemable noncontrolling interest	—	—	(1,019)	—	—	(1,019)	—	(1,019)	1,019
Other	6	—	55	(41)	—	14	(595)	(581)	(59)
Balances as of January 31, 2014	3,233	323	2,362	76,566	(2,996)	76,255	5,084	81,339	1,491
Consolidated net income	—	—	—	16,363	—	16,363	736	17,099	—
Other comprehensive income, net of income taxes	—	—	—	—	(4,172)	(4,172)	(546)	(4,718)	—
Cash dividends declared ($1.92 per share)	—	—	—	(6,185)	—	(6,185)	—	(6,185)	—
Purchase of Company stock	(13)	(1)	(29)	(950)	—	(980)	—	(980)	—
Purchase of redeemable noncontrolling interest	—	—	—	—	—	—	—	—	(1,491)
Other	8	1	129	(17)	—	113	(731)	(618)	—
Balances as of January 31, 2015	3,228	$ 323	$ 2,462	$ 85,777	$ (7,168)	$ 81,394	$ 4,543	$ 85,937	$ —

See accompanying notes.

Wal-Mart Stores, Inc.
Consolidated Statements of Cash Flows

(Amounts in millions)	Fiscal Years Ended January 31, 2015	2014	2013
Cash flows from operating activities:			
Consolidated net income	$ 17,099	$ 16,695	$ 17,756
Income from discontinued operations, net of income taxes	(285)	(144)	(52)
Income from continuing operations	16,814	16,551	17,704
Adjustments to reconcile income from continuing operations to net cash provided by operating activities:			
Depreciation and amortization	9,173	8,870	8,478
Deferred income taxes	(503)	(279)	(133)
Other operating activities	785	938	602
Changes in certain assets and liabilities, net of effects of acquisitions:			
Receivables, net	(569)	(566)	(614)
Inventories	(1,229)	(1,667)	(2,759)
Accounts payable	2,678	531	1,061
Accrued liabilities	1,249	103	271
Accrued income taxes	166	(1,224)	981
Net cash provided by operating activities	28,564	23,257	25,591
Cash flows from investing activities:			
Payments for property and equipment	(12,174)	(13,115)	(12,898)
Proceeds from the disposal of property and equipment	570	727	532
Proceeds from the disposal of certain operations	671	—	—
Other investing activities	(192)	(138)	(271)
Net cash used in investing activities	(11,125)	(12,526)	(12,637)
Cash flows from financing activities:			
Net change in short-term borrowings	(6,288)	911	2,754
Proceeds from issuance of long-term debt	5,174	7,072	211
Payments of long-term debt	(3,904)	(4,968)	(1,478)
Dividends paid	(6,185)	(6,139)	(5,361)
Purchase of Company stock	(1,015)	(6,683)	(7,600)
Dividends paid to noncontrolling interest	(600)	(426)	(282)
Purchase of noncontrolling interest	(1,844)	(296)	(132)
Other financing activities	(409)	(260)	(58)
Net cash used in financing activities	(15,071)	(10,789)	(11,946)
Effect of exchange rates on cash and cash equivalents	(514)	(442)	223
Net increase (decrease) in cash and cash equivalents	1,854	(500)	1,231
Cash and cash equivalents at beginning of year	7,281	7,781	6,550
Cash and cash equivalents at end of year	$ 9,135	$ 7,281	$ 7,781
Supplemental disclosure of cash flow information:			
Income taxes paid	8,169	8,641	7,304
Interest paid	2,433	2,362	2,262

See accompanying notes.

F

Specimen Financial Statements: Louis Vuitton

Louis Vuitton is a French company and is one of the leading international fashion houses in the world. Louis Vuitton has been named the world's most valuable luxury brand. Note that its financial statements are IFRS-based and are presented in euros (€). To access the company's complete financial statements, follow these steps:

1. Go to **www.lvmh.com/investor-relations**.
2. Select All publications, then the Reports tab, and then 2014 Consolidated financial statements.
3. Note that the comments (notes) to the financial statements begin on page 7.

CONSOLIDATED INCOME STATEMENT

(EUR millions, except for earnings per share)	Notes	2014	2013[1]	2012[1]
Revenue	23-24	30,638	29,016	27,970
Cost of sales		(10,801)	(9,997)	(9,863)
Gross margin		19,837	19,019	18,107
Marketing and selling expenses		(11,744)	(10,767)	(10,013)
General and administrative expenses		(2,373)	(2,212)	(2,151)
Income (loss) from joint ventures and associates	7	(5)	(23)	(19)
Profit from recurring operations	23-24	5,715	6,017	5,924
Other operating income and expenses	25	(284)	(119)	(182)
Operating profit		5,431	5,898	5,742
Cost of net financial debt		(115)	(101)	(138)
Other financial income and expenses		3,062	(97)	126
Net financial income (expense)	26	2,947	(198)	(12)
Income taxes	27	(2,273)	(1,753)	(1,821)
Net profit before minority interests		6,105	3,947	3,909
Minority interests	17	(457)	(511)	(484)
Net profit, Group share		5,648	3,436	3,425
Basic Group share of net earnings per share *(EUR)*	28	11.27	6.87	6.86
Number of shares on which the calculation is based		501,309,369	500,283,414	499,133,643
Diluted Group share of net earnings per share *(EUR)*	28	11.21	6.83	6.82
Number of shares on which the calculation is based		503,861,733	503,217,497	502,229,952

(1) The financial statements as of December 31, 2013 and 2012 have been restated to reflect the retrospective application as of January 1, 2012 of IFRS 11 Joint Arrangements. See Note 1.2.

CONSOLIDATED STATEMENT OF COMPREHENSIVE GAINS AND LOSSES

(EUR millions)	2014	2013[1]	2012[1]
Net profit before minority interests	6,105	3,947	3,909
Translation adjustments	534	(346)	(99)
Tax impact	104	(48)	(18)
	638	(394)	(117)
Change in value of available for sale financial assets	494	963	(27)
Amounts transferred to income statement	(3,326)	(16)	(14)
Tax impact	184	(35)	(6)
	(2,648)	912	(47)
Change in value of hedges of future foreign currency cash flows	(30)	304	182
Amounts transferred to income statement	(163)	(265)	13
Tax impact	57	(17)	(50)
	(136)	22	145
Gains and losses recognized in equity, transferable to income statement	(2,146)	540	(19)
Change in value of vineyard land	(17)	369	85
Amounts transferred to consolidated reserves	(10)	-	-
Tax impact	9	(127)	(28)
	(18)	242	57
Employee benefit commitments: change in value resulting from actuarial gains and losses	(161)	80	(101)
Tax impact	52	(22)	29
	(109)	58	(72)
Gains and losses recognized in equity, not transferable to income statement	(127)	300	(15)
Comprehensive income	3,832	4,787	3,875
Minority interests	(565)	(532)	(469)
Comprehensive income, Group share	3,267	4,255	3,406

(1) The financial statements as of December 31, 2013 and 2012 have been restated to reflect the retrospective application as of January 1, 2012 of IFRS 11 Joint Arrangements. See Note 1.2.

CONSOLIDATED BALANCE SHEET

ASSETS *(EUR millions)*	Notes	2014	2013[1][2]	2012[1]
Brands and other intangible fixed assets	3	13,031	12,596	11,322
Goodwill	4	8,810	9,058	7,709
Property, plant and equipment	6	10,387	9,621	8,694
Investments in joint ventures and associates	7	519	480	483
Non-current available for sale financial assets	8	580	7,080	6,004
Other non-current assets	9	489	457	519
Deferred tax	27	1,436	913	952
Non-current assets		**35,252**	**40,205**	**35,683**
Inventories and work in progress	10	9,475	8,492	7,994
Trade accounts receivable	11	2,274	2,174	1,972
Income taxes		354	223	201
Other current assets	12	1,916	1,856	1,813
Cash and cash equivalents	14	4,091	3,226	2,187
Current assets		**18,110**	**15,971**	**14,167**
Total assets		**53,362**	**56,176**	**49,850**

LIABILITIES AND EQUITY *(EUR millions)*	Notes	2014	2013[1][2]	2012[1]
Share capital	15.1	152	152	152
Share premium account	15.1	2,655	3,849	3,848
Treasury shares and LVMH-share settled derivatives	15.2	(374)	(451)	(414)
Cumulative translation adjustment	15.4	492	(8)	342
Revaluation reserves		1,019	3,900	2,731
Other reserves		12,171	16,001	14,340
Net profit, Group share		5,648	3,436	3,425
Equity, Group share		21,763	26,879	24,424
Minority interests	17	1,240	1,028	1,084
Total equity		**23,003**	**27,907**	**25,508**
Long-term borrowings	18	5,054	4,149	3,825
Non-current provisions	19	2,291	1,797	1,772
Deferred tax	27	4,392	4,280	3,884
Other non-current liabilities	20	6,447	6,404	5,456
Non-current liabilities		**18,184**	**16,630**	**14,937**
Short-term borrowings	18	4,189	4,674	2,950
Trade accounts payable		3,606	3,297	3,118
Income taxes		549	357	442
Current provisions	19	332	324	335
Other current liabilities	21	3,499	2,987	2,560
Current liabilities		**12,175**	**11,639**	**9,405**
Total liabilities and equity		**53,362**	**56,176**	**49,850**

(1) The financial statements as of December 31, 2013 and 2012 have been restated to reflect the retrospective application as of January 1, 2012 of IFRS 11 Joint Arrangements. See Note 1.2.
(2) The consolidated balance sheet as of December 31, 2013 has been restated to reflect the finalized purchase price allocation for Loro Piana. See Note 2.

CONSOLIDATED STATEMENT OF CHANGES IN EQUITY

(EUR millions)	Number of shares	Share capital	Share premium account	Treasury shares and LVMH-share settled derivatives	Cumulative translation adjustment	Revaluation reserves				Net profit and other reserves	Total equity		
						Available for sale financial assets	Hedges of future foreign currency cash flows	Vineyard land	Employee benefit commitments		Group share	Minority interests	Total
Notes		15.1		15.2	15.4							17	
As of December 31, 2011	**507,815,624**	**152**	**3,801**	**(485)**	**431**	**1,990**	**(15)**	**714**	**(28)**	**15,811**	**22,371**	**1,055**	**23,426**
Gains and losses recognized in equity					(89)	(47)	133	44	(60)	-	(19)	(15)	(34)
Net profit										3,425	3,425	484	3,909
Comprehensive income		**-**	**-**	**-**	**(89)**	**(47)**	**133**	**44**	**(60)**	**3,425**	**3,406**	**469**	**3,875**
Stock option plan and similar expenses										50	50	3	53
(Acquisition)/disposal of treasury shares and LVMH-share settled derivatives				24						(12)	12	-	12
Exercise of LVMH share subscription options	1,344,975		94								94	-	94
Retirement of LVMH shares	(997,250)		(47)	47							-	-	-
Capital increase in subsidiaries											-	8	8
Interim and final dividends paid										(1,447)	(1,447)	(317)	(1,764)
Changes in control of consolidated entities										(12)	(12)	(11)	(23)
Acquisition and disposal of minority interests' shares										(40)	(40)	(25)	(65)
Purchase commitments for minority interests' shares										(10)	(10)	(98)	(108)
As of December 31, 2012	**508,163,349**	**152**	**3,848**	**(414)**	**342**	**1,943**	**118**	**758**	**(88)**	**17,765**	**24,424**	**1,084**	**25,508**
Gains and losses recognized in equity					(350)	912	18	188	51	-	819	21	840
Net profit										3,436	3,436	511	3,947
Comprehensive income		**-**	**-**	**-**	**(350)**	**912**	**18**	**188**	**51**	**3,436**	**4,255**	**532**	**4,787**
Stock option plan and similar expenses										31	31	3	34
(Acquisition)/disposal of treasury shares and LVMH-share settled derivatives				(103)						(7)	(110)	-	(110)
Exercise of LVMH share subscription options	1,025,418		67								67	-	67
Retirement of LVMH shares	(1,395,106)		(66)	66							-	-	-
Capital increase in subsidiaries											-	8	8
Interim and final dividends paid										(1,500)	(1,500)	(228)	(1,728)
Acquisition of a controlling interest in Loro Piana[1]											-	235	235
Changes in control of consolidated entities										1	1	(1)	-
Acquisition and disposal of minority interests' shares										(73)	(73)	(76)	(149)
Purchase commitments for minority interests' shares[1]										(216)	(216)	(529)	(745)
As of December 31, 2013	**507,793,661**	**152**	**3,849**	**(451)**	**(8)**	**2,855**	**136**	**946**	**(37)**	**19,437**	**26,879**	**1,028**	**27,907**
Gains and losses recognized in equity					500	(2,648)	(122)	(15)	(96)	-	(2,381)	108	(2,273)
Net profit										5,648	5,648	457	6,105
Comprehensive income		**-**	**-**	**-**	**500**	**(2,648)**	**(122)**	**(15)**	**(96)**	**5,648**	**3,267**	**565**	**3,832**
Stock option plan and similar expenses										37	37	2	39
(Acquisition)/disposal of treasury shares and LVMH-share settled derivatives				27						(17)	10	-	10
Exercise of LVMH share subscription options	980,323		59								59	-	59
Retirement of LVMH shares	(1,062,271)		(50)	50							-	-	-
Capital increase in subsidiaries											-	3	3
Interim and final dividends paid										(1,579)	(1,579)	(328)	(1,907)
Distribution in kind of Hermès shares. See Note 8.			(1,203)							(5,652)	(6,855)	-	(6,855)
Changes in control of consolidated entities										(5)	(5)	11	6
Acquisition and disposal of minority interests' shares										(2)	(2)	32	30
Purchase commitments for minority interests' shares										(48)	(48)	(73)	(121)
As of December 31, 2014	**507,711,713**	**152**	**2,655**	**(374)**	**492**	**207**	**14**	**931**	**(133)**	**17,819**	**21,763**	**1,240**	**23,003**

(1) The consolidated balance sheet as of December 31, 2013 has been restated to reflect the finalized purchase price allocation for Loro Piana. See Note 2.

CONSOLIDATED CASH FLOW STATEMENT

(EUR millions)	Notes	2014	2013[1]	2012[1]
I. OPERATING ACTIVITIES AND OPERATING INVESTMENTS				
Operating profit		5,431	5,898	5,742
Income/(loss) and dividends from joint ventures and associates[a]	7	26	49	37
Net increase in depreciation, amortization and provisions		1,895	1,435	1,289
Other computed expenses		(188)	(29)	(59)
Other adjustments		(84)	(76)	(52)
Cash from operations before changes in working capital		**7,080**	**7,277**	**6,957**
Cost of net financial debt: interest paid		(116)	(111)	(152)
Income taxes paid[a]		(1,639)	(1,832)	(1,880)
Net cash from operating activities before changes in working capital		**5,325**	**5,334**	**4,925**
Change in working capital	14.1	(718)	(620)	(810)
Net cash from operating activities		**4,607**	**4,714**	**4,115**
Operating investments	14.2	(1,775)	(1,657)	(1,694)
Net cash from operating activities and operating investments (free cash flow)		**2,832**	**3,057**	**2,421**
II. FINANCIAL INVESTMENTS				
Purchase of non-current available for sale financial assets	8	(57)	(197)	(131)
Proceeds from sale of non-current available for sale financial assets	8	160	38	36
Dividends received[a]	8	69	71	179
Income tax related to financial investments[a]		(237)	(11)	(21)
Impact of purchase and sale of consolidated investments	2.4	(167)	(2,161)	(59)
Net cash from (used in) financial investments		**(232)**	**(2,260)**	**4**
III. TRANSACTIONS RELATING TO EQUITY				
Capital increases of LVMH SE	15.1	59	66	95
Capital increases of subsidiaries subscribed by minority interests	17	3	7	8
Acquisition and disposals of treasury shares and LVMH-share settled derivatives	15.2	1	(113)	5
Interim and final dividends paid by LVMH SE	15.3	(1,619)[b]	(1,501)	(1,447)
Income taxes paid related to interim and final dividends paid[a]		(79)	(137)	(73)
Interim and final dividends paid to minority interests in consolidated subsidiaries	17	(336)	(220)	(314)
Purchase and proceeds from sale of minority interests	2.4	10	(150)	(206)
Net cash from (used in) transactions relating to equity		**(1,961)**	**(2,048)**	**(1,932)**
Change in cash before financing activities		**639**	**(1,251)**	**493**
IV. FINANCING ACTIVITIES				
Proceeds from borrowings		2,407	3,095	1,028
Repayment of borrowings		(2,100)	(1,057)	(1,494)
Purchase and proceeds from sale of current available for sale financial assets	13	(106)	101	(67)
Net cash from (used in) financing activities		**201**	**2,139**	**(533)**
V. EFFECT OF EXCHANGE RATE CHANGES		27	47	(43)
NET INCREASE (DECREASE) IN CASH AND CASH EQUIVALENTS (I+II+III+IV+V)		867	935	(83)
CASH AND CASH EQUIVALENTS AT BEGINNING OF PERIOD	14	2,916	1,981	2,064
CASH AND CASH EQUIVALENTS AT END OF PERIOD	14	3,783	2,916	1,981
TOTAL INCOME TAXES PAID		(1,955)	(1,980)	(1,974)
Transactions included in the table above, generating no change in cash:				
- acquisition of assets by means of finance leases		5	7	5

(a) Restated to reflect the amended presentation of dividends received and income tax paid starting in 2014. See Note 1.4.

(b) The distribution in kind of Hermès shares had no impact on cash, apart from related income tax effects. See Note 8.

(1) The financial statements as of December 31, 2013 and 2012 have been restated to reflect the retrospective application as of January 1, 2012 of IFRS 11 Joint Arrangements. See Note 1.2.

G

Time Value of Money

APPENDIX PREVIEW

Would you rather receive $1,000 today or a year from now? You should prefer to receive the $1,000 today because you can invest the $1,000 and then earn interest on it. As a result, you will have more than $1,000 a year from now. What this example illustrates is the concept of the **time value of money**. Everyone prefers to receive money today rather than in the future because of the interest factor.

APPENDIX OUTLINE

LEARNING OBJECTIVES	
1 Compute interest and future values.	• Nature of interest • Future value of a single amount • Future value of an annuity
2 Compute present values.	• Present value variables • Present value of a single amount • Present value of an annuity • Time periods and discounting • Present value of a long-term note or bond
3 Use a financial calculator to solve time value of money problems.	• Present value of a single sum • Present value of an annuity • Useful financial calculator applications

LEARNING OBJECTIVE 1 **Compute interest and future values.**

NATURE OF INTEREST

Interest is payment for the use of another person's money. It is the difference between the amount borrowed or invested (called the **principal**) and the amount repaid or collected. The amount of interest to be paid or collected is usually stated as a rate over a specific period of time. The rate of interest is generally stated as an annual rate.

The amount of interest involved in any financing transaction is based on three elements:

1. **Principal (*p*):** The original amount borrowed or invested.
2. **Interest Rate (*i*):** An annual percentage of the principal.
3. **Time (*n*):** The number of periods that the principal is borrowed or invested.

Simple Interest

Simple interest is computed on the principal amount only. It is the return on the principal for one period. Simple interest is usually expressed as shown in Illustration G-1.

ILLUSTRATION G-1
Interest computation

$$\text{Interest} = \underset{p}{\text{Principal}} \times \underset{i}{\text{Rate}} \times \underset{n}{\text{Time}}$$

For example, if you borrowed $5,000 for 2 years at a simple interest rate of 12% annually, you would pay $1,200 in total interest, computed as follows.

$$\begin{aligned}\text{Interest} &= p \times i \times n \\ &= \$5{,}000 \times .12 \times 2 \\ &= \$1{,}200\end{aligned}$$

Compound Interest

Compound interest is computed on principal **and** on any interest earned that has not been paid or withdrawn. It is the return on (or growth of) the principal for two or more time periods. Compounding computes interest not only on the principal but also on the interest earned to date on that principal, assuming the interest is left on deposit.

To illustrate the difference between simple and compound interest, assume that you deposit $1,000 in Bank Two, where it will earn simple interest of 9% per year, and you deposit another $1,000 in Citizens Bank, where it will earn compound interest of 9% per year compounded annually. Also assume that in both cases you will not withdraw any cash until three years from the date of deposit. Illustration G-2 shows the computation of interest to be received and the accumulated year-end balances.

ILLUSTRATION G-2
Simple versus compound interest

Bank Two

Simple Interest Calculation	Simple Interest	Accumulated Year-End Balance
Year 1 $1,000.00 × 9%	$ 90.00	$1,090.00
Year 2 $1,000.00 × 9%	90.00	$1,180.00
Year 3 $1,000.00 × 9%	90.00	$1,270.00
	$ 270.00	

Citizens Bank

Compound Interest Calculation	Compound Interest	Accumulated Year-End Balance
Year 1 $1,000.00 × 9%	$ 90.00	$1,090.00
Year 2 $1,090.00 × 9%	98.10	$1,188.10
Year 3 $1,188.10 × 9%	106.93	$1,295.03
	$ 295.03	

$25.03 Difference

Note in Illustration G-2 that simple interest uses the initial principal of $1,000 to compute the interest in all three years. Compound interest uses the accumulated balance (principal plus interest to date) at each year-end to compute interest in the succeeding year—which explains why your compound interest account is larger.

Obviously, if you had a choice between investing your money at simple interest or at compound interest, you would choose compound interest, all other things—

especially risk—being equal. In the example, compounding provides \$25.03 of additional interest income. For practical purposes, compounding assumes that unpaid interest earned becomes a part of the principal, and the accumulated balance at the end of each year becomes the new principal on which interest is earned during the next year.

Illustration G-2 indicates that you should invest your money at the bank that compounds interest. Most business situations use compound interest. Simple interest is generally applicable only to short-term situations of one year or less.

FUTURE VALUE OF A SINGLE AMOUNT

The **future value of a single amount** is the value at a future date of a given amount invested, assuming compound interest. For example, in Illustration G-2, \$1,295.03 is the future value of the \$1,000 investment earning 9% for three years. The \$1,295.03 is determined more easily by using the following formula.

$$FV = p \times (1 + i)^n$$

ILLUSTRATION G-3
Formula for future value

where:

FV = future value of a single amount
p = principal (or present value; the value today)
i = interest rate for one period
n = number of periods

The \$1,295.03 is computed as follows.

$$\begin{aligned} FV &= \quad p \quad \times (1 + i)^n \\ &= \$1{,}000 \times (1 + .09)^3 \\ &= \$1{,}000 \times 1.29503 \\ &= \$1{,}295.03 \end{aligned}$$

The 1.29503 is computed by multiplying (1.09 × 1.09 × 1.09), where 1.09 is 1 plus the interest rate of 9%. Thus, 1.29503 represents the 9% rate compounded for three years. The amounts in this example can be depicted in the time diagram shown in Illustration G-4.

ILLUSTRATION G-4
Time diagram

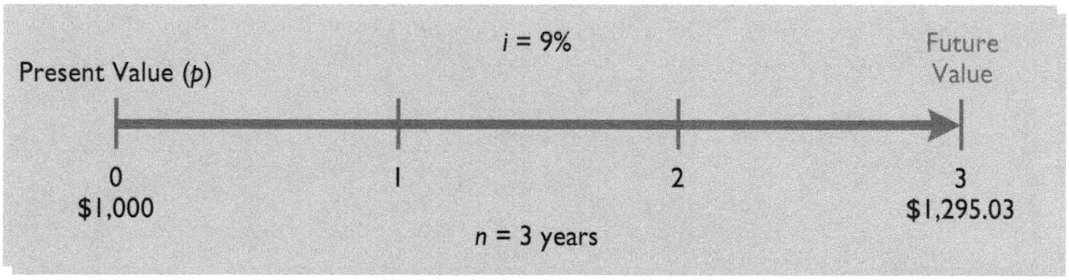

Another method used to compute the future value of a single amount involves a compound interest table. This table shows the future value of 1 for n periods. Table 1 (page G-4) is such a table.

In Table 1, n is the number of compounding periods, the percentages are the periodic interest rates, and the 5-digit decimal numbers in the respective columns are the future value of 1 factors. To use Table 1, you multiply the principal amount by the future value factor for the specified number of periods and interest rate. For example, the future value factor for two periods at 9% is 1.18810. Multiplying this factor by \$1,000 equals \$1,188.10—which is the accumulated balance at the end of year 2 in the Citizens Bank example in Illustration G-2. The

TABLE 1 Future Value of 1

(*n*) Periods	4%	5%	6%	7%	8%	9%	10%	11%	12%	15%
0	1.00000	1.00000	1.00000	1.00000	1.00000	1.00000	1.00000	1.00000	1.00000	1.00000
1	1.04000	1.05000	1.06000	1.07000	1.08000	1.09000	1.10000	1.11000	1.12000	1.15000
2	1.08160	1.10250	1.12360	1.14490	1.16640	1.18810	1.21000	1.23210	1.25440	1.32250
3	1.12486	1.15763	1.19102	1.22504	1.25971	1.29503	1.33100	1.36763	1.40493	1.52088
4	1.16986	1.21551	1.26248	1.31080	1.36049	1.41158	1.46410	1.51807	1.57352	1.74901
5	1.21665	1.27628	1.33823	1.40255	1.46933	1.53862	1.61051	1.68506	1.76234	2.01136
6	1.26532	1.34010	1.41852	1.50073	1.58687	1.67710	1.77156	1.87041	1.97382	2.31306
7	1.31593	1.40710	1.50363	1.60578	1.71382	1.82804	1.94872	2.07616	2.21068	2.66002
8	1.36857	1.47746	1.59385	1.71819	1.85093	1.99256	2.14359	2.30454	2.47596	3.05902
9	1.42331	1.55133	1.68948	1.83846	1.99900	2.17189	2.35795	2.55803	2.77308	3.51788
10	1.48024	1.62889	1.79085	1.96715	2.15892	2.36736	2.59374	2.83942	3.10585	4.04556
11	1.53945	1.71034	1.89830	2.10485	2.33164	2.58043	2.85312	3.15176	3.47855	4.65239
12	1.60103	1.79586	2.01220	2.25219	2.51817	2.81267	3.13843	3.49845	3.89598	5.35025
13	1.66507	1.88565	2.13293	2.40985	2.71962	3.06581	3.45227	3.88328	4.36349	6.15279
14	1.73168	1.97993	2.26090	2.57853	2.93719	3.34173	3.79750	4.31044	4.88711	7.07571
15	1.80094	2.07893	2.39656	2.75903	3.17217	3.64248	4.17725	4.78459	5.47357	8.13706
16	1.87298	2.18287	2.54035	2.95216	3.42594	3.97031	4.59497	5.31089	6.13039	9.35762
17	1.94790	2.29202	2.69277	3.15882	3.70002	4.32763	5.05447	5.89509	6.86604	10.76126
18	2.02582	2.40662	2.85434	3.37993	3.99602	4.71712	5.55992	6.54355	7.68997	12.37545
19	2.10685	2.52695	3.02560	3.61653	4.31570	5.14166	6.11591	7.26334	8.61276	14.23177
20	2.19112	2.65330	3.20714	3.86968	4.66096	5.60441	6.72750	8.06231	9.64629	16.36654

$1,295.03 accumulated balance at the end of the third year is calculated from Table 1 by multiplying the future value factor for three periods (1.29503) by the $1,000.

The demonstration problem in Illustration G-5 shows how to use Table 1.

ILLUSTRATION G-5
Demonstration problem—Using Table 1 for *FV* of 1

John and Mary Rich invested $20,000 in a savings account paying 6% interest at the time their son, Mike, was born. The money is to be used by Mike for his college education. On his 18th birthday, Mike withdraws the money from his savings account. How much did Mike withdraw from his account?

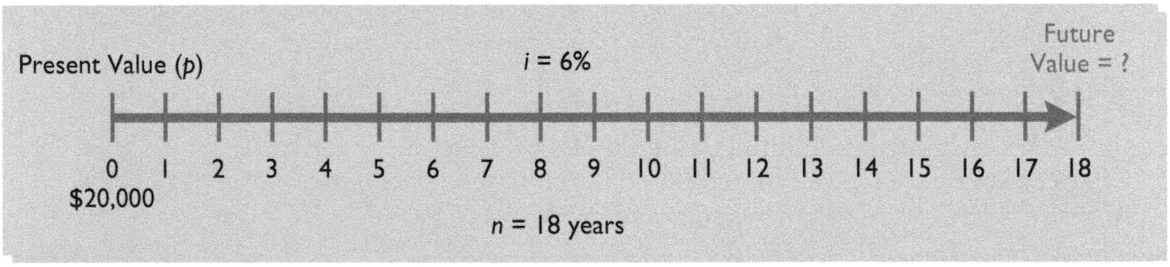

Answer: The future value factor from Table 1 is 2.85434 (18 periods at 6%). The future value of $20,000 earning 6% per year for 18 years is **$57,086.80** ($20,000 × 2.85434).

FUTURE VALUE OF AN ANNUITY

The preceding discussion involved the accumulation of only a single principal sum. Individuals and businesses frequently encounter situations in which a

series of equal dollar amounts are to be paid or received at evenly spaced time intervals (periodically), such as loans or lease (rental) contracts. A series of payments or receipts of equal dollar amounts is referred to as an **annuity**.

The **future value of an annuity** is the sum of all the payments (receipts) plus the accumulated compound interest on them. In computing the future value of an annuity, it is necessary to know (1) the interest rate, (2) the number of payments (receipts), and (3) the amount of the periodic payments (receipts).

To illustrate the computation of the future value of an annuity, assume that you invest $2,000 at the end of each year for three years at 5% interest compounded annually. This situation is depicted in the time diagram in Illustration G-6.

ILLUSTRATION G-6
Time diagram for a three-year annuity

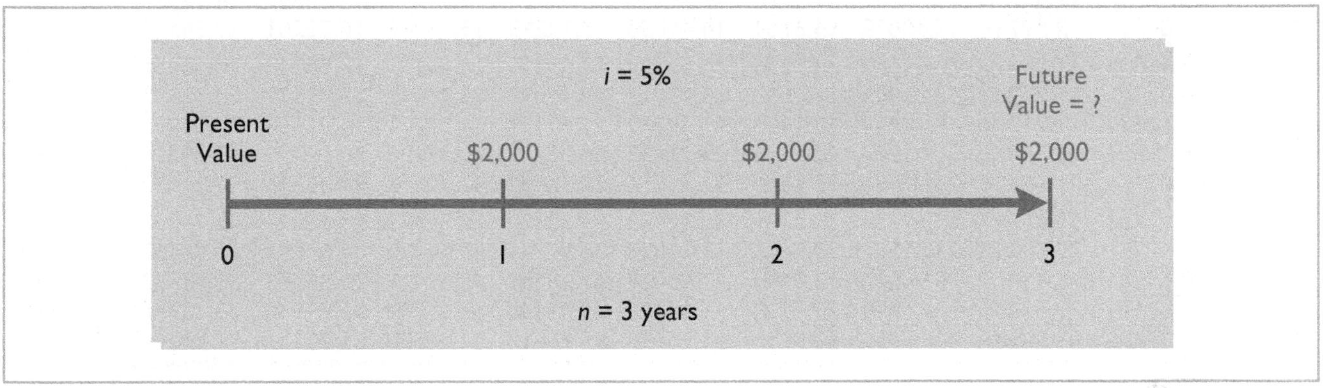

The $2,000 invested at the end of year 1 will earn interest for two years (years 2 and 3), and the $2,000 invested at the end of year 2 will earn interest for one year (year 3). However, the last $2,000 investment (made at the end of year 3) will not earn any interest. Using the future value factors from Table 1, the future value of these periodic payments is computed as shown in Illustration G-7.

ILLUSTRATION G-7
Future value of periodic payment computation

Invested at End of Year	Number of Compounding Periods	Amount Invested	×	Future Value of 1 Factor at 5%	=	Future Value
1	2	$2,000		1.10250		$2,205
2	1	2,000		1.05000		2,100
3	0	2,000		1.00000		2,000
				3.15250		**$6,305**

The first $2,000 investment is multiplied by the future value factor for two periods (1.1025) because two years' interest will accumulate on it (in years 2 and 3). The second $2,000 investment will earn only one year's interest (in year 3) and therefore is multiplied by the future value factor for one year (1.0500). The final $2,000 investment is made at the end of the third year and will not earn any interest. Thus, $n = 0$ and the future value factor is 1.00000. Consequently, the future value of the last $2,000 invested is only $2,000 since it does not accumulate any interest.

Calculating the future value of each individual cash flow is required when the periodic payments or receipts are not equal in each period. However, when the periodic payments (receipts) are **the same in each period**, the future value can be computed by using a future value of an annuity of 1 table. Table 2 (page G-6) is such a table.

Table 2 shows the future value of 1 to be received periodically for a given number of payments. It assumes that each payment is made at the **end** of each period. We can see from Table 2 that the future value of an annuity of 1 factor for

TABLE 2 Future Value of an Annuity of 1

(*n*) Payments	4%	5%	6%	7%	8%	9%	10%	11%	12%	15%
1	1.00000	1.00000	1.00000	1.0000	1.00000	1.00000	1.00000	1.00000	1.00000	1.00000
2	2.04000	2.05000	2.06000	2.0700	2.08000	2.09000	2.10000	2.11000	2.12000	2.15000
3	3.12160	3.15250	3.18360	3.2149	3.24640	3.27810	3.31000	3.34210	3.37440	3.47250
4	4.24646	4.31013	4.37462	4.4399	4.50611	4.57313	4.64100	4.70973	4.77933	4.99338
5	5.41632	5.52563	5.63709	5.7507	5.86660	5.98471	6.10510	6.22780	6.35285	6.74238
6	6.63298	6.80191	6.97532	7.1533	7.33592	7.52334	7.71561	7.91286	8.11519	8.75374
7	7.89829	8.14201	8.39384	8.6540	8.92280	9.20044	9.48717	9.78327	10.08901	11.06680
8	9.21423	9.54911	9.89747	10.2598	10.63663	11.02847	11.43589	11.85943	12.29969	13.72682
9	10.58280	11.02656	11.49132	11.9780	12.48756	13.02104	13.57948	14.16397	14.77566	16.78584
10	12.00611	12.57789	13.18079	13.8164	14.48656	15.19293	15.93743	16.72201	17.54874	20.30372
11	13.48635	14.20679	14.97164	15.7836	16.64549	17.56029	18.53117	19.56143	20.65458	24.34928
12	15.02581	15.91713	16.86994	17.8885	18.97713	20.14072	21.38428	22.71319	24.13313	29.00167
13	16.62684	17.71298	18.88214	20.1406	21.49530	22.95339	24.52271	26.21164	28.02911	34.35192
14	18.29191	19.59863	21.01507	22.5505	24.21492	26.01919	27.97498	30.09492	32.39260	40.50471
15	20.02359	21.57856	23.27597	25.1290	27.15211	29.36092	31.77248	34.40536	37.27972	47.58041
16	21.82453	23.65749	25.67253	27.8881	30.32428	33.00340	35.94973	39.18995	42.75328	55.71747
17	23.69751	25.84037	28.21288	30.8402	33.75023	36.97351	40.54470	44.50084	48.88367	65.07509
18	25.64541	28.13238	30.90565	33.9990	37.45024	41.30134	45.59917	50.39593	55.74972	75.83636
19	27.67123	30.53900	33.75999	37.3790	41.44626	46.01846	51.15909	56.93949	63.43968	88.21181
20	29.77808	33.06595	36.78559	40.9955	45.76196	51.16012	57.27500	64.20283	72.05244	102.44358

three payments at 5% is 3.15250. The future value factor is the total of the three individual future value factors as shown in Illustration G-7. Multiplying this amount by the annual investment of $2,000 produces a future value of $6,305.

The demonstration problem in Illustration G-8 shows how to use Table 2.

ILLUSTRATION G-8
Demonstration problem—Using Table 2 for *FV* of an annuity of 1

John and Char Lewis's daughter, Debra, has just started high school. They decide to start a college fund for her and will invest $2,500 in a savings account at the end of each year she is in high school (4 payments total). The account will earn 6% interest compounded annually. How much will be in the college fund at the time Debra graduates from high school?

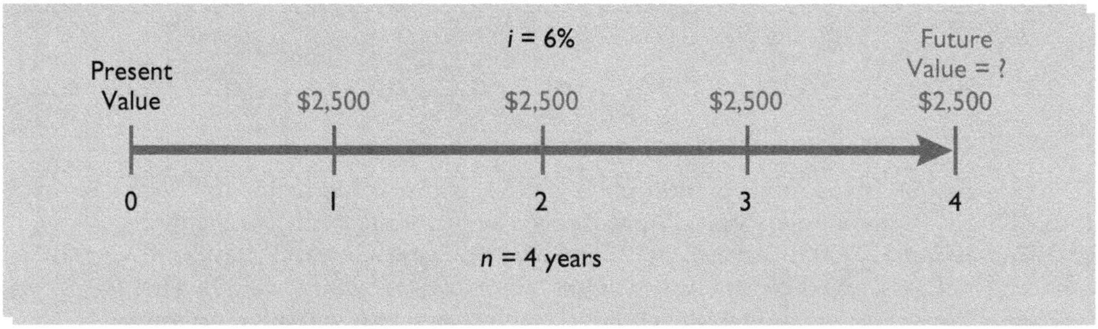

Answer: The future value factor from Table 2 is 4.37462 (4 payments at 6%). The future value of $2,500 invested each year for 4 years at 6% interest is **$10,936.55** ($2,500 × 4.37462).

Note that we can apply the same concepts in situations where the future value and interest rate are known, but the payment must be calculated. Suppose, for example, that in Illustration G-8 that the amount that Debra needs to accumulate in her college fund by the end of four years is $10,936.55. If Debra earns 6% on her four annual payments, we can solve for the amount of the annuity payments by dividing $10,936.55 by the future value factor of 4.37462 to determine the payment amount of $2,500.

LEARNING OBJECTIVE 2 **Compute present values.**

PRESENT VALUE VARIABLES

The **present value** is the value now of a given amount to be paid or received in the future, assuming compound interest. The present value, like the future value, is based on three variables: (1) the dollar amount to be received (future amount), (2) the length of time until the amount is received (number of periods), and (3) the interest rate (the discount rate). The process of determining the present value is referred to as **discounting the future amount.**

Present value computations are used in measuring many items. For example, the present value of principal and interest payments is used to determine the market price of a bond. Determining the amount to be reported for notes payable and lease liabilities also involves present value computations. In addition, capital budgeting and other investment proposals are evaluated using present value computations. Finally, all rate of return and internal rate of return computations involve present value techniques.

PRESENT VALUE OF A SINGLE AMOUNT

To illustrate present value, assume that you want to invest a sum of money today that will provide $1,000 at the end of one year. What amount would you need to invest today to have $1,000 one year from now? If you want a 10% rate of return, the investment or present value is $909.09 ($1,000 ÷ 1.10). The formula for calculating present value is shown in Illustration G-9.

$$\text{Present Value } (PV) = \textbf{Future Value } (FV) \div (1 + i)^n$$

ILLUSTRATION G-9
Formula for present value

The computation of $1,000 discounted at 10% for one year is as follows.

$$\begin{aligned} PV &= FV \div (1 + i)^n \\ &= \$1{,}000 \div (1 + .10)^1 \\ &= \$1{,}000 \div 1.10 \\ &= \$909.09 \end{aligned}$$

The future amount ($1,000), the discount rate (10%), and the number of periods (1) are known. The variables in this situation are depicted in the time diagram in Illustration G-10.

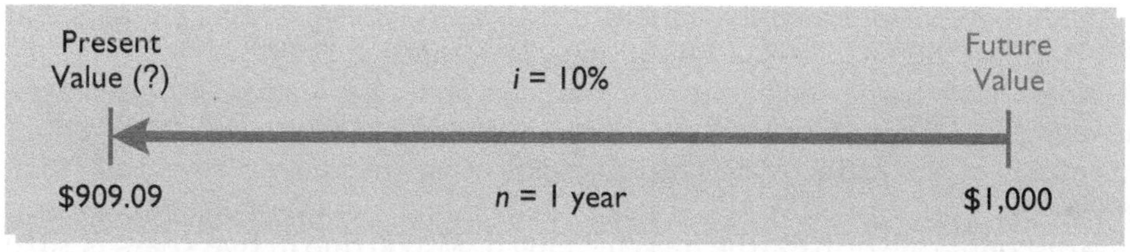

ILLUSTRATION G-10
Finding present value if discounted for one period

If the single amount of $1,000 is to be received **in two years** and discounted at 10% [$PV = \$1{,}000 \div (1 + .10)^2$], its present value is $826.45 [($1,000 ÷ 1.21), depicted in Illustration G-11.

ILLUSTRATION G-11
Finding present value if discounted for two periods

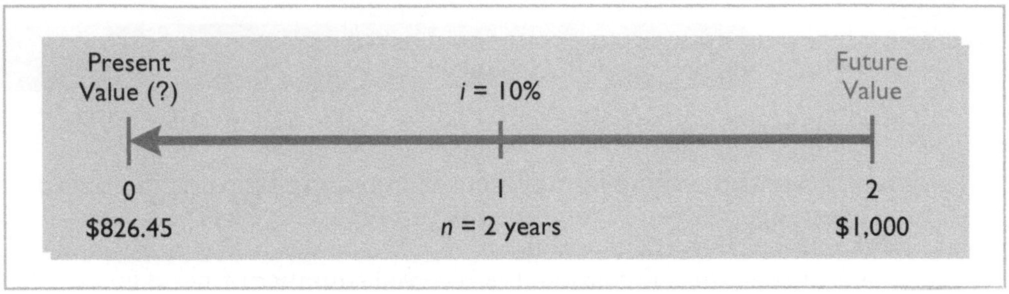

The present value of 1 may also be determined through tables that show the present value of 1 for *n* periods. In Table 3 (see below), *n* is the number of discounting periods involved. The percentages are the periodic interest rates or discount rates, and the 5-digit decimal numbers in the respective columns are the present value of 1 factors.

When using Table 3, the future value is multiplied by the present value factor specified at the intersection of the number of periods and the discount rate.

TABLE 3 Present Value of 1

(*n*) Periods	4%	5%	6%	7%	8%	9%	10%	11%	12%	15%
1	.96154	.95238	.94340	.93458	.92593	.91743	.90909	.90090	.89286	.86957
2	.92456	.90703	.89000	.87344	.85734	.84168	.82645	.81162	.79719	.75614
3	.88900	.86384	.83962	.81630	.79383	.77218	.75132	.73119	.71178	.65752
4	.85480	.82270	.79209	.76290	.73503	.70843	.68301	.65873	.63552	.57175
5	.82193	.78353	.74726	.71299	.68058	.64993	.62092	.59345	.56743	.49718
6	.79031	.74622	.70496	.66634	.63017	.59627	.56447	.53464	.50663	.43233
7	.75992	.71068	.66506	.62275	.58349	.54703	.51316	.48166	.45235	.37594
8	.73069	.67684	.62741	.58201	.54027	.50187	.46651	.43393	.40388	.32690
9	.70259	.64461	.59190	.54393	.50025	.46043	.42410	.39092	.36061	.28426
10	.67556	.61391	.55839	.50835	.46319	.42241	.38554	.35218	.32197	.24719
11	.64958	.58468	.52679	.47509	.42888	.38753	.35049	.31728	.28748	.21494
12	.62460	.55684	.49697	.44401	.39711	.35554	.31863	.28584	.25668	.18691
13	.60057	.53032	.46884	.41496	.36770	.32618	.28966	.25751	.22917	.16253
14	.57748	.50507	.44230	.38782	.34046	.29925	.26333	.23199	.20462	.14133
15	.55526	.48102	.41727	.36245	.31524	.27454	.23939	.20900	.18270	.12289
16	.53391	.45811	.39365	.33873	.29189	.25187	.21763	.18829	.16312	.10687
17	.51337	.43630	.37136	.31657	.27027	.23107	.19785	.16963	.14564	.09293
18	.49363	.41552	.35034	.29586	.25025	.21199	.17986	.15282	.13004	.08081
19	.47464	.39573	.33051	.27615	.23171	.19449	.16351	.13768	.11611	.07027
20	.45639	.37689	.31180	.25842	.21455	.17843	.14864	.12403	.10367	.06110

For example, the present value factor for one period at a discount rate of 10% is .90909, which equals the $909.09 ($1,000 × .90909) computed in Illustration G-10. For two periods at a discount rate of 10%, the present value factor is .82645, which equals the $826.45 ($1,000 × .82645) computed previously.

Note that a higher discount rate produces a smaller present value. For example, using a 15% discount rate, the present value of $1,000 due one year from now is $869.57, versus $909.09 at 10%. Also note that the further removed from the present the future value is, the smaller the present value. For example, using the same discount rate of 10%, the present value of $1,000 due in **five years** is $620.92. The present value of $1,000 due in **one year** is $909.09, a difference of $288.17.

The following two demonstration problems (Illustrations G-12 and G-13) illustrate how to use Table 3.

ILLUSTRATION G-12
Demonstration problem—Using Table 3 for *PV* of 1

Suppose you have a winning lottery ticket and the state gives you the option of taking $10,000 3 years from now or taking the present value of $10,000 now. The state uses an 8% rate in discounting. How much will you receive if you accept your winnings now?

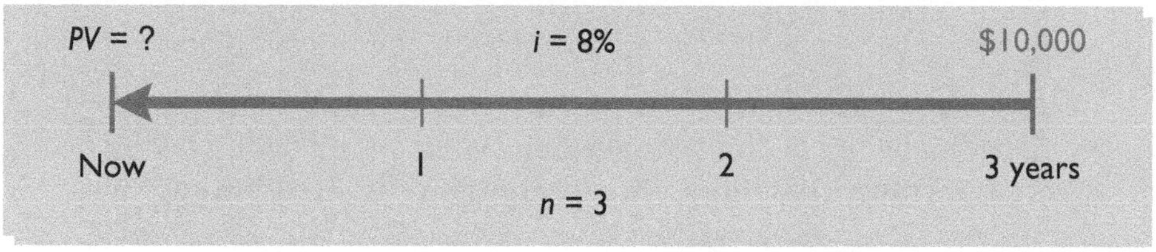

Answer: The present value factor from Table 3 is .79383 (3 periods at 8%). The present value of $10,000 to be received in 3 years discounted at 8% is **$7,938.30** ($10,000 × .79383).

ILLUSTRATION G-13
Demonstration problem—Using Table 3 for *PV* of 1

Determine the amount you must deposit today in your super savings account, paying 9% interest, in order to accumulate $5,000 for a down payment 4 years from now on a new car.

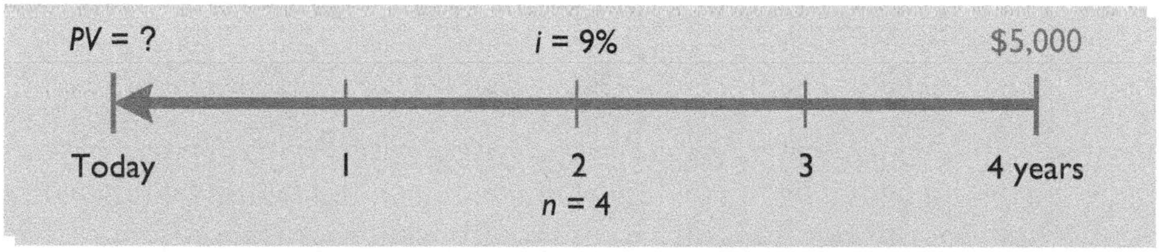

Answer: The present value factor from Table 3 is .70843 (4 periods at 9%). The present value of $5,000 to be received in 4 years discounted at 9% is **$3,542.15** ($5,000 × .70843).

PRESENT VALUE OF AN ANNUITY

The preceding discussion involved the discounting of only a single future amount. Businesses and individuals frequently engage in transactions in which a series of equal dollar amounts are to be received or paid at evenly spaced time intervals (periodically). Examples of a series of periodic receipts or payments are loan agreements, installment sales, mortgage notes, lease (rental) contracts, and pension obligations. As discussed earlier, these periodic receipts or payments are **annuities**.

The **present value of an annuity** is the value now of a series of future receipts or payments, discounted assuming compound interest. In computing the present value of an annuity, it is necessary to know (1) the discount rate, (2) the number of payments (receipts), and (3) the amount of the periodic receipts or payments. To illustrate the computation of the present value of an annuity, assume that you will receive $1,000 cash annually for three years at a time when the discount rate is 10%. This situation is depicted in the time diagram in Illustration G-14. Illustration G-15 shows the computation of its present value in this situation.

ILLUSTRATION G-14
Time diagram for a three-year annuity

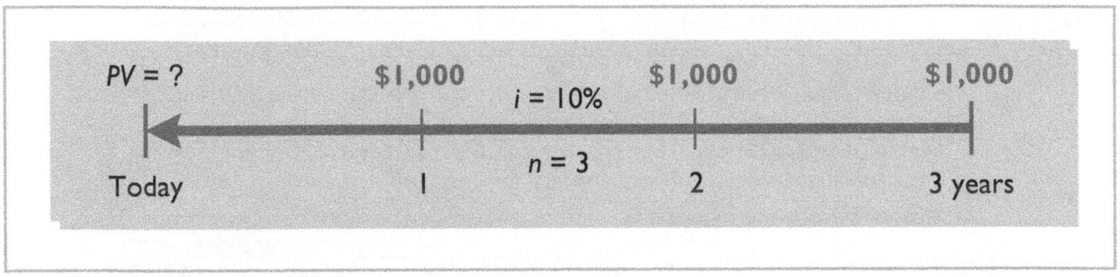

ILLUSTRATION G-15
Present value of a series of future amounts computation

Future Amount	×	Present Value of 1 Factor at 10%	=	Present Value
$1,000 (1 year away)		.90909		$ 909.09
1,000 (2 years away)		.82645		826.45
1,000 (3 years away)		.75132		751.32
		2.48686		$2,486.86

This method of calculation is required when the periodic cash flows are not uniform in each period. However, when the future receipts are the same in each period, an annuity table can be used. As illustrated in Table 4 below, an annuity table shows the present value of 1 to be received periodically for a given number of payments. It assumes that each payment is made at the end of each period.

TABLE 4 Present Value of an Annuity of 1

(*n*) Payments	4%	5%	6%	7%	8%	9%	10%	11%	12%	15%
1	.96154	.95238	.94340	.93458	.92593	.91743	.90909	.90090	.89286	.86957
2	1.88609	1.85941	1.83339	1.80802	1.78326	1.75911	1.73554	1.71252	1.69005	1.62571
3	2.77509	2.72325	2.67301	2.62432	2.57710	2.53130	2.48685	2.44371	2.40183	2.28323
4	3.62990	3.54595	3.46511	3.38721	3.31213	3.23972	3.16986	3.10245	3.03735	2.85498
5	4.45182	4.32948	4.21236	4.10020	3.99271	3.88965	3.79079	3.69590	3.60478	3.35216
6	5.24214	5.07569	4.91732	4.76654	4.62288	4.48592	4.35526	4.23054	4.11141	3.78448
7	6.00205	5.78637	5.58238	5.38929	5.20637	5.03295	4.86842	4.71220	4.56376	4.16042
8	6.73274	6.46321	6.20979	5.97130	5.74664	5.53482	5.33493	5.14612	4.96764	4.48732
9	7.43533	7.10782	6.80169	6.51523	6.24689	5.99525	5.75902	5.53705	5.32825	4.77158
10	8.11090	7.72173	7.36009	7.02358	6.71008	6.41766	6.14457	5.88923	5.65022	5.01877
11	8.76048	8.30641	7.88687	7.49867	7.13896	6.80519	6.49506	6.20652	5.93770	5.23371
12	9.38507	8.86325	8.38384	7.94269	7.53608	7.16073	6.81369	6.49236	6.19437	5.42062
13	9.98565	9.39357	8.85268	8.35765	7.90378	7.48690	7.10336	6.74987	6.42355	5.58315
14	10.56312	9.89864	9.29498	8.74547	8.24424	7.78615	7.36669	6.98187	6.62817	5.72448
15	11.11839	10.37966	9.71225	9.10791	8.55948	8.06069	7.60608	7.19087	6.81086	5.84737
16	11.65230	10.83777	10.10590	9.44665	8.85137	8.31256	7.82371	7.37916	6.97399	5.95424
17	12.16567	11.27407	10.47726	9.76322	9.12164	8.54363	8.02155	7.54879	7.11963	6.04716
18	12.65930	11.68959	10.82760	10.05909	9.37189	8.75563	8.20141	7.70162	7.24967	6.12797
19	13.13394	12.08532	11.15812	10.33560	9.60360	8.95012	8.36492	7.83929	7.36578	6.19823
20	13.59033	12.46221	11.46992	10.59401	9.81815	9.12855	8.51356	7.96333	7.46944	6.25933

Table 4 shows that the present value of an annuity of 1 factor for three payments at 10% is 2.48685.[1] This present value factor is the total of the three

[1]The difference of .00001 between 2.48686 and 2.48685 is due to rounding.

individual present value factors, as shown in Illustration G-15. Applying this amount to the annual cash flow of $1,000 produces a present value of $2,486.85.

The following demonstration problem (Illustration G-16) illustrates how to use Table 4.

ILLUSTRATION G-16
Demonstration problem—Using Table 4 for *PV* of an annuity of 1

Kildare Company has just signed a capitalizable lease contract for equipment that requires rental payments of $6,000 each, to be paid at the end of each of the next 5 years. The appropriate discount rate is 12%. What is the present value of the rental payments—that is, the amount used to capitalize the leased equipment?

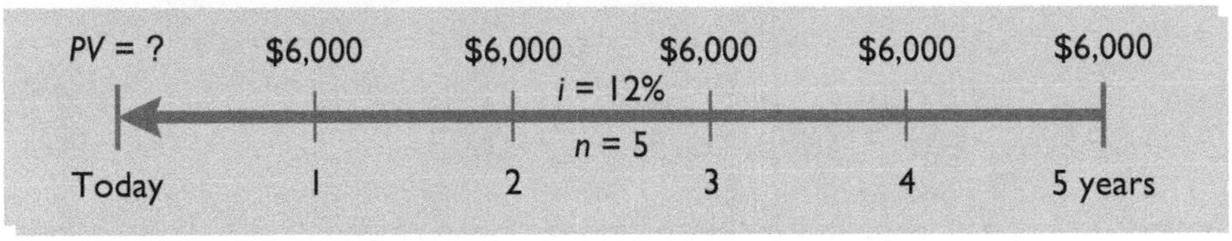

Answer: The present value factor from Table 4 is 3.60478 (5 payments at 12%). The present value of 5 payments of $6,000 each discounted at 12% is **$21,628.68** ($6,000 × 3.60478).

Note that the same concepts apply in situations when the price and interest rate are known, but the payment must be calculated. Suppose, for example, that in Illustration G-16 that the price of the lease contract is $21,628.68 and that Kildare Company wants to finance the lease contract by making five annual lease payments when the annual rate of interest is 12%. In this case, rather than solving for the present value, we need to solve for the amount of the annual payment. To do this, we divide the price (the present value) of $21,628.68 by the present value factor of 3.60478 to arrive at an annual payment of $6,000.

TIME PERIODS AND DISCOUNTING

In the preceding calculations, the discounting was done on an annual basis using an annual interest rate. Discounting may also be done over shorter periods of time such as monthly, quarterly, or semiannually.

When the time frame is less than one year, it is necessary to convert the annual interest rate to the applicable time frame. Assume, for example, that the investor in Illustration G-14 received $500 **semiannually** for three years instead of $1,000 annually. In this case, the number of periods becomes six (3 × 2), the discount rate is 5% (10% ÷ 2), the present value factor from Table 4 is 5.07569 (6 periods at 5%), and the present value of the future cash flows is $2,537.85 (5.07569 × $500). This amount is slightly higher than the $2,486.86 computed in Illustration G-15 because interest is computed twice during the same year. That is, during the second half of the year, interest is earned on the first half-year's interest.

PRESENT VALUE OF A LONG-TERM NOTE OR BOND

The present value (or market price) of a long-term note or bond is a function of three variables: (1) the payment amounts, (2) the length of time until the amounts are paid, and (3) the discount rate. Our example uses a five-year bond issue.

The first variable (dollars to be paid) is made up of two elements: (1) a series of interest payments (an annuity) and (2) the principal amount (a single sum). To compute the present value of the bond, both the interest payments and the principal amount must be discounted—two different computations. The time diagrams for a bond due in five years are shown in Illustration G-17.

ILLUSTRATION G-17
Time diagrams for the present value of a bond

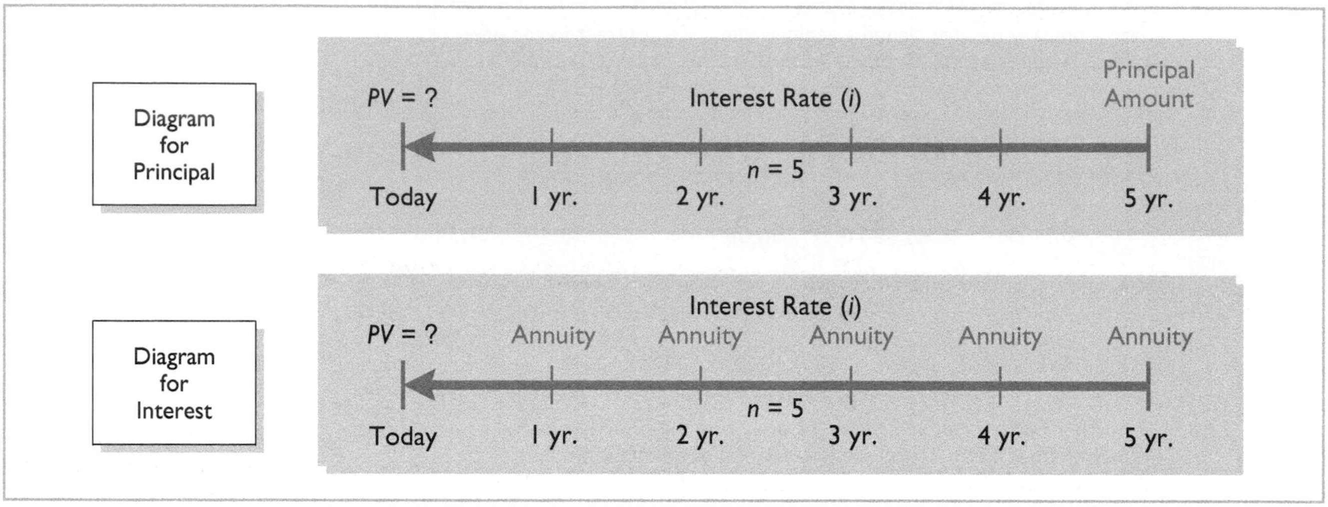

When the investor's market interest rate is equal to the bond's contractual interest rate, the present value of the bonds will equal the face value of the bonds. To illustrate, assume a bond issue of 10%, five-year bonds with a face value of $100,000 with interest payable **semiannually** on January 1 and July 1. If the discount rate is the same as the contractual rate, the bonds will sell at face value. In this case, the investor will receive (1) $100,000 at maturity and (2) a series of ten $5,000 interest payments [($100,000 × 10%) ÷ 2] over the term of the bonds. The length of time is expressed in terms of interest periods—in this case—10, and the discount rate per interest period, 5%. The following time diagram (Illustration G-18) depicts the variables involved in this discounting situation.

ILLUSTRATION G-18
Time diagram for present value of a 10%, five-year bond paying interest semiannually

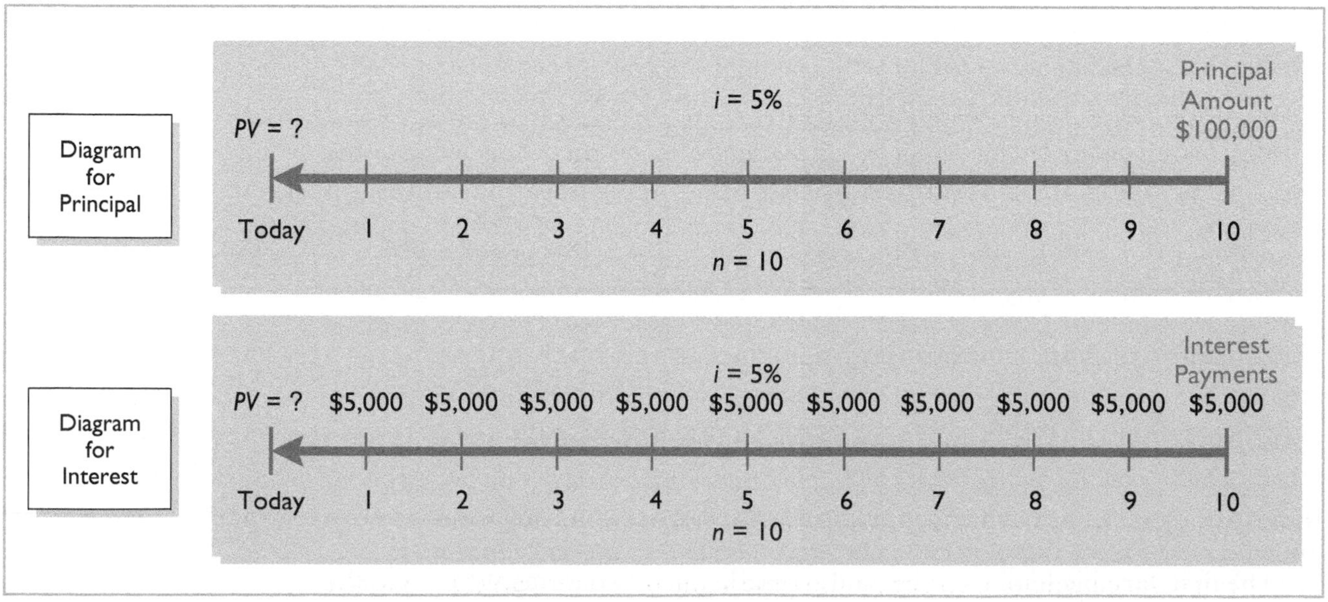

Illustration G-19 shows the computation of the present value of these bonds.

ILLUSTRATION G-19
Present value of principal and interest—face value

10% Contractual Rate—10% Discount Rate	
Present value of principal to be received at maturity	
$100,000 × *PV* of 1 due in 10 periods at 5%	
$100,000 × .61391 (Table 3)	$ 61,391
Present value of interest to be received periodically over the term of the bonds	
$5,000 × *PV* of 1 due periodically for 10 periods at 5%	
$5,000 × 7.72173 (Table 4)	38,609*
Present value of bonds	$100,000

*Rounded

Now assume that the investor's required rate of return is 12%, not 10%. The future amounts are again $100,000 and $5,000, respectively, but now a discount rate of 6% (12% ÷ 2) must be used. The present value of the bonds is $92,639, as computed in Illustration G-20.

ILLUSTRATION G-20
Present value of principal and interest—discount

10% Contractual Rate—12% Discount Rate	
Present value of principal to be received at maturity	
$100,000 × .55839 (Table 3)	$ 55,839
Present value of interest to be received periodically over the term of the bonds	
$5,000 × 7.36009 (Table 4)	36,800
Present value of bonds	$92,639

Conversely, if the discount rate is 8% and the contractual rate is 10%, the present value of the bonds is $108,111, computed as shown in Illustration G-21.

ILLUSTRATION G-21
Present value of principal and interest—premium

10% Contractual Rate—8% Discount Rate	
Present value of principal to be received at maturity	
$100,000 × .67556 (Table 3)	$ 67,556
Present value of interest to be received periodically over the term of the bonds	
$5,000 × 8.11090 (Table 4)	40,555
Present value of bonds	$108,111

The above discussion relied on present value tables in solving present value problems. Calculators may also be used to compute present values without the use of these tables. Many calculators, especially financial calculators, have present value (*PV*) functions that allow you to calculate present values by merely inputting the proper amount, discount rate, periods, and pressing the PV key. We discuss the use of financial calculators in the next section.

LEARNING OBJECTIVE ▶3

Use a financial calculator to solve time value of money problems.

Business professionals, once they have mastered the underlying time value of money concepts, often use a financial calculator to solve these types of problems. To use financial calculators, you enter the time value of money variables into the calculator. Illustration G-22 shows the five most common keys used to solve time value of money problems.[2]

ILLUSTRATION G-22
Financial calculator keys

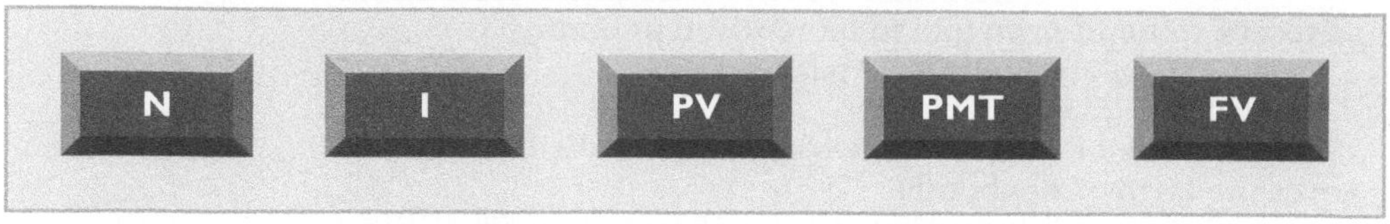

where:

N = number of periods
I = interest rate per period (some calculators use I/YR or i)
PV = present value (occurs at the beginning of the first period)
PMT = payment (all payments are equal, and none are skipped)
FV = future value (occurs at the end of the last period)

In solving time value of money problems in this appendix, you will generally be given three of four variables and will have to solve for the remaining variable. The fifth key (the key not used) is given a value of zero to ensure that this variable is not used in the computation.

PRESENT VALUE OF A SINGLE SUM

To illustrate how to solve a present value problem using a financial calculator, assume that you want to know the present value of $84,253 to be received in five years, discounted at 11% compounded annually. Illustration G-23 depicts this problem.

ILLUSTRATION G-23
Calculator solution for present value of a single sum

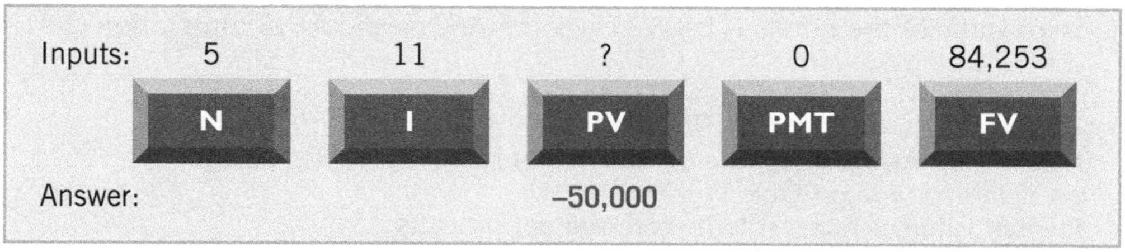

Illustration G-23 shows you the information (inputs) to enter into the calculator: N = 5, I = 11, PMT = 0, and FV = 84,253. You then press PV for the answer: −$50,000. As indicated, the PMT key was given a value of zero because a series of payments did not occur in this problem.

Plus and Minus

The use of plus and minus signs in time value of money problems with a financial calculator can be confusing. Most financial calculators are programmed so that the positive and negative cash flows in any problem offset each other. In the present value problem above, we identified the $84,253 future value initial investment as a positive (inflow); the answer −$50,000 was shown as a negative amount, reflecting a cash outflow. If the 84,253 were entered as a negative, then the final answer would have been reported as a positive 50,000.

Hopefully, the sign convention will not cause confusion. If you understand what is required in a problem, you should be able to interpret a positive or negative amount in determining the solution to a problem.

---

[2]On many calculators, these keys are actual buttons on the face of the calculator; on others, they appear on the display after the user accesses a present value menu.

Compounding Periods

In the previous problem, we assumed that compounding occurs once a year. Some financial calculators have a default setting, which assumes that compounding occurs 12 times a year. You must determine what default period has been programmed into your calculator and change it as necessary to arrive at the proper compounding period.

Rounding

Most financial calculators store and calculate using 12 decimal places. As a result, because compound interest tables generally have factors only up to five decimal places, a slight difference in the final answer can result. In most time value of money problems in this textbook, the final answer will not include more than two decimal places.

PRESENT VALUE OF AN ANNUITY

To illustrate how to solve a present value of an annuity problem using a financial calculator, assume that you are asked to determine the present value of rental receipts of $6,000 each to be received at the end of each of the next five years, when discounted at 12%, as pictured in Illustration G-24.

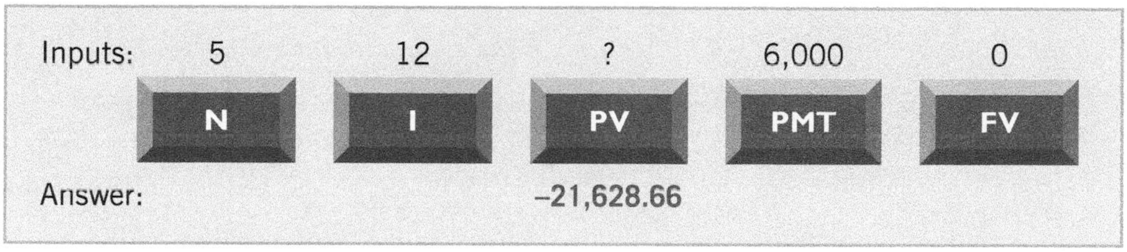

ILLUSTRATION G-24
Calculator solution for present value of an annuity

In this case, you enter N = 5, I = 12, PMT = 6,000, FV = 0, and then press PV to arrive at the answer of −$21,628.66.

USEFUL APPLICATIONS OF THE FINANCIAL CALCULATOR

With a financial calculator, you can solve for any interest rate or for any number of periods in a time value of money problem. Here are some examples of these applications.

Auto Loan

Assume you are financing the purchase of a used car with a three-year loan. The loan has a 9.5% stated annual interest rate, compounded monthly. The price of the car is $6,000, and you want to determine the monthly payments, assuming that the payments start one month after the purchase. This problem is pictured in Illustration G-25.

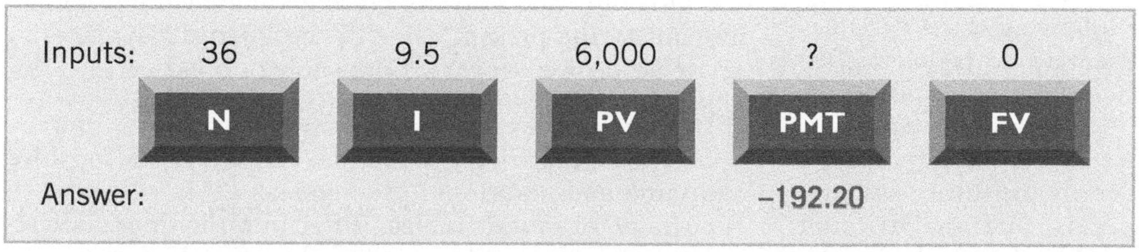

ILLUSTRATION G-25
Calculator solution for auto loan payments

To solve this problem, you enter N = 36 (12 × 3), I = 9.5, PV = 6,000, FV = 0, and then press PMT. You will find that the monthly payments will be $192.20. Note that the payment key is usually programmed for 12 payments per year. Thus, you must change the default (compounding period) if the payments are other than monthly.

Mortgage Loan Amount

Say you are evaluating financing options for a loan on a house (a mortgage). You decide that the maximum mortgage payment you can afford is $700 per month. The annual interest rate is 8.4%. If you get a mortgage that requires you to make monthly payments over a 15-year period, what is the maximum home loan you can afford? Illustration G-26 depicts this problem.

ILLUSTRATION G-26
Calculator solution for mortgage amount

Inputs:	180	8.4	?	–700	0
	N	I	PV	PMT	FV
Answer:			71,509.81		

You enter N = 180 (12 × 15 years), I = 8.4, PMT = −700, FV = 0, and press PV. With the payments-per-year key set at 12, you find a present value of $71,509.81—the maximum home loan you can afford, given that you want to keep your mortgage payments at $700. Note that by changing any of the variables, you can quickly conduct "what-if" analyses for different situations.

REVIEW

LEARNING OBJECTIVES REVIEW

1 Compute interest and future values. Simple interest is computed on the principal only, while compound interest is computed on the principal and any interest earned that has not been withdrawn.

To solve for future value of a single amount, prepare a time diagram of the problem. Identify the principal amount, the number of compounding periods, and the interest rate. Using the future value of 1 table, multiply the principal amount by the future value factor specified at the intersection of the number of periods and the interest rate.

To solve for future value of an annuity, prepare a time diagram of the problem. Identify the amount of the periodic payments (receipts), the number of payments (receipts), and the interest rate. Using the future value of an annuity of 1 table, multiply the amount of the payments by the future value factor specified at the intersection of the number of periods and the interest rate.

2 Compute present value. The following three variables are fundamental to solving present value problems: (1) the future amount, (2) the number of periods, and (3) the interest rate (the discount rate).

To solve for present value of a single amount, prepare a time diagram of the problem. Identify the future amount, the number of discounting periods, and the discount (interest) rate. Using the present value of a single amount table, multiply the future amount by the present value factor specified at the intersection of the number of periods and the discount rate.

To solve for present value of an annuity, prepare a time diagram of the problem. Identify the amount of future periodic receipts or payments (annuities), the number of payments (receipts), and the discount (interest) rate. Using the present value of an annuity of 1 table, multiply the amount of the annuity by the present value factor specified at the intersection of the number of payments and the interest rate.

To compute the present value of notes and bonds, determine the present value of the principal amount and the present value of the interest payments. Multiply the principal amount (a single future amount) by the present value factor (from the present value of 1 table) intersecting at the number of periods (number of interest payments) and the discount rate. To determine the present value of the series of interest payments, multiply the amount of the interest payment by the present value factor (from the present value of an annuity of 1 table) intersecting at the number of periods (number of interest payments) and the discount rate. Add the present value of the principal amount to the present value of the interest payments to arrive at the present value of the note or bond.

3 Use a financial calculator to solve time value of money problems. Financial calculators can be used to solve the same and additional problems as those solved with time value of money tables. Enter into the financial calculator the amounts for all of the known elements of a time value of money problem (periods, interest rate, payments, future or present value), and it solves for the unknown element. Particularly useful situations involve interest rates and compounding periods not presented in the tables.

GLOSSARY REVIEW

Annuity A series of equal dollar amounts to be paid or received at evenly spaced time intervals (periodically). (p. G-5).

Compound interest The interest computed on the principal and any interest earned that has not been paid or withdrawn. (p. G-2).

Discounting the future amount(s) The process of determining present value. (p. G-7).

Future value of an annuity The sum of all the payments (receipts) plus the accumulated compound interest on them. (p. G-5).

Future value of a single amount The value at a future date of a given amount invested, assuming compound interest. (p. G-3).

Interest Payment for the use of another person's money. (p. G-1).

Present value The value now of a given amount to be paid or received in the future, assuming compound interest. (p. G-7).

Present value of an annuity The value now of a series of future receipts or payments, discounted assuming compound interest. (p. G-9).

Principal The amount borrowed or invested. (p. G-1).

Simple interest The interest computed on the principal only. (p. G-2).

BRIEF EXERCISES

(Use tables to solve exercises BEG-1 to BEG-23.)

Compute the future value of a single amount. (LO 1), AP

BEG-1 Jozy Altidore invested $6,000 at 5% annual interest, and left the money invested without withdrawing any of the interest for 12 years. At the end of the 12 years, Jozy withdrew the accumulated amount of money. (a) What amount did Jozy withdraw, assuming the investment earns simple interest? (b) What amount did Jozy withdraw, assuming the investment earns interest compounded annually?

Use future value tables. (LO 1), C

BEG-2 For each of the following cases, indicate (a) what interest rate columns and (b) what number of periods you would refer to in looking up the future value factor.

(1) In Table 1 (future value of 1):

	Annual Rate	Number of Years Invested	Compounded
Case A	5%	3	Annually
Case B	12%	4	Semiannually

(2) In Table 2 (future value of an annuity of 1):

	Annual Rate	Number of Years Invested	Compounded
Case A	3%	8	Annually
Case B	8%	6	Semiannually

Compute the future value of a single amount. (LO 1), AP

BEG-3 Liam Company signed a lease for an office building for a period of 12 years. Under the lease agreement, a security deposit of $9,600 is made. The deposit will be returned at the expiration of the lease with interest compounded at 4% per year. What amount will Liam receive at the time the lease expires?

Compute the future value of an annuity.
(LO 1), AP

BEG-4 Bates Company issued $1,000,000, 10-year bonds and agreed to make annual sinking fund deposits of $78,000. The deposits are made at the end of each year into an account paying 6% annual interest. What amount will be in the sinking fund at the end of 10 years?

Compute the future value of a single amount and of an annuity.
(LO 1), AP

BEG-5 Andrew and Emma Garfield invested $8,000 in a savings account paying 5% annual interest when their daughter, Angela, was born. They also deposited $1,000 on each of her birthdays until she was 18 (including her 18th birthday). How much was in the savings account on her 18th birthday (after the last deposit)?

Compute the future value of a single amount.
(LO 1), AP

BEG-6 Hugh Curtin borrowed $35,000 on July 1, 2017. This amount plus accrued interest at 8% compounded annually is to be repaid on July 1, 2022. How much will Hugh have to repay on July 1, 2022?

Compute the annuity payment amount of a known future value.
(LO 1), AP

BEG-7 Sara has just graduated from college. She has determined that to purchase a home in 8 years she needs to accumulate $20,000 for a down payment. If Sara can earn 6% per year on her savings, what is the amount of the annual annuity payment that Sara must make at the end of each year for 8 years?

Use present value tables.
(LO 2), C

BEG-8 For each of the following cases, indicate (a) what interest rate columns and (b) what number of periods you would refer to in looking up the discount rate.

(1) In Table 3 (present value of 1):

	Annual Rate	Number of Years Involved	Discounts per Year
Case A	12%	7	Annually
Case B	8%	11	Annually
Case C	10%	8	Semiannually

(2) In Table 4 (present value of an annuity of 1):

	Annual Rate	Number of Years Involved	Number of Payments Involved	Frequency of Payments
Case A	10%	20	20	Annually
Case B	10%	7	7	Annually
Case C	6%	5	10	Semiannually

Determine present values.
(LO 2), AP

BEG-9 (a) What is the present value of $25,000 due 9 periods from now, discounted at 10%?
(b) What is the present value of $25,000 to be received at the end of each of 6 periods, discounted at 9%?

Compute the present value of a single amount investment.
(LO 2), AP

BEG-10 Messi Company is considering an investment that will return a lump sum of $900,000 6 years from now. What amount should Messi Company pay for this investment to earn an 8% return?

Compute the present value of a single amount investment.
(LO 2), AP

BEG-11 Lloyd Company earns 6% on an investment that will return $450,000 8 years from now. What is the amount Lloyd should invest now to earn this rate of return?

Compute the present value of an annuity investment.
(LO 2), AP

BEG-12 Robben Company is considering investing in an annuity contract that will return $40,000 annually at the end of each year for 15 years. What amount should Robben Company pay for this investment if it earns an 8% return?

Compute the present value of an annual investment.
(LO 2), AP

BEG-13 Kaehler Enterprises earns 5% on an investment that pays back $80,000 at the end of each of the next 6 years. What is the amount Kaehler Enterprises invested to earn the 5% rate of return?

Compute the present value of bonds.
(LO 2), AP

BEG-14 Dempsey Railroad Co. is about to issue $400,000 of 10-year bonds paying an 11% interest rate, with interest payable semiannually. The discount rate for such securities is 10%. How much can Dempsey expect to receive for the sale of these bonds?

Compute the present value of bonds.
(LO 2), AP

BEG-15 Assume the same information as BEG-14 except that the discount rate is 12% instead of 10%. In this case, how much can Dempsey expect to receive from the sale of these bonds?

BEG-16 Neymar Taco Company receives a $75,000, 6-year note bearing interest of 4% (paid annually) from a customer at a time when the discount rate is 6%. What is the present value of the note received by Neymar?

Compute the present value of a note.
(LO 2), AP

BEG-17 Gleason Enterprises issued 6%, 8-year, $2,500,000 par value bonds that pay interest semiannually on October 1 and April 1. The bonds are dated April 1, 2017, and are issued on that date. The discount rate of interest for such bonds on April 1, 2017, is 8%. What cash proceeds did Gleason receive from issuance of the bonds?

Compute the present value of bonds.
(LO 2), AP

BEG-18 Frazier Company issues a 10%, 5-year mortgage note on January 1, 2017, to obtain financing for new equipment. Land is used as collateral for the note. The terms provide for semiannual installment payments of $48,850. What are the cash proceeds received from the issuance of the note?

Compute the present value of a note.
(LO 2), AP

BEG-19 If Colleen Mooney invests $4,765.50 now and she will receive $12,000 at the end of 12 years, what annual rate of interest will Colleen earn on her investment? (*Hint:* Use Table 3.)

Compute the interest rate on a single amount.
(LO 2), AP

BEG-20 Tim Howard has been offered the opportunity of investing $36,125 now. The investment will earn 11% per year and at the end of that time will return Tim $75,000. How many years must Tim wait to receive $75,000? (*Hint:* Use Table 3.)

Compute the number of periods of a single amount.
(LO 2), AP

BEG-21 Joanne Quick made an investment of $10,271.38. From this investment, she will receive $1,200 annually for the next 15 years starting one year from now. What rate of interest will Joanne's investment be earning for her? (*Hint:* Use Table 4.)

Compute the interest rate on an annuity.
(LO 2), AP

BEG-22 Kevin Morales invests $7,793.83 now for a series of $1,300 annual returns beginning one year from now. Kevin will earn a return of 9% on the initial investment. How many annual payments of $1,300 will Kevin receive? (*Hint:* Use Table 4.)

Compute the number of periods of an annuity.
(LO 2), AP

BEG-23 Sophie Corp. purchased a new blending machine for $3,150.15. It paid $500 down and financed the remaining $2,650.15. It is required to pay 10 annual payments at the end of each year at an annual rate of interest of 11%. What is the amount of the annual payment?

Compute the annuity payment amount of a known present value.
(LO 2), AP

BEG-24 Carly Simon wishes to invest $18,000 on July 1, 2017, and have it accumulate to $50,000 by July 1, 2027. Use a financial calculator to determine at what exact annual rate of interest Carly must invest the $18,000.

Determine interest rate.
(LO 3), AP

BEG-25 On July 17, 2016, Keith Urban borrowed $42,000 from his grandfather to open a clothing store. Starting July 17, 2017, Keith has to make 10 equal annual payments of $6,500 each to repay the loan. Use a financial calculator to determine what interest rate Keith is paying.

Determine interest rate.
(LO 3), AP

BEG-26 As the purchaser of a new house, Carrie Underwood has signed a mortgage note to pay the Nashville National Bank and Trust Co. $8,400 every 6 months for 20 years, at the end of which time she will own the house. At the date the mortgage is signed, the purchase price was $198,000 and Underwood made a down payment of $20,000. The first payment will be made 6 months after the date the mortgage is signed. Using a financial calculator, compute the exact rate of interest earned on the mortgage by the bank.

Determine interest rate.
(LO 3), AP

BEG-27 Using a financial calculator, solve for the unknowns in each of the following situations.

(a) On June 1, 2016, Jennifer Lawrence purchases lakefront property from her neighbor, Josh Hutcherson, and agrees to pay the purchase price in seven payments of $16,000 each, the first payment to be payable June 1, 2017. (Assume that interest compounded at an annual rate of 7.35% is implicit in the payments.) What is the purchase price of the property?

Various time value of money situations.
(LO 3), AP

(b) On January 1, 2016, Gerrard Corporation purchased 200 of the $1,000 face value, 8% coupon, 10-year bonds of Sterling Inc. The bonds mature on January 1, 2026, and pay interest annually beginning January 1, 2017. Gerrard purchased the bonds to yield 10.65%. How much did Gerrard pay for the bonds?

Various time value of money situations.

(LO 3), AP

BEG-28 Using a financial calculator, provide a solution to each of the following situations.

(a) Lynn Anglin owes a debt of $42,000 from the purchase of her new sport utility vehicle. The debt bears annual interest of 7.8% compounded monthly. Lynn wishes to pay the debt and interest in equal monthly payments over 8 years, beginning one month hence. What equal monthly payments will pay off the debt and interest?

(b) On January 1, 2017, Roger Molony offers to buy Dave Feeney's used snowmobile for $8,000, payable in five equal annual installments, which are to include 7.25% interest on the unpaid balance and a portion of the principal. If the first payment is to be made on December 31, 2017, how much will each payment be?

H

Reporting and Analyzing Investments

APPENDIX PREVIEW

Some companies believe in aggressive growth through investing in the stock of existing companies. Besides purchasing stock, companies also purchase other securities such as bonds issued by corporations or by governments. Companies can make investments for a short or long period of time, as a passive investment, or with the intent to control another company. As you will see in this appendix, the way in which a company accounts for its investments is determined by a number of factors.

APPENDIX OUTLINE

LEARNING OBJECTIVES	
1 Explain how to account for debt investments.	• Why corporations invest • Accounting for debt investments
2 Explain how to account for stock investments.	• Holdings of less than 20% • Holdings between 20% and 50% • Holdings of more than 50%
3 Discuss how debt and stock investments are reported in the financial statements.	• Categories of securities • Balance sheet presentation • Presentation of realized and unrealized gain or loss • Statement of cash flows presentation

LEARNING OBJECTIVE 1 **Explain how to account for debt investments.**

WHY CORPORATIONS INVEST

Corporations purchase investments in debt or equity securities generally for one of three reasons. First, a corporation may **have excess cash** that it does not need for the immediate purchase of operating assets. For example, many companies experience seasonal fluctuations in sales. A Cape Cod marina has more sales in the spring and summer than in the fall and winter. The reverse is true for an Aspen ski shop. Thus, at the end of an operating cycle, many companies may have cash on hand that is temporarily idle until the start of another operating cycle. These companies may invest the excess funds to earn—through interest and dividends—a greater return than they would get by just holding the funds in the bank. Illustration H-1 shows the role that such temporary investments play in the operating cycle.

ILLUSTRATION H-1
Temporary investments and the operating cycle

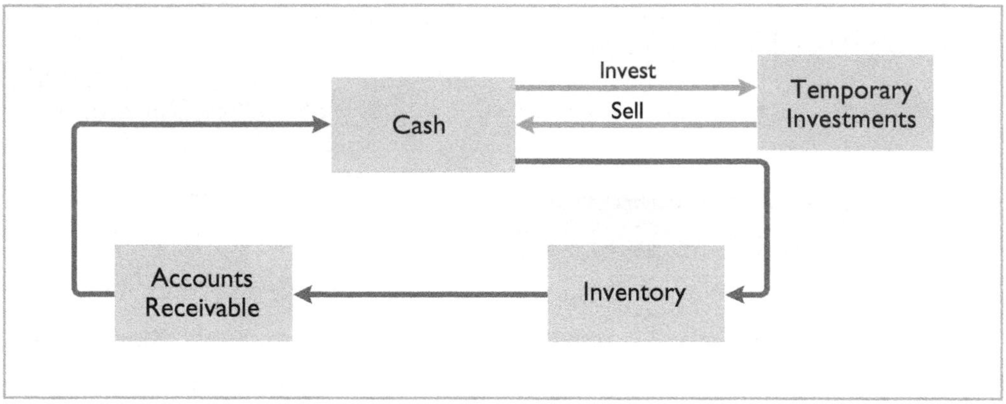

A second reason some companies such as banks purchase investments is to generate **earnings from investment income**. Although banks make most of their earnings by lending money, they also generate earnings by investing in primarily debt securities. Banks purchase investment securities because loan demand varies both seasonally and with changes in the economic climate. Thus, when loan demand is low, a bank must find other uses for its cash.

Some companies attempt to generate investment income through speculative investments. That is, they are speculating that the investment will increase in value and thus result in positive returns. Therefore, they invest mostly in the common stock of other corporations.

Third, companies also invest for **strategic reasons**. A company may purchase a noncontrolling interest in another company in a related industry in which it wishes to establish a presence. Or, a company can exercise some influence over one of its customers or suppliers by purchasing a significant, but not controlling, interest in that company. Another option is for a corporation to purchase a controlling interest in another company in order to enter a new industry without incurring the costs and risks associated with starting from scratch.

In summary, businesses invest in other companies for the reasons shown in Illustration H-2.

ILLUSTRATION H-2
Why corporations invest

Reason	Typical Investment
To house excess cash until needed 	Low-risk, highly liquid, short-term securities such as government-issued securities
To generate earnings 	Banks and financial institutions often purchase debt securities, while mutual funds and index funds purchase both debt and stock securities
To meet strategic goals 	Stocks of companies in a related industry or in an unrelated industry that the company wishes to enter

ACCOUNTING FOR DEBT INVESTMENTS

Debt investments are investments in government and corporation bonds. In accounting for debt investments, companies must make entries to record (1) the acquisition, (2) the interest revenue, and (3) the sale.

Recording Acquisition of Bonds

At acquisition, debt investments are recorded at cost. Cost includes all expenditures necessary to acquire these investments, such as the price paid plus brokerage fees (commissions), if any.

For example, assume that Kuhl Corporation acquires 50 Doan Inc. 8%, 10-year, $1,000 bonds on January 1, 2017, at a cost of $50,000. Kuhl records the investment as:

Jan. 1	Debt Investments	50,000	
	Cash		50,000
	(To record purchase of 50 Doan Inc. bonds)		

A = L + SE
+50,000
−50,000
Cash Flows
−50,000

Recording Bond Interest

The Doan Inc. bonds pay interest of $4,000 annually on January 1 ($50,000 × 8%). If Kuhl Corporation's fiscal year ends on December 31, it accrues the interest of $4,000 earned since January 1. The adjusting entry is:

Dec. 31	Interest Receivable	4,000	
	Interest Revenue		4,000
	(To accrue interest on Doan Inc. bonds)		

A = L + SE
+4,000
+4,000 Rev
Cash Flows
no effect

Kuhl reports Interest Receivable as a current asset in the balance sheet. It reports Interest Revenue under "Other revenues and gains" in the income statement.

Kuhl records receipt of the interest on January 1 as follows.

Jan. 1	Cash	4,000	
	Interest Receivable		4,000
	(To record receipt of accrued interest)		

A = L + SE
+4,000
−4,000
Cash Flows
+4,000

A credit to Interest Revenue at this time would be incorrect. Why? Because the company earned and accrued the interest revenue in the preceding accounting period.

Recording Sale of Bonds

When Kuhl Corporation sells the bond investments, it credits the investment account for the cost of the bonds. The company records as a gain or loss any difference between the net proceeds from the sale (sales price less brokerage fees) and the cost of the bonds.

Assume, for example, that Kuhl receives net proceeds of $54,000 on the sale of the Doan Inc. bonds on January 1, 2018, after receiving the interest due. Since the securities cost $50,000, Kuhl has realized a gain of $4,000. It records the sale as follows.

▼ HELPFUL HINT
The accounting for short-term debt investments and long-term debt investments is similar. Any exceptions are discussed in more advanced courses.

Jan. 1	Cash	54,000	
	Debt Investments		50,000
	Gain on Sale of Debt Investments		4,000
	(To record sale of Doan Inc. bonds)		

A = L + SE
+54,000
−50,000
+4,000 Rev
Cash Flows
+54,000

Kuhl reports the gain on the sale of debt investments under "Other revenues and gains" in the income statement and reports losses under "Other expenses and losses."

LEARNING OBJECTIVE **2**

Explain how to account for stock investments.

Stock investments are investments in the capital stock of corporations. When a company holds stock (and/or debt) of several different corporations, the group of securities is an **investment portfolio**.

The accounting for investments in common stock depends on the extent of the investor's influence over the operating and financial affairs of the issuing corporation (the **investee**). Illustration H-3 shows the general guidelines.

ILLUSTRATION H-3
Accounting guidelines for stock investments

Investor's Ownership Interest in Investee's Common Stock	Presumed Influence on Investee	Accounting Guidelines
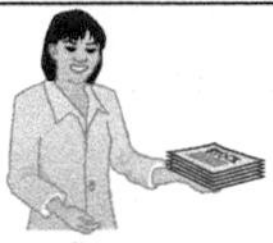 Less than 20%	Insignificant	Cost method
 Between 20% and 50%	Significant	Equity method
 More than 50%	Controlling	Consolidated financial statements

Companies are required to use judgment instead of blindly following the guidelines.[1] We explain and illustrate the application of each guideline next.

HOLDINGS OF LESS THAN 20%

In the accounting for stock investments of less than 20%, companies use the cost method. Under the **cost method**, companies record the investment at cost and recognize revenue only when cash dividends are received.

Recording Acquisition of Stock

At acquisition, stock investments are recorded at cost. Cost includes all expenditures necessary to acquire these investments, such as the price paid plus brokerage fees (commissions), if any.

Assume, for example, that on July 1, 2017, Sanchez Corporation acquires 1,000 shares (10% ownership) of Beal Corporation common stock at $40 per share. The entry for the purchase is:

A	=	L	+	SE
+40,000				
−40,000				

Cash Flows
−40,000

July 1	Stock Investments	40,000	
	Cash		40,000
	(To record purchase of 1,000 shares of Beal common stock)		

[1]Among the factors that companies should consider in determining an investor's influence are whether (1) the investor has representation on the investee's board of directors, (2) the investor participates in the investee's policy-making process, (3) there are material transactions between the investor and the investee, and (4) the common stock held by other stockholders is concentrated or dispersed.

Recording Dividends

During the time the company holds the stock, it makes entries for any cash dividends received. Thus, if Sanchez Corporation receives a $2 per share dividend on December 31, the entry is:

Dec. 31	Cash (1,000 × $2)	2,000	
	Dividend Revenue		2,000
	(To record receipt of a cash dividend)		

A	=	L	+	SE
+2,000				
				+2,000 Rev

Cash Flows
+2,000

Sanchez reports Dividend Revenue under "Other revenues and gains" in the income statement.

Recording Sale of Stock

When a company sells a stock investment, it recognizes the difference between the net proceeds from the sale (sales price less brokerage fees) and the cost of the stock as a gain or a loss.

Assume, for instance, that Sanchez Corporation receives net proceeds of $39,500 on the sale of its Beal Corporation stock on February 10, 2018. Because the stock cost $40,000, Sanchez has incurred a loss of $500. It records the sale as:

Feb. 10	Cash	39,500	
	Loss on Sale of Stock Investments	500	
	Stock Investments		40,000
	(To record sale of Beal common stock)		

A	=	L	+	SE
+39,500				
				−500 Exp
−40,000				

Cash Flows
+39,500

Sanchez reports the loss account under "Other expenses and losses" in the income statement and shows a gain on sale under "Other revenues and gains."

HOLDINGS BETWEEN 20% AND 50%

When an investor company owns only a small portion of the shares of stock of another company, the investor cannot exercise control over the investee. But when an investor owns between 20% and 50% of the common stock of a corporation, it is presumed that the investor has significant influence over the financial and operating activities of the investee. The investor probably has a representative on the investee's board of directors. Through that representative, the investor begins to exercise some control over the investee—and the investee company in some sense becomes part of the investor company.

For example, even prior to purchasing all of Turner Broadcasting, Time Warner owned 20% of Turner. Because it exercised significant control over major decisions made by Turner, Time Warner used an approach called the equity method. Under the **equity method, the investor records its share of the net income of the investee in the year when it is earned**. An alternative might be to delay recognizing the investor's share of net income until a cash dividend is declared. But that approach would ignore the fact that the investor and investee are, in some sense, one company, making the investor better off by the investee's earned income.

Under the **equity method**, the company initially records the investment in common stock at cost. After that, it adjusts the investment account **annually** to show the investor's equity in the investee. Each year, the investor does the following. (1) It increases (debits) the investment account and increases (credits) revenue for its share of the investee's net income.[2] (2) The investor also decreases (credits) the investment account for the amount of dividends received. The investment account is reduced for dividends received because payment of a dividend decreases the net assets of the investee.

[2]Conversely, the investor increases (debits) a loss account and decreases (credits) the investment account for its share of the investee's net loss.

Recording Acquisition of Stock

Assume that Milar Corporation acquires 30% of the common stock of Beck Company for $120,000 on January 1, 2017. The entry to record this transaction is:

A	=	L	+	SE
+120,000				
−120,000				

Cash Flows
−120,000

Jan. 1	Stock Investments	120,000	
	Cash		120,000
	(To record purchase of Beck common stock)		

Recording Revenue and Dividends

For 2017, Beck reports net income of $100,000. It declares and pays a $40,000 cash dividend. Milar must record (1) its share of Beck's income, $30,000 (30% × $100,000), and (2) the reduction in the investment account for the dividends received, $12,000 (30% × $40,000). The entries are:

A	=	L	+	SE
+30,000				+30,000 Rev

Cash Flows
no effect

(1)

Dec. 31	Stock Investments	30,000	
	Revenue from Stock Investments		30,000
	(To record 30% equity in Beck's 2017 net income)		

A	=	L	+	SE
+12,000				
−12,000				

Cash Flows
+12,000

(2)

Dec. 31	Cash	12,000	
	Stock Investments		12,000
	(To record dividends received)		

After Milar posts the transactions for the year, the investment and revenue accounts are as shown in Illustration H-4.

ILLUSTRATION H-4
Investment and revenue accounts after posting

Stock Investments

Jan. 1	120,000	Dec. 31	12,000
Dec. 31	30,000		
Dec. 31	Bal. 138,000		

Revenue from Stock Investments

		Dec. 31	30,000

During the year, the investment account increased by $18,000. This $18,000 is explained as follows: (1) Milar records a $30,000 increase in revenue from its stock investment in Beck, and (2) Milar records a $12,000 decrease due to dividends received from its stock investment in Beck.

Note that the difference between reported revenue under the cost method and reported revenue under the equity method can be significant. For example, Milar would report only $12,000 of dividend revenue (30% × $40,000) if it used the cost method.

HOLDINGS OF MORE THAN 50%

A company that owns more than 50% of the common stock of another entity is known as the **parent company**. The entity whose stock is owned by the parent company is called the **subsidiary (affiliated) company**. Because of its stock ownership, the parent company has a **controlling interest** in the subsidiary company.

When a company owns more than 50% of the common stock of another company, it usually prepares **consolidated financial statements**. Consolidated financial statements present the assets and liabilities controlled by the parent company. They also present the total revenues and expenses of the subsidiary companies. Companies prepare consolidated statements **in addition to** the financial statements for the individual parent and subsidiary companies.

As noted earlier, prior to acquiring all of Turner Broadcasting, Time Warner accounted for its investment in Turner using the equity method. Time Warner's net investment in Turner was reported in a single line item—Other investments. After the merger, Time Warner instead consolidated Turner's results with its own. Under this approach, Time Warner included the individual assets and liabilities of Turner with its own assets. That is, Turner's plant and equipment were added to Time Warner's plant and equipment, its receivables were added to Time Warner's receivables, and so on. A similar sort of consolidation went on when AOL merged with Time Warner.

▼ **HELPFUL HINT**
If the parent (A) has three wholly owned subsidiaries (B, C, and D), there are four separate legal entities but only one economic entity from the viewpoint of the shareholders of the parent company.

Consolidated statements are useful to the stockholders, board of directors, and management of the parent company. Consolidated statements indicate to creditors, prospective investors, and regulatory agencies the magnitude and scope of operations of the companies under common control. For example, regulators and the courts undoubtedly used the consolidated statements of AT&T to determine whether a breakup of the company was in the public interest. Illustration H-5 lists three companies that prepare consolidated statements and some of the companies they have owned.

ILLUSTRATION H-5
Examples of consolidated companies and their subsidiaries

PepsiCo	Cendant	The Walt Disney Company
Frito-Lay	Howard Johnson	Capital Cities/ABC, Inc.
Tropicana	Ramada Inn	Disneyland, Disney World
Quaker Oats	Century 21	Mighty Ducks
Pepsi-Cola	Coldwell Banker	Anaheim Angels
Gatorade	Avis	ESPN

LEARNING OBJECTIVE ▶3 **Discuss how debt and stock investments are reported in the financial statements.**

The value of debt and stock investments may fluctuate greatly during the time they are held. For example, in a 12-month period, the stock of Time Warner hit a high of 58½ and a low of 9. In light of such price fluctuations, how should companies value investments at the balance sheet date? Valuation could be at cost, at fair value, or at the lower-of-cost-or-market value.

Many people argue that fair value offers the best approach because it represents the expected cash realizable value of securities. **Fair value** is the amount for which a security could be sold in a normal market. Others counter that unless a security is going to be sold soon, the fair value is not relevant because the price of the security will likely change again.

CATEGORIES OF SECURITIES

For purposes of valuation and reporting at a financial statement date, debt and stock investments are classified into three categories of securities[3]:

INTERNATIONAL NOTE
A recent U.S. accounting standard gives companies the "option" of applying fair value accounting, rather than historical cost, to certain types of assets and liabilities. This makes U.S. accounting closer to international standards.

1. **Trading securities** are bought and held primarily for sale in the near term to generate income on short-term price differences.
2. **Available-for-sale securities** are held with the intent of selling them sometime in the future.
3. **Held-to-maturity securities** are debt securities that the investor has the intent and ability to hold to maturity.[4]

[3]The FASB is currently considering a new approach to reporting investment securities. If adopted, the new approach could significantly change the reporting of investments.

[4]This category is provided for completeness. The accounting and valuation issues related to held-to-maturity securities are discussed in more advanced accounting courses.

Illustration H-6 shows the valuation guidelines for these securities. **These guidelines apply to all debt securities and to those stock investments in which the holdings are less than 20%.**

ILLUSTRATION H-6
Valuation guidelines for securities

Trading
(both debt and stock)

At fair value with changes reported in net income

Available-for-Sale
(both debt and stock)

At fair value with changes reported in the stockholders' equity section

Held-to-Maturity
(debt only)

At amortized cost

Trading Securities

Trading securities are held with the intention of selling them in a short period of time (generally less than three months and sometimes less than a full day). **Trading** means frequent buying and selling. As indicated in Illustration H-6, companies adjust trading securities to fair value at the end of each period (an approach referred to as **mark-to-market** accounting). They report changes from cost **as part of net income**. The changes are reported as **unrealized gains or losses** because the securities have not been sold. The unrealized gain or loss is the difference between the **total cost** of trading securities and their **total fair value**. Companies classify trading securities as a current asset.

As an example, Illustration H-7 shows the costs and fair values for investments classified as trading securities for Pace Corporation on December 31, 2017. Pace has an unrealized gain of $7,000 because total fair value ($147,000) is $7,000 greater than total cost ($140,000).

ILLUSTRATION H-7
Valuation of trading securities

Trading Securities, December 31, 2017

Investments	Cost	Fair Value	Unrealized Gain (Loss)
Yorkville Company bonds	$ 50,000	$ 48,000	$(2,000)
Kodak Company stock	90,000	99,000	9,000
Total	$140,000	$147,000	$ 7,000

▼ HELPFUL HINT
Companies report an unrealized gain or loss in the income statement because of the likelihood that the securities will be sold at fair value since they are a short-term investment.

The fact that trading securities are a short-term investment increases the likelihood that Pace will sell them at fair value for a gain. Pace records fair value and the unrealized gain through an adjusting entry at the time it prepares financial statements. In this entry, the company uses a valuation allowance account, Fair Value Adjustment—Trading, to record the difference between the total cost and the total fair value of the securities. The adjusting entry for Pace is:

A	=	L	+	SE
+7,000				
				+7,000 Rev

Cash Flows
no effect

Dec. 31	Fair Value Adjustment—Trading	7,000	
	Unrealized Gain—Income		7,000
	(To record unrealized gain on trading securities)		

The use of the Fair Value Adjustment—Trading account enables the company to maintain a record of the investment cost. Actual cost is needed to determine the gain or loss realized when the securities are sold. The company adds the debit balance (or subtracts a credit balance) of the Fair Value Adjustment—Trading account to the cost of the investments to arrive at a fair value for the trading securities.

The fair value of the securities is the amount companies report on the balance sheet. They report the unrealized gain on the income statement under "Other revenues and gains." The term **income** in the account title indicates that the gain affects net income.

If the total cost of the trading securities is greater than total fair value, an unrealized loss has occurred. In such a case, the adjusting entry is a debit to Unrealized Loss—Income and a credit to Fair Value Adjustment—Trading. Companies report the unrealized loss under "Other expenses and losses" in the income statement.

The fair value adjustment account is carried forward into future accounting periods. No entries are made to this account during the period. At the end of each reporting period, a company adjusts the balance in the account to the difference between cost and fair value at that time. It closes the Unrealized Gain—Income account or Unrealized Loss—Income account at the end of the reporting period.

Available-for-Sale Securities

As indicated earlier, available-for-sale securities are held with the intent of selling them sometime in the future. If the intent is to sell the securities within the next year or operating cycle, a company classifies the securities as current assets in the balance sheet. Otherwise, it classifies them as long-term assets in the investments section of the balance sheet.

Companies also report available-for-sale securities at fair value. The procedure for determining fair value and unrealized gain or loss for these securities is the same as that for trading securities. To illustrate, assume that Elbert Corporation has two securities that are classified as available-for-sale. Illustration H-8 provides information on the cost, fair value, and amount of the unrealized gain or loss on December 31, 2017. There is an unrealized loss of $9,537 because total cost ($293,537) is $9,537 more than total fair value ($284,000).

ILLUSTRATION H-8
Valuation of available-for-sale securities

Available-for-Sale Securities, December 31, 2017

Investments	Cost	Fair Value	Unrealized Gain (Loss)
Campbell Soup Corporation 8% bonds	$ 93,537	$103,600	$10,063
Hershey Foods stock	200,000	180,400	(19,600)
Total	$293,537	$284,000	$ (9,537)

Both the adjusting entry and the reporting of the unrealized loss from Elbert's available-for-sale securities differ from those illustrated for trading securities. The differences result because these securities are not going to be sold in the near term. Thus, prior to actual sale it is much more likely that changes in fair value may reverse the unrealized loss. Therefore, Elbert does not report an unrealized loss in the income statement. Instead, the company reports it as an item of other comprehensive income in the comprehensive income statement, as discussed in Chapter 5. In the adjusting entry, Elbert identifies the fair value adjustment account with available-for-sale securities, and identifies the unrealized gain or loss account with stockholders' equity. The adjusting entry for Elbert to record the unrealized loss of $9,537 is:

▼ **HELPFUL HINT**
The entry is the same regardless of whether the securities are considered short-term or long-term.

Dec. 31	Unrealized Gain or Loss—Equity	9,537	
	Fair Value Adjustment—Available-for-Sale		9,537
	(To record unrealized loss on available-for-sale securities)		

A	=	L	+	SE
				−9,537 Eq
−9,537				

Cash Flows
no effect

If total fair value exceeds total cost, Elbert would record the adjusting entry as an increase (debit) to Fair Value Adjustment—Available-for-Sale and a credit to Unrealized Gain or Loss—Equity.

Elbert's unrealized loss of $9,537 would appear in the comprehensive income statement as shown in Illustration H-9.

ILLUSTRATION H-9
Comprehensive income statement

ELBERT CORPORATION Comprehensive Income Statement For the Year Ended December 31, 2017	
Net income	$118,000
Other comprehensive income	
Unrealized loss on available-for-sale securities	(9,537)
Comprehensive income	$108,463

ETHICS NOTE
Recently, the SEC accused investment bank Morgan Stanley of overstating the value of certain bond investments by $75 million. The SEC stated that, in applying fair value accounting, Morgan Stanley used its own more optimistic assumptions rather than relying on external pricing sources.

For available-for-sale securities, the company carries forward the Unrealized Gain or Loss—Equity account to future periods. At each future balance sheet date, the account is adjusted with the fair value adjustment account to show the difference between cost and fair value at that time.

BALANCE SHEET PRESENTATION

In the balance sheet presentation, companies must classify investments as either short-term or long-term.

Short-Term Investments

Short-term investments (also called **marketable securities**) are securities held by a company that are (1) **readily marketable** and (2) **intended to be converted into cash** within the next year or operating cycle, whichever is longer. Investments that do not meet **both criteria** are classified as **long-term investments**.

▼ HELPFUL HINT
Trading securities are always classified as short-term. Available-for-sale securities can be either short-term or long-term.

READILY MARKETABLE **An investment is readily marketable when it can be sold easily whenever the need for cash arises.** Short-term paper[5] meets this criterion because a company can readily sell it to other investors. Stocks and bonds traded on organized securities markets, such as the New York Stock Exchange, are readily marketable because they can be bought and sold daily. In contrast, there may be only a limited market for the securities issued by small corporations and no market for the securities of a privately held company.

INTENT TO CONVERT **Intent to convert means that management intends to sell the investment within the next year or operating cycle, whichever is longer.** Generally, this criterion is satisfied when the investment is considered a resource that the company will use whenever the need for cash arises. For example, a ski resort may invest idle cash during the summer months with the intent to sell the securities to buy supplies and equipment shortly before the next winter season. This investment is considered short-term even if lack of snow cancels the next ski season and eliminates the need to convert the securities into cash as intended.

Because of their high liquidity, companies list short-term investments immediately below Cash in the current assets section of the balance sheet. Short-term investments are reported at fair value. For example, Weber Corporation would report its trading securities as shown in Illustration H-10.

[5]Short-term paper includes (1) certificates of deposits (CDs) issued by banks, (2) money market certificates issued by banks and savings and loan associations, (3) Treasury bills issued by the U.S. government, and (4) commercial paper issued by corporations with good credit ratings.

ILLUSTRATION H-10
Balance sheet presentation of short-term investments

WEBER CORPORATION Balance Sheet (partial)	
Current assets	
Cash	$21,000
Short-term investments, at fair value	**60,000**

Long-Term Investments

Companies generally report long-term investments in a separate section of the balance sheet immediately below "Current assets," as shown in Illustration H-11. Long-term investments in available-for-sale securities are reported at fair value. Investments in common stock accounted for under the equity method are reported at equity.

ILLUSTRATION H-11
Balance sheet presentation of long-term investments

WEBER CORPORATION Balance Sheet (partial)		
Investments		
Bond sinking fund	$100,000	
Investments in stock of less than 20% owned companies, at fair value	**50,000**	
Investment in stock of 20%–50% owned company, at equity	**150,000**	
Total investments		$300,000

PRESENTATION OF REALIZED AND UNREALIZED GAIN OR LOSS

Companies must present in the financial statements gains and losses on investments, whether realized or unrealized. In the income statement, companies report gains and losses, as well as interest and dividend revenue, in the nonoperating activities section under the categories listed in Illustration H-12.

ILLUSTRATION H-12
Nonoperating items related to investments

Other Revenue and Gains	Other Expenses and Losses
Interest Revenue	Loss on Sale of Investments
Dividend Revenue	Unrealized Loss—Income
Gain on Sale of Investments	
Unrealized Gain—Income	

As discussed in Chapter 11, companies report the cumulative amount of other comprehensive income items from the current and previous years as a separate component of stockholders' equity. To illustrate, assume that Muzzillo Inc. has common stock of $3,000,000, retained earnings of $1,500,000, and an accumulated other comprehensive loss of $100,000. Illustration H-13 shows the financial statement presentation of the accumulated other comprehensive loss.

ILLUSTRATION H-13
Unrealized loss in stockholders' equity section

MUZZILLO INC. Balance Sheet (partial)	
Stockholders' equity	
Common stock	$3,000,000
Retained earnings	1,500,000
Total paid-in capital and retained earnings	4,500,000
Accumulated other comprehensive loss	**(100,000)**
Total stockholders' equity	$4,400,000

Note that the presentation of the accumulated other comprehensive loss is similar to the presentation of the cost of treasury stock in the stockholders' equity section. (It decreases stockholders' equity.) Accumulated other comprehensive income would be added in this section.

Companies must report, as part of a more inclusive measure called **comprehensive income**, items such as unrealized gains and losses on available-for-sale securities, which affect stockholders' equity but are not included in the calculation of net income. Comprehensive income is discussed more fully in Chapter 13.

STATEMENT OF CASH FLOWS PRESENTATION

As shown previously in Illustrations H-10, H-11, and H-13, the balance sheet presents a company's investment accounts at a point in time. The "Investing activities" section of the statement of cash flows reports information on the cash inflows and outflows during the period that resulted from investment transactions.

Illustration H-14 presents the cash flows from investing activities from a recent statement of cash flows of The Walt Disney Company. From this information, we learn that Disney received $1,530 million from the sale or redemption of investments during the year.

ILLUSTRATION H-14
Statement of cash flows presentation of investment activities

Real World

THE WALT DISNEY COMPANY
Statement of Cash Flows (partial)
(in millions)

Investing Activities	
Investments in parks, resorts and other property	$(1,566)
Acquisitions	(588)
Dispositions	—
Proceeds from sale of investments	**1,530**
Other	6
Cash used by investing activities	$ (618)

REVIEW

LEARNING OBJECTIVES REVIEW

1 Explain how to account for debt investments. Corporations invest for three common reasons: (a) they have excess cash, (b) they view investment income as a significant revenue source, and (c) they have strategic goals such as gaining control of a competitor or supplier or moving into a new line of business.

Entries for investments in debt securities are required when companies purchase bonds, receive or accrue interest, and sell bonds.

2 Explain how to account for stock investments. Entries for investments in common stock are required when companies purchase stock, receive dividends, and sell stock. When ownership is less than 20%, the cost method is used—the investment is recorded at cost. When ownership is between 20% and 50%, the equity method should be used—the investor records its share of the net income of the investee in the year it is earned. When ownership is more than 50%, consolidated financial statements should be prepared.

When a company owns more than 50% of the common stock of another company, consolidated financial statements are usually prepared. These statements are especially useful to the stockholders, board of directors, and management of the parent company.

3 Discuss how debt and stock investments are reported in the financial statements. Investments in debt and stock securities are classified as trading, available-for-sale, or held-to-maturity for valuation and reporting purposes. Trading securities are reported as current assets at fair value, with changes from cost reported in net income. Available-for-sale securities are also reported at fair value, with the changes from cost reported as items of other comprehensive income. Available-for-sale securities are classified as short-term or long-term depending on their expected realization.

Short-term investments are securities held by a company that are readily marketable and intended to be converted to cash within the next year or operating cycle, whichever is longer. Investments that do not meet both criteria are classified as long-term investments.

GLOSSARY REVIEW

Available-for-sale securities Securities that are held with the intent of selling them sometime in the future. (p. H-7).

Consolidated financial statements Financial statements that present the assets and liabilities controlled by the parent company and the total revenues and expenses of the subsidiary companies. (p. H-6).

Controlling interest Ownership of more than 50% of the common stock of another entity. (p. H-6).

Cost method An accounting method in which the investment in common stock is recorded at cost and revenue is recognized only when cash dividends are received. (p. H-4).

Debt investments Investments in government and corporation bonds. (p. H-3).

Equity method An accounting method in which the investment in common stock is initially recorded at cost, and the investment account is then adjusted annually to show the investor's equity in the investee. (p. H-5).

Fair value Amount for which a security could be sold in a normal market. (p. H-7).

Held-to-maturity securities Debt securities that the investor has the intent and ability to hold to maturity. (p. H-7).

Long-term investments Investments that are not readily marketable or that management does not intend to convert into cash within the next year or operating cycle, whichever is longer. (p. H-10).

Mark-to-market A method of accounting for certain investments that requires that they be adjusted to their fair value at the end of each period. (p. H-8).

Parent company A company that owns more than 50% of the common stock of another entity. (p. H-6).

Short-term investments (marketable securities) Investments that are readily marketable and intended to be converted into cash within the next year or operating cycle, whichever is longer. (p. H-10).

Stock investments Investments in the capital stock of corporations. (p. H-4).

Subsidiary (affiliated) company A company in which more than 50% of its stock is owned by another company. (p. H-6).

Trading securities Securities bought and held primarily for sale in the near term to generate income on short-term price differences. (p. H-7).

WileyPLUS Many additional resources are available for practice in WileyPLUS.

QUESTIONS

1. What are the reasons that companies invest in securities?
2. (a) What is the cost of an investment in bonds?
   (b) When is interest on bonds recorded?
3. Geena Jaymes is confused about losses and gains on the sale of debt investments. Explain these issues to Geena:
   (a) How the gain or loss is computed.
   (b) The statement presentation of gains and losses.
4. Heliy Company sells bonds that cost $40,000 for $45,000, including $1,000 of accrued interest. In recording the sale, Heliy books a $5,000 gain. Is this correct? Explain.
5. What is the cost of an investment in stock?
6. To acquire Gaines Corporation stock, Palmer Co. pays $61,500 in cash. What entry should be made for this investment, assuming the stock is readily marketable?
7. (a) When should a long-term investment in common stock be accounted for by the equity method?
   (b) When is revenue recognized under the equity method?
8. Stetson Corporation uses the equity method to account for its ownership of 30% of the common stock of Pike Packing. During 2017, Pike reported a net income of $80,000 and declares and pays cash dividends of $10,000. What recognition should Stetson Corporation give to these events?
9. What constitutes "significant influence" when an investor's financial interest is less than 50%?
10. Distinguish between the cost and equity methods of accounting for investments in stocks.
11. What are consolidated financial statements?
12. What are the valuation guidelines for trading and available-for-sale investments at a balance sheet date?

13. Pat Ernst is the controller of J-Products, Inc. At December 31, the end of its first year of operations, the company's investments in trading securities cost $74,000 and have a fair value of $70,000. Indicate how Pat would report these data in the financial statements prepared on December 31.
14. Using the data in Question 13, how would Pat report the data if the investments were long-term and the securities were classified as available-for-sale?
15. Boise Company's investments in available-for-sale securities at December 31 show total cost of $202,000 and total fair value of $210,000. Prepare the adjusting entry.
16. Using the data in Question 15, prepare the adjusting entry, assuming the securities are classified as trading securities.
17. Where is Accumulated Other Comprehensive Loss reported on the balance sheet?
18. Bargain Wholesale Supply owns stock in Cyrus Corporation, which it intends to hold indefinitely because of some negative tax consequences if sold. Should the investment in Cyrus be classified as a short-term investment? Why?

BRIEF EXERCISES

Journalize entries for debt investments.
(LO 1), AP

BEH-1 Craig Corporation purchased debt investments for $40,800 on January 1, 2017. On July 1, 2017, Craig received cash interest of $1,660. Journalize the purchase and the receipt of interest. Assume no interest has been accrued.

Journalize entries for stock investments.
(LO 2), AP

BEH-2 On August 1, Snow Company buys 1,000 shares of BCN common stock for $35,600 cash. On December 1, the stock investments are sold for $38,000 in cash. Journalize the purchase and sale of the common stock.

Journalize transactions under the equity method.
(LO 2), AP

BEH-3 Tote Company owns 25% of Toppe Company. For the current year, Toppe reports net income of $150,000 and declares and pays a $60,000 cash dividend. Record Tote's equity in Toppe's net income and the receipt of dividends from Toppe.

Prepare adjusting entry using fair value.
(LO 3), AP

BEH-4 Cost and fair value data for the trading securities of Lecler Company at December 31, 2017, are $62,000 and $59,600, respectively. Prepare the adjusting entry to record the securities at fair value.

Indicate statement presentation using fair value.
(LO 3), AN

BEH-5 For the data presented in BEH-4, show the financial statement presentation of the trading securities and related accounts.

Prepare adjusting entry using fair value.
(LO 3), AP

BEH-6 In its first year of operations, Machin Corporation purchased available-for-sale stock securities costing $72,000 as a long-term investment. At December 31, 2017, the fair value of the securities is $69,000. Prepare the adjusting entry to record the securities at fair value.

Indicate statement presentation using fair value.
(LO 3), AN

BEH-7 For the data presented in BEH-6, show the financial statement presentation of the securities and related accounts. Assume the securities are noncurrent.

Prepare investments section of balance sheet.
(LO 3), AP

BEH-8 Perth Corporation has these long-term investments: common stock of Vejas Co. (10% ownership) held as available-for-sale securities, cost $108,000, fair value $112,000; common stock of Penn Inc. (30% ownership), cost $210,000, equity $230,000; and a bond sinking fund of $150,000. Prepare the investments section of the balance sheet.

EXERCISES

Journalize debt investment transactions, and accrue interest.
(LO 1), AP

EH-1 Chopin Corporation had these transactions pertaining to debt investments:

Jan.	1	Purchased 90 10%, $1,000 Martine Co. bonds for $90,000 cash. Interest is payable semiannually on July 1 and January 1.
July	1	Received semiannual interest on Martine Co. bonds.
July	1	Sold 30 Martine Co. bonds for $32,000.

Instructions
(a) Journalize the transactions.
(b) Prepare the adjusting entry for the accrual of interest at December 31.

EH-2 Soylent Company had these transactions pertaining to stock investments:

Journalize stock investment transactions, and explain income statement presentation.
(LO 2, 3), AN

Feb.	1	Purchased 1,200 shares of BJ common stock (2% of outstanding shares) for $8,400.
July	1	Received cash dividends of $2 per share on BJ common stock.
Sept.	1	Sold 500 shares of BJ common stock for $5,400.
Dec.	1	Received cash dividends of $1 per share on BJ common stock.

Instructions
(a) Journalize the transactions.
(b) Explain how dividend revenue and the gain (loss) on sale should be reported in the income statement.

EH-3 Cooper Inc. had these transactions pertaining to investments in common stock:

Journalize transactions for investments in stock.
(LO 2), AP

Jan.	1	Purchased 1,200 shares of Gate Corporation common stock (5% of outstanding shares) for $59,200 cash.
July	1	Received a cash dividend of $7 per share.
Dec.	1	Sold 900 shares of Gate Corporation common stock for $47,200 cash.
	31	Received a cash dividend of $7 per share.

Instructions
Journalize the transactions.

EH-4 On January 1, Lyon Corporation purchased a 25% equity investment in Shane Corporation for $150,000. At December 31, Shane declared and paid a $80,000 cash dividend and reported net income of $380,000.

Journalize and post transactions under the equity method.
(LO 2), AP

Instructions
(a) Journalize the transactions.
(b) Determine the amount to be reported as an investment in Shane stock at December 31.

EH-5 These are two independent situations:

Journalize entries under cost and equity methods.
(LO 2), AP

1. Sosey Cosmetics acquired 12% of the 300,000 shares of common stock of Elite Fashion at a total cost of $14 per share on March 18, 2017. On June 30, Elite declared and paid a $75,000 dividend. On December 31, Elite reported net income of $244,000 for the year. At December 31, the market price of Elite Fashion was $16 per share. The stock is classified as available-for-sale.
2. Williams Inc. obtained significant influence over Kasey Corporation by buying 25% of Kasey's 30,000 outstanding shares of common stock at a total cost of $11 per share on January 1, 2017. On June 15, Kasey declared and paid a cash dividend of $35,000. On December 31, Kasey reported a net income of $120,000 for the year.

Instructions
Prepare all the necessary journal entries for 2017 for (a) Sosey Cosmetics and (b) Williams Inc.

EH-6 At December 31, 2017, the trading securities for Gwynn, Inc. are as follows.

Prepare adjusting entry to record fair value, and indicate statement presentation.
(LO 3), AP

Security	Cost	Fair Value
A	$18,100	$16,000
B	12,500	14,800
C	23,000	18,000
Total	$53,600	$48,800

Instructions
(a) Prepare the adjusting entry at December 31, 2017, to report the securities at fair value.
(b) Show the balance sheet and income statement presentation at December 31, 2017, after adjustment to fair value.

EH-7 Data for investments in stock classified as trading securities are presented in EH-6. Assume instead that the investments are classified as available-for-sale securities with the same cost and fair value data. The securities are considered to be a long-term investment.

Prepare adjusting entry to record fair value, and indicate statement presentation.
(LO 3), AN

Instructions

(a) Prepare the adjusting entry at December 31, 2017, to report the securities at fair value.
(b) Show the statement presentation at December 31, 2017, after adjustment to fair value.
(c) Pam Jenks, a member of the board of directors, does not understand the reporting of the unrealized gains or losses on trading securities and available-for-sale securities. Write a letter to Ms. Jenks explaining the reporting and the purposes it serves.

Prepare adjusting entries for fair value, and indicate statement presentation for two classes of securities.

(LO 3), AN

EH-8 Weston Company has these data at December 31, 2017, the end of its first year of operations.

Securities	Cost	Fair Value
Trading	$110,000	$122,000
Available-for-sale	100,000	96,000

The available-for-sale securities are held as a long-term investment.

Instructions

(a) Prepare the adjusting entries to report each class of securities at fair value.
(b) Indicate the statement presentation of each class of securities and the related unrealized gain (loss) accounts.

PROBLEMS

Journalize debt investment transactions.

(LO 1), AN

PH-1 Penn Farms is a grower of hybrid seed corn for Bend Genetics Corporation. It has had two exceptionally good years and has elected to invest its excess funds in bonds. The following selected transactions relate to bonds acquired as an investment by Penn Farms, whose fiscal year ends on December 31.

2017

Jan. 1	Purchased at par $600,000 of Dover Corporation 10-year, 7% bonds dated January 1, 2017, directly from the issuing corporation.
July 1	Received the semiannual interest on the Dover bonds.
Dec. 31	Accrual of interest at year-end on the Dover bonds.

Assume that all intervening transactions and adjustments have been properly recorded and the number of bonds owned has not changed from December 31, 2017, to December 31, 2019.

2020

Jan. 1	Received the semiannual interest on the Dover bonds.
Jan. 1	Sold $300,000 of Dover bonds at 110.
July 1	Received the semiannual interest on the Dover bonds.
Dec. 31	Accrual of interest at year-end on the Dover bonds.

Instructions

Journalize the listed transactions for the years 2017 and 2020.

Journalize investment transactions, prepare adjusting entry, and show financial statement presentation.

(LO 1, 2, 3), AN

GLS

PH-2 In January 2017, the management of Northern Company concludes that it has sufficient cash to purchase some short-term investments in debt and stock securities. During the year, the following transactions occurred.

Feb. 1	Purchased 1,200 shares of LAF common stock for $51,600.
Mar. 1	Purchased 500 shares of NCL common stock for $18,500.
Apr. 1	Purchased 70 $1,000, 8% TRC bonds for $70,000. Interest is payable semiannually on April 1 and October 1.
July 1	Received a cash dividend of $0.80 per share on the LAF common stock.
Aug. 1	Sold 200 shares of LAF common stock at $42 per share.
Sept. 1	Received $2 per share cash dividend on the NCL common stock.
Oct. 1	Received the semiannual interest on the TRC bonds.
Oct. 1	Sold the TRC bonds for $75,700.

At December 31, the fair values of the LAF and NCL common stocks were $39 and $30 per share, respectively.

Instructions

(a) Journalize the transactions and post to the accounts Debt Investments and Stock Investments. (Use the T-account form.)
(b) Prepare the adjusting entry at December 31, 2017, to report the investments at fair value. All securities are considered to be trading securities.
(c) Show the balance sheet presentation of investment securities at December 31, 2017.
(d) Identify the income statement accounts and give the statement classification of each account.

PH-3 On December 31, 2016, the end of its first year of operations, Botani Associates owned the following securities that are held as long-term investments.

Journalize transactions, prepare adjusting entry for stock investments, and show balance sheet presentation.

(LO 2, 3), AN

GLS

Common Stock	Shares	Cost
C Co.	1,000	$48,000
D Co.	5,000	36,000
E Co.	1,200	24,000

On this date, the total fair value of the securities was equal to its cost. The securities are not held for influence or control over the investees. In 2017, the following transactions occurred.

July 1	Received $2.00 per share semiannual cash dividend on D Co. common stock.
Aug. 1	Received $0.50 per share cash dividend on C Co. common stock.
Sept. 1	Sold 1,000 shares of D Co. common stock for cash at $9 per share.
Oct. 1	Sold 300 shares of C Co. common stock for cash at $53 per share.
Nov. 1	Received $1 per share cash dividend on E Co. common stock.
Dec. 15	Received $0.50 per share cash dividend on C Co. common stock.
31	Received $2.20 per share semiannual cash dividend on D Co. common stock.

At December 31, the fair values per share of the common stocks were C Co. $47, D Co. $7, and E Co. $24.

Instructions

(a) Journalize the 2017 transactions and post to the account Stock Investments. (Use the T-account form.)
(b) Prepare the adjusting entry at December 31, 2017, to show the securities at fair value. The stock should be classified as available-for-sale securities.
(c) Show the balance sheet presentation of the investments and the unrealized gain (loss) at December 31, 2017. At this date, Botani Associates has common stock $2,000,000 and retained earnings $1,200,000.

PH-4 Wellman Company acquired 30% of the outstanding common stock of Grinwold Inc. on January 1, 2017, by paying $1,800,000 for 60,000 shares. Grinwold declared and paid a $0.50 per share cash dividend on June 30 and again on December 31, 2017. Grinwold reported net income of $800,000 for the year.

Prepare entries under cost and equity methods, and prepare memorandum.

(LO 2), AN

Instructions

(a) Prepare the journal entries for Wellman Company for 2017, assuming Wellman cannot exercise significant influence over Grinwold. (Use the cost method.)
(b) Prepare the journal entries for Wellman Company for 2017, assuming Wellman can exercise significant influence over Grinwold. (Use the equity method.)
(c) The board of directors of Wellman Company is confused about the differences between the cost and equity methods. Prepare a memorandum for the board that explains each method and shows in tabular form the account balances under each method at December 31, 2017.

PH-5 Here is Kalvin Company's portfolio of long-term available-for-sale securities at December 31, 2016, the end of its first year of operations.

Journalize stock transactions, and show balance sheet presentation.

(LO 2, 3), AN

	Cost
1,400 shares of Batone Inc. common stock	$73,500
1,200 shares of Mendez Corporation common stock	84,000
800 shares of P. Tillman Corporation preferred stock	33,600

On December 31, the total cost of the portfolio equaled the total fair value. Kalvin had the following transactions related to the securities during 2017.

Jan.	20	Sold 1,400 shares of Batone Inc. common stock at $55 per share.
	28	Purchased 400 shares of $10 par value common stock of P. Wahl Corporation at $78 per share.
	30	Received a cash dividend of $1.25 per share on Mendez Corporation common stock.
Feb.	8	Received cash dividends of $0.40 per share on P. Tillman Corporation preferred stock.
	18	Sold all 800 shares of P. Tillman preferred stock at $35 per share.
July	30	Received a cash dividend of $1.10 per share on Mendez Corporation common stock.
Sept.	6	Purchased an additional 600 shares of the $10 par value common stock of P. Wahl Corporation at $82 per share.
Dec.	1	Received a cash dividend of $1.50 per share on P. Wahl Corporation common stock.

At December 31, 2017, the fair values of the securities were:

Mendez Corporation common stock	$65 per share
P. Wahl Corporation common stock	$77 per share

Kalvin uses separate account titles for each investment, such as Investment in Mendez Corporation Common Stock.

Instructions

(a) Prepare journal entries to record the transactions.
(b) Post to the investment accounts. (Use separate T-accounts for each investment.)
(c) Prepare the adjusting entry at December 31, 2017, to report the portfolio at fair value.
(d) Show the balance sheet presentation at December 31, 2017.

Prepare a balance sheet.
(LO 3), AP

PH-6 The following data, presented in alphabetical order, are taken from the records of Manfreid Corporation.

Accounts payable	$ 150,000
Accounts receivable	90,000
Accumulated depreciation—buildings	180,000
Accumulated depreciation—equipment	52,000
Allowance for doubtful accounts	6,000
Bonds payable (10%, due 2028)	350,000
Buildings	900,000
Cash	63,000
Common stock ($5 par value; 500,000 shares authorized, 240,000 shares issued)	1,200,000
Debt investments	400,000
Discount on bonds payable	20,000
Dividends payable	50,000
Equipment	275,000
Goodwill	190,000
Income taxes payable	70,000
Inventory	170,000
Land	410,000
Notes payable (due 2018)	70,000
Paid-in capital in excess of par value	464,000
Prepaid insurance	16,000
Retained earnings	310,000
Stock investments (Horton Inc. stock, 30% ownership, at equity)	240,000
Stock investments (short-term, at fair value)	128,000

Instructions

Prepare a balance sheet at December 31, 2017.

Payroll Accounting

APPENDIX PREVIEW

Payroll and related fringe benefits often make up a large percentage of current liabilities. Employee compensation is often the most significant expense that a company incurs. For example, Costco recently reported total employees of 103,000. Labor and fringe benefits costs approximated 70% of the company's total cost of operations.

Payroll accounting involves more than paying employees' wages. Companies are required by law to maintain payroll records for each employee, to file and pay payroll taxes, and to comply with state and federal tax laws related to employee compensation.

APPENDIX OUTLINE

LEARNING OBJECTIVES	
1 Record the payroll for a pay period.	• Determining the payroll • Recording the payroll
2 Record employer payroll taxes.	• FICA taxes • Federal unemployment taxes • State unemployment taxes • Recording employer payroll taxes • Filing and remitting payroll taxes
3 Discuss the objectives of internal control for payroll.	• Objectives of internal control for payroll • Internal control activities

LEARNING OBJECTIVE ▶1 **Record the payroll for a pay period.**

The term "payroll" **pertains to both salaries and wages of employees.** Managerial, administrative, and sales personnel are generally paid **salaries**. Salaries are often expressed in terms of a specified amount per month or per year rather than an hourly rate. Store clerks, factory employees, and manual laborers are normally paid **wages**. Wages are based on a rate per hour or on a piecework basis (such as per unit of product). Frequently, people use the terms "salaries" and "wages" interchangeably.

The term "payroll" **does not apply to payments made for services of professionals** such as certified public accountants, attorneys, and architects. Such professionals are independent contractors rather than salaried employees. Payments to them are called **fees**. This distinction is important because government regulations relating to the payment and reporting of payroll taxes apply only to employees.

DETERMINING THE PAYROLL

Determining the payroll involves computing three amounts: (1) gross earnings, (2) payroll deductions, and (3) net pay.

Gross Earnings

Gross earnings is the total compensation earned by an employee. It consists of wages or salaries, plus any bonuses and commissions.

Companies determine total **wages** for an employee by multiplying the hours worked by the hourly rate of pay. In addition to the hourly pay rate, most companies are required by law to pay hourly workers a minimum of 1½ times the regular hourly rate for overtime work in excess of eight hours per day or 40 hours per week. In addition, many employers pay overtime rates for work done at night, on weekends, and on holidays.

For example, assume that Michael Jordan, an employee of Academy Company, worked 44 hours for the weekly pay period ending January 14. His regular wage is $12 per hour. For any hours in excess of 40, the company pays at 1½ times the regular rate. Academy computes Jordan's gross earnings (total wages) as follows.

ILLUSTRATION I-1
Computation of total wages

Type of Pay	Hours	×	Rate	=	Gross Earnings
Regular	40	×	$12	=	$ 480
Overtime	4	×	18	=	72
Total wages					$552

This computation assumes that Jordan receives 1½ times his regular hourly rate ($12 × 1.5) for his overtime hours. Union contracts often require that overtime rates be as much as twice the regular rates.

ETHICS NOTE
Bonuses often reward outstanding individual performance, but successful corporations also need considerable teamwork. A challenge is to motivate individuals while preventing an unethical employee from taking another's idea for his or her own advantage.

An employee's **salary** is generally based on a monthly or yearly rate. The company then prorates these rates to its payroll periods (e.g., biweekly or monthly). Most executive and administrative positions are salaried. Federal law does not require overtime pay for employees in such positions.

Many companies have **bonus** agreements for employees. One survey found that over 94% of the largest U.S. manufacturing companies offer annual bonuses to key executives. Bonus arrangements may be based on such factors as increased sales or net income. Companies may pay bonuses in cash and/or by granting employees the opportunity to acquire shares of company stock at favorable prices (called stock option plans).

Payroll Deductions

As anyone who has received a paycheck knows, gross earnings are usually very different from the amount actually received. The difference is due to **payroll deductions**.

Payroll deductions may be mandatory or voluntary. **Mandatory deductions are required by law and consist of FICA taxes and income taxes.** Voluntary deductions are at the option of the employee. Illustration I-2 summarizes common types of payroll deductions. Such deductions do not result in payroll tax expense to the employer. The employer is merely a collection agent, and subsequently transfers the deducted amounts to the government and designated recipients.

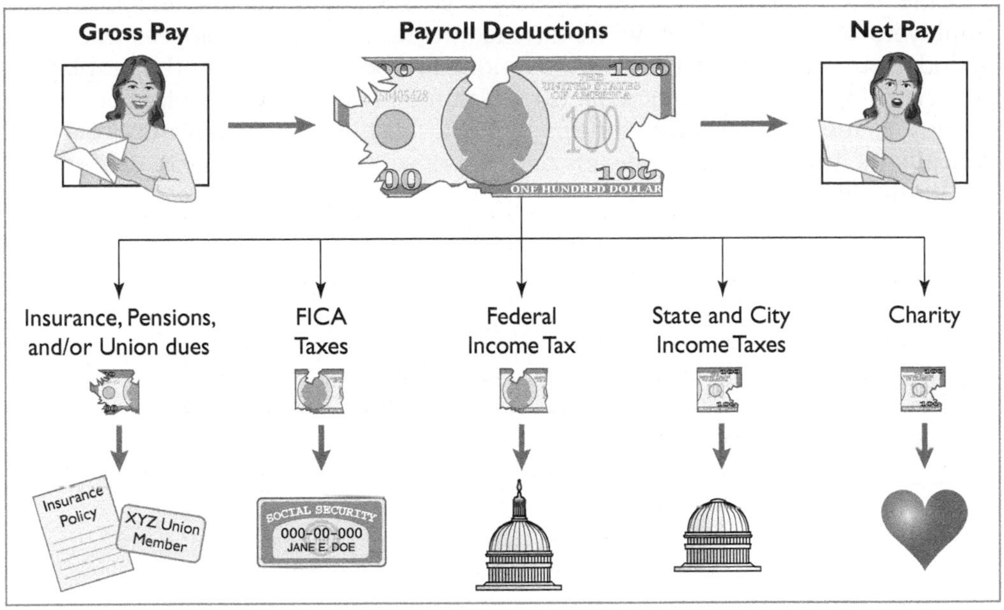

ILLUSTRATION I-2
Payroll deductions

FICA TAXES In 1937, Congress enacted the Federal Insurance Contribution Act (FICA). **FICA taxes are designed to provide workers with supplemental retirement, employment disability, and medical benefits.** In 1965, Congress extended benefits to include Medicare for individuals over 65 years of age. The benefits are financed by a tax levied on employees' earnings.

FICA taxes consist of a Social Security tax and a Medicare tax. They are paid by both employee and employer. The FICA tax rate is 7.65% (6.2% Social Security tax up to $117,000 plus 1.45% Medicare tax) of salary and wages for each employee.[1] In addition, the Medicare tax of 1.45% continues for an employee's salary and wages in excess of $117,000. These tax rate and tax base requirements are shown in Illustration I-3.

ILLUSTRATION I-3
FICA tax rate and tax base

Social Security taxes	
Employee and employer	**6.2%** on salary and wages up to **$117,000**
Medicare taxes	
Employee and employer	**1.45%** on all salary and wages without limitation

To illustrate the computation of FICA taxes, assume that Mario Ruez has total wages for the year of $100,000. In this case, Mario pays FICA taxes of $7,650 ($100,000 × 7.65%). If Mario has total wages of $124,000, Mario pays FICA taxes of $9,052, as shown in Illustration I-4.

[1]The $117,000 limit is based upon 2014 guidelines set by the Social Security Administration.

ILLUSTRATION I-4
FICA tax computation

Social Security tax	($117,000 × 6.2%)	$ 7,254
Medicare tax	($124,000 × 1.45%)	1,798
Total FICA taxes		**$9,052**

Mario's employer is also required to pay $9,052.

INCOME TAXES Under the U.S. pay-as-you-go system of federal income taxes, employers are required to withhold income taxes from employees each pay period. Four variables determine the amount to be withheld: (1) the employee's gross earnings, (2) marital status, (3) the number of allowances claimed by the employee, and (4) the length of the pay period. The number of allowances claimed typically includes the employee, his or her spouse, and other dependents.

Withholding tables furnished by the Internal Revenue Service indicate the amount of income tax to be withheld. Withholding amounts are based on gross wages and the number of allowances claimed. Separate tables are provided for weekly, biweekly, semimonthly, and monthly pay periods. Illustration I-5 shows the withholding tax table for Michael Jordan (assuming he earns $552 per week, is married, and claims two allowances). For a weekly salary of $552 with two allowances, the income tax to be withheld is $24 (highlighted in red)

ILLUSTRATION I-5
Withholding tax table

MARRIED Persons — **WEEKLY** Payroll Period
(For Wages Paid through December 2017)

If the wages are —		And the number of withholding allowances claimed is —										
At least	But less than	0	1	2	3	4	5	6	7	8	9	10
		The amount of income tax to be withheld is —										
500	**510**	34	27	19	11	4	0	0	0	0	0	0
510	**520**	35	28	20	12	5	0	0	0	0	0	0
520	**530**	37	29	21	13	6	0	0	0	0	0	0
530	**540**	38	30	22	14	7	0	0	0	0	0	0
540	**550**	40	31	23	15	8	0	0	0	0	0	0
550	**560**	41	32	24	16	9	1	0	0	0	0	0
560	**570**	43	33	25	17	10	2	0	0	0	0	0
570	**580**	44	34	26	18	11	3	0	0	0	0	0
580	**590**	46	35	27	19	12	4	0	0	0	0	0
590	**600**	47	36	28	20	13	5	0	0	0	0	0
600	**610**	49	38	29	21	14	6	0	0	0	0	0
610	**620**	50	39	30	22	15	7	0	0	0	0	0
620	**630**	52	41	31	23	16	8	1	0	0	0	0
630	**640**	53	42	32	24	17	9	2	0	0	0	0
640	**650**	55	44	33	25	18	10	3	0	0	0	0
650	**660**	56	45	34	26	19	11	4	0	0	0	0
660	**670**	58	47	35	27	20	12	5	0	0	0	0
670	**680**	59	48	37	28	21	13	6	0	0	0	0
680	**690**	61	50	38	29	22	14	7	0	0	0	0
690	**700**	62	51	40	30	23	15	8	0	0	0	0

In addition, most states (and some cities) require **employers** to withhold income taxes from employees' earnings. As a rule, the amounts withheld are a percentage (specified in the state revenue code) of the amount withheld for the federal income tax. Or they may be a specified percentage of the employee's earnings. For the sake of simplicity, we have assumed that Jordan's wages are subject to state income taxes of 2%, or $11.04 (2% × $552) per week.

There is no limit on the amount of gross earnings subject to income tax withholdings. In fact, under our progressive system of taxation, the higher the earnings, the higher the percentage of income withheld for taxes.

OTHER DEDUCTIONS Employees may voluntarily authorize withholdings for charitable organizations, retirement, and other purposes. All voluntary deductions from gross earnings should be authorized in writing by the employee. The authorization(s) may be made individually or as part of a group plan. Deductions for charitable organizations, such as the United Fund, or for financial arrangements, such as U.S. savings bonds and repayment of loans from company credit unions, are made individually. Deductions for union dues, health and life insurance, and pension plans are often made on a group basis. We assume that Jordan has weekly voluntary deductions of $10 for the United Fund and $5 for union dues.

Net Pay

Academy Company determines **net pay** by subtracting payroll deductions from gross earnings. Illustration I-6 shows the computation of Jordan's net pay for the pay period.

ALTERNATIVE TERMINOLOGY
Net pay is also called *take-home pay.*

ILLUSTRATION I-6
Computation of net pay

Gross earnings		$ 552.00
Payroll deductions:		
FICA taxes	$42.23	
Federal income taxes	24.00	
State income taxes	11.04	
United Fund	10.00	
Union dues	5.00	92.27
Net pay		$459.73

Assuming that Michael Jordan's wages for each week during the year are $552, total wages for the year are $28,704 (52 × $552). Thus, all of Jordan's wages are subject to FICA tax during the year. In comparison, let's assume that Jordan's department head earns $3,000 per week, or $156,000 for the year. Since only the first $117,000 is subject to Social Security taxes, the maximum FICA withholdings on the department head's earnings would be $9,516 [($117,000 × 6.20%) + ($156,000 × 1.45%)].

RECORDING THE PAYROLL

Recording the payroll involves maintaining payroll department records, recognizing payroll expenses and liabilities, and recording payment of the payroll.

Maintaining Payroll Department Records

To comply with state and federal laws, an employer must keep a cumulative record of each employee's gross earnings, deductions, and net pay during the year. The record that provides this information is the **employee earnings record**. Illustration I-7 (page I-6) shows Michael Jordan's employee earnings record.

Companies keep a separate earnings record for each employee and update these records after each pay period. The employer uses the cumulative payroll data on the earnings record to (1) determine when an employee has earned the maximum earnings subject to FICA taxes, (2) file state and federal payroll tax returns (as explained later), and (3) provide each employee with a statement of gross earnings and tax withholdings for the year. Illustration I-11 (page I-10) shows this statement.

Academy Company.xls

ACADEMY COMPANY
Employee Earnings Record
For the Year 2017

Name	Michael Jordan	**Address**	2345 Mifflin Ave.
Social Security Number	329-35-9547		Hampton, Michigan 48292
Date of Birth	December 24, 1994	**Telephone**	555-238-9051
Date Employed	September 1, 2015	**Date Employment Ended**	
Sex	Male	**Exemptions**	2
Single ______	**Married** x		

2017 Period Ending	Total Hours	Gross Earnings: Regular	Overtime	Total	Cumulative	Deductions: FICA	Fed. Inc. Tax	State Inc. Tax	United Fund	Union Dues	Total	Payment: Net Amount	Check No.
1/7	42	480.00	36.00	516.00	516.00	39.47	20.00	10.32	10.00	5.00	84.79	431.21	974
1/14	44	480.00	72.00	552.00	1,068.00	42.23	24.00	11.04	10.00	5.00	92.27	459.73	1028
1/21	43	480.00	54.00	534.00	1,602.00	40.85	22.00	10.68	10.00	5.00	88.53	445.47	1077
1/28	42	480.00	36.00	516.00	2,118.00	39.47	20.00	10.32	10.00	5.00	84.79	431.21	1133
Jan. Total		1,920.00	198.00	2,118.00		162.02	86.00	42.36	40.00	20.00	350.38	1,767.62	

ILLUSTRATION I-7
Employee earnings record

In addition to employee earnings records, many companies find it useful to prepare a **payroll register**. This record accumulates the gross earnings, deductions, and net pay by employee for each pay period. Illustration I-8 presents Academy Company's payroll register. It provides the documentation for preparing a paycheck for each employee. For example, it shows the data for Michael Jordan

ILLUSTRATION I-8
Payroll register

Academy Company.xls

ACADEMY COMPANY
Payroll Register
For the Week Ending January 14, 2017

Employee	Total Hours	Earnings: Regular	Over-time	Gross	Deductions: FICA	Federal Income Tax	State Income Tax	United Fund	Union Dues	Total	Paid: Net Pay	Check No.	Account Debited: Salaries and Wages Expense
Arnold, Patricia	40	580.00		580.00	44.37	61.00	11.60	15.00		131.97	448.03	998	580.00
Canton, Matthew	40	590.00		590.00	45.14	63.00	11.80	20.00		139.94	450.06	999	590.00
Mueller, William	40	530.00		530.00	40.55	54.00	10.60	11.00		116.15	413.85	1000	530.00
Bennett, Robin	42	480.00	36.00	516.00	39.47	35.00	10.32	18.00	5.00	107.79	408.21	1025	516.00
Jordan, Michael	44	480.00	72.00	552.00	42.23	24.00	11.04	10.00	5.00	92.27	459.73	1028	552.00
Milroy, Lee	43	480.00	54.00	534.00	40.85	46.00	10.68	10.00	5.00	112.53	421.47	1029	534.00
Total		16,200.00	1,010.00	17,210.00	1,316.57	3,490.00	344.20	421.50	115.00	5,687.27	11,522.73		17,210.00

in the wages section. In this example, Academy's total weekly payroll is $17,210, as shown in the salary and wages expense column (column N, row 31).

Note that this record is a listing of each employee's payroll data for the pay period. In some companies, a payroll register is a journal or book of original entry. Postings are made from it directly to ledger accounts. In other companies, the payroll register is a memorandum record that provides the data for a general journal entry and subsequent posting to the ledger accounts. Academy follows the latter procedure.

Recognizing Payroll Expenses and Liabilities

From the payroll register in Illustration I-8, Academy Company makes a journal entry to record the payroll. For the week ending January 14, the entry is as follows.

Jan. 14	Salaries and Wages Expense	17,210.00	
	FICA Taxes Payable		1,316.57
	Federal Income Taxes Payable		3,490.00
	State Income Taxes Payable		344.20
	United Fund Payable		421.50
	Union Dues Payable		115.00
	Salaries and Wages Payable		11,522.73
	(To record payroll for the week ending January 14)		

A	=	L	+	SE
				−17,210.00 Exp
		+1,316.57		
		+3,490.00		
		+344.20		
		+421.50		
		+115.00		
		+11,522.73		

Cash Flows
no effect

The company credits specific liability accounts for the mandatory and voluntary deductions made during the pay period. In the example, Academy debits Salaries and Wages Expense for the gross earnings of its employees. The amount credited to Salaries and Wages Payable is the sum of the individual checks the employees will receive.

Recording Payment of the Payroll

A company makes payments by check (or electronic funds transfer) either from its regular bank account or a payroll bank account. Each paycheck is usually accompanied by a detachable **statement of earnings** document. This shows the employee's gross earnings, payroll deductions, and net pay, both for the period and for the year-to-date. Academy Company uses its regular bank account for payroll checks. Illustration I-9 shows the paycheck and statement of earnings for Michael Jordan.

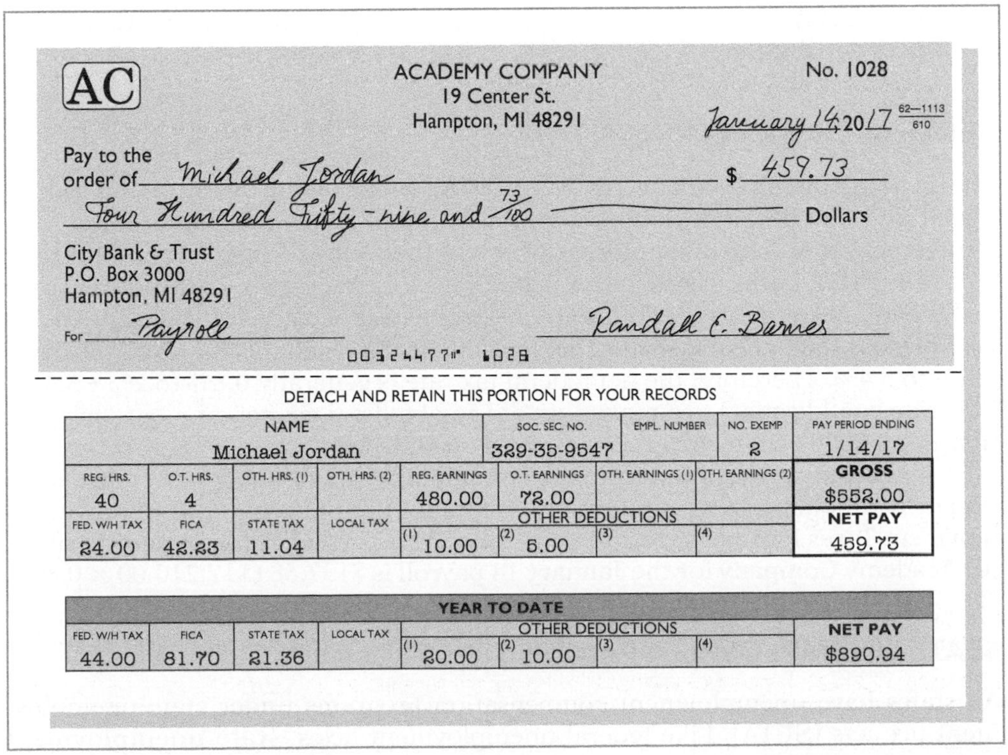

AC

ACADEMY COMPANY
19 Center St.
Hampton, MI 48291

No. 1028

January 14, 2017 62–1113/610

Pay to the order of Michael Jordan $ 459.73

Four Hundred Fifty-nine and 73/100 Dollars

City Bank & Trust
P.O. Box 3000
Hampton, MI 48291

For Payroll Randall E. Barnes

00324477" 1028

DETACH AND RETAIN THIS PORTION FOR YOUR RECORDS

NAME	SOC. SEC. NO.	EMPL. NUMBER	NO. EXEMP	PAY PERIOD ENDING
Michael Jordan	329-35-9547		2	1/14/17

REG. HRS.	O.T. HRS.	OTH. HRS. (1)	OTH. HRS. (2)	REG. EARNINGS	O.T. EARNINGS	OTH. EARNINGS (1)	OTH. EARNINGS (2)	GROSS
40	4			480.00	72.00			$552.00

FED. W/H TAX	FICA	STATE TAX	LOCAL TAX	OTHER DEDUCTIONS (1)	(2)	(3)	(4)	NET PAY
24.00	42.23	11.04		10.00	5.00			459.73

YEAR TO DATE

FED. W/H TAX	FICA	STATE TAX	LOCAL TAX	OTHER DEDUCTIONS (1)	(2)	(3)	(4)	NET PAY
44.00	81.70	21.36		20.00	10.00			$890.94

ILLUSTRATION I-9
Paycheck and statement of earnings

▼ **HELPFUL HINT**
None of the income tax liabilities result in payroll tax expense for the employer because the employer is acting only as a collection agent for the government.

Following payment of the payroll, the company enters the check numbers in the payroll register. Academy records payment of the payroll as follows.

A	=	L	+	SE
		−11,522.73		
−11,522.73				

Cash Flows
−11,522.73

Jan. 14	Salaries and Wages Payable	11,522.73	
	Cash		11,522.73
	(To record payment of payroll)		

Many medium- and large-size companies use a payroll processing center that performs payroll recordkeeping services. Companies send the center payroll information about employee pay rates and hours worked. The center maintains the payroll records and prepares the payroll checks. In most cases, it costs less to process the payroll through the center (outsource) than if the company did so internally.

LEARNING OBJECTIVE 2

Record employer payroll taxes.

Payroll tax expense for businesses results from three taxes that governmental agencies levy **on employers**. These taxes are (1) FICA, (2) federal unemployment tax, and (3) state unemployment tax. These taxes plus such items as paid vacations and pensions are collectively referred to as **fringe benefits**. As indicated earlier, the cost of fringe benefits in many companies is substantial.

FICA TAXES

Each employee must pay FICA taxes. In addition, employers must match each employee's FICA contribution. This means the employer must remit to the federal government 12.4% of each employee's first $117,000 of taxable earnings, plus 2.9% of each employee's earnings, regardless of amount. The matching contribution results in **payroll tax expense** to the employer. The employer's tax is subject to the same rate and maximum earnings as the employee's. The company uses the same account, FICA Taxes Payable, to record both the employee's and the employer's FICA contributions. For the January 14 payroll, Academy Company's FICA tax contribution is $1,316.57 ($17,210.00 × 7.65%).

FEDERAL UNEMPLOYMENT TAXES

▼ HELPFUL HINT
Both the employer and employee pay FICA taxes. Federal unemployment taxes and (in most states) the state unemployment taxes are borne entirely by the employer.

The Federal Unemployment Tax Act (FUTA) is another feature of the federal Social Security program. **Federal unemployment taxes** provide benefits for a limited period of time to employees who lose their jobs through no fault of their own. The FUTA tax rate is currently 6.2% of taxable wages. The taxable wage base is the first $7,000 of wages paid to each employee in a calendar year. Employers who pay the state unemployment tax on a timely basis will receive an offset credit of up to 5.4%. Therefore, the net federal tax rate is generally 0.8% (6.2% − 5.4%). This rate would equate to a maximum of $56 of federal tax per employee per year (0.8% × $7,000). State tax rates are based on state law.

The **employer** bears the entire federal unemployment tax. There is no deduction or withholding from employees. Companies use the account Federal Unemployment Taxes Payable to recognize this liability. The federal unemployment tax for Academy Company for the January 14 payroll is $137.68 ($17,210.00 × 0.8%).

STATE UNEMPLOYMENT TAXES

All states have unemployment compensation programs under state unemployment tax acts (SUTA). Like federal unemployment taxes, **state unemployment**

taxes provide benefits to employees who lose their jobs. These taxes are levied on employers.[2] The basic rate is usually 5.4% on the first $7,000 of wages paid to an employee during the year. The state adjusts the basic rate according to the employer's experience rating. Companies with a history of stable employment may pay less than 5.4%. Companies with a history of unstable employment may pay more than the basic rate. Regardless of the rate paid, the company's credit on the federal unemployment tax is still 5.4%.

Companies use the account State Unemployment Taxes Payable for this liability. The state unemployment tax for Academy Company for the January 14 payroll is $929.34 ($17,210.00 × 5.4%). Illustration I-10 summarizes the types of employer payroll taxes.

ILLUSTRATION I-10
Employer payroll taxes

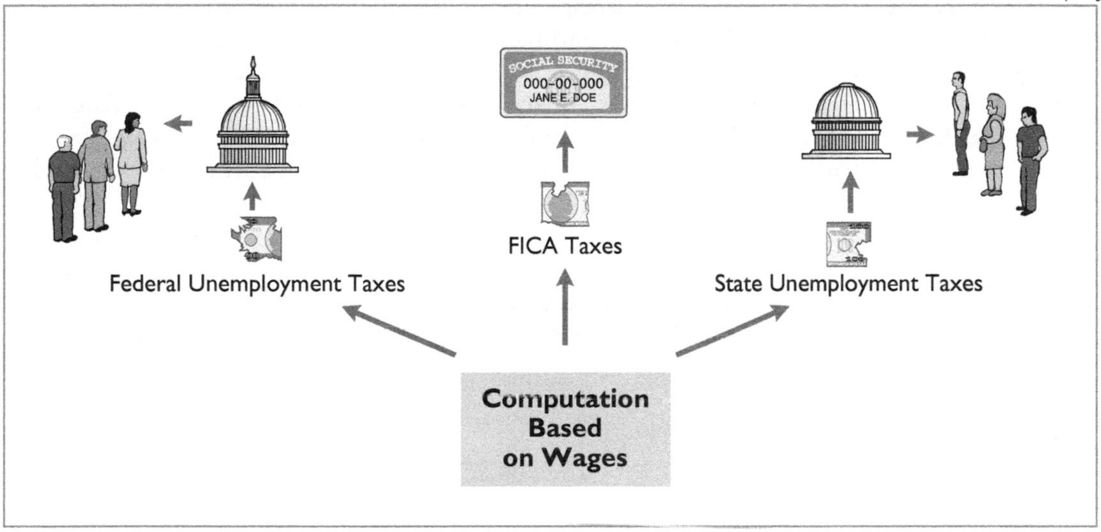

RECORDING EMPLOYER PAYROLL TAXES

Companies usually record employer payroll taxes at the same time they record the payroll. The entire amount of gross pay ($17,210.00) shown in the payroll register in Illustration I-8 is subject to each of the three taxes mentioned previously. Accordingly, Academy records the payroll tax expense associated with the January 14 payroll with the following entry.

Jan. 14	Payroll Tax Expense	2,383.59	
	FICA Taxes Payable		1,316.57
	Federal Unemployment Taxes Payable		137.68
	State Unemployment Taxes Payable		929.34
	(To record employer's payroll taxes on January 14 payroll)		

A	=	L	+	SE
				−2,383.59 Exp
		+1,316.57		
		+137.68		
		+929.34		

Cash Flows
no effect

Note that Academy uses separate liability accounts instead of a single credit to Payroll Taxes Payable. Why? Because these liabilities are payable to different taxing authorities at different dates. Companies classify the liability accounts in the balance sheet as current liabilities since they will be paid within the next year. They classify Payroll Tax Expense on the income statement as an operating expense.

FILING AND REMITTING PAYROLL TAXES

Preparation of payroll tax returns is the responsibility of the payroll department. The treasurer's department makes the tax payment. Much of the information for the returns is obtained from employee earnings records.

[2] In a few states, the employee is also required to make a contribution. *In this appendix, including the homework, we will assume that the tax is only on the employer.*

For purposes of reporting and remitting to the IRS, the company combines the FICA taxes and federal income taxes that it withheld. **Companies must report the taxes quarterly**, no later than one month following the close of each quarter. The remitting requirements depend on the amount of taxes withheld and the length of the pay period. Companies remit funds through deposits in either a Federal Reserve bank or an authorized commercial bank.

Companies generally file and remit federal unemployment taxes **annually** on or before January 31 of the subsequent year. Earlier payments are required when the tax exceeds a specified amount. Companies usually must file and pay state unemployment taxes by the **end of the month following each quarter**. When payroll taxes are paid, companies debit payroll liability accounts and credit Cash.

Employers also must provide each employee with a **Wage and Tax Statement (Form W-2)** by January 31 following the end of a calendar year. This statement shows gross earnings, FICA taxes withheld, and income taxes withheld for the year. The required W-2 form for Michael Jordan, using assumed annual data, is shown in Illustration I-11. The employer must send a copy of each employee's Wage and Tax Statement (Form W-2) to the Social Security Administration. This agency subsequently furnishes the Internal Revenue Service with the income data required.

ILLUSTRATION I-11
W-2 form

22222	Void ☐	a Employee's social security number 329-35-9547	For Official Use Only ▶ OMB No. 1545-0008

b Employer identification number (EIN) 36-2167852	1 Wages, tips, other compensation 26,300.00	2 Federal income tax withheld 2,248.00
c Employer's name, address, and ZIP code Academy Company 19 Center St. Hampton, MI 48291	3 Social security wages 26,300.00	4 Social security tax withheld 1,630.60
	5 Medicare wages and tips 26,300.00	6 Medicare tax withheld 381.35
	7 Social security tips	8 Allocated tips
d Control number	9 Advance EIC payment	10 Dependent care benefits
e Employee's first name and initial: Michael; Last name: Jordan; Suff.	11 Nonqualified plans	12a See instructions for box 12 Code
2345 Mifflin Ave. Hampton, MI 48292	13 Statutory employee ☐ Retirement plan ☐ Third-party sick pay ☐	12b Code
	14 Other	12c Code
f Employee's address and ZIP code		12d Code

15 State	Employer's state ID number	16 State wages, tips, etc.	17 State income tax	18 Local wages, tips, etc.	19 Local income tax	20 Locality name
MI	423-1466-3	26,300.00	526.00			

Form **W-2 Wage and Tax Statement** 2017

Department of the Treasury—Internal Revenue Service

For Privacy Act and Paperwork Reduction Act Notice, see back of Copy D.

Copy A For Social Security Administration — Send this entire page with Form W-3 to the Social Security Administration; photocopies are **not** acceptable.

Cat. No. 10134D

LEARNING OBJECTIVE ▶3

Discuss the objectives of internal control for payroll.

Chapter 7 introduced internal control. As applied to payrolls, the objectives of internal control are (1) to safeguard company assets against unauthorized payments of payrolls, and (2) to ensure the accuracy and reliability of the accounting records pertaining to payrolls.

Irregularities often result if internal control is lax. Frauds involving payroll include overstating hours, using unauthorized pay rates, adding fictitious employees to the payroll, continuing terminated employees on the payroll, and distributing duplicate payroll checks. Moreover, inaccurate records will result in incorrect paychecks, financial statements, and payroll tax returns.

Payroll activities involve four functions: hiring employees, timekeeping, preparing the payroll, and paying the payroll. For effective internal control, companies should assign these four functions to different departments or individuals. Illustration I-12 highlights these functions and illustrates their internal control features.

ILLUSTRATION I-12
Internal control for payroll

Payroll Function

Hiring Employees

Internal control feature: Human Resources department documents and authorizes employment.

Fraud prevented: Fictitious employees are not added to payroll.

Timekeeping

Internal control feature: Supervisors monitor hours worked through time cards and time reports.

Fraud prevented: Employee not paid for hours not worked.

Payroll Function

Preparing the Payroll

Internal control feature: Two (or more) employees verify payroll amounts; supervisor approves.

Fraud prevented: Payroll calculations are accurate and relevant.

Paying the Payroll

Internal control feature: Treasurer signs and distributes prenumbered checks.

Fraud prevented: Checks are not lost, misappropriated, or unavailable for proof of payment; endorsed check provides proof of payment.

REVIEW

LEARNING OBJECTIVES REVIEW

1 Record the payroll for a pay period. The computation of the payroll involves gross earnings, payroll deductions, and net pay. In recording the payroll, Salaries and Wages Expense is debited for gross earnings, individual tax and other liability accounts are credited for payroll deductions, and Salaries and Wages Payable is credited for net pay. When the payroll is paid, Salaries and Wages Payable is debited, and Cash is credited.

2 Record employer payroll taxes. Employer payroll taxes consist of FICA, federal unemployment taxes, and state unemployment taxes. The taxes are usually accrued at the time the payroll is recorded by debiting Payroll Tax Expense and crediting separate liability accounts for each type of tax.

3 Discuss the objectives of internal control for payroll. The objectives of internal control for payroll are (1) to safeguard company assets against unauthorized payments of payrolls, and (2) to ensure the accuracy and reliability of the accounting records pertaining to payrolls.

GLOSSARY REVIEW

Bonus Compensation to management personnel and other employees, based on factors such as increased sales or the amount of net income. (p. I-2).

Employee earnings record A cumulative record of each employee's gross earnings, deductions, and net pay during the year. (p. I-5).

Federal unemployment taxes Taxes imposed on the employer that provide benefits for a limited time period to employees who lose their jobs through no fault of their own. (p. I-8).

Fees Payments made for the services of professionals. (p. I-2).

FICA taxes Taxes designed to provide workers with supplemental retirement, employment disability, and medical benefits. (p. I-3).

Gross earnings Total compensation earned by an employee. (p. I-2).

Net pay Gross earnings less payroll deductions. (p. I-5).

Payroll deductions Deductions from gross earnings to determine the amount of a paycheck. (p. I-2).

Payroll register A payroll record that accumulates the gross earnings, deductions, and net pay by employee for each pay period. (p. I-6).

Salaries Specified amount per month or per year paid to managerial, administrative, and sales personnel. (p. I-1).

Statement of earnings A document attached to a paycheck that indicates the employee's gross earnings, payroll deductions, and net pay. (p. I-7).

State unemployment taxes Taxes imposed on the employer that provide benefits to employees who lose their jobs. (p. I-8).

Wage and Tax Statement (Form W-2) A form showing gross earnings, FICA taxes withheld, and income taxes withheld which is prepared annually by an employer for each employee. (p. I-10).

Wages Amounts paid to employees based on a rate per hour or on a piecework basis. (p. I-1).

WileyPLUS Many additional resources are available for practice in WileyPLUS.

QUESTIONS

1. What is the difference between gross pay and net pay? Which amount should a company record as wages or salaries expense?
2. Which payroll tax is levied on both employers and employees?
3. Are the federal and state income taxes withheld from employee paychecks a payroll tax expense for the employer? Explain your answer.
4. What do the following acronyms stand for: FICA, FUTA, and SUTA?
5. What information is shown on a W-2 statement?
6. Distinguish between the two types of payroll deductions and give examples of each.
7. What are the primary uses of the employee earnings record?
8. (a) Identify the three types of employer payroll taxes. (b) How are tax liability accounts and Payroll Tax Expense classified in the financial statements?
9. You are a newly hired accountant with Nolasco Company. On your first day, the controller asks you to identify the main internal control objectives related to payroll accounting. How would you respond?
10. What are the four functions associated with payroll activities?

BRIEF EXERCISES

Compute gross earnings and net pay.
(LO 1), AP

BEI-1 Beth Corbin's regular hourly wage rate is $16, and she receives an hourly rate of $24 for work in excess of 40 hours. During a January pay period, Beth works 45 hours. Beth's federal income tax withholding is $95, she has no voluntary deductions, and the FICA tax rate is 7.65%. Compute Beth Corbin's gross earnings and net pay for the pay period.

Record a payroll and the payment of wages.
(LO 1), AP

BEI-2 Data for Beth Corbin are presented in BEI-1. Prepare the journal entries to record (a) Beth's pay for the period and (b) the payment of Beth's wages. Use January 15 for the end of the pay period and the payment date.

Record employer payroll taxes.
(LO 2), AP

BEI-3 In January, gross earnings in Lugo Company totaled $80,000. All earnings are subject to 7.65% FICA taxes, 5.4% state unemployment taxes, and 0.8% federal unemployment taxes. Prepare the entry to record January payroll tax expense.

BEI-4 Swenson Company has the following payroll procedures.

Identify payroll functions.
(LO 3), AP

(a) Supervisor approves overtime work.
(b) The human resources department prepares hiring authorization forms for new hires.
(c) A second payroll department employee verifies payroll calculations.
(d) The treasurer's department pays employees.

Identify the payroll function to which each procedure pertains.

EXERCISES

EI-1 Maria Garza's regular hourly wage rate is $16, and she receives a wage of 1½ times the regular hourly rate for work in excess of 40 hours. During a March weekly pay period, Maria worked 42 hours. Her gross earnings prior to the current week were $6,000. Maria is married and claims three withholding allowances. Her only voluntary deduction is for group hospitalization insurance at $25 per week.

Compute net pay and record pay for one employee.
(LO 1), AP

Instructions
(a) Compute the following amounts for Maria's wages for the current week.
  (1) Gross earnings.
  (2) FICA taxes. (Assume a 7.65% rate on maximum of $117,000.)
  (3) Federal income taxes withheld. (Use the withholding table in Illustration I-5, page I-4.)
  (4) State income taxes withheld. (Assume a 2.0% rate.)
  (5) Net pay.
(b) Record Maria's pay.

EI-2 Employee earnings records for Slaymaker Company reveal the following gross earnings for four employees through the pay period of December 15.

Compute maximum FICA deductions.
(LO 1), AP

J. Seligman	$93,500	L. Marshall	$115,100
R. Eby	$113,600	T. Olson	$120,000

For the pay period ending December 31, each employee's gross earnings is $4,500. The FICA tax rate is 7.65% on gross earnings of $117,000.

Instructions
Compute the FICA withholdings that should be made for each employee for the December 31 pay period. (Show computations.)

EI-3 Ramirez Company has the following data for the weekly payroll ending January 31.

Prepare payroll register and record payroll and payroll tax expense.
(LO 1, 2), AP

	Hours							Federal	
Employee	**M**	**T**	**W**	**T**	**F**	**S**	**Hourly Rate**	**Income Tax Withholding**	**Health Insurance**
L. Helton	8	8	9	8	10	3	$12	$34	$10
R. Kenseth	8	8	8	8	8	2	14	37	25
D. Tavaras	9	10	8	8	9	0	15	58	25

Employees are paid 1½ times the regular hourly rate for all hours worked in excess of 40 hours per week. FICA taxes are 7.65% on the first $117,000 of gross earnings. Ramirez Company is subject to 5.4% state unemployment taxes and 0.8% federal unemployment taxes on the first $7,000 of gross earnings.

Instructions
(a) Prepare the payroll register for the weekly payroll.
(b) Prepare the journal entries to record the payroll and Ramirez's payroll tax expense.

EI-4 Selected data from a February payroll register for Sutton Company are presented below. Some amounts are intentionally omitted.

Compute missing payroll amounts and record payroll.
(LO 1), AP

Gross earnings:		State income taxes	$ (3)
Regular	$9,100	Union dues	100
Overtime	(1)	Total deductions	(4)
Total	(2)	Net pay	$7,595
Deductions:		Account debited:	
FICA taxes	$ 765	Salaries and wages expense	(5)
Federal income taxes	1,140		

FICA taxes are 7.65%. State income taxes are 4% of gross earnings.

Instructions

(a) Fill in the missing amounts.
(b) Journalize the February payroll and the payment of the payroll.

Determine employer's payroll taxes; record payroll tax expense.
(LO 2), AP

EI-5 According to a payroll register summary of Frederickson Company, the amount of employees' gross pay in December was $850,000, of which $80,000 was not subject to Social Security taxes of 6.2% and $750,000 was not subject to state and federal unemployment taxes.

Instructions

(a) Determine the employer's payroll tax expense for the month, using the following rates: FICA 7.65%, state unemployment 5.4%, and federal unemployment 0.8%.
(b) Prepare the journal entry to record December payroll tax expense.

PROBLEMS

Prepare payroll register and payroll entries.
(LO 1, 2), AP

PI-1 Mann Hardware has four employees who are paid on an hourly basis plus time-and-a-half for all hours worked in excess of 40 a week. Payroll data for the week ended March 15, 2017, are presented as follows.

Employee	Hours Worked	Hourly Rate	Federal Income Tax Withholdings	United Fund
Ben Abel	40	$15.00	$?	$5.00
Rita Hager	42	16.00	?	5.00
Jack Never	44	13.00	60.00	8.00
Sue Perez	46	13.00	61.00	5.00

Abel and Hager are married. They claim 0 and 4 withholding allowances, respectively. The following tax rates are applicable: FICA 7.65%, state income taxes 3%, state unemployment taxes 5.4%, and federal unemployment 0.8%.

Instructions

(a) Net pay $2,039.30
(b) Payroll tax expense $349.43
(d) Cash paid $578.02

(a) Prepare a payroll register for the weekly payroll. (Use the wage-bracket withholding table in the text for federal income tax withholdings.)
(b) Journalize the payroll on March 15, 2017, and the accrual of employer payroll taxes.
(c) Journalize the payment of the payroll on March 16, 2017.
(d) Journalize the deposit in a Federal Reserve bank on March 31, 2017, of the FICA and federal income taxes payable to the government.

Journalize payroll transactions and adjusting entries.
(LO 1, 2), AP
GLS

PI-2 The following payroll liability accounts are included in the ledger of Harmon Company on January 1, 2017.

FICA Taxes Payable	$ 760.00
Federal Income Taxes Payable	1,204.60
State Income Taxes Payable	108.95
Federal Unemployment Taxes Payable	288.95
State Unemployment Taxes Payable	1,954.40
Union Dues Payable	870.00
U.S. Savings Bonds Payable	360.00

In January, the following transactions occurred.

Jan. 10 Sent check for $870.00 to union treasurer for union dues.
12 Remitted check for $1,964.60 to the Federal Reserve bank for FICA taxes and federal income taxes withheld.
15 Purchased U.S. Savings Bonds for employees by writing check for $360.00.
17 Paid state income taxes withheld from employees.
20 Paid federal and state unemployment taxes.
31 Completed monthly payroll register, which shows salaries and wages $58,000, FICA taxes withheld $4,437, federal income taxes payable $2,158, state income taxes payable $454, union dues payable $400, United Fund contributions payable $1,888, and net pay $48,663.
31 Prepared payroll checks for the net pay and distributed checks to employees.

At January 31, the company also makes the following accrued adjustments pertaining to employee compensation.

1. Employer payroll taxes: FICA taxes 7.65%, federal unemployment taxes 0.8%, and state unemployment taxes 5.4%.
2. Vacation pay: 6% of gross earnings. (Use Vacation Benefit Expense to record the transaction.)

Instructions

(a) Journalize the January transactions.
(b) Journalize the adjustments pertaining to employee compensation at January 31.

(b) Payroll tax expense $8,033; Vacation benefit expense $3,480

PI-3 For the year ended December 31, 2017, Denkinger Electrical Repair Company reports the following summary payroll data.

Prepare entries for payroll and payroll taxes; prepare W-2 data.

(LO 1, 2), AP

Gross earnings:	
Administrative salaries	$200,000
Electricians' wages	370,000
Total	$570,000
Deductions:	
FICA taxes	$ 38,645
Federal income taxes withheld	174,400
State income taxes withheld (3%)	17,100
United Fund contributions payable	27,500
Health insurance premiums	17,200
Total	$274,845

Denkinger Company's payroll taxes are Social Security tax 6.2%, Medicare tax 1.45%, state unemployment 2.5% (due to a stable employment record), and 0.8% federal unemployment. Gross earnings subject to Social Security taxes of 6.2% total $490,000, and gross earnings subject to unemployment taxes total $135,000.

Instructions

(a) Prepare a summary journal entry at December 31 for the full year's payroll.
(b) Journalize the adjusting entry at December 31 to record the employer's payroll taxes.
(c) The W-2 Wage and Tax Statement requires the following dollar data.

(a) Salaries and wages payable $295,155
(b) Payroll tax expense $43,100

Wages, Tips, Other Compensation	Federal Income Tax Withheld	State Income Tax Withheld	FICA Wages	FICA Tax Withheld

Complete the required data for the following employees.

Employee	Gross Earnings	Federal Income Tax Withheld
Maria Sandoval	$59,000	$28,500
Jennifer Mingenback	26,000	10,200

J

Subsidiary Ledgers and Special Journals

APPENDIX PREVIEW

A reliable accounting information system is a necessity for any company. Whether companies use pen, pencil, or computers in maintaining accounting records, certain principles and procedures apply. The purpose of this appendix is to explain and illustrate two components of an accounting information system: subsidiary ledgers and special journals.

APPENDIX OUTLINE

LEARNING OBJECTIVES	
1 Describe the nature and purpose of a subsidiary ledger.	• Subsidiary ledger example • Advantages of subsidiary ledgers
2 Record transactions in special journals.	• Sales journal • Cash receipts journal • Purchases journal • Cash payments journal • Effects of special journals on the general journal • Cyber security

LEARNING OBJECTIVE 1

Describe the nature and purpose of a subsidiary ledger.

Imagine a business that has several thousand charge (credit) customers and shows the transactions with these customers in only one general ledger account—Accounts Receivable. It would be nearly impossible to determine the balance owed by an individual customer at any specific time. Similarly, the amount payable to one creditor would be difficult to locate quickly from a single Accounts Payable account in the general ledger.

Instead, companies use subsidiary ledgers to keep track of individual balances. A **subsidiary ledger** is a group of accounts with a common characteristic (for example, all accounts receivable). It is an addition to, and an expansion of, the general ledger. The subsidiary ledger frees the general ledger from the details of individual balances.

Two common subsidiary ledgers are as follows.

1. The **accounts receivable** (or **customers'**) **subsidiary ledger**, which collects transaction data of individual customers.
2. The **accounts payable** (or **creditors'**) **subsidiary ledger**, which collects transaction data of individual creditors.

In each of these subsidiary ledgers, companies usually arrange individual accounts in alphabetical order.

A general ledger account summarizes the detailed data from a subsidiary ledger. For example, the detailed data from the accounts receivable subsidiary ledger are summarized in Accounts Receivable in the general ledger. The general ledger account that summarizes subsidiary ledger data is called a **control account**. Illustration J-1 presents an overview of the relationship of subsidiary ledgers to the general ledger. In Illustration J-1, the general ledger control accounts and subsidiary ledger accounts are in green. Note that Cash and Common Stock in this illustration are not control accounts because there are no subsidiary ledger accounts related to these accounts.

ILLUSTRATION J-1
Relationship of general ledger and subsidiary ledgers

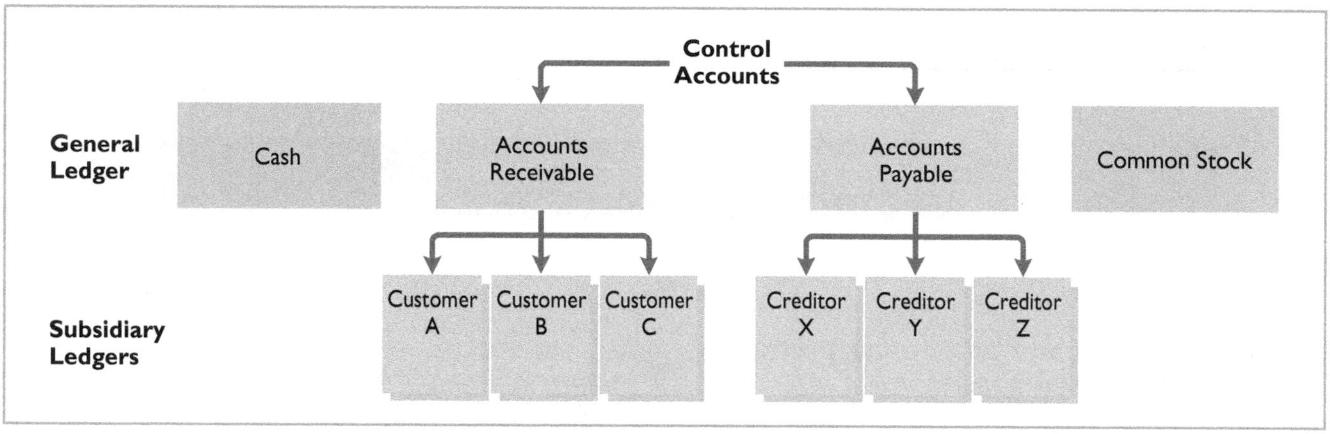

At the end of an accounting period, each general ledger control account balance must equal the composite balance of the individual accounts in the related subsidiary ledger. For example, the balance in Accounts Payable in Illustration J-1 must equal the total of the subsidiary balances of Creditors X + Y + Z.

SUBSIDIARY LEDGER EXAMPLE

Illustration J-2 lists sales and collection transactions for Pujols Enterprises.

ILLUSTRATION J-2
Sales and collection transactions

Credit Sales			Collections on Account		
Jan. 10	Aaron Co.	$ 6,000	Jan. 19	Aaron Co.	$4,000
12	Branden Inc.	3,000	21	Branden Inc.	3,000
20	Caron Co.	3,000	29	Caron Co.	1,000
		$12,000			$8,000

Illustration J-3 provides an example of a control account and subsidiary ledger based on these transactions. (Due to space considerations, the explanation column in these accounts is not shown in this and subsequent illustrations.)

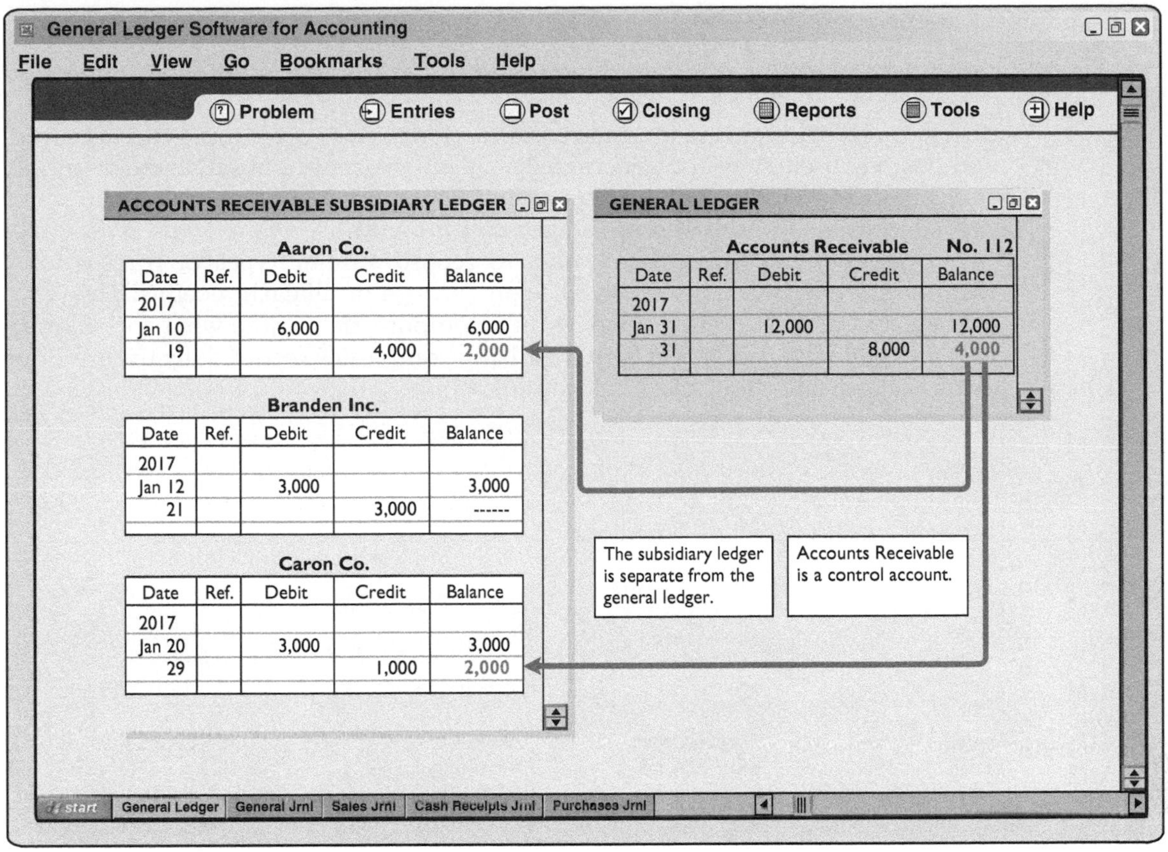

ILLUSTRATION J-3
Relationship between general and subsidiary ledgers

Pujols can reconcile the total debits ($12,000) and credits ($8,000) in Accounts Receivable in the general ledger to the detailed debits and credits in the subsidiary accounts. Also, the balance of $4,000 in the control account agrees with the total of the balances in the individual accounts (Aaron Co. $2,000 + Branden Inc. $0 + Caron Co. $2,000) in the subsidiary ledger.

As Illustration J-3 shows, companies make monthly postings to the control accounts in the general ledger. This practice allows them to prepare monthly financial statements. Companies post to the individual accounts in the subsidiary ledger daily. Daily posting ensures that account information is current. This enables the company to monitor credit limits, bill customers, and answer inquiries from customers about their account balances.

ADVANTAGES OF SUBSIDIARY LEDGERS

Subsidiary ledgers have several advantages:

1. **They show in a single account transactions affecting one customer or one creditor**, thus providing up-to-date information on specific account balances.
2. **They free the general ledger of excessive details.** As a result, a trial balance of the general ledger does not contain vast numbers of individual account balances.
3. **They help locate errors in individual accounts** by reducing the number of accounts in one ledger and by using control accounts.
4. **They make possible a division of labor in posting.** One employee can post to the general ledger while someone else posts to the subsidiary ledgers.

LEARNING OBJECTIVE **2**

Record transactions in special journals.

So far you have learned to journalize transactions in a two-column general journal and post each entry to the general ledger. This procedure is satisfactory in only very small companies. To expedite journalizing and posting, most companies use special journals **in addition to the general journal.**

Companies use **special journals** to record similar types of transactions. Examples are all sales of merchandise on account or all cash receipts. The types of transactions that occur frequently in a company determine what special journals the company uses. Most merchandising companies record daily transactions using the journals shown in Illustration J-4.

ILLUSTRATION J-4
Use of special journals and the general journal

Sales Journal	Cash Receipts Journal	Purchases Journal	Cash Payments Journal	General Journal
Used for: All sales of merchandise on account	Used for: All cash received (including cash sales)	Used for: All purchases of merchandise on account	Used for: All cash paid (including cash purchases)	Used for: Transactions that cannot be entered in a special journal, including correcting, adjusting, and closing entries

If a transaction cannot be recorded in a special journal, the company records it in the general journal. For example, if a company had special journals for only the four types of transactions listed above, it would record purchase returns and allowances that do not affect cash in the general journal. Similarly, **correcting, adjusting, and closing entries are recorded in the general journal**. In some situations, companies might use special journals other than those listed above. For example, when sales returns and allowances that do not affect cash are frequent, a company might use a special journal to record these transactions.

Special journals **permit greater division of labor** because several people can record entries in different journals at the same time. For example, one employee may journalize all cash receipts, and another may journalize all credit sales. Also, the use of special journals **reduces the time needed to complete the posting process**. With special journals, companies may post some accounts monthly, instead of daily, as we will illustrate later in this appendix. On the following pages, we discuss the four special journals shown in Illustration J-4.

▼ HELPFUL HINT
Postings are also made daily to individual ledger accounts in the inventory subsidiary ledger to maintain a perpetual inventory.

SALES JOURNAL

In the **sales journal**, companies record **sales of merchandise on account**. Cash sales of merchandise go in the cash receipts journal. Credit sales of assets other than merchandise go in the general journal.

Journalizing Credit Sales

To demonstrate use of a sales journal, we will use data for Karns Wholesale Supply, which uses a **perpetual inventory system**. Under this system, each entry in the sales journal results in one entry **at selling price** and another entry **at cost**. The entry at selling price is a debit to Accounts Receivable (a control account) and a credit of equal amount to Sales Revenue. The entry at cost is a debit to Cost of Goods Sold and a credit of equal amount to Inventory (a control account). Using a sales journal with two amount columns, the company can show on only one line a sales transaction at both selling price and cost. Illustration J-5 shows this two-column sales journal of Karns Wholesale Supply, using assumed credit sales transactions (for sales invoices 101–107).

SALES JOURNAL S1

Date	Account Debited	Invoice No.	Ref.	Accts. Receivable Dr. Sales Revenue Cr.	Cost of Goods Sold Dr. Inventory Cr.
2017					
May 3	Abbot Sisters	101		10,600	6,360
7	Babson Co.	102		11,350	7,370
14	Carson Bros.	103		7,800	5,070
19	Deli Co.	104		9,300	6,510
21	Abbot Sisters	105		15,400	10,780
24	Deli Co.	106		21,210	15,900
27	Babson Co.	107		14,570	10,200
				90,230	62,190

ILLUSTRATION J-5
Journalizing the sales journal—perpetual inventory system

Note that, unlike the general journal, an explanation is not required for each entry in a special journal. Also, the use of prenumbered invoices ensures that all invoices are journalized. Finally, the reference (Ref.) column is not used in journalizing. It is used in posting the sales journal, as explained next.

Posting the Sales Journal

Companies make daily postings from the sales journal **to the individual accounts receivable** in the subsidiary ledger. Posting **to the general ledger** is done **monthly**. Illustration J-6 (page J-6) shows both the daily and monthly postings.

A check mark (✓) is inserted in the reference posting column to indicate that the daily posting to the customer's account has been made. If the subsidiary ledger accounts were numbered, the account number would be entered in place of the check mark. At the end of the month, Karns posts the column totals of the sales journal to the general ledger. Here, the column totals are as follows. From the selling-price column, a debit of $90,230 to Accounts Receivable (account No. 112), and a credit of $90,230 to Sales Revenue (account No. 401). From the cost column, a debit of $62,190 to Cost of Goods Sold (account No. 505), and a credit of $62,190 to Inventory (account No. 120). Karns inserts the account numbers below the column totals to indicate that the postings have been made. In both the general ledger and subsidiary ledger accounts, the reference **S1** indicates that the posting came from page 1 of the sales journal.

General Ledger Software for Accounting

File Edit View Go Bookmarks Tools Help

Problem | Entries | Post | Closing | Reports | Tools | Help

SALES JOURNAL S1

Date	Account Debited	Invoice No.	Ref.	Accts. Receivable Dr. Sales Revenue Cr.	Cost of Goods Sold Dr. Inventory Cr.
2017					
May 3	Abbot Sisters	101	√	10,600	6,360
7	Babson Co.	102	√	11,350	7,370
14	Carson Bros.	103	√	7,800	5,070
19	Deli Co.	104	√	9,300	6,510
21	Abbot Sisters	105	√	15,400	10,780
24	Deli Co.	106	√	21,210	15,900
27	Babson Co.	107	√	14,570	10,200
				90,230	62,190
				(112) / (401)	(505) / (120)

At the end of the accounting period, the company posts totals to the general ledger.

The company posts individual amounts to the subsidiary ledger daily.

ACCOUNTS RECEIVABLE SUBSIDIARY LEDGER

Abbot Sisters

Date	Ref.	Debit	Credit	Balance
2017				
May 3	S1	10,600		10,600
21	S1	15,400		26,000

Babson Co.

Date	Ref.	Debit	Credit	Balance
2017				
May 7	S1	11,350		11,350
27	S1	14,570		25,920

Carson Bros.

Date	Ref.	Debit	Credit	Balance
2017				
May 14	S1	7,800		7,800

Deli Co.

Date	Ref.	Debit	Credit	Balance
2017				
May 19	S1	9,300		9,300
24	S1	21,210		30,510

GENERAL LEDGER

Accounts Receivable No. 112

Date	Ref.	Debit	Credit	Balance
2017				
May 31	S1	90,230		90,230

Inventory No. 120

Date	Ref.	Debit	Credit	Balance
2017				
May 31	S1		62,190	62,190[1]

Sales Revenue No. 401

Date	Ref.	Debit	Credit	Balance
2017				
May 31	S1		90,230	90,230

Cost of Goods Sold No. 505

Date	Ref.	Debit	Credit	Balance
2017				
May 31	S1	62,190		62,190

The subsidiary ledger is separate from the general ledger.

Accounts Receivable is a control account.

[1]The normal balance for Inventory is a debit. But, because of the sequence in which we have posted the special journals, with the sales journals first, the credits to Inventory are posted before the debits. This posting sequence explains the credit balance in Inventory, which exists only until the other journals are posted.

start | General Ledger | General Jrnl | Sales Jrnl | Cash Receipts Jrnl | Purchases Jrnl

ILLUSTRATION J-6
Posting the sales journal

Proving the Ledgers

The next step is to "prove" the ledgers. To do so, Karns must determine two things: (1) The total of the general ledger debit balances must equal the total of the general ledger credit balances. (2) The sum of the subsidiary ledger balances must equal the balance in the control account. Illustration J-7 shows the proof of the postings from the sales journal to the general and subsidiary ledger.

ILLUSTRATION J-7
Proving the equality of the postings from the sales journal

Postings to General Ledger

General Ledger

Credits	
Inventory	$62,190
Sales Revenue	90,230
	$152,420
Debits	
Accounts Receivable	$90,230
Cost of Goods Sold	62,190
	$152,420

Debit Postings to the Accounts Receivable Subsidiary Ledger

Subsidiary Ledger

Abbot Sisters	$26,000
Babson Co.	25,920
Carson Bros.	7,800
Deli Co.	30,510
	$90,230

Advantages of the Sales Journal

Use of a special journal to record sales on account has several advantages. First, the one-line entry for each sales transaction saves time. In the sales journal, it is not necessary to write out the four account titles for each transaction. Second, only totals, rather than individual entries, are posted to the general ledger. This saves posting time and reduces the possibilities of posting errors. Finally, a division of labor results because one individual can take responsibility for the sales journal.

CASH RECEIPTS JOURNAL

In the **cash receipts journal**, companies record all receipts of cash. The most common types of cash receipts are cash sales of merchandise and collections of accounts receivable. Many other possibilities exist, such as receipt of money from bank loans and cash proceeds from disposal of equipment. A one- or two-column cash receipts journal would not have space enough for all possible cash receipt transactions. Therefore, companies use a multi-column cash receipts journal.

Generally, a cash receipts journal includes the following columns: debit columns for Cash and Sales Discounts, and credit columns for Accounts Receivable, Sales Revenue, and "Other Accounts." Companies use the Other Accounts category when the cash receipt does not involve a cash sale or a collection of accounts receivable. Under a perpetual inventory system, each sales entry also is accompanied by an entry that debits Cost of Goods Sold and credits Inventory for the cost of the merchandise sold. Illustration J-8 (page J-8) shows a six-column cash receipts journal.

ILLUSTRATION J-8
Journalizing and posting the cash receipts journal

General Ledger Software for Accounting

File Edit View Go Bookmarks Tools Help

Problem | Entries | Post | Closing | Reports | Tools | Help

CASH RECEIPTS JOURNAL CR1

Date	Account Credited	Ref.	Cash Dr.	Sales Discounts Dr.	Accounts Receivable Cr.	Sales Revenue Cr.	Other Accounts Cr.	Cost of Goods Sold Dr. Inventory Cr.
2017								
May 1	Common Stock	311	5,000				5,000	
7			1,900			1,900		1,240
10	Abbot Sisters	√	10,388	212	10,600			
12			2,600			2,600		1,690
17	Babson Co.	√	11,123	227	11,350			
22	Notes Payable	200	6,000				6,000	
23	Carson Bros.	√	7,644	156	7,800			
28	Deli Co.	√	9,114	186	9,300			
			53,769	781	39,050	4,500	11,000	2,930
			(101)	(414)	(112)	(401)	(x)	(505)/(120)

The company posts individual amounts to the subsidiary ledger daily.

At the end of the accounting period, the company posts totals to the general ledger.

ACCOUNTS RECEIVABLE SUBSIDIARY LEDGER

Abbot Sisters

Date	Ref.	Debit	Credit	Balance
2017				
May 3	S1	10,600		10,600
10	CR1		10,600	--------
21	S1	15,400		15,400

Babson Co.

Date	Ref.	Debit	Credit	Balance
2017				
May 7	S1	11,350		11,350
17	CR1		11,350	--------
27	S1	14,570		14,570

Carson Bros.

Date	Ref.	Debit	Credit	Balance
2017				
May 14	S1	7,800		7,800
23	CR1		7,800	-------

Deli Co.

Date	Ref.	Debit	Credit	Balance
2017				
May 19	S1	9,300		9,300
24	S1	21,210		30,510
28	CR1		9,300	21,210

The subsidiary ledger is separate from the general ledger.

Accounts Receivable is a control account.

GENERAL LEDGER

Cash **No. 101**

Date	Ref.	Debit	Credit	Balance
2017				
May 31	CR1	53,769		53,769

Accounts Receivable **No. 112**

Date	Ref.	Debit	Credit	Balance
2017				
May 31	S1	90,230		90,230
31	CR1		39,050	51,180

Inventory **No. 120**

Date	Ref.	Debit	Credit	Balance
2017				
May 31	S1		62,190	62,190
31	CR1		2,930	65,120

Notes Payable **No. 200**

Date	Ref.	Debit	Credit	Balance
2017				
May 22	CR1		6,000	6,000

Common Stock **No. 311**

Date	Ref.	Debit	Credit	Balance
2017				
May 1	CR1		5,000	5,000

Sales Revenue **No. 401**

Date	Ref.	Debit	Credit	Balance
2017				
May 31	S1		90,230	90,230
31	CR1		4,500	94,730

Sales Discounts **No. 414**

Date	Ref.	Debit	Credit	Balance
2017				
May 31	CR1	781		781

Cost of Goods Sold **No. 505**

Date	Ref.	Debit	Credit	Balance
2017				
May 31	S1	62,190		62,190
31	CR1	2,930		65,120

start | General Ledger | General Jrnl | Sales Jrnl | Cash Receipts Jrnl | Purchases Jrnl

Companies may use additional credit columns if these columns significantly reduce postings to a specific account. For example, a loan company, such as Household International, receives thousands of cash collections from customers. Using separate credit columns for Loans Receivable and Interest Revenue, rather than the Other Accounts credit column, would reduce postings.

Journalizing Cash Receipts Transactions

To illustrate the journalizing of cash receipts transactions, we will continue with the May transactions of Karns Wholesale Supply. Collections from customers relate to the entries recorded in the sales journal in Illustration J-5 (page J-5). The entries in the cash receipts journal are based on the following cash receipts.

May	1	Stockholders invested $5,000 in the business.
	7	Cash sales of merchandise total $1,900 (cost, $1,240).
	10	Received a check for $10,388 from Abbot Sisters in payment of invoice No. 101 for $10,600 less a 2% discount.
	12	Cash sales of merchandise total $2,600 (cost, $1,690).
	17	Received a check for $11,123 from Babson Co. in payment of invoice No. 102 for $11,350 less a 2% discount.
	22	Received cash by signing a note for $6,000.
	23	Received a check for $7,644 from Carson Bros. in full for invoice No. 103 for $7,800 less a 2% discount.
	28	Received a check for $9,114 from Deli Co. in full for invoice No. 104 for $9,300 less a 2% discount.

Further information about the columns in the cash receipts journal is listed below.

Debit Columns:

1. **Cash.** Karns enters in this column the amount of cash actually received in each transaction. The column total indicates the total cash receipts for the month.
2. **Sales Discounts.** Karns includes a Sales Discounts column in its cash receipts journal. By doing so, it does not need to enter sales discount items in the general journal. As a result, the cash receipts journal shows on one line the collection of an account receivable within the discount period.

Credit Columns:

3. **Accounts Receivable.** Karns uses the Accounts Receivable column to record cash collections on account. The amount entered here is the amount to be credited to the individual customer's account.
4. **Sales Revenue.** The Sales Revenue column records all cash sales of merchandise. Cash sales of other assets (plant assets, for example) are not reported in this column.
5. **Other Accounts.** Karns uses the Other Accounts column whenever the credit is other than to Accounts Receivable or Sales Revenue. For example, in the first entry, Karns enters $5,000 as a credit to Common Stock. This column is often referred to as the sundry accounts column.

▼ HELPFUL HINT

A *subsidiary ledger* account is entered when the entry involves a collection of accounts receivable. A *general ledger* account is entered when the account is not shown in a special column (and an amount must be entered in the Other Accounts column). Otherwise, no account is shown in the Account Credited column.

Debit and Credit Column:

6. **Cost of Goods Sold and Inventory.** This column records debits to Cost of Goods Sold and credits to Inventory.

In a multi-column journal, generally only one line is needed for each entry. Debit and credit amounts for each line must be equal. When Karns journalizes the collection from Abbot Sisters on May 10, for example, three amounts are indicated. Note also that the Account Credited column identifies both general ledger and subsidiary ledger account titles. General ledger accounts are illustrated in the

May 1 and May 22 entries. A subsidiary account is illustrated in the May 10 entry for the collection from Abbot Sisters.

When Karns has finished journalizing a multi-column journal, it totals the amount columns and compares the totals to prove the equality of debits and credits. Illustration J-9 shows the proof of the equality of Karns' cash receipts journal.

ILLUSTRATION J-9
Proving the equality of the cash receipts journal

Debits		Credits	
Cash	$53,769	Accounts Receivable	$39,050
Sales Discounts	781	Sales Revenue	4,500
Cost of Goods Sold	2,930	Other Accounts	11,000
	$57,480	Inventory	2,930
			$57,480

Totaling the columns of a journal and proving the equality of the totals is called **footing** and **crossfooting** a journal.

Posting the Cash Receipts Journal

Posting a multi-column journal (Illustration J-8, page J-8) involves the following steps.

1. **At the end of the month**, the company posts all column totals, except for the Other Accounts total, to the account title(s) specified in the column heading (such as Cash or Accounts Receivable). The company then enters account numbers below the column totals to show that they have been posted. For example, Karns has posted cash to account No. 101, accounts receivable to account No. 112, inventory to account No. 120, sales revenue to account No. 401, sales discounts to account No. 414, and cost of goods sold to account No. 505.
2. The company **separately posts the individual amounts comprising the Other Accounts total** to the general ledger accounts specified in the Account Credited column. See, for example, the credit posting to Common Stock. The total amount of this column has not been posted. The symbol (X) is inserted below the total to this column to indicate that the amount has not been posted.
3. The individual amounts in a column, posted in total to a control account (Accounts Receivable, in this case), are posted **daily to the subsidiary ledger** account specified in the Account Credited column. See, for example, the credit posting of $10,600 to Abbot Sisters.

The symbol **CR**, used in both the subsidiary and general ledgers, identifies postings from the cash receipts journal.

Proving the Ledgers

After posting of the cash receipts journal is completed, Karns proves the ledgers. As shown in Illustration J-10, the general ledger totals agree. Also, the sum of the subsidiary ledger balances equals the control account balance.

ILLUSTRATION J-10
Proving the ledgers after posting the sales and the cash receipts journals

Schedule of Accounts Receivable
(from accounts receivable subsidiary ledger)

Abbot Sisters	$15,400
Babson Co.	14,570
Deli Co.	21,210
	$51,180

General Ledger

Debits	
Cash	$53,769
Accounts Receivable	51,180
Sales Discounts	781
Cost of Goods Sold	65,120
	$170,850

Credits	
Notes Payable	$ 6,000
Common Stock	5,000
Sales Revenue	94,730
Inventory	65,120
	$170,850

PURCHASES JOURNAL

In the **purchases journal**, companies record all purchases of merchandise on account. Each entry in this journal results in a debit to Inventory and a credit to Accounts Payable. For example, consider the following credit purchase transactions for Karns Wholesale Supply in Illustration J-11.

ILLUSTRATION J-11
Credit purchases transactions

Date	Supplier	Amount
5/6	Jasper Manufacturing Inc.	$11,000
5/10	Eaton and Howe Inc.	7,200
5/14	Fabor and Son	6,900
5/19	Jasper Manufacturing Inc.	17,500
5/26	Fabor and Son	8,700
5/29	Eaton and Howe Inc.	12,600

Illustration J-12 (page J-12) shows the purchases journal for Karns based on these transactions. When using a one-column purchases journal (as in Illustration J-12), a company cannot journalize other types of purchases on account or cash purchases in it. For example, using the purchases journal shown in Illustration J-12, Karns would have to record credit purchases of equipment or supplies in the general journal. Likewise, all cash purchases would be entered in the cash payments journal. As illustrated later, companies that make numerous credit purchases for items other than merchandise often expand the purchases journal to a multi-column format. (See Illustration J-14 on page J-13.)

Journalizing Credit Purchases of Merchandise

The journalizing procedure is similar to that for a sales journal. Companies make entries in the purchases journal from purchase invoices. In contrast to the sales journal, the purchases journal may not have an invoice number column because invoices received from different suppliers will not be in numerical sequence. To ensure that they record all purchase invoices, some companies consecutively number each invoice upon receipt and then use an internal document number column in the purchases journal.

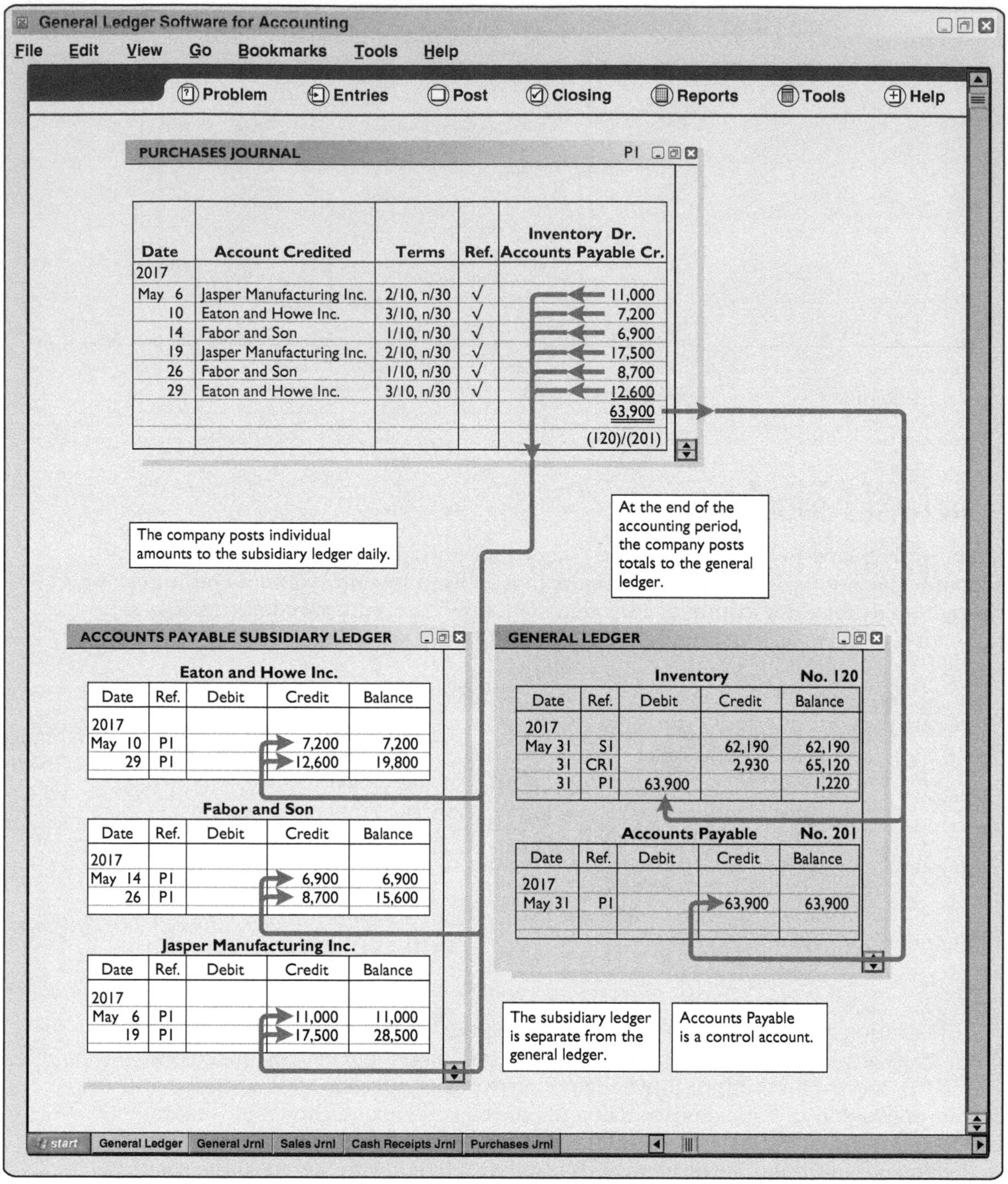

ILLUSTRATION J-12
Journalizing and posting the purchases journal

Posting the Purchases Journal

▼ **HELPFUL HINT**
Postings to subsidiary ledger accounts are done daily because it is often necessary to know a current balance for the subsidiary accounts.

The procedures for posting the purchases journal are similar to those for the sales journal. In this case, Karns makes **daily** postings to the **accounts payable ledger**; it makes **monthly** postings to Inventory and Accounts Payable in the general ledger. In both ledgers, Karns uses **P1** in the reference column to show that the postings are from page 1 of the purchases journal.

Proof of the equality of the postings from the purchases journal to both ledgers is shown in Illustration J-13.

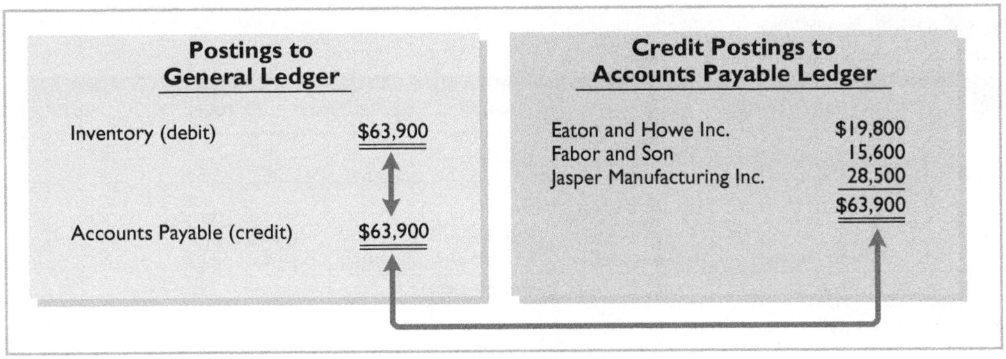

ILLUSTRATION J-13
Proving the equality of the purchases journal

Expanding the Purchases Journal

As noted earlier, some companies expand the purchases journal to include all types of purchases on account. Instead of one column for Inventory and Accounts Payable, they use a multi-column format. This format usually includes a credit column for Accounts Payable and debit columns for purchases of Inventory, Office Supplies, Store Supplies, and Other Accounts. Illustration J-14 shows a multi-column purchases journal for Hanover Co. The posting procedures are similar to those shown earlier for posting the cash receipts journal.

▼ HELPFUL HINT
A single-column purchases journal needs only to be footed to prove the equality of debits and credits.

ILLUSTRATION J-14
Multi-column purchases journal

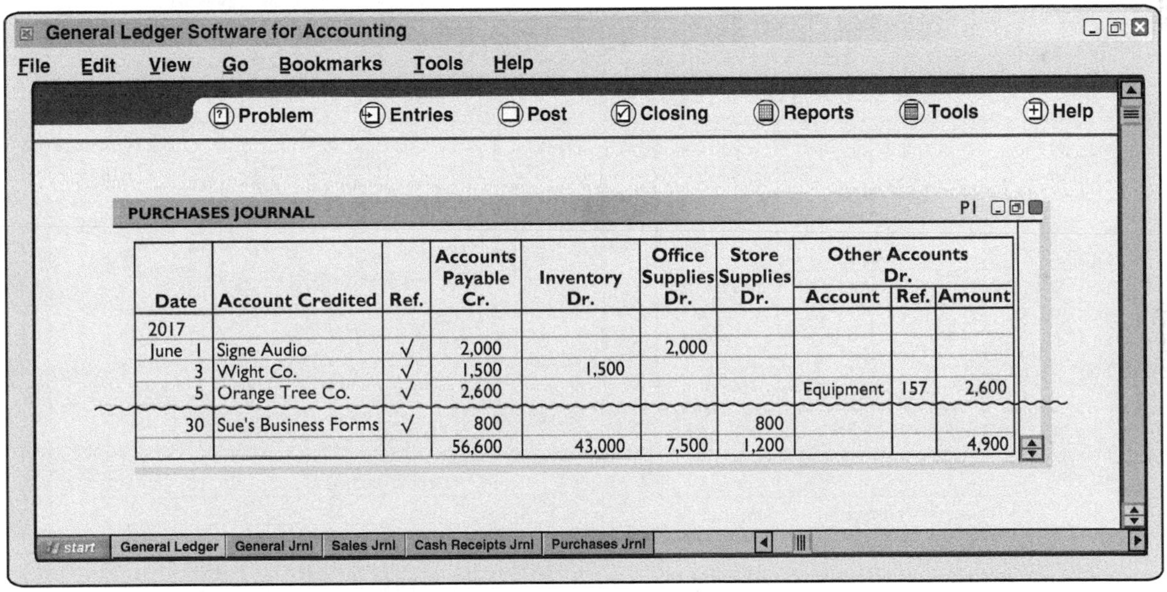

PURCHASES JOURNAL P1

Date	Account Credited	Ref.	Accounts Payable Cr.	Inventory Dr.	Office Supplies Dr.	Store Supplies Dr.	Other Accounts Dr. Account	Ref.	Amount
2017									
June 1	Signe Audio	√	2,000		2,000				
3	Wight Co.	√	1,500	1,500					
5	Orange Tree Co.	√	2,600				Equipment	157	2,600
30	Sue's Business Forms	√	800			800			
			56,600	43,000	7,500	1,200			4,900

CASH PAYMENTS JOURNAL

In a **cash payments (cash disbursements) journal**, companies record all disbursements of cash. Entries are made from prenumbered checks. Because companies make cash payments for various purposes, the cash payments journal has multiple columns. Illustration J-15 (page J-14) shows a four-column journal.

Journalizing Cash Payments Transactions

The procedures for journalizing transactions in this journal are similar to those for the cash receipts journal. Karns records each transaction on one line, and for each line there must be equal debit and credit amounts. The entries in the cash

General Ledger Software for Accounting

File Edit View Go Bookmarks Tools Help

Problem Entries Post Closing Reports Tools Help

CASH PAYMENTS JOURNAL CP1

Date	Ck. No.	Account Debited	Ref.	Other Accounts Dr.	Accounts Payable Dr.	Inventory Cr.	Cash Cr.
2017							
May 1	101	Prepaid Insurance	130	1,200			1,200
3	102	Inventory	120	100			100
8	103	Inventory	120	4,400			4,400
10	104	Jasper Manuf. Inc.	√		11,000	220	10,780
19	105	Eaton & Howe Inc.	√		7,200	216	6,984
23	106	Fabor and Son	√		6,900	69	6,831
28	107	Jasper Manuf. Inc.	√		17,500	350	17,150
30	108	Cash Dividends	332	500			500
				6,200	42,600	855	47,945
				(x)	(201)	(120)	(101)

The company posts individual amounts to the subsidiary ledger daily.

At the end of the accounting period, the company posts totals to the general ledger.

ACCOUNTS PAYABLE SUBSIDIARY LEDGER

Eaton and Howe Inc.

Date	Ref.	Debit	Credit	Balance
2017				
May 10	P1		7,200	7,200
19	CP1	7,200		-------
29	P1		12,600	12,600

Fabor and Son

Date	Ref.	Debit	Credit	Balance
2017				
May 14	P1		6,900	6,900
23	CP1	6,900		-------
26	P1		8,700	8,700

Jasper Manufacturing Inc.

Date	Ref.	Debit	Credit	Balance
2017				
May 6	P1		11,000	11,000
10	CP1	11,000		--------
19	P1		17,500	17,500
28	CP1	17,500		--------

The subsidiary ledger is separate from the general ledger.

Accounts Payable is a control account.

GENERAL LEDGER

Cash **No. 101**

Date	Ref.	Debit	Credit	Balance
2017				
May 31	CR1	53,769		53,769
31	CP1		47,945	5,824

Inventory **No. 120**

Date	Ref.	Debit	Credit	Balance
2017				
May 3	CP1	100		100
8	CP1	4,400		4,500
31	S1		62,190	57,690
31	CR1		2,930	60,620
31	P1	63,900		3,280
31	CP1		855	2,425

Prepaid Insurance **No. 130**

Date	Ref.	Debit	Credit	Balance
2017				
May 1	CP1	1,200		1,200

Accounts Payable **No. 201**

Date	Ref.	Debit	Credit	Balance
2017				
May 31	P1		63,900	63,900
31	CP1	42,600		21,300

Cash Dividends **No. 332**

Date	Ref.	Debit	Credit	Balance
2017				
May 30	CP1	500		500

start | General Ledger | General Jrnl | Sales Jrnl | Cash Receipts Jrnl | Purchases Jrnl

ILLUSTRATION J-15
Journalizing and posting the cash payments journal

payments journal in Illustration J-15 are based on the following transactions for Karns Wholesale Supply.

May 1	Issued check No. 101 for $1,200 for the annual premium on a fire insurance policy.
3	Issued check No. 102 for $100 in payment of freight when terms were FOB shipping point.
8	Issued check No. 103 for $4,400 for the purchase of merchandise.
10	Sent check No. 104 for $10,780 to Jasper Manufacturing Inc. in payment of May 6 invoice for $11,000 less a 2% discount.
19	Mailed check No. 105 for $6,984 to Eaton and Howe Inc. in payment of May 10 invoice for $7,200 less a 3% discount.
23	Sent check No. 106 for $6,831 to Fabor and Son in payment of May 14 invoice for $6,900 less a 1% discount.
28	Sent check No. 107 for $17,150 to Jasper Manufacturing Inc. in payment of May 19 invoice for $17,500 less a 2% discount.
30	Issued check No. 108 for $500 to stockholders as a dividend.

Note that whenever Karns enters an amount in the Other Accounts column, it must identify a specific general ledger account in the Account Debited column. The entries for checks No. 101, 102, 103, and 108 illustrate this situation. Similarly, Karns must identify a subsidiary account in the Account Debited column whenever it enters an amount in the Accounts Payable column. See, for example, the entry for check No. 104.

After Karns journalizes the cash payments journal, it totals the columns. The totals are then balanced to prove the equality of debits and credits.

Posting the Cash Payments Journal

The procedures for posting the cash payments journal are similar to those for the cash receipts journal. Karns posts the amounts recorded in the Accounts Payable column individually to the subsidiary ledger and in total to the control account. It posts Inventory and Cash only in total at the end of the month. Transactions in the Other Accounts column are posted individually to the appropriate account(s) affected. The company does not post totals for the Other Accounts column.

Illustration J-15 shows the posting of the cash payments journal. Note that Karns uses the symbol **CP** as the posting reference. After postings are completed, the company proves the equality of the debit and credit balances in the general ledger. In addition, the control account balances should agree with the subsidiary ledger total balance. Illustration J-16 shows the agreement of these balances.

ILLUSTRATION J-16
Proving the ledgers after postings from the sales, cash receipts, purchases, and cash payments journals

Schedule of Accounts Payable
(from accounts payable subsidiary ledger)

Eaton and Howe Inc.	$12,600
Fabor and Son	8,700
	$21,300

General Ledger

Debits	
Cash	$ 5,824
Accounts Receivable	51,180
Inventory	2,425
Prepaid Insurance	1,200
Cash Dividends	500
Sales Discounts	781
Cost of Goods Sold	65,120
	$127,030

Credits	
Notes Payable	$ 6,000
Accounts Payable	21,300
Common Stock	5,000
Sales Revenue	94,730
	$127,030

EFFECTS OF SPECIAL JOURNALS ON THE GENERAL JOURNAL

Special journals for sales, purchases, and cash substantially reduce the number of entries that companies make in the general journal. **Only transactions that cannot be entered in a special journal are recorded in the general journal.** For example, a company may use the general journal to record such transactions as granting of credit to a customer for a sales return or allowance, granting of credit from a supplier for purchases returned, acceptance of a note receivable from a customer, and purchase of equipment by issuing a note payable. Also, **correcting, adjusting, and closing entries are made in the general journal.**

The general journal has columns for date, account title and explanation, reference, and debit and credit amounts. When control and subsidiary accounts are not involved, the procedures for journalizing and posting of transactions are the same as those described in earlier chapters. When control and subsidiary accounts *are* involved, companies make two changes from the earlier procedures:

1. In **journalizing**, they identify both the control and the subsidiary accounts.
2. In **posting**, there must be a **dual posting**: once to the control account and once to the subsidiary account.

To illustrate, assume that on May 31, Karns Wholesale Supply returns $500 of merchandise for credit to Fabor and Son. Illustration J-17 shows the entry in the general journal and the posting of the entry. If Karns receives cash instead of credit on this return, then it would record the transaction in the cash receipts journal.

The general journal indicates two accounts (Accounts Payable, and Fabor and Son) for the debit, and two postings ("201/✓") in the reference column. One debit is posted to the control account and another debit to the creditor's account in the subsidiary ledger.

ILLUSTRATION J-17
Journalizing and posting the general journal

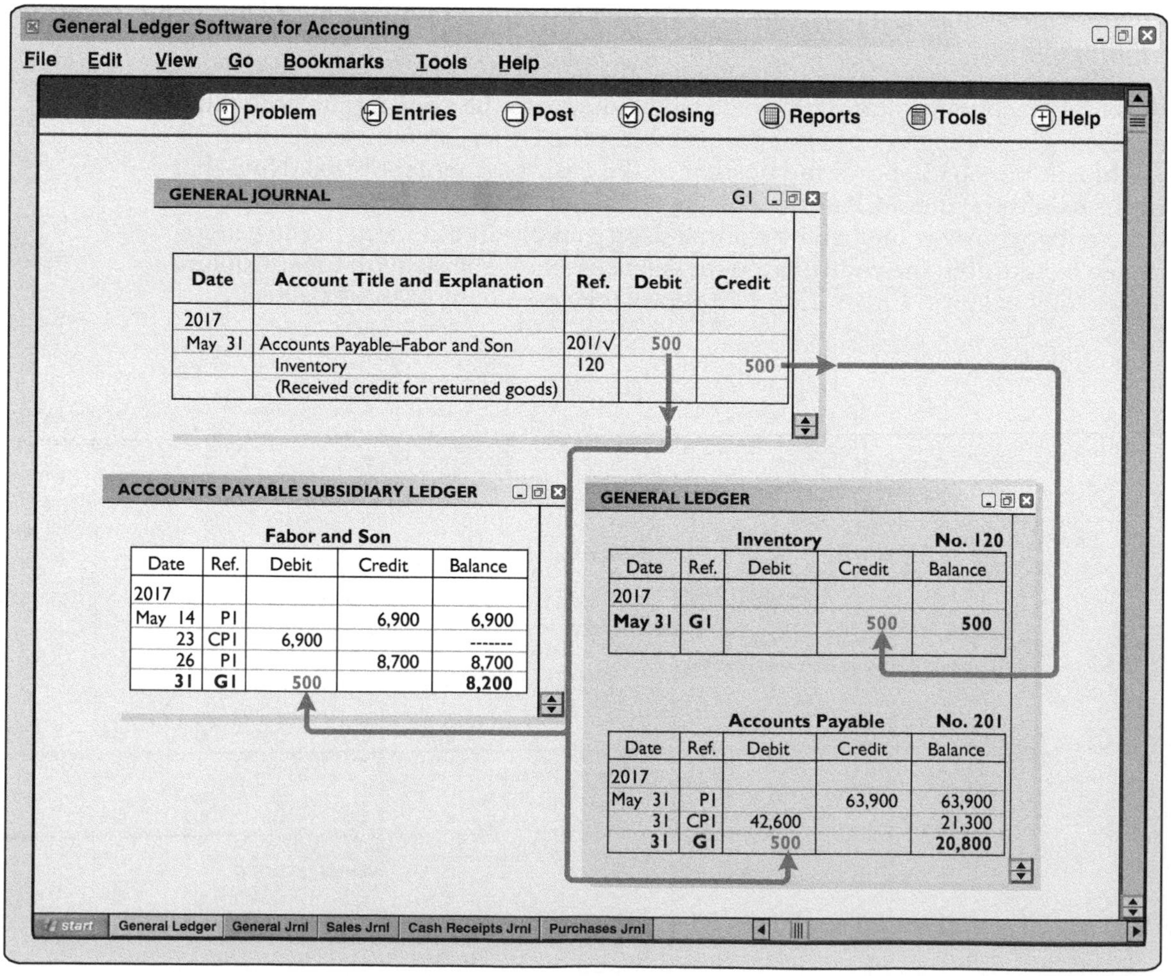

Date	Account Title and Explanation	Ref.	Debit	Credit
2017				
May 31	Accounts Payable–Fabor and Son	201/✓	500	
	Inventory	120		500
	(Received credit for returned goods)			

Fabor and Son

Date	Ref.	Debit	Credit	Balance
2017				
May 14	P1		6,900	6,900
23	CP1	6,900		-------
26	P1		8,700	8,700
31	G1	500		8,200

Inventory No. 120

Date	Ref.	Debit	Credit	Balance
2017				
May 31	G1		500	500

Accounts Payable No. 201

Date	Ref.	Debit	Credit	Balance
2017				
May 31	P1		63,900	63,900
31	CP1	42,600		21,300
31	G1	500		20,800

CYBER SECURITY: A FINAL COMMENT

Have you ever been hacked? With the increasing use of cell phones, tablets, and other social media outlets, a real risk exists that your confidential information may be stolen and used illegally. Companies, individuals, and even nations have all been victims of **cybercrime**—a crime that involves the Internet, a computer system, or computer technology.

For companies, cybercrime is clearly a major threat as the hacking of employees' or customers' records related to cybercrime can cost millions of dollars. Unfortunately, the numbers of security breaches are increasing. A security breach at Target, for example, cost the company a minimum of $20 million, the CEO lost his job, and sales plummeted.

Here are three reasons for the rise in the successful hacks of corporate computer records.

1. Companies and their employees continue to increase their activity on the Internet, primarily due to the use of mobile devices and cloud computing.
2. Companies today collect and store unprecedented amounts of personal data on customers and employees.
3. Companies often take measures to protect themselves from cyber security attacks but then fail to check if employees are carrying out the proper security guidelines.

Note that cyber security risks extend far beyond company operations and compliance. Many hackers target highly sensitive intellectual information or other strategic assets. Illustration J-18 highlights the type of hackers and their motives, targets and impacts.

Companies now recognize that cyber security systems that protect confidential data must be implemented. It follows that companies (and nations and individuals) must continually verify that their cyber security defenses are sound and uncompromised.

ILLUSTRATION J-18
Profiles of hackers

Malicious Actors	Motives	Targets	Impacts
Nation-state	• Economic, political, and/ or military advantage	• Trade secrets • Sensitive business information • Emerging technologies • Critical infrastructure	• Loss of competitive advantage • Disruption to critical infrastructure
Organized crime	• Immediate financial gain • Collect information for future financial gains	• Financial/payment systems • Personally identifiable information • Payment card information • Protected health information	• Costly regulatory inquiries and penalties • Consumer and shareholder lawsuits • Loss of consumer confidence
Hacktivists	• Influence political and/or social change • Pressure businesses to change their practices	• Corporate secrets • Sensitive business information • Information related to key executives, employees, customers, and business partners	• Disruption of business activities • Harm to brand and reputation • Loss of consumer confidence
Insiders	• Personal advantage, monetary gain • Professional revenge • Patriotism	• Sales, deals, market strategies • Corporate secrets, intellectual property • Business operations • Personnel information	• Trade secret disclosure • Operational disruption • Harm to brand and reputation • National security impact

Source: PriceWaterhouseCoopers, "Answering Your Cybersecurity Questions" (January 2014).

REVIEW

LEARNING OBJECTIVES REVIEW

1 Describe the nature and purpose of a subsidiary ledger. A subsidiary ledger is a group of accounts with a common characteristic. It facilitates the recording process by freeing the general ledger from details of individual balances.

2 Record transactions in special journals. Companies use special journals to group similar types of transactions. In a special journal, generally only one line is used to record a complete transaction.

In posting a multi-column journal:

(a) Companies post all column totals except for the Other Accounts column once at the end of the month to the account title specified in the column heading.

(b) Companies do not post the total of the Other Accounts column. Instead, the individual amounts comprising the total are posted separately to the general ledger accounts specified in the Account Credited (Debited) column.

(c) The individual amounts in a column posted in total to a control account are posted daily to the subsidiary ledger accounts specified in the Account Credited (Debited) column.

GLOSSARY REVIEW

Accounts payable (creditors') subsidiary ledger A subsidiary ledger that collects transaction data of individual creditors. (p. J-2).

Accounts receivable (customers') subsidiary ledger A subsidiary ledger that collects transaction data of individual customers. (p. J-2).

Cash payments (cash disbursements) journal A special journal that records all cash paid. (p. J-13).

Cash receipts journal A special journal that records all cash received. (p. J-7).

Control account An account in the general ledger that summarizes subsidiary ledger data. (p. J-2).

Cybercrime A crime that involves the Internet, a computer system, or computer technology. (p. J-17).

Purchases journal A special journal that records all purchases of merchandise on account. (p. J-11).

Sales journal A special journal that records all sales of merchandise on account. (p. J-4).

Special journals Journals that record similar types of transactions, such as all credit sales. (p. J-4).

Subsidiary ledger A group of accounts with a common characteristic. (p. J-1).

WileyPLUS Many additional resources are available for practice in WileyPLUS.

QUESTIONS

1. What are the advantages of using subsidiary ledgers?
2. (a) When do companies normally post to (1) the subsidiary accounts and (2) the general ledger control accounts? (b) Describe the relationship between a control account and a subsidiary ledger.
3. Identify and explain the four special journals discussed in this appendix. List an advantage of using each of these journals rather than using only a general journal.
4. Burguet Company uses special journals. It recorded in a sales journal a sale made on account to P. Starch for $435. A few days later, P. Starch returns $70 worth of merchandise for credit. Where should Burguet Company record the sales return? Why?
5. A $500 purchase of merchandise on account from Liu Company was properly recorded in the purchases journal. When posted, however, the amount recorded in the subsidiary ledger was $50. How might this error be discovered?

6. Why would special journals used in different businesses not be identical in format? What type of business would maintain a cash receipts journal but not include a column for accounts receivable?
7. The cash and the accounts receivable columns in the cash receipts journal were mistakenly over-added by $4,000 at the end of the month. (a) Will the customers' ledger agree with the Accounts Receivable control account? (b) Assuming no other errors, will the trial balance totals be equal?
8. One column total of a special journal is posted at month-end to only two general ledger accounts. One of these two accounts is Accounts Receivable. What is the name of this special journal? What is the other general ledger account to which that same month-end total is posted?
9. In what journal would the following transactions be recorded? (Assume that a two-column sales journal and a single-column purchases journal are used.)
   (a) Recording of depreciation expense for the year.
   (b) Credit given to a customer for merchandise purchased on credit and returned.
   (c) Sales of merchandise for cash.
   (d) Sales of merchandise on account.
   (e) Collection of cash on account from a customer.
   (f) Purchase of office supplies on account.
10. In what journal would the following transactions be recorded? (Assume that a two-column sales journal and a single-column purchases journal are used.)
    (a) Cash received from signing a note payable.
    (b) Investment of cash by stockholders.
    (c) Closing of the expense accounts at the end of the year.
    (d) Purchase of merchandise on account.
    (e) Credit received for merchandise purchased and returned to supplier.
    (f) Payment of cash on account due a supplier.
11. What transactions might be included in a multi-column purchases journal that would not be included in a single-column purchases journal?
12. Give an example of a transaction in the general journal that causes an entry to be posted twice (i.e., to two accounts), one in the general ledger, the other in the subsidiary ledger. Does this affect the debit/credit equality of the general ledger?
13. Give some examples of appropriate general journal transactions for an organization using special journals.

BRIEF EXERCISES

Identify subsidiary ledger balances. (LO 1), C

BEJ-1 Presented below is information related to Cortes Company for its first month of operations. Identify the balances that appear in the accounts receivable subsidiary ledger and the accounts receivable balance that appears in the general ledger at the end of January.

Credit Sales			**Cash Collections**		
Jan. 7	Adcock Co.	$10,000	Jan. 17	Adcock Co.	$7,000
15	Cruz Co.	7,000	24	Cruz Co.	6,000
23	Morissy Co.	9,000	29	Morissy Co.	9,000

Identify subsidiary ledger accounts. (LO 1), C

BEJ-2 Identify in what ledger (general or subsidiary) each of the following accounts is shown.
(a) Rent Expense.
(b) Accounts Receivable—Molina.
(c) Notes Payable.
(d) Accounts Payable—Unruh.

Identify special journals. (LO 2), C

BEJ-3 Identify the journal in which each of the following transactions is recorded.
(a) Cash sales.
(b) Payment of cash dividends.
(c) Cash purchase of land.
(d) Credit sales.
(e) Purchase of merchandise on account.
(f) Receipt of cash for services performed.

Identify entries to cash receipts journal. (LO 2), C

BEJ-4 Indicate whether each of the following debits and credits is included in the cash receipts journal. (Use "Yes" or "No" to answer this question.)
(a) Debit to Sales Revenue.
(b) Credit to Inventory.
(c) Credit to Accounts Receivable.
(d) Debit to Accounts Payable.

Identify transactions for special journals. (LO 2), C

BEJ-5 Kiner Co. uses special journals and a general journal. Identify the journal in which each of the following transactions is recorded.
(a) Purchased equipment on account.
(b) Purchased merchandise on account.
(c) Paid utility expense in cash.
(d) Sold merchandise on account.

Identify transactions for special journals. (LO 2), C

BEJ-6 Identify the special journal(s) in which the following column headings appear.
(a) Sales Discounts Dr.
(b) Accounts Receivable Cr.
(c) Cash Dr.
(d) Sales Revenue Cr.
(e) Inventory Dr.

Indicate postings to cash receipts journal.
(LO 2), C

BEJ-7 Merando Computer Components Inc. uses a multi-column cash receipts journal. Indicate which column(s) is/are posted only in total, only daily, or both in total and daily.
(a) Accounts Receivable.
(b) Sales Discounts.
(c) Cash.
(d) Other Accounts.

EXERCISES

Determine control account balances, and explain posting of special journals.
(LO 1, 2), AP

EJ-1 Lanley Company uses both special journals and a general journal as described in this appendix. On June 30, after all monthly postings had been completed, the Accounts Receivable control account in the general ledger had a debit balance of $314,000; the Accounts Payable control account had a credit balance of $77,000.

The July transactions recorded in the special journals are summarized below. No entries affecting accounts receivable and accounts payable were recorded in the general journal for July.

Sales journal	Total sales $161,400
Purchases journal	Total purchases $54,100
Cash receipts journal	Accounts receivable column total $131,000
Cash payments journal	Accounts payable column total $47,500

Instructions
(a) What is the balance of the Accounts Receivable control account after the monthly postings on July 31?
(b) What is the balance of the Accounts Payable control account after the monthly postings on July 31?
(c) To what account(s) is the column total of $161,400 in the sales journal posted?
(d) To what account(s) is the accounts receivable column total of $131,000 in the cash receipts journal posted?

Explain postings to subsidiary ledger.
(LO 1), AP

EJ-2 Presented below is the subsidiary Accounts Receivable account of Martha Nott.

Date	Ref.	Debit	Credit	Balance
2017				
Sept. 2	S31	61,000		61,000
9	G4		14,000	47,000
27	CR8		47,000	—

Instructions
Write a memo to Erica Grier, chief financial officer, that explains each transaction.

Post various journals to control and subsidiary accounts.
(LO 1, 2), AP

EJ-3 On September 1, the balance of the Accounts Receivable control account in the general ledger of Stark Company was $10,960. The customers' subsidiary ledger contained account balances as follows: Zeyen $1,440, Milo $2,640, Baez $2,060, and Dey $4,820. At the end of September, the various journals contained the following information.

Sales journal: Sales to Dey $800; to Zeyen $1,260; to Guy $1,330; to Baez $1,260.
Cash receipts journal: Cash received from Baez $1,310; from Dey $2,300; from Guy $380; from Milo $1,800; from Zeyen $1,240.
General journal: An allowance is granted to Dey $185.

Instructions
(a) Set up control and subsidiary accounts and enter the beginning balances. Do not construct the journals.
(b) Post the various journals. Post the items as individual items or as totals, whichever would be the appropriate procedure. (No sales discounts given.)
(c) Prepare a schedule of accounts receivable and prove the agreement of the controlling account with the subsidiary ledger at September 30, 2017.

EJ-4 Bill Porter Company has a balance in its Accounts Receivable control account of $10,200 on January 1, 2017. The subsidiary ledger contains three accounts: Connor Company, balance $4,000; Uhlig Company, balance $2,500; and Matson Company. During January, the following receivable-related transactions occurred.

Determine control and subsidiary ledger balances for accounts receivable.

(LO 1, 2), AP

	Credit Sales	Collections	Returns
Connor Company	$9,000	$8,000	$ –0–
Uhlig Company	7,000	2,500	3,000
Matson Company	8,300	9,000	–0–

Instructions

(a) What is the January 1 balance in the Matson Company subsidiary account?
(b) What is the January 31 balance in the control account?
(c) Compute the balances in the subsidiary accounts at the end of the month.
(d) Which January transaction would not be recorded in a special journal?

EJ-5 Gonzalez Company has a balance in its Accounts Payable control account of $8,250 on January 1, 2017. The subsidiary ledger contains three accounts: Rye Company, balance $3,000; Keyes Company, balance $1,875; and Colaw Company. During January, the following receivable-related transactions occurred.

Determine control and subsidiary ledger balances for accounts payable.

(LO 1, 2), AP

	Purchases	Payments	Returns
Rye Company	$6,750	$6,000	$ –0–
Keyes Company	5,250	1,900	2,300
Colaw Company	6,375	6,750	–0–

Instructions

(a) What is the January 1 balance in the Colaw Company subsidiary account?
(b) What is the January 31 balance in the control account?
(c) Compute the balances in the subsidiary accounts at the end of the month.
(d) Which January transaction would not be recorded in a special journal?

EJ-6 Norren Company uses special journals and a general journal. The following transactions occurred during September 2017.

Record transactions in sales and purchases journal.

(LO 2), AP

Sept. 2 Sold merchandise on account to J. Yancey, invoice no. 101, $780, terms n/30. The cost of the merchandise sold was $420.
10 Purchased merchandise on account from H. Heerey $600, terms 2/10, n/30.
12 Purchased office equipment on account from Y. Kojima $6,500.
21 Sold merchandise on account to K. Pricer, invoice no. 102 for $800, terms 2/10, n/30. The cost of the merchandise sold was $480.
25 Purchased merchandise on account from G. Jeanik $835, terms n/30.
27 Sold merchandise to D. Schaff for $700 cash. The cost of the merchandise sold was $400.

Instructions

(a) Prepare a sales journal (see Illustration J-6) and a single-column purchases journal (see Illustration J-12). (Use page 1 for each journal.)
(b) Record the transaction(s) for September that should be journalized in the sales journal and the purchases journal.

EJ-7 Milner Co. uses special journals and a general journal. The following transactions occurred during May 2017.

Record transactions in cash receipts and cash payments journal.

(LO 2), AP

May 1 M. Milner invested $48,000 cash in the business in exchange for common stock.
2 Sold merchandise to A. Belton for $6,340 cash. The cost of the merchandise sold was $4,200.
3 Purchased merchandise for $7,200 from E. Stein using check no. 101.
14 Paid salary to M. Hunt $700 by issuing check no. 102.
16 Sold merchandise on account to S. Spies for $900, terms n/30. The cost of the merchandise sold was $630.
22 A check of $9,000 is received from N. Feeney in full for invoice 101; no discount given.

Instructions

(a) Prepare a multi-column cash receipts journal (see Illustration J-8) and a multi-column cash payments journal (see Illustration J-15). (Use page 1 for each journal.)

(b) Record the transaction(s) for May that should be journalized in the cash receipts journal and cash payments journal.

Explain journalizing in cash journals.
(LO 2), AP

EJ-8 Eaton Company uses the columnar cash journals illustrated in the textbook. In April, the following selected cash transactions occurred.

1. Made a cash refund to a customer for the return of damaged goods.
2. Received collection from customer within the 3% discount period.
3. Purchased merchandise for cash.
4. Paid a creditor within the 3% discount period.
5. Received collection from customer after the 3% discount period had expired.
6. Paid freight on merchandise purchased.
7. Paid cash for office equipment.
8. Received cash refund from supplier for merchandise returned.
9. Paid cash dividend to stockholders.
10. Made cash sales.

Instructions

Indicate (a) the journal and (b) the columns in the journal that should be used in recording each transaction.

Journalize transactions in general journal and post.
(LO 1, 2), AP

EJ-9 Nolasco Company has the following selected transactions during March.

Mar.	2	Purchased equipment costing $9,400 from Brantly Company on account.
	5	Received credit of $410 from Dumont Company for merchandise damaged in shipment to Nolasco.
	7	Issued credit of $390 to Horst Company for merchandise the customer returned. The returned merchandise had a cost of $240.

Nolasco Company uses a one-column purchases journal, a sales journal, the columnar cash journals used in the text, and a general journal.

Instructions

(a) Journalize the transactions in the general journal.

(b) In a brief memo to the president of Nolasco Company, explain the postings to the control and subsidiary accounts from each type of journal.

Indicate journalizing in special journals.
(LO 2), AP

EJ-10 Below are some typical transactions incurred by Barone Company.

1. Payment of creditors on account.
2. Return of merchandise sold for credit.
3. Collection on account from customers.
4. Sale of land for cash.
5. Sale of merchandise on account.
6. Sale of merchandise for cash.
7. Received credit for merchandise purchased on credit.
8. Sales discount taken on goods sold.
9. Payment of employee wages.
10. Payment of cash dividend to stockholders.
11. Depreciation on building.
12. Purchase of office supplies for cash.
13. Purchase of merchandise on account.

Instructions

For each transaction, indicate whether it would normally be recorded in a cash receipts journal, cash payments journal, sales journal, single-column purchases journal, or general journal.

Explain posting to control account and subsidiary ledger.
(LO 1), AP

EJ-11 The general ledger of Raysom Company contained the following Accounts Payable control account (in T-account form). Also shown is the related subsidiary ledger.

GENERAL LEDGER

Accounts Payable

Feb. 15	General journal	1,400	Feb. 1	Balance	26,025
28	?	?	5	General journal	195
			11	General journal	550
			28	Purchases	13,400
			Feb. 28	Balance	9,800

ACCOUNTS PAYABLE LEDGER

Keyser

	Feb. 28	Bal. 4,600

Robillard

	Feb. 28	Bal. ?

Stine

	Feb. 28	Bal. 2,100

Instructions

(a) Indicate the missing posting reference and amount in the control account, and the missing ending balance in the subsidiary ledger.

(b) Indicate the amounts in the control account that were dual-posted (i.e., posted to the control account and the subsidiary accounts).

EJ-12 Selected accounts from the ledgers of Ramos Company at July 31 showed the following.

Prepare purchases and general journals.

(LO 1, 2), AP

GENERAL LEDGER

Equipment No. 153

Date	Explanation	Ref.	Debit	Credit	Balance
July 1		G1	3,900		3,900

Accounts Payable No. 201

Date	Explanation	Ref.	Debit	Credit	Balance
July 1		G1		3,900	3,900
15		G1		600	4,500
18		G1	380		4,120
25		G1	200		3,920
31		P1		8,500	12,420

Inventory No. 120

Date	Explanation	Ref.	Debit	Credit	Balance
July 15		G1	600		600
18		G1		380	220
25		G1		200	20
31		P1	8,500		8,520

ACCOUNTS PAYABLE LEDGER

Alaska Equipment Co.

Date	Explanation	Ref.	Debit	Credit	Balance
July 1		G1		3,900	3,900

Carolina Co.

Date	Explanation	Ref.	Debit	Credit	Balance
July 3		P1		2,400	2,400
20		P1		700	3,100

Florida Corp

Date	Explanation	Ref.	Debit	Credit	Balance
July 17		P1		1,400	1,400
18		G1	380		1,020
29		P1		1,600	2,620

Kentucky Co.

Date	Explanation	Ref.	Debit	Credit	Balance
July 14		P1		1,300	1,300
25		G1	200		1,100

Nevada Co.

Date	Explanation	Ref.	Debit	Credit	Balance
July 12		P1		500	500
21		P1		600	1,100

Oklahoma Inc.

Date	Explanation	Ref.	Debit	Credit	Balance
July 15		G1		600	600

Instructions

From the data prepare:

(a) The single-column purchases journal for July.
(b) The general journal entries for July.

Determine correct posting amount to control account.

(LO 1, 2), AP

EJ-13 Castro Products uses both special journals and a general journal as described in this appendix. Castro also posts customers' accounts in the accounts receivable subsidiary ledger. The postings for the most recent month are included in the subsidiary T-accounts below.

Dingel

Bal.	340	250
	280	

Lopez

Bal.	150	150
	240	

Epping

Bal.	–0–	145
	145	

Rivera

Bal.	120	120
	190	
	130	

Instructions

Determine the correct amount of the end-of-month posting from the sales journal to the Accounts Receivable control account.

Compute balances in various accounts.

(LO 2), AP

EJ-14 Selected account balances for Ramano Company at January 1, 2017, are presented below.

Accounts Payable	$19,000
Accounts Receivable	22,000
Cash	17,000
Inventory	13,500

Ramano's sales journal for January shows a total of $100,000 in the selling price column, and its one-column purchases journal for January shows a total of $72,000.

The column totals in Ramano's cash receipts journal are Cash Dr. $64,000; Sales Discounts Dr. $1,100; Accounts Receivable Cr. $48,000; Sales Revenue Cr. $6,000; and Other Accounts Cr. $11,100.

The column totals in Ramano's cash payments journal for January are Cash Cr. $55,000; Inventory Cr. $1,000; Accounts Payable Dr. $46,000; and Other Accounts Dr. $10,000. Ramano's total cost of goods sold for January is $63,600.

Accounts Payable, Accounts Receivable, Cash, Inventory, and Sales Revenue are not involved in the "Other Accounts" column in either the cash receipts or cash payments journal, and are not involved in any general journal entries.

Instructions

Compute the January 31 balance for Ramano in the following accounts.

(a) Accounts Payable.
(b) Accounts Receivable.
(c) Cash.
(d) Inventory.
(e) Sales Revenue.

PROBLEMS

Journalize transactions in cash receipts journal; post to control account and subsidiary ledger.

(LO 1, 2), AP

GLS

PJ-1 Parsons Company's chart of accounts includes the following selected accounts.

101 Cash
112 Accounts Receivable
120 Inventory
311 Common Stock
401 Sales Revenue
414 Sales Discounts
505 Cost of Goods Sold

On April 1, the accounts receivable ledger of Parsons Company showed the following balances: Park $1,550, Kolten $1,200, Hurt Co. $2,900, and Afzal $1,800. The April transactions involving the receipt of cash were as follows.

Apr.	1	Stockholders invested $7,200 additional cash in the business, in exchange for common stock.
	4	Received check for payment of account from Afzal less 2% cash discount.
	5	Received check for $990 in payment of invoice no. 307 from Hurt Co.
	8	Made cash sales of merchandise totaling $7,845. The cost of the merchandise sold was $4,347.
	10	Received check for $600 in payment of invoice no. 309 from Park.
	11	Received cash refund from a supplier for damaged merchandise $680.
	23	Received check for $1,500 in payment of invoice no. 310 from Hurt Co.
	29	Received check for payment of account from Kolten.

Instructions

(a) Journalize the preceding transactions in a six-column cash receipts journal with columns for Cash Dr., Sales Discounts Dr., Accounts Receivable Cr., Sales Revenue Cr., Other Accounts Cr., and Cost of Goods Sold Dr./Inventory Cr. Foot and crossfoot the journal.

(a) Balancing totals $21,815

(b) Insert the beginning balances in the Accounts Receivable control and subsidiary accounts, and post the April transactions to these accounts.

(c) Prove the agreement of the control account and subsidiary account balances.

(c) Accounts Receivable $1,360

PJ-2 Venson Company's chart of accounts includes the following selected accounts.

Journalize transactions in cash payments journal; post to control account and subsidiary ledgers.

(LO 1, 2), AP

GLS

101 Cash	201 Accounts Payable
120 Inventory	332 Cash Dividends
130 Prepaid Insurance	505 Cost of Goods Sold
157 Equipment	

On October 1, the accounts payable ledger of Venson Company showed the following balances: Coulsen Company $2,700, Flynn Co. $2,500, Noy Co. $2,100, and Trent Company $3,700. The October transactions involving the payment of cash were as follows.

Oct.	1	Purchased merchandise, check no. 63, $300.
	3	Purchased equipment, check no. 64, $1,200.
	5	Paid Coulsen Company balance due of $2,700, less 2% discount, check no. 65, $2,646.
	10	Purchased merchandise, check no. 66, $2,250.
	15	Paid Noy Co. balance due of $2,100, check no. 67.
	16	Paid cash dividend of $400, check no. 68.
	19	Paid Flynn Co. in full for invoice no. 610, $1,800 less 2% cash discount, check no. 69, $1,764.
	29	Paid Trent Company in full for invoice no. 264, $2,500, check no. 70.

Instructions

(a) Journalize the transactions above in a four-column cash payments journal with columns for Other Accounts Dr., Accounts Payable Dr., Inventory Cr., and Cash Cr. Foot and crossfoot the journal.

(a) Balancing totals $13,250

(b) Insert the beginning balances in the Accounts Payable control and subsidiary accounts, and post the October transactions to these accounts.

(c) Prove the agreement of the control account and the subsidiary account balances.

(c) Accounts Payable $1,900

PJ-3 The chart of accounts of Beldona Company includes the following selected accounts.

Journalize transactions in multi-column purchases journal; post to the general and subsidiary ledgers.

(LO 1, 2), AP

GLS

112 Accounts Receivable	401 Sales Revenue
120 Inventory	412 Sales Returns and Allowances
126 Supplies	505 Cost of Goods Sold
157 Equipment	610 Advertising Expense
201 Accounts Payable	

In July, the following selected transactions were completed. All purchases and sales were on account. The cost of all merchandise sold was 70% of the sales price.

July	1	Purchased merchandise from Dent Company $7,600.
	2	Received freight bill from Rensing Shipping on Dent purchase $400.
	3	Made sales to Dayley Company $1,300 and to Orsen Bros. $2,000.
	5	Purchased merchandise from Langer Company $3,200.
	8	Received credit on merchandise returned to Langer Company $300.
	13	Purchased store supplies from Abel Supply $910.
	15	Purchased merchandise from Dent Company $3,600 and from Goran Company $3,300.
	16	Made sales to Gentry Company $3,450 and to Orsen Bros. $1,570.
	18	Received bill for advertising from Wei Advertisements $600.
	21	Made sales to Dayley Company $310 and to Musky Company $2,800.
	22	Granted allowance to Dayley Company for merchandise damaged in shipment $65.
	24	Purchased merchandise from Langer Company $3,000.
	26	Purchased equipment from Abel Supply $900.
	28	Received freight bill from Rensing Shipping on Langer purchase of July 24, $380.
	30	Made sales to Gentry Company $5,600.

(a) Purchases journal—Accounts Payable $23,890
Sales journal—Sales revenue column total $17,030
(c) Accounts Receivable $16,965
Accounts Payable $23,590

Instructions

(a) Journalize the preceding transactions in a purchases journal, a sales journal, and a general journal. The purchases journal should have the following column headings: Date, Account Credited (Debited), Ref., Accounts Payable Cr., Inventory Dr., and Other Accounts Dr.

(b) Post to both the general and subsidiary ledger accounts. (Assume that all accounts have zero beginning balances.)

(c) Prove the agreement of the control and subsidiary accounts.

Journalize transactions in special journals.
(LO 1, 2), AP
GLS

PJ-4 Selected accounts from the chart of accounts of Rivera Company are shown below.

101 Cash	401 Sales Revenue
112 Accounts Receivable	412 Sales Returns and Allowances
120 Inventory	414 Sales Discounts
126 Supplies	505 Cost of Goods Sold
157 Equipment	726 Salaries and Wages Expense
201 Accounts Payable	

The cost of all merchandise sold was 60% of the sales price. During January, Rivera completed the following transactions.

Jan.	3	Purchased merchandise on account from Quayle Co. $10,000.
	4	Purchased supplies for cash $80.
	4	Sold merchandise on account to Gant $5,600, invoice no. 371, terms 1/10, n/30.
	5	Returned $300 worth of damaged goods purchased on account from Quayle Co. on January 3.
	6	Made cash sales for the week totaling $3,750.
	8	Purchased merchandise on account from Eubank Co. $4,500.
	9	Sold merchandise on account to Notson Corp. $6,400, invoice no. 372, terms 1/10, n/30.
	11	Purchased merchandise on account from Akers Co. $3,700.
	13	Paid in full Quayle Co. on account less a 2% discount.
	13	Made cash sales for the week totaling $6,260.
	15	Received payment from Notson Corp. for invoice no. 372.
	15	Paid semi-monthly salaries of $14,300 to employees.
	17	Received payment from Gant for invoice no. 371.
	17	Sold merchandise on account to Loeb Co. $1,200, invoice no. 373, terms 1/10, n/30.
	19	Purchased equipment on account from Barb Corp. $5,500.
	20	Cash sales for the week totaled $3,200.
	20	Paid in full Eubank Co. on account less a 2% discount.
	23	Purchased merchandise on account from Quayle Co. $7,800.
	24	Purchased merchandise on account from Fifer Corp. $5,100.
	27	Made cash sales for the week totaling $4,230.
	30	Received payment from Loeb Co. for invoice no. 373.
	31	Paid semi-monthly salaries of $14,300 to employees.
	31	Sold merchandise on account to Gant $9,330, invoice no. 374, terms 1/10, n/30.

Rivera Company uses the following journals.

1. Sales journal.
2. Single-column purchases journal.
3. Cash receipts journal with columns for Cash Dr., Sales Discounts Dr., Accounts Receivable Cr., Sales Revenue Cr., Other Accounts Cr., and Cost of Goods Sold Dr./ Inventory Cr.
4. Cash payments journal with columns for Other Accounts Dr., Accounts Payable Dr., Inventory Cr., and Cash Cr.
5. General journal.

Instructions

Using the selected accounts provided:

(a) Record the January transactions in the appropriate journal noted.
(b) Foot and crossfoot all special journals.
(c) Show how postings would be made by placing ledger account numbers and check-marks as needed in the journals. (Actual posting to ledger accounts is not required.)

(a) Sales journal $22,530
Purchases journal $31,100
Cash receipts journal balancing total $30,640
Cash payments journal balancing total $42,880

PJ-5 Presented below are the purchases and cash payments journals for Ramirez Co. for its first month of operations.

Journalize in sales and cash receipts journals; post; prepare a trial balance; prove control to subsidiary; prepare adjusting entries; prepare an adjusted trial balance.

(LO 1, 2), AP

PURCHASES JOURNAL **P1**

Date	Account Credited	Ref.	Inventory Dr. Accounts Payable Cr.
July 4	T. Donley		6,500
5	K. Farmer		8,100
11	M. Huang		5,920
13	D. Sampson		15,300
20	G. Young		7,900
			43,720

CASH PAYMENTS JOURNAL **CP1**

Date	Account Debited	Ref.	Other Accounts Dr.	Accounts Payable Dr.	Inventory Cr.	Cash Cr.
July 4	Supplies		600			600
10	K. Farmer			8,100	81	8,019
11	Prepaid Rent		6,000			6,000
15	T. Donley			6,500		6,500
19	Cash Dividends		2,500			2,500
21	D. Sampson			15,300	153	15,147
			9,100	29,900	234	38,766

In addition, the following transactions have not been journalized for July. The cost of all merchandise sold was 65% of the sales price.

July 1 A. Ramirez invested $80,000 in cash in exchange for common stock.
6 Sold merchandise on account to Edwards Co. $6,600 terms 1/10, n/30.
7 Made cash sales totaling $6,300.
8 Sold merchandise on account to Carmoni $3,600, terms 1/10, n/30.
10 Sold merchandise on account to L. Nunez $4,900, terms 1/10, n/30.
13 Received payment in full from Carmoni.
16 Received payment in full from L. Nunez.
20 Received payment in full from Edwards Co.
21 Sold merchandise on account to M. Putzi $5,000, terms 1/10, n/30.
29 Returned damaged goods to T. Donley and received cash refund of $450.

Instructions

(a) Open the following accounts in the general ledger.

101 Cash	131 Prepaid Rent
112 Accounts Receivable	201 Accounts Payable
120 Inventory	311 Common Stock
127 Supplies	332 Cash Dividends

401 Sales Revenue	631 Supplies Expense
414 Sales Discounts	729 Rent Expense
505 Cost of Goods Sold	

(b) Sales journal total $20,100
Cash receipts journal balancing totals $101,850

(e) Totals $120,220

(f) Accounts Receivable $5,000
Accounts Payable $13,820

(h) Totals $120,220

(b) Journalize the transactions that have not been journalized in the sales journal, the cash receipts journal (see Illustration J-8), and the general journal.
(c) Post to the accounts receivable and accounts payable subsidiary ledgers. Follow the sequence of transactions as shown in the problem.
(d) Post the individual entries and totals to the general ledger.
(e) Prepare a trial balance at July 31, 2017.
(f) Determine whether the subsidiary ledgers agree with the control accounts in the general ledger.
(g) The following adjustments at the end of July are necessary.
(1) A count of supplies indicates that $170 is still on hand.
(2) Recognize rent expense for July, $500.
Prepare the necessary entries in the general journal. Post the entries to the general ledger.
(h) Prepare an adjusted trial balance at July 31, 2017.

Journalize in special journals; post; prepare a trial balance.

(LO 1, 2), AP

GLS

PJ-6 The post-closing trial balance for Bensen Co. is as follows.

BENSEN CO.
Post-Closing Trial Balance
December 31, 2016

	Debit	Credit
Cash	$ 41,500	
Accounts Receivable	15,000	
Notes Receivable	45,000	
Inventory	20,000	
Equipment	7,500	
Accumulated Depreciation—Equipment		$ 1,500
Accounts Payable		43,000
Common Stock		84,500
	$129,000	$129,000

The subsidiary ledgers contain the following information: (1) accounts receivable—M. Cedeno $2,500, J. Deitz $7,500, and E. Divine $5,000; (2) accounts payable—B. Forrest $10,000, L. Gold $18,000, and A. Pele $15,000. The cost of all merchandise sold was 60% of the sales price.

The transactions for January 2017 are as follows.

Jan. 3 Sell merchandise to T. Raynor $4,600, terms 2/10, n/30.
5 Purchase merchandise from P. Weng $2,800, terms 2/10, n/30.
7 Receive a check from E. Divine $3,500.
11 Pay freight on merchandise purchased $300.
12 Pay rent of $1,000 for January.
13 Receive payment in full from T. Raynor.
14 Post all entries to the subsidiary ledgers. Issued credit of $300 to M. Cedeno for returned merchandise.
15 Send A. Pele a check for $14,850 in full payment of account, discount $150.
17 Purchase merchandise from E. Nanco $1,600, terms 2/10, n/30.
18 Pay sales salaries of $2,500 and office salaries $2,000.
20 Give L. Gold a 60-day note for $18,000 in full payment of account payable.
23 Total cash sales amount to $9,100.
24 Post all entries to the subsidiary ledgers. Sell merchandise on account to J. Deitz $7,400, terms 1/10, n/30.
27 Send P. Weng a check for $950.
29 Receive payment on a note of $37,000 from W. Lague.
30 Post all entries to the subsidiary ledgers. Return merchandise of $300 to E. Nanco for credit.

Instructions

(a) Open general and subsidiary ledger accounts for the following.

101 Cash	311 Common Stock
112 Accounts Receivable	401 Sales Revenue
115 Notes Receivable	412 Sales Returns and Allowances
120 Inventory	414 Sales Discounts
157 Equipment	505 Cost of Goods Sold
158 Accumulated Depreciation—Equipment	726 Salaries and Wages Expense
200 Notes Payable	729 Rent Expense
201 Accounts Payable	

(b) Record the January transactions in a sales journal, a single-column purchases journal, a cash receipts journal (see Illustration J-8), a cash payments journal (see Illustration J-15), and a general journal.

(c) Post the appropriate amounts to the general ledger.

(d) Prepare a trial balance at January 31, 2017.

(e) Determine whether the subsidiary ledgers agree with controlling accounts in the general ledger.

(b) Sales journal $12,000
Purchases journal $4,400
Cash receipts journal (balancing) $54,200
Cash payments journal (balancing) $21,750

(d) Totals $138,250

(e) Accounts Receivable $18,600
Accounts Payable $13,150

COMPREHENSIVE PROBLEM

CPJ-1 Zweifel Company has the following opening account balances in its general and subsidiary ledgers on January 1 and uses the periodic inventory system. All accounts have normal debit and credit balances.

General Ledger

Account Number	Account Title	January 1 Opening Balance
101	Cash	$32,750
112	Accounts Receivable	13,000
115	Notes Receivable	42,000
120	Inventory	20,000
125	Supplies	1,000
130	Prepaid Insurance	2,000
157	Equipment	6,450
158	Accumulated Depreciation—Equip.	1,500
201	Accounts Payable	35,000
311	Common Stock	70,000
320	Retained Earnings	10,700

Schedule of Accounts Receivable
(from accounts receivable subsidiary ledger)

Customer	January 1 Opening Balance
G. Dukes	$1,800
M. Hall	7,200
L. Longhini	4,000

Schedule of Accounts Payable
(from accounts payable subsidiary ledger)

Creditor	January 1 Opening Balance
O. Kitson	$ 9,000
D. Markoff	15,000
L. Quinn	11,000

In addition, the following transactions have not been journalized for January 2017.

Jan. 3 Sell merchandise on account to W. Rayms $3,600, invoice no. 510, and M. Fischer $1,800, invoice no. 511.
5 Purchase merchandise on account from K. Zapfel $3,000 and J. Liotta $2,400.
7 Receive checks for $4,000 from L. Longhini and $2,000 from M. Hall.
8 Pay freight on merchandise purchased $180.
9 Send checks to O. Kitson for $9,000 and L. Quinn for $11,000.
9 Issue credit of $240 to M. Fischer for merchandise returned.
10 Cash sales total $15,500 from January 1 to January 10. Make one journal entry for these sales.
11 Sell merchandise on account to G. Dukes for $1,900, invoice no. 512, and to L. Longhini $900, invoice no. 513.

12 Pay rent of $1,000 for January.
13 Receive payment in full from W. Rayms and M. Fischer.
15 Pay cash dividend of $650.
16 Purchase merchandise on account from L. Quinn for $15,000, from O. Kitson for $13,900, and from K. Zapfel for $1,500.
17 Pay $400 cash for office supplies.
18 Return $200 of merchandise to O. Kitson and receive credit.
20 Cash sales total $17,750 from January 11 to January 20. Make one journal entry for these sales.
21 Issue $15,000 note to D. Markoff in payment of balance due.
21 Receive payment in full from L. Longhini.
22 Sell merchandise on account to W. Rayms for $3,700, invoice no. 514, and to G. Dukes for $800, invoice no. 515.
23 Send checks to L. Quinn and O. Kitson in full payment.
25 Sell merchandise on account to M. Hall for $3,500, invoice no. 516, and to M. Fischer for $6,100, invoice no. 517.
27 Purchase merchandise on account from L. Quinn for $12,500, from J. Liotta $1,200, and from K. Zapfel for $2,800.
28 Pay $200 cash for office supplies.
31 Cash sales total $22,920 from January 21 to January 31. Make one journal entry for these sales.
31 Pay sales salaries of $4,300 and office salaries of $3,100.

Instructions

(a) Record the January transactions in the appropriate journal—sales, purchases, cash receipts, cash payments, and general.

(b) Post the journals to the general and subsidiary ledgers. Add and number new accounts in an orderly fashion as needed.

(c) Trial balance totals $199,270
Adj. T/B totals $199,425

(c) Prepare a trial balance at January 31, 2017, using a worksheet. Complete the worksheet using the following additional information.
(1) Office supplies at January 31 total $580.
(2) Insurance coverage expires on October 31, 2017.
(3) Annual depreciation on the equipment is $1,500.
(4) Interest of $30 has accrued on the note payable.
(5) Inventory at January 31 is $12,600.

(d) Net income $8,775
Total assets $127,255

(d) Prepare a multiple-step income statement and a retained earnings statement for January and a classified balance sheet at the end of January.

(e) Prepare and post the adjusting and closing entries.

(f) Post-closing T/B totals $128,880

(f) Prepare a post-closing trial balance, and determine whether the subsidiary ledgers agree with the control accounts in the general ledger.

K

Accounting for Partnerships

APPENDIX PREVIEW

In this appendix, we discuss reasons why businesses select the partnership form of organization. We also explain the major issues in accounting for partnerships.

APPENDIX OUTLINE

LEARNING OBJECTIVES	
1 Discuss and account for the formation of a partnership.	• Characteristics of partnerships • Organizations with partnership characteristics • Advantages and disadvantages of partnerships • The partnership agreement • Accounting for a partnership formation
2 Explain how to account for net income or net loss of a partnership.	• Dividing net income or net loss • Partnership financial statements
3 Explain how to account for the liquidation of a partnership.	• No capital deficiency • Capital deficiency
4 Prepare journal entries when a partner is either admitted or withdraws.	• Admission of a partner • Withdrawal of a partner

LEARNING OBJECTIVE 1

Discuss and account for the formation of a partnership.

A **partnership** is an association of two or more persons to carry on as co-owners of a business for profit. Partnerships are sometimes used in small retail, service, or manufacturing companies. Accountants, lawyers, and doctors also find it desirable to form partnerships with other professionals in the field.

CHARACTERISTICS OF PARTNERSHIPS

Partnerships are fairly easy to form. People form partnerships simply by a verbal agreement or more formally by written agreement. We explain the principal characteristics of partnerships in the following sections.

Association of Individuals

Association of Individuals

A partnership is a legal entity. A partnership can own property (land, buildings, equipment) and can sue or be sued. **A partnership also is an accounting entity.** Thus, the personal assets, liabilities, and transactions of the partners are excluded from the accounting records of the partnership, just as they are in a proprietorship.

The net income of a partnership is not taxed as a separate entity. But, a partnership must file an information tax return showing partnership net income and each partner's share of that net income. Each partner's share is taxable at **personal tax rates**, regardless of the amount of net income each withdraws from the business during the year.

Mutual Agency

Mutual Agency

Mutual agency means that each partner acts on behalf of the partnership when engaging in partnership business. The act of any partner is binding on all other partners. This is true even when partners act beyond the scope of their authority, so long as the act appears to be appropriate for the partnership. For example, a partner of a grocery store who purchases a delivery truck creates a binding contract in the name of the partnership, even if the partnership agreement denies this authority. On the other hand, if a partner in a law firm purchased a snowmobile for the partnership, such an act would not be binding on the partnership. The purchase is clearly outside the scope of partnership business.

Limited Life

Limited Life

Corporations have unlimited life. Partnerships do not. A partnership may be ended voluntarily at any time through the acceptance of a new partner or the withdrawal of a partner. It may be ended involuntarily by the death or incapacity of a partner. **Partnership dissolution** occurs whenever a partner withdraws or a new partner is admitted. Dissolution does not necessarily mean that the business ends. If the continuing partners agree, operations can continue without interruption by forming a new partnership.

Unlimited Liability

Unlimited Liability

Each partner is **personally and individually liable** for all partnership liabilities. Creditors' claims attach first to partnership assets. If these are insufficient, the claims then attach to the personal resources of any partner, irrespective of that partner's equity in the partnership. Because each partner is responsible for all the debts of the partnership, each partner is said to have **unlimited liability**.

Co-Ownership of Property

Co-Ownership of Property

Partners jointly own partnership assets. If the partnership is dissolved, each partner has a claim on total assets equal to the balance in his or her respective capital account. This claim does not attach to **specific assets** that an individual partner contributed to the firm. Similarly, if a partner invests a building in the partnership valued at $100,000 and the building is later sold at a gain of $20,000, the partners all share in the gain.

Partnership net income (or net loss) is also co-owned. **If the partnership contract does not specify to the contrary, all net income or net loss is shared equally by the partners.** As you will see later, though, partners may agree to unequal sharing of net income or net loss.

ORGANIZATIONS WITH PARTNERSHIP CHARACTERISTICS

If you are starting a business with a friend and each of you has little capital and your business is not risky, you probably want to use a partnership. As indicated above, the partnership is easy to establish and its cost is minimal. These types of partnerships are often called **regular partnerships**. However if your business is risky—say, roof repair or performing some type of professional service—you will want to limit your liability and not use a regular partnership. As a result, special forms of business organizations with partnership characteristics are now often used to provide protection from unlimited liability for people who wish to work together in some activity.

The special partnership forms are limited partnerships, limited liability partnerships, and limited liability companies. These special forms use the same accounting procedures as those described for a regular partnership. In addition, for taxation purposes, all the profits and losses pass through these organizations (similar to the regular partnership) to the owners, who report their share of partnership net income or losses on their personal tax returns.

Limited Partnerships

In a **limited partnership**, one or more partners have **unlimited liability** and one or more partners have **limited liability** for the debts of the firm. Those with unlimited liability are **general partners**. Those with limited liability are **limited partners**. Limited partners are responsible for the debts of the partnership up to the limit of their investment in the firm.

The words "Limited Partnership," "Ltd.," or "LP" identify this type of organization. For the privilege of limited liability, the limited partner usually accepts less compensation than a general partner and exercises less influence in the affairs of the firm. If the limited partners get involved in management, they risk their liability protection.

INTERNATIONAL NOTE
Much of the funding for successful new U.S. businesses comes from "venture capital" firms, which are organized as limited partnerships. To develop its own venture capital industry, China has taken steps to model its partnership laws to allow for limited partnerships like those in the United States.

Limited Liability Partnership

Most states allow professionals such as lawyers, doctors, and accountants to form a **limited liability partnership** or "LLP." The LLP is designed to protect innocent partners from malpractice or negligence claims resulting from the acts of another partner. LLPs generally carry large insurance policies as protection against malpractice suits. These professional partnerships vary in size from a medical partnership of three to five doctors, to 150 to 200 partners in a large law firm, to more than 2,000 partners in an international accounting firm.

▼ HELPFUL HINT
In an LLP, *all* partners have limited liability. There are no general partners.

Limited Liability Companies

A hybrid form of business organization with certain features like a corporation and others like a limited partnership is the **limited liability company** or "LLC." An LLC usually has a limited life. The owners, called **members**, have limited liability like owners of a corporation. Whereas limited partners do not actively participate in the management of a limited partnership (LP), the members of a limited liability company (LLC) can assume an active management role. For income tax purposes, the IRS usually classifies an LLC as a partnership.

Illustration K-1 (page K-4) summarizes different forms of organizations that have partnership characteristics.

ADVANTAGES AND DISADVANTAGES OF PARTNERSHIPS

Why do people choose partnerships? One major advantage of a partnership is to combine the skills and resources of two or more individuals. In addition, partnerships are easily formed and are relatively free from government regulations and restrictions. A partnership does not have to contend with the "red

ILLUSTRATION K-1
Different forms of organizations with partnership characteristics

	Major Advantages	**Major Disadvantages**
Regular Partnership  General Partners	Simple and inexpensive to create and operate.	Owners (partners) personally liable for business debts.
Limited Partnership  General Partner / Limited Partners	Limited partners have limited personal liability for business debts as long as they do not participate in management. General partners can raise cash without involving outside investors in management of business.	General partners personally liable for business debts. More expensive to create than regular partnership. Suitable mainly for companies that invest in real estate.
Limited Liability Partnership 	Mostly of interest to partners in old-line professions such as law, medicine, and accounting. Owners (partners) are not personally liable for the malpractice of other partners.	Unlike a limited liability company, owners (partners) remain personally liable for many types of obligations owed to business creditors, lenders, and landlords. Often limited to a short list of professions.
Limited Liability Company  *Source: www.nolo.com.*	Owners have limited personal liability for business debts even if they participate in management.	More expensive to create than regular partnership.

tape" that a corporation must face. Also, partners generally can make decisions quickly on substantive business matters without having to consult a board of directors.

On the other hand, partnerships also have some major disadvantages. **Unlimited liability** is particularly troublesome. Many individuals fear they may lose not only their initial investment but also their personal assets if those assets are needed to pay partnership creditors.

Illustration K-2 summarizes the advantages and disadvantages of the regular partnership form of business organization. As indicated previously, different types of partnership forms have evolved to reduce some of the disadvantages.

ILLUSTRATION K-2
Advantages and disadvantages of a partnership

Advantages	**Disadvantages**
Combining skills and resources of two or more individuals	Mutual agency
Ease of formation	Limited life
Freedom from governmental regulations and restrictions	Unlimited liability
Ease of decision-making	

THE PARTNERSHIP AGREEMENT

Ideally, the agreement of two or more individuals to form a partnership should be expressed in a written contract, called the **partnership agreement** or **articles of co-partnership**. The partnership agreement contains such basic information as the name and principal location of the firm, the purpose of the business, and date of inception. In addition, it should specify relationships among the partners, such as:

ETHICS NOTE

A well-developed partnership agreement specifies in clear and concise language the process by which the partners will resolve ethical and legal problems. This issue is especially significant when the partnership experiences financial distress.

1. Names and capital contributions of partners.
2. Rights and duties of partners.
3. Basis for sharing net income or net loss.
4. Provision for withdrawals of assets.
5. Procedures for submitting disputes to arbitration.
6. Procedures for the withdrawal or addition of a partner.
7. Rights and duties of surviving partners in the event of a partner's death.

We cannot overemphasize the importance of a written contract. The agreement should attempt to anticipate all possible situations, contingencies, and disagreements. The help of a lawyer is highly desirable in preparing the agreement.

ACCOUNTING FOR A PARTNERSHIP FORMATION

We now turn to the basic accounting for partnerships. The major accounting issues relate to forming the partnership, dividing income or loss, and preparing financial statements.

When forming a partnership, each partner's initial investment in a partnership is entered in the partnership records. The partnership should record these investments at the **fair value of the assets at the date of their transfer to the partnership**. All partners must agree to the values assigned.

To illustrate, assume that A. Rolfe and T. Shea combine their proprietorships to start a partnership named U.S. Software. The firm will specialize in developing financial modeling software. Rolfe and Shea have the following assets prior to the formation of the partnership.

ILLUSTRATION K-3
Book and fair values of assets invested

	Book Value		Fair Value	
	A. Rolfe	**T. Shea**	**A. Rolfe**	**T. Shea**
Cash	$ 8,000	$ 9,000	$ 8,000	$ 9,000
Equipment	5,000		4,000	
Accumulated depreciation—equipment	(2,000)			
Accounts receivable		4,000		4,000
Allowance for doubtful accounts		(700)		(1,000)
	$11,000	$12,300	$12,000	$12,000

Items under ***owners' equity (OE)*** *in the accounting equation analyses are not labeled in this partnership appendix. Nearly all affect partners'* ***capital*** *accounts.*

The partnership records the investments as follows.

Investment of A. Rolfe

Cash	8,000	
Equipment	4,000	
A. Rolfe, Capital		12,000
(To record investment of Rolfe)		

A = L + OE
+8,000
+4,000
+12,000

Cash Flows
+8,000

Investment of T. Shea

Cash	9,000	
Accounts Receivable	4,000	
Allowance for Doubtful Accounts		1,000
T. Shea, Capital		12,000
(To record investment of Shea)		

A = L + OE
+9,000
+4,000
−1,000
+12,000

Cash Flows
+9,000

Note that the partnership records neither the original cost of the equipment ($5,000) nor its book value ($5,000 – $2,000). It records the equipment at its fair value, $4,000. The partnership does not carry forward any accumulated depreciation from the books of previous entities (in this case, the two proprietorships).

In contrast, the gross claims on customers ($4,000) are carried forward to the partnership. The partnership adjusts the allowance for doubtful accounts to $1,000, to arrive at a cash (net) realizable value of $3,000. A partnership may start with an allowance for doubtful accounts because it will continue to collect existing accounts receivable, some of which are expected to be uncollectible. In addition, this procedure maintains the control and subsidiary relationship between Accounts Receivable and the accounts receivable subsidiary ledger.

After formation of the partnership, the accounting for transactions is similar to any other type of business organization. For example, the partners record all transactions with outside parties, such as the purchase or sale of inventory and the payment or receipt of cash, the same as would a sole proprietor.

The steps in the accounting cycle described in Chapter 4 also apply to a partnership. For example, the partnership prepares a trial balance and journalizes and posts adjusting entries. A worksheet may be used. There are minor differences in journalizing and posting closing entries and in preparing financial statements, as we explain in the following sections. The differences occur because there is more than one owner.

LEARNING OBJECTIVE 2 **Explain how to account for net income or net loss of a partnership.**

DIVIDING NET INCOME OR NET LOSS

Partners equally share partnership net income or net loss unless the partnership contract indicates otherwise. The same basis of division usually applies to both net income and net loss. It is customary to refer to this basis as the **income ratio**, the **income and loss ratio**, or the **profit and loss (P&L) ratio**. Because of its wide acceptance, we use the term **income ratio** to identify the basis for dividing net income and net loss. The partnership recognizes a partner's share of net income or net loss in the accounts through closing entries.

Closing Entries

As in the case of a proprietorship, a partnership must make four entries in preparing closing entries. The entries are:

1. Debit each revenue account for its balance, and credit Income Summary for total revenues.
2. Debit Income Summary for total expenses, and credit each expense account for its balance.
3. Debit Income Summary for its balance, and credit each partner's capital account for his or her share of net income. Or, credit Income Summary, and debit each partner's capital account for his or her share of net loss.
4. Debit each partner's capital account for the balance in that partner's drawings account, and credit each partner's drawings account for the same amount.

The first two entries are the same as in a corporation. The last two entries are different because (1) there are two or more owners' capital and drawings accounts, and (2) it is necessary to divide net income (or net loss) among the partners.

To illustrate the last two closing entries, assume that AB Company has net income of $32,000 for 2017. The partners, L. Arbor and D. Barnett, share net income and net loss equally. Drawings for the year were Arbor $8,000 and Barnett $6,000. The last two closing entries are as follows.

		Debit	Credit
Dec. 31	Income Summary	32,000	
	L. Arbor, Capital ($32,000 × 50%)		16,000
	D. Barnett, Capital ($32,000 × 50%)		16,000
	(To transfer net income to partners' capital accounts)		
Dec. 31	L. Arbor, Capital	8,000	
	D. Barnett, Capital	6,000	
	L. Arbor, Drawings		8,000
	D. Barnett, Drawings		6,000
	(To close drawings accounts to capital accounts)		

A	=	L	+	OE
				−32,000
				+16,000
				+16,000

Cash Flows
no effect

A	=	L	+	OE
				−8,000
				−6,000
				+8,000
				+6,000

Cash Flows
no effect

Assume that the beginning capital balance is $47,000 for Arbor and $36,000 for Barnett. After posting the closing entries, the capital and drawings accounts will appear as shown in Illustration K-4.

ILLUSTRATION K-4
Partners' capital and drawings accounts after closing

L. Arbor, Capital

Debit		Credit	
12/31 Clos.	8,000	1/1 Bal.	47,000
		12/31 Clos.	16,000
		12/31 Bal.	55,000

D. Barnett, Capital

Debit		Credit	
12/31 Clos.	6,000	1/1 Bal.	36,000
		12/31 Clos.	16,000
		12/31 Bal.	46,000

L. Arbor, Drawings

Debit		Credit	
12/31 Bal.	8,000	12/31 Clos.	8,000

D. Barnett, Drawings

Debit		Credit	
12/31 Bal.	6,000	12/31 Clos.	6,000

As in a proprietorship, the partners' capital accounts are permanent accounts. Their drawings accounts are temporary accounts. Normally, the capital accounts will have credit balances, and the drawings accounts will have debit balances. Drawings accounts are debited when partners withdraw cash or other assets from the partnership for personal use.

Income Ratios

As noted earlier, the partnership agreement should specify the basis for sharing net income or net loss. The following are typical income ratios.

▼ HELPFUL HINT
A proportion such as 4:4:2 has a denominator of 10 (4 + 4 + 2). Thus, the basis for sharing net income or loss is 4/10, 4/10, and 2/10.

1. A fixed ratio, expressed as a proportion (6:4), a percentage (70% and 30%), or a fraction (2/3 and 1/3).
2. A ratio based either on capital balances at the beginning of the year or on average capital balances during the year.
3. Salaries to partners and the remainder on a fixed ratio.
4. Interest on partners' capital balances and the remainder on a fixed ratio.
5. Salaries to partners, interest on partners' capital, and the remainder on a fixed ratio.

The objective is to settle on a basis that will equitably reflect the partners' capital investment and service to the partnership.

A **fixed ratio** is easy to apply, and it may be an equitable basis in some circumstances. Assume, for example, that Hughes and Lane are partners. Each contributes the same amount of capital, but Hughes expects to work full-time in the partnership and Lane expects to work only half-time. Accordingly, the partners agree to a fixed ratio of 2/3 to Hughes and 1/3 to Lane.

A **ratio based on capital balances** may be appropriate when the funds invested in the partnership are considered the critical factor. Capital ratios may also be equitable when the partners hire a manager to run the business and do not plan to take an active role in daily operations.

The three remaining ratios (items 3, 4, and 5) give specific recognition to differences among partners. These ratios provide salary allowances for time worked and interest allowances for capital invested. Then, the partnership allocates any remaining net income or net loss on a fixed ratio.

Salaries to partners and interest on partners' capital are not expenses of the partnership. Therefore, these items do not enter into the matching of expenses with revenues and the determination of net income or net loss. For a partnership, as for other entities, salaries and wages expense pertains to the cost of services performed by employees. Likewise, interest expense relates to the cost of borrowing from creditors. But partners, as owners, are not considered either **employees** or **creditors**. When the partnership agreement permits the partners to make monthly withdrawals of cash based on their "salary," the partnership debits these withdrawals to the partner's drawings account.

Salaries, Interest, and Remainder on a Fixed Ratio

Under income ratio (5) in the list above, the partnership must apply salaries and interest **before** it allocates the remainder on the specified fixed ratio. **This is true even if the provisions exceed net income. It is also true even if the partnership has suffered a net loss for the year.** The partnership's income statement should show, below net income, detailed information concerning the division of net income or net loss.

To illustrate, assume that Sara King and Ray Lee are co-partners in the Kingslee Company. The partnership agreement provides for (1) salary allowances of $8,400 to King and $6,000 to Lee, (2) interest allowances of 10% on capital balances at the beginning of the year, and (3) the remaining income to be divided equally. Capital balances on January 1 were King $28,000, and Lee $24,000. In 2017, partnership net income is $22,000. The division of net income is as shown in Illustration K-5.

ILLUSTRATION K-5
Division of net income schedule

KINGSLEE COMPANY
Division of Net Income
For the Year Ended December 31, 2017

Net income $ 22,000

Division of Net Income

	Sara King	Ray Lee	Total
Salary allowance	$ 8,400	$6,000	$14,400
Interest allowance on partners' capital			
Sara King ($28,000 × 10%)	2,800		
Ray Lee ($24,000 × 10%)		2,400	
Total interest allowance			5,200
Total salaries and interest	11,200	8,400	19,600
Remaining income, $2,400 ($22,000 − $19,600)			
Sara King ($2,400 × 50%)	1,200		
Ray Lee ($2,400 × 50%)		1,200	
Total remainder			2,400
Total division of net income	$12,400	$9,600	$22,000

A	=	L	+	OE
				−22,000
				+12,400
				+9,600

Cash Flows
no effect

Kingslee records the division of net income as follows.

Dec. 31	Income Summary	22,000	
	Sara King, Capital		12,400
	Ray Lee, Capital		9,600
	(To close net income to partners' capital)		

Now let's look at a situation in which the salary and interest allowances **exceed** net income. Assume that Kingslee Company's net income is only $18,000. In this case, the salary and interest allowances will create a deficiency of $1,600 ($18,000 – $19,600). The computations of the allowances are the same as those in the preceding example. Beginning with total salaries and interest, we complete the division of net income as shown in Illustration K-6.

ILLUSTRATION K-6
Division of net income—income deficiency

	Sara King	Ray Lee	Total
Total salaries and interest	$11,200	$8,400	$19,600
Remaining deficiency ($1,600)			
($18,000 – $19,600)			
Sara King ($1,600 × 50%)	(800)		
Ray Lee ($1,600 × 50%)		(800)	
Total remainder			(1,600)
Total division	$10,400	$7,600	$18,000

PARTNERSHIP FINANCIAL STATEMENTS

The financial statements of a partnership are similar to those of a proprietorship. The differences are due to the number of owners involved. The income statement for a partnership is identical to the income statement for a proprietorship except for the division of net income, as shown earlier.

The owners' equity statement for a partnership is called the **partners' capital statement**. It explains the changes in each partner's capital account and in total partnership capital during the year. Illustration K-7 shows the partners' capital statement for Kingslee Company. It is based on the division of $22,000 of net income in Illustration K-5. The statement includes assumed data for the additional investment and drawings. The partnership prepares the partners' capital statement from the income statement and the partners' capital and drawings accounts.

ILLUSTRATION K-7
Partners' capital statement

KINGSLEE COMPANY
Partners' Capital Statement
For the Year Ended December 31, 2017

	Sara King	Ray Lee	Total
Capital, January 1	$28,000	$24,000	$52,000
Add: Additional investment	2,000		2,000
Net income	12,400	9,600	22,000
	42,400	33,600	76,000
Less: Drawings	7,000	5,000	12,000
Capital, December 31	$35,400	$28,600	$64,000

▼ **HELPFUL HINT**
As in a proprietorship, partners' capital may change due to (1) additional investment, (2) drawings, and (3) net income or net loss.

The balance sheet for a partnership is the same as for a proprietorship except for the owners' equity section. For a partnership, the balance sheet shows the capital balances of each partner. Illustration K-8 (page K-10) shows the owners' equity section for Kingslee Company.

ILLUSTRATION K-8
Owners' equity section of a partnership balance sheet

KINGSLEE COMPANY
Balance Sheet (partial)
December 31, 2017

Total liabilities (assumed amount)		$115,000
Owners' equity		
Sara King, capital	$35,400	
Ray Lee, capital	28,600	
Total owners' equity		64,000
Total liabilities and owners' equity		$179,000

LEARNING OBJECTIVE 3

Explain how to account for the liquidation of a partnership.

Liquidation of a business involves selling the assets of the firm, paying liabilities, and distributing any remaining assets. Liquidation may result from the sale of the business by mutual agreement of the partners, from the death of a partner, or from bankruptcy. **Partnership liquidation** ends both the legal and economic life of the entity.

From an accounting standpoint, the partnership should complete the accounting cycle for the final operating period prior to liquidation. This includes preparing adjusting entries and financial statements. It also involves preparing closing entries and a post-closing trial balance. Thus, only balance sheet accounts should be open as the liquidation process begins.

In liquidation, the sale of noncash assets for cash is called **realization**. Any difference between book value and the cash proceeds is called the **gain or loss on realization**. To liquidate a partnership, it is necessary to:

ETHICS NOTE
The process of selling noncash assets and then distributing the cash reduces the likelihood of partner disputes. If instead the partnership distributes noncash assets to partners to liquidate the firm, the partners would need to agree on the value of the noncash assets, which can be very difficult to determine.

1. Sell noncash assets for cash and recognize a gain or loss on realization.
2. Allocate gain/loss on realization to the partners based on their income ratios.
3. Pay partnership liabilities in cash.
4. Distribute remaining cash to partners on the basis of their **capital balances**.

Each of the steps must be performed in sequence. The partnership must pay creditors **before** partners receive any cash distributions. Also, an accounting entry must record each step.

When a partnership is liquidated, all partners may have credit balances in their capital accounts. This situation is called **no capital deficiency**. Or, one or more partners may have a debit balance in the capital account. This situation is termed a **capital deficiency**. To illustrate each of these conditions, assume that Ace Company is liquidated when its ledger shows the following assets, liabilities, and owners' equity accounts.

ILLUSTRATION K-9
Account balances prior to liquidation

Assets		Liabilities and Owners' Equity	
Cash	$ 5,000	Notes Payable	$15,000
Accounts Receivable	15,000	Accounts Payable	16,000
Inventory	18,000	R. Arnet, Capital	15,000
Equipment	35,000	P. Carey, Capital	17,800
Accum. Depr.—Equipment	(8,000)	W. Eaton, Capital	1,200
	$65,000		$65,000

NO CAPITAL DEFICIENCY

The partners of Ace Company agree to liquidate the partnership on the following terms. (1) The partnership will sell its noncash assets to Jackson Enterprises for $75,000 cash. (2) The partnership will pay its partnership liabilities. The income ratios of the partners are 3:2:1, respectively. The steps in the liquidation process are as follows.

▼ HELPFUL HINT
The income ratios' denominator for Ace Company is 6 (3 + 2 + 1).

1. Ace sells the noncash assets (accounts receivable, inventory, and equipment) for $75,000. The book value of these assets is $60,000 ($15,000 + $18,000 + $35,000 − $8,000). Thus, Ace realizes a gain of $15,000 on the sale. The entry is:

(1)

Cash	75,000	
Accumulated Depreciation–Equipment	8,000	
Accounts Receivable		15,000
Inventory		18,000
Equipment		35,000
Gain on Realization		15,000
(To record realization of noncash assets)		

A	=	L	+	OE
+75,000				
+8,000				
−15,000				
−18,000				
−35,000				
				+15,000

Cash Flows
+75,000

2. Ace allocates the $15,000 gain on realization to the partners based on their income ratios, which are 3:2:1. The entry is:

(2)

Gain on Realization	15,000	
R. Arnet, Capital ($15,000 × 3/6)		7,500
P. Carey, Capital ($15,000 × 2/6)		5,000
W. Eaton, Capital ($15,000 × 1/6)		2,500
(To allocate gain to partners' capital accounts)		

A	=	L	+	OE
				−15,000
				+7,500
				+5,000
				+2,500

Cash Flows
no effect

3. Partnership liabilities consist of Notes Payable $15,000 and Accounts Payable $16,000. Ace pays creditors in full by a cash payment of $31,000. The entry is:

(3)

Notes Payable	15,000	
Accounts Payable	16,000	
Cash		31,000
(To record payment of partnership liabilities)		

A	=	L	+	OE
		−15,000		
		−16,000		
−31,000				

Cash Flows
−31,000

4. Ace distributes the remaining cash to the partners on the basis of **their capital balances**. After posting the entries in the first three steps, all partnership accounts, including Gain on Realization, will have zero balances except for four accounts: Cash $49,000; R. Arnet, Capital $22,500; P. Carey, Capital $22,800; and W. Eaton, Capital $3,700, as shown below.

ILLUSTRATION K-10
Ledger balances before distribution of cash

Cash		R. Arnet, Capital		P. Carey, Capital		W. Eaton, Capital	
Bal. 5,000	(3) 31,000		Bal. 15,000		Bal. 17,800		Bal. 1,200
(1) 75,000			(2) 7,500		(2) 5,000		(2) 2,500
Bal. 49,000			Bal. 22,500		Bal. 22,800		Bal. 3,700

Ace records the distribution of cash as follows.

(4)

R. Arnet, Capital	22,500	
P. Carey, Capital	22,800	
W. Eaton, Capital	3,700	
Cash		49,000
(To record distribution of cash to partners)		

A	=	L	+	OE
				−22,500
				−22,800
				−3,700
−49,000				

Cash Flows
−49,000

After posting this entry, all partnership accounts will have zero balances.

ALTERNATIVE TERMINOLOGY
The schedule of cash payments is sometimes called a *safe cash payments schedule.*

A word of caution: **Partnerships should not distribute remaining cash to partners on the basis of their income-sharing ratios.** On this basis, Arnet would receive three-sixths, or $24,500, which would produce an erroneous debit balance of $2,000. The income ratio is the proper basis for allocating net income or loss. **It is not a proper basis for making the final distribution of cash to the partners.**

Schedule of Cash Payments

The **schedule of cash payments** shows the distribution of cash to the partners in a partnership liquidation. The schedule of cash payments is organized around the basic accounting equation. Illustration K-11 shows the schedule for Ace Company. The numbers in parentheses in column B refer to the four required steps in the liquidation of a partnership. They also identify the accounting entries that Ace must make. The cash payments schedule is especially useful when the liquidation process extends over a period of time.

ILLUSTRATION K-11
Schedule of cash payments, no capital deficiency

ACE Company.xls

ACE COMPANY
Schedule of Cash Payments

Item		Cash	+	Noncash Assets	=	Liabilities	+	R. Arnet, Capital	+	P. Carey, Capital	+	W. Eaton, Capital
Balances before liquidation		5,000	+	60,000	=	31,000	+	15,000	+	17,800	+	1,200
Sale of noncash assets and allocation of gain	(1)&(2)	75,000	+	(60,000)	=			7,500	+	5,000	+	2,500
New balances		80,000	+	–0–	=	31,000	+	22,500	+	22,800	+	3,700
Pay liabilities		(31,000)			=	(31,000)						
New balances	(3)	49,000	+	–0–	=	–0–	+	22,500	+	22,800	+	3,700
Cash distribution to partners	(4)	(49,000)			=			(22,500)	+	(22,800)	+	(3,700)
Final balances		–0–		–0–		–0–		–0–		–0–		–0–

CAPITAL DEFICIENCY

A capital deficiency may result from recurring net losses, excessive drawings, or losses from realization suffered during liquidation. To illustrate, assume that Ace Company is on the brink of bankruptcy. The partners decide to liquidate by having a "going-out-of-business" sale. They sell merchandise at substantial discounts, and sell the equipment at auction. Cash proceeds from these sales and collections from customers total only $42,000. Thus, the loss from liquidation is $18,000 ($60,000 − $42,000). The steps in the liquidation process are as follows.

A	=	L	+	OE
+42,000				
+8,000				
				−18,000
−15,000				
−18,000				
−35,000				

Cash Flows
+42,000

1. The entry for the realization of noncash assets is:

(1)

Cash	42,000	
Accumulated Depreciation—Equipment	8,000	
Loss on Realization	18,000	
Accounts Receivable		15,000
Inventory		18,000
Equipment		35,000
(To record realization of noncash assets)		

2. Ace allocates the loss on realization to the partners on the basis of their income ratios. The entry is:

(2)		
R. Arnet, Capital ($18,000 × 3/6)	9,000	
P. Carey, Capital ($18,000 × 2/6)	6,000	
W. Eaton, Capital ($18,000 × 1/6)	3,000	
Loss on Realization		18,000
(To allocate loss on realization to partners)		

A	=	L	+	OE
				−9,000
				−6,000
				−3,000
				+18,000

Cash Flows
no effect

3. Ace pays the partnership liabilities. This entry is the same as the previous one.

(3)		
Notes Payable	15,000	
Accounts Payable	16,000	
Cash		31,000
(To record payment of partnership liabilities)		

A	=	L	+	OE
		−15,000		
		−16,000		
−31,000				

Cash Flows
−31,000

4. After posting the three entries, two accounts will have debit balances—Cash $16,000 and W. Eaton, Capital $1,800. Two accounts will have credit balances—R. Arnet, Capital $6,000 and P. Carey, Capital $11,800. All four accounts are shown below.

ILLUSTRATION K-12
Ledger balances before distribution of cash

Cash		R. Arnet, Capital		P. Carey, Capital		W. Eaton, Capital	
Bal. 5,000	(3) 31,000	(2) 9,000	Bal. 15,000	(2) 6,000	Bal. 17,800	(2) 3,000	Bal. 1,200
(1) 42,000			**Bal. 6,000**		**Bal. 11,800**	**Bal. 1,800**	
Bal. 16,000							

Eaton has a capital deficiency of $1,800 and so owes the partnership $1,800. Arnet and Carey have a legally enforceable claim for that amount against Eaton's personal assets. Note that the distribution of cash is still made on the basis of capital balances. But, the amount will vary depending on how Eaton settles the deficiency. Two alternatives are presented in the following sections.

Payment of Deficiency

If the partner with the capital deficiency pays the amount owed the partnership, the deficiency is eliminated. To illustrate, assume that Eaton pays $1,800 to the partnership. The entry is:

(a)		
Cash	1,800	
W. Eaton, Capital		1,800
(To record payment of capital deficiency by Eaton)		

A	=	L	+	OE
+1,800				
				+1,800

Cash Flows
+1,800

After posting this entry, account balances are as follows.

ILLUSTRATION K-13
Ledger balances after paying capital deficiency

Cash		R. Arnet, Capital		P. Carey, Capital		W. Eaton, Capital	
Bal. 5,000	(3) 31,000	(2) 9,000	Bal. 15,000	(2) 6,000	Bal. 17,800	(2) 3,000	Bal. 1,200
(1) 42,000			**Bal. 6,000**		**Bal. 11,800**		(a) 1,800
(a) 1,800							**Bal. –0–**
Bal. 17,800							

A	=	L	+	OE
				−6,000
				−11,800
−17,800				

Cash Flows
−17,800

The cash balance of $17,800 is now equal to the credit balances in the capital accounts (Arnet $6,000 + Carey $11,800). Ace now distributes cash on the basis of these balances. The entry is:

R. Arnet, Capital	6,000	
P. Carey, Capital	11,800	
Cash		17,800
(To record distribution of cash to the partners)		

After posting this entry, all accounts will have zero balances.

▼ **HELPFUL HINT**
The ratios with all three partners were 3:2:1 and the denominator was therefore 6. Leaving out Eaton, the denominator changes to 5 (3 + 2).

Nonpayment of Deficiency

If a partner with a capital deficiency is unable to pay the amount owed to the partnership, the partners with credit balances must absorb the loss. The partnership allocates the loss on the basis of the income ratios that exist between the partners with credit balances.

The income ratios of Arnet and Carey are 3:2, or 3/5 and 2/5, respectively. Thus, Ace would make the following entry to remove Eaton's capital deficiency.

A	=	L	+	OE
				−1,080
				−720
				+1,800

Cash Flows
no effect

(a)

R. Arnet, Capital ($1,800 × 3/5)	1,080	
P. Carey, Capital ($1,800 × 2/5)	720	
W. Eaton, Capital		1,800
(To record write-off of capital deficiency)		

After posting this entry, the cash and capital accounts will have the following balances.

ILLUSTRATION K-14
Ledger balances after nonpayment of capital deficiency

Cash

Debit		Credit	
Bal.	5,000	(3)	31,000
(1)	42,000		
Bal.	**16,000**		

R. Arnet, Capital

Debit		Credit	
(2)	9,000	Bal.	15,000
(a)	1,080		
		Bal.	**4,920**

P. Carey, Capital

Debit		Credit	
(2)	6,000	Bal.	17,800
(a)	720		
		Bal.	**11,080**

W. Eaton, Capital

Debit		Credit	
(2)	3,000	Bal.	1,200
		(a)	1,800
		Bal.	**-0-**

The cash balance ($16,000) now equals the sum of the credit balances in the capital accounts (Arnet $4,920 + Carey $11,080). Ace records the distribution of cash as:

A	=	L	+	OE
				−4,920
				−11,080
−16,000				

Cash Flows
−16,000

R. Arnet, Capital	4,920	
P. Carey, Capital	11,080	
Cash		16,000
(To record distribution of cash to the partners)		

After posting this entry, all accounts will have zero balances.

LEARNING OBJECTIVE 4

Prepare journal entries when a partner is either admitted or withdraws.

We have now explained how the basic accounting for a partnership works. We next look at how to account for a common occurrence in partnerships—the addition or withdrawal of a partner.

ADMISSION OF A PARTNER

The admission of a new partner results in the **legal dissolution** of the existing partnership and the beginning of a new one. From an economic standpoint, however, the admission of a new partner (or partners) may be of minor significance in the continuity of the business. For example, in large public accounting or law firms, partners are admitted annually without any change in operating policies. **To recognize the economic effects, it is necessary only to open a capital account for each new partner.** In the entries illustrated below, we assume that the accounting records of the predecessor firm will continue to be used by the new partnership.

A new partner may be admitted either by (1) purchasing the interest of one or more existing partners or (2) investing assets in the partnership. The former affects only the capital accounts of the partners who are parties to the transaction. The latter increases both net assets and total capital of the partnership.

Purchase of a Partner's Interest

The **admission** of a partner **by purchase of an interest** is a personal transaction between one or more existing partners and the new partner. Each party acts as an individual separate from the partnership entity. The individuals involved negotiate the price paid. It may be equal to or different from the capital equity acquired. The purchase price passes directly from the new partner to the partners who are giving up part or all of their ownership claims.

▼ HELPFUL HINT
In a purchase of an interest, the partnership is not a participant in the transaction. In this transaction, the new partner contributes *no* cash to the partnership.

Any money or other consideration exchanged is the personal property of the participants and **not** the property of the partnership. Upon purchase of an interest, the new partner acquires each selling partner's capital interest and income ratio.

Accounting for the purchase of an interest is straightforward. The partnership records only the changes in partners' capital. **Partners' capital accounts are debited for any ownership claims sold.** At the same time, the new partner's capital account is credited for the capital equity purchased. Total assets, total liabilities, and total capital remain unchanged, as do all individual asset and liability accounts.

To illustrate, assume that L. Carson agrees to pay $10,000 each to C. Ames and D. Barker for 33⅓% (one-third) of their interest in the Ames–Barker partnership. At the time of the admission of Carson, each partner has a $30,000 capital balance. Both partners, therefore, give up $10,000 of their capital equity. The entry to record the admission of Carson is:

C. Ames, Capital	10,000	
D. Barker, Capital	10,000	
L. Carson, Capital		20,000
(To record admission of Carson by purchase)		

The effect of this transaction on net assets and partners' capital is shown below.

ILLUSTRATION K-15
Ledger balances after purchase of a partner's interest

Net Assets		C. Ames, Capital		D. Barker, Capital		L. Carson, Capital	
60,000		10,000	30,000	10,000	30,000		20,000
			Bal. 20,000		Bal. 20,000		

Note that net assets remain unchanged at $60,000, and each partner has a $20,000 capital balance. Ames and Barker continue as partners in the firm, but the capital interest of each has changed. The cash paid by Carson goes directly to the individual partners and not to the partnership.

Regardless of the amount paid by Carson for the one-third interest, the entry is exactly the same. If Carson pays $12,000 each to Ames and Barker for one-third of the partnership, the partnership still makes the entry shown above.

Investment of Assets in a Partnership

The admission of a partner by an investment of assets is a transaction between the new partner and the partnership. Often referred to simply as **admission by investment**, the transaction **increases both the net assets and total capital of the partnership**.

Assume, for example, that instead of purchasing an interest, Carson invests \$30,000 in cash in the Ames-Barker partnership for a 33 1/3% capital interest. In such a case, the entry is:

Cash	30,000	
L. Carson, Capital		30,000
(To record admission of Carson by investment)		

ILLUSTRATION K-16
Ledger balances after investment of assets

Illustration K-16 shows the effects of this transaction on the partnership accounts.

Net Assets		C. Ames, Capital		D. Barker, Capital		L. Carson, Capital	
60,000			30,000		30,000		30,000
30,000							
Bal. 90,000							

Note that both net assets and total capital have increased by \$30,000.

Remember that Carson's one-third capital interest might not result in a one-third income ratio. The new partnership agreement should specify Carson's income ratio, and it may or may not be equal to the one-third capital interest.

The comparison of the net assets and capital balances in Illustration K-17 shows the different effects of the purchase of an interest and admission by investment.

ILLUSTRATION K-17
Comparison of purchase of an interest and admission by investment

Purchase of an Interest		Admission by Investment	
Net assets	\$60,000	Net assets	\$90,000
Capital		Capital	
C. Ames	\$20,000	C. Ames	\$30,000
D. Barker	20,000	D. Barker	30,000
L. Carson	20,000	L. Carson	30,000
Total capital	\$60,000	Total capital	\$90,000

When a new partner purchases an interest, the total net assets and total capital of the partnership **do not change**. When a partner is admitted by investment, both the total net assets and the total capital **change** by the amount of the new investment.

In the case of admission by investment, further complications occur when the new partner's investment differs from the capital equity acquired. When those amounts are not the same, the difference is considered a **bonus** either to (1) the existing (old) partners or (2) the new partner.

BONUS TO OLD PARTNERS For both personal and business reasons, the existing partners may be unwilling to admit a new partner without receiving a bonus. In an established firm, existing partners may insist on a bonus as compensation for the work they have put into the company over the years. Two accounting factors underlie the business reason. First, total partners' capital equals the **book value** of the recorded net assets of the partnership. When the new partner is admitted, the fair values of assets such as land and buildings may be higher than their book values. The bonus will help make up the difference between fair value and book value. Second, when the partnership has been profitable, goodwill may exist. But, the partnership balance sheet does not report goodwill. The new partner is usually willing to pay the bonus to become a partner.

A bonus to old partners results when the new partner's investment in the firm is greater than the capital credit on the date of admittance. The bonus results in **an increase in the capital balances of the old partners. The partnership allocates the bonus to them on the basis of their income ratios before the admission of the new partner.** To illustrate, assume that the Bart-Cohen partnership, owned by Sam Bart and Tom Cohen, has total capital of $120,000. Lea Eden acquires a 25% ownership (capital) interest in the partnership by making a cash investment of $80,000. The procedure for determining Eden's capital credit and the bonus to the old partners is as follows.

1. **Determine the total capital of the new partnership.** Add the new partner's investment to the total capital of the old partnership. In this case, the total capital of the new firm is $200,000, computed as follows.

Total capital of existing partnership	$120,000
Investment by new partner, Eden	80,000
Total capital of new partnership	$200,000

2. **Determine the new partner's capital credit.** Multiply the total capital of the new partnership by the new partner's ownership interest. Eden's capital credit is $50,000 ($200,000 × 25%).
3. **Determine the amount of bonus.** Subtract the new partner's capital credit from the new partner's investment. The bonus in this case is $30,000 ($80,000 − $50,000).
4. **Allocate the bonus to the old partners on the basis of their income ratios.** Assuming the ratios are Bart 60%, and Cohen 40%, the allocation is Bart $18,000 ($30,000 × 60%) and Cohen $12,000 ($30,000 × 40%).

The entry to record the admission of Eden is:

Cash	80,000	
Sam Bart, Capital		18,000
Tom Cohen, Capital		12,000
Lea Eden, Capital		50,000
(To record admission of Eden and bonus to old partners)		

A	=	L	+	OE
+80,000				
				+18,000
				+12,000
				+50,000

Cash Flows
+80,000

BONUS TO NEW PARTNER A bonus to a new partner results when the new partner's investment in the firm is less than his or her capital credit. This may occur when the new partner possesses special attributes that the partnership wants. For example, the new partner may be able to supply cash that the firm needs for expansion or to meet maturing debts. Or the new partner may be a recognized expert in a relevant field. Thus, an engineering firm may be willing to give a renowned engineer a bonus to join the firm. The partners of a restaurant may offer a bonus to a sports celebrity in order to add the athlete's name to the partnership. A bonus to a new partner may also result when recorded book values on the partnership books are higher than their fair values.

A bonus to a new partner results in a **decrease in the capital balances of the old partners. The amount of the decrease for each partner is based on the income ratios before the admission of the new partner.** To illustrate, assume that Lea Eden invests $20,000 in cash for a 25% ownership interest in the Bart–Cohen partnership. The computations for Eden's capital credit and the bonus are as follows, using the four procedures described in the preceding section.

ILLUSTRATION K-18
Computation of capital credit and bonus to new partner

1. Total capital of Bart–Cohen partnership		$120,000
Investment by new partner, Eden		20,000
Total capital of new partnership		$140,000
2. **Eden's capital credit** (25% × $140,000)		$ 35,000
3. **Bonus to Eden** ($35,000 − $20,000)		$ 15,000
4. Allocation of bonus to old partners:		
Bart ($15,000 × 60%)	$9,000	
Cohen ($15,000 × 40%)	6,000	$ 15,000

A	=	L	+	OE
+20,000				
				−9,000
				−6,000
				+35,000

Cash Flows
+20,000

The partnership records the admission of Eden as follows.

	Debit	Credit
Cash	20,000	
Sam Bart, Capital	9,000	
Tom Cohen, Capital	6,000	
Lea Eden, Capital		35,000
(To record Eden's admission and bonus)		

WITHDRAWAL OF A PARTNER

Now let's look at the opposite situation–the withdrawal of a partner. A partner may withdraw from a partnership **voluntarily**, by selling his or her equity in the firm. Or, he or she may withdraw **involuntarily**, by reaching mandatory retirement age or by dying. The withdrawal of a partner, like the admission of a partner, legally dissolves the partnership. The legal effects may be recognized by dissolving the firm. However, it is customary to record only the economic effects of the partner's withdrawal, while the firm continues to operate and reorganizes itself legally.

As indicated earlier, the partnership agreement should specify the terms of withdrawal. The withdrawal of a partner may be accomplished by (1) payment from partners' personal assets or (2) payment from partnership assets. The former affects only the partners' capital accounts. The latter decreases total net assets and total capital of the partnership.

Payment from Partners' Personal Assets

Withdrawal by payment from partners' personal assets is a personal transaction between the partners. **It is the direct opposite of admitting a new partner who purchases a partner's interest.** The remaining partners pay the retiring partner directly from their personal assets. **Partnership assets are not involved in any way, and total capital does not change.** The effect on the partnership is limited to changes in the partners' capital balances.

To illustrate, assume that partners Morz, Nead, and Odom have capital balances of $25,000, $15,000, and $10,000, respectively. Morz and Nead agree to buy out Odom's interest. Each of them agrees to pay Odom $8,000 in exchange for one-half of Odom's total interest of $10,000. The entry to record the withdrawal is:

A	=	L	+	OE
				−10,000
				+5,000
				+5,000

Cash Flows
no effect

	Debit	Credit
J. Odom, Capital	10,000	
A. Morz, Capital		5,000
M. Nead, Capital		5,000
(To record purchase of Odom's interest)		

The effect of this entry on the partnership accounts is shown below.

Net Assets

50,000	

A. Morz, Capital

	25,000
	5,000
	Bal. 30,000

M. Nead, Capital

	15,000
	5,000
	Bal. 20,000

J. Odom, Capital

10,000	10,000
	Bal. –0–

ILLUSTRATION K-19
Ledger balances after payment from partners' personal assets

Note that net assets and total capital remain the same at $50,000.

What about the $16,000 paid to Odom? You've probably noted that it is not recorded. The entry debited Odom's capital only for $10,000, not for the $16,000 that she received. Similarly, both Morz and Nead credit their capital accounts for only $5,000, not for the $8,000 they each paid.

After Odom's withdrawal, Morz and Nead will share net income or net loss equally unless they indicate another income ratio in the partnership agreement.

Payment from Partnership Assets

Withdrawal by payment from partnership assets is a transaction that involves the partnership. **Both partnership net assets and total capital decrease as a**

result. Using partnership assets to pay for a withdrawing partner's interest is the **reverse** of admitting a partner through the investment of assets in the partnership.

Many partnership agreements provide that the amount paid should be based on the fair value of the assets at the time of the partner's withdrawal. When this basis is required, some maintain that any differences between recorded asset balances and their fair values should be (1) recorded by an adjusting entry, and (2) allocated to all partners on the basis of their income ratios. This position has serious flaws. Recording the revaluations violates the historical cost principle, which requires that assets be stated at original cost. It also violates the going-concern assumption, which assumes the entity will continue indefinitely. The terms of the partnership contract should not dictate the accounting for this event.

In accounting for a withdrawal by payment from partnership assets, the partnership should not record asset revaluations. Instead, it should consider any difference between the amount paid and the withdrawing partner's capital balance as **a bonus** to the retiring partner or to the remaining partners.

BONUS TO RETIRING PARTNER A partnership may pay a bonus to a retiring partner when:

1. The fair value of partnership assets is more than their book value,
2. There is unrecorded goodwill resulting from the partnership's superior earnings record, or
3. The remaining partners are eager to remove the partner from the firm.

The partnership deducts the bonus from the remaining partners' capital balances on the basis of their income ratios at the time of the withdrawal.

To illustrate, assume that the following capital balances exist in the RST partnership: Roman $50,000, Sand $30,000, and Terk $20,000. The partners share income in the ratio of 3:2:1, respectively. Terk retires from the partnership and receives a cash payment of $25,000 from the firm. The procedure for determining the bonus to the retiring partner and the allocation of the bonus to the remaining partners is as follows.

1. **Determine the amount of the bonus.** Subtract the retiring partner's capital balance from the cash paid by the partnership. The bonus in this case is $5,000 ($25,000 – $20,000).
2. **Allocate the bonus to the remaining partners on the basis of their income ratios.** The ratios of Roman and Sand are 3:2. Thus, the allocation of the $5,000 bonus is: Roman $3,000 ($5,000 × 3/5) and Sand $2,000 ($5,000 × 2/5).

▼ **HELPFUL HINT**
Compare this entry to the one on the next page.

The partnership records the withdrawal of Terk as follows.

B. Terk, Capital	20,000	
F. Roman, Capital	3,000	
D. Sand, Capital	2,000	
Cash		25,000
(To record withdrawal of and bonus to Terk)		

A	=	L	+	OE
				−20,000
				−3,000
				−2,000
−25,000				

Cash Flows
−25,000

The remaining partners, Roman and Sand, will recover the bonus given to Terk as the partnership sells or uses the undervalued assets.

BONUS TO REMAINING PARTNERS The retiring partner may give a bonus to the remaining partners when:

1. Recorded assets are overvalued.
2. The partnership has a poor earnings record.
3. The partner is eager to leave the partnership.

In such cases, the cash paid to the retiring partner will be less than the retiring partner's capital balance. **The partnership allocates (credits) the bonus to the capital accounts of the remaining partners on the basis of their income ratios.**

▼ HELPFUL HINT
Compare this entry to the one on the previous page.

To illustrate, assume instead that the partnership pays Terk only $16,000 for her $20,000 equity when she withdraws from the partnership. In that case:

1. The bonus to remaining partners is $4,000 ($20,000 − $16,000).
2. The allocation of the $4,000 bonus is Roman $2,400 ($4,000 × 3/5) and Sand $1,600 ($4,000 × 2/5).

Under these circumstances, the entry to record the withdrawal is as follows.

A	=	L	+	OE
				−20,000
				+2,400
				+1,600
−16,000				

Cash Flows
−16,000

B. Terk, Capital	20,000	
F. Roman, Capital		2,400
D. Sand, Capital		1,600
Cash		16,000
(To record withdrawal of Terk and bonus to remaining partners)		

Note that if Sand had withdrawn from the partnership, Roman and Terk would divide any bonus on the basis of their income ratio, which is 3:1 or 75% and 25%.

Death of a Partner

The death of a partner dissolves the partnership. However, partnership agreements usually contain a provision for the surviving partners to continue operations. When a partner dies, it usually is necessary to determine the partner's equity at the date of death. This is done by (1) determining the net income or loss for the year to date, (2) closing the books, and (3) preparing financial statements. The partnership agreement may also require an independent audit and a revaluation of assets.

The surviving partners may agree to purchase the deceased partner's equity from their personal assets. Or they may use partnership assets to settle with the deceased partner's estate. In both instances, the entries to record the withdrawal of the partner are similar to those presented earlier.

To facilitate payment from partnership assets, some partnerships obtain life insurance policies on each partner, with the partnership named as the beneficiary. The partnership then uses the proceeds from the insurance policy on the deceased partner to settle with the estate.

REVIEW

▶ LEARNING OBJECTIVES REVIEW

1 Discuss and account for the formation of a partnership. The principal characteristics of a partnership are (a) association of individuals, (b) mutual agency, (c) limited life, (d) unlimited liability, and (e) co-ownership of property. When formed, a partnership records each partner's initial investment at the fair value of the assets at the date of their transfer to the partnership.

2 Explain how to account for net income or net loss of a partnership. Partnerships divide net income or net loss on the basis of the income ratio, which may be (a) a fixed ratio, (b) a ratio based on beginning or average capital balances, (c) salaries to partners and the remainder on a fixed ratio, (d) interest on partners' capital and the remainder on a fixed ratio, and (e) salaries to partners, interest on partners' capital, and the remainder on a fixed ratio.

The financial statements of a partnership are similar to those of a proprietorship. The principal differences are as follows. (a) The partnership shows the division of net income on the income statement. (b) The owners' equity statement is called a partners' capital statement. (c) The partnership reports each partner's capital on the balance sheet.

3 Explain how to account for the liquidation of a partnership. When a partnership is liquidated, it is necessary to record the (a) sale of noncash assets, (b) allocation of the gain or loss on realization, (c) payment of partnership liabilities, and (d) distribution of cash to the partners on the basis of their capital balances.

4 Prepare journal entries when a partner is either admitted or withdraws. The entry to record the admittance of a new partner by purchase of a partner's interest affects only partners' capital accounts. The entries to record the admittance by investment of assets in the partnership (a) increase both net assets and total capital and (b) may result in recognition of a bonus to either the old partners or the new partner.

The entry to record a withdrawal from the firm when the partners pay from their personal assets affects only partners' capital accounts. The entry to record a withdrawal when payment is made from partnership assets (a) decreases net assets and total capital and (b) may result in recognizing a bonus either to the retiring partner or the remaining partners.

GLOSSARY REVIEW

Admission by investment Admission of a partner by investing assets in the partnership, causing both partnership net assets and total capital to increase. (p. K-15).

Admission by purchase of an interest Admission of a partner in a personal transaction between one or more existing partners and the new partner; does not change total partnership assets or total capital. (p. K-15).

Capital deficiency A debit balance in a partner's capital account after allocation of gain or loss. (p. K-10).

General partners Partners who have unlimited liability for the debts of the firm. (p. K-3).

Income ratio The basis for dividing net income and net loss in a partnership. (p. K-6).

Limited liability company A form of business organization, usually classified as a partnership for tax purposes and usually with limited life, in which partners, who are called members, have limited liability. (p. K-3).

Limited liability partnership A partnership of professionals in which partners are given limited liability and the public is protected from malpractice by insurance carried by the partnership. (p. K-3).

Limited partners Partners whose liability for the debts of the firm is limited to their investment in the firm. (p. K-3).

Limited partnership A partnership in which one or more general partners have unlimited liability and one or more partners have limited liability for the obligations of the firm. (p. K-3).

No capital deficiency All partners have credit balances after allocation of gain or loss. (p. K-10).

Partners' capital statement The owners' equity statement for a partnership which shows the changes in each partner's capital account and in total partnership capital during the year. (p. K-9).

Partnership An association of two or more persons to carry on as co-owners of a business for profit. (p. K-1).

Partnership agreement A written contract expressing the voluntary agreement of two or more individuals in a partnership. (p. K-5).

Partnership dissolution A change in partners due to withdrawal or admission, which does not necessarily terminate the business. (p. K-2).

Partnership liquidation An event that ends both the legal and economic life of a partnership. (p. K-10).

Schedule of cash payments A schedule showing the distribution of cash to the partners in a partnership liquidation. (p. K-12).

Withdrawal by payment from partners' personal assets Withdrawal of a partner in a personal transaction between partners; does not change total partnership assets or total capital. (p. K-18).

Withdrawal by payment from partnership assets Withdrawal of a partner in a transaction involving the partnership, causing both partnership net assets and total capital to decrease. (p. K-18).

QUESTIONS

1. The characteristics of a partnership include the following: (a) association of individuals, (b) limited life, and (c) co-ownership of property. Explain each of these terms.
2. Kevin Mathis is confused about the partnership characteristics of (a) mutual agency and (b) unlimited liability. Explain these two characteristics for Kevin.
3. Lance Kosinski and Matt Morrisen are considering a business venture. They ask you to explain the advantages and disadvantages of the partnership form of organization.
4. Why might a company choose to use a limited partnership?
5. Newland and Palermo form a partnership. Newland contributes land with a book value of $50,000 and a fair value of $60,000. Newland also contributes equipment with a book value of $52,000 and a fair value of $57,000. The partnership assumes a $20,000 mortgage

on the land. What should be the balance in Newland's capital account upon formation of the partnership?

6. W. Jenson, N. Emch, and W. Gilligan have a partnership called Outlaws. A dispute has arisen among the partners. Jenson has invested twice as much in assets as the other two partners, and he believes net income and net losses should be shared in accordance with the capital ratios. The partnership agreement does not specify the division of profits and losses. How will net income and net loss be divided?
7. Mutt and Jeff are discussing how income and losses should be divided in a partnership they plan to form. What factors should be considered in determining the division of net income or net loss?
8. M. Elston and R. Ogle have partnership capital balances of $40,000 and $80,000, respectively. The partnership agreement indicates that net income or net loss should be shared equally. If net income for the partnership is $42,000, how should the net income be divided?
9. S. Pletcher and F. Holt share net income and net loss equally. (a) Which account(s) is (are) debited and credited to record the division of net income between the partners? (b) If S. Pletcher withdraws $30,000 in cash for personal use instead of salary, which account is debited and which is credited?
10. Partners T. Greer and R. Parks are provided salary allowances of $30,000 and $25,000, respectively. They divide the remainder of the partnership income in a ratio of 3:2. If partnership net income is $40,000, how much is allocated to Greer and Parks?
11. Are the financial statements of a partnership similar to those of a proprietorship? Discuss.
12. How does the liquidation of a partnership differ from the dissolution of a partnership?
13. Roger Fuller and Mike Rangel are discussing the liquidation of a partnership. Roger maintains that all cash should be distributed to partners on the basis of their income ratios. Is he correct? Explain.
14. In continuing their discussion from Question 13, Mike says that even in the case of a capital deficiency, all cash should still be distributed on the basis of capital balances. Is Mike correct? Explain.
15. Norris, Madson, and Howell have income ratios of 5:3:2 and capital balances of $34,000, $31,000, and $28,000, respectively. Noncash assets are sold at a gain and allocated to the partners. After creditors are paid, $103,000 of cash is available for distribution to the partners. How much cash should be paid to Madson?
16. Before the final distribution of cash, account balances are Cash $27,000; S. Shea, Capital $19,000 (Cr.); L. Seastrom, Capital $12,000 (Cr.); and M. Luthi, Capital $4,000 (Dr.). Luthi is unable to pay any of the capital deficiency. If the income-sharing ratios are 5:3:2, respectively, how much cash should be paid to L. Seastrom?
17. Why is Apple not a partnership?
18. Susan Turnbull decides to purchase from an existing partner for $50,000 a one-third interest in a partnership. What effect does this transaction have on partnership net assets?
19. Jerry Park decides to invest $25,000 in a partnership for a one-sixth capital interest. How much do the partnership's net assets increase? Does Park also acquire a one-sixth income ratio through this investment?
20. Jill Parsons purchases for $72,000 Jamar's interest in the Tholen-Jamar partnership. Assuming that Jamar has a $68,000 capital balance in the partnership, what journal entry is made by the partnership to record this transaction?
21. Jaime Keller has a $41,000 capital balance in a partnership. She sells her interest to Sam Parmenter for $45,000 cash. What entry is made by the partnership for this transaction?
22. Andrea Riley retires from the partnership of Jaggard, Pester, and Riley. She receives $85,000 of partnership assets in settlement of her capital balance of $81,000. Assuming that the income-sharing ratios are 5:3:2, respectively, how much of Riley's bonus is debited to Pester's capital account?
23. Your roommate argues that partnership assets should be revalued in situations like those in Question 21. Why is this generally not done?
24. How is a deceased partner's equity determined?

BRIEF EXERCISES

Journalize entries in forming a partnership.

(LO 1), AP

BEK-1 Barbara Ripley and Fred Nichols decide to organize the ALL-Star partnership. Ripley invests $15,000 cash, and Nichols contributes $10,000 cash and equipment having a book value of $3,500. Prepare the entry to record Nichols's investment in the partnership, assuming the equipment has a fair value of $4,000.

Prepare portion of opening balance sheet for partnership.

(LO 1), AP

BEK-2 Penner and Torres decide to merge their proprietorships into a partnership called Pentor Company. The balance sheet of Torres Co. shows:

Accounts receivable	$16,000	
Less: Allowance for doubtful accounts	1,200	$14,800
Equipment	20,000	
Less: Accumulated depreciation—equip.	7,000	13,000

The partners agree that the net realizable value of the receivables is $14,500 and that the fair value of the equipment is $11,000. Indicate how the accounts should appear in the opening balance sheet of the partnership.

BEK-3 Rod Dall Co. reports net income of $75,000. The income ratios are Rod 60% and Dall 40%. Indicate the division of net income to each partner, and prepare the entry to distribute the net income.

Journalize the division of net income using fixed income ratios.

(LO 2), AP

BEK-4 PFW Co. reports net income of $45,000. Partner salary allowances are Pitts $15,000, Filbert $5,000, and Witten $5,000. Indicate the division of net income to each partner, assuming the income ratio is 50:30:20, respectively.

Compute division of net income with a salary allowance and fixed ratios.

(LO 2), AP

BEK-5 Nabb & Fry Co. reports net income of $31,000. Interest allowances are Nabb $7,000 and Fry $5,000, salary allowances are Nabb $15,000 and Fry $10,000, and the remainder is shared equally. Show the distribution of income.

Show division of net income when allowances exceed net income.

(LO 2), AP

BEK-6 After liquidating noncash assets and paying creditors, account balances in the Mann Co. are Cash $21,000; A, Capital (Cr.) $8,000; B, Capital (Cr.) $9,000; and C, Capital (Cr.) $4,000. The partners share income equally. Journalize the final distribution of cash to the partners.

Journalize final cash distribution in liquidation.

(LO 3), AP

BEK-7 Gamma Co. capital balances are Barr $30,000, Croy $25,000, and Eubank $22,000. The partners share income equally. Tovar is admitted to the firm by purchasing one-half of Eubank's interest for $13,000. Journalize the admission of Tovar to the partnership.

Journalize admission by purchase of an interest.

(LO 4), AP

BEK-8 In Eastwood Co., capital balances are Irey $40,000 and Pedigo $50,000. The partners share income equally. Vernon is admitted to the firm with a 45% interest by an investment of cash of $58,000. Journalize the admission of Vernon.

Journalize admission by investment.

(LO 4), AP

BEK-9 Capital balances in Pelmar Co. are Lango $40,000, Oslo $30,000, and Fernetti $20,000. Lango and Oslo each agree to pay Fernetti $12,000 from their personal assets. Lango and Oslo each receive 50% of Fernetti's equity. The partners share income equally. Journalize the withdrawal of Fernetti.

Journalize withdrawal paid by personal assets.

(LO 4), AP

BEK-10 Data pertaining to Pelmar Co. are presented in BEK-9. Instead of payment from personal assets, assume that Fernetti receives $24,000 from partnership assets in withdrawing from the firm. Journalize the withdrawal of Fernetti.

Journalize withdrawal paid by partnership assets.

(LO 4), AP

EXERCISES

EK-1 Mark Rensing has prepared the following list of statements about partnerships.

Identify characteristics of partnership.

(LO 1), C

1. A partnership is an association of three or more persons to carry on as co-owners of a business for profit.
2. The legal requirements for forming a partnership can be quite burdensome.
3. A partnership is not an entity for financial reporting purposes.
4. The net income of a partnership is taxed as a separate entity.
5. The act of any partner is binding on all other partners, even when partners perform business acts beyond the scope of their authority.
6. Each partner is personally and individually liable for all partnership liabilities.
7. When a partnership is dissolved, the assets legally revert to the original contributor.
8. In a limited partnership, one or more partners have unlimited liability and one or more partners have limited liability for the debts of the firm.
9. Mutual agency is a major advantage of the partnership form of business.

Instructions

Identify each statement as true or false. If false, indicate how to correct the statement.

Journalize entry for formation of a partnership.

(LO 1), AP

EK-2 K. Decker, S. Rosen, and E. Toso are forming a partnership. Decker is transferring $50,000 of personal cash to the partnership. Rosen owns land worth $15,000 and a small building worth $80,000, which she transfers to the partnership. Toso transfers to the partnership cash of $9,000, accounts receivable of $32,000, and equipment worth $39,000. The partnership expects to collect $29,000 of the accounts receivable.

Instructions

(a) Prepare the journal entries to record each of the partners' investments.

(b) What amount would be reported as total owners' equity immediately after the investments?

Journalize entry for formation of a partnership.

(LO 1), AP

EK-3 Suzy Vopat has owned and operated a proprietorship for several years. On January 1, she decides to terminate this business and become a partner in the firm of Vopat and Sigma. Vopat's investment in the partnership consists of $12,000 in cash, and the following assets of the proprietorship: accounts receivable $14,000 less allowance for doubtful accounts of $2,000, and equipment $30,000 less accumulated depreciation of $4,000. It is agreed that the allowance for doubtful accounts should be $3,000 for the partnership. The fair value of the equipment is $23,500.

Instructions

Journalize Vopat's admission to the firm of Vopat and Sigma.

Prepare schedule showing distribution of net income and closing entry.

(LO 2), AP

XLS

EK-4 McGill and Smyth have capital balances on January 1 of $50,000 and $40,000, respectively. The partnership income-sharing agreement provides for (1) annual salaries of $22,000 for McGill and $13,000 for Smyth, (2) interest at 10% on beginning capital balances, and (3) remaining income or loss to be shared 60% by McGill and 40% by Smyth.

Instructions

(a) Prepare a schedule showing the distribution of net income, assuming net income is (1) $50,000 and (2) $36,000.

(b) Journalize the allocation of net income in each of the situations above.

Prepare journal entries to record allocation of net income.

(LO 2), AP

EK-5 Coburn (beginning capital, $60,000) and Webb (beginning capital $90,000) are partners. During 2017, the partnership earned net income of $80,000, and Coburn made drawings of $18,000 while Webb made drawings of $24,000.

Instructions

(a) Assume the partnership income-sharing agreement calls for income to be divided 45% to Coburn and 55% to Webb. Prepare the journal entry to record the allocation of net income.

(b) Assume the partnership income-sharing agreement calls for income to be divided with a salary of $30,000 to Coburn and $25,000 to Webb, with the remainder divided 45% to Coburn and 55% to Webb. Prepare the journal entry to record the allocation of net income.

(c) Assume the partnership income-sharing agreement calls for income to be divided with a salary of $40,000 to Coburn and $35,000 to Webb, interest of 10% on beginning capital, and the remainder divided 50%–50%. Prepare the journal entry to record the allocation of net income.

(d) Compute the partners' ending capital balances under the assumption in part (c).

Prepare partners' capital statement and partial balance sheet.

(LO 2), AP

EK-6 For National Co., beginning capital balances on January 1, 2017, are Nancy Payne $20,000 and Ann Dody $18,000. During the year, drawings were Payne $8,000 and Dody $5,000. Net income was $40,000, and the partners share income equally.

Instructions

(a) Prepare the partners' capital statement for the year.

(b) Prepare the owners' equity section of the balance sheet at December 31, 2017.

Prepare a classified balance sheet of a partnership.

(LO 2), AP

EK-7 Terry, Nick, and Frank are forming The Doctor Partnership. Terry is transferring $30,000 of personal cash and equipment worth $25,000 to the partnership. Nick owns land worth $28,000 and a small building worth $75,000, which he transfers to the partnership. There is a long-term mortgage of $20,000 on the land and building, which the partnership assumes. Frank transfers cash of $7,000, accounts receivable of $36,000, supplies worth

$3,000, and equipment worth $27,000 to the partnership. The partnership expects to collect $32,000 of the accounts receivable.

Instructions

Prepare a classified balance sheet for the partnership after the partners' investments on December 31, 2017.

Prepare cash payments schedule.

(LO 3), AP

EK-8 Sedgwick Company at December 31 has cash $20,000, noncash assets $100,000, liabilities $55,000, and the following capital balances: Floyd $45,000 and DeWitt $20,000. The firm is liquidated, and $105,000 in cash is received for the noncash assets. Floyd and DeWitt income ratios are 60% and 40%, respectively.

Instructions

Prepare a schedule of cash payments.

Journalize transactions in a liquidation.

(LO 3), AP

EK-9 Data for Sedgwick Company are presented in EK-8. Sedgwick Company now decides to liquidate the partnership.

Instructions

Prepare the entries to record:

(a) The sale of noncash assets.
(b) The allocation of the gain or loss on realization to the partners.
(c) Payment of creditors.
(d) Distribution of cash to the partners.

Journalize transactions with a capital deficiency.

(LO 3), AP

EK-10 Prior to the distribution of cash to the partners, the accounts in the VUP Company are Cash $24,000; Vogel, Capital (Cr.) $17,000; Utech, Capital (Cr.) $15,000; and Pena, Capital (Dr.) $8,000. The income ratios are 5:3:2, respectively. VUP Company decides to liquidate the company.

Instructions

(a) Prepare the entry to record (1) Pena's payment of $8,000 in cash to the partnership and (2) the distribution of cash to the partners with credit balances.
(b) Prepare the entry to record (1) the absorption of Pena's capital deficiency by the other partners and (2) the distribution of cash to the partners with credit balances.

Journalize admission of a new partner by purchase of an interest.

(LO 4), AP

EK-11 K. Kolmer, C. Eidman, and C. Ryno share income on a 5:3:2 basis. They have capital balances of $34,000, $26,000, and $21,000, respectively, when Don Jernigan is admitted to the partnership.

Instructions

Prepare the journal entry to record the admission of Don Jernigan under each of the following assumptions.

(a) Purchase of 50% of Kolmer's equity for $19,000.
(b) Purchase of 50% of Eidman's equity for $12,000.
(c) Purchase of 33 1/3% of Ryno's equity for $9,000.

Journalize admission of a new partner by investment.

(LO 4), AP

EK-12 S. Pagan and T. Tabor share income on a 6:4 basis. They have capital balances of $100,000 and $60,000, respectively, when W. Wolford is admitted to the partnership.

Instructions

Prepare the journal entry to record the admission of W. Wolford under each of the following assumptions.

(a) Investment of $90,000 cash for a 30% ownership interest with bonuses to the existing partners.
(b) Investment of $50,000 cash for a 30% ownership interest with a bonus to the new partner.

Journalize withdrawal of a partner with payment from partners' personal assets.

(LO 4), AP

EK-13 N. Essex, C. Gilmore, and C. Heganbart have capital balances of $50,000, $40,000, and $30,000, respectively. Their income ratios are 4:4:2. Heganbart withdraws from the partnership under each of the following independent conditions.

1. Essex and Gilmore agree to purchase Heganbart's equity by paying $17,000 each from their personal assets. Each purchaser receives 50% of Heganbart's equity.

2. Gilmore agrees to purchase all of Heganbart's equity by paying $22,000 cash from her personal assets.
3. Essex agrees to purchase all of Heganbart's equity by paying $26,000 cash from his personal assets.

Instructions

Journalize the withdrawal of Heganbart under each of the assumptions above.

Journalize withdrawal of a partner with payment from partnership assets.

(LO 4), AP

EK-14 B. Higgins, J. Mayo, and N. Rice have capital balances of $95,000, $75,000, and $60,000, respectively. They share income or loss on a 5:3:2 basis. Rice withdraws from the partnership under each of the following conditions.

1. Rice is paid $64,000 in cash from partnership assets, and a bonus is granted to the retiring partner.
2. Rice is paid $52,000 in cash from partnership assets, and bonuses are granted to the remaining partners.

Instructions

Journalize the withdrawal of Rice under each of the assumptions above.

Journalize entry for admission and withdrawal of partners.

(LO 4), AP

EK-15 Foss, Albertson, and Espinosa are partners who share profits and losses 50%, 30%, and 20%, respectively. Their capital balances are $100,000, $60,000, and $40,000, respectively.

Instructions

(a) Assume Garrett joins the partnership by investing $88,000 for a 25% interest with bonuses to the existing partners. Prepare the journal entry to record his investment.
(b) Assume instead that Foss leaves the partnership. Foss is paid $110,000 with a bonus to the retiring partner. Prepare the journal entry to record Foss's withdrawal.

PROBLEMS

Prepare entries for formation of a partnership and a balance sheet.

(LO 1, 2), AP

GLS

PK-1 The post-closing trial balances of two proprietorships on January 1, 2017, are presented below.

	Sorensen Company		Lucas Company	
	Dr.	Cr.	Dr.	Cr.
Cash	$ 14,000		$12,000	
Accounts receivable	17,500		26,000	
Allowance for doubtful accounts		$ 3,000		$ 4,400
Inventory	26,500		18,400	
Equipment	45,000		29,000	
Accumulated depreciation—equipment		24,000		11,000
Notes payable		18,000		15,000
Accounts payable		22,000		31,000
Sorensen, capital		36,000		
Lucas, capital				24,000
	$103,000	$103,000	$85,400	$85,400

Sorensen and Lucas decide to form a partnership, Solu Company, with the following agreed upon valuations for noncash assets.

	Sorensen Company	Lucas Company
Accounts receivable	$17,500	$26,000
Allowance for doubtful accounts	4,500	4,000
Inventory	28,000	20,000
Equipment	25,000	15,000

All cash will be transferred to the partnership, and the partnership will assume all the liabilities of the two proprietorships. Further, it is agreed that Sorensen will invest an additional $5,000 in cash, and Lucas will invest an additional $19,000 in cash.

Instructions

(a) Prepare separate journal entries to record the transfer of each proprietorship's assets and liabilities to the partnership.
(b) Journalize the additional cash investment by each partner.
(c) Prepare a classified balance sheet for the partnership on January 1, 2017.

(a) Sorensen, Capital $40,000
Lucas, Capital $23,000

(c) Total assets $173,000

PK-2 At the end of its first year of operations on December 31, 2017, NBS Company's accounts show the following.

Journalize divisions of net income and prepare a partners' capital statement.

(LO 2), AP

Partner	Drawings	Capital
Art Niensted	$23,000	$48,000
Greg Bolen	14,000	30,000
Krista Sayler	10,000	25,000

The capital balance represents each partner's initial capital investment. Therefore, net income or net loss for 2017 has not been closed to the partners' capital accounts.

Instructions

(a) Journalize the entry to record the division of net income for the year 2017 under each of the following independent assumptions.
 (1) Net income is $30,000. Income is shared 6:3:1.
 (2) Net income is $40,000. Niensted and Bolen are given salary allowances of $15,000 and $10,000, respectively. The remainder is shared equally.
 (3) Net income is $19,000. Each partner is allowed interest of 10% on beginning capital balances. Niensted is given a $15,000 salary allowance. The remainder is shared equally.
(b) Prepare a schedule showing the division of net income under assumption (3) above.
(c) Prepare a partners' capital statement for the year under assumption (3) above

(a) (1) Niensted $18,000
(2) Niensted $20,000
(3) Niensted $17,700

(c) Niensted $42,700

PK-3 The partners in Crawford Company decide to liquidate the firm when the balance sheet shows the following.

Prepare entries with a capital deficiency in liquidation of a partnership.

(LO 3), AP

GLS

CRAWFORD COMPANY
Balance Sheet
May 31, 2017

Assets		Liabilities and Owners' Equity	
Cash	$ 27,500	Notes payable	$ 13,500
Accounts receivable	25,000	Accounts payable	27,000
Allowance for doubtful accounts	(1,000)	Salaries and wages payable	4,000
Inventory	34,500	A. Jamison, capital	33,000
Equipment	21,000	S. Moyer, capital	21,000
Accumulated depreciation—equipment	(5,500)	P. Roper, capital	3,000
	$101,500		$101,500

The partners share income and loss 5:3:2. During the process of liquidation, the following transactions were completed in the following sequence.

1. A total of $51,000 was received from converting noncash assets into cash.
2. Gain or loss on realization was allocated to partners.
3. Liabilities were paid in full.
4. P. Roper paid his capital deficiency.
5. Cash was paid to the partners with credit balances.

Instructions

(a) Prepare the entries to record the transactions.
(b) Post to the cash and capital accounts.
(c) Assume that Roper is unable to pay the capital deficiency.
 (1) Prepare the entry to allocate Roper's debit balance to Jamison and Moyer.
 (2) Prepare the entry to record the final distribution of cash.

(a) Loss on realization $23,000
Cash paid: to Jamison $21,500; to Moyer $14,100

PK-4 At April 30, partners' capital balances in PDL Company are G. Donley $52,000, C. Lamar $48,000, and J. Pinkston $18,000. The income sharing ratios are 5:4:1, respectively. On May 1, the PDLT Company is formed by admitting J. Terrell to the firm as a partner.

Journalize admission of a partner under different assumptions.

(LO 4), AP

Instructions

(a) Journalize the admission of Terrell under each of the following independent assumptions.

(a) (1) Terrell $9,000

(1) Terrell purchases 50% of Pinkston's ownership interest by paying Pinkston $16,000 in cash.

(2) Terrell $16,000

(2) Terrell purchases $33^1/_3$% of Lamar's ownership interest by paying Lamar $15,000 in cash.

(3) Terrell $54,000

(3) Terrell invests $62,000 for a 30% ownership interest, and bonuses are given to the old partners.

(4) Terrell $48,000

(4) Terrell invests $42,000 for a 30% ownership interest, which includes a bonus to the new partner.

(b) Lamar's capital balance is $32,000 after admitting Terrell to the partnership by investment. If Lamar's ownership interest is 20% of total partnership capital, what were (1) Terrell's cash investment and (2) the bonus to the new partner?

Journalize withdrawal of a partner under different assumptions.

(LO 4), AP

PK-5 On December 31, the capital balances and income ratios in TEP Company are as follows.

Partner	Capital Balance	Income Ratio
Trayer	$60,000	50%
Emig	40,000	30%
Posada	30,000	20%

Instructions

(a) Journalize the withdrawal of Posada under each of the following assumptions.

(a) (1) Emig, Capital $15,000

(1) Each of the continuing partners agrees to pay $18,000 in cash from personal funds to purchase Posada's ownership equity. Each receives 50% of Posada's equity.

(2) Emig, Capital $30,000

(2) Emig agrees to purchase Posada's ownership interest for $25,000 cash.

(3) Bonus $4,000

(3) Posada is paid $34,000 from partnership assets, which includes a bonus to the retiring partner.

(4) Bonus $8,000

(4) Posada is paid $22,000 from partnership assets, and bonuses to the remaining partners are recognized.

(b) If Emig's capital balance after Posada's withdrawal is $43,600, what were (1) the total bonus to the remaining partners and (2) the cash paid by the partnership to Posada?

L

Accounting for Sole Proprietorships

APPENDIX PREVIEW

Chapter 1 identified three forms of business organization. Two forms, the sole proprietorship and the partnership, were discussed only briefly. Emphasis was placed on the corporate form in Chapter 1 as well as in subsequent chapters. The purpose of this appendix is to discuss and illustrate the accounting for the operations and financial condition of a sole proprietorship.

APPENDIX OUTLINE

LEARNING OBJECTIVES	
1 Identify the differences in equity accounts between a corporation and a sole proprietorship.	• Owner's capital account • Drawing account
2 Understand what accounts increase and decrease owner's equity.	• Owner's equity in a sole proprietorship • Recording transactions of a proprietorship
3 Describe the differences between a retained earnings statement and an owner's equity statement.	• Using the adjusted trial balance • Reporting equity
4 Explain the process of closing the books for a sole proprietorship.	• Preparing a post-closing trial balance for a proprietorship

LEARNING OBJECTIVE 1

Identify the differences in equity accounts between a corporation and a sole proprietorship.

The primary difference between accounting and reporting for a sole proprietorship and a corporation involves accounting for equity transactions. Because a sole proprietorship has a single owner rather than numerous stockholders, a sole proprietorship uses a permanent **owner's capital account**, such as "Sally Jones, Capital," instead of Common Stock and Retained Earnings. In a sole proprietorship, there is no need to separate owner's investments from net income retained for dividends because the sole proprietor does not declare or receive dividends. Instead, withdrawals by the owner of cash or other assets from the business for personal use are recorded in a temporary **drawing** account. The different equity accounts are contrasted as shown in Illustration L-1.

ILLUSTRATION L-1
Equity section of the balance sheet—corporation vs. proprietorship

Corporation	Sole Proprietorship
Stockholders' equity	Owner's equity
Common stock	Owner's name, capital
Retained earnings	

For purposes of comparing the accounting for a corporation with a sole proprietorship, the illustrations in this appendix assume a sole proprietorship owned by R. Neal and named Sierra Company. **Except for equity transactions, we use the same accounts, amounts, and transactions as those of Sierra Corporation presented in Chapters 1 through 4.**

LEARNING OBJECTIVE 2

Understand what accounts increase and decrease owner's equity.

OWNER'S EQUITY IN A SOLE PROPRIETORSHIP

The ownership claim on total assets is known as **owner's equity**. It is equal to total assets minus total liabilities.

Increases in Owner's Equity

In a proprietorship, owner's equity is increased by owner's investments and revenues.

INVESTMENTS BY OWNER **Investments by owner** are the assets the owner puts into the business. These investments increase owner's equity.

REVENUES **Revenues** are the gross increase in owner's equity resulting from business activities entered into for the purpose of earning income.

Decreases in Owner's Equity

In a proprietorship, owner's equity is decreased by owner's drawings and expenses.

DRAWINGS An owner may withdraw cash or other assets for personal use. These withdrawals could be recorded as a direct decrease of owner's equity. However, it is generally considered preferable to use a separate classification called **drawings** to determine the total withdrawals for each accounting period. **Drawings decrease owner's equity.**

EXPENSES **Expenses** are the cost of assets consumed or services used in the process of earning revenue. They are **decreases in owner's equity that result from operating the business.**

In summary, owner's equity is increased by an owner's investments and by revenues from business operations. In contrast, owner's equity is decreased by an owner's withdrawals of assets and by expenses. These relationships are shown in Illustration L-2. **Net income** results when revenues exceed expenses. A **net loss** occurs when expenses exceed revenues.

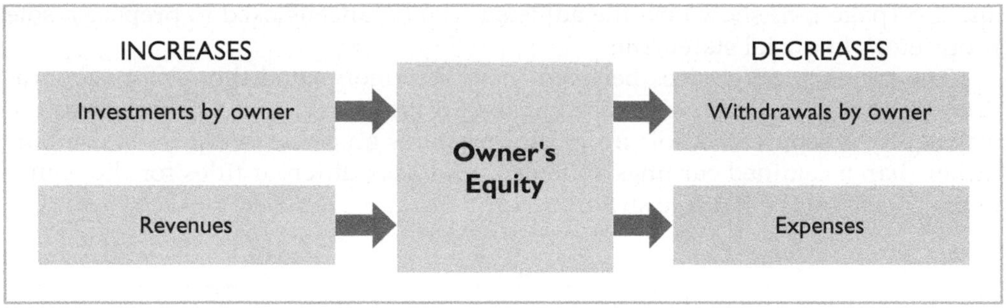

ILLUSTRATION L-2
Increases and decreases in owner's equity

RECORDING TRANSACTIONS OF A PROPRIETORSHIP

Chapter 3 described the basic steps employed in the accounting process as follows:

- Analyze transactions.
- Record transactions in the journal.
- Post journal entries to the general ledger.
- Prepare a trial balance.

These same steps apply to all forms of business. Illustration 3-3 (page 99) presented the impact of Sierra's transactions on its accounting equation. Illustration L-3 shows how the same transactions would have been recorded for a sole proprietor. The only differences are related to the accounts used to record equity transactions. Those differences are highlighted here in red.

ILLUSTRATION L-3
Summary of transactions

	Assets							=	Liabilities					+	Owner's Equity	
	Cash	+	Supplies	+	Prepaid Insurance	+	Equipment	=	Notes Payable	+	Accounts Payable	+	Unearned Service Revenue	+	R. Neal, Capital	
(1)	+$10,000							=							+$10,000	Investment by owner
(2)	+5,000								+$5,000							
	15,000							=	5,000					+	10,000	
(3)	−5,000						+$5,000									
	10,000					+	5,000	=	5,000					+	10,000	
(4)	+1,200												+$1,200			
	11,200					+	5,000	=	5,000			+	1,200	+	10,000	
(5)	+10,000														+10,000	Service Revenue
	21,200					+	5,000	=	5,000			+	1,200	+	20,000	
(6)	−900														−900	Rent Expense
	20,300					+	5,000	=	5,000			+	1,200	+	19,100	
(7)	−600				+$600											
	19,700			+	600	+	5,000	=	5,000			+	1,200	+	19,100	
(8)			+$2,500								+$2,500					
	19,700	+	2,500	+	600	+	5,000	=	5,000	+	2,500	+	1,200	+	19,100	
(10)	−500			+											−500	Drawings
	19,200	+	2,500	+	600	+	5,000	=	5,000	+	2,500	+	1,200	+	18,600	
(11)	−4,000														−4,000	Sal./Wages Expense
	$15,200	+	$2,500	+	$600	+	$5,000	=	$5,000	+	$2,500	+	$1,200	+	$14,600	
	$23,300								$23,300							

LEARNING OBJECTIVE 3

Describe the differences between a retained earnings statement and an owner's equity statement.

Chapter 4 described accounting for adjusting entries. A sole proprietor makes the same types of adjustments as a corporation. After recording and posting all of the adjustments, an adjusted trial balance is prepared. Illustrations L-4 (page L-4) and L-5 (page L-5) show how the adjusted trial balance is used to prepare a sole proprietor's financial statements.

The primary differences between these statements and those of a corporation (presented in Illustrations 4-27 and 4-28, pages 172 and 173) relate to the way equity is reported. A sole proprietor prepares an **owner's equity statement** rather than a retained earnings statement and uses different titles for the equity items shown on the balance sheet.

ILLUSTRATION L-4
Preparation of the income statement and owner's equity statement from the adjusted trial balance

SIERRA COMPANY
Adjusted Trial Balance
October 31, 2017

Account	Debit	Credit
Cash	$15,200	
Accounts Receivable	200	
Supplies	1,000	
Prepaid Insurance	550	
Equipment	5,000	
Accumulated Depreciation—Equipment		$ 40
Notes Payable		5,000
Accounts Payable		2,500
Interest Payable		50
Unearned Service Revenue		800
Salaries and Wages Payable		1,200
R. Neal, Capital		10,000
R. Neal, Drawing	500	
Service Revenue		**10,600**
Salaries and Wages Expense	**5,200**	
Supplies Expense	**1,500**	
Rent Expense	**900**	
Insurance Expense	**50**	
Interest Expense	**50**	
Depreciation Expense	**40**	
	$30,190	$30,190

SIERRA COMPANY
Income Statement
For the Month Ended October 31, 2017

Revenues		
Service revenue		$10,600
Expenses		
Salaries and wages expense	$5,200	
Supplies expense	1,500	
Rent expense	900	
Insurance expense	50	
Interest expense	50	
Depreciation expense	40	
Total expenses		7,740
Net income		$ 2,860

SIERRA COMPANY
Owner's Equity Statement
For the Month Ended October 31, 2017

R. Neal, Capital, October 1	$ -0-
Add: Investments by owner	10,000
R. Neal, Capital	10,000
Net income	2,860
	12,860
Less: Drawings	500
R. Neal, Capital, October 31	$12,360

To balance sheet

LEARNING OBJECTIVE 4

Explain the process of closing the books for a sole proprietorship.

At the end of the accounting period, the temporary account balances are transferred to the permanent owner's equity account, Owner's Capital, through the preparation of closing entries. **Closing entries** for a proprietorship formally recognize in the ledger the transfer of net income (or net loss) and owner's drawing to owner's capital. The results of these entries are shown in the owner's equity statement.

Journalizing and posting closing entries is a required step in the accounting cycle. (See Illustration 4-30 on page 176 for Sierra Corporation.)

SIERRA COMPANY
Adjusted Trial Balance
October 31, 2017

Account	Debit	Credit
Cash	$15,200	
Accounts Receivable	200	
Supplies	1,000	
Prepaid Insurance	550	
Equipment	5,000	
Accumulated Depreciation—Equipment		$ 40
Notes Payable		5,000
Accounts Payable		2,500
Interest Payable		50
Unearned Service Revenue		800
Salaries and Wages Payable		1,200
R. Neal, Capital		10,000
R. Neal, Drawing	500	
Service Revenue		10,600
Salaries and Wages Expense	5,200	
Supplies Expense	1,500	
Rent Expense	900	
Insurance Expense	50	
Interest Expense	50	
Depreciation Expense	40	
	$30,190	$30,190

SIERRA COMPANY
Balance Sheet
October 31, 2017

Assets		
Cash		$15,200
Accounts receivable		200
Supplies		1,000
Prepaid insurance		550
Equipment	$5,000	
Less: Accumulated depreciation—equipment	40	4,960
Total assets		$21,910
Liabilities and Owner's Equity		
Liabilities		
Notes payable		$ 5,000
Accounts payable		2,500
Interest payable		50
Unearned service revenue		800
Salaries and wages payable		1,200
Total liabilities		9,550
Owner's equity		
R. Neal, capital		12,360
Total liabilities and owner's equity		$21,910

Capital balance at Oct. 31 from owner's equity statement in Illustration L-4

ILLUSTRATION L-5
Preparation of the balance sheet from the adjusted trial balance

In preparing closing entries for a proprietorship, each income statement account could be closed directly to owner's capital. However, to do so would result in excessive detail in the permanent owner's capital account. Instead, the revenue and expense accounts are closed, in the same manner as for a corporation, to another temporary account, **Income Summary**. Only the net income or net loss is transferred from this account to Owner's Capital.

Closing entries for a proprietorship may be prepared directly from the adjusted balances in the ledger, from the income statement and balance sheet columns of the worksheet, or from the income and owner's equity statements. Separate closing entries could be prepared for each nominal account, but the following four entries accomplish the desired result more efficiently:

1. Debit each revenue account for its balance, and credit Income Summary for total revenues.
2. Debit Income Summary for total expenses, and credit each expense account for its balance.
3. Debit Income Summary and credit Owner's Capital for the amount of net income.
4. Debit Owner's Capital for the balance in the Owner's Drawing account, and credit Owner's Drawing for the same amount.

▼ HELPFUL HINT
Owner's Drawing is closed directly to Owner's Capital and *not* to Income Summary because Owner's Drawing is not an expense.

The four entries are referenced in the diagram of the closing process shown in Illustration L-6 (page L-6) and in the journal entries in Illustration L-7 (page L-6). The posting of closing entries is shown in Illustration L-8 (page L-7).

If there were a net loss because expenses exceeded revenues, entry 3 in Illustration L-6 would be reversed: credit Income Summary and debit Owner's Capital.

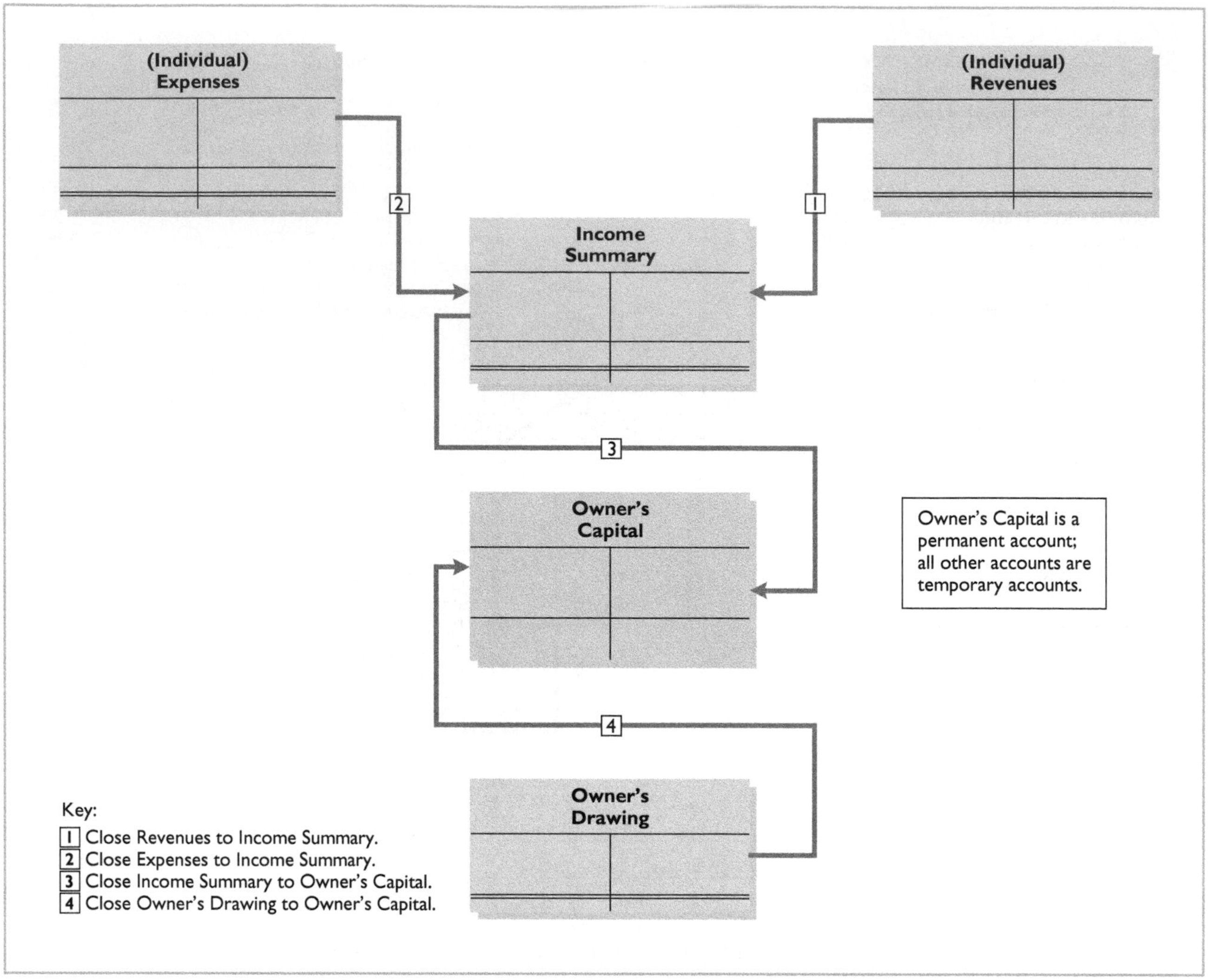

ILLUSTRATION L-6
Diagram of closing process

GENERAL JOURNAL

Date	Account Titles and Explanation	Debit	Credit
	Closing Entries		
2017	(1)		
Oct. 31	Service Revenue	10,600	
	Income Summary		10,600
	(To close revenue account)		
	(2)		
31	Income Summary	7,740	
	Salaries and Wages Expense		5,200
	Supplies Expense		1,500
	Rent Expense		900
	Insurance Expense		50
	Interest Expense		50
	Depreciation Expense		40
	(To close expense accounts)		
	(3)		
31	Income Summary	2,860	
	R. Neal, Capital		2,860
	(To close net income to owner's capital)		
	(4)		
31	**R. Neal, Capital**	500	
	R. Neal, Drawing		500
	(To close drawings to owner's capital)		

▼ HELPFUL HINT
Income Summary is a very descriptive title. Total revenues are closed to Income Summary, total expenses are closed to Income Summary, and the balance in Income Summary is a net income or net loss.

ILLUSTRATION L-7
Closing entries journalized

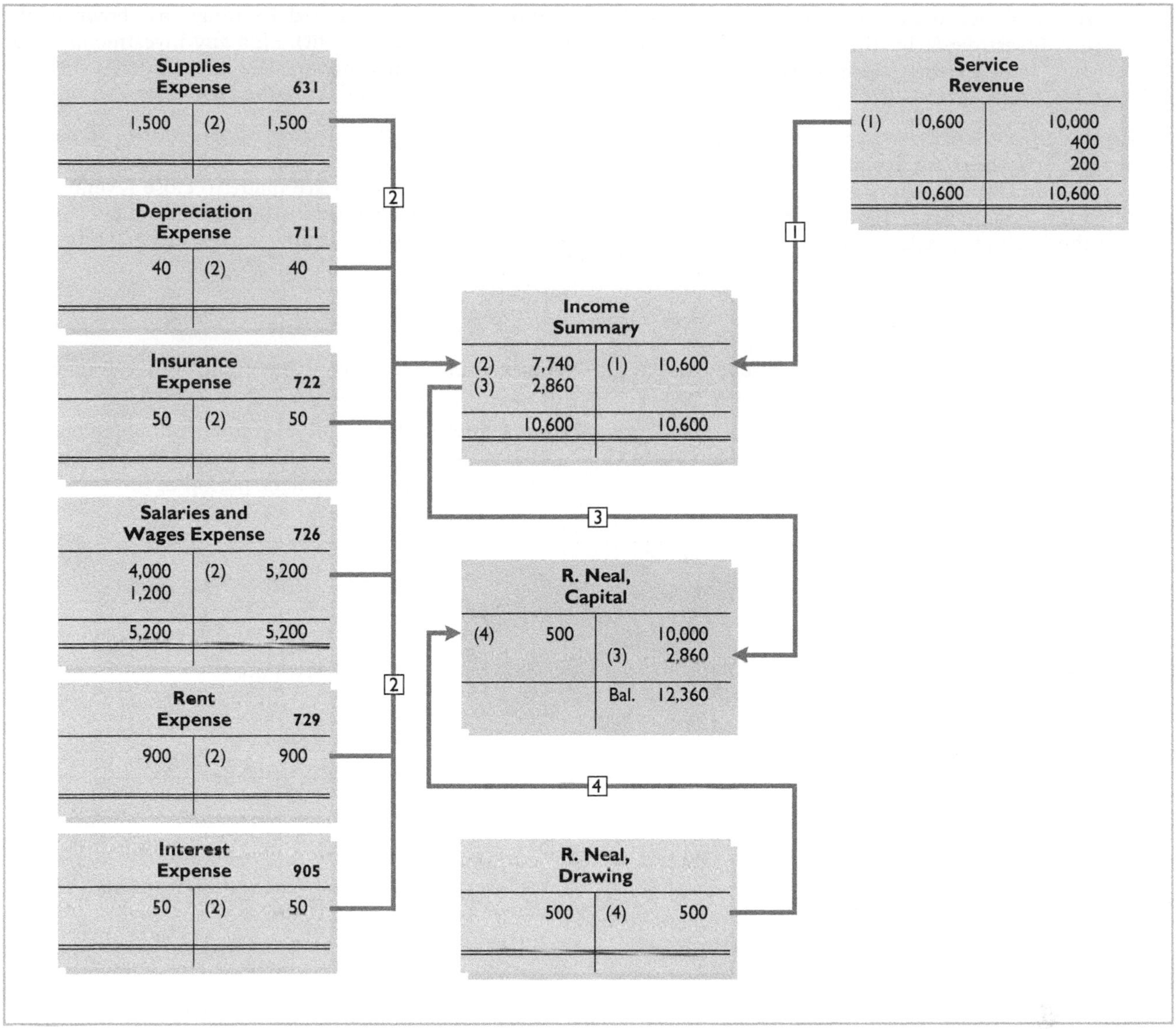

ILLUSTRATION L-8
Posting of closing entries

PREPARING A POST-CLOSING TRIAL BALANCE FOR A PROPRIETORSHIP

After all closing entries are journalized and posted, the **post-closing trial balance** is prepared from the ledger. A post-closing trial balance is a list of all permanent accounts and their balances after closing entries are journalized and posted. As with a corporation, **the purpose of a proprietorship post-closing trial balance is to prove the equality of the permanent account balances that are carried forward into the next accounting period**. Since all temporary accounts will have zero balances, **the post-closing trial balance will contain only permanent—balance sheet—accounts**.

REVIEW

▶ LEARNING OBJECTIVES REVIEW

1 Identify the differences in equity accounts between a corporation and a sole proprietorship. A sole proprietorship uses a permanent owner's equity capital account instead of Common Stock and Retained Earnings. Withdrawals of cash or other assets by the owner for personal use are recorded in a temporary drawing account.

2 Understand what accounts increase and decrease owner's equity. Investments by the owner and revenue increase owner's equity. Owner's drawings and expenses decrease owner's equity.

3 Describe the differences between a retained earnings statement and an owner's equity statement. A sole proprietor prepares an owner's equity statement rather than a retained earnings statement. The owner's equity statement shows the beginning balance in the owner's capital account (instead of Retained Earnings, as shown in the retained earnings statement), plus any investments made by the owner, plus net income, less any drawings (in place of Dividends, shown in the retained earnings statement).

4 Explain the process of closing the books for a sole proprietorship. In closing the books for a sole proprietorship, separate entries are made to close revenues and expenses to Income Summary, Income Summary to Owner's Capital, and Owner's Drawing to Owner's Capital.

GLOSSARY REVIEW

Drawings Withdrawal of cash or other assets from a sole proprietorship for the personal use of the owner. (p. L-2)

Investments by owner The assets put into the business by a sole proprietor. (p. L-2)

Owner's equity The ownership claim on the total assets of a sole proprietorship. (p. L-2)

Owner's equity statement The financial statement prepared for a sole proprietorship to summarize the changes in owner's equity for a specific period of time. (p. L-4)

WileyPLUS Many additional resources are available for practice in WileyPLUS.

QUESTIONS

1. What is the basic accounting equation for a sole proprietorship?
2. What are the differences in the equity accounts of a sole proprietorship versus those of a corporation?
3. What items affect owner's equity, and in what direction?
4. In February 2017, Ken Moran invested an additional $10,000 in his business, Moran's Pharmacy, which is organized as a proprietorship. Moran's accountant, Terry Baden, recorded this receipt as an increase in cash revenues. Is this treatment appropriate? Why or why not?
5. What are the steps in preparing an owner's equity statement?
6. Identify the account(s) debited and credited in each of the required closing entries for a sole proprietorship, assuming the company has net income for the year.

BRIEF EXERCISES

Determine effect of transactions on basic accounting equation.

(LO 2), C

BEL-1 Presented below are three business transactions. On a sheet of paper, list the letters (a), (b), (c) with columns for assets, liabilities, and owner's equity. For each column, indicate whether the transactions increased (+), decreased (−), or had no effect (NE) on assets, liabilities, and owner's equity.

(a) Invested cash in the business.
(b) Withdrawal of cash by owner.
(c) Received cash from a customer who had previously been billed for services performed.

Determine effect of transactions on owner's equity.

(LO 2), C

BEL-2 Presented below are three transactions. Mark each transaction as affecting owner's investment (I), owner's drawing (D), revenue (R), expense (E), or not affecting owner's equity (NOE).

(a) Received cash for services performed.
(b) Paid cash to purchase equipment.
(c) Paid employee salaries.

Indicate debit and credit effects and normal balance.

(LO 2), C

BEL-3 For each of the following accounts, indicate the effects of (a) a debit and (b) a credit on the accounts and (c) the normal balance of the account.

1. Accounts Payable.
2. Advertising Expense.
3. Service Revenue.
4. Accounts Receivable.
5. A. L. Brislin, Capital.
6. A. L. Brislin, Drawing.

EXERCISES

EL-1 An analysis of the transactions made by Rodriguez & Co., a certified public accounting firm, for the month of August is shown below. Each increase and decrease in owner's equity is explained.

Analyze transactions and compute net income.

(LO 2), AP

	Cash	+ Accounts Receivable	+ Supplies	+ Equipment	= Accounts Payable	+ Owner's Equity Rodriguez, Capital
1.	+$12,000					+$12,000 Investment
2.	−2,000			+$5,000	+$3,000	
3.	−750		+$750			
4.	+2,600	+$3,700				+6,300 Service Revenue
5.	−1,500				−1,500	
6.	−2,000					−2,000 Drawings
7.	−650					−650 Rent Expense
8.	+450	−450				
9.	−2,900					−2,900 Sal./Wag. Expense
10.					+500	−500 Utilities Expense

Instructions

(a) Describe each transaction that occurred for the month.
(b) Determine how much owner's equity increased for the month.
(c) Compute the amount of net income for the month.

EL-2 Presented below is information related to the sole proprietorship of Kurt Cooper, attorney.

Prepare an owner's equity statement.

(LO 3), AP

Legal service revenue—2017	$360,000
Total expenses—2017	211,000
Assets, January 1, 2017	85,000
Liabilities, January 1, 2017	62,000
Assets, December 31, 2017	168,000
Liabilities, December 31, 2017	70,000
Drawings—2017	?

Instructions

Prepare the 2017 owner's equity statement for Kurt Cooper's legal practice.

EL-3 The adjusted trial balance of Lorenz Company at the end of its fiscal year is:

Prepare income statement, owner's equity statement, and balance sheet.

(LO 1, 2, 3, 4), AP

LORENZ COMPANY
Adjusted Trial Balance
July 31, 2017

No.	Account Titles	Debit	Credit
101	Cash	$ 14,940	
112	Accounts Receivable	8,780	
157	Equipment	15,900	
167	Accumulated Depreciation—Equipment		$ 5,400
201	Accounts Payable		4,220
208	Unearned Rent Revenue		1,800
301	J. D. Lorenz, Capital		45,200
306	J. D. Lorenz, Drawing	14,000	
404	Service Revenue		65,100
429	Rent Revenue		6,500
711	Depreciation Expense	4,000	
720	Salaries and Wages Expense	55,700	
732	Utilities Expense	14,900	
		$128,220	$128,220

Instructions

(a) Prepare an income statement and an owner's equity statement for the year. Lorenz did not make any capital investments during the year.
(b) Prepare a classified balance sheet at July 31.

PROBLEMS

Prepare income statement, owner's equity statement, and balance sheet.

(LO 1, 2, 3, 4), AP

PL-1 On May 1, Steven Rumford started Skyline Flying School, a company that provides flying lessons, by investing $45,000 cash in the business. Following are the assets and liabilities of the company on May 31, 2017, and the revenues and expenses for the month of May.

Cash	$ 6,500	Notes Payable	$30,000
Accounts Receivable	7,200	Rent Expense	1,200
Equipment	64,000	Maintenance and Repairs Expense	400
Service Revenue	8,600	Gasoline Expense	2,500
Advertising Expense	500	Insurance Expense	400
		Accounts Payable	800

Steven Rumford made no additional investment in May, but he withdrew $1,700 in cash for personal use.

Instructions

(a) Net income $ 3,600
Owner's equity $46,900
Total assets $ 77,700
(b) Net income $ 1,200
Owner's equity $44,500

(a) Prepare an income statement and owner's equity statement for the month of May and a balance sheet at May 31.

(b) Prepare an income statement and owner's equity statement for May assuming that the data above need to be adjusted for the following items: (1) $900 worth of services were performed and billed but not collected at May 31, and (2) $3,300 of gasoline expense was incurred but not paid.

Prepare financial statements, closing entries, and post-closing trial balance.

(LO 1, 2, 3, 4), AP

GLS

PL-2 The adjusted trial balance columns of the worksheet for Whitmore Company are as follows.

WHITMORE COMPANY
Adjusted Trial Balance
For the Year Ended December 31, 2017

Account No.	Account Titles	Adjusted Trial Balance Debit	Adjusted Trial Balance Credit
101	Cash	$ 20,800	
112	Accounts Receivable	15,400	
126	Supplies	2,300	
130	Prepaid Insurance	4,800	
151	Equipment	44,000	
152	Accumulated Depreciation—Equipment		$ 18,000
200	Notes Payable		20,000
201	Accounts Payable		8,000
212	Salaries and Wages Payable		3,000
230	Interest Payable		1,000
301	B. Whitmore, Capital		36,000
306	B. Whitmore, Drawing	12,000	
400	Service Revenue		79,000
610	Advertising Expense	12,000	
631	Supplies Expense	3,700	
711	Depreciation Expense	6,000	
722	Insurance Expense	4,000	
726	Salaries and Wages Expense	39,000	
905	Interest Expense	1,000	
	Totals	$165,000	$165,000

Instructions

(a) Net income $13,300
Current assets $43,300
Current liabilities $22,000

(d) Post-closing trial balance $87,300

(a) Prepare an income statement, owner's equity statement, and a classified balance sheet. $10,000 of the notes payable become due in 2018. B. Whitmore did not make any additional investments in the business during 2017.

(b) Prepare the closing entries.

(c) Post the closing entries. Use the three-column form of account. Income summary is No. 350.

(d) Prepare a post-closing trial balance.

PL-3 The adjusted trial balance columns of the worksheet for Rick Pool Company, owned by Rick Pool, are as follows.

Prepare financial statements, closing entries, and post-closing trial balance.

(LO 1, 2, 3, 4), AP

RICK POOL COMPANY
Adjusted Trial Balance
For the Year Ended December 31, 2017

Account No.	Account Titles	Adjusted Trial Balance Debit	Adjusted Trial Balance Credit
101	Cash	$ 13,600	
112	Accounts Receivable	15,400	
126	Supplies	1,500	
130	Prepaid Insurance	2,800	
151	Equipment	34,000	
152	Accumulated Depreciation—Equipment		$ 8,000
200	Notes Payable		16,000
201	Accounts Payable		6,000
212	Salaries and Wages Payable		3,000
230	Interest Payable		500
301	Rick Pool, Capital		25,000
306	Rick Pool, Drawing	10,000	
400	Service Revenue		88,000
610	Advertising Expense	12,000	
631	Supplies Expense	5,700	
711	Depreciation Expense	4,000	
722	Insurance Expense	5,000	
726	Salaries and Wages Expense	42,000	
905	Interest Expense	500	
	Totals	$146,500	$146,500

Instructions

(a) Prepare an income statement, owner's equity statement, and a classified balance sheet (*Note:* $10,000 of the notes payable become due in 2018.) Rick Pool did not make any additional investments in the business during the year.

(b) Prepare the closing entries. Use J14 for the journal page.

(c) Post the closing entries. Use the three-column form of account. Income Summary is No. 350.

(d) Prepare a post-closing trial balance.

(a) Net income $18,800
Current assets $33,300
Current liabilities $19,500

(d) Post-closing trial balance $67,300

M

Pricing

APPENDIX PREVIEW

Few management decisions are more important than setting prices. Intel, for example, must sell computer chips at a price that is high enough to cover its costs and ensure a reasonable profit. But if the price is too high, the chips will not sell. In this appendix, we examine two types of pricing situations. The first part of this appendix addresses pricing for goods sold or services provided to external parties. The second part of this appendix addresses pricing decisions managers face when they sell goods to other divisions within the company.

APPENDIX OUTLINE

LEARNING OBJECTIVES	
1 Compute a target cost when the market determines a product price.	• Target costing
2 Compute a target selling price using cost-plus pricing.	• Cost-plus pricing • Variable-cost pricing
3 Use time-and-material pricing to determine the cost of services provided.	• Calculate labor rate • Calculate material loading charge
4 Determine a transfer price using the negotiated, cost-based, and market-based approaches.	• Negotiated transfer prices • Cost-based transfer prices • Market-based transfer prices • Effect of outsourcing on transfer pricing • Transfers between divisions in different countries
5 Determine prices using absorption-cost pricing and variable-cost pricing.	• Absorption-cost pricing • Variable-cost pricing

LEARNING OBJECTIVE 1

Compute a target cost when the market determines a product price.

Establishing the price for any good or service is affected by many factors. Take the pharmaceutical industry as an example. Its approach to profitability has been to spend heavily on research and development in an effort to find and patent a few new drugs, price them high, and market them aggressively. However, the AIDS crisis in Africa placed the drug industry under considerable pressure to lower prices on drugs used to treat the disease. For example, Merck Co. lowered the price of its AIDS drug Crixivan to $600 per patient in these countries. This compares with the $6,016 it typically charged in the United States.[1] As a consequence, individuals in the United States questioned whether prices in the U.S. market were too high. The drug companies countered that to cover their substantial financial risks to develop these products, they need to set the prices high. Illustration M-1 indicates the many factors that can affect pricing decisions.

ILLUSTRATION M-1
Pricing factors

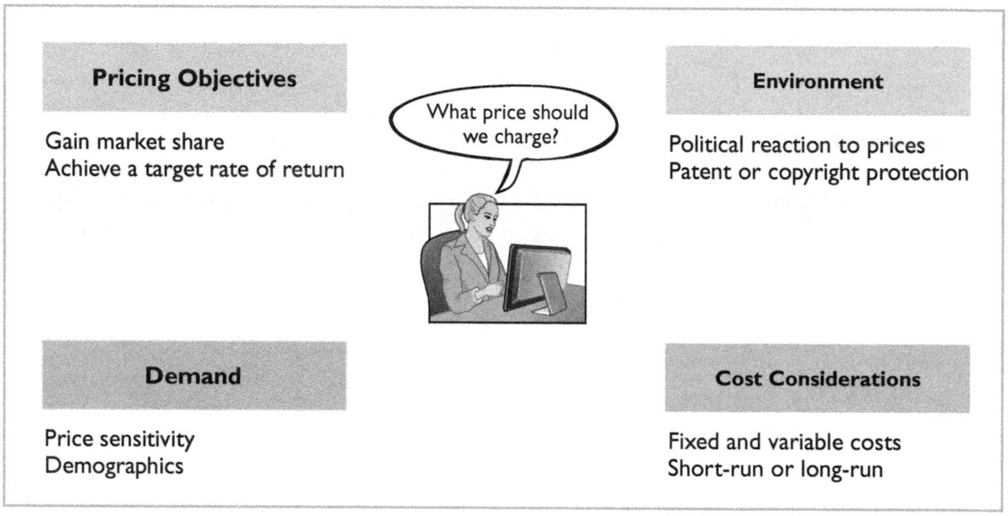

In the long run, a company must price its product to cover its costs and earn a reasonable profit. But to price its product appropriately, it must have a good understanding of market forces at work. In most cases, a company does not set the prices. Instead, the price is set by the competitive market (the laws of supply and demand). For example, a company such as ChevronTexaco or Exxon-Mobil cannot set the price of gasoline by itself. These companies are called **price takers** because the price of gasoline is set by market forces (the supply of oil and the demand by customers). This is the case for any product that is not easily differentiated from competing products, such as farm products (corn or wheat) or minerals (coal or sand).

In other situations, the company sets the prices. This would be the case where the product is specially made for a customer, as in a one-of-a-kind product such as a designer dress by Versace or Armani. A company also sets the price when there are few or no other producers capable of manufacturing a similar item. An example would be a company that has a patent or copyright on a unique process, such as the case of computer chips by Intel. Finally, a company can set prices when it effectively differentiates its product or service from others. Even in a competitive market like coffee, Starbucks has been able to differentiate its product and charge a premium for a cup of java.

[1] "AIDS Gaffes in Africa Come Back to Haunt Drug Industry at Home," *Wall Street Journal* (April 23, 2001), p. 1.

TARGET COSTING

Automobile manufacturers like Ford or Toyota face a competitive market. The price of an automobile is affected greatly by the laws of supply and demand, so no company in this industry can affect the price to a significant degree. Therefore, to earn a profit, companies in the auto industry must focus on controlling costs. This requires setting a **target cost** that provides a desired profit. Illustration M-2 shows the relationship of target cost to market price and desired profit.

Market Price	−	Desired Profit	=	Target Cost

ILLUSTRATION M-2
Target cost as related to price and profit

Assuming it reaches sales targets, if General Motors can produce its automobiles for its target cost (or less), it will meet its profit goal. If it cannot achieve its target cost, it will fail to achieve the desired profit, which will disappoint its stockholders.

In a competitive market, a company chooses the segment of the market it wants to compete in—that is, its market niche. For example, it may choose between selling luxury goods or economy goods in order to focus its efforts on one segment or the other. Once the company has identified the segment of the market in which it wants to compete, it conducts market research. This determines the features its product should have, and what the market price is for a product with those features. Once the company has determined this price, it can determine its target cost by setting a desired profit. The difference between the market price and the desired profit is the target cost of the product (shown in Illustration M-2). After the company determines the target cost, it assembles a team of employees with expertise in a variety of areas (production and operations, marketing, and finance). The team's task is to design and develop a product that can meet quality specifications while not exceeding the target cost. The target cost includes all product and period costs necessary to make and market the product or service.

LEARNING OBJECTIVE ▶2 **Compute a target selling price using cost-plus pricing.**

COST-PLUS PRICING

As discussed, in a competitive product environment, the price of a product is set by the market. In order to achieve its desired profit, the company focuses on achieving a target cost. In a less competitive environment, companies have a greater ability to set the product price. Commonly, when a company sets a product price, it does so as a function of, or relative to, the cost of the product or service. This is referred to as **cost-plus pricing**. Under cost-plus pricing, a company first determines a cost base and then adds a **markup** to the cost base to determine the **target selling price**.

If the cost base includes all of the costs required to produce and sell the product, then the markup represents the desired profit. This can be seen in Illustration M-3, where the markup represents the difference between the selling price and cost—the profit on the product.

Selling Price	−	Cost	=	Markup (Profit)

ILLUSTRATION M-3
Relation of markup to cost and selling price

The size of the markup (profit) depends on the return the company hopes to generate on the amount it has invested. In determining the optimal markup, the company must consider competitive and market conditions, political and legal issues, and other relevant factors. Once the company has determined its cost base and its desired markup, it can add the two together to determine the target selling price. The basic cost-plus pricing formula is expressed as follows.

ILLUSTRATION M-4
Cost-plus pricing formula

Cost	+	Markup	=	Target Selling Price

To illustrate, assume that Thinkmore Products, Inc. is in the process of setting a selling price on its new video camera pen. It is a functioning pen that records up to 2 hours of audio and video. The per unit variable cost estimates for the video camera pen are as follows.

ILLUSTRATION M-5
Variable cost per unit

	Per Unit
Direct materials	$23
Direct labor	17
Variable manufacturing overhead	12
Variable selling and administrative expenses	8
Variable cost per unit	$60

To produce and sell its product, Thinkmore incurs fixed manufacturing overhead of $350,000 and fixed selling and administrative expenses of $300,000. To determine the cost per unit, we divide total fixed costs by the number of units the company expects to produce. Illustration M-6 shows the computation of fixed cost per unit for Thinkmore, assuming the production of 10,000 units.

ILLUSTRATION M-6
Fixed cost per unit, 10,000 units

	Total Costs	÷	Budgeted Volume	=	Cost per Unit
Fixed manufacturing overhead	$350,000	÷	10,000	=	$35
Fixed selling and administrative expenses	300,000	÷	10,000	=	30
Fixed cost per unit					$65

Management is ultimately evaluated based on its ability to generate a high return on the company's investment. This is frequently expressed as a return on investment (ROI) percentage, calculated as income divided by the average amount invested in a product or service. A higher percentage reflects a greater success in generating profits from the investment in a product or service. Chapter 22 provides a more in-depth discussion of the use of ROI to evaluate the performance of investment center managers.

To achieve a desired return on investment percentage, a product's markup should be determined by calculating the desired return on investment (ROI) per unit. This is calculated by multiplying the desired ROI percentage times the amount invested to produce the product, and then dividing this by the number of units produced. Illustration M-7 shows the computation used to determine a markup amount based on a desired ROI per unit for Thinkmore, assuming that the company desires a 20% ROI and that it has invested $2,000,000.

ILLUSTRATION M-7
Calculation of markup based on desired ROI per unit

$$\frac{\text{Desired ROI Percentage} \times \text{Amount Invested}}{\text{Units Produced}} = \text{Markup (Desired ROI per Unit)}$$

$$\frac{20\% \times \$2{,}000{,}000}{10{,}000 \text{ units}} = \$40$$

Thinkmore expects to receive income of $400,000 (20% × $2,000,000) on its $2,000,000 investment. On a per unit basis, the markup based on the desired ROI per unit is $40 ($400,000 ÷ 10,000 units). Given the per unit costs shown above, Illustration M-8 computes the sales price to be $165.

ILLUSTRATION M-8
Computation of selling price, 10,000 units

	Per Unit
Variable cost	$ 60
Fixed cost	65
Total cost	125
Markup (desired ROI per unit)	40
Selling price per unit	$165

In most cases, companies like Thinkmore use a markup percentage on cost to determine the selling price. The formula to compute the markup percentage to achieve a desired ROI of $40 per unit is as follows.

ILLUSTRATION M-9
Computation of markup percentage

Markup (Desired ROI per Unit)	÷	Total Unit Cost	=	Markup Percentage
$40	÷	$125	=	32%

Using a 32% markup on cost, Thinkmore would compute the target selling price as follows.

ILLUSTRATION M-10
Computation of selling price—markup approach

Total Unit Cost	+	(Total Unit Cost	×	Markup Percentage)	=	Target Selling Price per Unit
$125	+	($125	×	32%)	=	$165

Thinkmore should set the price for its video camera pen at $165 per unit.

Limitations of Cost-Plus Pricing

The cost-plus pricing approach has a major advantage: It is simple to compute. However, the cost model does not give consideration to the demand side. That is, will customers pay the price Thinkmore Products computed for its video camera pen? In addition, sales volume plays a large role in determining per unit costs. The lower the sales volume, for example, the higher the price Thinkmore must charge to meet its desired ROI. To illustrate, if the budgeted sales volume was 5,000 instead of 10,000, Thinkmore's variable cost per unit would remain the same. However, the fixed cost per unit would change as follows.

ILLUSTRATION M-11
Fixed cost per unit, 5,000 units

	Total Costs	÷	Budgeted Volume	=	Cost per Unit
Fixed manufacturing overhead	$350,000	÷	5,000	=	$ 70
Fixed selling and administrative expenses	300,000	÷	5,000	=	60
Fixed cost per unit					$130

As indicated in Illustration M-6 (page M-4), the fixed cost per unit for 10,000 units was $65. However, at a lower sales volume of 5,000 units, the fixed cost per unit increases to $130. Thinkmore's desired 20% ROI now results in a $80 ROI per unit [(20% × $2,000,000) ÷ 5,000]. Thinkmore computes the selling price at 5,000 units as follows.

ILLUSTRATION M-12
Computation of selling price, 5,000 units

	Per Unit
Variable cost	$ 60
Fixed cost	130
Total cost	190
Markup (desired ROI per unit)	80
Selling price per unit	$270

As shown, the lower the budgeted volume, the higher the per unit price. The reason: Fixed costs and ROI are spread over fewer units, and therefore the fixed cost and ROI per unit increase. In this case, at 5,000 units, Thinkmore would have to mark up its total unit costs 42.11% to earn a desired ROI of $80 per unit, as shown below.

$$42.11\% = \frac{\$80 \text{ (desired ROI per unit)}}{\$190 \text{ (total unit cost)}}$$

The target selling price would then be $270, as indicated earlier:

$$\$190 + (\$190 \times 42.11\%) = \$270$$

The opposite effect will occur if budgeted volume is higher (say, at 12,000 units) because fixed costs and ROI can be spread over more units. As a result, the cost-plus model of pricing will achieve its desired ROI only when Thinkmore sells the quantity it budgeted. If actual volume is much less than budgeted volume, Thinkmore may sustain losses unless it can raise its prices.

VARIABLE-COST PRICING

In determining the target price for Thinkmore Products' video camera pen, we calculated the cost base by including all costs incurred. This approach is referred to as **full-cost pricing**. Instead of using full costs to set prices, some companies simply add a markup to their variable costs (thus excluding fixed manufacturing and fixed selling and administrative costs). Using **variable-cost pricing** as the basis for setting prices avoids the problem of using uncertain cost information (as discussed above for Thinkmore) related to fixed-cost-per-unit computations. Variable-cost pricing also is helpful in pricing special orders or when excess capacity exists.

The major disadvantage of variable-cost pricing is that managers may set the price too low and consequently fail to cover their fixed costs. In the long run, failure to cover fixed costs will lead to losses. As a result, companies that use variable-cost pricing must adjust their markups to make sure that the price set will provide a fair return. The use of variable costs as the basis for setting prices is discussed in a later section.

LEARNING OBJECTIVE ▶3 Use time-and-material pricing to determine the cost of services provided.

Another variation on cost-plus pricing is **time-and-material pricing**. Under this approach, the company sets two pricing rates—one for the **labor** used on a job and another for the **material**. The labor rate includes direct labor time and other employee costs. The material charge is based on the cost of direct parts and materials used and a **material loading charge** for related overhead costs. Time-and-material pricing is widely used in service industries, especially professional firms such as public accounting, law, engineering, and consulting firms, as well as construction companies, repair shops, and printers.

To illustrate a time-and-material pricing situation, assume the following data for Lake Holiday Marina, a boat and motor repair shop.

ILLUSTRATION M-13
Total annual budgeted time and material costs

LAKE HOLIDAY MARINA
Budgeted Costs for the Year 2017

	Time Charges	Material Loading Charges*
Mechanics' wages and benefits	$103,500	—
Parts manager's salary and benefits	—	$11,500
Office employee's salary and benefits	20,700	2,300
Other overhead (supplies, depreciation, property taxes, advertising, utilities)	26,800	14,400
Total budgeted costs	$151,000	$28,200

*The material loading charges exclude the invoice cost of the materials.

Using time-and-material pricing involves three steps: (1) calculate the per hour labor charge, (2) calculate the charge for obtaining and holding materials, and (3) calculate the charges for a particular job.

STEP 1: CALCULATE THE LABOR RATE. The first step for time-and-material pricing is to determine a charge for labor time. The charge for labor time is expressed as a rate per hour of labor. This rate includes (1) the direct labor cost of the employees, including hourly pay rate plus fringe benefits; (2) selling, administrative, and similar overhead costs; and (3) an allowance for a desired profit or ROI per hour of employee time. In some industries, such as repair shops for autos and boats, the same hourly labor rate is charged regardless of which employee performs the work. In other industries, the rate that is charged is adjusted according to classification or level of the employee. A public accounting firm, for example, would charge different rates for the services of an assistant, senior, manager, or partner; a law firm would charge different rates for the work of a paralegal, associate, or partner.

Illustration M-14 shows computation of the hourly charges for Lake Holiday Marina during 2017. The marina budgets 5,000 annual labor hours in 2017, and it desires a profit margin of $8 per hour of labor.

ILLUSTRATION M-14
Computation of hourly time-charge rate

Lake Holiday Marina.xls

	A	B	C	D	E	F
1	Per Hour	Total Cost	÷	Total Hours	=	Per Hour Charge
2	Hourly labor rate for repairs					
3	Mechanics' wages and benefits	$103,500	÷	5,000	=	$20.70
4	Overhead costs					
5	Office employee's salary and benefits	20,700	÷	5,000	=	4.14
6	Other overhead	26,800	÷	5,000	=	5.36
7	Total hourly cost	$151,000	÷	5,000	=	30.20
8	Profit margin					8.00
9	Rate charged per hour of labor					$38.20
10						

To determine the labor charge for a job, the marina multiplies this rate of $38.20 by the number of hours of labor used.

STEP 2: CALCULATE THE MATERIAL LOADING CHARGE. The charge for materials typically includes the invoice price of any materials used on the job plus a material loading charge. The **material loading charge** covers the costs of purchasing, receiving, handling, and storing materials, plus any desired profit margin on the materials themselves. The material loading charge is expressed as a **percentage** of the total estimated costs of parts and materials for the year. To determine this percentage, the company does the following. (1) It estimates its total annual costs for purchasing, receiving, handling, and storing materials. (2) It divides this amount by the total estimated cost of parts and materials. (3) It adds a desired profit margin on the materials themselves.

Illustration M-15 shows computation of the material loading charge used by Lake Holiday Marina during 2017. The marina estimates that the total invoice cost of parts and materials used in 2017 will be $120,000. The marina desires a 20% profit margin on the invoice cost of parts and materials.

ILLUSTRATION M-15
Computation of material loading charge

Lake Holiday Marina.xls

	A	B	C	D	E	F
1		Material Loading Charges	÷	Total Invoice Cost, Parts and Materials	=	Material Loading Percentage
2	Overhead costs					
3	Parts manager's salary and benefits	$11,500				
4	Office employee's salary	2,300				
5		13,800	÷	$120,000	=	11.50%
6						
7	Other overhead	14,400	÷	120,000	=	12.00%
8		$28,200	÷	120,000	=	23.50%
9	Profit margin					20.00%
10	Material loading percentage					43.50%
11						

The marina's material loading charge on any particular job is 43.50% multiplied by the cost of materials used on the job. For example, if the marina used $100 of parts, the additional material loading charge would be $43.50.

STEP 3: CALCULATE CHARGES FOR A PARTICULAR JOB. The charges for any particular job are the sum of (1) the labor charge, (2) the charge for the materials, and (3) the material loading charge. For example, suppose that Lake Holiday Marina prepares a price quotation to estimate the cost to refurbish a used 28-foot pontoon boat. Lake Holiday Marina estimates the job will require 50 hours of labor and $3,600 in parts and materials. Illustration M-16 shows the marina's price quotation.

ILLUSTRATION M-16
Price quotation for time and material

LAKE HOLIDAY MARINA Time-and-Material Price Quotation		
Job: Marianne Perino, repair of 28-foot pontoon boat		
Labor charges: 50 hours @ $38.20		$1,910
Material charges		
Cost of parts and materials	$3,600	
Material loading charge (43.5% × $3,600)	1,566	5,166
Total price of labor and material		$7,076

Included in the $7,076 price quotation for the boat repair are charges for labor costs, overhead costs, material costs, material handling and storage costs, and a profit margin on both labor and parts. Lake Holiday Marina used labor hours as a basis for computing the time rate. Other companies, such as machine shops, plastic molding shops, and printers, might use machine hours.

LEARNING OBJECTIVE 4

Determine a transfer price using the negotiated, cost-based, and market-based approaches.

In today's global economy, growth is often vital to survival. Some companies grow "vertically," meaning they expand in the direction of either their suppliers or customers. For example, a manufacturer of bicycles like Trek may acquire a bicycle component manufacturer or a chain of bicycle shops. A movie production company like Walt Disney or Time Warner may acquire a movie theater chain or a cable television company.

In addition to customer sales, divisions within vertically integrated companies often transfer goods or services to other divisions in the company. When goods are transferred between divisions of the same company, the price used to record the transaction is the **transfer price**. Illustration M-17 (page M-10) shows transfers between divisions for Aerobic Bicycle Company. As shown, the Component Division sells goods to the Company's Assembly Division, as well as to outside parties. Units sold to the Assembly Division are recorded at the transfer price.

ILLUSTRATION M-17
Transfer pricing example

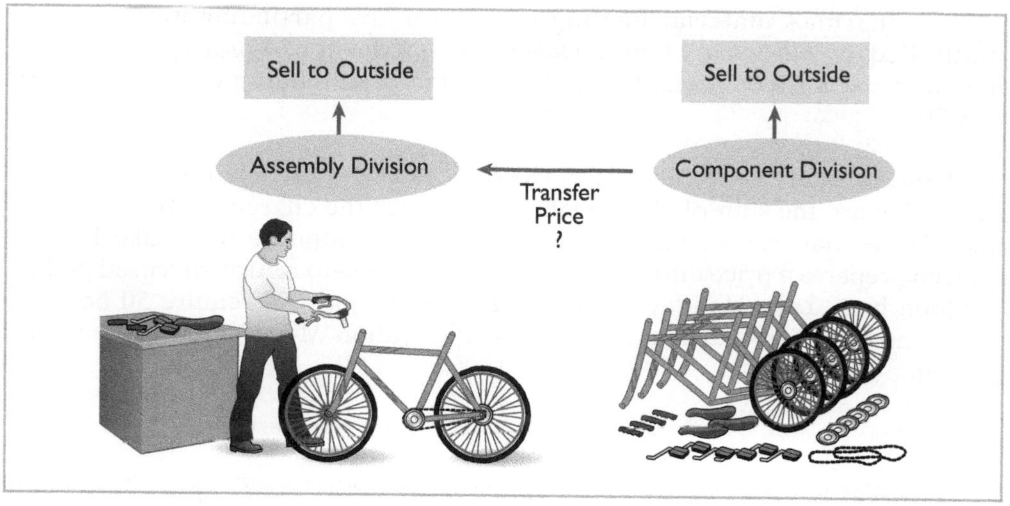

The primary objective of transfer pricing is the same as that of pricing a product to an outside party. The objective is to maximize the return to the company. An additional objective of transfer pricing is to measure divisional performance accurately. Setting a transfer price is complicated because of competing interests among divisions within the company. For example, in the case of the bicycle company shown in Illustration M-17, setting the transfer price high will benefit the Component Division (the selling division) but will hurt the Assembly Division (the purchasing division).

There are three possible approaches for determining a transfer price:

1. Negotiated transfer prices.
2. Cost-based transfer prices.
3. Market-based transfer prices.

Conceptually, a negotiated transfer price should work best, but due to practical considerations, companies often use the other two methods.

NEGOTIATED TRANSFER PRICES

A **negotiated transfer price** is determined through agreement of division managers. To illustrate negotiated transfer pricing, we examine Alberta Company. Until recently, Alberta focused exclusively on making rubber soles for work boots and hiking boots. It sold these rubber soles to boot manufacturers. However, last year the company decided to take advantage of its strong reputation by expanding into the business of making hiking boots. As a consequence of this expansion, the company is now structured as two independent divisions, the Boot Division and the Sole Division. The company compensates the manager of each division based on achievement of profitability targets for that division.

The Boot Division manufactures leather uppers for hiking boots and attaches these uppers to rubber soles. During its first year, the Boot Division purchased its rubber soles from an outside supplier so as not to disrupt the operations of the Sole Division. However, top management now wants the Sole Division to provide at least some of the soles used by the Boot Division. Illustration M-18 shows the computation of the contribution margin per unit for each division when the Boot Division purchases soles from an outside supplier.

Boot Division		Sole Division	
Selling price of boots	$90	Selling price of sole	$18
Variable cost of boot (not including sole)	35	Variable cost per sole	11
Cost of sole purchased from outside supplier	17		
Contribution margin per unit	**$38**	**Contribution margin per unit**	**$ 7**

Total contribution margin per unit $45 ($38 + $7)

ILLUSTRATION M-18
Computation of contribution margin for two divisions, when Boot Division purchases soles from an outside supplier

This information indicates that the contribution margin per unit for the Boot Division is $38 and for the Sole Division is $7. The total contribution margin per unit is $45 ($38 + $7).

Now let's ask the question, "What would be a fair transfer price if the Sole Division sold 10,000 soles to the Boot Division?" The answer depends on how busy the Sole Division is—that is, whether it has excess capacity.

No Excess Capacity

As indicated in Illustration M-18, the Sole Division charges outside customers $18 and derives a contribution margin of $7 per sole. The Sole Division has **no excess capacity** and produces and sells 80,000 units (soles) to outside customers. Therefore, the Sole Division must receive from the Boot Division a payment that will at least cover its variable cost per sole **plus** its lost contribution margin per sole. (This lost contribution margin is often referred to as **opportunity cost.**) If the Sole Division cannot recover that amount—called the **minimum transfer price**—it should not sell its soles to the Boot Division. The minimum transfer price that would be acceptable to the Sole Division is $18, as shown below.

Variable Cost	+	Opportunity Cost	=	Minimum Transfer Price
$11	+	$7	=	$18

ILLUSTRATION M-19
Minimum transfer price—no excess capacity

From the perspective of the Boot Division (the buyer), the most it will pay is what the sole would cost from an outside supplier. In this case, therefore, the Boot Division would pay no more than $17. As shown in Illustration M-20, an acceptable transfer price is not available in this situation.

ILLUSTRATION M-20
Transfer price negotiations—no deal

Excess Capacity

What happens if the Sole Division **has excess capacity**? For example, assume the Sole Division can produce 80,000 soles but can sell only 70,000 soles in the open market. As a result, it has available capacity of 10,000 units. Because it has excess capacity, the Sole Division could provide 10,000 units to the Boot Division without losing its $7 contribution margin on these units. Therefore, the minimum price it would now accept is $11, as shown below.

ILLUSTRATION M-21
Minimum transfer price formula—excess capacity

Variable Cost	+	Opportunity Cost	=	Minimum Transfer Price
$11	+	$0	=	$11

In this case, the Boot Division and the Sole Division should negotiate a transfer price within the range of $11 to $17, as shown in Illustration M-22.

ILLUSTRATION M-22
Transfer pricing negotiations—deal

Given excess capacity, Alberta Company will increase its overall net income if the Boot Division purchases the 10,000 soles internally. This is true as long as the Sole Division's variable cost is less than the outside price of $17. The Sole Division will receive a positive contribution margin from any transfer price above its variable cost of $11. The Boot Division will benefit from any price below $17. At any transfer price above $17 the Boot Division will go to an outside supplier, a solution that would be undesirable to both divisions as well as to the company as a whole.

Variable Costs

In the minimum transfer price formula, **variable cost is defined as the variable cost of units sold *internally***. In some instances, the variable cost of units sold internally will differ from the variable cost of units sold externally. For example, companies often can avoid some variable selling expenses when units are sold internally. In this case, the variable cost of units sold internally will be lower than that of units sold externally.

Alternatively, the variable cost of units sold internally could be higher than normal if the internal division requests a special order that requires more expensive materials or additional labor. For example, assume that the Boot Division designs a new high-margin, heavy-duty boot. The sole for this boot will use denser rubber with an intricate lug design. Alberta Company is not aware of any supplier that currently makes such a sole, nor does it feel that any other supplier can meet its quality expectations. As a consequence, there is no available market price to use as the transfer price.

We can, however, employ the formula for the minimum transfer price to assist in arriving at a reasonable solution. After evaluating the special sole, the Sole Division determines that its variable cost would be $19 per sole. The Sole Division is at full capacity. The Sole Division's opportunity cost at full capacity is the $7 ($18 − $11) per sole that it earns producing the standard sole and selling it to an outside customer. Therefore, the minimum transfer price that the Sole Division would be willing to accept for the special-order sole is as follows.

ILLUSTRATION M-23
Minimum transfer price formula—special order

Variable Cost	+	Opportunity Cost	=	Minimum Transfer Price
$19	+	$7	=	$26

The transfer price of $26 provides the Sole Division with enough revenue to cover its increased variable cost and its opportunity cost (contribution margin on its standard sole).

Summary of Negotiated Transfer Pricing

Under negotiated transfer pricing, the selling division establishes a minimum transfer price, and the purchasing division establishes a maximum transfer price. This system provides a sound basis for establishing a transfer price because both divisions are better off if the proper decision-making rules are used. However, companies often do not use negotiated transfer pricing because:

- Market price information is sometimes not easily obtainable.
- A lack of trust between the two negotiating divisions may lead to a breakdown in the negotiations.
- Negotiations often lead to different pricing strategies from division to division, which is cumbersome and sometimes costly to implement.

Many companies, therefore, often use simple systems based on cost or market information to develop transfer prices.

COST-BASED TRANSFER PRICES

An alternative to negotiated transfer pricing is cost-based pricing. A **cost-based transfer price** is based on the costs incurred by the division producing the goods or services. A cost-based transfer price can be based on variable costs alone, or on variable costs plus fixed costs. Also, in some cases the selling division may add a markup.

The cost-based approach sometimes results in improper transfer prices. Improper transfer prices can reduce company profits and provide unfair evaluations of division performance. To illustrate, assume that Alberta Company requires the division to use a transfer price based on the variable cost of the sole. With no excess capacity, the contribution margins per unit for the two divisions are as follows.

ILLUSTRATION M-24
Cost-based transfer price—10,000 units

Boot Division		Sole Division	
Selling price of boots	$90	Selling price of sole	$11
Variable cost of boot (not including sole)	35	Variable cost per sole	11
Cost of sole purchased from sole division	11		
Contribution margin per unit	**$44**	**Contribution margin per unit**	**$ 0**

Total contribution margin per unit $44 ($44 + $0)

This cost-based transfer system is a bad deal for the Sole Division as it reports no profit on the transfer of 10,000 soles to the Boot Division. If the Sole Division could sell these soles to an outside customer, it would make $70,000 [10,000 × ($18 − $11)]. The Boot Division, on the other hand, is delighted: its contribution margin per unit increases from $38 to $44, or $6 per boot. Thus, this transfer price results in an unfair evaluation of these two divisions.

Further examination of this example reveals that this transfer price reduces the company's overall profits. The Sole Division lost a contribution margin per unit of $7 (Illustration M-18, page M-11), and the Boot Division experiences only a $6 increase in its contribution margin per unit. Overall, Alberta Company loses $10,000 [10,000 boots × ($7 − $6)]. Illustration M-25 illustrates this deficiency.

ILLUSTRATION M-25
Cost-based transfer price results—no excess capacity

The overall results change if the Sole Division **has excess capacity**. In this case, the Sole Division continues to report a zero profit on these 10,000 units but does not lose the $7 per unit of contribution margin (because it had excess capacity). The Boot Division gains $6. So overall, the company is better off by $60,000 (10,000 × $6). However, with a cost-based system, the Sole Division continues to report a zero profit on these 10,000 units.

We can see that a cost-based system does not reflect the division's true profitability. What's more, **it does not provide adequate incentive for the Sole Division to control costs**. The division's costs are simply passed on to the next division.

Notwithstanding these disadvantages, the cost system is simple to understand and easy to use because the information is already available in the accounting system. In addition, market information is sometimes not available, so the only alternative is some type of cost-based system. As a result, it is the most common method used by companies to establish transfer prices.

MARKET-BASED TRANSFER PRICES

The **market-based transfer price** is based on existing market prices of competing goods or services. A market-based system is often considered the best approach because it is objective and generally provides the proper economic incentives. For example, if the Sole Division can charge the market price, it is indifferent as to whether soles are sold to outside customers or internally to the Boot Division—it does not lose any contribution margin. Similarly, the Boot Division pays a price for the soles that is at or reasonably close to market.

When the Sole Division has no excess capacity, the market-based system works reasonably well. The Sole Division receives market price, and the Boot Division pays market price.

If the Sole Division has excess capacity, however, the market-based system can lead to actions that are not in the best interest of the company. The minimum transfer price that the Sole Division should receive is its variable cost plus opportunity cost. If the Sole Division has excess capacity, its opportunity cost is zero. However, under the market-based system, the Sole Division transfers the goods at the market price of $18, for a contribution margin per unit of $7 ($18 − $11). The Boot Division manager has to accept the $18 sole price. This price may not accurately reflect a fair cost of the sole, given that the Sole Division had excess capacity. As a result, the Boot Division may overprice its boots in the market if it uses the market price of the sole plus a markup in setting the price of the boot. This action can lead to losses for Alberta overall.

As indicated earlier, in many cases, there simply is not a well-defined market for the good or service being transferred. When this is the case, a reasonable market value cannot be developed, so companies often resort to a cost-based system.

EFFECT OF OUTSOURCING ON TRANSFER PRICING

An increasing number of companies rely on **outsourcing**. Outsourcing involves contracting with an external party to provide a good or service, rather than performing the work internally. Some companies have taken outsourcing to the extreme by outsourcing all of their production. Many of these so-called **virtual companies** have well-established brand names though they do not manufacture any of their own products. Companies use incremental analysis (Chapter 20) to determine whether outsourcing is profitable. When companies outsource, fewer components are transferred internally between divisions. This reduces the need for transfer prices.

TRANSFERS BETWEEN DIVISIONS IN DIFFERENT COUNTRIES

As more companies "globalize" their operations, an increasing number of intercompany transfers are between divisions that are located in different countries. One estimate suggests that 60% of trade between countries is simply transfers between company divisions. Differences in tax rates across countries can complicate the determination of the appropriate transfer price.

LEARNING OBJECTIVE ▶5

Determine prices using absorption-cost pricing and variable-cost pricing.

In determining the target price for Thinkmore Products' video camera pen earlier in the appendix, we calculated the cost base **by including all costs incurred**. This approach is referred to as **full-cost pricing**. Using total cost as the basis of the markup makes sense conceptually because, in the long run, the price must cover all costs and provide a reasonable profit. However, total cost is difficult to determine in practice. This is because period costs (selling and administrative expenses) are difficult to trace to a specific product. Activity-based costing can be used to overcome this difficulty to some extent.

In practice, companies sometimes use two other cost approaches: (1) absorption cost pricing or (2) variable-cost pricing. Absorption-cost pricing is more popular than variable-cost pricing.[2] We illustrate both approaches because both have merit.

[2]For a discussion of cost-plus pricing, see Eunsup Skim and Ephraim F. Sudit, "How Manufacturers Price Products," *Management Accounting* (February 1995), pp. 37–39; and V. Govindarajan and R.N. Anthony, "How Firms Use Cost Data in Pricing Decisions," *Management Accounting* (65, no. 1), pp. 30–36.

ABSORPTION-COST PRICING

Absorption-cost pricing is consistent with generally accepted accounting principles (GAAP). The reason: It includes both variable and fixed manufacturing costs as product costs. **It excludes from this cost base both variable and fixed selling and administrative costs.** Thus, companies must somehow provide for selling and administrative costs plus the target ROI. They do this through the markup.

The **first step** in absorption-cost pricing is to compute the unit **manufacturing cost**. For Thinkmore Products, this amounts to $87 per unit at a volume of 10,000 units, as shown in Illustration M-26.

ILLUSTRATION M-26
Computation of unit manufacturing cost

	Per Unit
Direct materials	$23
Direct labor	17
Variable manufacturing overhead	12
Fixed manufacturing overhead ($350,000 ÷ 10,000)	35
Total unit manufacturing cost (absorption cost)	$87

In addition, Thinkmore provides the following information regarding selling and administrative expenses per unit and desired ROI per unit.

ILLUSTRATION M-27
Other information

Variable selling and administrative expenses	$ 8
Fixed selling and administrative expenses ($300,000 ÷ 10,000)	30
Total selling and administrative expenses per unit	$38
Desired ROI per unit (see Illustration M-7)	$40

The **second step** in absorption-cost pricing is to compute the markup percentage using the formula in Illustration M-28. Note that when companies use manufacturing cost per unit as the cost base to compute the markup percentage, the **percentage must cover the desired ROI and also the selling and administrative expenses.**

ILLUSTRATION M-28
Markup percentage—absorption-cost pricing

Desired ROI per Unit	+	Selling and Administrative Expenses per Unit	=	Markup Percentage	×	Manufacturing Cost per Unit
$40	+	$38	=	MP	×	$87

Solving, we find:

$$MP = (\$40 + \$38) \div \$87 = 89.66\%$$

The **third** and final **step** is to set the target selling price. Using a markup percentage of 89.66% and absorption-cost pricing, Thinkmore computes the target selling price as shown in Illustration M-29.

ILLUSTRATION M-29
Computation of target price—absorption-cost pricing

Manufacturing Cost per Unit	+	(Markup Percentage	×	Manufacturing Cost per Unit)	=	Target Selling Price
$87	+	(89.66%	×	$87)	=	$165

Using a target price of $165 will produce the desired 20% return on investment for Thinkmore on its video camera pen at a volume level of 10,000 units, as shown in Illustration M-30.

ILLUSTRATION M-30
Proof of 20% ROI—absorption-cost pricing

THINKMORE PRODUCTS, INC.
Budgeted Absorption-Cost Income Statement

Revenue (10,000 camera pens × $165)	$1,650,000
Cost of goods sold (10,000 camera pens × $87)	870,000
Gross profit	780,000
Selling and administrative expenses [10,000 camera pens × ($8 + $30)]	380,000
Net income	$ 400,000

Budgeted ROI

$$\frac{\text{Net income}}{\text{Invested assets}} = \frac{\$400{,}000}{\$2{,}000{,}000} = 20\%$$

Markup Percentage

$$\frac{\text{Net income + Selling and administrative expenses}}{\text{Cost of goods sold}} = \frac{\$400{,}000 + \$380{,}000}{\$870{,}000} = 89.66\%$$

Because of the fixed cost element, if Thinkmore sells more than 10,000 units, the ROI will be greater than 20%. If it sells fewer than 10,000 units, the ROI will be less than 20%. The markup percentage is also verified by adding $400,000 (the net income) and $380,000 (selling and administrative expenses) and then dividing by $870,000 (the cost of goods sold or the cost base).

Most companies that use cost-plus pricing use either absorption cost or full cost as the basis. The reasons for this tendency are as follows.

1. Absorption-cost information is most readily provided by a company's cost accounting system. Because absorption-cost data already exist in general ledger accounts, it is cost-effective to use the data for pricing.
2. Basing the cost-plus formula on only variable costs could encourage managers to set too low a price to boost sales. There is the fear that if managers use only variable costs, they will substitute variable costs for full costs, which can lead to suicidal price cutting.
3. Absorption-cost or full-cost pricing provides the most defensible base for justifying prices to all interested parties—managers, customers, and government.

VARIABLE-COST PRICING

Under **variable-cost pricing**, the cost base consists of all of the **variable costs** associated with a product, including variable selling and administrative costs. **Because fixed costs are not included in the base, the markup must provide for all fixed costs (manufacturing, and selling and administrative) and the target ROI.** Variable-cost pricing is more useful for making short-run decisions because it considers variable-cost and fixed-cost behavior patterns separately.

The **first step** in variable-cost pricing is to compute the unit variable cost. For Thinkmore Products, this amounts to $60 per unit, as shown in Illustration M-31 (page M-18).

ILLUSTRATION M-31
Computation of unit variable cost

	Per Unit
Direct materials	$23
Direct labor	17
Variable manufacturing overhead	12
Variable selling and administrative expense	8
Total unit variable cost	$60

The **second step** in variable-cost pricing is to compute the markup percentage. Illustration M-32 shows the formula for the markup percentage. For Thinkmore, fixed costs include fixed manufacturing overhead of $35 per unit ($350,000 ÷ 10,000) and fixed selling and administrative expenses of $30 per unit ($300,000 ÷ 10,000).

ILLUSTRATION M-32
Computation of markup percentage—variable-cost pricing

Desired ROI per Unit	+	Fixed Cost per Unit	=	Markup Percentage	×	Variable Cost per Unit
$40	+	($35 + $30)	=	MP	×	$60

Solving, we find:

$$MP = \frac{\$40 + (\$35 + \$30)}{\$60} = 175\%$$

The **third step** is to set the target selling price. Using a markup percentage of 175% and the contribution approach, Thinkmore computes the selling price as shown in Illustration M-33.

ILLUSTRATION M-33
Computation of target price—variable-cost pricing

Variable Cost per Unit	+	(Markup Percentage	×	Variable Cost per Unit)	=	Target Selling Price
$60	+	(175%	×	$60)	=	$165

Using a target price of $165 will produce the desired 20% return on investment for Thinkmore on its video camera pen at a volume level of 10,000 units, as shown in Illustration M-34.

ILLUSTRATION M-34
Proof of 20% ROI—contribution approach

THINKMORE PRODUCTS, INC.
Budgeted Variable-Cost Income Statement

Revenue (10,000 camera pens × $165)		$1,650,000
Variable costs (10,000 camera pens × $60)		600,000
Contribution margin		1,050,000
Fixed manufacturing overhead (10,000 camera pens × $35)	$350,000	
Fixed selling and administrative expenses (10,000 camera pens × $30)	300,000	650,000
Net income		$ 400,000

Budgeted ROI

$$\frac{\text{Net income}}{\text{Invested assets}} = \frac{\$400,000}{\$2,000,000} = 20\%$$

Markup Percentage

$$\frac{\text{Net income + Fixed costs}}{\text{Variable costs}} = \frac{\$400,000 + \$650,000}{\$600,000} = 175\%$$

Under any of the three pricing approaches we have looked at (full-cost, absorption-cost, and variable-cost), the desired ROI will be attained only if the budgeted sales volume for the period is attained. None of these approaches guarantees a profit or a desired ROI. Achieving a desired ROI is the result of many factors, some of which are beyond the company's control, such as market conditions, political and legal issues, customers' tastes, and competitive actions.

Because absorption-cost pricing includes allocated fixed costs, it does not make clear how the company's costs will change as volume changes. To avoid blurring the effects of cost behavior on net income, some managers therefore prefer variable-cost pricing. The specific reasons for using variable-cost pricing, even though the basic accounting data are less accessible, are as follows.

1. Variable-cost pricing, being based on variable cost, is more consistent with cost-volume-profit analysis used by managers to measure the profit implications of changes in price and volume.
2. Variable-cost pricing provides the type of data managers need for pricing special orders. It shows the incremental cost of accepting one more order.
3. Variable-cost pricing avoids arbitrary allocation of common fixed costs (such as executive salaries) to individual product lines.

REVIEW

LEARNING OBJECTIVES REVIEW

1 Compute a target cost when the market determines a product price. To compute a target cost, the company determines its target selling price. Once the target selling price is set, it determines its target cost by setting a desired profit. The difference between the target price and desired profit is the target cost of the product.

2 Compute a target selling price using cost-plus pricing. Cost-plus pricing involves establishing a cost base and adding to this cost base a markup to determine a target selling price. The cost-plus pricing formula is expressed as follows: Target selling price = Cost + (Markup percentage × Cost).

3 Use time-and-material pricing to determine the cost of services provided. Under time-and-material pricing, two pricing rates are set—one for the labor used on a job and another for the material. The labor rate includes direct labor time and other employee costs. The material charge is based on the cost of direct parts and materials used and a material loading charge for related overhead costs.

4 Determine a transfer price using the negotiated, cost-based, and market-based approaches. The negotiated price is determined through agreement of division managers. Under a cost-based approach, the transfer price may be based on variable cost alone or on variable costs plus fixed costs. Companies may add a markup to these numbers. The cost-based approach often leads to poor performance evaluations and purchasing decisions. The advantage of the cost-based system is its simplicity. A market-based transfer price is based on existing competing market prices and services. A market-based system is often considered the best approach because it is objective and generally provides the proper economic incentives.

5 Determine prices using absorption-cost pricing and variable-cost pricing. Absorption-cost pricing uses total manufacturing cost as the cost base and provides for selling and administrative costs plus the target ROI through the markup. The target selling price is computed as: Manufacturing cost per unit + (Markup percentage × Manufacturing cost per unit).

Variable-cost pricing uses all of the variable costs, including selling and administrative costs, as the cost base and provides for fixed costs and target ROI through the markup. The target selling price is computed as: Variable cost per unit + (Markup percentage × Variable cost per unit).

GLOSSARY REVIEW

Absorption-cost pricing An approach to pricing that defines the cost base as the manufacturing cost; it excludes both variable and fixed selling and administrative costs. (p. M-16).

Cost-based transfer price A transfer price that uses as its foundation the costs incurred by the division producing the goods. (p. M-13).

Cost-plus pricing A process whereby a product's selling price is determined by adding a markup to a cost base. (p. M-3).

Full-cost pricing An approach to pricing that defines the cost base as all costs incurred. (p. M-6).

Market-based transfer price A transfer price that is based on existing market prices of competing products. (p. M-14).

Markup The amount added to a product's cost base to determine the product's selling price. (p. M-3).

Material loading charge A charge added to cover the cost of purchasing, receiving, handling, and storing materials, plus any desired profit margin on the materials themselves. (p. M-8).

Negotiated transfer price A transfer price that is determined by the agreement of the division managers. (p. M-10).

Outsourcing Contracting with an external party to provide a good or service, rather than performing the work internally. (p. M-15).

Target cost The cost that will provide the desired profit on a product when the seller does not have control over the product's price. (p. M-3).

Target selling price The selling price that will provide the desired profit on a product when the seller has the ability to determine the product's price. (p. M-3).

Time-and-material pricing An approach to cost-plus pricing in which the company uses two pricing rates, one for the labor used on a job and another for the material. (p. M-7).

Transfer price The price used to record the transfer of goods between two divisions of a company. (p. M-9).

Variable-cost pricing An approach to pricing that defines the cost base as all variable costs; it excludes both fixed manufacturing and fixed selling and administrative costs. (pp. M-6, M-17).

WileyPLUS Many additional resources are available for practice in WileyPLUS.

QUESTIONS

1. What are the two types of pricing environments for sales to external parties?
2. In what situation does a company place the greatest focus on its target cost? How is the target cost determined?
3. What is the basic formula to determine the target selling price in cost-plus pricing?
4. Benz Corporation produces a filter that has a per unit cost of $18. The company would like a 30% markup. Using cost-plus pricing, determine the per unit selling price.
5. What is the basic formula for the markup percentage?
6. What are some of the factors that affect a company's desired ROI?
7. Stanley Corporation manufactures an electronic switch for dishwashers. The cost base per unit, excluding selling and administrative expenses, is $60. The per unit cost of selling and administrative expenses is $15. The company's desired ROI per unit is $6. Calculate its markup percentage on total unit cost.
8. Sheen Co. manufactures a standard cabinet for a Blu-ray player. The variable cost per unit is $16. The fixed cost per unit is $9. The desired ROI per unit is $6. Compute the markup percentage on total unit cost and the target selling price for the cabinet.
9. In what circumstances is time-and-material pricing most often used?
10. What is the material loading charge? How is it expressed?
11. What is a transfer price? Why is determining a fair transfer price important to division managers?
12. When setting a transfer price, what objective(s) should the company have in mind?
13. What are the three approaches for determining transfer prices?
14. Describe the cost-based approach to transfer pricing. What is the strength of this approach? What are the weaknesses of this approach?
15. What is the general formula for determining the minimum transfer price that the selling division should be willing to accept?
16. When determining the minimum transfer price, what is meant by the "opportunity cost"?
17. In what circumstances will a negotiated transfer price be used instead of a market-based price?
18. What costs are excluded from the cost base when absorption-cost pricing is used to determine the markup percentage?
19. Marie Corporation manufactures a fiber optic connector. The variable cost per unit is $16. The fixed cost per unit is $9. The company's desired ROI per unit is $3. Compute the markup percentage using variable-cost pricing.

BRIEF EXERCISES

BEM-1 Ortega Company manufactures computer hard drives. The market for hard drives is very competitive. The current market price for a computer hard drive is $45. Ortega would like a profit of $10 per drive. How can Ortega accomplish this objective?

Compute target cost.
(LO 1)

BEM-2 Mussatto Corporation produces snowboards. The following per unit cost information is available: direct materials $12, direct labor $8, variable manufacturing overhead $6, fixed manufacturing overhead $14, variable selling and administrative expenses $4, and fixed selling and administrative expenses $12. Using a 30% markup percentage on total per unit cost, compute the target selling price.

Use cost-plus pricing to determine selling price.
(LO 2)

BEM-3 Jaymes Corporation produces high-performance rotors. It expects to produce 50,000 rotors in the coming year. It has invested $10,000,000 to produce rotors. The company has a required return on investment of 12%. What is its ROI per unit?

Compute ROI per unit.
(LO 2)

BEM-4 Morales Corporation produces microwave ovens. The following per unit cost information is available: direct materials $36, direct labor $24, variable manufacturing overhead $18, fixed manufacturing overhead $40, variable selling and administrative expenses $14, and fixed selling and administrative expenses $28. Its desired ROI per unit is $30. Compute its markup percentage using a total-cost approach.

Compute markup percentage.
(LO 2)

BEM-5 During the current year, Chudrick Corporation expects to produce 10,000 units and has budgeted the following: net income $300,000, variable costs $1,100,000, and fixed costs $100,000. It has invested assets of $1,500,000. The company's budgeted ROI was 20%. What was its budgeted markup percentage using a full-cost approach?

Compute ROI and markup percentage.
(LO 2)

BEM-6 Rooney Small Engine Repair charges $42 per hour of labor. It has a material loading percentage of 40%. On a recent job replacing the engine of a riding lawnmower, Rooney worked 10.5 hours and used parts with a cost of $700. Calculate Rooney's total bill.

Use time-and-material pricing to determine bill.
(LO 3)

BEM-7 The Heating Division of Kobe International produces a heating element that it sells to its customers for $45 per unit. Its variable cost per unit is $25, and its fixed cost per unit is $10. Top management of Kobe International would like the Heating Division to transfer 15,000 heating units to another division within the company at a price of $29. The Heating Division is operating at full capacity. What is the minimum transfer price that the Heating Division should accept?

Determine minimum transfer price.
(LO 4)

BEM-8 Use the data from BEM-7 but assume that the Heating Division has sufficient excess capacity to provide the 15,000 heating units to the other division. What is the minimum transfer price that the Heating Division should accept?

Determine minimum transfer price with excess capacity.
(LO 4)

BEM-9 Use the data from BEM-7 but assume that the units being requested are special high-performance units and that the division's variable cost would be $27 per unit (rather than $25). What is the minimum transfer price that the Heating Division should accept?

Determine minimum transfer price for special order.
(LO 4)

BEM-10 Using the data in BEM-4, compute the markup percentage using absorption-cost pricing.

Compute markup percentage using absorption-cost pricing.
(LO 5)

BEM-11 Using the data in BEM-4, compute the markup percentage using variable-cost pricing.

Compute markup percentage using variable-cost pricing.
(LO 5)

EXERCISES

Compute target cost.
(LO 1), AP

EM-1 Mesa Cheese Company has developed a new cheese slicer called Slim Slicer. The company plans to sell this slicer through its catalog, which it issues monthly. Given market research, Mesa believes that it can charge $20 for the Slim Slicer. Prototypes of the Slim Slicer, however, are costing $22. By using cheaper materials and gaining efficiencies in mass production, Mesa believes it can reduce Slim Slicer's cost substantially. Mesa wishes to earn a return of 40% of the selling price.

Instructions

(a) Compute the target cost for the Slim Slicer.
(b) When is target costing particularly helpful in deciding whether to produce a given product?

Compute target cost.
(LO 1), AP

EM-2 Eckert Company is involved in producing and selling high-end golf equipment. The company has recently been involved in developing various types of laser guns to measure yardages on the golf course. One small laser gun, called LittleLaser, appears to have a very large potential market. Because of competition, Eckert does not believe that it can charge more than $90 for LittleLaser. At this price, Eckert believes it can sell 100,000 of these laser guns. Eckert will require an investment of $8,000,000 to manufacture, and the company wants an ROI of 20%.

Instructions

Determine the target cost for one LittleLaser.

Compute target cost and cost-plus pricing.
(LO 1, 2), AP

EM-3 Leno Company makes swimsuits and sells these suits directly to retailers. Although Leno has a variety of suits, it does not make the All-Body suit used by highly skilled swimmers. The market research department believes that a strong market exists for this type of suit. The department indicates that the All-Body suit would sell for approximately $100. Given its experience, Leno believes the All-Body suit would have the following manufacturing costs.

Direct materials	$ 25
Direct labor	30
Manufacturing overhead	45
Total costs	$100

Instructions

(a) Assume that Leno uses cost-plus pricing, setting the selling price 25% above its costs. (1) What would be the price charged for the All-Body swimsuit? (2) Under what circumstances might Leno consider manufacturing the All-Body swimsuit given this approach?
(b) Assume that Leno uses target costing. What is the price that Leno would charge the retailer for the All-Body swimsuit?
(c) What is the highest acceptable manufacturing cost Leno would be willing to incur to produce the All-Body swimsuit, if it desired a profit of $25 per unit? (Assume target costing.)

Use cost-plus pricing to determine selling price.
(LO 2), AP

EM-4 Kaspar Corporation makes a commercial-grade cooking griddle. The following information is available for Kaspar Corporation's anticipated annual volume of 30,000 units.

	Per Unit	Total
Direct materials	$17	
Direct labor	$ 8	
Variable manufacturing overhead	$11	
Fixed manufacturing overhead		$300,000
Variable selling and administrative expenses	$ 4	
Fixed selling and administrative expenses		$150,000

The company uses a 40% markup percentage on total cost.

Instructions

(a) Compute the total cost per unit.
(b) Compute the target selling price.

EM-5 Schopp Corporation makes a mechanical stuffed alligator that sings the Martian national anthem. The following information is available for Schopp Corporation's anticipated annual volume of 500,000 units.

Use cost-plus pricing to determine various amounts.

(LO 2), AP

	Per Unit	Total
Direct materials	$ 7	
Direct labor	$11	
Variable manufacturing overhead	$15	
Fixed manufacturing overhead		$3,000,000
Variable selling and administrative expenses	$14	
Fixed selling and administrative expenses		$1,500,000

The company has a desired ROI of 25%. It has invested assets of $28,000,000.

Instructions

(a) Compute the total cost per unit.
(b) Compute the desired ROI per unit.
(c) Compute the markup percentage using total cost per unit.
(d) Compute the target selling price.

EM-6 Alma's Recording Studio rents studio time to musicians in 2-hour blocks. Each session includes the use of the studio facilities, a digital recording of the performance, and a professional music producer/mixer. Anticipated annual volume is 1,000 sessions. The company has invested $2,352,000 in the studio and expects a return on investment (ROI) of 20%. Budgeted costs for the coming year are as follows.

Use cost-plus pricing to determine various amounts.

(LO 2), AP

	Per Session	Total
Direct materials (CDs, etc.)	$ 20	
Direct labor	$400	
Variable overhead	$ 50	
Fixed overhead		$950,000
Variable selling and administrative expenses	$ 40	
Fixed selling and administrative expenses		$500,000

Instructions

(a) Determine the total cost per session.
(b) Determine the desired ROI per session.
(c) Calculate the markup percentage on the total cost per session.
(d) Calculate the target price per session.

EM-7 Gibbs Corporation produces industrial robots for high-precision manufacturing. The following information is given for Gibbs Corporation.

Use cost-plus pricing to determine various amounts.

(LO 2), AP

	Per Unit	Total
Direct materials	$380	
Direct labor	$290	
Variable manufacturing overhead	$ 72	
Fixed manufacturing overhead		$1,500,000
Variable selling and administrative expenses	$ 55	
Fixed selling and administrative expenses		$ 324,000

The company has a desired ROI of 20%. It has invested assets of $54,000,000. It anticipates production of 3,000 units per year.

Instructions

(a) Compute the cost per unit of the fixed manufacturing overhead and the fixed selling and administrative expenses.

(b) Compute the desired ROI per unit. (Round to the nearest dollar.)
(c) Compute the target selling price.

Use time-and-material pricing to determine bill.
(LO 3), AP

EM-8 Second Chance Welding rebuilds spot welders for manufacturers. The following budgeted cost data for 2017 is available for Second Chance.

	Time Charges	Material Loading Charges
Technicians' wages and benefits	$228,000	—
Parts manager's salary and benefits	—	$42,500
Office employee's salary and benefits	38,000	9,000
Other overhead	15,200	24,000
Total budgeted costs	$281,200	$75,500

The company desires a $30 profit margin per hour of labor and a 20% profit margin on parts. It has budgeted for 7,600 hours of repair time in the coming year, and estimates that the total invoice cost of parts and materials in 2017 will be $400,000.

Instructions
(a) Compute the rate charged per hour of labor.
(b) Compute the material loading percentage. (Round to three decimal places.)
(c) Pace Corporation has requested an estimate to rebuild its spot welder. Second Chance estimates that it would require 40 hours of labor and $2,000 of parts. Compute the total estimated bill.

Use time-and-material pricing to determine bill.
(LO 3), AP

EM-9 Rey Custom Electronics (RCE) sells and installs complete security, computer, audio, and video systems for homes. On newly constructed homes it provides bids using time-and-material pricing. The following budgeted cost data are available.

	Time Charges	Material Loading Charges
Technicians' wages and benefits	$150,000	—
Parts manager's salary and benefits	—	$34,000
Office employee's salary and benefits	30,000	15,000
Other overhead	15,000	42,000
Total budgeted costs	$195,000	$91,000

The company has budgeted for 6,250 hours of technician time during the coming year. It desires a $38 profit margin per hour of labor and an 80% profit on parts. It estimates the total invoice cost of parts and materials in 2017 will be $700,000.

Instructions
(a) Compute the rate charged per hour of labor.
(b) Compute the material loading percentage.
(c) RCE has just received a request for a bid from Buil Builders on a $1,200,000 new home. The company estimates that it would require 80 hours of labor and $40,000 of parts. Compute the total estimated bill.

Use time-and-material pricing to determine bill.
(LO 3), AP

EM-10 Wasson's Classic Cars restores classic automobiles to showroom status. Budgeted data for the current year are as follows.

	Time Charges	Material Loading Charges
Restorers' wages and fringe benefits	$270,000	
Purchasing agent's salary and fringe benefits		$ 67,500
Administrative salaries and fringe benefits	54,000	21,960
Other overhead costs	24,000	77,490
Total budgeted costs	$348,000	$166,950

The company anticipated that the restorers would work a total of 12,000 hours this year. Expected parts and materials were $1,260,000.

In late January, the company experienced a fire in its facilities that destroyed most of the accounting records. The accountant remembers that the hourly labor rate was $70.00 and that the material loading charge was 83.25%.

Instructions

(a) Determine the profit margin per hour on labor.
(b) Determine the profit margin on materials.
(c) Determine the total price of labor and materials on a job that was completed after the fire that required 150 hours of labor and $60,000 in parts and materials.

EM-11 Chen Company's Small Motor Division manufactures a number of small motors used in household and office appliances. The Household Division of Chen then assembles and packages such items as blenders and juicers. Both divisions are free to buy and sell any of their components internally or externally. The following costs relate to small motor LN233 on a per unit basis.

Determine minimum transfer price.

(LO 4), AP

Fixed cost per unit	$ 5
Variable cost per unit	$11
Selling price per unit	$35

Instructions

(a) Assuming that the Small Motor Division has excess capacity, compute the minimum acceptable price for the transfer of small motor LN233 to the Household Division.
(b) Assuming that the Small Motor Division does not have excess capacity, compute the minimum acceptable price for the transfer of the small motor to the Household Division.
(c) Explain why the level of capacity in the Small Motor Division has an effect on the transfer price.

EM-12 The Cycle Division of Ayala Company has the following per unit data related to its most recent cycle called Roadbuster.

Determine effect on income from transfer price.

(LO 4), AP

Selling price		$2,200
Variable cost of goods sold		
Body frame	$300	
Other variable costs	900	1,200
Contribution margin		$1,000

Presently, the Cycle Division buys its body frames from an outside supplier. However Ayala has another division, FrameBody, that makes body frames for other cycle companies. The Cycle Division believes that FrameBody's product is suitable for its new Roadbuster cycle. Presently, FrameBody sells its frames for $350 per frame. The variable cost for FrameBody is $270. The Cycle Division is willing to pay $280 to purchase the frames from FrameBody.

Instructions

(a) Assume that FrameBody has excess capacity and is able to meet all of the Cycle Division's needs. If the Cycle Division buys 1,000 frames from FrameBody, determine the following: (1) effect on the income of the Cycle Division; (2) effect on the income of FrameBody; and (3) effect on the income of Ayala.
(b) Assume that FrameBody does not have excess capacity and therefore would lose sales if the frames were sold to the Cycle Division. If the Cycle Division buys 1,000 frames from FrameBody, determine the following: (1) effect on the income of the Cycle Division; (2) effect on the income of FrameBody; and (3) effect on the income of Ayala.

EM-13 Benson Corporation manufactures car stereos. It is a division of Berna Motors, which manufactures vehicles. Benson sells car stereos to Berna, as well as to other vehicle manufacturers and retail stores. The following information is available for Benson's standard unit: variable cost per unit $37, fixed cost per unit $23, and selling price to outside

Determine minimum transfer price.

(LO 4), AP

customer $86. Berna currently purchases a standard unit from an outside supplier for $80. Because of quality concerns and to ensure a reliable supply, the top management of Berna has ordered Benson to provide 200,000 units per year at a transfer price of $35 per unit. Benson is already operating at full capacity. Benson can avoid $3 per unit of variable selling costs by selling the unit internally.

Instructions

Answer each of the following questions.

(a) What is the minimum transfer price that Benson should accept?

(b) What is the potential loss to the corporation as a whole resulting from this forced transfer?

(c) How should the company resolve this situation?

Compute minimum transfer price.

(LO 4), AP

EM-14 The Bathtub Division of Kirk Plumbing Corporation has recently approached the Faucet Division with a proposal. The Bathtub Division would like to make a special "ivory" tub with gold-plated fixtures for the company's 50-year anniversary. It would make only 5,000 of these units. It would like the Faucet Division to make the fixtures and provide them to the Bathtub Division at a transfer price of $160. If sold externally, the estimated variable cost per unit would be $140. However, by selling internally, the Faucet Division would save $6 per unit on variable selling expenses. The Faucet Division is currently operating at full capacity. Its standard unit sells for $50 per unit and has variable costs of $29.

Instructions

Compute the minimum transfer price that the Faucet Division should be willing to accept, and discuss whether it should accept this offer.

Determine minimum transfer price.

(LO 4), AP

EM-15 The Appraisal Department of Jean Bank performs appraisals of business properties for loans being considered by the bank and appraisals for home buyers that are financing their purchase through some other financial institution. The department charges $160 per home appraisal, and its variable costs are $130 per appraisal.

Recently, Jean Bank has opened its own Home-Loan Department and wants the Appraisal Department to perform 1,200 appraisals on all Jean Bank–financed home loans. Bank management feels that the cost of these appraisals to the Home-Loan Department should be $150. The variable cost per appraisal to the Home-Loan Department would be $8 less than those performed for outside customers due to savings in administrative costs.

Instructions

(a) Determine the minimum transfer price, assuming the Appraisal Department has excess capacity.

(b) Determine the minimum transfer price, assuming the Appraisal Department has no excess capacity.

(c) Assuming the Appraisal Department has no excess capacity, should management force the department to charge the Home-Loan Department only $150? Discuss.

Determine minimum transfer price under different situations.

(LO 4), AP

EM-16 Crede Inc. has two divisions. Division A makes and sells student desks. Division B manufactures and sells reading lamps.

Each desk has a reading lamp as one of its components. Division A can purchase reading lamps at a cost of $10 from an outside vendor. Division A needs 10,000 lamps for the coming year.

Division B has the capacity to manufacture 50,000 lamps annually. Sales to outside customers are estimated at 40,000 lamps for the next year. Reading lamps are sold at $12 each. Variable costs are $7 per lamp and include $1 of variable sales costs that are not incurred if lamps are sold internally to Division A. The total amount of fixed costs for Division B is $80,000.

Instructions

Consider the following independent situations.

(a) What should be the minimum transfer price accepted by Division B for the 10,000 lamps and the maximum transfer price paid by Division A? Justify your answer.

(b) Suppose Division B could use the excess capacity to produce and sell externally 15,000 units of a new product at a price of $7 per unit. The variable cost for this new product is $5 per unit. What should be the minimum transfer price accepted by Division B for the 10,000 lamps and the maximum transfer price paid by Division A? Justify your answer.

(c) If Division A needs 15,000 lamps instead of 10,000 during the next year, what should be the minimum transfer price accepted by Division B and the maximum transfer price paid by Division A? Justify your answer.

(CGA adapted)

EM-17 Twyla Company is a multidivisional company. Its managers have full responsibility for profits and complete autonomy to accept or reject transfers from other divisions. Division A produces a subassembly part for which there is a competitive market. Division B currently uses this subassembly for a final product that is sold outside at $2,400. Division A charges Division B market price for the part, which is $1,500 per unit. Variable costs are $1,100 and $1,200 for Divisions A and B, respectively.

Determine minimum transfer price under different situations.

(LO 4), AP

The manager of Division B feels that Division A should transfer the part at a lower price than market because at market, Division B is unable to make a profit.

Instructions

(a) Calculate Division B's contribution margin if transfers are made at the market price, and calculate the company's total contribution margin.

(b) Assume that Division A can sell all its production in the open market. Should Division A transfer the goods to Division B? If so, at what price?

(c) Assume that Division A can sell in the open market only 500 units at $1,500 per unit out of the 1,000 units that it can produce every month. Assume also that a 20% reduction in price is necessary to sell all 1,000 units each month. Should transfers be made? If so, how many units should the division transfer and at what price? To support your decision, submit a schedule that compares the contribution margins under the following three different alternatives. Alternative 1: maintain price, no transfers; Alternative 2: cut price, no transfers; and Alternative 3: maintain price and transfers.

(CMA-Canada adapted)

EM-18 Information for Schopp Corporation is given in EM-5.

Compute total cost per unit, ROI, and markup percentages using absorption-cost pricing and variable-cost pricing.

(LO 5), AP

Instructions

Using the information given in EM-5, answer the following.

(a) Compute the total cost per unit.

(b) Compute the desired ROI per unit.

(c) Using absorption-cost pricing, compute the markup percentage.

(d) Using variable-cost pricing, compute the markup percentage.

EM-19 Rap Corporation produces outdoor portable fireplace units. The following per unit cost information is available: direct materials $20, direct labor $25, variable manufacturing overhead $14, fixed manufacturing overhead $21, variable selling and administrative expenses $9, and fixed selling and administrative expenses $11. The company's ROI per unit is $24.

Compute markup percentage using absorption-cost pricing and variable-cost pricing.

(LO 5), AP

Instructions

Compute Rap Corporation's markup percentage using (a) absorption-cost pricing and (b) variable-cost pricing.

EM-20 Information for Gibbs Corporation is given in EM-7.

Compute various amounts using absorption-cost pricing and variable-cost pricing.

(LO 5), AP

Instructions

Using the information given in EM-7, answer the following.

(a) Compute the cost per unit of the fixed manufacturing overhead and the fixed selling and administrative expenses.

(b) Compute the desired ROI per unit. (Round to the nearest dollar.)

(c) Compute the markup percentage and target selling price using absorption-cost pricing. (Round the markup percentage to three decimal places.)
(d) Compute the markup percentage and target selling price using variable-cost pricing (Round the markup percentage to three decimal places.)

PROBLEMS

Use cost-plus pricing to determine various amounts.

(LO 2), AP

PM-1 National Corporation needs to set a target price for its newly designed product M14–M16. The following data relate to this new product.

	Per Unit	Total
Direct materials	$25	
Direct labor	$40	
Variable manufacturing overhead	$10	
Fixed manufacturing overhead		$1,440,000
Variable selling and administrative expenses	$ 5	
Fixed selling and administrative expenses		$ 960,000

These costs are based on a budgeted volume of 80,000 units produced and sold each year. National uses cost-plus pricing methods to set its target selling price. The markup percentage on total unit cost is 40%.

Instructions

(a) Variable cost per unit $80

(a) Compute the total variable cost per unit, total fixed cost per unit, and total cost per unit for M14–M16.
(b) Compute the desired ROI per unit for M14–M16.
(c) Compute the target selling price for M14–M16.
(d) Compute variable cost per unit, fixed cost per unit, and total cost per unit assuming that 60,000 M14–M16s are produced and sold during the year.

Use cost-plus pricing to determine various amounts.

(LO 2), AP

PM-2 Lovell Computer Parts Inc. is in the process of setting a selling price on a new component it has just designed and developed. The following cost estimates for this new component have been provided by the accounting department for a budgeted volume of 50,000 units.

	Per Unit	Total
Direct materials	$50	
Direct labor	$26	
Variable manufacturing overhead	$20	
Fixed manufacturing overhead		$600,000
Variable selling and administrative expenses	$19	
Fixed selling and administrative expenses		$400,000

Lovell Computer Parts management requests that the total cost per unit be used in cost-plus pricing its products. On this particular product, management also directs that the target price be set to provide a 25% return on investment (ROI) on invested assets of $1,000,000.

Instructions

(Round all calculations to two decimal places.)

(a) Compute the markup percentage and target selling price that will allow Lovell Computer Parts to earn its desired ROI of 25% on this new component.

(b) Target selling price $146.25

(b) Assuming that the volume is 40,000 units, compute the markup percentage and target selling price that will allow Lovell Computer Parts to earn its desired ROI of 25% on this new component.

Use time-and-material pricing to determine bill.

(LO 3), AP

PM-3 Sutton's Electronic Repair Shop has budgeted the following time and material for 2017.

SUTTON'S ELECTRONIC REPAIR SHOP
Budgeted Costs for the Year 2017

	Time Charges	Material Loading Charges
Shop employees' wages and benefits	$108,000	—
Parts manager's salary and benefits	—	$25,400
Office employee's salary and benefits	23,500	13,600
Overhead (supplies, depreciation, advertising, utilities)	26,000	16,000
Total budgeted costs	$157,500	$55,000

Sutton's budgets 5,000 hours of repair time in 2017 and will bill a profit of $10 per labor hour along with a 25% profit markup on the invoice cost of parts. The estimated invoice cost for parts to be used is $100,000.

On January 5, 2017, Sutton's is asked to submit a price estimate to fix a 72-inch flat-screen TV. Sutton's estimates that this job will consume 4 hours of labor and $200 in parts.

Instructions

(a) Compute the labor rate for Sutton's Electronic Repair Shop for the year 2017.

(b) Compute the material loading charge percentage for Sutton's Electronic Repair Shop for the year 2017.

(c) Prepare a time-and-material price quotation for fixing the flat-screen TV.

(c) $526

Determine minimum transfer price with no excess capacity and with excess capacity.

(LO 4), AP

PM-4 Word Wizard is a publishing company with a number of different book lines. Each line has contracts with a number of different authors. The company also owns a printing operation called Quick Press. The book lines and the printing operation each operate as a separate profit center. The printing operation earns revenue by printing books by authors under contract with the book lines owned by Word Wizard, as well as authors under contract with other companies. The printing operation bills out at $0.01 per page, and a typical book requires 500 pages of print. A manager from Business Books, one of the Word Wizard's book lines, has approached the manager of the printing operation offering to pay $0.007 per page for 1,500 copies of a 500-page book. The book line pays outside printers $0.009 per page. The printing operation's variable cost per page is $0.004.

Instructions

Determine whether the printing should be done internally or externally, and the appropriate transfer price, under each of the following situations.

(a) Assume that the printing operation is booked solid for the next 2 years, and it would have to cancel an obligation with an outside customer in order to meet the needs of the internal division.

(b) Assume that the printing operation has available capacity.

(c) The top management of Word Wizard believes that the printing operation should always do the printing for the company's authors. On a number of occasions, it has forced the printing operation to cancel jobs with outside customers in order to meet the needs of its own lines. Discuss the pros and cons of this approach.

(d) Calculate the change in contribution margin to each division, and to the company as a whole, if top management forces the printing operation to accept the $0.007 per page transfer price when it has no available capacity.

(d) Loss to company ($750)

Determine minimum transfer price with no excess capacity.

(LO 4), AP

PM-5 Gutierrez Company makes various electronic products. The company is divided into a number of autonomous divisions that can either sell to internal units or sell externally. All divisions are located in buildings on the same piece of property. The Board Division has offered the Chip Division $21 per unit to supply it with chips for 40,000 boards. It has been purchasing these chips for $22 per unit from outside suppliers. The Chip Division receives $22.50 per unit for sales made to outside customers on this type of chip. The variable cost of chips sold externally by the Chip Division is $14.50. It estimates that it will save $4.50 per chip of selling expenses on units sold internally to the Board Division. The Chip Division has no excess capacity.

Instructions

(b) Total loss to company $160,000

(a) Calculate the minimum transfer price that the Chip Division should accept. Discuss whether it is in the Chip Division's best interest to accept the offer.
(b) Suppose that the Chip Division decides to reject the offer. What are the financial implications for each division, and for the company as a whole, of this decision?

Determine minimum transfer price under different situations.

(LO 4), AP

PM-6 Comm Devices (CD) is a division of Worldwide Communications, Inc. CD produces pagers and other personal communication devices. These devices are sold to other Worldwide divisions, as well as to other communication companies. CD was recently approached by the manager of the Personal Communications Division regarding a request to make a special pager designed to receive signals from anywhere in the world. The Personal Communications Division has requested that CD produce 12,000 units of this special pager. The following facts are available regarding the Comm Devices Division.

Selling price of standard pager	$95
Variable cost of standard pager	$50
Additional variable cost of special pager	$30

Instructions

For each of the following independent situations, calculate the minimum transfer price, and discuss whether the internal transfer should take place or whether the Personal Communications Division should purchase the pager externally.

(a) The Personal Communications Division has offered to pay the CD Division $105 per pager. The CD Division has no available capacity. The CD Division would have to forgo sales of 10,000 pagers to existing customers in order to meet the request of the Personal Communications Division. (*Note*: The number of special pagers to be produced does not equal the number of existing pagers that would be forgone.)

(b) Minimum transfer price $140

(b) The Personal Communications Division has offered to pay the CD Division $150 per pager. The CD Division has no available capacity. The CD Division would have to forgo sales of 16,000 pagers to existing customers in order to meet the request of the Personal Communications Division. (*Note*: The number of special pagers to be produced does not equal the number of existing pagers that would be forgone.
(c) The Personal Communications Division has offered to pay the CD Division $100 per pager. The CD Division has available capacity.

Compute the target price using absorption-cost pricing and variable-cost pricing.

(LO 5), AP

PM-7 Stent Corporation needs to set a target price for its newly designed product EverReady. The following data relate to this new product.

	Per Unit	Total
Direct materials	$20	
Direct labor	$40	
Variable manufacturing overhead	$10	
Fixed manufacturing overhead		$1,600,000
Variable selling and administrative expenses	$ 5	
Fixed selling and administrative expenses		$1,120,000

The costs shown above are based on a budgeted volume of 80,000 units produced and sold each year. Stent uses cost-plus pricing methods to set its target selling price. Because some managers prefer absorption-cost pricing and others prefer variable-cost pricing, the accounting department provides information under both approaches using a markup of 50% on absorption cost and a markup of 80% on variable cost.

Instructions

(a) Markup $45
(b) Markup $60

(a) Compute the target price for one unit of EverReady using absorption-cost pricing.
(b) Compute the target price for one unit of EverReady using variable-cost pricing.

Compute various amounts using absorption-cost pricing and variable-cost pricing.

(LO 5), AP

PM-8 Anderson Windows Inc. is in the process of setting a target price on its newly designed tinted window. Cost data relating to the window at a budgeted volume of 4,000 units are as follows.

	Per Unit	Total
Direct materials	$100	
Direct labor	$ 70	
Variable manufacturing overhead	$ 20	
Fixed manufacturing overhead		$120,000
Variable selling and administrative expenses	$ 10	
Fixed selling and administrative expenses		$102,000

Anderson Windows uses cost-plus pricing methods that are designed to provide the company with a 25% ROI on its tinted window line. A total of $1,016,000 in assets is committed to production of the new tinted window.

Instructions

(a) Compute the markup percentage under absorption-cost pricing that will allow Anderson Windows to realize its desired ROI. (a) 45%

(b) Compute the target price of the window under absorption-cost pricing, and show proof that the desired ROI is realized.

(c) Compute the markup percentage under variable-cost pricing that will allow Anderson Windows to realize its desired ROI. (Round to three decimal places.)

(d) Compute the target price of the window under variable-cost pricing, and show proof that the desired ROI is realized.

(e) Since both absorption-cost pricing and variable-cost pricing produce the same target price and provide the same desired ROI, why do both methods exist? Isn't one method clearly superior to the other?

COMPANY INDEX

A
ABC, Inc., H-7
Abitibi Consolidated Inc., 30
Acer Inc., 282
Adelphia, 61
adidas, 398–399, 414, 517, 564, 720
Advanced Micro Devices, 790
Ag-Chem, 341
Ahold NV, 212
AIG, 7
Airbus, 475
AirTran Airways, 435–436
Alaskan Airlines, 789
Alcoa, 641
Allegiant Airlines, 717
Alliance Atlantis Communications Inc., 464
Alternative Distributor Corp., 369
Amazon.com, Inc., 13, 35, 38, 83, 145, 209, 216, 218, 261, 310–311, 368, 416, 440, 472, 529–530, 584, 608, 641, 696, 698, 719, 883, 902–903, 928, 982, 1021, D-1–D-3
AMD, 611
American Airlines, 160, 423, 481, 705, 853, 891
American Cancer Society, 538
American Eagle Outfitters, 68–69, 77
American Express Company, 378, 396, 507, 978
American Greetings Corporation, 311
American LaFrance, 748
American Van Lines, 1070
Anaheim Angels, H-7
Anytime Fitness, 973
AOL, H-7
Apple Inc., 5, 28, 37, 39, 71, 83, 89, 129, 144, 153, 209, 248, 260, 310, 355, 367, 392, 405, 416, 446, 459, 472, 488, 515, 529, 537, 572, 583, 591, 609–610, 628, 640, 660, 683, 696, 698, A-1–A-5, K-22
Armani, M-2
Armour, 984
AT&T, 652, 705, 885, H-7
Aviation Partners, 475
Avis, H-7

B
Baan NV, 212
BabyCakes NYC, 1015, 1018, 1038–1039
Balanced Scorecard Institute, 1164
Bank of America, 370, 384
Bank One Corporation, 99
Barnes & Noble, 530–531, 690
Barnes & Noble.com, 440
Barriques, 316–318, 324, 328
Ben & Jerry's, 586–587, 748, 794
Berkshire Hathaway, 555
Best Buy, 44, 45, 52–58, 60, 63, 76, 162, 263, 444, 472–473
Beverly Hills Fan Company, 1012
BHP Billiton, 444
Blockbuster, Inc., 19
Bob Evans Farms, 71, 685
Bob's Red Mill, 1015
Boeing, 74, 85–86, 424, 437, 475, 521, 716, 719, 748, 981
Boeing Capital Corporation, 428
Boise Cascade Corporation, 451
Borders Group, 530–531
BorderStylo LLC, 441
Box, 605
BP, 279
Briggs and Stratton, 1092
Bright-Farms, 886
Bristol-Myers Squibb, 173, 277, 653
Buck Knives, 990
Burlington Northern Railroad, 938
Burton Snowboards, 710

C
Calico Corners, 406
Callaway Golf Company, 75–76
Cal State–Northridge Stdt Union, 30
Campbell Soup Company, 35, 277, 432, 459, 705, 1180–1181, 1202
Canadian National Railway Company (CN), 517
Canwest Global Communications Corp., 629
Capital Cities, H-7
Cargill Inc., 538
Carnival Corporation, 1167
Carrefour SA, 261
Caterpillar, Inc., 267–268, 279, 284–285, 314, 396, 424, 538, 709, 794, 855
Caterpillar Financial Services, 396
CBS, 442
Cendant, H-7
Center Ice Consultants, 790
Century 21, H-7
Cerberus, 479
Chase, 1136
ChevronTexaco, M-2
Chicago Bears, 104
Chicago Cubs, 104
Chieftain International, Inc., 145
Chrysler, 479, 1133
Cisco Systems, 175, 653, 935, 1077
Citibank Visa, 401
Citicorp, 6
Citigroup, 5, 53, 152, 532
Clark Equipment Company, 845
Clark-Hurth, 845
Clif Bar & Company, 5, 41

The Clorox Company, 252, 975
CN (Canadian National Railway Company), 517
CNH Global, 285
The Coca-Cola Company, 5, 42, 406, 443, 447–448, 634, 697, 709, 720, 789, 920, 1092
Coldwell Banker, H-7
Columbia Sportswear Company, 3, 8–10, 18–20, 38, 44, 83, 144–145, 209, 261, 310, 368, 416, 472, 529, 583–584, 629, 640, 696, B-1–B-4
Commonwealth Edison, 552
Compumotor, 845
Computer Associates International, Inc., 1114–1115
ConAgra Foods, 172–173, 230, 549
ConocoPhilips, 444
Conservation International, 1133
Continental Bank, 428
Costco Wholesale Corp., 226, 594, I-1
Countrywide Financial Corporation, 393
Craig Consumer Electronics, 270
Credit Suisse Group, 110
Current Designs, 702–705, 708–709, 713–715, 722–723, 741–742, 784, 831, 877–879, 918, 969, 1009–1010, 1059, 1111–1112, 1161, 1200
Curves, 973
Cyan, 605
Cypress Semiconductor Corporation, 629

D

Daimler-Benz, 479
DaimlerChrysler, 479
Dayton Hudson, 342
Deere & Company, 304–305, 391–392
Dell, 268–269, 705, 718, 855, 1166
Dell Financial Services, 428
Del Monte Foods Company, 971
Deloitte & Touche, 19
Delta Air Lines, Inc., 60, 152, 160, 341, 437, 448–449, 987, 1135
Dewey & LeBoeuf LLP, 8
Dick's Sporting Goods, 235–236, 238–239, 712
Discover, 396
Disney, *See* The Walt Disney Company
Disneyland, H-7
Disney World, H-7
Dow Chemical, 13, 709, 790
Duke Energy Co., 6, 885, 1070, 1082
Dun & Bradstreet, 654
Dunkin' Donuts, Inc., 60
DuPont Co., 237, 376, 486, 790
Dynegy, 6, 603

E

EarthLink, 552
Eastman Kodak, 590
eBay, 230
Eli Lilly, 319, 1092
Enron Corporation, 6, 7, 230, 495, 499, 532, 539, 653, 705
Ernst & Young, 368
Eskimo Pie Corporation, 29
ESPN, H-7
Ethan Allen, 983
E*Trade, 935
ExxonMobil Corporation, 5, 56, 279, 333, 748, 790, 984, 1166, M-2

F

Facebook, 12, 536–539, 541–544, 546, 549–550, 557, 561, 707, 938
Fannie Mae, 99, 164
FASB (Financial Accounting Standards Board), 368–369
Federal Express, 464, 705
FedEx Corporation, 410–411, 971
Fiat/Chrysler, 42
Financial Accounting Standards Board (FASB), 368–369
Fireeye, 605
Fitch, 662
Flightserve, 897
FMCC (Ford Motor Credit Corp.), 396
Ford Motor Company, 6, 110, 217, 269, 281, 376, 396, 444, 478–479, 497, 500–501, 803, 891, 929, 1082, M-3
Ford Motor Credit Corp. (FMCC), 396
Fox Broadcasting, 442, 1072
Frito-Lay, H-7

G

Gap, Inc., 83–84
Gatorade, H-7
GE, *see* General Electric
GE Capital, 396
General Dynamics Corp., 649
General Electric (GE), 6, 224, 319, 376, 396, 418, 521, 538, 549, 707, 720, 764, 798, 856
General Mills, 432, 654, 658–659, 668–676, 790, 848
General Motors (GM), 5, 6, 56, 92, 308, 406, 478–479, 482, 486, 495–498, 501, 507, 538, 652, 684, 705, 718, 749, 856, 974, M-3
Glassmaster Company, 1163
Global Crossing, 495
Global Reporting Initiative, 721
GM, *see* General Motors
Goldman Sachs, 6, 763
Gold's Gym, 835
Goodyear, 988
Google Inc., 12, 44, 48, 50, 56, 439, 441, 536–537, 555, 557, 648, 660
Grant Thornton LLP, 30
Green Bay Packers, 91, 146
Groupon, Inc., 150, 151, 180–181, 557
Gulf Craft, 818
Gulf Oil, 541

H

H. J. Heinz Company, 67–68, 75
Hard Candy, 835
Harley-Davidson, 855
HealthSouth, 7
Hechinger Co., 530
Hershey, 793–794
Hewlett-Packard (HP), 53, 705, 717, 719, 856, 929, 981, 1135
hhgregg, 52, 55–56
Hilton Hotels, 428, 719, 835, 885
Holland America Line, 1167, 1175, 1186–1187
Home Depot, 269, 530
Honda, 1080
Honeywell International, 652
Host Marriott Corporation, 584
Household International, J-9
Howard Johnson, H-7
HP, *see* Hewlett-Packard
H&R Block, 791
Hughes Aircraft Co., 649
Human Rights Watch, 720

I

IBM, 40, 230, 538, 542n.1, 555, 571, 608, 650, 652, 719, 1122
Ice Pro, 790
InBev, 418

The Institute of Management Accountants (IMA), 744
Institutional Shareholder Services, 540
Intel Corporation, 42, 237, 342, 376, 394, 440, 611, 718, 790, 804, 929, M-1–M-2
InterContinental, 428
International Outsourcing Services, LLC, 107
iSuppli, 755
IT&T, 3

J
J. Walter Thompson, 790
JCPenney Company, 342, 377, 405, 594
JetBlue Airways, 423–424, 426, 428, 444–447, 610
Jiffy Lube, 791
Jif Peanut Butter, 818
John Deere Capital Corporation, 428
Jones Soda Co., 788–790, 804–806
Jostens, Inc., 1135
J.P. Morgan Leasing, 428
JPMorgan Chase Bank, 35, 99, 384

K
Kaiser, 790
Kansas Farmers' Vertically Integrated Cooperative, Inc. (K-VIC), 121–122
Kellogg Company, 33, 561, 608, 654, 664–666, 748, 790, 797, 799–803, 807–812, 891, 1129
Kmart Stores, 262, 393, 1011
Kohl's Corporation, 594
Kohl's Department Stores, 355
Komag, 937–938
Kraft Foods, 107, 1129
Krispy Kreme Doughnuts, Inc., 134
Kroger, 236, 277
K-VIC (Kansas Farmers' Vertically Integrated Cooperative, Inc.), 121–122

L
Laser Recording Systems, 209–210
LDK Solar Co., 282, 608
Lease Finance Corporation, 428
Leslie Fay, 270, 313
Limited Brands, 71
Linens 'n Things, Inc., 392–393
Lockheed, 437
Louis Vuitton, 43, 89, 149, 213, 265, 315, 373, 421, 477, 535, 589, 645, 701, 706, F-1–F-5
Lucent, 705

M
McDonald's Corporation, 6, 42, 439, 460, 507, 521–522, 634, 1120
McDonnell Douglas, 85–86, 719
McKesson Corporation, 216, 313, 341, 385
Macy's, 934, 1082
Madison Square Garden, 1021
Manitowoc Company, 286–287
Marriott Hotels, 428, 432, 442, 885, 1070
Marriott International, 584
Massachusetts General Hospital, 884
MasterCard, 385, 396
Mattel Corporation, 346–347
Maxwell Car Company, 479
Mayo Clinic, 763, 790
MEC (Mountain Equipment Cooperative), 238–239
Medtronic, Inc., 488
Merck and Co., 31, 236, M-2
Merrill Lynch, 6
Method Products, 975, 981, 991
MF Global Holdings Ltd, 91, 101–102, 119, 539
Microsoft, 5, 56, 92, 108, 224, 230, 237, 424, 439, 444, 537, 561, 591, 608, 610, 684, 704
Mighty Ducks, H-7
Minnesota Mining and Manufacturing Company (3M), 376. *See also* 3M Company
Mobile Iron, 605
Moody's, 654, 662
Morgan Stanley, H-10
Morrow Snowboards, Inc., 219
The Motley Fool, 45
Motorola, 277, 649
Mountain Equipment Cooperative (MEC), 238–239
MSN.com, 668
Museum of Contemporary Art, 1037

N
NationsBank, 370
NBC, 442
NBCUniversal, 1072
NEC, 212
Nestlé, 42
Netflix, 641, 698
New York Stock Exchange, 4
NFL, 442
Nike, Inc., 34, 50, 56, 237, 343, 374–376, 382, 395–399, 414, 439, 460, 538, 544, 547, 549, 555, 557, 560–562, 564, 610, 660, 688, 719, 885, 936
Nordstrom, Inc., 76, 386, 424, 689
The North Face, 35
Northwest Airlines, 427
Novartis AG, 499

O
Oakley, Inc., 300
Office Depot, Inc., 216, 251, 283, 411
Office Max, 173
Oracle Corporation, 30
Oral-B Laboratories, 974

P
Packard Bell, 394
PairGain Technologies, 45
Pandora, 937
Parker Hannifin, 845
Parmalat, 371, 602
PCAOB (Public Company Accounting Oversight Board), 369
Penske Automotive Group, 1135
PepsiCo, Inc., 5, 107, 237, 280, 304, 634, 697, 789, 790, H-7
Pepsi-Cola, H-7
Phantom Tac, 720
Philip Morris International, 488
Pilgrim's Pride, 173, 230
Pratt and Whitney, 764
Precor, 834–835, 847, 854–855
PricewaterhouseCoopers, 40, 763
Princeton University, 1037
Procter & Gamble, 6, 544, 649, 712, 975, 1077, 1122
Promodes SA, 261
Prudential Real Estate, 6
Public Company Accounting Oversight Board (PCAOB), 369

Q
Quad Graphics, 748
Quaker Oats, 280, 818, H-7

R
Radio Shack, 235
Ramada Inn, H-7
RBC Financial Group, 194
Reebok, 548, 885

Reebok International Ltd., 277
REI (Recreational Equipment Incorporated), 215, 216, 220, 227–229, 231, 235–236, 238–239
Rolling Stones, 901
Royal Ahold, 371
Royal Dutch Shell, 279, 790

S
SafeNet, 543
Safeway, 236, 320, 923
Saks Fifth Avenue, 235
Salvation Army, 538
San Diego Zoo, 1075
SAP, 718
Sara Lee Corporation, 559, 709
Satyam Computer Services, 371
Schering-Plough, 719
The Scotts Company, 416–417
Sears, Roebuck & Co., 194, 385
Sears Holdings Corporation, 230, 385, 437
Seattle Seahawks, 789
Sharp, 1180
Shell, 442
Sherwin Williams, 790
Siebel Systems, 1079
Siemens AG, 1092
Simon Properties, 488
Skechers, 393–395, 398–399
Skechers USA, 374, 384, 660
Skype, 230
SkyTrax, 423
Smart Balance, 972
Snap Fitness, 973
Sony, 42, 108, 284
Southwest Airlines, 30, 33, 47, 194, 423, 424, 434–435, 445–447, 499, 525–526, 608, 660, 884
Sportsco Investments, 30
Sports Illustrated, 481
Sprint Corporation, 481
Standard Oil Company of California, 451
Standard & Poor's, 531, 547, 551, 654, 662
Stanley Black & Decker Manufacturing Company, 277
Staples, Inc., 685
Starbucks, 277, 313, 557, 608, 720, 1118–1119, 1133, 1138–1139, M-2
Subway, 442
Sunbeam, 978
SUPERVALU, 573

T
Target Corporation, 81–82, 236, 269, 283–284, 333, 342, 393, 594, 695, 975, J-17
Tecumseh Products Company, 1202
Tektronix Inc., 558
Tempur Sealy International, 890
Tesla Motors, Inc., 48
Texas Instruments, Inc., 75
The Walt Disney Company, H-7, H-12
3M Company, 407, 522, 931
Tiffany and Co., 236
Time Warner, 6, 1018–1019, H-7, M-9
Tootsie Roll, 92
Topps Company, Inc., 686
Toronto Blue Jays, 194
Toyota, 42, 442, 497, 718, 720, M-3
Trek, 6, 983, M-9
Tribeca Grand Hotel, 1064–1065, 1089–1090
Tropicana, H-7
True Value Hardware, 269
Turner Broadcasting, H-5, H-7
Tweeter Home Entertainment, 63
Twitter, 938

U
U-Haul, 887
Ultimate Electronics, 194
Unilever, 494, 975, 1136
United Air Lines, 6, 160, 423, 482, 590, 884, 929, 1135, 1137
United Parcel Service (UPS), 652
U.S. Navy, 1122
United States Steel Corp., 486, 608, 891
United Stationers, 216
UPS (United Parcel Service), 652
USAir, 486
US Bancorp Equipment Finance, 428
USX, 790

V
Valujet, 423
Verizon Communications Inc., 488, 652, 1174
Versace, M-2
VF Corporation, 20, 38, 83, 144–145, 209, 261, 310, 368, 416, 472, 529, 583–584, 640, 696, C-1–C-3
Visa, 385, 386, 396, 401
Vodafone/Mannesmann, 42

W
Wachovia, 378
Walgreen Company, 216, 277, 577
Wal-Mart Stores, Inc., 38, 81–83, 145, 209, 215, 216, 235–237, 261, 269, 281, 283–284, 310–311, 333, 368, 393, 416, 424, 472, 529–530, 561, 584, 594, 610, 641, 695, 696, 698, 719, 1136, E-1–E-5
The Walt Disney Company, 6, 49, 60, 436, 444, 746–748, 758, 767–768, 790, M-9
Warner Brothers, 790, 818
Waste Management Company, 99
Wells Fargo Bank, 318, 378, 384
Wells Fargo & Company, 576
Wendy's, 424
Wendy's International, 277, 585
Wenonah Canoe, 702–703, 741
Whirlpool, 709
Whole Foods Market, 922–923, 939–940
Winnebago Industries, Inc., 300
World Bank, 1122
WorldCom, 7, 173, 325, 427, 495, 539, 653, 659

X
Xerox, 38, 173, 705
XM Satellite Radio Holdings, 1028

Y
Yahoo! Inc., 78, 654
Young & Rubicam, 790

Z
Zoom Kitchen, 932

SUBJECT INDEX

Please note: any entries for pages within Appendices I-M may be found at the book's companion website, www.wiley.com/college/kimmel.

A
Absorption costing, 940–948
  decision-making concerns and, 946–948
  example of, 940–942
  for inventory costing, 946–947
  net income effects of, 942–946
  variable costing compared to, 940–948
Absorption-cost pricing, M-16–M-17
Accelerated depreciation, 432, 450
Accounts-
  chart of accounts, 109–110
  debit and credit procedures, 101–104
  debits and credits, 101–106
  defined, 100
  journalizing transactions, 106–109
  permanent, 175
  posting to, 109–118
  T-accounts, 100–101
  temporary, 175
Accounting cycle, 92, 177–178
Accounting equation, 93–94
Accounting information system, 9, 92–122
  journalizing transactions, 106–109
  posting to ledger accounts, 109–118
  recording transactions, 100–106
  transactions analysis, 92–100
  trial balance preparation, 119–122
Accounting principle, changes in, 651–652
Accounting time periods, 61, 152
Accounting transactions, 92–93
Accounts payable-
  operating activities and, 10
  on statement of cash flows, 600
Accounts payable subsidiary ledger, J-2, J-12
Accounts receivable, 10, 376–387
  disposing of, 385–387
  recognizing, 376–378
  valuing and recording, 378–384
Accounts receivable subsidiary ledger, J-2
Accounts receivable turnover, 395–396, 661, 668–669
Accruals, 163–170
  expenses, 164–167
  revenues, 163–164
Accrual accounting, 152–181
  adjusted trial balance, 170–174
  adjusting entries for accruals, 163–170
  adjusting entries for deferrals, 156–162
  cash basis of accounting vs., 153–154
  closing entries, 175–177, 179–180
  expense recognition principle, 152–153
  need for adjusting entries in, 154–155
  revenue recognition principle, 152, 153
  types of adjusting entries in, 155–156
Accrued interest, 165–166
Accrued salaries, 166–167
Accumulated appreciation, 159–160
Accumulated depreciation, 48
Accumulated other comprehensive income, 558
Activity base, 757, 758
Activity-based costing (ABC), 718, 836–855
  benefits and limitations of, 845–850
  incremental analysis and, 978–979
  for manufacturing, 840–845
  for service industries, 850–853
  traditional costing compared to, 836–837
Activity-based management (ABM), 848–489
Activity-based overhead rate, 841
Activity flowcharts, 847–848
Activity index, 884
Additions and improvements, for plant assets, 427
Adjusted cash balance per books, 338
Adjusted trial balance, 170–174
  preparing, 170–171
  preparing financial statements from, 171–172
  quality of earnings and, 172–173
Adjusting entries, J-16
  for accruals, 163–170
  for deferrals, 156–162
  improper, 173
  need for, 154–155
  for sales discounts, 226
  types of, 155–156
Administrative expenses, 10
Affiliated companies, H-6
Aging schedule, 393, 394
Aging the accounts receivable, 382

Allowances-
for doubtful accounts, 380
merchandise sales, 225–226
in periodic inventory system, 240
in perpetual inventory system, 221, 225–226
purchase, 221–222
sales, 225–226, 240
Allowance method, for uncollectable accounts, 379–384
Alternative accounting methods, quality of earnings and, 652
Amortization-
of bonds at discount, 491
bonds at premium and, 492–493
effective-interest method, 504–507
of intangible assets, 440
quality of earnings and, 652
straight-line method, 502–504
Amount due at maturity, for interest-bearing notes, 390
Annual depreciation, prorating, 432
Annually recurring expenditures, for equipment, 426
Annual rate of return method, 1184–1185
Annual reports, 18–20, A-1. *See also* Financial statements
Annuity, G-5, G-9
future value of, G-4–G-7
present value of, G-9–G-11
Articles of co-partnership, K-5
Assets. *See also specific types of assets, e.g.*- Intangible assets
debit and credit procedures for, 102
leased, 428
overstating, 602
in partnerships, K-5–K-6, K-18–K-20
useful life of, 158
Asset turnover, 662, 674
Auditors, 19, 325
Auditor's report, 19
Authorized stock, 543
Auto loans, G-15
Available-for-sale securities, 650, H-7, H-9–H-10
Average collection period, 395, 661, 669
Average-cost method, 276–277, 289
Average operating assets, reducing, 1088

B
Background checks, 325
Bad debt expense, 378, 380, 384. *See also* Uncollectable accounts
Bad information, bad loans and, 393
Balanced scorecard, 718–719, 1135–1137
Balance sheet(s), 13–14
budgeted, 1033–1034
consolidated, A-3, B-2, C-1, D-3, E-3, F-3
cost flow methods and, 278–279
fair value of securities on, H-9
horizontal analysis of, 656
inventory errors and, 290–291
liabilities on, 495
long-term investments and, H-11
for manufacturer, 714–715
for partnerships, K-9–K-10
short-term investments and, H-10–H-11
stockholders' equity on, 558–560
vertical analysis of, 657
Bank accounts, 333–340
bank statements, 333–334
electronic funds transfers, 333
errors and, 335–337
reconciling, 334–340
Bank charges expense, 338–339
Bank errors, 335–337
Bank line of credit, 497
Bank reconciliation, 334–340
defined, 333
entries from, 338–339
illustrated, 337–338
procedure for, 335–337
Bank statements, 333–334
Basic accounting equation, 13
Batch-level activities, 846
Beginning work in process inventory, 713
Behavioral decision-making errors, 987
Behavioral principles, performance evaluations and, 1079
Benchmarks, 849
Benford's Law, 659
Board of directors, 539, 707
Bonds, 485–494
accounting for, H-3
accounting for redemptions, 493–494
additional cost of borrowing, 491
amortizing the discount, 491
amortizing the premium, 492–493
bond certificate, 486, 487
carrying (book) value of, 490, 494
contractual interest rate for, 486, 489–490
convertible and callable bonds, 486
discount or premium on bonds, 489–490
effective-interest amortization method, 504–507
face value of, 486, 489
green, 494
interest expense with, 491
interest payable, as a current liability, 489
interest payments and, 487
issuing at a discount, 490–491
issuing at face value, 489
issuing at premium, 492–493
issuing procedures for, 486
market for, 488
market interest rates for, 486, 490
market price of, 486–488
maturity date for, 486
present value of, G-11–G-13
principal for, 487
recording acquisition of, H-3
recording interest on, H-3
recording sale of, H-3
redeeming at maturity, 493
redeeming before maturity, 493–494
secured and unsecured bonds, 486
straight-line amortization method, 502–504
zero-coupon, 490
Bond financing, advantages of common stock and, 562–563
Bonding employees, 325
Bond market, 488
Bonds payable-
as debt securities, 9
on statement of cash flows (direct method), 617
on statement of cash flows (indirect method), 603
Bonuses, I-2, K-16–K-20
Book errors, bank reconciliation and, 337, 338

Book (carrying) value-
for bonds, 490, 494
declining-balance method for, 449
defined, 160
depreciation and, 429
in incremental analysis, 987
of partnerships, K-16
Borrowing, additional cost of, 491
Break-even analysis, 896–899, 925
contribution margin technique in, 897
graphic presentation of, 898–899
mathematical equation in, 896
Break-even point, 893, 896, 902, 936–937
Break-even sales-
in dollars, 931–932
in units, 929–930
Budgetary control, 1066–1076, 1089–1090
concept of, 1066–1067
flexible budgets, 1069–1076
static budget reports, 1067–1069
Budgetary slack, 1019
Budget committees, 1018
Budgeted balance sheet, 1033–1034
Budgeted income statements, 1028–1030
Budgeting, 1016–1039
accounting information in, 1016
benefits of, 1016
budgetary optimism and, 1022
budgeted balance sheet, 1033–1034
budgeted income statement, 1028–1030
budget period length, 1017
cash budgets, 1030–1035
direct labor budgets, 1026–1027
direct materials budgets, 1023–1026
financial budgets, 1019–1020, 1030–1035
human behavior and, 1018–1019
long-range planning and, 1019
manufacturing overhead budget, 1027–1028
master budget, 1019–1020
for merchandising companies, 1035–1036, 1038
for nonmanufacturing companies, 1035–1038
for not-for-profit organizations, 1037
operating budgets, 1019
participative, 1018–1019
process of, 1017–1018
production budgets, 1022–1023, 1025
sales budgets, 1021–1022, 1025
selling and administrative expense budget, 1028
for service companies, 1036–1037
standards and, 1121
Budget reports, 1066
Budget variance, 1067
Buildings, 426
construction of, 426
depreciation and, 429
interest costs and, 426
purchase of, 426
on statement of cash flows (direct method), 617
on statement of cash flows (indirect method), 603
Burden, 709
Business activities, 8–10
financing, *see* Financing activities
investing, *see* Investing activities
operating, *see* Operating activities
Business careers, 6
Business documents, recording sales and, 224
Business environment, 926–927
Business ethics, 719. *See also* Ethics
Business organization, forms of, 4–5
Business size, internal controls and, 327
Buying, leasing vs., 428
Buy or make decisions, 981–983
By-laws, of corporations, 541

C

Calculators, *see* Financial calculators
Callable bonds, 486
Canceled checks, 334
Capital-
corporate, 544
legal, 543
paid-in, 544, 545, 553, 555
venture, K-3
working, 54, 661
Capital acquisition, by corporations, 539
Capital budgeting, 1168–1187
annual rate of return method for, 1184–1185
cash flow information for, 1168–1169
cash payback technique in, 1169–1171
discounted cash flow method comparisons, 1183
intangible benefits in, 1176–1178
internal rate of return method for, 1182–1184
limited resources and, 1179
net present value method in, 1171–1176
post-audit of investment projects, 1180–1181
profitability index for mutually exclusive projects, 1178–1181
risk analysis in, 1180
sensitivity analysis and, 1180
Capital deficiency, partnership liquidation and, K-10, K-12–K-14
Capital expenditures, 427
defined, 424
free cash flow and, 57
improperly capitalized, 424–425
Capital leases, 428, 499
Capital stock, 50. *See also* Common stock
Captive finance companies, 396
Carrying value, 160. *See also* Book value
Cash-
advance receipt from customer, 95
depreciation of assets and, 430
fraud and, 327
increases and decreases in, 101
insurance policy purchase with, 114
investing, 9
managing and monitoring, 341–343
note issued in exchange for, 94–95
overstating, 602
payment of employee salaries with, 98, 116

payment of rent with, 114
purchase of insurance policy for, 97
purchase of office equipment for, 95
receipt in advance from customer, 113
restricted, 341
services performed for, 96, 113
stockholders' investment of, 94, 111
Cash basis of accounting, accrual-basis accounting vs., 153–154
Cash budget(s), 344–347, 1030–1035
cash disbursements section, 1030–1031
cash management and, 1033
cash receipts section, 1030
financing section, 1031
Cash controls, 327–332, 340–347
cash budgeting, 344–347
cash disbursements controls, 330–331
cash receipt controls, 328–330, 332
managing and monitoring cash, 341–343
petty cash fund, 347–348
reporting cash, 340–341
Cash disbursements controls, 330–331
petty cash fund, 331, 347–348
voucher system, 330–331
Cash disbursements journal, *see* Cash payments journal
Cash dividends, 549–551
adequate cash and, 549–550
declaration date for, 550
declared, 550
entries for, 550–551
free cash flow and, 57
payment date for, 550
payout ratio and, 676
record date for, 550
retained earnings and, 549
Cash equivalents, 340
Cash equivalent price, 425
Cash flows, 14–15. *See also* Statement of cash flows
ability to generate, 592
in capital budgeting evaluation, 1168–1169
classification of, 592–593
equal annual cash flows, 1172–1173
from financing activities, 592
inventory costing and, 279–280. *See also* Cost flow methods
negative cash and, 608
from operating activities, 592–593
product life cycle and, 607
simplifying assumptions and, 1175
unequal annual cash flows, 1173
Cash payback technique, 1169–1171
Cash payments-
for income tax, 616
for interest, 616
major classes of, 613
for operating expenses, 615
on statement of cash flows, 614–616
Cash payments journal, J-12–J-15
journalizing transactions, J-13–J-15
posting, J-15
Cash (net) realizable value, 380, 389
Cash receipts-
acceleration of, 396–398
major classes of, 613
on statement of cash flows, 613–614
Cash receipts controls, 328–330, 332
mail receipts, 330
over-the-counter receipts, 328–330
Cash receipts journal, J-7–J-11
journalizing transactions, J-8–J-10
posting of, J-8, J-10
proving of, J-10–J-11
Cash register documents, 224
Cash reporting, 340–341
cash equivalents and, 340
restricted cash and, 341
Cash sales, credit cards and, 385
Certified public accountant (CPA), 19
Change in accounting principle, 651–652
Changes in equity, consolidated statement of, F-4
Channel stuffing, 653
Chart of accounts, 109–110
Checks, outstanding, 335–337
Check register, 330
Chief executive officer (CEO), 540, 707
Chief financial officer (CFO), 707
Classified balance sheet, 46–51
current assets on, 46–48
current liabilities on, 50
intangible assets on, 48–49
long-term investments on, 48
long-term liabilities and, 50
property, plant, and equipment on, 48
ratio analysis for, 53–56
stockholder's equity on, 50
Closing entries, 175–177, 179–180, J-16
for partnerships, K-6–K-8
post-closing trial balance, 176–177
preparing, 175–176
for sole proprietorships, L-4–L-7
Code of ethical standards, 719
Collaboration, competition vs., 1077
Collection agent, 481
Collection monitoring, 393–394, 396
Collusion, 327
Combined statement of comprehensive income, 651
Commercial paper, 341
Common costs, 1084
Common-size analysis, 657
Common stock, 9
accounting for issues of, 545–546
bond financing vs., 562–563
debit and credit procedures and, 102–103
earnings per share and, 675
on statement of cash flows (direct method), 617
on statement of cash flows (indirect method), 604
stockholder rights and, 541
stockholders' equity and, 50
Company evaluation, statement of cash flows in, 607–611
Company officers, 5
Comparability, 59, 60
Comparative analysis, 654
Comparative balance sheets, statement of cash flows and, 595
Competition, collaboration vs., 1077

Complete statement of comprehensive income, 651
Completion percentages, process costing and, 797
Compounding periods, financial calculators and, G-15
Compound interest, G-2–G-3
Comprehensive income, 231, 650–651, H-12
  complete statement of, 651
  components of, 648
  format for, 650
Comprehensive income statement, 231–232
Comprehensive income statements, consolidated, A-2, B-2, C-2, D-2, E-2
Concentration of credit risk, 394
Confirmatory value, 60
Conservatism, 282
Consigned goods, 270–271
Consistency, 59, 60
Consolidated financial statements-
  balance sheets, A-3, B-2, C-1, D-3, E-3, F-3
  income statements, B-1, C-2, E-1, F-1
  statement of cash flows, A-5, B-3, C-3, D-1, E-5, F-5
  statement of changes in equity, F-4
  statement of comprehensive gains and losses, F-2
  statement of shareholders' equity, A-4
  statement of shareholders' equity and redeemable noncontrolling interest, E-4
  statement of stockholders' equity, B-4, C-3, D-3
  statements of comprehensive income, A-2, B-2, C-2, D-2, E-2
  statements of operations, A-2, B-1, D-2
  stock holdings in another entity and, H-6–H-7
Construction, building, 426
Contingencies, 498–499
Continuous 12-month budgets, 1017
Continuous life, of corporations, 539
Contra account, 490
Contractual interest rate, for bonds, 486, 489–490
Contra revenue account, 226
Contribution margin (CM), 892
  cost structure and, 936
  defined, 924
  per unit of limited resource, 933
  transfer pricing and, M-14
Contribution margin ratio, 894–895, 897, 925
Control accounts, 752, 761, J-2
Controllable margin, 1085, 1087
Controllable revenues and costs, 1078–1079, 1084–1085
Controller, 540, 707
Controlling, as management function, 705
Controlling interest, H-6
Conversion costs-
  defined, 797
  equivalent units for, 809
Conversion rates, 928
Convertible bonds, 486
Copyrights, 441
Corporate capital, 544
Corporate life cycle, 607–608
Corporate social responsibility, 540, 720–721
Corporations, 538–541
  characteristics of, 538–541
  classification of, 538
  corporate capital, 544
  description of, 4–5
  earnings from investment income and, H-2
  excess cash in, H-1–H-2
  formation of, 541
  hacks of computer records, J-17
  investing by, H-1–H-2
  organization of, 539–540
  S corporation, 541
  social responsibility of, 720–721
  stockholder rights and, 541–542
  stock issue considerations for, 542–544
  strategic reasons for investment, H-2
Correcting entries, J-16
Cost accounting systems, 748
  activity-based costing, 837–839. *See also* Activity-based costing (ABC)
  job order cost system, 748–749. *See also* Job order costing
  operations costing, 803–804
  process cost system, 748. *See also* Process costing
  traditional, 836–837, 851
Cost-based transfer prices, M-13–M-14
Cost behavior analysis, 884–888
  fixed costs in, 885
  high-low method and, 888–891
  mixed costs in, 887–891
  relevant range in, 886–887
  segregating costs in, 891
  variable costs in, 884–885
Cost centers, responsibility accounting and, 1082, 1083
Cost constraint, 62
Cost control, in activity-based costing, 846–848
Cost drivers, in activity-based costing, 838, 840–841
Cost factors, depreciation and, 430
Cost flow-
  in job order cost accounting, 749–750
  in process costing, 793
Cost flow assumptions, 272–277
Cost flow methods, 271–281
  assumptions of, 272–277
  average-cost, 276–277
  balance sheet effects of, 278–279
  first-in, first-out, 274–275
  income statement effects of, 277–278
  last-in, first-out, 275–276
  for perpetual inventory system, 287–289
  specific identification, 272
  tax effects of, 279
Cost method, for stock holdings of less than 20%, H-4
Cost of capital, 1174
Cost of goods available for sale, 273
Cost of goods manufactured, 712–716
Cost of goods manufactured schedule, 714, 766
Cost of goods purchased, 712
Cost of goods sold, 10, 216
  assigning job costs to, 761
  on multi-step income statement, 229
  under periodic inventory system, 233–234
  stated at standard cost, 1134

Cost of living adjustments (COLAs), 1123
Cost per unit, 1121, 1123
Cost-plus contracts, 763
Cost-plus pricing, M-3–M-6
Cost pools-
  assigning overhead to, 840
  multiple, advantage of, 845–846
Cost reconciliation schedules, 802, 804, 810–811
Cost structure, 935
  break-even point and, 936–937
  contribution margin ratio and, 936
  degree of operating leverage and, 937–938
  margin of safety ratio and, 937
  operating leverage and, 935–939
Cost-volume-profit (CVP) analysis, 884–903, 924–940
  basic computations in, 925–926
  basic concepts in, 924–925
  break-even analysis in, 896–899
  break-even point in, 896, 902
  business environment changes and, 926–927
  contribution margin ratio in, 894–895
  cost behavior analysis in, 884–888
  high-low method for mixed costs in, 888–891
  income statement in, 892–895
  margin of safety in, 901–902
  operating leverage in, 935–939
  sales mix and break-even in, 929–933
  sales mix with limited resources in, 933–935
  target net income in, 899–902
  unit contribution margin in, 893–894
Cost-volume-profit (CVP) graph, 898–899
Covenant-lite debt, 500
CP (cash payments journal postings), J-15
CR (cash receipts journal postings), J-10
Credit(s) (Cr.), 101
  for accrued expenses, 164
  for accrued revenues, 163
  in bank transactions, 333
  for manufacturing work in process costs, 752
  for prepaid expenses, 157
  for unearned revenues, 160
Credit, extending, 392–393
Credit balance, 101, 766
Credit card sales, 385–386, 396
Credit extension, for receivables, 392–393
Creditors, 6, 9
Creditors' subsidiary ledger, J-2
Credit procedures, *see* Debit and credit procedures
Credit purchases, journalizing, J-11–J-12
Credit risk, concentration of, 394
Credit sales, journalizing, J-5
Credit terms, 222
Crossfooting, journal, J-10
Cumulative dividends, 552
Current assets-
  on classified balance sheet, 46–48
  composition of, 55
Current income statement, 595
Current liabilities, 480–485
  bond interest payable as, 489
  on classified balance sheet, 50
  current maturities of long-term debt, 482
  notes payable, 480–481
  payroll and payroll taxes payable, 483–485
  sales taxes payable, 481
  on statement of cash flows, 601
  unearned revenues, 481–482
Current maturities of long-term debt, 482
Current performance measurement, 811–812
Current-period sales, 655
Current ratio, 54–55, 496–497, 661, 668
Curvilinear costs, 886
Customers-
  cash receipts from, 613–614
  as external users, 6
  receipt of cash in advance from, 95
Customers' subsidiary ledger, J-2
Cutoff rate, 1174
Cybercrime, J-17
Cyber security, J-17

D

Days in inventory, 283, 399, 661, 669–670
Death of partners, K-20
Debit(s) (Dr.), 101
  for accrued expenses, 164
  for accrued revenues, 163
  in bank transactions, 333
  for manufacturing work in process costs, 752
  for prepaid expenses, 157
  for unearned revenues, 160
Debit and credit procedures, 101–104
  for assets and liabilities, 102
  for stockholders' equity, 102–104
  stockholders' equity relationships, 104–105
Debit balance-
  in allowance account, 383
  definition of, 101
  for manufacturing overhead, 766
Debt-
  during economic downturns, 497
  liabilities as, 13. *See also* Liability(-ies)
Debt covenants, 500
Debt investments-
  bonds, H-3. *See also* Bonds
  categories of, H-7
  defined, H-3
Debt masking, 498
Debt to assets ratio, 56, 661, 670–671
Debt to equity ratio, 671
Debt vs. equity decisions, 562–563
Decentralization, responsibility accounting and, 1077
Decision making-
  absorption costing and, 946–948
  capital budgeting and, 1169
  by management, 976–979. *See also* Incremental analysis
Declaration date, for cash dividends, 550
Declared dividends, 550
Decline phase, corporate life cycle and, 608
Declining-balance depreciation method, 432–433, 449–450
Declining book value, 449
Defaulted notes, 391
Deferrals, 156–162
  prepaid expenses, 156–160
  unearned revenues, 160–161

Degree of operating leverage, 937–938
Deposits in transit, 335–337
Depreciation, 48, 429–436
  accelerated-depreciation methods, 432, 450
  accumulated, 159–160
  adjusting entries for, 158–160
  annual rate of, 432
  book value and, 429
  cash accumulation and, 430
  comparison of methods, 434
  declining-balance method, 432–433, 449–450
  depreciable cost, 431
  depreciation schedule, 431–432
  disclosure in notes, 434–435
  double-declining-balance method and, 433, 450
  factors in computing, 430
  fair value and, 429
  income taxes and, 434
  land and, 429
  obsolescence and, 430
  periodic revision of, 435–436
  plant asset classes and, 429
  proration of, 432
  quality of earnings and, 652
  on statement of cash flows, 598–599, 616
  straight-line method, 431–432
  units-of-activity method and, 450–451
Developing countries, notes receivable and, 390
Differential analysis, *see* Incremental analysis
Direct fixed costs, profit centers and, 1084
Directing, as management function, 705
Direct labor, 709
Direct labor budgets, 1026–1027
Direct labor cost per unit, 1123
Direct labor costs, 836, 837
Direct labor efficiency standard, 1123
Direct labor price standard, 1123
Direct labor quantity standard, 1123
Direct labor rate standard, 1123
Direct labor variances, 1129–1131
Direct materials, 708
Direct materials budgets, 1023–1025
Direct materials cost per unit, 1123
Direct materials price standard, 1122
Direct materials quantity standard, 1122
Direct materials variances, 1125–1129
Direct method (statement of cash flows), 596, 611–618
  investing and financing activities in, 617–618
  net change in cash, 618
  operating activities, 613–616
Direct write-off method for uncollectable accounts, 378–379
Disbursements, cash, 330–331
Discontinued operations, 649
Discounts (in general)-
  discount period, 222
  of future amount, G-7
  in periodic inventory system, 239
  in perpetual inventory system, 222–223, 226–227
  purchase, 222–223
  sales, 226–227
  time periods and, G-11
Discounts (bond), 489–490
  amortization of, 491
  effective-interest amortization method, 505–506
  straight-line amortization method, 502–503
Discounted cash flow, 1171, 1183
Discount period, 222
Discount rate, 1171, 1174
Dishonor of notes receivable, 391
Disposals, of plant assets, 437–439
Dividends, 549–556
  cash dividends, 549–551
  cumulative, 552
  debit and credit procedures and, 103
  guarantee of, 552
  payment of, 98, 116
  on preferred stocks, 553
  reporting of, 550–551
  statement of cash flows and, 592
  stock dividends, 553–554
  stock investments between 20% and 50% and, H-6
  stock investments of less than 20% and, H-5
Dividends in arrears, 552
Dividend record, in measuring corporate performance, 560–561
Documentation procedures, 322–323, 427
Dollar-value last-in, first-out, 273n.1
Double-declining-balance method, 433, 450
Double-entry system, 101–102
Double taxation, of corporate income, 540
Down payments, leasing and, 428
Drawing account, for sole proprietorships, L-2
Dual posting, J-16
Duties, segregation of, 321–322

E

Earnings, quality of, 172–173, 652–654
Earnings management, 172, 436
Earnings performance, in measuring corporate performance, 561–562
Earnings per share (EPS), 53, 662, 675
Economic downturns, debt risks with, 497
Economic entity assumption, 61
Effective-interest amortization method, 504–507
Electronic data processing (EDP) systems, 92
Electronic funds transfers (EFTs), 333, 338
Employees-
  background checks of, 325
  bonding of, 325
  hiring of, 98
  requiring vacations for, 325
  rotating duties of, 325
Employee earnings record, I-5–I-8
Employee safety, 1178
Employee salaries, payment of cash for, 116
Employer payroll taxes, I-8–I-10
Ending inventory-
  direct materials budget and, 1024
  production requirements and, 1023
Ending units in process, 802

Ending work in process inventory, 713
Enterprise resource planning (ERP) systems, 718
Equal annual cash flows, net present value and, 1172–1173
Equal Employment Opportunity Act, 1120
Equipment, 426–427
  depreciation of, 429
  purchase of, 112
  repair, retain, or replace decisions for, 987–988
  on statement of cash flows (direct method), 617
  on statement of cash flows (indirect method), 603
Equity method, for stock investments between 20% and 50%, H-5, H-7
Equivalents, cash, 340–341
Equivalent units of production-
  defined, 796
  FIFO method, 806–812
  for production cost report, 800–801
  weighted average method, 796–798
Errors, 119
  bank, 335–337
  behavioral decision-making, 987
  inventory, 290–291
Estimated uncollectables, 380
Ethics-
  appearance of liquidity, 55
  bad debt expense, 384
  bonuses, I-2
  in business activities, 719
  cash flow from operations, 603
  changes in accounting principles, 651–652
  completion percentages, 797
  convenient overstatement, 110
  depreciation, 430
  earnings management, 230
  economic entity assumption, 61
  employee safety, 1178
  errors and irregularities, 119
  falsifying inventory, 269, 270
  in financial reporting, 7–8
  financial restatements, 341
  fraudulent documents, 107
  improper adjusting entries, 164
  income statements, 12
  inflating corporate income figures, 540
  lease accounting, 499
  make-or-buy decisions, 982
  manipulating net income, 272
  occupational fraud, 332
  overstating bond investment value, H-10
  partnership agreements, K-5
  in partnership liquidations, K-10
  petty cash funds, 331, 347
  quality of financial reporting, 224
  quality of reported net income, 592
  reporting liabilities, 495
  reporting receivables, 376
  solving ethical dilemmas, 7
  standards and, 1121
  telecommunications service, 716
  treasury stock purchases, 548
  unrealistic budgeting, 1019
Euronext, 543
Excess capacity, transfer pricing and, M-12
Exclusive right, 49
Expenses, 10
  accrued, adjusting entries for, 164–167
  debit and credit procedures and, 104
  on income statements, 227
  payroll, I-7
  in sole proprietorships, L-2
  stockholders' equity and, 96
Expense recognition principle, in accrual accounting, 152–153
External users, of financial information, 6

F

Face value-
  of bonds, 486, 489
  of notes receivable, 389
Facility-level activities, 846
Factoring, 385–387
Factory labor costs-
  assigning, to work in process, 755–757
  cost accumulation and, 751
  in process cost system, 794
Factory overhead, 709
Fair Labor Standards Act, 1120
Fair value-
  depreciation and, 429
  in partnerships, K-5
  of securities, H-7–H-9
Fair value adjustment, H-8–H-9
Fair value per share, 554
Fair value principle, 61
Faithful representation, 60
Favorable variances, 1126
Federal Insurance Contribution Act (FICA), 483n.1, 485, I-3
Federal Trade Commission, 6
Federal unemployment taxes, I-8
Fees, I-2
FICA taxes, I-3–I-4, I-8
Finance directors, 5
Financial accounting, managerial accounting compared to, 704, 705
Financial Accounting Standards Board (FASB), 59, 390
Financial analysis, 648–676
  horizontal analysis in, 655–657, 659
  quality of earnings in, 652–654
  ratio analysis in, 660–664, 666–676
  sustainability of income in, 648–652
  vertical analysis in, 657–659
Financial budgets, 1019–1020, 1030–1035. *See also* Budgeting
  budgeted balance sheet, 1033–1034
  cash budget, 1030–1035
Financial calculators-
  auto loans, G-15
  compounding periods, G-15
  mortgage loans, G-16
  plus and minus signs, G-14
  present value of annuity, G-15
  present value of single sum, G-14–G-15
  rounding, G-15
  time value of money problems, G-13–G-16
Financial information-
  decision-making process and, 976
  external users of, 6
  internal users of, 5
  usefulness of, 59–60
Financial pressure, fraud and, 318
Financial ratio fraud, 659
Financial reporting, 58–62
  assumptions in, 60–61
  cost constraint for, 62
  ethics in, 7–8
  fair value principle in, 61
  full disclosure principle in, 62
  historical cost principle in, 61

Financial reporting (*continued*)
measurement principles in, 61
qualities of useful information, 59–60
standard-setting environment and, 58–59
Financial statements, 11–17
in annual reports, A-1–A-5
balance sheet, 13–14
classified balance sheet, 46–51, 53–56
consolidated, *see* Consolidated financial statements
depreciation on, 159–160
income statement, 11–12, 52–53
interrelationships of, 15–16
inventory error effects on, 289–291
for manufacturers, 712–716
notes to, 18
prepared from adjusted trial balance, 171–172
ratio analysis and, 51–58
receivables on, 391–392
retained earnings statement, 12–13
statement of cash flows, 14, 57
Financing activities, 120
cash flows and, 14
cash flows from, 592
corporations and, 9
primary types of, 120
on statement of cash flows (direct method), 617–618
on statement of cash flows (indirect method), 603–604
Finished goods, assigning costs to, 760–761
Finished goods inventory, 268
First-in, first-out (FIFO) method, 274–275, 287–288, 652
computing equivalent units under, 806–812
weighted-average method and, 811–812
Fiscal year, 60
Fixed assets, 9. *See also* Plant assets
Fixed costs-
in cost behavior analysis, 885
in cost-volume-profit analysis, 891
Fixed manufacturing costs, 1068
Fixed selling and administrative expenses, 1068
Flexible budgets, 1069–1076
case study, 1072–1074
development of, 1072
Flexible budgets reports, 1074–1075
Flexible manufacturing, 1080
Flow of costs, for merchandising company, 217–219
FOB destination, 221
FOB shipping point, 221
Footing, journal, J-10
Form 10-K, A-1
Form W-2 (Wage and Tax Statement), I-10
Franchises, 442
Fraud, 318. *See also* Internal controls
altered inventory figures and, 271
and bank reconciliation, 335
documentation procedures and, 323, 427
human resource controls and, 225, 326, 484–485
independent internal verification and, 325, 377, 427, 484–485, 543, 602, 659
internal control systems and, 318–319
occupational, 332
physical controls and, 323
responsibility establishment and, 320
Sarbanes-Oxley Act and, 318–319
segregation of duties and, 321–322, 377
stealing merchandise, 225
susceptibility of cash to, 327
Fraud triangle, 318
Free cash flow, 57
as solvency ratio, 661, 671–672
statement of cash flows and, 609–611
Free on board (FOB), 221
Freight costs-
incurred by buyer, 221
incurred by seller, 221
in periodic inventory system, 240
in perpetual inventory system, 221
Fringe benefits, I-8
Full costing, *see* Absorption costing
Full-cost pricing, M-6, M-15
Full disclosure principle, 62, 594
Fund availability, capital budgeting decisions and, 1169
Future value-
of an annuity, G-4–G-7
of a single amount, G-3–G-4

G

Gain-
consolidated statement of comprehensive gains and losses, F-2
realized and unrealized, H-11–H-12
on sale of plant assets, 437–438
General journal, 107
posting to, J-5
showing adjusting entries, 168
special journals' effects on, J-16
use of special journals and, J-4
General ledger, 109
after adjustments, 169
subsidiary ledgers' relationship to, J-2–J-3
Generally accepted accounting principles (GAAP), 11, 42
adjusting entries, 212–213
cash-basis accounting, 154
classified balance sheet format, 87–88
financial statement analysis, 699–700
fraud, internal control, and cash, 371–372
income statement presentation, 699–700
inventories, 314
liabilities, 533–544
long-lived assets, 475–476
merchandising, 264–265
pro forma income, 652–653
receivables, 419–420
recording process, 148–149
sale of receivables, 385
standard-setting environment and, 58–59
statement of cash flows, 643–644
stockholders' equity, 587–588
General partners, K-3
Globalization, M-15
Going concern assumption, 61
Goods in transit, 270
Goodwill, 49, 442
Government regulations, for corporations, 540
Government units, budgeting and, 1037

Graphic presentation-
of break-even analysis, 898–899
of target net income, 900–901
Green bonds, 494
Green marketing, 237
Gross earnings, I-2
Gross margin, 229. *See also* Gross profit
Gross profit, on multi-step income statement, 228, 229
Gross profit rate, 234–235, 238
expressed as percentage, 234
industry competitiveness and, 674–675
as profitability ratio, 662
Growth phase, corporate life cycle and, 607–608

H

Hacktivists, J-17
Held-to-maturity securities, H-7
High-low method, 888–891
High-volume businesses, profit margin and, 673
Hiring new employees, 98
Historical cost principle, 61, 424
Honor of notes receivable, 390
Horizontal analysis, 655–657, 659
Human behavior, budgeting and, 1018–1019
Human element, internal controls and, 327
Human resource controls, 325–326
employee hirings and, 484–485
fraud and, 225, 326, 484–485
Hurdle rate, 1174

I

Ideal standards, normal standards vs., 1121
Idle cash, 343
Impairments of plant assets, 436
Improperly capitalized expenditures, 424–425
Improper recognition, quality of earnings and, 653
Incentives, creating, 719
Income and loss ratio, K-6
Income from operations, 228, 230
Income measurement process, for merchandising company, 216
Income ratio, K-6
Income statements, 11–12
budgeted, 1028–1030
comprehensive, 231–232
consolidated, B-1, C-2, E-1, F-1
cost flow methods and, 277–278
cost of goods sold under periodic system, 233–234
cost-volume-profit, 892–895
cost-volume-profit analysis and, 924
format for, 228
gross profit on, 228
horizontal analysis of, 656–657
income from operations on, 228
inventory errors and, 289–290
for manufacturer, 712–714
multiple-step income statements, 228–231
net income on, 11–12, 228, 229
nonoperating activities on, 230
ratio analysis for, 52–53
revenues and expenses on, 227
showing variances on, 1134–1135
single-step, 227–228
sustainable income information on, 648
vertical analysis and, 658
Income taxes, 10, I-4–I-5
cash payments for, 616
depreciation and, 434
on statement of cash flows, 601
Income taxes payable, 10
Incremental analysis, 976–991
for accepting orders at special prices, 979–980
activity-based costing and, 978–979
for eliminating unprofitable segment or product decisions, 988–990
key cost concepts in, 977
for make-or-buy decisions, 981–983
in management decision-making, 976–979
opportunity costs and, 982
qualitative factors in, 978
for repair, retain, or replace equipment decisions, 987–988
for sell vs. process further decisions, 983–986
types of, 979
Independent contractors, I-2
Independent internal verification-
fraud and, 271, 377, 427, 484–485, 543, 602, 659
as internal control, 324–325
Indirect fixed costs, profit centers and, 1084
Indirect manufacturing costs, 709
Indirect materials, 710
Indirect method (statement of cash flows), 595–606
depreciation expense in, 598–599
investing and financing activities in, 603–604
loss on disposal of plant assets, 599
net change in cash in, 604–605
net income to net cash conversions, 598
operating activities in, 598–603
Industries-
gross profit rate by, 235
industry-average comparisons, 51, 654
profit margins by, 235
Inflation, cost flow methods and, 278
Information security, J-17
Insiders, hacking by, J-17
Institute of Management Accountants (IMA), 719
Insurance, adjusting entries for, 158
Insurance policies, 97, 114
Intangible assets, 439–443
accounting for, 440
on classified balance sheet, 48–49
copyrights, 441
franchises, 442
goodwill, 442
patents, 440
research and development costs, 441
trademarks and trade names, 441
types of, 49
Intangible benefits, in capital budgeting, 1176–1178
Intent to convert, as investment criterion, H-10
Intercompany comparative analysis, 654, 658
Intercompany comparison, 51
Interest, G-1–G-3
accrued, 165–166

Interest (*continued*)
adjusting entries for, 165–166
on bonds, 486, 487, 489
on building costs, 426
cash payments for, 616
compound, G-2–G-3
expense, 10
interest-bearing notes, 390
interest rate, G-2
on notes receivable, 388
in partnerships, K-8–K-9
passing up discount and, 223
payable, 10
recording bond interest, H-3
simple, G-2
Interest expense, 10
Interest payable, 10
Interest rate, G-2
Interest revenue, 10
Internal auditors, 325
Internal audit staff, 707
Internal controls, 318–346. *See also individual controls*
for bank accounts, 333–340
for cash, 327–332, 340–347. *See also* Cash controls
components of, 319
defined, 319
documentation procedures, 322–323
fraud and, 318–319. *See also* Fraud
human resource controls, 325–326
independent internal verification, 324–325
limitations of, 326–327
for payroll, I-10–I-11
physical controls, 323–324
principles of control activities, 320–326
responsibility establishment, 320
segregation of duties, 321–322
Internal rate of return (IRR), 1171, 1182–1184
Internal Revenue Service, 6
Internal users, of financial information, 5
Internal verification, independent, *see* Independent internal verification
International Accounting Standards Board (IASB), 59, 390
International Financial Reporting Standards (IFRS), 11, 42–43
adjusting entries, 212–213
classified balance sheet format, 87–88
financial statement analysis, 699–700
fraud, internal control, and cash, 371–372
income statement presentation, 699–700
inventories, 314
liabilities, 533–544
long-lived assets, 475–476
merchandising, 264–265
receivables, 419–420
recording process, 148–149
standard-setting environment and, 59
statement of cash flows, 643–644
stockholders' equity, 587–588
Internet business, 928
Intracompany comparisons, 51, 654
Introductory phase, corporate life cycle and, 607
Inventoriable costs, 710
Inventory, 10
analysis of, 283–284
cash management and levels of, 343
classifying, 268–269
consigned goods, 270–271
cost flow methods for, 271–281
determining ownership of goods, 270–271
determining quantities, 269–271
errors in, 289–291
falsifying, 269, 270
financial statement presentation of, 281
goods in transit, 270
inventory turnover, 283–286
just-in-time, 268–269
LIFO reserve adjustments, 284–285
lower-of-cost-or-market valuation, 281–282
in manufacturing companies, 268
perpetual inventory systems, 287–289
on statement of cash flows, 600
taking physical inventory, 269
Inventory analysis, 283–284
Inventory costing. *See also* Cost flow methods
absorption costing for, 946–947
change in methods and, 652
quality of earnings and methods of, 652
Inventory errors-
balance sheet effects of, 290–291
income statement effects of, 289–290
Inventory turnover, 283–286, 661, 669
Investing activities, 9, 10, 120
cash flows and, 14
on statement of cash flows (direct method), 617–618
on statement of cash flows (indirect method), 603–604
Investment(s), 9
available-for-sale securities, H-7
balance sheet presentation and, H-10–H-11
cash flows and, 592
corporations' reasons for investing, H-1–H-2
held-to-maturity securities, H-7
intent to convert and, H-10
nonoperating items related to, H-11
in partnerships, K-15–K-18
presentation of realized and unrealized gain or loss, H-11–H-12
readily marketable, H-10
security categories, H-7
statement of cash flows presentation, H-12
trading securities, H-7–H-9
valuing and reporting of, H-7–H-12
Investment centers-
responsibility accounting for, 1082, 1085–1088
responsibility reporting and, 1082
return on investment for, 1086–1088
Investment portfolios, H-4
Irregularities, 119
Item controllability, 1078–1079

J

Job cost sheet, 752. *See also* Manufacturing costs assignment

Job order costing, 748–768
accumulating manufacturing costs in, 750–752
advantages and disadvantages of, 764–765
assigning costs to cost of goods sold, 761
assigning costs to finished goods, 760–761
assigning costs to work in process, 752–760
cost accounting systems, 748
cost flows in, 749–750, 761–762
flow of documents and, 762
job order cost system, 748–749
process costing compared to, 748, 791–792
for service companies, 763–764
standard costs in, 1139–1141
under- or overapplied manufacturing overhead, 765–767
Joint costs, 985
Joint products, 984, 985
Journal(s), 106–108
general, *see* General journal
special, *see* Special journals
Journalizing transactions, 106–109, 111–118, J-16
Just-in-time (JIT) inventory, 268–269, 283, 718
Just-in-time (JIT) processing, 855–856

K
Korean discount, 59

L
Labor price variance, 1130, 1131
Labor quantity variance, 1130, 1131
Labor unions, 6
Land-
costs related to, 425
depreciation and, 429
on statement of cash flows (direct method), 617
on statement of cash flows (indirect method), 603
Land improvements, 425, 429
Large stock dividends, 554
Last-in, first-out (LIFO) method, 275–276, 279–280, 288, 652
Last in still here (LISH) assumption, 274
Lean manufacturing, 718
Leasing, 428, 499
Ledger(s), 106, 109
general, *see* General ledger
posting to, 109–118
subsidiary, *see* Subsidiary ledgers
Ledger accounts, 1141
Legal capital, 543
Legal liability-
organizational forms and, 4
partnerships and, K-2
Leveraging, 673
Liability(-ies), 480–501. *See also* Bonds
analysis of, 496–500
balance sheet presentation of, 13, 495
bank line of credit, 497
bonds, 485–494
cash management and, 343
contingencies and, 498–499
credit balances and, 102
current, 50, 480–485, 601
debt covenants, 500
debt masking and, 498
defined, 9
leasing and, 428, 499
liquidity ratios for, 496–497
off-balance-sheet financing, 499
payroll, I-7
solvency ratios and, 497–498
times interest earned and, 497
Liability (legal), *see* Legal liability
Licenses, for corporations, 541
LIFO conformity rule, 279
LIFO reserve, 284–285
Limited liability companies (LLCs), 4, 541, K-3
Limited liability of corporate stockholders, 538
Limited liability partnerships (LLPs), 541, K-3
Limited life, of intangible assets, 440
Limited partnerships (Ltd., LP), 541, K-3
Limited resources-
capital investments and, 1179
determining sales mix with, 933–935
Linear costs, 886–887
Line of credit, liabilities and, 497
Line positions, 707
Liquidation-
defined, K-10
of partnerships, K-10–K-14
Liquidation preference, preferred stocks and, 552
Liquid investments, 343
Liquidity-
defined, 53
excessive, 55
of receivables and, 394–395
Liquidity ratios, 52–55, 660–661, 667–670
accounts receivable turnover, 395–396, 668–669
average collection period, 395, 669
current ratio, 54–55, 668
days in inventory, 283, 669–670
inventory turnover, 283, 669
for liabilities, 496–497
working capital, 54
London Stock Exchange, 543
Long-lived assets, 424–451
analysis of, 445–447
depreciation of plant assets, 429–436
disposal of plant assets, 437–439
expenditures for plant assets, 424–429
financial statement presentation of, 443–444
intangible assets, 439–443
plant assets, 424–439
Long-range planning, budgeting and, 1019
Long-term debt, current maturities of, 482
Long-term investments-
balance sheet presentation of, H-11
classification as, H-10
on classified balance sheet, 48
Long-term liabilities, 485. *See also* Bonds
on classified balance sheet, 50
defined, 480
Long-term notes, present value of, G-11–G-13
Long-term notes payable, 507–508
Long-term notes receivable, 390
Loss-
consolidated statement of comprehensive gains and losses, F-2
on disposal of plant assets, 616
net, 10, K-2, K-6–K-10, L-2
profit and loss (P&L) ratio, K-6

Loss- (*continued*)
realized, H-11–H-12
on sale of plant assets, 437
Lower-of-cost-or-market (LCM), 281–282
Low-volume businesses, profit margin and, 673

M
Machine hours, 758, 836
Machine time used, 794
Madoff's ponzi scheme, 339
Mail receipts, 330
Major expenditures, cash management and, 343
Make or buy decisions, 981–983
Management, corporate, 539–540
Management acceptance, effective budgeting and, 1017
Management by exception, 1078–1079
Management decision making-
activity-based costing and, 848–849
process of, 976–979. *See also* Incremental analysis
Management discussion and analysis (MD&A), 18
Management functions, 704–705
Managerial accounting, 704–723
balanced scorecard and, 718–719
business ethics and, 719
corporate social responsibility and, 720–721
financial accounting compared to, 704, 705
financial statements for manufacturers, 712–716
management functions and, 704–705
manufacturing cost concepts in, 708–712
organizational structure and, 706–707
trends in, 716–721
value chain focus in, 717–718
Manufacturing, employment in, 709
Manufacturing cost concepts, 708–712
direct labor, 709
direct materials, 708
fixed costs, 1068
manufacturing overhead, 708, 709
product vs. period costs, 710
Manufacturing costs accumulation, 749–752
factory labor costs, 751
manufacturing overhead costs, 751
raw material costs, 750–751
Manufacturing costs assignment, 749
factory labor costs, 755–757, 794
in job order costing, 752–760
manufacturing overhead costs, 757–760, 794
materials costs, 793–794
in process costing, 793–795
raw materials costs and, 753–755
transfer to cost of goods sold, 795
transfer to finished goods, 795
transfer to next department, 795
Manufacturing costs incurred in prior period, 713
Manufacturing costs in financial statements, 712–716
balance sheets, 714–715
cost of goods manufactured, 713–716
cost of goods manufactured schedule, 714
income statements, 712–714
Manufacturing overhead, 708, 709
assigning, to work in process, 757–760, 794
causes of variances, 1132–1133
cost accumulation and, 751
in process cost system, 794
standards for, 1123–1124
under- or overapplied, 765–767
Manufacturing overhead budgets, 1027–1028
Manufacturing overhead cost per unit, 1124
Manufacturing overhead variances, 1131–1133
Manufacturing processes, 790
Margin (income) measure, return on investment and, 1087
Margin of safety, 901–902, 926
Margin of safety ratio, 901, 937
Marketable securities, H-10
Market-based transfer price, M-14–M-15
Marketing expenses, 10
Marketing managers, 5
Marketing return on investment, 445
Market interest rates, for bonds, 486, 487, 490
Market price-
of bonds, 486–488
of stock, 543
Mark-to-market accounting, H-8
Markup, M-3, M-17
Master budgets, 1019–1020. *See also* Budgeting
Matching principle, 152. *See also* Expense recognition principle
Materials-
equivalent units for, 809
in process cost system, 793–794
Materiality, 60, 1078
Material loading charge, M-7–M-9
Materials price variance, 1127, 1128
Materials quantity variance, 1127, 1129
Materials requisition slips, 753
Matrix for direct labor variances, 1131
Matrix for direct materials variances, 1128
Maturity date-
for bonds, 486
for notes receivable, 388
redeeming bonds at, 493
Maturity phase, corporate life cycle and, 608
Maturity value, for interest-bearing notes, 390
Measurement principles, financial reporting and, 61
Medicare tax, I-3–I-4
Merchandise inventory, 268. *See also* Inventory
Merchandise purchases-
discounts, 222–223
freight costs and, 221
in periodic inventory system, 239
in perpetual inventory systems, 219–223
returns and allowances, 221–222
transaction summary, 223
Merchandise purchases budget, 1038

Merchandise sales, 224–227
discounts, 226–227
in periodic inventory system, 240–241
in perpetual inventory systems, 224–227
returns and allowances, 225–226
Merchandising operations, 216–239
budgeting for, 1035–1036
comprehensive income statements for, 231–232
flow of costs in, 217–219
gross profit rate for, 234–235, 238
income measurement process for, 216
multiple-step income statements for, 228–231
operating cycles for, 216–217, 342
periodic inventory system and, 218, 233–234, 239–241
perpetual inventory system and, 217–227
profit margin for, 235–236, 238
Merchandising profit, 229
Minimum rate of return, 1091
Minimum transfer price, M-11
Mixed costs, in cost behavior analysis, 888–891
Modified accelerated cost recovery system (MACRS), 434
Monetary unit assumption, 61
Money market funds, 341
Monthly responsibility reports, 1085
Mortgage, 507
Mortgage loans, G-16
Mortgage notes payable, 507
Moving-average method, 289
Moving decisions, 990
Multiple-product case, sell or process further and, 984–986
Multiple-step income statements, 228–231
Mutual agency, K-2
Mutually exclusive projects, profitability index for, 1178–1180

N

Nasdaq stock market, 543
National credit card sales, 385–386
Nation-states, hacking by, J-17
Negative cash, 608
Negotiated transfer prices, M-10–M-13
Net 30, 222
Net cash provided by operating activities, 57, 592
Net change in cash-
direct method, 618
indirect method, 604–605
Net income-
on income statements, 11, 228, 229
manipulating, 272
to net cash conversions, 598
net cash provided (used) by operating activities vs., 592
in partnerships, K-2, K-6–K-10
per share, 675
in sole proprietorships, L-2
Net loss, 10
in partnerships, K-2, K-6–K-10
retained earnings and, 557
in sole proprietorships, L-2
Net pay, I-5
Net present value (NPV), 1171
Net present value (NPV) method, 1171–1176
discount rate choice for, 1174
for equal annual cash flows, 1172–1173
mutually exclusive projects and, 1178–1180
simplifying assumptions in, 1175
for unequal annual cash flows, 1173
Net (cash) realizable value, 380, 389
Net sales-
horizontal analysis of, 655
on multi-step income statement, 229
New employee hiring, 115
New York Stock Exchange, 543
No capital deficiency, partnership liquidation and, K-11–K-12
No excess capacity, transfer pricing and, M-11
Nominal accounts, 175
Noncash activities, statement of cash flows and, 593–594
Noncash current assets, on statement of cash flows, 599–601
Noncontrollable costs, responsibility accounting and, 1079
Nonfinancial information, decision-making process and, 976
Nonfinancial measures, various industries and, 1135
Nonlinear cost behavior, 886
Nonmanufacturing companies, budgeting for, 1035–1038
Nonoperating items-
on multi-step income statements, 230–231
related to investments, H-11
Non-recurring charges, 649
Non-value-added activities, 847
No-par stock, 544–546
Normal balances, 102
Normal capacity, 1124
Normal standards, ideal standards vs., 1121
Note issued in exchange for cash, 94–95
Notes payable, 9
accounting for, 480–481
issuance of, 112
long-term, 507–508
Notes receivable, 376, 387–391
accrual of interest receivable, 390
computing interest on, 388
determining maturity date of, 388
dishonor of, 391
disposing of, 389–391
honor of, 390
promissory notes, 387
recognizing, 388–389
valuing, 389
Notes to financial statements, 18
Not-for-profit organization budgeting, 1037
NSF (not sufficient funds) checks, 334, 338

O

Obligations, ability to meet, 592
Obsolescence-
depreciation and, 430
leasing and, 428
Occupational fraud, 332
Off-balance-sheet financing, 499
Office equipment, purchased for cash, 95
One-time items, 172, 173
Open Standards Benchmarking Collaborative, 1122
Operating activities, 9–10, 120
cash flows and, 14, 592–593

Operating activities (*continued*)
on statement of cash flows (direct method), 613–616
on statement of cash flows (indirect method), 598–603
Operating assets, reducing, 1088
Operating asset valuation, return on investment and, 1087
Operating budgets, 1019–1020. *See also* Budgeting
budgeted income statement, 1028–1030
direct labor budget, 1026–1027
direct materials budget, 1023–1025
manufacturing overhead budget, 1027–1028
sales budget, 1021–1022, 1025
selling and administrative expense budget, 1028
Operating cycles, 46
for merchandising company, 216–217
for service company, 216, 217
temporary investments and, H-2
Operating expenses-
cash payments for, 615
improper capitalization of, 653
on multi-step income statement, 229
Operating leases, 499
Operating leverage, cost structure and, 935–939
Operations-
consolidated statements of, A-2, D-2
income from, 228
Operations costing, 803–804
Opportunity, for fraud, 318
Opportunity costs, 977, 982, M-11
Orders accepted at special prices, 979–980
Ordinary repairs, 427
Organizational structure, 706–707, 1016
Organization charts, 539–540, 706
Organized crime, hacking by, J-17
Other expenses and losses, 230
Other receivables, 376
Other revenues and gains, 230
Outsourcing, transfer pricing and, M-15
Outstanding checks, 335–337
Overapplied manufacturing overhead, 765–767
Overhead-
in activity-based costing, 836, 840–842, 1124. *See also* Activity-based costing (ABC)
allocated to products, 841–842
allocation of, 765
assigned to cost pools, 840
computing accurate unit costs and, 836–837
manufacturing. *see* Manufacturing overhead
Overhead controllable variances, 1132, 1142–1143
Overhead rate-
activity-based, 841
predetermined, 757, 836
standard predetermined, 1123
Overhead volume variances, 1132, 1143
Overstated cash/assets, 602
Over-the-counter receipts, 328–330
Owner's capital account, L-2
Owner's equity, in sole proprietorships, L-2–L-3
Owner's equity statement, L-3–L-4
Ownership of goods, determining, 270–271
Ownership rights, of corporations, 538–539

P

Paid-in capital, 544
stock dividends and, 553
stockholders' equity and, 544, 545
stock splits and, 555
Paper profit, 278
Parent company, H-6
Participative budgeting, 1018–1019
Partners' capital statement, K-9
Partnerships, 4, K-1–K-20
admission of a partner, K-14–K-18
advantages and disadvantages of, K-3–K-4
capital deficiency and, K-12–K-14
characteristics of, K-2
dissolution of, K-2, K-14
dividing net income or net loss in, K-6–K-10
financial statements of, K-9–K-10
formation of, K-5–K-6
limited liability companies, K-3
limited liability partnerships, K-3
limited partnerships, K-3
liquidation of, K-10–K-14
no capital deficiency and, K-11–K-12
partnership agreements, K-5
salaries, interest, and remainder on a fixed ratio, K-8–K-9
withdrawal of a partner, K-18–K-20
Partnership agreement, K-5
Partnership dissolution, K-2, K-14
Par value per share, 554
Par value stock, 543–544
Patents, 440
Payment date, for cash dividends, 550
Payment period, for receivables, 393
Payout ratio, 560–561, 662, 676
Payroll, 483–485, I-1
Payroll accounting, I-1–I-11
determining payroll, I-2–I-5
employer payroll taxes, I-8–I-10
gross earnings and, I-2
internal control for, I-10–I-11
maintaining records, I-5–I-7
net pay and, I-5
payroll deductions and, I-2–I-5
recording payroll, I-5–I-8
recording payroll payment, I-7–I-8
Payroll deductions, I-2–I-5
FICA taxes, I-3–I-4
income taxes, I-4–I-5
voluntarily authorized withholdings, I-5
Payroll recording, I-5–I-8
Payroll registers, I-6–I-8
Payroll taxes, I-8–I-10
FICA, I-8
filing and remitting, I-9–I-10
recording, I-9
unemployment, I-8–I-9
Payroll tax expense, I-8
Payroll taxes payable, 483–485
Pension portfolios, 652
Percentage, gross profit rate as, 234
Percentage of base amount, 657
Percentage of net sales, 658
Percentage-of-receivables basis, 382

Performance evaluations, 1085–1089
behavioral principles and, 1079
controllability of item and, 1078–1079
management by exception and, 1078–1079
materiality and, 1078
reporting principles and, 1079
Performance standards, 849
Period costs, 710
Periodic inventory system, 218, 233–234, 710
cost flow assumptions in, 273
cost of goods sold under, 233–234
defined, 218
freight costs in, 240
perpetual inventory system compared to, 233, 241
purchase discounts in, 241
purchase returns and allowances in, 240
recording merchandise transactions in, 239–241
sales discounts and, 241
sales returns and allowances and, 240
Periodicity assumption, 61, 152
Permanent accounts, 175
Perpetual inventory system, 217–227, J-5
average-cost and, 289
cost accounting systems and, 748
cost flow assumptions in, 273
cost flow methods in, 287–289
first-in, first-out, 287–288
last-in, first-out, 288
periodic system compared to, 233, 241
recording purchases under, 219–223
recording sales under, 224–227
Petty cash funds, 347–348
establishment of, 347
internal controls and, 331
making payments from, 347
replenishment of, 348
Phantom profit, 278
Physical controls, 225, 323–324
Physical custody, segregating recordkeeping from, 322
Physical inventory, 269
Physical unit flow, computing, 800, 808–809
Planning, as management function, 705
Plant assets, 48, 424–439. *See also* Depreciation
accounting for, 424–429
additions and improvements, 427
analyzing, 444–447
asset turnover, 445–446
buildings, 426
buying or leasing, 428
capital expenditures and, 427
cash equivalent price for, 425
on classified balance sheet, 48
depreciation methods for, 429–436
determining cost of, 424–427
disposal of, 437–439
earnings management and, 436
equipment, 426–427
expenditures during useful life, 427
expense capitalization, 424–425
gain on sale of, 437–438
historical cost principle, 424
impairments of, 436
land, 425
land improvements, 425
loss on disposal of, 599, 616
loss on sale of, 437, 438
ordinary repairs and, 427
profit margin for, 446–447
retirement of, 438
return on assets, 444–445
sale of, 437–438
Ponzi schemes, 339
Post-audit, of investment projects, 1180–1181
Post-closing trial balance, 176–177, L-7
Post-dated checks, 340
Posting to ledger, 109–118
chart of accounts and, 109–110
illustration of, 111–118
posting procedure, 110
Predetermined overhead rate, 757, 836, 1123
Predictive value, 60
Preferred stock, 546
cumulative dividends on, 552
dividend preferences for, 552–553
liquidation preference and, 552
Premiums (bonds), 489–490
effective-interest amortization method, 506–507
issuing bonds at, 492–493
straight-line amortization method, 503–504
Prenumbered documents, 322
Prepaid expenses, 156
adjusting entries for, 156–160
depreciation, 158–160
insurance, 158
on statement of cash flows, 600–601
supplies, 157–158
Present value, G-7
of an annuity, G-9–G-11, G-15
of equal net annual cash flows, 1172–1173
of long-term note or bond, G-11–G-13
of single amount, G-7–G-9
of single sum, G-14–G-15
of unequal annual cash flows, 1173
Present value variables, G-7
Price-earnings (P-E) ratio, 660, 662, 675–676
Price takers, M-2
Pricing, M-1–M-19
absorption-cost pricing, M-16–M-17
cost-plus pricing, M-3–M-6
pricing factors, M-2
target costing, M-2–M-3
time-and-material, M-7–M-9
transfer pricing, M-9–M-15
variable-cost pricing, M-6–M-7, M-17–M-19
Principal-
bonds and, 487
interest rate and, G-1, G-2
Process costing, 790–806
cost-benefit trade-offs with, 803
cost flow in, 793
equivalent units computation (FIFO method), 806–812
equivalent units computation (weighted-average method), 796–798
job order costing compared to, 748, 791–792
manufacturing costs assignment in, 793–795
production cost reports, 799–804
reasons for, 748
for service companies, 791
uses of, 790
Products, unprofitable, 988–990
Product costs, 710, 711

Product costing, 716–717
Production budget, 1022–1023, 1025
Production cost reports, 799–804
  cost reconciliation schedules, 802, 804
  equivalent units of production computation, 800–801
  physical unit flow computation, 800
  preparing, 802–803, 811
  unit production costs, 801–802
Production department-
  labor variances and, 1130, 1131
  materials price variances and, 1129
Production requirements formula, 1022
Production supervisors, 5
Product-level activities, 846
Product life cycle, 607
Profitability evaluation-
  annual rate of return method, 1184–1185
  cash payback technique, 1170–1171
  discounted cash flow method, 1183
  gross profit rate, 234–235
  internal rate of return method, 1182–1184
  net present value method, 1171–1176
  profit margin, 235–236
Profitability index, 1181
  computing, 1179
  for mutually exclusive projects, 1178–1180
Profitability ratios, 52, 661–662, 667, 672–676
  asset turnover, 445–446, 662, 674
  earnings per share, 53, 662, 675
  gross profit rate, 234–235, 662, 674–675
  payout ratio, 560–561, 662, 676
  price-earnings ratio, 660, 675–676
  profit margin, 235–236, 662, 673
  return on assets, 444–445, 662, 673
  return on common stockholders' equity, 561–562, 662, 672
Profit and loss (P&L) ratio, K-6
Profit centers-
  direct and indirect fixed costs and, 1084
  responsibility accounting for, 1083–1085
  responsibility reporting and, 1082
Profit margins, 235–236, 238
  plant assets and, 446–447
  as profitability ratio, 662, 673
Pro forma income, 652–653
Project relationships, capital budgeting decisions and, 1169
Project risk, capital budgeting decisions and, 1169
Promissory notes, 387
Property, plant, and equipment, 9. *See also* Plant assets
Property ownership, partnerships and, K-2
Property taxes payable, 10
Proration, of depreciation, 432
Public Company Accounting Oversight Board (PCAOB), 59
Pull approach, 856
Purchase discounts-
  paying interest and, 223
  in periodic inventory system, 241
  in perpetual inventory system, 222–223
Purchase invoices, 220
Purchase of an interest (in partnerships), K-15
Purchase returns and allowances, 221–222, 240
Purchases journal, J-11–J-13
  expanding of, J-12
  journalizing credit merchandise purchases, J-11–J-12
  posting of, J-12–J-13
Purchasing activities, internal controls and, 321
Purchasing department, materials price variances and, 1128
Purchasing on account, 97
Push approach, 855

Q

Qualitative factors, in decision making, 978
Quality of earnings, 652–654
  adjusted trial balance and, 172–173
  alternative accounting methods and, 652
  cost flow methods and, 280
  improper recognition and, 653
  price-earnings ratio and, 660
  pro forma income and, 652–653
Quality of earnings ratio, 237
Quarterly dividend rates, 549

R

Rating agencies, 662
Ratio, 51
Ratio analysis, 51–58, 660–664, 666–676
  classified balance sheet, 53–56
  comprehensive illustration of, 666–676
  income statement, 52–53
  liquidity ratios, 660–661, 667–670
  profitability ratios, 661–662, 667, 672–676
  solvency ratios, 661, 667, 670–672
  statement of cash flows, 57
Rationalization, fraud and, 318
Raw materials, 268, 710
Raw materials costs-
  assigning, to work in process, 753–755
  cost accumulation and, 750–751
  direct materials price standard and, 1122
  skyrocketing of, 1024
Readily marketable investments, H-10
Real accounts, 175
Realization, gain and loss on, K-10
Realized gain or loss, H-11–H-12
Reasonable assurance, internal controls and, 326–327
Receivables, 376–399
  accounts receivable, 376–387
  cash management and, 342
  financial statement presentation of, 391–392
  management of, 392–397
  notes receivable, 387–391
  types of, 376
Record date, for cash dividends, 550
Recording estimated uncollectables, 380
Recording transactions, 100–118
  debit and credit procedures, 101–104
  debit/credit rules, 105
  debits and credits, 101

illustration of, 111–118
journalizing, 106–109
posting to ledger, 109–118
stockholders' equity relationships, 104–105
T-accounts, 100–101
Recordkeeping, segregating physical custody and, 322
Recovery of uncollectable account, 381
Redemptions, bond, 493–494
Regular partnerships, K-3
Regulations, 1120
Regulatory agencies, 6
Related activities, segregation of, 321–322, 340
Relevance, information, 60
Relevant costs, in incremental analysis, 977, 988–990
Relevant range, 886–887
Remanufacturing, 798
Rent, 96–97, 114
Repair, equipment, 987–988
Replacement, equipment, 987–988
Reporting principles, performance evaluations and, 1079
Required rate of return, 1172, 1174
Research and analysis, effective budgeting and, 1016–1017
Research and development (R&D) costs, 441
Residual income, 1091–1092
Responsibility accounting, 1076–1089
competition vs. collaboration and, 1077
controllable vs. noncontrollable revenues and costs, 1078–1079
for cost centers, 1083
decentralization and, 1077
for investment centers, 1082, 1085–1088
performance evaluation principles, 1078–1080
for profit centers, 1083–1085
responsibility centers and, 1082–1085
responsibility reporting systems, 1080–1082
Responsibility centers, 1082–1085
cost centers, 1082, 1083
investment centers, 1082, 1085–1088
profit centers, 1082–1085
Responsibility establishment, internal controls and, 320
Responsibility reporting systems, 1080–1082, 1086–1087
Restricted cash, 341
Restructuring charges, 649
Retailers, 216
Retained earnings, 12, 557–558
cash dividends and, 549
common stock and, 544
in corporations, 544
debit and credit procedures and, 102
net losses and, 557
restrictions on, 558
in sole proprietorships, L-3–L-4
on statement of cash flows (direct method), 617
on statement of cash flows (indirect method), 604
stock dividends and, 553
stockholders' equity and, 50
stock splits and, 555
Retained earnings statement, 12–13
Retaining equipment, 987–988
Retirement of plant assets, 438
Returns-
in periodic inventory system, 240
in perpetual inventory system, 221, 225–226
purchase, 221–222
sales, 225–226, 240
Return on assets, 444–445, 662, 673
Return on common stockholders' equity, 561–562, 662, 672
Return on investment (ROI), 1091, M-4–M-5
balanced scorecard and, 1135
improving, 1087–1088
increasing controllable margin and, 1087
for investment centers, 1086–1088
margin (income) measure and, 1087
reduction of average operating assets and, 1088
residual income compared to, 1091–1092
valuation of operating assets and, 1087
Returns policy, 226
Revenue(s), 10
accrued, 163–164
adjusting entries for, 160–161, 163–164
debit and credit procedures and, 104
on income statements, 227
inflating, 173
stockholders' equity and, 96
unearned, 160–161
Revenue expenditures, 424
Revenue recognition principle, 152, 153
Revised depreciation, 435–436
Risk-
capital budgeting and, 1169, 1180
cybercrime and, J-17
Risk-free investments, 343

S

Safe cash payments schedule, K-12
Safety, employee, 1178
Salaries, I-1, I-2. *See also* Payroll accounting
accrued, 166–167
adjusting entries for, 166–167
in partnerships, K-8–K-9
payment of cash for, 98, 116
Sales-
internal controls and, 321
for merchandising operations, 216
on multi-step income statement, 229
in periodic inventory system, 255
in perpetual inventory systems, 226–227
of plant assets, 437–438
of receivables to a factor, 385
Sales budget, 1021–1022, 1025
Sales discounts, 226–227
Sales dollars, 896, 897
Sales forecasting, 1017, 1021
Sales invoices, 224
Sales journal, J-4–J-7
advantages of, J-7
journalizing credit sales, J-5
posting of, J-5–J-6
proving of, J-7
Sales mix, 929–935
break-even, 929–933
determining with limited resources, 933–935

Sales returns and allowances, 225–226, 240
Sales revenue, 10
Sales taxes payable, 10, 481
Sales units, 896
Salvage value, depreciation and, 430
Sarbanes-Oxley Act (SOX), 7, 99, 318–319, 326, 540, 719
Schedule of cash payments, K-12
S corporation, 541
Secured bonds, 486
Securities-
  available-for-sale, 650, H-7, H-9–H-10
  balance sheet presentation, H-10–H-11
  bonds, H-3
  categories of, H-7
  comprehensive income and, 650–651
  held-to-maturity, H-7
  realized and unrealized gain or loss, H-11–H-12
  statement of cash flows presentation, H-12
  stocks, H-4–H-7
  trading securities, 650, H-7–H-10
Securities and Exchange Commission (SEC), 6, 59, 498, 540
Segments-
  responsibility accounting and, 1077
  unprofitable, 988–990
Segregation of duties, 321–322, 377
Selling and administrative expense budget, 1028
Selling and administrative expenses, fixed, 1068
Selling expenses, 9
Sell or process further decisions, 983–986
  multiple-product case and, 984–986
  single-product case and, 983–986
Sensitivity analysis, capital investments and, 1180
Separate legal existence, of corporations, 538
Service companies-
  activity-based costing for, 850–853
  budgeting for, 1036–1037
  expected input and, 1037
  expected output and, 1037
  job order costing for, 763–764
  managerial accounting for, 716–717
  operating cycles for, 216, 217
  process costing for, 791
Services performed for cash, 96
Service revenues, 10, 764
Shareholders, 4
Short-term investments, balance sheet presentation of, H-10–H-11
Simple interest, G-2
Single-product case, sell or process further and, 984
Single-step income statement, 227–228
Skilled labor, 890
Small stock dividends, 554
Socially responsible business, 15
Social responsibility, 540, 720–721
Social Security taxes, 483n.1, 485, I-3–I-4
Sole proprietorships, 4, L-1–L-7
  closing the books for, L-4–L-7
  drawing account for, L-2
  financial statements for, L-3–L-5
  income summary account for, L-5
  owner's capital account in, L-2
  owner's equity in, L-2–L-3
  recording transactions of, L-3
Solvency, 55–56
Solvency ratios, 52, 55–56, 667, 670–672
  debt to assets ratio, 56, 661, 670–671
  debt to equity ratio, 671
  free cash flow, 57, 661, 671–672
  for liabilities, 497–498
  times interest earned, 497, 661, 671
Source document, recording process and, 106
Special journals, J-4–J-17
  cash payments journal, J-12–J-15
  cash receipts journal, J-7–J-11
  dual posting and, J-16
  effects on general journal, J-16
  purchases journal, J-11–J-13
  sales journal, J-4–J-7
  use of, J-4
Special prices, accepting orders at, 979–980
Specific identification method, 272
Split-off points, 985
Staff positions, 707
Stakeholders, in ethical dilemmas, 7
Standards, budgets and, 1121
Standard costs, 1120–1139. *See also* Variances
  case study of, 1122–1124
  cost controls and, 1124
  direct labor variances and, 1129–1131
  direct materials variances and, 1125–1129
  ideal vs. normal standards, 1121
  manufacturing overhead variances and, 1131–1133
  normal capacity and, 1124
  reporting variances, 1133–1138
  setting, 1121–1124
  total standard cost per unit, 1124
Standard cost accounting system, 1139–1141
  journal entries in, 1142–1141
  ledger accounts in, 1141
Standard hours allowed, 1132, 1142
Standard manufacturing overhead rates, 1124
Standard predetermined overhead rate, 1123
Standard-setting environment, 58–59
Stated rate, for bonds, 486
Stated value per share, 554
Statement of cash flows, 14, 592–611, A-5, F-5
  additional information for, 595
  classification of cash flows, 592–593
  comparative balance sheets and, 595
  consolidated, A-5, C-3, D-1, F-5
  corporate life cycle and, 607–608
  current income statement and, 595
  direct method for, 596, 611–618. *See also* Direct method

in evaluating a company, 607–611
format of, 594–595
free cash flow and, 609–611
indirect method for, 595–606. *See also* Indirect method
investments on, H-12
preparation of, 595–596
ratio analysis for, 57
significant noncash activities and, 593–594
T-account approach to, 618–620
usefulness of, 592
Statements of cash flows, consolidated, B-3, E-5
Statement of changes in equity, consolidated, F-4
Statement of comprehensive gains and losses, consolidated, F-2
Statement of earnings document, I-7
Statements of equity, consolidated, B-4
Statement of shareholders' equity, consolidated, A-4
Statement of shareholders' equity and redeemable noncontrolling interest, consolidated, E-4
Statement of stockholders' equity, consolidated, C-3
Statements of stockholders' equity, consolidated, B-4, C-3, D-3
State unemployment taxes, I-8–I-9
Static budgets, 1069–1071
Static budget reports, 1067–1069
Stock-
amounts received from issuing, 12
common, *see* Common stock
preferred, 546, 552–553
Stock certificates, 541–542
Stock dividends, 12, 553–554
preparing entries for, 565
stockholders' equity and, 554
stock splits differentiated from, 555
Stockholders, 4
claims of creditors vs., 9
as external users, 6
investment of cash by, 94, 111
limited liability of, 538
rights of, 541–542
Stockholders' equity, 538–564
accounting for common stock, 545–546
accounting for preferred stock, 546
accounting for treasury stock, 547–549
balance sheet presentation of, 13, 558–560
on classified balance sheet, 50
common stock and, 102–103
corporate capital, 544
corporate form of organization and, 538–541
debit and credit procedures for, 102–104
debt vs. equity decision and, 562–563
dividend record and, 560–561
dividends, 103, 549–556
earnings performance and, 561–562
financial statement presentation of, 558–560
investment transactions, 94–97
preferred stock, 546
reporting of, 104–105
retained earnings and, 103, 557–558
return on common stockholders' equity, 561–562
revenues and expenses and, 104
stock issue considerations and, 542–544
stock splits and, 555–556
Stock investments, H-4
accounting for, H-4–H-7
categories of, H-7
holdings between 20% and 50%, H-5–H-6
holdings of less than 20% and, H-4–H-5
holdings of more than 50% and, H-6–H-7
Stock issue considerations, 542–544
authorized stock, 543
direct and indirect issuance, 543
market price, 543
par and no-par value stocks, 543–544
Stock quotes, reading, 546
Stock splits, 555–556
Stock value considerations, 545–546
Straight-line amortization, 502–504
bond discount, 502–503
bond premium, 503–504
Straight-line depreciation, 431–432
Subsidiary (affiliated) company, H-6
Subsidiary ledgers, 752, J-1–J-3
advantages of, J-3
control account and, J-2
defined, J-1
Sunk costs, 977, 985, 987
Suppliers, cash payments to, 614–615
Supplies-
adjusting entries for, 157–158
operating activities and, 10
purchase on account, 97, 115
Sustainability reports, 444
Sustainable income, 648–652
change in accounting principle and, 651–652
comprehensive income and, 650–651
discontinued operations and, 649
"non-recurring" charges and, 649
unusual items and, 648

T

T-account approach, to statement of cash flows, 618–620
Take-home pay, I-5
Target cost, M-2–M-3
Target net income, 899–902
contribution margin technique for, 900
in CVP analysis, 925
graphic presentation of, 900–901
mathematical equation for, 899–900
Target selling price, M-3
Taxes. *See also* Income taxes
for corporations, 540
cost flow methods and, 279
FICA, I-3–I-4
income, 10, I-4–I-5
organizational forms and, 4
payroll, I-3–I-4, I-8–I-10
taxing authorities, 6
Tax advantages, leasing and, 428
Temporary accounts, 175
Temporary investments, operating cycle and, H-2

Theory of constraints, 718, 934
Time-and-material pricing, M-7–M-9
  labor rate calculation, M-7–M-8
  material loading charge calculation, M-7–M-9
  particular job charge calculations, M-9
Timeliness, 59, 60
Time periods-
  discounting and, G-11
  interest rates and, G-1, G-2
Times interest earned, 497, 661, 671
Time tickets, 755
Time value of money, 486, 1171, G-1–G-16
  future value of an annuity, G-4–G-7
  future value of a single amount, G-3–G-4
  nature of interest, G-1–G-3
  present value of annuity, G-9–G-11
  present value of long-term note or bond, G-11–G-13
  present value of single amount, G-7–G-9
  present value variables, G-7
  time diagram, G-2
  time periods and discounting, G-11
  using financial calculators for, G-13–G-16
Tokyo Stock Exchange, 543
Total amounts, 1121
Total cost of trading securities, H-8
Total cost of work in process, 713
Total costs accounted for, 802
Total costs to be accounted for, 802
Total fair value of securities, H-8
Total labor variance, 1129
Total manufacturing costs, 711
Total materials variance, 1127
Total overhead variance, 1131
Total quality management (TQM), 718
Total standard cost per unit, 1124
Total units accounted for, 800
Total wages, I-2
Traceable costs, 1084
Trademarks, 441
Trade names, 441
Trade receivables, 376
Trading on the equity, 673
Trading securities, 650, H-7–H-10
Traditional costing systems, 836–837, 851
Transaction analysis, 92–100
  accuracy and, 99
  balancing accounting equation, 93
  hiring new employees, 98
  investment of cash by stock holders, 94
  note issued in exchange for cash, 94–95
  payment of cash for employee salaries, 98
  payment of dividends, 98
  payment of rent, 96–97
  purchase of insurance policy for cash, 97
  purchase of office equipment for cash, 95
  purchase of supplies on account, 97
  receipt of cash in advance from customer, 95
  services performed for cash, 96
  summary of transactions, 99
Transferable ownership rights, corporations and, 538–539
Transfer pricing, M-9–M-15
  cost-based transfer prices, M-13–M-14
  market-based transfer prices, M-14–M-15
  negotiated transfer prices, M-10–M-13
  outsourcing effects on, M-15
  with transfer between divisions in different countries, M-15
  variable costs and, M-12–M-13
Transfer process costs-
  transfer to cost of goods sold, 795
  transfer to finished goods, 795
  transfer to next department, 795
Treasurer, 540, 707
Treasury bills, 341
Treasury stock-
  accounting for, 547–549
  purchase of, 547–548
Trial balance, 119–122, 154
  adjusting entries and, 154. *See also* Adjusted trial balance
  example, 120–121
  limitations of, 119–120
  post-closing, 176–177
Triple bottom line, 720

U

Uncollectable accounts-
  allowance method for, 379–384
  bad debt expense, 378
  direct write-off method for, 378–379
  estimated, 380
  recording the write-off of, 380–381
  recovery of, 381
Underapplied manufacturing overhead, 765–767
Understandability, 59, 60
Unearned revenues, 160–161, 481–482
Unemployment taxes, I-8–I-9
Unequal annual cash flows, net present value and, 1173
Unfavorable variances, 1156
Unit amounts, 1121
Units completed, 802
Unit contribution margin, 893–894, 897, 929–930
Unit cost comparison, in activity-based costing, 842–843
Unit-level activities, 845
Units-of-activity (units-of-production) method, for depreciation, 450–451
Unit production costs, computing, 801–802, 809–810
Unit selling prices, 896
Units started and completed, 806
Unit variable costs, 896
Unlimited liability, in partnerships, K-2–K-4
Unprofitable segments or products, eliminating, 988–990
Unqualified opinions, 19
Unrealized gains or losses-
  investments and, H-11–H-12
  securities and, H-11–H-12
  on trading securities, H-8
Unsecured bonds, 486
Useful life-
  of assets, 158
  depreciation and, 430
  of intangible assets, 440

V

Vacations, requiring, 325
Value-added activities, 847

Value chain, 717–718
Variable costs-
  in cost behavior analysis, 884–885
  in cost-volume-profit analysis, 891
  in transfer pricing, M-12–M-13
Variable costing, 940–949
  absorption costing compared to, 940–948
  decision-making concerns and, 946–948
  example of, 940–942
  net income effects of, 942–946
  potential advantages of, 948
Variable cost pricing, M-6–M-7, M-17–M-19
Variances, 1125
  analyzing and reporting, 1125–1126
  direct labor variances, 1129–1131
  direct materials variances, 1126–1129
  favorable, 1126
  income statement presentation of, 1134–1135
  manufacturing overhead variances, 1131–1133
  overhead controllable variance, 1132
  overhead volume variance, 1132
  reporting, 1133–1134
  significant, 1134
  unfavorable, 1125
Variance accounts, 1139–1141
Venture capital, K-3
Verifiability, 59, 60
Verification, independent internal, *see* Independent internal verification
Vertical analysis, 657–659
Virtual companies, M-15
Voluntarily authorized withholdings, I-5
Voucher register, 330
Voucher system controls, 330–331

W

Wages, I-1–I-2. *See also* Payroll accounting
Wage and Tax Statement (Form W-2), I-10
Wages payable, 10
Weighted-average method-
  equivalent units computation, 796–798
  FIFO and, 811–812
Weighted-average unit contribution margins, 929–930
Weighted-average unit cost, 276–277
Wholesalers, 216
Withholding tax table, I-4
Worker efficiency, labor quantity variances and, 1131
Working capital, 54, 661
Work in process, 268
  assigning manufacturing costs to, 752–760
  inventory, 759
Worksheets, 182–183
Write-downs, 282, 436
Write-offs-
  allowance method, 380–381
  direct method, 378–379

Y

Year-end balance, job order costing and, 767

Z

Zero-coupon bonds, 490

ACCOUNT CLASSIFICATION AND PRESENTATION			
Account Title	**Classification**	**Financial Statement**	**Normal Balance**
A			
Accounts Payable	Current Liability	Balance Sheet	Credit
Accounts Receivable	Current Asset	Balance Sheet	Debit
Accumulated Depreciation—Buildings	Plant Asset—Contra	Balance Sheet	Credit
Accumulated Depreciation—Equipment	Plant Asset—Contra	Balance Sheet	Credit
Administrative Expenses	Operating Expense	Income Statement	Debit
Allowance for Doubtful Accounts	Current Asset—Contra	Balance Sheet	Credit
Amortization Expense	Operating Expense	Income Statement	Debit
B			
Bad Debt Expense	Operating Expense	Income Statement	Debit
Bonds Payable	Long-Term Liability	Balance Sheet	Credit
Buildings	Plant Asset	Balance Sheet	Debit
C			
Cash	Current Asset	Balance Sheet	Debit
Common Stock	Stockholders' Equity	Balance Sheet	Credit
Copyrights	Intangible Asset	Balance Sheet	Debit
Cost of Goods Sold	Cost of Goods Sold	Income Statement	Debit
D			
Debt Investments	Current Asset/ Long-Term Investment	Balance Sheet	Debit
Depreciation Expense	Operating Expense	Income Statement	Debit
Discount on Bonds Payable	Long-Term Liability—Contra	Balance Sheet	Debit
Dividend Revenue	Other Income	Income Statement	Credit
Dividends	Temporary account closed to Retained Earnings	Retained Earnings Statement	Debit
Dividends Payable	Current Liability	Balance Sheet	Credit
E			
Equipment	Plant Asset	Balance Sheet	Debit
F			
Freight-Out	Operating Expense	Income Statement	Debit
G			
Gain on Disposal of Plant Assets	Other Income	Income Statement	Credit
Goodwill	Intangible Asset	Balance Sheet	Debit
I			
Income Summary	Temporary account closed to Retained Earnings	Not Applicable	(1)
Income Tax Expense	Income Tax Expense	Income Statement	Debit
Income Taxes Payable	Current Liability	Balance Sheet	Credit
Insurance Expense	Operating Expense	Income Statement	Debit
Interest Expense	Other Expense	Income Statement	Debit
Interest Payable	Current Liability	Balance Sheet	Credit
Interest Receivable	Current Asset	Balance Sheet	Debit
Interest Revenue	Other Income	Income Statement	Credit
Inventory	Current Asset	Balance Sheet (2)	Debit

Account Title	Classification	Financial Statement	Normal Balance
		L	
Land	Plant Asset	Balance Sheet	Debit
Loss on Disposal of Plant Assets	Other Expense	Income Statement	Debit
		M	
Maintenance and Repairs Expense	Operating Expense	Income Statement	Debit
Mortgage Payable	Long-Term Liability	Balance Sheet	Credit
		N	
Notes Payable	Current Liability/ Long-Term Liability	Balance Sheet	Credit
		P	
Patents	Intangible Asset	Balance Sheet	Debit
Paid-in Capital in Excess of Par Value—Common Stock	Stockholders' Equity	Balance Sheet	Credit
Paid-in Capital in Excess of Par Value—Preferred Stock	Stockholders' Equity	Balance Sheet	Credit
Preferred Stock	Stockholders' Equity	Balance Sheet	Credit
Premium on Bonds Payable	Long-Term Liability—Contra	Balance Sheet	Credit
Prepaid Insurance	Current Asset	Balance Sheet	Debit
Prepaid Rent	Current Asset	Balance Sheet	Debit
		R	
Rent Expense	Operating Expense	Income Statement	Debit
Retained Earnings	Stockholders' Equity	Balance Sheet and Retained Earnings Statement	Credit
		S	
Salaries and Wages Expense	Operating Expense	Income Statement	Debit
Salaries and Wages Payable	Current Liability	Balance Sheet	Credit
Sales Discounts	Revenue—Contra	Income Statement	Debit
Sales Returns and Allowances	Revenue—Contra	Income Statement	Debit
Sales Revenue	Revenue	Income Statement	Credit
Selling Expenses	Operating Expense	Income Statement	Debit
Service Revenue	Revenue	Income Statement	Credit
Stock Investments	Current Asset/Long-Term Investment	Balance Sheet	Debit
Supplies	Current Asset	Balance Sheet	Debit
Supplies Expense	Operating Expense	Income Statement	Debit
		T	
Treasury Stock	Stockholders' Equity	Balance Sheet	Debit
		U	
Unearned Service Revenue	Current Liability	Balance Sheet	Credit
Utilities Expense	Operating Expense	Income Statement	Debit

(1) The normal balance for Income Summary will be credit when there is a net income, debit when there is a net loss. The Income Summary account does not appear on any financial statement.
(2) If a periodic system is used, Inventory also appears on the income statement in the calculation of cost of goods sold.

The following is a sample chart of accounts. It does not represent a comprehensive chart of all the accounts used in this textbook but rather those accounts that are commonly used. This sample chart of accounts is for a company that generates both service revenue as well as sales revenue. It uses the perpetual approach to inventory. If a periodic system was used, the following temporary accounts would be needed to record inventory purchases: Purchases, Freight-In, Purchase Returns and Allowances, and Purchase Discounts.

CHART OF ACCOUNTS

Assets	Liabilities	Stockholders' Equity	Revenues	Expenses
Cash	Notes Payable	Common Stock	Service Revenue	Administrative Expenses
Accounts Receivable	Accounts Payable	Paid-in Capital in Excess of Par Value—Common Stock	Sales Revenue	Amortization Expense
Allowance for Doubtful Accounts	Unearned Service Revenue	Preferred Stock	Sales Discounts	Bad Debt Expense
Interest Receivable	Salaries and Wages Payable	Paid-in Capital in Excess of Par Value—Preferred Stock	Sales Returns and Allowances	Cost of Goods Sold
Inventory	Interest Payable	Treasury Stock	Interest Revenue	Depreciation Expense
Supplies	Dividends Payable	Retained Earnings	Gain on Disposal of Plant Assets	Freight-Out
Prepaid Insurance	Income Taxes Payable	Dividends		Income Tax Expense
Prepaid Rent	Bonds Payable	Income Summary		Insurance Expense
Land	Discount on Bonds Payable			Interest Expense
Equipment	Premium on Bonds Payable			Loss on Disposal of Plant Assets
Accumulated Depreciation—Equipment	Mortgage Payable			Maintenance and Repairs Expense
Buildings				Rent Expense
Accumulated Depreciation—Buildings				Salaries and Wages Expense
Copyrights				Selling Expenses
Goodwill				Supplies Expense
Patents				Utilities Expense

RAPID REVIEW
Chapter Content

ACCOUNTING CONCEPTS (Chapters 2–4)

Fundamental Qualities	Enhancing Qualities	Assumptions	Principles	Constraint
Relevance	Comparability	Monetary unit	Historical cost	Materiality
Faithful representation	Consistency	Economic entity	Fair value	
	Verifiability	Periodicity	Full disclosure	
	Timeliness	Going concern	Revenue recognition	
	Understandability	Accrual basis	Expense recognition	

BASIC ACCOUNTING EQUATION (Chapter 3)

Basic Equation: **Assets = Liabilities + Stockholders' Equity**

Expanded Basic Equation: Assets = Liabilities + Common Stock + Retained Earnings + Revenues − Expenses − Dividends

Debit / Credit Rules:

	Assets	Liabilities	Common Stock	Retained Earnings	Revenues	Expenses	Dividends
Dr.	+	−	−	−	−	+	+
Cr.	−	+	+	+	+	−	−

INVENTORY (Chapters 5 and 6)

Ownership

Freight Terms	Ownership of goods on public carrier resides with:
FOB Shipping point	Buyer
FOB Destination	Seller

ADJUSTING ENTRIES (Chapter 4)

	Type	Adjusting Entry	
Deferrals	1. Prepaid expenses	Dr. Expenses	Cr. Assets
	2. Unearned revenues	Dr. Liabilities	Cr. Revenues
Accruals	1. Accrued revenues	Dr. Assets	Cr. Revenues
	2. Accrued expenses	Dr. Expenses	Cr. Liabilities

Note: Each adjusting entry will affect one or more income statement accounts and one or more balance sheet accounts.

Interest Computation

Interest = Face value of note × Annual interest rate × Time in terms of one year

CLOSING ENTRIES (Chapter 4)

Purpose

1. Update the Retained Earnings account in the ledger by transferring net income (loss) and dividends to retained earnings.
2. Prepare the temporary accounts (revenue, expense, dividends) for the next period's postings by reducing their balances to zero.

ACCOUNTING CYCLE (Chapter 4)

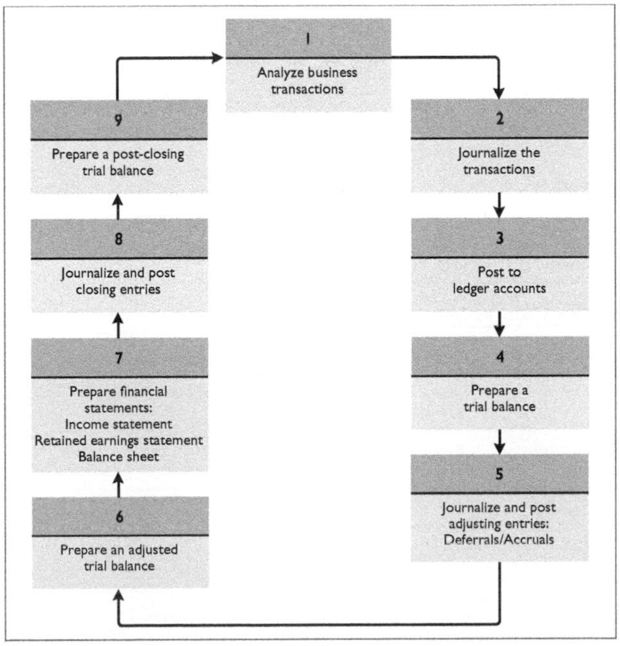

Perpetual vs. Periodic Journal Entries

Event	Perpetual	Periodic
Purchase of goods	Inventory Cash (A/P)	Purchases Cash (A/P)
Freight (shipping point)	Inventory Cash	Freight-In Cash
Return of purchased goods	Cash (or A/P) Inventory	Cash (or A/P) Purchase Returns and Allowances
Sale of goods	Cash (or A/R) Sales Revenue Cost of Goods Sold Inventory	Cash (or A/R) Sales Revenue No entry
Return of sold goods	Sales Returns and Allowances Accounts Receivable Inventory Cost of Goods Sold	Sales Returns and Allowances Accounts Receivable No entry
End of period	No entry	Closing or adjusting entry required

FRAUD, INTERNAL CONTROL, AND CASH (Chapter 7)

Principles of Internal Control

Establishment of responsibility
Segregation of duties
Documentation procedures
Physical controls
Independent internal verification
Human resource controls

The Fraud Triangle

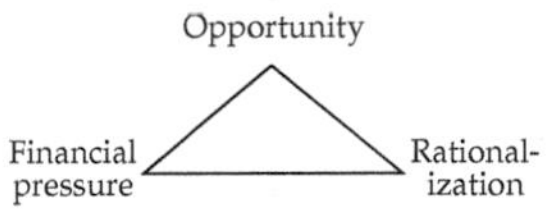

Bank Reconciliation

Bank	Books
Balance per bank statement	Balance per books
Add: Deposits in transit	Add: Unrecorded credit memoranda from bank statement
Deduct: Outstanding checks	Deduct: Unrecorded debit memoranda from bank statement
Adjusted cash balance	Adjusted cash balance

Note: 1. Errors should be offset (added or deducted) on the side that made the error.
2. Adjusting journal entries should only be made for items affecting books.

STOP AND CHECK: Does the adjusted cash balance in the Cash account equal the reconciled balance?

RAPID REVIEW
Chapter Content

RECEIVABLES (Chapter 8)

Two Methods to Account for Uncollectible Accounts

Direct write-off method	Record bad debt expense when the company determines a particular account to be uncollectible.
Allowance method	At the end of each period, estimate the amount of uncollectible receivables. Debit Bad Debt Expense and credit Allowance for Doubtful Accounts in an amount that results in a balance in the allowance account equal to the estimate of uncollectibles. As specific accounts become uncollectible, debit Allowance for Doubtful Accounts and credit Accounts Receivable.

Steps to Manage Accounts Receivable

1. Determine to whom to extend credit.
2. Establish a payment period.
3. Monitor collections.
4. Evaluate the receivables balance.
5. Accelerate cash receipts from receivables when necessary.

PLANT ASSETS (Chapter 9)

Computation of Annual Depreciation Expense

Straight-line	$\frac{\text{Cost} - \text{Salvage value}}{\text{Useful life (in years)}}$
***Declining-balance**	Book value at beginning of year × Declining balance rate* *Declining-balance rate = 1 ÷ Useful life (in years)
***Units-of-activity**	$\frac{\text{Cost} - \text{Salvage value}}{\text{Useful life (in units)}}$ × Units of activity during year

Note: If depreciation is calculated for partial periods, the straight-line and declining-balance methods must be adjusted for the relevant proportion of the year. Multiply the annual depreciation expense by the number of months expired in the year divided by 12 months.

BONDS (Chapter 10)

Premium	Market interest rate < Contractual interest rate
Face Value	Market interest rate = Contractual interest rate
Discount	Market interest rate > Contractual interest rate

Computation of Annual Bond Interest Expense

Interest expense = Interest paid (payable) + Amortization of discount
(OR − Amortization of premium)

***Straight-line amortization**	$\frac{\text{Bond discount (premium)}}{\text{Number of interest periods}}$	
***Effective-interest amortization (preferred method)**	Bond interest expense	Bond interest paid
	Carrying value of bonds at beginning of period × Effective-interest rate	Face amount of bonds × Contractual interest rate

STOCKHOLDERS' EQUITY (Chapter 11)

No-Par Value vs. Par Value Stock Journal Entries

No-Par Value	Par Value
Cash Common Stock	Cash Common Stock (par value) Paid-in Capital in Excess of Par Value

Comparison of Dividend Effects

	Cash	Common Stock	Retained Earnings
Cash dividend	↓	No effect	↓
Stock dividend	No effect	↑	↓
Stock split	No effect	No effect	No effect

*Items with asterisk are covered in appendix.

STATEMENT OF CASH FLOWS (Chapter 12)

Cash flows from operating activities (**indirect method**)

Net income			
Add:	Amortization and depreciation	$X	
	Losses on disposals of assets	X	
	Decreases in current assets	X	
	Increases in current liabilities	X	
Deduct:	Increases in current assets	(X)	
	Decreases in current liabilities	(X)	
	Gains on disposals of assets	(X)	
Net cash provided (used) by operating activities			$X

Cash flows from operating activities (**direct method**)

Cash receipts		
(Examples: from sales of goods and services to customers, from receipts of interest and dividends)	$X	
Cash payments		
(Examples: to suppliers, for operating expenses, for interest, for taxes)	(X)	
Net cash provided (used) by operating activities		$X

FINANCIAL STATEMENT ANALYSIS (Chapter 13)

Discontinued operations	Income statement (presented separately after "Income from continuing operations")
Changes in accounting principle	In most instances, use the new method in current period and restate previous years' results using new method. For changes in depreciation and amortization methods, use the new method in the current period, but do not restate previous periods.

Income Statement and Comprehensive Income

Sales	$XX
Cost of goods sold	XX
Gross profit	XX
Operating expenses	XX
Income from operations	XX
Other revenues (expenses) and gains (losses)	XX
Income before income taxes	XX
Income tax expense	XX
Income before irregular items	XX
Irregular items (net of tax)	**XX**
Net income	**XX**
Other comprehensive income items (net of tax)	**XX**
Comprehensive income	**$ XX**

MANAGERIAL ACCOUNTING (Chapter 14)

Characteristics of Managerial Accounting

Primary users	Internal users
Reports	Internal reports issued as needed
Purpose	Special purpose for a particular user
Content	Pertains to subunits, may be detailed, use of relevant data
Verification	No independent audits

Types of Manufacturing Costs

Direct materials	Raw materials directly associated with finished product
Direct labor	Work of employees directly associated with turning raw materials into finished product
Manufacturing overhead	Costs indirectly associated with manufacture of finished product

RAPID REVIEW
Chapter Content

JOB ORDER AND PROCESS COSTING (Chapters 15 and 16)

Types of Accounting Systems

Job order	Costs are assigned to each unit or each batch of goods
Process cost	Costs are applied to similar products that are mass-produced in a continuous fashion

Job Order and Process Cost Flow

Job Order Cost Flow	Process Cost Flow
Direct Materials Direct Labor Manufacturing Overhead	Direct Materials Direct Labor Manufacturing Overhead
↓	↓
Work in Process Inventory Job No. 101 Job No. 102 Job No. 103	Work in Process
↓	↓
Finished Goods Inventory	Finished Goods Inventory
↓	↓
Cost of Goods Sold	Cost of Goods Sold

ACTIVITY-BASED COSTING (Chapter 17)

1. **Identify and classify the activities** involved in the manufacture of specific products and **assign overhead to cost pools**.

↓

2. **Identify the cost driver** that has a strong correlation to the costs accumulated in each cost pool.

↓

3. **Compute the activity-based overhead rate** for each cost pool.

↓

4. **Allocate overhead costs to products** using the overhead rates determined for each cost pool.

COST-VOLUME-PROFIT (Chapters 18 and 19)

Types of Costs

Variable costs	Vary in total directly and proportionately with changes in activity level
Fixed costs	Remain the same in total regardless of change in activity level
Mixed costs	Contain both a fixed and a variable element

CVP Income Statement Format

	Total	Per Unit
Sales	$xx	$xx
Variable costs	xx	xx
Contribution margin	xx	$xx
Fixed costs	xx	
Net income	$xx	

Unit contribution margin	=	Unit selling price − Unit variable costs
Break-even point in units	=	Fixed costs ÷ Unit contribution margin*
Break-even point in dollars	=	Fixed costs ÷ Contribution margin ratio*
Required sales in units for target net income	=	(Fixed costs + Target net income) ÷ Unit contribution margin
Degree of operating leverage	=	Contribution margin ÷ Net income

*For multiple products, use weighted-average.

INCREMENTAL ANALYSIS (Chapter 20)

1. Identify the relevant costs associated with each alternative. **Relevant costs** are those costs and revenues that differ across alternatives. Choose the alternative that maximizes net income.
2. **Opportunity costs** are those benefits that are given up when one alternative is chosen instead of another one. Opportunity costs are relevant costs.
3. **Sunk costs** have already been incurred and will not be changed or avoided by any future decision. Sunk costs are not relevant costs.

BUDGETS (Chapter 21)

Components of the Master Budget

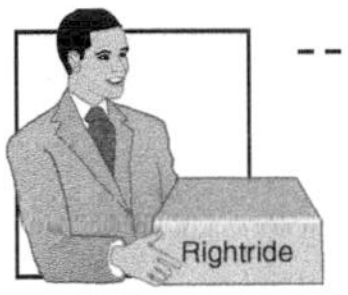

Operating Budgets

Sales Budget

↓

Production Budget

↓

Direct Materials Budget | **Direct Labor Budget** | **Manufacturing Overhead Budget**

↓

Selling and Administrative Expense Budget

↓

Budgeted Income Statement

↓

Financial Budgets

Capital Expenditure Budget → **Cash Budget** → **Budgeted Balance Sheet**

RESPONSIBILITY ACCOUNTING (Chapter 22)

Types of Responsibility Centers

Cost	Profit	Investment
Expenses only	Expenses and Revenues	Expenses and Revenues and ROI

Return on Investment

Return on investment (ROI)	=	Investment center controllable margin ÷ Average investment center operating assets

RAPID REVIEW
Chapter Content

STANDARD COSTS (Chapter 23)

Standard Cost Variances

Total materials variance = Materials price variance + Materials quantity variance

Total labor variance = Labor price variance + Labor quantity variance

Total overhead variance = Overhead controllable variance + Overhead volume variance

Materials price variance = $AQ \times AP$ − $AQ \times SP$

Materials quantity variance = $AQ \times SP$ − $SQ \times SP$

Labor price variance = $AH \times AR$ − $AH \times SR$

Labor quantity variance = $AH \times SR$ − $SH \times SR$

* **Overhead controllable variance** = Actual overhead − Overhead budgeted

* **Overhead volume variance** = Fixed overhead rate × (Normal capacity hours − Standard hours allowed)

*Appendix coverage

Balanced Scorecard

Linked process across perspectives:

Financial → Customer → Internal Process → Learning and Growth

CAPITAL BUDGETING (Chapter 24)

Annual Rate of Return

Annual rate of return = Expected annual net income ÷ Average investment

Cash Payback

Cash payback period = Cost of capital investment ÷ Annual cash inflow

Discounted Cash Flow Approaches

Net Present Value	Internal Rate of Return
Compute net present value (a dollar amount). If net present value is zero or positive, accept the proposal. If net present value is negative, reject the proposal.	Compute internal rate of return (a percentage). If internal rate of return is equal to or greater than the minimum required rate of return, accept the proposal. If internal rate of return is less than the minimum rate, reject the proposal.

INVESTMENTS (Appendix H)

Comparison of Long-Term Bond Investment and Liability Journal Entries

Event	Investor	Investee
Purchase / issue of bonds	Debt Investments Cash	Cash Bonds Payable
Interest receipt / payment	Cash Interest Revenue	Interest Expense Cash

Comparison of Cost and Equity Methods of Accounting for Long-Term Stock Investments

Event	Cost	Equity
Acquisition	Stock Investments Cash	Stock Investments Cash
Investee reports earnings	No entry	Stock Investments Investment Revenue
Investee pays dividends	Cash Dividend Revenue	Cash Stock Investments

PRICING (Appendix M)

External Pricing

Markup percentage = Desired ROI per unit ÷ Total unit cost

Target selling price per unit = Total unit cost + (Total unit cost × Markup percentage)

Transfer Pricing

Minimum transfer price = Variable cost + Opportunity cost

RAPID REVIEW
Financial Statements

Order of Preparation	Date
1. Income statement	For the period ended
2. Retained earnings statement	For the period ended
3. Balance sheet	As of the end of the period
4. Statement of cash flows	For the period ended

Income Statement (perpetual inventory system)

Name of Company Income Statement For the Period Ended		
Sales revenues		
Sales	$ X	
Less: Sales returns and allowances	X	
Sales discounts	X	
Net sales		$ X
Cost of goods sold		X
Gross profit		X
Operating expenses		
(Examples: store salaries, advertising, delivery, rent, depreciation, utilities, insurance)		X
Income from operations		X
Other revenues and gains		
(Examples: interest, gains)	X	
Other expenses and losses		
(Examples: interest, losses)	X	X
Income before income taxes		X
Income tax expense		X
Net income		$ X

Income Statement (periodic inventory system)

Name of Company Income Statement For the Period Ended			
Sales revenues			
Sales		$ X	
Less: Sales returns and allowances		X	
Sales discounts		X	
Net sales			$ X
Cost of goods sold			
Beginning inventory		X	
Purchases	$ X		
Less: Purchase returns and allowances	X		
Net purchases	X		
Add: Freight in	X		
Cost of goods purchased		X	
Cost of goods available for sale		X	
Less: Ending inventory		X	
Cost of goods sold			X
Gross profit			X
Operating expenses			
(Examples: store salaries, advertising, delivery, rent, depreciation, utilities, insurance)			X
Income from operations			X
Other revenues and gains			
(Examples: interest, gains)		X	
Other expenses and losses			
(Examples: interest, losses)		X	X
Income before income taxes			X
Income tax expense			X
Net income			$ X

Name of Company Comprehensive Income Statement For the Period Ended	
Net income	$XX
Other comprehensive income	XX
Comprehensive income	$XX

Retained Earnings Statement

Name of Company Retained Earnings Statement For the Period Ended	
Retained earnings, beginning of period	$ X
Add: Net income (or deduct net loss)	X
	X
Deduct: Dividends	X
Retained earnings, end of period	$ X

STOP AND CHECK: Net income (loss) presented on the retained earnings statement must equal the net income (loss) presented on the income statement.

Balance Sheet

Name of Company Balance Sheet As of the End of the Period			
Assets			
Current assets			
(Examples: cash, short-term investments, accounts receivable, inventory, prepaids)			$ X
Long-term investments			
(Examples: investments in bonds, investments in stocks)			X
Property, plant, and equipment			
Land		$ X	
Buildings and equipment	$ X		
Less: Accumulated depreciation	X	X	X
Intangible assets			X
Total assets			$ X
Liabilities and Stockholders' Equity			
Liabilities			
Current liabilities			
(Examples: notes payable, accounts payable, accruals, unearned revenues, current portion of notes payable)			$ X
Long-term liabilities			
(Examples: notes payable, bonds payable)			X
Total liabilities			X
Stockholders' equity			
Common stock			X
Retained earnings			X
Total liabilities and stockholders' equity			$ X

STOP AND CHECK: Total assets on the balance sheet must equal total liabilities plus stockholders' equity; and, ending retained earnings on the balance sheet must equal ending retained earnings on the retained earnings statement.

Statement of Cash Flows

Name of Company Statement of Cash Flows For the Period Ended	
Cash flows from operating activities	
Note: May be prepared using the direct or indirect method	
Net cash provided (used) by operating activities	$ X
Cash flows from investing activities	
(Examples: purchase / sale of long-term assets)	
Net cash provided (used) by investing activities	X
Cash flows from financing activities	
(Examples: issue / repayment of long-term liabilities, issue of stock, payment of dividends)	
Net cash provided (used) by financing activities	X
Net increase (decrease) in cash	X
Cash, beginning of the period	X
Cash, end of the period	$ X

STOP AND CHECK: Cash, end of the period, on the statement of cash flows must equal cash presented on the balance sheet.

RAPID REVIEW

Tools for Analysis

Liquidity

Working capital	Current assets – Current liabilities	p. 54
Current ratio	$\frac{\text{Current assets}}{\text{Current liabilities}}$	p. 54
Inventory turnover	$\frac{\text{Cost of goods sold}}{\text{Average inventory}}$	p. 283
Days in inventory	$\frac{\text{365 days}}{\text{Inventory turnover}}$	p. 283
Accounts receivable turnover	$\frac{\text{Net credit sales}}{\text{Average net accounts receivable}}$	p. 395
Average collection period	$\frac{\text{365 days}}{\text{Accounts receivable turnover}}$	p. 395

Solvency

Debt to assets ratio	$\frac{\text{Total liabilities}}{\text{Total assets}}$	p. 56
Times interest earned	$\frac{\text{Net income + Interest expense + Income tax expense}}{\text{Interest expense}}$	p. 497
Free cash flow	Net cash provided by operating activities – Capital expenditures – Cash dividends	p. 57

Profitability

Earnings per share	$\frac{\text{Net income – Preferred dividends}}{\text{Weighted-average common shares outstanding}}$	p. 53
Price-earnings ratio	$\frac{\text{Market price per share}}{\text{Earnings per share}}$	p. 660
Gross profit rate	$\frac{\text{Gross profit}}{\text{Net sales}}$	p. 234
Profit margin	$\frac{\text{Net income}}{\text{Net sales}}$	p. 235
Return on assets	$\frac{\text{Net income}}{\text{Average total assets}}$	p. 444
Asset turnover	$\frac{\text{Net sales}}{\text{Average total assets}}$	p. 446
Payout ratio	$\frac{\text{Cash dividends declared on common stock}}{\text{Net income}}$	p. 560
Return on common stockholders' equity	$\frac{\text{Net income – Preferred dividends}}{\text{Average common stockholders' equity}}$	p. 561